C#

Primer Plus

Klaus Michelsen

SAMS

201 West 103rd St., Indianapolis, Indiana, 46290 USA

C# Primer Plus

International Standard Book Number: 0-672-32152-1

Library of Congress Catalog Card Number: 2001089509

Printed in the United States of America

First Printing: November 2001

04 03 02 01 4 3 2 1

Trademarks

All terms mentioned in this book that are known to be trademarks or service marks have been appropriately capitalized. Sams Publishing cannot attest to the accuracy of this information. Use of a term in this book should not be regarded as affecting the validity of any trademark or service mark.

Warning and Disclaimer

Every effort has been made to make this book as complete and as accurate as possible, but no warranty or fitness is implied. The information provided is on an "as is" basis.

ASSOCIATE PUBLISHER
Jeff Koch

ACQUISITIONS EDITOR
Neil Rowe

DEVELOPMENT EDITOR
Kevin Howard

MANAGING EDITOR
Matt Purcell

PROJECT EDITOR
George E. Nedeff

COPY EDITOR
Pat Kinyon

INDEXER
Rebecca Salerno

PROOFREADER
Plan-It Publishing

TECHNICAL EDITOR
Brad Shannon

TEAM COORDINATOR
Denni Bannister

MEDIA DEVELOPER
Dan Scherf

INTERIOR DESIGNER
Gary Designer

COVER DESIGNER
Alan Clements

PAGE LAYOUT
Plan-It Publishing
Brad Lenser

CONTENTS AT A GLANCE

TABLE OF CONTENTS

ABOUT THE AUTHOR

Klaus Michelsen has a Masters degree in Economics from Aarhus University in Denmark. His studies included artificial intelligence and courses in advanced computer science at Sydney University in Australia. Since his first programming assignment for a shoe shop when he was 18, he has, during his 15 years of programming experience, been exposed to many different technologies and programming languages, including Java™, Visual J++, C++, MS Access, VB, Eiffel, and Pascal. Klaus has been working with C# and .NET since their introduction in the year 2000.

DEDICATION

To Deborah,

My friend, my love, my wife.

ACKNOWLEDGMENTS

I would like to thank my wife Deborah who, despite my obstinate tendency to turn into a hermit during this project and my countless late nights of writing frenzies, is still putting up with me. Without you and your boundless support, this book project would have been impossible. Without you and our young boy Julian, any project in my life would seem meaningless. I love you!

I would like to thank the team of editors, coordinators, and technicians at Sams Publishing for putting their hard work and invaluable expertise into this project. I'm especially grateful to Neil Rowe, Acquisitions Editor, for initially contacting me, encouraging me to engage in this project, and for his solid support during the whole process. Thanks for taking a chance with a new writer; it has changed my life forever.

I would like to thank my mother Vita Lund Michelsen, for her strong support and incessant encouragement throughout my life and in particular during the months I was writing. Thanks to my sister Kirsten for keeping the spirits up on the other side of the world, even during difficult times; this gave me peace of mind to focus on the book.

Lastly, thanks to my two dogs, Charlie and Honey, and the great composers Mozart and Beethoven who all kept me company on many a late night.

TELL US WHAT YOU THINK!

As the reader of this book, *you* are our most important critic and commentator. We value your opinion and want to know what we're doing right, what we could do better, what areas you'd like to see us publish in, and any other words of wisdom you're willing to pass our way.

As an Associate Publisher for Sams Publishing, I welcome your comments. You can fax, email, or write me directly to let me know what you did or didn't like about this book—as well as what we can do to make our books stronger.

Please note that I cannot help you with technical problems related to the topic of this book, and that due to the high volume of mail I receive, I might not be able to reply to every message.

When you write, please be sure to include this book's title and author as well as your name and phone or fax number. I will carefully review your comments and share them with the author and editors who worked on the book.

Fax: 317-581-4770

Email: `feedback@samspublishing.com`

Mail: Jeff Koch
Associate Publisher
Sams Publishing
201 West 103rd Street
Indianapolis, IN 46290 USA

INTRODUCTION

Philosophy, Goals, and Audience

Forming a group of grammatically correct sentences in the English language by combining verbs, nouns, and other language elements is relatively easy compared to the task of constructing sentences that together form a spellbinding, classical novel.

C#, like any other programming language, also consists of a basic set of language elements. To form valid C# "sentences," these elements must be put together according to C#'s rules of syntax. This is relatively easy compared to the task of creating a group of C# "sentences" that together form a successful, robust, and bug-free program.

Not only does this book teach you C#'s language elements from the ground up, it also explains their optimal use and shows you how they are combined to form robust and valuable programs. The latter is achieved by including proven fundamental programming techniques (with an emphasis on object-oriented programming) as part of the introduction of the C# language. To maintain this dual focus and to avoid any superfluous distractions, only the parts of .NET directly relevant to C# are discussed. Accordingly, this book is not about .NET's ASP+, Web Services, or Win Forms but about making you a proficient C# programmer.

This book is targeted at the beginner and requires no mathematical skills other than some simple algebra. An absolute beginner should read the book from cover to cover.

If you've had limited experience with another programming language, you can still benefit from this book. In that case, you might want to concentrate only on the .NET and C# related parts in Chapters 1 and 2 and skip the discussions about abstraction and encapsulation (if your experience include object-oriented programming) in Chapter 3.

Learning a new programming language is, in my view, best facilitated by combining several different teaching tools, so that any one aspect can be viewed and attacked from different angles. Consequently, this tutorial not only contains the basic text describing the various C# elements but also a generous number of figures, source code examples (with accompanying sample output and analysis), case studies, Note boxes, Tip boxes, Common Pitfall boxes, Syntax boxes, and review questions (with answers located in Appendix A, "Answers to Quizzes and Exercises").

It is important to realize that learning to program is not about learning a lot of dry theory and concepts by heart. Instead, it is about experimenting, learning from mistakes, unleashing your creativity, and having fun. As a result, each chapter ends with a set of programming exercises with which you can experiment, test, and improve your skills.

How This Book Is Organized

This book is divided into 23 chapters and 6 appendixes. Five appendixes (Appendix B–F) are located on SAMS Web site at `www.samspublishing.com`.

Chapter 1: "Computers and Computer Programming: Basic Concepts" starts with an overview of the fundamental computer hardware and software concepts required to begin learning C# and computer programming. The last part of the chapter introduces .NET and highlights important services provided by this essential C# programming platform.

Chapter 2: "Your First C# Program" introduces you to the basic software development phases that successful programmers go through to produce robust computer programs and gives you an initial feel for object-oriented programming. The chapter culminates by showing you the mechanics of writing, compiling, and running a simple C# program.

Chapters 3 and 4: Often, an enjoyable and efficient way to learn about an unknown location you visit for the first time is to join a guided tour. Chapter 3, "A Guided Tour Through C#: Part I," and Chapter 4, "A Guided Tour Through C#: Part II," take you to the main attractions of the C# language needed to write simple C# programs. Rather than getting bogged down by details and theory, the aim in these two chapters is to kick start your ability to write simple C# programs and allow you to play and experiment with the language. This is achieved by letting the contents of a few simple C# programs dictate the hands-on and fast-paced story line of these two chapters.

Chapter 5: The first part of Chapter 5, "Your First Object-Oriented Program," builds on the practical knowledge you acquired from Chapters 3 and 4 to give you a deeper insight into the basic structure of the C# language. The second part elaborates on the object-oriented programming knowledge you have gained up until now and turns it into an object-oriented elevator simulation program.

Chapter 6: By now, you will know how to write simple object-oriented C# programs. However, many aspects of the C# language have intentionally been ignored to keep the fast track of the previous chapters free from obscuring and distracting elements. Chapter 6, "Types Part I: The Simple Types," and the remaining chapters of the book are devoted to letting you expand the basic kinds of C# programs you have mastered in the first five chapters. This is done through a systematic and thorough discussion of the many exciting and powerful elements in C# that you now have enough knowledge to appreciate, absorb, and use in the programs with which you might already be experimenting and playing.

Chapter 6 discusses the type concept in general and the simple types, used in most C# programs, in particular. It also introduces an important notation form that is used throughout the rest of the book to describe the syntax of the various C# elements.

Chapter 7: Types allow you to specify attributes about the data kept in a program. Operators in general act on these data. Without operators, program data remain motionless and in most cases useless. Chapter 7, "Types Part II: Operators, Enumerators, and Strings," provides an overview of the different kinds of operators found in C# and looks closer at the main arithmetic operators. Furthermore, the chapter discusses the derived types—`string` (used to represent text) and `enum` (used to handle unchanging values). Several useful and interesting `string`-related program examples are presented and discussed.

Chapter 8: Branching statements allow programs to behave intelligently by reacting differently to different circumstances. Chapter 8, "Flow of Control Part I: Branching Statements and Related Concepts," contains elaborate discussions of the entire set of C# branching statement constructs—`if`, `if-else`, and `switch`—along with their close associates—comparison and logical operators—that also are pivotal for implementing the iteration statements presented in Chapter 9.

Chapter 9: Iteration statements are used to perform the same actions over and over again until some condition is no longer true. C#'s iteration statements, consisting of the `while` loop, the `do-while` loop, and the `for` loop, are discussed in Chapter 9, "Flow of Control Part II: Iteration Statements." Their treatment is elaborated by introducing the useful idea of nested iteration statements. Finally, the structured programming concept that contains proven principles about how to construct robust software on the very detailed design level is presented.

Chapter 10: An array is used to represent a small or large group of similar data items. Chapter 10, "Arrays Part I: Array Essentials," presents arrays and shows how they can be accessed efficiently by using the iteration statements presented in Chapter 9. It also introduces the `foreach` iteration statement specifically targeted at arrays and other collections of data items. The array is a reference type—an important object-oriented concept. For that reason, arrays are used as examples in this chapter for teaching about reference types.

Chapter 11: Chapter 10 only deals with one-dimensional arrays designed for storing data elements that can be viewed as sitting on a line one after the other. Sometimes, data are better represented in two-dimensional tables. Our ability to represent these types of data with two-dimensional arrays is discussed in Chapter 11, "Arrays Part II: Multidimensional Arrays," together with arrays of three or more dimensions. The symbiotic relationship between multidimensional arrays and nested loops is a great example of how data structures and program logic go hand in hand. The chapter concludes by describing a couple famous algorithms for sorting and searching arrays and shows examples of how you can save countless programming hours by reusing the pre-built program parts found in .NET.

Chapter 12: Classes and objects are at the core of object-oriented programming. Classes are written by the programmer in the source code and act as blueprints for objects generated while the program is running. Objects collaborate to provide the functionality of a C# program. The first part of Chapter 12, "Class Anatomy Part I: `static` Class Members and Method Adventures," provides an overview of the ingredients that make up a class. The chapter then continues, as do Chapters 13 and 14, with a detailed look at each of those ingredients. Initially, the chapter looks at static class members that belong to a class rather than any particular object. This is followed by a closer look at method overloading—a mechanism used to write different versions of methods all of same name but with different interfaces and implementations.

Chapter 13: "Class Anatomy Part II: Object Creation and Garbage Collection" looks at how new objects are initialized and old useless objects are disposed of. The latter is achieved through a built-in mechanism called garbage collection that automatically frees the memory (needed by the newly-created objects of the program) otherwise occupied by the useless objects.

Chapter 14: Properties, indexers and user-defined operator overloading are among the C# elements presented in Chapter 14, "Class Anatomy Part III: Writing Intuitive Code." They can, if used correctly, make the source code appear simpler and more intuitive.

Chapter 15: Namespaces assist you in organizing your classes while you write the source code as well as in keeping the classes easily accessible for other programmers when they reuse your classes. Chapter 15, "Namespaces, Compilation Units, and Assemblies," discusses namespaces, compilation units, and assemblies. It also demonstrates the flexibility by which they can be combined and shows you how their overall layout can be tailor-made to suit many different application configurations.

Chapter 16: Inheritance allows you to derive class A from class B and thereby let class A automatically inherit the features of class B. Features specific to class A can then be added manually in the code. Inheritance is a core concept in object-oriented programming with many virtues and is discussed at length in Chapter 16, "Inheritance Part I: Basic Concepts."

Chapter 17: "Inheritance Part II: `abstract` Functions, Polymorphism, and Interfaces," discusses polymorphism and how it allows you to program on a high abstraction level by letting you program against a few simple interfaces while the program takes care of the underlying complexities. Polymorphism is made possible by inheritance and abstract functions. Interfaces are also discussed in this chapter; they allow you to implement polymorphism across the rigid structures of one or more inheritance hierarchies.

Chapter 18: "Structs" looks at structs, which are lightweight alternatives to their close cousins—classes.

Chapter 19: An exception is an abnormal condition in your program and causes a special exception object to be generated by .NET during the execution of the troubled program. Chapter 19, "Exception Handling," introduces exception handling and shows you how to avoid abrupt user-unfriendly program terminations, among other things.

Chapter 20: Conventionally, you must decide which actions a program will execute while you are writing the source code. Delegates allow you to postpone those decisions until the program is running. This allows your programs to be more dynamic with the ability to adjust to a variety of situations. Chapter 20, "Delegates and Events," discuss delegates and their relationship to events. Delegates form the basis for events that, through event-driven programming, have become an important part of many modern application types, especially graphical user interfaces (GUIs).

Chapter 21: "Preprocessing, XML Documentation and Attributes" explains how to conveniently exclude parts of your source code from being included in the finished program through the use of preprocessor directives. This is useful when you want to generate different application versions from the same source code. The chapter continues by looking at C#'s ability to extract XML-formatted source code documentation automatically and directly from the comments you insert into your source code. The chapter ends by presenting attributes and their ability to let you add additional declarative information to C#'s code elements.

Chapter 22: Files let you store data permanently on a disk. They allow programs to read them repeatedly and can be sent over networks to remote computers. Chapter 22, "File I/O Basics," contains a brief introduction to file I/O, which is short for file input (file flowing into a program) and file output (file flowing out of a program).

Chapter 23: When a method asks itself to be executed it is called a recursive method. The use of recursive methods is called recursion and this is covered in Chapter 23, "Recursion Fundamentals." Superficially, recursion seems to represent circular, impossible, and useless logic. However, as this chapter demonstrates through meticulous explanations, the recursion concept can be used to solve important computational problems.

Appendix A: "Answers to Review Questions and Exercises" contains the answers to the review questions and the programming exercises posed at the end of each chapter.

Appendix B: "Operator Precedence"

Appendix C: "Reserved Words In C#"

Appendix D: "Number Systems" discusses the binary, octal and hexadecimal number systems.

Appendix E: "Unicode Character Set"

Appendix F: "Using DOS Commands In The Console Window"

Conventions

To help you differentiate between different types of information presented in this book, we have used different text styles and layout.

- Important words and new terminology appear as *Important words.*
- Text written onscreen by the computer looks as follows:

  `I'm your trusted computer`
- Text written onscreen and typed by you looks as follows:

  `Hello computer, are you there?`
- While writing text onscreen special keys pressed by you, such as the enter key, are symbolized by **`<enter>`**.
- Code shown as part of code examples has the following appearance:

  `private static void Main()`
- The line continuation symbol ➥ is positioned at the beginning of a source code line and indicates that the preceding line of code was too long to fit the page. The previous line and the line following ➥ should be regarded as one line.

C# On The Internet

Even though C# is a relatively new programming language, many useful sources of C# information exist on the Internet. In my view the following three resources are particularly valuable:

- `http://msdn.microsoft.com/net` This is the .NET part of the Microsoft Developer Network (MSDN) Web site. Here you will find the latest language specifications, documentation, and technical articles about C# and .NET.
- `http://www.devx.com/dotnet/resources/` This site contains a comprehensive list of .NET and C# resources on the Internet.
- `http://discuss.develop.com/dotnet.html` While this discussion group is not targeted at beginners, it is frequented by some of the key C# and .NET designers from Microsoft, along with many other highly-qualified C# programmers. As you read through this book, you will likely begin to appreciate the interesting and useful contributions found here.

Contacting the Author

Please contact me if you have any general comments, criticism, praise, or questions (I can't guarantee replies to all questions though) related to the book. Criticism accompanied by reasons and suggestions how the issues can be rectified are particularly valuable to me.

If you want to report specific mistakes (whether they be typing mistakes, code bugs, or meaningless sentences) please make sure you include a page number and even line number if possible.

My e-mail address is `kmichelsen@ozemail.com.au`.

CHAPTER 1

COMPUTERS AND COMPUTER PROGRAMMING: BASIC CONCEPTS

You will learn about the following in this chapter:

- The fundamental nature of computers and computer languages and why this makes computer programming an exciting and creative activity
- The fundamental computer hardware and software concepts necessary to begin learning about C#
- How the computer hardware, despite its simple underlying bit operations, is able to stage sophisticated applications
- Why modern computer languages like C# need compilers and why this makes programming much more enjoyable than with the early compiler-less languages
- .NET and its significance when programming with C#
- How C# and .NET solve some commonly encountered problems found with traditional approaches
- How C# and .NET allows programmers using different computer languages to seamlessly work together on the same project

Just as a writer uses a spoken language to write stories, the computer programmer needs a computer programming language to write computer programs. A spoken language with many grammatical subtleties and a vast vocabulary is highly expressive, but it can be difficult to master and error prone. Accordingly, the evolution of a spoken language continuously strikes a balance between the expressive, complicated, and error prone on one hand, and the constrained, simple, and fool proof on the other.

Designers of programming languages face a similar challenge when they set out to design a new computer language. A powerful programming language can be difficult to learn and too complicated to use, leaving a trail of errors behind. On the other hand, an overly simple language is easy to learn and use, but can restrain the programmer's creativity.

C# (pronounced C sharp) is a new, exciting programming language aimed at striking an optimal balance between expressiveness and simplicity while allowing the programmer to construct sophisticated programs of high performance.

Generations of people are constantly adjusting their spoken language to reflect their current way of life. While the core parts of the English language change very little, many new words and expressions have emerged (the word software springs to mind) over the past hundred years, and many have been left behind.

In 1998, Anders Hejlsberg (designer of Delphi and Turbo Pascal), and his team at Microsoft began to design the first version of the C# language. C# was, like modern English, not created in a vacuum but is an evolutionary step forward from the previous languages that inspired its designers. This has resulted in a language firmly based on a solid core of features that has proven invaluable to most programmers over time. It also adds many new features to accommodate for the needs, possibilities, and challenges that today's programmers encounter.

Computers have been spreading through our society in the past twenty years like rings in the water. Most professions today rely directly or indirectly on computers to accomplish at least parts of their tasks. Even in their spare time, people are turning to the computer as an important source of entertainment. Why is the computer so useful and popular? One reason is the universal range of computer applications that can be created with a computer language such as C#. A light bulb is merely meant for emitting light, a chair is made for sitting, but a computer can be a word-processor one moment, a drawing tool assisting architects the next, and then suddenly turn into a weather forecasting tool utilized by a meteorologist.

The potential for what a computer can do, by tinkering with this universality, is limited only by the programmer's imagination, creativity, and programming expertise combined with the physical limitations of the computer (the screen, speed, and so on). This fact is one of the reasons why computer programming is an exciting and challenging undertaking, considered by many to be an art form offering the same aesthetic pleasures as those experienced by composers and poets.

After a program is finished and handed over to the end user, the universality accessed by the programmer is substituted by the relatively narrow set of features contained in this program which could be a chess game, an image processing application, or a human heart simulator. The artist's soft, malleable clay has been fired and turned into a rigid (hopefully) beautiful sculpture that can be enjoyed by its audience (end users).

In effect, computer programming is significantly different from merely using a computer. Programming a computer entails writing exact instructions for it to execute. The computer in return, blindly follows any valid instructions (no, "Wash the dishes!" is still an invalid instruction.). Even if instructed to do a seemingly illogical calculation like 2 + 2 over and over again a million times, the computer will not question the programmer's sanity. Instead, it will obediently perform the task exactly as described.

C# Is an Object-Oriented Programming Language

Combining simple instructions and thereby utilizing the universality of computers to construct end user applications is linked to one fundamental element—Complexity.

Since the 1940s, when the early computer pioneers were still struggling to fit a computer with the computing-power of a simple calculator into a large room, many valuable principles and paradigms have evolved to deal with the many different facets of complexity in software construction. In particular, one important methodology has emerged during the 1990s called object-oriented programming (OOP).

Our world can be viewed as a collection of objects interacting with each other to accomplish various tasks. For example, a person object can apply a pencil object to write on a paper object. This allows another person object to read the message on the paper object.

OOP imitates this world view by allowing the programmer to create artificial worlds of objects interacting and collaborating with each other to provide the features of a computer program. This approach gives the programmer the powerful ability to divide (and conquer) a seemingly complex programming problem into a set of objects, each significantly simpler than the overall problem. Along with many other advantages, OOP effectively deals with complexity and allows programmers to create better programs in a shorter period of time.

C# provides elaborate support for writing object-oriented programs. Teaching object-oriented programming is arguably best facilitated by learning an object-oriented language, such as C#, simultaneously. This book will provide a complete introduction to C# and utilize its concreteness to clarify the often fuzzy concepts of OOP and, conversely, will employ OOP to explain the design of C#.

Later in this chapter and in Chapter 2, "Your First C# Program," you will take a closer look at C#'s roots, design goals, and core features. However, because C# is closely related to the basic organization of a computer, you can best prepare for this future discussion by first spending time on some important fundamental computer concepts.

Computer Organization

A computer consists of two parts—hardware and software. *Hardware* is made up of the physical, tangible parts of the computer. *Software* is made up of *programs*, also called *applications* that contain instructions for the computer to run or execute.

A computer needs software just as much as hardware to be of any real use. Computer hardware without accompanying software is a bit like a book with empty pages. The cover, the back, and the pages inside constitute the hardware of the book, but the book is pretty useless without any text (the software).

Hardware

When a user interacts with a computer, he or she provides ***input*** for it (see Figure 1.1). In response, the computer processes the input returning (hopefully) valuable ***output*** to the user. Input can be in the form of commands given, text and numbers typed, and images scanned. Output could be the results of spreadsheet calculations, a letter printed out on a printer, or a car moving onscreen during a racing car game.

For the user to provide input, the computer has several ***input devices*** as part of its hardware—the keyboard and the mouse being the most familiar.

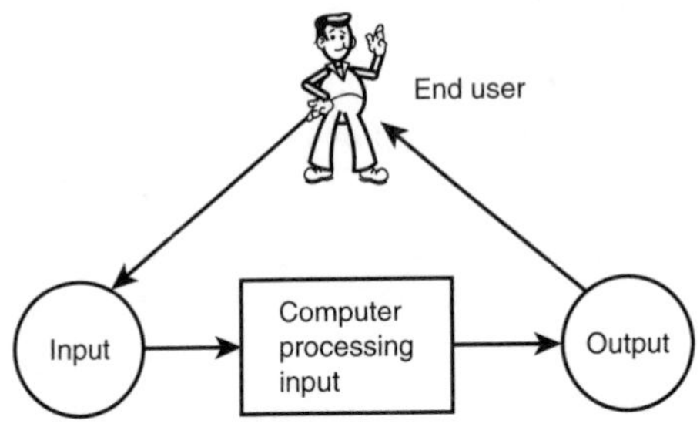

FIGURE 1.1
Input is processed and is returned as output.

To the user, output is typically provided with devices such as screens and printers. Other input or ***output devices*** are available, some of which are very specialized.

Two additional important hardware components, which are less obvious to the ordinary user, are the processor and the memory.

The processor is the device inside the computer that follows a program's instructions. Other terms used for the processor are CPU (Central Processing Unit) or chip. Many different commercial chips are available. A well-known example would be the Pentium chip.

The processor can only carry out simple instructions, such as very simple arithmetic calculations and moving items like numbers around among different locations. However, the speed with which the processor can perform these tasks is amazing and allows it to work through intricate combinations of instructions to perform very complex operations.

Computer memory can be divided into two categories—auxiliary memory and main memory.

Auxiliary memory consists of devices used by the computer to store data permanently. When needed, the data can be retrieved from these devices.

Typical examples of auxiliary memory are floppy disks, compact disks, and disk drives.

Main memory holds the running program and the results of the computer's intermediate calculations. It is also referred to as RAM or Random Access Memory.

Main memory is where a program, or parts of a program currently executing, is stored. It also holds much of the data being manipulated by the program. Examples of data could be the wind speed in different parts of a simulated tornado or the current location of a race car in a car game application. C# conveniently allows the programmer to name the data values of the program and simply refer to the values by their name. For example, he or she could call the tornado wind speed `windSpeed` or the car location `carLocation`. Thus, most of the time, the programmer is not exposed to the underlying mechanisms of main memory; it is all taken care of by C#. However, the programmer must, to a limited degree, still decide how these values are represented by main memory to write a valid program. Furthermore, if appropriately done, he or she can design leaner and faster programs. Consequently, the nature of the main memory discussed shortly consequently contains important aspects for you to understand.

The Nature of Main Memory

The main memory contains millions of tiny electrical circuits. The circuits are like light switches in that they can be in one of two states—1 for "on" or 0 for "off." This two-stateness originates from the relative ease with which physical devices containing just two stable states can be designed and manufactured.

At the machine level of the computer, it is only possible to do the following 3 things:

- Set a circuit to 1
- Set a circuit to 0
- Check the state of a circuit

These very primitive operations might seem too restrictive to allow the computer to perform complicated tasks such as word processing and playing games. However, the great advantage of main memory is its astonishing speed and the ability to assign various meanings to individual or groups of circuits.

To illustrate how you can use just one circuit (either 1 or 0) to contain important information, consider a computer game with two difficulty levels—Novice and Advanced. When the user starts the game, the program asks whether the user wants to play at the Novice or Advanced level. If the user chooses Novice, the computer will, if programmed accordingly, set a specific circuit to 0. If the user chooses Advanced, the circuit will be set to 1. So whenever the running program needs to know the current difficulty level during a game (maybe to determine whether your enemy in the game should be good at martial arts or not), the computer can check the state of the circuit.

By applying other interpretations to the state of a circuit, any meaning can be assigned to it by the program. Other examples could be connected (1) or not connected (0) to the network, ready (1) or not ready (0), underlined (1) or not underlined (0), bold (1) or not bold (0).

New Term: Bit

A *bit* is a circuit or a digit that can have exactly two values, such as 1 and 0.

So far, I have explained how concepts with only two states can possibly be represented. Far more complex information, such as a number like 6574635, or a sentence such as "This sentence is more complex." also needs to be represented in the main memory. Let's see how the numbers 0, 1, 2, 3 can be represented in the main memory. To represent a number, we form a group of several circuits and combine their states. In this case, we need to combine two circuits and then decide on the interpretation, as shown in Figure 1.2. It is important to notice that the interpretation is arbitrary and not necessarily calculated. Consequently, we could have written 20 instead of 3 in the lower-right square of the figure but, because we have decided to represent 0, 1, 2 and 3, stick to 3 for the moment.

FIGURE 1.2
Representing 0, 1, 2, and 3 with 2 bits.

State of circuit 1	State of circuit 2	Interpretation
0	0	0
0	1	1
1	0	2
1	1	3

When circuit 1 is 0 and circuit 2 is 0, we have decided the value to be 0 and so forth.

The computer program could easily apply another interpretation representing, for example, four colors, such as yellow, red, blue, and green.

How many numbers can we represent with 3 circuits? Figure 1.3 shows us the different combinations.

FIGURE 1.3
Representing 0, 1, 2, 3, 4, 5, 6, and 7 with 3 bits.

State of circuit 1	State of circuit 2	State of circuit 3	Interpretation
0	0	0	0
0	0	1	1
0	1	0	2
0	1	1	3
1	0	0	4
1	0	1	5
1	1	0	6
1	1	1	7

By involving more circuits and changing the interpretations of the states of the circuits, it is possible to represent any number, letter, color, and so on that we want.

The Number Systems

The system of 1s and 0s used by computer hardware internally to represent numbers requires a new way for us humans to think about numbers. Suddenly, the symbols 1, 0 (10) inside the computer at the machine level are not equal to the number of fingers we have on our two hands; they merely represent the number of legs on a human, if interpreted as in the previous example. We were taught the fundamentals of arithmetic at an early age and most of us do not question the meaning of 10 anymore. Our ingrained way of thinking about 10 assumes two things:

- The presence of the 10 digits: 0, 1, 2, 3, 4, 5, 6, 7, 8, 9. Our number system is for that reason called ***base 10*** or the ***decimal number system***. 10 (as in base 10) can also be found by adding one to the highest digit (9).
- Each position in which a digit is written has a specific ***positional value***. For example, in the decimal number 853, we say that 3 is written in the ones position, five is written in the tens position, and 8 is written in the hundreds position. Accordingly, we read it eight hundred and fifty three.

The number system used by the computer is called the ***binary number system*** or ***base 2*** because only two digits (0 and 1) are used to represent various numbers. Appendix D, "Number Systems," provides a detailed discussion of the binary number system.

Consider the binary number 1010100001. By applying the positional values as described in Appendix D, we can convert this number to base 10:

$1x2^9+0x2^8+1x2^7+0x2^6+1x2^5+0x2^4+0x2^3+0x2^2+0x2^1+1x2^0 = 673$

1010100001 has a relatively large number of digits compared to its base-10 counterpart.

In general, binary numbers tend to be considerably longer than their corresponding decimal numbers. Consequently, programmers manipulating numbers at the machine level find it very cumbersome to work with base 2 numbers. Luckily, it is possible to abbreviate binary numbers in a convenient manner using two other number systems called the ***octal number system (base 8)*** and the ***hexadecimal number system (base 16)***.

For a more detailed discussion of the octal and hexadecimal number systems and how to abbreviate binary numbers, please see Appendix D, "Number Systems."

Bytes

To keep track of the data stored in memory, the computer needs to know what is stored where. This is facilitated in main memory through a very long list of numbered locations called ***bytes***. Each byte contains a list of eight bits so, instead of the 2 and 3 bits shown in Figures 1.2 and 1.3, we now are dealing with the equivalent of eight circuits. How many different numbers can then be represented by 1 byte? This is one of the questions at the end of the chapter.

One byte is limited to store data, such as relatively small numbers or a restricted set of characters. If larger numbers or texts with many characters need to be stored, the computer provides the necessary memory space by grouping together several adjacent bytes.

An ***address*** is attached to each byte and used by the computer to locate a particular byte when its data needs to be recovered. In the case of several adjacent bytes holding one piece of larger data (such as a large number or a string of text) as mentioned previously, these bytes are considered to have only one single memory location, represented by the address of the first byte in this group of bytes. Figure 1.4 illustrates how bytes can be positioned in the main memory of a typical computer.

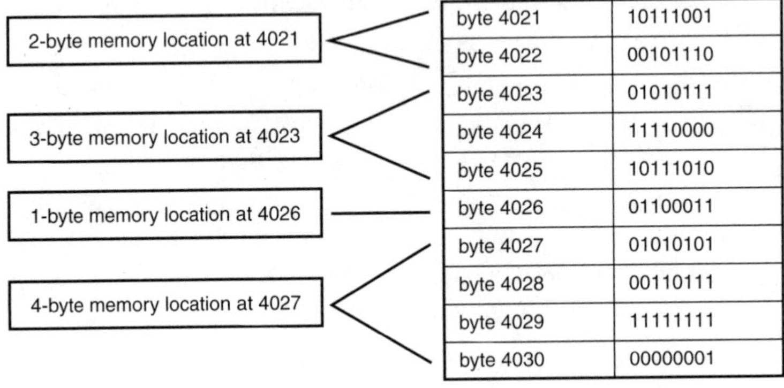

FIGURE 1.4
Bytes and their locations.

The memory locations and their boundaries are determined by the software running on the computer, so they are not directly influenced by the hardware. In Chapter 2 and Chapter 3, "A Guided Tour Through C#: Part I," I will introduce the idea of a ***named variable*** as a convenient means of referring to specific locations in memory. This enables us to abstract away from the arcane memory addresses and allows us to give meaningful names to the data we are working with in our programs. For example, to represent a population size inside a program, we can simply call this size `populationSize` at our convenience instead of having to write something similar to "4 bytes at location 4027."

Files

Equipped with the knowledge of bits and bytes, let us return to the permanent auxiliary memory for a moment. This memory stores large collections of bits called *files* on the various storage devices mentioned earlier (floppy disks, hard disks, and so on). Each file usually has an arbitrary name (for example, `MyDocument`) and an extension that indicates the type of file we are dealing with (such as .doc, indicating a document written in the Microsoft Word processor). So, a fully qualified name could look like `MyDocument.doc`.

Files can contain almost any sort of data. Examples could be an image, a sound file, a computer program, a letter, or just a list of numbers. Various conventions are used to encode and interpret the contents of a file similar to the interpretations used for bits and bytes in main memory discussed earlier. Conventions you might have encountered are MPEG (extension `.mpg`) for storing multimedia files, JPEG for storing images (extension `.jpg`).

A specific type of file you will encounter frequently in this book is a text file with the extension `.cs` (for `c` sharp). These files contain C# source code. A source code file could, for example, be called `MyProgram.cs`. Files are frequently arranged into groups of files called *folders* or *directories*. These help the user organize files into coherent groups.

Software

Computer programming is essentially about constructing the software that bridges the gap between the very primitive operations of the hardware presented in the previous section (which are pretty useless to the typical computer user) and programs like word processors and spreadsheet programs that feature specialized functionality targeted at various users' specific needs.

Overall Process of Executing a C# Program

What happens when a C# program is running on the computer? Even though C# abstracts away from the underlying hardware, it is obviously still utilizing the functionality of the computers processor and memory systems at some point.

Figure 1.5 depicts the main parts involved to execute a C# program. First, you need to write the C# program and then store it in the auxiliary memory, typically on a hard disk (see 1 in Figure 1.5). For example, your program could be called `MyFirstProgram.cs`. Notice the previously mentioned `.cs` extension that is required for all C# program files.

FIGURE 1.5
The elements of executing a C# program.

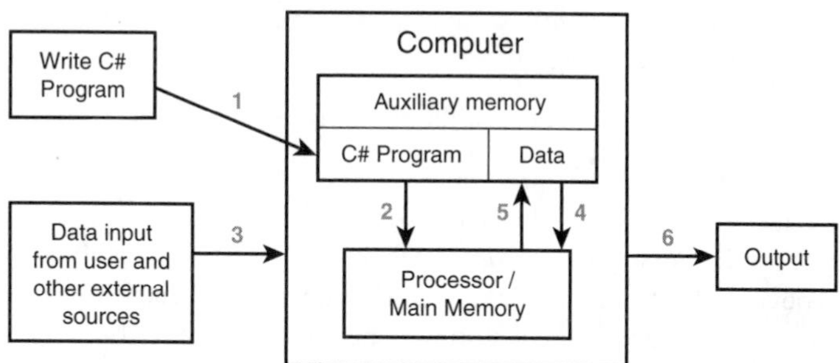

When prompted, the program or the parts of the program that are to be executed will be loaded into the main memory (2 in Figure 1.5). Through a complex set of operations, the main memory will now collaborate with the processor and execute the operations specified by the program. This is also referred to as *running* or *executing* the program.

The lifeblood of the program is the data that it processes. It can get the data from the user (3 in Figure 1.5) in the form of keys pressed on the keyboard and mouse movements and clicks or from other external sources, such as networks and the Internet. Data is also often read in from files kept in the auxiliary memory of the computer (4 in Figure 1.5). For example, if the C# program is a word processor, this data could be the unfinished letter you stored yesterday (5 in Figure 1.5) while you were working on the word processor. When you need to finish it today, you request to have it loaded back into the word processing C# program. After you are finished with the letter, you then store it back into the auxiliary memory. The computer provides output (6 in Figure 1.5) all along by showing the letters of the document on the screen. Perhaps you want to print out the letter, the output is then provided through a printer.

The Operating System

There is one important piece of software not mentioned in the previous discussion—the operating system. Examples of commercial operating systems are Windows 2000, Linux, DOS, MacOS (Apple), and UNIX. Even though they are very different, they all have important things in common. The operating system is involved in most operations performed by the computer. In fact, the operating system conducts the entire operation of the computer. It is the first program to be loaded into the computer when it is turned on, and it is so closely fused with the computer that it is easy to mistake it as *being* the computer. Examples of particular operations performed by the operating system are the retrieval of a program prompted by a command (in the form of a mouse click on an icon or a command typed in with the keyboard) and the initiation of a program's execution. In this scenario, the retrieval and initiation are closely controlled by the operating system.

Programming Languages and Compilers

The first computers manufactured in the 1940s were monstrosities to program. They were programmed with ***machine language*** that contained sequences of bits directly controlling a processor's simple operations. Programming on the level of bits is an enormously time consuming and tedious task. The following is a fraction of a program that calculates the greatest common divisor of two integers:

27bdffd0 afbf0014 0c1002a8 00000000 0c1002a8 afa2001c 8fa4001c and so on, and so on.

Yes, I agree—total gobbledygook. As you can imagine, programmers soon began to yearn for a less machine-like, more human-like language to increase their productivity. This resulted in the so-called ***assembly languages*** where one encounters slightly more human commands such as `move`, `getint`, and `putint`. Even though assembly languages were slightly easier to read and understand, there was still a one to one correspondence between them and machine language. The programmer still had to think in terms of low-level processor operations. As computers evolved and the demand for more complex programs increased, programmers began to wish for a totally machine-independent language. In the mid-1950s, this resulted in probably the first high-level language called FORTRAN. It was suddenly possible to articulate numerical computations by expressions resembling mathematical algebra such as the following:

```
AVERAGE = (20 + 30) / 2
```

which calculates the average of 20 and 30.

The popularity of these abstractions away from the machine language was immense, and many other high-level languages soon followed. Today, the number of high-level languages is estimated to more than two thousand. One of the latest additions is C#.

No matter how far we abstract away from the basic computer operations with various high-level languages, we still need to end up with machine language code comprehensible (and hence executable) by the computer hardware. Systems programs called ***compilers*** have traditionally performed the job of turning a high-level language into low-level machine language.

Figure 1.6 is a simple illustration of how the source code of a typical high-level language is turned into an executable program. The text you write that contains high-level language instructions is called a ***source program*** or ***source code***. In the case of C#, this source code is kept in a `.cs` file. To turn the source code into machine language, you need a compiler to compile it. The result of this compilation is called an ***executable program*** consisting of machine language.

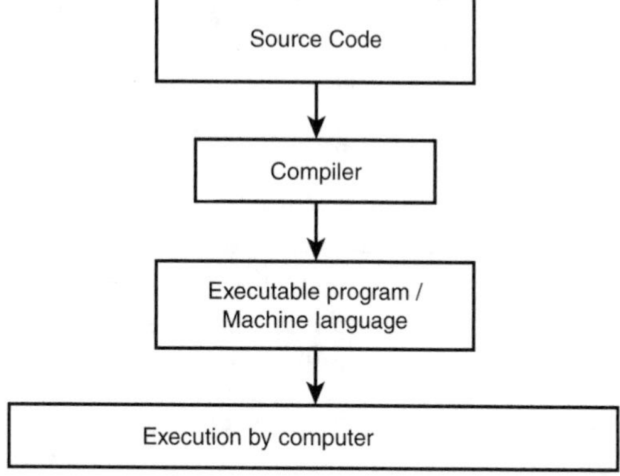

FIGURE 1.6
The traditional compiling process.

Note

The word *program* is often used to describe two different things—an entire executable program *or* a piece of source code. In this book, I will strive to use either *source code*, *source program*, or simply *code* to denote a piece of source code. An executable program will be referred to as an *executable program, application*, or just a *program*.

Introducing .NET

Before continuing with the discussion of C# and its execution environment, we need to introduce an important technology closely related to C# called .NET (pronounced dot net).

While C# refers to a language with a set of rules for how to write a source program, .NET is somewhat harder to identify. .NET is an umbrella term for many important services provided during the construction and execution of a C# program. In fact, C# is totally dependent on .NET and, consequently, many of the features and constructs of C# can be traced directly back to .NET. The following are a few important services provided by .NET:

- .NET provides the means to execute the instructions contained in a C# program. This part of .NET is called an ***execution engine***.
- .NET helps promote a so-called ***type safe*** environment (more about this in Chapter 6, "Types Part I: The Simple Types") where only certain types of values meant for specific memory locations will be allowed. Metaphorically speaking, .NET ensures the matching of triangular shapes with triangular holes and round shapes with round holes.

- .NET frees the programmer from the tedious and error-prone job of managing the computer memory used by the program.
- .NET provides a secure environment, attempting to make life harder for computer hackers and their like.
- The .NET Framework holds a library containing a vast amount of pre-written program parts that you can make use of in your programs. The .NET Framework library can save you vast amounts of time when constructing various parts of a program. You are, in effect, reusing program components already constructed and thoroughly tested by professional programmers at Microsoft.
- Getting a program ready for use (also called *deployment*) has been simplified in .NET.
- .NET provides cross language interoperability. Any language targeting .NET can seamlessly work together with other languages of this platform. At the time of this writing, about 15 languages are being ported to the .NET platform. Because the same .NET runtime is used to execute all languages targeting the .NET platform, the .NET runtime is often called the *Common Language Runtime (CLR)*.

A program constructed with the intent of reuse is called a component or a software *component*.

These points only represent a superficial listing of a platform featuring many state-of-the-art technologies.

Compiling C# Source Code in .NET

The traditional compilation process for converting the source code of high-level languages into executable programs as described in the previous section has several disadvantages. Two of these are discussed next.

Problem 1:

We need a different high-level language compiler for every make of computer because different types of computers have different machine language configurations. Consequently, if you want to run your FORTRAN program on four computers of different makes, you will need four different FORTRAN compilers. Furthermore, whenever a computer manufacturer makes changes to its computer hardware or extends its line of computers for sale, costly and time-consuming compiler adjustments and additions will be necessary.

Problem 2:

Most programmers have a preferred programming language, and many "multilingual" programmers have a preferred programming language for specific kinds of programming tasks. As you gradually get acquainted with the world of programming, you will no doubt encounter quite a few programmers with a nearly religious attachment to their favored languages. This is all very well.

However, a problem appears when programmers with different preferences have to collaborate to write the source code for one single project. Perhaps the best solution would be to allow each programmer to use his or her favorite language, but this is very difficult when following the compilation process illustrated in Figure 1.6. Different languages represent the same functionality in different ways at the machine level, due in part to different compiler configurations. This, in turn, makes collaboration between different languages impossible.

An attempt has been made to solve this problem by introducing so-called component systems (such as CORBA and COM) that provide standards for the interactions between different parts of a program. Programmer A can then write a component called *X* in, say, a language such as Visual Basic that can interact with Programmer B's component *Y* written in the C++ language.

The commercial success of these component systems has been enormous. However, apart from introducing several other problems, the components involved in the program cannot interact on the same detailed level as if all parts of the program were written in the same language.

C# and .NET provide interesting solutions to the two problems described. Let's have a look at the overall elements involved when compiling under .NET, as shown in Figure 1.7.

FIGURE 1.7
The .NET compilation process.

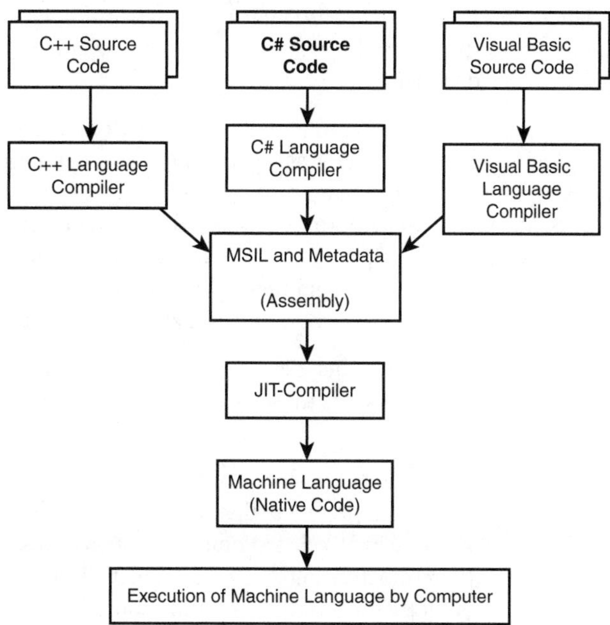

First, notice that two other languages (C++ and Visual Basic) are displayed in Figure 1.7. So whether we write in C# or in any other language targeted at .NET, the programming does not change the overall process of compiling under .NET. After the source code is written, we still need to compile it, but, as you can see, the source code is compiled into another language called *Microsoft Intermediate Language (MSIL)* instead of compiling into machine language right away. In fact, all language compilers targeting the .NET platform will need to compile into this ***intermediate language***. The idea of an intermediate language is not new. It was already applied in connection with another high-level language, called Pascal, by utilizing what the designers called a "UCSD Pascal p-machine." Similar ideas are also being used in languages like Smalltalk and Java.

As the name implies, MSIL is somewhere in between high-level languages and machine languages (also called ***native code***), allowing it to be efficiently translated into machine language by a so-called ***JIT-Compiler*** (Just in Time-Compiler). The output from a JIT-Compiler is similar to that of a conventional compiler, but the JIT-Compiler uses a slightly different strategy. Instead of using memory and time to convert all of the MSIL, it only converts the parts that are actually needed during execution. So in effect, the code is compiled, on the run, and the unused parts of the MSIL code (this can be a substantial amount) did not waste the JIT-Compiler's time.

So what are some of the advantages of the .NET architecture? Until now, we only seem to have complicated matters. Well, by inserting the MSIL between the high-level language and the machine language, we have essentially decoupled those two languages. The MSIL remains unchanged, no matter on what kind of computer system it is being used. The JIT-Compiler is the only part that needs to be changed or adjusted when changes in the computer system are being made. Each computer will have its own JIT-Compiler that translates from MSIL to machine language suited for that particular computer configuration. As a result, we only ever need to compile our high-level languages into one, non-changing language. This solves *Problem 1* mentioned earlier.

Now, for a simplified explanation to how Problem 2 is solved. Notice the ***Metadata*** next to the MSIL in Figure 1.7. Metadata is emitted by the high-level language compiler and contains detailed descriptions of all the elements in your source code. Metadata is also defined as data about data. So detailed is this information that source code from other high-level languages will be able to utilize your source code as if it was written in exactly the same language. It is now possible for a Visual Basic programmer to work with a C++ programmer and a C# programmer on the same project, collaborating as if all were using just one single language.

Metadata and MSIL add many other exciting features to C# and .NET in addition to the two already mentioned. We will discuss those aspects when relevant as we advance through the book.

It is important to know about the existence of MSIL, but in your everyday programming, you are not directly aware of MSIL's presence. If you use the compiler suggested in this book, you will typically give two commands, one to compile your program (into MSIL/Metadata) and one to run the program (thereby activating the JIT-Compiler). Running the program can just be viewed as an execution of the final output from the compilers. The MSIL is not exposed during this process.

Summary

In this chapter, you have learned about basic concepts related to computer hardware and software. We have also discussed some of the ways C# and .NET aims to solve previous programming problems and some of the exciting new possibilities these technologies present to us.

The following are the important points covered in this chapter:

A programming language like C# allows the programmer to tap into the universality of the computer and write a diverse set of applications that can be used by an end user. A program bridges the gap between the primitive set of operations performed by the computer hardware and useful applications.

C# is an object-oriented programming language that is highly suited to deal with complex programming tasks. It strikes an optimal balance between simplicity and expressiveness, while based on proven useful concepts. C# is tightly connected with .NET.

Main memory consists of long lists of numbered locations called bytes. Each byte contains 8 circuits. A circuit can be 0 or 1. Understanding the binary system helps us understand how numbers are manipulated by the main memory.

When a program is executed, the computer's main memory holds the part of the program that currently is being executed together with the data being manipulated by the program. The end user interacts with this process through input and output devices.

Despite the limited set of basic operations that the circuits can be engaged in, the main memory's high speed and its ability to interpret groups of circuits in different ways makes the computer the ultimate manipulator of abstract object-oriented worlds.

Early, low-level programming languages were difficult to use because they were based on how the hardware worked not on how the programmer reasoned. Today, compilers perform the tedious task of turning a program written in a high-level language like C# into machine code.

.NET provides a host of important services during the construction and execution of a C# program.

.NET uses a common language, called MSIL, that all languages working under .NET must compile too, before it is compiled to machine code. This decoupling between hardware and high-level language allows for language interoperability and dissolves rigid relationships between high-level language compilers and hardware.

Review Questions

1. Give a reason why computers pervade our society today.
2. What are the differences between being a computer programmer and an end user?
3. Give a brief description of how the world is viewed from an object-oriented programmer's point of view.
4. What are the two basic parts of a computer?
5. What is software?
6. How does the computer user interact with the computer?
7. What is a processor?

8. Name the two computer memory categories. Briefly describe each one of them.
9. What data would be involved in calculating the average monthly rainfall in New York during year 2000?
10. What are bits and bytes?
11. How many different numbers can be represented by one byte?
12. How does the main memory organize the data it is storing?
13. What are files used for?
14. What is a source program?
15. How can you recognize a C# source program file?
16. Describe what a compiler does?
17. List a few of the services provided by .NET
18. What is MSIL? How does it improve the .NET architecture over previous architectures?

CHAPTER 2

YOUR FIRST C# PROGRAM

You will learn about the following in this chapter:

- The fundamental process of software development and related basic techniques
- Algorithms and how their set of exact instructions can be represented with the help of a popular notation form called pseudocode.
- The three types of errors you will meet as a computer programmer
- Essential concepts of object-oriented programming and how this paradigm attempts to solve programming problems related to earlier programming styles
- Source code reuse along with component-oriented programming and how C# and .NET facilitates these important concepts.
- The assembly and why it is a core concept in .NET
- Why you should reuse the vast amount of functionality and expertise collected in the .NET Framework class library
- How the most important computer language predecessors of C# have evolved over the past sixty years
- How C# and .NET relate and their overall design goals
- How to write, compile, and execute a specific C# program

Software Development

Because programming is a creative process that involves human intuition and judgment, it is difficult to prescribe an exact procedure to follow when developing software. Fortunately, many useful techniques and principles have evolved over the past 50-odd years that are followed by most developers to write better programs with fewer errors in a shorter amount of time. These techniques, some of which are briefly presented in the next section, are valid for most high-level languages, including C#.

The Software Development Process

A *software development process* is a set of activities where the end product is a computer program. Numerous distinct activities have been identified in the last 20 years as being part of the software development process. We will just discuss the most important steps in this section.

1. Software Specification—Defining the requirements of the software.
2. Software Design—Conception or contrivance of a method for turning the software specification into an operational program. It links the software specification with writing the exact program text in a high-level language such as C#.
3. Writing the Software—Constructing and writing the text, which constitutes the source code of the program.
4. Software Validation and Debugging—The software must be validated to ensure that it does what was defined during the software specification phase.

These steps should be performed in the sequence presented here. However, it is often necessary to go back to a previous step before continuing. Let's take a closer look at each step.

1. Software Specification—

   Why do we need software requirements? First, if we don't know what the program is supposed to do, how can we even start thinking about ways to implement it? It is the first step toward a solution. Often, one will find the solution hidden inside the specification. There are many other reasons for software specifications, whose discussion is beyond the scope of this book.

   An example of a very simple software specification could be, "The program must be able to calculate the average of two numbers."

2. Software Design—Software design can involve many diverse activities, depending on the size and nature of a project. A large project might have several stages as shown in the following:

   2a. *Division of the overall project into various subsystems*—Examples of subsystems are user interfaces, report formatters, and database interfaces. Note that the programs we construct in this book are too small to involve this stage. Thus, every program here can be regarded being part of a subsystem already.

   2b. *Segregating each subsystem into modules*—The term module is a flexible word that has different meanings in different contexts. Here, a *module* is defined as a collection of data and routines that can act on that data. A module will have a host of suitable services assigned to it that, when collaborating with the other modules in the subsystem, will be able to fulfill its requirements.

   A routine generally only has a very narrow purpose. It consists of a set of specific instructions executed one after the other. Examples of routines would be "Find the square root of a number." or "Find the largest number in this list of numbers." Various high-level languages use different terms, such as *procedure*, *function*, and *subroutine* for this concept. In the C# world, a routine is referred to as a *method*.

2c. *Identify the data and methods in each module*—The services offered by the module are divided into suitable subparts that are small enough to be accomplished by one method. Each subpart will then be assigned a method and, consequently, each method will get its functionality specified. Finally, the designers identify the data that must be represented by this module.

2d. *Internal method design*—This design level is usually left to the individual programmer. Algorithms are constructed here to accomplish very specific tasks. The first actual valid statements might be written here using a language such as C#.

At this point, we are moving into or getting very close to the next step—writing the software.

New Term: Algorithm

An algorithm is a set of exact instructions used to solve a problem. The instructions must be expressed accurately so that by following them blindly, as the computer would, the desired result is still accomplished.

3. Writing the Software—The actual statements are written in C#. This part of the design process is always needed on projects of any size and nature.
4. Software validation and debugging—Various tests should be performed on the program, during and after writing the program, to make sure that it does what it is intended to do. You are, in effect, detecting the errors in the program. This activity is referred to as *testing*.

   To write a correct program, you need to be careful with the design of all program elements and of the translation into C# source code. However, unless you are superhuman, errors (also called *bugs*) tend to creep into programs from many unexpected angles. Eliminating bugs in a program is called *debugging*. Sometimes, the terms testing and debugging are used interchangeably but, strictly speaking, this is incorrect.

Small informal projects, such as many of the programs you will encounter throughout this book, will often involve only design levels 3 and 4 and can be done while the programmer sits in front of the computer. Design might then be taking place inside the head of the programmer, be in the form of scribbling a few diagrams on a piece of paper, and/or looking up a few standard algorithms in a textbook.

Note

Regardless of the project size, careful design will always be beneficial to the software construction process and the end result.

Note

In the OOP discussions of this book, the term object refers to a module; a method to a routine and instance variables are part of the data.

Now we'll look at some of the concepts often encountered by programmers during the design of algorithms. These will be particularly useful when we introduce the first concepts of C#.

Algorithms and Pseudocode

The hardest part of designing a program using a language, such as C#, is not trying to work out how to express a specific algorithm in C#. The hardest part is to construct the algorithm itself. Often, complex algorithms are the result of many years of research. The majority of those complex algorithms could be implemented by a proficient C# programmer in a few hours or days.

Expressing algorithms is often facilitated through a "language" called pseudocode. To illustrate what pseudocode is and how it can be a useful way to express algorithms, consider the following situation.

An alien, from planet Blipos, is visiting earth for a brief period of time. He needs to know how the average of an arbitrary list of numbers is calculated. This will allow him to perform a few very important calculations on his spaceship computer so he can take off again. The computer is to be programmed in his favorite language, C#.

His mind, being between a man's and a machine's, is a bit peculiar. He understands English but will only understand instructions if they are exactly to the point. He is not able to make any assumptions. Phrases such as "Sum up the numbers and then divide by the amount of numbers in the list." are too vague. Determining the "amount of numbers in the list" would be one of his problems in this particular case. His big advantage, though, is the ease with which he converts precisely given instructions into C# source code.

How can we best explain to the alien the method of finding the average of any list of numbers? The following shows what we might tell him.

"Here are the steps to calculate the average of a list of numbers. Please start with step 1 and follow the steps in the sequence they are presented. You must remember to repeat the sequence: 3.a, 3.b, 3.c and 3.d for every number in the list, as stated in 3."

1. Take a piece of paper and a pencil.
2. Write two zero's on the paper, one on the left side and one on the right. Call the left zero Sum and the right zero ListSize.
3. Repeat the following sequence (3a-3d) *for each* number in the list:

   3.a. Add the number to the Sum on the paper.

   3.b. Replace the old Sum on the paper with the result of 3.a.

   3.c. Add 1 to the ListSize.

   3.d. Replace the old ListSize on the paper with the result of 3.c.

4. Divide the Sum by the ListSize and write this number down.

5. Read the number you wrote down in 4. It is the average.
6. End of calculation.

When the alien receives these instructions, he quickly tries out the algorithm on this simple list of numbers {1,2,3,4,5} because he knows by heart that the average of this particular list is 3. He grabs a piece of paper. Figure 2.1 shows what he wrote.

FIGURE 2.1
How the alien calculated the average of {1, 2, 3, 4, 5}.

Sum		ListSize
~~0~~		~~0~~
~~1~~		~~1~~
~~3~~		~~2~~
~~6~~		~~3~~
~~10~~		~~4~~
15		5
	3	

To get a good first-hand understanding of what it "feels" like to be a computer executing an algorithm, pretend for a moment that you are the alien and choose a short list of numbers. Follow each step of the algorithm given to the alien blindly and find the average of the numbers.

The test performed by our alien doesn't prove the correctness of the algorithm, but it seems to satisfy the alien, who, with a big smile, runs back to the spaceship where it is easy for him to convert the algorithm into C# source code. It is then fed into the space shuttle computer.

Five minutes later, our alien happily leaves earth in his spaceship and continues his extraterrestrial voyage.

The algorithm presented to the alien consists of a mixture of English and a high-level programming language like C#. Often, programmers (who are sometimes accused of having a thinking process somewhere between that of a man and a machine) use this "language" to express algorithms. It is referred to as *pseudocode*.

Note

Generally, the steps of the pseudocode are processed one after the other in the order in which they are written.

The next phase after constructing the pseudocode is to convert it into C# source code consisting of instructions to the computer that follow the language rules of C#. This is a relatively easy task, because each step of the pseudocode more or less becomes one C# instruction, and because the instructions are written in the same sequence as their corresponding pseudocode steps.

Note

Generally, the instructions of the C# source code are executed one after the other by the computer, in the order in which they are written.

Most algorithms need to store some intermediate results, such as Sum and ListSize in our alien example. When the algorithm is translated into C#, those intermediate results are referred to as *variables* and will be stored in the computer's main memory during execution instead of on the paper in the example. I will introduce variables further in Chapter 3, "A Guided Tour Through C#: Part I."

The Three Different Types of Errors

Our alien was able to take off with the spaceship in this case. But what if he was unable to leave due to an unknown error. Well, with a laser gun pointed at our heads by an enraged alien, we would have to consider several possibilities quickly. By knowing the three different types of errors described below, we would certainly be able to locate the problem faster.

- *Syntax error*—Refers to a grammatical mistake in the C# source code. There are very strict rules for how to write a C# program. These rules form the grammar for C#. This grammar is equivalent to the grammar of the English language, but much more concise. The grammar rules for a programming language are called the *syntax* of the language.

  It is easy to make a syntax error. Even omitting a semicolon when expected will cause a syntax error.

  During its compilation process, the C# compiler will look for syntax errors and print error messages on the screen. It will even try to tell you what caused the error and where it thinks the error is located. However, this information is not always correct because the compiler only makes informed guesses.

  A syntax error reported by the spaceship's computer would have been due to a mistake made by the alien when he converted the pseudocode to C# code; in which case, he would owe us an apology for groundless threats.

- *Logic error*—Had there been a mistake in the underlying logic presented with the pseudocode, we would refer to this as a *logic error*. Given that the alien converted all instructions exactly as shown in the pseudocode into a valid C# program without any syntax errors, he would, accordingly and unknowingly, have brought the logic error along into the C# program.

  For example, if line 3.c would mistakenly read "Add 2 to the ListSize," we would get a ListSize twice as big as the correct size and, as a result, end up with a calculated average only half of the correct average. This would most likely be a large enough error to prevent the alien's spaceship from taking off. In this case, we would apologize and plead for mercy.

- *Runtime error*—If the computer detects and reports an error message during the execution of the program, we refer to this as a *runtime error*. In this case, the computer will stop executing the program, and report the type of error along with its approximate location. However, the system might misinterpret the problem in many cases and lead you in the wrong direction.

  A runtime error could be caused by either a logic error or an incorrect conversion into the C# language from pseudocode. Even for our alien friend with his abilities to convert pseudocode into C# code, it would be possible to introduce bugs resulting in runtime errors. For example, the alien might not realize how large the Sum number can get during a specific calculation and, through a declaration in C#, allocate too little main memory for the Sum number. When the Sum number gets larger than this allocated main memory, a runtime error might be reported.

  Hopefully, we would be able to explain this possibility to the alien and save our lives.

Unfortunately, it looks as if we have, in fact, made an error in the pseudocode that could easily cause a runtime error. Consider a scenario where the list of numbers is empty. We then end up with Sum and ListSize being zero, dividing zero by zero in step 4. This is considered an invalid operation by the computer, and you will receive the following message, "The application has generated an exception that could not be handled." Fortunately, all the calculations in the spaceship must have involved lists of one or more numbers for it to take off. But we might not be as lucky next time.

Note

The test performed by the alien of the "average calculating" algorithm by using the list {1,2,3,4,5} seemed to ascertain the correctness of the algorithm. However, we have just seen one instance proving the algorithm to be faulty. This is a good example of how delicate software testing is.

It is impossible to prove that a program is correct simply by testing it. On the other hand, a program can be proven to be incorrect if errors are detected.

Object-Oriented Programming: A First Encounter

OOP and C# cannot be fully understood if studied in a vacuum. They are both part of a vibrant computer science and programming community. The ideas behind their designs are highly influenced by previous programming paradigms and computer languages. By viewing OOP in the light of preceding programming techniques, it is easier to understand its architecture and the problems it attempts to solve. One of the major predecessors to OOP is process-oriented programming.

Process-Oriented Programming and Its Innate Problems

One of the traditional approaches to the design of computer programs has been the *process-oriented* style. It prioritizes the actions performed by a software element highly while the data is kept aside, ready to be manipulated by an action. It implies a series of instructions executed one after the other and will most likely contain numerous branching points where only one of several directions is chosen, depending on specific conditions fulfilled in the program. Each instruction more or less resembles a line of pseudocode, as presented earlier in the alien example, and most instructions manipulate data.

In the old fashioned, process-oriented programs, the data can be reached by all parts of the program, as illustrated in Figure 2.2 and can be accessed by any instruction as needed.

Note

Large parts of the source code written in many object-oriented languages, including C#, are constructed using the same primitive language constructs as those used in process-oriented programming.

This approach is fine for very small projects but, for larger complex programs, the programmer is faced with the formidable task of keeping track of all the different branches belonging to the program because all parts are more or less interconnected. Furthermore, one specific piece of data can be manipulated and changed from all parts of the program. When programming one part of the program, it is difficult to know whether the data you are working with is going to be affected by other parts of the program. The situation will quickly reach chaotic levels (Figure 2.2 already looks pretty chaotic) when several programmers are working together.

Object-Oriented Programming and Its Advantages

How can we attempt to overcome this problem? Well, a typical human way of coping with complexity is to break a problem into simpler pieces. Let's try to break the previous illustration into four smaller, self-contained pieces. The result is displayed in Figure 2.3. We have now separated the whole set of instructions into four separate modules. In the OO world, such modules are called *objects*. The data has also been divided into four pieces so that each object contains only the data on which it acts. The four objects now collaborate to execute the program by sending messages to each other activating each others' sets of instructions and exchanging data. Not only have we now reduced the complexity of the program considerably, we have also created four self-contained modules, each of which can be "taken out" of the program, modified, and "slotted back" again. With relative ease each module can now be created and maintained by a different programmer.

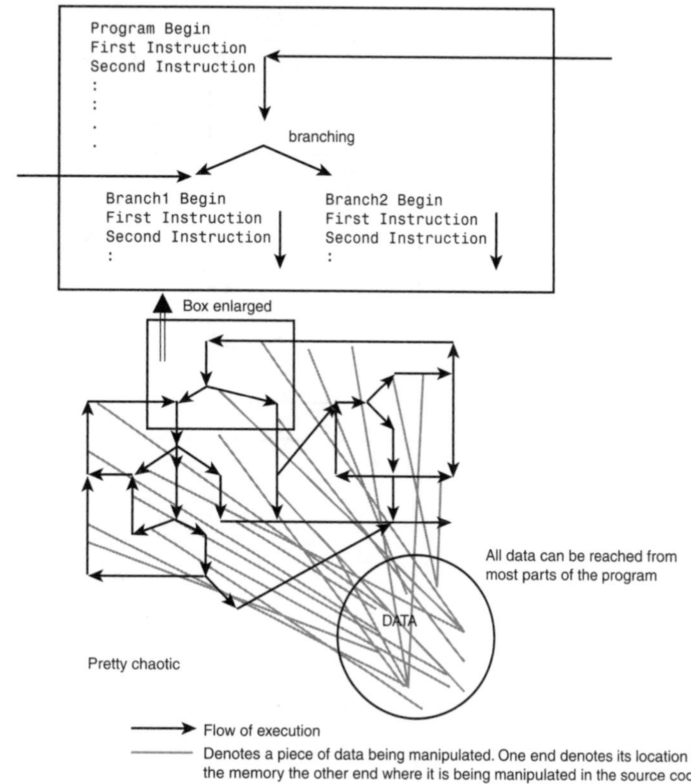
Program Begin
First Instruction
Second Instruction
branching
Branch1 Begin
First Instruction
Second Instruction
Branch2 Begin
First Instruction
Second Instruction
Box enlarged
All data can be reached from most parts of the program
DATA
Pretty chaotic
Flow of execution
Denotes a piece of data being manipulated. One end denotes its location in the memory the other end where it is being manipulated in the source code.
A small part of the flow of execution displayed has been enlarged (at Box enlarged) for illustrative purposes.

FIGURE 2.2
A program.

As you can see, objects are used to combine data with the methods (instructions) operating on the data. In the object-oriented world, data and processes are given equal importance. But how do we know which objects a program should contain? Which data do we need? Which instructions are necessary? To answer these questions we first need to find out what an object is.

We are surrounded by objects in our daily lives. Examples are books, houses, cars, dogs, people, tables, spiders, plates, and cups. Objects are often able to take part in certain actions. A car, for example, is able to "have its door opened," "have its door closed," "have its engine started," "move forward," "accelerate," "turn," and "brake."

Each object interacts with its surroundings and has an impact on other objects. A "person" object reaching out and opening the door of a "car" object, or a "car" object containing a "person" object transporting him or her from point A to point B, are examples of such interactions. The process-oriented methodology would, if representing a program with cars and people, focus on the actions ("open door," "close door," and so one). *Object-oriented programming* (*OOP*), on the other hand, focuses on the "car" object and the "person" object and so it is a methodology emphasizing the objects involved to solve a particular problem.

FIGURE 2.3
Dividing the process-oriented program into self-contained modules.

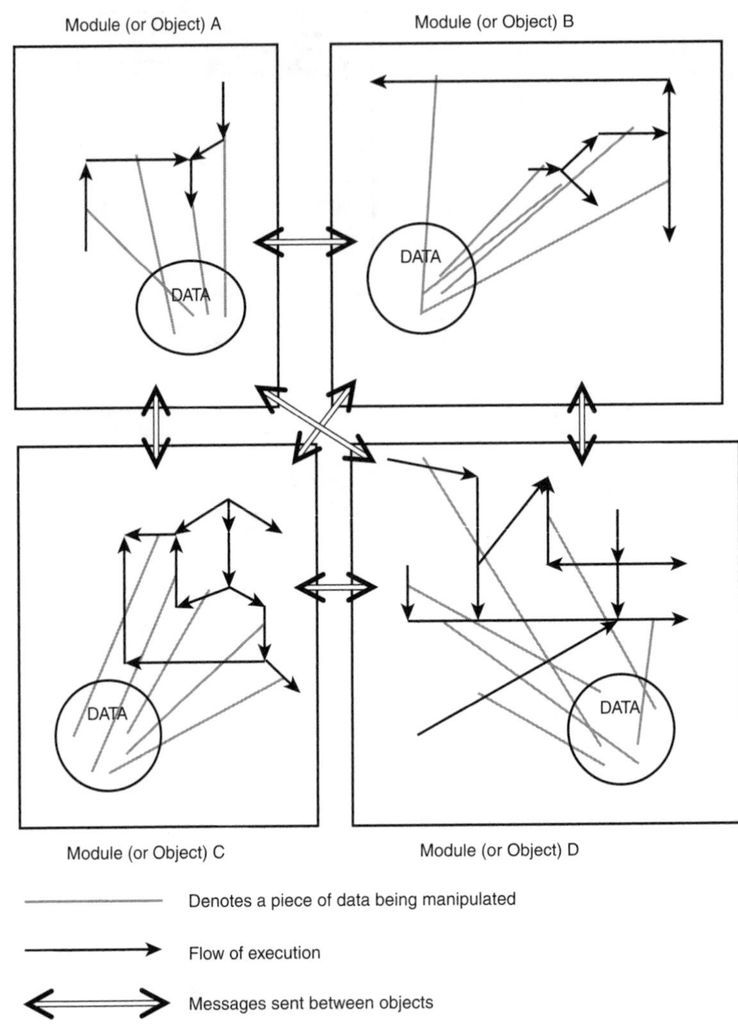

To illustrate these concepts further, consider the following scenario.

A company, Big Finance Ltd., intends to build a ten-story office building and wants to install an elevator system. Big Finance Ltd. would like to determine the size and number of elevators needed. You, an enthusiastic object-oriented (OO) programmer in a small software company, have been asked to design a program that can simulate the elevator system and thereby answer the company's questions.

New Term: Computer Simulation

A computer simulation attempts to mimic the process of a real-world or theoretical system over time inside a computer. By collecting data from this artificial system, a successful simulation will enable us to gain valuable insights into the real system. Before the simulation can be executed, a model of the system must be designed and implemented on the computer. This model is often a simplified version of the real system, but it is relevant to the insights we want to gain.

One of the first computer languages specifically targeted at this problem domain was Simula. Simula is considered to be the first object-oriented programming language because it enabled the programmer to represent abstractions of real-world objects as artificial objects inside a computer simulation program. Simulations and Simula have played an important role in forming the original ideas leading to OOP as we know it today.

To bridge the gap between the real world and the simulation inside the computer, we must first identify the objects involved. This is typically one of the first steps taken in OOP and relates directly to step 2b of the software development process discussed previously, which segregates each subsystem into objects (modules). Try for a moment to imagine the elevator system in action; which objects are involved? Usually, a good strategy is to notice the nouns you encounter when describing a problem because the nouns identify the objects involved. In this example, we can describe the elevator system as follows with the relevant objects on bolded type.

A number of **elevators** are located in a **building** with ten **floors**. Each elevator can access all floors. When a **person** wants to get on an elevator, he or she needs to press the **button** on the floor where he or she is located, and so on.

The next stage relates to step 2c of the software development process where the attributes (data) and behavior (methods) of each module (object) are identified. For example, the "Elevator" object could have the following attributes: a "maximum speed," "current location," "current speed," and "maximum number of people it can contain." Behaviors would include "ascend," "descend," "stop," and "open door." Having identified the relevant attributes and behaviors of each object in the real world, we are ready to represent these in the computer simulation program. To this end, we need to extend our OOP terminology with a few more important terms.

Each part of a C# program that represents an object of the real world is suitably called an *object*.

The relevant attributes of an object of the real world must be represented in the corresponding object of a C# program. These attributes are then referred to as *instance variables*, which are said to represent the *state* of an object. Instance variables are equivalent to the data of Figure 2.3.

The behavior of a real-world object is represented in an object of a C# program in the form of *methods*. Each method contains instructions similar to those making up the "average-calculating" algorithm presented earlier. The methods of an object act on the instance variables of this same object. Methods are equivalent to the flows of execution in Figure 2.3.

Note

An object in an object-oriented program does not have to represent an object of a physical nature. It can also represent objects of a conceptual nature. Examples of conceptual objects are holiday, computer course, voyage, and spirit.

Class is another important OOP term. A *class* specifies the common features (instance variables and methods) of a group of similar objects. Consequently, all objects of the same class have the same instance variables and methods. A programmer is free to choose the instance variables and methods he or she wants to include in a class. These choices all depend on what he or she finds relevant for the particular program he or she is creating.

Let's illustrate the meaning of class with an example. Consider the concept of a car. In the real world, we see, touch, and drive tangible specific cars. Examples could be the blue Volvo in the parking lot with a maximum speed of 100 mph, or the neighbor's black BMW with a maximum speed of 150 mph. Both these tangible cars are referred to as objects.

To enable a description of a particular car object in a C# program, a programmer decides to include the following four instance variables in a class that he or she calls `Car`: `Brand name`, `Location`, `Maximum speed`, and `Current speed` (see Figure 2.4). Notice that Color is not included because the programmer found this irrelevant in his or her program. He or she further chooses to equip the class with the methods called `Open door`, `Close door`, `Move forward`, `Reverse`, `Accelerate`, `Break`, and `Turn`.

Each instance variable of the `Car` class can be viewed as representing an empty box waiting to be filled out in a specific `Car` object. Figure 2.4 shows our two cars from above when described through the instance variable templates provided by the `Car` class.

The content of each instance variable may or may not vary from object to object, as demonstrated in Figure 2.4, but each method defined by the `Car` class is identical in all `Car` objects.

The object, class, and their related concepts are introduced at this early stage merely to let your mind gradually get used to the idea of OOP and also as a preparation for the later elaborate and hands-on presentation of these subjects.

Software Reuse

When you start out writing programs, each program might seem like an entirely separate project, designed and constructed from scratch. However, this is not a prudent way to create computer programs, and it's not the way most programs are created today.

There is a much better alternative—reuse of pre-constructed and pre-tested programs or parts of programs.

A high degree of reuse means far less code to write and allows you to tap into well-designed, well-tested software components written by highly skilled experts.

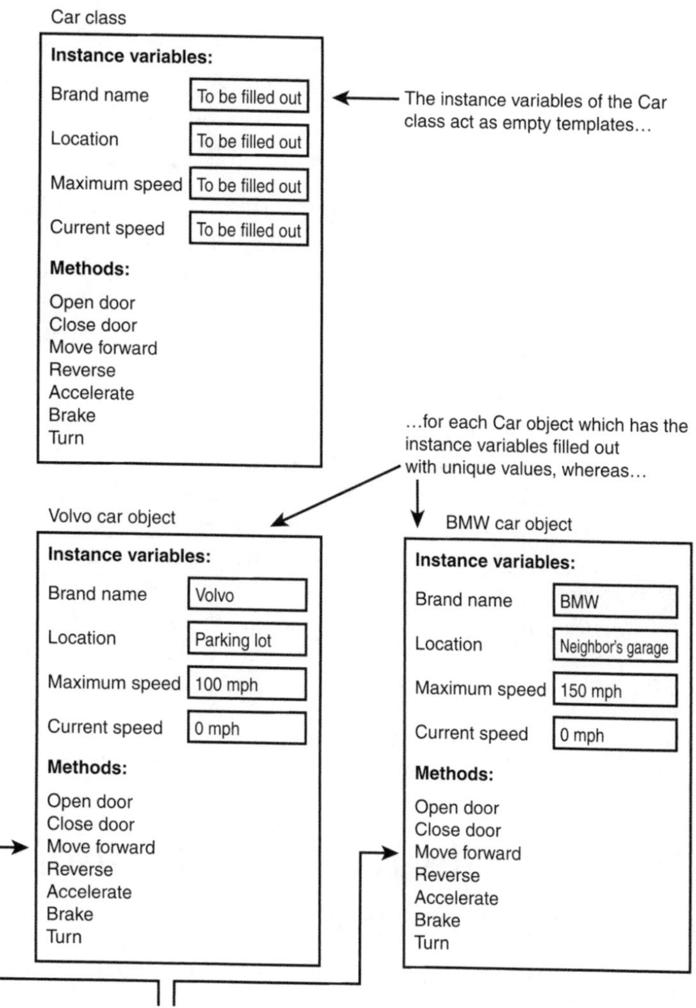

FIGURE 2.4
The class acts as a template for its objects.

Note

Even the simplest C# programs, including the first few you will encounter in this book, rely on software reuse under the hood.

The following example illustrates the value of reuse.

You want to build a simple radio. You can follow two paths to accomplish this task.

You can build every component you need from scratch (resistors, transistors, chips and so on). You will need a lot of knowledge, talent, money, and time to build each of these sophisticated components yourself. In fact, you might not finish the project for many years.

Alternatively, you could purchase the electronic components you need from the local electronics retail shop. For a relatively small cost, you utilize the expertise and big investments involved in manufacturing the components and, before you know it, you will have built a brand new radio.

Software reuse can take many shapes; the following are only two of many:

- *Reuse of individuals lines of code* This is a simple form of reuse and involves copying lines of code from one part of a program to another. However, because the same code is replicated perhaps many places in the same program, the benefits are somewhat limited.
- *The "class" as a unit of reuse* One of the major enticements of an object-oriented language like C# is the elaborate support for code reuse. The `class` in particular turns out to be a very good reuse unit.

  To illustrate this fact, recall the elevator simulation example presented earlier. Due to the success of this project, another company called Very Big Finance Ltd. has requested that we perform a simulation involving a larger building and more elevators. Initially, it seems we have to dispose of the previous project entirely and start from scratch. However, closer scrutiny reveals that the new elevators are more or less unchanged. Due to its object-oriented design, the `Elevator` class from the previous project contains and encapsulates all the attributes and methods needed for it to function as an elevator in this new project. Consequently, it is relatively easy to slot the `Elevator` into our new program and reuse it here as a software component.

Reuse is at the core of .NET and C# programming, and we will frequently return to this topic throughout the book. In fact, this is an important part of the next section.

The Assembly, the Basic Unit of Code Reuse in .NET

The increasing popularity of software reuse has resulted in a new term, *Component-Oriented Programming*, that not only encompasses object-oriented programming, but also has built-in mechanisms facilitating code reuse. To understand the mechanisms provided by .NET to facilitate component-oriented programming, we need to have a look at the nature of classes and code reuse.

Note

Code reuse in this discussion will refer to reuse at the class level as previously described. It can involve more than one class.

1. *Classes often collaborate*—Objects of a class often collaborate with objects of other classes to accomplish their tasks. For example, in the Elevator simulation, the objects of the `Building`, `People`, `Elevator`, `Button`, and so on classes collaborate to run a full simulation.

2. *Categories of classes*—A class can often be said to belong to the same category as another class. For example, one class might enable you to calculate the square root of a number and provide various logarithmic functions. Another class might enable you to calculate certain trigonometric expressions, such as sine and cosine. Both classes can be said to belong to a `Math` category.

3. *Class libraries*—Collecting classes belonging to the same category into the same container makes it easier to browse through large numbers of classes. Such collections of classes are often referred to as *class libraries*.

4. *Classes and resources*—Classes or class libraries often rely on various resources that cannot be regarded as computer programs. Examples of resources are images and sounds.

5. *Classes and files*—Classes and class libraries exist inside the computer and, consequently, must have a physical existence (electrical signals in the memory and processor of the computer). Their dormant existence is in the form of files. When the classes are activated and their functionality used, they are compiled and executed in the main memory and processor of the computer.

The unit of reuse in .NET is called an *assembly*. For that reason, an assembly can be said to be a component. Any program in .NET and C# consists of one or more assemblies. We will see how the assembly accommodates for the nature of classes and their reuse to facilitate component-oriented programming. But first, we need to take a closer look at the assembly itself.

An *assembly* is a logical self-describing package. It consists of MSIL, metadata, and optional resources, such as graphical images. Any program written under .NET, whether it is a component for reuse only or a freestanding executable program, is an assembly.

An assembly can be viewed from two perspectives:

- From the assembly developer's point of view, looking at the assembly from the inside at the detailed source code level.

- From the assembly users point of view, he or she is looking at the assembly from the outside in search for suitable components to be reused in his or her current project.

The Assembly Developer's Viewpoint

Notice that in the compilation process shown in Figure 1.7 (see page 19), you can regard the output from all the language compilers to be assemblies.

An assembly is produced by the C# compiler, as shown shortly in Figure 2.5. The less important parts of this discussion have been dimmed in the figure, but they have been included so you can relate the concepts to the overall compilation and execution process.

Initially, the developer writes the C# source code (see 1 in Figure 2.5). Perhaps he or she wants to reuse the code from other already existing assemblies in the executable program. This is accomplished by instructing the compiler to include the relevant assemblies in the compilation process (see 2 in Figure 2.5). Depending on the programmer's preference, the compilation results in either a Portable Executable File (PE File with extension `.exe`) or a Dynamic Link Library File (DLL File with extension `.dll`). A PE file can be executed as is simply by executing it, but it can also be used as a component for reuse in other programs. On the other hand, a DLL file cannot be executed on its own. It is a component made for reuse only and can only be put into use if slotted into another application.

MSIL is generated during the compilation, and will be part of the assembly.

The compiler further emits a manifest consisting of metadata to represent the assembly. It holds descriptive information about the classes, methods, and resources exposed from within the assembly. This enables programmers to browse through the relevant details of each assembly, allowing him or her to judge whether it is suitable for reuse in his or her project. Each assembly might be dependent on other assemblies. The manifest specifies the assemblies on which its assembly depends. The latter are established in step 2 in Figure 2.5 and maintained in step 2 of Figure 2.6, which appears shortly. The connections illustrated with arrows are specified in the manifest.

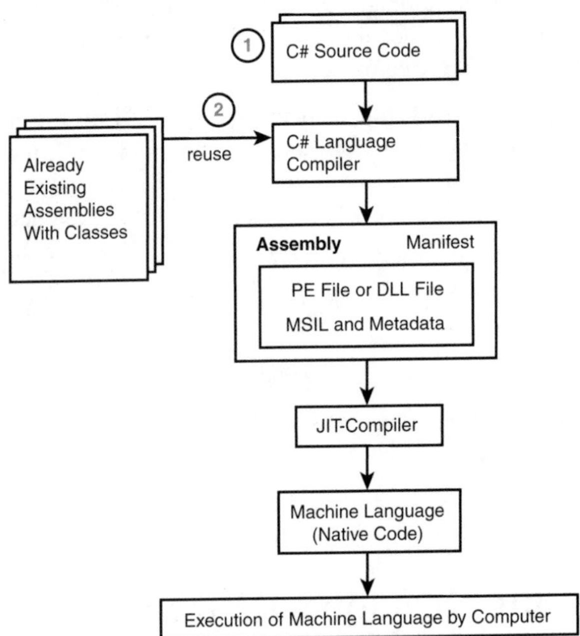

FIGURE 2.5
Creating an assembly by reusing existing assemblies.

Note

An assembly might be dependent on other assemblies to provide its functionality, as mentioned earlier; this is specified in the manifest. But the manifest also indirectly connects its assembly to these assemblies. The term *indirectly* is used here because the connections provided by the manifest are of a descriptive nature.

The Assembly User's Viewpoint

Even though the assembly is based on separate files, it is one logic entity when looked at from the outside.

The manifest allows the runtime to expose classes and their methods to the assembly user (see Figure 2.6). The assembly user can then choose whichever functionality he or she needs to reuse from the assembly.

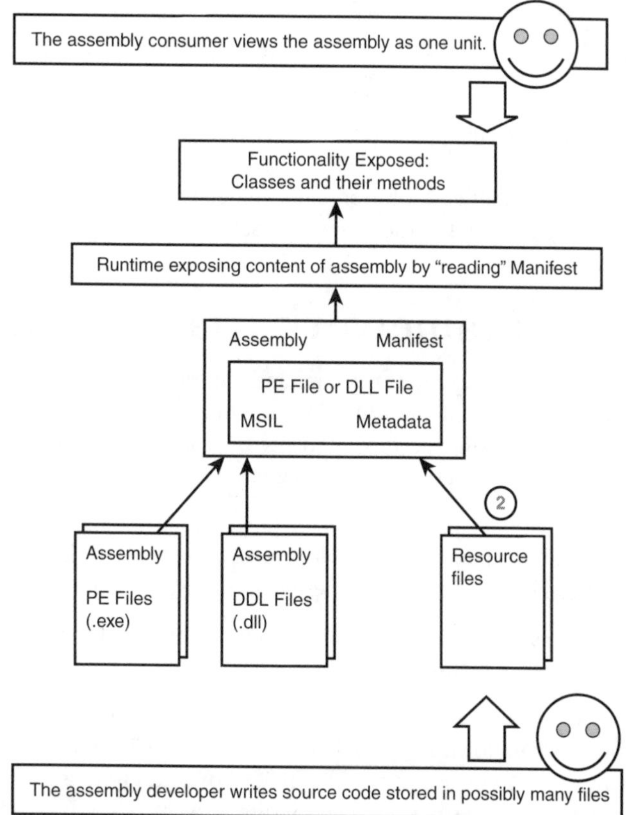

FIGURE 2.6
The views of the assembly user and developer.

The decoupling of the logical entity seen from the outside and the physical elements (files) on the inside gives the developer of the assembly much more freedom in terms of the number of files needed, the sizes of these files, and their location.

We can now begin to appreciate the assembly as the unit of reuse in .NET. Through its self-describing abilities using metadata, it exposes the functionality it provides to its user and further specifies the classes and resources it needs to provide those services.

Let's return to the five points concerning the nature of classes and reuse and look at how assemblies and .NET deal with each of those points.

Re.1 *Classes often collaborate*—Each class residing inside an `.exe/.dll` file can, through the accompanying metadata, expose its functionality and thereby resolve dependencies to other classes.

Re.2 *Categories of classes*—It's easy to form different assemblies containing various categories of classes.

Re.3 *Class libraries*—The container referred to in this point is an assembly in the .NET world. Utilizing the metadata provided in the manifest, it becomes easy to browse through classes, methods, and instance variables of the container (assembly).

Re.4 *Classes and resources*—Simply by including the various resource files needed by the classes of an assembly, they are ready to be used.

Re.5 *Classes and files*—As we have seen, the physical representation of the assembly is extremely flexible. The developer has great flexibility in terms of how many files to use and the content and location of each file. These choices do not affect the view and functionality provided to the assembly user.

The .NET Framework Class Library

Over the years, many types of routines and algorithms have been used over and over again by programmers writing different kinds of programs. For example, it is often necessary to sort a list of numbers or names according to size or alphabetic order. Other examples could be specialized engineering calculations, mathematical calculations, and so on; yes, the list is very long.

Many software companies and developers have recognized this fact. Their response has been to develop class libraries containing these commonly used functions.

The success has been staggering. It is difficult to find an application today that does not contain parts from a reused class library.

Likewise, Microsoft has provided a class library as part of .NET called the .NET Framework class library, also known as the Base Class Library (BCL). It contains many hundreds of classes, providing a vast number of functions. BCL allows you to reuse the expertise of the Microsoft programmers who have designed and written this library. Object-oriented principles, along with the assembly technology and its related concepts, are some of the core mechanisms used in this library that, as a result, provide unprecedented reusability and ease of use.

C# does not specify its own class library. C# is completely fused with the BCL. Consequently, it is not possible to run a C# program without the BCL and the .NET runtime.

All classes written in C# are based on one specific class in the BCL, and many C# constructs are merely representations of classes and their functions in the class library.

It is much easier to access the underlying services of the operating system with the BCL. Rather than having to use arcane commands and complicated expressions, the services are exposed in a much more user-friendly fashion. The comprehensive support for windows-based Graphical User Interface (GUI) development provided by the BCL is one example.

C#: History and Design Goals

Recall how OOP's predecessor—process-oriented programming—provided us with a better understanding for the philosophy behind OOP. By looking at the background for C#, we can similarly appreciate and gain a further understanding for the design goals of this language.

C#'s Background

Before we begin the practical parts of creating a C# program, it is useful to take a look at C#'s roots and design goals.

Currently, there are more than 2000 different high-level languages. Each was designed to fulfill certain requirements related to a specific problem domain and some of them provided inspiration for the designers of C#.

New Term: Problem Domain

The problem domain is the realm or range of a specific set of related problems.

Some examples are computer simulations and nuclear physics.

One of the main incentives to invent new languages has been the growing need to develop complex applications. Users have increasingly demanded feature-packed, easy-to-use programs running on faster, more sophisticated computers. Ironically though, the easier a program is to use, the harder it is to program. Today's user-friendly interfaces, also called GUIs, contain windows, menus, icons, and all the other features most of us now take for granted. These are based on extremely intricate underlying applications.

Note

Progress in the theory of computing, especially in the formal understanding of semantics, modules, program abstractions, and processes, has been a major factor in allowing the evolution of languages to continue.

The meaning or an interpretation of the meaning of a word, sign, sentence, and so on is referred to as *semantics* of a language.

Figure 2.7 presents a genealogical tree of selected high-level languages preceding C#. They might well be considered the most important in terms of popularity or influence on other languages.

The date for each language is approximate and indicates when a broader audience knew about the language.

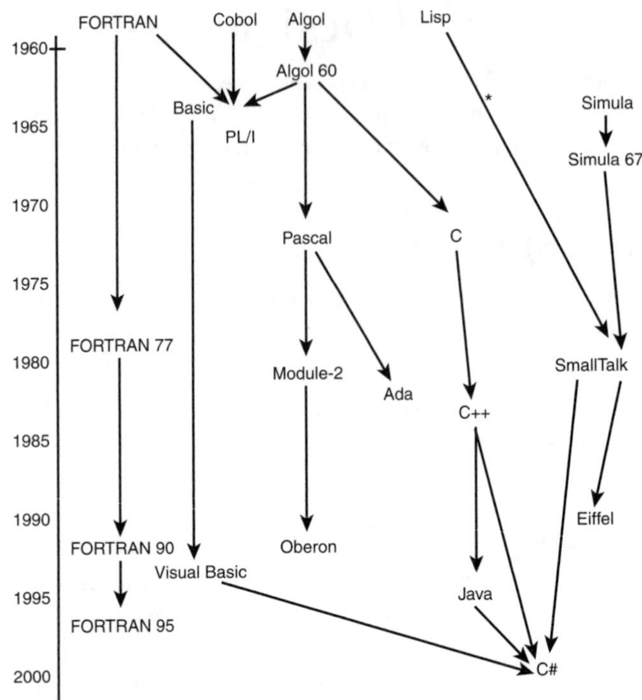

FIGURE 2.7
Genealogical tree of influential high-level languages.

Note

A few technical terms are used in this discussion with which you will probably not be familiar. They are included for completeness and should not interfere with the overall understanding of this section.

According to the designers of C#, a wide spectrum of many different languages have influenced them. In this section, we will only look at a few selected obvious predecessors to C#.

The origins of C# can be traced all the way back to FORTRAN and Algol.

Developed in the 1950s, FORTRAN is the first high-level imperative language. The acronym FORTRAN stands for FORmula TRANslator, reflecting that the main purpose of FORTRAN was to translate mathematical formulas into sequences of assembly language instructions.

Algol 60 was considered a major step forward in clarity and conciseness compared to previous languages. It is *the* original block structured language and has had an enormous influence on most programming languages. The block is also an important aspect of C#. Chapter 3 will introduce you to this concept, which is used in numerous languages today.

The C designers got their basic ideas from the Algol family of languages and were, to a large degree, influenced by C's intended use as a programming language to write the UNIX operating system. Despite this limited initial use, C became one of the most popular imperative languages due to its concise syntax and fast execution.

Pascal was very popular during the 1970s and 1980s, especially in academic circles and for teaching purposes. It was designed in the late 1960s as a response to Algol 68's (a direct descendant of Algol) very complicated design.

FORTRAN, Algol, Pascal, and C are all referred to as *procedural programming languages* and are linked to the process-oriented programming style. A procedural language has at its core a set of procedures that acts upon data. Each procedure contains a set of instructions executed in a step-by-step fashion. The procedures are somewhat separate from the data, as illustrated previously in Figure 2.2. This means that much of the programmer's time is devoted to checking which procedures act on what data and when. As the complexity of the application increases, it becomes increasingly difficult for the programmer to use this method; hence, the need for a new paradigm is apparent.

Ideas of encapsulating the procedures together with the data they were acting on, already illustrated in Figure 2.3, led to object-oriented programming. This was perceived as the new model for which many frustrated programmers had been waiting.

The common predecessor of most object-oriented languages is Simula, designed in the 1960s. Simula was built on the ideas of Algol60 and was targeted at writing simulation programs, such as the Elevator simulation presented earlier in this chapter. This emphasis on simulations introduced the paradigm of writing programs reflecting the objects (nouns) of the problem domain and their actions (verbs) and attributes, all of which are now at the core of object-oriented principles.

Lisp is the earliest functional language and is used extensively for computer programs related to artificial intelligence. Lisp is very different from languages like C++ and C#, but it contains one mechanism that has been adopted by many languages, including C#—automatic reclamation of memory, also called *garbage collection*.

Smalltalk extended the ideas of Simula. It is considered *the* quintessential object-oriented language. Everything in SmallTalk is an object, or part of an object and all actions are considered to be "messages" sent between these objects. Later, you will see why everything in C# can also be viewed as being an object or part of an object.

Several attempts were made to turn C into an object-oriented language, but Bjarne Stroustrup's C++ turned out to be the most successful by far. C++ is largely a superset of C. It provides what most programmers would regard as improvements, such as type checking, overloaded routines, and object-oriented programming features.

C++ is a very powerful language due to its inheritance of C's features that support operating system development. Unfortunately, the acquisition of power and freedom is directly related to the responsibility, complexity, and risk of "pressing the red button," in other words, creating plentiful bugs.

Java is based largely on a subset of C++ and is considerably simpler. It was designed for the construction of architecture-neutral, highly portable programs. An intermediate language, called *byte code*, which is comparable to MSIL, is interpreted by a Java virtual machine (JVM) during execution. It features a type-safe reference model, a simplified inheritance model, multi-threading, and extensive class libraries.

Basic is a very simple language. Basic is short for Beginner's All-purpose Symbolic Instruction Code.

Visual Basic was created by Microsoft and is very different from Basic. It is the most widely used programming language today. Part of its huge success is due to its Rapid Application Development (RAD) capabilities when integrated with the Microsoft's Visual Studio development environment. RAD allows programmers to design GUI-based programs rapidly by dragging and dropping visual components in a visual design environment.

C#'s Design Goals

C# was designed in cooperation with .NET to

- *Let C and C++ programmers feel familiar with C#* C# has many operators, keywords, and concepts in common with C++, which makes it immediately familiar to C++ programmers.
- *Be simpler, safer and more productive than C++* This is achieved through mechanisms such as garbage collection, structured exception handling, and type safety, and by letting the underlying runtime take care of many other error prone, tedious, and time consuming housekeeping tasks.
- *Be a true component-oriented language* Creating a component is as easy as creating a program, because any program you create is also a component. No other special files are required. This concept is known as *one stop programming*.
- Metadata and attributes allow each component to be self-describing in terms of the functionality it exposes and the resources and other components it needs so, in effect, allows it to easily be slotted into a broad variety of computing environments.
- *Be a true OO language, such as SmallTalk, where everything is an object* The ability in a language to treat every variable as an object has several advantages. SmallTalk supports this paradigm but, unfortunately, with one important drawback—slow program execution. Java and C++ do not support this model, perhaps because of this latter problem. However, the C# designers have done some pretty ingenious thinking by allowing the support of "everything is an object" while avoiding the performance compromise found in SmallTalk.
- *Provide full support for RAD, similar to Visual Basic* Constructs, such as properties that are also found in Visual Basic, allows C# to be fully integrated with Visual Studio.NET and its Integrated Development Environment (IDE). This allows C# to fully support RAD.

- *Be totally integrated with the .NET platform* C# was designed from the ground up to interoperate with and leverage all the relevant features of .NET. The result is a seamless integration between C# and .NET.
- *Interoperate with other languages at the object-oriented level* For example, it is now possible to write a class in Visual Basic, derive a class from this Visual Basic class in C++, and then instantiate this C++ class in C#. MSIL and metadata make this level of interoperability possible, as discussed in a previous section.
- *Interoperate fully with already existing code, such as COM and DLLs* By writing wrapper classes, the programmer allows the program to call COM objects. Conversely, you can also allow .NET objects to be used as COM objects. Through a feature called *platform invoke*, it is possible to call native DLL functions.

What Kind of Programs Can I Write with C#?

As you have seen, numerous programming languages exist today. Even though you can use most languages to create any computer program you want, many languages have been designed to accommodate for a more or less specific range of problems.

Currently, C# and .NET are only working on top of the Windows operating system, but they provide the programmer with powerful means to program this operating system. Consequently, this short section will revolve around Windows-related technologies. It is important to understand that C# is a multi-purpose language and can be used, within the Windows platform, to create many kinds of weird and wonderful programs.

The following is a brief list of just a few of the numerous programming categories where C# will get powerful support from .NET and make the C# programmer productive.

- *Console applications* A console application utilizes one simple window to communicate with the user. There are no fancy graphics or animations; the communication is character based, reducing the complexity of the application, usually encountered in graphical rich applications. Even though you are not likely to find many (if any at all) modern commercial console-based applications, it is a great place to start when learning to program. It allows you to focus on the language constructs and quickly bring you the understanding needed to create more complex graphical programs.

  However, programming for the console window is not restricted to novice programmers; professional programmers often use the console window to test applications and components.

  Notice that even though console applications generally require the least support (of the four categories previously mentioned) from .NET, the programmer still has access to a wide array of useful components in the BCL.

  Later in this chapter, I introduce you to console-based programming, which is used in many parts of the book.

- *Windows applications with WinForms* If you have ever worked with a computer, you have probably experienced a windows-based application. In contrast to a console application, it contains a graphics-rich user interface (GUI) where commands are given with a mouse by clicking on icons and buttons and interaction is through various text and list boxes.

  If you had to write a windows-based application from scratch without being able to reuse any prewritten components, you would have to add months and years to your development time, in fact you might not finish before a new and better technology arrives.

  The .NET Framework class library contains a comprehensive set of components called WinForms for creating advanced windows-based applications. WinForms gives the C# programmer easy access to the underlying windows services of the Windows operating system.

- *ASP.NET applications* ASP.NET (Active Server Pages.NET) covers an array of components that facilitate the creation of browser-based applications.

  A *browser* is an application that allows the user to examine documents, encoded with formats such as Hypertext Markup Language (HTML), in a form suitable for display. Browsers are widely used to display information found on the Internet.

- *Web Services* Web Services is an important new technology that promises to change the way we use the Internet and our perception of how we program and use computer applications.

  > Web Services are simply components or applications delivered to your computer via the Internet. Web Services residing on different computers, all linked to the Internet, can be pieced together to form new Web Services. This opens up new exciting avenues for computer programmers.
  >
  > It lets the developer assemble a component or application not only by using the components from the .NET Framework class libraries and his or her own source code but also from Web Services found on the Internet.
  >
  > It allows individual developers or software companies to build Web Services and make them available on the Internet perhaps by charging a fee.

C# is an exciting, feature-packed language with powerful support from the .NET platform, so let's roll our sleeves up and get ready for some real C# programming.

The Mechanics of Creating a C# Program

In this section. I will show you the practical steps you need to take to write, compile, and run simple C# programs.

Currently, you have two major options for developing and running C# programs. You can either obtain the .NET Software Development Kit (SDK) for free from Microsoft or purchase the feature-packed Visual Studio .NET program.

The SDK contains everything you need to compile, run, and test C# programs. It includes the Common Language Runtime, sample code, a C# language compiler, JIT compilers, and documentation. The only thing not included is a text editor to type and edit your C# programs. We will provide some tips on choosing an editor a little later in this section.

Visual Studio .NET is Microsoft's comprehensive development environment. It includes an Integrated Development Environment (IDE), advanced C# editor, support for RAD, extensive support for debugging, and many additional features that improve the developers productivity.

It is important to notice that the SDK and Visual Studio .NET use the same C# compiler, JIT compilers and runtime to compile and execute programs. Accordingly, you can run exactly the same programs and they will execute with the same speed no matter which package you use. Visual Studio .NET simply provides you with numerous additional powerful tools to facilitate the designing and writing of C# programs.

This book assumes you are using the SDK with a simple text editor like Notepad.

Before Getting Started

Before we begin this discussion, we need to go through a couple of important practicalities to ready your computer for running the C# programs. You need to do the following:

- Check that your computer fulfills the requirements stated for the .NET platform.
- Software requirements for .NET SDK At the time of this writing, you can run the .NET SDK with one of the following operating systems: Microsoft Windows 2000, Microsoft Windows XP, Microsoft Windows NT 4.0, Microsoft Windows Millenium Edition, or Microsoft Windows 98. You also need Internet Explorer 5.01 and Data Access Components 2.6 installed on your computer.
- *Minimum hardware requirements* Your computer must at least have a Pentium class processor running at 133 MHz, 128 MB RAM, and 900MB of free disk space. Your screen should have a resolution of minimum 800×600 with 256 colors.
- At this moment, due to .NET's instability (it is still only a beta release), Microsoft only recommends the installation of .NET on a non-production computer, which simply means a computer that is not used for any critical tasks.

Note

Some of the requirements I have mentioned are likely to change. Please check with Microsoft's Web sites, `http://www.microsoft.com` and `http://msdn.microsoft.com`, for the latest facts on these issues.

- *Install the .NET platform on your computer* You can either download the .NET SDK on `http://msdn.microsoft.com/downloads` or order it on a CD-ROM from Microsoft. To install the .NET SDK, you need to follow the instructions of the included installation program. The details of this procedure are likely to change and so they are not discussed here. However, by following the instructions exactly as given by the installation program and accompanying Help files, such as `readme.txt` and `readme.1st`, the process should be easy and trouble free.

Choosing a Text Editor

Text editors used for writing source code range from the simple no frills Notepad editor to sophisticated editors, such as those found in Visual Studio .NET. The more elaborate editors are specifically targeted at writing code and, consequently, provide many features that can help the programmer. We will not delve into any of those features; we'll assume that you are using the freely available Notepad, which can be found on any Windows platform.

When choosing a text editor, you need to be aware of the following important details:

- All C# source files must be saved with no formatting. If you use a word processor to create the source code, you must save the file as Text Only. Different editors use different names for Text Only, such as Plain Text, ASCII Text, and DOS Text.
- Even though advanced word processors are helpful when writing letters, books, and so on, they are not targeted at program development. They're not helpful for this purpose.
- Editors, such as Notepad, might add an extra `.txt` file extension to the filename of any C# source file you save—even if you have already specified the `.cs` extension. Only files with the extension `.cs` are recognized by the C# compiler and accepted for compilation, so this would create an error message when you attempt to compile the source code file. You can avoid this problem by placing quotation marks around the filename and its extension (`.cs`) when saving the file. For example, if you want your source code file to be called `Shakespeare.cs`, as the program shown later, you can type **`"Shakespeare.cs"`** in the Save As window instead of just `Shakespeare.cs`, as illustrated in Figure 2.12 shown later.
- In many ways, it can be advantageous to start out with a simple text editor like Notepad because you can focus on learning C# instead of being sidetracked by the numerous features of a sophisticated C# editor. The many hundred pages of documentation accompanying Visual Studio.NET illustrate this point.

The Seven Steps to Writing a Simple C# Program

After you have successfully installed the .NET SDK and chosen a suitable editor you are ready to write and run your C# programs. This can be accomplished by performing the following seven steps (shown here by using pseudocode):

1. Open the command console.

2. Use the chosen text editor to type and edit the C# source code and save this text as a `.cs` file.
3. Use the C# language compiler to turn this source code into a PE (`.exe`) or DLL (`.dll`) file.
4. If the compiler detects any syntax errors in step 3, go back to step 2 and correct these errors. Continue through steps 3, 4, and so on.
5. Run the program.
6. Verify that the output matches your expectations. If this is not the case, go back to step 2 and correct the mistakes in the C# code. Then continue through steps 3, 4, and so on.
7. Time to celebrate your first C# program.

Let's take a closer look at each of these steps.

Opening and Using the Command Console (Step 1)

The command console is like a control center. It allows the user to operate the computer completely by typing special commands with the keyboard.

Throughout this book, you will be using the command line console to launch Notepad, create directories, copy files, initiate the C# compiler, execute your programs, and view their output. The source code itself is written inside Notepad.

You can open the command console by first selecting Run option on the Start menu and then typing **cmd** (see Figure 2.8) in the text field. Click OK. You should then see the command console appear, as shown in Figure 2.9. In general, commands are typed after the `C:\>` prompt and executed by pressing the Enter key on the keyboard. In this text, we refer to the `C:\>` prompt, but this could also be `D:\>` or `E:\>`, depending on the disk drive you are using.

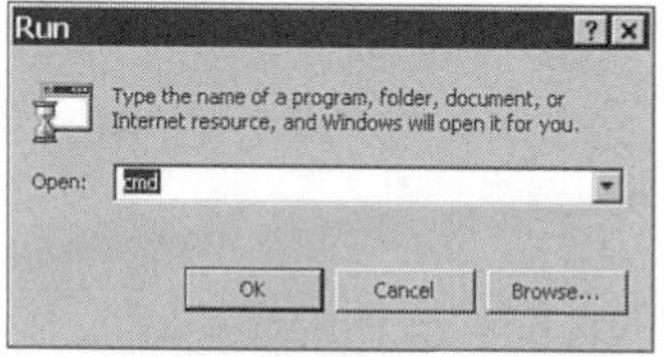

FIGURE 2.8
Type **`cmd`** in the Run window.

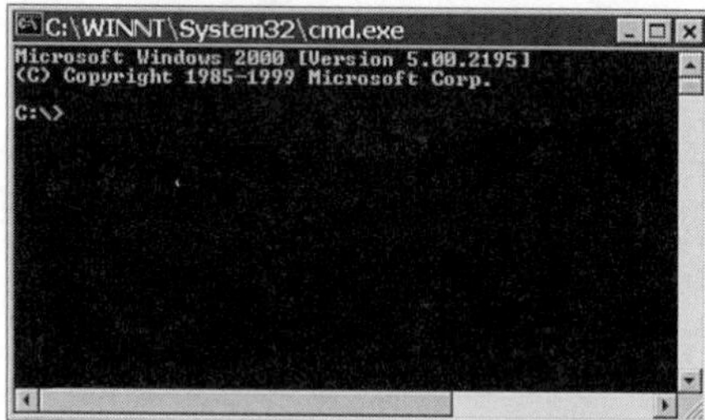

FIGURE 2.9
The command console window.

Appendix F, "Using DOS Ccommands in the Console Window" explains the basic command console options you will need.

Note

The conventions used in this book for explaining how to give commands in the command console are illustrated by this example:

```
C:\>cd mydirectory <enter>
```

The `C:\>` part, and any other text that is printed by the computer, is written with normal text. The part you type, in this case **`cd mydirectory,`** is bolded. Any named keys are indicated with <> angle braces. **`<enter>`** here for example means that you have to press the Enter key.

Before writing the C# source code, you need to create a directory where it can be stored. Create a directory called MyC#Programs for this purpose with the following command:

```
C:\>md MyC#Programs<enter>
```

Enter this new directory by typing the following:

```
C:\>cd MyC#Programs<enter>
```

Typing and Saving the C# Source Code (Step 2)

Use the chosen text editor to type and edit the C# source code and save this text as a `.cs` file.

First you need to start Notepad by typing the following command in the console window::

```
C:\>MyC#Programs>notepad<enter>
```

You will see Notepad appear, as shown in Figure 2.10.

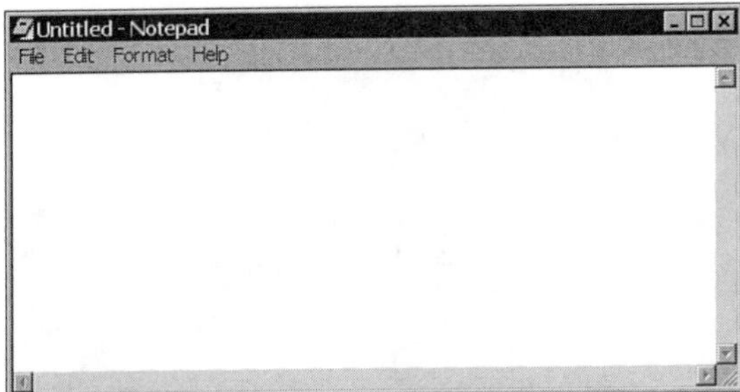

FIGURE 2.10
The Notepad window.

You are now ready to write the C# program in the text editor.

Our first C# program will print out the following lines on the command console:

```
Though this be madness
yet there is method in it
William Shakespeare
```

Even though the quote was written many years ago, before the advent of computers, it might still be a good description of what most people feel like when they learn a new programming language.

Listing 2.1 contains a C# program that will print the quote by Shakespeare on the command console.

The line numbers and colons appearing on the left side of Listing 2.1 are not part of the program. They are included to help me refer to specific lines by referring to their numbers and are not to be included when you type in the program with the editor. However, all other details, such as semicolons, parenthesis, and braces, must be entered exactly as shown. The C# compiler is case sensitive, meaning Main, main, and maiN are all different. Consequently, you must capitalize all letters exactly as written in Listing 2.1.

Note

Typing mistakes will likely cause syntax errors and will be reported by the compiler.

You are not meant to understand the C# program shown in Listing 2.1. It is only intended to show you the mechanics of how to write, compile, and run a C# program. However, it can still be enlightening to read through the code and make a guess about what is happening in each line. Later, you can compare your guesses with the brief explanations of each line that I provide.

LISTING 2.1 Source code of `Shakespeare.cs`

```
01: using System;
02: public class Shakespeare
03: {
04:     public static void Main()
05:     {
06:         Console.WriteLine("Though this be madness");
07:         Console.WriteLine("yet there is method in it");
08:         Console.WriteLine("William Shakespeare");
09:     }
10: }
```

After you have finished typing the program, your Notepad window should look like Figure 2.11.

Save the program by selecting Save As on the File menu of Notepad and typing **`Shakespeare.cs`** in the File Name text box. Your screen should now look similar to Figure 2.12. Then click the Save button.

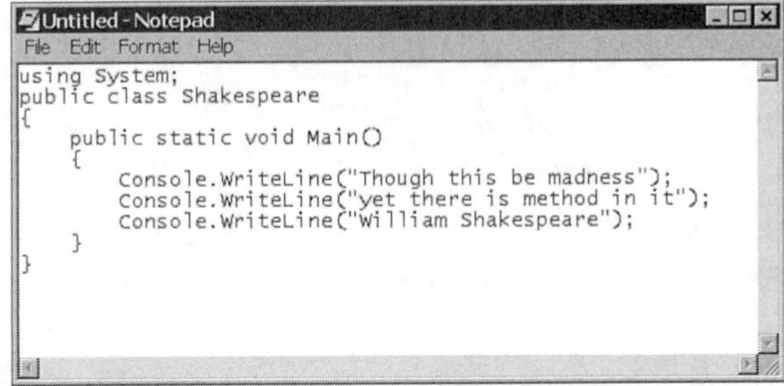

Untitled - Notepad
File Edit Format Help
using System;
public class Shakespeare
{
public static void Main()
{
Console.WriteLine("Though this be madness");
Console.WriteLine("yet there is method in it");
Console.WriteLine("William Shakespeare");
}
}

FIGURE 2.11
Notepad window displaying the *Shakespeare.cs* source code.

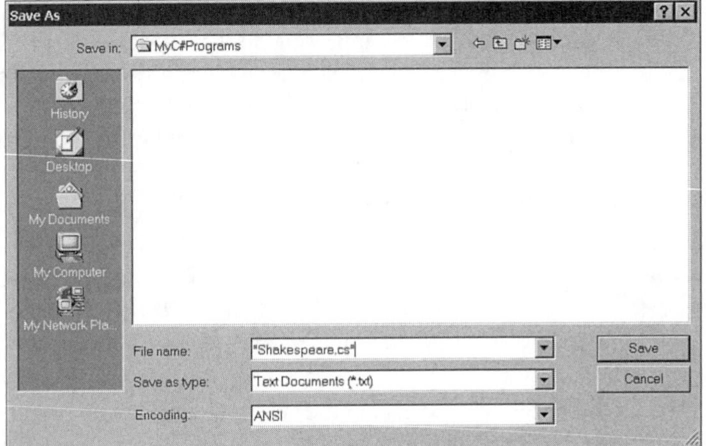

FIGURE 2.12
Saving the *Shakespeare.cs* source code.

You are now ready to activate the C# compiler and turn the brand new `Shakespeare.cs` file into a PE file.

Note

When your source code is ready to be compiled, you can turn it into a PE file (`.exe` file extension) or a DLL file (`.dll` file extension), depending on the command you give the compiler.

Turn the Source Code into a PE (.exe) File (Step 3)

Initiate the C# compiler by giving the following command:

```
C:\MyC#Programs>csc Shakespeare.cs<enter>
```

Now hold your breath and wait with excitement…if the compiler detected no syntax errors, it will print two lines stating the compiler version and a copyright message, similar to what is shown in Figure 2.13. Notice that the compiler version and other details might vary, the important part is that no error messages or other complaints were printed.

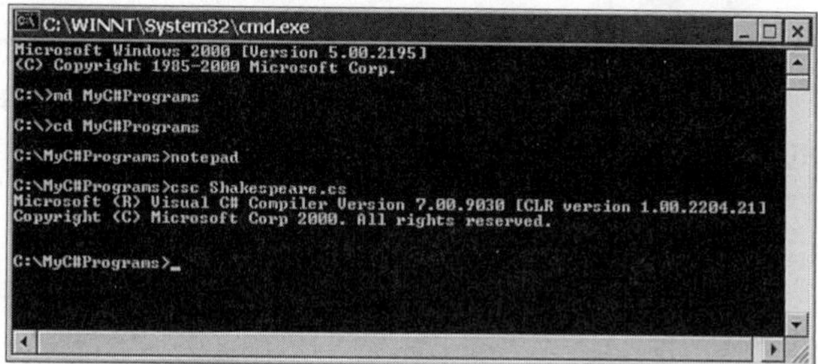

FIGURE 2.13
No errors detected by the compiler.

Note

A successful compilation does not mean your source code is free of errors (bugs). It merely means that the source code represents a valid C# program free of syntax errors.

In the event of a successful compilation, the compiler creates a file called `Shakespeare.exe` and saves it in the same folder that contains `Shakespeare.cs`. `Shakespeare.exe` is a PE file and is also an assembly containing MSIL and a manifest (metadata).

But what if a typing error had sneaked its way into the source code?

If the Compiler Detects Syntax Errors (Step 4)

Let's have a bit of fun with the compiler and watch how it responds to a syntax error.

- Start Notepad again by typing the following:

  ```
  C:\MyC#Programs>notepad Shakespeare.cs<enter>
  ```

  Create an error in the code by removing the semicolon from the end of line 1 of Listing 2.1. Line 1 should now look like the following:

  ```
  01:  using System
  ```

- Save the `Shakespeare.cs` file by selecting Save from the File menu of Notepad.
- Initiate the compiler as shown in the next line and see if it can find the missing semicolon.

  ```
  C:\MyC#Programs>csc Shakespeare.cs<enter>
  ```

- You should see the following line as part of the output from the compiler:

  ```
  Shakespeare.cs(2,1): error CS1002:   ;   expected
  ```

  It did, in fact, catch the syntax error! Notice the parentheses `(2,1)` in the compiler output. This is an indication of where the compiler thinks the error is located and can often be of great help when correcting errors. 2 refers to the line number and 1 to the character number.

But wait, we removed the semicolon from position (1,13). Shouldn't the compiler have given this position instead? Well, the compiler looks a bit differently at the source code than we humans do. Whether we put a semicolon in position (1,13) or position (2,1) is not significant for the compiler. Its only concern is whether the semicolon is *between* `System` in line 1 and `public` in line 2. For that matter, we could put the semicolon in position (1,14), (1,15), or so on.

To enhance the understanding for humans viewing the source code, various styles are being used when writing it. Listing 2.1 follows a specific style of presenting the source code. For example, putting the semicolon in position (1,13) looks much better and clearer than putting it in position (1,34). Style is discussed further in Chapter 3.

Let's return to our `Shakespeare.cs` file. Use Notepad to put the missing semicolon back so that the source file looks exactly like Listing 2.1 again. Compile the source code as already shown and verify that the compiler reports no errors. It is now time to execute your `Shakespeare.exe` file.

Run the Program (Step 5)

To run the PE file `Shakespeare.exe`, you type the following command:

```
C:\MyC#Programs>Shakespeare<enter>
```

The JIT compiler is activated and machine language is emitted that is then executed, resulting in the now familiar lines

Though this be madness
yet there is method in it
William Shakespeare

Verify the Output (Step 6)

Did you get the correct output? If the answer is no, then go back to step 2 of the seven steps. Compare your source code with Listing 2.1 and find the mistake. Correct the code with the editor. Even if you only change a semicolon in the source code, you still need to go through step 3, 4 and so on until the program is working.

If the answer is yes, then congratulations! You have successfully executed your first C# program. You can move to the last step.

Time to Celebrate (Step 7)

Now it's time to celebrate !

A Brief Source Code Analysis

We will go deeper into the C# syntax and structure in Chapter 3, "A Guided Tour through C#: Part I" but, for now it can be educational to have a quick look through the source code and compare it with the pseudocode provided in Listing 2.2. This listing is the Shakespeare.cs program written in pseudocode and with line numbers corresponding exactly to Listing 2.1. In other words, line 1 of Listing 2.2 briefly explains line 1 of Listing 2.1, line 2 of Listing 2.2 explains line 2 of Listing 2.1, and so on.

LISTING 2.2 Pseudocode for the Shakespeare Program

```
01:   Facilitate use of classes belonging to the System part of the BCL
02:   Begin definition of a class called Shakespeare
03:   Begin block in which the Shakespeare class definition is written.
04:           Indicate with Main where the program execution will start
05:           Begin block, which will be executed when Main is started.
06:                   Print: "Though this be madness" on the console and move down
                      ➥one line
07:                   Print: "yet there is method in it" on the console and move
                      ➥down one line
08:                   Print: "William Shakespeare" on the console and move down one
                      ➥line
09:          End block, which was executed when Main was started
10: End block in which the Shakespeare class definition is written.
```

Note on Syntax Errors and Compilers

In the following chapters, you are going to use the C# compiler extensively and will most likely experience it reporting numerous syntax errors in the command console due to incorrectly constructed statements or typing mistakes.

Fortunately, syntax errors are slowly becoming easier to detect and remove due to improved compiler diagnostics and error messages. The days when the programmer had to spend several hours tracking one syntax error down are nearly gone.

To improve your syntax error elimination abilities, keep the following tips in mind:

- *Line numbers in compiler error messages are not always correct* You experienced this problem first-hand in the Listing 2.1 example when the compiler reported position (2,1) instead of (1,13). Always look directly before and after the error position when you search for the mistake.

  Understanding the compiler will enable you to find errors in the future more efficiently. After you find the true error, analyze why the compiler reported the wrong position and learn from the experience.

- *Several compiler error messages can be caused by just one real error* Most compilers do not stop at reporting just the single real error. One syntax error might change the meaning of other parts of the program and trick the compiler to burst over with error messages. Consequently, if you can find the error of just one of many compiler error messages, fix that particular error and recompile.

- *Compiler messages often need interpretation* Compilers are very exact contraptions. They try to report exactly what is wrong with your source code. However, you have to read between the lines sometimes to understand what an error message really means.
- *Hide parts of the source code temporarily during compilation* Troublesome errors can often be found and eliminated by dividing the code into sections and having the compiler check the source code with various parts removed.

  When the part containing the problem is removed, the compiler will be silent. You can then inspect the removed section more closely. Some parts of code are easily hidden for the compiler by turning them into comments with `//`, or `/*`, `*/` as described in Chapter 3, "A guided tour through C#: Part I".

The three best ways to learn to program are writing programs, writing programs, and writing more programs. Only through hands-on practice can you acquire the mind of a proficient programmer. In Chapter 3, you will get the opportunity to write and analyze more programs to familiarize yourself with C#.

Summary

In this chapter, we have looked at the fundamental steps of the software development process. You have also learned about some of the advantages of object-oriented programming, about the design goals of C# and .NET, and have been presented with the basic mechanics for creating a C# program.

The following are the essential points we have covered in this chapter:

The software development process described in this chapter only contains a core subset of the many different approaches used in today's software development processes. The core steps are software specification, software design, writing the software, and validating and debugging the software.

An algorithm precisely specifies a series of actions performed in a sequential manner by the computer to solve a computational problem. Algorithms are often expressed using pseudocode, which is a mixture of human language and a high level programming language. Designing an algorithm is usually significantly harder than implementing an existing algorithm in C#.

When you write, compile, and run C# programs, you will bump into three types of errors—syntax errors, logic errors, and runtime errors.

Whereas the earlier process-oriented programs consisted of large monolithic source code mammoths, object-oriented programs consists of smaller, self-contained modules (objects) that communicate and collaborate with each other to provide the functionality of a program.

An object consists of data (represented by instance variables that represents the state of an object) and methods (representing the object's behavior) acting on those data.

The class acts as a template for its objects.

Software reuse is a valuable and important part of software construction today. A piece of software constructed for reuse is called a *software component*. C# provides powerful support for component-oriented programming. The basic unit of reuse in C# is the assembly.

Many class libraries exist and are packed with classes with the sole purpose of being reused in other programs. The .NET Framework class library contains many hundreds of classes at your disposal, ready to be reused.

C# and .NET constitute an evolutionary step forward by building on problems and solutions experienced by previous programmers and their languages.

C# and .NET provide powerful support for the development of many different types of programs. These include Web services, browser-based applications, Windows-based programs, and simple console-based applications, along with a host of other types of programs.

To begin writing C# applications, you need a text editor, such as Notepad, and the .NET Software Development Kit (SDK) installed on your computer.

Review Questions

1. What are the four core activities in the software development process? Describe each activity briefly.
2. What is an algorithm and how can it be expressed?
3. Why do computers need a very precise set of instructions to solve a problem?
4. In what order are instructions in pseudocode and C# executed?
5. What are the three different errors programmers encounter? Describe each of them briefly.
6. Why is computer testing a tricky undertaking?
7. Briefly describe process-oriented programming.
8. Briefly describe object-oriented programming. What are the advantages of object-oriented programming compared to process-oriented programming?
9. What is an object? What does it consist of?
10. What is the relationship between a class and its objects?
11. How are the objects of a specific programming problem often identified?
12. What is a software part meant for reuse called?
13. What is the basic unit of reuse in .NET? Describe this unit.
14. Which part of .NET offers software components for reuse?
15. What are some of the design goals of C# and .NET?

16. What are the main steps required for running a simple C# program?
17. Can a C# program that has been accepted by the compiler still contain errors?

Programming Exercises

1. Write the pseudocode for an algorithm that determines the maximum number of two given numbers. Hint: Use the following logic: If `number1` is greater than `number2`, `number1` is the maximum number; otherwise, `number2` is greater than or equal to `number1`.
2. Write the pseudocode for an algorithm that determines the maximum number in a given list of numbers. The list can contain any amount of numbers. Hint: Keep a variable called `maxSoFar` (written on the paper, with zero as the initial value). Go through the list one by one and compare each number with `maxSoFar`. Any number found to be greater than `maxSoFar` becomes equal to `maxSoFar`. At the end of the list, `maxSoFar` represents the largest number in the list.
3. Change the average-calculating pseudocode in the section "Algorithms and Pseudocode" so that it doesn't perform division by zero, even when no numbers are provided.
4. Write, compile, and run a C# program that writes the following on the console:

```
Our alien friend
lives on planet Blipos
far far away
```

CHAPTER 3

A GUIDED TOUR THROUGH C#: PART I

You will learn about the following in this chapter:

- The advantages of applying two important OOP concepts—abstraction and encapsulation
- Why the C# keywords `public` and `private` play an important role in implementing encapsulation
- The basic C# elements needed to write simple C# applications
- How to write a user interactive application using simple keyboard input and screen output
- Single line comments and why comments are important in your source code
- The special meaning of keywords
- How to define the beginning and the end of a class and method body by using C#'s block construct
- How to use C#'s `if` statement to make your program respond in different ways to different user input
- The `string` class and its ability to let your programs store and process text
- The special role played by the `Main` method
- The `static` keyword and why `Main` must always be declared `public` and `static`
- How to use variables
- How to call a method and thereby use its functionality
- Several useful classes from the .NET Framework class libraries and how to reuse these in the C# source code
- Statements in C#—the declaration, assignment, method call, and `if` statements
- General C# concepts based on the knowledge gained from the C# source code example
- How to access and use the .NET Framework Documentation so you can explore and reuse the .NET Framework's comprehensive collection of classes

Introduction

Each language construct of a C# program does not exist in isolation. It has its own vital part to play but is also closely interrelated with other elements. This makes it difficult to look at any one aspect of C# without requiring the knowledge of others. Due to this circular dependence among the elements of C#, this chapter, along with Chapter 4, "A Guided Tour Through C#: Part II," and Chapter 5, "Your First Object-Oriented C# Program," presents an overview of several important features, to give you an introductory feel for the language.

The presentation is facilitated by C# source code examples containing several essential elements of C#. Each element will be presented, discussed, and related to other parts of the C# program in a practically related fashion. This will enable you to start writing your own programs during this chapter. I hope you will grab this opportunity to play with and explore C#. Some of the most important parts of this and the following two chapters are the programming exercises at the end of each chapter. You don't become a proficient C# programmer just by learning lots of definitions by heart but by doing and unleashing your creativity. So have a go at these exercises and use your imagination to come up with other ideas of how to improve the programs or, even better, create your own programs.

Abstraction and Encapsulation

Object-oriented programming is at the core of C#. Practically speaking, everything in C# is an object. Even the simple program you encountered in Chapter 2, "Your First C# Program" relies on OO principles. So before we dive into the first C# example, it is useful to expand on our OO introduction by looking at two core concepts of OO called abstraction and encapsulation.

Abstraction

Consider an airplane. Initially, it seems an impossible task to represent an airplane in a computer program. Just think about all the details—intricately designed jet engines, extremely complex onboard computers, entertainment systems. It is dizzying. However, by looking at the role we want the airplane to play in our application, we can significantly reduce the features to be represented. Perhaps we just need an airplane to be a position on a map. Perhaps we need to test the aerodynamic characteristics of an airplane in which case we only need to represent its outer shape. Perhaps an interior designer is making a 3D presentation of the airplane's interiors, in which case, he needs to represent only the interior surfaces of the airplane.

In every airplane role mentioned, it is possible to identify the key characteristics of the airplane relevant to that particular application. Essentially, we are coping with the intricacies of the airplane by abstracting away from them.

Abstraction is one of the fundamental concepts utilized by programmers to cope with complexity.

When an object (or system) is specified or depicted in a simpler, less detailed fashion than its real counterpart, this specification is called an *abstraction*. Highlighting the properties that are relevant to the problem at hand, while ignoring the irrelevant and unduly complicating properties, creates a useful abstraction in OOP.

When creating an abstraction, it is important to include only the features that are part of the object being specified. The behavior of an object must not go beyond that of the expected. For example, creating an abstract car with the ability to draw architectural plans should be avoided. It creates confusion among yourself and other programmers trying to understand your source code.

Note

Recall the elevator simulation discussion from Chapter 2, "Your First C# Program." When designing an elevator simulation program, we must first ignore (by abstraction) all the unnecessary characteristics and parameters of the real world. For example, the color of each elevator and the hairstyle of each person in them can be disregarded. On the other hand, important information is the speed of each elevator, the number of people wanting to catch an elevator, and the floors to which they want to travel.

The simulation enables us to calculate statistics concerning waiting times and eventually an estimate for the number and types of elevators needed to service the building, just as Big Finance Ltd. requested in Chapter 2.

You have already seen one example of an abstraction in the C# program example in Chapter 2. It contained a class called `Shakespeare`.

Lacking arms, legs, inner organs, and a brain, the class had very little resemblance to the writer and person named Shakespeare, but it could still recite one very short quote of Shakespeare. Thus, because a very tiny piece of Shakespeare could be found in it, we still dared to call our class `Shakespeare`. Our `Shakespeare` class was an abstraction of the real writer and person—Shakespeare.

Encapsulation

Whereas abstraction focuses on reducing the complexity of how we view the real world, encapsulation concentrates on the design of our C# source code. It is a powerful mechanism for reducing complexity and protecting data of individual objects on the programming level.

Encapsulation is the process of combining data and the actions (methods) acting on the data into a single entity, just as you saw in Chapter 2. In OOP and hence C#, such an entity is equivalent to an *object*.

Encapsulation is a mechanism for hiding instance variables and irrelevant methods of a class from other objects. Only methods, which are necessary to use an object of the class, are exposed.

The term encapsulation might sound like a sophisticated academic term, but despite this first impression, we can find parallels to it from our everyday life. We might not refer to it as encapsulation, but the analogies are so striking that an example from the real world might be instructive. The example provided here returns to the world of elevators.

Encapsulation in a Real World Elevator System

Any useful elevator has a mechanism, such as buttons, that allow a passenger to select his or her destination floor. Pressing a button is a very *easy* action to perform for the user of the elevator. However, for the elevator faced with many conflicting simultaneous requests from many different people, it can be a complicated matter deciding which floor to go to and fulfill the request of each traveler expediently. Many conditions complicate the design of an elevator; some examples are provided in the following Note.

The Complicated Life of an Elevator

Modern elevators rely on sophisticated algorithms residing inside computers that control every move they make. Here are a few reasons why it is a complicated matter to decide the next move of an elevator.

A person called A might enter the elevator at floor 3 and request to go to floor 30. However, another person, B, has already pressed the button on floor 1 requesting to be picked up there. If the elevator goes directly to floor 30 with person A (but without B), person A will get there as fast as he or she could ever expect. However, person B has to wait. Perhaps, by merely moving two floors down, the elevator could have taken both people to a higher floor at the same time, saving time and power. Instead, the elevator has to go all the way up to floor 30 and then back down to pick up B. With many people constantly requesting elevators and destination floors, the matter gets much more complex.

At least a couple of other aspects complicate matters further for our trusted elevator:

- Several elevators are probably working together to transport people between the different floors. They consequently need a "team" approach to fulfill as many requests as possible. Densely populated buildings with large amounts of traffic between floors require approximately two elevators for every three floors. Thus, a 60-floor building would require about 40 elevators.
- Certain floors are more likely to be visited and have pick-me-up requests than other floors. These probabilities might vary throughout the day. If the elevators can somehow remember these patterns, they can optimize the efficiency of the sequence of floors visited.

Sophisticated algorithms have been constructed running inside computers that control the movements of the elevators, allowing them to serve as many people as possible, fast and efficiently.

This was a bit of elevator talk, but it leads us to an essential observation.

It is *easy* for a person to *press a* button and thereby use the hidden complex services (algorithms, engines, hydraulics, gears, wires, data about current speed, maximum speed, and so on) provided by the elevator. Thus, the ignorant passenger, in terms of elevator technology, can easily utilize the services of the elevator to accomplish his or her tasks of the day.

Not only is this concealment of elevator data, algorithms, and mechanics an advantage for travelers who do not want to deal with complex matters that are irrelevant to them; but it also improves the reliability of the elevator itself. No unauthorized and incompetent person can gain access to the inner control mechanisms of the elevator. Imagine if the elevator was equipped with a small "cockpit" where anybody traveling in the elevator could tinker with the maximum speed, or make the elevator believe it was on an incorrect floor, or force it to move to a floor other than the one calculated by its control algorithms. A chaotic situation would soon prevail.

A final advantage of segregating the buttons from the underlying elevator mechanisms is the capability of making changes to these mechanisms without altering the buttons and, hence, the way it is operated. In this way, an elevator can contain the same buttons that everyone has become accustomed to using for many years, while many underlying hardware and software upgrades have taken place to keep the system up to date.

Encapsulation in an Elevator Simulation

Let's look at how the previously discussed issues relate to an object-oriented C# elevator simulation program.

An elevator simulation program written in C# will probably have `Elevator` and `Person` objects along with others. Even though now inside a computer program, a `Person` object will still be able to perform the equivalent of "pressing the button" of an `Elevator` object and giving it a floor request.

Each `Elevator` object of the simulation probably contains, like its real counterpart, many complex methods and many sensitive data. For example, many `Elevator` objects might, to make the simulation particularly realistic, be equipped with algorithms (similar to the algorithms of real world elevators) to calculate the most efficient sequence of floors visited.

Now the important analogy—each `Person` object (and the programmer implementing it) of the simulation should still not need or be allowed to "know" about the inner complexities (source code) of any `Elevator` object. All they should "care" about, just like their real counterparts, is to get from one floor to another. They don't want to be confused about unnecessary complexities either. They should not be allowed to tinker with the inner workings (data and source code) of the `Elevator` object, and the programmers implementing the elevator should be able to change and upgrade the source code without interfering with how the `Elevator` object is used (operated).

To accomplish this concealment in the OO world, we say that we *encapsulate* (hide) the underlying data and source code that is irrelevant for all but the `Elevator` objects themselves.

When we write and create the `Elevator` objects in C#, we somehow need a way to tell the program and the other objects, including the `Person` objects, that the data and source code are hidden. C# has a special word for this purpose called `private`. Thus, by *declaring* the data and relevant source code to be `private`, we are able to prevent any other object from gaining access to these parts of our `Elevator` object.

Convention

Any words with a special meaning in C# as well as references made to parts of source code presented in this book appear in a special font, such as `private`.

`private` and `public`

The word `private` has a special meaning to the C# compiler. It is used to hide method and instance variables (residing inside an object) from other objects.

Likewise, the word `public` has a special (albeit opposing) meaning to the C# compiler. `public` is used to allow other objects access to methods and instance variables of a specific object.

Because `private` and `public` control the accessibility of the methods and instance variables belonging to an object, these two words are referred to as *access modifiers*.

However, if we hide *all* the instance variables and methods of an object, none of its methods can be accessed, rendering the object completely useless. For example, a `Person` object needs somehow the ability to "express" its floor request. A method with this capacity could arbitrarily be called `NewFloorRequest`. What would happen if we declared `NewFloorRequest` to be `private`? Well, an `Elevator` object that had just "loaded" a "passenger" (a `Person` object) with these characteristics would not be able to access the `NewFloorRequest` method, which is the only means to find out the floor to which this "passenger" "wanted" to "travel." This would be the equivalent of a real person without any arms, who is unable to reach out and press a button. In the C# source code, we somehow need a way to put "arms" on our `Person` object and buttons on our `Elevator` object, so contact can be made between the two objects.

We do this by exposing methods like `NewFloorRequest`. Instead of marking this method with the `private` word, we use another special word from C# called `public`.

A `Person` object can now "walk into" an `Elevator` object. When ready, the `Elevator` object can send a message to the `Person` object and, via the `NewFloorRequest` method, receive the desired destination floor of this `Person`. Figure 3.1 illustrates this scenario. Notice the double lined arrow. It represents the message sent to the `Person` object. The single lined arrow going in the opposite direction represents the value (the floor number request) returned to the `Elevator` object from the `Person` object. The double lined arrow represents a method call. Programmers say that the `Elevator` object is *calling* the `NewFloorRequest` method.

The `Elevator` object, like its real counterpart, might need to somehow keep track of, for example, the speed at which it is traveling and its maximum speed; these are the *instance variables* (data) of the object, as mentioned previously. Just like the elevators of the real world, the `Elevator` objects of the C# simulation do not want any interference from other objects to mistakenly change their instance variables. Therefore, the `Elevator` objects declare them to be `private`, as shown in Figure 3.1, making them inaccessible for other objects.

Encapsulation in a Typical Class

Recall the objects displayed in Figure 2.3 of Chapter 2. They are equivalent to the objects shown in Figure 3.1. A generalized object using C#'s access modifiers and indicating the encapsulating `public` layer is displayed in Figure 3.2. Notice how the `public` area of this generic object can be viewed to surround the `private` area like a protective shell. The object still contains the instructions executed by the computer (flow of execution or algorithms); they have now been divided into a `public` part and a `private` part. All the data (or instance variables) are hidden inside in the `private` area.

FIGURE 3.1
`Elevator` object requesting information from *`Person`* object.

◇ `private` Instance variables
● `private` methods
○ `public` methods

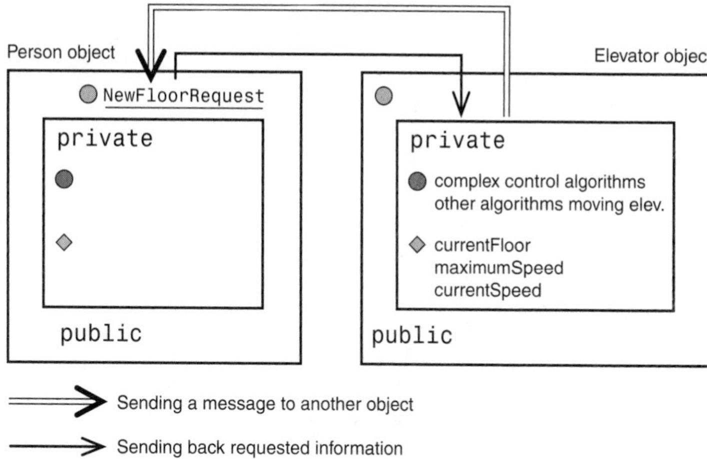

FIGURE 3.2
A generic object.

○ `public` methods
● `private` methods
◇ `private` Instance variables

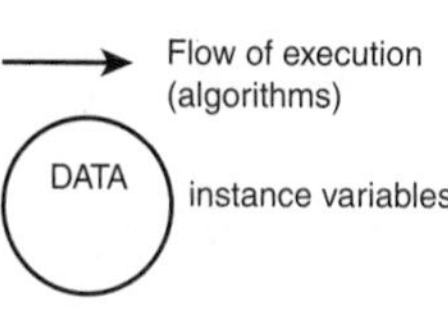

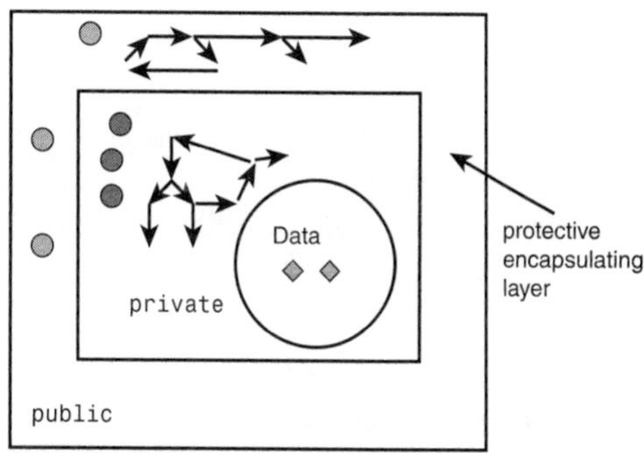

Class and Object

The class works as a template for the creation of objects. The blueprint of an elevator is to the elevator designer what the class is to the programmer.

All objects of the same class contain the same methods and the same instance variables. Consequently, a class is a logical construct; but an object has the ability to perform the actions specified by the class.

All objects of the same class are called *instances of a class*. When an object is formed during the execution of a program (as when a tangible elevator is manufactured), we say it is *created* or *instantiated*.

We can now depict a typical generic class as illustrated in Figure 3.3. Simply viewed, the class consists of data (instance variables) and algorithms (methods). When you write the source code for a class, you specify the methods and the instance variables that you want this class, and all objects derived from it, to contain. All instance variables and methods are collectively referred to as *members* or *fields* of the class.

FIGURE 3.3
A generic class illustrates encapsulation.

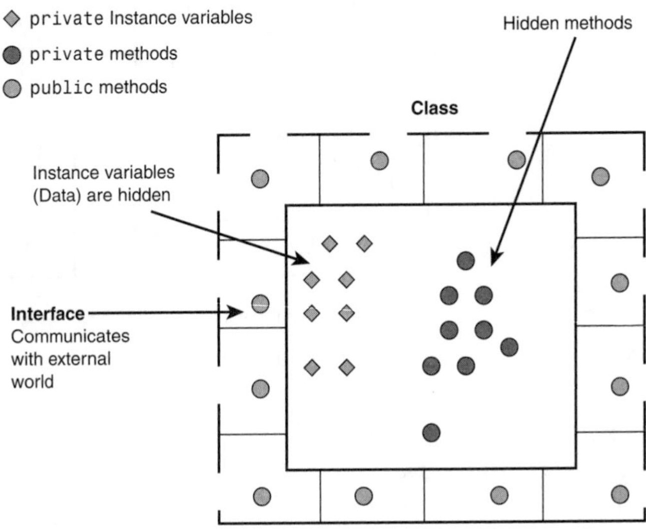

Encapsulation entails a layer that is meant to communicate with the outside world. Only through this part can the outside world communicate with the object. It further allows for a hidden part to exist inside this layer. This protective layer is denoted an *interface* and should only consist of methods.

Helper Methods

`private` methods can only be called by methods belonging to that same object. They provide functionality and support for other (often `public`) methods in the object and are frequently called *helper methods* or *utility methods*.

Note

The main advantages of encapsulation are as follows:

- *It provides for an abstraction layer*—Encapsulation saves the programmer who uses a class the need to know about the details of how this particular class is implemented.
- *It decouples the user interface of the object with its implementation*—It is possible to upgrade the implementation of an object while maintaining its user interface.
- *It covers the object with a protective wrapper*—Encapsulation protects the data inside the object from unwanted access that, otherwise, could cause the data to be corrupted and misused.

Only Methods Should Be Part of an Object's Interface, not Instance Variables

Instance variables positioned in the interface (this is possible in C#) effectively break the protective wrapper and allow for other objects to tinker with those exposed pieces of data. If access to specific data is needed, it should always be through a method (or properties and indexers, as discussed in later chapters).

A Note on Learning Object-Oriented Programming

Object-oriented programming and its related concepts might seem a bit fuzzy and overwhelming to you right now. This is perfectly normal, so don't despair.

In my experience, learning OOP is not like learning the content of, say, a history book by heart. While reading the history book, you gradually learn the material. It seems that an hour spent studying gives you an hour's worth of knowledge (unless the subject is complex and interrelated with other historical events), resulting in a nearly linear relationship between the amount of hours spent studying and the amount of knowledge you have acquired (see Figure 3.4).

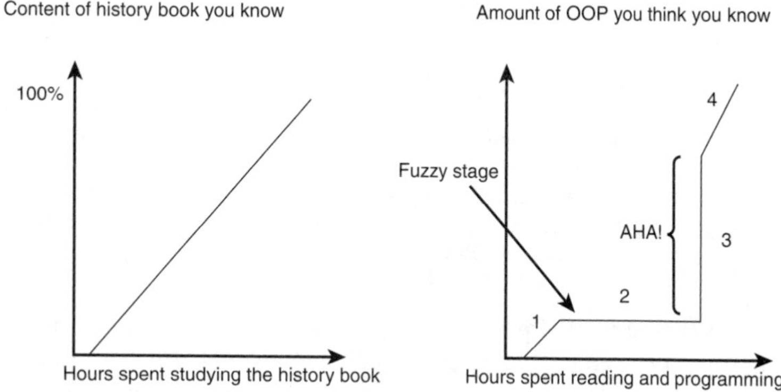

FIGURE 3.4
Comparing learning by heart and learning OOP.

This is most often not the case when learning OOP because of its interrelated and dynamic aspects and because OOP implies more than just a bunch of statements being executed one after the other. Initially, you will likely learn the names of several concepts (see 1 in Figure 3.4) but without much understanding for their real purpose. You might spend some time in this fuzzy, perhaps frustrating stage. Despite your studying efforts, you might not feel you are really gaining an increased understanding for the underlying logic; new concepts presented seem to confuse rather than enlighten (see 2 in Figure 3.4). However, your mind is constantly absorbing new aspects, information, and subtleties whenever you read the theory and work through the examples. Suddenly, at a specific moment in time (perhaps at night just after waking up from your favorite dream about abstraction and encapsulation), you experience this quantum leap in understanding, this AHA! Experience. All of a sudden, the pieces of the puzzle form a meaningful picture (see 3 in Figure 3.4). Equipped with this fundamental understanding, it becomes much easier to learn the new, more advanced OOP concepts (see 4 in Figure 3.4).

So don't get frustrated—have fun instead. Attack the OOP concepts from different angles, theoretically as well as experimentally, with the C# language.

An Interactive Hello World! Program

While you are digesting the OO information from the previous section, in the next few sections, I will present and analyze a C# source code example accompanied by an introduction to many of the fundamental aspects and features of the C# language. This will be a step toward your first object-oriented C# program presented in the last section of Chapter 5, which constitutes a simple, but working C# elevator simulation source program, directly related to our earlier, somewhat theoretical OO discussion.

Presenting `Hello.cs`

By tradition, the first program written in a new language prints the two words Hello World! onscreen. Because this is your second program (the first program `Shakespeare.cs` was in Chapter 2), we will write a similar program but slightly more advanced. Instead of merely printing out Hello World!, the user can interact with the program in Listing 3.1 and choose whether Hello World! is printed onscreen.

Note

Any professional interactive application allocates large amounts of source code dealing with invalid user input. Metaphorically speaking, the program attempts to prevent any user from inputting squares where the program expects triangles. To keep the source programs presented in this book compact and focused at the relevant features presented, most parts of the book do not include any user input validation code.

A central facet of programming should be aimed at making programs user friendly. The end user of a program and the programmer are often different people. As the programmer, you cannot expect the user to know how to interact with your program. You must enable the program to guide the user and make the program easy to use, as shown in the sample output after Listing 3.1. There are two possible outputs from the program, depending on whether the user wants Hello World! to be printed. The text typed in by the user is shown in boldface. Notice how the sentence:

```
Type y for yes; n for no.
```

guides the user through the program.

LISTING 3.1 Source Code for `Hello.cs`

```
 // This is a simple C# program
class Hello
{
     // The program begins with a call to Main()
    public static void Main()
```

LISTING 3.1 continued

```
06:     {
07:         string answer;
08:
09:         System.Console.WriteLine("Do you want me to write the two words?");
10:         System.Console.WriteLine("Type y for yes; n for no. Then <enter>");
11:         answer = System.Console.ReadLine();
12:         if (answer == "y")
13:             System.Console.WriteLine("Hello World!");
14:         System.Console.WriteLine("Bye Bye!");
15:     }
16: }
```

Sample output 1 results when the user answers **y** (yes):

```
Do you want me to write the two words?
Type y for yes; n for no. Then <enter>.
y <enter>
Hello World!
Bye Bye!
```

Sample output 2 results when the user answers **n** (no):

```
Do you want me to write the two words?
Type y for yes; n for no. Then <enter>.
n <enter>
Bye Bye!
```

Listing 3.2 provides a brief analysis of each source code line in Listing 3.1. There is a one-to-one correspondence between the line numbers in the two listings. Each line of Listing 3.1 is thoroughly discussed in the following sections. Listing 3.2 is only meant as a quick reference when you return to Listing 3.1 for a reminder about how a particular construct is written.

LISTING 3.2 Analysis of Source Code for `Hello.cs`

```
01: Make comment: This is a simple C# program
02: Begin the definition of a class named Hello
03: Begin the block of the Hello class definition
04:     Make comment: The program begins with a call to Main()
05:     Begin the definition of a method called Main()
06:     Begin the block of the Main() method definition
07:         Declare a variable called answer, which can store text
08:         Empty line
09:         Print out: Do you want me to write the two words? Move down
                one line
10:         Print out: Type y for yes; n for no. Then <enter>  Move down one
                line
11:         Store users answer in the answer variable. Move down one line.
12, 13:     If answer stores a 'y' then print: Hello World!
            If answer does not store a 'y' then jump over
            ➥line 13 and continue with line 14.
14:         Print out: Bye Bye! Move down one line.
15:     End block containing Main() method definition
16: End block containing Hello class definition
```

Convention

Output printed on the command console from the program is presented as `Bye Bye!`

It's time to start up good old Notepad and type in the source code. You can call the source file `Hello.cs`. Compile `Hello.cs`, run the program by typing **`Hello`** after the console prompt, and compare the output with what is shown in the sample output from Listing 3.1.

If the Screen Disappears Before You Can Read All the Output

You might have decided to use a text editor other than Notepad, perhaps even an Integrated Development Environment (IDE) configured for C#. This is fine. However, you might encounter a small problem with some systems with the command console disappearing too early, certainly before you ever get a chance to read the onscreen output.

Fortunately, there is a simple solution to this problem. Put the following line of code at the end of the `Main` method (just before the brace that ends the block containing the `Main` method):

```
System.Console.ReadLine();
```

When the program encounters this statement, it will wait for you to press the Enter key, allowing you time to study the output onscreen.

The program in Listing 3.1 is relatively simple, but it contains many essential ingredients of a typical C# program. Let's take a closer look at each part of the program. After you have mastered the concepts presented in this section, they can be applied to most C# programs you will write.

Basic Elements of `Hello.cs`

Every line number contained in this section refers to the line numbers of Listing 3.1.

Comments

Line 1 contains a *comment*. The compiler ignores the contents of a comment. It is used purely to describe or explain the elements of the program to anyone reading through the source code. In this case, the comment simply tells you that the source code you are looking at represents a simple C# program.

```
01:  // This is a simple C# program
```

Comments

Comments are extremely valuable for your source code. They are as important as the other elements of the source code. Not only do they enable other people to understand your code, they also act as your own valuable reminders in source code you haven't seen for some time. It is only too easy to forget the structure and logic behind your own source code.

The double forward slash (//) tells the compiler to ignore the rest of the line. In line 1, the comment is on its own line, but it can also be on the same line as code. Consequently lines 1 and 2 could have been combined as follows:

```
class Hello  // This is a simple C# program
```

but the following is invalid:

```
// This is a simple C# program  class Hello
```

The whole line is suddenly regarded as a comment and so `class Hello` will be ignored completely by the compiler.

Defining a Class

To explain line 2, I must briefly introduce the concept keyword also called reserved word. A *keyword* has a special predefined meaning in the C# language and is recognized by the compiler.

```
02: class Hello
```

Line 2 uses the keyword `class` to declare that a class is being defined. `Hello` is the name of the class and must be positioned immediately after `class`.

Every language, including spoken languages, contains words with a special meaning. In English, we call it a vocabulary; in science it's called terminology.

Likewise, the C# language has its own vocabulary made up of *keywords*, also referred to as *reserved words*. Listing 3.1 introduces the following keywords: `class`, `public`, `static`, `void`, `string`, and `if`. It's wise to spend a moment locating these in Listing 3.1. You can find the remaining C# keywords in Appendix C, "Reserved Words in C#." which is found on www.samspublishing.com.

Keywords have very special meanings to the compiler. They cannot, as the term reserved word indicates, be used for other objectives in C#.

`class`, for instance, cannot be used as a name for any element in C#, such as a method or a variable.

Let's give an example from the English language of why this makes sense. Look at the sentence, "Running is very helpful. Running fixed the washing machine today."

Hmm…what is going on here? Well, the parents of Running didn't quite follow the traditional conventions when they named their son Running. Their strange naming preferences distorted our ability to communicate for a moment. Despite our brain's amazing capacity of deciphering information, we still were confused with the use of the word Running. Did Running refer to the English *keyword* running (as a verb) or the son's name Running?

In contrast to our brain, the compiler is a very exact and non-forgiving creature. If for instance line 2 of Listing 3.1 was changed to `class class`; instead of `class Hello`, the compiler would be even more confused than us, causing it to report an error.

Notice that a keyword can be part of a name, so **classVariable** is an acceptable name.

The technical term for a name like **Hello** is *identifier*. Identifiers are, apart from classes, also used to name elements like methods and instance variables.

Had we implemented our **Elevator** class from the elevator simulation, we would most likely have used the identifier **Elevator** instead of **Hello**.

Identifiers (Names)

Names in source code are often called identifiers. Many elements, such as classes, objects, methods and, variables must have identifiers. In contrast to the keywords of C#, which were decided by its designers, you as a programmer decide each identifier.

A few rules apply here. An identifier must consist entirely of letters, digits (0–9), or the underscore character (_). An identifier cannot start with a digit and cannot be one of the keywords displayed in Appendix C which you can find on www.samspublishing.com.

Examples:

Legal identifiers:

```
Elevator
_elevator
My2Elevators,
My_Elevator
MyElevator
```

Illegal identifiers:

```
Ele vator
6Elevators
```

C# is case sensitive, so lowercase and uppercase letters are considered to be different characters. **Hello** and **hello** are as different to the compiler as **Hello** and **Bye**.

Braces and Blocks of Source Code

Line 3 contains a brace ({). It indicates the beginning of a block.

A *block* is a piece of C# source code enclosed within braces. } indicates the end of a block. After a block of code has been created, it becomes a logical unit. Braces, which are used to indicate blocks of code, always work together in pairs. Whenever you see a {, you know there must be a matching } somewhere. The matching } to line 3 is found in line 16. We have another matching pair of braces in lines 6 and 15.

```
03: {
```

Because { of line 3 is positioned immediately after line 2, the compiler knows that the entire definition of the **Hello** class is contained in between { of line 3 and } of line 16. Methods and instance variables can now be inserted in this class definition block, as shown in Figure 3.5, by making sure that all method and instance variable declarations are written between the two braces.

FIGURE 3.5
The class definition.

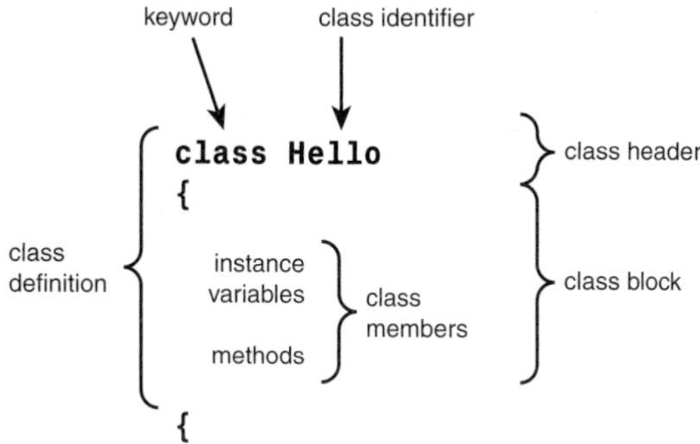

Tip

The following is a way to help prevent missing braces. Whenever you need to indicate the start of a block with a left brace ({), immediately type the right brace (}) under the left brace. Then position the cursor between the two braces and write the source code for this particular block.

In line 4

```
04:        // The program begins with a call to Main()
```

we recognize the `//` indicating the beginning of a comment.

The `Main()` Method and Its Definition

Line 5 indicates the beginning of the definition for a method called `Main`. There is no special C# keyword such as "method" indicating that we are dealing with a method. The compiler, though, works this out by recognizing the parentheses `()` after `Main`.

```
05:        public static void Main()
```

The `Main` method has a special meaning in C#. Any C# application begins its execution at the `Main` method. This method is called by the .NET runtime when the program is started.

For example, a sophisticated spreadsheet program written in C# might contain thousands of methods with different identifiers, but only a method named `Main` will be called by the .NET runtime to start the program.

I will not attempt to provide you with the exact meaning of all the parts of line 5, because this involves a detailed understanding of how C# deals with certain object-oriented principles.

However, Figure 3.3, presented earlier in this chapter, can certainly help illuminate parts of line 5. Remember that a class consists of an interface made up of `public` methods and a hidden part consisting of `private` methods and `private` instance variables.

`public`, in line 5, is an access modifier. This keyword allows the programmer to control the visibility of a class member. By using `public` in line 5 somewhere in front of `Main`, we indicate that `Main` is a `public` method and so it is part of the interface of the `Hello` class. As a result, `Main` can be called from outside a `Hello` object.

Figure 3.6 illustrates the major elements of a method definition.

FIGURE 3.6
A method definition.

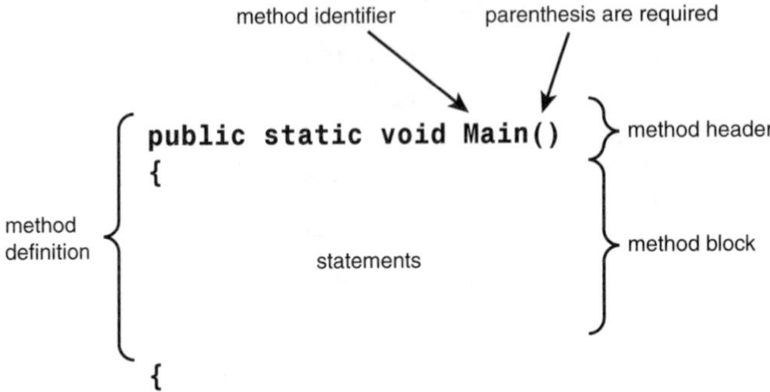

The *Main* Method

Every C# program must contain a method called `Main`. When a program is executed, the .NET runtime will look for a `Main` method as a first step. When found, it will execute this method; thus, it is always the first method to be executed in a program. An error is reported if no `Main` method is found.

`Main` is in Listing 3.1 located inside of the `Hello` class and the .NET runtime is located outside. When .NET attempts to execute the `Main` method, it will be regarded as just another object trying to access a method of the class. Therefore, we need to expose the `Main` method and make it part of the interface of its class.

A `Main` method must always be declared `public` to let .NET gain access to it.

Typically Main will cause other methods located in other objects to be executed but, as you can see, our first simple examples merely contain one class with one Main method

To get an initial feel for the meaning of the `static` keyword, recall our discussion about the differences between a class and an object. A class is just a specification of how to create an object, just like an architectural drawing is only a plan of how to create a real house. A class usually cannot take any actions. Well, the `static` keyword lets us cheat a bit here. It enables us to use methods of a class without instantiating any objects first.

When `static` is part of a method header, we tell the class that it does not need to be instantiated for an object outside the class to use the method. In this case, it allows us to specify that `Main` can be used without first instantiating a specific object based on the `Hello` class. This is necessary here because `Main` is called by the .NET runtime before any objects are created.

Note

A `Main` method must always be declared `public` and `static`.

If the meaning of `static` seems a bit fuzzy and incomprehensible, don't worry. We will return to this concept in more detail later.

To fully understanding the meaning of `void` in line 5, you need to know a bit more about how methods work. At this point, I will only give you a brief explanation. `void` indicates that `Main()` does not return a value to the caller.

In line 6, { indicates the beginning of `Main()`'s block, which contains the source code comprising the method. The matching } ending this block can be found in line 15.

```
06:        {
```

Tip

Choose meaningful variable names in your source code to improve clarity and readability. Avoid abbreviations; don't be afraid to choose long variable names. Which is clearer to you, `avgSpPHr` or `averageSpeedPerHour`?

Source code that can be understood simply by reading it rather than having to consult manuals and look through excessive amounts of comments is said to be *self-documenting*.

Variables: Representing Data Stored in Computer Memory

`answer` in line 7 is a variable. `answer` is the identifier of this variable.

A *variable* is a named memory location representing a stored piece of data. The keyword `string` dictates `answer` to be of type `string`.

```
07:            string answer;
```

The programmer can arbitrarily choose the identifier `answer`, whereas `string` is unchangeable because it is a keyword.

By typing `answer` after `string`, as in line 7, we say in technical terms that we have declared `answer` to be a variable of type `string`.

Note

Any variable used in a C# program must be declared.

We use the `answer` variable in lines 11 and 12. A variable of type `string` can contain text. For example, "Coco is a dog," "Julian is a boy," "y," or "n" are all examples of text and so are valid data storable in `answer`. In C#, strings of characters are denoted with `" "` (double quotes). I have illustrated the parts that make up a variable, such as `answer`, in Figure 3.7.

The figure shows that a variable consists of three things:

- Its *identifier*, which is `answer` in this case.

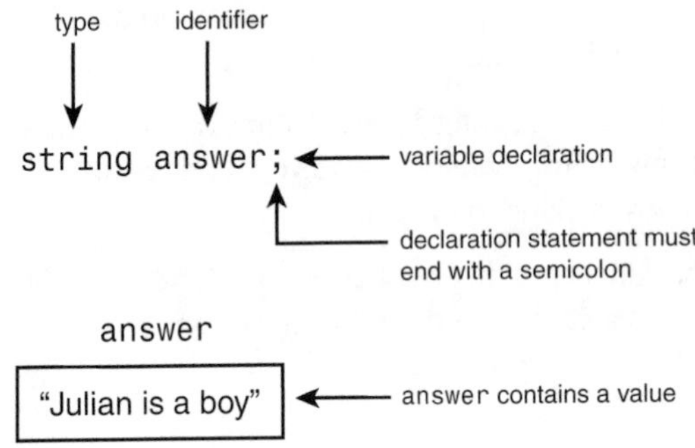

FIGURE 3.7
A variable's type, identifier, and value.

- Its *type* or the kind of information it can hold, which in this case is `string`, meaning a sequence of characters.
- Its *value*, which is the information presently stored. In the illustration, the current value is `"Julian is a boy"`.

I have not revealed all the facts about the `string` type here. String is actually a *reference* type so does not itself hold the text it seems to store; it merely refers to the memory location holding the text. For now, however, we can happily continue disregarding this knowledge. We will return to this aspect in Chapter 6, "Types Part I: The Simple Types."

The only thing left to explain in line 7 is the semicolon character (`;`). Any task accomplished by a C# program can be broken down into a series of instructions. A simple instruction is called a *statement*. All statements must be terminated with a semicolon character. Line 7 is a declaration statement so a semicolon character must terminate the line.

Line 8 is an empty line.

```
08:
```

The C# compiler will simply ignore an empty line. The empty line is inserted to improve the look and readability of the source code.

Invoking Methods of the .NET Framework

The program in line 9

```
09:         System.Console.WriteLine("Do you want me to write the two words?");
```

instructs the computer to print out the following:

```
Do you want me to write the two words?
```

For now, you can consider `System.Console.WriteLine` to be a peculiar way of saying "print whatever is shown in parenthesis after `WriteLine` onscreen and then move down one line."

Briefly, this is what happens behind the curtains of line 9. `System.Console` is a class from the .NET Framework. Recall that the .NET Framework is a class library containing numerous useful classes written by professional programmers from Microsoft. Here, we are essentially reusing a class referred to as `System.Console` in our program to print out text onscreen.

`System.Console` contains a method, named `WriteLine`, that is called with the command `System.Console.WriteLine`. `WriteLine` carries out an action; it prints the text inside the parenthesis `("Do you want me to write the two words?")`.

When a method is called to perform a task, we say the method is being *invoked*. The item inside the parenthesis (in this case, the text: `"Do you want me to write the famous words?"`) is called an argument. An *argument* provides information needed by the invoked method to carry out its task. The argument is passed to the `WriteLine` method when invoked. `WriteLine` then has access to this data for its own statements. We can then describe the action of `WriteLine` as follows, "When `WriteLine` is invoked, print out the argument passed to it."

Line 9 is a statement, like line 8, and so it must end with a semicolon.

There is one problem with line 9 that we briefly need to address. It might not be obvious, but we are using a method of the class `System.Console` in line 9. How can we use the method of a class? Several times now we have emphasized classes as mere plans and objects as the doers. However, by using the keyword `static` (mentioned earlier) to cheat a little bit, it becomes possible to use the method of a class. The programmer who implemented the `WriteLine` method used `static` to make `WriteLine` available for use without first having to instantiate `System.Console`.

The General Mechanics of Method Invocation

The instructions of a method reside inside its method definition in the form of statements.

To invoke a method means to initiate the statements it has been instructed to perform. They will be performed in a sequential manner, beginning at the topmost statement and in the same sequence as they are written in the source code.

Methods can only be defined inside classes. A method is an action that an object is able to perform. It is invoked by writing the object name (or the class name if the method is declared `static`) followed by a period (full stop) `.`, called a *dot*, followed by the method name and ending with a pair of parenthesis `()` that may or may not contain arguments. Arguments are data passed to the method.

A call to a non-static method residing in an object generally looks like the following:

```
ObjectName.MethodName(Optional_Arguments)
```

A call to a static method includes the class name as in the following:

```
ClassName.MethodName(Optional_Arguments)
```

By substituting the general terms with actual names, we can form the following valid statement, which is identical to line 14 of Listing 3.1.

```
System.Console.WriteLine("Bye Bye!");
```

When the method has finished, it will return to the position from which it was invoked. The program flow when invoking a method, as in line 14 of Listing 3.1, is shown in Figure 3.8. The following individual steps can be identified in the figure. The numbers correspond to those shown in the figure.

1. Execute statements prior to line 14.
2. Execute line 14.
3. Call `System.Console.WriteLine` with the argument `"Bye Bye!";`.
4. Execute the statements inside `System.Console.WriteLine(...)`.
5. Return to statement just after line 14.
6. Execute the rest of the statements in the `Main` method.

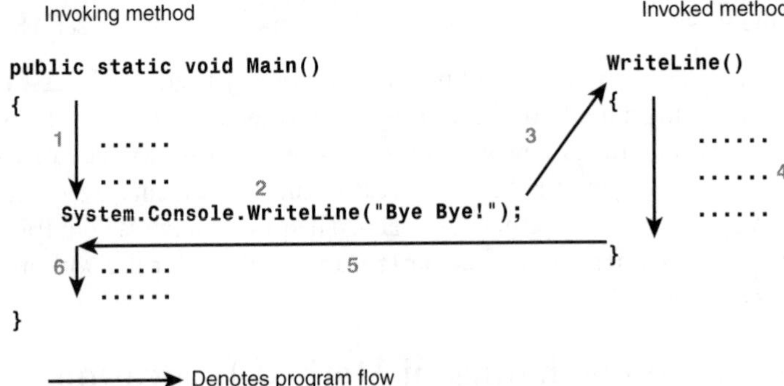

FIGURE 3.8
Program flow when invoking a method.

Line 10 contains another method call to `WriteLine`

```
10:          System.Console.WriteLine("Type y for yes; n for no. Then <enter>");
```

The result of this method call is as follows:

```
Type y for yes; n for no. Then <enter>.
```

is printed onscreen, and the cursor is moved down one line.

Message: Another Term for Method Invocation

Consider line 9 of Listing 3.1. It contains a statement invoking the `WriteLine` method. Another term is often used in object-oriented programming circles to denote the invocation of an object.

When a method of object A contains a statement that is invoking the method of an object called B, we say A is sending a message to B. In line 10, our class `Hello` is sending a message to the `System.Console` class. The message is

```
WriteLine("Type y for yes; n for no. Then <enter>")
```

In general, objects are thought of as performing actions triggered by messages received. In our example, the action taken is to print

```
Type y for yes; n for no. Then <enter>
```

on the console.

Assigning a Value to a Variable

In line 11, we again reuse the `System.Console` class. This time, we use another of its `static` methods called `ReadLine`, which will pause the execution and wait for a response from the user. The response must be in the form of text entered and the Enter key pressed. As its name suggests, `ReadLine` will read the input from the user.

```
11:            answer = System.Console.ReadLine();
```

When the Enter key is pressed, the text typed in by the user will be stored in the `answer` variable. Consequently, if the user types 'y', `answer` will contain a `"y"`. If the user types 'n', `answer` will contain an `"n"`. This is because of the equals sign (=) placed after `answer`.

The equals sign (=) is used differently in C# than in standard arithmetic. In arithmetic, the equals sign usually denotes the equality of items to the left and right of the sign. For example, 4=2+2 is a valid expression in arithmetic and can be said to be true. In C#, the meaning is quite different. Instead, the equals sign says "Make `answer` equal to `System.Console.ReadLine()`" or, in other words, "Store the text read from the keyboard in `answer`."

The mechanism of giving `answer` a new value is called *assignment*. The text typed in by the user is said to be assigned to the `answer` variable. Line 11 is called an *assignment statement* and the equals sign (=) is called an *assignment operator* when used in this context. The equals sign is involved in other contexts and then it will have different appropriate names.

An Advantage of Declaring Variables

Initially, variable declarations seem to complicate matters and be a waste of typing and time. Why can't we just use the variable when needed without any previous declaration? Well, in extremely short programs, such as the one presented, we could easily live without declarations. However, variable declarations have important benefits when writing larger programs. Consider a programming language like an older version of BASIC (not Visual Basic) where variable declarations are not required. Without further ado, BASIC allows us to involve, say, `MyVariable` in an assignment statement as in the following:

```
MyVariable = 100
MyVarable = 300
System.Console.WriteLine(MyVariable)
```

Initially, we stored `100` in `MyVariable` and later wanted to store `300` instead. However, due to a spelling mistake in the second line shown, we ended up storing `300` in `MyVarable`, leaving `MyVariable` with the same value 100. This mistake was not picked up by the BASIC compiler, but would have been unveiled by the C# compiler, where all variables used throughout the program are checked for matching declarations.

Now, try and put your trusty C# compiler to the test. Change the spelling of `answer` in line 11 or 12 and observe its reaction when you compile the now faulty program.

Branching with the `if` Statement

You saw one use for the equals sign in line 11. In line 12, it is used in a different context, this time resembling that of arithmetic's standard use of the equals sign.

```
12:            if (answer == "y")
13:                System.Console.WriteLine("Hello World!");
```

C# uses two adjacent equals signs (==), called an *equality operator*, to denote a comparison between what is on its left with what is on its right. Consequently, the two following expressions articulate the same question:

Using standard arithmetic:

> 2 + 3 = 6 meaning "Is 2 + 3 equal to 6?"
>
> Answer: false

Is the same as

Using the C# language

> `2 + 3 == 6` meaning "Is 2 + 3 equal to 6?"
>
> Answer: `false`

In line 12, we ask the question `answer == "y"`, meaning "Is `answer` equal to `"y"`?" The answer can be either `true` or `false`.

An expression that can only have the two values—`true` or `false`—is said to be a *Boolean expression*.

Caution

It is easy to confuse the equality operator == with the assignment operator =. The assignment operator = can be read "gets the value of" or "gets," whereas the equality operator == should be read "is equal to." To avoid confusion, some programmers refer to the assignment operator as *equals equals* or *double equals*.

By putting the keyword `if` in front of the Boolean expression `answer == "y"` and surrounding this expression by parenthesis, we are saying that only if `answer == "y"` is `true` should the line immediately after line 12 (in this case line 13) be executed. Conversely, if `answer == "y"` is `false`, jump over line 13 and continue with line 14. In Figure 3.9 I have zoomed in on lines 12–14 and indicated the execution flow with arrows.

Lines 12 and 13 contain a vital element for controlling the output of the computer and, in fact, achieve two different outputs as shown previously in sample output 1 and 2.

Note a couple of important details:

- Regardless of whether we answer `y` or `n`, the program writes the line "Bye Bye!" at the end.

- Only the answer `y` will trigger the program to print Hello World!. Any other answer, such as horse, Peter, Y, yes, n, N, and so on will make the Boolean expression false and ignore line 13.

Line 12 and 13 constitute an `if` statement. The `if` statement is said to control the flow of the execution because the execution at this point can choose to follow two different directions. The `if` statement is said to belong to a category of statements called branching statements.

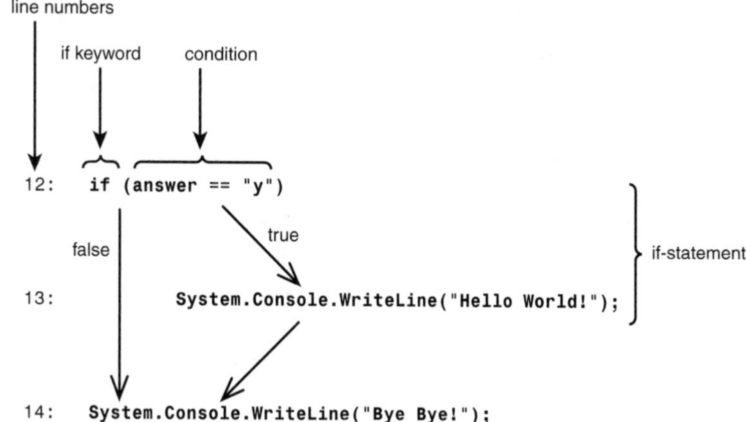

FIGURE 3.9
The flow of execution in an `if` statement.

Caution

The left and right parenthesis enclosing the condition of the if statement, as shown in the following:

```
if (answer == "y")
```

are always required. Omitting them will produce a syntax error.

Ending the `Main()` Method and the `Hello` Class

The `}` on line 15 ends the `Main` method block started in line 6.

```
15:        }
```

Caution

The braces `{}` must occur in pairs. Failing to comply with this rule triggers a compiler error.

In line 16, `}` ends the `Hello` class definition block.

```
16: }
```

This concludes the analysis of Listing 3.1.

A Few Fundamental Observations

The previous sections were able to extract many fundamental C# constructs and mechanisms from Listing 3.1, despite its simple appearance. This section looks at a few general C# concepts by summarizing and building on the knowledge you have gained from Listing 3.1.

C#'s Source Code Format

Blank lines, space characters, tab characters, and carriage returns are collectively known as *whitespace*. To a large degree, the C# compiler ignores whitespace. Consequently, you can use blank lines, space characters, tab characters, and carriage returns interchangeably. Let's look at an example. From the C# compilers point of view, the three lines of source code in Figure 3.10 are all identical to line 5 of Listing 3.1.

```
05:         public static void Main()
```

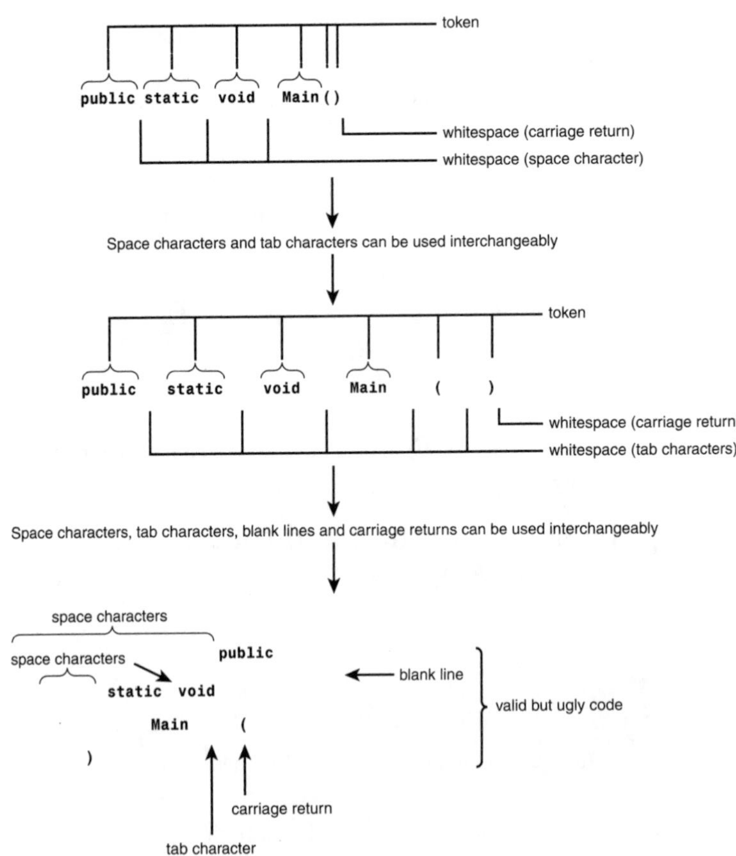

FIGURE 3.10
Whitespace is ignored by the compiler.

Notice how distorted the third line in Figure 3.10 has become; it is still valid code but incomprehensible and ugly.

The indivisible elements in a line of source code are called *tokens*. One token must be separated from the next by whitespace, commas, or semicolons. However, it is unacceptable to separate the token itself into smaller pieces by using whitespace or separators.

A *token* is a particular instance of a word with a special meaning attached to it. The term token is also frequently used in the scientific fields of logic and linguistics.

Don't break up tokens with whitespace; this causes invalid code as shown below, which contains three invalid versions of line 5: `public static void Main():`

```
pub lic   stati c   void  Main()
```

```
public static void Ma

in()
```

```
public static vo id Main()
```

On the other hand, it is possible to aggregate statements and source code on the same line, as shown in the following line.

```
class Hello { public static void Main() {  string answer;
```

The following is better-styled original code:

```
02: class Hello
03: {
04:       // The program begins with a call to Main()
05:     public static void Main()
06:     {
07:         string answer;
```

Although C# provides much freedom when formatting your source code, you can increase its clarity considerably by following a reasonable style. It is possible to write valid but ugly source code, as you have seen in a few of the previous examples. Ugly here refers to messy, unclear, confusing source code that is difficult for another person to comprehend.

Listing 3.1 follows a certain style that is adhered to by a large proportion of the programming community. Let's have a look at a few general guidelines. Line numbers from Listing 3.1 are provided as examples.

- Have one statement per line (lines 7, 9, 10, 11, and 14).

  However, note the `if` statement; it's an exception. It should be spread over several lines (in the case of Listing 3.1 it is spread over two lines).

- After an opening brace (`{`) move down one line and indent (lines 4, and 7).

- Indent matching pairs of braces identically (lines 3, 16 and lines 6, 15).

- While observing the two previous rules, indent lines between matching pairs of braces identically. (Lines 4, 5 and lines 7–14). Keep in mind that statements after `if` conditions should be indented (line 13).

- Put in blank lines to separate distinctive logic parts of the source code (line 8).
- Do not use whitespace around the parentheses associated with a function name (line 5).

Competent programmers apply other conventions, to improve the style of their source code. We will discuss these in the following chapters whenever relevant.

A Brief Tour Around the .NET Framework

We have already made extensive use of the .NET Framework class library in Listing 3.1. It's especially visible in lines 9, 10, 11, 13, and 14 with `System.Console.WriteLine` and `System.Console.ReadLine`. There is extensive support for equipping your program with a wide variety of functionality from this class library. But how do we know which particular classes and methods we have access to and can reuse and how do we know their characteristics and the functionality they provide? We can find answers to these questions in the comprehensive documentation provided for the class library. The simple aim of this section is to show you how to locate this documentation and confirm the existence of `System.Console.WriteLine` and `System.Console.ReadLine` inside the myriad of other classes and methods.

At the time of writing, the following set of commands can be used to locate the .NET Framework documentation. This might change in later versions of the Software Development Kit (SDK).

Open up the directory with the path `D:\Program Files\Microsoft.Net\FrameworkSDK`.

Notice that `D:\` could be another letter, depending on where your documentation has been installed.

You should then see a window displaying the contents of the FrameworkSDK folder, similar to that shown in Figure 3.11.

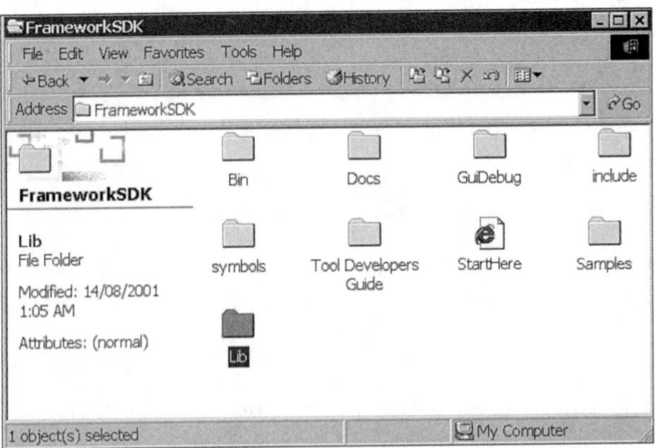

FIGURE 3.11
Contents of the FrameworkSDK folder.

Double-click the StartHere icon to bring up the start page of the .NET Framework Reference. Display the start page of the .NET Framework Documentation by clicking the hyperlink called

.NET Framework SDK documentation situated in the Documentation section. Expand the appearing .NET Framework SDK node on the left hand side of the window. Locate the .NET Framework Reference node and expand it. Among many other appearing nodes one is called .NET Framework Class Library which you can expand to display a window similar to that shown in Figure 3.12.

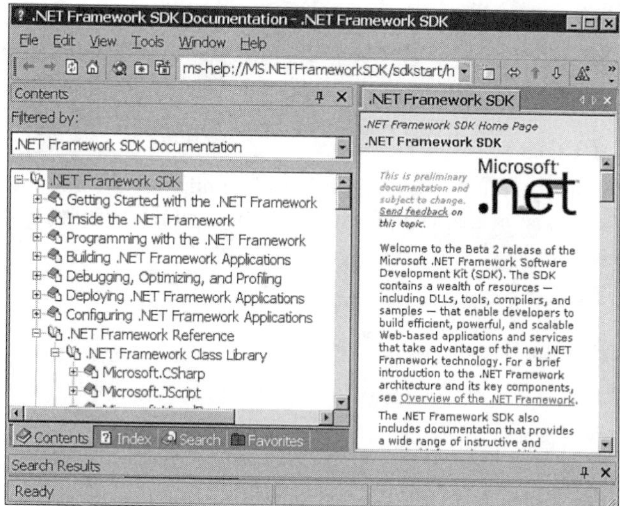

FIGURE 3.12
The .NET Framework Class Library Documentation.

You are now free to browse the documentation for the class library.

To locate the `Console` class, expand the System node and scroll down to find and expand the Console Class node. You can now find the `WriteLine` and `ReadLine` methods by clicking the Console Members node. Click the `ReadLine` hyperlink in the right part of the window to see the window shown in Figure 3.13.

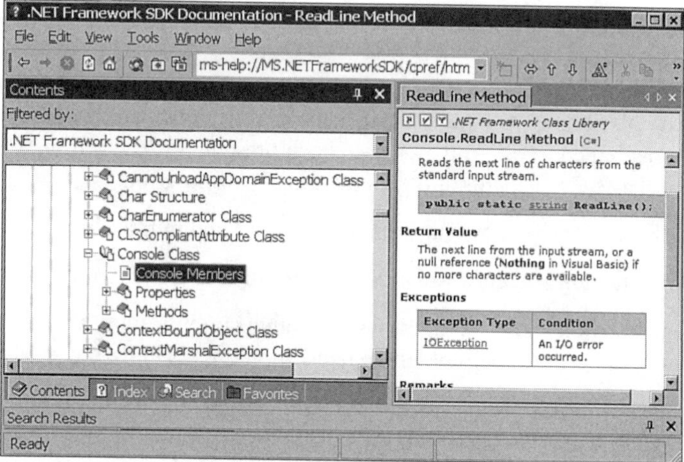

FIGURE 3.13
Displaying the *`Console.ReadLine`* specifications.

Under the headline `Console.ReadLine` Method, you can read a short description of `ReadLine`. You can locate the `WriteLine` method in the same fashion.

Many of the terms mentioned in the .NET Framework Reference will not make any sense to you right now. However, eventually this reference is most likely going to be an important source of information.

As you are presented with more classes from the library, try to locate them and use the new terms introduced in the coming chapters to familiarize yourself with this very powerful set of tools.

C# Statements

As mentioned earlier, each method in C# contains a collection of statements. Many types of statements exist in C#. The following is a brief summary of the statements we encountered in Listing 3.1.

- Declaration statements (line 7)
- Assignment statements (line 11)
- Method call statements (lines 9, 10, 11, 13, and 14)

Declaration statements create a variable that can be used in the program. They announce the type and identifier of the variable.

Even though declaration statements may seem superfluous, they introduce several features that help eliminate bugs in computer programs.

An assignment statement uses the assignment operator =. It assigns a value to a storage location that is represented by the identifier of the variable.

A method call activates a method. It can send arguments to the invoked method that utilizes these to perform its actions. When the invoked method terminates, the program will return to the statement immediately following the method call statement.

Summary

In this chapter, you have learned about abstraction and encapsulation, two important object-oriented concepts. You have also been presented with a simple C# program and learned about its basic C# elements and general underlying concepts.

The following are the important points covered in this chapter:

Abstraction and encapsulation are important concepts in object-oriented programming.

Abstraction allows programmers, through simplification, to cope with complexity. Only attributes relevant to the problem at hand should be included in an abstraction.

Encapsulation packs data and their associated actions into the class entity. Only relevant parts of an object are exposed to the outside world. This keeps the data inside an object non-corrupted and provides for a simpler interface to the outside world. `public` and `private` are two important C# keywords used when implementing the encapsulation concept.

The method of one object can call the method of another object. In OO terminology, we say that a message is sent between two objects.

A class is written in the source code and is an inactive blueprint for its dynamic object counterparts that are created inside the main memory during the execution of a program.

Comments are ignored by the compiler but are used to make the code clearer for the person reading through the source code.

The keywords in C# were chosen by C#'s designers so their names and predefined meaning never change. In contrast, identifiers vary between programs, are decided by the programmer, and are used to name C# constructs, such as classes, methods, and instance variables.

A block forms a logical unit in a program. Among other functions, blocks are used to indicate which parts of a program belong to which classes and methods.

Every program must have one `Main` method. The `Main` method is called by the .NET runtime and is the first part of a program to be executed.

A variable has a name (identifier), is of a specific type, and represents a memory location containing a value.

A variable of type `string` can be used to store text.

Any set of actions performed by C# can be broken down into simple instructions called statements.

The predefined functionality in the .NET Framework class library can be conveniently accessed from the C# source code.

Methods are defined inside classes and contain statements. When a method is called, its statements are executed in the same sequence as they are written in the source code.

The equals sign is used in two different fashions, as an assignment operator (=) and as an equality operator (==).

The `if` statement is able to change the program's flow of execution. The path followed depends on the Boolean value of its condition.

To make the C# source code clear for the reader, follow a certain format and style.

The .NET Framework class library has comprehensive documentation attached.

Three common statements found in C# are declaration statements, assignment statements, and method call statements.

Review Questions

1. How does abstraction help the programmer to cope with complexity?
2. Is the idea behind encapsulation confined to software design? Give an example from everyday life.
3. What are the advantages of using encapsulation in software construction?
4. Which two C# keywords are important for implementing encapsulation?
5. What are the differences between a class and its objects?
6. What is the significance of the class interface?
7. How do you specify the beginning of a comment?
8. Why use comments if the compiler ignores them?
9. What are keywords and identifiers?
10. How is a block specified in C#? What are blocks used for?
11. Can you write a program without a `Main` method? Why or why not?
12. What are the essential parts of a variable?
13. What is a simple C# instruction called? How is it terminated?
14. Which class and which method can you call in the .NET Framework class library to print text on the console? Write a statement that prints "My dog is brown."
15. How is a method called? What happens when a method is called?
16. What is an assignment? Which symbol is used to perform an assignment?
17. What is the advantage of declaring variables?
18. How can you make the program decide between two paths of execution?
19. What is whitespace? Does the compiler care much about whitespace?
20. Do all programmers have to follow the same style to write valid C# programs?

Programming Exercises

In the following exercises, you are meant to change and add parts to the program in Listing 3.1 to make it perform the suggested actions.

1. Instead of printing "Bye Bye!" as the last text on the command console before the program finishes, change the source code so that the program writes "Bye Bye. Have a good day!"

2. Instead of typing a **y** to have the program print "Hello World!", have the user type **Yes**. Have the program inform the user about this by changing line 10.

3. Instead of using the variable name `answer` to hold the input from the user, change the name to `userInput`.

4. Let the program print out an additional line under `"Bye Bye. Have a good day!"` saying `"The program is terminating."`

5. Declare another variable of type `string` called `userName`. Before the program prints "Do you want me to write the famous words?", have the program request the user to type in his or her name. After the user has entered his or her name, have the program read this name and store it in the `userName` variable. Then have the program print "Hello" followed by the content of the username. Tip: the last printout can be accomplished by typing

```
System.Console.WriteLine("Hello" + userName);
```

A typical execution of the program should result in the following output:

```
Please type your name
Deborah<enter>
Hello Deborah
Do you want me to write the famous words?
Type Yes for yes; n for no. Then <enter>.
Yes<enter>
Hello World!
Bye Bye. Have a good day!
The program is terminating.
```

CHAPTER 4

A GUIDED TOUR THROUGH C#: PART II

You will learn about the following in this chapter:

- More fundamental C# elements building on those presented in Chapter 3, "A Guided Tour Through C#: Part I," through a source code driven presentation
- The namespace concept and an understanding for how this feature can help organize and access C# components
- The `int` type for storing whole numbers
- How to write and call your own user-defined methods
- Multiline comments and their different styles
- How C# evaluates simple expressions
- How methods can be used to simplify your source code

Introduction

A new source code example containing a simple calculator is presented in this chapter, along with several new elements of the C# language.

Essential Elements of `SimpleCalculator.cs`

You have already met the `string` type in Chapter 3, "A Guided Tour through C#: Part I." The calculator program you will see shortly introduces another type called `int`, which is a commonly used type for variables holding whole numbers. You will further see how you can define and use your own methods. The important namespace concept, enabling classes and other types to be organized into a single coherent hierarchical structure while providing easy access, is also presented. `WriteLine` will show off by revealing its versatility, and you will finally meet the handy `Math` class and apply a couple of methods from this part of the .NET Framework class library.

Presenting `SimpleCalculator.cs`

The source code in Listing 4.1 calculates the sum, product, minimum, and maximum value of two numbers entered by the user. The program prints the answers on the command console.

LISTING 4.1 Source Code for `SimpleCalculator.cs`

```
using System;

/*
 * This class finds the sum, product,
 * min and max of two numbers
 */
public class SimpleCalculator
{
    public static void Main()
    {
        int x;
        int y;

        Console.Write("Enter first number: ");
        x = Convert.ToInt32(Console.ReadLine());
        Console.Write("Enter second number: ");
        y = Convert.ToInt32(Console.ReadLine());
        Console.WriteLine("The sum is: " + Sum(x, y));
        Console.WriteLine("The product is: " + Product(x, y));
        Console.WriteLine("The maximum number is: " + Math.Max(x, y));
        Console.WriteLine("The minimum number is: " + Math.Min(x, y));
    }

     // Sum calculates the sum of two int's
    public static int Sum(int a, int b)
    {
        int sumTotal;

        sumTotal = a + b;
        return sumTotal;
    }

     // Product calculates the product of two int's
    public static int Product(int a, int b)
    {
        int productTotal;

        productTotal = a * b;
        return productTotal;
    }
}
```

The following is the sample output when the user enters **3** and **8**:

```
Enter first number: 3<enter>
Enter second number: 8<enter>
```

```
The sum is: 11
The product is: 24
The maximum number is: 8
The minimum number is: 3
```

A quick reference to the source code in Listing 4.1 is provided in Listing 4.2. You will most likely recognize several constructs from `Shakespeare.cs` in Chapter 2, "Your First C# Program," and `Hello.cs` in Chapter 3, and you will probably begin to form a picture of what the fundamental elements of a typical C# program look like.

LISTING 4.2 Brief Analysis of Listing 4.1

```
01: Allow this program to use shortcuts
    ➥when accessing classes in System namespace
02: Empty line
03: Begin multi-line comment
04:     Second line of multi-line comment: This class finds the sum, product,
05:     Third line of multi-line comment: min and max of two numbers
06: End multi-line comment
07: Begin the definition of a class named SimpleCalculator
08: Begin the block of the SimpleCalculator class definition
09:     Begin the definition of a method called Main()
10:     Begin the block of the Main() method definition
11:         Declare a variable called x which
            ➥can store whole numbers (integers).
12:         Declare a variable called y which
            ➥can store whole numbers (integers).
13:         Empty line
14:         Print out: Enter first number:
15:         Store users answer in the x variable. Move down one line
16:         Print out: Enter second number:
17:         Store users answer in the y variable. Move down one line
18:         Print out: The sum is: followed by the
            ➥value returned from the Sum method.
19:         Print out: The product is: followed by the
            ➥value returned from the Product method.
20:         Print out: The maximum number is: followed by the
            ➥value returned by the Max method of the Math class.
21:         Print out: The minimum number is: followed by the
            ➥value returned by the Min method of the Math class
22:     End the block containing the Main() method definition
23:     Empty line
24:     Make comment: Sum calculates the sum of two int's
25:     Begin the definition of a the method Sum(int a, int b)
26:     Begin the block of the Sum(int a, int b) method definition
27:         Declare a local variable called sumTotal which
            ➥can store whole integers.
28:         Empty line
29:         Find the sum of a and b; store this result in sumTotal
30:         Terminate the method; return the value of sumTotal to the caller.
31:     End the block of the Sum(int a, int b) method
32:     Empty line.
```

LISTING 4.2 continued

```
33:     Make comment: Product calculates the product of two int's
34:     Begin the definition of a the method Product(int a, int b)
35:     Begin the block of the Product(int a, int b) method definition
36:         Declare a local variable called productTotal which
            ➥can store whole integers
37:         Empty line
38:         Find the product of a and b; store this result in productTotal.
39:         Terminate the method; return the
            ➥value of productTotal to the caller
40:     End the block of the Product(int a, int b) method
41: End block containing SimpleCalculator class definition
```

By now, I assume you are comfortable writing source code in Notepad and compiling it with the `csc` command of the command console; therefore, I will let you write and run the source code in Listing 4.1 in peace now.

A Closer Look at `SimpleCalculator.cs`

`SimpleCalculator.cs` is probably not a program people would rush to buy in their local software store, but it certainly contains a few essential ingredients that would be part of most C# best-selling computer programs. The following section will take a closer look at Listing 4.1 to uncover them.

Introducing Namespaces

We need to introduce the namespace concept to get an initial understanding for line 1. To this end, we move to a seemingly unrelated place—your home.

```
01: using System;
```

Have you ever, like me, had the feeling of an invisible spirit at play that constantly turns your home into a place resembling a test site for new explosives, despite your best efforts to the contrary?

There seems to be a large number of different objects in a home causing the mess to relentlessly get out of hand—shirts, spoons, knives, shampoo, books, CDs, apples, pots, and Picasso paintings all pile up.

How, then, do we manage to make our home neat and tidy before the family arrives at Christmas? Containers are the solution to our problem. We form small hierarchies of containers inside other containers holding similar kinds of objects. For example, a kitchen knife (the object) would be positioned in the kitchen (here regarded as being a container) in the upper-left drawer container, in the cutlery tray container, in the knife compartment container, together with other more-or-less similar knives.

Not only do these containers help us to make our home nice and tidy, they also allow us to get an overview of where different objects are stored in the house. We are even able to show our guests where to find different objects. When everything is tidy around Christmas time, we can confidently tell our new friend Fred how to find a knife. If we turned our home into a small hotel with new visitors arriving on a daily basis, we might further create a little system for how to tell new guests where to find different objects. In this referencing system, we could decide to simply put a dot (period) between each container name. A guest looking for a knife then might only need the message `Kitchen.UpperLeftDrawer.CutleryTray.KnifeCompartment`.

As a final bonus, we avoid name collision problems. For example, we can differentiate between a knife used for fishing found in the garage and a knife used for eating found in the kitchen, even though they are both referred to as knife. This is simply done by specifying where each particular knife is positioned. Accordingly, the kitchen knife specified by `Kitchen.UpperLeftDrawer.CutleryTray.KnifeCompartment.Knife` would likely be different from our fishing knife referenced by `Garage.FishingCupboard.UpperRightDrawer.KnifeBox.Knife`.

The kitchen contains not only drawers and boxes, it also can contain objects like chairs and tables. Similarly, every container can contain not only other containers but also objects.

The practical container system described here is similar in concept to the namespace idea. The *namespaces* act as containers for the many classes we construct and must keep track of. Namespaces help us organize our source code when developing our programs (keeping our "home" of classes "nice and tidy," allowing us to know where each class is kept). They also allow us to tell our "guest" users where classes are kept, so they (other programmers) easily can access and reuse our classes. Name collisions between classes created by different programmers, perhaps from different software companies, are eliminated, because each class can be uniquely referenced through its namespace name.

Recall the .NET Framework documentation viewed previously. If you had a good look, you would have encountered a myriad of classes. In fact, the .NET Framework contains several thousand classes. Consequently, the .NET Framework is heavily dependent on namespaces to keep its classes organized and accessible.

The .NET Framework contains an important namespace called `System`. It holds specific classes fundamental to any C# program. Many other `System` classes are frequently used by most C# programs. It also includes our familiar `Console` class used extensively in Listing 3.1 (lines 9–11 and 13–15) of Chapter 3 and lines 14–21 in Listing 4.1.

Tip

Avoid giving names to classes that are identical to important, often-used namespace identifiers, such as `System`, `Collections`, `Forms`, and `IO`.

Listings 3.1 and 4.1 represent two different options available when accessing classes of the `System` (or any other) namespace in your source code:

- Without `using System;` in the source code, as in line 1 of Listing 3.1—We must then reference the `System` namespace explicitly every time we use one of its classes, as in Listing 3.1, line 14:

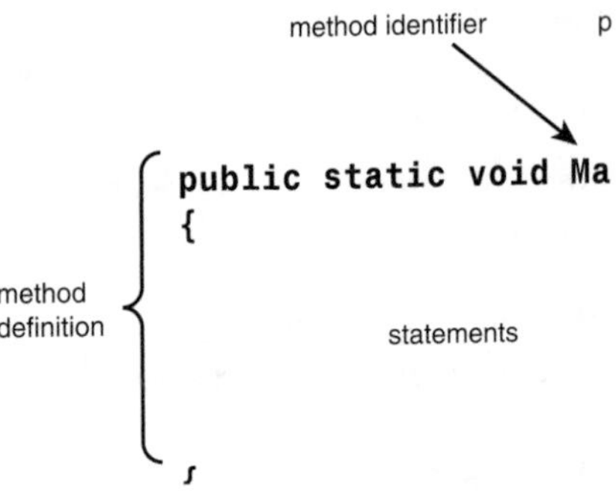

- With `using System;`, as in line 1 of Listing 4.1—We can use any class of the `System` namespace without the repetitive tedious chore of explicitly typing `System`. The previous example of code could then be truncated to the following (just like lines 14–21 of Listing 4.1).

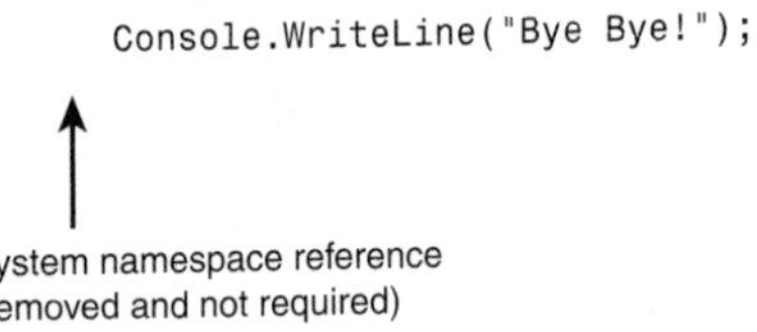

`using` essentially frees us from the burden of writing fully-qualified namespace names in numerous places of our source code. It also enhances the readability of our code by abbreviating otherwise lengthy references.

Note

`using` can only be applied to namespaces and not classes, so the following line is invalid:

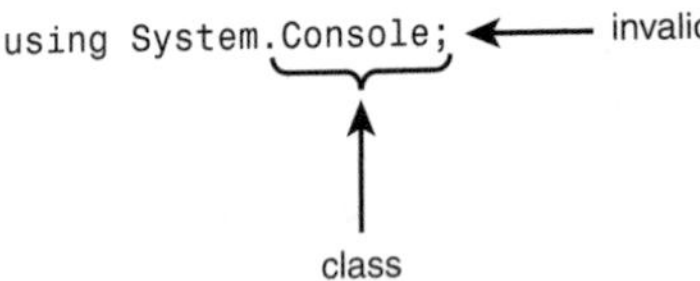

Multi-Line Comments

You have already met the double slash `//` used for single line comments in lines 1 and 4 of Listing 3.1. `/*` (forward slash star) indicates the beginning of a multi-line comment. Anything written between `/*` and the matching `*/` is a comment and is ignored by the compiler (as in line 3 of Listing 4.1).

```
03: /*
```

// could be used for multi-line comments, but you would have to include // in every line of the comment, as shown in the following:

```
//This comment spans
//over two lines
```

/* */ could likewise be used for a single line comment:

```
/* This is a single line comment */
```

Most programmers seem to prefer // for one or at most only a few lines of comments, whereas /* */ facilitates elaborate comments spanning numerous lines.

A few different multi-line commenting styles are often seen. The start comment /* and end comment */ have been highlighted so it is easier for you to locate the beginning and end of each comment.

```
/*  Many attempts to communicate
    are nullified by saying too much.

                       Robert Greenleaf      */


/*
 * I have made this rather
 * long letter because I haven't
 * had the time to make it shorter.
 *
 *          Blaise Pascal
 */


/**********************************************
 * It's a damn good program.
 * If you have any comments,
 * write them on the back
 * of the cheque.
 *
 *   Adapted from Erle Stanley Gardner
**********************************************/
```

Probably not the typical content of a comment, but these comments illustrate three different popular multi-line commenting styles and possess wisdom applicable when commenting source code.

The actual text of the multi-line comment is seen in lines 4 and 5 of Listing 4.1:

```
04:  * This class finds the sum, product,
05:  * min and max of two numbers
```

In line 6, */ matches /* of line 3 and terminates the multi-line comment.

```
06:  */
```

Tip

Making good comments is like adding salt to your food; you have to add the right amount. Excessive use of comments obscures the readability of the code and gives the reader more to read than necessary. It is as damaging as too few comments.

Rather than merely restating what the code does by using different words, try to describe the overall intent of the code.

Coding nightmare:

Poor comment. It only repeats in a verbose fashion what is expressed very precisely in C# in the next line.

```
/*
 * The next line adds s1 to s2. s3 is then
 * again added to the previous result and finally s4 is
 * added to the latter result. This result is then stored in
 * the ss variable. s1, s2, s3 and s4 all represent different
 * speeds  of a car. ss is the sum of those speeds.
 */
ss = s1 + s2 + s3 + s4;
```

Inferior choice of identifiers

```
/*
 * The next line takes the ss variable from above and divides
 * it by 4 it then stores this result in the variable a which
 * then is the average of s1, s2, s3 and s4.
 */
a = ss / 4;
```

Another poor comment.

Bad identifier choice.

Let's see how we can improve this source code:

Improved code ☺

the comment states the *intent* of the code briefly

```
//Calculate the average speed of a car

speedSum = speed1 + speed2 + speed3 + speed4;
averageSpeed = speedSum / 4;
```

Good choice of identifiers makes the code self documenting

Declaring a Variable of Type `int`

Line 11 contains a statement declaring a variable called `x`. Remember how we previously declared a variable of type `string` in Listing 3.1 line 7, enabling it to contain a string of characters (text). This time, we have exchanged the keyword `string` with the keyword `int`. It dictates the type of `x` to be a specific kind of integer taking up 32 bits of memory (4 bytes).

```
11:         int x;
```

Integers, in general are whole numbers, such as 8, 456, and –3123. This contrasts with *floating-point* numbers that include a fraction. 76.98, 3.876, and –10.1 are all examples of floating point numbers. Because `x` now takes up 32 bits of memory, it can represent numbers in the –2147483648–2147483647 range. We will not examine this fact closely now, but observe the following calculation:

$2^{32} /2 = 2147483648$

The first 2 is the bit size, the 32 is the number of bits, and the /2 shows that half of the available numbers are allocated for positive numbers, and half for negative numbers.

Binary numbers are discussed at length in Appendix D, "Number Systems," which is found on `www.samspublishing.com`, while integers and their range will be discussed thoroughly in Chapter 6, "Types Part I: The Simple Types."

Line 12 declares a variable called `y` to be of type `int`.

```
12:         int y;
```

`x` and `y` are usually considered to be unacceptable names for variables because identifiers must be meaningful and reflect the content of the variable. In this particular case, however, `x` and `y` are involved in generic arithmetic calculations and do not represent any particular values, such as average rainfall or the number of newborns in Paris. Any math whiz kid would immediately accept `x` and `y` as valid name choices in a mathematical equation with equivalent generic characteristics.

Converting from Type `string` to Type `int`

Any user response typed on the console, followed by Enter, and received by `Console.ReadLine()` is considered to be of type `string` by the C# program. Even a number like 432 is initially presumed to merely be a set of characters and could easily be ABC or #@$ instead.

A number represented as a `string` cannot be stored directly in a variable of type `int`; so we must first convert the `string` variable to a variable of type `int` before commencing.

By using the `ToInt32` method of the `Convert` class as in line 15, the program attempts to convert any user input to an `int` number. After successful conversion, the part on the right side of the equals sign in line 15 will represent the corresponding `int` number, and be stored in `x`. However, the conversion can only take place if the user input matches an `int` number. Thus, inputs such as **`57.53`** or **`three hundred`** will trigger an error, whereas **`109`** or **`64732`** are accepted.

```
15:         x = Convert.ToInt32(Console.ReadLine());
```

Creating and Invoking Your Own Methods

Before line 18 can be understood properly, we need to jump ahead and look at lines 25–31.

```
25:     public static int Sum(int a, int b)
26:     {
27:         int sumTotal;
28:
29:         sumTotal = a + b;
30:         return sumTotal;
31:     }
```

Until now, we have happily used pre-fabricated methods, such as **`Console.ReadLine()`** and **`Console.WriteLine()`**. Despite the vast array of functionality found in the .NET Framework and other available commercial class libraries, you will, when creating new unique source code, need to supply specialized functionality by writing your own user-defined methods.

Lines 25–31 are an example of a user-defined method called **`Sum`**.

Briefly explained, **`Sum`**, when called, receives two numbers. It adds the two numbers together and returns the result to the caller.

The definition for the **`Sum()`** method, with its method header, braces **`{}`**, and method body, follows the same general structure as the definition for the **`Main`** method.

Tip

Generally, classes represent objects, whereas methods represent actions. Try to adhere to the following when you name classes and methods:

Use nouns (**`Car`**, **`Airplane`**, and so on) when naming classes.

Use verbs for method names (**`DriveForward`**, **`MoveLeft`**, **`TakeOff`**, and so on).

The method header of line 25 is, in many ways, similar to the method header of **`Main`** in line 9 (recall the access modifier **`public`** and its ability to let a method be included in the interface of the class to which it belongs).

We have also previously introduced **`static`**, in line 5 of Listing 3.1, and will abstain from any further description of this keyword right now.

However, **`void`** has been replaced by **`int`**, and we see what looks like two variable declarations separated by a comma residing inside a pair of parentheses **`(int a, int b)`** located after **`Sum`**. This deserves an explanation.

Line 25 can be regarded as the interface of the **`Sum`** method. This interface facilitates the communication between the method calling **`Sum`** (in this case **`Main`**) and the method body of **`Sum`**.

In everyday language, an *interface* can be described as a feature or circumstance that enables separate (and sometimes incompatible) elements to communicate effectively.

Figure 4.1 zooms in on the process involved when **`Sum(int a, int b)`** of line 25 is invoked from line 18 **`Sum(x, y)`** of the **`Main()`** method. The two arrows marked Zoom simply indicate which parts have graphically been blown up and zoomed in on.

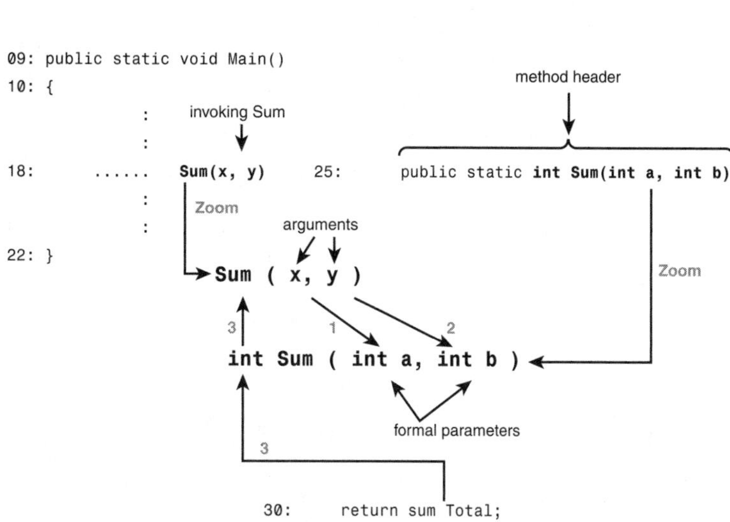

FIGURE 4.1
Invoking a user-defined method.

`a` and `b` in `Sum`'s method header are called formal parameters. A *formal parameter* is used in the method body as a stand-in for a value that will be stored here when the method is called. In this case, the values of the arguments `x` and `y` of line 18 will be plugged into `a` and `b` indicated with arrows 1 and 2, just as though the two assignment statements `a=x;` and `b=y;` were executed.

`a` and `b` can now be used inside the method body (in this case line 29) just like any regular declared variable initially holding the values of `x` and `y`.

The `int` in line 25 replacing `void` not only tells us that `Sum` returns a value of some sort, but also that this value is of type `int`. This leads us to line 30, where we find the C# keyword `return`.

```
30:         return sumTotal;
```

`return` belongs to a type of statement called a return statement. When a *return statement* is executed, the method is terminated. The flow of execution is returned to the caller and brings along the value residing in the expression after `return` (in this case the value of `sumTotal`. See the arrows with number three in Figure 4.1).

Accordingly, the type of `sumTotal` must be compatible with the return type specified in the method header (in this case `int`), as illustrated in Figure 4.2.

No Data Are Returned from a *void* Method

When the keyword `void` is positioned in front of the method name in the method header, it indicates that when the runtime has finished executing the statements of the method, it will not return any data to the caller. Consequently the `void` keyword has the opposite meaning from the keyword `int` when put in front of the method name in the method header. The latter indicates that the method will always return a value of type `int`.

FIGURE 4.2
Return type of method header must match type of return expression.

```
25:    public static int Sum(int a, int b)
26:    {
27:        int sumTotal;
28:
29:        sumTotal = a + b;
30:        return sumTotal;
31:    }
```

compatible types required because...

...sumTotal is returned to invoking method

return statement

Tip

When you program in C#, think in terms of building blocks. Classes, objects, and methods are meant for this approach. Break down your programs into manageable building blocks. In a C# program, you typically use classes and methods that are

- From class libraries (NET Framework or other commercially available packages). Many class libraries can be obtained for free over the Internet.
- Written by yourself and, as a result, contain user-defined classes and methods.
- Created by other programmers, perhaps your fellow students or colleagues at work.

Don't attempt to reinvent the wheel. Before throwing time and money into creating new classes and methods, check to see if equivalent functionality has already been implemented, tested by professional programmers, and made available in the form of highly efficient and robust software components.

An Assignment Statement

Line 29 is an assignment statement. `a` and `b` are added together using the `+` operator. The result is stored in the `sumTotal` variable due to the assignment operator `=` (see Figure 4.3). Let's illustrate this by using the sample output example of from Listing 4.1, where the input provided was **3** and **8**. When `Sum` is called, `3` and `8` are transferred to `a` and `b`, through `x` and `y` of `Main`. After the execution of line 29, `sumTotal` holds the value 11.

```
29:          sumTotal = a + b;
```

Combining Strings and Method Calls

In line 18, we first need to focus on the `Sum(x, y) part`, which, as already shown, invokes the `Sum` method defined in lines 25–31 and sends the two arguments `x` and `y` along. Notice that we do not need to include *`ObjectName`* or *`ClassName`* as specified in the previously given conventions, *`ObjectName.MethodName(Optional_Arguments)`* and *`ClassName.MethodName(Optional_Arguments)`*, because the invoker and the invoked method reside inside the same class—`SimpleCalculator`.

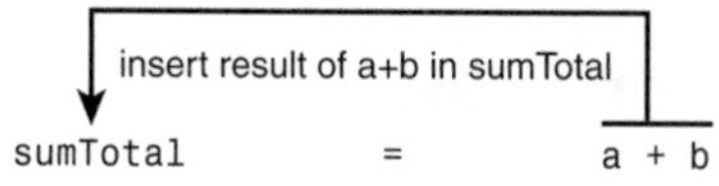

FIGURE 4.3
Assigning the result of a calculation to a variable.

insert result of a+b in sumTotal

```
sumTotal        =        a + b
```

```
18:          Console.WriteLine("The sum is: " + Sum(x, y));
```

After the `Sum` method returns, you can virtually substitute `Sum(x, y)` with `sumTotal` from line 30. In our example, `Sum(x, y)` will represent the value 11 (see Figure `4.4`).

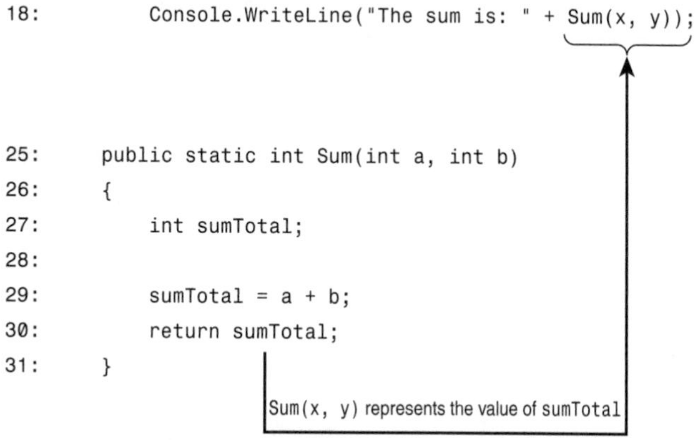

FIGURE 4.4
`Sum(x, y)` represents the value of `sumTotal` when `Sum` returns.

```
18:          Console.WriteLine("The sum is: " + Sum(x, y));

25:      public static int Sum(int a, int b)
26:      {
27:          int sumTotal;
28:
29:          sumTotal = a + b;
30:          return sumTotal;
31:      }
```

`Sum(x, y)` represents the value of `sumTotal`

Even though `Sum(x, y)` resides inside another method call in the form of `Console.WriteLine()`, C# can easily cope and correctly resolves the sequence of events that need to take place. When the value of `Sum(x, y)` is needed, the call will be made. Line 18 could then, after lines 25–31 have been executed and the flow has returned to line 18, be thought of as:

```
Console.WriteLine("The sum is: " + 11);
```

Because `11` is inside the parentheses of a call to `WriteLine`, it is automatically converted to a `string`. Consequently, we can now look at line 18 as follows:

```
Console.WriteLine("The sum is: " + "11");
```

We still have one odd detail to sort out—the + symbol between `"The sum is: "` and `"11"`. When the + symbol is positioned between two numeric values, it adds them together in standard arithmetic fashion. However, when the C# compiler finds the + symbol surrounded by strings, it changes its functionality. It is then used to connect the two strings surrounding it, which results in `"The sum is: 11"`. In general, connecting or pasting together two strings to obtain a larger string is called *concatenation*, so the + symbol in this case is referred to as a *concatenation operator*.

Finally, line 18 has essentially been transformed to look like the following:

```
Console.WriteLine("The sum is: 11");
```

This is familiar to us and says, "Print out `The sum is: 11` on the console." Fortunately, this is exactly what we see when running the program.

The + Symbol: Adding or Concatenating?

The + operator can be used for different purposes. One moment it is used for a string concatenation; the next it is involved in adding numbers together. Due to this flexibility of the + operator, we say it is *overloaded*. Overloaded operators are very useful, but they come at a price; hard to trace bugs and mysterious results can sometimes appear.

For example, when + acting as a string concatenation operator is confused with + acting as an addition operator, the program produces unexpected results. Consider the following line of code:

```
Console.WriteLine("x + 8 = " + x + 8);
```

If `x` has the value 6, which output would you expect?

The actual output is `x + 8 = 68`, whereas many would have expected `x + 8 = 14`.

Why is that? Well first, `"x + 8 = " + x` is concatenated to `"x + 8 = 6"` which again is concatenated with `8` to form `x + 8 = 68`.

A correct result printing `x + 8 = 14` can be produced with the following code:

```
"x + 8 = " + (x + 8)
```

KISS

The C# compiler is capable of resolving extremely complicated, nested, convoluted statements and programs. Programmers with a bit of experience sometimes attempt to show off by stretching this power to create some warped, weird, and intricate programs that nobody apart from themselves can understand. This kind of programming practice is acceptable if you want to have a bit of fun in your free time at home, but it has no place in properly constructed software.

Be humble! Follow the KISS principle—Keep It Simple Stupid.

Lines 34–40 are very similar to lines 25–31, the only differences being different method and variable names and, instead of calculating the sum, the `Product` method calculates the product of two numbers. Note that the asterisk (`*`) character is used to specify multiplication.

```
34:     public static int Product(int a, int b)
35:     {
36:         int productTotal;
37:
38:         productTotal = a * b;
39:         return productTotal;
40:     }
```

Lines 18 and line 19 are conceptually identical.

```
19:         Console.WriteLine("The product is: " + Product(x, y));
```

Tip

The order in which the methods of a class are defined is arbitrary and has no relation to when you can call those methods in your source code and when they will be executed. Accordingly, you could change the order in which the `Sum` and `Product` definitions appear in the definition of the `SimpleCalculator` class.

The `Math` Class: A Useful Member of the .NET Framework

Line 20 is similar in concept to lines 18 and 19. However, here we utilize the `Math` class (instead of `Sum` and `Product`) of the `System` namespace in the .NET Framework class library to find the greater of two numbers using the `Max` method.

```
20:         Console.WriteLine("The maximum number is: " + Math.Max(x, y));
```

The `Math` class contains many useful math-related methods, such as trigonometry and logarithms.

Tip

It is permissible to spread one long statement over several lines as long as no tokens are separated into smaller pieces of text. However, if not thoughtfully done, breaking up statements into several lines can easily obscure the readability of the source code. To avoid this problem, choose logical breaking points, such as after an operator or after a comma. When statements are separated into more than one line, indent all successive lines.

For example, we might decide that line 20 of Listing 4.1 is too long

```
20:         Console.WriteLine("The maximum number is: " + Math.Max(x, y));
```

and break it up after the concatenation operator (+) so that `Math.Max(x,y));` is moved down to the next line and indented

```
20:         Console.WriteLine("The maximum number is: " +
            Math.Max(x, y));
```

Analogous to line 20, `Math.Min(x, y)` in line 21 finds the smaller of `x` and `y`.

```
21:         Console.WriteLine("The minimum number is: " + Math.Min(x, y));
```

This ends our tour through Listing 4.1.

Simplifying Your Code with Methods

We have already discussed how the construction of an object-oriented program can be simplified by breaking it down into suitable classes. The following case study looks at how the design of an individual class can be simplified by breaking its functionality down into suitable methods. It exemplifies and stresses the importance of thinking in terms of building blocks on the method level also.

Methods As Building Blocks: Encapsulating Your Helper Methods with the `private` keyword.

We can expect the internal parts of each class in a program to be less complex than the overall program, but the programmer is still often confronted with individual classes of relatively high complexity. Fortunately, it is possible to reduce this complexity by dividing its functionality into methods. Let's look at an example.

Notice that this discussion is relevant to step 2c (Identification of methods in each class) and step 2d (Internal method design) of the Software Design phase in the Software Development Process presented in Chapter 2.

Consider a map represented in your source code by a class called `Map`. One of the services of this class is to calculate the distance between a list of 6 specified locations (here referred to as `L1`, `L2`, `L3`, `L4`, `L5`, and `L6`) on the map. Every location in the map constitutes a set of 2 coordinates (x and y), where `L1` has the coordinates (x1, y1), `L2` has the coordinates (x2, y2), and so on. The distance between two locations, say `L1` (x1, y1) and `L2` (x2, y2), can be calculated by using Pythagoras's formula:

$$\text{distance} = \sqrt{(x1 - x2)^2 + (y1 - y2)^2}$$

which can be used to calculate the distance of a path beginning at `L1` and going through `L2`, `L3` and on to `L6`. The formula for this calculation is

Total distance =

L1 to L2 + L2 to L3 + L3 to L4 + L4 to L5 + L5 to L6 =

$$\sqrt{(x1 - x2)^2 + (y1 - y2)^2} + \sqrt{(x2 - x3)^2 + (y2 - y3)^2} +$$
$$\sqrt{(x3 - x4)^2 + (y3 - y4)^2} + \sqrt{(x4 - x5)^2 + (y4 - y5)^2} + \sqrt{(x5 - x6)^2 + (y5 - y6)^2}$$

We can implement this distance calculation in two ways:

- By using just one method, without any attempt to break up the problem into a couple of simpler methods.
- By thinking in terms of methods as building blocks, we can divide the functionality into several methods.

To keep the examples simple, I will only provide the very important parts of the C# code.

Let's have a closer look at each implementation.

- By using only one method:

```
totalDistance =
    Math.Sqrt(Math.Pow(x1-x2,2) + Math.Pow(y1-y2,2)) +
    Math.Sqrt(Math.Pow(x2-x3,2) + Math.Pow(y2-y3,2)) +
    Math.Sqrt(Math.Pow(x3-x4,2) + Math.Pow(y3-y4,2)) +
    Math.Sqrt(Math.Pow(x4-x5,2) + Math.Pow(y4-y5,2)) +
    Math.Sqrt(Math.Pow(x5-x6,2) + Math.Pow(y5-y6,2));
```

  where `Math.Sqrt(x)` calculates the square root of `x` and `Math.Pow(a, b)` raises `a` to the power of `b`.

  This coding nightmare is one statement spread over six lines of source code. Let's try to simplify this massive statement.

- Breaking down the functionality into two methods:

  Because we are repeatedly calculating distances between two locations, we can separate the functionality into two methods—a helper method calculating distances between two locations and a method calculating the total distance between the six locations. We will simply call our helper method `Distance` and let it contain four formal parameters `a1`, `b1` (representing the first location) `a2`, `b2` (representing the second location). When `Distance` is called, it returns the distance between the location arguments sent to it.

  We can now write the calculation in only four lines of code.

```
TotalDistance =
    Distance(x1,y1,x2,y2) + Distance(x2,y2,x3,y3) +
    Distance(x3,y3,x4,y4) + Distance(x4,y4,x5,y5) +
    Distance(x5,y5,x6,y6);
```

In this way, we were able to obtain a significant reduction in the complexity of this calculation. Another advantage is that we don't have to remember Pythagoras's formula and try to get it right numerous times; instead, we simply need to call the `Distance` method.

Note

By implementing a class called `Location` to represent specific locations in the form of objects, naming these location objects L1, L2, and so on will reduce the previous statement to

```
TotalDistance =
    Distance(L1,L2) + Distance(L2,L3) +
    Distance(L3,L4) + Distance(L4,L5) +
    Distance(L5,L6);
```

Indeed, this is a much simpler and self-documenting statement. To understand and construct this type of statement, we need to put more meat into your understanding for methods and OOP.

If none of our other objects in the program are interested in a `Distance` method, we need to make things less complex when looking at the class from the outside. As a result, we declare this helper method to be `private`.

As we attempt to reduce the complexity of the individual class by breaking its complicated tasks into subtasks, we also create the need for `private` methods.

Tip

A method attempting to solve several tasks is likely to be overly complex and should probably be broken down into smaller, simpler methods. So don't be afraid of creating many small methods.

A method that accomplishes one clear task is said to be *cohesive*.

A good guideline for whether you have created a set of cohesive methods is the ease with which you can name each method. Methods with one distinct task are easier to name than multipurpose methods.

Summary

This chapter presented you with another C# source code example with the ability to perform simple calculations. Many essential constructs and concepts were extracted from this program to extend the knowledge you gained from the previous chapter.

The following are the important elements covered in this chapter:

A variable of type `int` can be used to store whole numbers and can take part in standard arithmetic calculations.

Namespaces help programmers keep their classes organized and accessible to other programmers for reuse purposes.

The `System` namespace in the .NET Framework class library contains many fundamental classes.

Use comments to describe the overall intent of the source code instead of merely restating what the code does.

A `string` value consisting of digits that form a whole number can be converted to a value of type `int`. Conversely, a value of type `int` can also be converted to a value of type `string`.

A method is defined by writing its method header (which includes access modifier, return type, name and formal parameters), by indicating its method body with `{}` and by writing the statements of the method inside the method body.

A method call must include the name of the called method and an argument list that matches the formal parameter list of the called method. When a method is called, the values held by the arguments are assigned to the formal parameters of the called method. A method can return a value, in which case, the method call can be regarded as holding this value just after the method called returns.

When positioned between two numeric values, the `+` operator will perform a standard arithmetic addition but, if positioned between two `string`s, will perform a `string` concatenation.

The `Math` class found in the `System` namespace of the .NET Framework class library contains many helpful methods to perform various mathematical calculations.

Instead of using just one method to solve a complex computational problem, break the problem into several simpler methods. Every method should accomplish just one clear task. Such a method is described as being *cohesive*.

Review Questions

1. What are namespaces used for in C# and .NET?
2. What is the advantage of including the keyword `using` followed by the name of a namespace in the beginning of a program?
3. Which namespace contains classes related to mathematical calculations and console input/output.
4. How should comments be applied in the source code?
5. Describe a variable of type `int`.
6. Why are `x` and `y` often regarded as unacceptable variable identifiers? Why are they acceptable in Listing 4.1?
7. What are the fundamental parts of a method?
8. Why is `MoveLeft` a bad name for a class? For which C# construct would it be better suited?
9. How do you specify that a method does not return a value?
10. How do you specify that a method returns a value of type `int`?
11. What are arguments (in method calls)?
12. What are formal parameters?
13. How do arguments and formal parameters relate?
14. Does the `+` operator only perform arithmetic additions?
15. How can you break down the inner complexities of a class?
16. What is a cohesive method?

Programming Exercises

Make the following changes to the program in Listing 4.1:

1. Change the multi-line comments in lines 3–6 to two single line comments.
2. Apart from addition and multiplication, allow the user to perform a subtraction. Among other changes, you need to add a `Subtract` method. (The symbol – is used to perform subtractions in C#).
3. Instead of calculating the sum and the product of *two* numbers, make the program perform the calculations on *three* numbers. (You can ignore the `Max` and `Min` functions here.) Hint: You need to declare another `int` variable in `Main`. The `Sum`, `Product`, and `Subtract` methods must accept three arguments instead of two. You must allow the user to input a third number, and you must include the third argument when these methods are called.
4. Create two methods called `MyMax` and `MyMin` that both take three arguments and find the maximum and minimum value of these arguments. Hint: `Math.Max(Math.Max(a, b),c)` returns the max of `a`, `b` and `c`.

CHAPTER 5

YOUR FIRST OBJECT-ORIENTED C# PROGRAM

You will learn about the following in this chapter:

- The atomic elements of a C# source program
- The conventional styles used for naming classes, methods, and variables
- Operators, operands, and expressions (introductory)
- How to write and instantiate your own custom-made classes
- How the theoretical OO discussion about `Elevators` and `Person` classes in Chapter 3, "A Guided Tour Through C#: Part I," can be implemented to form a fully working C# program
- What a simple object-oriented program looks like and its important elements
- How to initialize the instance variables of your newly created objects
- The ability of objects to contain instance variables that contain other objects
- How programmers implement relationships between classes to let them collaborate and form object-oriented programs
- The Unified Modeling Language (UML) and how it can be used to graphically illustrate and model relationships among classes
- Three common types of relationships among classes called association, aggregation, and composition

Introduction

You have now been presented with two source programs—Listing 3.1 of Chapter 3 and Listing 4.1 of Chapter 4, "A Guided Tour through C#: Part II." The associated presentation of the C# language constructs has been somewhat guided by the contents of each particular line of code and, consequently, touched on many diverse but interrelated aspects simultaneously. To make up for this fast tour through C#, the first part of this chapter provides an overview of the very basic elements of C#.

The last part of the chapter contains the first object-oriented C# program of the book. It builds on previous theoretical OO discussions, in particular the `Elevator` simulation discussion in the beginning of Chapter 3. Among other things, it allows you to see how the relationship between the `Elevator` and the `Person` classes discussed in this earlier section is implemented in C#.

Lexical Structure

When the C# compiler receives a piece of source code to compile, it is faced with the seemingly daunting task of deciphering a long list of characters (more specifically Unicode characters, presented in Appendix E, "Unicode Character Set") which can be found at `www.samspublishing.com` and turn them into matching MSIL with exactly the same meaning as the original source code. To make sense of this mass of source code, it must recognize the atomic elements of C#—the unbreakable pieces making up the C# source code. Examples of atomic elements are a brace (`{`), a parenthesis (`(`), and keywords like `class` and `if`. The task performed by the compiler, associated with differentiating opening and closing braces, keywords, parentheses, and so on is called *lexical analysis*. Essentially, the lexical issues dealt with by the compiler pertain to how source code characters can be translated into tokens that are comprehensible to the compiler.

C# programs are a collection of identifiers, keywords, whitespace, comments, literals, operators, and separators. You have already met many of these C# elements. The following provides a structured overview of these and, whenever relevant, will introduce a few more aspects.

Identifiers and CaPitaLIzaTioN Styles

Identifiers are used to name classes, methods, and variables. We have already looked at the rules any identifier must follow to be valid and how well-chosen identifiers can enhance the clarity of source code and make it self-documenting. Now we will introduce another aspect related to identifiers—namely CaPitaLIzaTioN sTyLe.

Often programmers choose identifiers that are made up of several words to increase the clarity and the self-documentation of the source code. For example, the words could be child-births-per-year. However, because of the compiler's sensitivity to whitespace, any identifier broken up into words by means of whitespace will be misinterpreted. For example, a variable to represent the average speed per hour cannot be named `average speed per hour`. We need to discard whitespace to form one proper token, while maintaining a style allowing the reader of the source code to distinguish the individual words in the identifier. Some computer languages have agreed on the convention `average_speed_per_hour`. In C#, however, most programmers utilizes an agreed-upon sequence of upper- and lowercase characters to distinguish between individual words in an identifier.

A couple of important capitalization styles are applied in the C# world:

- *Pascal casing*—The first letter of each word in the name is capitalized, as in AverageSpeedPerHour.
- *Camel casing*—Same as Pascal casing, with the exception of the first word of the identifier that is lowercase, as in averageSpeedPerHour.

Pascal casing is recommended when naming classes and methods, whereas Camel casing is used for variables.

Tip

Not all computer languages are case sensitive. In these languages, `AVERAGE` and `average` are identical to the compiler. For compatibility with these languages, you should avoid using case as the distinguishing factor between `public` identifiers accessible from other languages.

Literals

Consider the following two lines of source code:

```
int number;
number = 10;
```

`number` is clearly a variable. In the first line, we declare `number` to be of type `int`. In the second line, we assign `10` to `number`. But what is `10`? Well, `10` is incapable of changing its value and is named a *literal*. Literals are not confined to numbers. They can also be characters, such as B, $, and z or text, such as "This is a literal." Literals can be stored by any variable with a type compatible with that of the literal.

Comments and Source Code Documentation

The main characteristic of comments is the compiler's ability to totally ignore them. We have so far seen two ways of making comments—single line with `//` and multi-line using `/* */`.

In fact, there is a third type that allows you to write the documentation as part of the source code as shown in this chapter, but with the added ability of extracting this documentation into separate Extensible Markup Language (XML) files. For now, you can appreciate a particular useful end result of this feature; you just need to take a look at the .NET Framework class library documentation, which was created by extracting XML files from the comments/documentation sitting inside the original source code.

Separators

Separators are used to separate various elements in C# from each other. You have already met many of them. An example is the commonly used semicolon `;` that is required to terminate a statement. Table 5.1 summarizes the separators we have presented to so far.

TABLE 5.1 Important Separators in C#

Name	Symbol	Purpose
Braces	{ }	Used to confine a block of code for classes, methods, and the, yet to be presented, branching and looping statements.
Parentheses	( )	Contains lists of formal parameters in method headers and lists of arguments in method invocation statements. Also required to contain the Boolean expression of an `if` statement and other, yet to be presented, branching and looping statements.
Semicolon	;	Terminates a statement.
Comma	,	Separates formal parameters inside the parentheses of a method header and separates arguments in a method invocation statement.
Period (dot operator)	.	Used to reference namespaces contained inside other namespaces and to specify classes inside namespaces and methods (if accessible) inside classes and objects. It can also be used to specify instance variables inside classes and objects (if accessible), but this practice should be avoided.

Operators

Operators are represented by symbols such as `+` , `=` , `==`, and `*`. Operators act on ***operands***, which are found next to the operator. For example

```
SumTotal + 10
```

contains the `+` operator surrounded by the two operands `sumTotal` and `10`. In this context, the `+` operator combines two operands to produce a result and so it is classified as a ***binary operator***. Some operators act on only one operand; they are termed ***unary operators***.

Operators, together with their operands, form ***expressions***. A literal or a variable by itself is also an expression, as are combinations of literals and variables with operators. Consequently, expressions can be used as operands as long as the rules, which apply to each individual operator, are adhered to, as shown in the following example:

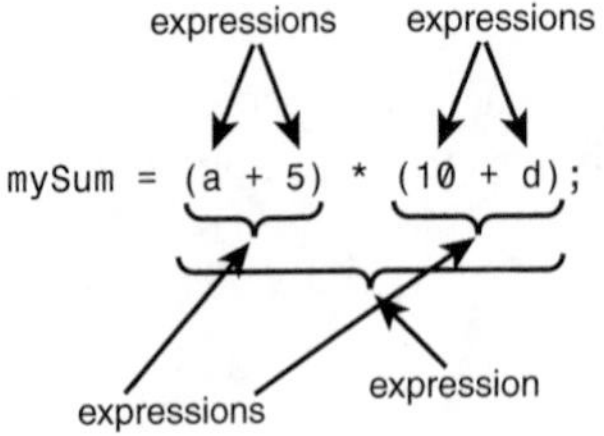

`a`, `5`, and `10`, `d` are all expressions acted on by the `+` operator. However, `(a + 5)` and `(10 + d)` are also expressions acted on by the `*` operator. Finally, `(a + 5) * (10 + d)` can be regarded as one expression. The assignment operator = acts on this latter expression and the expression `mySum`. Expressions are often nested inside each other to form hierarchies of expressions, as in the previous example.

Operators can be divided into the following categories—assignment, arithmetic, unary, equality, relational, logical, conditional, shift, and primary operators.

We will spend more time on operators in later chapters, but the following is a quick summary of the operators you have encountered so far:

- *Assignment operator* (=)—Causes the operand on its left side to have its value changed to the expression on the right side of the assignment operator as in

  ```
  29:          sumTotal = a + b;
  ```

  where `a + b` can be regarded as being one operand.
- Binary *arithmetic operators* (+ and *)—The following example

  ```
  a * b
  ```

  multiplies `a` and `b` without changing their values.
- *Concatenation operator* (+)—Concatenates two strings into one string.
- *Equality operator* (==)—Compares two expressions to test whether they are equal. For example,

  ```
  leftExpression == rightExpression
  ```

  will only be true if the two expressions are equal; otherwise, it is false.

Keywords

Appendix C at `www.samspublishing.com` lists all 77 different keywords of C#. We have so far met the keywords `if`, `class`, `public`, `static`, `void`, `string`, `int`, and `return`. The syntax (language rules) of the operators and separators combined with the keywords form the definition of the C# language.

Some Thoughts on Elevator Simulations

The C# program presented after the following case study is a first attempt (prototype) to implement an object-oriented elevator simulation. The case study introduces a few goals, problems, and solutions of a simple elevator simulation and attempts to put you in the right frame of mind for the following practical C# example. It is also meant as a reminder of our encapsulation discussion in the beginning of Chapter 3.

Concepts, Goals and Solutions in an Elevator Simulation Program: Collecting Valuable Statistics for Evaluating an Elevator System

This case study looks at a strategy for collecting important information from a particular elevator simulation to answer the question, "Is the elevator system that we are simulating performing its task of transporting passengers between various floors properly?" In other words, if we took a real elevator system, extracted all its relevant characteristics, and turned it into a computer simulation, how well would this system perform?

Statistics

A numerical fact or datum, especially one computed from a sample, is called a *statistic*.

Statistics is the science that deals with the collection, classification, analysis, and interpretation of numerical facts or data, and that, by use of mathematical theories of probability, imposes order and regularity on aggregates of more or less disparate elements.

The term statistics is also used to refer to the numerical facts or data themselves.

Two statistics considered important by most elevator travelers when rating an elevator system are

- The time a typical person has to wait on a floor after having pressed the button to call the elevator
- The average time it takes to travel one floor

An attempt to collect these numbers from an elevator simulation could be done as follows.

Because the `Person` objects are "traveling" through the elevator system, it is ultimately these objects that the `Elevator` objects must service. Consequently, the `Person` objects will "know" how well the system is working and are able to collect some of the essential statistics required. An analogous strategy in the real world would be to interview the users of the elevator system and gather some of their elevator system experiences.

Each `Person` object of the elevator simulation program could be implemented to have a couple of instance variables keeping track of its total waiting time outside the elevator (to answer the first bullet) and an average traveling time per floor (addressing the second bullet). They would give a good indication of how well the elevator system is working and be part of the statistics collected for each simulation. We could call these variables `totalWaitingTime` and `averageFloorTravelingTime`.

Calculating `totalWaitingTime` would require a method located inside `Person` containing instructions to start the computer's built-in stopwatch every time the person has "pressed a button" on a particular `Floor` object calling an elevator. As soon as the `Elevator` object "arrives," the stopwatch is stopped and the time is added to the current value of `totalWaitingTime`.

Similarly, the `averageFloorTravelingTime` is calculated by another method inside `Person` starting the stopwatch as soon as the `Person` object has "entered" the `Elevator` object. When the `Person` has reached its "destination," the stopwatch is stopped and the time divided by the number of floors "traveled" to get the average traveling time per floor. This result is stored in a list together with other `averageFloorTravelingTime` sizes. When the final `averageFloorTravelingTime` statistic needs to be calculated, a method will calculate the average of the numbers stored in the list.

All these calculations involving starting and stopping stopwatches, summing numbers, calculating averages, and so on are not of any interest to other objects in the simulation, and they would complicate matters unduly for other programmers were they exposed to them. Consequently, we should hide all the methods involved here by declaring them to be `private`.

Each `Person` object must also be able to report its `totalWaitingTime` and `averageFloorTravelingTime` sizes. We can do this through two `public` methods arbitrarily named `getTotalWaitingTime` and `getAverageFloorTravelingTime`. Any other object calling any of these two methods will receive the corresponding statistic.

Another programmer who is also working on this project is writing a class to collect the important statistics of each simulation. He or she calls this class `StatisticsReporter`. He or she must ensure that all `Person` objects are "interviewed" at the end of a simulation by letting the `StatisticsReporter` collect their `totalWaitingTime` and `averageFloorTravelingTime` statistics. The `StatisticsReporter` can now simply do this by calling the `getTotalWaitingTime` and `getAverageFloorTravelingTime` methods of each `Person` object involved in a particular simulation.

To summarize:

- `getTotalWaitingTime` and `getAverageFloorTravelingTime` are part of an interface that is hiding or encapsulating all the irrelevant complexities for our happy programmer of the `StatisticsReporter`.
- Likewise, the instance variables of the `Person` objects should be hidden by declaring them `private`. This prevents any other objects, including the `StatisticsReporter`, from mistakenly changing any of these sizes. In other words, the `getTotalWaitingTime` and `getAverageFloorTravelingTime` methods "cover," by means of encapsulation, the instance variables `totalWaitingTime` and `averageFloorTravelingTime` as a protective wrapper by allowing only the `StatisticsReporter` to get the values of these and not to set them.

Object-Oriented Programming: A Practical Example

So far, our discussion about object-oriented programming has been somewhat theoretical. We have discussed the difference between classes and objects and how objects need to be instantiated before they can actually perform any actions. You have seen a couple of simple classes in Listings 3.1 of Chapter 3 and 4.1 of Chapter 4, but they didn't contain any real objects; they were passive containers only created to hold the `Main` method. Actually, none of these programs can be regarded as being particularly object-oriented. Because they only have methods containing sequences of statements one executed after the other, they resemble programs written in the procedural programming style.

By merely adding plenty of methods and statements to the `SimpleCalculator` class of Listing 4.1, it would be possible, albeit extremely cumbersome, to write a valid and full-blown sophisticated spreadsheet application without ever being concerned about writing any other classes, learning any theoretical object-oriented principles, or ever using any mentionable object-oriented C# features. The structure of this program would be closer to a program written in a procedural language like C or Pascal than it would to a typical object-oriented C# program.

Conversely and surprisingly, it would also be possible to write an object-oriented program in C or Pascal, but it would be awkward because these languages, as opposed to C#, do not have any built-in support for this paradigm.

To make our previous object-oriented discussions more practical and to avoid the risk of constructing a non-object-oriented full-size spreadsheet program, I have provided an example illustrating a couple important C# features closely related to our theoretical discussion about classes, objects, and instantiation.

Presenting `SimpleElevatorSimulation.cs`

Listing 5.1 contains the source code for a simple elevator simulation program. Its goal is to illustrate what a custom-made object looks like in C# and how it is instantiated from a custom written class. In particular, it shows how an `Elevator` object is created and how it calls a method of the `Person` object named `NewFloorRequest` and triggers the latter to return the number of the requested "floor," enabling the `Elevator` to fulfill this request.

Many abstractions were made during the design stage of the source code in Listing 5.1, allowing us to make the program simple and be able to concentrate on the essential object-oriented parts of the source code.

The following is a brief description of the overall configuration of the elevator's system used for this simulation, highlighting the major differences to a real elevator system.

- The `Building` class has one `Elevator` object called `elevatorA`.
- One `Person` object residing inside the `passenger` variable is "using" `elevatorA`.
- The `Elevator` object can "travel" to any "floor" that is within the range specified by the `int` type (–2147483648 to 2147483647). However, a `Person` object is programmed to randomly choose floors between 1 and 30.
- The elevator will instantly "travel" to the "destination floor."
- The "movements" of `elevatorA` will be displayed on the console.
- After the `passenger` has "entered" `elevatorA`, "he" or "she" will stay in `elevatorA` throughout the simulation and simply choose a new floor whenever a previous request has been satisfied.

- Only the `Elevator`, `Person`, and `Building` classes are used in this simulation, leaving out `Floor`, `StatisticsReporter`, and other classes considered important for a full-blown simulation.
- At the end of each simulation, the total number of floors traveled by `elevatorA` will be displayed on the console. This number could be a very important statistic in a serious elevator simulation.

So, despite the simplicity and high abstraction of this simulation, we are actually able to extract one important statistic from it and, without too many additions, you would be able to create a small but useful simulation enabling the user to gain valuable insights into a real elevator system.

Please take a moment to examine the source code in Listing 5.1. Try first to establish a bigger picture when looking through the code. For example, notice the three class definitions (`Elevator`, `Person` and `Building`) that constitute the entire program (apart from lines 1–4). Then notice the methods defined in each of these three classes and the instance variables of each class.

Note

Recall that the order in which the methods of a class are written in the source code is independent of how the program is executed. The same is true for the order of the classes in your program. You can choose any order that suits your style. In Listing 5.1, I chose to put the class containing the `Main` method last, and yet `Main` is the first method to be executed.

Typical output from Listing 5.1 is shown following the listing. Because the requested floor numbers are randomly generated, the `"Departing floor"` and `"Traveling to"` floors (except for the first departing floor, which will always be 1) and the `"Total floors traveled"` will be different on each run of the program.

LISTING 5.1 Source Code for `SimpleElevatorSimulation.cs`

```
01:  // A simple elevator simulation
02:
03: using System;
04:
05: class Elevator
06: {
07:     private int currentFloor = 1;
08:     private int requestedFloor = 0;
09:     private int totalFloorsTraveled = 0;
10:     private Person passenger;
11:
12:     public void LoadPassenger()
13:     {
14:         passenger = new Person();
15:     }
```

LISTING 5.1 continued

```

    public void InitiateNewFloorRequest()
    {
        requestedFloor = passenger.NewFloorRequest();
        Console.WriteLine("Departing floor: " + currentFloor
            + " Traveling to floor: " + requestedFloor);
        totalFloorsTraveled = totalFloorsTraveled +
            Math.Abs(currentFloor - requestedFloor);
        currentFloor = requestedFloor;
    }

    public void ReportStatistic()
    {
        Console.WriteLine("Total floors traveled: " + totalFloorsTraveled);
    }
}

class Person
{
    private System.Random randomNumberGenerator;

    public Person()
    {
        randomNumberGenerator = new System.Random();
    }

    public int NewFloorRequest()
    {
         // Return randomly generated number
        return randomNumberGenerator.Next(1,30);
    }
}

class Building
{
    private static Elevator elevatorA;

    public static void Main()
    {
        elevatorA = new Elevator();
        elevatorA.LoadPassenger();
        elevatorA.InitiateNewFloorRequest();
        elevatorA.InitiateNewFloorRequest();
        elevatorA.InitiateNewFloorRequest();
        elevatorA.InitiateNewFloorRequest();
        elevatorA.InitiateNewFloorRequest();
        elevatorA.ReportStatistic();
    }
}
```

```
Departing floor: 1 Traveling to floor: 2
Departing floor: 2 Traveling to floor: 24
```

```
Departing floor: 24 Traveling to floor: 15
Departing floor: 15 Traveling to floor: 10
Departing floor: 10 Traveling to floor: 21
Total floors traveled: 48
```

Overall Structure of the Program

Before we continue with the more detailed analysis of the program, look at Figure 5.1. It connects the illustration used in Figure 3.1, shown in Chapter 3, with the concrete C# program of Listing 5.1.

The `Elevator` and `Person` classes of Listing 5.1 define abstracted versions of our now familiar counterparts from the real world. They are graphically depicted next to their C# counterparts in Figure 5.1. Each part of the `Elevator` and `Person` classes written in the C# source code (indicated by braces) has been linked to its graphical counterpart with arrows. Notice how the `public` methods of the two classes (the interface) encapsulate the hidden `private` instance variables. In this case, no `private` methods were needed.

The `Building` class has one `Elevator`, which is represented by its `elevatorA` instance variable declared in line 51. It also holds the `Main` method where the application commences. This class is never instantiated in the program. It is used by the .NET runtime to access `Main` and start the program.

Just as in the previous listings, I will provide a brief explanation of the lines in the source code. Many lines have not been shown because they have already been explained in a previous example.

LISTING 5.2 Brief Analysis of Listing 5.1

```
05: Begin the definition of a class named Elevator

07: Declare an instance variable called currentFloor to be of type int; set
    ➥its access level to private and its initial value to 1.

10: Declare passenger to be a variable, which can hold an
    ➥object of class Person. The class Person is said to play the role
    ➥of passenger in its association with the Elevator class.

12: Begin the definition of a method called LoadPassenger. Declare
    ➥it public to be part of the interface of the Elevator class.

14: Instantiate (create) a new object of class Person by using the
    ➥keyword new. Assign this object to the passenger variable.

17: Begin the definition of a method called InitiateNewFloorRequest. Declare
    ➥it public to be part of the interface of the Elevator class.

19: Call the NewFloorRequest method of the passenger object; assign the
    ➥number returned by this method to the requestedFloor variable.
```

LISTING 5.2 *continued*

```
20-21: Print information about the "movement" of the operator
       ➥on the command console.

22-23: Calculate the number of floors traveled by the elevator on one
       ➥particular trip (line 23). Add this result to the total number
       ➥of floors already traveled by the elevator.
24: Let the Elevator "travel" to the requested floor by assigning the
    ➥value of requestedFloor to currentFloor.

29: Whenever the ReportStatistics method is called, print out the
    ➥totalFloorsTraveled variable.

33: Begin the definition of a class named Person.

35: Declare randomNumberGenerator to be a variable, which can hold an
    ➥object of class System.Random.

37: Begin the definition of a special method called a constructor, which will
    ➥be invoked automatically whenever a new object of class
    ➥Person is created.

39: Create a new object of class System.Random by using the
    ➥C# keyword: new; assign this object to the
    ➥randomNumberGenerator variable.

42: Begin the definition of a method called NewFloorRequest. public declares
    ➥it to be part of the interface of the Person class. int specifies
    ➥it to return a value of type int.

43: The Person decides on which floor "he" or "she" wishes to travel to
    ➥by returning a randomly created number between 1 and 30.

51: The Building class declares an instance variable of type Elevator
    ➥called elevatorA. The Building class is said to have a "has-a"
    ➥(or a composition) relationship with the Elevator class.

53: Begin the definition of the Main method where the program will commence.


55: Instantiate an object of class Elevator with the keyword new; assign
    ➥this object to the elevatorA variable.

56: Invoke the LoadPassenger method of the elevatorA object.

57-61: Invoke the InitiateNewFloorRequest method of the
       ➥elevatorA object 5 times.

62: Invoke the ReportStatistic method of the elevatorA object.
```

FIGURE 5.1
Linking Figure 3.1 with actual C# program.

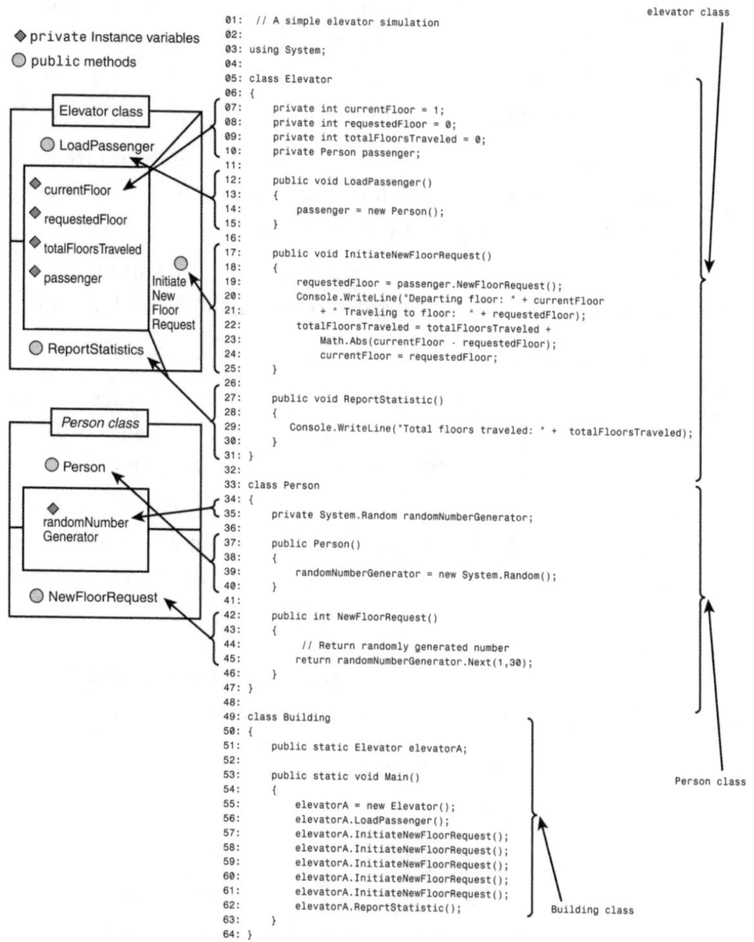

private Instance variables
public methods
Elevator class
LoadPassenger
currentFloor
requestedFloor
totalFloorsTraveled
passenger
Initiate New Floor Request
ReportStatistics
Person class
Person
randomNumber Generator
NewFloorRequest
elevator class
Person class
Building class
01: // A simple elevator simulation
02:
03: using System;
04:
05: class Elevator
06: {
07:     private int currentFloor = 1;
08:     private int requestedFloor = 0;
09:     private int totalFloorsTraveled = 0;
10:     private Person passenger;
11:
12:     public void LoadPassenger()
13:     {
14:         passenger = new Person();
15:     }
16:
17:     public void InitiateNewFloorRequest()
18:     {
19:         requestedFloor = passenger.NewFloorRequest();
20:         Console.WriteLine("Departing floor: " + currentFloor
21:             + " Traveling to floor: " + requestedFloor);
22:         totalFloorsTraveled = totalFloorsTraveled +
23:             Math.Abs(currentFloor - requestedFloor);
24:             currentFloor = requestedFloor;
25:     }
26:
27:     public void ReportStatistic()
28:     {
29:        Console.WriteLine("Total floors traveled: " + totalFloorsTraveled);
30:     }
31: }
32:
33: class Person
34: {
35:     private System.Random randomNumberGenerator;
36:
37:     public Person()
38:     {
39:         randomNumberGenerator = new System.Random();
40:     }
41:
42:     public int NewFloorRequest()
43:     {
44:          // Return randomly generated number
45:         return randomNumberGenerator.Next(1,30);
46:     }
47: }
48:
49: class Building
50: {
51:     public static Elevator elevatorA;
52:
53:     public static void Main()
54:     {
55:         elevatorA = new Elevator();
56:         elevatorA.LoadPassenger();
57:         elevatorA.InitiateNewFloorRequest();
58:         elevatorA.InitiateNewFloorRequest();
59:         elevatorA.InitiateNewFloorRequest();
60:         elevatorA.InitiateNewFloorRequest();
61:         elevatorA.InitiateNewFloorRequest();
62:         elevatorA.ReportStatistic();
63:     }
64: }

A Deeper Analysis of `SimpleElevatorSimulation.cs`

The following sections discuss important subjects related to Listing 5.1.

Defining a Class to Be Instantiated in Our Own Program

You are already familiar with how a class is defined. I still highlight line 5 because this is the first time you define your own class that is being instantiated and therefore used to create an object in your program.

```
05: class Elevator
```

Initializing Variables

The new feature presented in line 7 is the combination of a declaration statement and an assignment statement. This is called an *initialization*. `private int currentFloor;` is a straightforward declaration and, by adding `= 1` at the end, you effectively assign 1 to `currentFloor` during or immediately after the creation of the object to which this instance variable belongs.

```
07:        private int currentFloor = 1;
```

A variable often needs an initial value before it can be utilized in the computations in which it takes part. `currentFloor` in line 7 is a good example. We want the elevator to start at floor number 1 so we initialize it to this value.

When a variable is assigned a value before it takes part in any computations, we say it is being ***initialized***. Two important methods exist to initialize an instance variable. You can

- Assign the variable an initial value in its declaration (as in line 7).
- Utilize a C# feature called a constructor. The source code contained in a ***constructor*** is executed when an object of a class is being created, which is the ideal time for any initializations. Constructors are informally presented shortly.

Instance variables that are not explicitly initialized in the source code are automatically assigned a default value by the C# compiler. For example, had we not assigned the value 1 to `currentFloor` in line 7, C# would have given it the default value 0.

Initialize All Your Variables Explicitly

Do not rely on the C# compiler to initialize your variables. Explicit initializations make the code clearer and avoid the source code relying on compiler initializations and their default values, which can change in the future and introduce errors into your source code.

Tip

It is possible to declare a class member without explicitly stating its accessibility by leaving out the `public` or `private` keyword. The accessibility is then, by default, `private`.

Nevertheless, use the `private` keyword to declare all `private` class members to enhance clarity.

Declaring a Variable Representing an Object of a Specific Class

Line 10 states that the instance variable `passenger` can hold an object created from the `Person` class.

```
10:        private Person passenger;
```

We haven't yet put a particular `Person` object here; we would need an assignment statement to do this, which you will see a bit further in this section. So far, we are merely expressing that an `Elevator` object is able to "transport" one `passenger`, which must be a `Person`. For example, no `Dog`, `Airplane`, or `Submarine` objects can be stored in the `Elevator`, had we ever defined such classes in our program.

Now, jump down to lines 33–47 for a moment. By defining the **Person** class in these lines, you have effectively created a new custom-made type. So, instead of merely being able to declare a variable to be of type **int** or type **string**, you can also declare it to be of type **Person**, which is exactly what you do in line 10.

Note

int and **string** are built-in, pre-defined types. The classes you write and define in your source code are custom-made types.

Notice that line 10 is closely linked with lines 14, 19, and 33–47. Line 14 assigns a new **Person** object to **passenger**; line 19 utilizes some of the functionality of the **passenger** variable (and hence a **Person** object) by calling one of its methods, and lines 33–47 define the **Person** class.

Tip

The sequence of class member declarations and definitions is arbitrary. However, try to divide the class members into sections containing members with similar access modifiers to improve clarity.

The following is one example of a commonly used style:

```
class ClassName
{
        declarations of private instance variables
        private method definitions
        public method definitions
}
```

Instance Variables Representing the State of an Elevator Object

Lines 7–10 contain the list of instance variables I found relevant to describe an **Elevator** object for this simulation.

```
07:     private int currentFloor = 1;
08:     private int requestedFloor = 0;
09:     private int totalFloorsTraveled = 0;
10:     private Person passenger;
```

The state of any **Elevator** object is described by the instance variables declared in the following lines:

- *Line 7*—The **currentFloor** variable keeps track of the floor on which an **Elevator** object is situated.
- *Line 8*—A new floor request will be stored in the **requestedFloor** variable. The **Elevator** object will attempt to fulfill this request as swiftly as possible (line 24), depending on the speed of your computer's processor.

- *Line 9*—When the `Elevator` object is created, you can regard it to be "brand new." It has never moved up or down, so `totalFloorsTraveled` initially must contain the value 0. This is achieved by initializing it to the value 0.

  The amount of floors traveled is added to `totalFloorsTraveled` (lines 22-23), just before a trip is finished (line 24).

- *Line 10*—The passenger(s) of the elevator are ultimately the decision makers of the floor numbers visited by the elevator. The `Person` object residing inside `passenger` chooses which floors our `Elevator` object must visit. A request is obtained from the `passenger` in line 19 and assigned to the `requestedFloor` variable.

Abstraction and the Choice of Instance Variables

Recall the discussion about abstraction in the beginning of Chapter 3. The goal associated with abstraction is to identify the essential characteristics of a class of objects that are relevant to our computer program.

During the process of deciding which instance variables to include in a class definition, and the declaration of them in the source code, the programmer is applying the conceptual idea of abstraction in a very practical, hands-on manner.

For example, I could have attempted to include an instance variable such as `color` of type `string` in the `Elevator` class, declared as follows:

```
private string color;  <---- probably useless for our purposes
```

But where can I make any use of it? I could perhaps assign the `string red` to it and write a method that would print the following:

```
My color is: red
```

on the command console whenever called; but the exercise would be irrelevant to what we are trying to achieve in our simple little simulation so it is wasteful and complicates our `Elevator` class unnecessarily.

Another programmer might have included an instance variable of the `Elevator` class that measures the number of trips performed by the elevator; the programmer might call it `totalTrips` and declare it as follows:

```
private int totalTrips;  <---- potentially useful
```

The `Elevator` class could then be designed so that a method would add 1 to `totalTrips` every time a request had been fulfilled. This instance variable would enable us to keep track of another, perhaps important, statistic and so it has the potential of being useful.

As you can see, there are many different ways to represent a real world object when deciding which instance variables to include. The choice of instance variables depends on the individual programmer and what he or she wants to do with each object.

Enabling `Elevator` Object to Load a New Passenger

An `Elevator` object must be able to load a new `Person` object. This is accomplished by the `LoadPassenger` method residing inside an `Elevator` object (see line 12). `LoadPassenger()` is accessed from outside its object, and so it must be declared `public`. The call to `LoadPassenger` is made in line 56 of Listing 5.1.

```
12:     public void LoadPassenger()
```

Talking About Classes and Objects

Consider the following declaration statement:

```
private Person passenger;
```

You will come across many different, more or less correct, ways to describe what this sentence is about and, in particular, how to identify an object. In my opinion, the following is a good description but perhaps a bit cumbersome:

"`passenger` is a variable declared to hold an object of class `Person`."

Due to this lengthy description, I often use the following expression:

"`passenger` is a variable declared to hold a `Person` object."

In Chapter 6, "Types Part I: The Simple Types," you will see why the following description is probably the most correct but also the longest:

"`passenger` is a variable declared to hold a reference to an object of class `Person`."

Creating a New Object with the `new` Keyword

Line 14 goes hand-in-hand with line 10.

```
14:         passenger = new Person();
```

`new`, as applied in this line, is a keyword in C# used to instantiate a new object. It will create a new instance (object) of the `Person` class. This new object of class `Person` is then assigned to the `passenger` variable. `passenger` now contains a `Person` object that can be called and used to perform actions.

Note

When an object is instantiated, an initialization of this object's instance variables is often needed. A *constructor* is a special kind of method that performs this initialization task.

To specify that a method is a constructor, it must have the same name as its class. Thus, a constructor for the `Person` class is called `Person()` (see line 37). Whenever a new `Person` object is created with the keyword `new`, the `Person()` constructor is automatically called to perform the necessary initializations. This explains the parentheses in line 14, which are always required when any method, and any constructor, is called.

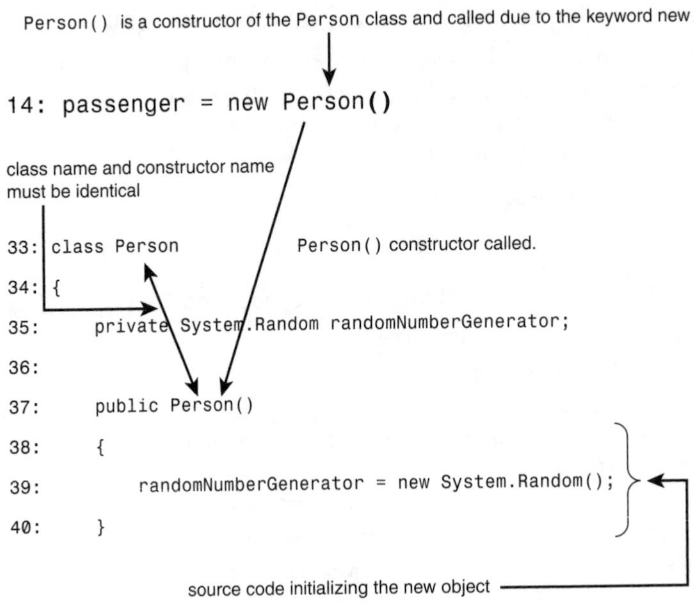

Person() is a constructor of the Person class and called due to the keyword new

```
14: passenger = new Person()
```

class name and constructor name must be identical

Person() constructor called.

```
33: class Person
34: {
35:     private System.Random randomNumberGenerator;
36:
37:     public Person()
38:     {
39:         randomNumberGenerator = new System.Random();
40:     }
```

source code initializing the new object

Letting an Elevator Object Receive and Fulfill Passenger Requests

By calling the `InitiateNewFloorRequest` method, the `Elevator` object is briefly instructed to:

- Get a new request from the `passenger` (line 19)
- Print out its departure and destination floor (lines 20-21)
- Update the `totalFloorsTraveled` statistic (lines 21-22)
- Fulfill the request of the `passenger` (line 24).

```
17:     public void InitiateNewFloorRequest()
18:     {
19:         requestedFloor = passenger.NewFloorRequest();
20:         Console.WriteLine("Departing floor: " + currentFloor
21:             + " Traveling to floor: " + requestedFloor);
22:         totalFloorsTraveled = totalFloorsTraveled +
23:         Math.Abs(currentFloor - requestedFloor);
24:         currentFloor = requestedFloor;
25:     }
```

Let's begin with line 19:

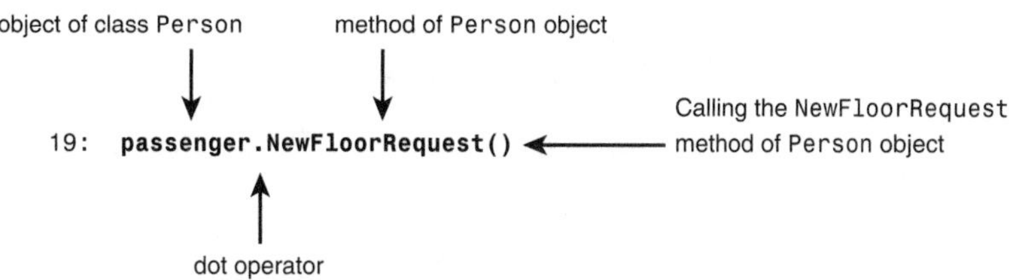

Here, we are using the following syntax introduced earlier:

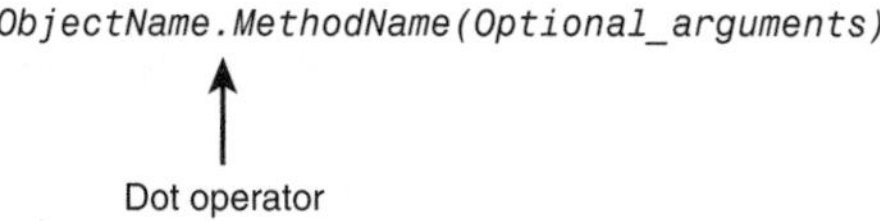

where the dot operator (`.`) is used to refer to a method residing inside an object. You have already used the dot operator many times. For example you used the dot operator when you called the `WriteLine` method of the `System.Console` with `System.Console.WriteLine("Bye Bye!")`. This time, however, instead of calling a prewritten method of the .NET Framework you are calling your own custom-made method from the `Person` class.

Note

You can see the fixed class definition in the source code. An object, on the other hand, is dynamic and comes to life during execution of the program.

Instead of calling a method residing inside the same object, you are calling a method residing in another object. Here, the `Elevator` object is said to send a message to the `Person` object. A call to a method residing in another object is similar to calling a local method. In Figure 5.2, I have linked Figure 3.1 with the general mechanism illustrated in Figure 4.1. The upper half of the figure illustrates the call to `NewFloorRequest`, following the same graphical style as in Figure 4.1. Step 1 symbolizes the call to `NewFloorRequest`. There are no formal parameters specified for `NewFloorRequest`, so no arguments are passed to the method. This step is equivalent to step 1 of the lower half of the figure. After the `NewFloorRequest` has terminated, it returns a value of type `int`, as symbolized by the arrow marked 2. The graphics equivalent of step 2 is shown in the lower half of this figure. As seen previously (line 18 of Listing 4.1 in Chapter 4), after step 2 is completed, you can substitute `passenger.NewFloorRequest()` with this value of type `int`. Finally, this value can be assigned to the variable `requestedFloor` with the assignment operator `=`.

FIGURE 5.2
Invoking a method of another object.

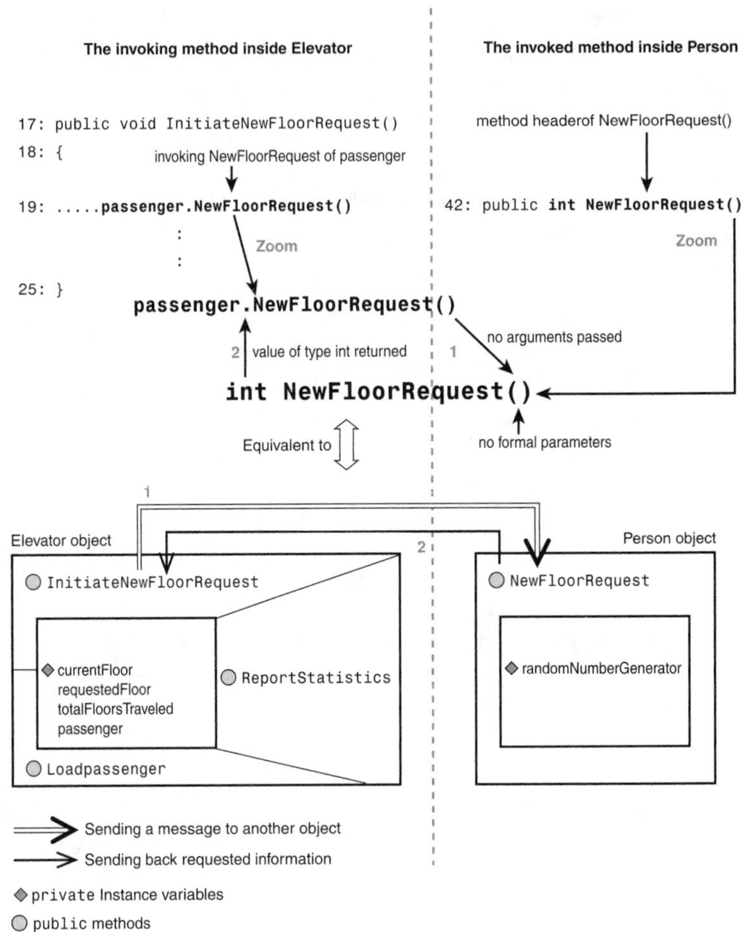

After the newly received request from its `passenger` in line 19, the `Elevator` object has a current position held by the `currentFloor` variable and a different floor held in `requestedFloor` to which it must travel. If the `Elevator` is "brand new" and has just been created, `currentFloor` will have a value of 1. If the `Elevator` has already been on one or more "rides," `currentFloor` will be equal to the destination of the latest "ride." Line 20 will print out the value of the `currentFloor` by using the now familiar `WriteLine` method. The newly received `passenger` request is then printed in line 21.

Note that lines 22 and 23 represent just one statement; you can verify this by locating the single semicolon found at the end of line 23. The statement has been spread over two lines due to lack of space. Line 23 has been indented relative to line 22; this indicates to the reader that we are dealing with only one statement.

Absolute Value

The *absolute value* of a positive number is the number itself.

The absolute value of a negative number is the number with the negative sign removed.

For example,

The absolute value of (-12) is 12.

The absolute value of 12 is 12.

In Mathematics, absolute value is indicated with two vertical lines, surrounding the literal or variable, as shown in the following:

```
|-12| = 12
```

The use of *Math.Abs()*

The `Abs` method of the `Math` class residing inside the .NET Framework returns the absolute value of the argument sent to it. Consequently, the method call `Math.Abs(99)` returns `99`, whereas `Math.Abs(-34)` returns 34.

When calculating the distance traveled by the elevator, we are interested in the positive number of floors traveled, irrespective of whether the elevator is moving up or down. If we calculate the number of floors traveled using the following expression:

```
currentFloor - requestedFloor
```

we will end up with a negative number of floors traveled whenever `requestedFloor` is larger than `currentFloor`. This negative number is then added to `totalFloorsTraveled`; so the number of floors traveled in this case has mistakenly been deducted rather than added from `totalFloorsTraveled`. We can avoid this problem by adding the absolute value of (`currentFloor - requestedFloor`), as has been done in line 23:

```
Math.Abs(currentFloor - requestedFloor);
```

The statement can be broken down into the following sub-instructions:

1. `Math.Abs(currentFloor - requestedFloor)`—Calculate the number of floors traveled on the next elevator ride.
2. `totalFloorsTraveled + Math.Abs(currentFloor - requestedFloor)`—Add the number of floors traveled on the next elevator ride to the current value of `totalFloorsTraveled`.
3. Assign the result of 2 to `totalFloorsTraveled`.

Having `totalFloorsTraveled` on both sides of the assignment operator might seem odd at first. However, this is a very useful operation adding the number of floors traveled on the latest elevator ride to the original value of `totalFloorsTraveled`. `totalFloorsTraveled` is the "odometer" of the elevator, constantly keeping track of the total amount of floors it has traveled. More details about this type of statement will be provided in Chapter 6.

Surprisingly, the simple assignment statement in line 24 represents the "elevator ride". It satisfies the request from `passenger`. By assigning the value of the `requestedFloor` variable to currentFloor, we can say that the elevator has "moved" from the currentFloor value it contained prior to this assignment to the requestedFloor.

The Person Class: The Template for an Elevator Passenger

Line 33 begins the definition of the second custom written class, which will be used as a template to create an object.

```
33: class Person
```

As we have seen, a Person object is created and kept inside an Elevator object from which its NewFloorRequest method is called, telling the Elevator object where its passenger wants to go next.

In Line 35, an object of the Person class has been enabled to make floor requests by equipping it with an object containing a method that can generate random numbers. This object is kept in the randomNumberGenerator variable. The class this object is instantiated from is found in the .NET class library and is called System.Random(). Line 35 declares the randomNumberGenerator to contain an object of type System.Random.

```
35:     private System.Random randomNumberGenerator;
```

Because randomNumberGenerator is an instance variable of the Person class, it is declared private. Note that after this declaration, the randomNumberGenerator is still empty; no object has yet been assigned to this variable. We must assign an object to the randomNumberGenerator before any random numbers can be generated by this variable; lines 37–40 fulfill this important task by containing a constructor for the Person class.

The constructor concept has already been discussed and I won't drill further into this subject now. It is not important to fully understand the constructor mechanism now, as long as you are aware that the essential part is line 39, where a new object of class System.Random is assigned to the randomNumberGenerator of any newly created object of class Person.

```
37:     public Person()
38:     {
39:         randomNumberGenerator = new System.Random();
40:     }
```

The NewFloorRequest defined in lines 42–46 will, when called, generate and return a random number that indicates passenger's next floor request. Line 45 finds a random number between 1 and 30 (specified in the parentheses .Next(1,30)). The return keyword sends this random number back to the caller which, in this case, is the InitiateNewFloorRequest method of the Elevator object. The details of the System.Random class will not be discussed any further here. If you want to investigate this class further, please use the .NET Framework Documentation.

```
42:     public int NewFloorRequest()
43:     {
44:         // Return randomly generated number
45:         return randomNumberGenerator.Next(1,30);
46:     }
```

Note

The programmer who implements the `Elevator` class makes use of the `NewFloorRequest` method of a `Person` object. However, he or she should not need to look at the method definition to use the method. He or she would most likely not be interested in how a `Person` object decides on the values returned and would happily be unaware of random number generators and the like. The method header and a short description of the intent of the method is all that he or she needs to know. Information of how the intent is accomplished has no place here.

The method header forms a contract with the user of the method. It gives the name of the method and how many arguments should be sent along with the method call. The method then promises to return either no value (if stated void) or one value of a specific type.

So as long as we don't tinker with the method header (don't change the name of the method, the number and type of its formal parameters, or its return type), we can create all sorts of intricate processes for the `Person` object to decide on the next destination floor.

The `Main()` Method: Conducting the Simulation

In lines 53–63, we find our old friend the unavoidable `Main` method.

```
53:     public static void Main()
54:     {
55:         elevatorA = new Elevator();
56:         elevatorA.LoadPassenger();
57:         elevatorA.InitiateNewFloorRequest();
58:         elevatorA.InitiateNewFloorRequest();
59:         elevatorA.InitiateNewFloorRequest();
60:         elevatorA.InitiateNewFloorRequest();
61:         elevatorA.InitiateNewFloorRequest();
62:         elevatorA.ReportStatistic();
63:     }
```

Even if `Main()` is positioned at the end of the program in this case, it contains, as always, the statements that are to be executed first when the program is started. You can view `Main()` to be a "control tower" of the whole program. It uses the overall functionality provided by the other classes in the program to direct the general flow of execution.

Briefly, the `Main method` initially creates an `Elevator` object and assigns it to `elevatorA` (line 55); instructs it to load in a passenger (line 56); asks elevatorA to request a "next floor request" along with its fulfillment five times (lines 57–61); and finally, it asks the `Elevator` object to report the statistic it has collected over those five trips (line 62).

Note how relatively easy it is to conduct this simulation from the `Main` method. All the hard detailed work is performed in the `Elevator` and `Person` classes.

Class Relationships and UML

The three user-defined classes, along with the `System.Random` class of Listing 5.1, collaborate to provide the functionality of our simple elevator simulation program. The `Building` class contains an `Elevator` object and calls its methods, the `Elevator` object employs a `Person` object to direct its movements, and the `Person` object uses a `System.Random` object to decide the next floor. In well-constructed, object-oriented programs, classes collaborate in similar ways—each contributing with its own unique functionality—for the whole program to work.

If two classes are to collaborate, they must have a relationship (interact) with each other. Several different relationships can exist between two classes, and it is up to the designer of the program to decide which particular relationships should be implemented for the program at hand. This design phase typically takes place when the classes of the program have been identified (stage 2b of the design process described in Chapter 2, "Your First C# Program"). The following section discusses a few commonly found relationships.

`Building-Elevator` and `Elevator-Person` form two kinds of relationships that we will use as examples.

The `Building-Elevator` *Relationship*

A typical building is composed of many different parts, such as floors, walls, ceilings, a roof, and sometimes elevators. In our case, we can say that the **`Building`** we are simulating has an **`Elevator`** as one of its parts. This is sometimes referred to as a whole/part relationship. We have implemented this relationship in Listing 5.1 by declaring an instance variable of type **`Elevator`** inside the **`Building`** class as in line 51:

```
51:     private static Elevator elevatorA;
```

This allows **`Building`** to hold an **`Elevator`** object and call its **`public`** methods. A class can have many different instance variables holding many objects of different classes. For example, we could also have equipped **`Building`** with instance variables representing a number of **`Floor`** objects. This concept of constructing a class (**`Building`**) with other classes (**`Elevator`** or **`Floors`** or both and many others) is generally called *aggregation*, and the accompanying relationships *aggregation relationships*.

If the aggregation relationship (as in the case of the **`Building-Elevator`** relationship), is reflecting a situation where one class is an integral part of the other, we can further call this aggregation a ***composition***. (In a moment you will see why the Elevator-Person relationship is an aggregation but not a composition). The composition relationship can be illustrated with a Unified Modeling Language (UML) class diagram as shown in Figure 5.3. The two rectangular boxes symbolize classes and the line connecting them with the black diamond (pointing at the whole class) illustrates a composition relationship between the classes. Both classes are marked with the number 1 to indicate that one **`Building`** has one **`Elevator`**.

The Unified Modeling Language (UML): The Lingua Franca of OO Modeling

Pseudocode is a useful aid in expressing algorithms that are implemented in single methods because they are read from top to bottom, like the runtime executes the program, and because it abstracts away from the hard-coded rigor of a computer language (semicolons, parentheses, and so on). However, classes can consist of many methods, and larger programs consist of many classes. Pseudocode is not a suitable tool to illustrate models of how the classes of a program relate, because classes break free of the sequential procedural-oriented way of thinking (every class can potentially have a relationship with any other class defined in the program) and because the format of the pseudocode is much too detailed to provide an overview of a large OO program.

To model class relationships and the overall architecture of an OO program effectively, we need a language that allows us to abstract away from the internal details of methods and, instead, provide us with the means to express class relationships and OO concepts on a suitable level of detail. For this purpose, most OO programmers today, irrespective of their programming language, use a graphical diagramming language called the Unified Modeling Language (UML). UML is a feature-rich language and requires a whole book to be amply presented; accordingly, this book only presents a small subset of UML.

You can get detailed information about UML from the non-profit organization Object Management Group (OMG) (`www.omg.org`) at `www.omg.org/uml`. Many good UML books have been written including *The Unified Modeling Language User Guide* by the originators of UML, Grady Booch, James Rumbaugh, and Ivar Jacobson.

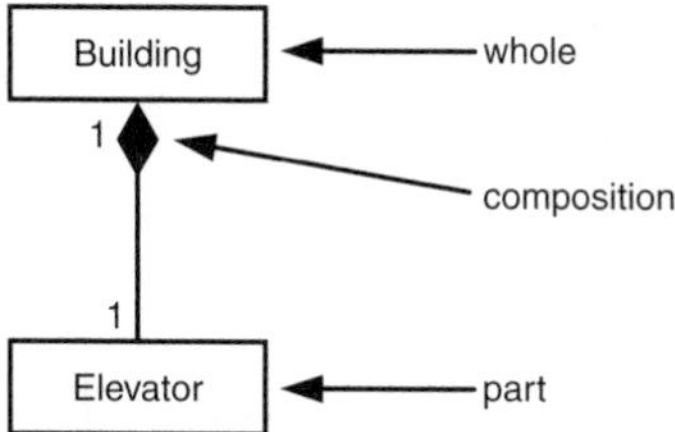

FIGURE 5.3
UML diagram symbolizing composition.

The `Elevator-Person` *Relationship*

A button is an integral part of an elevator, but a passenger is not. (The elevator is still fully operational without a passenger, but not without its buttons). So even though the passenger in our implementation (for abstraction reasons) has been made a permanent part of the `Elevator` (the same `Person` object stays inside the `Elevator` throughout the simulation), it is not a composition relationship, merely an aggregation. The relationship is illustrated with UML in Figure 5.4. Notice that an open diamond, in contrast to the filled diamond in Figure 5.3, symbolizes aggregation.

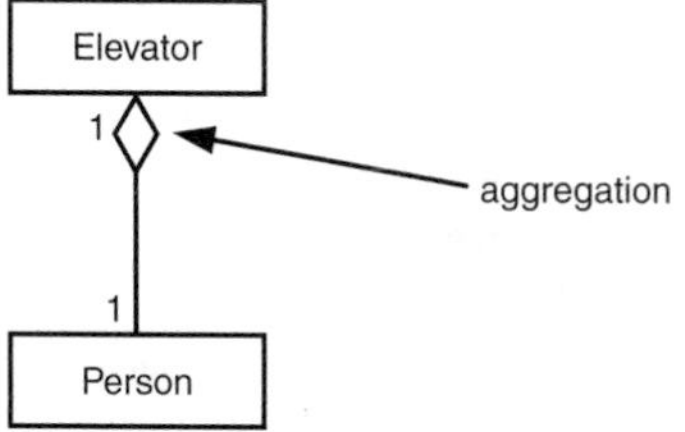

FIGURE 5.4
UML diagram symbolizing aggregation.

The whole UML class diagram for the program in Listing 5.1 is shown in Figure 5.5. UML allows us, as shown, to divide the rectangle representing a class into three compartments—the upper compartment contains the name of the class, the middle compartment the instance variables (or attributes), and the lower compartment the methods (behavior) belonging to the class.

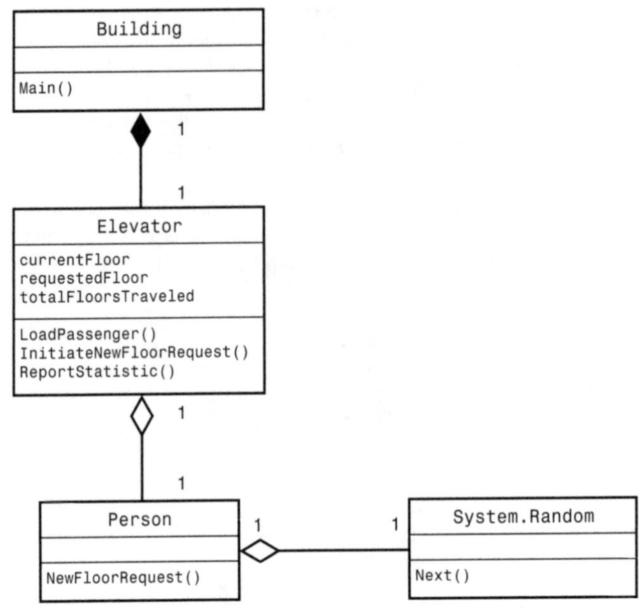

FIGURE 5.5
UML class diagram for Listing 5.1.

Associations

Permanent relationships between classes, such as the aggregation and composition relationships discussed in the previous sections, are generally called ***structural relationships*** or, more formally, ***associations***. However, other types of associations exist that are not aggregations (and therefore not compositions either). To give an example of the latter, consider the following scenario: In an attempt to make our elevator simulation more realistic, we change our original list of abstractions shown earlier by allowing many `Person` objects to enter, travel, and exit the `Elevator` object instead of just the one `Person` object that permanently stays there at the moment. Any one `Person` object could then no longer be said to be a permanent part of the `Elevator` object, and we would just say that the `Elevator` class is associated with the `Person` class. An association is shown with a simple line as in Figure 5.6.

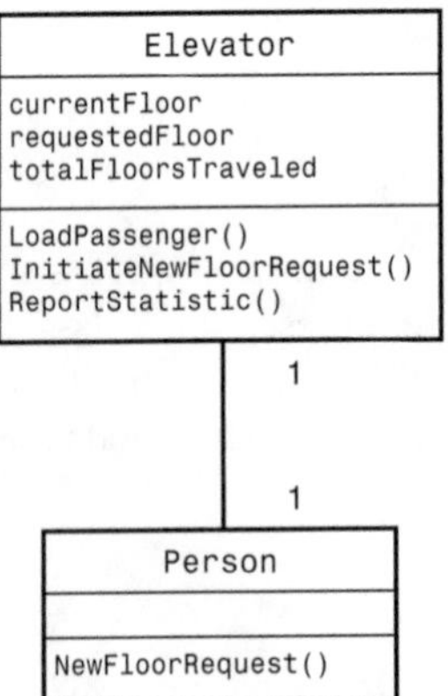

FIGURE 5.6
Elevator/Person class association.

Other example of associations that are not aggregations are

- `Employee` works for `Company`
- `BankCustomer` interacts with the `BankTeller`

Note 

Associations that precisely connect two classes are called binary associations; they are the most common kind of association.

Summary

This chapter consists of two main parts. The first part is about the lexical structure of a C# source program. The second part provides an example of an object-oriented program, which relates directly to the discussion in Chapter 3 about abstraction and encapsulation.

The following are the most important points covered in this chapter:

A C# source program can be viewed as a collection of identifiers, keywords, whitespace, comments, literals, operators, and separators.

C# is a case-sensitive language. To improve the clarity for other readers of the code, it is important to adhere to a certain capitalization style. Pascal Casing (`ThisIsPascalCasing`) and Camel Casing (`thisIsCamelCasing`) are the preferred styles and are used for different C# constructs.

A literal has the value that is written in the source code (what you see is what you get). Values like 10 and "This is a dog" are examples of literals.

Separators, such as semicolons (`;`), commas (`,`), and periods (`.`), separate different elements in C# from each other.

Operators act on operands. Operands combine with operators to form expressions.

Instance variables must be initialized when an object is created. This is either done automatically by the runtime, by a declaration initialization, or by an instance constructor.

An object can hold a reference to another object in an instance variable. Such a permanent relationship is called an association.

An object is created by using the `new` keyword.

In an object-oriented program, classes collaborate to provide the functionality of the program.

Two classes can collaborate by having a relationship.

Common association relationships are aggregations and compositions.

The Unified Modeling Language (UML) is by far the most popular graphical modeling language used to express and illustrate object-oriented program designs.

Review Questions

1. What is lexical analysis?
2. What are the atomic parts of a C# program?
3. What is Pascal casing and camel casing? For which parts of the C# program should they be used?
4. What is the main difference between variables and literals?
5. What are operators and operands? How do they relate?
6. Is `50` an expression? Is `(50 + x)`? Is `public`?
7. Give examples of typical keywords in C#.
8. Why is pseudocode not well suited for expressing the overall design of an object-oriented program?
9. What kind of relationship does a `BankCustomer` object have with a `BankTeller` object? How is this expressed in UML?
10. What kind of relationship does a `Heart` object have with a `HumanBody` object. How is this expressed in UML?
11. What kind of relationship does a `LightBulb` have with a `Lamp` object. How is this expressed in UML?
12. How is an association relationship implemented in C#?
13. How can instance variables be initialized when an object is created?
14. Describe `passenger` when declared as in the following line:

```
private Person passenger;
```

Programming Exercises

Enable the program in Listing 5.1 to exhibit the following functionality by changing its source code:

1. Print "The simulation has commenced" on the command console right after the program is started.
2. Print "The simulation has ended" as the last thing just before the program is terminated.
3. Instead of merely choosing floors between 1 and 30, the `Person` class chooses floors between 0 and 50.
4. On its first ride, `Elevator` starts at floor number 0 instead of floor number 1.
5. The `Elevator object` does 10 journeys instead of the 5 it is doing now.

6. `Elevator` is currently counting the total floors traveled with the `totalFloorsTraveled` variable. Declare an instance variable inside the `Elevator` class that keeps track of the number of trips this elevator completes. You could call this variable `totalTripsTraveled`. The `Elevator` should update this variable by adding one to `totalTripsTraveled` after every trip. Update the `ReportStatistics` method of the `Elevator` class to print out not only `totalFloorsTraveled` but also `totalTripsTraveled`, accompanied by an explanation for what is being printed.

7. Add an instance variable to the `Elevator` class that can hold the name of the elevator. You can call it `myName`. Which type should you use for this instance variable? Should you use `private` or `public` when you declare it? Write a constructor by which you can set the value of this variable as you create the `Elevator` object with `new` and assign it to a variable. (Hint: The constructor is a method and must have the same name as its class. This constructor must have a formal parameter of type `string` in its header.) Adjust the call to the constructor when using the keyword `new` by inserting the name of the `Elevator` as an argument (between the parenthesis—instead of `new Elevator()`, write `new Elevator("ElevatorA")`.

   Every time the `Elevator` completes a trip, it should print its name along with its departing and arrival floor. In other words, instead of printing

   ```
   Departing floor: 2 Traveling to floor: 24
   ```

   it should print

   ```
   ElevatorA: Departing floor: 2 Traveling to floor: 24
   ```

   where `ElevatorA` is the name of the `Elevator` residing inside `myName`.

CHAPTER 6

TYPES PART I: THE SIMPLE TYPES

You will learn about the following in this chapter:

- The importance of types in C# and why it is important to be familiar with them
- The implications of C# being a strongly typed language
- Two important ways of dividing the types in C#—simple types versus derived types and value types versus reference types
- All the main types found in C#
- Simple predefined types in C#
- How C# determines the type of a literal
- How to best apply each simple type, and how to avoid common pitfalls during this process
- Compatibilities between the various simple types and understanding for implicit and explicit conversions between these types
- A syntax notation form used in the rest of the book to effectively and concisely describe the syntax of C#
- How to work with symbolic constants, their advantages, and when to apply them
- How to format numbers when converting them to strings to improve their readability and compactness when displayed as output

Introduction

In Chapter 3, "A Guided Tour through C#: Part I," Chapter 4, "A Guided Tour through C#: Part II," and Chapter 5, "Your First Object-Oriented Program," you met two of the predefined types in C#, `int` and `string`. You saw how it was possible to specify whether a variable was meant to hold whole numbers, by declaring it to be of type `int`, or to represent text, by declaring it to be of type `string`.

In the simple elevator simulation program, you were shown how to define and use *your own* custom-made, types such as the `Elevator` and `Person` classes. In particular, you encountered the possibility of combining the following ingredients to construct the `Elevator` class.

- Two of the predefined types in C#, `int` and `string`
- The pre-fabricated types from .NET's class library (`Console` and `Math` classes)
- Your own custom-made `Person` type

This idea of combining and extending different types by using them as building blocks to form new types is a core concept and a major strength of object-oriented programming. To make you a better object-oriented programmer, you need a proficient understanding of the predefined building blocks found in C#.

The predefined types of C# can conveniently, albeit artificially, be divided into two major groups—simple types and derived types:

- *Simple types*—A pivotal set of building blocks is found in C#'s set of simple types, of which `int` is just one example. Simple types allow you to work with numbers and single characters in your source code. They provide you with the basis to represent information, such as the speed of an airplane in an aviation simulation or calculating the movement of an animated spaceship. C# provides a broad range of simple types (13 to be exact) that allow you to match each piece of information with a suitable type.
- *Derived predefined types*—`string` is an example of a pre-defined type and represents a more complex variety of types, often with elaborate functionality.

This chapter thoroughly discusses the comprehensive set of simple types used to represent single numbers and also introduces the simple type `bool`, which allows you to represent the states `true` and `false`.

Types in C#: An Overview

Before we begin our discussion of the various types found in C#, we need to clarify what a type is and its significance in C#.

What Is a Type?

In our everyday language, the word type usually signifies a number of persons or items sharing one or more particular characteristics. This often causes a group of people of the same type to be regarded as a more or less precisely defined group.

In C#, all values belonging to a specific *type* can be said to share a set of predefined characteristics.

Important characteristics for a variable of a simple type are the values that can be represented, its internal memory requirements, and its predefined behavior when applied in various computations. For example, each variable of type `int` can store integers of the size –2147483648 to 2147483647, and will occupy 32 bits of internal memory.

Note

Recall from Chapter 1, "Computers and Computer Programming: Basic Concepts," how computer software has the ability to interpret a single bit or a combination of several bits of computer memory in many different ways. By specifying a variable to be of type `int`, we are instructing the program to interpret the underlying bits as representing a value of type `int`.

Further, a clearly specified set of operations can be performed on a variable of type `int`. For example, it would not make sense to perform arithmetic calculations on a value of type `string`, whereas this would be perfectly natural with a value of type `int`. C# supports this logic through operator overloading, as demonstrated in Chapter 4. When the + operator combines two operands of type `int`, C# performs standard arithmetic addition, whereas two operands of type `string` are concatenated.

C# contains several other pre-defined overloaded operators and it is possible to extend these built-in features by specifying your own user-defined overloading processes.

By understanding the type concept, we can begin to glimpse the power of types in C#. The next sections will elaborate on this power.

C#: A Strongly Typed Language

Every value in C# must have a type. Due to the wealth of types found in C#, you will often need to combine values of different types in the same statement of a source program. To help the programmer apply this range of types correctly, speed up development time, and increase the robustness of the finished application, C# contains succinctly defined rules for the compatibility between various types when they are mixed. The compiler acts as the police; it reinforces these rules to the best of its ability, by reporting errors and warnings.

The procedure performed by the C# compiler to ensure that the compatibility rules of a program are adhered to is called *type checking*.

The following three examples illustrate typical circumstances under which the C# compiler attempts to ensure that values of different types work together smoothly:

1. An Assignment statement;
2. A method call passing arguments to the called method;
3. An expression.

- An *assignment statement*—Whenever a value is assigned to a variable in an assignment statement, the compiler checks the compatibility between the type of the variable and the type of the value assigned to it; if non-compatible, you will bump into an error message.

  Let's illustrate. You could attempt to write the following lines of code

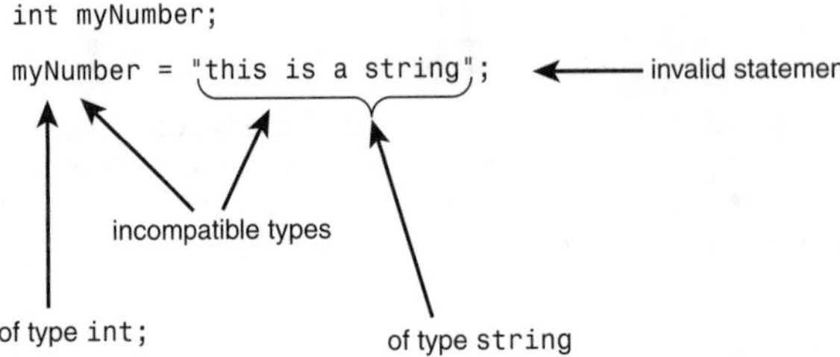

but the second line would result in a compiler error, due to incompatible types.

A breach of the type compatibility rules is termed a *type clash*.

- *Method call passing arguments*—Passing arguments to formal parameters during method invocations is another area of potential type clashes and, consequently, is scrutinized by the compiler. The following example would result in an error during compilation:

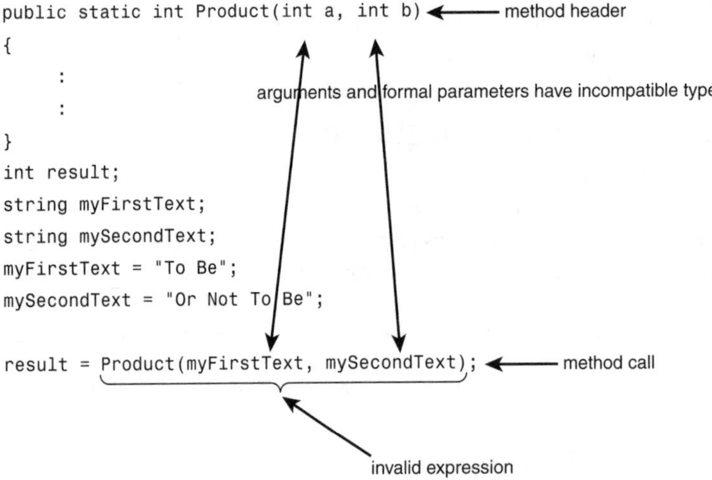

  The error is caused by a type clash between the arguments and the formal parameters. The method call to `Product` contains arguments of type `string`, but the formal parameters of `Product`'s method header expect to receive arguments of type `int`.

- *Expressions*—Any expression in C# has a specific type. When expressions are nested inside each other, the compiler chooses the type logically suited for expressions at higher levels, while simultaneously checking that these choices are sound. Take a look at the following code snippet:

```
string text1;
string text2;
int number1;
int number2;
int result;
number1 = 5;
```

```
07:  number2 = 14;
08:  text1 = " If you want to C#'er, ";
09:  text2 = "go to the optometrist";
10:  result = (number1 + number2) + (text1 + text2);
```

Let's zoom in on line 10 for a moment, as shown in Figure 6.1.

FIGURE 6.1
A nested expression.

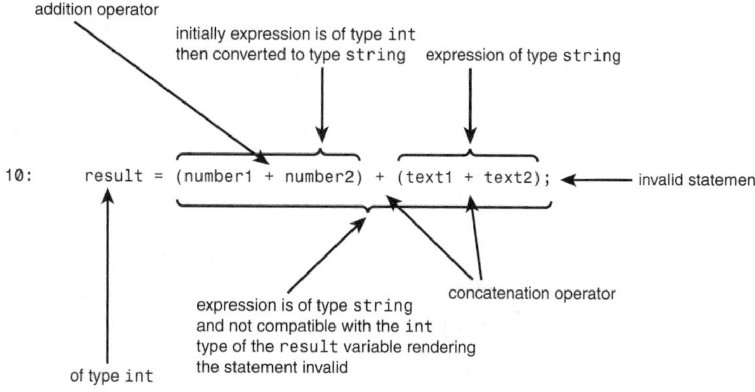

Line 10 contains a few nested expressions. Recall that any literal or variable is an expression, so `number1`, `number2`, `text1`, and `text2` are all expressions in their own right. `number1` and `number2` are both of type `int` and, when combined with the + operator, they form a new expression—`(number1 + number2)`, which is also of type `int`. The expression `(text1 + text2)` is formed to be of type `string`. When `(number1 + number2)` is combined with `(text1 + text2)` by using the + operator, the compiler faces a dilemma. How can it add an expression of type `int` to an expression of type `string`? The only way out is to implicitly convert `(number1 + number2)` to type `string`, which can then be concatenated with `(text1 + text2)`.

However, `result` on the left side of the equality operator = is of type `int` and incompatible with `string`, which finally triggers a compiler error.

The statement would have been valid if `result` had been of type `string`. `result` would then have received the value `"19 If you want to C#'er, go to the optometrist"`.

Implicit conversions are conversions from one type to another that are performed automatically by the C# compiler.

For an implicit conversion to take place, it must not incur any loss of data and must not require any further need for a detailed examination of the particular values involved.

A computer language that attempts to prohibit the use of any value in any process of which is not meant to participate, is termed a *strongly typed computer language*.

C# is a strongly typed language.

All expressions and statements in C# are, where relevant, checked for compatibilities between the involved values, in a fashion similar to the examples previously provided.

The Advantages of Types

Why should we as programmers appreciate the type system found in C#? Considering what I have mentioned so far about types in C#, we can appreciate the extreme power and high information content of the following declaration statement:

```
int distance;
```

With this statement, we tell the C# compiler the following:

- We only want to store whole numbers in `distance`.
- We only want to store numbers of a certain magnitude in `distance`.
- The program needs to allocate only a limited amount of memory to hold a value in `distance`.
- Whenever we, for example, use the `+` symbol in connection with `distance`, the program implicitly assumes that we want to perform an addition operation. This holds for all other arithmetic operators (multiplication, subtraction, and so on).
- If we try to assign this variable to a variable of an incompatible type, it is probably because we have made a mistake, so the compiler will direct our attention to the problem by returning an error or warning message.

Yes, an impressive amount of information; all contained in one small, unpretentious statement. In fact, our ability to use types and write declaration statements such as the one previously shown allows us to let the compiler take over many tedious chores. This can significantly reduce the amount of source code we have to write.

The Power of Declarative Information

Consider the following two statements:

```
int distance;   <------------ declaration statement (1)

    and

sum = number1 + number2;   <--- assignment statement (2)
```

The declaration statement (1) consists of declarative information, which tells the computer what to do. The assignment statement (2) tells the computer how to do something. As you have already seen, the declaration statement is extremely powerful and contains a lot more information than the assignment statement (2), which merely tells the computer how to calculate sum.

In general, telling someone (including the computer) *what* to do (do the dishes, for example) is a lot easier than telling him or her (it) *how* to do it (stopper the drain, open the tap, get the dishwashing liquid, take the first plate, and so on).

C# includes an exciting feature called *attributes* that allows programmers to expand and custom design the declarative information he or she can communicate to the computer. Attributes are discussed further in Chapter 21, "Preprocessing, XML Documentation and Attributes."

The Types of C#

You have now seen how the types of C# can be divided into simple types and derived types. Another equally important, and certainly more correct, way to group the types of C# is according to whether a type is a value type or a reference type.

Value Types and Reference Types

The distinction between simple types and derived types is, strictly speaking, not correct. C# uses a class-like value type, called a `struct`, to represent its simple types. This allows every simple type to have pre-defined methods attached to it. For this reason, it is possible to call the predefined method `ToString` of 5 by writing

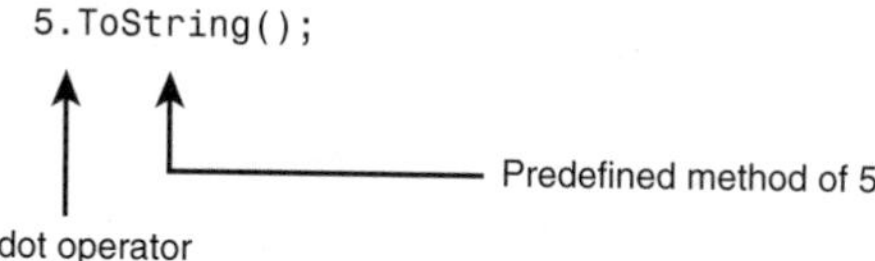

which returns the string `"5"`. In many ways, what we have defined in the previous section as a simple type is just as complex as many derived types.

Note

`ToString` is a commonly used method name in the .NET Framework. It is, as its name implies, used to return a value of type `string` from a value. The `string` often describes core information about this value. You can locate the `ToString` method of 5, used in the example, in the .NET Framework documentation by looking at the methods of the `System.Int32` struct.

Nonetheless, the distinction between simple types and derived types is convenient and originates from previous languages, such as C++ and Java, which do not contain C#'s sophisticated simple types. These languages contain true simple types, meaning a number is a number without any extra functionality attached. Later, when we return to a more detailed discussion of the struct mechanism, we will see why C# can be regarded as a fully object-oriented programming language where everything, including the simple types, can be viewed as being an object.

A variable of a *value type* holds the actual value stored in it. If we could zoom in on the actual value kept in the memory, it would store this particular value here. The `int` type is a typical example of a value type. If we declared a variable of type `int` called `myNumber` and assigned it the literal 345, we could depict it as shown in Figure 6.2.

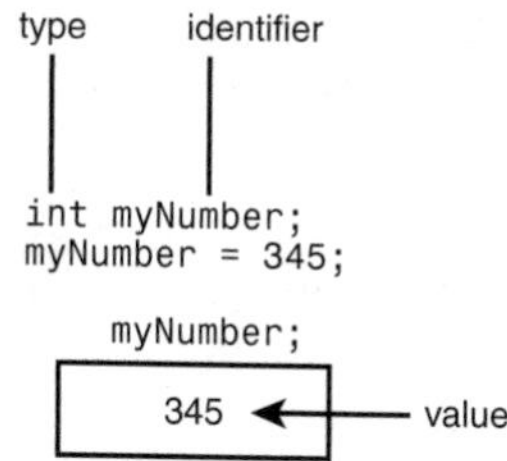

FIGURE 6.2
`int` is a value type.

All this is fairly straightforward and probably not surprising to you, but it is worth keeping in mind when we look at the other major set of types, the reference types.

A variable of a *reference type* contains a reference to an object in the computer memory and so does not, itself, contain the object. The reference consists of the location (or address) of the referred to object. To illustrate what a reference type is, we need first to turn our attention to our old friend the `string` type.

Hmm…our otherwise trusty `string` type actually turns out to have a hidden agenda; here is one important revelation about it: `string` is a reference type.

A variable of type `string` does not itself contain a `string` but is declared to hold a reference to a `string` located somewhere else in the computer memory.

Consider the following line of code:

```
string myText;  <—— declare myText to be of type string
```

This declaration statement actually says, "Allow `myText` to hold a reference to a `string`."

We can now use `myText` in the following assignment statement:

```
myText = "Lets go to the C to catch a #";
```

which assigns the address of the string `"Lets go to the C to catch a #"` to `myText`.

If you tried to zoom in on the underlying memory of `myText`, you would not find any text, just a memory address, also called a reference. This is illustrated in Figure 6.3, where I have arbitrarily located the text at the address 4027, which is the address held by `myText`.

Note

Fortunately, you never see the actual address when using references in your source code.

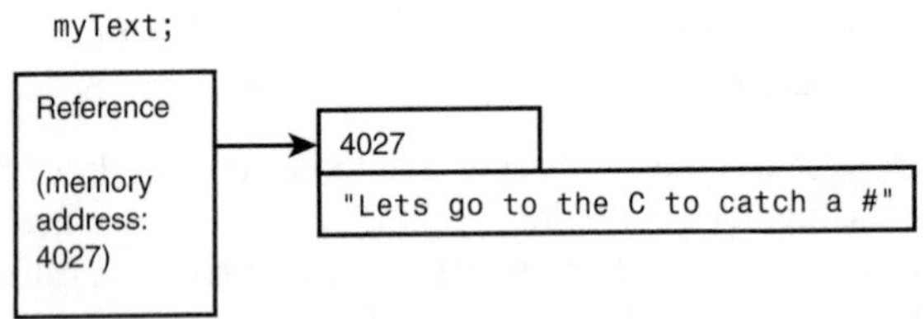

FIGURE 6.3
`string` is a reference type.

The `string` class is a good example of a reference type, but we could also have used our `Elevator` or `Person` classes from Listing 5.1 in Chapter 5 as examples of reference types.

Note

All classes are reference types.

The memory address referring to where an object is stored in the computer memory is termed a *reference* to that object.

Under many circumstances, the differences between working with value types and reference types are negligible. Our ability to work with `string` in the previous chapters without understanding the reference concept is an example of this fact. However, there are marked differences in other cases in the behavior of the two kinds of types, of which the object-oriented programmer must be aware. The source code in Listing 6.1 illustrates a typical scenario of this kind.

LISTING 6.1 Source Code of `ReferenceTest.cs`

```
using System;

/*
 * This class gives an example of
 * a difference between reference
 * types and value types
 */

class Person
{
    private int age = 0;

    public void SetAge(int newAge)
    {
        age = newAge;
    }

    public int GetAge()
    {
        return age;
    }
}

class ReferenceTester
{
    public static void Main()
    {
        Person julian;
        Person deborah;

        julian = new Person();
        deborah = new Person();
        julian.SetAge(2);
        deborah.SetAge(33);
        Console.WriteLine("Julian's age: " + julian.GetAge());
        Console.WriteLine("Deborah's age: " + deborah.GetAge());
        julian = deborah;
        Console.WriteLine("Julian's age: " + julian.GetAge());
        Console.WriteLine("Deborah's age: " + deborah.GetAge());
```

LISTING 6.1 continued

```
40:            julian.SetAge(10);
41:            Console.WriteLine("Julian's age: " + julian.GetAge());
42:            Console.WriteLine("Deborah's age: " + deborah.GetAge());
43:        }
44: }
```

```
Julian's age: 2
Deborah's age: 33
Julian's age: 33
Deborah's age: 33
Julian's age: 10
Deborah's age: 10
```

Line 9 defines a simple class called `Person` that contains just one instance variable representing age (line 11).

In lines 13–21, a couple of methods called `SetAge` and `GetAge` permits access to the value of `age`.

The class `ReferenceTester` holds the `Main` method, which declares two variables (`julian` and `deborah` in lines 28 and 29) to hold references to objects of class `Person`.

Lines 31 and 32 each create a new instance of the `Person` class with the `new` keyword. Here comes the first important point: Line 31 assigns a reference pointing at the newly created `Person` object to the `julian` variable. Line 32 assigns another reference, this time to the `deborah` variable. This reference points to the new `Person` object created in this line, which is different to the Person object created in line 31.

In lines 33 and 34, the age instance variables of the two objects are given the values 2 and 33 respectively. Thus, after line 34, we can illustrate the references from `julian` and `deborah` as in Figure 6.4.

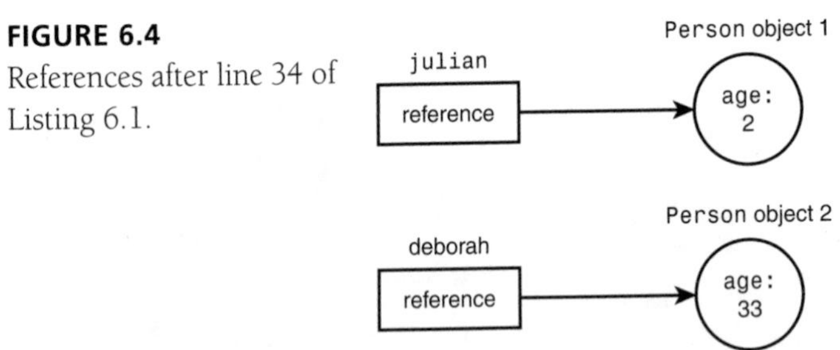

FIGURE 6.4
References after line 34 of Listing 6.1.

Lines 35 and 36 print out the ages of `julian` and `deborah`.

In line 37, the program assigns the value of `deborah` to the `julian` variable. However, because this value is a reference type, we are merely telling `julian` to reference the same object as `deborah`, leading to the situation displayed in Figure 6.5.

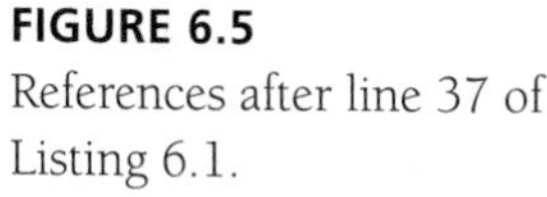

FIGURE 6.5
References after line 37 of Listing 6.1.

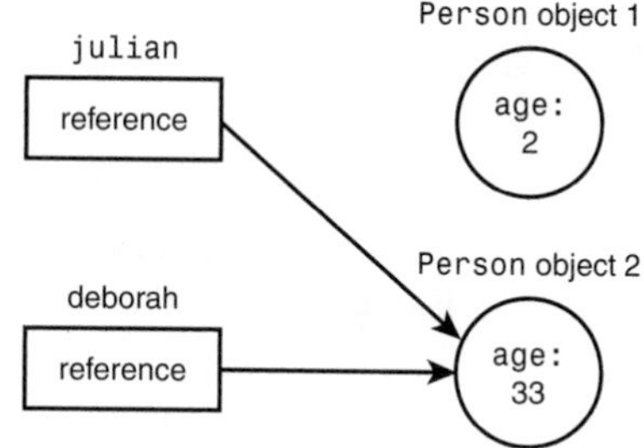

Thus, `julian` and `deborah` are now referencing exactly the same object. This is partly confirmed by the output provided by lines 38 and 39 where both `julian` and `deborah` are shown to be the same age—33. However, the convincing and often surprising result is found through lines 40–42. The program changes the age of `julian` to 10 in line 40 but, according to the sample output, it also changes the age of `deborah` to 10, confirming that `julian` and `deborah` are, in fact, pointing at the same object.

It is important to be aware of the differences between value types and reference types. Not only will this allow you to pinpoint and fix problems in your source code more quickly, but it also allows you to create speedier, more sophisticated programs.

The Main Types of C#: An Overview

Equipped with the knowledge of value types and reference types, it is useful to look at an outline of the main types found in C#, as shown in Table 6.1. Even though we have only discussed a few of the types mentioned in Table 6.1 so far, they are shown at this point of the book as an overview and a reference when you continue through the book.

TABLE 6.1 Overview of the Main Types in C#

Value Types	Reference Types
Simple types (`int` is an example)	Class types (`Elevator` and `Person` from Listing 5.1 are examples `string` type
Enum types*	Array types*
Struct types*	Interface types* Delegate types*

* not yet discussed

The following are some brief explanations of the types available in C#:

- *Simple types*—The now familiar `int` type is just one of the 13 simple types found in C#. The simple types are used to hold numeric values and single characters. They are discussed thoroughly in the next section of this chapter.

- *Enum types*—These types provide the means for creating symbolic constants, especially for sets of related constants, such as the days of the week (Monday, Tuesday, and so on), the months of the year (January, February, March, and so on), or a set of colors (Green, Red, Blue).
- *Struct types*—This type contains methods and data just like classes. Even though they are similar to classes, they also have a few important differences. One of the most important differences is that class types are reference types, whereas structures are value types. All simple types are struct types.
- *Class types*—A class defines a category of objects and is a blueprint used for creating objects. Classes contain members that, among others, can be instance variables that describe the state of an object and methods that specify the behavior of an object. Classes can inherit members from other classes. The class concept is pivotal to object-oriented programming.
- *Array type*—Variables of type array are objects dedicated to storing small or large collections of data. Each data item in an array must be of the same type. For example, if you wanted to represent the daily rainfall in London over the last 100 days, you would likely use an array.
- *Interface types*—An interface stipulates abstract behavior by specifying one or more method headers but without the accompanying implementation that is found with non-abstract methods in a class. Classes can implement interfaces and must concretize the abstract behavior stated by the interface by defining the implementation. Interfaces allow the programmer to implement advanced object-oriented concepts.
- *Delegate types*—Like interfaces, delegates are used to specify behavior, but they only specify the method header for a single method. An instance of a delegate type contains one method, and the delegate constitutes a reference to this method. The delegates (or method references) can be passed around in a program and be executed. Delegates are vital for implementing event-driven programs in C#.

The .NET Common Type System (CTS)

The .NET Common Type System (CTS) is an integral part of the .NET Framework. It defines all the types described in this section and contains the rules for how applications running under the .NET runtime can apply these types. As its name implies, all programming languages that target the .NET platform, including C#, are based on the types defined by the CTS.

Simple Types

Simple types are also called *primitive types* and belong to a group of built-in predefined types found in C#. Examples of such values are single numbers (the `int` type) and individual characters.

Our path to appreciating the variety of simple types provided begins with an understanding of the relationship between the information you want to store from the "real" world and the variables in your source code.

Variables constitute a central part of a C# program. They enable the programmer to symbolically represent values stored in the computer memory. In fact, the identifier of a variable (such as `count` or `age`) is a symbol representing an underlying value somewhere in memory. A name, such as `taxPercentage`, is far easier to understand in a piece of source code than a memory address such as "4 bytes at address 3024."

Variables enable a program to absorb input from external sources, such as users and databases, and provide easy access to those data in your source code. By manipulating these variables, it becomes possible to eventually extract valuable information from the program in the form of output.

Programmers need to store many different kinds of information from the real world (and from results of temporary calculations in the programs) in the variables of their computer programs. Some examples are the average yearly rainfall in San Francisco, the number of newborn babies in Paris in 1996, the height of a particular door in an architectural drawing of a CAD program, or the name of a famous movie star.

When we choose a variable to be of a specific type, we are specifying the kind of value this variable can hold and the kind of operations in which it can be involved. Each simple type exposes specific characteristics in terms of

- *What it allows the variable to store*—Examples are integer numbers, floating-point numbers, and single characters.
- *Its size range*—An example size range for `int` is –2147483648 to 2147483647.
- *The amount of internal memory used*—The memory consumption can easily vary between 8 and 64 bits to represent one variable, depending on its type. For example, a variable of type `int` takes up 32 bits of memory.
- *The kind of operations that may be performed on it*—Earlier examples showing `int` values suited for addition and `string` values suited for concatenation illustrate this point.

Accordingly, it is important to choose a type well suited for the problem at hand. For example, the name of a famous actor could not be represented by an `int` variable, and the average rainfall in San Francisco would be hard to represent with a value of a type meant for characters.

Using types eating up superfluous amounts of internal memory is a problem often found when the characteristics of each piece of information has not been properly analyzed. Consider a person's age. Peoples' ages usually vary between 0 and approximately 120. So, if you need to store the age of each person in the State of California who receives Social Security benefits, why use a 32-bit int variable with the range of –2147483648 to 2147483647 if another 8-bit integer type exists with the range 0–255? For each one thousand people being stored, you would save 1,000 × (32–8) = 24,000 bits of memory, not to mention the advantage of the higher processing speeds that accompany the leaner 8-bit integer-based variable.

Fortunately, C# provides a rich assortment of simple types that make it possible to choose a suitable type to represent a number or a single character. The next section takes a closer look at each of these types.

Overview of the Simple Types

C# defines 13 simple types, which are listed in Table 6.2. I have chosen to give a complete overview at this early stage to provide a handy reference. You will likely return to this table many times while writing your programs.

Note

Even though the `bool` type (last row of Table 6.2) is considered a simple type, it goes hand in hand with the control of flow.

TABLE 6.2 The Simple Types in C#

C# Keyword	.NET CTS Type	Kind Of Value	Memory Used	Range and Precision
`sbyte`	`System.SByte`	Integer	8 bits	–128 to 127
`byte`	`System.Byte`	Integer	8 bits	0 to 255
`short`	`System.Int16`	Integer	16 bits	–32768 to 32767
`ushort`	`System.UInt16`	Integer	16 bits	0 to 65535
`int`	`System.Int32`	Integer	32 bits	–2147483648 to 2147483647
`uint`	`System.UInt32`	Integer	32 bits	0 to 4294967295
`long`	`System.Int64`	Integer	64 bits	–9223372036854775808 to 9223372036854775807
`ulong`	`System.UInt64`	Integer	64 bits	0 to 18446744073709551615
`char`	`System.Char`	Integer (Single character)	16 bits	All Unicode characters
`float`	`System.Single`	floating point	32 bits	$(+/-)1.5\times10^{-45}$ to $(+/-)3.4\times10^{38}$ Approximately 7 significant digits
`double`	`System.Double`	floating point	64 bits	$(+/-)5.0\times10^{-324}$ to $(+/-)3.4\times10^{30}$ 15–16 significant digits

TABLE 6.2 continued

C# Keyword	.NET CTS Type	Kind Of Value	Memory Used	Range and Precision
decimal	System.Decimal	High precision decimal number	128 bits	(+/-)1.0×10^{-28} to (+/-)7.9×10^{28}
bool	System.Boolean	true or false	1 bit	Not applicable

Before I describe what each column represents, please identify the `int` type in the fifth row from the top. This should give you a good idea of the content of each column.

The following is a brief summary of what each column of Table 6.2 represents:

- *Keyword column*—Keyword refers to the symbol used in the C# source code when declaring a variable. An example is the familiar declaration statement using the keyword `int`.

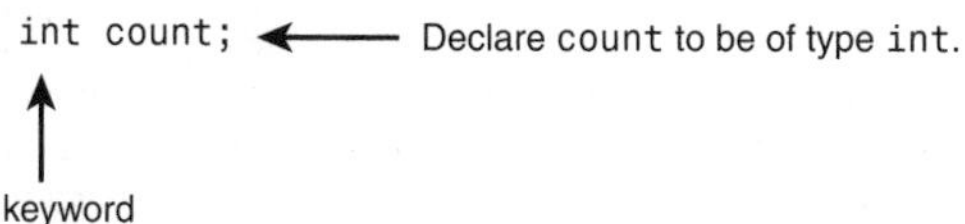

- *.NET CTS type column*—The `System` namespace of the .NET Framework contains all the simple types. Each of the keywords shown in the keyword column is an alias for the type it specifies in the .NET Common Type System (CTS). For example, the keyword `int` refers to its CTS name `System.Int32`. Thus, you could use either the short alias or the long full name in your source code. Accordingly, the following two statements are identical:

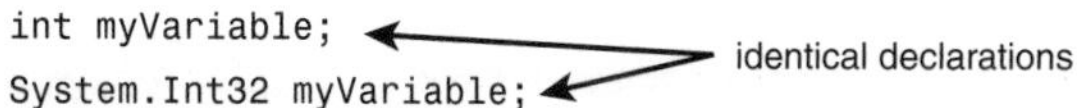

  The latter is a cumbersome style, so the use of the alias is recommended.

- *The Kind of value column*—Specifies the four different groups of simple types contained in C#— integer, floating-point, true/false, and high-precision. Briefly
  - Integers are whole numbers.
  - Floating-point numbers can represent numbers with fractions.
  - High-precision numbers also represent fractions but with higher precision.
  - `bool` type values can contain only two values—`true` and `false`.
- *Memory used*—The amount of internal computer memory used by a value of each type. Notice that 8 bits equals 1 byte.

- *The Range and precision column*—Displays the range and precision a value of the corresponding type can hold. Notice that even though the `char` type is designed for single character values, it is regarded as being an integer type. More about this when I return to the `char` type later in this chapter.

When looking through the table, you will discover nine integer types in total. They differ from each other in three different ways—the range, the amount of computer memory they occupy, and whether negative numbers can be stored.

You will also find the three types `float`, `double`, and `decimal` that are used to store numbers containing a fractional part, such as 6.87, 9.0, and 100.01. The main attributes setting them apart are their range, memory use, and precision.

Syntax Box 6.1 Syntax and the Variable Declaration Statement

The syntax of a computer language provides the rules to follow when writing a valid computer program. When you learn a computer language, you need to know its syntax. Until now, I have relied on descriptions (based on the English language) and examples to portray the syntax of C#. However, syntax is very exact (to the semicolon), so a description of it is enhanced by a similarly exact notation form. One such notation form will be described in this Syntax Box and used throughout the rest of the book in similarly marked Syntax Boxes.

Notice that this notation is not a substitute for examples and thorough descriptions in this book but should merely be regarded as an enhancement of these. The notation form is useful for quick references and will even enable you to learn new language constructs merely by looking through very few lines of syntax notation.

The notation form I have chosen to use is a simplified version of a notation form frequently used to describe computer language syntax called Backus-Naur Form or BNF. This form was originally developed by J. Backus and P. Naur for the definition of the Algol 60 language.

The syntax notation form consists of the following elements:

- The *::=* symbol that means "is defined by"
- Meta variables (place holders) of the form *<Word>*
- The optional symbol consisting of two square bracket *[ ]* that encloses optional items *[<this is optional>]*
- Three periods **...** indicate an unlimited amount of items
- The vertical line | used to indicate alternative items

The following text describes each element in more detail.

To precisely describe a construct of the C# language (for example, a variable declaration statement) is to *define* the construct. The symbol *::=* (two semicolons immediately followed by an equals sign) is used to indicate "is defined by."

We also need a way to denote and represent words (such as keywords and identifiers) used in a C# program. To this, end we use symbols called *meta variables* or *syntactic variables*. They take the form *<Word>* and act as placeholders.

As an example, consider our familiar variable declaration statement:

```
int myNumber;
```

In the previous chapters, you have seen several examples of variable declaration statements. Examples are great teaching tools, but they don't provide for exact definitions, such as the following notation:

```
Variable_declaration_statement  ::=

                <Type> <Variable_identifier>;
```

In this case, the `::=` indicates that what follows is a definition of a *`variable_declaration_statement`*. `<Type>` is a syntactic variable and can be replaced by `int`, `string`, or any valid type name in C#. For example, all the keywords of each simple type listed in Table 6.2 could take the place of `<Type>`.

The second syntactic variable, *`<Variable_identifier>`*, can be replaced by a variable name such as `myNumber`.

Finally, the declaration statement must end with a semicolon.

The following gives you an example where the three periods `...` and the optional symbol *[ ]* are needed to precisely define a C# construct.

Apart from declaring the two integer variables `number1` and `number2` as follows

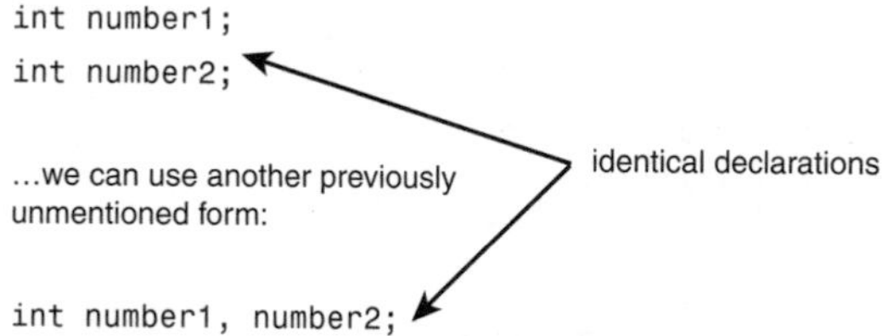
int number1;
int number2;
...we can use another previously unmentioned form:
identical declarations
int number1, number2;

we could have declared as many `int` variables as we wanted by using the following form:

```
int number1, number2, number3,... ;
```

The three dots `...` between `number3` and the semicolon indicate that we can declare as many `int` variables that we want.

Note that the following

```
, number2, number3, ...
```

is optional. Consequently, we can write the declaration statement more correctly as follows by using the optional symbol

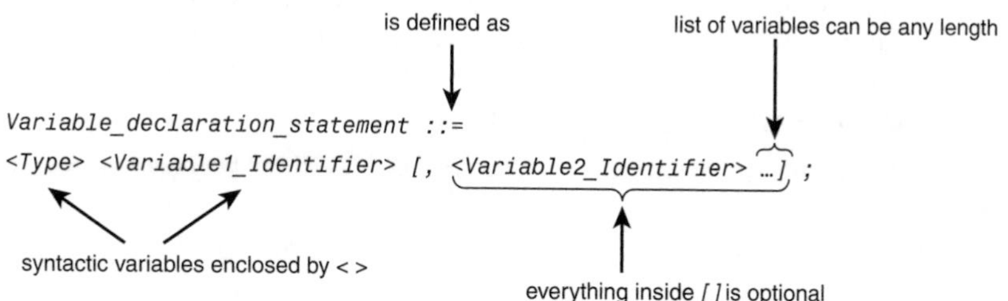
is defined as
list of variables can be any length
Variable_declaration_statement ::=
<Type> <Variable1_Identifier> [, <Variable2_Identifier> ...] ;
syntactic variables enclosed by < >
everything inside [ ] is optional

Finally, we need to be able to express when several alternative items can be used in one position. As you have seen previously, the keywords `public` and `private` are used when declaring the methods and instance variables of a class, such as

```
private int currentFloor;
```

Even though it is regarded as poor programming practice, it is also possible to declare an instance variable to be public, as in the following:

```
public int currentFloor;
```

We could also leave out any of the access specifiers altogether and write

```
int currentFloor;
```

defaulting `currentFloor` to have `private` access.

Our ability to use either `private` *or* `public` is denoted by a vertical line (|) and can be expressed as `private | public`. Because the specification is optional, we can write *[*`private | public`*]*, and the full variable declaration can now be defined as follows

```
Variable_declaration_statement ::=

        [public | private] <Type> <Variable1_Identifier>
➥ [, <Variable2_Identifier> ...];
```

Sometimes a language element can be defined in different ways. For example as you will see later an expression can be defined not only as a literal but also as a variable identifier and a numerical expression. This can be expressed with our notation form by using several ::= symbols after expression as shown in the following lines:

```
<Expression>
          ::= <Literal>
          ::= <Variable_Identifier>
          ::= <Numerical_Expression>
```

Note

The contents of the Syntax Boxes are not targeted at advanced programmers who are going to write the source code for a C# compiler and who therefore need exact detailed information about every aspect of C#'s syntax. Instead they are meant as an aid to learn C# and to introduce the idea of syntax notation. For that reason, each definition does not cover all the gory details and possibilities about the particular C# construct it defines but is kept as simple and accessible as possible.

Syntax and Semantics

Where syntax relates to the form of a language construct, *semantics* is concerned about the meaning of the construct. For example "adding `myNumber` together with `yourNumber` and assigning the result to `ourSum`" explains the semantics of the following statement

```
ourSum = myNumber + yourNumber;
```

whereas the syntax is about the symbols we use (=, +, ;) and how the variables are written and combined with these symbols.

Integer Types

C# defines nine integer types as shown in Table 6.2. Integers are whole numbers with no fractional part, such as 34, 0 and –7653. Because there are an infinite number of integers (8773662727363625256362562776365257635928272 62 is also an integer) and a finite amount of computer memory allocated with each simple type, we can only represent a subset (an extremely useful subset, fortunately) of all integers.

Each integer type uses a specific amount of internal memory. A larger range occupies more memory.

Some types (such as `int`), called *signed types*, can store both negative and positive values. Other types, called *unsigned types*, can represent only positive values (including zero). There are four signed types (`sbyte`, `short`, `int`, and `long`) and four unsigned types (`byte`, `ushort`, `uint`, and `ulong`).

Note

The `char` type is also considered to be an integer type, despite its special properties dedicated to representing Unicode characters. Because `char` is the odd one out and goes hand-in-hand with the `string` type, I will first present the eight previously mentioned integers.

Bit Refresher

A bit represents just two values—0 and 1. Accordingly, two bits can represent 2×2 different values = 4. 3 bits can represent 2×2×2 = 8 values. x bits can represent 2^x values, and 8 bits can represent 2^8 = 256 values.

16 bits—65,536 values
32 bits—4,294,967,296 values
64 bits—18,446,744,073,709,551,616 value

For a detailed discussion about the binary number system and how it relates to other number systems, please refer to Appendix D, "Number Systems."

Signed Integer Types

The smallest signed integer type is `sbyte`. It occupies 8 bits and has a range from –128 to 127. Half of the 256 values that can be represented by an 8-bit based type are dedicated to negative values, the other half are dedicated to 0 and positive values.

`sbyte` variables are declared by using the keyword `sbyte`, as shown in the following:

```
sbyte myNumber;
```

You can find the other signed integer types in Table 6.2.

Tip

When you start programming, `int` is good choice for most variables; it can be used for most purposes without consuming excessive amounts of memory. However, you should make it a habit to analyze each variable carefully and choose its type accordingly.

Unsigned Integer Types

Each of the four signed integer types has a corresponding unsigned type that consumes the same amount of memory as its counterpart. Because the negative part is eliminated, the memory to hold those values can be used to hold larger positive numbers instead. For example, `sbyte` can represent the range –128 to 127, whereas its unsigned counterpart `byte` can hold integers in the range 0 to 255 (127 + |–128|). Table 6.3 displays the signed integer types along with their unsigned counterparts.

TABLE 6.3 Signed Integer Types and Their Unsigned Counterparts

Signed	Unsigned	Memory Use
`sbyte`	`byte`	8 bits
`short`	`ushort`	16 bits
`int`	`uint`	32 bits
`long`	`ulong`	64 bits

Tip

You should use unsigned types for amounts, which are never negative. Examples could be the number of births in a country in one year, the population of a city, and number of books in a library.

Integer Literals

Different from variables, literals cannot change their value. A literal number like 5 is always 5, never 3 or 8, so numbers such as 3, 1009, and –487 are all examples of literals.

All integer literals are of a specific type, just like all variables you declare must be of a certain type. The C# compiler follows precisely specified rules when determining the type of a literal. It will look at the size of the literal and an optional suffix immediately following the literal.

If no suffix is specified, the compiler will choose the first of the following types where the literal can "fit": `int`, `uint`, `long`, and `ulong`. If we combine this fact with the ranges provided in Table 6.2, we can deduct which literals are determined to be which types. This is specified in Figure 6.6.

FIGURE 6.6
Literals and their types—no suffix.

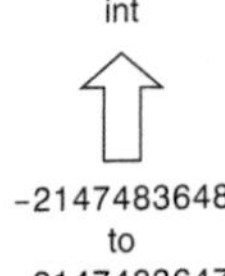

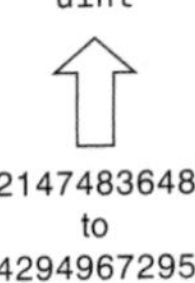

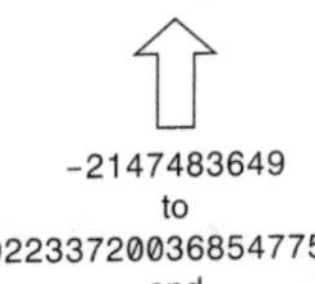

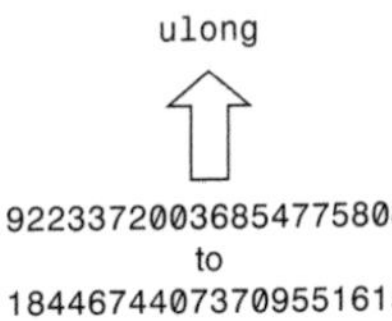

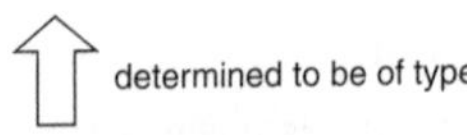

According to Figure 6.6, the literal

- 43200 is an `int`
- 2507493742 is a `uint`

- –25372936858775201 is a `long`
- 270072036654375827 is a `long`
- 17016748093204541685 is a `ulong`

U, L, or UL can be used to suffix a literal.

If a literal is suffixed by U (such as 75U), the compiler will choose the first of the types `uint` or `ulong` that can contain the value of the literal within its range. This is illustrated in Figure 6.7.

FIGURE 6.7
Literals and their types—with the suffix U.

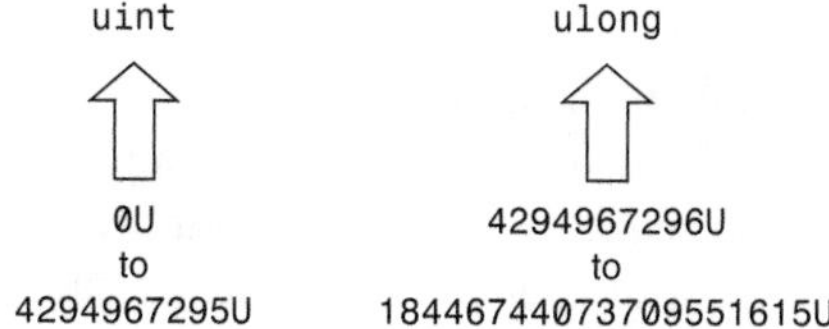

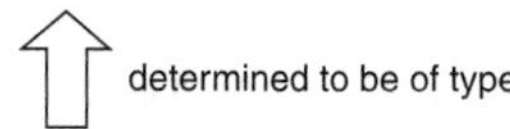

If the literal is suffixed by L (such as 453L), the compiler will choose the first of the `long` or `ulong` types that will contain the value of the literal. This is illustrated in Figure 6.8.

FIGURE 6.8
Literals and their types—with the suffix L.

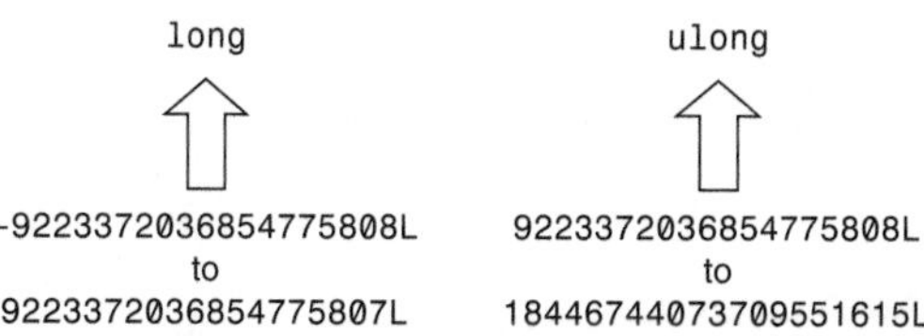

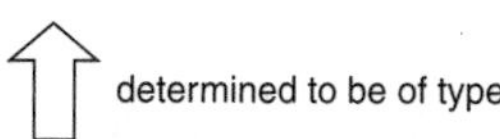

If the programmer writes the suffix UL after the literal, the compiler has no options; it specifies that the literal must be of type `ulong`.

Note

The compiler lets you choose among a few options when typing the suffixes:

- Instead of U, you can use u.
- L and l (lowercase L) have the same meaning. However, because it is easy to confuse 1 (one) with l (lowercase L), L is recommended.
- Many different options exist to represent UL. You can use any combination of upper- and lowercase U and L. For example, Ul, lu, and uL are all valid suffixes representing the same meaning.

C# allows you to write integer literals in two different number bases—decimal numbers (base 10) and hexadecimal numbers (base 16). See Appendix D which can be found at `www.samspublishing.com` for a discussion of the various number bases. A base 10 literal begins with any of the digits 1–9, whereas 0x in front of the number indicates a hexadecimal number. For example, 99 is a base 10 number, but 0x99 is a hexadecimal number that is equal to 153 in base 10.

```
int aNumber;
aNumber = 99;      ← Assigning 99 from base 10
aNumber = 0x99;    ← Assigning 99 from base 16
```

Integer literals cannot contain commas (32,000 is invalid) or decimal points (3.0 and 76.97 are both invalid).

```
aNumber = 32,000;
```

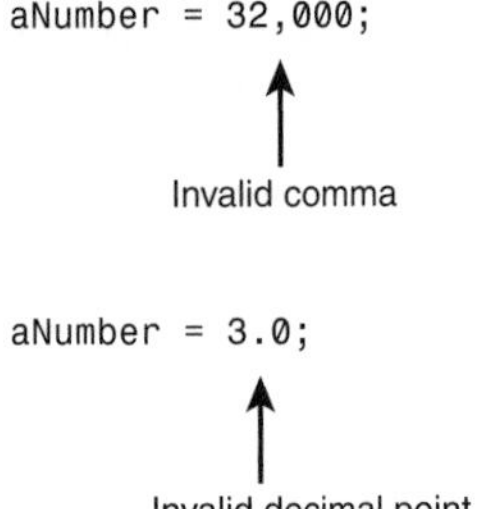

To specify that an integer is negative, add a minus sign in front of the number, such as –30. If you want to emphasize that an integer is positive, you can put a + sign in front of the integer literal, but this is not required, so +55 is identical to 55.

Assignment Statements

An assignment statement, as stated in Chapter 3, assigns a value to a variable. For example, if `populationSize` is of type `int`, you can assign the value 387675 by using the following assignment statement:

```
populationSize = 387675;
```

When used in an assignment statement, the equals sign is called *assignment operator*. By using our newly introduced syntax notation form, we can write the general assignment statement for a simple type as follows:

Syntax Box 6.2 The Assignment Statement with Simple Types

```
Assignment_statement ::=
                    <Variable_Identifier> = <Expression> ;
```

where

```
<Expression>
          ::= <Literal>
          ::= <Variable_Identifier>
          ::= <Numerical_Expression>
```

Note that `<Numerical_expression>` refers to a valid combination of number values and operators. `(count * 4) + (distance - 100)` is a numerical expression.

An expression can be a literal, such as 3876, a variable like `populationSize`, or any valid combination of literals, variables, and operators. Consequently,

```
6 + 5
```

is an expression, just as

```
(5 + populationSize) - (200 - populationSize)
```

When the computer executes the assignment statement, the right side of the assignment operator is first evaluated; the resulting value is then assigned to the variable on the left side of the operator. For example, take the assignment statement shown in Figure 6.9, where `distance1` has the value 100 and `distance2` has the value 200.

FIGURE 6.9
Two steps in an assignment statement.

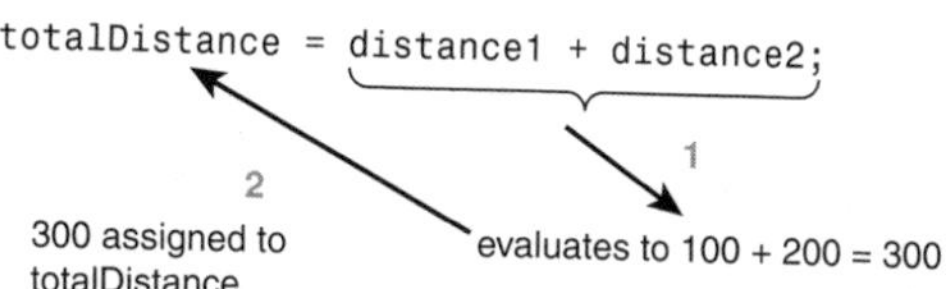

The computer will first add the two variables `distance1` and `distance2` together (see 1 in Figure 6.9) and then assign the result of 300 to `totalDistance` (see 2 in Figure 6.9).

Due to this sequence of events, it is possible and often useful to position identical variable identifiers on both sides of the assignment operator, as in the following:

```
count = count + 1;
```

At first glance, this assignment looks peculiar, but when executed in two sequences as previously shown, we realize that all we are effectively doing is adding 1 to the original value of `count`. Had the value of `count` prior to the statement been 100, it would now be 101. It is possible to replicate this logic with the minus sign (–). For example, the following statement

```
count = count - 1;
```

will deduct 1 from the original value of `count`.

The two predefined operators (++ and --) are available to express these statements in a more compact fashion. The following statement will add 1 to the original value of the operand:

```
count++; <—— equivalent to count = count + 1;
```

whereas

```
count--; <—— equivalent to count = count - 1;
```

deducts 1 from the original value of `count`. The program in Listing 6.8 presented later, which is part of the Blipos Clock case study, makes use of these operators.

Integer Type Compatibilities

The large number of integer types available enables you to choose a suitable type for each variable in your program. However, many different types often coexist in the same program, and several types are often involved in the same statement. This can cause problems related to incompatible types. In the following section, I will concentrate on the issues related to the assignment statement.

To illustrate a typical situation involving different types in an assignment statement, let's have a look at the example in Listing 6.2.

LISTING 6.2 Source Code of `Compatibility.cs`

```
//Compatible and incompatible types

using System;

public class Compatibility
{
    public static void Main()
    {
        int totalMinutesOnMobile;
        uint totalPopulation;
        ushort averageMinutesOnMobile;

        totalPopulation = 347638;
        averageMinutesOnMobile = 10;

         // uint cannot be implicitly converted to int.
        totalMinutesOnMobile = totalPopulation * averageMinutesOnMobile;

        Console.WriteLine("Total Minutes On Mobiles: " +
        ➥totalMinutesOnMobile);
    }
}
```

The following compile error is reported:

```
Compatibility.cs(17,32): error CS0029: Cannot implicitly convert type 'uint' to
'int'
```

Suppose you have written this source code snippet for use in an application facilitating the research and strategic planning in the marketing department of a large mobile phone company. To represent the total number of people in a city, you have chosen a `uint` variable called `totalPopulation` (line 10). The source code further contains a variable of type `ushort` called `averageMinutesOnMobile` (line 11) representing the average approximate number of minutes each person in the city is talking on a mobile phone in one day. Notice how `uint` and `ushort` have been chosen to suit the information they represent.

You would now like to calculate the total number of minutes the whole population is on the mobile phone. This can be done by multiplying `totalPopulation` with `averageMinutesOnMobile` and then assigning the result to `totalMinutesOnMobile` expressed in C# (line 17) and shown in Figure 6.10.

FIGURE 6.10
Invalid statement due to incompatible types.

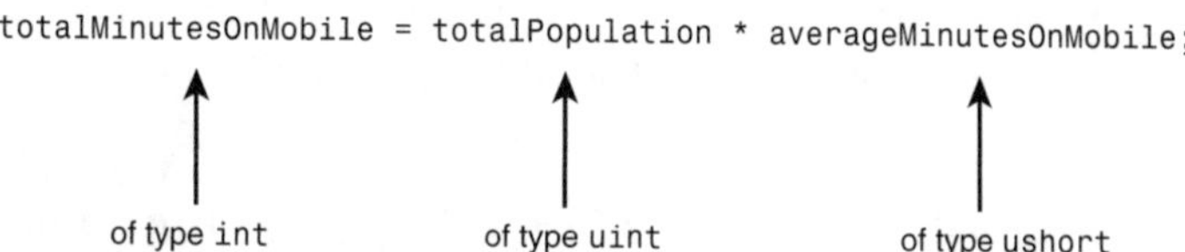

What happens if, as specified in line 9, we use the `int` type for `totalMinutesOnMobile`? Well, during compilation before the actual program has started running, the compiler is unaware of the values that will eventually be stored in our variables. Thus, it deduces that because `totalPopulation` is a `uint` and has a range of 0 to 4294967295, there is a legitimate chance that this variable might hold a large value, such as 4000000000. On the other hand, `totalMinutesOnMobile` has a range of –2147483648 to 2147483647 and is, therefore, not capable of holding the large value of 4000000000 we might assign to it from `totalPopulation`. The result would be a loss of data. Consequently, the compiler triggers the following compiler error:

```
"Cannot implicitly convert type 'uint' to 'int' "
```

even though our specific execution of the program would use population values considerably smaller than 2147483647.

If, instead of `int`, we had chosen the `uint` type for `totalMinutesOnMobile` (exchanging `int` in line 9 with `uint`), the compiler would have accepted the statement, despite the remaining difference between the source type `ushort` and the destination type `uint`.

Without hesitation, it would *implicitly convert* (automatic conversion performed by the compiler) the source type `ushort` with the range 0 to 65535 to the destination type `uint` with the larger range, because there is no danger of data loss. This is illustrated in Figure 6.11.

Note, though, that the result of the right-side multiplication could still exceed the upper limit (4294967295) of the destination variable. In the (unlikely) case of a city with a population of 4000000000 with an average mobile use of 10 minutes, the result of the multiplication would be 40000000000 and so it would exceed the capacity of `totalMinutesOnMobile` and trigger a runtime error. The compiler merely looks at each variable separately and does not take the actual mathematical calculation into consideration.

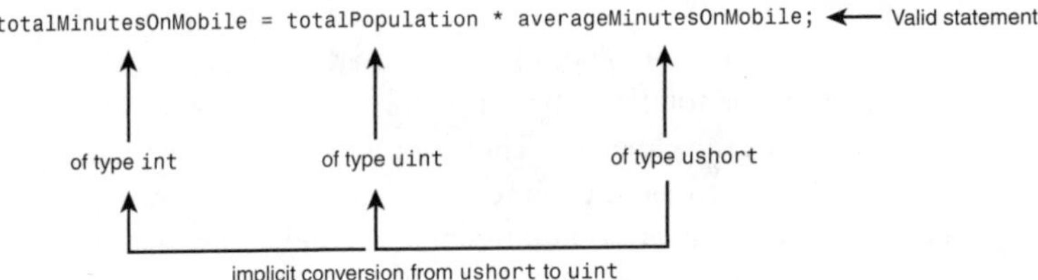

FIGURE 6.11
Implicit conversion of *ushort* to *uint*.

Incorrect assignments, similar to the kind previously described, can be of two types:

- The source value might exceed the upper limit of the destination type. This is termed *overflow*; for example, assigning 300 to a variable of type `byte` will result in an overflow.
- If the source value is less than the lower limit of the destination type, the result is an *underflow*; for example, assigning –40000 to a variable of type `short` results in an underflow.

Automatic Overflow/Underflow Checking During Runtime

It is possible to instruct the compiler to generate checks for overflow and underflow problems during runtime. This can be accomplished in the following way, illustrated by an example.

First, you need to type in the source code from Listing 6.3. Listing 6.3 is the result of changing the following lines of Listing 6.2:

1. Line 5 to

   ```
   public class Overflow
   ```

2. Line 9 to

   ```
   uint totalMinutesOnMobile;
   ```

3. Line 13 to

   ```
   totalPopulation = 4000000000;
   ```

By changing lines 9 and 13, we are causing an overflow. Then, when you instruct the compiler to compile the program, you need to include an additional command apart from the standard command you have used previously. Instead of merely typing

```
C:\>csc Overflow.cs <enter>
```

you need to type

```
C:\>csc /checked+ Overflow.cs <enter>
```

The `/checked+` part is called a *compiler command*. It instructs the compiler to generate checks for overflow and underflow problems during runtime. Notice the `+` after `/checked;`, it says "Yes, do make the check," whereas a `-` after `/checked` (`/checked-`) switches off this kind of check.

Note

If you don't provide the `/checked` compiler command when compiling, the setting defaults to `/checked-`.

LISTING 6.3 Source Code for `Overflow.cs`

```
01: //Compatible and incompatible types
02:
03: using System;
04:
05: public class Overflow
06: {
07:     public static void Main()
08:     {
09:         uint totalMinutesOnMobile;
10:         uint totalPopulation;
11:         ushort averageMinutesOnMobile;
12:
13:         totalPopulation = 4000000000;
14:         averageMinutesOnMobile = 10;
15:
16:          // uint cannot be implicitly converted to int.
17:         totalMinutesOnMobile = totalPopulation * averageMinutesOnMobile;
18:
19:         Console.WriteLine("Total Minutes On Mobiles: " +
            ➥totalMinutesOnMobile);
20:     }
21: }
```

Now compile the program with the `/checked+` command, shown earlier, and run the program. The program is prematurely interrupted by a runtime error and the following text is shown on the console:

```
Exception occurred: System.OverflowException… etc.
```

As expected, this is an `OverflowException` thrown by the runtime and caused by line 17 that attempted to assign 40000000000 to `totalMinutesOnMobile`.

Tip

It is often useful to have the `/checked` option switched on (`/checked+`) when you design and write software. However, because it causes a slight loss in performance, it might not be appropriate for the released version of the program.

Note

Exceptions are generated in C# when abnormal situations, such as an overflow or underflow, occur in your program.

The `/checked+` compiler command will generate underflow and overflow checks for the entire compiled source code. However, you might want to control which parts of the program are always being checked and which parts are never checked regardless of the compiler commands given. To this end, you can apply the keywords `checked` and `unchecked` in the C# source code itself. They can be applied to create checked and unchecked blocks of code (in which case, they are referred to as statements) or be applied to single expressions (in which case, they act as operators).

Syntax Box 6.3 `checked` and `unchecked` Statements

```
Checked_statement::=
        checked
        {
              <Statements>
        }

Unchecked_statement::=
        unchecked
        {
              <Statements>
        }
```

Note—The `checked` and `unchecked` statements must reside inside a method body. They cause all statements (<*statements*>) in the block they designate to be evaluated in a checked and unchecked environment.

```
Checked_expression::=
          checked (<Expression>)

Checked_expression::=
          unchecked (<Expression>)
```

Listing 6.4 illustrates the use of the `checked` keyword.

LISTING 6.4 Source Code for `TravelingFullCheck.cs`

```
using System;

class Traveling
{
    public static void Main()
    {
        checked
        {
            int totalTime;
            int totalEnergy;
            int totalRadiation;
            int distance = 2100000;
            int timeFactor = 100000;
            int energyFactor = 20;
            int radiationFactor = 40000;
```

LISTING 6.4 continued

```
16:
17:                 totalTime = distance * timeFactor;
18:                 totalEnergy = distance * energyFactor;
19:                 totalRadiation = distance * radiationFactor;
20:
21:                 Console.WriteLine("Total time: " + totalTime);
22:                 Console.WriteLine("Total energy: " + totalEnergy);
23:                 Console.WriteLine("Total radiation: " + totalRadiation);
24:             }
25:         }
26: }
```

When the code contains the `checked` keyword in line 7, irrespective of the compiler setting, the following output results:

```
Exception occurred: System.OverflowException… etc.
```

If you substitute `checked` in line 7 with `unchecked` you will see the following odd looking output

```
Total time: -453397504
Total energy: 42000000
Total radiation: -1899345920
```

Listing 6.4 contains a `checked` block spanning from line 8 to line 24 with the keyword `checked` in line 7. The two statements in lines 17 and 19 contain overflowing expressions causing the `OverflowException` (with checked block) or the incorrect results as output (with unchecked block) shown in the sample output.

We could fine-tune Listing 6.4 by using the `checked/unchecked` operators instead of the checked/unchecked statements. This is shown in Listing 6.5.

LISTING 6.5 Source Code for `TravelingPartlyChecked.cs`

```
using System;

class Traveling
{
    public static void Main()
    {
        int totalTime;
        int totalEnergy;
        int totalRadiation;
        int distance = 2100000;
        int timeFactor = 100000;
        int energyFactor = 20;
        int radiationFactor = 40000;

        totalTime = unchecked(distance * timeFactor);
        totalEnergy = checked(distance * energyFactor);
        totalRadiation = distance * radiationFactor;

```

LISTING 6.5 continued

```
19:         Console.WriteLine("Total time: " + totalTime);
20:         Console.WriteLine("Total energy: " + totalEnergy);
21:         Console.WriteLine("Total radiation: " + totalRadiation);
22:     }
23: }
```

If compiler option is set to `/checked+`

```
Exception occurred: System.OverflowException… etc.
```

If compiler option is set to `/checked-`

```
Total time: -453397504
Total energy: 42000000
Total radiation: -1899345920
```

The expression in line 15 of Listing 6.5 generates an overflow and is left `unchecked`; the expression in line 16 is `checked` but stays within the range of the `int` type, so no exceptions are generated from these two lines. Line 17 generates an overflow and has no specification. Consequently, an exception will be generated by line 17 only in the case when the source code is compiled with the `/checked+` option.

An expression consisting merely of literals on the right side of the assignment operator, such as in line 2 shown next

```
01:  long mySum;
02:  mySum = 2147483647 + 1;
```

only literals

can be fully evaluated and checked for overflow/underflow at compile time. The compiler checks all these expression at compile time, unless the expression is explicitly `unchecked` in the source code. If a problem is encountered, such as in the previous expression, a compiler warning or error will be generated during compile time

```
warning CS0220: The operation overflows at compile time in checked mode.
```

Don't Ignore Compiler Warnings

Unlike a compiler error, a compiler warning does not prevent a program from being executed. However, warnings are useful hints to more-or-less obvious problems in your program. The best practice is to identify the problems and remove all compiler warnings.

The Implicit Conversion Path

The compiler has a very precise idea of which integer types it agrees to implicitly convert, based on a general rule deduced from the previous discussion and stated in the following Note.

When Are Implicit Conversions of Integer Types Performed?

Every destination type accepted for an implicit conversion must be able to fully represent the range of the source type.

If we follow the rule of acceptable implicit conversions, we can draw a type hierarchy, shown in Figure 6.12, that indicates the possible implicit conversion pathways.

Not all paths have explicitly been shown with a single arrow. To determine whether an implicit conversion is acceptable, you might need to follow several arrows and go through several type boxes. For example, to convert from `byte` to `long`, you start at the `byte` box and follow the arrows over `short` and `int` and finally arrive at `long`.

FIGURE 6.12
Implicit conversion paths for the integer types.

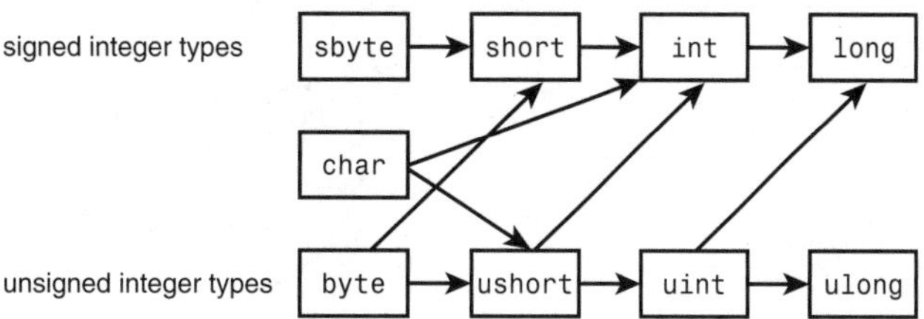

Where:

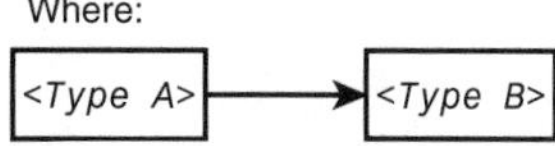

Means: It is possible to implicitly convert from Type A to Type B

Note

Even though `char` has a larger range than the `sbyte`, `byte`, and `ushort` type, spanning across all their possible values, *no* implicit conversion path exists back to the `char` type from any of these types.

Overflow and Underflow Behavior of Integer Variables

In the previous section, you saw how the compiler could be instructed to check for overflow and underflow during runtime. But what happens if we switch this capability off and the program experiences an overflow or underflow?

To answer this question, we will move our attention to planet Blipos, where our alien friend from Chapter 2, "Your First C# Program" has invited us to visit him. In his invitation, which arrived by i-mail (intergalactic mail), he explains that the Bliposians have a very different way of measuring time than do humans on planet Earth. Instead of 60 seconds in a minute, 60 minutes in an hour, and 24 hours in day, they have 256 seconds in a minute and 65,535 minutes in a full day. One full day consists of 32,768 minutes of darkness displayed as negative values and 32,767 minutes with daylight displayed as positive values (notice how these numbers relate to the ranges of the `byte` and `short` types).

It turns out that the method by which the Bliposians measure seconds resembles the behavior of a variable of type `byte` in that both will return to the beginning of the range of values (0) whenever the end of the range has been reached (255). Similarly, when the minutes counter on a Blipos clock has reached 32,767, it will display –32768 the next second, which is comparable to the behavior of a variable of type `short` when it overflows. Figure 6.13 illustrates these points.

FIGURE 6.13
Overflow behavior for variables of type *byte* and *short*.

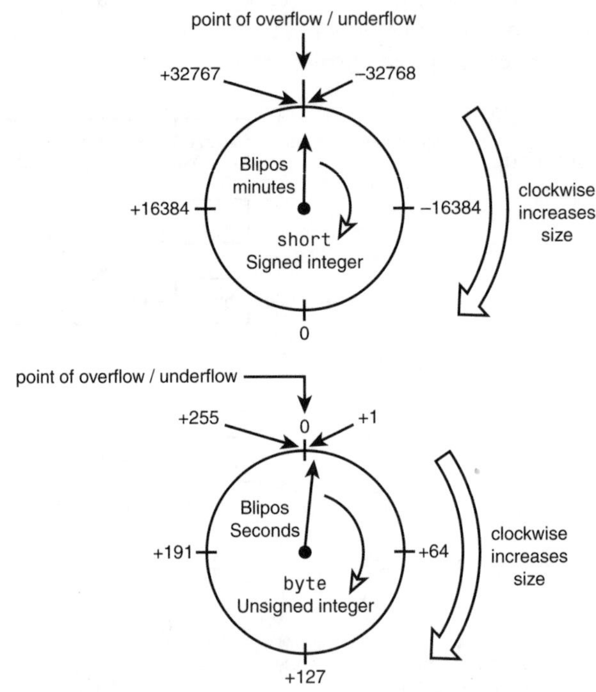

Overflow and Underflow of the *byte* and *short* Variables
Overflow of *byte* and *short*

`byte` Adding 1 to a variable of type `byte` with a value of 255 will result in a value of 0.

`short` Adding 1 to a variable of type `short` with a value of 32,767 will result in a value of –32,768.

Underflow *byte* and *short*

`byte` Deducting 1 from a variable of type `byte` with a value of 0 will result in a value of 255.

`short` Deducting 1 from a variable of type `short` with a value of –32,768 will result in a value of 32,767.

1 doesn't have to be exclusively used in these examples. For example, adding 8 to a variable of type `byte` containing a value of 255 will change its value to 7.

The remaining integer types follow the same logic of overflow and underflow with their relevant ranges substituted for the ranges of byte and short used in this presentation.

To get accustomed to the time measuring system used on planet Blipos, we decide to write a computer program resembling a Blipos clock. This program, presented in the following case study, not only illustrates how the `byte` and `short` integers handle overflow and underflow, it is also meant as an OOP and Software Development Process refresher. Additionally, it introduces a few useful features from C# not mentioned previously. These are local variables, two new comparison operators, the type `cast`, and the `while` loop. The introductions are brief and informal and attempt to put you in the right frame of mind for the next few chapters.

The Blipos Clock

Recall the Software Development Process from Chapter 2. We will be using relevant elements from this set of recommended activities. The complete source code is provided in Listing 6.8 and will be referenced throughout the discussion.

Software Specification:

The program must show the user how time keeping is performed on Blipos. We will not try to create a fully autonomic clock, merely construct a "clock" that can be set initially through appropriate commands and then adjusted by increments and decrements of 1 second or 50 seconds. After each adjustment, the new time of the clock will be shown onscreen in the form of: `Sec: sss Min: mmmmm`, where `sss` is an integer between 0 and 255 and `mmmmm` is an integer between –32768 and +32767. The user can make any adjustments one after the other by entering different keys. Entering a `T` (for terminate) will stop the program.

Software Design:

Segregating each subsystem into objects (modules).

We can identify one obvious object in the software specification—a Blipos clock (class name `BliposClock`) representing a clock that follows the same rules for time keeping as a clock on Blipos. This clock will encapsulate the instance variables `seconds` and `minutes`, which represent the time of the clock.

Identify the methods in each module.

The `BliposClock` has several public methods that allow it to be manipulated in suitable ways. According to the specification, it should be possible to

- Set the clock.
- Move it one second forward, one second backward, 50 seconds forward, and 50 seconds backward.
- Ask it to show its current time.

The `Main` method is the control center of the program. It creates an instance of the `BliposClock` class and repeatedly allows the user to give commands to this object, adjusting its time, until the user enters a `T`, which terminates the loop and the program. Every time the user has changed the time, the clock object is asked to display its current time.

Internal Method Design:

We will focus on solving two important problems to get the program ticking:

- *Problem 1*—We attempt to utilize the overflow/underflow mechanism to implement the behavior of `seconds`. Just as the seconds of a digital watch "overflow" when the seconds counter reaches 59 and returns to 00, our watch will overflow when it reaches 255 seconds and return to 0.

  The following problem must be solved to write any of the methods in the program that increment or decrement the `seconds` instance variable of a `BliposClock` object.

  Every time the `seconds` instance variable overflows, it must trigger the `minutes` instance variable to be incremented by 1, just like our watch increments the minutes display whenever the seconds counter "overflows" at 59 seconds. Conversely, `minutes` must be decremented by 1 every time `seconds` underflows. The important question is how do we detect when the overflow and underflow is taking place so we can adjust the `minutes` variable correctly?

- *Problem 2*—The program must somehow repeat itself in a loop until the user enters the letter `T`. How is this implemented?

The following is the solution to Problem 1, detecting an overflow.

When the `seconds` variable is incremented without an accompanying overflow, the following is true:

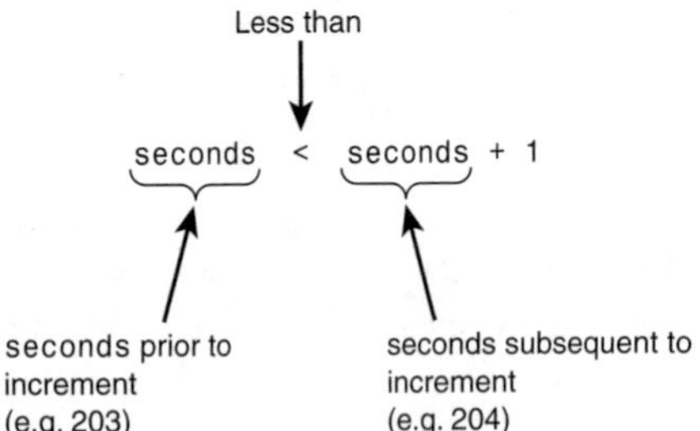

In other words, prior to the increment, `seconds` is less than `seconds` subsequent to the increment if no overflow takes place.

But if an overflow takes place, this no longer holds; instead, the following statement becomes true:

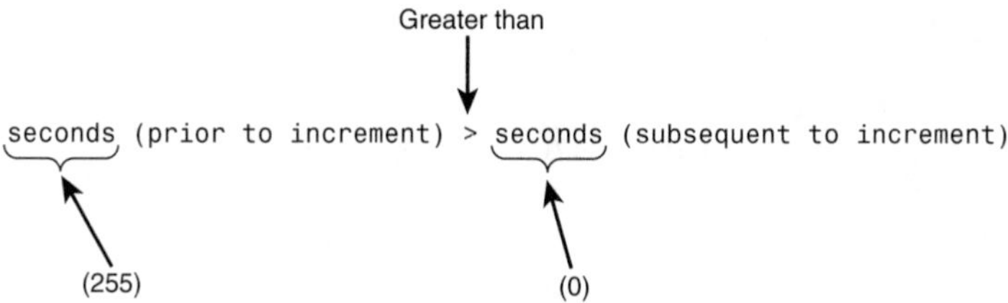

Thus, by "remembering" the value of **seconds** prior to its increment, we can use this piece of memory (here conveniently called **originalSeconds**) to compare to the new value of **seconds** and determine whether an overflow has taken place.

The algorithm used to check for overflow and adjust minutes is shown in Listing 6.6 using pseudocode.

LISTING 6.6 Pseudocode: Overflow Detection Algorithm

```
Algorithm inside OneForward method which increments seconds by one.

01: Set the variable originalSeconds equal to seconds
02: Increment seconds by 1
03: If originalSeconds is greater than seconds then perform line 4 else
    ➥jump over line 4 to line 5.
04:          Increment minutes by 1 (seconds have just overflown)
05: End
```

The same logic applies to detection of underflow in the **OneBackward** method. Have a look at the **OneForward** and **OneBackward** methods in lines 24–32 and 34–42 of Listing 6.8 and compare with the pseudocode. To remember the original value of **seconds** before it is incremented, we use the local variable **originalSeconds**.

Local Variables

Because **originalSeconds** is declared within a method body, we call it a *local variable*. A local variable is confined to the method body where it is declared. Consequently, **originalSeconds** declared in **OneBackward** is entirely different from **originalSeconds** in **OneForward**. They only share the same name.

The **FastForward** and **FastBackward** methods apply the same overall logic as **OneBackward** and **OneForward**.

The method of applying intermediate values, such as **originalSeconds**, to solve a programmatic problem is commonly used in programming.

The solution for Problem 2, creating a loop for user input, can be expressed by pseudocode, as presented in Listing 6.7.

LISTING 6.7 Pseudocode: A Loop for User Input

```
01: Begin loop
02:       Pause program and wait for user input. Read the command
          ➥given by the user and store it in a variable,
          ➥here called command.
03:       If command is an "F" then move the clock one second forward.
04:       If command is a "B" then move the clock one second backwards.
05:       If command is an "A" then move the clock forward by 50 seconds.
06:       If command is a "D" then move the clock backward by 50 seconds.
07:       Show the time of the clock
08: Repeat loop if command is not equal to "T" (for Terminate), by
    ➥starting at first statement after Begin in line 01. If
    ➥command is equal to "T" then terminate the loop.
```

Notice how lines 2–7 are repeated as long as the `command` variable does not hold the value `T`.

Compare this algorithm with lines 97–109 of Listing 6.8. To implement the loop in Listing 6.7, a `do-while` loop is applied. Line 1 of the pseudocode corresponds to `do` of line 97, and line 8 corresponds to line 109 of Listing 6.8. Notice that `!=` in line 109 means "is not equal to." The `do-while` loop will repeat lines 99–108 until the condition inside the parenthesis after `while` in line 109 is `false`. This occurs when the user has given the **`T`** command.

Take a moment to look through the source code in Listing 6.8. Even though it contains a few new C# elements, most of it should be familiar to you by now. All the new features are briefly explained shortly.

To illustrate overflow and underflow in the sample output presented after the source code, I set the clock to 253 seconds and 32,767 minutes. By entering `f`, the clock is moved forward by one second to 254 seconds and 32,767 minutes. However, when the `seconds` instance variable of the clock reaches 255 with an attempt to increment it, an overflow takes place and its value returns to the beginning of `byte`'s range (0). The overflow is detected by the program, triggering the `minutes` instance variable of `myClock` to be incremented by 1. But `minutes` is of type `short`, so this variable also experiences an overflow, this time resulting in new value of –32,767. By entering `f` again, we simply increment `seconds` by one without affecting `minutes`. If we enter `b` twice, the clock is adjusted backwards, triggering an underflow and causing seconds to return from 255 to 0.

Finally, the sample output demonstrates the effect of entering `a` and `d`, adjusting the clock 50 seconds forward and 50 seconds backward, respectively.

LISTING 6.8 Source Code for `BliposClock.cs`

```
01: using System;
02:
03: /*
04:  * The Blipos clock has 256 seconds in a minute and
05:  * 65536 minutes in a day. The night lasts for
06:  * 32768 minutes and is represented by negative minute values.
07:  * The daylight lasts 32767 minutes represented by positive
```

LISTING 6.8 continued

```
 * values. When minutes equals 0 it is neither day nor night.
 * The clock can tick forwards, backwards, be adjusted,
 * move fast forwards and fast backwards
 */

class BliposClock
{
    private byte seconds;
    private short minutes;

    public BliposClock()
    {
        seconds = 0;
        minutes = 0;
    }

    public void OneForward()
    {
        byte originalSeconds = seconds;

        seconds++;
        if(originalSeconds > seconds)
              // Overflow of seconds variable
            minutes++;
    }

    public void OneBackward()
    {
        byte originalSeconds = seconds;

        seconds--;
        if (originalSeconds < seconds)
              // Underflow of seconds variable
            minutes--;
    }

    public void FastForward()
    {
        byte originalSeconds = seconds;

        seconds = (byte)(seconds + 50);
        if (originalSeconds > seconds)
              // Overflow of seconds variable
            minutes++;
    }

    public void FastBackward()
    {
        byte originalSeconds = seconds;

        seconds = (byte)(seconds - 50);
        if (originalSeconds < seconds)
```

LISTING 6.8 continued

```
            // Underflow of seconds variable
            minutes—;
    }

    public void SetSeconds(byte sec)
    {
        seconds = sec;
    }

    public void SetMinutes(short min)
    {
        minutes = min;
    }

    public void ShowTime()
    {
        Console.WriteLine("Sec: " + seconds + " Min: " + minutes);
    }
}

class RunBliposClock
{
    public static void Main()
    {
        string command;

        Console.WriteLine("Welcome to the Blipos Clock. " +
            "256 seconds per minute " +
            "65536 minutes per day");
        BliposClock myClock = new BliposClock();
        Console.WriteLine("Please set the clock");
        Console.Write("Enter Seconds: ");
        myClock.SetSeconds(Convert.ToByte(Console.ReadLine()));
        Console.Write("Enter minutes: ");
        myClock.SetMinutes(Convert.ToInt16(Console.ReadLine()));
        Console.WriteLine("Enter orward ackward " +
            "dd fifty educt fifty (T)erminate");
        do
        {
            command = Console.ReadLine().ToUpper();
            if (command == "F")
                myClock.OneForward();
            if (command == "B")
                myClock.OneBackward();
            if(command == "A")
                myClock.FastForward();
            if(command == "D")
                myClock.FastBackward();
            myClock.ShowTime();
        } while (command != "T");
        Console.WriteLine("Thank you for using the Blipos Clock");
    }
}
```

```
Welcome to the Blipos Clock. 256 seconds per minute 65536 minutes per day
Please set the clock
Enter Seconds: 253<enter>
Enter minutes: 32767<enter>
Enter orward ackward dd fifty educt fifty (T)erminate
f<enter>
Sec: 254 Min: 32767
f<enter>
Sec: 255 Min: 32767
f<enter>          (Overflowing here. This comment is not part of output).
Sec: 0 Min: -32768
f<enter>
Sec: 1 Min: -32768
b<enter>
Sec: 0 Min: -32768
b<enter>          (Underflow is taking place here)
Sec: 255 Min: 32767
a<enter>          (Overflow is taking place here)
Sec: 49 Min: -32768
d<enter>          (Underflow is taking place here)
Sec: 255 Min: 32767
t<enter>
Thank you for using the Blipos Clock
```

Lines 18–22 constitute the constructor of the `BliposClock` class. Whenever a new object of this class is created, this constructor will be called and will initialize the instance variables `seconds` and `minutes` to 0.

The method header of a method called `OneForward` is in line 24. It increments the `seconds` instance variable of `BliposClock` by 1 and increments `minutes` by 1 if `seconds` overflows.

Line 26 declares a local variable called `originalSeconds` of type `byte` and assigns it the value of the instance variable `seconds`.

Line 28 uses the increment operator `++` to increase the value of `seconds` by 1.

Line 29 is the first line of an `if` statement. It applies the comparison operator `>` (greater than) to determine whether `originalSeconds` is greater than `second`.

If `originalSeconds` is greater than `seconds`, line 31 executes and increments `minutes` by 1.

Line 34 is the method header of `OneBackward`, which, when called, will decrease the `seconds` instance variable by 1 and decrement `minutes` by 1 if `seconds` underflows.

Line 38 decrements the instance variable `seconds` by 1, using the *decrement operator* `--`.

Lines 39–41 use the comparison operator `<` (less than) to determine whether `originalSeconds` is less than `seconds`. If this is the case, decrement `minutes` by 1 with the decrement operator.

In lines 44–52, the `FastForward` method increases `seconds` by 50 and increments `minutes` by 1 if `seconds` experiences any overflow during this operation.

In line 48, the expression `(seconds + 50)` is of type `int` and cannot be assigned to `seconds` of type `byte`. Consequently, we use the *type cast* `(byte)` in `(byte)(seconds + 50)`, which produces the value `(seconds + 50)` of type `byte`. Type casts are discussed in more detail in a later section of this chapter titled "Explicit Type Conversions."

Line 89 creates an object of class `BliposClock` and assigns the reference of this object to `myClock`.

The code block surrounded by the braces in lines 98 and 109 (lines 99–108) is repeated as long as `(command != "T")` is `true` due to the `do-while` loop. `!=` is a comparison operator called "not equal to," so as long as `command` is not equal to `"T"`, the code block of lines 99–108 will be repeated. As soon as the user types a `T`, the loop is terminated.

Lines 100–107 consist of several `if` statements to determine which command the user has given. For example, entering a `D` (or `d`) will move the clock `FastBackward`.

Do Not Rely on Overflow/Underflow to Implement Logic

The source code in Listing 6.8 has been created as a teaching tool to illustrate overflow and underflow through this mechanism's resemblance to the workings of a clock. However, it is not generally recommendable to rely on overflow and underflow in your source code to implement the logic of a program. C# might well one day change the way it handles overflow/underflow or perhaps change the ranges of the involved types and, consequently, introduce bugs into your programs.

Working with Integer Types

The next two sections provide a few useful hints when you apply integer types in your programs.

Preventing Overflow and Underflow Exceptions

Even though you can always fall back on the compiler to create checks for overflow and underflow during the design and testing of your program, the best way to avoid these kinds of exceptions is to think through each of the expressions that involve integers in your program.

Try to figure out the largest and smallest value each expression of type integer can possibly reach. For example, if you have an expression such as `(pricePerKilo * amountOfKilos)`, you will have to work out the probable minimum and maximum values of the two involved variables. By calculating max `pricePerKilo` with max `amountOfKilos`, you can find the probable maximum value for the whole expression. Similar logic is applied to find the minimum amount of the expression. In these calculations, you will have to consider future possible values of the involved variables. So even though `pricePerKilo` has fluctuated between 20 and 100 for the last 10 years, that doesn't necessarily mean it cannot suddenly reach 200 the next year.

It is important to check every sub-expression of a larger expression, not just the overall end result. Consider the simple source code in Listing 6.9. What is the output? An initial guess might be 1,000,000, but this is not the case here. Why? First, all the sub-parts of the expression in line 9 are of type `int`. Second, to calculate this expression, the sub-expression `1000000 * 1000000` will have to be calculated first. This is where our problems start. The result of this calculation is, in reality, 1,000,000,000,000, which is larger than the maximum possible `int` value of 2147483647, so the initial multiplication causes an overflow with the result of –727379968. The program finally divides this number by 1,000,000, producing the unexpected and incorrect result of 727.

LISTING 6.9 Source Code for `OverflowingSubExpression.cs`

```
01: using System;
02:
03: class OverflowingSubExpression
04: {
05:     public static void Main()
06:     {
07:         int result;
08:
09:         result = 1000000 * 1000000 / 1000000;
10:         Console.WriteLine("Result of calculation: " + result);
11:     }
12: }
```

Because of these incorrect results the compiler generates the following error message if you attempt to compile Listing 6.9:

```
OverflowingSubExpression.cs(9.18): error CS0220: The operation overflows at
 compile time in checked mode
```

Only literals are involved in line 9 of Listing 6.9. Because literals stay unchanged during the execution of a program, the compiler can identify the problem in line 9 at compile time.

Disappearing Fractions

What is the result of the expression `(4 / 10) x 10`? Under normal circumstances, it would be 4, but calculating this expression using integers in the source code returns a 0. The result of the sub-expression `(4 / 10)` is 0.4, which is represented as a 0 when using integers so the fraction .4 has been discarded. Multiplying 0 by 10 results in 0.

To prevent this type of error, you can attempt to rearrange the expression. In this case, you could write the expression as `(4 * 10) / 10`. If a reordering turns out to be impossible, you should probably resort to the floating-point or decimal types, which are designed to handle numbers with fractions.

Floating-Point Types

Floating-point types differ from integer types in many important ways. In contrast to variables of type integer, floating-point variables let you store numbers with a fraction, such as 2.99 (the price of the "Mock Chicken Salad" I happen to be eating right now) or a number like 3.1415926535897931, which is an approximation of the mathematical constant Pi (π).

Floating-point numbers also enable you to represent a much wider range of values than the most expansive integer type `long`. Even the number 9,223,372,036,854,775,807 (the maximum in the range of `long`) pales compared to the largest possible floating-point number, which is equivalent to 17 with 307 zeros behind it. Similarly, floating-point numbers also let you store extremely large negative numbers.

Two Floating-Point Notations Used in C#

Floating-point numbers are often used when representing very large or small numbers. When writing numbers of such magnitude, it is often convenient to use a notation called *scientific notation*, also called *e-notation* or *floating-point notation*.

This notation expresses the number 756,000,000,000,000 as shown in Figure 6.14, but this notation cannot be used in C# source code.

FIGURE 6.14
Scientific notation.

756,000,000,000,000 can be expressed as: 7.56×10^{14}

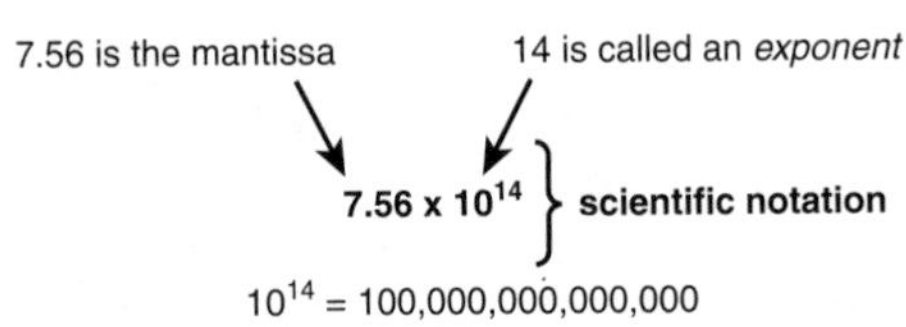

0.000000456 can be expressed as: 4.56×10^{-7}

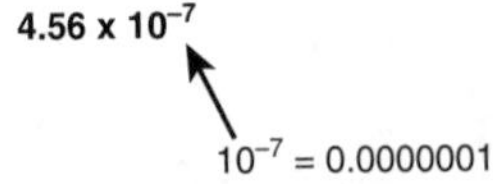

C# allows you to write floating-point numbers using two different notations. You can use the form we are familiar with from everyday life with a decimal point followed by digits (for example 134.87 and 0.0000345), or you can use the scientific notation shown here. However, because it is difficult to write exponents with the keyboard (it took me a while before I knew how to type the ^{7} in 10^7 using MS Word), the multiplication sign and the 10 has been removed and replaced with an E (or e) with the exponent written after the E. For example, the number 0.000000456 (equal to 4.56×10^{-7}) can be written in C# as `+4.56E-7`. Figure 6.15 looks closer at each part of this notation form.

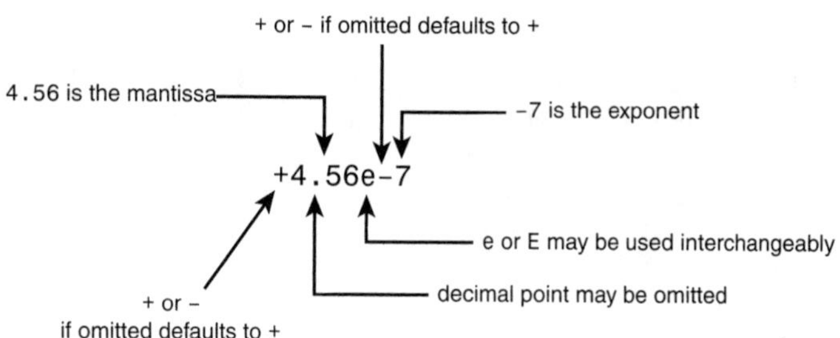

FIGURE 6.15
A closer look at scientific notation.

The following are a few floating-point numbers written as they look in a C# program using our familiar everyday notation:

```
56.78       // floating-point every day notation
0.645       // floating-point
7.0         // also floating-point.
```

Notice that even though the fraction in the last line is 0, the decimal point still triggers the compiler to treat `7.0` as a floating-point number.

The following are a few floating-point numbers in C# using e-notation:

```
456E-7      //same as 4.56e-7
8e3         //same as +8.0e+3 still floating-point.
-8.45e8     //a negative value
1.49e8      //distance between the earth and the sun
8.88e11     //distance from earth to planet Blipos in miles.
9.0e-28     //the mass of an electron in grams
```

The Floating (Decimal) Point

You might wonder why these types are called floating-point types. Well actually the (decimal) point in a floating-point number is "floating," meaning that it can be moved to the right or left in an otherwise unchanging sequence of digits. Let's look at this mechanism a bit closer.

You can think of a floating-point number as consisting of two parts, a *base value* and a *scaling factor* that moves the decimal point of the base value to the right or the left. Consider a base value of 0.871254; a scaling factor of 100 (10^2) would move the decimal point two places to the right, resulting in the number 87.1254. A scaling factor of 10000 (10^4) produces the number 8712.54 by moving the decimal point four places to the right. Conversely, it would be possible to move the decimal point to the left and create a smaller fraction closer to 0. For example, with a scaling factor of 0.001 (10^{-3}), we would move the decimal point three places to the left, producing 0.000871254.

Note

Even though we can scale the base value 0.871254 up or down, the digits and their sequence (871254) remain unchanged.

Interpreting the E-Notation

4.56E+7 means "Take the mantissa 4.56 and move the decimal point 7 places to the right; insert zeros as placeholders when the decimal point moves away from the digit farthest to the right."

`4.56E-7` means "Take the mantissa 4.56 and move the decimal point 7 places to the left; insert zeros as placeholders when the decimal point moves away from the digit farthest to the left."

Note

The maximum number of digits that can be represented by the base value varies between the two floating-point types found in C# and so is an important factor for determining the range and the accuracy of each type.

The Two Floating-Point Types

C# has two floating-point types, `float` and `double`. Two main attributes distinguish these two types—the number of significant digits they can represent (related to the base value concept already discussed) and the range of the exponents (related to the scaling factor concept).

***float* and *double* in a Nutshell**

Variables of the `float` type can hold values from –3.4E38 to 3.4E38. They can get as close to zero (without holding zero itself) as 1.5e–45 or –1.5e–45. Values are represented with approximately 7 significant digits. A `float` occupies 32 bits (4 bytes) of memory.

A variable of the `double` type can hold values from –1.7E308 to 1.7E308. It can get as close to zero (without holding zero itself) as 5.0E–324 or –5.0E–324. Values are represented with 15–16 significant digits. A `double` occupies 64 bits (8 bytes) of memory.

The definitions of and operations on C#'s floating-point types follow the IEEE 754 specifications, a commonly used standard. More details are available at IEEE's Web site at `http://www.ieee.org`.

The differing number of significant digits between the two types influence their accuracy. Thus, to write a number that can accurately be represented by the `double` type, it must contain less than approximately 17 significant digits. For example, the number 123,456,789,012,345 consists of 15 significant digits. If we tried to squeeze (explicitly convert) this number into a variable of type `float`, it would only be able to represent it as 123,456,700,000,000 containing only 7 significant digits. The remaining eight zeros are merely used as placeholders. This is illustrated in Figure 6.16.

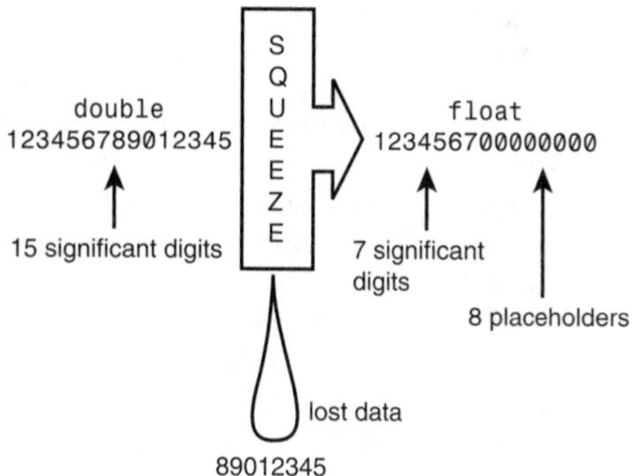

FIGURE 6.16
"Squeezing" a ***double*** into a ***float***.

Note

The ranges and number of significant digits for `float` and `double`, shown in the "Float and Double in a Nutshell" Note, are only approximations. When I tried to "squeeze" 123,456,789,012,345 into a `float` on my computer, it represented the number as 123,456,788,000,000 deviating from 123,456,700,000,000 previously stated.

Recall how an overflowing/underflowing integer value could generate an exception and then cause the program to terminate. In contrast, operations on floating-point values never produce exceptions during abnormal situations; instead, one of the following results is produced, depending on the operation performed:

- Positive zero (+0) or negative zero (-0)
- Positive infinity (∞) or negative infinity (–∞)
- NaN (`Not a Number`)

Each of these results, and the situations triggering them, are summarized in the following Note. Please note that the information provided here is of a more technical nature and is not required to understand any parts introduced later in the book.

Abnormal Floating-Point Operations and Their Results (Optional)

- If an attempt is made to assign a value `x` to a variable of type `float`, where `x` can be defined as –1.5E–45 > `x` > 1.5E-45 and `x` ≠ 0 (in other words, if `x` is very close to zero, without being zero), `x` cannot be represented properly by the `float` variable. The result of the operation is a positive zero (if `x` is positive) or a negative zero (if `x` is negative).
- If an attempt is made to assign a value `x` to a variable of type `double`, where `x` can be defined as –5.0E–324 > `x` > 5.0E–324 and `x` ≠ 0 (in other words, if `x` is very close to zero, without being zero), `x` cannot be represented properly by the `double` variable. The result of the operation is a positive zero (if `x` is positive) or a negative zero (if `x` is negative).

- If an attempt is made to assign a value x to a variable of type `float`, where x can be defined as –3.4E38 > x or x > 3.4E38 (in other words, if the magnitude of x is too large either in a negative direction or in a positive direction), the result of this operation becomes negative infinity (denoted `-Infinity` in output from the C# program) or positive infinity (denoted `Infinity` in output from the C# program).
- If an attempt is made to assign a value x to a variable of type `double`, where x can be defined as –1.7E308 > x or x > 1.7E308 (in other words, if the magnitude of x is too large either in a negative direction or in a positive direction), the result of this operation becomes negative infinity (denoted `-Infinity` in output from the C# program) or positive infinity (denoted `Infinity` in output from the C# program)
- If an attempt is made to perform an invalid operation on a floating-point type, the result is `NaN`. An example of an invalid operation is `(0.0/0.0)`.

For more details about positive/negative zero, positive/negative infinity, and NaN, please refer to the C# Language Specification and other technical references at www.msdn.microsoft.com.

Floating-Point Literals

When you write floating-point numbers, like `5.87` or `8.24E8`, in your C# program, they are regarded to be of type `double` by default. To specify a value of type `float`, you must append an `f` (or `F`) to the number. Thus, `5.87f` and `8.24E8F` are both literals of type `float`. Conversely, it is also possible to explicitly specify that a literal number is of type `double` by using the suffix `d` (or `D`) as in `5.87d` or `8.24E8D`.

Note

When you assign a literal to a variable of type `float`, you must specify the literal to be of type `float` by adding the `f` (or `F`) suffix. The compiler will not automatically perform the conversion, rendering the following two lines of source invalid:

```
float distance;
distance = 8.24E8;
```

Incorrect: 8.24E8 is of type double. and should be changed to 8.24E8f

Working with Floating-Point Values

The following section presents a few issues and some guidelines to avoid the most commonly encountered problems when applying floating-point values.

Fractions with Infinite Numbers of Decimal Places

An important issue when attempting to represent numbers with fractions is that many of these numbers have an infinite number of decimal digits, making `float`'s and `double`'s 7 and 15 significant digits look pretty meager. For example, Pi and the fractions 1/3 and 1/7 have an infinite number of decimal digits.

Note

The symbol π (Pi) in Mathematics is used to represent the ratio of the circumference of a circle to its diameter. Pi is an irrational number, so even though its value can be approximated to 3.1415926535897931, it is impossible to represent Pi exactly with a finite number of decimal places.

By utilizing modern computers, the digits of Pi's first 100,000,000 decimal places have been found.

Equality Between Floating-Point Values

What is the result of the calculation 10×0.1? In the world of Mathematics, it is equal to 1. Not so in the world of floating-point numbers. Many expressions considered to be equal in Mathematics are not always the same when calculated using floating-point values. This is caused by the curious fact that a floating-point value calculated in one way often differs from the apparently same floating-point value calculated in a different way.

Look at Listing 6.10. What would you expect the output to be?

LISTING 6.10 Source Code for `NonEquality.cs`

```
01: using System;
02:
03: class NonEquality
04: {
05:     public static void Main()
06:     {
07:         double mySum;
08:
09:         mySum = 0.2f + 0.2f + 0.2f + 0.2f + 0.2f;
10:         if (mySum == 1.0)
11:             Console.WriteLine("mySum is equal to 1.0");
12:         Console.WriteLine("mySum holds the value " + mySum);
13:     }
14: }
```

```
mySum holds the value 1.0000000149011612
```

In line 9 of Listing 6.10, `0.2f` is added together five times and the result is assigned to the `mySum` variable of type `double`. In Mathematics, 5×0.2 is well known to be exactly 1. However, when we compare `mySum` to `1.0` with the equality comparison operator `==` in line 10, this condition turns out to be `false` and so line 11 is never executed. Instead, `mySum` is stated to be equal to 1.0000000149011612, as shown in the previous sample output.

The problem originates in the limited precision of the `float` type. When the five `0.2f` values carrying a mere precision of 7 digits are added together and assigned to the `double` variable `mySum`, their limited accuracy is exposed by `mySum`'s additional 9 significant digits.

Tip

Avoid using the equality comparison operator with floating-point values. If you must perform such a comparison, allow for a certain range of inaccuracy. Alternatively, when comparing values for equality, you should allow for a certain range of inaccuracy.

Following the previous Tip, we decide that +/- 0.0001 is accurate enough in our last comparison, so we rewrite line 10 of Listing 6.10 as follows:

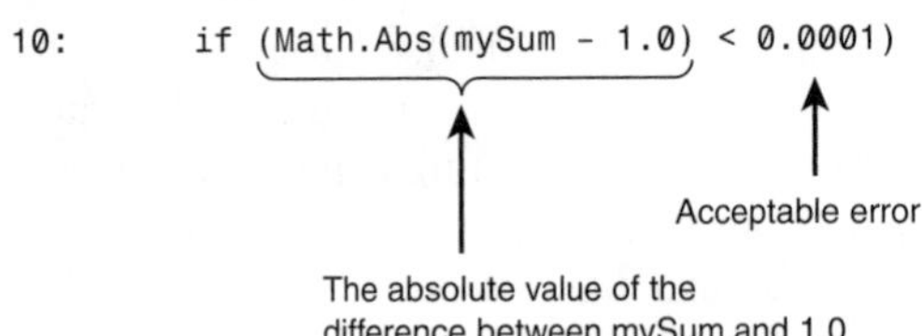

Strictly speaking, you should also change line 11 to

```
11:  Console.WriteLine("mySum is close to 1.0");
```

The output is now changed to

```
mySum is close to 1.0
mySum holds the value 1.0000000149011612
```

Adding or Subtracting Floating-Point Numbers with Different Magnitudes

Consider a variable of type `float` with the value `1234567000`. As we have seen before, the last three zeros are mere placeholders. So, if you attempted to add or subtract a number with a very different magnitude, such as 5, it would not be registered by the variable in this case. Listing 6.11 illustrates this point. The calculation 1234567000–5 is, by standard arithmetic, equal to 1234566995, which differs from our incorrect result in the sample output for Listing 6.11.

LISTING 6.11 Source Code for `DifferentMagnitudes.cs`

```
using System;

class DifferentMagnitudes
{
    public static void Main()
    {
        float distance = 1234567000f;

        distance = distance - 5f;
        Console.WriteLine("New distance: " + distance);
    }
}
```

```
New distance: 1.234567E+09
```

Obviously our operation in line 9 of the source code in Listing 6.11 is useless.

Tip

Additions and subtractions involving floating-point values should not involve numbers of very different magnitudes.

The `decimal` Type

In many ways, the `decimal` type is similar to the floating-point types in that it allows us to represent numbers with fractions and utilizes the idea of base value, significant digits, and scalar value. However, it is significantly more precise, has a smaller range, and takes up much more memory. Thus, the `decimal` type is useful for calculations in need of extreme accuracy.

A *Decimal* Type is Not a Floating-Point Type

Even though `decimal` type values are used to represent fractions like floating-point types, they are not considered to be part of these types. The `decimal` type does not support positive/negative zeros, positive/negative infinites, or NaN as the floating-point types. Instead, values between –1.0E–28 and 1.0E–28 will all simply be zero, and values out of range will generate overflow/underflow exceptions.

For `decimal` overflow/underflow operations, it is not possible to switch the compiler check on or off with the `/checked` compiler switch or the checked or unchecked operators/statements, as is the case for overflowing/underflowing integers.

The following Note lists the characteristics of the `decimal` type.

The *decimal* Type in a Nutshell

Variables of type `decimal` can represent values from approximately –7.9E28 to 7.9E28. They can get as close to zero (without holding zero itself) as –1.0E–28 or 1.0E–28. Values are represented with a staggering 28 significant digits. A `decimal` occupies 128 bits (16 bytes) of memory.

The `decimal` type solves the problem encountered on Listing 6.11 where the inaccuracy of `0.2f` was revealed. In fact, `decimal` types can represent numbers such as 0.1 and 0.2 with 100% accuracy.

Use Integer Types Where You Can

Floating-point and `decimal` numbers let you represent numbers with fractions and with a greater range than integers, but this comes with a price—increased memory requirements and slower performance.

Writing Numbers of Type `decimal`

As stated previously, any number written with a decimal point or with the e-notation is of type `double` by default. Thus, if we want a literal to be of type `decimal`, we need to specify this explicitly by appending the number with an `m` (or `M`). As you will see shortly, integer values are implicitly converted to type `decimal` if required. Consequently, integer literals, such as 10, 756, and –963, need not carry the `m` suffix.

Floating-Point, `decimal`, and Integer Value Compatibilities

The previous sections introduced the complete range of predefined types that enable you to represent numeric values in a program. We have already looked at the compatibilities between each of the integer types. Next, I have extended this discussion to floating-point and `decimal` types and linked these with the integer types.

- `float` *and* `double` *compatibilities*—Any value of type `float` can be represented by a value of type `double`; consequently, `float` type values are implicitly converted to values of type `double`.

  Implicit conversions from `double` to `float` are not possible.

- *Floating-points and* `decimal` *compatibilities*—The floating-point types have larger ranges than the `decimal` type. This might produce overflow/underflow exceptions during conversions from floating-point values to `decimal` values. Consequently, no implicit conversions are provided from any of the floating-point types to the `decimal` type.

  On the other hand, the `decimal` type has a higher number of significant digits (higher precision) than any of the floating-point types, ruling out any implicit conversions from the `decimal` type to the floating-point types.

- *Integers and floating-points. Integers and* `decimals`—The compiler will implicitly convert any of the integer types to both of the two floating-point types and the `decimal` type, despite the fact that conversions from `int`, `uint`, or `long` to `float` and from `long` to `double` could incur a loss of precision. However, because the range of `float` and `double` is far broader than any of the integer types, there is no loss of magnitude.

Based on this information and Figure 6.12 (presenting the integer type compatibilities), it is possible to illustrate how all the types discussed so far in this chapter relate in terms of possible implicit conversion paths. This is done in Figure 6.17. Please note that even though the `char` type has not been discussed yet, it is included in the figure for completeness. The `char` type will be discussed in Chapter 7 "Types Part II: Operators, Enumerators, and Strings."

Explicit Type Conversions

Apart from the implicit conversions that are happily and automatically performed by the compiler, C# also lets you force the compiler to perform type conversions by moving against the flow of the arrows shown in Figure 6.17. This requires a type cast explicitly written in the C# source.

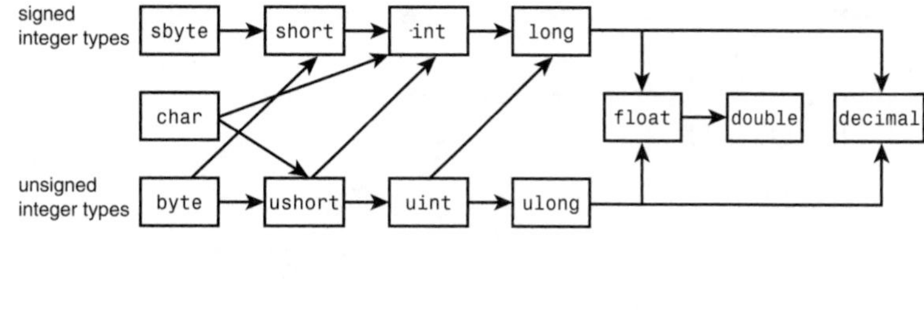

FIGURE 6.17
Implicit conversion paths for the numeric types.

Where:

<Type A> → <Type B>

Means: It is possible to implicitly convert from Type A to Type B

More specifically, a *cast operator* consists of two parentheses enclosing a type `(<Type>)`. It must be placed in front of the value you want to cast. For this reason, type casts are also termed *explicit conversions*. Let's illustrate the type cast with the following code snippet:

```
01:  float weight;
02:  int sum;
03:  weight = 10f;
04:  sum = weight;
```

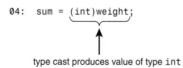

produces value of type `float`

Line 4 contains an invalid statement because we attempt to let the compiler perform an implicit conversion against the implicit conversion path, by assigning a variable of type `float` to a variable of type `int`. However, if the programmer is confident that in any execution of this program, the value of `weight` can be represented by `sum` of type `int` or, if this is not the case, the incurred data loss will not be harmful, he or she might want to enforce an explicit type conversion in line 4. This is done by placing the type cast operator `(int)` in front of `weight` in line 4, which then looks like the following:

```
04:  sum = (int)weight;
```

type cast produces value of type `int`

Line 4 now contains the expression `(int)weight`, which is called a type cast.

Note

The type cast `(int)weight` does not change anything about `weight`. Its type and its value remain untouched. `(int)weight` merely produces a value of type `int` instead of a value of type `float`.

If the value of **weight** is 15.0, the cast produces 15. If the value of **weight** is 15.98, the cast also produces the value 15; the 0.98 has been lost on the way to the variable **sum**. Note here that 15.98 has not been rounded off; instead, the fraction .98 has been removed. In computer language, this is called *truncating*.

Syntax Box 6.4 The Type Cast

```
Type_cast::=
        (<Type>) <Expression>
```

Examples—

```
(ushort) 6046

(decimal)((number1 + number2) / 2)
```

Where number1 and number2 arbitrarily could be chosen to be variables of type double.

Constants: Symbolic Names for Literals

Often, a source program will make use of unchanging numbers, such as 3.141592 (Pi), 186,000 (the approximate speed of light in miles/seconds), perhaps the maximum speed of an elevator or, other values more specific to your program, that you might expect not to change during the lifetime of a program. C# allows you to declare names for the literals or other expressions in your program representing such constants and allows you to use the name instead of writing the actual value. For example, instead of writing,

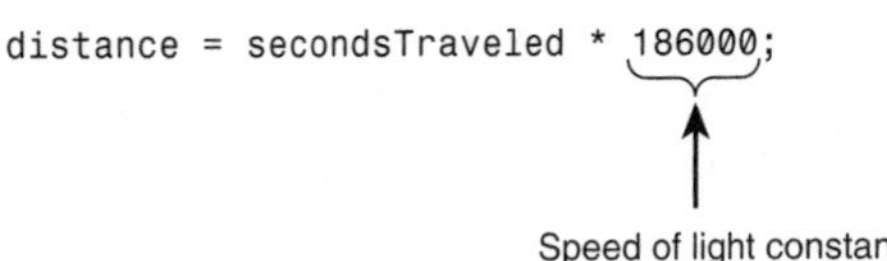

you could give **186000** the name **SpeedOfLight** and write the same statement as follows:

```
distance = secondsTraveled * SpeedOfLight;
```

SpeedOfLight looks very similar to a variable in that it has a name and a value. In fact, we could have declared it to be a straightforward variable with the following line:

```
int SpeedOfLight = 186000;
```

This would allow us to use **SpeedOfLight** in our **distance** calculation. However, there is a problem attached to using a variable here. We might accidentally change the value **SpeedOfLight** somewhere else in our program. To solve this problem, we can specify the value of **SpeedOfLight** to remain unchanged by using the **const** keyword.

Line 7 of Listing 6.12 demonstrates the use of `const` by declaring the name `MassOfElectron` (line 7) to represent the constant value `9.0E-28` (mass of electron in grams). `MassOfElectron` is applied in line 16 to calculate the total mass of a given number of electrons.

LISTING 6.12 Source Code for `MassCalculator.cs`

```
01: using System;
02:
03: // Calculates the mass of a given number of electrons
04:
05: class MassCalculator
06: {
07:     const decimal MassOfElectron = 9.0E-28m;
08:
09:     public static void Main()
10:     {
11:         decimal totalMass;
12:         int electronAmount;
13:
14:         Console.WriteLine("Enter number of electrons");
15:         electronAmount = Convert.ToInt32(Console.ReadLine());
16:         totalMass = MassOfElectron * electronAmount;
17:         Console.WriteLine("Mass of " + electronAmount +
18:             " electrons: " + totalMass + " grams");
19:     }
20: }
```

```
Enter number of electrons
2000<enter>
Mass of 2000 electrons: 1.8E-24 grams
```

A name that represents a constant value is called a *constant*.

Syntax Box 6.5 Declaring a Constant

```
Constant_declaration_statement ::=
[public | private] const <Type> <Constant_Identifier> = <Constant_expression>;
```

Notes:

The *<Constant_expression>* here can consist of just one literal, as in the following:

```
public const double Pi = 3.14159;
```

Constant_expression

It can also consist of a mixture of literals, other constants from the source code, and operators, as long as the expression can be calculated at compile time.

```
public const double Pi = 3.14159;
public const double TwicePi = 2 * Pi;
```

Valid since both 2 and Pi are known at compile time

The constant declaration can be placed in a class definition, making the constant a class member. Constants here are always `static` and so can only be accessed by other objects outside the class by using the classname (followed by the dot operator and the name of the constant) and not the instantiated object names. Listing 6.13 demonstrates this point.

LISTING 6.13 Source Code for `ConstantMass.cs`

```
01: using System;
02:  // Calculates the mass of 100 electrons;
03: class Constants
04: {
05:     public const decimal MassOfElectron = 9.0E-28m;
06: }
07:
08: class MassCalculator
09: {
10:     public static void Main()
11:     {
12:         decimal totalMass;
13:
14:         totalMass = 100 * Constants.MassOfElectron;
15:         Console.WriteLine(totalMass);
16:     }
17: }
```

```
9E-26
```

Listing 6.13 contains two classes, `Constants` and `MassCalculator`. The `Constants` class merely holds the `MassOfElectron` constant. The `MassCalculator` class needs access to this constant for its calculation of the mass of 100 electrons. Line 14 correctly contains the *class-name* `Constants` followed by the dot operator (`.`) and the name of the constant inside the `Constant` class `MassOfElectron`, which specifies the constant `Constants.MassOfElectron`. On the other hand, an attempt to access the `MassOfElectron` constant by first instantiating the `Constants` class, as shown the following two lines, would be invalid.

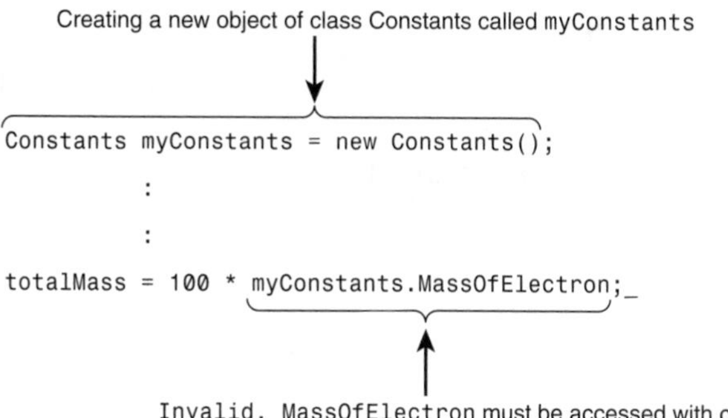
Creating a new object of class Constants called myConstants
Constants myConstants = new Constants();
:
:
totalMass = 100 * myConstants.MassOfElectron;_
Invalid. MassOfElectron must be accessed with class name

Note

C# has a feature similar to constants called `readonly` fields. However, whereas constants must be known at compile time and will have the same value throughout the entire execution of a program, the value of a `readonly` field can be assigned at the time an object is created and will stay unchanged throughout the life of the object. This is a useful feature. It goes hand in hand with the constructor and initialization mechanisms surrounding object creation.

Tip

Use a named constant consistently throughout the code for every value in the code; don't use the named constant for some of the values and literals for the remaining. For example, if `MaxSpeed` represents the constant value `200` in a program, you must use `MaxSpeed` everywhere for this value, never the literal `200`.

The inconsistent use of constants is a bug-laden procedure. Imagine if one day you had to change the maximum speed (`MaxSpeed`) in a program with inconsistent use of named constants. You would most likely forget to change the literals and merely change the `MaxSpeed` declaration.

The Advantages of Using Constants

You have seen how to declare and use constants. But why do we need them? This section discusses a few compelling reasons for employing constants in your programs:

- *Understanding the meaning of a value*—Instead of looking at a number like `200` somewhere in a program, `MaximumSpeed` gives the reader of the program a much better understanding for what the number represents. It makes the program self documenting.
- *Changes only need to be made in one place*—Some constants can be used numerous places throughout the source code. Using literals would force you to trace all the values down one-by-one, in case you had to change the value of the constant. This is an error-prone and time-consuming process. You might overlook certain literals or inadvertently change literals with the same value but which do not represent the constant.

  By having one named constant in the source, you only need to change the value in one place.

Formatting Numeric Values

Until now, we have been content with printing numbers using the default plain format applied when, for example, writing

```
Console.WriteLine("Distance traveled: " + 10000000.432);
```

which simply prints

```
Distance traveled: 10000000.432
```

on the console. However, by changing the appearance of a number through embedded commas, the use of scientific notation and a limited number of `decimal` digits, it is possible to improve its readability and compactness when printed onscreen. Table 6.4 displays a few examples.

TABLE 6.4 Examples of Formatted Numbers

Name of variable	Plain Number	Formatted number with improved readability / compactness
profit	3000000000.44876	$3,000,000,000.45
distance	7000000000000000	7.00E+015
mass	3.8783902983789877362	3.8784
length	20000000	20,000,000

In this section, we will discuss C#'s built-in features for formatting numbers when converted into strings.

Standard Formatting

Recall that each numeric type is based in the .NET Framework and here represented by a `struct`, allowing it to contain useful pre-written functionality. The `ToString` method is one of the methods providing this functionality. It enables us to convert any of the simple types to a string and to conveniently specify suitable formats during this conversion. Figure 6.18 shows an example utilizing the `ToString` method of the `decimal` type to convert 20000000.45965981m of type `decimal` to a `string` with commas embedded and only two decimal places shown.

The `ToString` method as we use it here takes one argument of type string that allows us to specify the desired `string` format. The argument consists of a character, called a *format character*, (N in this case), that indicates the format followed by an optional number called a *precision specifier*, (2 in this case) which has different meanings depending on the format character applied. Table 6.5 displays the different format characters available and their corresponding formats.

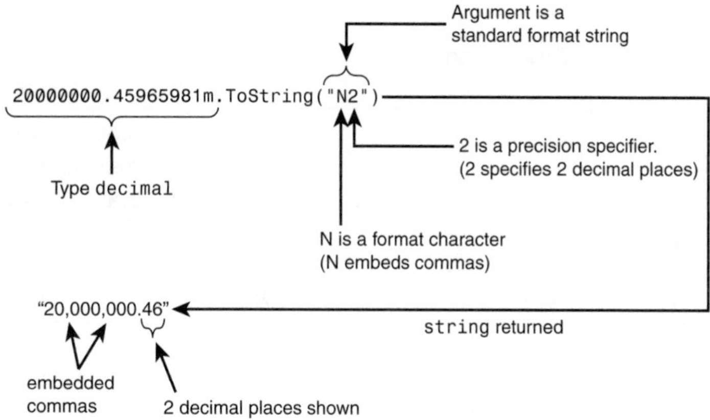

FIGURE 6.18
Formatting a literal of type ***decimal***.

TABLE 6.5 Available Format Characters

Format Character	Description	Example
C, c	*Currency*. Formatting is specific to local settings. Local settings contain information about the type of currency used and other parameters, which can vary from country to country.	`2000000.456m.ToString("C")` Returns: `"$2,000,000.46"` (If the operating system is set to American standards.)
D, d	*Integer*. Precision specifier sets the minimum number of digits. The output will be padded with leading zeros if the number of digits of the actual number is less than the precision specifier. (Note: Only available for the integer types)	`45687.ToString("D8")` Returns: `"00045678"`
E, e	*E-Notation*. (Scientific) Precision specifier determines the amount of decimal digits, which defaults to 6.	`345678900000.ToString("E3")` Returns: `"3.457E+011"` `345678912000.ToString("e")` Returns: `"3.456789e011"`
F, f	*Fixed-point*. Precision specifier that indicates the number of decimal digits.	`3.7667892.ToString("F3")` Returns: `"3.765"`

TABLE 6.5 continued

Format Character	Description	Example

G, g	*General.*
	The most compact format of either E or F will be chosen. Precision specifier sets the maximum amount of digits number can be represented by.
		`65432.98765.ToString("G")`
		Returns: `"65432.98765"`
		`65432.98765.ToString("G7")`
		Returns: `"65432.99"`
		`65432.98765.ToString("G4")`
		Returns: `"6.543E4"`

N, n	*Number.* Generates a number with embedded commas. Precision specifier sets the number of decimal digits.	`1000000.123m.ToString("N2")` Returns: `"1,000,000.12"`

X, x	*Hexadecimal.*
	The precision specifier sets the minimum number of digits represented in the string. Leading zeros will be padded to the specified width.
		`950.ToString("x")`
		Returns: `"3b6"`
		`950.ToString("X6")`
		Returns: `"0003B6"`

Notes:

The format character can be specified either in uppercase or lowercase. However, it only makes a difference in the case of E (e-notation) and X (hexadecimal). E specifies E to be used as in "3.0E+010"; e specifies e to be used as in "3.0e+010".

X specifies uppercase letters to be used to represent the hexadecimal value as in "FFA5". x specifies lowercase letters as in "ffa5".

The `ToString` method provides us with powerful means to format numeric values. However, its use becomes somewhat longwinded and cumbersome if we write several formatted numbers embedded in a `string`. The following lines illustrate how unclear the call to `WriteLine` becomes and how difficult it is to keep track of which part is static text and which part is a formatted number:

```
Console.WriteLine("The length is: " + 10000000.4324.ToString("N2") +
➥ "  The width is: " + 65476356278.098746.ToString("N2") +
➥ "  The height is: " + 4532554432.45684.ToString("N2"));
```

Providing the following output:

```
The length is: 10,000,000.43  The width is: 65,476,356,278.10
➥The height is 4,532,554,432.46
```

The statement would be much clearer if we could somehow separate the static text and the numbers and just indicate, with small discreet specifiers, the position and format of each number. C# provides an elegant solution to this problem.

If we disregard the formatting part for a moment and decide to let {<N>} be such a specifier, where <N> refers to the position of a number in a list of numbers positioned after the static text in the call to WriteLine, we can write the previous lines as follows:

```
Console.WriteLine("The length is: {0} The width is: {1} The height is: {2}",
        10000000.4324, 65476356278.098746, 4532554432.45684);
```

where {0} refers to the first value (100000000.4324) in the list of numbers after the string; {1} refers to the second value (65476356278.098746), and {2} to the third value. Certainly, this has provided us with a much clearer statement.

Because the yet to be explored string class together with the WriteLine method provides these features, I will end this part of the story here. When we look at strings in Chapter 7, I will finish the story and discuss how you can combine format characters and precision specifiers with the WriteLine method to not only specify where a certain number is positioned but also how it is formatted.

The bool Type: A Brief Encounter

The bool type (see last row of Table 6.2) is named after George Boole (1815–1864) an English mathematician who devised a formal way of representing and working with Boolean expressions, called Boolean algebra.

Just like a value of type short can hold any value between –32768 and 32767, a value of type bool can hold one of the literal values true and false, which are keywords in C#.

Whereas conventional algebra of arithmetic expresses the rules abided by addition, multiplication, and negation of numbers, Boolean algebra describes the rules obeyed by the logic operators "and," "or," and "not" when combined with the two values true and false.

Boolean algebra, together with the bool type, form the foundation of a powerful system of logic enabling you to think and reason effectively about the design of computer programs. Consequently, it is impossible to create C# programs of much substance without applying the bool type together with at least some of the rules found in Boolean algebra.

An expression that returns either the value true or false is termed a *Boolean expression*.

The following is an example of a Boolean expression

```
(length > 100)
```

returns true if the variable length is greater than 100 and false if length is smaller than or equal to 100.

true and false represent our intuitive understanding of the concepts true and false and allow us to specify the correctness of a claim (represented by a variable) by simply declaring a bool variable

```
bool isFinished;
```

and assigning it the literal value true (or false) as in the following:

```
isFinished = true;
```

This also allows us to assign any value from an expression that will return either `true` or `false`. For example, we could declare the `bool` variable `distanceIsGreaterThanTen`

```
bool distanceIsGreaterThanTen;
```

and assign it the value of the Boolean expression `(distance > 10)` as in the following:

```
distanceIsGreaterThanTen = (distance > 10);
```

It also allows us to let it be part of the condition of an `if` statement such as the following:

```
if(distanceIsGreaterThanTen)
    Console.WriteLine("Distance is greater than ten");
```

which only prints "Distance is greater than ten" if `distanceIsGreaterThanTen` contains the value `true`.

Statements controlling the flow of a program, such as `if` statements and `do-while` loops, go hand in hand with the `bool` type and Boolean algebra. This section is just a brief introduction to the comprehensive treatment of the subject found in Chapter 8, "Flow of Control Part 1: Branching Statements And Related Concepts."

Summary

This chapter provided an overview of the type system in C# and looked at the simple types in particular.

The important points we have discussed are as follows:

In object-oriented programming, types are used as building blocks to form other types.

Two ways can be used to divide the predefined types in C#: Simple types vs. derived types and value types vs. reference types. The former is often more convenient, the latter is the most correct.

All values belonging to a specific type share a set of predefined characteristics.

Every value must be of a specific type. There are strict rules in C# for the operations a value of a specific type can take part in. For that reason C# is termed a strongly typed language.

A strongly typed language allows us to write powerful declarative statements in the source code.

A variable of a value type holds the actual data stored in it. A reference type holds a reference to another part of the memory where the data are stored. `int` is a value type, `string` is a reference type.

It is possible for more than one value of the same reference type to reference the same object.

Important predefined value types in C# are the simple types, and enum types. All value types are structs.

Important predefined reference types are strings, arrays, interfaces, and delegates. All reference types are classes.

You can define your own classes and structs.

The syntax of a computer language provides the rules to follow for writing a valid source program. Syntax is exact and is best expressed with an exact notation form. A Backus-Naur resembling notation form was introduced for use in the rest of the book.

C# has thirteen predefined simple types that allow you to find a suitable type for most simple values you need to represent. Of those thirteen types, nine are integers, two are floating-point, one is high precision, and one is Boolean.

A predefined implicit conversion path exists between the different simple numeric types. The compiler automatically performs implicit conversions. Explicit conversions, written explicitly in the source code, are needed to move against the direction of this path.

An integer type variable overflows when its value becomes larger than the maximum range specified by the type. Its value is then set to the minimum specified by the range. Underflow is the same process reversed.

Working with the simple types presents several subtle issues you should be aware of to prevent errors in the source code.

The value of a constant is specified in the source code and cannot be changed after compilation. An identifier in the source code represents the value.

C# allows you to format numeric values for printout, providing improved readability.

Values of type bool can represent just two values: `true` and `false.`

Review Questions

1. Why are there two ways to categorize the types in C#?
2. Why does C# have other simple types than `int`?
3. Which kind of attributes distinguish the different types from each other?
4. What does it mean to be a strongly typed language like C#?
5. Is it possible to assign a value of type `int` to a variable of type `short,` without an explicit conversion? Why or why not?
6. How do you specify a literal to be of type `float`?
7. Write a line of code that declares a `private` instance variable called distance, which is of type `float` and is initialized to `100.5`.
8. A variable of type `byte` is holding the value `255`. The program now attempts to increment the value by one. What happens: If the compiler switch is set to `unchecked`? If it is set to `checked?`
9. Which simple type would you use for a variable storing an arbitrary person's weight (in pounds)? (1 pound is approximately 0.45 kilos)?

10. Which simple type would you use for storing account balances that would be involved in interest rate calculations requiring extremely high precision?

11. Suppose `myNumber` and `yourNumber` are both of type `float`. Write a statement that adds these values together as `int`s and assigns them to an `int` variable.

12. If `number1` and `number2` are of type `int` and `text1` is of type `string`, what is the type of the following expression?

    ```
    number1 + text1 + number2
    ```

13. Is the following expression `true` or `false` when evaluated in C# and why? `((10 * 0.2f) == 2.0)`

14. When should you use constants in your source code? What are their advantages?

15. Write a statement that prints 30000000.326m onscreen with this format: $30,000,000.33

Programming Exercises

Change the program `BliposClock.cs` in Listing 6.8 to exhibit the functionality presented in the next four points:

1. Enable the clock to be adjusted by plus/minus 100 seconds by giving the commands `H` and `M`.

2. A year on Blipos has 256 days. The first day of the year has number 0. The civilization is very old on Blipos; their current year is 4,294,967,296. Allow the Blipos clock to show the date on Blipos as ddd/y,yyy,yyy,yyy. Which types would you choose for ddd and yyyyyyyyyy?

3. Allow the user to set and adjust the day and year of the Blipos clock so that it becomes possible to move forward and backward in time by one day and one year.

4. The emperor's birthday is celebrated on the 100th day of each year. Enable the Blipos clock to write "Happy birthday emperor!" onscreen whenever the date is shown to be the 100th day of the year.

5. Write a program containing a method called `AverageAge` that calculates the average of three ages provided to it as arguments. Enable the user to enter three ages (as whole numbers) and use `AverageAge` to calculate the average age and print the result with a precision of three decimals. Which return type would you use for `AverageAge`? How can you format the output?

CHAPTER 7

TYPES PART II: OPERATORS, ENUMERATORS, AND STRINGS

You will learn about the following in the chapter:

- C#'s arithmetic operators.
- How an arithmetic expression is evaluated in terms of finding its value and associated type. In particular, how the precedence and associativity rules are applied.
- The flowchart as a means to describe an algorithm.
- How the C# compiler determines the type of a numerical expression.
- A method to access the metadata of a C# program and determine the type of any expression.
- How to work with enumerated constants and provide an understanding for their advantages.
- The simple type `char`.
- The `string` type and its underlying characteristics.
- How to use the most important `string` methods.
- How the built-in methods of the `string` type can be utilized to create powerful text processing components.

Introduction

The variety of types presented in the previous chapter allows you to create tailor-made formations of types suited to represent the data of your program's problem domain. However, without operators, these structures are like motionless skeletons unable to respond or perform useful tasks. Operators act; they let you create the muscles and the brain of your program. By mastering these fundamental C# elements, you will soon create program bodies that can run and even perform acrobatics.

C# offers access to a broad range of operators. Apart from some operators dedicated for special purposes, we can divide the remaining operators into four main categories—arithmetic, relational, logical, and bit-wise.

Arithmetic operators are applied to values of simple numeric types and form the basis for performing arithmetic calculations in C#, of which distance[ts]mass is an example.

Relational operators provide us with the ability to compare values, as in `(sum < 100)` using the less than (<) relational operator. Relational operators always form Boolean expressions that, per definition, evaluate to either `true` or `false`.

Logical operators let us to combine two or more Boolean expressions (any value of type `bool`). They go hand-in-hand with the relational operators and allow us, through `if` and loop statements, to control the flow of execution in a program and build "brainy" applications. For that reason, they are discussed along with the relational operators and flow of control in Chapter 8, "Flow of Control Part I: Branching Statements and Related Concepts."

Bit-wise operators allow us to manipulate individual bits of an operand. The discussion of these operators is beyond the scope of this book.

This chapter focuses on the main arithmetic operators and is considered an integral part of the types discussion begun in Chapter 6, "Types Part I: The Simple Types," due to the close relationship between operators and types.

Even though the `string` and `enumerator` types are considered derived types, they both play a fundamental role in C#'s type system and, consequently, are included in the latter half of this chapter.

Arithmetic Operators and Numerical Expressions

You have already seen numerous examples of how C# performs arithmetic calculations by evaluating arithmetic expressions, such as the following:

- `100 * Constants.MassOfElectron`
- `((distance1 + distance2) / 2)`

These examples give you a general idea of how a correct expression is put together and how it is evaluated. However, you can only create expressions that efficiently solve the computational problems of your particular program, if you know the different underlying building blocks of a C# expression and how these are combined to form valid expressions. The following sections are aimed at providing you with this knowledge.

Arithmetic operators (such as addition (+), subtraction (-), multiplication (*), and division (/)) combine with numbers called *operands* to form arithmetic expressions. Arithmetic expressions written in C# are fairly easy to interpret; they more or less follow the arithmetic rules we are used to from school.

Binary Operators

The four basic arithmetic operators mentioned in the preceding section all need one operand on their left sides and one operand on their right sides. An arithmetic operator combining *two* operands to form an expression, such as

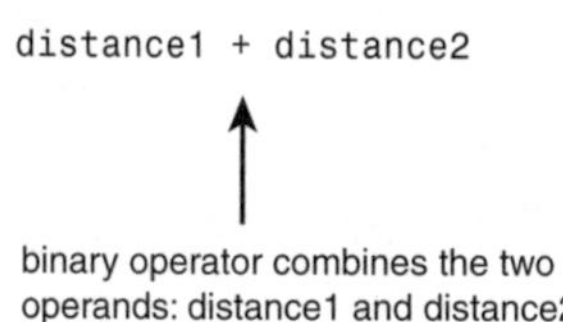

is called a *binary operator*. An operand can, in this context, take many forms. It can be a simple literal, such as 345.23, a variable, a constant representing a numerical value, *or a numerical expression* as in the following:

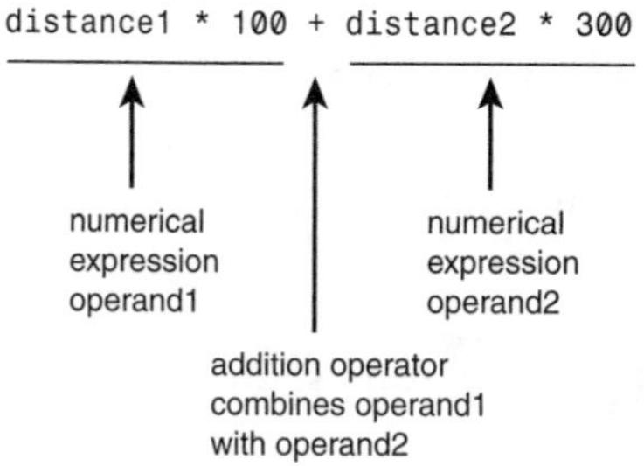

An operand can even be a method call. In this case, the method being called must have a return value. The following call to the `Average` method illustrates

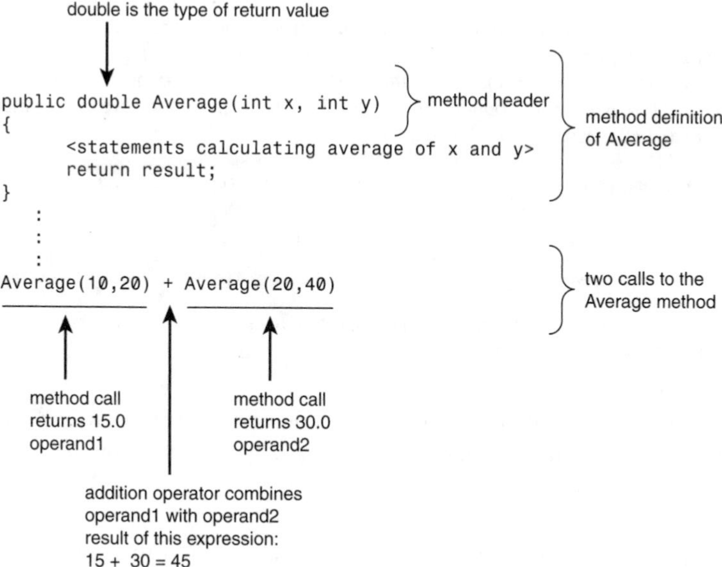

These two method calls are both resolved before the addition operator is applied, and can then be regarded as the numbers 15.0 and 30.0, both of type `double`, the type of `Average`'s return values as specified in its method header.

We can concisely express the five forms of an operand, by utilizing the syntax notation introduced in the previous chapter. This is done in Syntax Box 7.1.

Syntax Box 7.1 The Operand

An operand can be defined in five different ways:

Operand

```
::= <Literal>
::= <Numerical_variable_identifier>
::= <Numerical_constant_identifier>
::= <Numerical_expression>
::= <Method_call>
```

Note: The method called with *<Method_call>* must have a return value.

Additionally, our perception of a numerical expression can be formalized as in Syntax Box 7.2.

Syntax Box 7.2 The Numerical Expression

```
Numerical_expression

        ::= <Operand> <Binary_operator> <Operand>

        ::= <Numerical_expression> <Binary_operator> <Numerical_expression>
```

Notes:

- The latter definition (*<Numerical_expression> <Binary_operator> <Numerical_expression>*) can be deduced by combining the first definition (*<Operand> <Binary_operator> <Operand>*) with the fourth definition of an operand `Operand ::=` *<Numerical_expression>* found in Syntax Box 7.1. This is illustrated here by substituting *<Operand>* with *<Numerical_expression>*:

```
Numerical_expression ::= <Operand> <Binary_operator> <Operand>
                             ↓             ↓              ↓
              <Numerical_expression> <Binary_operator> <Numerical_expression>
```

- There are other definitions for numerical expressions involving other operators not yet presented. These will be mentioned in due time.

Because an operator surrounded by two operands forms a numerical expression, and an operand itself can be defined as a numerical expression, one way to define a numerical expression is as follows:

```
Numerical_expression::=
          <Numerical_expression> <Binary_operator> <Numerical_expression>
```

Consequently, any expression using more than two operands can always be divided into sub-expressions, each consisting of only two operands and one binary operator. After the result of each of these sub-expressions has been found, the results can be used to calculate the next level of sub-expressions. Consider the following expression:

```
4 * 5 + 40 * 10 - 20 * 40 / 10 + 70
```

At first, the expression seems to contain an overwhelming number of operators and operands (numbers), until we realize that it is composed of many sub-expressions. Figure 7.1 shows how we can apply our definition of a numerical expression to calculate the given expression.

FIGURE 7.1
An expression hierarchy.

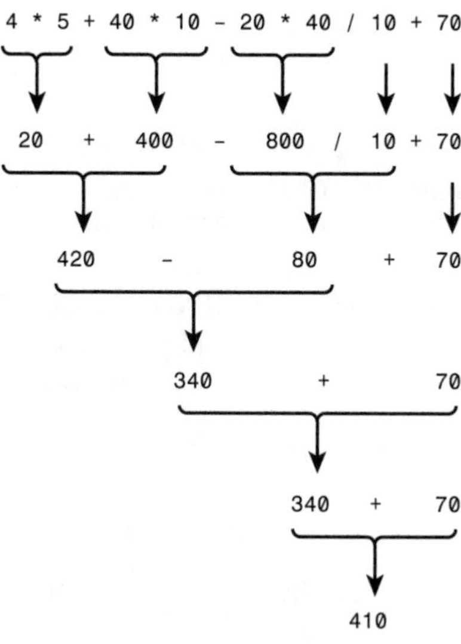

——— underlines two operands and one operator, together forming an expression.

In Figure 7.1, notice how multiplications are performed before additions, in accordance with the rules we learned in school. This fact is highlighted in Figure 7.2.

FIGURE 7.2
Multiplication has higher precedence than addition.

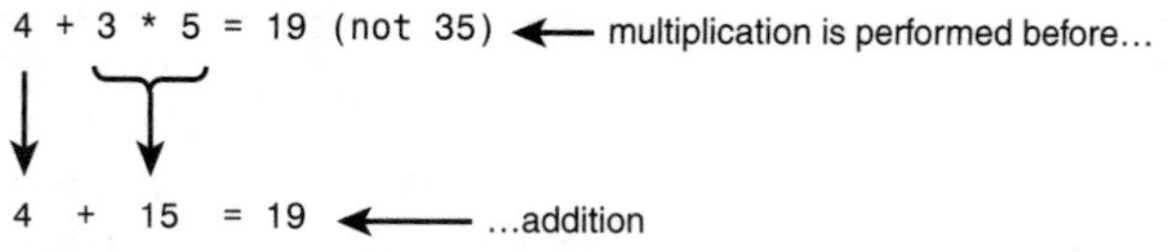

```
4 + 3 * 5 = 19 (not 35) ← multiplication is performed before...
4 +  15   = 19 ← ...addition
```

Consequently, when an operand (such as number 3 in Figure 7.2) can be processed by more than one operator (+ or *, in this case), C# uses *precedence rules* to decide which operator is applied first. These rules determine how expressions, such as the one shown in Figure 7.1, are divided into sub-expression.

Note

For simplicity, I have used literals in the numerical expressions of Figures 7.1 and 7.2. Obviously, I could have used a combination of any of the operand definitions given in Syntax Box 7.1.

C# contains arithmetic operators other than the four binary operators previously mentioned. Each of them carries an exact precedence in relation to the others.

Table 7.1 gives an overview of the operators discussed in this chapter along with their precedence. A listing of the operators presented in this book can be found in Appendix B, "Operator Precedence."

Note

Table 7.1 shows several operators not yet presented; they have been included at this stage as a handy reference and overview when you read through the rest of the section.

Please locate the four binary operators presented so far in Table 7.1. Observe that the multiplication (*) and division (/) operators both have a higher precedence than the addition (+) and subtraction (-) operators. This fits in nicely with our numerical expression examples and their results in Figures 7.1 and 7.2.

TABLE 7.1 Arithmetic Operators—Precedence and Associativity

Precedence	Category	Symbol	Name	Associativity
1.	Primary	`(`*`<Numeric _expression>`*`)`	Parenthesis	
	Primary	`++ (postfix)` (e.g. `count++`)	Increment Operator Postfix	Right-Left
	Primary	`-- (postfix)` (e.g. `count--`)	Decrement Operator Postfix	Right-Left
2.	Unary	+	Unary plus	Right-Left
	Unary	-	Unary minus	Right-Left
	Unary	++ (prefix) (e.g. `++count`)	Increment operator	Right-Left
	Unary	-- (prefix) (e.g. `--count`)	Decrement operator	Right-Left

TABLE 7.1 continued

Precedence	Category	Symbol	Name	Associativity
3.	Binary	*	Multiplication	Left-Right
	Binary	/	Division	Left-Right
	Binary	%	Modulus	Left-Right
4.	Binary	+	Addition	Left-Right
	Binary	-	Subtraction	Left-Right

Notes:

In the Precedence column, the lower the number, the higher the precedence.

For an introduction to the Associativity concept please see the next section.

Associativity

If you look at the precedence of the multiplication and division operators in Table 7.1, you will find them to have equal precedence. Now, consider the following expression:

`100 / 5 * 2`

If division is applied first: (100 / 5) * 2 = 40

If multiplication is applied first: 100 / (5 * 2) = 10

Which result?

How does C# determine which operator is applied first? It cannot get any help from the precedence rules because the two operators have identical precedence. C# then resorts to the rules of associativity. An operator can either have left-to-right or right-to-left associativity. When two operators (such as (/) and (*)) with the same precedence can be applied to the same operand (such as 5 in the previous expression), left-to-right associativity will cause the leftmost operator to be applied first; whereas right-to-left associativity will cause the rightmost operator to be applied first. According to Table 7.1, all the binary operators presented here have left-to-right associativity. Consequently, C# will apply the division operator first in the previous expression, returning a result of 40.

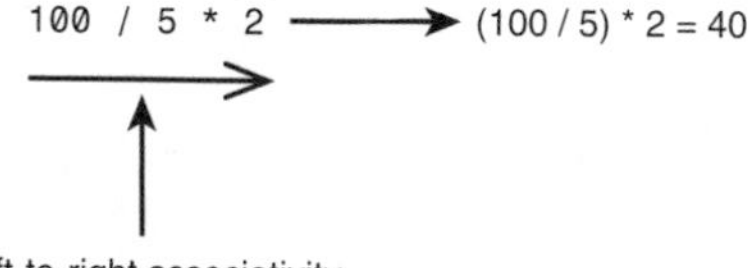

Parentheses and Precedence

If the precedence and associativity rules do not correspond with your calculations, you can apply the parentheses operator `( <Numerical_expression> )` to control the order in which each operator is applied in an arithmetic expression.

Syntax Box 7.3 The Parentheses Operator

```
Parenthesized_expression ::=
                    ( <Numerical_expression> )
```

Parentheses in C# are used in the same way as in algebra and arithmetic to accomplish this task. Because of their higher precedence level (as shown in Table 7.1), they have first priority over any precedence rules set for most other operators. The next example illustrates.

We want to construct a statement that finds the average time two people spend exercising every day. Our first attempt,

```
averageExerciseTime = exercisePerson1 + exercisePerson2 / 2;  ← incorrect
```

does not achieve our goal because `exercisePerson2` is first divided by 2, and then `exercisePerson1` is added. Fortunately, we can change the order by which the two operators are applied by using the parentheses operator

```
averageExerciseTime = (exercisePerson1 + exercisePerson2) / 2;  ← correct
```

which assigns the correct value to `averageExerciseTime`.

You might need to form more complex expressions involving nested parentheses. It is often possible to enhance the readability of these expressions by introducing a temporary variable. Let's look at an example.

A sports drink company, Unlimited Energy Limited, is considering putting a new sports drink on the market in San Francisco and New York. They want to make an estimate of the total amount of time the people of San Francisco and New York combined spend exercising. The only currently available data are in the form of `exercisePerson1` and `exercisePerson2`, as shown earlier. The junior marketing consultant has figured out that by finding the average exercise time and multiplying this amount by the total number of people in San Francisco and New York, it is possible to get an (albeit very inaccurate) estimate of the total exercise time of all people in the two cities combined. The result of this calculation will be called `totalExerciseTime`. A first attempt to calculate this size is as follows:

```
totalExerciseTime = (((exercisePerson1 + exercisePerson2) / 2) * (numPeopleSanFrancisco + numPeopleNewYork));
```

Correct but unclear

However, the expression on the right of the assignment operator = is somewhat complicated; it must be broken down from inside out to be understood. First, the average exercise time of the two persons is calculated in `((exercisePerson1 + exercisePerson2) / 2)` and then `(numPeopleSanFrancisco + numPeopleNewYork)` is calculated. Finally, these two results are multiplied together. So the statement is correct and fulfills our goal but has one problem; it is hard to understand for a programmer reading through the code, and so it is difficult to maintain. Let's try to improve the readability while getting the same result:

```
averageExerciseTime = (exerciseTimePerson1 + exercisePerson2) / 2;
totalPeople = numPeopleSanFrancisco + numPeopleNewYork;
totalExerciseTime = averageExerciseTime * totalPeople;
```

Correct and clearer

By separating the complex statement into three statements and adding the temporary variable `totalPeople` in the second line, the calculation has become easier to understand without altering the final value assigned to `totalExerciseTime`.

Tip

To increase the clarity and the self-documenting ability of source code, avoid deeply nested expressions. Instead, use temporary variables and more statements if necessary.

Temporary variables do take up a bit of computer memory and can slow down the code slightly. In most cases, though, the slowdown is unnoticeable and insignificant. Furthermore, computer memory and speed is increasing daily, whereas computer programmers and their time have become extremely sought after and highly valued as scarce resources. In fact, too scarce to spend time looking at unclear code.

Tip

Clarify your code by using parentheses, even if they are not needed. The following statement might do exactly what you want but when a programmer reads through your code, will he or she remember all the precedence and associativity rules?

```
distance * speed / 4 * time + speed * energy
```

correct but how is this expression interpreted?

By applying a few parentheses, there is no doubt how the expression is calculated:

```
(((distance * speed) / 4) * time) + (speed * energy)
```

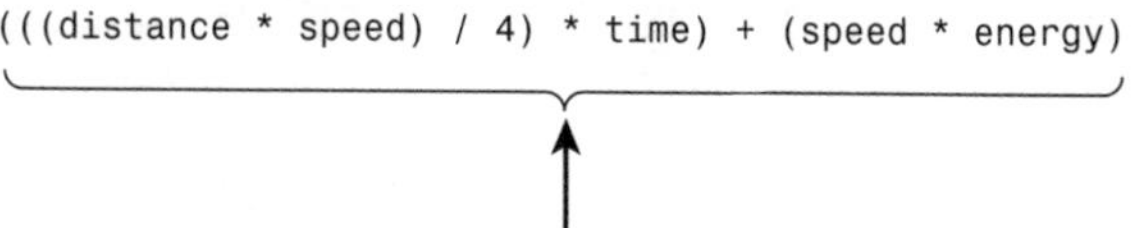

same result as above and no doubt about interpretation

The Modulus Operator (%)

The modulus operator, represented by the percent symbol ((%), is the last unmentioned binary operator of Table 7.1. The *modulus operator* has the same precedence as the division and multiplication operators. It can only be used with integer numbers and returns the remainder of dividing the first (left) operand with the second (right) operand. For example `20 % 7` is 6 because 7 goes into 20 two times, 2 * 7 = 14 and 20 - 14 = 6, which is the remainder. An often-used algebraic notation to denote a modulus calculation is the abbreviation *mod*. Thus, 20 % 7 in mathematics is often written 20 mod 7. Table 7.2 gives an overview of the five binary operators and how typical arithmetic expression are written in C#.

TABLE 7.2 The Binary Operators: Arithmetic and C#

Operation	Symbol	Arithmetic Expression	C# Expression
Addition	+	cost + 100	`cost + 100`
Subtraction	-	20–sum	`20 - sum`
Multiplication	*	price×tax or price tax	`price * tax`
Division	/	p/q or p÷q or $\frac{p}{q}$	`p/q`
Modulus	%	x mod y	`x % y`

The modulus operator is useful for solving many more programmatic problems than its simple appearance seems to indicate. For example, consider a program containing an algorithm that, among other things, is counting numbers (1, 2, 3, 4, 5, 6, 7, and so on) with a variable called `count`. You want to detect every number counted that is divisible by two. To solve this programmatic problem, you merely need to ask if `(count % 2)` is equal to zero, because the numbers 2, 4, 6, and so on have a remainder of 0 when divided by two. This method also applies when finding numbers divisible by 3, 4, 5, and so on.

Another useful application is conversions from one unit to another, such as converting inches to feet and inches or dollars to quarters, dimes, nickels, and pennies.

The following case study shows the modulus operator in action. It is used to find every 7th number in a list of numbers {1, 2, 3, 4, 5, 6, 7, and so on} representing days in a day-counting algorithm.

Case Study:Day Counter Algorithm for Elevator Simulation

Software Specification

The algorithm described here could be part of the internal timekeeper system of an elevator simulation program. It simulates "days" passing by and, consequently, determines which day it is inside the simulation and perhaps whether it is a busy day or a holiday. It also enables the user of the simulation program to determine the total amount of "days" the "elevator system" will run during one particular simulation.

Our algorithm must count the "days" for which the simulated elevator system has been running. Additionally, it is required to report how many "weeks" and "days" for which the simulation has lasted. For example, if the system has run for 23 days, we want the algorithm to report 3 weeks and 2 days.

Finally, the algorithm must provide a signal to the elevator control system whenever the current "day" is a "Sunday." The latter is important because the system goes into a "low-traffic" mode on "Sundays" for efficiency purposes.

Software Design:

We will jump straight to the algorithm design stage of the software design process, because the specification only involves a very small isolated piece of software (the algorithm), rendering the class and method identification stages superfluous.

Algorithm Design of Internal Method:

Which variables should the algorithms contain? The algorithm will certainly have to know the total running time (in days) of the elevator system. We can call this variable `maxSimulationDays` and, because it is holding a whole positive number of days, we choose it to be of the unsigned integer type `uint`. The simulation will further have to keep track of the current number of days the elevator system has been running. This will be represented by the `dayCounter` variable, also of type `uint`.

We then need a loop. Every time the loop is repeated, the `dayCounter` will be incremented by one, the weeks and days will be reported, a Sunday check will be made and an alert reported if it turns out to be Sunday.

The loop will stop when the value of `dayCounter` has reached the value of `maxSimulationDays`.

How do we then convert the amount held by `dayCounter` into weeks and days? The number of weeks is a straightforward division, `(dayCounter / 7)` which, because we are dealing with integers, will return the whole number of times 7 goes into `dayCounter`. We then need to find the few remaining days, yes, this is where the modulus operator comes into the picture. The calculation `(dayCounter % 7)` will do the trick. We now just need a way to detect every Sunday. A Sunday is simply set to be every 7th day counted. But how can the algorithm detect every 7th day passing by? Clearly, the days 7, 14, 21, 28, … are all divisible by 7. Consequently, if `(dayCounter % 7)` is equal to 0, it's Sunday.

Let's look at the resulting algorithm presented with pseudocode in Listing 7.1. It keeps track of the current day, reports of running time in weeks and days, and alerts when the current day is a Sunday.

LISTING 7.1 Pseudocode for "Day Counter Algorithm"

```
Set the variable dayCounter to 0
Set the maxSimulationDays to total days the elevator system should run for
While dayCounter is less than maxSimulationDays repeat the following block
```

LISTING 7.1 continued

```
04: {
05:     Increase dayCounter by one
06:     Calculate and report number of weeks in dayCounter
➥report remaining number of days.
07:     If dayCounter is divisible by 7 send message ("It's Sunday")
➥to the elevator controller and print: "Hey Hey It's Sunday!"
08:     If used as part of larger simulation program then
➥start elevator simulation lasting one day
09: }
10: Let user know that the simulation has ended
```

The algorithm contains a loop (lines 3–9) that repeats lines 5–8 as long as `dayCounter` is less than the `maxSimulationDays`.

It's time to construct the C# code based on the pseudocode. I decided to put the algorithm into the `Main()` method of the program because we are merely testing a freestanding prototype algorithm. Here is an overview of how the lines of the pseudocode correspond to the lines of the C# source code in Listing 7.2, the final source code.

Pseudocode line	Equivalent C# source code line
01	16
02	21–23
03	24
04	25
05	26
06	27–30
07	31–33
08	34
09	37
10	38

LISTING 7.2 Source code for `DayCounter.cs`

```
01: using System;
02:
03: /*
04:  * The DayCounter class contains a prototype for
05:  * a "Day counter" algorithm with potential use
06:  * in an elevator simulation.
07:  * It keeps track of the current day in simulation
08:  * It reports of running time in days and weeks
```

LISTING 7.2 continued

```
 * and alerts when current day is a Sunday
 */

class DayCounter
{
    public static void Main()
    {
        uint dayCounter = 0;
        uint maxSimulationDays;
        uint weeks;
        byte remainderDays;

        Console.Write("Please enter the number of days " +
            "the simulation should run for ");
        maxSimulationDays = Convert.ToUInt32(Console.ReadLine());
        while(dayCounter < maxSimulationDays)
        {
            dayCounter++;
            weeks = dayCounter / 7;
            remainderDays = (byte)(dayCounter % 7);
            Console.WriteLine("Weeks: " + weeks +
                "   Days: " + remainderDays);
            if(remainderDays == 0)
                 // TODO send "it's Sunday" message to controller
                Console.WriteLine("\t\tHey Hey It's Sunday!");
             // TODO start simulation lasting for one day.
             // Let the program pause for 200 milliseconds
            System.Threading.Thread.Sleep(200);
        }
        Console.WriteLine("Simulation ended");
    }
}
```

In the following output, the user specifies the simulated elevator system to run for 15 days.

```
Please enter the number of days the simulation should run for 15<enter>
Weeks: 0   Days: 1
Weeks: 0   Days: 2
Weeks: 0   Days: 3
Weeks: 0   Days: 4
Weeks: 0   Days: 5
Weeks: 0   Days: 6
Weeks: 1   Days: 0
                Hey Hey It's Sunday!
Weeks: 1   Days: 1
Weeks: 1   Days: 2
Weeks: 1   Days: 3
Weeks: 1   Days: 4
Weeks: 1   Days: 5
Weeks: 1   Days: 6
Weeks: 2   Days: 0
                Hey Hey It's Sunday!
Weeks: 2   Days: 1
Simulation ended
```

Lines 24–37 contain a `while` loop. The braces in lines 25 and 37 surround the block of the `while` loop, which is repeatedly executed as long as the condition `(dayCounter < maxSimulationDays)` (meaning `dayCounter` less than `maxSimulationDays`) is `true`. When this condition is evaluated to be `false` in line 24, the program will continue with line 38.

Line 26 increases the value of `dayCounter` by one.

Line 27 calculates the number of whole weeks in `dayCounter`. Because all variables involved in this calculation are of type `uint`, a whole number will be assigned to `weeks`.

Line 28 calculates the remaining days of a week using the modulus operator (%). `RemainderDays` is of type `byte` and the `(dayCounter % 7)` expression is of type `uint`, so an explicit cast is required using the `(byte)` cast operator.

Because `remainderDays` is equal to `(dayCounter % 7)` due to line 28, we need to ask whether `remainderDays` is equal to zero to find out whether today is Sunday. This is done with an `if` statement in line 31.

Programmers often use `TODO` as a reminder for them of things that still remain to be done in a program. `TODO` marked comments in the program can easily be tracked down by the `find` command of the source code editor. Line 32 is simply stating that in case this program was part of a real simulation source program, this is where the `It's Sunday` message would be sent to the elevator controller system of the program.

Note that you could use any arbitrary sequence of letters instead of `TODO`, such as `REMINDME`. However, `TODO` is now so ingrained in the programming community that a sophisticated IDE, such as Visual Studio .NET, recognizes `TODO` comments and also automatically inserts them at relevant places.

Line 33 uses the TAB (`\t`) escape character twice to indent the text "Hey Hey It's Sunday!" which is printed out accordingly.

For now, just think of line 36 as a peculiar way of saying pause the program here for 200 milliseconds. The pause will cause the program to write its output in a slower and, in my opinion, more pleasant manner. Feel free to adjust the number 200 if you want to speed up (by decreasing the number) or slow down the program (by increasing the number).

Note

The previous implementation (like most algorithms) could have been designed in several different ways that rely less on the modulus operator. However, the algorithm presented certainly constitutes a valid efficient algorithm.

Unary Operators

In contrast to binary operators, unary operators are only applied to one operand. The following sections look closer at the unary plus (+), the unary minus (-), the increment (++), and the decrement (--) operators.

Unary Plus and Unary Minus

The unary minus operator shown in the following

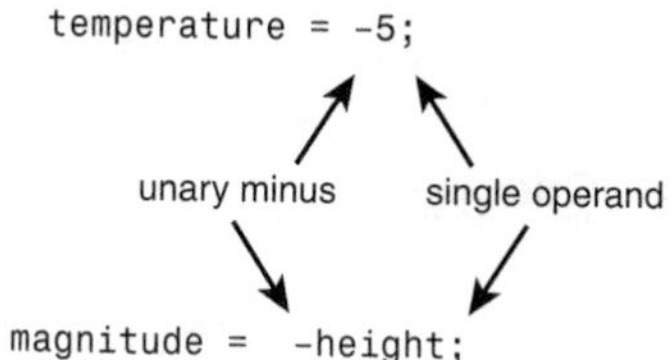
temperature = -5;
unary minus
single operand
magnitude = -height;

is not just a minus sign, as in the literals (like –18) we write on a piece of paper. It is an operator and will change the sign of the numerical expression to which it is applied. Consequently, if the variable `height` has the value 10, `- height` will return the value –10. If the value is –10, the result will be 10.

Note

When the unary minus operator is applied to a variable, it does not change the value held by this variable, it merely changes the value returned from this variable.

Because unary minus is applicable to an operand, and an operand is defined in five different ways (see Syntax Box 7.1), it can be applied to the full range of numerical expressions. The following is a valid expression:

```
- ((distance1 + 400) * (distance2 +100))
```

the unary minus is applicable to any numerical_expression

The unary operators shown in Table 7.1 have a higher precedence than any of the binary operators mentioned previously. An example illustrates why this makes sense:

```
int count = 10;
```

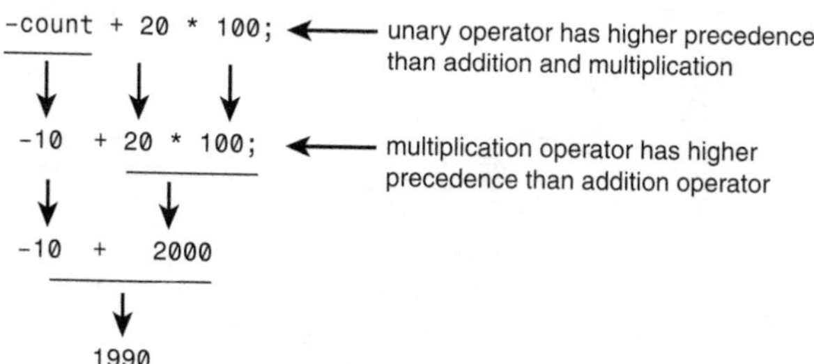
-count + 20 * 100;
unary operator has higher precedence than addition and multiplication
-10 + 20 * 100;
multiplication operator has higher precedence than addition operator
-10 + 2000
1990

`-count` is the first operation to take place that is intuitively how we understand a negation sign to work. If the unary minus operator had a lower precedence than any of the involved binary operators, the result would have been

```
-(10 + 20 * 100) = -2010
```

The unary plus (+) operator has no effect on the operand on which it is applied. For example, `+10` is equal to `10` and `+count` is equal to `count`.

Syntax Box 7.4 Unary Plus and Minus Operators

```
Unary_plus_expression ::=
               + <Numerical_expression>

Unary_minus_expression ::=
               - <Numerical_expression>
```

Increment and Decrement Operators

You have already learned about the increment operator (++) in Chapter 6, "Types Part I: The Simple Types." As you saw, it is a convenient operator when you want to increment a variable by one. If you declare a variable `count` as

```
int count = 10;
```

you can either add one to `count` by writing

```
count = count + 1;
```

resulting in count being equal to 11, or you can use the increment operator (++)

```
++count;
```

Note

The ++ symbol of the example presented here is positioned in front of, not after, the variable, as in previous examples. Both configurations increment the variable. However, they hold subtle differences discussed later. This is also true for the decrement operator (--) operator.

Similarly, you can deduct one from the value of `count` by applying the decrement operator (--):

```
--count;
```

Note

The increment and decrement operators are not an essential part of the C# language. Any construct written in C# with these operators can be rewritten without them to perform exactly the same tasks. In fact, many languages do not include these operators as part of their operator repertoire.

They are inherited from C#'s predecessors C and C++ (this explains the ++ in C++). You will constantly bump into them because they are commonly used in the programming community.

The increment/decrement operator can be part of a longer arithmetic expressions.

The operation performed by the operator can then be divided into two sub-operations:

- Increase the value of the variable it is applied to by one.
- Return the value of the variable to which it is applied.

Line 12 of Listing 7.3 uses the increment operator as part of a longer expression.

LISTING 7.3 Source Code for `Library.cs`

```
01: using System;
02:
03: class Library
04: {
05:     public static void Main()
06:     {
07:         int numProgrammingBooks = 2;
08:         int numStatisticsBooks = 1;
09:         int numActionBooks = 504;
10:         int totalBooks;
11:
12:         totalBooks = ++numActionBooks + numProgrammingBooks +
13:             numStatisticsBooks;
14:         Console.WriteLine("Number of action books: " +
15:             numActionBooks);
16:         Console.WriteLine("Total number of books: " +
17:             totalBooks);
18:     }
19: }
```

```
Number of actions books: 505
Total number of books: 508
```

Line 12 is an assignment statement. The increment operator is applied to the variable `numActionBooks`. When this statement is executed, the following actions will take place in the order they are displayed.

1. `numActionBooks` is incremented by one.
2. The new value of `numActionBooks` is returned and used in the rest of the expression to be added to `numProgrammingBooks` and `numStatisticsBooks`.
3. The sum of the three variables is assigned to `totalBooks`.

The decrement operator works in exactly the same manner in an expression with the obvious difference of decrementing by one instead of incrementing by one.

Note

Increment/decrement operators can only be applied to variables because the increment/decrement operators change the underlying value of a variable. Consequently,

```
++count
```

has the same effect as

```
count = count + 1;
```

An assignment takes place when an increment/decrement operator is applied. It only makes sense to assign a value to a variable. For example, the following constitutes an illogical statement:

```
20 = 20 + 1; ←—— Invalid. Impossible to assign a value to a literal.
```

which makes us realize that

```
++20;
```

is also unsound.

When the operator is positioned in front of the variable, it is called *prefix form*. When it is appended behind the variable, it is called *postfix form*. The difference between the two forms lies in the sequence of the two sub-operations performed by the operator.

Note

The sequence of steps performed by the prefix form of the increment/decrement operators is reversed when in the postfix form.

Prefix form: (++count)

1. Increase the value of the variable it is applied to by one.
2. Return the value of the variable to which it is applied.

Postfix form: (count++)

1. Return the value of the variable to which it is applied.
2. Increase the value of the variable it is applied to by one.

You can see the difference between the two forms by changing line 12 of Listing 7.3 to

++ has been changed from suffix to postfix

```
12:    totalBooks =  numActionBooks++ + numProgrammingBooks +
13:      numStatisticsBooks;
```

which results in the following output:

```
Number of actions books: 505 ←—— Unchanged
Total number of books: 507 ←——— Changed from 508 to now 507
```

The total number of books is not 508, as in the previous output, but 507, because the value of `numActionBooks` was not incremented until *after* its value had been used in the expression to calculate the total number of books.

Note

According to Table 7.1, the precedence of the postfix increment/decrement operators is 1, whereas their prefix counterparts only have a precedence of 2. What is the significance of this difference? Consider the following extract from a previous line, but with all the whitespace removed:

```
                                      (numActionBooks++) + numProgrammingBooks  (1)
numActionBooks+++numProgrammingBooks
                                                              which version?
                                      NumActionBooks + (++numProgrammingBooks) (2)
```

How does the compiler evaluate this statement? It can either apply the postfix increment operator to `numActionBooks` (marked 1) or apply the prefix increment operator to `numProgrammingBooks` (marked 2). This is where the difference in precedence comes to the rescue; it removes the apparent ambiguity of the expression. Because of the higher precedence of the postfix increment, version 1 can be chosen without hesitation:

```
(numActionBooks++) + numProgrammingBooks
```

Precedence, in this context, is used to determine which variable the operator acts on and not when the increment/decrement operation takes place. We can still rely on the postfix increment/decrement operators to perform their increment/decrement operations after the other operations of the expression have taken place.

Tip

Overuse of the increment/decrement operators as part of longer arithmetic expressions can severely obscure the readability of the source code. In fact, many professional programmers never use them in this way.

Their ability to be part of expressions is presented in this section so you can understand other programmer's source code.

Thus, instead of writing:

```
12:        totalBooks = ++numActionBooks + numProgrammingBooks +
13:            numStatisticsBooks;
```

as in Listing 7.3, it would be clearer first to make the increment of `numActionBooks` in a separate statement, and then let `numActionBooks` be part of calculating the total number of books:

```
11:     ++numActionBooks;
12:         totalBooks = numActionBooks + numProgrammingBooks +
13:             numStatisticsBooks;
```

When a statement only consists of a variable and an increment/decrement operator, such as in line 11, the prefix and the postfix version generate exactly the same results. Only when the variable appears as part of a longer expression do we see a difference between the two versions.

Increment and decrement operators are frequently used to increase or decrease the loop counters of a loop, as we shall see in the next chapter.

Syntax Box 7.5 The Increment and Decrement Operators

```
Prefix_increment_expression ::=
                 ++ <Variable_Identifier>

Prefix_decrement_expression ::=
                 --<Variable_Identifier>

Postfix_increment_expression ::=
                   <Variable_identifier>++

Postfix_decrement_expression ::=
                   <Variable_identifier>--
```

Determining the Type of an Expression

Several examples were presented in the previous chapter of how the many simple types found in C# impose a complicated life for the compiler. We saw how the C# compiler attempts to handle the often tricky situations of assignment statements by performing implicit conversions, and how the programmer can interfere by using explicit conversions in the form of type casts.

In this section, we will look at how operators affect the type of the value returned from a numerical expression. This will enable you to determine the type of expressions, such as

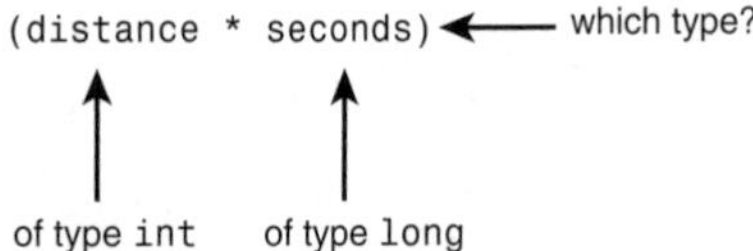

which mixes together two types. Because any expression only has one value with one type, a choice must be made.

The rules used to determine the type of an expression based on its elements and its relevant context are called *type inference rules.*

For the uninitiated, even the simple unary minus operator can produce values with unexpected types, just as in the following expression where `height` is of type `byte`.

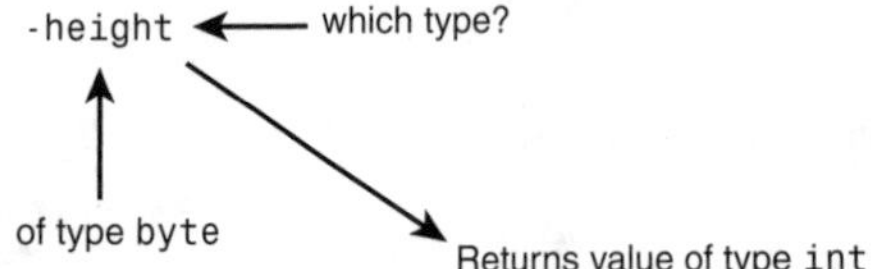

Surprisingly, the value returned from `-height` is of type `int`.

Automatic conversions are often performed in numerical expressions written in C#. A lack of understanding of these conversions and their accompanying results will often leave you mystified and can cause you to waste time on seemingly unfixable errors—errors that could have been removed with simple remedies.

Note

Automatic type conversions are performed by the C# compiler when

- A value of one type is assigned to a variable of another type and an implicit conversion path exists between the involved types.
- Arguments are passed to a method during a method call, and an implicit conversion path exists between the arguments and the formal parameters.
- Certain operators are acting on values of certain types.
- Various types are mixed together in one expression.

We have already dealt with the first two points in Chapter 6 and will discuss the last two aspects in the following section.

We will first look at the very simple expressions formed when applying one of the unary plus or minus operators on an operand.

Conversions and the Unary Plus/Minus Operators

Internally, C# only supports the use of the unary plus and minus operators on numbers of the `int`, `uint`, `long`, `ulong`, `float`, `double`, and `decimal` types; leaving out `byte`, `sbyte`, `short`, and `ushort`.

You can still use the unary operators on those latter integer types. However, in these cases, it forces C# to convert to the nearest type it can deal with, which is `int`. Thus, whenever you apply either the unary plus or the unary minus operator to a value of type `byte`, `sbyte`, `short`, or `ushort`, the operation will return a value of type `int`.

For example, the following code snippet:

```
short height = 40;
short negativeHeight;

negativeHeight = -height; <—— causes compiler error
     ↑              ↑
type short       type int
```

will cause the C# compiler to report the following error:

```
Cannot implicitly convert type 'int' to 'short'.
```

To prevent this error, you will need a cast explicitly converting `-height` to type `short` as in the following:

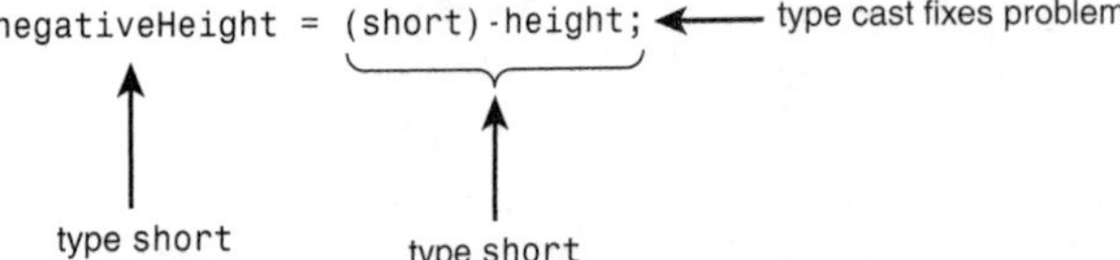

When a conversion is made from one type to another type with a broader range and/or higher precision, it is termed a *numeric promotion*.

A value of type `short` converted to a value of type `int` is an example of a numeric promotion.

Unary Numeric Promotions

Whenever the unary plus (+) or the unary minus operator (-) are applied to an operand of type `sbyte`, `byte`, `short`, `ushort`, or `char`, the numerical expression will have the type `int`.

If the unary minus operator is applied to an operand of type `uint`, the expression will be of type `long`.

Combining Different Types in One Expression

Recall that even the most complicated expressions involving binary operators can be divided into sub-expressions, each consisting of two operands and an operator; and remember how operator precedence and associativity rules determine to which operand each operator is applied. Along with the values passed through the various levels of this sub-expression hierarchy are also the types of these values, as illustrated in Figure 7.3.

FIGURE 7.3
Types from sub-expressions transferred through expression hierarchy.

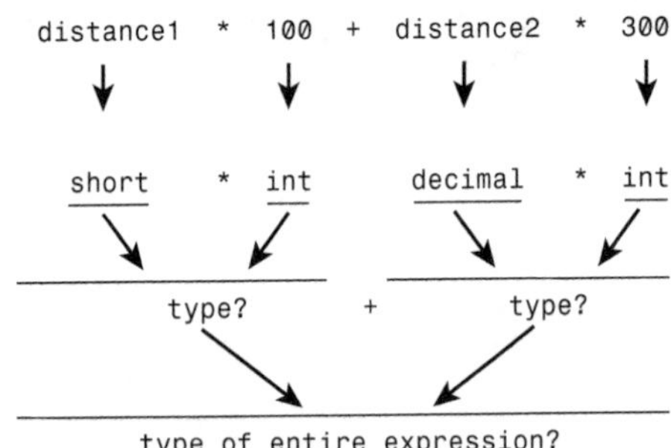

Note: The variable `distance1` is here of type short and `distance2` is of type `decimal`, whereas `100` and `300` are both of type `int`.

Consequently, if we can somehow determine the type of any expression involving just two operands and one binary operator, we can also determine the type of any expression, irrespective of its number of operators and operands. This allows us to simplify our discussion considerably. We now only need to ask how does the C# compiler determine the type of an expression consisting of two operands of any primitive type and one of the following binary operators +, -, *, / and %? Let's attempt to get an answer for this important question.

To determine the type of a two-operand-one-operator expression, the C# compiler will go through a neatly designed algorithm, presented in Figure 7.4 using a flowchart.

The Flowchart

A *flowchart* is a graphical diagram sometimes used by programmers to illustrate an algorithm. Instead of merely relying on text like pseudocode, a flowchart contains symbols to express how the algorithm is executed.

Flowcharts can contain numerous specialized symbols, but the four basic symbols presented in Figure 7.4 let you illustrate most algorithms.

FIGURE 7.4
The four basic flowchart symbols.

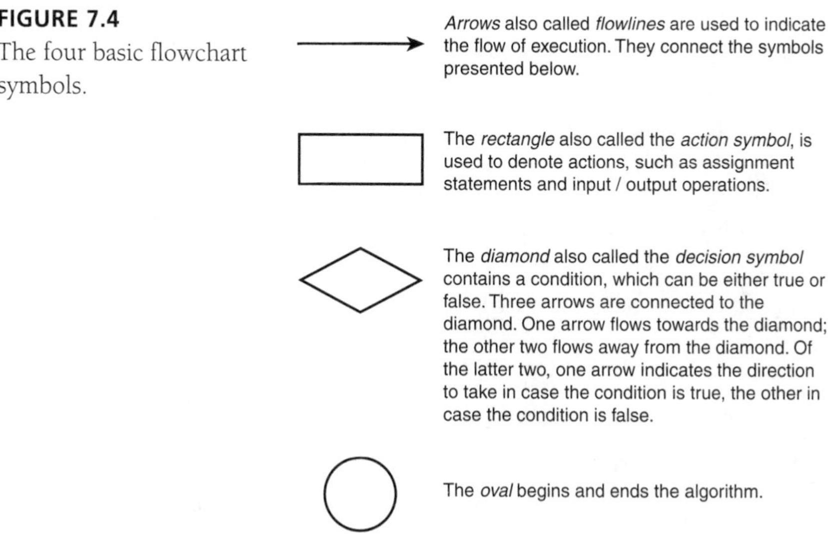

Arrows also called *flowlines* are used to indicate the flow of execution. They connect the symbols presented below.
The *rectangle* also called the *action symbol*, is used to denote actions, such as assignment statements and input / output operations.
The *diamond* also called the *decision symbol* contains a condition, which can be either true or false. Three arrows are connected to the diamond. One arrow flows towards the diamond; the other two flows away from the diamond. Of the latter two, one arrow indicates the direction to take in case the condition is true, the other in case the condition is false.
The *oval* begins and ends the algorithm.

Figure 7.5 provides a simple example of a flowchart. You start at the oval marked Begin and arrive at a decision symbol containing the condition "The person is a male." If this condition is `true`, Man will be printed; if the condition is `false`, Woman will be printed.

If you can trace this flowchart, you can also trace much larger flowcharts; simply move through them symbol-by-symbol and arrow-by-arrow.

FIGURE 7.5
Man or woman?

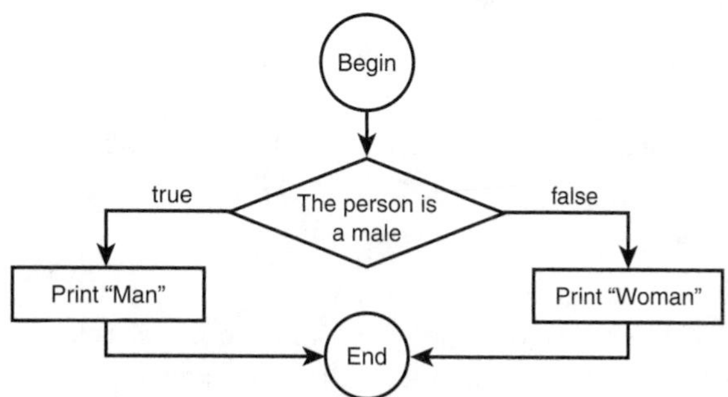

The type-determination algorithm in Figure 7.6 needs to know the types of the two operands involved, and depending on this specific combination of types, it will report the chosen type for the expression or report an error because two incompatible types were used.

To demonstrate how to use the flowchart in Figure 7.6, let's trace it with a couple of examples.

The first example contains an expression with the operand types `short` and `double`. We begin at the oval marked Begin and follow the arrow to the diamond, containing the condition "One of the operands is of type `decimal`." Because none of our types are of type `decimal`, this condition is `false`, so we follow the arrow marked false. We arrive at a new diamond with the condition "One of the operands is of type `double`." This is `true`, so we move along the arrow marked true and find ourselves in an action symbol with the text "Set the (sub) expression to be of type `double`." Lastly, we follow the arrow out and down to the oval marked End. The conclusion: An expression with operands of type `short` and `double` has a value of type `double`.

Now it's your turn. Try the following combinations of types:

- `decimal` and `short`
- `double` and `decimal`
- `short` and `ulong`
- `byte` and `short`

Let's have a look at the answers (the last three perhaps are surprising).

- `decimal` and `short` results in an expression of type `decimal`.
- `double` and `decimal` causes the compiler to report the following error:

  `"Operator cannot be applied to operands of type decimal and double".`

  This is caused by the inability of the compiler to implicitly convert a type `double` to a type `decimal` and a type `decimal` to a type `double`. Thus, if `distance` is of type `decimal` and `speed` is of type `double`, the following expression is invalid:

  ```
  (distance / speed)        Invalid
  ```

  Fortunately, there is a simple remedy for this problem—type cast `speed` to be of type `decimal`, resulting in the following line:

  ```
  (distance / (decimal)speed)        Valid
  ```

- `short` and `ulong` triggers an error with the following comment:

  ```
  "Operator is ambiguous on operand of type ulong combined with operand
  ➥of type sbyte, short, int or long" .
  ```

  Thus, the type `ulong` does not get along with any of the signed integer types (`sbyte`, `short`, `int`, and `long`) in the same expression. This is because none of the integer types can simultaneously accommodate the vast range of positive values found in `ulong` and the negative values of the signed integer types.

- `byte` and `short` results in an expression of type `int`, just like any expression with a combination of the integer types `sbyte`, `byte`, `short`, and `ushort`. This is similar to the unary plus and minus operators returning the type `int` when applied to operands of type `sbyte`, `byte`, `short`, and `ushort`.

Note

The algorithm depicted in Figure 7.6 does not attempt to illustrate how the actual algorithm inside the C# compiler is implemented. Figure 7.6 is only meant as an aid for us to determine the type of an expression.

FIGURE 7.6
Finding the type of two operands and a binary operator.

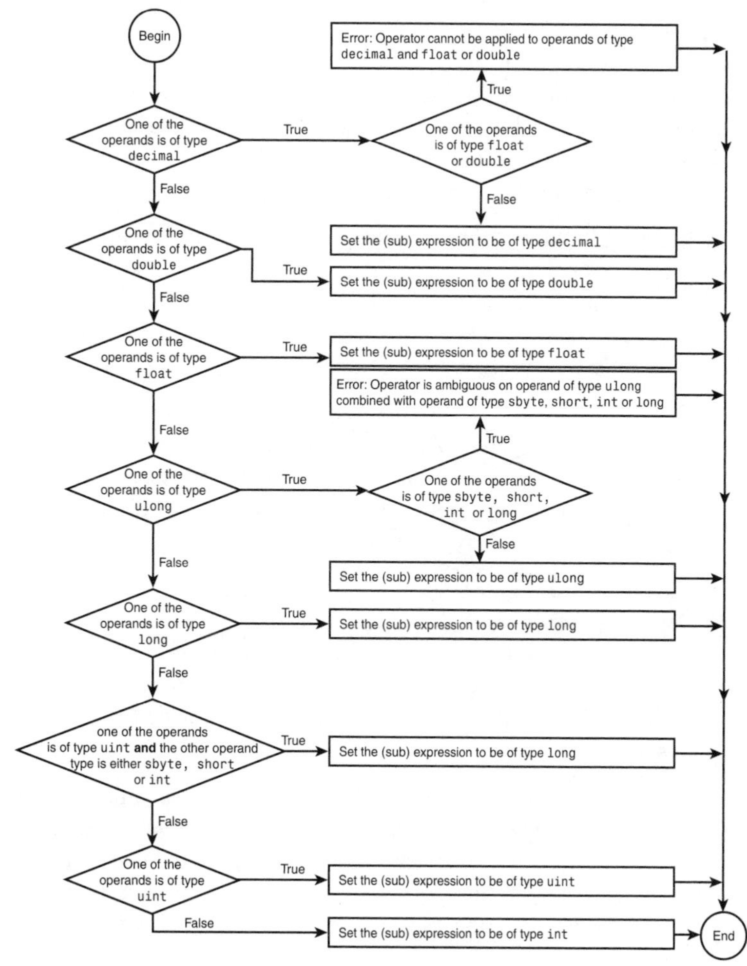

Note

Notice that no matter which of the five operators appear in the expression, the chosen type will remain unchanged.

The next section provides an overview of why metadata is a groundbreaking concept and gives you a peek at how it is accessed. In particular, you will see how we can check the answers found in the flowchart of Figure 7.6 with a relatively simple program.

Accessing the Metadata of a Component: A Brief Introduction

We form expressions by combining many different kinds of operands (constants, instance variables, method calls, and so on) from different origins. Sometimes, an operand belongs to the current object; sometimes it is fetched from another object. Irrespective of its origin, each operand's type must be carefully checked to ensure that the final expression returns a meaningful result. Finding the type of an operand has been easy in our examples. With all classes written in a small confined world of familiar C# source code, we have simply found it by looking at the method header or the variable declaration in the relevant class definition. We have then deciphered the meaning of recognizable type keywords, like `int` and `double`, and thereby revealed the attributes (range and so on) of the operand in question.

But what if our source code became a component traveling in the outside diverse world, for use in contexts where `int` and `double` are meaningless words, but where the ability to determine the attributes of a type still are important? Perhaps our component would provide data to a database or exchange data with other components written in other computer languages with different syntax and different configuration, or perhaps even be part of a Web service sent across the Internet.

If our component could describe its types in a flexible, user-friendly manner and thereby avoid the need for other contexts to decipher its internal rigid hard-coded standards, it would be able to seamlessly integrate with many different environments. C#'s built-in support for metadata allows for this separation of implementation and contextual details.

Chapter 1, "Computers and Computer Programming: Basic Concepts" and Chapter 2, "Your First C# Program" introduced the metadata concept and discussed the compiler's ability to automatically emit metadata relevant to an assembly (program). Metadata contains detailed descriptions of the methods, instance variables, and many other important characteristics of each type in a program. One of the attributes provided is simply the name of the type, such as `System.Int32` or `System.Decimal`.

The process of accessing metadata during runtime is called *reflection*. It is not the aim here to provide a thorough discussion of this advanced subject. Instead, we will merely provide an example of how reflection can be used to expose the name of a type. Not only does this allow us to check our findings in Figure 7.6 of the previous section, it also gives you a glimpse of what metadata is from a practical perspective and how it can be accessed.

Our goal here is to determine the type of a few expressions in an actual program through reflection.

Recall the `ToString` method discussed in Chapter 6. The `ToString` method is just one of several useful methods belonging to each of the simple types. If you browse through the fields of the simple types in the .NET Framework Reference, you will find another valuable method called **GetType**.

When we call the **GetType** method for an expression, it returns an object of class **Type** that gives us access to all the metadata kept about the type of this expression.

Note

The **GetType** method is available for any value of C#, whether this value is of a predefined simple type, a value type, or an object of a reference type. Even your own custom-made classes are equipped with this (and several other) methods for free by C#. When I present an important OOP concept called inheritance later, you will see how this is made possible.

The **Type** class is part of the .NET Framework class library and is located in the **System** namespace. An object of class **Type** is packed with methods and properties, such as the few mentioned in Table 7.3, that are ready to answer questions posed about the metadata of a particular type.

TABLE 7.3 Three Examples of Information Accessible via an Object of Class ***Type***

Property	Brief Explanation
FullName	Returns the fully qualified name of the type, including the namespace
IsPrimitive	Returns **true** if the type is a simple type; otherwise, **false**
IsClass	Returns **true** if the type is a class; otherwise, **false**

Note

FullName, **IsPrimitive**, and **IsClass** are not methods. They are properties. A property is an important C# construct not yet discussed. It allows you to access instance variables of an object from outside the object without violating the rules of encapsulation discussed previously. A detailed discussion of properties will be provided in Chapter 14, "Class Anatomy Part III: Writing Intuitive Code." Properties are in many ways similar to methods, so, for now, you can merely regard the three properties of Table 7.3 as being methods. The only difference you need to be aware of is that properties, when called, do not require parentheses after their name as the methods do.

Property names should, according to Microsoft's style guidelines, be written with Pascal casing.

Listing 7.4 illustrates how we can utilize the three properties shown in Table 7.3 to access information about simple types.

LISTING 7.4 Source Code for **MetadataAccessor.cs**

```
using System;
/*
```

LISTING 7.4 continued

```
03:  * This class demonstrates how the metadata of
04:  * a given type can be accessed.
05:  */
06: class MetadataAccessor
07: {
08:     public static void Main()
09:     {
10:         Type anyType;
11:         byte age = (byte)37;
12:         short energy = (short)4000;
13:         ushort height = (ushort)190;
14:         decimal mass = 398.98765m;
15:
16:         anyType = age.GetType();
17:         Console.WriteLine("The type of the age variable is: "
18:             + anyType.FullName);
19:         if(anyType.IsPrimitive)
20:             Console.WriteLine("The age variable is a simple type");
21:         if(anyType.IsClass  == false)
22:         Console.WriteLine("The age variable is not a class type");
23:         anyType = 100.GetType();
24:         Console.WriteLine("The type of the literal 100 is: " +
25:             anyType.FullName);
26:         anyType = 200.45.GetType();
27:         Console.WriteLine("The type of the literal 200.45 is: " +
28:             anyType.FullName);
29:         anyType = (age * mass).GetType();
30:         Console.WriteLine("The type of expression (age * mass) is: " +
31:             anyType.FullName);
32:         anyType = (age + height).GetType();
33:         Console.WriteLine("The type of the expression " +
34:             "(age + height) is: " + anyType.FullName);
35:         anyType = ((age * mass) * (energy + height)).GetType();
36:         Console.WriteLine("The type of the expression " +
37:             "((age * mass) * (energy + height)) is: " +
38:             anyType.FullName);
39:     }
40: }
```

```
The type of the age variable is: System.Byte
The age variable is a simple type
The age variable is not a class type
The type of the literal 100 is: System.Int32
The type of the literal 200.45 is: System.Double
The type of expression (age * mass) is: System.Decimal
The type of the expression (age + height) is: System.Int32
The type of the expression ((age * mass) * (energy + height)) is: System.Decimal
```

Line 10 declares `anyType` to hold a reference to an object of class `Type`. The `anyType` variable will reference the object from which we will receive information about the metadata of a particular type.

Line 16 calls the GetType() method of the age variable by using the dot operator. GetType() returns an object of class Type holding the metadata about age's type—in this case, byte. The Type object is assigned to the anyType variable. anyType is now ready to provide information about the metadata of the byte type.

Lines 17 and 18 call the FullName property of anyType, which is returned and printed on the console. As expected (see the previous output), the type is System.Byte.

Lines 19 and 20 represent an if statement. The IsPrimitive property (see Table 7.3) is utilized to detect whether byte is a simple (primitive) type. If this is the case, anyType.IsPrimitive will be true, causing the program to print "The age variable is a simple type". As expected, this is what we see in the output.

Lines 21 and 22 utilize the bool value false in the condition of the if statement. If anyType.IsClass returns the bool value false, the condition (anyType.IsClass == false) will be true and the string "The age variable is not a class type" is printed on the console. byte is a value type (a struct) not a class, so anyType.IsClass is false and (anyType.IsClass == false) is true, causing the text to be printed as shown in the previous output.

Line 23 accesses GetType() directly from the literal 100 and assigns the returned object to anyType.

Lines 24 and 25 confirm, through their output, that the type of 100 is System.Int32.

Lines 29–31 demonstrate our ability to access the Type object of the value returned from an expression combining two variables with an operator. In this case, we are confirming that the type of a value returned from an expression combining values of type byte and type decimal is, indeed, of type decimal (System.Decimal).

Line 34 shows that a longer expression can be investigated by the GetType() method. In fact, any expression of any complexity can be scrutinized in this fashion.

Listing 7.4 uses a somewhat longwinded way of accessing the metadata of a value to emphasize the process involved.

Instead of writing

```
10:         Type anyType;
    ...
16:         anyType = age.GetType();
17:         Console.WriteLine("The type of the age variable is: "
18:             + anyType.FullName);
```

which highlights the idea of a Type object being returned and assigned to anyType, ready to be "questioned," we could discard lines 10 and 16 and simply write

```
17:         Console.WriteLine("The type of the age variable is: "
18:             + age.GetType().FullName);
```

After age.GetType() has returned the Type object, we can regard age.GetType() as being the Type object. Consequently, it is possible to write age.GetType().FullName as in line 18.

Allowing Different Languages to Collaborate

The `FullName` property will always return the name of a type in the long .NET form (`System.Int32`), not the short C# form (`int`). This is because all programming languages that work on top of .NET can call `GetType`, `Type`, and `FullName`. Just as `int` is merely an alias for `System.Int32`, other languages would use other aliases to refer to this same type. For example, the Eiffel# language uses `INTEGER` as an alias for `System.Int32`.

Each language that works on top of the .NET platform uses the same simple types provided by the Common Type System of the .NET platform. So, whether we reflect on a component written in Eiffel, Visual Basic, Perl, or any other .NET language, we will only get names and other attributes of types with which we are familiar. This is a very unifying and powerful concept that makes it possible for components and programmers with different language backgrounds to work together on the same projects and on a detailed level.

Enumerated Constants

Recall the discussion from the previous chapter about constants and the advantages of representing a single constant number like 3.1415... with the name Pi. Sometimes, we need to represent a finite set of related constants all known prior to the compilation of the program. Examples could be the days of the week {Monday, Tuesday, Wednesday, Thursday, Friday, Saturday, Sunday} or the months of the year {January, February, March, and so on}. Enumerators are useful for creating symbolic constants representing those values.

For example, if you want to represent the five colors just mentioned, you can declare `Color` to be an enumeration with the five colors Green, Blue, Red, Yellow and Purple. In C#, you express this with the following declaration statement:

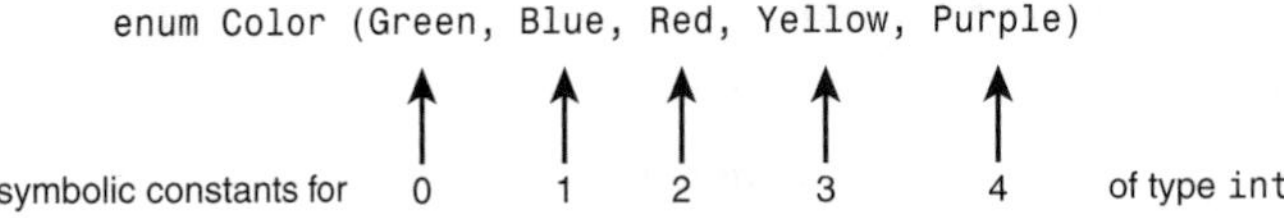

The `enum` keyword here specifies the following:

- `Color` is the name of a new custom-made type. It is called an *enumeration*, just like the `Elevator` from our elevator simulation is a custom-made type called a class.
- By using the dot . operator, `Color.Green` is a symbolic constant for the `int` value 0, `Color.Blue` is a symbolic constant for the `int` value 1, `Color.Red` is a symbolic constant for the `int` value 2.... These symbolic constants are called enumerators or members of the enumeration.

`int` values counting from 0 and up by increments of 1 (0, 1, 2, and so on) are assigned to the enumeration members by default. It is possible to override these defaults by explicitly specifying the underlying type for all values represented by the enumeration, and by stating the value of each member. Members without an explicitly stated value will be assigned default values by counting up from the previous value in increments of 1. For example, by writing

```
enum Color : byte {Green = 10, Blue, Red = 20, Yellow, Purple}
```

`Color.Green` is set to represent the value 10, `Color.Blue` the value 11, `Color.Red` the value 20, `Color.Yellow` the value 21, and `Color.Purple` the value 22; all values being of type `byte`.

An *enumerated type* specifies a finite set of named numeric constants that are known at compile time.

Syntax Box 7.6 The Enumeration Declaration

```
Enumeration_Declaration::=
        [<Access_modifier>] enum <Enum_Name> [: <Integer_Type>]
        ➥ {<Enum_Member_Name1> [= <Integer_Value1>]
        ➥ [,<Enum_Member_Name2> [= <Integer_ Value2>] ]... }
```

where:

```
Access_modifier
                ::= public
                ::= private
                ::= protected
                ::= internal
                ::= protected internal
```

Notes:

- `<Integer_Type>` can be any of the integer types (`byte`, `sbyte`, `short`, `ushort`, `int`, `uint`, `long`, and `ulong`).
- The keyword `enum` is an alias for `System.Enum`.
- Only the access modifiers `public` and `private` have been discussed so far. You can ignore the other three for the moment.

Having specified the enumeration, it is possible to declare a variable of that type. For example

```
Color wall;
```

declares `wall` to be of type `Color`. `wall` can now hold any of the five enumerators `Color.Green`, `Color.Blue`, and so on. Consequently, it is possible to perform the following assignment:

```
wall = Color.Red;
```

Notice that only the five enumerator values can validly be assigned to `wall`. As a result, even though `Color.Red` has the value 20 in this example, it is not possible to assign 20 to `wall`, as attempted in the following:

```
wall = 20; <—— Error. Cannot implicitly convert type int to type Color.
```

This will trigger a compiler error.

Improve the Readability with Enumerated Types

Languages that do not have the enumerator feature often rely on error-prone and unclear schemes for representing groups of constants. For instance, to represent the five colors mentioned in our example, an often used procedure is to say, "1 stands for green, 2 stands for red, 3 stands for blue, and so on." In this case, a check for whether the color of `wall` is green by using an `if` statement would require you to write the following:

```
if (wall == 1) <—— unclear that 1 signifies green
```

instead of

```
if (wall == Color.Green) <—— clear and self-documenting
```

The latter is much clearer and can intuitively be understood without any accompanying comments.

In conclusion, to improve the clarity and self-documenting abilities of your source code, use enumerations when you know all the possible values of a variable before the program is compiled.

Listing 7.5 provides an example of an enumerator representing the days of the week. The program simply moves through the days of the week. Whenever the current day is a Thursday or a Sunday, the program announces that fact.

LISTING 7.5 Source Code for `EnumDayCounter.cs`

```
using System;

enum Day {Monday, Tuesday, Wednesday,
    Thursday, Friday, Saturday, Sunday}

public class SimpleDayCounter
{
    public static void Main()
    {
        Day currentDay = Day.Monday;
        int counter = 1;
        while (counter < 8)
        {
            Console.WriteLine(counter);
            if(currentDay == Day.Thursday)
                Console.WriteLine("\tIt's Thursday");
            if(currentDay == Day.Sunday)
                Console.WriteLine("\tIt's Sunday");
            counter++;
            currentDay++;
        }
    }
}
```

```
1
2
3
4
```

```
    It's Thursday
5
6
7
    It's Sunday
```

Lines 3 and 4 define the enumerated type `Day` to have seven members, ranging from `Day.Monday` representing 0 to `Day.Sunday` representing 6.

The `Main()` method of the class `SimpleDayCounter` contains a `while` loop. It will repeat itself seven times because of

- Line 11, where `counter` is set to 1
- Line 12, where the loop only is repeated if the condition `(counter < 8)` is `true`
- Line 19, which increments `counter` by 1 every time the loop is repeated

Line 10 declares `currentDay` to be of type `Day` and assigns it the enumerator value `Day.Monday`.

Line 15 checks whether `currentDay` is equal to `Day.Thursday`. If this is the case, `"It's Thursday"` is printed onscreen by line 16. Similarly, if `currentDay` is equal to `Day.Sunday`, line 18 prints `"It's Sunday"` onscreen.

Line 20 illustrates our ability to use the increment operator `++` to increment the value of `currentDay` by 1. If `currentDay` prior to applying the `++` operator is holding the value `Day.Monday` that is equal to 0, `currentDay` will have the value 1 after applying the `++` operator. Because 1 is represented by `Day.Tuesday`, `currentDay` will now hold this enumerator.

Note

The increment operator does not look for the next enumerator in the list, but merely increments the integer value by 1 of the variable (in this case, `currentDay`) of which it is applied. The increment operator `++` is only suitable in Listing 7.5 because the enumerators (days) represent a sequence of numbers, all with increments of 1.

Enumerated Types Make It Easier to Modify Your Source Code

Not only does the dubious scheme mentioned in the previous Tip box (0 stands for Monday; 1 stands for Tuesday, and so on.) produce unclear code, it also generates source code that is difficult to modify.

For example, there happens to be 8 days in a week on planet Blipos. The additional day is between Tuesday and Wednesday called Cosday, so their week looks like {Monday, Tuesday, Cosday, Wednesday, Thursday, Friday, Saturday, Sunday}. Imagine if we wanted to convert our day counting program to be useful on planet Blipos. Had we not used enumerators in Listing 7.5 but, instead, followed the dubious scheme (0 is for Monday, and so on) mentioned earlier, we would be forced to change all the 2s representing Wednesdays to 3s, all the 3s representing Thursdays to 4s, and so on to let 2 represent Cosday. Alternately, we could have let 7 represent Cosday to avoid all the changes, but this would lead to a very confusing program. Most programmers would expect Cosday to be represented by number 2.

On the other hand, if we had to make a similar modification to our enumerator-based source code of Listing 7.5, we would need to make only one single modification in the definition of `Day`, as follows:

```
enum Day {Monday, Tuesday, Cosday, Wednesday,
    Thursday, Friday, Saturday, Sunday}
```

Enumerator Operators

Listing 7.5 showed how to apply the operators assignment (=), equals (==), and increment (++) to enumerators. Numerous other operators can be used with enumerators; they are listed in Table 7.4.

TABLE 7.4 Operators Applicable to Enumerators

Binary	`+, -`
Unary	`++, --, ~`
Comparison operators	`==, !=, <, >, <=, >=`
Logical	`&, |, ^`
Assignment	`=, +=, -=`
Primary	`sizeof`

You have not met all of the symbols displayed in Table 7.4. The operators relevant to enumerators are included here for completeness and overview; they will be discussed in relation to enumerators in due time.

The binary operators + and - cannot be applied to two enumerator types. Instead, they are meant to combine one enumerator operand with one integer value operand, such as the following:

```
currentDay = currentDay + 1;
```

This statement is equivalent to

```
currentDay++;
```

The binary operators (+) and (-) do not look for the next enumerator in the list (just like the increment and decrement operators). They only add or subtract the integer value from the value the enumerator represents.

Conversions

Only explicit conversions are possible for converting to (from) any `integer` type (not `char`, though) from (to) an `enum` type by using the cast operator `(<Type>)`. However, the number 0 (zero) is an exception. It can be implicitly converted to an enumerator type; the reason is displayed in the Tip box.

It is also possible to explicitly convert one enumerator type to another enumerator type.

Tip

The only numeric value that can be implicitly converted to an enumerator type is 0.

To reset or initialize an enumeration variable is the equivalent of assigning it the first member of the enumeration. If the first member of any enumeration is always set to have the value 0, it's possible to utilize the value 0 when initializing an enumeration. For example to initialize `currentDay`, we can simply write

```
currentDay = 0;
```

Therefore, always define one of the members of the enumeration to represent the value 0.

The Methods of `System.Enum`

The `enum` keyword is an alias for `System.Enum` located in the .NET Framework class library. `System.Enum` provides numerous valuable methods relevant for enumerations. You can study them by looking at the .NET Framework Documentation. It is beyond the scope of this book to provide a discussion of these, but the incomplete list of functionality that follows should give you an idea of `System.Enums` usefulness. You can

- Convert strings to enumerated values.
- Convert enumerated values into readable text.
- Determine whether a particular value is one of the defined values of an enumeration.
- Check the underlying type of the enumeration.
- Determine the symbolic name of an enumeration member representing a particular value.

To fully understand how the `enum` methods are applied, you will need a more detailed understanding of C# and OOP presented over the next few chapters.

Characters and Text

The `string` type constitutes an example of a *derived type*. By using individual characters of the *simple type* `char` as building blocks, the programmer can represent text by putting together a string of characters. Due to `char` type's imperative nature in relation to `string`, this type will be presented here, prior to the `string` type discussion.

The `char` Type

The `char` type (see Table 6.2 of Chapter 6) is used to represent Unicode characters, each taking up 16 bits of memory. Unicode is an international, standardized character set enabling computers to represent the characters found in most human languages. For more information about Unicode, see Appendix E, "Unicode Character Set."

A `char` literal can be

- A standard letter represented with single quotes, such as the lowercase `'a'` or the uppercase `'E'`.

  You could accordingly assign the character `'T'` to a variable, as shown in the following:

  ```
  char myChar;
  myChar = 'T';
  ```

- A single digit, such as `'4'`. Notice that to the C# compiler, a single digit character is not a number but just another character and so it cannot participate in any arithmetic calculations without prior conversions.
- A special character, such as `'@'`, `'$'` or `'&'`.
- Represented in Unicode format by writing `\u` (backslash u) followed by the hexadecimal code of the character, as shown in Appendix E, see samspublishing.com. For example, if you look up the hexadecimal code for `'T'` you will find `0x54`. Thus `'T'` can be represented as `'\u0054'`. Consequently, instead of the two previous source code lines, `'T'` can be assigned to `myChar` by writing

  ```
  char myChar;
  myChar = '\u0054';
  ```

- An escape character, which is written with a backslash followed by a character. `'\n'` is an example of an escape character. The sequence of characters forming an escape character (\ and n in \n) is called an escape sequence.

We need to explore the escape character concept a little further to realize its usefulness. Suppose that you wanted to print a string containing quotation marks as part of the text. An example could be

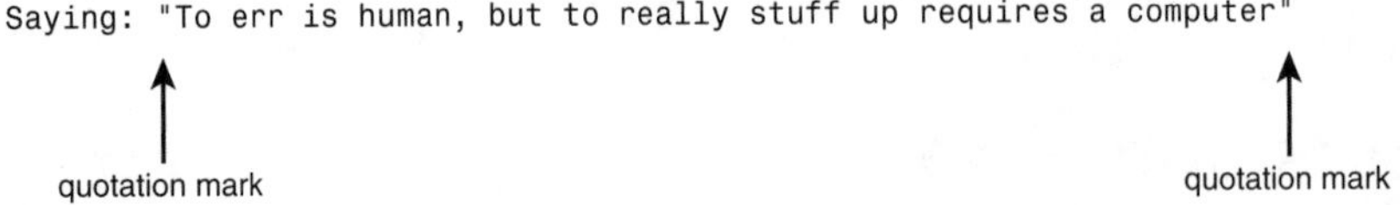

Our usual method of printing to the console

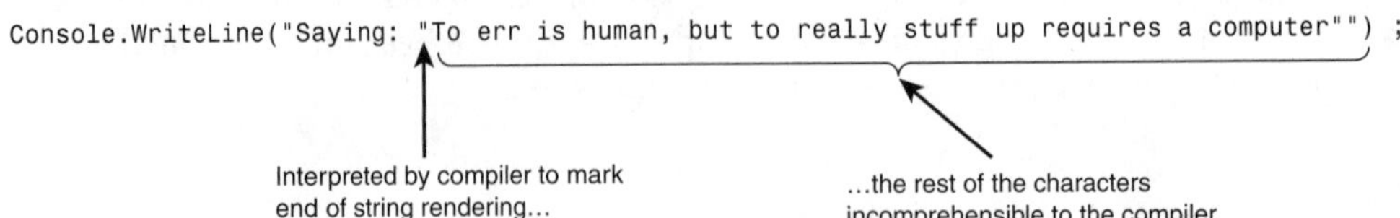

is invalid and generates a compiler error. The problem is that the compiler views the second quotation mark as a termination point for the string and thus stops "reading" at this point. So the remaining text:

```
To err is human, but to really stuff up requires a computer""
```

merely becomes incomprehensible garbage. The compiler follows very strict syntax when interpreting your string, and does not comprehend that the quotation mark is inserted to signify a quotation. Fortunately, you can make the computer understand your intentions by using the escape character `\"` (backslash double quote) as in the following:

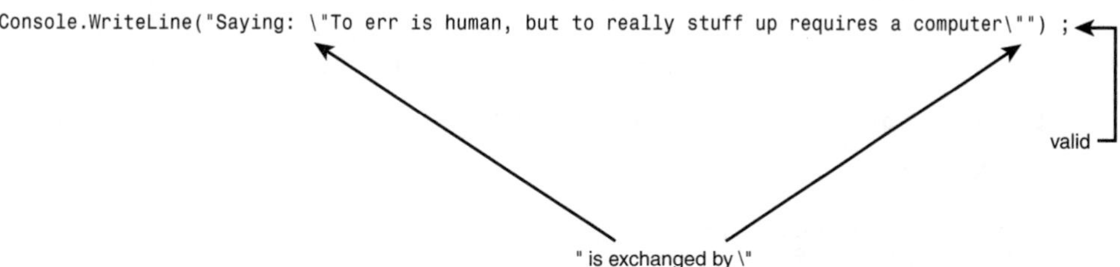
Console.WriteLine("Saying: \"To err is human, but to really stuff up requires a computer\"") ;
valid
" is exchanged by \"

Creating a valid statement.

Note

The word escape in escape sequence originates from the escape characters typical ability to "escape" from the conventional connotation of a character.

The full list of escape sequences is displayed in Table 7.5. Each of the escape sequences has a special meaning. For example, `\n` will move the cursor to the next line when inside a string. You can also represent an escape sequence by its Unicode value displayed in the right column of the table.

TABLE 7.5 Escape Sequences

Escape sequence	Meaning	Unicode Value
`\'`	Single quote	`\u0027`
`\"`	Double quote	`\u0022`
`\\`	Backslash	`\u005C`
`\0`	Null	`\u0000`
`\a`	Alert (Beep)	`\u0007`
`\b`	Backspace	`\u0008`
`\f`	Form feed	`\u000C`
`\n`	New line	`\u000A`

TABLE 7.5 continued

Escape sequence	Meaning	Unicode Value
\r	Carriage return	\u000D
\t	Horizontal Tab	\u0009
\v	Vertical Tab	\u000B

In the third row of Table 7.5, you will find the escape sequence `\\`. You might wonder about its purpose. Suppose that you needed to write the path `C:\MyFiles\temp\BliposClock.cs` of your Windows files system as a `string` literal. You might try to write the following:

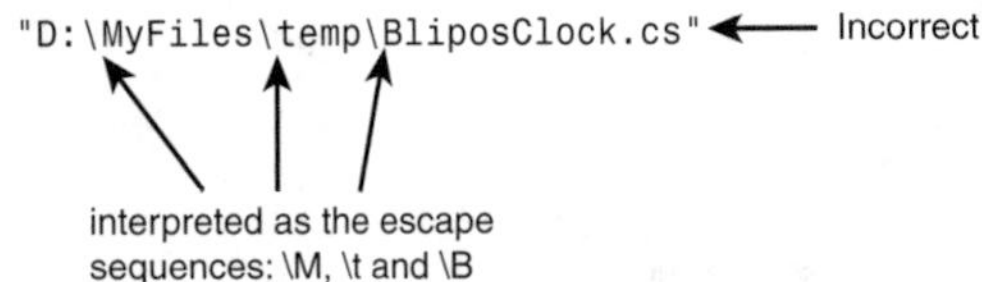
"D:\MyFiles\temp\BliposClock.cs"
Incorrect
interpreted as the escape
sequences: \M, \t and \B

However, the compiler would believe all the backslash characters were attempts to include escape characters in the string. In this case, it would see `\M`, `\t`, and `\G`, of which only `\t` is valid. This would cause an error message saying Invalid Escape Sequence Provided. By employing the `\\` escape sequence, you can ask the compiler to include a genuine backslash character inside the string. Thus, the correct way to write the file path is

```
"D:\\MyFiles\\temp\\BliposClock.cs"
```

In "The `string` Type" section later in this chapter, we will see an alternative way to handle this problem by using verbatim `strings`.

The Double Life of `char`

The `char` type lives a bit of a double life. It represents characters but is considered to be part of the integer family and its underlying value is an unsigned integer with the range 0–65536. It can take part in arithmetic calculations and implicitly be converted to an `int`, `long`, `ushort`, `uint`, and `ulong`, as shown previously in Figure 6.17 of Chapter 6. Note, though, that it is the underlying integer value that will be used for these calculations and conversions, not the digits, letters, and so on it is representing. Listing 7.6 demonstrates the double life of the two characters `'4'` and `'9'` with the underlying integer values 52 and 57. By adding these two characters together, we do not add together the numbers 4 and 9, but instead 52 and 57. The result, 109, is the underlying value for the character `'m'`.

LISTING 7.6 Code of `CharacterArithmetic.cs`

```
using System;

/*
 *  This class demonstrates how char variables can be added
```

LISTING 7.6 continued

```
05:  *  together as if they were 'normal' integers.
06:  */
07:
08: public class Characters
09: {
10:     public static void Main()
11:     {
12:         char firstSymbol;
13:         char secondSymbol;
14:         int intFirstSymbol;
15:         int intSecondSymbol;
16:         int result;
17:
18:         firstSymbol = '\u0034';
19:         secondSymbol = '\u0039';
20:         Console.WriteLine("firstSymbol as character: " + firstSymbol);
21:         Console.WriteLine("secondSymbol as character: " + secondSymbol);
22:         intFirstSymbol = firstSymbol;
23:         intSecondSymbol = secondSymbol;
24:         Console.WriteLine("firstSymbol as int: " + intFirstSymbol);
25:         Console.WriteLine("secondSymbol as int: " + intSecondSymbol);
26:         result = firstSymbol + secondSymbol;
27:         Console.WriteLine("Result as int: " + result);
28:         Console.WriteLine("Result as character: " + (char)result);
29:     }
30: }
```

```
firstSymbol as character: 4
secondSymbol as character: 9
firstSymbol as int: 52
secondSymbol as int: 57
Result as int: 109
Result as character: m
```

The literal `'\u0034'` in line 18 is the Unicode value for the character `'4'`. `'\u0039'` in line 19 represents the character '`9`'.

Line 20 prints the `firstSymbol` variable, which is being treated as a `char` variable and results in the output: `'4'`

In lines 22 and 23, `firstSymbol` and `secondSymbol` are implicitly converted to type `int` by assigning them to the `int` variables `intFirstSymbol` and `intSecondSymbol`.

`intFirstSymbol` and `intSecondSymbol` are printed in lines 24 and 25. The resulting output is the base 10 equivalents of 0x34 and 0x39, which are 52 and 57, respectively.

In line 26, `firstSymbol` and `secondSymbol` are implicitly converted to type `int` and added together. The result is assigned to the variable `result`. Note that the characters `'4'` and `'9'` are not converted to the numbers 4 and 9 but, instead, 52 is added to 57, resulting in 109 which is stored in `result`.

By adding the cast operator `(char)` in front of `result` in line 28, we perform an explicit conversion and tell the compiler to write `result` as a `char` type. In this case, the program converts 109 in base 10 to the equivalent Unicode character, which is `'m'`.

The `string` type

Single characters are not much fun on their own but, when put together, they constitute a powerful communication tool. The `string` type does exactly this for us, providing a powerful means of representing and working with strings of characters. `string`s are consequently used in most of your programs for names, descriptions, addresses, headings, and so on.

The word string is an alias for the .NET Framework class `String` located in the `System` namespace. Whenever you declare a variable to be of type `string`, you are, in fact, specifying this variable to be able to hold a reference to a `System.String` object, which then encapsulates your text. Consequently, the following two lines of source code have exactly the same meaning.

```
string someText;          <-- identical to the compiler
System.String someText;   <--
```

The string class comes packed with an entire host of features all based in the .NET Framework class library. You will see many examples of these features in this section.

`string` Literals and `string` Objects

The specification of a `string` literal, such as

```
"This is a string"
```

is familiar. The two double quotes enable the compiler to treat the individual characters between them as one single item. A string literal is an object of class `string`.

Recall how new objects of classes usually must be created with the use of the `new` keyword, such as the following:

```
Elevator elevator1 = new Elevator();
```

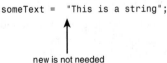

new keyword creates object of class Elevator

However, you can assign a `string` literal to a variable of type `string` simply by writing

```
someText =  "This is a string";
```

new is not needed

omitting the use of `new`. This is a convenient feature. Due to `string` types fundamental place in C# programming and to improve its ease of use, it has been given special abilities, such as the one mentioned here.

`string` is a reference type. Consequently, the latter assignment results in `someText` referring to a `string` object holding the text "This is a string" as follows:

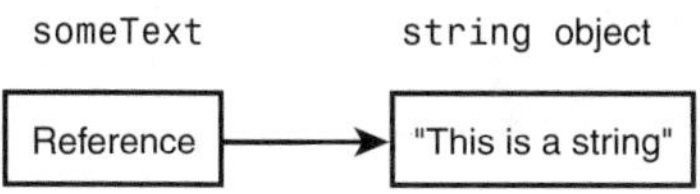

It is possible to let `someText` refer to another `string` object. For example, we can write

```
someText = "I'm the new string in the block";
```

which will move the reference from the `string` object holding the `"This is a string"` to the new object as follows:

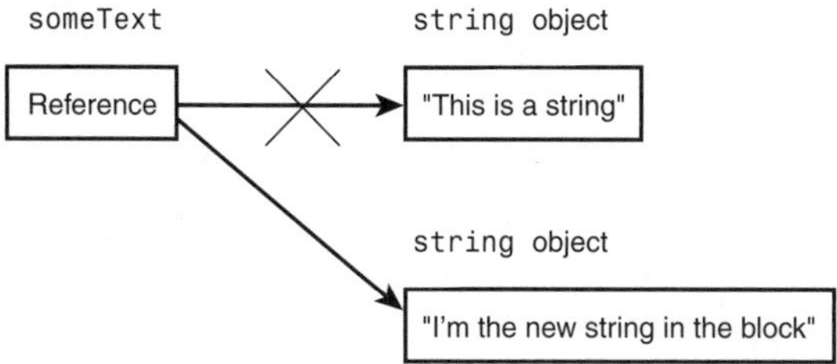

Verbatim Strings

From the previous `char` type section, recall how the problem of representing the backslash character `'\'` in a string could be solved. C# offers an elegant alternative to this procedure: By specifying a string literal to be interpreted literally (what you see is what you get), you can prevent the compiler from viewing the backslash `\` character as a "begin-escape-sequence" symbol. A factually interpreted `string` is called a *verbatim* `string` literal and is indicated by putting an `@` in front of the `string` literal. For example, to represent the previous path (`"D:\MyFiles\temp\BliposClock.cs"`), you can use the following instead of using the `\\` escape sequence as used in the `char` section:

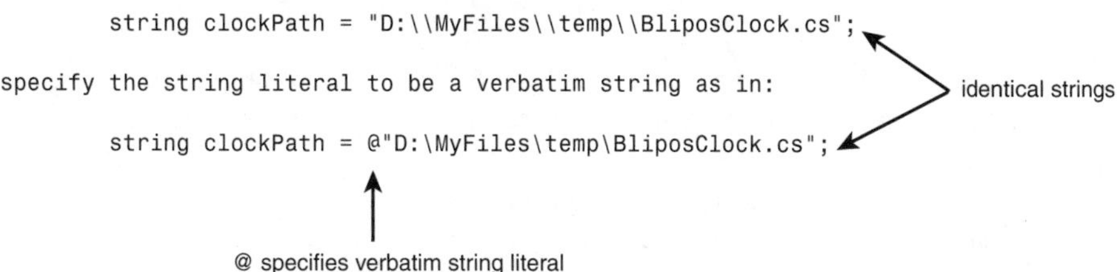

This produces exactly the same output.

Working with Strings

The `string` (`System.String`) class contains a vast array of useful methods that enable you to, for example,

- Concatenate two or more `strings`.
- Compare two `strings`.
- Access individual characters or sub-`strings` of a particular `string`.
- Insert part of one `string` into another `string`.
- Copy a `string`.
- Find the number of characters in a `string`.

To utilize these methods, we need a system by which we can identify individual characters and sub-`strings` in a `string`. For example, we might need to specify that we want to copy the sub-`string` `"and"` from the following string:

`".NET and C#."`

The `string` class uses a sequentially numbered index starting with 0 (not 1), as illustrated in Figure 7.7, to accomplish this. Notice how the periods and blanks are counted as part of the index and that the period in ".NET" is located at position 0.

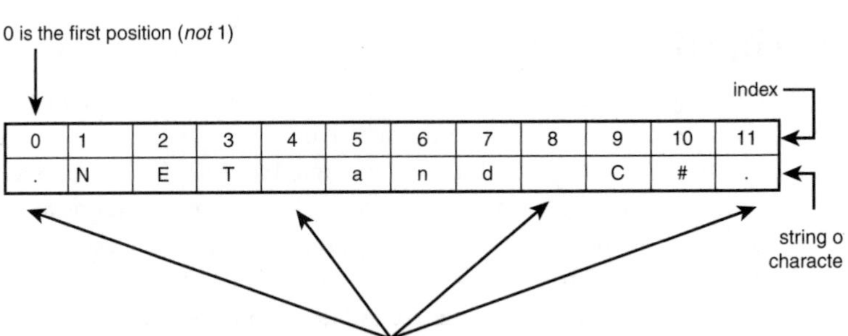
The string ".NET and C#." has 12 characters. Its index begins at 0 and ends at 11.
0 is the first position (*not* 1)
index
0 1 2 3 4 5 6 7 8 9 10 11
. N E T a n d C # .
the periods and the blanks are all characters and counted as part of the index

FIGURE 7.7
The underlying index of the `string` class.

Thus, to reach the sub-string `"and"`, we could write the equivalent of "get 3 characters starting at position 5." In C#, this is written as line 3 in the following code snippet:

```
01:        string andString;
02:        string myString = ".NET and C#";
03:        andString = myString.SubString(5, 3);
```

Line 3 utilizes the `SubString` method (see Table 7.6) of the `string` class to copy `"and"` from `myString` to `andString`. In particular, `myString.SubString (5, 3)` instructs the program to return a sub-`string` from `myString`, beginning at index 5 and including 3 characters.

Table 7.6 lists some of the `string` class methods and properties along with explanations and examples. The remaining methods can be found in the .NET Framework Documentation.

TABLE 7.6 Selected Methods and Properties of the *`string`* Class

Method/Property	Explanation	Example
`salutation.IndexOf (<Any_String>)`	Returns the position of the first occurrence of the sub-`string` *<Any_String>* in `salutation`. –1 is returned if *<Any_String>* is not found.	`salutation.IndexOf("Morn")` returns 5 `salutation.IndexOf("Hello")` returns –1
`salutation.Length`	Returns the number of characters in the `string`.	`salutation.Length` returns 13
`salutation[<index>]` Where *<index>* is a positive integer	Returns the character at the *<index>* of `string`.	`salutation[3]` returns `'d'`
`salutation.Equals (<Any_String>)`	If `salutation` and *<Any_String>* represents identical `strings`, this method returns `true`; otherwise, `false`. Note: the comparison operator == provides same comparison. Thus, `salutation.Equals (<Any_String>)` is equivalent to `salutation ==` *<Any_String>*.	`salutation.Equals("Good Morning!")` Returns `true` `salutation.Equals("Good Afternoon!")` Returns `false`. `salutation == "Good Morning!"` Returns `true`.
`salutation.ToUpper()`	Returns a `string` with the same sequence of characters as `salutation`, but all letters are converted to uppercase.	`salutation.ToUpper()` Returns `"GOOD MORNING!"`
`salutation.ToLower()`	Returns a `string` with the same sequence of characters as `salutation`, but all letters are converted to lowercase.	`salutation.ToLower()` Returns `"good morning!"`
`salutation.LastIndexOf (<Any_String>)`	Returns the position of the last occurence of the sub-`string` *<Any_String>* in `salutation`. –1 is returned if *<Any_String>* is not found.	`salutation.LastIndexOf("o")` Returns 6.

TABLE 7.6 continued

Method/Property	Explanation	Example
`salutation.CompareTo (<Any_String>)`	Compares `salutation` with `<Any_String>` by utilizing the corresponding Unicode value of each character. If `salutation` is less than `<Any_String>`, it returns a negative value. If `salutation` is greater than `<Any_String>`, it returns a positive value. If the two strings are equal, it returns zero. Only if both `strings` consist of either upper- or lowercase letters will the comparison constitute a valid lexicographic (alphabetic) evaluation.	`salutation. CompareTo ("Afternoon")` Returns a positive value `salutation. CompareTo ("Night")` Returns a negative value `salutation. CompareTo("Good Morning!")` Returns zero. `salutation. CompareTo("good Morning")` Returns a positive value `salutation. CompareTo("GOOD MORNING!"` Returns a negative value.
`salutation. Substring (<Index_Start>)`	Returns the sub-`string` of `salutation` starting from `<Index_Start>` continuing to the end of `salutation`.	`salutation. Substring(6)` Returns `"orning!"`
`salutation. Substring (<Index_Start> , <Length>)`	Returns the sub-`string` of `salutation` starting from `<Index_Start>` and including `<Length>` number of characters.	`salutation. Substring(6,3)` Returns `"orn"`
`salutation.Insert (<Index_Insert> , <Any_String>)`	Returns a `string` with `<Any_String>` inserted at position `<Index_Insert>` of `salutation`.	`salutation.Insert (5, "Better Best ")` Returns `"Good Better Best Morning!"`
`string.Copy (salutation)`	Returns a new copy of `salutation`.	`String.Copy (salutation)` Returns `"Good Morning!"`
`Format_Specifier ::=` *`{<Argument_Index> [,<Width>] [:<FormatString>] }`* Notes: `<Argument_Index>` is the zero-based index of the argument to be formatted. `<Width>` is the width (in	Allows you to construct `strings` containing normal static text with special markers, called *Format_Specifiers*, embedded at suitable positions. Each format specifier indicates where an argument (specified in the `Console.WriteLine()` method call) is to be inserted, along with an optional width and format.	`Console.WriteLine ("N1: N2: {0} {1} N3: {2}", 15, 28, 39);`Prints: `N1: 15 N2: 28 N3: 39` `Console.WriteLine ("Amount: {0:C}", 50000000.456);` Prints: `Amount:` $50,000,000.46

TABLE 7.6 continued

Method/Property	Explanation	Example

number of space characters) of the section containing the parameter. A negative number indicates the parameter to be left-aligned, a positive to be right-aligned. *<FormatString>* is a `string` of special formatting codes with conventions identical to that of the `ToString` methods of the numeric types.		`Console.WriteLine ("Distance1: {0:E2} Distance2: {1:E4}", 75463728991, 901100000000);`
		Prints:
		`Distance1: 7.55E+010`
		`Distance2: 9.0110E+011`
		
		`Console.WriteLine ("Mass: {0,10} grams. Energy: {1,10} joules",100, 300);`
		Prints: `Mass: 100 grams`
		`Energy: 300 joules`
		
		`Console.WriteLine ("Mass: {0,-10} grams Energy: {1,-10} joules", 100, 300);`
		Prints: `Mass: 100`
		`Energy: 300 joules`

Note: salutation is a string declared as

```
string salutation = "Good Morning!";
```

OOP, Encapsulation, and *System.String*

The `System.String` (`string`) class relies heavily on object-oriented principles in general, and encapsulation in particular, to provide power and ease of use to the programmer, and protects its state (the instance variables) from untimely access.

`System.String` is a complex class with hidden (`private`) methods and instance variables. Only useful methods, such as those presented in Table 7.6 are declared `public` by the designers of `System.String`, and so are made accessible.

Embedding Formatted Numbers in a `string`

This section should be read in conjunction with the last row of Table 7.6.

Recall how the `ToString` method of each numeric simple type allowed you to improve the readability and compactness of a number when converting it to a `string`. For example, you could write

```
Console.WriteLine("Distance traveled: " + 10000000.432.ToString("N2"));
```

This produces the following output:

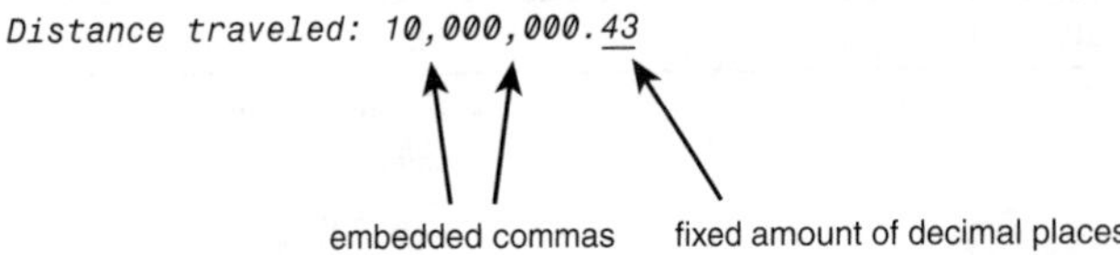

The `ToString` method clearly provides you with elaborate ways of formatting one single number. However, as we realized by the end of the `ToString` method discussion in Chapter 6, it results in a somewhat longwinded and unclear way of combining static text with formatted numbers. Fortunately, as you saw, format specifiers come to the rescue. The path to an understanding of the format specifier begins with the well-known `Console.WriteLine()`method.

A Glimpse of Overloaded Methods

Consider the following valid calls to a method `Sum` found close to each other in the same source program:

```
Sum(10, 20)  ———→ returns 30

Sum(5, 15, 30)  ———→ returns 50
```

Notice that they have the same name but different numbers of arguments. The previous brief discussions of methods told you that the number of arguments must match the number of formal parameters specified. So why are the previous calls valid? It is possible to define different versions of the same method name, but with differing numbers and types of formal parameters. A method name of the same class and different versions is called an *overloaded method*. By looking at the number of arguments and their types in the method call, C# will automatically apply the matching version of the method. This is illustrated in the following with the method header and definition on the left and the method call on the right.

Matching number of arguments and types.

```
Sum(int num1, int num2)        Sum(10, 20)

{

  return (num1 + num2);

}
```

Matching number of arguments and types.

```
Sum(int num1, int num2, int num3)     Sum(5, 15, 30)

{

   return (num1 + num2 + num3);

}
```

Letting multiple methods share the same name is a powerful feature and is used frequently in the .NET Framework class library. Chapter 12, "Class Anatomy Part I: Static Class Members And Method Adventures" will show you how to implement overloading in your own programs in more detail.

`Console.WriteLine` is an overloaded method representing many different versions. One version takes the following arguments:

```
Console.WriteLine(<Format>, <Value0>, <Value1>...)
```

where

- *<Format>* represents static text with markers called format specifiers (see Table 7.6).
- *<Value0>*, *<Value1>*... represents values that are to be inserted in *<Format>* at positions indicated by the format specifiers.

A format specifier is indicated by curly brackets (`{}`). It must always contain an index that references one of the subsequent `<Value>`s and specifies the value to be inserted at its location of the `string`. The following call to the `Console.WriteLine` method

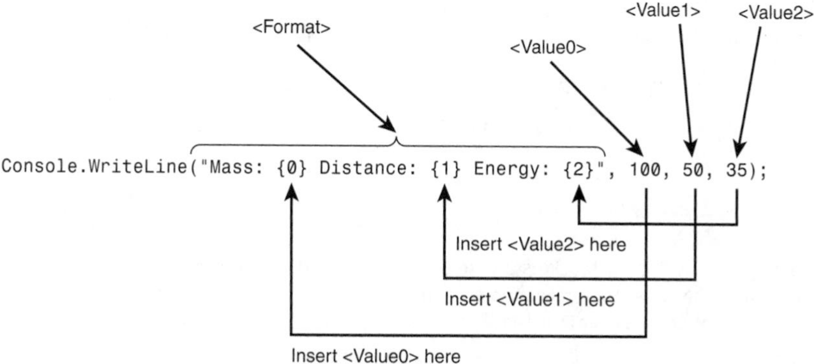

prints the following to the console:

```
Mass: 100  Distance: 50  Energy:  35
```

As an option, the format specifier also lets you specify the width of the region where a *<Value>* is to be printed. It is indicated by putting a comma after the index followed by a number specifying the width in characters. A positive number will right-align the *<Value>*, a negative number will left-align the *<Value>*. For example,

```
Console.WriteLine("Distance: {0,10} miles", 100);
```

prints

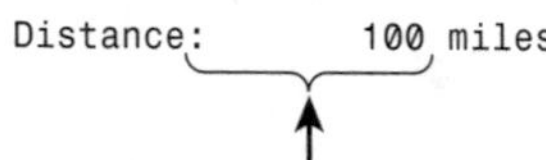

whereas, the following

```
Console.WriteLine("Distance: {0,-10} miles", 100);
```

Negative number specifies left alignment

prints

```
Distance: 100       miles
```

Width of region set to 10 characters.
Number is left aligned.

Finally, you can determine the format of the value by including an optional format character in the format specifier that can be followed by the optional precision specifier. The format character must follow a semicolon. It has exactly the same meaning as when used with the `ToString` method. For example, you can write

```
Console.WriteLine("Distance: {0,-12:E2}  Mass: {1,-12:N}", 100000000, 5000000);
```

which generates the following output:

```
Distance: 1.00E+008    Mass: 5,000,000.00
```

Tip

To print strings with curly brackets on the console, simply omit the *<Value0>*, *<Value1>* after the static text of the `Console.WriteLine` call. The C# compiler will choose another version (due to overloading) of `Console.WriteLine` that ignores `{}` brackets and prints them as is. For example,

```
Console.WriteLine("Number {0} is black, number {1} is red");
```

prints the following

```
Number {0} is black, number {1} is red
```

on the console.

The Immutability of `strings`

When a `string` object has been created, the set of characters it represents cannot be modified. For that reason, the `string` is said to be *immutable*. Consequently, none of the `string` methods will modify an existing `string`; instead, they create and return a *new* modified `string`. For example, if you want to change the characters of a `string` to uppercase by using the `string` method `ToUpper`, you cannot utilize the following procedure:

```
string myText = "the sun is shining";

myText.ToUpper(); <------------ Incorrect and invalid.
```

There are two problems with this latter statement. First, `myText.ToUpper()` returns a `string`, but none is being assigned or otherwise utilized. Additionally, `ToUpper()` does not change the `string` of `myText` to uppercase characters but, instead, returns a string containing the uppercase characters corresponding to the string of myText.

A successful conversion of myText to uppercase can be done as follows:

```
string myText = "the sun is shining";
myText = myText.ToUpper(); <———— correct
```

To understand why this is correct, recall why `count = count + 1;` works, as discussed earlier in this chapter. The right side of the assignment operator is processed first and, when finished, the result is assigned to `myText`. This same procedure can be utilized for many of the `string` methods.

Constructing strings with *System.Text.StringBuilder*

The immutability of the `string` class can sometimes lead to inconvenient and inefficient code when you are constructing longer strings from many small fragments of text because you will have to write lines like the following (where `myText` and `newText` are of type `string`):

```
myText = myText + newText;
```

The `StringBuilder` class located in the `System.Text` namespace offers an elegant and faster alternative to the `string` class, during string construction, because the text it represents can be updated. This is illustrated in Listing 7.7. Line 2 allows you to write shortcuts to classes in the `System.Text` namespace. Line 9 creates a new `StringBuilder` instance containing the text "Once upon a time" and assigns its reference to `fairyTaleBeingWritten`. Lines 10 and 11 append new text to this instance. Once constructed, `fairyTaleBeingWritten's` text is transferred to the `string finalFairyTale` in line 12.

`StringBuilder` contains other useful methods. You can explore them further in the .NET Framework documentation.

LISTING 7.7 Source code of StringMaker.cs

```
01: using System;
02: using System.Text;
03:
04: class StringMaker
05: {
06:     public static void Main()
07:     {
08:         string finalFairyTale;
09:         StringBuilder fairyTaleBeingWritten = new
            ➥StringBuilder("Once upon a time");
10:         fairyTaleBeingWritten.Append(" a beautiful princess");
11:         fairyTaleBeingWritten.Append(" lived in a big castle");
12:         finalFairyTale = fairyTaleBeingWritten.ToString();
13:         Console.WriteLine(finalFairyTale);
14:     }
15: }
```

```
Once upon a time a beautiful princess lived in a big castle
```

Working with strings

At the time of writing, the string class contains approximately fifty methods, a selected few of which are presented in Table 7.6. All methods are explained in the .NET Framework Reference and for this reason, I will not attempt an exhaustive presentation of each and every method here. To demonstrate the usability of the string methods, I have provided a few elaborate text-analyzing source code examples. The examples can be viewed as simple precursors to important components, such as spell checkers, thesauruses, word and character counters, and so on, found in all professional word processors like MS-Word. However, the underlying logic behind the presented algorithms are applied in many other contexts.

Accessing and Analyzing Individual Characters of a string

The source code in Listing 7.8 performs an analysis of a given text entered by the user. Specifically, it prints the following statistics on the console.

1. The number of vowels
2. The number of consonants
3. The number of letters
4. The number of digits
5. The number of words
6. The average word length

Designing a Text-Analyzing Algorithm

The text provided by the user is stored in a variable of type string.

To determine the previous first four points, you must access and evaluate each individual character of the given text.

Before scrutinizing each character, you need to declare three counters: a vowel counter, a letter counter, and a digit counter. Each counter must be initialized to zero. You are now ready for the following loop:

> For each individual character do the following:
>
> If it is a vowel, increment the vowel counter by 1.
>
> If it is a letter, increment the letter counter by 1.
>
> If it is a digit, increment the digit counter by 1.

Because a letter can be either a vowel or a consonant, the number of consonants can be calculated with the expression

> number of letters – number of vowels.

To calculate point 5 (number of words), assume that the number of words is equal to the number of spaces plus one.

For example, the next line contains seven spaces and eight words.

This line contains seven spaces and eight words.

So, while we are checking each individual character to assess points 1–4, it is also useful to count the number of whitespace characters. At the end, when all characters have been accessed, you simply add one to this number to determine the number of words.

Finally, the average word length can be found by calculating

`(("number of letters" + "number of digits") / "number of words")`

Note that a number is also counted as a word.

The Final C# Program: `TextAnalyzer.cs`

You are now ready to write the C# program. It is displayed in Listing 7.8.

Note

For the program to work correctly, you must only include one space character between each word of the text fed into the program.

LISTING 7.8 Code of `TextAnalyzer.cs`

```
using System;
/*
 * This program will provide the following
 * information about a text:
 * The number of vowels
 * The number of consonants
 * The number of digits
 * The number of words
 * The average word length
 */
class TextAnalyzer
{
    public static void Main()
    {
        string myText;
        int numVowels = 0;
        int numLetters = 0;
        int numDigits = 0;
        int numWhitespaceChars = 0;
        int numWords = 0;
        char ch;
        int index = 0;

        Console.WriteLine("Please enter text to be analyzed:");
```

LISTING 7.8 continued

```
25:         myText = Console.ReadLine();
26:         myText = myText.ToUpper();
27:
28:         while (index < myText.Length)
29:         {
30:             ch = myText[index];
31:              //All letters have been converted to uppercase
32:              //so only need to check for uppercase vowels.
33:             if(ch == 'A' || ch == 'E' || ch == 'I' ||
34:                  ch == 'O' || ch == 'U' || ch == 'Y')
35:                 numVowels++;
36:             if(char.IsLetter(ch))
37:                 numLetters++;
38:             if(char.IsDigit(ch))
39:                 numDigits++;
40:             if(char.IsWhiteSpace(ch))
41:                 numWhitespaceChars++;
42:             index++;
43:         }
44:
45:         numWords = numWhitespaceChars + 1;
46:
47:         Console.WriteLine("Text analysis:");
48:         Console.WriteLine("Number of vowels: {0:N0}", numVowels);
49:         Console.WriteLine("Number of consonants: {0:N0}",
50:             (numLetters - numVowels));
51:         Console.WriteLine("Number of letters: {0:N0}", numLetters);
52:         Console.WriteLine("Number or digits: {0:N0}", numDigits);
53:         Console.WriteLine("Number of words: {0:N0}", numWords);
54:         Console.WriteLine("Average word length: {0:N2}",
55:             ((numLetters + numDigits) / (float)numWords));
56:     }
57: }
```

```
Please enter text to be analyzed:
Now go, write it before them in a table, and note it in a book. Isaiah 30:8<enter>
Text analysis:
Number of vowels: 25
Number of consonants: 27
Number of letters: 52
Number of digits: 3
Number of words: 17
Average word length: 3.24
```

Lines 16–19 contain counters of the vowels, letters, digits, and white space characters; they are all initialized to 0.

The `index` variable declared in line 22 is used to specify the individual character accessed.

Because the `string` is mutable it is not possible to modify the `string` of characters inside a particular `string`. However, it is possible to let it return a modified `string`. In this case, the original `string` of `myText` returns a set of corresponding uppercase characters that are assigned back to `myText` in line 25. The end result is that all letters of `myText` are converted to uppercase letters.

Lines 28, 29, 42 and 43 represent the important ingredients for the `while` loop starting in line 28. The `while` loop is repeated exactly `myText.Length` times for the following reasons:

- `index` has a starting value of 0 when the program execution reaches line 28 for the first time.
- `index` is incremented by 1 in line 42 every time the loop is repeated.
- According to line 28, the `while` loop is repeated as long as `index` is less than `myText.Length`.

The `while` loop block begins at line 30 and ends at line 42.

The character with position `index` is accessed and assigned to the `ch` variable in line 30. Keeping the `while` loop just described in mind, the program is accessing every single character one after the other.

Lines 33-41 examine the `ch` variable.

The parallel vertical lines `||` in lines 33 and 34 symbolize the logic operator `"OR"`. `||` is discussed further in Chapter 8, "Flow Of Control Part I: Branching Statements And Related Concepts." For now, you can regard lines 33 and 34 as saying "If `ch` holds one of the 6 vowels ('A', 'E', 'I', 'O', 'U', 'Y'), increment `numVowels` by one in line 35."

Lines 36-37 use the static method of `char` called `IsLetter` to determine whether `ch` is a character. If this is, the case `numLetters` is incremented by one.

Lines 38 and 39 use another of `char`'s static methods, `IsDigit`, to determine whether `ch` is a digit. If this is the case, increment `numDigits` by one.

Lines 40 and 41 use the static method of `char` called `IsWhiteSpace` to determine whether `ch` is a space; in which case, `numWhiteSpaceChars` is incremented by one.

Notice that none of the punctuation characters (, ., ;, :, and so on) are counted by any of the mentioned counters.

When execution has reached line 45, `numWhitspaceChars` is equal to the total number of spaces in the text. But, because the number of words is equal to the number of spaces + 1, we must add 1 to `numWhitespaceChars` to calculate `numWords.`

Lines 47–55 print the results of the various counts to the console.

Sorting `strings` in Alphabetical Order

Electronic address books, telephone books, encyclopedias, and dictionaries all represent items relying on the ability to sort a list of words in alphabetical order.

This section presents a simple program for sorting just three words in alphabetical order. Its underlying algorithm is a precursor to the famous sorting algorithm called Bubble Sort, which is presented in Chapter 11, "Arrays Part II: Multidimensional Arrays. Searching And Sorting

Arrays". After you understand the underlying logic for these algorithms, you will be able to sort not only words, but also any set of elements that are comparable, such as numbers, dates, and so on.

At the heart of most conventional word sorting programs lays the ability to compare just two words and detect which of these two words comes first in the alphabet. This ability allows us to sort any length of strings by using more-or-less sophisticated sorting algorithms.

The `string` *Method* `CompareTo()`

The built-in `string` method `CompareTo` (see Table 7.6) provides us with an ability to compare the Unicode values of the characters constituting two `strings`. Thus, if we restrict our `strings` to contain either uppercase letters only or lowercase letters only (see the following Note), we can perform a valid lexicographic (using alphabetic sequence) comparison.

Note

A comparison between two characters in the `CompareTo` method is made by comparing the Unicode values of the two characters. The list of Unicode values found in Appendix E reveals that any uppercase letter has a smaller Unicode value than any lowercase letter. However, within the uppercase and lowercase letters respectively, the Unicode values are sequenced in alphabetical order. Thus, only when two `strings` consist entirely of uppercase or lowercase letters can a reliable lexicographic comparison be performed.

For example,

`"W"` is less than `"w"`
`"Z"` is less than `"a"`
`"stormy Weather"` is less than `"stormy weather"`

Note

Comparing for equality as in `string1 == string2`, does not help us to sort `strings`. We do not get the vitally important information of which `string` has the greatest value.

Before looking at Listing 7.10 with the final source code, we need to address a couple of issues.

A Closer Look at the `CompareTo` *Method*

The algorithm used by `CompareTo` when comparing two `strings` compares successive characters with identical index in each `string`, starting with the first character. The algorithm will continue this procedure until one of the following two situations occur:

- *Two corresponding characters are detected to be unequal*—In this case, the `string` containing the character (of the two corresponding characters) with the smallest Unicode value will be the smallest `string`.

  For example, `"many"` is greater than `"mane"` because `y` is greater than `e`.

- *The end of the shortest `string` is reached*—The shorter `string` will then be the smallest `string`.

  For example, `"AAA"` is greater than `"AA"`.

Swapping the Contents of Two Variables

Swapping the values of two variables is a frequently used piece of functionality in a source program. This is utilized in Listing 7.10 as part of its sorting algorithm.

To explain the swapping process used here, consider that we want to swap the contents of the variables A and B.

A first hunch to swap the values would be to assign for example B to A. However, A is then equal to B and it is impossible to assign the original value of A to B. Thus, before we perform this first assignment, we must preserve the original value of A. To do this, we employ a temporary variable, called `temp`, which is assigned the value of A. Thus, we can write the following:

```
temp = A;
A = B;
```

Now A holds the value of B, so we are half way. We now need to move the original value of A over to B. Fortunately, `temp` is holding the original A value, so the full swap can be accomplished by writing

```
B = temp;
```

Designing a Simple Sorting Algorithm

Sorting algorithms are fundamental to computer programming. Large portions of the output from today's applications are sorted one way or another. Internally, an initial sorting of data can often speed up subsequent processes. Consequently, sorting is an essential and intensely studied process that, over the years, has produced numerous ingenious, weird, wonderful, and extremely fast sorting algorithms.

Note

The database is just one of many types of applications that rely heavily on sorting algorithms. For example, invoices are sorted in order of their invoicing date or their total amount, and customers are sorted in terms of how much they buy or by their names.

Listing 7.9 is a primitive sorting algorithm, but it is relatively simple and gives you an idea about what sorting is all about. The sorting algorithm utilized is written with pseudocode. It sorts the three values held by `num1`, `num2`, and `num3` in ascending order. In this example, they initially hold the values 30, 20, and 10 (descending order), respectively. After having been processed by the sorting algorithm, their values are 10, 20 and 30 (ascending order), respectively. Consequently, after the sorting has been applied, `numA` will have the smallest value, `numB` will have the middle value, and `numC` will have the greatest value, regardless of the starting values.

LISTING 7.9 Pseudocode for Sorting Algorithm used in Listing 7.10

```
01: set numA equal to 30
02: set numB equal to 20
03: set numC equal to 10
04:
05: repeat as long as: num2 and num3 were swapped in last loop (Note:
   ➥ first loop is always performed)
06: {
07:       if numA is greater than numB then
08:              swap numA and numB
09:       if numB is greater than numC then
10:              swap numB and numC
11: }
```

Why does it work? Tracing is a good way to get an initial understanding for this algorithm, so this will be the first part of our analysis. Recall our first encounter with the alien from planet Blipos in Chapter 2. When the alien checked our average calculating algorithm, he was effectually tracing it. *Tracing* simply means to execute the algorithm as if you were the computer. You need to keep track of the variable values and any changes made to these as you "execute" the algorithm. Let's get started tracing Listing 7.9.

After lines 1-3, the values of the variables are

numA = 30
numB = 20
numC = 10

Line 5 indicates we have to perform the loop at least once, so let's begin.

Because `numA(30)` is greater than `numB(20)`, we swap these two variables in lines 7 and 8.

The variables now hold the following values:

numA = 20
numB = 30
numC = 10

Because `numB(30)` is greater than `numC(10)`, we swap these two variables in lines 9 and 10.

The variables now hold the values

numA = 20
numB = 10
numC = 30

We return to line 5. Do we need to repeat the loop? Yes, because `numB` and `numC` were swapped in the previous loop.

Because `numA(20)` is greater than `numB(10)`, we swap these two variables in lines 7 and 8.

```
numA(10)
numB(20)
numC(30)
```

In lines 9 and 10, because **numB** is not greater than **numC**, we do not swap the two variables.

We return to line 5. Because **numB** and **numC** were not swapped in the last loop, we stop the algorithm and the tracing. The three numbers have finally been sorted as requested.

So, even though **numA** and **numB** are correctly sorted after lines 7 and 8, lines 9 and 10 might spoil this by swapping a value into **numB** from **numC** that is smaller than **numA**. Consequently, we must repeat the loop until **numB** and **numC** are not swapped. At the same time, every swap is beneficial and able to transport number 10 initially in **numC** up to **numA** and 30 down to **numC**. In fact, the algorithm seems to work like a pump with the ability to "pump" small numbers upward until they are blocked by even smaller numbers. This is illustrated in Figure 7.8.

FIGURE 7.8
A "pumping" algorithm.

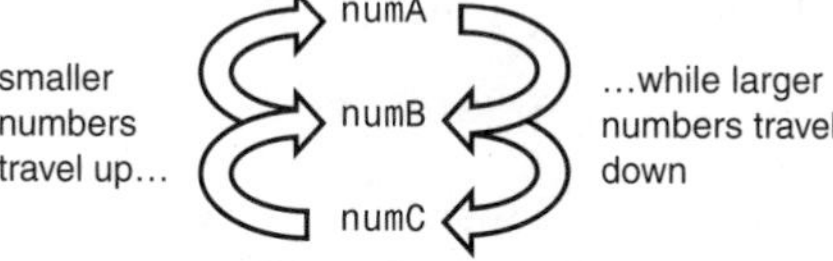

The Final C# String Sorter Program

It's time to have a look at the final source code in Listing 7.10.

Note

Notice that you must either input words with only upper- or lowercase letters to achieve a reliable alphabetical sort. This issue is discussed earlier in this section.

LISTING 7.10 Code of `StringSorter.cs`

```
using System;
/*
 * The Main method of the StringSorter class
 * Reads in 3 user specified strings
 * and sorts them in alphabetic order.
 */
class StringSorter
{
    public static void Main()
    {
        string string1;
        string string2;
        string string3;
        string tempString;
        bool changes = true;

        Console.Write("Enter first string: ");
        string1 = Console.ReadLine();
        Console.Write("Enter second string: ");
```

LISTING 7.10 continued

```
20:         string2 = Console.ReadLine();
21:         Console.Write("Enter third string: ");
22:         string3 = Console.ReadLine();
23:         while(changes)
24:         {
25:             changes = false;
26:             if(string1.CompareTo(string2) > 0)
27:             {
28:                  //The next 3 lines
29:                  //swap string1 and string2
30:                 tempString = string1;
31:                 string1 = string2;
32:                 string2 = tempString;
33:             }
34:             if(string2.CompareTo(string3) > 0)
35:             {
36:                  //The next 3 lines
37:                  //swap string2 and string3
38:                 tempString = string2;
39:                 string2 = string3;
40:                 string3 = tempString;
41:                 changes = true;
42:             }
43:         }
44:         Console.WriteLine("The strings in alphabetic order:");
45:         Console.WriteLine(string1);
46:         Console.WriteLine(string2);
47:         Console.WriteLine(string3);
48:     }
49: }
```

```
Enter first string: monkey<enter>
Enter second string: elephant<enter>
Enter third string: bird<enter>
The strings in alphabetic order:
bird
elephant
monkey
```

Line 14 declares the `tempString` variable of type `string` utilized for swapping two `string` variables.

Line 15 declares a variable of type `bool` with the name `changes`. It is used to keep track of whether `string2` and `string3` were swapped in the previous loop (more details will follow). A variable, such as `changes`, that "remembers" whether a certain event has taken place is called a *flag*.

Note

You have previously seen how a single statement can be positioned immediately after an `if` keyword and its associated condition as follows:

```
if (myNumber > 10)
     Console.WriteLine("myNumber is greater than 10");
Console.WriteLine("I'm always printed irrespective of myNumber's size");
```

But what if we want more than one statement to be executed only when the `if` condition `myNumber > 10` is true? C# allows you to substitute a single statement with a block of statements enclosed by curly braces ({}). All statements inside this block will be executed when the `if` condition is `true`. None of them will be executed if the condition is `false`:

```
if (myNumber > 10)
{
     Console.WriteLine("myNumber is greater than 10");
     Console.WriteLine("I'm also only printed if myNumber > 10 is true");
}
Console.WriteLine("I'm always printed");
```

The braces in lines 27 ({) and 33 (}) enclose the block of statements to be executed if the condition `(string1.CompareTo(string2) > 0)` of the `if` statement is `true`. Consequently, if this condition is `true`, all the statements in lines 30–32 will be executed. On the other hand, if `the condition` is `false`, the execution will jump over this block and continue at line 34. The same logic applies for the block enclosed by the braces of lines 35 and 42.

As long as `changes` in line 23 is holding the value `true`, the `while` loop will be repeated. To make sure that `changes` is really `true` due to a swap of `string2` with `string3` in the previous loop, `changes` is set to `false` in the beginning of every loop and then later changed to `true` in line 41 if the swap really took place. Without line 25, `changes` would always stay `true` and the loop would repeat itself forever; we would end up with a so-called *infinite loop*.

In lines 26–33, if the condition `(string1.CompareTo(string2) > 0)` is `true`, it means `string1` is larger than `string2`. Because we need to "pump" the smaller values "up," we need to swap the two values. This is performed in lines 30–32 with the help of the `tempString` as discussed earlier.

Lines 34–42 represent the same logic as lines 26–33 with the small addition that `changes` will be set to `true` in case of a swap.

Note

Many algorithms and programs can be divided into three separate phases:

1. A phase that declares and initializes the variables and constants of the program (lines 11–15 in this example).

2. A processing phase where the user inputs information and information is acquired from various sources, such as files, networks, the Internet, and so on. The main part of the processing takes place in this phase (lines 17–43).
3. A completion phase where final calculations are performed and the requested results provided as output (lines 44–47).

Extracting Sub-`strings` from a `string`

Instead of analyzing individual characters, as the `TextAnalyzer.cs` source code of Listing 7.10 does, the `WordExtractor.cs` source code presented in Listing 7.12 extracts individual words from a `string` and prints words with a specified minimum length. `WordExtractor.cs` is heavily dependent on the functionality of the `string` method `SubString`.

Note

The ability to isolate and recognize individual words in a sequence of characters is used in many different types of applications:

- Any sophisticated word-processing features, such as spell check and thesaurus facilities, rely on the ability to recognize individual words.
- Computer language compilers (which are programs themselves) must, as one of the first steps during their compilation process, isolate the tokens existing in the source code to recognize keywords, operators, and other language elements.
- Browsers understand HTML formatted documents by breaking down the HTML text into understandable parts.
- The whole XML-revolution would not be possible without programs that can break XML-documents into smaller word-resembling parts.
- Search engines like Yahoo and AltaVista must isolate and recognize the words you ask them to search for in the millions of documents they access on the Internet.

Designing a Word Extraction Algorithm

To construct an algorithm for extracting words, we must first define what a word is. In this case, I have defined a word to be any of the following three definitions:

1. A sequence of non-whitespace characters surrounded by whitespace characters on the left and the right. For example, in "The monkey is funny+," "monkey" and "is" can be regarded as words according to this definition, because they are both surrounded by whitespace characters. "The" does not have a whitespace character on its left side, and "funny" lacks whitespace on its left side.
2. A sequence of non-whitespace characters surrounded by:
   - The beginning of the text on the left
   - Whitespace character on the right

   Consequently, in "The monkey is funny," "The" can be defined as a word.

3. A sequence of non-whitespace characters surrounded by:
   - A whitespace character on the left
   - The end of the text on the right

   As a result, in "The monkey is funny," "funny" is defined as a word.

By using these definitions, we have included all the sub-`string`s of a text that we conventionally refer to as words. Equipped with a definition for what our algorithm is looking for, we can begin to form an idea of what it could look like.

The basic strategy utilized in the algorithm presented here employs two variables of type `int` that are used as text markers. We will call these two variables `wordBegin` and `wordEnd`. A number contained in any of these two markers refers to an index of a `string` and, thereby, an individual character. To illustrate how these markers can access important information in our text, consider the following assignment statement:

```
string myText = "My dog is white";
```

Recall that we can view `myText` as a collection of indexed characters as follows:

0	1	2	3	4	5	6	7	8	9	10	11	12	13	14
M	y		d	o	g		i	s		w	h	i	t	e

By assigning suitable values to the two markers `wordBegin` and `wordEnd`, we can now

- Access individual characters with the character access feature (using square brackets `[]`) of `string`, as in the following:

  ```
  char ch;
  wordEnd = 10;
  ch = myText[wordEnd];
  ```

  which assigns the letter `'w'` to the character variable `ch`.

- Access sub-`string`s enclosed by the two markers by using the `SubString` method of the `string` class. `wordBegin` indicates the beginning of a sub-`string`; `wordEnd` indicates the end. For example,

  ```
  int wordLength;
  wordBegin = 3;
  wordEnd = 6;
  wordLength = wordEnd - wordBegin;
  Console.WriteLine(myText.SubString(wordBegin, wordLength);
  ```

  prints the text "dog" to the console.

By making sure that `wordBegin` always points at the first character of a word, it is possible to let `wordEnd` move ahead character by character from the position of `wordBegin` and "look" for the end of the word. This is illustrated in Figure 7.9. According to our previous definitions of a word, `wordEnd` has found the end of a word whenever any of the two following events take place:

- `wordEnd` points at a whitespace character.

- `wordEnd` reaches the end of the text.

A newly detected word can then be extracted with the `SubString` method because, at this particular moment, we know that `wordBegin` and `wordEnd` mark the beginning and end of a word.

The last step of one cycle is to move the `wordBegin` marker to the first character of the next word. This can be achieved by assigning the `wordEnd` index number plus one to `wordBegin`. To realize why this makes sense, observe that when `wordEnd` is detecting a word it is pointing at the space just before the next word. Notice that the latter only holds if the end of the text has not been reached. In that case, however, the algorithm is stopped before an attempt is made to move `wordBegin`.

FIGURE 7.9
Three important stages when finding the next word in a `string`.

Stage 1:

Initial state: `wordBegin` is at the beginning of a word. `wordEnd` is set to start its search

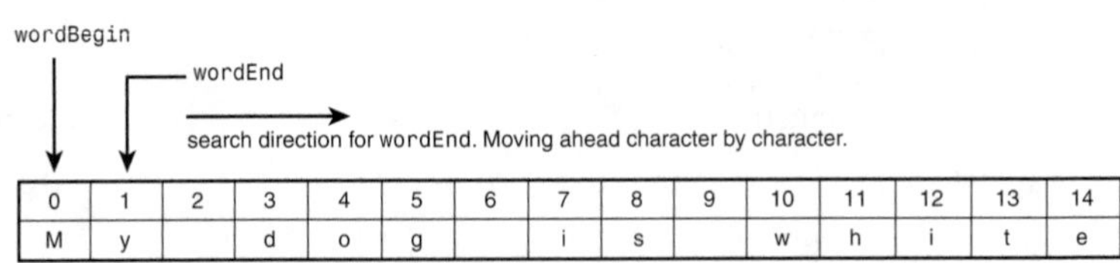

Stage 2:

First whitespace character and hence first word encountered by `wordEnd`

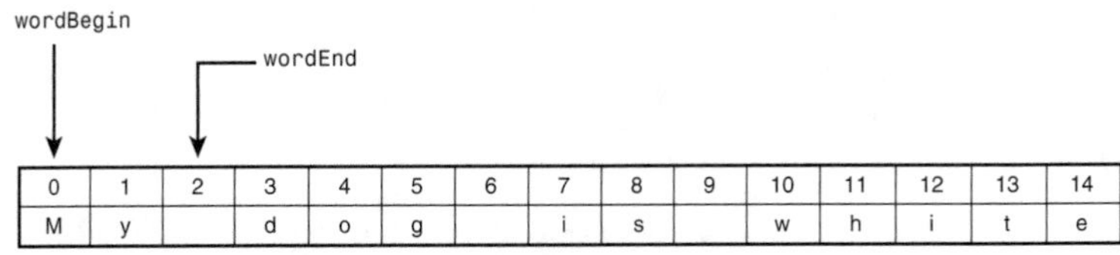

Stage 3:

Move `wordBegin` and `wordEnd` to the beginning of the next word

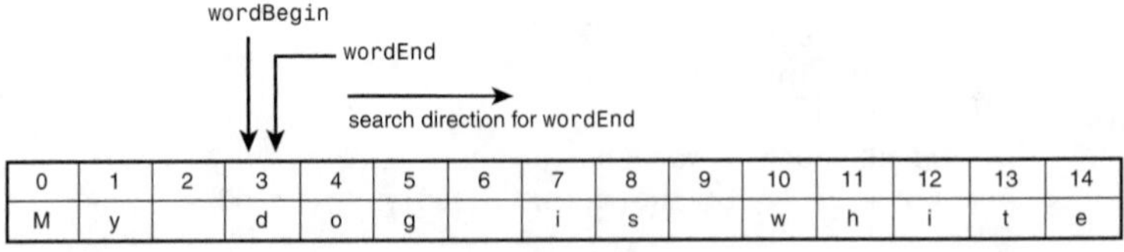

Repeat step 1, 2 and 3 until `wordEnd` reaches the end of the `string`.

Listing 7.11 illustrates with pseudocode the algorithm conceived on the basis of the previous discussion. Notice that it includes the ability to print only detected words that are longer than a certain specified minimum length. This is specified in lines 9 and 14.

LISTING 7.11 Pseudocode for `WordExtractor` Algorithm

```
01: Initialize the following variables to 0: wordBegin, wordEnd, wordLength.
02: User sets minLenght variable. (the minimum length of a word to be printed)
03: Repeat the following block as long as wordEnd has not reached the end of
    ➥string.
04: {
05:        move wordEnd one character forward.
06:        if wordEnd is pointing at a whitespace character then
           ➥execute the following block
07:        {
08:             // A new word has been found enclosed by wordBegin and wordEnd
09:            if new word length is same length or longer than minLength
               ➥then print the word to the console.
10:            Set wordBegin to point at the first character of the next word.
11:        }
12: }
13: wordEnd has reached the end of the string so wordBegin and
    ➥wordEnd now encloses the last word of the string.
14: If the last word is the same length or longer than minLength
    ➥then print the word on the console.
15: End
```

In line 1, setting `wordBegin` and `wordEnd` to zero sets both of them to point at the first index of the given `string`, as illustrated in stage 1 of Figure 7.9.

Line 3 causes the block between the curly brackets of lines 4 and 12 to be repeated as long as `wordEnd` is not at the end of the `string`.

Line 5 is the first step of stage 2 in Figure 7.9. `wordEnd` moves forward character by character. When combined with Lines 3, 4, and 12, line 5 causes `wordEnd` to point at every single character of the text one by one.

When the condition in line 6 is `true`, stage 2 of Figure 7.9 has been reached and the execution of the block enclosed by lines 7 and 11 commences.

Line 9 ensures that only words with a minimum length specified by the user in `minLength` are printed to the console.

Line 10 is related to stage 3 of Figure 7.9. `wordBegin` jumps forward to point at the beginning of the next word.

Lines 13–16 are self-explanatory.

The Final C# Word Extractor Program

The C# code of `WordExtractor.cs` can now be written. It is displayed in Listing 7.12.

LISTING 7.12 Code of `WordExtractor.cs`

```
using System;
/*
 * Locates words in a given text with a minimum
```

LISTING 7.12 continued

```
 * number of characters and prints those
 * on the console.
 * The text and the minimum word length is
 * provided as input from the user.
 */
public class WordExtractor
{
    public static void Main()
    {
        string myText;
        int minLength = 0;
        int wordBegin = 0;
        int wordEnd = 0;
        int wordLength = 0;
        int adjTextLength = 0;
        char ch;

        Console.WriteLine("Enter text:");
        myText = Console.ReadLine();
        Console.WriteLine("Enter minimum length" +
            " of words to be displayed");
        minLength = Convert.ToInt32(Console.ReadLine());
         //Adjust text length to match zero based index
        adjTextLength = myText.Length - 1;

         //Repeat while-block as long as end of text
         //has not been reached
        while(wordEnd < adjTextLength)
        {
            wordEnd++;
            ch = myText[wordEnd];
             //If ch is whitespace character then new word
             //has been found. wordBegin then indicates
             //beginning of word and wordEnd the end of the word
            if(char.IsWhiteSpace(ch))
            {
                 //Write word on console if number of characters is
                 //the same length or longer than minLength
                wordLength = wordEnd - wordBegin;
                if(wordLength >= minLength)
                {
                    Console.WriteLine
                    (myText.Substring(wordBegin, wordLength));
                }
                 //Jump over whitespace and begin
                 //at first character of next word
                wordBegin = wordEnd + 1;
            }
        }

         //Write out last word of myText if number of
         //characters is greater than or equal to minLength
```

LISTING 7.12 continued

```
56:          wordLength = wordEnd - wordBegin + 1;
57:          if(wordLength >= minLength)
58:          {
59:              Console.WriteLine
60:              (myText.Substring(wordBegin, wordEnd - wordBegin + 1));
61:          }
62:      }
63: }
```

```
Enter text:
When he who hears does not know what he who speaks means
➥and when he who speaks does not know what he himself means
➥that is philosophy  Voltaire<enter>
Enter minimum length of words to be displayed
5<enter>
hears
speaks
means
speaks
himself
means
philosophy
Voltaire
```

The block enclosed by lines 32 and 52 is equivalent to the block enclosed by lines 4 and 12 in Listing 7.11. `wordEnd` must start at zero (achieved by line 15) and be incremented by one (line 33) until it reaches the last index of `myText` (achieved by lines 27 and 31). If we mistakenly used `(wordEnd < myText.Length)` as the condition in line 31, the loop would repeat itself one times too many, because the underlying string index of `myText` is zero based. (It commences at zero.) Instead we use `adjTextLength` which is equal to `myText.Length` - 1.

The character of the current index held by `wordEnd` is assigned to the `ch` variable of type `char` in line 34.

If `ch` holds a whitespace character when line 38 is executed, a new word has been found and the statements between the curly brackets of lines 39 and 51 are executed.

Lines 43–47 print the detected word (by using the `SubString` method of the string class in line 46) if its length is the same or longer than specified in `minLength`.

When the while loop spanning lines 31–52 terminates, `wordEnd` has reached the end of the `string`. `wordLength` of the last word is calculated in line 56. `wordEnd` does not, at this moment, point at the space after the last word (there is no space) but at the last character of the word. Thus, the word length calculated by `wordEnd - wordBegin` must be adjusted by adding 1.

If the word length of the last word is longer than or equal to the minimum length specified by `minLength`, then lines 59-60 print this word to the console.

Summary

In this chapter, you learned about the main arithmetic operators along with the `string`, `char`, and enumerator types.

What follows are the important points covered in this chapter.

Arithmetic operators combine with operands to form arithmetic expressions.

Binary operators operate on two operands. Unary operators operate on one operand.

An operand can be any arithmetic expression, so any longer arithmetic expression can be broken into simple expressions consisting of binary and unary operators and their operands. The compiler evaluates any arithmetic expression by following this process while observing the precedence and associativity rules of the included operators. This evaluation process often gives the same result as when we apply the arithmetic rules we learned in school.

Apply parentheses when the precedence and associativity rules do not correspond with your calculations. (This also makes the code more clear.)

The modulus operator is useful for solving many more computational problems than its simple appearance indicates.

Any expression written with increment (++) and decrement (`--`) operators can be written without these unary operators. If not used with caution, they can easily lead to unclear and erroneous code.

To find the type of an expression the types of its sub-expressions are passed through, the expression hierarchy, just like the values of its sub-expressions, are passed through to find its value. If we know the type of any two operands and their binary operator and any one operand and its unary operator, we can combine these types to find the type of any longer expression.

A flowchart is a diagramming technique often used to express algorithms. A flowchart was used to describe the process followed by the compiler when it determines the type of two operands and a binary operator.

C#'s built-in support for metadata allows for a separation between hard-coded rigid standards pertaining to the C# language and a user friendly, flexible description of the source code and its types. This allows C# components to be useful in many different environments.

Enumerated constants are useful when we need to represent a finite set of related constants whose values are known before the program is compiled.

A value of type `char` represents a Unicode character. A value of type `string` represents a list of `char` values. The `string` class contains many valuable methods to manipulate strings of characters.

Review Questions

1. How are the following expressions evaluated in C#:

    a. 5 + 10 * 2

    b. 5 * 6 / 3

    c. 12 / 4 * 6

    d. 20 % 8

    e. `myIntVariable++`

    f. `--myIntVariable`

2. Suppose you need to add `number1` and `number2` together and multiply this result by `number3`. The first attempt:

    ```
    number1 + number2 * number3
    ```

    gave a wrong result. Fix the problem.

3. The following expression is correct but unclear for the reader of the code. Make it more clear.

    ```
    num1 + num2 / num3 * num4 - num5 * num6 / num7
    ```

4. Write an `if` statement that checks whether a number (call it `myNumber`) of type `int` is even or odd. Only if `myNumber` is even should it write "The number is even" onscreen.

5. What is the type of the following expression if `weight` is of type `short`?

    ```
    -weight
    ```

6. Improve the clarity of the following statement by separating it into three statements without altering the effects of the code:

    ```
    totalBacteria = ++bacteriaInBody1 + bacteriaInBody2++;
    ```

7. Draw a flowchart that illustrates the following logic. A person wants to go for a walk. If it rains, he asks his wife if they have an umbrella. If they have an umbrella he will go out; otherwise, he will stay inside. If it does not rain, he will go out whether they have an umbrella or not.

8. Which construct would be suitable to represent the following values in a C# program: {Red, Green, Blue, Yellow, Purple}

9. Write a statement that prints the following text on the console (including the quotation marks)?

    ```
    And then he said: "This is a great moment"
    ```

10. Suppose `myString` contains 20 characters. Write an expression that returns a sub-string from `myString` beginning at character number 10 and including 5 characters.

11. Suppose `distance1` is 100, `distance2` is 200, and `distance3` is 400. Write a statement that uses embedded formatted numbers to include the three variables in a string so that the final text reads

    ```
    The first distance is 100 meters, the second distance is 200 meters
    and the third distance is 400 meters.
    ```

Programming Exercises

Change the `DayCounter.cs` source program in Listing 7.2 to exhibit the following functionality:

1. Apart from reporting every Sunday, it should also report every Saturday. Hint: At the moment, the program is detecting every 7, 14, 21, 28, and so on. Which numbers does it need to detect to find all the Saturdays? Those would be 6, 13, 20, 27, and so on. How do they relate to the Sunday numbers? How can this be implemented?
2. Let's say that every year in the simulation has 365 days. Change the program to let it report the running time in days, weeks, and years, instead of just the days and weeks reported currently.
3. Recall the Blipos Clock case study in Chapter 6, "Types Part I: The Simple Types." Instead of relying on the overflow/underflow mechanism of the integer types, rewrite the `BliposClock` class to use the modulus operator to accomplish exactly the same tasks.

CHAPTER 8

FLOW OF CONTROL PART I: BRANCHING STATEMENTS AND RELATED CONCEPTS

You will learn about the following in this chapter:

- The main structures used to control the order in which the statements of a program are executed
- The `if-else` statement
- The comparison operators and how they allow programs to make meaningful decisions when combined with control structures like the `if-else` statement
- How the nested and multibranch `if-else` statements can help you solve important computational problems
- The logical operators and how they allow you to implement more powerful yet simpler programs
- The infamous `goto` statement, why it should be avoided in most situations, and the few cases where it can be useful in C#
- The `switch` statement
- The scope and lifetime concepts and their implications
- The conditional operator

Introduction to Flow of Control

In the Shakespeare.cs program presented in Chapter 2, "Your First C# Program," all statements were executed sequentially in the order they were written in the source code. This is called *sequential execution*. Normally, statements in a method are executed sequentially; that is, if none of the constructs, presented in this and the next chapter that are specifically designed to redirect this otherwise linear flow of events, are encountered.

A program based purely on sequential execution will, during each execution, always perform exactly the same actions; it is unable to react in response to current conditions.

But life is seldom that simple. Often, programs need to alter the flow of control in a program.

The *flow of control* is the order in which statements of a program are executed. Other terms used are *ordering* and *control flow*.

For example, the `Hello.cs` program of Listing 3.1 in Chapter 3, "A Guided Tour Through C#: Part 1," was able to let user input (yes or no) influence its flow of control by deciding whether the statement printing "Hello World!" should be executed. Implementing this type of logic calls for the ability to *use* a given condition to decide between two or more alternative branches. The `if` statement, informally presented in the `Hello.cs` program, together with the yet to be presented `switch` statement, form the group of statements used for this exact purpose and are collectively called branching statements.

A *branch* is a segment of a program made up of one statement or a group of statements.

A *branching statement* chooses to execute just one of several statements or blocks of statements. The choice made depends on a given condition. Branching statements are also called selection statements or alternation statements.

Note

C# supports less obvious ways of directing the flow of control through a couple of mechanisms called virtual method invocation (or dynamic binding) and delegate invocation. Due to the advanced object-oriented nature of these constructs, their treatment has been deferred to Chapter 17, "Inheritance Part II: Abstract Functions, Polymorphism, and Interfaces," and Chapter 20, "Delegates and Events."

Frequently, programs need to repeat the same actions over and over until a given condition is met. The `BliposClock.cs` program in Listing 6.8 in Chapter 6, "Types, Part I: The Simple Types" utilized the `do-while` loop to repeatedly let the user move the simulated Blipos Clock backward and forward until a given input (`"T"` for terminated) was provided. Without the ability to repeatedly reuse the same statements, the length of the `BliposClock.cs` program would be directly proportional to the number of times the user would want to adjust the clock. If the repeated sequence contained ten lines of code and the user wanted to adjust the clock one thousand times, this part of the program would have to occupy a staggering ten thousand lines of code. Apart from wasting valuable programmer time and computer memory, this latter approach would force the user to provide exactly one thousand clock adjustments every time the program was executed.

The familiar `while` and `do-while` statements, together with the hitherto not presented `for` statement, fortunately solve these serious problems. They belong to a group of statements called iteration statements.

An *iteration statement* repeats a statement or a block of statements until a given termination condition is met. Iteration statements are also referred to as *loop statements* or *repetition statements*.

Note

Whenever the flow of control is not directed by a branching or an iteration statement or something similar, C# executes all statements in a sequential fashion.

Note

Recursion, like iteration, constitutes a mechanism that repeatedly performs the same set of operations. However, in contrast to iteration statements, the repetition is accomplished by letting a method call itself over and over again until some termination condition is met. This seemingly peculiar process can be valuable for solving many computational problems of a recursive nature. Recursion is purely done through method calls and not associated with any special C# keywords. Due to the advanced nature of recursion, it is not presented until Chapter 23, "Recursion Fundamentals."

Not only do the branching and loop statements allow a program to respond appropriately to a variety of different user input, they also allow us to implement the underlying rules and logic governing complex systems, such as airplane navigation systems, the neurons of the brain, or ant colonies.

In fact, any program of much use involves one or more of the constructs already mentioned.

An essential element of branching and looping is the ability to compare values. In C#, this is facilitated through the use of comparison operators. The equality (==) operator presented in the `Hello.cs` program of Listing 3.1 in Chapter 3, "A Guided Tour Through C#: Part I" is an example of a comparison operator. It allows the program to check whether the statement "user input is equal to 'y'" is true or false and triggers the `if` statement to execute the appropriate statements.

Often, several comparisons must be combined before a decision can be made. For example, you might only go for a walk if the sun is shining *and* you are not working. The word "and" allows us to combine two individual comparisons and make a final conclusion. In C#, "and" belongs to a group of operators termed logical operators.

This chapter focuses on the branching statements, along with the closely related comparison and logical operators. The next chapter concludes the treatment of flow of control by looking at the iteration statements.

Branching with the `if` Statement

The `if` statement comes in different varieties. We will first look at the very basic `if` statement version (termed the simple `if` statement) with which you are already familiar.

The Simple `if` Statement

The syntax of the simple `if` statement is displayed in Syntax Box 8.1.

Syntax Box 8.1 Simple `if`-Statement

```
Simple_if-statement::=
                        if(<Boolean_expression>)
                            <Statement>;
```

Note

Recall from Chapter 6 that a Boolean expression is always evaluated to one of the two `bool` values—`true` and `false`.

The `<Statement>` immediately after the Boolean expression will only be executed if the Boolean expression of the `if` statement is evaluated to `true`.

For example, the Big Bucks Bank offers an account to its customers with the following specifications:

> The account only pays interest *if* the balance is over $1000, in which case it pays 10% of the current balance.

We can express these conditions in a flowchart, as illustrated in Figure 8.1.

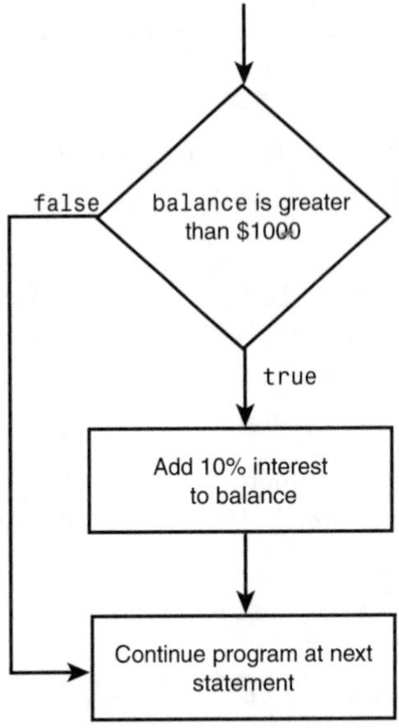

FIGURE 8.1
Calculating the interest for the account of the Big Bucks Bank.

The rules of the flowchart can be written in C# by using the simple `if` statement:

```
if (balance > 1000)
    balance = balance + (0.1 * balance);    //executed only if balance > 1000
```

which will only execute the second line if the Boolean expression `balance > 1000` is `true`.

Note

A Boolean expression must be enclosed by parentheses when it is part of an `if` statement, as shown in Syntax Box 8.1. This is common for all branching and looping statements. However, Boolean expressions separate from these constructs do not have this requirement.

Note

C# allows you to include so-called *empty statements*, also called *null statements*, in your code. An empty statement, as the name implies, does nothing. Recall that every statement must end with a semicolon. An empty statement is simply specified by a single semicolon (here often termed the do-nothing operator) located in a position where a statement is expected. For example, the semicolon of the second line in the following code snippet terminates an empty statement, whereas the two semicolons in the first and third lines terminate statements that both perform a computation:

```
distance = speed * time;
;
totalTime = time1 + time2;
```

What's the point of having a statement that does nothing? Well, sometimes a statement is required in the source code, but no operation is needed. However, this is not the main issue here. The important part is as follows.

The existence of the empty statement can lead to well-hidden bugs if mistakenly positioned after the rightmost parentheses enclosing the Boolean expression of an `if` statement. Let's use the already mentioned bank account example to illustrate. If, by mistake, you put a semicolon in the first line of the `if` statement as indicated in Figure 8.2, it would create an empty statement here, because a statement is expected in this position. The C# compiler would now regard the empty statement as the statement to execute whenever `balance > 1000` is `true` and would not consider the second line to be part of the `if` statement anymore. It would merely be interpreted as the next statement after the `if` statement. As a result, the second line would always be executed.

FIGURE 8.2
Inserting an empty statement in an *if* statement by mistake. Programmers view.

```
if(balance >1000);
        balance = balance + (0.1 * balance);
```


Recall that the compiler, as indicated in Figure 8.2, ignores indentation. Incorrect indentation can easily fool us into believing that an `if` statement represents the correct logic when this is not the case. For that reason, it is often difficult to spot errors produced by the inadvertent use of the empty statement. If we write the `if`-statement of Figure 8.2 according to the compiler's interpretation of the statement, it becomes much easier to spot the problem. To achieve this effect, we simply need to move the semicolon one line down and indent it, as shown in Figure 8.3.

FIGURE 8.3
Inserting an empty statement in an *if* statement by mistake. Compilers view.

```
if(balance > 1000)
  ;
balance = balance + (0.1 * balance);
```


In most cases, the C# compiler will detect the empty statement after an `if` statement and issue a warning, which might look like

```
EmptyStatement.cs(8,20): warning CS0642: Possible mistaken null statement
```

Compound Statements

The previous simple `if` statement only allowed us to execute one statement in case of a `true` Boolean expression. What if we need to execute more than one statement? For example, we might want the computer to print a message every time interest is added to our account *as well as* adding the interest. C# accommodates for this requirement by letting us substitute the single `<statement>` of Syntax Box 8.1 with a compound statement. The latter is defined in Syntax Box 8.2.

Syntax Box 8.2 The Compound Statement

A *compound statement* is simply another term for the familiar block of statements that you have seen in many previous examples.

```
Compound_statement::=
{
    <Statements>
}
```

This allows us to write

```
if (balance > 1000)
{
    balance = balance + (0.1 * balance);
    Console.WriteLine("Interest added");
}
```

All statements of compound statement are executed only if the Boolean expression is true.

which adds the interest *and* prints the message if the Boolean expression is `true`. If the Boolean expression is `false`, none of the statements of the compound statement will be executed.

The Optional `else` Clause

Big Bucks Bank offers another bank account to its customers with the following interest rates:

> If the balance is positive, pay 10% interest of the balance to the customer; *otherwise*, charge the customer 15% interest of the balance.

This interest payment rule is illustrated by a flowchart in Figure 8.4.

To implement this flowchart, we need to somehow express in C# that a choice is made among two alternative actions. This can be accomplished by extending the `if` statement with the optional `else` clause, as shown in Syntax Box 8.3.

FIGURE 8.4
Choosing among two alternative actions.

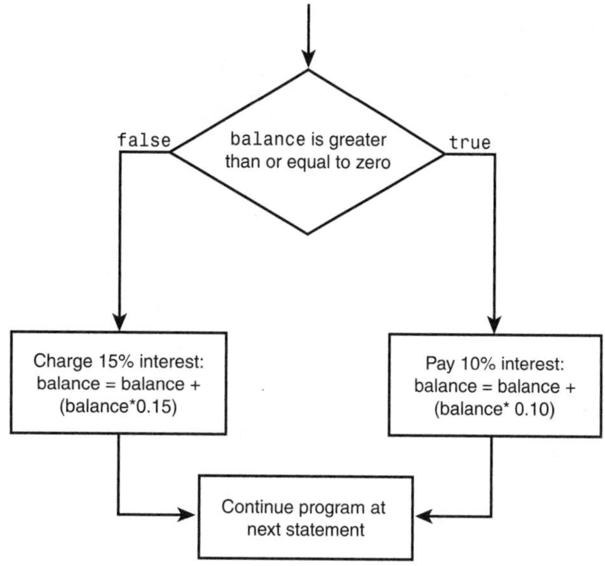

Syntax Box 8.3 `if-else` Statement

```
if-else_statement::=
if(<Boolean_expression>)
      <Statement1>; | <Compound_statement1>
[else
      <Statement2>; | <Compound_statement2>]
```

Notes:

- *<Statement1>; | <Compound_statement1>* is only executed if *<Boolean_expression>* is `true`.
- *<Statement2>; | <Compound_statement2>* is only executed if *<Boolean_expression>* is `false`.
- The *[symbol in front of else and the]* symbol after *<Compound_statement2>* symbolize that everything in between these two symbols is optional, as usual.
- Recall that the vertical line |, as in *<Statement>; | <Compound_statement>*, is surrounded by alternatives (see Syntax Box 6.1 of Chapter 6). In this case, it specifies that we can either use a *<Statement>* or a *<Compound_statement>*.

The flowchart in Figure 8.4 can then be expressed in C# as

```
          ┌────────────── greater-than-or-equal-to
          ▼
if (balance >= 0)
     balance = balance + (balance * 0.1);  ← only executed if (balance >= 0) is true
else
     balance = balance + (balance * 0.15); ← only executed if (balance >=0) is false
```

> **Note**
>
> The mathematical symbol for greater-than-or-equal-to is ≥ but does not exist on a conventional computer keyboard. In C#, the equivalent to ≥ was therefore chosen to be >=. The comparison operators != and <= were chosen for that same reason.

According to Syntax Box 8.3, it is possible to substitute the single statements by compound statements. This has been put into practice in lines 13–22 of Listing 8.1, which implements the bank account rule of Figure 8.4, along with a simple user interface.

LISTING 8.1 BankAccount.cs

```
01: using System;
02:
03: class BankAccount
04: {
05:     public static void Main()
06:     {
07:         const decimal InterestRatePaid = 0.1m;
08:         const decimal InterestRateCharged = 0.15m;
09:         decimal balance;
10:
11:         Console.Write("Please enter account balance: ");
12:         balance = Convert.ToDecimal(Console.ReadLine());
13:         if(balance >= 0)
14:         {
15:             Console.WriteLine("Interest paid: {0,13:C}", (balance *
                  ➥InterestRatePaid));
16:             balance = balance + (balance * InterestRatePaid);
17:         }
18:         else
19:         {
20:             Console.WriteLine("Interest charged: {0,10:C}", -(balance *
                  ➥InterestRateCharged));
21:             balance = balance + (balance * InterestRateCharged);
22:         }
23:         Console.WriteLine("New balance: {0,15:C}", balance);
24:     }
25: }
```

Sample 1 positive balance:

```
Please enter account balance: 1000<enter>
Interest paid:       $100.00
New balance:       $1,100.00
```

Sample 2 negative balance:

```
Please enter account balance: -1000<enter>
Interest charged:    $150.00
New balance:      $1,1500.00
```

Lines 15 and 16 will only be executed if `balance >= 0` (line 13) is `true`; otherwise, lines 20 and 21 will be executed.

Line 23 is the next statement after the `if-else` statement, so it will always be executed.

Indentation Style

Notice how the `if-else` statement in lines 13–22 of Listing 8.1 applies a certain indentation style. It aligns the opening and closing braces under the `if` keyword and indents the statements as follows:

```
if (<Boolean_expression>)
{
    <statements>
}
```

There are many possible indentation styles, but together with the style of Listing 8.1, two other variations seem to dominate in the programming community:

The braces and the statements are all indented:

```
if (<Boolean_expression>)
    {
        <statements>
    }
```

The opening brace is positioned in the same line after the (*<Boolean_expression>*), the *<statements>* are indented, and the closing brace is aligned under `if`

```
if (<Boolean_expression>) {
    <statements>
}
```

Every different style shown here has pros and cons, so you are free to choose your preferred style. The most important thing to remember is to be consistent—always use the same style throughout a software project.

Comparison Operators and Boolean Expressions

You have already seen a few of the comparison operators in action. This section presents the six fundamental comparison operators found in C# and explains how they form Boolean expressions.

A comparison operator allows two data values to be compared and generates a result of type `bool`. If the comparison is true, it produces the `bool` value `true`, and it produces the value `false` if the comparison is untrue.

The six comparison operators, can be divided into two categories—relational and equality. They are all listed in Table 8.1.

TABLE 8.1 The Six Fundamental Comparison Operators

Math Notation	C# Syntax	Name	Example	Category	Explanation
>	>	Greater-than	x > y	Relational	Returns `true` if x is greater than y; otherwise, returns `false`
≥	>=	Greater-than-or-equal-to	x >= y	Relational	Returns `true` if x is greater than or equal to y; otherwise, returns `false`
<	<	Less-than	x < y	Relational	Returns `true` if x is less than y, otherwise; returns `false`
≤	<=	Less-than-or-equal-to	x <= y	Relational	Returns `true` if x is less than or equal to y; otherwise, returns `false`
=	==	Equal-to	x == y	Equality	Returns `true` if x is equal to y; otherwise, returns `false`
≠	!=	Not-equal-to	x != y	Equality	Returns `true` if x is not equal to y; otherwise, returns `false`

`x` in the examples is usually referred to as the left operand and `y` is called the right operand.

C# contains one comparison operator not discussed in this chapter called the `is` operator. This operator is directly related to object-oriented programming and, for this reason, is not discussed until Chapter 17.

All comparison operators return one of the `bool` operators (`true` and `false`). Because a Boolean expression is an expression that is evaluated to be either `true` or `false`, comparison operators form Boolean expressions. This relationship is formally displayed in Syntax Box 8.4. Notice that each comparison operator combines exactly two operands to form a Boolean expression. Relational operators form relational expressions, and equality operators form equality expression.

Syntax Box 8.4 Comparison Operators and Boolean Expressions

```
Boolean_expression::= <Relational_expression>
                  ::= <Equality_expression>
                  ::= <bool_Value>

<Relational_expression>::= <Operand> <Relational_operator> <Operand>

<Equality_expression>::= <Operand> <Equality_operator> <Operand>

<Operand> ::= <Literal>
          ::= <Numerical_variable_identifier>
          ::= <Numerical_constant_identifier>
          ::= <Numerical_expression>
```

```
            ::= <Method_call>

<Relational_operator> ::=  >
                      ::=  >=
                      ::=  <
                      ::=  <=

<Equality_operator> ::=  ==
                    ::=  !=

<Comparison_operator> ::= <Relational_operator>
                      ::= <Equality_operator>
```

Notes:

When a `<Method_call>` is part of the Boolean expression, the method that is called must have a return value.

Only the equality operators can be applied to values of type `bool`.

It is possible to store the result of a Boolean expression in a variable of type `bool`. For example

```
01: bool isPositive;
02: decimal balance = 100;
03: isPositive = (balance > 0);
```

assigns `true` to `isPositive` in line 3.

A Boolean expression can simply be a value of type `bool` (`<bool_Value>`) as indicated in Syntax Box 8.4. Consequently, it is possible to utilize a variable of type `bool` in an `if` statement as shown by continuing the code example:

```
04: if (isPositive)
05:        WriteLine("The account has a positive balance");
```

According to Syntax Box 8.4, comparison operators can combine operands, which also comprise numerical expressions. Thus, the following comparison is valid:

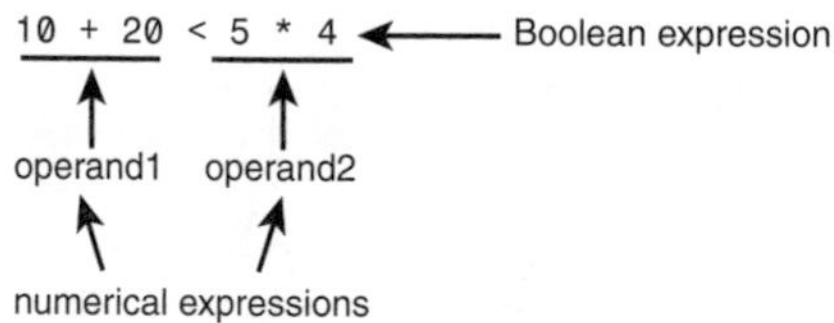

But how is this expression evaluated? For an answer, we need to look at the precedence rules of the operators involved. According to Appendix B, "Operator Precedence" (located at this book's Web site at `www.samspublishing.com`), the relational and equality operators all have lower precedence than any of the arithmetic operators. As a result, arithmetic operations are always performed before comparisons, leading to the following evaluation of our example:

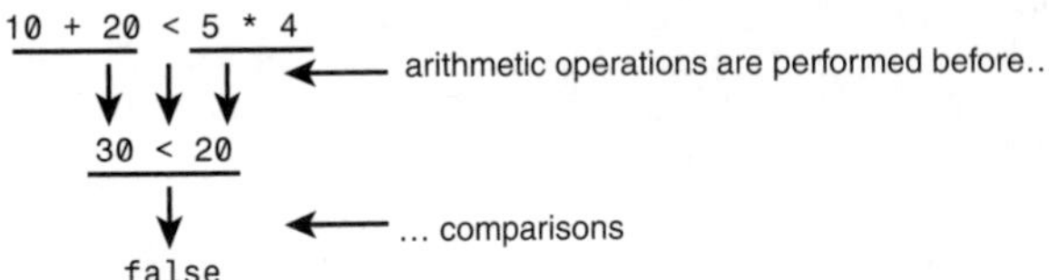

Tip

Even though the Boolean expression

```
10 + 30 < 5 * 4
```

might accomplish exactly what we intended, a couple of parentheses

```
(10 + 30) < (5 * 4)
```

enhances the readability and remove any ambiguity from the reader's mind as to how the expression is evaluated.

When two values of different types are compared with a comparison operator, the compiler follows exactly the same rules of implicit conversion and type promotion as when two values are combined with an arithmetic binary operator. These rules were illustrated in Figure 7.6 of Chapter 7, "Types Part II: Operators, Enumerators and Strings."

The following are a few examples of invalid comparisons. You can locate the problem by tracing the flowchart of Figure 7.6, of Chapter 7.

```
decimal energy = 1000.89m;
ulong mass = 200;
long distance = 10000;
short count = 500;
double length = 2000.98;
bool state;

state = (energy > length);←invalid cannot compare decimal with double
state = (count != energy);←invalid cannot compare short with ulong
state = (mass >= distance);←invalid cannot compare long with ulong
```

Nested `if` Statements

An **`if-else`** statement lets you choose between just two different sets of actions. But sometimes, life presents us with three or more alternatives. Fortunately, the definition of an **`if-else`** statement allows you to nest **`if`** statements inside each other and thereby let a program choose between as many alternative actions as your mind can comprehend.

An **`if`** statement, as the name implies, is a statement in itself. Consequently, it can be positioned inside another **`if`** statement in the position where a statement is expected or as one of the statements in a compound statement. This is illustrated in Figure 8.5, which is based on the syntax of the **`if-else`** statement from Syntax Box 8.3.

FIGURE 8.5
Creating nested *`if`* statements.

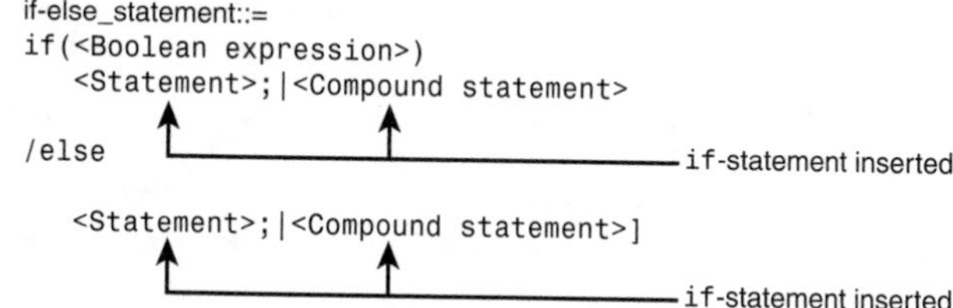

Let's take a look at an example. The logic behind a simple nested `if` statement is illustrated by a flowchart in Figure 8.6. Notice the two decision symbols, one cascading directly from the other.

Two decision symbols, one after the other, are a sign that nested `if` statements can be utilized to implement the given logic. The first decision symbol determines whether a given number is positive. If `false`, an appropriate message is printed. If `true`, the trailing decision symbol evaluates whether the number is divisible by three. If `true` a fitting, message is printed.

FIGURE 8.6
Two directly connected decision symbols.

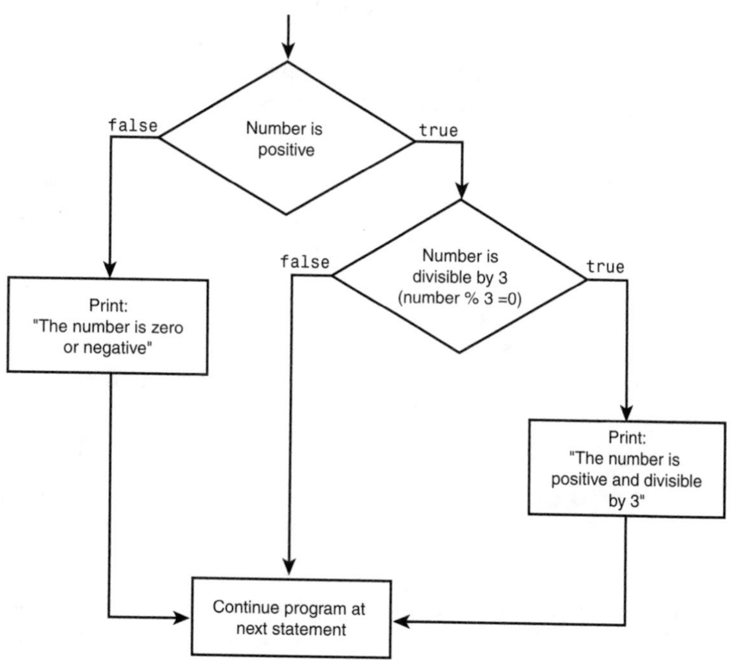

Figure 8.7 shows a code snippet containing one `if` statement nested inside another to implement the two cascading decision symbols of Figure 8.6.

Notice the braces enclosing the inner `if` statement in Figure 8.7. They play an important role in specifying the correct logic implemented and here is why. When you use nested `if-else` statements in your code, it is often questionable which `else` clause belongs to which `if` statement. Fortunately, the compiler has a very clear idea of how to match `if`s with `else`s; the rules abided by are displayed in the following Note.

FIGURE 8.7
One *if* statement nested inside another *if* statement.

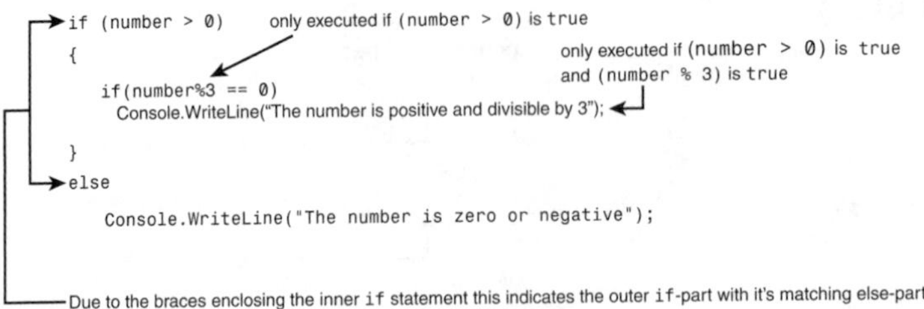

if (number > 0)
only executed if (number > 0) is true
{
only executed if (number > 0) is true
and (number % 3) is true
if(number%3 == 0)
Console.WriteLine("The number is positive and divisible by 3");
}
else
Console.WriteLine("The number is zero or negative");
Due to the braces enclosing the inner if statement this indicates the outer if-part with it's matching else-part

Pairing *else* Clauses with `if` Statements in Nested `if-else` Statements

In an `if-else` statement, an `else` is always paired with the nearest unmatched preceding `if` that is located in the same block.

The logic would be significantly different if we had left out the braces in Figure 8.7; `else` would then have been paired with the inner `if` statement, as shown in Figure 8.8, because this would be the nearest unmatched preceding `if` and *located in the same block*. The latter italicized phrase is where the braces make the important difference. In Figure 8.7, they dictate the inner `if` statement to be in a different block than the `else` clause and so they prevent any pairing between the two.

Figure 8.8 shows an `if-else` statement without the braces, which no longer represents the logic of the flowchart in Figure 8.6. The indentation correctly emphasizes that the `else` clause now matches the inner `if` statement.

FIGURE 8.8
One *if* statement nested inside another *if* statement—no braces, correct indentation, incorrect logic.

```
if (number > 0)
    if(number%3 == 0)
        Console.WriteLine("The number is positive and divisible by 3");
    else
        Console.WriteLine("The number is zero or negative");
```

Only executed if (number > 0) is true and (number % 3 == 0) is true

Only executed if (number > 0) is true and (number%3 == 0) is false

The matching if and else.

This message does not correspond with the implemented logic number is greater than zero if this statement is executed

Had we applied the incorrect indentation shown in Figure 8.9, where the `else` keyword is aligned with the `if` keyword of the outer `if` statement, we could mistakenly have convinced ourselves that the `else` clause is paired with the outer `if` statement.

FIGURE 8.9
One *if* statement nested inside another *if* statement—no braces, incorrect indentation.

```
if (number > 0)
    if(number%3 == 0)
        Console.WriteLine("The number is positive and
        divisible by 3");
else
    Console.WriteLine("The number is zero or negative");
```

The next example presents four `if` statements nested inside each other. They are used to accommodate a request from the financial controller of Big Bucks Bank. She believes that accounts with a balance between either $5,000 and $20,000 or between $60,000 and $75,000 hold special characteristics relevant for the cash management strategy of the bank. Therefore, the bank decides to write a program that can divide bank accounts into the following three categories:

A. $5000 \leq \text{balance} \leq 20000$

B. $60000 \leq \text{balance} \leq 75000$

C. Neither A nor B

The flowchart of Figure 8.10 determines whether a balance belongs to category A, B, or C. Notice the four decision symbols directly connected to each other; a clear sign of the need for four `if` statements nested inside each other.

FIGURE 8.10
Determining the category of balance.

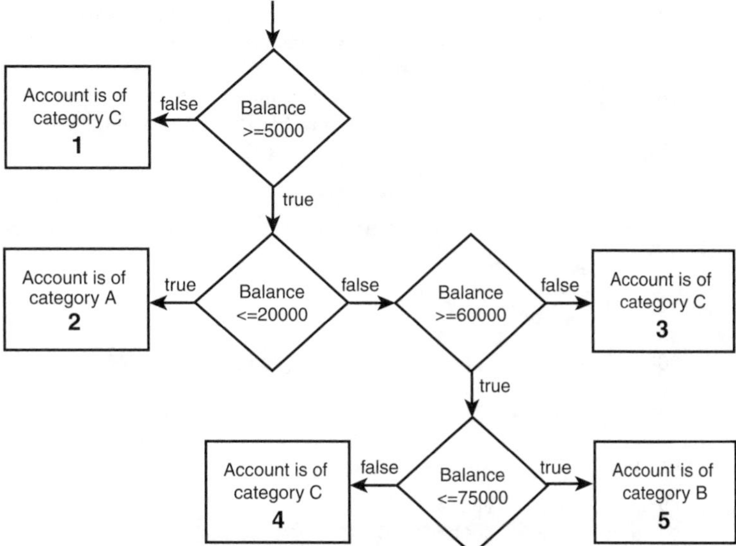

Listing 8.2 contains a prototype program that implements the logic of Figure 8.10. It simply asks the user to enter a balance and will determine to which of the three mentioned categories the balance belongs.

LISTING 8.2 `BalanceAssessment.cs`

```
using System;

class BalanceAssessment
{
    public static void Main()
    {
```

LISTING 8.2 continued

```
07:         decimal balance;
08:
09:         Console.Write("Enter balance: ");
10:         balance = Convert.ToDecimal(Console.ReadLine());
11:         if(balance >= 5000)
12:         {
13:             if(balance <= 20000)
14:             {
15:                  //5000 <= balance <= 20000
16:                 Console.WriteLine("5000 <= balance <= 20000. Category A");
17:             }
18:             else
19:             {
20:                 if(balance >= 60000)
21:                 {
22:                     if(balance <= 75000)
23:                          //60000 <= balance <= 75000
24:                         Console.WriteLine("60000 <= balance <= 75000.
                        ➥ Category B");
25:                     else
26:                          //balance > 75000
27:                         Console.WriteLine("balance > 75000. Category C");
28:                 }
29:                 else
30:                      //20000 < balance < 60000
31:                     Console.WriteLine("20000 < balance < 60000. Category C");
32:             }
33:         }
34:         else
35:              //balance < 5000
36:             Console.WriteLine("balance < 5000. Category C");
37:     }
38: }
```

Output sample 1:

```
Enter balance: 1000<enter>
balance < 5000. Category C
```

Output sample 2:

```
Enter balance: 7000<enter>
5000 <= balance <= 20000. Category A
```

Output sample 3:

```
Enter balance: 71000<enter>
60000 <= balance <= 75000. Category B
```

Listing 8.2 contains four nested `if` statements. The first outermost `if` statement starts at line 11 and matches the first decision symbol in Figure 8.10. If `(balance >= 5000)` is `false`, we know that `balance` must be in the C category, and the program jumps to the matching `else` clause beginning in line 34; this is equivalent to action symbol **1** in Figure 8.10 If `(balance >= 5000)` is `true`, the category is still undecided, so we move to the second level of nested `if` statements in line 13. Notice that for the entire block between the braces in lines 12 and 33, we know that `balance` is greater than or equal to 5000. This knowledge is already helpful when combined with `(balance <= 20000)` of line 13. If this Boolean expression is `true`, we can, with certainty, conclude that `5000   balance   20000`. This is equivalent to action symbol **2** of Figure 8.10. If, on the other hand, `(balance <= 20000)` is `false`, `balance` can still either be in the B or C category, so the flow of execution moves to the third level of `if` statements, commencing in line 20. Inside the block spanning lines 19–32, we can be confident that `balance > 20000`. Thus, if the Boolean expression (`balance >= 60000`) of line 20 is `false`, `balance` must be between 20000 and 60000 and belong to category C. Action symbol **3** corresponds to this situation. At line 22, we know that `(balance >= 60000)` is `true`, so if the condition (`balance <= 75000`) in line 22 is `true`, we know that `60000 <= balance <= 75000`, equivalent to action symbol **4** in Figure 8.10. Finally, if `(balance <= 75000)` is `false`, `balance` is larger than 75000 and part of category C. This is indicated by action symbol **5** in Figure 8.10.

Whew…this was quite an intricate affair. Fortunately, there are a couple of ways by which we can simplify Listing 8.2. One, which you will meet now, provides a standardized system for writing `if-else` statements; the other significantly simplifies the source code by applying logical operators. The latter approach will be demonstrated in the "Logical Operators" section later in this chapter.

Multibranch `if-else` Statements

Notice how the value of `balance` in Listing 8.2 determines which of the five different print statements the program will execute. Letting the value of a variable determine which statement (or compound statement) to execute of several possible alternatives is so commonplace in the programming world that a standardized system has been devised for writing the nested `if-else` structures used to implement this functionality. The resulting structures are called *multibranch* `if-else` *statements*.

Let's have a look at how we can turn Listing 8.2 into this standard style. We start by changing the flowchart of Figure 8.10 to form a new flowchart that yields the same results but follows a couple of standard conventions:

- Only the `false` arrow flowing away from a decision symbol can flow to another decision symbol.
- Every `true` arrow flowing away from a decision symbol flows to an action symbol and from the action symbol to the next statement in the program.

By inspecting Figure 8.10, we realize that the first and third decision symbols do not comply with the stated conventions because the `true` arrow leads to another decision symbol. Consequently, we need to call the `true` arrow `false` and the `false` arrow `true`, but without altering the logic. This can be accomplished by exchanging the greater-than-or-equal-to symbol (>=) with the smaller-than (<) symbol, as shown in Figure 8.11. We have likewise flip-flopped the `false/true` arrows of the third decision symbol while simultaneously exchanging the => symbol with the < symbol. The final complying flowchart is displayed in Figure 8.11.

FIGURE 8.11
The logic behind a multi-branch *`if-else`* statement.

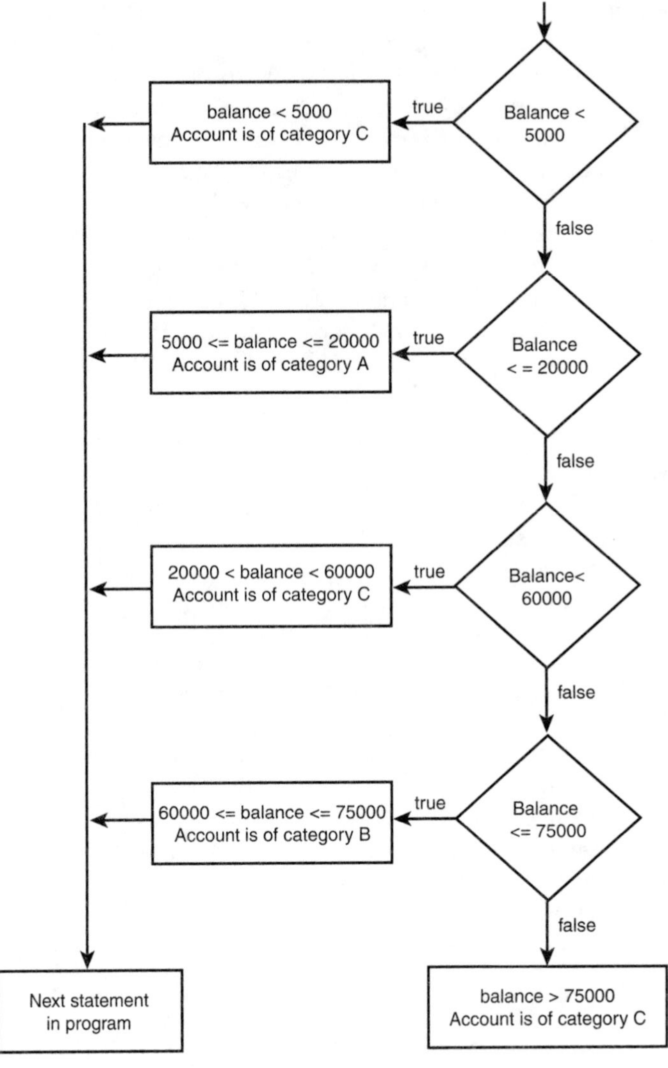

We are now ready to implement the logic expressed with the flowchart of Figure 8.11. By using nested `if-else` statements and adhering to the style of indentation used up to now, we end up with the source code displayed in Listing 8.3, which represents exactly the same functionality (and therefore generates the same output) as the program of Listing 8.2.

LISTING 8.3 `PreMultibranch.cs`

```
using System;

class PreMultibranch
{
```

LISTING 8.3 continued

```
05:     public static void Main()
06:     {
07:         decimal balance;
08:
09:         Console.Write("Enter balance: ");
10:         balance = Convert.ToDecimal(Console.ReadLine());
11:         if(balance < 5000)
12:             Console.WriteLine("balance < 5000. Category C");
13:         else
14:             if(balance <= 20000)
15:                 Console.WriteLine("5000 <= balance <= 20000. Category A");
16:             else
17:                 if(balance < 60000)
18:                     Console.WriteLine("20000 < balance < 60000. Category C");
19:                 else
20:                     if(balance <= 75000)
21:                         Console.WriteLine("60000 <= balance <= 75000 ");
22:                     else
23:                         Console.WriteLine("Balance is in category C");
24:     }
25: }
```

The output from Listing 8.3 is identical to that of Listing 8.2.

The program evaluates the Boolean expressions found in lines 11, 14, 17, and 20 in a sequential manner, starting with line 11. As long as the Boolean expressions are `false`, execution moves to the next indented `if-else` statement. When a Boolean expression is found to be `true`, the statement immediately after is executed. When that happens, we know that all previous Boolean expressions except the last one are `false`. This allows us to make certain deductions about the state of the program—in this case, about the value of `balance`. For example, if one sample run of the program results in the statement of line 21 being executed, we know that (`balance < 60000`) of line 17 is `false` *and* that (`balance <= 75000`) of line 20 is `true`. In turn, this allows us to deduce that (`60000  balance  75000`).

Programmers have devised a standard indentation style when writing multibranch `if-else` statements that reflects their purpose and the way they think about these structures. To fully comply with this style, we need to change the indenting of Listing 8.3 to that shown in Listing 8.4, which still represents exactly the same functionality.

LISTING 8.4 `MultibranchBalanceAssessment.cs`

```
using System;

class MultibranchBalanceAssessment
{
    public static void Main()
    {
        decimal balance;

        Console.Write("Enter balance: ");
        balance = Convert.ToDecimal(Console.ReadLine());
```

LISTING 8.4 continued

```
11:         if(balance < 5000)
12:             Console.WriteLine("balance < 5000. Category C");
13:         else if(balance <= 20000)
14:             Console.WriteLine("5000 <= balance <= 20000. Category A");
15:         else if(balance < 60000)
16:             Console.WriteLine("20000 < balance < 60000. Category C");
17:         else if(balance <= 75000)
18:             Console.WriteLine("60000 <= balance <= 75000. Category B");
19:         else
20:             Console.WriteLine("balance > 75000. Category C");
21:     }
22: }
```

The output from Listing 8.4 is identical to that of Listing 8.3.

Listing 8.4 represents exactly the same program as Listing 8.3, but it conforms to the indenting style associated with multibranch if-else statements. Each nested if(<*Boolean_expression*>) has simply been moved up one line and positioned next to the previous else keyword. The step wise indenting seen in Listing 8.3 is replaced with statements following a vertical line. Because multibranch if-else statements can be extended to contain any number of if-else statements, the indenting style in Listing 8.4 will not, as the style of Listing 8.3, cause you to eventually indent yourself out of the screen (or paper).

Syntax Box 8.5 The Multibranch if-else Statement

```
Multibranch_if-else_Statement::=

if (<Boolean_expression_1>)
     <Statement_1>; | <Compound_statement_1>
else if (<Boolean_expression_2>)
     <Statement_2>; | <Compound_statement_2>
          ......
else if (<Boolean_expression_n>)
     <Statement_n>; | <Compound_statement_n>
else
     <Default_statement>; | <Default_compound_statement>
```

Note: The <*Default_statement*>; | <*Default_compound_statement*> part is only executed if all previous Boolean expressions are false.

Only Use the default_statement for Genuine Defaults in Multibranch if-else Statements

Line 20 of Listing 8.4 contains what Syntax Box 8.5 denotes a <*Default_statement*>. Whenever this line is executed, we can with confidence say that balance is greater than 75000 because all other options have been effectively eliminated. This matches perfectly well with the message printed by line 20.

Listing 8.5 presents an example of the incorrect use of the default option. It asks the user to enter one of the three letters (A, B, or C) and responds by simply telling the user which letter was entered.

LISTING 8.5 `ChooseAction.cs`

```
01: using System;
02:
03: class ChooseAction
04: {
05:     public static void Main()
06:     {
07:         string choice;
08:
09:         Console.Write("Enter either A, B or C: ");
10:         choice = Console.ReadLine();
11:         if(choice == "A")
12:             Console.WriteLine("You entered an A");
13:         else if (choice == "B")
14:             Console.WriteLine("You entered a B");
15:         else
16:             Console.WriteLine("You entered a C");       //unsound
17:     }
18: }
```

Sample output 1:

```
Enter either A, B or C: B<enter>
You entered a B
```

Sample output 2:

```
Enter either A, B or C: F<enter>
You entered a C.
```

Line 16 is a default statement and mistakenly expects the letter entered by the user to always be a C if it is not an A and not a B. The sample output exposes the problem. As long as the user enters one of the letters (A, B, or C), there is no problem. However, any other letter, such as F, is incorrectly defaulted through `else` in line 15 to be a C.

Let's improve the code in Listing 8.5. First, we need to make sure that the message in line 16 corresponds with all previous Boolean expressions of the multibranch `if-else` statement. This can be achieved by explicitly testing for the letter C in line 15. Consequently, we change line 15 to

```
15:         else if (choice == "C")
```

The *<Default_statement>* is now unused, so we can put it to good use by letting it detect incorrect user input, as shown in lines 17 and 18 of Listing 8.6. If the flow of execution reaches line 18, we can be confident that the letter entered is not an A, B, or C. Otherwise, it would have been detected by any of the three Boolean expressions in lines 11, 13, and 15.

LISTING 8.6 Incomplete Code Snippet

```
        else if (choice == "C")
            Console.WriteLine("You entered a C");
        else
             Console.WriteLine("Invalid input. Letter was not A, B or C");
    }
}
```

Tip

This leads us to a second general recommendation when constructing multibranch `if-else` statements—detect errors with the *<Default_statement>* if it is unused.

Tip

Avoid too deeply nested `if-else` statements. In many cases, programmers cannot understand more than three to four levels of nested `if-else` statements.

Deep nesting can be prevented by

- Redesigning the Boolean expression. This process can often be facilitated through the use of logical operators, as shown in the forthcoming section.
- Breaking the code into simpler methods.

Logical Operators

So far, our Boolean expressions have consisted of only simple conditions, such as `balance <= 20000` in line 13 of Listing 8.4 or `(choice == "A")` in line 11 of Listing 8.5, with only one comparison operator. However, it is often beneficial to combine several simple conditions (sub-Boolean expressions) into one larger Boolean expression. *Logical operators* allow us to do exactly that.

C# contains three logical operators that are semantically equivalent to "and," "or," and "not" in our everyday language. The latter are used in Figure 8.12 as a general introduction to C#'s equivalents. Notice that each phrase could be part of a normal conversation, and that we intuitively understand their meaning.

The equivalents to and, or, and not from spoken English, are in the world of logic called *logical AND*, *logical OR*, and *logical NOT*. Logical AND is in C# symbolized by `&&` (two adjacent ampersands); logical OR is symbolized by `||` (two vertical lines); logical NOT is written as `!` (exclamation point).

The science of *logic* investigates the rules governing reliable deductions.

FIGURE 8.12
Three logical "operators" of the English language—and, or, and not.

1.

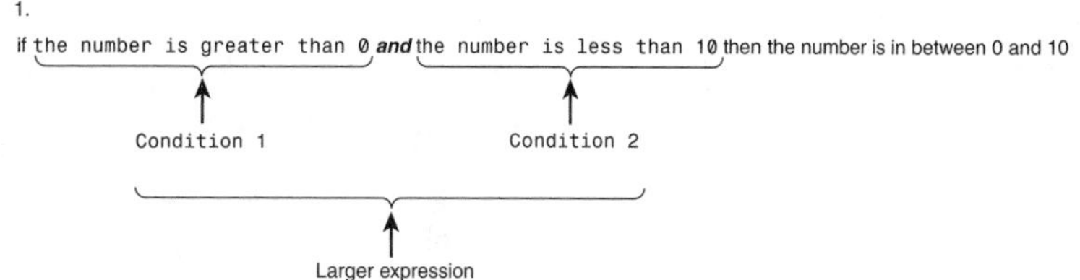

2.

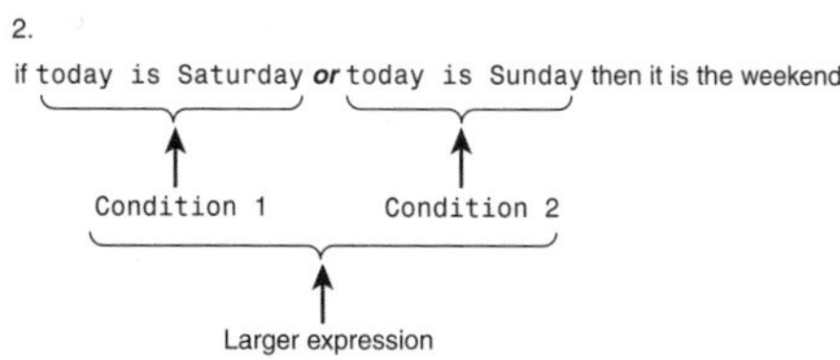

3.

Often it is also useful to negate a Boolean expression such as in this example...

If today is ***not*** the weekend then today is a working day.

...which is easier than saying: if today is Monday or today is Tuesday or today is Wednesday or today is Thursday or today is Friday then today is a working day.

Note

It is important to realize that the meaning associated with `&&` (AND), `||` (OR), and `!` (NOT) when used in C# does not deviate significantly from the meaning of and, or, and not in everyday speech. C# has merely formalized the meaning to iron out any ambiguities found in spoken language.

A *logical operator* (`&&`, `||`, `!`) can only be applied to expressions of type `bool` and will always return a value of type `bool`. Another common term for logical operator is *Boolean operator*.

Table 8.2 provides a brief overview of the three operators. Notice that AND, OR, and NOT are sometimes referred to as conjunction, disjunction, and negation.

TABLE 8.2 Three Commonly Used Logical Operators

Logical operator	Other term used	C# Symbol	Number of operands	Example
AND	Conjunction	`&&`	2 (binary)	`(5<3) && (10<20)`
OR	Disjunction	`||`	2 (binary)	`(mass < 800) || (distance > 1000)`
NOT	Negation	`!`	1 (unary)	`!(mass > 8000)`

Note

C# contains three additional logical operators apart from those mentioned in Table 8.2. They are called *logical bitwise operators* and are symbolized by single ampersand (`&`), single vertical line (`|`) arrow pointing up (`^`). The two former operators `&` and `|` have the same logical meaning as their close relatives `&&` and `||`, respectively, but with subtle differences during their evaluation. The last logical operator `^` is called the exclusive operator.

Because the logical bitwise operators are used less frequently than their cousins in Table 8.2. They will not be part of the main discussion here, but are presented at the end of this section.

The Logical AND Operator: &&

The logical AND operator (`&&`) is a binary operator and it combines *two* sub-Boolean expressions to form one larger Boolean expression (see Syntax Box 8.6).

Syntax Box 8.6: Forming Larger Boolean Expressions with the && Operator

```
Larger_Boolean_expression::=
                    <Sub_Boolean_expression1> && <Sub_Boolean_expression2>
```

By combining the two possible values (`true` and `false`) of `<Sub_Boolean_expression1>` with the two possible values of `<Sub_Boolean_expression2>`, we can form a *truth table* (see Table 8.3) with the four (2×2) different possible combinations and their resulting values when combined by the AND operator (`&&`).

A *truth table* provides a complete list of all the possible combinations of values of the variables in a Boolean expression and the resulting value for each combination. Tables 8.3, 8.4, 8.5, 8.6, 8.7, 8.8, and 8.9 are all examples of truth tables.

TABLE 8.3 Truth Table for the Logical AND (`&&`) Operator

Value of *sub_expression1*	Value of *sub_expression2*	Value of larger Boolean expression: *sub_expression1 && sub_expression2*	Example
false	false	false	(5>10) && (10<3)
false	true	false	(5==2) && (10>2)
true	false	false	(5!=0) && (3!=3)
true	true	true	(7>4) && (9<10)

Notice that only when *both* the original expressions of Table 8.3 are `true` does the resulting expression represent the value `true`; otherwise, the value is `false`.

Note

According to Appendix B (located at this book's Web site at www.samspublishing.com), all the comparison operators have higher precedence than the `&&` and `||` operators, so the parentheses applied in the examples of Table 8.3 are redundant. `(5>10) && (10<3)` is equivalent to `5>10 && 10<3`. However, the intent of the former is clearer.

Recall the `balance` assessment program of Listing 8.4 presented earlier. As promised, it is possible to significantly simplify this program with the use of logical operators; let's see how.

The basic strategy is to reduce the number of required nested `if` statements by letting the Boolean expression of each `if` statement more precisely express the logic we are implementing. Recall our three categories from the Big Bucks Bank:

A. $5000 \leq \text{balance} \leq 20000$

B. $60000 \leq \text{balance} \leq 75000$

C. Neither A nor B

The Boolean expression of each `if` statement in Listing 8.4 was only partly able to describe (express) each category and had to be combined with Boolean expressions of other nested `if` statements to complete the picture. If we can somehow express the mathematical notation $5000 \leq \text{balance} \leq 20000$ in one Boolean expression, we can write the logic shown in Figure 8.13 and reduce the number of nested `if` statements from four to two.

FIGURE 8.13
A simpler but invalid implementation of the logic in Listing 8.4.

```
if (5000 <=balance <=20000)
      //balance is in category A
else if ( 60000 <=balance <=75000)
      //balance is in category B
else
      //balance is in category C
```


The code in Figure 8.13 has certainly simplified the multibranch `if-else` statement, but it has one serious drawback—the Boolean expressions are invalid. It is not possible to use the mathematical notation $5000 \leq \text{balance} \leq 20000$ in the C# source code as in the following:

```
if (5000 <= balance <= 20000)     //Invalid
```

Any such comparisons must be broken down into sub-expressions with only one comparison operator and then connected fittingly with logical operators. Fortunately, it is possible by following this valid system to state the meaning contained in any logic expression.

But how do we express `5000 <= balance <= 20000` in this system, and how can we show that our new expression is correct? Well, many simpler expressions can be formed out of intuition and common sense, whereas more complicated expressions require knowledge from the science of logic. In our case, we try with common sense and convince ourselves that the meaning of

```
5000 <= balance <= 20000
```

had it been valid, is equivalent to

```
(5000 <= balance) && (balance <= 20000)
```

To prove that our common sense is correct, and that the two expressions in fact are identical, we can compare their truth tables. The truth table for `5000 <= balance <= 20000` is shown in Table 8.4. Notice that each of the first two columns must be filled out in the standard fashion introduced in Table 8.3, so they contain exactly the same entries.

TABLE 8.4 Truth Table for the Proposition `5000 <= balance <= 20000`

5000 ≤ balance	balance ≤ 20000	5000 ≤ balance ≤ 20000
false	false	false
false	true	false
true	false	false
true	true	true

The truth table for `&&` is simply constructed by copying the values given in `&&`'s truth table of Table 8.3 and inserting `balance >= 5000` and `balance <= 20000` in the place of the subexpressions. This results in Table 8.5.

TABLE 8.5 Truth Table for the Proposition `5000 ≤ balance` AND `balance ≤ 20000`

balance >= 5000	balance <= 20000	5000 <= balance && balance <= 20000
false	false	false
false	true	false
true	false	false
true	true	true

Because the entries of the two tables are identical, we conclude that our common sense indeed was correct, in that

```
5000 ≤ balance ≤ 20000
```

is equivalent to

```
5000 <= balance && balance <=  20000
```

and, consequently, we can simplify the nested `if` statements of our Big Bucks Bank application in a similar fashion to that shown in Figure 8.13. Lines 11–16 of Listing 8.7 present the resulting multibranch `if-else` statements.

LISTING 8.7 `CompactBalanceAssessment.cs`

```
01: using System;
02:
03: class CompactBalanceAssessment
04: {
05:     public static void Main()
06:     {
07:         decimal balance;
08:
09:         Console.Write("Enter balance: ");
10:         balance = Convert.ToDecimal(Console.ReadLine());
11:         if(balance >= 5000 && balance <= 20000)
12:             Console.WriteLine("Balance is in category A");
13:         else if(balance >= 60000 && balance <= 75000)
14:             Console.WriteLine("Balance is in category B");
15:         else
16:             Console.WriteLine("Balance is in category C");
17:     }
18: }
```

The output is the same as that from Listing 8.4.

By utilizing the `&&` operator in lines 11 and 13, we reduce the number of nested `if-else` statements from four to two. This is possible since we have shown that:

> `balance >= 5000 && balance <= 20000` is logically equivalent to
> `5000 >= balance >= 20000`

and that:

> `balance >= 5000 && balance <= 20000` is logically equivalent to
> `5000 >= balance >= 20000`

The Logical OR Operator: ||

The logical operator OR, written with two vertical lines `||`, is a binary operator and, as such, combines two operands, as shown in Syntax Box 8.7.

Syntax Box 8.7 Forming Larger Boolean Expressions with the || Operator

```
Larger_Boolean_expression::=
                    <Sub_Boolean_expression1> || <Sub_Boolean_expression2>
```

The truth table of the logical OR operator shown in Table 8.6 tells us that only if both sub-expressions are `false` (first row) will the larger expression be `false`; otherwise, it will be `true`. This nicely fits in with our usual connotation of the word "or." For example in the following sentence

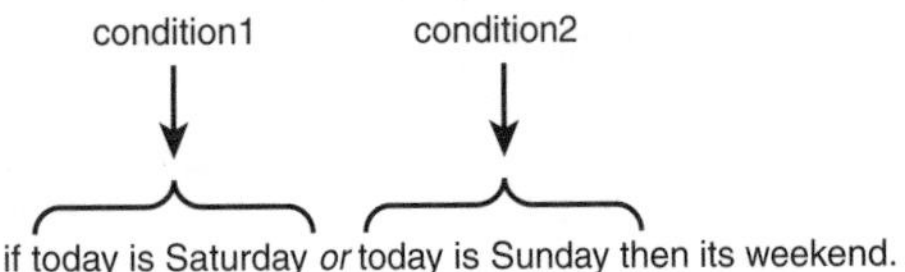

both conditions need to be `false` for today not to be a weekend.

TABLE 8.6 Truth Table for the Logical OR (||) Operator

Value of sub- `expression1`	Value of sub-`expression2`	`sub-expression1 || sub-expression2`
`false`	`false`	`false`
`false`	`true`	`true`
`true`	`false`	`true`
`true`	`true`	`true`

Example:

Sometimes theatres and cinemas offer discounted tickets to people who fit into a certain age category. In this case, a person must be either less than 15 or more than 65 years old to get a discounted ticket. Listing 8.8 utilizes the `||` operator along with this rule to determine whether a person is entitled to a discount.

LISTING 8.8 `DiscountOrNot.cs`

```
using System;

class DiscountOrNot
{
    public static void Main()
    {
        int age;

        Console.Write("Enter your age: ");
```

LISTING 8.8 continued

```
10:         age = Convert.ToInt32(Console.ReadLine());
11:         if ((age < 15) || (age > 65))
12:             Console.WriteLine("Congratulations! You get a discount");
13:         else
14:             Console.WriteLine("Sorry no discount for you");
15:     }
16: }
```

```
Enter your age: 10<enter>
Congratulations! You get a discount
```

Line 11 utilizes the `||` operator to determine whether `age` is less than 15 or greater than 65. If this is the case, line 12 is executed; otherwise, the flow of control is passed to line 14.

You might use as many logical operators in one Boolean expression as you want, but must then keep in mind that the `&&` operator has a higher precedence than the `||` operator. Consequently, you might need to apply parentheses to get a correct result.

Example:

A programmer wants to implement a simple program that sifts through a list of cars for sale in a database to locate cars with suitable characteristics. In this case, the programmer is interested in the `price`, `age`, and `maxSpeed`. The `price` is the main concern, so as long as the `price` is less than $5,000.00, she is happy if just one of the following two criteria is `true`:

- `age` < 10 years
- `maxSpeed` > 120 mph.

The following is a first attempt to implement these rules:

```
if (price < 5000 && age < 10 || maxSpeed > 120)  //Incorrect first attempt
```

However, due to the higher precedence of the `&&` operator, the Boolean expression is evaluated as

```
  if ((price < 5000 && age < 10) || maxSpeed > 120)
```

which represents a different logic. It locates all cars with a `maxSpeed` greater than 120, disregarding the `price` and `age`. All other cars will only be selected if both (`price < 5000`) and (`age < 10`) are `true`. To rectify the problem, we need to apply a couple of parentheses, forcing the `||` operator to be applied first:

```
if (price < 5000 && (age < 10 || maxSpeed > 120))  //Correct
```

Let's compare the truth tables (see Table 8.7) of the invalid and the valid car evaluation expressions to pinpoint the differences between them. Notice that the differences between the two expressions appear in the second and fourth rows, the rest are identical.

TABLE 8.7 Comparing Truth Tables of the Two Car Evaluation Expressions

Price < 5000	Age < 10	MaxSpeed > 120	(price < 5000 && age < 10 || maxSpeed > 120)	(price < 5000 && (age < 10 || maxSpeed > 120))
false	false	false	false	false
false	false	true	true	false
false	true	false	false	false
false	true	true	true	false
true	false	false	false	false
true	false	true	true	true
true	true	false	true	true
true	true	true	true	true

Note

To write down all the combinations of `true` and `false` for the sub-expression in a truth table, use the system applied in Table 8.7. The leftmost column has `false` written in the four top rows and `true` in the four bottom rows. The next column has two `false`s and two `true`s, and every second row is `false` in the thirdmost column.

Short Circuit Evaluation and the Bitwise Operators & and |

When the program evaluates a Boolean expression containing the `&&` operator, such as

```
(distance == 1000) && (mass ==3000)
```

it will first evaluate `(distance == 1000)`. If this part turns out to be `false`, the compiler knows that according to the `&&` truth table, the whole expression must be `false`, irrespective of the value the second part (`(mass == 3000)`). To save time, the compiler skips the evaluation of `(mass == 3000)`. This mechanism is referred to as *short-circuiting*.

Similarly, if the program contains the following `||` expression

```
(distance == 1000) || (mass == 3000)
```

and the first part (`(distance == 1000)`) is evaluated to be `true`, the latter part will be ignored, because its value, according to the OR truth table, will not make any difference to the value of the full expression.

C# contains two additional logical operators called *bitwise AND* symbolized with a single ampersand (`&`) and *bitwise OR* symbolized by a single vertical line (`|`). The truth tables for `&`

and `|` are identical to those of `&&` and `||`, respectively. However, `&` and `|` do *not* cause short circuit evaluation and will, therefore, perform a fraction slower than their short-circuiting equivalents.

In most cases, `&&` and `||` will be the preferred operators to use, but in rare instances, you might want the program to complete the evaluation of a Boolean expression, even if it is not needed to determine the value of the overall Boolean expression.

For example, recall the increment (++) and decrement (--) arithmetic operators from Chapter 7. Just as they can be part of a longer arithmetic expression, they can also be part of a Boolean expression, such as the following:

```
if ((++distance == 1000) && (++count <= 10))
```

whenever `(++count <= 10)` is evaluated, `count` is first incremented by one and then compared with `10`. However, due to the short-circuiting nature of `&&`, `(++count <= 10)` is only evaluated if `(++distance == 1000)` is `true`. As a consequence, `count` will only be incremented by one when `distance` is equal to `1000`, which was probably not what the programmer had in mind. To make sure that the increment always takes place when this line is executed, the programmer can make use of the bitwise operator `&`:

```
if ((++distance == 1000) & (++count <= 10))
```

Tip

Even though source code with increment and decrement operators applied inside longer expression might look smart and sophisticated at first glance, they usually represent bug-prone code, difficult to read and, hence, not worthwhile. Thus, instead of writing

```
if ((++distance == 1000) & (++count <= 10))
```

break the line up into three lines:

```
++distance;
++count;
if ((distance == 1000) && (count <= 10))
```

There is no doubt as to how these three lines are processed.

Sometimes, programmers use a certain style for constructing a Boolean expression that requires short-circuit evaluation to avoid runtime errors. This is exemplified in the following line:

```
if ((speed != 0)  && ((distance / speed) > 100))
```

In general, division by zero produces an infinitely large value and a runtime exception. Thus, if `speed` in the expression is equal to zero, the second part of the expression (`((distance / speed) > 100)`) generates a runtime exception. However, because `(speed != 0)`, along with the short circuiting of the `&&` operator, only allows the second part to be executed if `speed` is different from zero, the line will never generate a runtime exception due to this problem. This would obviously not be the case had we applied the bitwise `&` operator instead.

The Bitwise Exclusive OR Operator: ^

The `||` operator is sometimes referred to as *inclusive OR* and is, in many cases, equivalent to the meaning of "or" in our spoken language. For example, if I ask you

Would you like salt or pepper?

"or" has the same meaning as `||`. It is implicitly understood that you can choose just the salt or just the pepper or even both; all three cases would lead to `true`, similar to our truth table for `||` (see Table 8.6). Only if you decide against both offers does the proposition become `false`. But what about the next question:

Would you like to go to the cinema or the theatre tonight?

where the intent is to either go to the cinema or the theatre but not both. Thus, if you choose neither or if you choose both, the proposition is `false`. Only if you choose just the cinema or just the theatre will it be `true`. This meaning of "or" is referred to as *exclusive OR* and is symbolized by ^ in C#. The truth table is shown in Table 8.8.

TABLE 8.8 Truth Table for the Logical Exclusive OR Operator: ^

Value of sub- `expression1`	Value of sub-`expression2`	`sub-expression1 ^ sub-expression2`
`false`	`false`	`false`
`false`	`true`	`true`
`true`	`false`	`true`
`true`	`true`	`false`

Note

The ambiguous connotation of "or" in our spoken language can sometimes have important implications.

Consider this scenario: Your house is damaged by fire and, during the fire, a thief takes all your belongings. After this ordeal, you rush to check your insurance policy and are relieved when you see the following line:

"...and you are insured against theft or fire..."

Then it suddenly strikes you (because you've just been reading your favorite chapter about logical operators in some book about C#) that the insurance company might interpret "or" in the contract as exclusive "or." You're freaked out by the thought of the implications: Because the two misfortunes happened at the same time, you get zilch compensation. Only if the house is on fire exclusively, or if the house is broken into exclusively will you get a payment.

The Logical NOT Operator: !

The logical NOT (`!`)operator is, as opposed to the binary operators `&&` and `||`, a unary operator, as shown in Syntax Box 8.8. Just as the unary minus operator - reverses the sign of a numerical expression, the logical NOT operator inverts the truth value of the Boolean expression to which it is applied. In other words, if the value of `myBooleanExpression` is `true`, `!myBooleanExpression` is `false`, and vice versa. This is displayed in Table 8.9.

Syntax Box 8.8 Forming Boolean Expressions with the `!` Operator

```
Boolean_expression::= !<Sub_Boolean_expression>
```

Note

A popular name for the `!` operator is *bang*. Thus, `!isReady` is pronounced "bang is Ready."

Note

The `!` operator does not change the value of the expression to which it is applied. It merely changes the value generated by the expression.

TABLE 8.9 Truth Table for the Logical NOT (`!`) Operator

Value of *sub-expression*	*!sub-expression*
`false`	`true`
`true`	`false`

In many cases, Boolean expressions are clearer if they don't involve negations. Fortunately, it is often possible to steer clear of the negation operator by rearranging the operands and by carefully selecting the comparison operators applied in a Boolean expression. Table 8.10 provides a few examples.

TABLE 8.10 Negated Boolean Expressions and Their Non-Negated Equivalent Counterparts

Boolean expression with ! operator	Clearer equivalent Boolean expression without the ! operator
`!(x == 10)`	`(x != 10)`
`!(x > 10)`	`(x <= 10)`
`!(x <= 10)`	`(x > 10)`

Note

As opposed to && and ||, the ! operator has a higher precedence than any of the arithmetic or comparison operators. Thus, you should always enclose a Boolean expression involving those operators in parentheses before negating it. For example

```
! (10 > 20)  //Valid

! 10 > 20    //Invalid
```

The first expression is valid because the parentheses enclose a Boolean expression.

However, the second expression is interpreted as `(! 10) > 20`, applying the `!` operator to `10`, which is an `int` and a non-Boolean expression. As a result, a compiler error is triggered in this case.

If you are constructing an `if-else` statement and are trying to remove an `!` operator stalking the associated Boolean expression, the following method might be helpful.

Consider the following two code snippets.

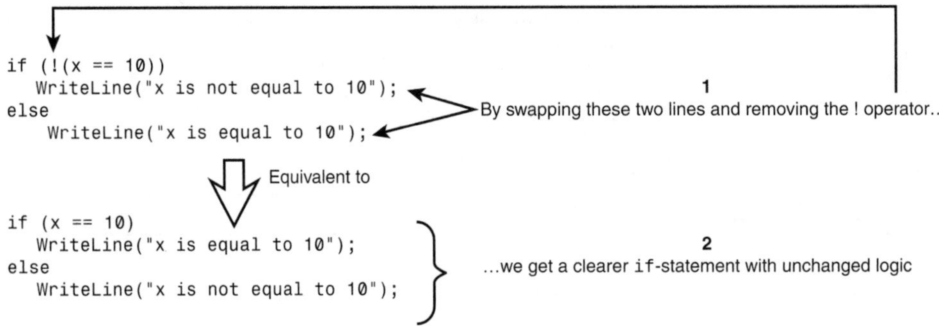

The only effect of the `!` operator in this `if-else` statement is to redirect the flow from the `true` `if` part to the `false` `else` part and vice versa. Thus, by removing the `!` operator as well as swapping the contents of the `if` part and the `else` part, the logic of the `if-else` statements remains unchanged.

Until now, we have merely tried to avoid our poor and lonely `!` operator. Isn't it useful for anything? Yes, it is useful in cases where it is impossible to exchange one comparison operator with another or swapping statements in `if-else` statements as demonstrated above. We bump into those cases when working with methods returning a value of type `bool`. Recall our `TextAnalyzer.cs` program from Listing 7.8, in Chapter 7. It utilized a whole host of methods found in the `System.Char` structure, one of which was the `IsWhiteSpace()` method. It returned the value `true` if the character provided as an argument was a whitespace character; otherwise, it returned `false`. But what if we wanted to count the non-whitespace characters of a text? Because there is no `IsNotWhiteSpace()` method or something similar, we can utilize the `!` operator instead to simulate such a method. This is done in line 17 of Listing 8.9, which counts all non-whitespace characters of a text.

LISTING 8.9 `CharacterCounter.cs`

```
01: using System;
02:
03: class CharacterCounter
04: {
05:     public static void Main()
06:     {
07:         string myText;
08:         int charCount = 0;
09:         char ch;
10:         int index = 0;
11:
12:         Console.WriteLine("Enter some text");
13:         myText = Console.ReadLine();
14:         while (index < myText.Length)
15:         {
16:             ch = myText[index];
17:             if (!char.IsWhiteSpace(ch))
18:                 charCount++;
19:             index++;
20:         }
21:         Console.WriteLine("Number of non-white-space characters:
            ➥ {0:N0}", charCount);
22:     }
23: }
```

Sample 1:

```
Enter some text
Beethoven<enter>
Number of non-white-space characters: 9
```

Sample 2:

```
Enter some text
B e e   th  o   v    e   n<enter>
Number of non-white-space characters: 9
```

As long as `(index < myText.Length)` in line 14 is `true`, the compound statement of the `while` statement spanning from line 15 to line 20 is repeated. Because `index` is initialized to 0 in line 10, and every repetition of the compound statement increments `index` by 1 in line 19, the loop is repeated `myText.Length` times, allowing the algorithm to analyze every position of `myText` in lines 17 and 18. We are able to detect all non-whitespace characters by applying the `!` operator in line 17. Every time a non-whitespace character is encountered, `charCount` is incremented by one.

The Scope of Variables

The majority of the source code presented in the previous chapters has mainly used the block construct and its accompanying matching braces to mark out the context of a class or to delineate the context of methods, the `Main()` method in particular.

With the introduction of **`if-else`** statements and their ability to contain blocks of code (compound statements), you will begin to create programs containing several layers of nested blocks inside and next to each other. It is, therefore, important to introduce a new concept closely related to the block construct called scope. The scope determines which segments (and hence variables) of the source code are visible (and hence accessible) to other parts of the source code. Scope is the technical term used for the informal word context.

Scope is the segment of the source code where a particular variable identifier can be used. Variables can only be used inside their scope. The block of source code in which a variable is declared defines the scope of the variable.

Two of the major scopes in C# are those marked out by the class block and the method block, as illustrated in Figure 8.14. Even though the distinction between these two blocks might be somewhat artificial, the class scope contains several distinctive characteristics not found within the method scope. For example, it is only possible to insert **`if-else`** statements inside the method scope. Consequently, the class scope discussion is deferred until the detailed discussion of the class concept in Chapter 12, "Class Anatomy Part I: **`static`** Class Members and Method Adventures." The rest of the discussion here is focused on the method scope and blocks (scopes) nested inside it.

FIGURE 8.14
Class block and the `Main()` method block.

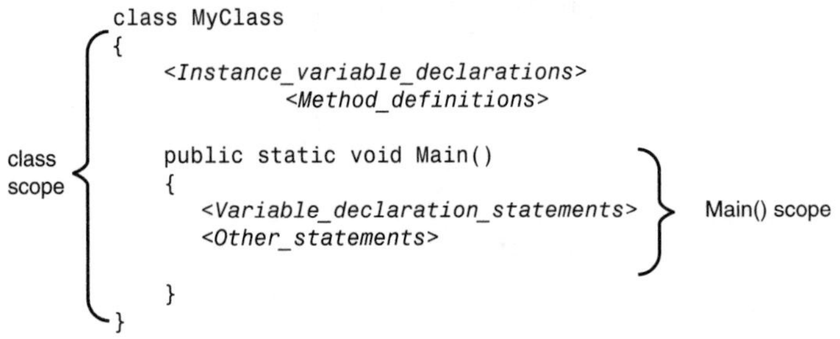

```
class MyClass
{
    <Instance_variable_declarations>
            <Method_definitions>

    public static void Main()
    {
        <Variable_declaration_statements>
        <Other_statements>

    }
}
```

class scope

Main() scope

You don't need constructs like the **`if-else`** statements to create a block inside another block. A new block, and thereby a new scope, can simply be created by inserting a couple of matching braces, as shown in Figure 8.15. When a block, here named B, is inserted inside another block A, the scope formed by block B is said to be the *inner scope*, and the scope formed by block A is the *outer scope*. Inner and outer are relative terms, thus making the scope of block A inner relative to the outer `Main()` block scope. Notice that the names A and B are used merely for illustrative purposes; blocks created simply by adding a couple of braces do not carry any name tags and cannot be referenced as such.

A *local variable* is a variable declared within a method.

Variables declared inside a method block are not accessible from outside this block and are referred to as local variables.

As a rule of thumb, variables declared inside a block are only accessible from code written within this block (including that of other inner blocks inserted here) and after the declaration of the variable. A variable can be declared at any position within a block.

FIGURE 8.15
Blocks can be inserted anywhere inside the method scope.

```
...
public static void Main()
{
   //Main() Block
  ...
   {
      // Block A <------ inner relative to Main(), but outer relative to B
       ...
      {
          // Block B
          ...
      }
      ...
   }
  ...
}
...
```

Figure 8.16 illustrates the effect of these rules. It contains two blocks of code. One block belongs to the `Main()` method, and the other to an `if` statement, which is positioned inside the `Main()` block. Because `distance` is declared at the beginning of the outer scope, it is accessible throughout the code of `Main()`, including the code inside the inner `if` statement block. On the other hand, because `mass` is not declared until towards the end of `Main()`, it is only accessible in the relatively small segment of code between this declaration and the end of the `Main()` scope. The `energy` variable is declared inside the `if` statement block and is only accessible within this block.

FIGURE 8.16
Blocks, scope, and accessibility.

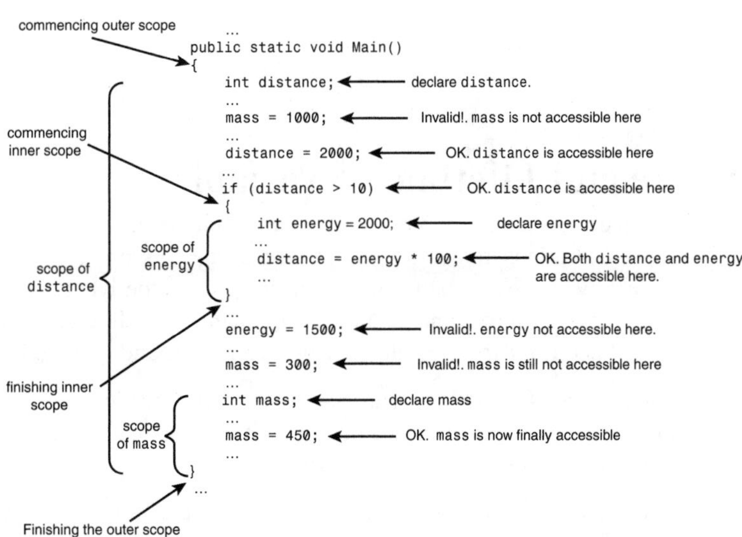

It is an error to declare a variable in an inner scope with a name identical to that of a variable in an outer scope (see Figure 8.17). The reason for this is that this would give a different meaning to the variable name of the outer scope.

FIGURE 8.17
Two variables with the same name cannot be declared in two nested blocks.

```
public static void Main()
{
        int distance;
          ...
        {
                int distance; //invalid. Same name as
                              //distance in outer scope.
                  ...
        }
        ...
}
```

On the other hand, it is possible, albeit perhaps confusing, to declare two variables with the same name in two blocks both residing inside the same block but existing next to each other, rather than nested inside each other. Figure 8.18 illustrates.

FIGURE 8.18
Two variables with the same name but in different adjacent blocks.

```
public static void Main()
{
          ...
        {
                int distance;
                  ...
        }
        {
                int distance;
                  ...
        }
          ...
}
```

Scope and Lifetime of Variables

Recall our discussion about variable names (identifiers) as a convenient means to reference specific locations in memory. When discussing the scope concept, it is important to separate the ability to use a certain name to reference the underlying data residing inside the memory (the scope) from the time the underlying memory itself exists. The latter is referred to as the *lifetime of a variable*. The difference between scope and lifetime is illustrated in Figure 8.19.

The lifetime of a variable is the time between the creation and the destruction of a variable. From the time a variable is created, its value is retained somewhere in the computer memory. This preservation lasts until its destruction.

The reference from a name of a variable to the data in memory, which it represents is often referred to as a *binding*.

Note

As a general rule, variables in C# are created when the program flow enters their scope and destroyed when it leaves their scope. As a result, the lifetime of a variable is confined to its scope.

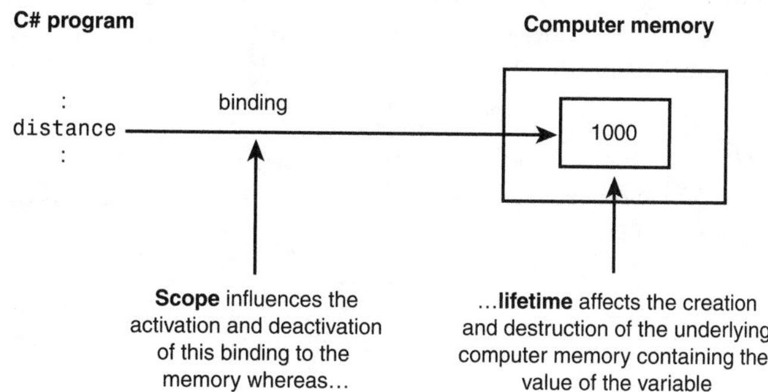
C# program
Computer memory
:
distance
:
binding
1000
Scope influences the activation and deactivation of this binding to the memory whereas...
...**lifetime** affects the creation and destruction of the underlying computer memory containing the value of the variable

FIGURE 8.19
Scope and lifetime.

Even though the rule put forth in the previous note seems obvious, it does not hold for all computer languages. Some languages allow the program flow to enter and leave the scope of a variable numerous times while preserving the value of the variable. Thus, every time the scope is re-entered, the variable has the same value it had just before leaving the scope at the previous visit.

The `goto` Statement

The `goto` statement transfers program control to a position specified by the programmer. Consequently, it interferes with the usual sequential execution of a program.

The `goto` statement has had a long controversial history. One of the first languages to include this language construct was an early version of FORTRAN. However, in the late 1960s, most of the 1970s, and even presently at rare occasions, the pros and cons of this semi-structured language element are hotly debated among programmers and language designers.

Note

Most programmers and computer language experts agree that *indiscriminate* use of the `goto` statement leads to ugly, unclear code that takes longer to write, contains more bugs, and is difficult to debug and maintain. As a general rule, `goto` is a superfluous language element in C#; however, it can be useful when constructing `switch` statements, as demonstrated in the next section. Because of this, the `goto` examples provided here are merely meant as illustrations of how `goto` works and are not examples of good programming practice. The `goto` presentation is included for completeness, to warn you against its use, to let you use it in the `switch` statement, and to let you know what's going on if you should stumble on the (hopefully) odd `goto` statement inserted by another programmer.

There are three varieties of `goto` statements. One variation (the `goto` label statement) is used in the general source code and is discussed in this section; the other two (the `goto case` and `goto default` statements) are specifically targeted at the `switch` statement and are discussed in the next section.

The **goto** label construct consists of a **goto**-label statement and an associated label statement. When the **goto** statement is executed, it transfers the flow of control to the associated label, as illustrated in Figure 8.20.

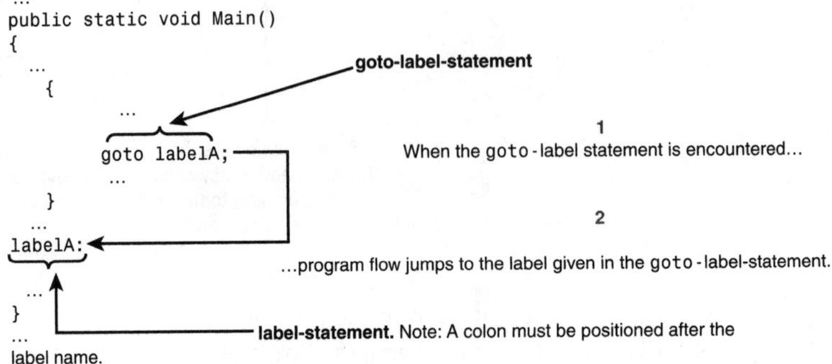

FIGURE 8.20
Transfer of control with the *goto* label statement.

Syntax Box 8.9 The goto-label-statement

```
goto_label_statement::=
         goto <Label>;

Label_statement::=
        <Label_identifier>:
                <Statement>; | <Compound_statement>
```

Note:

A <*Statement*> or <*Compound statement*> must follow the label statement. Consequently, it is an error to position a label statement at the end of a block of code as in the following:

```
{
  ...
    {
        ...
        goto labelB;
        ...
    }
    ...
    labelB:   //Invalid.
}
```

To satisfy the compiler, you can simply insert an empty statement (a semicolon) after the label statement.

In an attempt to curb the amount of damage that a **goto** label statement can cause, the following restrictions apply.

The **goto** label statement and its associated label statement must be within the same method, *and* the **goto** label statement must be within the scope of the label-statement.

Practically speaking, these rules only permit the **goto** label statement to transfer control *out* of a nested scope, not inside a nested scope. Thus, the following is invalid:

```
{
    goto labelC;────┐
    :               │
    {               │
        :           │
        labelC; ◄───┘   Invalid: Attempting to transfer control into a nested scope.
        :
    }
    :
}
```

whereas the following is accepted by the compiler:

```
{
   ...
  {
       ...
       goto labelD;─┐
       ...          │
  }                 │
  labelD; ◄─────────┘   Valid. Transferring control out of the nested scope.
  ...
}
```

The **goto** statement belongs to a group of statements know as *jump statements*. Jump statements cause the flow of control to *jump* to another part of the program. Other jump statements found in C# are **break**, **continue**, **return**, and **throw**. You have only met the **return** statement so far, which terminates a method. **break** and **continue** will be introduced later in this chapter, and **throw** will be introduced in Chapter 19, "Exception Handling."

The switch Statement

The **switch** statement enables a program to select from multiple actions, based on the value of a *controlling expression* also called a **switch** *expression*. The logic implemented by the **switch** statement is, therefore, somewhat similar to that of a multibranch **if-else** statement. To demonstrate the similarities and differences between a **switch** statement and a multibranch **if-else** statement, let's have a look at an example.

The program of Listing 8.10 implements the logic behind a "talking" dishwasher by using a multibranch **if-else** statement. By choosing one of the numbers 1, 2, or 3, the user can select one of the three programs featured by the dishwasher—1: Economy, 2: Intensive, 3: Universal. Every time a choice has been made, the dishwasher responds with a suitable comment.

LISTING 8.10 DishwasherMultibranch.cs

```
01: using System;
02:
03: class DishwasherMultibranch
04: {
05:     public static void Main()
06:     {
07:         int programSelection;
08:
09:         Console.WriteLine("Please select a dishwashing program: ");
10:         Console.WriteLine("1: Economy   2: Intensive    3: Universal");
11:         programSelection = Convert.ToInt32(Console.ReadLine());
12:
13:         if(programSelection == 1)
14:         {
15:             Console.WriteLine("You have selected the Economy program");
16:             Console.WriteLine("Nice environmentally friendly choice");
17:         }
18:         else if (programSelection == 2)
19:         {
20:             Console.WriteLine("You have selected the Intensive program");
21:             Console.WriteLine("Good for week old unwashed dishes");
22:         }
23:         else if (programSelection == 3)
24:         {
25:             Console.WriteLine("You have selected the Universal program");
26:             Console.WriteLine("OK! I'm ready for anything. Just try me out.");
27:         }
28:         else
29:             Console.WriteLine("Invalid selection. You must choose a number " +
30:                 "between 1 and 3");
31:     }
32: }
```

Sample output 1:

```
Please select a dishwashing program: 2<enter>
You have selected the Intensive program
Good for week old unwashed dishes
```

Sample output 2:

```
Please select a dishwashing program: 9<enter>
Invalid selection. You must choose a number between 1 and 3.
```

I assume you are already familiar with the syntax and semantics of the multibranch `if-else` statement, so I will only highlight aspects relevant to the `switch` statement discussion.

Notice that each of the Boolean expressions in lines 13, 18, and 23 of the multibranch `if-else` statement

```
programSelection == 1
programSelection == 2
programSelection == 3
```

can be written in the following general form

```
<Controlling expression> == <constant expression>
```

In this context, it is important to observe that

- The controlling expression remains the same; it's always represented by the `int` variable `programSelection`.
- The constant expression is, as the name implies, always a constant. In this case, it is represented by the *constants* 1, 2, and 3, respectively.
- The only comparison operator used is the equals (==) operator.

Thus, the program compares (for equality) the value of a single expression (in this case, `programSelection`) with several constant expressions (here 1, 2, and 3) to decide which statements to execute. The `switch` statement is tailor-made and confined to this type of scenario.

The `switch` statement condenses the type of multibranch `if-else` statements shown in Listing 8.10 through a somewhat rigid structure specialized for only this type of logic. Listing 8.11, along with its accompanying analysis, explains how this is done by implementing exactly the same functionality as the program in Listing 8.10, but this time with a `switch` statement.

LISTING 8.11 `DishwasherSwitch.cs`

```
using System;

class Dishwasher
{
    public static void Main()
    {
        int programSelection;

        Console.WriteLine("Please select a dishwashing program: ");
        Console.WriteLine("1: Economy   2: Intensive   3: Universal");
        programSelection = Convert.ToInt32(Console.ReadLine());

        switch(programSelection)
        {
            case 1:
                Console.WriteLine("You have selected the Economy program");
                Console.WriteLine("Nice environmentally friendly choice");
                break;
            case 2:
                Console.WriteLine("You have selected the Intensive program");
                Console.WriteLine("Good for week old unwashed dishes");
                break;
            case 3:
                Console.WriteLine("You have selected the Universal program");
                Console.WriteLine("OK! I'm ready for anything. Just try me
                  ➥out.");
                break;
            default:
```

LISTING 8.11 continued

```
28:                     Console.WriteLine("Invalid selection. You must choose a number
                        ➥" +
29:                         "between 1 and 3");
30:                     break;
31:             }
32:         }
33: }
```

The output is the same as the output of Listing 8.10.

The `switch` statement is located between line 13 containing the required `switch` keyword and line 31 with the ending brace matching that of line 14. Notice how `programSelection` only appears in one position—next to the `switch` keyword (line 13), instead of in every single control expression as in Listing 8.10. The three constants, `1`, `2`, and `3`, are now positioned after the required keyword `case` in lines 15, 19, and 23 and before a colon. There is no need to write the equality operator anywhere; it is implicitly understood that if `programSelection` is *equal* to 1, lines 16–18 will be executed. If `programSelection` is *equal* to 2, lines 20–22 are executed, and so on.

Braces to indicate blocks of statements, as seen with the multibranch `if-else` statements, are redundant. All statements between `case` and `break` are executed as if they resided inside a block.

Each of the lines 15, 19, 23, and 27 only act as line labels, not as delineators between choices. Thus, execution does not automatically end at the next `case` or `default` section. For example, execution must be stopped by a `break` statement, as in this example. Consequently, the `break` statements in lines 18, 22, 26, and 30 ends the `switch` statement and transfers the control to the next line after the `switch` statement (in this case, line 32).

The default case of the multibranch `if-else` statements specified by lines 28–30 of Listing 8.10 is in the `switch` statement implemented by the optional `default` section, as shown in lines 27–30.

Note

If a `switch` statement does not contain the optional default section and none of the constant values are matching that of the control expression, the flow of control will continue from the next line after the closing brace of the `switch` statement.

Note

Not only is the `switch` statement often clearer and easier to write than a multibranch `if-else` statement, the `switch` statement is also more efficient in most cases and, thus, creates faster running code.

The general syntax for the `switch` statement is displayed in Syntax Box 8.10.

Syntax Box 8.10 The `switch` Statement

```
switch (<Switch_expression>)
{
     case <Constant_expression> :
            [<Statement>;
             <Statement>;                                       ...
              <Statement>;
              <break_statement>; | <goto_statement>;]

      case <Constant_expression> :
            [<Statement>;
             <Statement>;
                   ...
              <Statement>;
              <break_statement>; | <goto_statement>;]

     <Any number of case fragments can be included>

      [default:
             [ <Statement>;
               <Statement>;                               ...
               <Statement>;
               <break_statement>; | <goto_statement>; ] ]
}

<Zero or one default section may be included>
```

Notes:

- The term `<Switch expression>` used next to the `switch` keyword is the official term for what has been termed a control expression.
- `case` and `default` sections are both referred to as `switch` sections.
- The `<Constant_expression>` following the `case` keyword in a case section is referred to as a *case value* or a *case label*. Each case value must be unique.
- The `<brake_statement>` and `<goto_statement>` constitute the most common way to terminate a switch section.

Tip

Position the default section last.

Even though the case sections and the default section can appear in any sequence, it is considered a better style to position the default section at the end of the `switch` statement.

The notion of the flow of control moving from one `switch` section through to the next `switch` section is called *fall through*. The most common way to prevent fall through is by applying the `break` and `goto` statements.

Apart from the syntax just described, there are several rules you must follow when constructing `switch` statements. Let's have a look at each of them and their consequences.

switch Statement Rule 1

A switch section can consist of zero or more statements. Only switch sections containing zero statements are allowed to let the flow of control continue (fall through) to the next switch section.

By inserting case sections with zero statements one after the other, it is possible to let multiple constant values cause the same statements to be executed. This is illustrated in the code snippet in Listing 8.12. If letter of line 1 is equal to either 'a' or 'A', the statements in lines 5 and 6 will be executed. Similarly, if letter is equal to 'b', 'B', 'c', 'C', lines 11 and 12 are executed.

LISTING 8.12 Several Letters Causing the Same Statement to Be Executed—Incomplete Code

```
01: switch(letter)
02: {
03:     case 'a':
04:     case 'A':
05:         Console.WriteLine("The letter is either a or A");
06:         break;
07:     case 'b':
08:     case 'B':
09:     case 'c':
10:     case 'C':
11:         Console.WriteLine("The letter is either b, B, c or C");
12:         break;
13:     default:
14:         Console.WriteLine("Invalid input");
15          break;
16: }
```

Note that this is only an extract from a complete program and does not compile on its own.

Only the case sections commencing with case 'A': and case 'C': (lines 4 and 10) contain any statements, the rest in lines 3, 7, 8, and 9 have zero statements. In the latter cases, the flow of control is said to *fall through* down to the next case section. Consequently, if letter holds the character 'b', the flow of control falls through all the way down to case 'C':, executing the statements of this section.

switch Statement Rule 2

If there are one or more statements in a case section, the flow of control must not be able to reach the end of this section; in other words, a fall through is not permitted.

Typically, this is prevented through the use of a break or goto statement, but other constructs, such as the return statement, associated with the termination of methods, can also be used.

Listing 8.13 provides an example of an invalid switch section. The case 'a': section beginning in line 3 triggers a compiler error by allowing the flow of control to fall through and run all the way down to line 6.

LISTING 8.13 Invalid Code—Fall Through Not Permitted

```
...
switch(letter)
{
    case 'a':
        Console.WriteLine("You typed the letter: a");
        Console.WriteLine("a is for apple");
    case 'b':
        Console.WriteLine("You typed the letter: b");
        Console.WriteLine("b is for boat");
        break;
```

Note

The reason for disallowing fall through in switch sections with one or more statements originates from the bad experiences of programmers working with the `switch` statements of C++ and Java. Both these languages contain very similar `switch` statements to that of C#, but with one notable difference—they both allow fall through, disregarding the number of statements involved. By mistakenly omitting a `break` statement, one or more `switch` sections might then be executed unknowingly and incorrectly. In other words, it is very easy to introduce bugs into the code when fall through is permitted. As a result, the designers of C# decided to eliminate this source of bugs in C#.

Why does C++ and Java allow fall through if it is a source of bugs? Sometimes it can be useful to let the value of a `switch` expression execute not only its own associated `switch` section but also another or several other `switch` sections. By intentionally omitting the `break` statement in C++ and Java, the programmer can implement this logic. But if C# does not allow fall through, how can similar logic be implemented with C#? This is where the `goto` statement comes into the picture.

Recall the `goto` statement and its ability to jump to a label statement positioned somewhere in the source code. C# allows the `default` keyword and the `case` keyword, along with its associated constant expression, to act as label statements for the `goto` statement. Apart from simulating a fall through, it is possible to redirect the flow from inside any `switch` section to the beginning of any `switch` section with the `goto` statement, irrespective of the sequence in which the `switch` statements appear in the source code.

Listing 8.14 illustrates this feature by calculating the manufacturing cost of the three different ice creams manufactured by Chilling Sensations Ltd.—Bare Minimum, Standard, and Mumbo Jumble. Bare Minimum is just a very basic ice cream. Standard has exactly the same ingredients as Bare Minimum plus a few extra goodies. Mumbo Jumble is a deluxe ice cream identical to Standard but with quite a few additional scrumptious and decadent ingredients added. The manufacturing costs are specified as follows:

- *Bare Minimum*—The cost of manufacturing Bare Minimum.
- *Standard*—The cost of Bare Minimum plus the cost of the additional ingredients of Standard.
- *Mumbo Jumble*—The cost of Standard plus the cost of the additional ingredients of Mumbo Jumble.

Listing 8.14 prints out the calculated manufacturing costs for the ice cream specified by the user, as shown in the sample output that follows the listing.

LISTING 8.14 `IceCreamManufacturer.cs`

```
01: using System;
02:
03: class IceCreamManufacturer
04: {
05:     public static void Main()
06:     {
07:         const decimal BareMinimumCost = 1.2m;
08:         const decimal StandardCost = 1.5m;
09:         const decimal MumboCost = 2.1m;
10:         int iceCreamType;
11:         decimal totalCost;
12:
13:         Console.WriteLine("Please enter ice cream type: \n" +
14:             "1: Mumbo Jumble  2: Standard  3: Bare Minimum");
15:         iceCreamType = Convert.ToInt32(Console.ReadLine());
16:         totalCost = 0;
17:
18:         switch(iceCreamType)
19:         {
20:             case 1:
21:                 totalCost = totalCost + MumboCost;
22:                 goto case 2;
23:             case 2:
24:                 totalCost = totalCost + StandardCost;
25:                 goto case 3;
26:             case 3:
27:                 totalCost = totalCost + BareMinimumCost;
28:                 Console.WriteLine("Total manufacturing cost: {0:C}",
                    ➥totalCost);
29:                 break;
30:             default:
31:                 Console.WriteLine("Invalid selection");
32:                 break;
33:         }
34:     }
35: }
```

```
Please enter ice cream type:
1: Mumbo Jumble  2: Standard  3: Bare Minimum
1<enter>
Total manufacturing cost: $4.80
```

The `goto case` statement of line 22 lets the execution continue at `case 2:` in line 23, imitating a fall through. The same happens in line 25. So when the user, for example, requests to have the costs calculated for the `Mumbo Jumble` by entering 1, execution inside the `switch` statement commences at line 20 followed by all statements between line 20 and line 29, allowing the program to perform what amounts to the following calculation—`totalCost = MumboCost`

+ `StandardCost` + `BareMinimumCost`, which is the cost of a Mumbo Jumble. Similarly, if 2 is entered to calculate the cost of Standard, the equivalent of the calculation `totalCost = BareMinimumCost + StandardCost` is performed.

Note

Because a `switch` statement is a type of statement, it can be inserted at the position where a statement is expected in a `switch` section, resulting in nested `switch` statements. Even when constructing nested `switch` statements, it is only possible to let `goto-case` statements refer to `case` sections contained within the same `switch` statement as the `goto-case` statement. However, you can utilize the standard `goto` label statement to jump to an outer `switch` statement.

In general, though, stay away from the `goto` label statement and avoid nested `switch` statements with more than a couple of levels.

Listing 8.14 illustrated the use of `goto-case` statements. If you want to jump to a `default` section, simply exchange the case and constant expression with the keyword `default`, as shown in Syntax Box 8.11.

Syntax Box 8.11 The goto-Case-Statement and goto-Default-Statement

```
goto_case_statement::=
        goto case <Constant_expression>;

goto_default_statement::=
        goto default;
```

`switch` Statement Rule 3

The governing type of the `switch` statement is determined by the `switch` expression. If the `switch` expression is of type `byte`, `sbyte`, `short`, `ushort`, `int`, `uint`, `long`, `ulong`, `char`, `string`, or `enum`, that is the governing type. If this is not the case, there must exist an implicit conversion path specified by the programmer to one of the types `byte`, `sbyte`, `short`, `ushort`, `int`, `uint`, `long`, `ulong`, `char`, `string`. (To see how user-defined implicit conversion paths are specified, see Chapter 14, "Class Anatomy Part III, Writing Intuitive Code.")

Thus, the floating point and decimal types are not permitted as `switch` expression types. If you need to implement the functionality of a `switch` statement but are faced with one of those types, you must resort to the multibranch `if-else` statement.

The `enum` type is, with its associated finite set of related constants, a very suitable type for a `switch` expression. Listing 8.15 determines the number of days in a particular month of a particular year by utilizing a `switch` expression of type `enum`. As the sample output illustrates, the user can type in the relevant year and the name of the month to receive the correct number of days.

LISTING 8.15 DaysInMonth.cs

```
using System;

class DaysInMonth
{
    enum Month {January, February, March, April, May, June,
        July, August, September, October, November, December}

    public static void Main()
    {
        Month currentMonth;
        int year;
        int dayCount = 0;

        Console.Write("Enter year: ");
        year = Convert.ToInt32(Console.ReadLine());
        Console.Write("Enter month: ");
         //Convert user input to enum type Month
        currentMonth = (Month)Enum.Parse(typeof(Month),
        ➥ Console.ReadLine(), true);
        switch (currentMonth)
        {
            case Month.January:
            case Month.March:
            case Month.May:
            case Month.July:
            case Month.August:
            case Month.October:
            case Month.December:
                dayCount = 31;
                break;
            case Month.April:
            case Month.June:
            case Month.September:
            case Month.November:
                dayCount = 30;
                break;
            case Month.February:
                 //Determine if year is a leap year
                if (((year % 4 == 0) && !(year % 100 == 0)) || (year % 400 == 0))
                    dayCount = 29;
                else
                    dayCount = 28;
                break;
            default:
                Console.WriteLine("Invalid month");
                break;
        }
        Console.WriteLine("Number of days in {0} of year {1}: {2}",
            currentMonth, year, dayCount);
    }
}
```

```
Enter year: 2000<enter>
Enter month: November<enter>
Number of days in November of year 2001: 30
```

Lines 5 and 6 declare the `enum Month` to contain our familiar months of the year as its members.

Line 18 is only explained very briefly. It utilizes the static method of the `System.Enum` class called `Parse()` to convert the string input from the user (via `Console.ReadLine()`) into one of the valid values of type `Month`. `true` specified at the end of the line simply indicates that uppercase and lowercase characters are treated as identical characters. In other words, if the user inputs January or january, this string value is converted to `Month.January` and inserted into the variable `currentMonth`. All months containing 31 days are lined up in lines 21–27 letting the execution fall through down to line 28 where the appropriate number of days (31) is assigned to `dayCount`. The same idea is used in lines 30–35 for the months with 30 days. The tricky part, of course, is calculating the days in February of a particular year. The rules are as follows. If the year is a leap year, February contains 29 days; otherwise, it contains just 28 days. A year is a leap year if one of the following two conditions is `true`:

- The year is divisible by 4 and not divisible by 100
- The year is divisible by 400

These rules are implemented in lines 38–41. Recall how the modulus operator `%` allows the program to determine whether a number is divisible by another number. For example `400 % 4` is equal to 0 because the remainder is 0, meaning that 400 is divisible by 4.

Notice how easy it becomes to interpret the `switch` statement when combined with the `enum` type. There is no doubt as to what each `switch` section represents.

`switch` Statement Rule 4

The constant expression of each `switch` section must represent a value of the same type as, or a value implicitly convertible to, the governing type.

The following code snippet is invalid because there is no implicit conversion path specified from `int` to `string`:

```
...
string choice;
    ...
    switch (choice)
    {
      case 1:                    Cannot implicitly convert constant value of type int to type string
        Console.WriteLine("You chose 1");
        break;
      case 2:
        Console.WriteLine("You chose 2");
        break;
      default:
        Console.WriteLine("You chose neither 1 nor 2");
        break;
    }
...
```

whereas the next piece of source code is acceptable because `int` can be implicitly converted to `long`:

```
long choice;
  ...
  switch (choice)
  {
      case 1:
          Console.WriteLine("You chose 1");
          break;
      case 2:
          Console.WriteLine("You chose 2");
          break;
      default:
          Console.WriteLine("You chose neither 1 nor 2");
          break;
  }
```

OK can implicitly convert constant value of type `int` to type `long`

Working with `switch` Statements

The following are a few general guidelines when using `switch` statements.

Limit the Number of Statements in Each `switch` Section

Some `switch` statements might contain numerous `switch` sections. Many statements inside each `switch` section will clutter up the code and make it unclear. Instead, complicated actions requiring large numbers of statements can be collected inside methods and called from the `switch` section to reduce the number of statements here.

Order the Cases by Occurrence, by Number, or by Letter (Alphabetically)

The simple `switch` statements presented in this section merely included a few `switch` sections and could, therefore, be noted by a glimpse of the eye. However, some `switch` statements might contain large numbers of `switch` sections, leading to source code being exceedingly unclear and difficult to navigate. Introducing a scheme in which the case labels are ordered can improve the readability and save you and your fellow programmers precious time sifting through pages and pages of code.

There are several possible schemes available:

- *By occurrence*—If you position the `switch` sections you expect to be executed most frequently at the top of the of the `switch` section, you save other programmers from reading through code dealing with exceptional circumstances. You might also speed up the code by saving the computer from sifting through rarely processed case labels before finding the sought after `switch` section.
- *Alphabetically or by number*—To facilitate navigation through the different case labels, position them in alphabetical or numerical order.

Use the Default Section for the Same Purposes as the Default Statement of the Multibranch `if-else` Statements

Recall the two general rules mentioned during the multibranch **`if-else`** statement discussion about the default statement following the last **`else`** clause. They also apply to the default section of the **`switch`** statement and are just briefly summarized here:

- Only use the default section for genuine defaults.
- Detect errors with the default section if unused.

Because the discussion of these two recommendations in relation to the **`switch`** statement merely is a repeat of the discussion in the multibranch **`if-else`** statement section, please refer to that section for further details.

The Conditional Operator

As shown in Syntax Box 8.12 the *conditional operator* combines three expressions with the two symbols—question mark **`?`** and colon **`:`**. It will return either the value of **`ExpressionA`** or the value of **`ExpressionB`**, depending on whether the Boolean expression to the left of the question mark is **`true`** or **`false`**. If **`true`**, the value of **`ExpressionA`** is returned; otherwise, the value of **`ExpressionB`** is returned.

Syntax Box 8.12 The Conditional Operator

```
<Boolean_expression> ? <ExpressionA> : <ExpressionB>
```

Note

The conditional operator is the only operator in C# to combine three expressions, so it is also referred to as the ternary operator.

Let's have a look at a couple of examples. The Boolean expression of the following expression is **`true`**, so the value of the overall expression is 100.

```
(3 < 10) ? 100 : 200
```

In the next line

```
(3 > 20) ? 200 : 300
```

the value of the expression is 300 because **`(3 > 20)`** is **`false`**, causing the value after the colon to be returned.

Sometimes a simple **`if-else`** statement can be substituted with the conditional operator and create shorter more compact code. Consider the following **`if-else`** statement

```
if (distance1 > distance2)
      maxDistance = distance1;
else
      maxDistance = distance2;
```

It says that if *distance1* is greater than `distance2`, assign `distance1` to `maxDistance`; otherwise, assign `distance2` to `maxDistance`. This can be expressed in one line by using the conditional operator:

```
maxDistance = (distance1 > distance2) ? distance1 : distance2;
```

which, like its `if-else` statement counterpart, assigns the larger value of `distance1` and `distance2` to `maxDistance`.

Note

The conditional operator always returns a value, so it can only be used instead of certain types of `if-else` statements, such as the one shown in the previous example.

Summary

The bulk of this chapter focused on the `if-else` and `switch` branching statements and their related language elements—the comparison and logical operators. Together they allow you to write decision-making programs that can react in different ways to different data.

The most important points discussed in this chapter are reviewed in this section.

A branching statement is a language construct that uses a given condition (Boolean expression) to decide between two or more alternative directions (branches) to follow in a program.

A program without any branching or iteration statements is executed sequentially, in the order (from top to bottom) that the statements are written in the source code.

The `if` statement is the fundamental branching statement in C#. It contains a Boolean expression that controls whether a statement (single or compound) will be executed.

By combining an `if` statement with an `else` block, the program can choose between executing just one of two alternative statements (single or compound).

A comparison operator allows two expressions to be compared and generates a result of type `bool` (`true` or `false`). C# contains six comparison operators of which four are relational and two are equality based.

By nesting `if` statements inside each other, you can make a construct that can choose between executing any number of different (single or compound) statements.

Sometimes nested `if` else statements are difficult to construct, maintain, and comprehend. By using a standardized system, nested `if-else` statements can be converted to multibranch `if-else` statements that are simpler and easier understand.

A logical operator (also called Boolean operator) allows you to combine two Boolean expressions into one Boolean expression. As a result, any number of Boolean expressions can be combined to form one Boolean expression. C# contains the three commonly used logical operators `&&` ("and"), `||` ("or"), and `!` ("not") and the less frequently applied logical operators `&` (bitwise "and"), `|` (bitwise "or"), and `^` (bitwise "exclusive or"). Logical operators more or less have the same meaning as and, or, and not in our every day spoken language and allow you to construct simpler programs while maintaining their logic expressiveness.

The segment of the source code where a particular variable identifier can be used to access the variables underlying value is called the variables scope. A variables scope is outlined by the block in which the variable is declared.

A block A can be inserted inside another block B. Block A then forms an outer scope relative to block B, which forms an inner scope. Inner and outer are relative terms.

The time between the creation and destruction of a variable is called the variables lifetime. As a general rule, a variable in C# is created when execution enters its scope and destroyed when execution leaves its scope.

The `goto` statement transfers control (jumps) to another part of the program and, therefore, belongs to a group of statements called jump statements. It is a controversial, error-prone construct and should only be used sparingly with the `switch` statement.

The `switch` statement is tailor-made to select from multiple (single or compound) statements and is somewhat similar to a condensed multibranch `if-else` statement but with a narrower set of applications. If applicable, the `switch` statement is often clearer, simpler, and more efficient than a corresponding multibranch `if-else` statement.

The conditional operator is also called the tertiary operator because it is the only operator in C# that combines three expressions. It allows you to let a Boolean expression determine which of two values (expressions) this conditional operator will return.

Review Questions

1. Which general type of statement would you use to implement each of the following logical descriptions:

    a. If `number` is greater than 100, write "greater than 100" onscreen; otherwise, write "less than or equal to 100."

    b. Repeatedly check each letter of a string until no more letters are left in the string.

2. Suppose that your program contains three variables called **rainfall**, **wind**, and **temperature**, all of type **double**. For each of the following points, write a few lines of code that implement the described logic (you don't need to write the whole program):

   a. If **rainfall** is greater than 100, write "Heavy rainfall" onscreen.

   b. If **rainfall** is greater than 100 or **wind** is greater than 120, write "Bad weather" onscreen.

   c. If **rainfall** is equal to 0 and **wind** is less than 10 and **temperature** is between 23 and 27 (Celsius), write "Nice weather."

   d. If **rainfall** is equal to 0, write "It is not raining"; otherwise, write "It is raining."

3. No matter which value **rainfall** has, the following lines will always write "It's raining" onscreen. Why?

```
if(rainfall > 10);
    Console.WriteLine("It's raining");
```

4. What is the purpose of nested **if** statements?

5. Write logical expressions (using C#'s comparison operators and logical operators) that represent the following conditions:

   a. **rainfall** is between 100 and 150.

   b. **number** is odd and not equal to 23.

   c. **number** is even and smaller than 100, or **weight** is less than 100.

6. A method with the header **bool IsEven(int number)** returns **true** if the argument passed to its parameter **number** is even; otherwise, it returns **false**. Write a Boolean expression containing a call to **IsEven** that is **true** if the number passed along with the call is odd.

7. To what does the term scope refer?

8. What is one of the few correct uses of the **goto** statement?

9. Rewrite the following **if-else** multibranch statement using a **switch** statement.

```
if(timeOfDay == "morning")
    Console.WriteLine("Good Morning");
else if(timeOfDay == "midday")
    Console.WriteLine("Good Day");
else if(timeOfDay == "evening")
    Console.WriteLine("Good evening");
else
    Console.WriteLine("Invalid time");
```

10. To what does "falling through" in relation to the **switch** statement refer? How can "falling through" be prevented?

11. Your program contains variables called `cost1`, `cost2`, and `minimumCost`. Write a statement involving the conditional operator that assigns the smaller of the values in `cost1` and `cost2` to `minimumCost`.

Programming Exercises

1. The currency on planet Blipos is called sopilbs. The aliens on Blipos pay the following amount of tax depending on their income:

   - 0% of income less than or equal to 10000 sopilbs
   - 5% of income that is greater than 10000 and less than or equal to 25000 sopilbs
   - 10% of income that is greater than 25000 and less than or equal to 50000 sopilbs
   - 15% of income that is greater than 50000 and less than or equal to 100000 sopilbs
   - 20% of income that is greater than 100000 sopilbs

   So if an alien earns 60000 sopilbs, it will have to pay the following amount in tax: 0 * 10000 + 0.05 * 15000 + 0.1 * 25000 + 0.15 * 10000 = 4750.

   Write a program that accepts a certain income as input and from that amount calculates and outputs the tax payable.

2. Write a program (using a `switch` statement) that accepts one of the exam scores A, B, C, D, and E. In response, the program will output the corresponding percentage score, which is A: 90–100; B: 80–89; C: 70–79; D: 60–69; E: 0–59.

3. Write a program that can find a number between 0 and 100. The user decides on a number and the program repeatedly makes a guess and constantly narrows in on the number until the number is found. Hint: Let the computer guess on the number in the middle of the possible maximum number and the possible minimum number. For example, the first guess should be 50. If the user indicates the number to be greater, the next guess should be 75, and so on.

CHAPTER 9

FLOW OF CONTROL PART II: ITERATION STATEMENTS

You will learn about the following in this chapter:

- The essential nature of iteration statements and the typical situations where they are called for
- The `while`, `do-while`, and `for`-loops and how to work with these iteration statements
- How the jump statements `break` and `continue` can be applied to exert additional control over the iteration statements
- The combination assignment operators
- How iteration statements can be positioned inside each other to form nested loops and the usefulness of these types of constructs
- The concept of structured programming and its advantages

Without the ability to repeatedly perform the same set of operations, as facilitated by the iteration statements, the time it would take a program to run from its first statement to its last statement would be directly proportional to the length of the program. Often, computer users work on their computer for many hours (days), letting the computer solve the same tasks repeatedly, but typically involving different data during each repeated execution. Writing a document using a word processor is an example. Each time a character is typed the program repeats some actions. This would require immensely sized programs that no programmer would ever want to program were it not for the presence of the iteration statements. Consequently, iteration is one of the cornerstones in computing without which programmers would find it hard to create programs of much use.

The imperative nature of the iteration statements is reflected by their early introduction in this book and casual use in many examples prior to their thorough discussion in this chapter. In Chapter 2, "Your First C# Program," you were presented (using pseudocode) with an average-calculating algorithm based on iteration to help our alien friend from planet Blipos. Chapter 6,

"Types Part I: The Simple Types" provided you with an informal introduction to the `do-while` loop as a means to create a Blipos clock, and Chapter 7, "Types Part II: Operators, Enumerators and Strings" utilized the `while`-loop to: create a day counter program, analyze text, order words in alphabetical order and to extract words of a certain length from a string.

It is interesting to note that in each program the iteration algorithm was employed to handle data of a repetitive nature. For example, the list of numbers analyzed by the average calculating algorithm in Chapter 2 could be written as

```
{number1, number2, number3, number4...}
```

and the series of times generated by the Blipos clock could, in a general form, be written as

```
{time1, time2, time3, time4...}
```

The remaining examples are listed in Table 9.1.

TABLE 9.1 The Repetitive Nature of Data Related to Iterative Statements

Name of example	Type of sequence processed	Analyzing or Generating
Average-calculating algorithm	A list of numbers	Analyzing
Blipos clock	A series of seconds and minutes	Generating
Day counter program	A sequence of days	Generating
Text analyzer	A string of characters	Analyzing
Word extractor	A string of characters (and ultimately a list of words)	Analyzing

Also note, as indicated in Table 9.1, that each example either uses the iteration statement to analyze a sequence of given data or to generate a sequence of data. Analyzing and generating data are important uses for the loop statements.

Traversing, Analyzing, and Generating Sequences of Data

When a program visits each element of a list of elements, programmers say the list is being *traversed*. Traversal is one of the most fundamental uses of iteration statements. The general loop construct for analyzing a list of data can be depicted by a flow chart or pseudocode as in Figure 9.1. Notice how the depiction matches our definition of an iteration statement presented in the beginning of the previous chapter: "An iteration statement repeats a statement or a block of statements until a given termination condition is met."

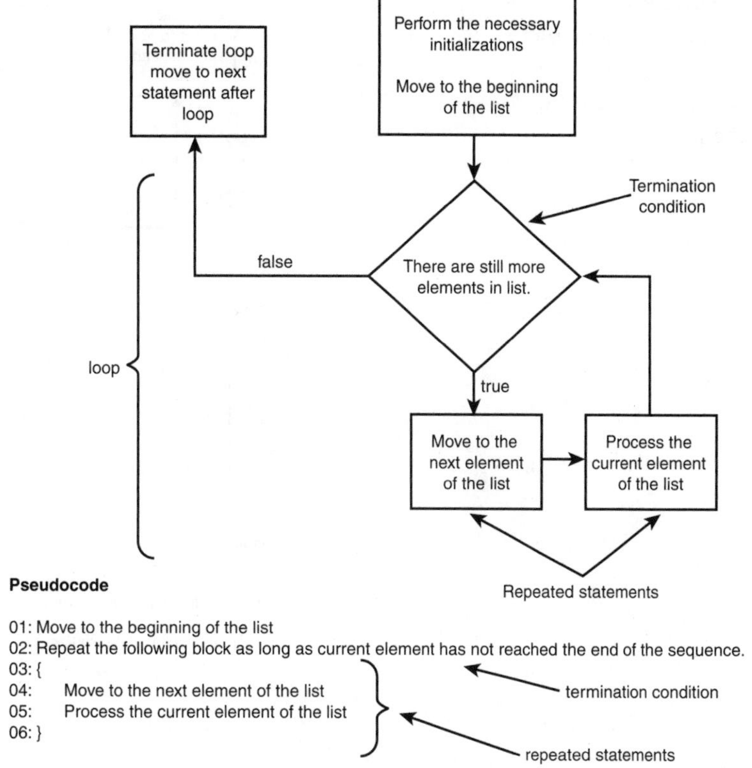
Terminate loop move to next statement after loop
Perform the necessary initializations
Move to the beginning of the list
Termination condition
false
There are still more elements in list.
loop
true
Move to the next element of the list
Process the current element of the list
Repeated statements
Pseudocode
Move to the beginning of the list
Repeat the following block as long as current element has not reached the end of the sequence.
{
Move to the next element of the list
Process the current element of the list
}
termination condition
repeated statements

FIGURE 9.1
An iteration construct used for *analyzing* a sequence of data elements.

Figure 9.2 illustrates the general framework for a loop generating a list of data elements. Notice how it is merely a variation of the same theme as that shown in Figure 9.1.

There are many variations of the iteration theme, apart from the few already presented. For example, only every second element might be visited, perhaps the algorithm works faster if the list is processed from the end and backwards, or perhaps the best way is to start in the middle and work towards the beginning and end simultaneously, and so on. Fortunately, C# contains three different iteration constructs that cater to any need you might encounter. Let's have a closer look at their syntax and general form before we explore their practical use.

The `while` Loop Statement

The `while` loop repeats a statement or compound statement again and again, here referred to as *loop body*, as long as its associate loop condition, consisting of a Boolean expression, is `true` (see Syntax Box 9.1). When the loop condition is `false` while being evaluated, flow of control moves to the line immediately following the `while` loop.

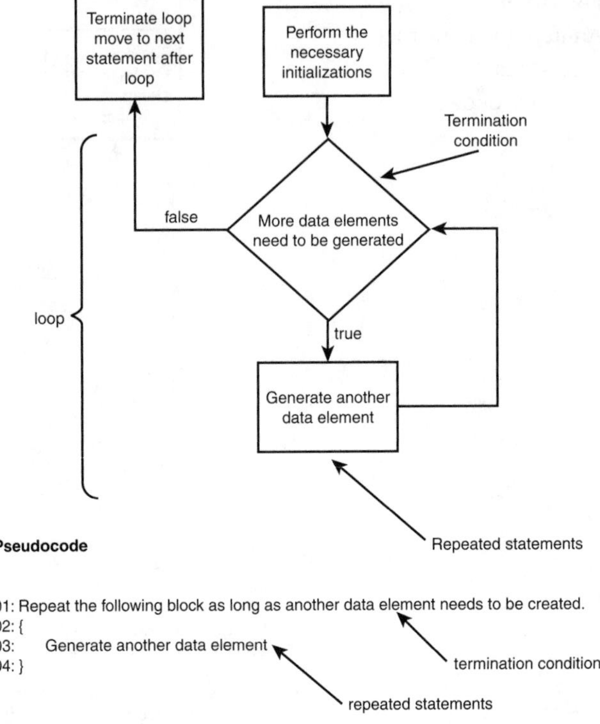

FIGURE 9.2
An iteration construct used for *generating* a sequence of data elements.

Syntax Box 9.1 The `while`-Loop

```
while_statement:=
while (<Loop_condition>)
    <Loop_body>
```

where:

```
<Loop_condition>::= <Boolean_expression>

<Loop_body>::= <Statement>;
           ::= <Compound_statement>
```

Note:

- The loop body is repeated as long as `<Loop_condition>` is `true`.

The keyword `while` is suitably chosen; we can even use it to describe the semantics of the `while` loop in plain English:

While (the loop condition is `true`) repeat the loop body over and over again.

Note

One of the best ways to learn the inner logic of the various loop constructs presented here is to trace the examples given, just as you have traced the pseudocode and source code presented in earlier chapters. In particular, try to focus on the variable(s) involved in the loop condition of the iteration. Look at its (their) initial values and the positions where it (they) is altered; this will provide you with the key information needed to determine how many times the loop will repeat itself.

Listing 9.1 presents a simple example utilizing the `while` loop to print out the numbers from 0 to 4.

LISTING 9.1 A `while` loop—Incomplete Source Code

```
01: int index;
02: index = 0;
03: while (index < 5)
04: {
05:     Console.WriteLine(index);
06:     index++;
07: }
```

```
0
1
2
3
4
```

The `while` statement begins with the keyword `while` in line 3 and is followed by its associated loop condition `index < 5` enclosed by parentheses. The loop body in lines 5 and 6 is enclosed by a matching pair of braces in lines 4 and 7 and constitute a compound statement that is executed repeatedly.

`index` is part of the *loop condition* in line 3 and acts as a loop termination controller. Thus, to facilitate our analysis, we need to focus on the source code locations that change the value of `index`. The hotspots are as follows:

- Initialization of `index` to 0 in line 2 (called *loop initialization*)
- Incrementing `index` by 1 in line 6 (called *loop update*)

As long as `index < 5` is `true`, the loop body is repeated. Because `index`, due to its initialization of line 2, has the value 0, when line 3 is executed for the first time, `index < 5` is `true` and the loop body executed. Thus, line 5 prints out a 0 (see sample output) and line 6 increments `index` by 1 to hold the value 1. Flow of control then returns to line 3. Because `index` is 1, `(index < 5)` is still `true`, causing another printout and increment of `index`.

Notice that every time the loop body is repeated, `index` is nearing the point where `index < 5` becomes `false` due to line 6. After four repetitions, `index` is equal to 4 and `index < 5` is still `true` causing 4 to be printed out in line 5 and index to be incremented to 5 in line 6. The flow of control once again jumps back to line 3 where `index < 5` this time is `false`, prompting the loop to terminate and move to the next statement after the `while` loop, which in this case would be line 8.

Verify that the Loop Eventually Terminates

The analysis of Listing 9.1 convinced us that every repeated execution of the loop body gradually carried the loop variable closer to terminating the loop. In general, it is recommended that you mentally trace the execution of a loop to ensure that, under any set of circumstances, it will terminate.

A loop construct, such as the `while` loop, that contains its loop condition at the beginning of the loop is called an *entry-condition* loop.

Note

The loop condition of any of the iteration statements in C# is only evaluated *once* during each repeated execution of the loop body.

```
x = 100
while (x > 10)
{
   :
   x = 5;
   Console.WriteLine("Hello there");
   :
}
```

1 Even though...

2 ...this makes the loop condition `false`...

3 ...the rest of the statements in the loop body are still executed because the loop condition is only evaluated once after each repeated execution of the loop body

The Boolean expression is tested at the beginning of the `while` loop; thus, if the Boolean expression is `false` initially, the loop body is never executed. This is an essential feature as demonstrated in Listing 9.2. The program presented in Listing 9.2 lets the user choose, by inputting an integer value, the number of times a piece of music should be played again. Each piece of music being played is simply symbolized by printing Play onscreen. When the user enters a 0, the `while` loop never executes its loop body, appropriately preventing Play from being written onscreen even once.

LISTING 9.2 `PlayItAgain.cs`

```
using System;

class PlayItAgain
{
    public static void Main()
    {
        int counter;
        Console.WriteLine("Play");
```

LISTING 9.2 continued

```
09:         Console.Write("Sam says: Play it again how many times? ");
10:         counter = Convert.ToInt32(Console.ReadLine());
11:         while(counter > 0)
12:         {
13:             Console.WriteLine("Play");
14:             counter--;
15:         }
16:         Console.WriteLine("That's it folks!");
17:     }
18: }
```

Sample output 1:

```
Play
Sam: Play it again how many times? 3<enter>
Play
Play
Play
That's it folks!
```

Sample output 2:

```
Play
Sam: Play it again how many times? 0<enter>
That's it folks!
```

`counter` plays the same pivotal role for the `while` statement here as `index` does for the `while` statement in Listing 9.1, but with a few notable adjustments. Instead of starting at zero like `index`, `counter` begins at the number provided by the end user, which ultimately is the number of times the word Play will be displayed onscreen. To accommodate for this modification and still allow the `while` loop to function correctly, the comparison operator of the Boolean expression in line 11 has been reversed from less-than (in line 3 of Listing 9.1) to greater-than, and instead of incrementing it by 1, `counter` is now being decremented by 1 in line 14. Through these adjustments, we can utilize the number entered by the end user as is and, at the same time, preserve the overall logic found in Listing 9.1—every time the loop statements are repeated, `counter` moves closer towards making `(counter > 0) false`. In this case, it takes `counter` (its initial value) repetitions to make `counter > 0` equal to `false`.

Tip

Always position the loop initializations immediately before the loop.

The previous two examples, demonstrating the use of the `while` statement, positioned the initialization statements immediately before the `while` loop. This is not a coincidence but represents an important rule of thumb—loop initializations should always be positioned immediately before the loop. Not only does this allow the reader easy access to this important code while looking at the loop, it further stands as a reminder to include the loop initialization in any modifications made to the loop itself.

The majority of computational problems requiring a loop construct as part of its solution call for a loop statement with the exit point at the beginning, such as the `while` loop, to be implemented correctly and elegantly. However, in certain contexts, a loop construct with the exit point after the loop body can provide for a more elegant solution. The `do-while` loop presented in the next section provides this type of functionality.

The `do-while` Loop Statement

The `do-while` loop is analogous to the `while` loop in that the loop body is repeatedly executed over and over again as long as the Boolean expression is `true`. However, there is one important difference—the loop body, located between the keywords `do` and `while` (see Syntax Box 9.2), is executed before the Boolean expression is evaluated. Consequently, the loop body of the `do-while` loop is always executed at least once, even if the Boolean expression is `false` initially.

Syntax Box 9.2 The `do-while` Statement

```
do_while_statement:=
     do
       <Loop_body>
     while (<Loop_condition>);
```

where:

```
<Loop_body>::= <Statement>;
           ::= <Compound_statement>

<Loop_condition>::= <Boolean expression>
```

Note:

- The `<Loop_body>` is repeated as long as `<Loop_condition>` is `true`.

A loop construct, such as the `do-while` loop, that has its loop condition at the end of the loop is called an *exit condition* loop.

Tip

The choice between the `while` loop and the `do-while` loop depends on the computational problem at hand. However, for the majority of the cases, the entry condition `while` loop is the correct choice. For example, if the loop is used to traverse a list of numbers (or a list of any other kind of objects), the list might well be empty, in which case the loop statements should never be executed. Thus, a `do-while` loop applied here would lead to flawed code.

Even though not as commonly called for as the `while`-loop, the `do-while` loop is highly compatible with a few distinct types of computational problems. One such problem is found in program parts that requests, receives, processes and evaluates user input repeatedly. Often the user input is used in the loop condition. In this scenario the user input must be received *before* it can be utilized here; in other words, the loop body, which fetches the user input, must be executed before the loop condition can be evaluated. This fits perfectly well with our exit condition `do-while` loop.

Listing 9.3 is used to illustrate this point. It contains the source code of a letter-guessing game. The program randomly picks a letter between A and Z; the aim of the game is to find the secret letter simply by typing in single letters. To help the player (the user) along, the program will let him or her know whether the secret letter is earlier or later in the alphabet than each guess. In the sample output after Listing 9.3, the secret letter was N and was found after the fifth guess, but this will vary between different games.

LISTING 9.3 `AlphabetGame.cs`

```
using System;

class AlphabetGame
{
    public static void Main()
    {
        string secretLetter;
        string letterGuess;
        Random Randomizer = new Random();
         // Choose the secretLetter randomly from the full
         // alphabet ranging from Unicode 65 (reprenting 'A') to
         // Unicode 91 (representing 'Z')
        secretLetter = ((char)Randomizer.Next(65, 91)).ToString();
        Console.WriteLine("Guess my secret letter \n" +
            "I will tell you if the secret letter \n" +
            "is Earlier or Later in the alphabet than your guess");
        do
        {
            letterGuess = Console.ReadLine().ToUpper();
             // Is secretLetter earlier or later than letterGuess?
            if (secretLetter.CompareTo(letterGuess) < 0)
                Console.WriteLine("   Earlier\n");
            if (secretLetter.CompareTo(letterGuess) > 0)
                Console.WriteLine("   Later\n");
        } while (secretLetter != letterGuess);
        Console.WriteLine("You got it! \n\nEnd of Game");
    }
}
```

```
Guess my secret letter
I will tell you if the secret letter
is Earlier or Later in the alphabet than your guess
M<enter>
     Later

S<enter>
     Earlier
```

```
P<enter>
     Earlier

O<enter>
     Earlier

N<enter>
You got it!
End of Game.
```

The first part of line 9, before the assignment operator, declares `Randomizer` to hold a reference to an object of type `System.Random`. The latter half applies the keyword `new` to create a new object of type `System.Random`, which is then assigned to `Randomizer`, enabling it to generate random numbers. This is utilized in line 13, where `Randomizer.Next(65, 91)` produces a random number greater than or equal to 65 and less than 91. The Unicode numbers 65 and 90 represent the characters A and Z, respectively, with the rest of the alphabet in between (see Appendix E, "Unicode Character Set"). The randomly chosen number is cast to be of type `char` and turned into a `string` before it is assigned to `secretLetter` of type `string`. End result—line 13 assigns a randomly chosen letter between A and Z to `secretLetter`.

The program is now ready to

1. Assign the user input (the guess) to `letterGuess` (line 19).
2. Compare `letterGuess` with `secretLetter` (lines 21 and 23).
3. Provide an appropriate response to the user (lines 22 and 24).
4. Determine if the loop should be terminated (line 26).

Because this sequence of actions must be repeated until the user enters the secret letter, an iteration statement is appropriate for implementing this functionality. The question then is should we use the `while` or the `do-while` construct? To answer this question, first have a look at the pseudocode in Figure 9.3. It summarizes the process described previously with an attempt to apply the `while` loop. Notice that the repeated part (the loop body) is repeated as long as `secretLetter` is not equal to `letterGuess`. However, the fact that `letterGuess` is utilized in the loop condition, but not assigned a value until the loop body is executed, poses a problem for our `while` loop and, in fact, renders the pseudocode incorrect.

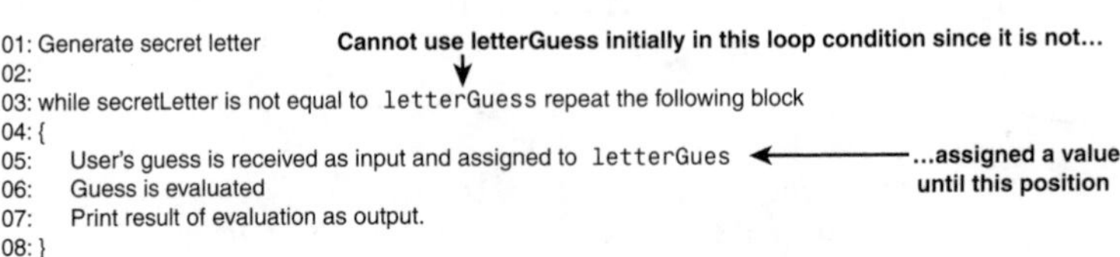

Generate secret letter
Cannot use letterGuess initially in this loop condition since it is not...
while secretLetter is not equal to letterGuess repeat the following block
{
User's guess is received as input and assigned to letterGues
Guess is evaluated
Print result of evaluation as output.
}
...assigned a value until this position

FIGURE 9.3
Pseudocode of *AlphabetGame* applying *while* loop—invalid solution.

If the `while` loop was the only available loop statement in C#, we could have worked around the problem and come up with a fully working, but inelegant program. Figure 9.4 presents the pseudocode behind such an attempt. By using the variable `notGuessed` of type `bool` with an initial value of `true` in the loop condition, we are able to execute the loop body at least once and obtain the first guess from the user. By making **`notGuessed false`** whenever the user guesses the **`secretLetter`**, the loop is terminated at the appropriate moment. In reality, then, line 9 has become our loop condition. Yes, it does work, and yes, it is pretty ugly and graceless.

FIGURE 9.4
Pseudocode of *`AlphabetGame`* applying *`while`* loop—valid but ugly code.

```
01: Generate secret letter
02: Declare variable called notGuessed to be of type bool.
03: Set notGuessed to be true.
04: while notGuessed is true repeat the following block  <---  loop body is repeatedly executed until
05: {                                                         notGuessed is false, which happens...
06:     Receive user guess as input. Assign it to letterGuess
06:     Evaluate letterGuess
07:     Print result of evaluation as output.
08:     if secretLetter is equal to letterGuess then set notGuessed to false <--... when secretLetter is found
08: }
09: Print: "You got it!. End of game."
```

Fortunately, the **`do-while`** loop, due to its *exit* condition, seamlessly supports the logic we want to represent in our **`AlphabetGame`**. The associated pseudocode is shown in Figure 9.5 and forms the basis for Listing 9.3.

FIGURE 9.5
Pseudocode of *`AlphabetGame`* applying *`do-while`* loop—valid and elegant.

```
01: Generate a random letter between A and Z. Assign it to secretLetter
02: {                                                         This works because
03:     Receive user guess as input. Assign it to letterGuess <--- letterGuess is assigned a value before...
04:     Compare letterGuess with secretLetter
05:     Print result of evaluation as output.
06: }
07: while letterGuess is not equal to secretLetter repeat the block above <---...it is evaluated in loop condition
08: Print: "You got it. End of game"
```

Line 3 of the pseudocode is implemented in line 19 of Listing 9.3. Notice that the letter is converted to uppercase, with the built-in **`ToUpper()`** method, allowing the user to input lower- and uppercase letters without making any difference. The comparisons between **`letterGuess`** and **`secretLetter`** along with appropriate feedback takes place in lines 21–24. Because **`secretLetter`** and **`letterGuess`** are of type **`System.String`**, we can utilize the built-in method **`CompareTo()`** presented in Chapter 4. The loop condition is located in line 25 and will cause the loop to terminate whenever **`secretLetter`** is equal to **`letterGuess`**.

The `for` Loop Statement

As we have seen in many previous examples involving iteration, the three key components of a loop are as follows:

- *Loop condition*—When evaluated to **`true`**, will cause the loop body to be repeated.
- *Loop initialization*—During the loop initialization the variable(s) taking part in the loop condition are assigned initial suitable values. This process only takes place once before the loop commences.
- *Loop update*—Updates the variables of the loop condition. This is repeatedly done during every loop.

These are exemplified in Figure 9.6, which uses the source code of the `while` loop shown earlier. Notice that only the loop condition is restrained by the rules of syntax to a specific position, namely inside a pair of parentheses positioned right after the `while` keyword. On the other hand, the loop initialization and loop update can be positioned anywhere. This is fine for a simple loop with a small loop body, such as the one shown here, but if initializations and updates are scattered around large amounts of code, it can become difficult to locate and remain conscious about these loop hotspots. All too often, this results in `while` or `do-while` loops that, during alterations, only have one or two key components modified without the necessary adjustments for the third components.

FIGURE 9.6
The three key components of a loop.

```
int index;
 index=0;  <------------ Loop intialization
 while (index<5)  <------------ Loop condition
  {
       Console.WriteLine(index);
       index++;  <------------ Loop update
 }
```

The `for` loop addresses this potential problem by providing exact syntactic rules for the location of all three loop control elements. As Syntax Box 9.3 shows, all three elements must be enclosed in parentheses next to the `for` keyword and separated by semicolon.

Syntax Box 9.3 The `for`-Loop Statement

```
for ( [<Initialization_statements>] ; [<Loop_condition>] ;
    ➥ [<Update_statements>] )
    <Loop_body>
```

where:

```
<Loop_body>::= <statement>;
          ::= <Compound_statement>


<Initialization_statements>::= <Initialization_statement1>,
                               <Initialization_statement2>...

<Loop_condition>::= <Boolean_expression>

<Update_statements>::= <Update_statement1>, <Update_statement2>...
```

Note:

- Use commas, as shown, to separate more than one initialization statement. The same applies if more than one update statement is specified. Semicolons are used to separate the loop statements from the loop condition and the loop condition from the update statements.
- The initialization statements, along with the loop condition and the update statements, are all optional. Consequently

```
for ( ; ; )
{
    // do something
}
```

constitutes a valid `for`-loop. Notice that the two semicolons must still be included.

The syntax of the `for` loop allows us to implement the same semantics as the code of Figure 9.6. This is done in Figure 9.7. It is important to notice that the timing of events taking place in the `for` loop are the same as those of the displayed `while` loop, which means

- The loop initialization takes place only once on entry to the loop.
- The loop condition is evaluated at the beginning of each iteration.
- The loop update is performed at the end of each iteration.

FIGURE 9.7
A `for` loop and its corresponding `while` loop.

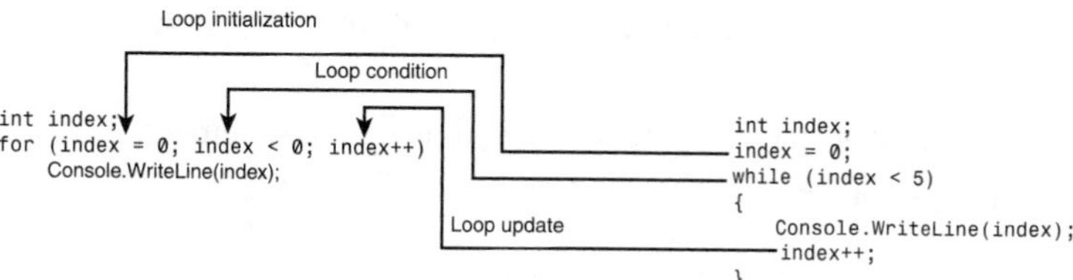

Note

The `for` and `while` loop constructs are both entry condition loops. The `do-while` loop is the only exit condition loop in C#.

Note

The loop body of the `for` statement can, like that of the `while` and `do-while` loops, be either a single or compound statement. The three different loop constructs are always counted as a single statement, disregarding the number of statements it contains in the loop body.

The following discusses the implications of the notes written in Syntax Box 9.3.

1. Each of the three loop parts in the `for` loop is optional, however the parentheses after the `for` keyword must always contain three semicolons.

Example: Figure 9.7 showed us how a `while` loop can be converted to fit into the conventional framework of a `for` loop. Conversely, Figure 9.8 illustrates how the `for` loop can mimic the syntax of the `while` loop, the only difference being the `for` keyword and a couple of semicolons. The loop initialization `index = 0` of the `for` loop has been removed from its position inside the parentheses to line 2, and the loop update `index++` removed to line 6.

FIGURE 9.8
for loop looking like a *while* loop.

Identical semantics

```
int index;
index = 0
for ( ; index < 5; )
{
    Console.WriteLine(index);
    index++;
}
```

```
int index;
index = 0;
while (index < 5)
{
  Console.WriteLine(index);
  index++;
}
```

It is even possible to omit the loop condition and leave the parentheses empty apart from the obligatory semicolons. A missing loop condition is interpreted by the compiler to be a loop condition that is always `true`, making `for( ; ; )` equivalent to `for( ; true; )`. The following would thus constitute an infinite loop:

```
for (  ;  ; )
{
    Console.WriteLine("I'm repeated infinitely many times");
}
```

Notice that the following `while` and `do-while` statements also constitute infinite loops:

```
while(true)
{
    Console.WriteLine("Pyyyhhhh, this is hard work");
}


do
{
    Console.WriteLine("As spoken out of my mouth");
} while (true)
```

You might, with good reason, wonder if a loop condition that is always `true` has any practical use. It turns out that it can be used together with the `break` statement you already met during the `switch` statement discussion, but more about this later in the section "The Jump Statements `break` and `continue`".

2. The loop initialization and loop update can consist of several statements separated by commas, but only a maximum of one loop condition is permitted.

Because of this, it is possible to include as many initializations and updates as you want within the parentheses after the `for` keyword.

The program in Listing 9.4 utilizes this feature to determine a number positioned between the initial values of `i` and `j` (in this case 0 and 21) for which it is true that it is one third from `i` towards `j` (and two thirds from `j` towards `i`). The loop body of the `for` loop prints the values of `i` and `j` as they get closer to the solution. In this case, the answer is 7, as shown in the final line of the sample output.

LISTING 9.4 OneThird.cs

```
01: using System;
02:
03: class OneThird
04: {
05:     public static void Main()
06:     {
07:         int i;
08:         int j;
09:
10:         Console.WriteLine("Value of\n i   j\n");
11:         for (i=0, j=21; i <= j; i++, j=j-2)
12:             Console.WriteLine(" {0}   {1}", i, j);
15:     }
16: }
```

```
Value of
 i   j

0    21
1    19
2    17
3    15
4    13
5    11
6    9
7    7
```

Line 11 specifies the `for` loop to enclose two initialization statements (`i = 0 , j = 21`) and two update statements (`i++ , j = j - 2`), in each case separated by the comma operator (see the following Note), whereas the loop body of line 12 merely performs a simple printout. Because `j` is decremented by 2 every time `i` is incremented by 1, `i` will be greater than `j`, and will make the loop condition `i <= j false`, approximately when `i` is one third toward the original value of `j` and `j` is two thirds towards the original value of `i`.

The Comma Operator

The language element allowing us to squeeze two or more expressions into the space of one `for` statement is called the *comma operator*. The effect of the comma operator, as in the following

```
for (i=0, j=21; i <= j; i++, j=j-2)   //combining i=0, j=21 and

                                      //combining i++ and j=j-2
```

is to combine two or more statements to count as one and, hence, fit where just one statement is expected.

The comma operator should not be confused with:

- The role the comma plays in a declaration statement, such as

  ```
  int count, distance;
  ```

  where it is used to separate the two variable identifiers that are declared to be of type `int`.

- Its use as a separator for formal parameters in a method header:

  ```
  public static int Sum(int a, int b)
  ```

- The separation of method arguments in a method call

  ```
  Sum(10, 20);
  ```

  Notice that instead of declaring `i` and `j` in lines 7 and 8 of Listing 9.4, it is possible to declare them inside the `for` statement as part of the initialization, as in the following:

  ```
          for (int i=0, j=21; i <= j; i++, j=j-2)
  ```

  According to the scope rules discussed previously, the scope of `i` and `j` is then confined to that of the loop body of the `for` loop, which is acceptable because `i` and `j` are only used within this scope.

  The compiler can confuse the comma operator and the comma separator, so it is not possible to separate two variable declarations (they contain the comma separator) with the comma operator, as shown next.

  ```
          for (int i=0, int j=21; i <= j; i++, j=j-2)  //Invalid
  ```

  The left most comma can either be a comma separator or a comma separator, the compiler has no way of telling which one it is.

Note

You can only have a maximum of one loop condition in the `for` statement, but because the loop condition is a Boolean expression, you can still use the logical operators (`&&`, `||`, `!`, `&`, `|`, `^`) to form longer Boolean expressions.

Tip

Only use the loop initialization and loop update for variables that are part of the loop condition.

The comma operator allows you to insert an infinite number of expressions into the space of the loop initializations and loop updates. It can be tempting to cram initializations and updates in here other than those directly linked to the variable(s) of the loop condition. Listing 9.5 illustrates this. It creates a table of heights and widths and, for each pair, calculates the resulting area.

LISTING 9.5 `AreaCalculatorUgly.cs`

```
using System;

class AreaCalculator
{
    public static void Main()
    {
        int i;
        int width;
        int height;

        Console.WriteLine("height   width     area\n");
```

LISTING 9.5 continued

```
12:         for (height = 1000, width = 100, i=0; i <= 10;
13:             height = height + 100, width = width + 10, i++)
14:         {
15:             Console.WriteLine("{0}      {1}       {2}",
16:                 height, width, height * width);
17:         }
18:     }
19: }
```

```
height   width       area

1000     100       100000
1100     110       121000
1200     120       144000
1300     130       169000
1400     140       196000
1500     150       225000
1600     160       256000
1700     170       289000
1800     180       324000
1900     190       361000
2000     200       400000
```

Note that lines 12 and 13 not only contain the loop initialization and loop updates for the loop condition variable `i`, they also contain initializations and updates for `width` and `height`. Consequently, the only thing left for the loop body to do is to print out the values calculated in the loop initialization and updates. Notice that it becomes hard to distinguish between the elements dealing with the control of the loop (the variable `i`) and those that are merely part of the processes performed during each loop. The ability and advantage of the `for` statement to enable a separation between the loop controlling parts and other processes performed during one loop has been misused, resulting in cluttered, unclear, ugly code. Listing 9.6 shows an improved version with exactly the same functionality as Listing 9.5.

LISTING 9.6 `AreaCalculatorImproved.cs`

```
using System;

class AreaCalculator
{
    public static void Main()
    {
        int i;
        int width;
        int height;

        height = 1000;
        width = 100;
        Console.WriteLine("height   width       area\n");
        for (i=0; i <= 10; i++)
        {
```

LISTING 9.6 continued

```
16:             Console.WriteLine("{0}      {1}      {2}",
17:                 height, width, height * width);
18:             height = height + 100;
19:             width = width + 10;
20:         }
21:     }
22: }
```

The output is the same as that from Listing 9.5.

The initializations and updates of `height` and `width` have been removed from the pair of parentheses following the `for` keyword. The initializations have been put in lines 11 and 12 prior to the `for` statement, and the updates have become part of the loop body where they belong.

The simple appearance of line 14 of this listing, compared to that of lines 12 and 13 in Listing 9.5, allows the reader to easily grasp the essential workings of this `for` loop.

`i` and `j` As Names for Counting Variables

The use of `i` and `j` as names for counting variables has a long (in terms of computing history) history behind it. The tradition was established with the FORTRAN language in that it only allowed variables with the names `i`, `j`, `k`, `l`, `m`, and `n` to be used for counting purposes. The impact of this tradition is widespread throughout the programming community where you will often encounter those names used for counting variables.

The Jump Statements `break` and `continue`

The following section discusses how the `break` and `continue` statements can be used to influence the flow of execution during the execution of a loop statement.

The `break` Statement

Occasionally programmers want to terminate a loop somewhere inside its loop body rather than at the beginning or at the end of the loop. They can achieve this by using the `break` statement that was introduced along with the `switch` statement in the previous chapter.

The *break* Statement and the Iteration Statements

The `break` statement can be used to terminate an iteration statement and will, when executed, cause the flow of control to jump out to the next statement immediately following the iteration statement. The `break` statement can be positioned anywhere inside the loop body to implement this effect.

Syntax Box 9.4 The break Statement

break_statement::= *break;*

The `break` statement is applied in line 20 of Listing 9.7 as part of a program that enables the user to transfer individually chosen characters from a given text into another text (see the sample output after Listing 9.7). Initially, the user enters a text. Each individual letter is then displayed one-by-one and for each letter the user can choose to either insert the letter into the new text or skip the letter. This repeated set of actions can be terminated at any time by pressing the letter T, causing the extracted letters to be displayed.

LISTING 9.7 `TransferLetters.cs`

```
01: using System;
02:
03: class TransferLetters
04: {
05:     public static void Main()
06:     {
07:         string myText;
08:         string answer;
09:         string newText = "";
10:
11:         Console.WriteLine("Enter some text:");
12:         myText = Console.ReadLine();
13:         Console.WriteLine("Type I<enter> to insert, " +
14:             "<enter> to skip and T<enter> to terminate");
15:         for (int i=0; i<myText.Length; i++)
16:         {
17:             Console.Write(myText[i] + " ");
18:             answer = Console.ReadLine().ToUpper();
19:             if (answer == "T")
20:                 break;
21:             if (answer == "I")
22:                 newText = newText + myText[i];
23:         }
24:         Console.WriteLine("The new text is: " + newText);
25:     }
26: }
```

```
Enter some text:
There is one way to find out if a man is honest - ask him. If he says yes you
➥ know he is crooked. - Groucho Marx<enter>
Type I<enter> to insert, <enter> to skip and T<enter> to terminate
T <enter>
h <enter>
e <enter>
r <enter>
e <enter>
  <enter>
i <enter>
```

```
s <enter>
  <enter>
o i<enter>
n i<enter>
e i<enter>
   i<enter>
w i<enter>
a i<enter>
y i<enter>
   T <enter>
The new text is: one way
```

We are faced with two contrasting requirements when choosing an iteration statement for this program.

On one hand, we need an entry condition loop because `myText`, which is visited character by character, might be empty, in which case we never want to execute the loop body.

On the other hand, we need an exit condition loop because we only know if the user wants to terminate the loop if at least the first character of `myText` has been presented. This calls for the loop body to be executed at least partially.

There are many ways to solve this computational problem. In this case, I chose to use the `for` loop to accommodate for the entry condition requirement and the `break` statement (after all, this listing is supposed to demonstrate the `break` statement) along with an `if` statement (see lines 19 and 20) to act instead of an exit condition. The `for` loop beginning in line 15 ensures that the loop body is repeated at most `myText.Length` times. If the user enters a t (or T) after one of the individual characters printed on the console by line 17, the Boolean expression of line 19 is evaluated to be `true` triggering the `break` statement of line 20 to be executed. The `for` statement is then terminated and the flow of control moves to line 24.

Note

The `break` statement is most frequently used together with an `if` statement, as shown in Listing 9.7, acting as an internal loop condition.

The `continue` Statement

The continue statement makes the flow of execution skip the rest of a loop body to continue with the next loop. This ability is sometimes useful.

The *`continue`* Statement and the Iteration Statements

When the `continue` statement is executed inside the loop body of an iteration statement, it causes the flow of control to jump over the remaining statements in the loop body and begin at the next iteration. If used with a `while` or a `do-while` loop, the loop condition will be the first part of this next iteration to be evaluated. In a `for` loop, the flow of control is passed to the loop update.

Syntax Box 9.5 The `continue` Statement

Continue_statement::= `continue;`

Note:

- The `continue` statement can only be utilized inside an iteration loop.

The `continue` statement does not interfere with the number of times the loop body is repeated as does the `break` statement, but merely influences the flow of control in any one particular iteration. Listing 9.8 utilizes the `continue` statement in line 10 to prevent the program from printing every fourth number.

LISTING 9.8 `Counting.cs`

```
01: using System;
02:
03: class Counting
04: {
05:     public static void Main()
06:     {
07:         for (int i = 0; i <= 20; i++)
08:         {
09:             if (i % 4 == 0)
10:                 continue;
11:             Console.Write(i + ", ");
12:         }
13:     }
14: }
```

```
1, 2, 3, 5, 6, 7, 9, 10, 11, 13, 14, 15, 17, 18, 19,
```

`i` is declared and initialized to zero in line 7. The `for` loop then increments it by 1 and repeatedly executes the loop body until `i` is greater than 20. Whenever `i` is a multiple of 4 (as tested for in line 9), the `continue` statement is executed and jumps over the remaining part of the loop body (in this case, line 11) and back to the loop update (`i++`) in line 7 to begin another iteration. As a result all numbers between zero and twenty, except those that are multiples of 4, are printed onscreen.

Structured Programming and Structured Constructs

Structured programming is a methodology that attempts to minimize the complexity associated with designing, writing, and modifying individual algorithms, so it is focused on the very detailed level of programming.

The fundamental idea of *structured programming* is simple: Only use control constructs that have one entry and one exit point. In C#, those structured constructs are represented by `while`, `do-while`, `for`, `if-else`, and `switch`.

The basic ideas associated with structured programming were conceived during the 1960s and 1970s. Before the advent of this important methodology, the `goto` statement had been applied to implement much of the logic in a program. However, it soon became apparent that many of the problems experienced by programmers were caused by the indiscriminate use of this jump statement, leading to what is often called spaghetti code (see Figure 9.9).

FIGURE 9.9
Convoluted spaghetti code made possible with the *goto* statement.

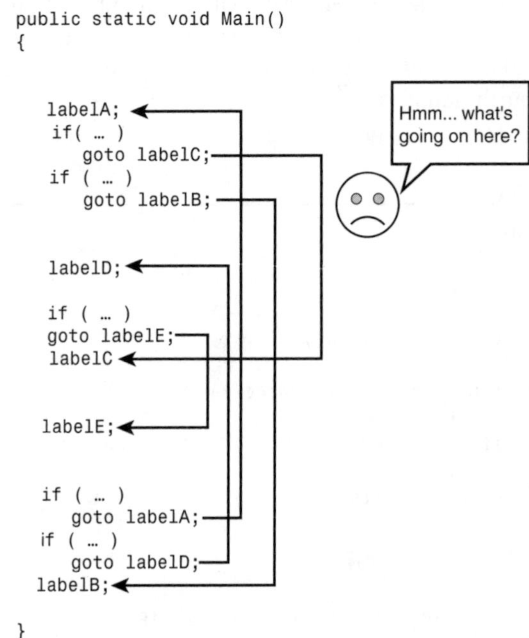

Fortunately, a better alternative was discovered in the form of the structured programming constructs for which it is true that the flow of control only has a single entry point and a single exit point. The `while`, `do-while`, `for`, `if-else`, and `switch` statements all belong to this category, as illustrated in Figure 9.10. Each of those constructs can be viewed as a black box from outside of their scope. From this viewpoint, the programmer can always be certain that the flow of control enters at the top in one entry point and exits at the bottom from one exit point. Consequently, when the construct is terminated, the next statement to follow is executed.

Recall how classes and objects used in object-oriented programming are used to break down the overall problem domain of a programming project into simpler, self-contained pieces. Each piece can be created, viewed, and modified separately. Well, this age-old strategy of breaking complex problems into simpler solvable parts is also at play in structured programming, but this time at the very detailed level of a program. Whereas the uncontrolled use of `goto` statements forces us to look at numerous aspects of an algorithm simultaneously, the structured constructs allow us to break an algorithm up into smaller self-contained pieces that, to a certain degree, can be viewed and analyzed separately, as they solve separate parts of a problem. Figure 9.11 illustrates this point.

FIGURE 9.10
Structured programming constructs in C#.

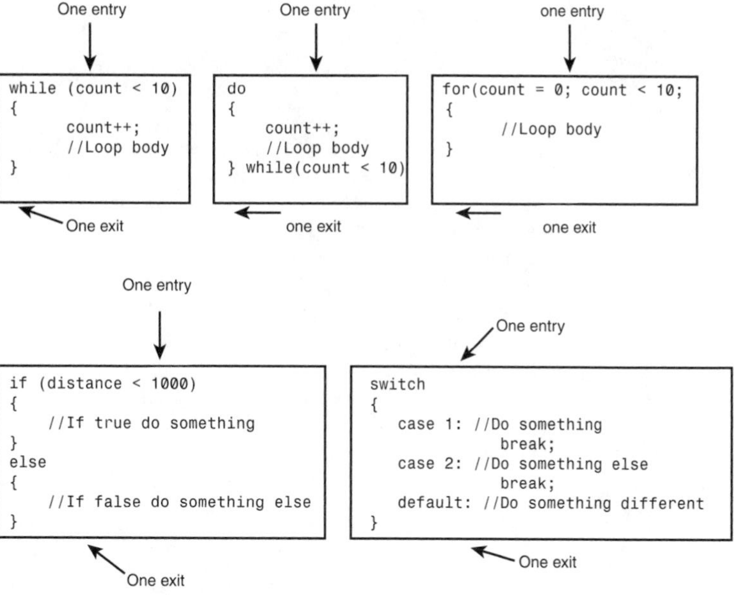

FIGURE 9.11
A structured method can be read from start to finish.

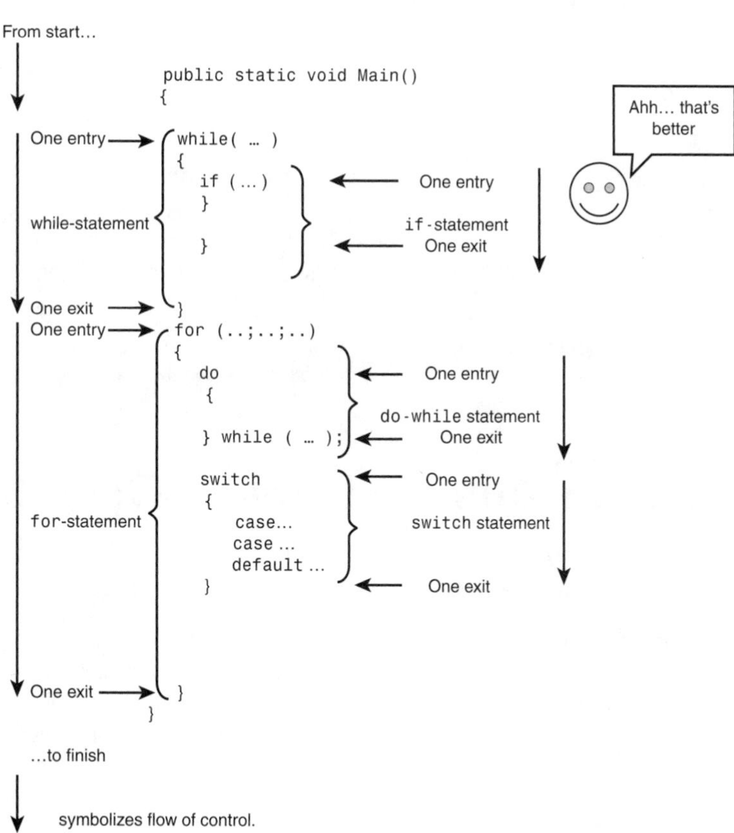

Caution

Flowcharts can lead to an apparent need for goto statements.

Expressing the flow of control visually with a flowchart can be a great aid in understanding and communicating the inner logic of a specific algorithm. However, there is at least one drawback of designing algorithms with flowcharts. It is very easy to call for the use of `goto` statements in the resulting source code. This is so because an arrow in a flowchart represents transfer of control from one part of the program to another. It is tempting and easy to get carried away and draw arrows to all kinds of weird and wonderful places when drawing a flowchart. Many of these jumps can, unless utmost care is taken, only be accomplished in the resulting C# source code through the use of the `goto` statement and not any of the structured programming elements.

This is one of the reasons why many programmers prefer pseudocode to flowcharts. They force the programmer to think in terms of structured programming elements, because pseudocode is written as lines of text from start to finish; erratic jumps do not easily fit in with this format.

Note

During the 1960s and 70s, computer scientists showed that any logic implemented by using `goto` statements could be implemented by a combination of the structured constructs discussed here. Because programmers then had no excuse for using `goto` statements in languages containing the structured constructs, the structured programming movement became synonymous with a crusade against the evil `goto` statement.

***break*, *continue*, and Structured Programming**

The effects achieved by applying the `break` and `continue` statements inside iteration statements can be achieved by a combination of the basic structured constructs (`while`, `do-while`, `for`, `if-else`, and `switch`). Some programmers believe `break` and `continue` breach the intent of structured programming and never use them. Other programmers argue that `break` and `continue`, when correctly applied, produce faster programs. Often, the best route to follow in this situation is first to write the source as clearly and correctly as possible (minimizing the use of `break` and `continue`), disregarding the speed of execution. If needed, tuning can then be performed at a later stage.

Combination Assignment Operators

The following assignment, found in line 18 of Listing 9.6

```
height = height + 100;
```

as you know, increments the variable `height` by 100. Frequently, and in particular in connection with iteration statements, variables are incremented with a specific amount. C# offers a condensed way of writing this type of assignment through the plus-equals (+=) operator. It allows us to express the previous assignment statement as

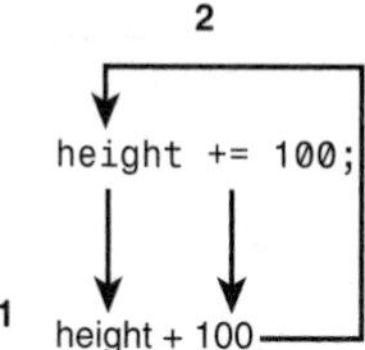

where the left operand is added to the right operand (step 1) and the result is then assigned to the left operand (step 2).

C# contains five combination assignment operators, one for each of the binary operators `+`, `-`, `*`, `/`, and `%`. They are all displayed in Table 9.2.

TABLE 9.2 The Combination Assignment Operators

Operator	Name	Example	Equivalent to
`+=`	Addition assignment	`height += 100;`	`height = height + 100;`
`-=`	Subtraction assignment	`sum -= 10;`	`sum = sum - 10;`
`*=`	Multiplication assignment	`length *= 3;`	`length = length * 3;`
`/=`	Division assignment	`height /= 2;`	`height = height / 2;`
`%=`	Modulus assignment	`days %= 7;`	`days = days % 7;`

Syntax Box 9.6 `Combination assignment`

```
Combination_assignment::=
<Variable> <Combination_assignment_operator> <Expression>
```

Note:

- The left operand must be a variable, whereas the right operand can be any expression for which it is true that an implicit conversion path exists from its type to the type of the left operand.

Listing 9.9 demonstrates the four combination assignment operators `+=`, `-=`, `*=`, and `/=` in action and allows the program to print out a counting table as shown in the sample output.

LISTING 9.9 CountingTable.cs

```
01: using System;
02:
03: class CountingTable
04: {
05:     public static void Main()
06:     {
07:         int countUp = 0;
08:         int countDown = 100;
09:         int fastUp = 1;
10:         int fastDown = 1024;
11:
12:         Console.WriteLine("+=      -=      *=      /=");
13:         for (int i = 0; i < 10; i++)
14:         {
15:             countUp += 5;
16:             countDown -= 20;
17:             fastUp *= 2;
18:             fastDown /= 2;
19:             Console.WriteLine("{0,2}   {1,4}   {2,4}   {3,4}",
20:                 countUp, countDown, fastUp, fastDown);
21:         }
22:     }
23: }
```

```
+=      -=      *=      /=
 5      80       2     512
10      60       4     256
15      40       8     128
20      20      16      64
25       0      32      32
30     -20      64      16
35     -40     128       8
40     -60     256       4
45     -80     512       2
50    -100    1024       1
```

The program utilizes a `for` loop to repeat the loop body in lines 15–20 ten times. For every repetition, the four combination assignment operators are used to update the four different variables in lines 15–18. As the `for` loop progresses through the ten loops, the value of each variable is printed (lines 19 and 20) to form the table shown in the sample output.

Nested Iteration Statements

The loop body of any iteration statement can consist of one or more statements. Because each iteration statement is a statement in itself, it can be nested inside the loop body of another iteration statement. An infinite number of iteration statements can be nested inside each other.

A *nested loop* consists of one loop (called an *inner loop*) residing inside another loop (called an *outer loop*).

Every time the outer loop executes its loop body once, the inner loop executes all of its loops. To illustrate this process, let's first have a look at an example containing only a single `for` loop and no nested loops yet. In a moment, we will expand this example with a nested `for` loop. Our first modest aim here is to construct a program that prints out five stars along a vertical line onscreen. Because a line is only one dimensional, the program is called `StarsOneDimension.cs`; it is displayed in Listing 9.10.

LISTING 9.10 `StarsOneDimension.cs`

```
01: using System;
02:
03: class StarsOneDimension
04: {
05:     public static void Main()
06:     {
07:         for (int i = 0; i < 5; i++)
08:         {
09:             Console.Write("*");
10:             Console.WriteLine();
11:         }
12:     }
13: }
```

```
*
*
*
*
*
```

The loop body of the `for` loop is repeated five times. During each loop, a star (*) is printed on the console (line 9) and the cursor moved to the next line (line 10).

Our next goal is slightly more ambitious. We still want to write out 5 lines, but this time each line must contain seven stars instead of one. This, in effect, creates a picture of 5 × 7 stars in two dimensions. The picture is created by a program suitably called `StarsTwoDimensions.cs` displayed in Listing 9.11.

LISTING 9.11 `StarsTwoDimensions.cs`

```
using System;

class StarsTwoDimensions
{
    public static void Main()
    {
        for (int i = 0; i < 5; i++)
        {
            for (int j = 0; j < 7; j++)
            {
                Console.Write("*");
            }
            Console.WriteLine();
```

LISTING 9.11 continued

```
14:         }
15:     }
16: }
```

```
*******
*******
*******
*******
*******
```

The problem we achieve to solve can be expressed through pseudocode consisting of an outer and an inner loop:

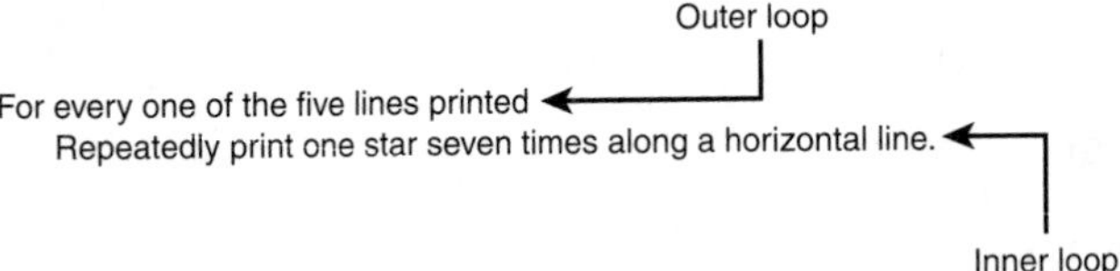

To express the logic of the pseudocode in C#, we exchange line 9 of Listing 9.10, which merely printed out one star, with a statement that prints out seven stars next to each other. This one statement is here in the form of a `for` statement spanning lines 9–12 and repeating itself seven times.

Listing 9.11 prints in two dimensions. Had we inserted another `for` statement inside the inner `for` statement, and had the console been equipped with 3D image technology, we could have printed in three dimension. In the next chapters, we will look at how arrays of three dimensions can be traversed using this same idea of three nested loop statements inside each other.

Case Study: The Letter Guessing Game

The following case study explores how two `do-while` statements, one nested inside the other, can be utilized to create a letter guessing game.

Software specification:

The object of the Guess Two Letters game is to let the user guess a sequence of two letters randomly selected by the computer program from the four letters A, B, C, and D. Repeat letters are permitted.

The user starts by entering two letters. The program compares this guess with its secret combination and responds by providing two numbers that evaluates the guess:

- The first number indicates how many letters of the guess were the correct letter and the correct position. This number is called `CC`.
- The second number indicates how many letters were the correct letter but wrong position. This number is called `CW`.

The user then enters another combination of letters, triggering another response. This sequence of events is repeated until the user has worked out the correct sequence of letters.

The following is an example:

Secret combination generated by program: BD

Guess	Response		Comment
	CC	CW	
AB	0	1	B is correct letter but wrong position
BC	1	0	B is correct letter and correct position
DB	0	2	Both letters are correct but wrong position
BD	2	0	Both letters are correct and in correct positions

The user found the correct combination using four guesses.

The program we aim to design must be able to play the Guess Two Letters game and provide the same type of output as just shown. Further, the program must provide a suitable comment related to how many guesses it took the user to guess the combination. For example, if less than 8 guesses were used, write `Well Done!` In the case of 8 or more guesses, write `Finally!`. And lastly, whenever a game is over, the program must let the user choose whether he or she wants to terminate the program or continue with yet another game. Then, the game can be played *repeatedly* until the user decides to quit the program.

Software design:

Only one algorithm belonging to the `Main()` method is needed in this program, rendering the class and method identification stages of the software development process superfluous. As a result, we will jump straight to the internal method design of the `Main()` method.

Internal method design:

Observe that the word *repeated* is mentioned twice in the previous software specification, indicating a need for two loops. In fact, we need an outer loop repeating a whole game and its inner loop repeating the guess-response events. The overall algorithm is described with pseudocode in Listing 9.12. I chose exit condition `do-while` loops over the entry condition `while` and `for` loops because both the inner and outer loops require user input to evaluate its loop's condition, calling for a minimum of one execution of the loop body, as shown previously in Listing 9.3.

LISTING 9.12 The Fundamental Pseudocode Behind Listing 9.13

```
do
{
    generate secret combination
    do
    {
        let user enter guess
        compare guess with secret combination
```

LISTING 9.12 continued

```
            provide feedback about the guess
            increment guess counter by one
        } while guess is wrong
        print the total number of guesses entered by user plus
        ➥ a fitting comment
        determine if user wants to play another game
    } while user still wants to play another game
```

The C# source code corresponding to the pseudocode of Listing 9.12 is shown in Listing 9.13.

LISTING 9.13 `GuessTwoLetters.cs`

```
using System;

class GuessTwoLetters
{
    public static void Main()
    {
        string letterCode;
        string letterGuess;
        string letters = "ABCD";
        int ccCounter;
        int cwCounter;
        int guessCounter = 0;
        string anotherGame;
        Random Randomizer = new Random();
        do
        {
            guessCounter = 0;
            letterCode = letters[Randomizer.Next(0,4)].ToString() +
                         letters[Randomizer.Next(0,4)].ToString();
            Console.WriteLine("\nChoose two of the four
                ➥ letters A, B, C, D\n" +
                "CC: Correct letter Correct position\n" +
                "CW: Correct letter Wrong position\n" +
                "Please enter letter guesses\n\n" +
                "   CC CW");
            do
            {
                ccCounter = 0;
                cwCounter = 0;
                letterGuess = Console.ReadLine().ToUpper();
                 // Determine how many positions of the guess contains a
                 // correct letter in a correct position (CC's)
                if(letterGuess[0] == letterCode[0])
                    ccCounter++;
                if(letterGuess[1] == letterCode[1])
                    ccCounter++;
                 // If no CC's were found determine how many positions
                 // of the guess contains a correct letter
                 ➥ but incorrect position
```

LISTING 9.13 continued

```
                if(ccCounter == 0)
                {
                    if(letterGuess[0] == letterCode[1])
                        cwCounter++;
                    if(letterGuess[1] == letterCode[0])
                        cwCounter++;
                }
                Console.WriteLine("   {0}  {1} ", ccCounter,
                ➥ cwCounter + "\n");
                guessCounter++;
            } while (letterCode != letterGuess);
             // Use conditional operator to provide suitable comment
            Console.WriteLine((guessCounter < 8) ?
            ➥ "Well done! " : "Finally! ");
            Console.WriteLine("You guessed the code in {0} guesses",
            ➥guessCounter);
            Console.WriteLine("\nDo you wish to play another game? Y(es)
            ➥N(o)");
            anotherGame = Console.ReadLine().ToUpper();
        } while (anotherGame == "Y" || anotherGame == "YES");
         Console.WriteLine("Great playing with you. Hope you had fun!");
    }
}
```

```
Choose two of the four letters A, B, C, D
CC: Correct letter Correct position
CW: Correct letter Wrong position
Please enter letter guesses

   CC CW
AB<enter>
   0  0

CD<enter>
   1  0

CC<enter>
   2  0

Well done!
You guessed the code in 3 guesses

Do you wish to play another game? Y(es)  N(o)
N<enter>
Great playing with you. Hope you had fun!
```

The overall structure of Listing 9.13 can perhaps best be understood by relating it to the pseudocode, which has been done in Table 9.3.

TABLE 9.3 The Pseudocode and Its Corresponding C# Line Numbers

Line numbers: Pseudocode	Line numbers–C# source code
01–13: Outer loop	15–53
04–10: Inner loop	25–47
03: Generate secret combination	18, 19
06: Let the user enter guess	29
07: Compare guess with secret combination	30–44
08: Provide feedback about quality of guess	45
09: Increment guess counter by one	46
11: Print total number of guesses	49–50
12: Determine if user wants to play again	51–52

The important goal of this code is to demonstrate the use of two nested `do-while` loops. However, there are a few other points worth noticing

- *Randomly generating the secret letter combination*—Because we are restricted to the four letters A, B, C, and D, the program declares a `string` type variable called `letters` made up of these four letters (see line 9). By choosing a number randomly between 0 and 3, through the `Randomizer.Next(0, 4)` command, and by using this number to select an index of `letters` as in `letters[Randomizer.Next(0,4)]` (see lines 18 and 19), we are, in effect, generating a random value of type `char` that might be any of the four given letters. Because we want to combine this value with another randomly created letter to finally create a `string` of two letters, we need to turn the value of type `char` into a value of type `string`. This is done by applying the built-in `ToString()` method with the dot operator to form `letters[Randomizer.Next(0,4)].ToString()`. Finally, the program combines the two randomly created `strings` with the concatenation operator `+`. The end result is assigned to `letterCode.`

  - *Comparing* `letterGuess` *with* `letterCode`
  - Determining the number of correct letters in correct positions (lines 32–35).

    If the first letter of the `letterGuess` is a correct letter in a correct position, it must be true that the letter at index 0 of `letterGuess` is equal to the letter at index 0 of `letterCode`, or more succinctly—`letterGuess[0] == letterCode[0]`. Thus, if this is `true`, `ccCounter` is incremented by one (see line 33). Exactly the same argument holds for the second letter in index 1 (see lines 34–35).

  - Determining the number of correct letters in wrong positions (lines 38—44).

    If the `ccCounter` is equal to 2 after lines 32–35 have been processed, the guess is obviously correct and the game is over. However, the implications of `ccCounter` being equal to 1, meaning if just one of the letters in `letterGuess` is a correct letter in a correct position, is not quite so apparent. In this case, the number of correct letters but wrong position must be zero. Figure 9.12 exemplifies this point. In the first instance, the `letterCode` is `AB` and the `letterGuess` `AC`. Because there is a perfect match between the two A's, position 0 of `letterCode` and `letterGuess` is disregarded in any further analysis. Consequently, we are only left with position 1 in both variables. If the letter in position 1 of `letterGuess` is the correct letter, it must also be in the correct position. But because `ccCounter` is only equal to one, it must be an incorrect letter altogether.

What if the second guess is an A, wouldn't this count as a correct letter, wrong position? No. The second part of Figure 9.12 explains why.

FIGURE 9.12
When one letter is a correct letter and the correct position.

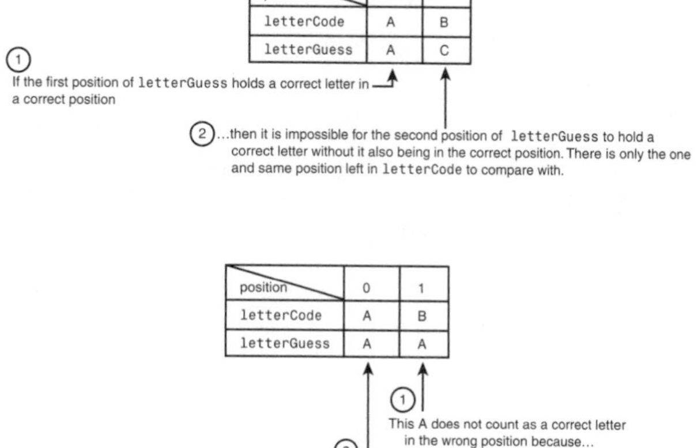

Due to the arguments put forth, the `cwCounter` can only be greater than zero if the `ccCounter` is zero. This explains the `if` statement commencing in line 38 and its corresponding Boolean expression, which ensures that `ccCounter` is equal to zero before beginning the analysis of correct letters but incorrect positions.

Printing appropriate comment at end of game related to total number of guesses.

If the user needs more than seven guesses to find the correct `letterCode`, the program will write `Finally!` as an additional comment. Less than 8 guesses are saluted by the more encouraging `Well done!`.

The `guessCounter` is incremented by one in line 46 for every new guess. When line 49 is executed, a game has just been finished and `guessCounter` contains the total number of guesses required. Line 49 utilizes the conditional operator `?` as an argument to the `WriteLine` method to print out `Well done!` if `guessCounter` is smaller than eight; otherwise, it will print out `Finally!`.

Programming Exercises

Extend the program of Listing 9.13 to include the following features:

1. Instead of choosing from only four letters (A, B, C, and D) when generating the `letterCode`, let the program choose between the five letters A, B, C, D, and E.

2. If the user could not guess the `letterCode` after 5 guesses, let the program reveal the letter held in position zero.
3. If the user did not detect the `letterCode` after 7 guesses, let the program reveal the combination and end the game.
4. Let the program keep track of the number of guesses required for each game so that the average number of guesses can be printed out just before the program is terminated.
5. Let the program keep track of the maximum and minimum number of guesses of any one game. Print these statistics at the end of a game.
6. Enable the program to play with three letters instead of two.

Note: No answers are provided for these programming exercises.

Keep Variable Declarations Outside the Loop Body If Possible

None of the iteration statement examples presented in this section contain any declaration statements inside their loop body. Instead, they are positioned outside, usually at the beginning of the method. This is not coincidental. Declaration statements residing inside a loop body will, like any other statement, be executed repeatedly. This can, depending on the inner workings of the compiler, slow down the program because variables can be created, destroyed, and recreated every time the loop is repeated.

Caution

Unintentional use of the empty statement with loop statements.

The empty statement is, as you might recall, conceived when a semicolon is placed where a statement is expected. We saw in the previous chapter how it can cause trouble for the `if` statement. Unfortunately, it might cause exactly the same type of problem for the `while` and `for` constructs as shown next, using the `while` statement as an example:

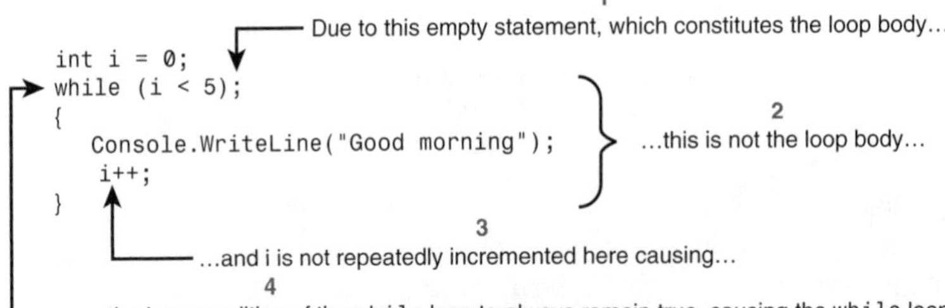

The compiler can detect the unintentional empty statement and report a warning with the following message:

```
EmptyStatement.cs(8,22): warning CS0642: Possible mistaken null statement
```

Intentional Use of the Empty Statement with Loop Statements

Occasionally, programmers make use of the empty statement when constructing a loop. The following example illustrates:

```
...
int i;
int j;
                              Empty statement
i = 30;                              |
j = 0;                               v
for ( ; i > j; i--, j++)             ;

Console.WriteLine("Midtpoint between i and j:"+i);
...
```

Because all the processing takes place within the loop update of the `for` statement, there is no need for a loop body. The loop condition `i > j` is initially `true`, causing the `for` statement to execute the empty statement (even though there is very little going on here) and the loop update repeatedly. As the loop update causes `i` to be decremented by one and `j` incremented by one, the loop condition will eventually be `false` when `i` is equal to `j`, which is half way between the two numbers (in this case 30 and 0), the result is thus 15. This programming practice does not produce clear code and should in most cases be avoided. It is mentioned here so you can recognize it when you stumble upon it in other programmers code.

Summary

This chapter explored the fundamental aspects of iteration and how to implement this essential programming tool by using C#'s three types of iteration statements—`while`, `do-while`, and `for` loops.

Important points mentioned in this chapter are reviewed in this section.

An iteration statement repeats a statement or block of statements as long as its loop condition is `true`.

Iteration statements are often used to generate or analyze (traverse) a sequence of data elements.

The `while` loop statement consists of the `while` keyword, a loop condition, and a loop body (consisting of one or more statements) that is repeatedly executed until the loop condition is `false`. The `while` loop is an entry condition loop, so its loop body may never be executed even once.

The `do-while` loop statement is an exit condition loop. As a result, its loop body will be executed at least once. Entry condition loops are more frequently used than exit condition loops. However, `do-while` loops are particularly suited for receiving and processing repeated user input.

The `for` loop is, like the `while` loop, an entry condition loop, but as opposed to the `while` loop, it confines the important parts of a loop (loop condition, loop initialization, and loop update) to one place in the source code. This makes it easier to focus on the parts that need to be modified to make the `for` loop work correctly. The `for` loop is a flexible construct that allows you, with the use of the comma operator, to include more than one loop initialization and more than one loop update.

The `break` statement can be used to jump out of an iteration statement to continue execution at the statement following the iteration statement.

The `continue` statement jumps over the rest of the statements in the loop body and continues with the next loop.

Structured programming is focused on how to write the detailed parts of computer programs found inside individual methods. Its basic philosophy is simply stated as "Only use control constructs that have one entry and one exit point." This basic rule can easily be broken when using the error-prone `goto` statement.

The combination assignment operator plus equals (+=) allows you to write

```
number += 10;
```

instead of

```
number = number + 10;
```

The same ability runs parallel for the combinations assignment operators—`-=`, `*=`, `/=`, `%=`.

Iteration statements can be nested inside each other to any required level. Two nested iteration statements are suited for generating and processing two-dimensional data. Three nested iteration statements are suited for three-dimensional data and so forth.

Review Questions

1. What is the major difference between the `while` and the `do-while` statements? Why is the `while` statement most often the preferred type of statement?

2. What is the output from the following piece of source code? (Mentally trace the code.)

```
int counter = 0;
while(counter < 4)
{
    counter++;
    Console.Write(counter + " ");
}
```

3. What is the output from the following `do-while` construct? (Trace the code.)

```
int counter = 4;
do
{
    Console.Write(counter + " ");
```

```
    counter--;
} while(counter > 0);
Console.WriteLine("Value of counter: {0}", counter);
```

4. What is the output from the following `for` loop construct? (Trace the code.)

```
for(int i = 0; i < 0; i += 2)
{
    Console.Write(i + " ");
}
```

5. Write a `for` loop that generates the following output:

```
12  9  6  3  0  -3
```

6. Is the following `for` loop valid (disregarding that it is not shown to be part of a complete program). If so, what output will it generate?

```
for(int i = 1, j = 1; i < 5; i++, j += 2)
{
    Console.Write("  {0}", i * j);
}
```

7. What is the output from the following nested pair of `for` loops? (Trace the source code.)

```
for(int i = 1; i < 4; i++)
{
    for(int j = 1; j < 5; j++)
    {
        Console.Write(" {0}", i + j);
    }
}
```

8. Consider the following `for` loop:

```
for(int counter = 1;  ; counter++)
{
    Console.WriteLine("The value of counter: {0}", counter);
    Console.WriteLine("This value of counter * 10: {0}, counter * 10);
}
```

Syntactically, this `for` loop is valid. However, it is an infinite loop as it stands now, because it lacks a loop condition. Change the `for` loop so that at its fourth repeated loop it terminates between the two `WriteLine` statements. Thus, at its fourth repeated loop, it should only write

```
The value of counter: 4
```

and then terminate. Hint: You can use the `break` statement.

9. Consider the following for loop shown previously in Listing 9.8:

```
for(int i = 0; i <= 20; i++)
{
    if(i % 4 == 0)
        continue;
    Console.Write(i + ", ");
}
```

Rewrite the `for` loop and eliminate the `continue` statement while keeping the semantics of the `for` loop intact.

10. Name one advantage of pseudocode over flowcharts in relation to constructing structured programs.

Programming Exercises

1. The factorial is an important mathematical function. The factorial of a number *n* is written *n!*. *n!* is calculated as the product of the integers from 1 to *n*. For example $4! = 4 \times 3 \times 2 \times 1$. Furthermore $1! = 1$, and $0! = 1$. Write a program that receives an integer from the user, calculates its factorial, and returns this value as output. Allow the user (through a loop construct) to perform as many calculations as he or she wants during one program. After each calculation, the program must ask the user whether he or she wants to perform another calculation.

2. Write a program that generates the following output:

```
*
**
***
****
*****
******
*******
********
```

3. Write a program that generates the following output:

```
*
########
**
#######
***
######
****
#####
*****
####
******
###
*******
##
********
#
```

CHAPTER 10

ARRAYS PART I: ARRAY ESSENTIALS

You will learn about the following in this chapter:

- Why the idea of putting many values of the same type into the same data structure (the array) is so compelling
- How to declare, define, initialize, and apply one-dimensional arrays
- How arrays are effectively accessed with loop statements
- The iteration statement `foreach` and how this statement, compared to the `for`-loop, can simplify access to an array
- The implications of the fact that an array is a reference type.
- How arrays can be provided as arguments to methods and as return values from methods
- The implications of letting the values of an array be references to objects
- The ability to let arrays be instance variables of classes and the associated advantages

In previous chapters we have worked with only a few variables in the sample programs presented. The elevator simulation program in Chapter 5, "Your First Object-Oriented Program," dealt with just one or two elevators interacting with merely one person, and a later example contained only one `accountBalance`. However, our programs often need to represent much larger numbers of similar items. Some skyscrapers can contain 30 or more elevators, transporting thousands of people every day, and banks have to manage tens of thousands of account balances.

How can we effectively and conveniently represent large amounts of similar data items in our source code? We could, as a first hunch, attempt to declare the items one by one in a similar fashion to what we have done before. For a bank simulation program attempting to represent an unchanging amount of different account balances, say 3000, it could look like the following:

```
decimal accountBalance1;
decimal accountBalance2;
```

```
     ...
decimal accountBalance1000;
decimal accountBalance1001;
     ...
decimal accountBalance3000;
```

which declares 3000 different variables of type `decimal` using 3000 lines of source code.

However, this approach poses a couple of serious problems:

- Not only is it a nuisance, but it is also time and memory consuming to write the thousands of source code lines required.
- It is impossible to traverse the list of variables by using a loop statement, because we are dealing with 3000 *different* names. A loop construct needs a *single* name combined with an index that can be incremented to access different values; just like the `string` type allows a loop to traverse its characters through a single name and an index enclosed in square brackets (example: `myText[i]` allows the counter `i` to determine which character we access).

  Thus, if we needed to, say, perform a routine addition of interest to *all* the accounts, we would have to write each visit explicitly in the code, such as

  ```
  accountBalance1 = accountBalance1 + accountBalance1 * interestRate;
  accountBalance2 = accountBalance2 + accountBalance2 * interestRate;
    ...
  accountBalance3000 = accountBalance3000 + accountBalance3000 * interestRate
  ```

  requiring another 3000 lines of code.

To solve these problems, we need a construct that can hold and represent an entire collection of similar data items and that possesses the following characteristics:

- The construct can be declared simply by using one or two lines of source code, disregarding the number of items it is meant to represent.
- Each item in the collection can be accessed via just one name plus a unique index (such as `accountBalances[0]`), allowing a simple loop construct to traverse the entire list.

The array class presented and discussed in this chapter holds those and many other qualities, making it suitable to represent small and large collections of data items of the same type.

Declaring and Defining an Array

In certain respects, the array is very similar to the `string` type, which, for that reason, is often referred to as an *array of characters*. I expect you to be reasonably familiar with the `string` class by now and I will briefly use it here to familiarize you with the array concept.

Recall how a variable of type `string` is able to hold a collection of characters, all neatly ordered and indexed, facilitating easy access to each character as in

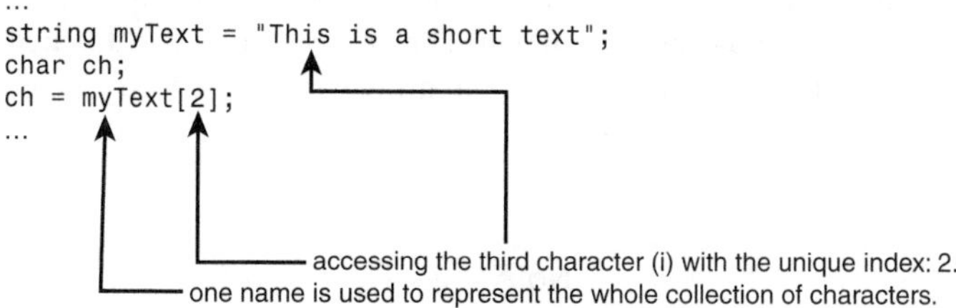
...
string myText = "This is a short text";
char ch;
ch = myText[2];
...
accessing the third character (i) with the unique index: 2.
one name is used to represent the whole collection of characters.

which assigns the letter `i` to `ch`. Or as in

```
string myText = "To b or not to be said the bee";
int bCounter = 0;
for(int i=0; i<myText.Length; i++)
{
   if(myText[i].ToString().ToUpper() == "B")
        bCounter++;
}
Console.WriteLine("Number of b's in text: " + bCounter);
```

By initializing i to 0 and incrementing it by one for every loop...
...the program can access each individual character...
...and count the number of b's

which counts the number of `b`s in `myText` and generates the following output:

```
Number of b's in text: 3
```

Notice that `myText` is the only name needed to access any of the individual characters in the collection of characters it represents, as long as we combine it with an index enclosed by square brackets. This uniform compact method of referencing individual characters, as you will see shortly, is identical to that of referencing individual data elements in an array.

The `string` and array are both class types and reference types. Whereas the underlying class for the `string` type is the .NET class `System.String`, an array originates from the `System.Array` class. Consequently, an array is an object, which, like the `string` object, has many built-in methods useful for accessing and manipulating collections of data items.

There are many similarities between `strings` and arrays, but, while the `string` type along with its built-in methods is specialized in and restricted to represent collections of characters, an array can be declared to hold a collection of *any* type of values, including any of the simple types `int`, `long`, `decimal` and so on, and any group of objects, such as elevators, persons, strings, Blipos Clocks, and so on.

An *array* is a named data structure (or object) that maps a list of index numbers with a collection of data storage locations called *array elements*. All array elements must be of the same type. The type of the array elements is called the *array element type*, also referred to as the *base type* of the array.

Array elements are sometimes called *indexed variables*, *subscripted variables*, or simply *elements*.

A variable of type `array` is declared in the source code by specifying the array element type followed by an empty pair of square brackets and the name of the array. The following line of source code

```
decimal [] accountBalances;
```

declares a variable of the name `accountBalances` with the ability to hold a reference to an array object containing a collection of `decimal` numbers. The only syntactical difference between declaring a single variable of, say, `decimal` and an array variable of base type `decimal` is the pair of square brackets.

Note

Sometimes, programmers position the square brackets immediately next to the type name as in the following

```
decimal[]  accountBalances;
```

to highlight the notion of an array. Whichever style you choose, remember to be consistent.

The previous declaration merely creates an empty container with the ability to hold a reference to an array object. The array object itself, with its collection of `decimal` values, is not yet created, and no memory has so far been allocated for this purpose.

An object of type `array`, must, like any other class (with the exception of `strings`), be created by applying the keyword `new`, which you have used before to create `Elevator` and `Person` objects. The single line of code in Figure 10.1 instantiates an array object (of class `System.Array`) that will hold a collection of five decimal values and assigns its reference to `accountBalances`.

The name of a valid type, such as `int` or—as in this case—`decimal` must follow the `new` keyword. A pair of square brackets enclosing an integer number, specifying the number of array elements in the array object created, follows. This number must be implicitly convertible to type `int`. As usual, a semicolon terminates the whole statement.

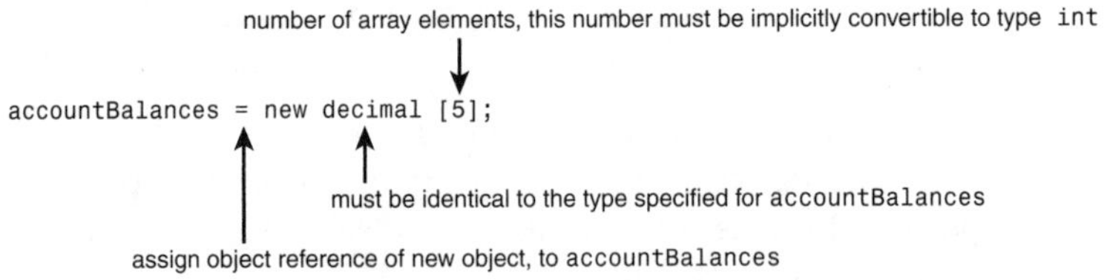

FIGURE 10.1
Creating an array object of five elements.

```
accountBalances = new decimal [5];
```

number of array elements, this number must be implicitly convertible to type int
must be identical to the type specified for accountBalances
assign object reference of new object, to accountBalances

Note

Instead of separating the declaration statement from the instantiation statement into two lines, it is possible to combine them in the same line, as follows:

```
decimal [] accountBalances = new decimal [5];
```

Note

You might encounter a syntax significantly different from that already shown to declare array variables and create new array objects. This syntax refers to the class and method names from the .NET Framework directly in the source code, as demonstrated in the following line

```
System.Array rainfall = System.Array.CreateInstance( Type.GetType
➥("System.Decimal"), 5 );
```

that declares an array variable called `rainfall` and assigns it a reference to a new array object of base type `decimal`. The syntax shown in this Note is not applied in this book, but merely presented so you can recognize it if you stumble upon it in source code written by other programmers.

After the array variable `accountBalances` has been declared and assigned a new array object, the state of affairs can be illustrated, as in Figure 10.2. `accountBalances` now contains a reference pointing to a specific object of class `System.Array` located somewhere in the computer memory. This object has the capacity to hold a collection of five `decimal` values. Because each `decimal` takes up 128 bits (or 16 bytes), this part of the array object will occupy 5 × 128 bits = 640 bits (or 80 bytes). The reference itself takes up 4 bytes of memory.

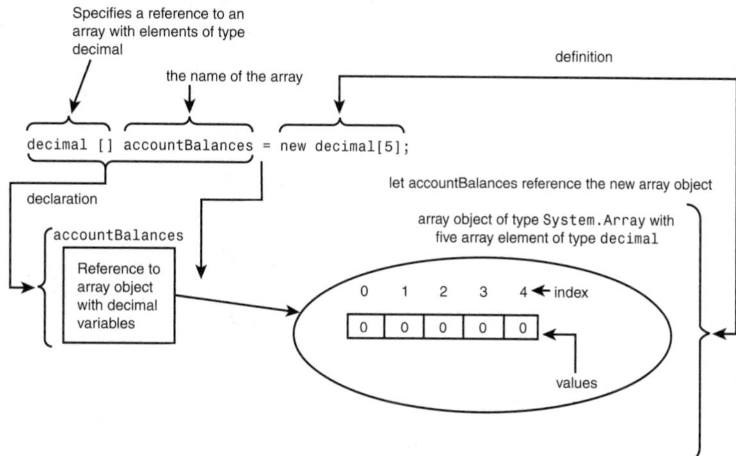

FIGURE 10.2
Array variable referencing array object.

An *array length* is the total number of array elements an array can hold. Another term used instead of length is *size*.

It is possible, as you will see shortly, to specify and assign initial values to elements of the array at the same time as it is being created. When an array is created without any initial values, as in the previous examples, its array elements are automatically assigned default values. The default values vary according to the array element type:

- Numerical values of type `short`, `int`, `float`, `decimal` and so on are assigned the value zero.
- Values of type `char` are assigned the Unicode character `\u0000`.

- Values of type `bool` are initialized to the value `false`.
- Values of reference types are initialized to `null`.

In our example, the array element type is `decimal`, so all values are initialized to zero, as indicated in Figure 10.2. It is generally a good idea to perform your own initializations in the source code rather than relying on default values provided by the compiler. Not only does it make the code clearer for programmers who are not up to date with the particular default values provided, it also prevents the program from being susceptible to default values that might change over time or differ between various compilers from different compiler makers.

The *null* Value

When a reference is not referencing any particular object, it references the `null` object. `null` is compatible with all reference types. It is represented by the keyword `null` in C#. If you want a reference to point to nothing, you can assign it the value `null` as in the following:

```
elevator3 = null;
```

The general syntax for declaring and creating a single array is shown in Syntax Box 10.1.

Syntax Box 10.1 Single array declaration and instantiation

```
Array_declaration::= <Base_type> [] <Array_identifier>;

Array_creation::= new <Base_type> [<Array_length>]

Array_reference_assignment::= <Array_identifier> = new <Base_type>
                              ➥ [<Array_length>];
                            ::= <Array_declaration> = new <Base_type>
                              ➥ [<Array_length>];
```

Notes:

- The *<Base_type>* of the declaration must be identical to the *<Base_type>* of the instantiation.
- *<Array_length>* must be positive and of a type implicitly convertible to type `int`. It can be a literal, constant, or variable.
- The square brackets `[]` do not indicate an option in this case (otherwise they would have been printed as *[]*); the square brackets must be written as part of the syntax.

When the array has been declared and a reference to an array object assigned, we are ready to access its individual array elements.

Accessing Individual Array Elements

An individual array element is accessed in the same manner as an individual character of a `string` variable—by writing the array variable name followed by a pair of square brackets containing the index value of the element. The following line

```
accountBalances[0] = 1000m;
```

assigns the value 1000 of type `decimal` to the first element of array elements contained in the object referenced by `accountBalances`. The index can be any numerical expression with a non-negative value of a type implicitly convertible to type `int`, and must be evaluated to a value less than the length of the array.

Note

The index values of the individual array elements begin at zero *not one*; the array is said to be *zero based*. Thus, `accountBalances[0]` represents the first array element of the collection represented by `accountBalances`. The index of the last array element is equal to the array length minus one. Consequently, `accountBalances[4]` refers to the fifth and last array element in our example.

Sometimes, the first array element (`accountBalances[0]`) is mistakenly referred to as the "zero'eth" element. The problem with this name appears when we then have to find a suitable name for `accountBalances[1]`. The logical but incorrect name would be "first element." If, instead of this incorrect naming scheme, you get into the habit of calling `accountBalances[0]` for the first element, you should quickly get accustomed to calling `accountBalances[4]` for the fifth element.

Note

Recall that `strings` are immutable. This prevents us from changing any of the characters in a `string`. On the other hand, the array is mutable, allowing us to assign values to individual elements of an array.

`accountBalances[0]` can be regarded as any other variable of type `decimal` in the sense that we can assign and retrieve values from this element and let it take part in any suitable expression. For example, to print the value of a ten percent interest from `accountBalances[0]`, we can write the following:

```
Console.WriteLine(accountBalances[0] * 0.1m);
```

Let's put all the pieces we have mentioned so far together into a simple program. The source code presented in Listing 10.1 declares an array of five account balances. It lets the user assign an amount to the first two array elements and adds a ten percent interest to those. The amounts of these two first account balances are finally printed out. To keep the source code short, the three remaining account balances `accountBalances[2]`, `accountBalances[3]`, and `accountBalances[4]` are not accessed in this program.

LISTING 10.1 SimpleAccountBalances.cs

```
using System;

class SimpleAccountBalances
{
    public static void Main()
    {
```

LISTING 10.1 continued

```
07:         const decimal interestRate = 0.1m;
08:         decimal [] accountBalances;
09:
10:         accountBalances = new decimal [5];
11:
12:         Console.WriteLine("Please enter two account balances: ");
13:         Console.Write("First balance: ");
14:         accountBalances[0] = Convert.ToDecimal(Console.ReadLine());
15:         Console.Write("Second balance: ");
16:         accountBalances[1] = Convert.ToDecimal(Console.ReadLine());
17:
18:         accountBalances[0] = accountBalances[0] + accountBalances[0]
            ➥ * interestRate;
19:         accountBalances[1] = accountBalances[1] + accountBalances[1]
            ➥ * interestRate;
20:
21:         Console.WriteLine("New balances after interest: ");
22:         Console.WriteLine("First balance: {0:C}", accountBalances[0]);
23:         Console.WriteLine("Second balance: {0:C}", accountBalances[1]);
24:     }
25: }
```

```
Please enter two account balances:
First balance: 1000<enter>
Second balance: 2000<enter>
New balances after interest:
First balance: $1,100.00
Second balance: $2,200.00
```

Line 8 declares `accountBalances` to hold a reference to an array with array elements of type `decimal`. Line 10 instantiates an object of class `System.Array`, allocates space for it in memory, and assigns its reference to the `accountBalances` variable. Lines 14 and 16 assign the amounts provided by the user to the array elements with index 0 and 1, respectively. If the user enters the amounts 1000 and 2000, as shown in the sample output, the array object can be depicted as shown in Figure 10.3, which further shows how each array element is accessed syntactically. Lines 18 and 19 add the interest (determined by the `const interestRate` in line 7) to the two account balances. Their values after this interest update are finally printed out in lines 22 and 23.

The syntax used for accessing individual array elements, as presented earlier and used in Listing 10.1 is formalized in Syntax Box 10.2.

Syntax Box 10.2 Accessing Array Elements

```
Array_element_access::= <Array_identifier> [<Numerical_expression>]
```

Notes:

- The square brackets `[ ]` do not indicate an option in this case (then they would have looked like *[ ]*) but the actual square brackets that must enclose the index in the form of a *<Numerical_expression>*.

- *<Numerical_expression>* can be any expression with a type implicitly convertible to type `int`. According to Figure 6.17, of Chapter 6, "Types Part I: The Simple Types," showing the implicit conversion paths of the simple numeric types in C#, it is possible to use expressions of type `sbyte`, `byte`, `short`, `ushort`, and `char`. Any other type must either have a user-defined implicit conversion path specified, or be explicitly converted with the cast operator.

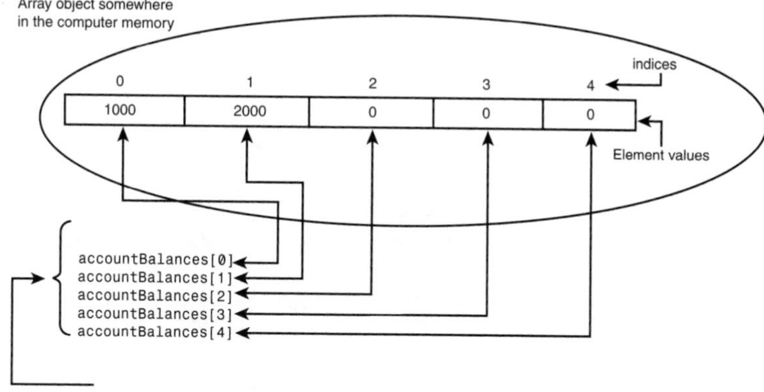

FIGURE 10.3
The two values assigned to *accountBalances*.

Note

It is important to differentiate between the three different contexts in which the square brackets are used in relation to arrays:

- To declare an array variable

  `decimal [] accountBalances;`

- To enclose the array length when creating an array object

  `new decimal [5]`

- To access individual array elements

  `accountBalances[0]`

Listing 10.1 showed you how to use the array element reference `accountBalances[0]` in a program just like any other variable of type `decimal`. Even though this is useful as an initial demonstration of how individual array elements are accessed and used, it doesn't demonstrate the real power of arrays. To that end, we can combine the array with a loop statement, such as in Listing 10.2. The functionality of the program is very similar to that of Listing 10.1, but the implementation differs significantly. By combining the `for` loop construct with the array `accountBalances`, the program

- Allows the user to enter five account balances
- Adds interest to each single account balance
- Prints out the resulting five balances

LISTING 10.2 AccountBalanceTraversal.cs

```
01: using System;
02:
03: class AccountBalanceTraversal
04: {
05:     public static void Main()
06:     {
07:         const decimal interestRate = 0.1m;
08:
09:         decimal [] accountBalances;
10:
11:         accountBalances = new decimal [5];
12:
13:         Console.WriteLine("Please enter {0} account balances:",
            ➥ accountBalances.Length);
14:         for (int i = 0; i < accountBalances.Length; i++)
15:         {
16:             Console.Write("Enter balance with index {0}: ", i);
17:             accountBalances[i] = Convert.ToDecimal(Console.ReadLine());
18:         }
19:
20:         Console.WriteLine("\nAccount balances after adding interest\n");
21:         for (int i = 0; i < accountBalances.Length; i++)
22:         {
23:             accountBalances[i] = accountBalances[i]
24:                 + (accountBalances[i] * interestRate);
25:             Console.WriteLine("Account balance with index {0}: {1:C}",
26:                 i, accountBalances[i]);
27:         }
28:     }
29: }
```

```
Please enter five account balances:
Enter balance with index 0: 10000<enter>
Enter balance with index 1: 20000<enter>
Enter balance with index 2: 15000<enter>
Enter balance with index 3: 50000<enter>
Enter balance with index 4: 100000<enter>

Account balances after adding interest

Account balance with index 0: $11,000.00
Account balance with index 1: $22,000.00
Account balance with index 2: $16,500.00
Account balance with index 3: $55,000.00
Account balance with index 4: $110,000.00
```

Once again, `accountBalances` refers to an array object holding 5 `decimal` values (lines 9 and 11).

The `for` loop spanning lines 14–18 is repeated five times. The variable `i` starts at 0 and is incremented by 1 for every repeated execution of the loop body. Execution stops when the loop condition `i < accountBalances.Length` becomes `false`. `accountBalances.Length` is equivalent to the `Length` property found in the `string` class, and is just one of many useful properties and methods built into an object of type `System.Array`. It returns the array length, in this case 5, and causes `i < accountBalances.Length` to be `false` when `i` is equal to 5. Consequently `i` is equal to 4 when the loop body is executed for the last time. This fits nicely with the functionality we want to implement with the loop body in lines 16 and 17, to repeatedly get a new amount from the user and insert it into an array element with an index starting at 0 and incremented by 1 for every new amount. All 5 array elements: `accountBalances[0]`, `accountBalances[1]`, `accountBalances[2]`, `accountBalances[3]`, and `accountBalances[4]` are each assigned a new amount from the user.

The `for` loop of lines 21–27 contains exactly the same loop initialization, loop condition, and loop update as the previous `for` loop, resulting in the same loop behavior. Through the statement in lines 23 and 24, each account balance gets interest added to its amount. The balance, along with its corresponding index value, is then provided as output through lines 25 and 26.

Notice that the scope of the variable `i` declared in line 14 is confined to lines 14–18 and is entirely different from the `i` declared in line 21 with a scope confined to lines 21–27.

Let's pause for a moment and appreciate the advantages of using an array in this program. Even with an attempt to represent and process a much larger array in the source code, the length of the source code would remain unchanged due to our ability to access the array with loops. In fact, we would only need to adjust the number of array elements allocated for the array object to hold in line 11. Consequently, if we need to read in and process 3000 account balances, we just need to change line 11 to the following:

```
11:        accountBalances = new decimal [3000];
```

Tip

Use the `Length` property instead of literals or constants to specify the length of an array in the source code. This will allow you to let the program adjust itself whenever you change the size of any array utilized, only requiring a single adjustment in the code. For example

```
decimal [] accountBalances = new decimal [5];
...
Console.WriteLine("Please enter {0} account balances:", accountBalances.Length);
...
...
Console.WriteLine("Please enter {0} account balances:", 5);
...
```

1
Whenever the size of this array is changed...
2
...the number returned from this property will automatically return the new size, whereas...
3
...the literal 5 would be incorrect and have to be changed manually in the code.

Using Singular or Plural Names for Array Identifiers

Consider the word `accountBalances` of Listing 10.2. It is clearly in its plural form, as opposed to the singular form `accountBalance`. The programming community finds it difficult to agree which form is more correct. The proponents of the singular form claim that

```
accountBalance[2]
```

is preferred, because we refer to just one element, whereas the proponents of the plural form believe that

```
accountBalances.Length
```

is more suitable because `accountBalances` represent several account balances.

So even though this book uses the plural form, it is due to my personal preference rather than a general recommendation.

Array Indexes Out of Range

The minimum valid index value when referencing an array element is 0, as in `accountBalances[0]` of Listing 10.2. The maximum value is the array length minus 1, as in `accountBalances[4]`. A common mistake is to write an expression representing an index value, which is evaluated to be either smaller than zero or larger than the maximum valid index, causing the index to be *out of range*.

When an index, provided to access an array element, is either smaller than the valid minimum index value, or larger than the maximum valid index, this index is said to be *out of range*.

An out of range index will trigger the .NET runtime to throw an *exception* (see the following Note) during program execution, not surprisingly called an `IndexOutOfRangeException`.

Exceptions in C#

When the runtime executes a program, it might, in exceptional cases, encounter unusual or erroneous situations in which case it will generate an exception. When this happens, the runtime is said to *throw an exception*. An exception will, if not dealt with suitably, cause the program to terminate abruptly. Chapter 19, "Exception Handling," discusses exception handling at length.

Some of the most common causes for out of range exceptions are found when combining loop constructs with arrays. I have provided two typical scenarios.

1) An incorrect loop condition that causes the loop body to be executed one time too many.

Consider the following `for` loop:

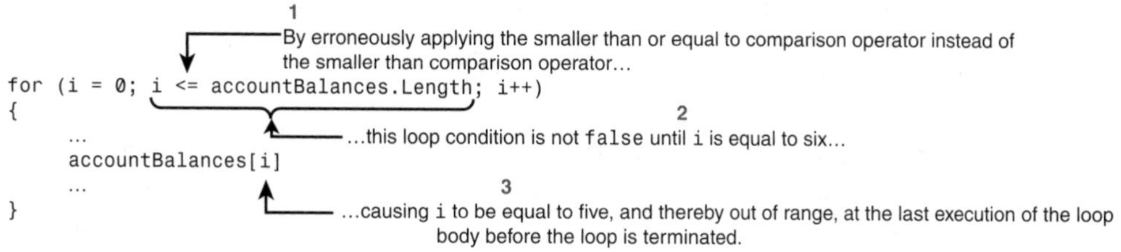

```
for (i = 0; i <= accountBalances.Length; i++)
{
    ...
    accountBalances[i]
    ...
}
```

1 By erroneously applying the smaller than or equal to comparison operator instead of the smaller than comparison operator...

2 ...this loop condition is not `false` until `i` is equal to six...

3 ...causing `i` to be equal to five, and thereby out of range, at the last execution of the loop body before the loop is terminated.

The less-than-or-equal-to comparison operator used in the `for` loop condition causes this Boolean expression to be `true`, even when `i` is equal to 5. `i` is 5 when the loop body is executed for the last time, prompting an `IndexOutOfRangeException`. To fix the problem, we simply need to exchange the less-than-or-equal-to operator <= with the less-than operator <.

2) *Relying solely on the user to end the entry of values into an array before its end is reached will sooner or later invite the user to cause an out of range error.*

Loops are frequently utilized to let a user input a list of values into an array. Lines 13–18 of Listing 10.2 represent an example of this functionality. The user is in this case forced to assign a value to every single array element (5 elements in our example). Sometimes, however, the user might want to enter less than this total number of values and, thus, terminate the input phase before the end of the array has been reached. How can this be implemented?

One possible strategy is to use a sentinel value (also called a *dummy value* or a *signal value*).

A *sentinel value* is a special value signaling to the program that the user has ended the entry of values. By typing in the sentinel value after all the proper values have been entered, the user is able to control the number of values he or she wants to enter into an array.

For this technique to work, the sentinel value must be distinctly different from the range of values normally entered into the array. For example, if the values are all expected to be positive, the sentinel value could be a negative number.

Let's see how lines 13–18 of Listing 10.2 can be changed by applying a sentinel value to let the user determine the number of values entered. Listing 10.3 provides the pseudocode outlining a first *flawed* attempt to implement this logic. Any account balance is presumed to be positive, permitting us to apply a negative value as a sentinel value. This is reflected in line 2 that terminates the loop if the entered value is negative. The flawed logic resides in the fact that the user is solely responsible for terminating the input loop, permitting him or her to attempt to insert more values than there are array elements and causing an out of range exception.

LISTING 10.3 Pseudocode Demonstrating Incorrect Use of Sentinel Value

```
01:  Enter the value for the first array element
02:  While the user did not enter a negative value
03:  {
```

LISTING 10.3 continued

```
        Assign this value into the corresponding array element.
        Add one to the index counter
        Enter the next value
}
```

The program of Listing 10.4 is similar in functionality to that of Listing 10.2, but utilizes the logic presented in the pseudocode of Listing 10.3 to let the user enter values into the array elements of `accountBalances` (see lines 12–23). The user can end the data entry at any point before all five values have been entered, simply by entering a negative value. This works fine (see Sample output 1) as long as the user remembers to enter the sentinel value (in this case minus one) before the end of the array has been reached. However, in Sample output 2, the user forgets to end the data entry after inputting the fifth value and attempts to enter a sixth value (500 in this case). The .NET runtime responds by generating an `IndexOutOfRangeException` as reported on the console.

LISTING 10.4 `BalancesIncorrectSentinel.cs`

```
01: using System;
02:
03: class BalancesIncorrectSentinel
04: {
05:     public static void Main()
06:     {
07:         const decimal interestRate = 0.1m;
08:         decimal [] accountBalances;
09:         decimal newValue;
10:         accountBalances = new decimal [5];
11:
12:         Console.WriteLine("Please enter max five account balances, " +
13:             "terminate with negative value:");
14:         Console.Write("Enter balance 1: ");
15:         newValue = Convert.ToDecimal(Console.ReadLine());
16:         int j = 0;
17:         while (newValue >= 0)
18:         {
19:             accountBalances[j] = newValue;
20:             j++;
21:             Console.Write("Enter balance {0}: ", (j + 1));
22:             newValue = Convert.ToDecimal(Console.ReadLine());
23:         }
24:
25:         Console.WriteLine("\nAccount balances after adding interest\n");
26:         for (int i = 0; i < accountBalances.Length; i++)
27:         {
28:             accountBalances[i] = accountBalances[i] + (accountBalances[i]
                ➥ * interestRate);
29:             Console.WriteLine("Account balance with index {0}: {1:C}", i,
                ➥ accountBalances[i]);
30:         }
31:     }
32: }
```

Sample output 1:

```
Please enter max five account balances, terminate with negative value:
Enter balance 1: 1000<enter>
Enter balance 2: 3000<enter>
Enter balance 3: 2000<enter>
Enter balance 4: -1<enter>

Account balances after adding interest

Account balance with index 0: $1,100.00
Account balance with index 1: $3,300.00
Account balance with index 2: $2,200.00
Account balance with index 3: $0.00
Account balance with index 4: $0.00
```

Sample output 2:

```
Please enter max five account balances, terminate with negative value:
Enter balance 1: 3000<enter>
Enter balance 2: 200<enter>
Enter balance 3: 5000<enter>
Enter balance 4: 300<enter>
Enter balance 5: 1000<enter>
Enter balance 6: 500<enter>

Exception occurred: System.IndexOutOfRangeException: An exception of type

System.IndexOutOfRangeException was thrown at BalancesIncorrectSentinel.Main()
```

Note

To help you determine where in the program an exception is thrown, the name of the method (in this case, `BalancesIncorrectSentinel.Main()`) is printed on the console as part of the error message.

Lines 17–23 utilize a `while` loop to enter values into `accountBalances`. Whenever `newValue >= 0` is `false`, meaning when the user enters a negative value, the loop is terminated. Even though the counter `j` is incremented for every repetition of the loop, it is not involved in the loop condition. The sentinel value is the sole value responsible for the termination of the loop. The number of repetitions of the loop body is unknown prior to the execution of this `while` loop, which, for that reason, is called an indefinite loop.

If a sentinel value is the sole factor controlling the termination of a loop, as in lines 16–23 of Listing 10.4, the number of repetitions is not known prior to its execution. The loop is thus often referred to as an *indefinite loop*.

Fortunately, there is a simple remedy to rectify the problem of lines 16–23. By using the counter `j` in the loop condition, we can let the repetitions stop if either the user enters a negative value, *or* `j` is greater than or equal to the length of `accountBalances`. This has been done in Listing 10.5 by using a `break` statement (line 22), which is executed to terminate the loop if `j >= accountBalances.Length` is `true` in line 21.

LISTING 10.5 Improving Lines 16–23 of Listing 10.4

```
16: int j = 0;
17: while (newValue >= 0)
18: {
19:     accountBalances[j] = newValue;
20:     j++;
21:     if (j >= accountBalances.Length)
22:         break;
23:     Console.Write("Enter balance {0}: ", (j + 1));
24:     newValue = Convert.ToDecimal(Console.ReadLine());
25: }
```

The Fixed Length of Arrays

After an array object has been created, its length cannot be changed. So the following line

```
decimal [] accountBalances = new decimal[5];
```

creates an array object that will have a fixed length of 5 throughout its lifetime.

Therefore, the array is not suited to represent collections for which the number of elements varies during runtime.

For example, a program written for a real world bank that manages a fluctuating number of account balances (as opposed to our simulated bank used in the examples here with a fixed number of account balances) would not be served well by attempting to represent the account balances with an array. The .NET Framework contains data structures in its `System.Collections` namespace that are tailor-made to hold collections of similar elements, such as the array, and with an ability to dynamically grow or shrink during runtime.

Adjusting for the Zero-Based Array Index

The index of any array commences at 0; this cannot be altered. Occasionally, however, you might want a program to give the user the impression that a different and more suitable numbering scheme is being applied to a collection of data items. For example, it might often be more convenient to think of the first item in a collection as having index 1, rather than index 0. By making appropriate adjustments in the source code, you can accomplish this objective.

As an example, let's adjust Listing 10.2 to give the user the impression that the first account balance is number 1 (instead of 0) and the last number is 5 (instead of 4). First, we need to locate all lines of code that prints the index (the variable `i` in this case) onscreen—lines 16 and 23 in this case. Then we need to add 1 to the value of `i`, turning 0 into 1 and 4 into 5:

```
16:             Console.Write("Enter balance with index {0}: ", (i + 1));

25:             Console.WriteLine("Account balance with index {0}: {1:C}",
26:                 (i + 1), accountBalances[i]);
```

The first couple of lines of output from the altered program will now look like

```
Please enter five account balances:
Enter balance with index 1:
```

In case we entered the same values as in the sample output of Listing 10.2, the first couple of sample output lines providing the account balances after adding interest would look like the following:

```
Account balance with index 1: $11,000.00
Account balance with index 2: $22,000.00
...
```

providing the index number 1 instead of 0, 2 instead of 1 and so on.

Instead of receiving an index as output, the reader must sometimes provide a number as input representing an index to, for example, access the information contained in a corresponding array element. This number will also have to be adjusted before it can be used to access the corresponding array element inside the program. In our case, the program would have to subtract 1 from the number entered by the user, as shown in the following lines of code, that can be inserted after line 27 of Listing 10.2. The code allows the user to access one of the balances indexed 0 to 4 by entering a number between 1 and 5.

```
int myIndex;
Console.Write("Enter number of account to get balance: ");
myIndex = Convert.ToInt32(Console.ReadLine()) - 1;
Console.WriteLine("Balance of account balance number: {0} is: {1}",
      myIndex + 1, accountBalances[myIndex]);
```

Initializing Arrays

The array elements of an array can be initialized, with values of your choice, at the time the array is being created. To accomplish this, you first need to write the declaration of the array variable as usual. However, instead of creating the array object using the `new` keyword, as in the following

```
new int [6];
```

you can specify the list of initialization values explicitly by enclosing them in braces, and assigning this list to the array variable with the assignment operator. The following line follows this procedure:

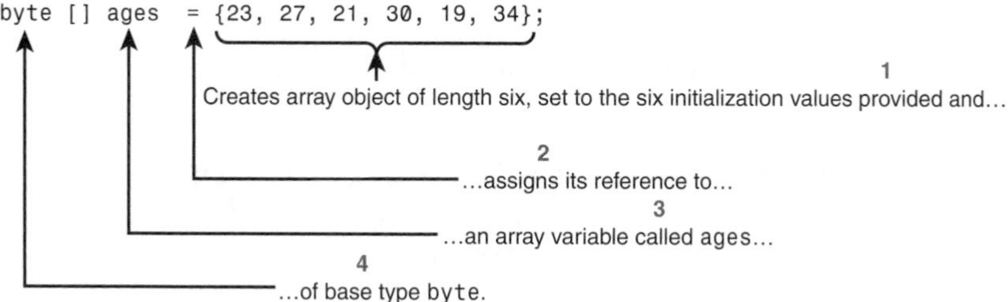
byte [] ages = {23, 27, 21, 30, 19, 34};
1
Creates array object of length six, set to the six initialization values provided and...
2
...assigns its reference to...
3
...an array variable called ages...
4
...of base type byte.

The array object is automatically created with just enough array elements (six, in this example) to hold the values specified within the braces. Because the number of values provided inside the braces determines the length of the array, there is no need to specify the length explicitly. Only values implicitly convertible to the base type specified in the declaration (**byte** in this case) can be included within the braces.

Note

It is possible to specify the length of the array in addition to providing the initialization values enclosed in braces, as in the following line that is equivalent to the previous line.

```
byte [] ages  =  new byte [6] {23, 27, 21, 30, 19, 34};
```

`new int [6]` is redundant, but it might, in some cases, be wise to explicitly specify the length in this way; it has two advantages:

- It clearly states the length of the array to the reader of the code. This can be handy if the list provided is long.
- The compiler compares the length of the array, as stated in the square brackets, with the number of initialization values provided within the braces. Any discrepancies will be reported as an error. Thus, the compiler will detect and report any mistakenly omitted or added values.

When you utilize the braces to initialize an array, you must provide an initialization value for all the array elements. If you don't want to assign a value to every single element, you can use one of two procedures:

- Supply the initialization values in the braces as before, but let all elements you don't want to assign be set to the default initialization value (in this case, 0), or provide your own "missing value" value. For example, if you did not know the last three initialization values provided earlier (30, 19, and 34), you could write the following:

  ```
  byte [] ages  = {23, 27, 21, 0, 0, 0};
  ```

- Use the standard assignment operator as in the following:

  ```
  byte [] ages = new byte [6];
  ages[0] = 23;
  ages[1] = 27;
  ages[2] = 21;
  ages[3] = 0;
  ages[4] = 0;
  ages[5] = 0;
  ```

  which again only sets the first, second, and third elements.

Syntax Box 10.3 Declaration and Manual Initialization of an Array

```
Array_declaration_with_manual_initialization::=
<Base_type> [] <Array_identifier> = [new <Base_type> [<Array_length>]...]
➥ {<Value1>, <Value2>,...<ValueN>};
```

Notes:

- `<Value1>`, `<Value2>`, and so on must all be implicitly convertible to type `<Base_type>`.
- The number of values assigned to the array (here, symbolized by *N*) is equal to the length of this array.

Traversing an Entire Array with the `foreach` Statement

Instead of using the `for` loop to traverse an entire array, you can apply C#'s `foreach` statement as a convenient alternative. For example, to print every array element value of the array `childbirths` declared and defined as

```
uint [] childbirths =  {1340, 3240, 1003, 4987, 3877};
```

you can write the following `foreach` statement:

```
foreach (uint temp in childbirths)
{
      Console.WriteLine(temp);
}
```

to provide the following output:

```
1340
3240
1003
4987
3877
```

This deserves a closer look. The `foreach` statement consists of a header and a loop body (see Figure 10.4). The loop body can either be a single statement or a compound statement. The first two words inside the parentheses of the header must consist of a type and an identifier. Together they declare the *iteration variable* of the `foreach` statement. In this case, the iteration variable is called `temp` (for temporary). To the right of the iteration variable, you must write the keyword `in`, which is followed by the array variable name representing the array to be traversed (here, called `childbirths`). Observe that the type specified for the iteration variable must be implicitly convertible to the base type of the specified array. The loop body is executed once for every array element in the specified array. The iteration variable can be used in the loop body. During the first execution of the loop body, its value will be equal to the value of the first array element. For every new execution of the loop body, it will hold the value of the next array element. When the `foreach` statement is terminated, the iteration variable will have traversed the entire collection of array element values.

Syntax Box 10.4 The `foreach` Statement

```
foreach_statement::=
foreach ( <Type> <Iteration_variable_identifier> in <Array_identifier>)
    [ <Statement> | <Compound_statement> ]
```

When executing the `foreach` statement, C# automatically determines the number of iterations. It also assigns the value of each array element to the iteration variable without the need for the programmer to provide explicit indexes. The loop counters, loop conditions, and loop updates needed when applying the conventional `for` loop are superfluous, providing for an easier, cleaner, and less bug-prone implementation.

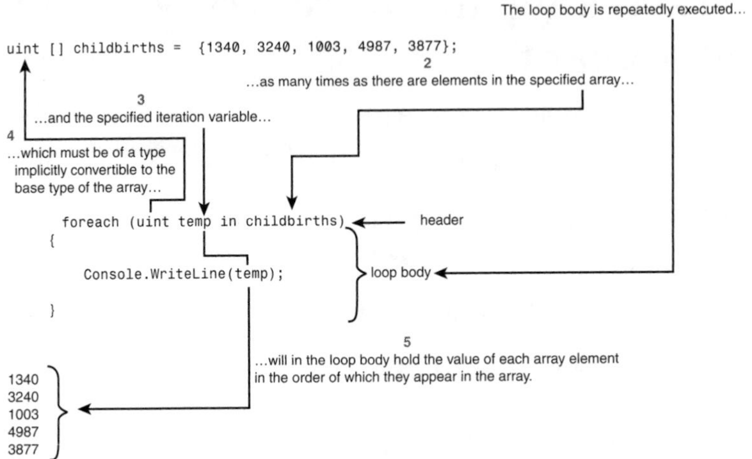

FIGURE 10.4
The *foreach* statement.

Note

The `foreach` statement can also be used with the collection classes found in the `System.Collection` namespace of the .NET Framework.

Note

Because the `foreach` statement hides loop counters, loop updates, and access to array elements under the hood, it is difficult, to follow the detailed mechanics of this type of loop by viewing the code. The `for` loop in contrast spells out all the gory details. The `for` loop also provides more flexibility in terms of limiting the access to various parts of the array (for example, when only access to every second or every third array element is needed). For those reasons, the `for` loop has been used throughout this chapter, even in situations where the `foreach` statement could have provided a cleaner implementation.

`System.Array` Is a Reference Type

The `System.Array` class is a reference type like `System.String`. Consequently an array variable containing a reference is separate from the array object it is referencing. A reference type variable can be assigned different references, just as a variable of a numeric type can be assigned different numbers. So an array variable can reference different array objects at different segments in a program by assigning different references to it. Recall the state of affairs after the following statement

```
decimal [] accountBalances = new  decimal[5];
```

as illustrated earlier in Figure 10.2. The `accountBalances` variable is referencing an array object of base type `decimal` and length 5. Suppose that later in the program you want `accountBalances` to reference another object of length 3000. This can be achieved by assigning a different reference to `accountBalances`:

```
accountBalances = new decimal[3000];
```

As illustrated in Figure 10.5, the object containing 5 elements and the object of length 3000 are completely separate entities. After the latter new object has been assigned, the former old object becomes garbage (assuming `accountBalances` was the only reference to this old object, see the following Note) and is eventually disposed of, along with its five `decimal` values. `accountBalances` can now only be used to access array elements of the new object of length 3000.

Note

Recall from our previous discussion about reference types in Chapter 6, "Types, Part I: The Simple Types" that an object can be referenced by any number of variables. An object only becomes garbage and disposed of when no variables are referencing it anymore, because it can then no longer be referenced; it is out of reach. More about garbage collection in Chapter 13, "Class Anatomy Part II: Object Creation and Garbage Collection."

FIGURE 10.5
Reassigning a new array object to an array variable.

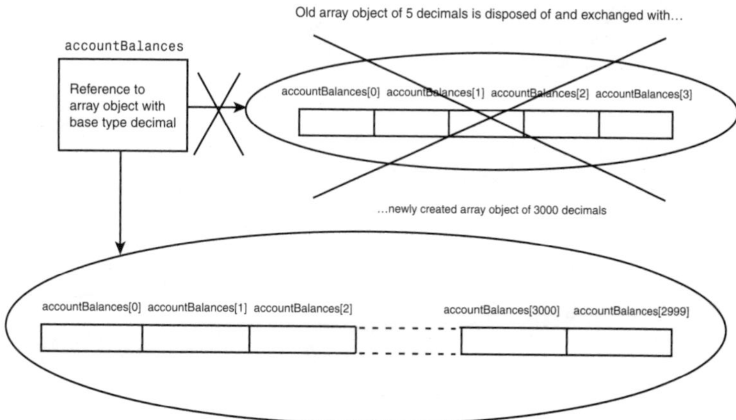

Matching the Base Type Specified in the Array Variable Declaration

Even though different array objects can be assigned to one array variable, the base type of any array object assigned to it must always match the type specified in the original array variable declaration. Consequently, any array object assigned to `accountBalances` must be of base type `decimal`.

Note

The `new` keyword causes the runtime to allocate memory to hold a given number of elements of a given type. However, if the memory needed is greater than the memory available (this depends on the computer's hardware, other programs running, and other more technical matters), the runtime will throw an exception called `OutOfMemoryException`.

Due to the properties of reference types, it is possible to assign a reference held by one array variable to another array variable. This will let both array variables hold the same reference and cause them to reference exactly the same array object. Let's look at an example—the array used here could be used in a program to store the ages of a list of people. The first line

```
byte [] ages  = new byte [6];
```

creates the array variable `ages` and lets it reference a `new` array object of length six created after the assignment operator. It is now possible to write

```
byte [] sameAges = ages;
```

that will assign the reference of `ages` to `sameAges`, causing both array variables to reference exactly the same array object. This is illustrated in Figure 10.6.

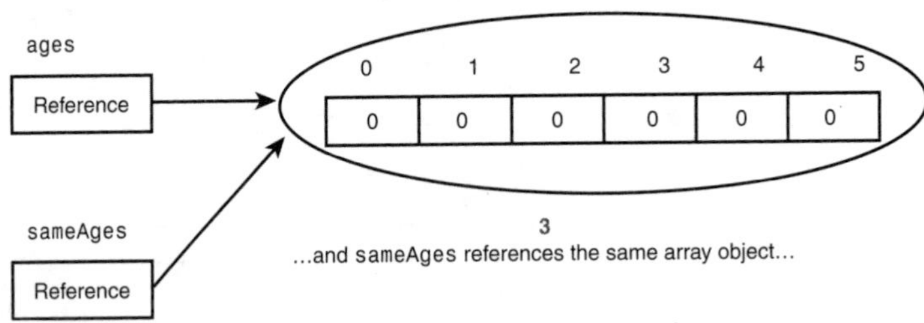

FIGURE 10.6
Two array variables pointing at the same array object.

`ages[0]` is now exactly the same element as `sameAges[0]`. Consequently, the two lines

```
ages[0] = 99;
Console.WriteLine("Age of first person: " + sameAges[0]);
```

will print the following

Age of first person: 99

Generally Speaking: Have Only One Array Variable Reference Per Array Object

To have several array variables reference the same array object simultaneously can result in overly-complicated code and difficult-to-trace bugs, because seemingly separate variables can alter each other's values in different parts of a program. As a rule of thumb, use only one array variable reference per array object.

Arrays and Equality

Occasionally, we want to determine whether two array variables are equal to each other. We might attempt to answer this question by using the equality operator (==) as in the following:

```
int [] myArray = new int [6];
int [] yourArray = new int [6];

if (myArray == yourArray)
    Console.WriteLine("myArray is equal to yourArray");
```

But how does the equality operator == of C# compare two array variables (as in line 3 of the code sample) containing references to array objects? There are two possible options—reference equality, where the references of the two array variables are compared, and value equality, where the array elements of the referenced array objects are compared. Let's have a closer look at each option before revealing which one the == operator of C# applies:

- *Reference equality*—If values of a reference type, such as `System.Array`, are compared for reference equality, the references held by the two variables are compared. If they are identical, meaning if they reference the same object (see the upper part of Figure 10.7), the comparison is `true`. If they reference different objects, even if those objects are of similar length and contain matching pairs of array elements holding identical values, the comparison is `false` (see the lower part of Figure 10.7).
- *Value equality*—If two array variables are compared for value equality, the array elements of the referenced array objects are compared with each other. Thus, the length of each array must be identical, and each matching pair of array elements must have identical values for this comparison to be `true`. The upper part of Figure 10.8 represents two arrays that are (value) equal because the two referenced array objects are of identical length and contain identical sets of array elements. In the lower part of Figure 10.8, `myArray` has had a few of its array elements changed and does not match the corresponding array elements in `yourArray` anymore. As a result, the two arrays here are not (value) equal.

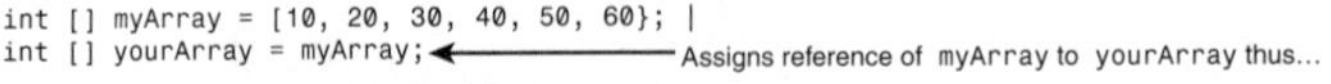

int [] myArray = [10, 20, 30, 40, 50, 60}; |
int [] yourArray = myArray;
Assigns reference of myArray to yourArray thus...

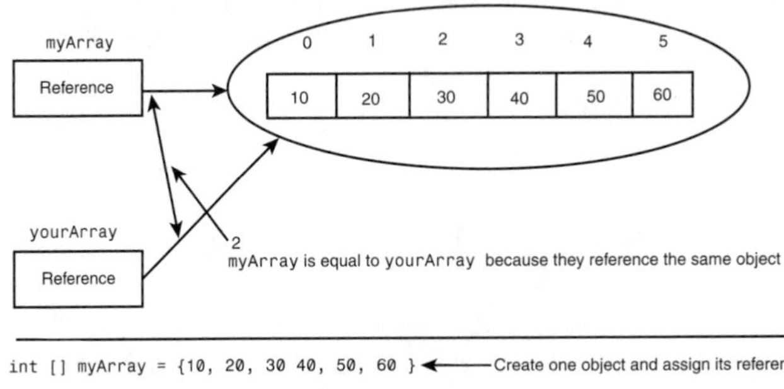

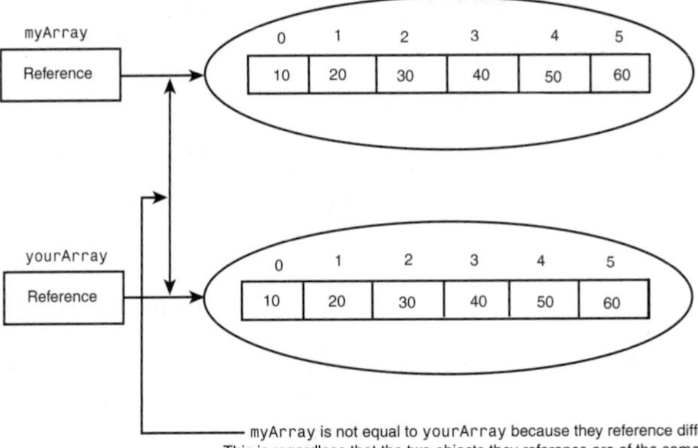

FIGURE 10.7
Reference equality.

The equals comparison operator (==) of C# supports reference equality between array variables. The implications are illustrated with the following source code:

```
int [] myArray = {10, 20, 30, 40, 50, 60};
int [] yourArray = myArray;
if (myArray == yourArray)
...                                 true
```

```
int [] myArray = {10, 20, 30, 40, 50, 60};
int [] yourArray = {10, 20, 30, 40, 50, 60};
Create another object. Assign its reference to yourArray
if (myArray == yourArray)
...                                 false
```

Instead of performing reference equality comparisons by using the == operator, you might want to compare two arrays for value equality instead. One way to accomplish this task is by writing a method specialized in comparing two arbitrary arrays for value equality. The next section looks at how arrays and methods can cooperate and provides an understanding of how an array-comparing method can be written, along with a specific source code example.

FIGURE 10.8
Value equality.

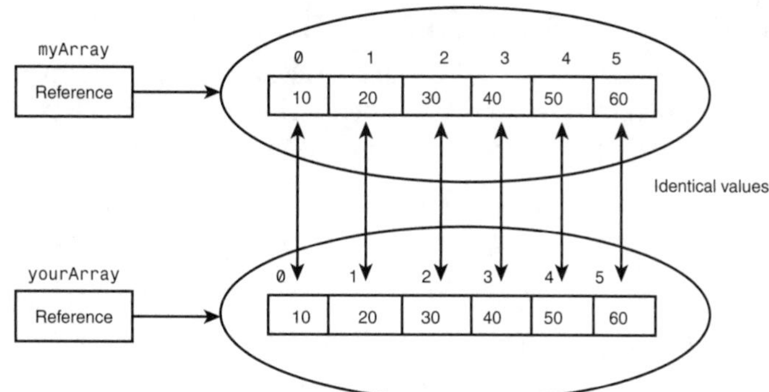

myArray is value equal to yourArray because they reference array objects of the same length and because each array element with the same index contains the same value.

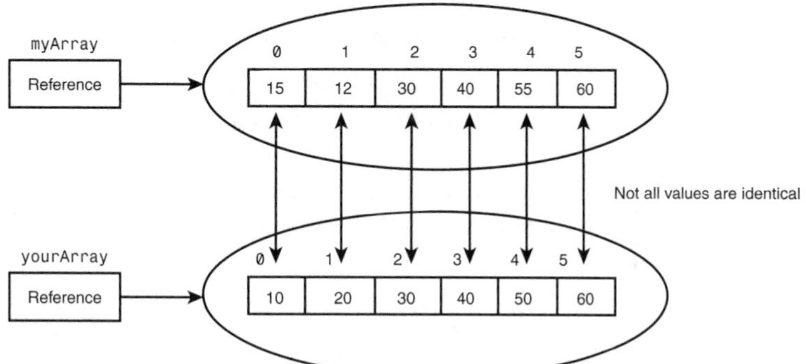

myArray is not (value) equal to yourArray because the array elements values of the array object referenced by myArray do not match their counterparts in the array object referenced by yourArray.

Note

Whereas the equals operator (==) compares for reference equality when applied to array variables, recall that it supports value equality when values of type `string` are compared (see Chapter 7, "Types Part II: Operators, Enumerators and Strings."

Arrays and Methods

Array elements, such as `accountBalances[0]`, as well as array object references, such as `accountBalances`, can be arguments in a method call, as well as return values from a method. The next few sections show you how and discuss the implications and possibilities.

Array Elements As Method Arguments

Recall that an array element, like `accountBalances[0]` of base type `decimal`, can be applied in any position of the source code where a simple variable of type `decimal` can be used. This also allows for array elements to be used as method arguments in method calls.

For example, the following line is a method header of the `MaxAmount` method specifying that method calls must provide two arguments both of type `decimal`.

```
private static decimal MaxAmount(decimal a, decimal b)
```

Because the two following arrays are both of base type `decimal`

```
decimal [] person1Sales = {40000, 10000, 25000, 50000, 33000, 60000};
decimal [] person2Sales = {80000, 3000, 110000, 40000, 33000, 59000};
```

their array elements can be used as arguments in a method call to `MaxAmount` as follows

```
...MaxArray(person1Sales[0], person2Sales[0]...
```

Listing 10.6 completes this example and represents a fully working program. The sales figures of two sales people are kept in the two arrays `person1Sales` and `person2Sales` (see lines 7 and 8) for the first six months of the current year. The company wants to see the maximum individual sales for each month. This is achieved by comparing corresponding pairs of array elements from the two arrays in the `MaxAmount` method (lines 18–24) that return the greater of the two values passed to it as arguments.

LISTING 10.6 `MaxSales.cs`

```
01: using System;
02:
03: class MaxSales
04: {
05:     public static void Main()
06:     {
07:         decimal [] person1Sales = {40000, 10000, 25000, 50000,
            ➥ 33000, 60000};
08:         decimal [] person2Sales = {80000, 3000, 110000, 40000,
            ➥ 33000, 59000};
09:
10:         Console.WriteLine("Max individual sales for each of the
            ➥ first six months: ");
11:         for (int i = 0; i < 6; i++)
12:         {
13:             Console.WriteLine("Month {0}: {1,11:C}",
14:                 i+1, MaxAmount(person1Sales[i], person2Sales[i]));
15:         }
16:     }
17:
18:     private static decimal MaxAmount(decimal a, decimal b)
19:     {
20:         if (a > b)
21:             return a;
```

LISTING 10.6 continued

```
22:         else
23:             return b;
24:     }
25: }
```

```
Max individual sales for each of the first six months:
Month 1:  $80,000.00
Month 2:  $10,000.00
Month 3: $110,000.00
Month 4:  $50,000.00
Month 5:  $33,000.00
Month 6:  $60,000.00
```

The `MaxAmount` method (lines 18–24) has two formal parameters (`a` and `b`), both of type `decimal`. It returns the maximum value of `a` and `b` back to the caller.

The method call `MaxAmount(person1Sales[i], person2Sales[i])` of line 14 resides inside a `for` loop that repeats itself six times, once for every month. During the first repetition, `i` is equal to 0. The two expressions `person1Sales[i]` and `person2Sales[i]` become `person1Sales[0]` and `person2Sales[0]`, which again are evaluated to 40000 and 80000. The method call can now be perceived as `MaxAmount(40000, 80000);`, returning the value 80000 (see the sample output) because 80000 is greater than 40000. Observe that the indexed expressions `person1Sales[i]` and `person2Sales[i]` of line 14 are evaluated to determine which array element value to send off to the method. At the next repetition of the loop body, `i` holds the value 1 and the method call becomes `MaxAmount(10000, 3000)` returning the value 10000. This cycle of events are repeated six times.

Note

There is no indication in the method header of `MaxAmount` (see line 18 of Listing 10.6) that this method accepts array elements as arguments. In fact, it is irrelevant from any method's point of view whether the arguments passed to it originates from a literal, constant, variable, or an array element, as long as the value passed along is of the specified type, in this case `decimal`.

Array References As Method Arguments

As shown in Chapter 4, "A Guided Tour through C#: Part II" it is possible to pass values of simple types as arguments to a method. It turns out that a reference to an array object can also constitute an argument.

To specify that a method accepts arguments of type array-object-reference, we need to include a suitable formal parameter in the method header. An example is given in the following line:

```
public static int Sum (uint [] numbers)
```

The declaration of the formal parameter is identical to the conventional declaration of an array variable; this time, the declaration is merely inserted between the parentheses containing the formal parameters of the method header. In this case, the method header declares `numbers` to be a formal parameter of type reference-to-array-object-of-base-type-`uint`.

Figure 10.9 shows the rest of the `Sum` method (lines 25–33) along with the events that take place when a method call passes a reference to this method with an argument.

Line 1 declares `populationSizes` to be an array variable holding a reference to an array object of base type `uint`, and assigns it an array object of length 3. Lines 2–4 initializes the three array elements of `populationSizes`. When the method call `Sum(populationSizes)` (line 10) is executed, the reference held by `populationSizes` is passed on to `numbers` of the `Sum` method, which is then referencing an identical array object during its execution. As a result, it is able to calculate the sum of, in this case, the array elements of `populationSizes` through its access to the entire set of individual array elements (lines 27—31). The resulting sum is passed back by the `return totalSum;` statement (line 32).

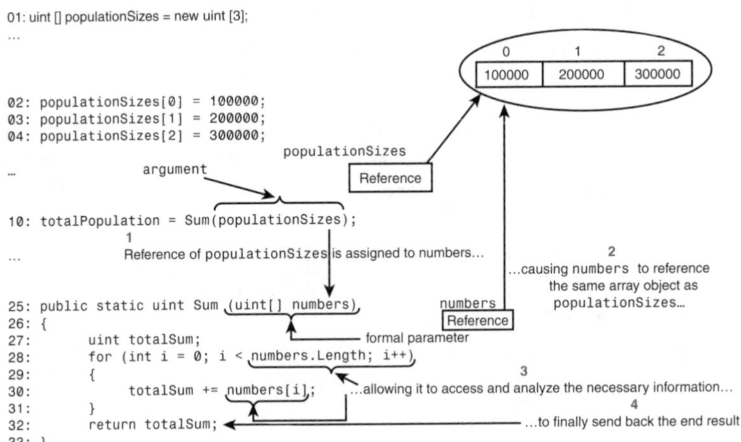

FIGURE 10.9
Providing an array reference as argument with method call.

Note

An argument of an array variable provided for a method call does not include any square brackets, making the following line incorrect:

```
Sum(populationSizes[])     //Incorrect. [] should not be included
```

Listing 10.7 provides the complete source code of a program that utilizes C#'s ability to provide array object references as method call arguments. The method `AverageAge` (lines 27–35) calculates the average of any array object (of any length) of base type `byte` passed to it as a reference. The user is asked to enter two sets of ages—one for a scout camp containing six scouts and one for the crewmembers of a space shuttle containing six astronauts. The averages of the two sets are calculated and printed onscreen in each instance.

LISTING 10.7 `AverageAgeCalculator`

```
01: using System;
02:
```

LISTING 10.7 continued

```
class AverageAgeCalculator
{
    public static void Main()
    {
        byte[] agesScoutCamp = new byte[4];
        byte[] agesSpaceShuttle = new byte [6];

        Console.WriteLine("Enter ages for {0} scouts: ",
        ➥ agesScoutCamp.Length);
        for (int i = 0; i < agesScoutCamp.Length; i++)
        {
            Console.Write("Enter age for scout number {0}: ", i + 1);
            agesScoutCamp[i] = Convert.ToByte(Console.ReadLine());
        }
        Console.WriteLine("Average age of scouts: " +
        ➥ AverageAge(agesScoutCamp));

        Console.WriteLine("\nEnter ages for {0} astronauts",
        ➥ agesSpaceShuttle.Length);
        for (int i = 0; i < agesSpaceShuttle.Length; i++)
        {
            Console.Write("Enter age for astronaut number {0}: ", i + 1);
            agesSpaceShuttle[i] = Convert.ToByte(Console.ReadLine());
        }
        Console.WriteLine("Average age of astronauts: " +
        ➥ AverageAge(agesSpaceShuttle));
    }

    public static byte AverageAge(byte[] ages)
    {
        int ageSum = 0;
         // The sum of all ages is assigned to ageSum
        for (int i = 0; i < ages.Length; i++)
            ageSum += ages[i];
         // Calculate the average age and return it back to the caller
        return (byte)(ageSum / ages.Length);
    }
}
```

```
Enter ages for 4 scouts:
Enter age for scout number 1: 10<enter>
Enter age for scout number 2: 9<enter>
Enter age for scout number 3: 8<enter>
Enter age for scout number 4: 9<enter>
Average age of scouts: 9

Enter ages for 6 astronauts
Enter age for astronaut number 1: 34<enter>
Enter age for astronaut number 2: 38<enter>
Enter age for astronaut number 3: 30<enter>
Enter age for astronaut number 4: 35<enter>
Enter age for astronaut number 5: 33<enter>
Enter age for astronaut number 6: 34<enter>
Average age of astronauts: 34
```

Lines 7 and 8 declare and define the two arrays holding the ages of two groups of people—4 scouts in a scout camp and 6 crew members of a space shuttle.

Lines 10–15 reads in the ages for the children of the scout camp from the user and assigns each age to an array element of the `agesScoutCamp` variable. An identical procedure is utilized in lines 18–23, this time for the space shuttle crew. Line 16 utilizes the functionality of the `AverageAge` method to calculate and print the average age of the scouts contained in the array `agesScoutCamp`. The array object to be analyzed by the method is provided by sending it the `agesScoutCamp` reference as an argument. It is received by the formal parameter `ages` of type `byte[]` in line 27 and used for the necessary average calculations in the `AverageAge` method of lines 27–35. A similar set of events is used in line 24 to calculate and print the average age of the space shuttle crew members.

A reference contained in an array variable takes up just 4 bytes of memory. This is in stark contrast to the size of the object itself. For example, an array object containing 100 `decimal` values occupies (100 × 16) 1600 bytes. Thus, when a reference is passed from one array variable to another, or from method argument to formal parameter, only 4 bytes are transferred in contrast to the 1600 bytes given here as an example. Not only does this save memory, it also speeds up the execution of a program.

Cloning an Array Object

Passing array object references to other parts of the program, whether this be as method arguments or simply to other array variables, can be a very efficient way of passing around data in a program as mentioned in the previous section, but it poses certain risks as explained in the following text.

1) Methods that accidentally change your array.

When a method has been passed a reference to an array object, it cannot only access, but also can *change* the value of each array element. The change might be deliberate or accidental. An example of the latter is provided here. Suppose that Listing 10.7 contained a flaw in line 32, as shown in the two code lines following this paragraph, causing every array element to be incremented by 10, instead of leaving it unchanged as the original correct line 32 did. All array elements contained in any array passed to this method would then have their values incremented by 10, accidentally and possibly without the programmer's awareness.

```
31:   for (int i = 0; i < ages.Length; i++)
32:   ages[i] += 10;   //ages[i] is accidentally incremented by 10
```

Tip

When passing your array references around to other methods, perhaps written by other more or less trusted programmers, you need to take extra care in ensuring that only deliberate changes are being made to your arrays during those calls.

2) More than one array variable referencing the same array object can lead to overly complicated code.

To have several array variables reference the same array object can result in overly complicated code and difficult to trace bugs, because seemingly separate variables can alter each other's values in different parts of a program. This problem has already been hinted at earlier in this chapter.

It is possible to use **System.Array**'s built in method **Clone()** to make a full copy of an array object and thereby avoid the problems previously mentioned. To illustrate the **Clone()** methods effects and how it is applied, we first declare our familiar **accountBalances** array referencing an array object with four array elements by writing the following:

```
decimal [] accountBalances = {3000, 4000, 1000, 2000};
```

We then declare another array variable called **balancesClone** of the same base type:

```
decimal [] balancesClone;
```

The situation after this last statement has been executed, is depicted in Figure 10.10. **accountBalances** references an object of four array elements, and **balanceClone** is referencing null because it has not yet been assigned any array object.

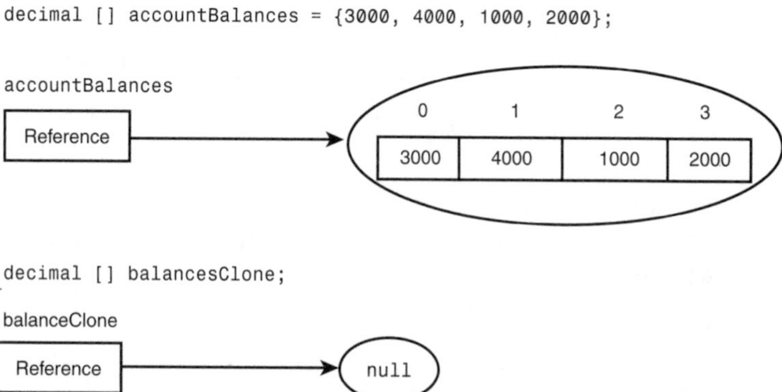

FIGURE 10.10
Declaring two array variables and creating one array object.

The next line (shown after this paragraph) calls the **Clone()** method by applying the dot operator to **accountBalances** followed by **Clone()**. The result is the creation of a new array object identical to, but separate from, the array object referenced by **accountBalances**; its reference is assigned to **balancesClone**.

```
balancesClone = (decimal []) accountBalances.Clone();
```

First, notice that the **Clone()** method is called in the usual manner by writing the name of the array variable (in this case, **accountBalances**) followed by the dot operator and finally the name of the method, which is **Clone()** in this case.

Second, observe that we had to apply the cast operator **(decimal [])** in front of the method call. To fully understand why, you need to know more aspects of OOP. For now, I will merely give you this brief analogous explanation—the method call **accountBalances.Clone()** returns an anonymous container enclosing a value of type **decimal []**. To unwrap this value so it can be assigned to **balancesClone**, we need to apply the **(decimal [])** cast operator.

The process involved in executing the previous statement and its final result is illustrated in Figure 10.11.

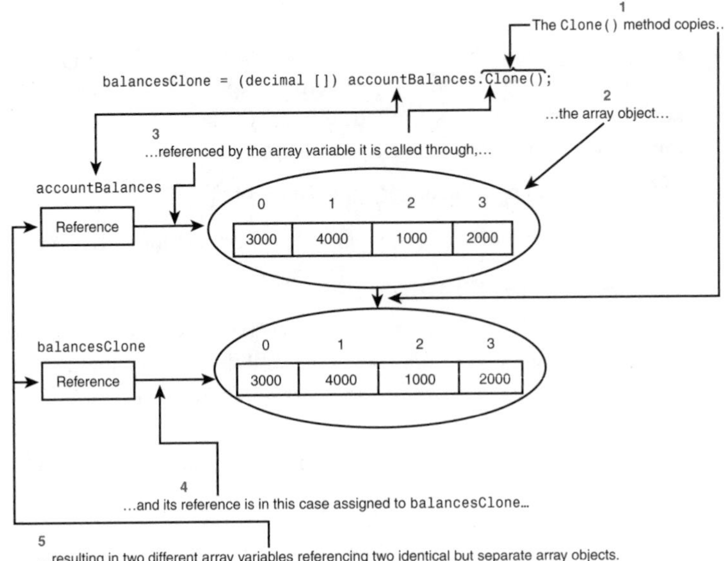

FIGURE 10.11
The effects of calling the `Clone()` method.

Because **`accountBalances`** and **`balancesClone`** are referencing separate array objects, **`accountBalances[0]`** and **`balancesClone[0]`** refer to different array elements. As a result, we can write the following

```
balancesClone[0] = 20000;
```

without affecting the value in **`accountBalances[0]`**.

Listing 10.8 contains a source program demonstrating how the **`Clone()`** method is applied and highlights the difference between this approach of copying an array and the familiar procedure of assigning an array object reference with the assignment operator = . Overall, the program contains five initial speeds (could be car speeds in a racing game) in an array. Each initial speed must be altered by multiplying it by an acceleration factor. We want to keep track of the original speeds as well as the current speeds, so the original speeds are copied to a new array of speeds that are subject to the changes. The question is which copy mechanism should we use—the **`Clone()`** method (as in line 12), or simply the assignment operator (line 21)?

LISTING 10.8 `ArrayCloning.cs`

```
01: using System;
02:
03: class ArrayCloning
04: {
05:     public static void Main()
06:     {
```

LISTING 10.8 continued

```
07:         const float accellerationFactor = 1.1f;
08:         float [] initialSpeeds  = {50, 100, 35, 60, 20};
09:         float [] currentSpeeds;
10:
11:         Console.WriteLine("Assigning a clone:");
12:         currentSpeeds = (float[])initialSpeeds.Clone();
13:         for (int i = 0; i < currentSpeeds.Length; i++)
14:         {
15:             currentSpeeds[i] = currentSpeeds[i] * accellerationFactor;
16:             Console.WriteLine("Current speed {0,2}: {1,4}   Initial
                ➥ speed {2,2}: {3,4}",
17:                 i+1, currentSpeeds[i], i+1, initialSpeeds[i]);
18:         }
19:
20:         Console.WriteLine("\nAssigning a reference:");
21:         currentSpeeds = initialSpeeds;
22:         for (int i = 0; i < currentSpeeds.Length; i++)
23:         {
24:             currentSpeeds[i] = currentSpeeds[i] * accellerationFactor;
25:             Console.WriteLine("Current speed {0,2}: {1,4}   Initial
                ➥ speed {2,2}: {3,4}",
26:                 i+1, currentSpeeds[i], i+1, initialSpeeds[i]);
27:         }
28:     }
29: }
```

```
Assigning a clone:
Current speed  1:   55   Initial speed  1:   50
Current speed  2:  110   Initial speed  2:  100
Current speed  3: 38.5   Initial speed  3:   35
Current speed  4:   66   Initial speed  4:   60
Current speed  5:   22   Initial speed  5:   20
Assigning a reference:
Current speed  1:   55   Initial speed  1:   55
Current speed  2:  110   Initial speed  2:  110
Current speed  3: 38.5   Initial speed  3: 38.5
Current speed  4:   66   Initial speed  4:   66
Current speed  5:   22   Initial speed  5:   22
```

Line 8 declares an array called **`initialSpeeds`** of base type **`float`**. It is initialized to contain 5 different speeds. The entire collection of speeds is to be changed by multiplying them by an acceleration factor. The program must keep track of the current speed resulting from the acceleration but, at the same time, cannot "forget" about the speeds initially stored in **`initialSpeeds`**. Consequently, we need two separate speed array objects—one containing the initial speeds and the other containing the current speeds. **`currentSpeeds`** declared in line 9 is used for the latter purpose. Line 12 uses the **`Clone()`** method to create a new identical but separate array object with the same values as those referenced by **`initialSpeeds`**. The reference to this new object is assigned to **`currentSpeeds`**. Line 15 multiplies each array element of **`currentSpeeds`** with the **`accellerationFactor`** constant (declared in line 7), and the content of both **`currentSpeeds`** and **`initialSpeeds`** are printed in lines 16 and 17. As you can see from the sample output, **`currentSpeeds`** have changed, whereas **`initialSpeeds`** correctly has been left untouched.

The next part of the program (from line 21) begins by assigning the reference contained inside `initialSpeeds` to `currentSpeeds`, but without creating an accompanying new array object, so the two array variables are referencing the same array object. The problem with this approach is exposed through lines 22–27. Line 24 once again applies the acceleration factor to the array elements of `currentSpeeds`, but this time the array elements of `initialSpeeds` are affected, which is seen in the latter half of the sample output created by lines 25 and 26.

In the previous example, each array element holds values of type `int`, which is a value type. As mentioned earlier, arrays can also be declared to let its array elements hold values of a reference type. In this case, each array element will reference an object. Two important terms are used in connection with copying array objects of this kind—shallow copy and deep copy.

When an array object of a reference base type is *shallow copied*, the objects referenced by the array variables are not copied. Only the references themselves are copied to the new array elements. Thus, each array element of the new array object will reference the same object as the corresponding array element in the original array object.

The array elements of the *deep copy* will, like the shallow copy, contain copies of the references found in the original array object. However, in contrast to the shallow copy, the referenced objects will also be new copies. The objects referenced by the array elements of the deep array copy will be separate from the objects referenced by the original array.

Methods specialized in copying array objects provide either a shallow or deep copy.

For example, the `Clone()` method generates a shallow copy of the array it is called through.

A Method to Perform Array Value Equality Comparisons

Recall our earlier discussion about reference and value equality. Equipped with an understanding for how array object references are passed as arguments to a method, we can now design a method that determines whether two arrays are value equal to each other. The `ValueEquals` method (lines 21–41) of Listing 10.9 contains this functionality. The `Main()` method demonstrates how `ValueEquals` is used. It declares two array variables each referencing different objects, but with identical sets of array elements (lines 7 and 8). The following sample output verifies the difference between value equality as performed by the `ValueEquals` method, and reference equality performed by the equals comparison operator ==.

LISTING 10.9 `ValueEquality.cs`

```
01: using System;
02:
03: class ValueEquality
04: {
05:     public static void Main()
06:     {
07:         int [] myArray = {10, 20, 30, 40, 50, 60};
```

LISTING 10.9 continued

```
08:         int [] yourArray = {10, 20, 30, 40, 50, 60};
09:
10:         if (ValueEquals (myArray, yourArray))
11:             Console.WriteLine("myArray is value equal to yourArray");
12:         else
13:             Console.WriteLine("myArray is not value equal to yourArray");
14:
15:         if (myArray == yourArray)
16:             Console.WriteLine("myArray is reference equal to yourArray");
17:         else
18:             Console.WriteLine("myArray is not reference equal to
                ➥ yourArray");
19:     }
20:
21:     private static bool ValueEquals (int [] array1, int [] array2)
22:     {
23:         bool areValueEqual = true;
24:
25:         if (!(array1.Length == array2.Length))
26:         {
27:             areValueEqual = false;
28:         }
29:         else
30:         {
31:             for (int i = 0; i < array1.Length; i++)
32:             {
33:                 if (!(array1[i] == array2[i]))
34:                 {
35:                     areValueEqual = false;
36:                     break;
37:                 }
38:             }
39:         }
40:         return areValueEqual;
41:     }
42: }
```

```
myArray is value equal to yourArray
myArray is not reference equal to yourArray
```

Let's first look at the `ValueEquals` method spanning lines 21–41. Its header specifies two formal parameters (`array1` and `array2`), both array variables of base type `int`. When `ValueEquals` is called, we must provide two array references as arguments (see line 10). The inner logic of `ValueEquals` follows the definition of value equal. First, the lengths of the two arrays must be identical (checked in lines 25–28), and second, each array element of one array (`array1`) must be identical to the array element with the corresponding index in the other array (`array2`) (see line 33). If any of these conditions are `false`, the two arrays are not value equal and the `bool` variable `areValueEqual` is set to `false` in line 27 or line 35. Notice that because the initial value of `areValueEqual` is set to `true` (in line 27), it will remain `true` until the method is terminated (in line 40) unless any of the previous conditions trigger it to be set to `false`. As specified in the method header, the method returns a value of type `bool`. This value will, when the method returns, be identical to the final value of `areEqualValue`, and only `true` if `array1` and `array2` are value equal.

The `Main()` method demonstrates the use of `ValueEquals` by declaring two array variables referencing two different array variables that are value equal. As expected (see sample output), the Boolean expression `ValueEquals (myArray, yourArray)` in line 10 returns the value `true`, whereas `myArray == yourArray` is `false`.

Command Line Arguments

Recall that the `Main()` method is special in that it is automatically invoked by the .NET runtime when program execution commences. It holds another special feature—it is possible to enter data (here called arguments) into the `Main()` method from the console window (or a Windows application) when the program initially is started. To enable this functionality, we need to include a formal parameter of type reference-to-array-object of base type `string` in the method header of `Main()` as in the following:

```
public static void Main(string [] args)
```

where the array variable, as per tradition, is called `args`.

Passing arguments from the console into `Main()` can now be done simply by typing these next to the text you usually type (typically just the name of the program) to invoke the program. For example, to pass the arguments

Planet Blipos is far away

into the `Main()` method of the program in Listing 10.10 called `ConsoleArguments.cs`, you must write the following commands in the console window, after having created the `ConsoleArguments.cs` file with the editor. First, the program is compiled as usual:

```
C:\MyC#Programs>csc ConsoleArguments.cs<enter>
```

Then, the arguments are typed next to the name of the program as follows:

```
C:\MyC#Programs>ConsoleArguments Planet Blipos is far away<enter>
```

In this case, our program simply prints the content of the `args` array variable back to the screen, resulting in the sample output shown after the listing.

LISTING 10.10 `ConsoleArguments.cs`

```
using System;

class ConsoleArguments
{
    public static void Main(String [] args)
    {
        for (int i = 0; i < args.Length; i++)
        {
            Console.WriteLine(args[i]);
```

LISTING 10.10 continued

```
10:         }
11:     }
12: }
```

```
Planet
Blipos
is
far
away
```

The text entered after the name of the program (in this case, `Planet Blipos is far away`) is analyzed by the .NET runtime and automatically divided into separate words. A word is defined to have whitespace or begin/end-of-text on either side. Every word is then assigned to an array element of **`args`** in the order in which it was written. Thus, immediately after the method body of `Main()` has begun executing (line 7), the array object referenced by **`args`** has the following content, which is verified by the sample output generated by lines 7–10.

args[0]	args[1]	args[2]	args[3]	args[4]
Planet	Blipos	is	far	away

Note

args of

```
public static void Main(String [] args)
```

is merely an identifier. Consequently, you can use any other name for this parameter, providing that you follow the usual rules for variable naming (avoid using keywords and so on).

It is possible to enter several words into the same array element by using quotation marks. For example, the following command

```
C:\MyC#Programs>ConsoleArguments "Wolfgang Amadeus Mozart" was
➥ a composer <enter>
```

results in the following output:

```
Wolfgang Amadeus Mozart
was
a
composer
```

obviously assigning the string `"Wolfgang Amadeus Mozart"` to the first array element, despite the whitespace between Wolfgang, Amadeus, and Mozart.

Sometimes, the user might want to pass numbers to a program. This can be achieved by letting the program convert the relevant array elements of **`args`** from type **`string`** to the suitable numerical type. For example, the program of Listing 10.11 reads in two numbers and prints out their sum.

LISTING 10.11 SumOfArguments.cs

```
01: using System;
02:
03: class SumOfArguments
04: {
05:     public static void Main(string[] args)
06:     {
07:         int x;
08:         int y;
09:
10:         x = Convert.ToInt32(args[0]);
11:         y = Convert.ToInt32(args[1]);
12:         Console.WriteLine(
13:             "The sum of the two arguments is: {0}", (x+y));

14:     }
15: }
```

```
C:\MyC#Programs>SumOfArguments 100 200<enter>
The sum of the two arguments is: 300
```

The two numeric arguments (100 and 200 in this example) reside inside the first and second array elements in the form of strings. To involve the numbers in any calculations, they must first be converted to an appropriate numeric type, in this case `int`. The conversions are performed in lines 10 and 11 and assigned to the two `int` variables `x` and `y`. Line 13 prints out the sum of x and y.

Using Arrays As Return Values from Methods

C# allows a method to return an array object reference back to the caller. Figure 10.12 shows the relevant parts of a source program making use of this feature. Two methods are defined here—`Main` (lines 5–40) and `GetTenRandomNumbers` (lines 50–71). The latter will, when called, return a reference to an array containing ten random numbers. These numbers could be used for various mathematical analyses (irrelevant for this demonstration and therefore not shown) performed in the `Main` method.

Recall that the return type for a method is specified just prior to the method name of the method header, such as in the following:

```
private static int Sum (int a, int b)
```

where the method header in this case specifies `Sum` to return a value of type `int`.

By exchanging `int` with the array type name `int []`, as in the following (the method name has also changed, but this is irrelevant in this context):

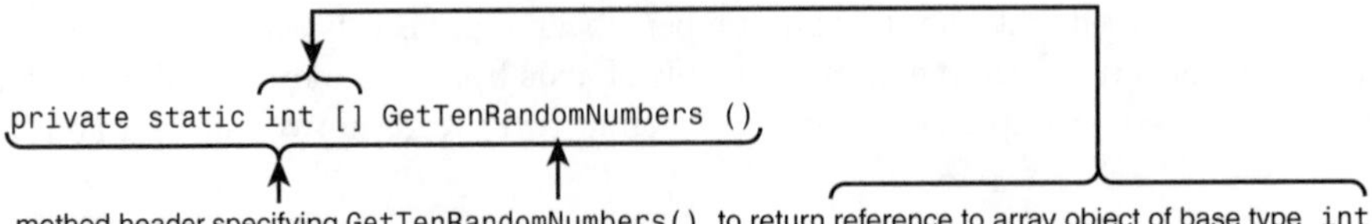
private static int [] GetTenRandomNumbers ()
method header specifying GetTenRandomNumbers() to return reference to array object of base type int

of line 50, we specify the method `GetTenRandomNumbers()` to return a reference to an array of base type `int`. After `GetTenRandomNumbers()` has been defined, it is possible to insert its method call anyplace where a reference to array of base type `int` is expected. Consequently, it becomes possible to assign its return value to `randomNumbers` (declared in line 10), which is of a compatible type, by writing

```
randomNumbers = GetTenRandomNumbers();
```

as done in line 20 of Figure 10.12. `randomNumbers` now references an array object with ten random numbers. Each of its array elements can be called in the usual manner as follows:

```
randomNumbers[0]
```

Notice that because `randomArray` is declared within the scope of `GetTenRandomNumbers()` (see line 55 of Figure 10.12), its scope is confined to this method. However, even though the new array object, whose reference is assigned to `randomArray` in the same line, is created within the same scope, this same array object happily lives on outside the scope of `GetTenRandomNumbers()` through the reference passed back to the caller (via line 70), which, in this case, resides in the `Main()` method.

Note

In general, the lifetime of an array object is not determined by the scope of where it is created, but whether any references are referencing it. Consequently, array objects created inside the scope of a method can live outside the confines of this method by returning its references.

FIGURE 10.12
Returning a reference to an array object of base type *int*.

```
...
05: public static void Main()
06: {
 ...
10:     int [] randomNumbers;
 ...
20:     randomNumbers = GetTenRandomNumbers();
 ...
     // Statements utilizing the random numbers
     // contained in randomNumbers and accessed
     // with the familiar syntax (e.g. randomNumbers[0])
 ...
40: }
 ...
50: private static int [] GetTenRandomNumbers ()
51: {
 ...
55:     int [] randomArray = new int [10];
 ...
     //Statements filling the local array variable
     //randomArray with ten random numbers
 ...
70:     return randomArray;
71: }
 ...
```

1 randomNumbers is declared to hold a reference to an array object of base type int...
2 ...and can thus be assigned...
3 ...the reference to the array object of base type int...
4 ...which is created here...
5 ...and filled with suitable values here...
6 ...and which reference is returned back to the caller here.

Listing 10.12 contains a fully-working program to exemplify the previous discussion. The program is similar to that of Listing 10.6, but this time the maximum individual sales of `person1Sales` and `person2Sales` (declared in lines 7 and 8) are determined via a separate method called `MaxArray` that assigns the maximum values to a locally created array. The reference to this array is returned from `MaxArray` to the `Main` method where it is used to print out the content of the array object and the maximum individual sales figures (see the sample output following the listing).

LISTING 10.12 `ReturnMaxSalesArray.cs`

```
01: using System;
02:
03: class ReturnMaxSalesArray
04: {
05:     public static void Main()
06:     {
07:         decimal [] person1Sales = {40000, 10000, 25000, 50000, 33000,
           ➥ 60000};
08:         decimal [] person2Sales = {80000, 3000, 110000, 40000, 33000,
           ➥ 59000};
09:         decimal [] maxSales;
10:
11:         maxSales = MaxArray(person1Sales, person2Sales);
12:         Console.WriteLine("Max individual sales for each of the first
           ➥ six months: ");
13:         for (int i = 0; i < 6; i++)
14:         {
15:             Console.WriteLine("Max sales month {0}: {1,12:C}", (i+1),
               ➥ maxSales[i]);
16:         }
17:     }
18:
19:     private static decimal [] MaxArray (decimal [] sales1,
       ➥ decimal [] sales2)
20:     {
21:         decimal [] maxSales = new decimal[sales1.Length];
22:
23:         for (int i = 0; i < maxSales.Length; i++)
24:         {
25:             maxSales[i] = MaxAmount(sales1[i], sales2[i]);
26:         }
27:         return maxSales;
28:     }
29:
30:     private static decimal MaxAmount(decimal a, decimal b)
31:     {
32:         if (a > b)
33:             return a;
34:         else
35:             return b;
36:     }
37: }
```

```
Max individual sales for each of the first six months:
Max sales month 1:   $80,000.00
Max sales month 2:   $10,000.00
Max sales month 3:  $110,000.00
Max sales month 4:   $50,000.00
Max sales month 5:   $33,000.00
Max sales month 6:   $60,000.00
```

Lines 7–9 declare three array variables. Lines 30—36 contain the method `MaxAmount` that is identical to `MaxAmount` of Listing 10.6. It returns the greater of the two arguments passed to it. Lines 19–28 contain the definition for the method `MaxArray`. According to the method header of line 19, it has two formal parameters `sales1` and `sales2` and a return value, all of type reference to an array object of base type `decimal`. In line 25, `MaxArray` compares each pair of corresponding array elements from `sales1` and `sales2` by applying `MaxAmount`. In each instance, the greatest value is assigned to the corresponding array element of the local array variable `maxSales` declared in line 21. After the `for` loop repeatedly has executed its loop body `maxSales.Length` times (6 in this case), the reference to the array object, created in line 21 with the `new` keyword and now containing the max individual sales, is returned to the caller with the `return` keyword in line 27.

Line 11 calls the `MaxArray` method and passes two arguments along, `person1Sales` and `person2Sales`. Flow of execution then moves to the beginning of the `MaxArray` method, where `sales1` and `sales2` now are referencing the same array objects as `person1Sales` and `person2Sales`, respectively. The array elements referenced by these two array variables are then processed according to `MaxArray`'s description previously discussed. As a result, a reference to an array object containing the maximum individual sales of `person1Sales` and `person2Sales` is returned from this method call and assigned to `maxSales`. It is now easy, through the `for` loop of lines 13–16, to print out the values of this array.

Syntax Box 10.5 Method Returning an Array Object Reference

```
Typical_anatomy_of_method_returning_an_array_object_reference::=

public static <Base_type> [] <Method_identifier> ( <Formal_Parameter_list> )
{
      ...
      <Base_type> [] <Local_array_identifier> = new <Base_type> [<Array_length>];
      ...
      <Statements assigning values to array elements of <Local_array_identifier> >
      ...
      return <Local_array_identifier>;
}
```

Notes:

- The method need not be declared `public` or `static`. These keywords are merely included because they are often used to declare a method.
- The method must, like any other method, be positioned within a `class` or a `struct` definition.

Arrays and Classes

As briefly mentioned earlier, the base type of an array is not only confined to be of a primitive type, but can be any declarable type, including a class. The coming section provides examples of how to work with object references stored in array elements and the trailing section combines this ability with C#'s capability of letting arrays be instance variables in classes.

Array Elements Referencing Objects

The source program of Listing 10.13 shown later utilizes an array of elevators (line 35) to effectively control a *collection* of elevators. It is used to demonstrate the syntax and mechanics involved when array elements hold references to objects. Recall the elevator simulation example from Chapter 5. It defined an `Elevator` similar to that found in lines 3–29 of Listing 10.13, but only employed one of this kind. The `Main()` method (lines 33–54) in contrast manages 10 elevators.

To better focus on the important issues surrounding arrays of objects, the program has omitted some of the aspects included in the example of Chapter 5. There are, for example, no `Person` objects here; instead, the elevators are manipulated directly from the `Main()` method, where each `Elevator` object is accessed through the array of elevators.

Lines 3–29 define a bare bones `Elevator` class. It can keep track of its current floor position (through `currentFloorNumber` declared in line 5) and its total number of floors traveled (`floorsTraveled` of line 6). Both instance variables are initialized to zero by the constructor defined in lines 8–12. A constructor is, as you might recollect, automatically called and executed during the process of creating a new object, and is a handy mechanism to perform various initializations.

An `Elevator` object can be moved to a new floor (`MoveToFloor` lines 14–18), return the total number of floors traveled (`GetFloorsTraveled` lines 20–23), and can return its current floor location (lines 25–28). We are now able to create and manage a large group of `Elevator` objects. This can effectively be done by keeping their references neatly ordered and indexed inside an array of base type `Elevator`. Our humble aim here is merely to control 10 `Elevator` objects inside the `Main()` method. To declare the elevator array, we exchange the name of the primitive types we have utilized so far with the name of our custom designed type—`Elevator`. Thus,

```
Elevator [] elevators
```

of line 35 specifies `elevators` to be an array variable of base type `Elevator`. So far, `elevators` only references `null`, as illustrated in Figure 10.13, so it needs to be assigned a reference to an array object of base type `Elevator` and length `10`.

As usual, this can be done with the `new` keyword. For example, after line 35

```
Elevator [] elevators = new Elevator[10];
```

elevators is referencing an array object with ten array elements of type reference-to-**Elevator**-object. However, because none of them have yet been assigned a reference to a particular **Elevator** object, they are all **null**, as illustrated in Figure 10.14.

```
Elevator [] elevators
```

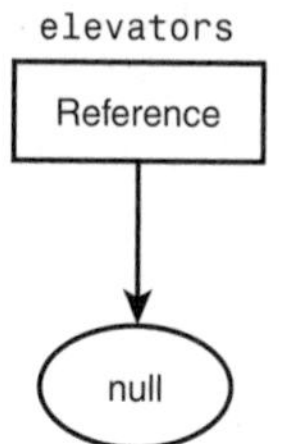

FIGURE 10.13
The newly declared *elevators* array variable referencing *null*.

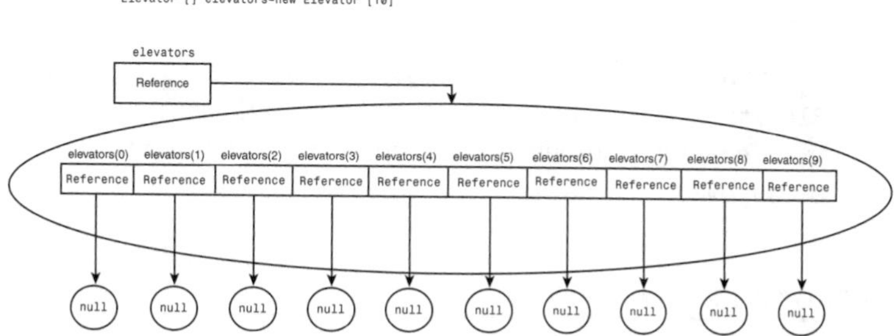

FIGURE 10.14
All array elements referencing *null*.

For each array element in **elevators**, we need to create an **Elevator** object and assign its reference to this array element (lines 36–39). As the **for** loop increments **i** from 0 to 9, each **elevators** element is assigned a reference to a freshly created **Elevator** object through the following loop body found in line 38:

```
elevators[i] = new Elevator();
```

Each array element is now referencing an **Elevator** object, as illustrated in Figure 10.15.

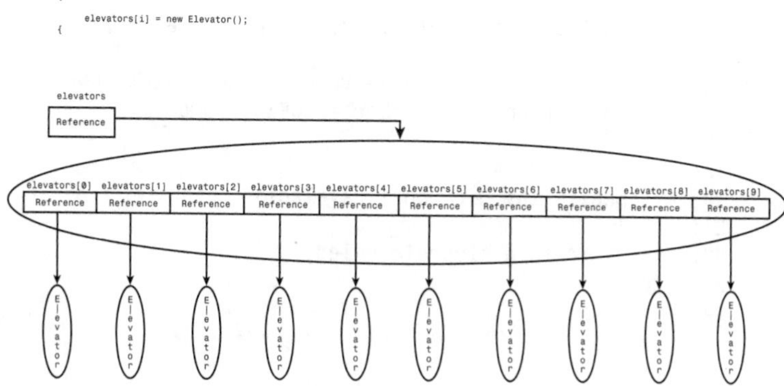

FIGURE 10.15
Situation after assigning new *Elevator* objects to *elevators* array elements.

Finally, the 10 **elevators** are ready to be accessed and used.

To identify a particular **Elevator** object, we need to specify the relevant index in square brackets after the array variable name. The first **Elevator** object can, for example, be referenced by writing the following:

```
elevators[0]
```

To call a method of the referenced object, we simply need to apply the dot operator followed by the name of the method, as in line 41:

```
elevators[0].MoveToFloor(10);
```

which calls the **MoveToFloor** method of the first **Elevator** object in **elevators** and passes along the argument **10**.

Lines 41–44 "moves" the first and the fifth elevator a couple of times each. We could have involved **elevators** in a much more elaborate set of movements involving all 10 elevators and sophisticated movement-generating algorithms, but this would sidetrack us from the issues discussed here.

Lines 46—53 calls the **GetFloorsTraveled** and **GetCurrentFloorNumber** methods of each **Elevator** object and provides an overview of the current state of each object. As you can see from the sample output, as expected, only the first and the fifth elevator are shown to have been moved.

LISTING 10.13 ElevatorArray.cs

```
01: using System;
02:
03: class Elevator
04: {
05:     private int currentFloorNumber;
06:     private int floorsTraveled;
07:
08:     public Elevator()
09:     {
10:         currentFloorNumber = 0;
11:         floorsTraveled = 0;
12:     }
13:
14:     public void MoveToFloor(int toFloorNumber)
15:     {
16:         floorsTraveled += Math.Abs(currentFloorNumber - toFloorNumber);
17:         currentFloorNumber = toFloorNumber;
18:     }
19:
20:     public int GetFloorsTraveled()
21:     {
22:         return floorsTraveled;
23:     }
24:
```

LISTING 10.13 continued

```
    public int GetCurrentFloorNumber()
    {
        return currentFloorNumber;
    }
}

class ElevatorArray
{
    public static void Main()
    {
        Elevator [] elevators = new Elevator[10];
        for (int i = 0; i < elevators.Length; i++)
        {
            elevators[i] = new Elevator();
        }

        elevators[0].MoveToFloor(10);
        elevators[4].MoveToFloor(20);
        elevators[0].MoveToFloor(5);
        elevators[4].MoveToFloor(7);

        Console.WriteLine("Total floors traveled and current location
        ➥ for each elevator\n");
        Console.WriteLine("              Floors traveled   Current location");
        for (int i = 0; i < elevators.Length; i++)
        {
            Console.WriteLine("Elevator
            ➥ {0,2}:       {1,4}              {2,4}",
                (i + 1), elevators[i].GetFloorsTraveled(),
                elevators[i].GetCurrentFloorNumber());
        }
    }
}
```

Total floors traveled and current location for each elevator

```
              Floors traveled   Current location
Elevator  1:        15                 5
Elevator  2:         0                 0
Elevator  3:         0                 0
Elevator  4:         0                 0
Elevator  5:        33                 7
Elevator  6:         0                 0
Elevator  7:         0                 0
Elevator  8:         0                 0
Elevator  9:         0                 0
Elevator 10:         0                 0
```

Arrays As Instance Variables in Classes

The typical framework for a class definition seen so far in this book looks like the following:

```
class AnyClass
{
      <Instance Variables>
      <Methods>
      <Others>
}
```

The instance variables we have declared in our classes have up till now, mostly consisted of primitive types, but they can also be objects, such as `System.Array` objects. The following example illustrates.

Consider a simulation involving a `Building` class. Somehow, we want it to be implemented so that it "contains" numerous `Elevator` and `Floor` objects, just like its real counterpart. The following definition of the `Building` class contains declarations of two instance variables, both of type `System.Array`, called `elevators` and `floors`, respectively, making this request possible:

```
class Building
{
    private Elevator [] elevators;
    private Floor [] floors;
    <Other instance variables>
    <Methods>
    <Others>
}
```

We can now, from within one of the methods of the `Building` class, assign new array objects with a specified number of elevators and floors to these two array variables. If we wanted to create a building containing 10 elevators and 30 floors, we could instantiate a `Building` object and initialize `elevators` and `floors` with the following statements:

```
elevators = new Elevator[10];
floors = new Floor[30];
```

Let's look at another example in more detail, this time involving banks and account balances.

So far, we have made extensive use of the `accountBalances` array to demonstrate several aspects of the array. The idea of a collection of account balances (represented by an array of values of a primitive type like `decimal`) as an instance variable in a `Bank` class is good (I hope) to demonstrate the syntax and semantics of arrays in a simple context. However, to tackle the complexities contained in software for a real world bank we need to make this approach more object-oriented. How can this be done? Rather than a list of account balances, a bank can be perceived to contain a collection of accounts. We can thus create an `Account` class written briefly as follows:

```
class Account
{
      <Instance variable>
      <Methods>
}
```

...and a `Bank` class with a collection of `Account` objects as in:

```
class Bank
{
      private Account [] accounts;
      <Other instance variables>
      <Methods>
}
```

The following case study continues the story and shows you how to build a relatively simple bank simulation program by using an array of accounts as an instance variable in a `Bank` class.

Case Study: Bank Simulation Program

The final complete source code of this case study is provided in Listing 10.14, later in this case study, and will be referenced throughout the discussion.

Software specification:

The program written in this case study will simulate a bank holding several bank accounts. The accounts of the bank can be accessed and manipulated via a simple user interface provided from the console window. In particular, the user must, by giving simple commands, be able to

- Initially specify the number of accounts managed by the bank
- Deposit money into a specified account
- Withdraw money from a specified account
- Set the interest rate of a specific account
- Add interest to all accounts
- Print all account balances
- Print total interest paid to each account
- Print interest rate of each account
- End the simulation

Software design:

Segregating each subsystem into objects (modules):

Two obvious classes can be identified—`Account` (lines 3–51) and `Bank` (lines 53–144), along with the class `BankSimulation` (lines 146–205); it contains the `Main()` method that glues together the various parts of the program and responds to user input.

Identify the instance variables of the classes:

According to the software specification, an `Account` object must keep track of the following information:

- Its balance
- Its current interest rate
- The total interest paid to it

Consequently, the `Account` class must contain the following instance variables (see lines 5–7):

```
private decimal balance;
private decimal currentInterestRate;
private decimal totalInterestPaid;
```

The `Bank` class contains a collection of accounts. All information relevant for the `Bank` can be found within the account objects. Consequently, the `Bank` class merely needs a single instance variable—an array of accounts. The declaration looks like the following (see line 55):

```
private Account [] accounts;
```

The `BankSimulation` class merely needs one instance variable—a `Bank` object (declared in line 148).

Identify the methods in each module:

- `Account` *class*—All instance variables should be initialized at the creation time of the object to which they belong. The constructor of lines 9–14 accomplishes this task. Recall that a constructor is a method with the same name as the class in which it resides. It is invoked during the creation of a new `Account` object. In our case, it initializes all instance variables to zero.

  All instance variables of `Account` are declared `private` to prevent any access from outside the object. As a consequence, we must define special methods, called accessor and mutator methods, to get and set the instance variables that must be retrieved and/or set directly. `currentInterestRate` requires two accessor methods, here called `SetInterestRate` (lines 16–19) and `GetInterestRate` (lines 21–24). `balance` is updated via the `Deposit` (lines 32–35) and `Withdraw` (lines 37–40) methods; however, the value must be returned via an accessor-method here called `GetBalance` (lines 42–45). `totalInterestPaid` is updated through the `UpdateInterest` method (lines 26–30) but must be returned with an accessor method, here called `GetTotalInterestPaid` (lines 47–50).

Note

In Chapter 14, "Class Anatomy Part III: Writing Intuitive Code," you will be introduced to properties that constitute a better way to access instance variables than accessor and mutator methods. For now, though, we can live happily without properties.

- `Bank` *class*—Whenever a new `Bank` object is created, we must create the `Account` objects it will manage, and assign their references to the array elements of `accounts`. This task could be performed by a standard method that is called after the creation of a `Bank` object. However, because this procedure must be performed for any new `Bank` object for it to be of any use, I decided to let a constructor perform the task (see lines 57–66). When a new `Bank` is created, as in line 154, the user will automatically be asked to enter the number of bank accounts controlled by the bank. Notice that the number of accounts once decided cannot be changed during the entire execution of the bank simulation.

The newly created account objects residing inside accounts are now ready to be accessed. All the methods of the `Bank` class are devoted to updating or retrieving information from a single account or the entire collection of accounts and are, consequently, heavily dependent on the methods exposed by the `Account` class.

The following methods work in a very similar manner in that they all ask the user to enter a specific account number and then permit the user to perform the requested action on the particular account.

- `Deposit` (lines 68–79)
- `Withdraw` (lines 81–92)
- `SetInterestRate` (lines 94–103)

In contrast, the subsequent four methods traverse through the entire collection of accounts to update a particular instance variable in each `Account`, or simply to access information for printing purposes:

- `PrintAllInterestRates` (lines 105–113)
- `PrintAllBalances` (lines 115–123)
- `PrintTotalInterestPaidAllAccounts` (lines 125–133)
- `UpdateInterestAllAccounts` (lines 135–143)

- `BankSimulation` *class*—The `BankSimulation` class provides a container for a `Bank` object and the `Main()` and `PrintMenu` methods. The latter evolves around a `do-while` loop combined with a `switch` statement to respond to user commands. Notice how relatively simple the `Main()` method is. All major tasks have been delegated to other methods either residing inside `BankSimulation` (the `PrintMenu` method) or inside the other objects of the simulation (`Bank` and `Account`).

Internal method design:

None of the methods in this program involve any elaborate algorithms, so I will just highlight a couple of smaller issues here in connection with the methods of the `Bank` class:

1. `accounts[0]` contains a reference to an `Account` object. A method of this object can be called by applying the dot operator to `accounts[0]` as in the following:

   ```
   accounts[0].GetBalance()
   ```

   which returns the balance of the first `Account` object.

2. The user is led to believe that the first account is of index one (line 203). We must adjust for this when indexes entered or viewed by the user are used as indexes to access individual accounts. For example, in the `Deposit` method (lines 68–79) the user enters the account number of the account into which he or she wants to deposit money. The number is assigned to `accountNumber`, but will be one too big for our zero-based collection. The adjustments are performed in lines 76 and 78 by deducting one from `accountNumber` before it is passed as an index.

LISTING 10.14 `BankSimulation.cs`

```
01: using System;
02:
03: class Account
04: {
05:     private decimal balance;
06:     private decimal currentInterestRate;
07:     private decimal totalInterestPaid;
08:
09:     public Account()
10:     {
11:         balance = 0;
12:         currentInterestRate = 0;
13:         totalInterestPaid = 0;
14:     }
15:
16:     public void SetInterestRate(decimal newInterestRate)
17:     {
18:         currentInterestRate = newInterestRate;
19:     }
20:
21:     public decimal GetInterestRate()
22:     {
23:         return currentInterestRate;
24:     }
25:
26:     public void UpdateInterest()
27:     {
28:         totalInterestPaid += balance * currentInterestRate;
29:         balance += balance * currentInterestRate;
30:     }
31:
32:     public void Withdraw (decimal amount)
33:     {
34:         balance -= amount;
35:     }
36:
37:     public void Deposit (decimal amount)
38:     {
39:         balance += amount;
40:     }
41:
```

LISTING 10.14 continued

```
    public decimal GetBalance()
    {
        return balance;
    }

    public decimal GetTotalInterestPaid()
    {
        return totalInterestPaid;
    }
}

class Bank
{
    private Account [] accounts;

    public Bank()
    {
        Console.WriteLine("Congratulations! You have created
        ➥ a new bank");
        Console.Write("Please enter number of accounts in bank: ");
        accounts = new Account[Convert.ToInt32(Console.ReadLine())];
        for (int i = 0; i < accounts.Length; i++)
        {
            accounts[i] = new Account();
        }
    }

    public void Deposit()
    {
        int accountNumber;
        decimal amount;
        Console.Write("Deposit. Please enter account number: ");
        accountNumber = Convert.ToInt32(Console.ReadLine());
        Console.Write("Enter amount to deposit: ");
        amount = Convert.ToDecimal(Console.ReadLine());
        accounts[accountNumber - 1].Deposit(amount);
        Console.WriteLine("New balance of account {0}: {1:C}",
            accountNumber, accounts[accountNumber - 1].GetBalance());
    }

    public void Withdraw()
    {
        int accountNumber;
        decimal amount;
        Console.Write("Withdraw. Please enter account number: ");
        accountNumber = Convert.ToInt32(Console.ReadLine());
        Console.Write("Enter amount to withdraw: ");
        amount = Convert.ToDecimal(Console.ReadLine());
        accounts[accountNumber - 1].Withdraw(amount);
        Console.WriteLine("New balance of account {0}: {1:C}",
            accountNumber, accounts[accountNumber - 1].GetBalance());
    }
```

LISTING 10.14 continued

```

    public void SetInterestRate()
    {
        int accountNumber;
        decimal newInterestRate;
        Console.Write("Set interest rate. Please enter
        ➥ account number: ");
        accountNumber = Convert.ToInt32(Console.ReadLine());
        Console.Write("Enter interest rate: ");
        newInterestRate = Convert.ToDecimal(Console.ReadLine());
        accounts[accountNumber - 1].SetInterestRate(newInterestRate);
    }

    public void PrintAllInterestRates()
    {
        Console.WriteLine("Interest rates for all accounts:");
        for (int i = 0; i < accounts.Length; i++)
        {
            Console.WriteLine("Account {0,-3}: {1,-10}",
                (i + 1), accounts[i].GetInterestRate());
        }
    }

    public void PrintAllBalances()
    {
        Console.WriteLine("Account balances for all accounts:");
        for (int i = 0; i < accounts.Length; i++)
        {
            Console.WriteLine("Account {0,-3}: {1,12:C}",
                (i + 1), accounts[i].GetBalance());
        }
    }

    public void PrintTotalInterestPaidAllAccounts()
    {
        Console.WriteLine("Total interest paid for each
        ➥ individual account");
        for (int i = 0; i < accounts.Length; i++)
        {
            Console.WriteLine("Account {0,-3}: {1,12:C}",
                (i + 1), accounts[i].GetTotalInterestPaid());
        }
    }

    public void UpdateInterestAllAccounts()
    {
        for (int i = 0; i < accounts.Length; i++)
        {
            Console.WriteLine("Interest added to account
            ➥ number {0,-3}: {1,12:C}",
                (i + 1), accounts[i].GetBalance() *
                ➥ accounts[i].GetInterestRate());
```

LISTING 10.14 continued

```
                accounts[i].UpdateInterest();
            }
        }
}

class BankSimulation
{
    private static Bank bigBucksBank;

    public static void Main()
    {
        string command;

        bigBucksBank = new Bank();
        do
        {
            PrintMenu();
            command = Console.ReadLine().ToUpper();
            switch (command)
            {
                case "D":
                    bigBucksBank.Deposit();
                    break;
                case "W":
                    bigBucksBank.Withdraw();
                    break;
                case "S":
                    bigBucksBank.SetInterestRate();
                    break;
                case "U":
                    bigBucksBank.UpdateInterestAllAccounts();
                    break;
                case "P":
                    bigBucksBank.PrintAllBalances();
                    break;
                case "T":
                    bigBucksBank.PrintTotalInterestPaidAllAccounts();
                    break;
                case "I":
                    bigBucksBank.PrintAllInterestRates();
                    break;
                case "E":
                    Console.WriteLine("Bye Bye!");
                    break;
                default:
                    Console.WriteLine("Invalid choice");
                    break;
            }
        } while (command != "E");
    }

    private static void PrintMenu()
```

LISTING 10.14 continued

```
    {
        Console.WriteLine("\nWhat would you like to do?\n" +
            "D)eposit\n" +
            "W)ithdraw\n" +
            "S)et interest rate\n" +
            "U)pdate all accounts for interest\n" +
            "P)rint all balances\n" +
            "T)otal interest paid printed for all accounts\n" +
            "I)nterest rates printed for all accounts\n" +
            "E)nd session\n" +
            "Note: First account has account number one");
    }
}
```

```
Congratulations! You have created a new bank
Please enter number of accounts in bank: 7<enter>

What would you like to do?
D)eposit
W)ithdraw
S)et interest rate
U)pdate all accounts for interest
P)rint all balances
T)otal interest paid printed for all accounts
I)nterest rates printed for all accounts
E)nd session
Note: First account has account number one
S<enter>
Set interest rate. Please enter account number: 2<enter>
Enter interest rate: 0.1<enter>

What would you like to do?
...
D<enter>
Deposit. Please enter account number: 2<enter>
Enter amount to deposit: 100000<enter>
New balance of account 2: $100,000.00

What would you like to do?
...
U<enter>
Interest added to account number 1  :         $0.00
Interest added to account number 2  :    $10,000.00
Interest added to account number 3  :         $0.00
Interest added to account number 4  :         $0.00
Interest added to account number 5  :         $0.00
Interest added to account number 6  :         $0.00
Interest added to account number 7  :         $0.00

What would you like to do?
...
```

```
P<enter>
Account balances for all accounts:
Account 1  :        $0.00
Account 2  :  $110,000.00
Account 3  :        $0.00
Account 4  :        $0.00
Account 5  :        $0.00
Account 6  :        $0.00
Account 7  :        $0.00

What would you like to do?
...
E<enter>
Bye Bye!
```

Notes:

- After every task has been accomplished, the 8 choices eposit, W)ithdraw, and so on) are printed onscreen. To save paper, these choices are only shown here once and then replaced by three dots.
- The sample output does not demonstrate all of the functionalities found in the `BankSimulation.cs` program.

Summary

In this chapter, you learned about the fundamentals of declaring, creating, and working with one-dimensional arrays.

The essential points discussed in this chapter are reviewed in this section.

Arrays can be useful for representing and accessing a small or a large number of similarly typed data items. Regardless of the number of items an array represents, it only needs one or two lines to be declared, and a loop construct can easily access different array element by referencing a single array name with a varying index.

Loop constructs a highly suited to traverse arrays.

When an array is created, its elements are initially and automatically assigned a default value. This value depends on the array element type.

After an array has been created, its length cannot be altered; this is one of the reasons why arrays sometimes are not the preferred means to represent a small or a large number of data items. In those cases, collection types with the ability to alter their length dynamically during runtime are called needed.

A reference is referencing the `null` object if it does not reference any particular other object. Any reference type can reference the `null` object.

The array has a zero-based index, meaning that the first array element has the index zero. It is possible to make your program pretend that the first index is 1 (or any other index you might find convenient).

If you attempt to access an array element with an index smaller than zero or larger than the array's length minus one, the runtime will generate an `IndexOutOfRangeException`.

It is possible to specify the initial values of an array's elements directly in the source code; the values must be enclosed by curly braces.

The traditional loop constructs (especially the `for` loop) provide tremendous power to the hands of the programmer, because the programmer has direct control over loop counters and the indexes used to access individual array elements. However, sometimes this detailed control is not necessary. In those cases, the `foreach` statement provides a handy and simple alternative to the traditional loop constructs (`for`, `while`, and `do-while`).

The array is a class type (`System.Array`) and therefore a reference type. This means that arrays follow the rules of any reference type. One array object can be referenced by several array references, and array references can be passed to methods as arguments and returned back to the caller from a method. The equals operator (==) support reference equality between array variables.

An array element, like any other variable, can be used as an argument in a method call.

If you assign an array reference variable to another array reference variable, you are merely assigning it a copy of the reference. After this assignment, the two array variables will reference the same array object. If you want to create a totally new array instead, but with identical array elements, you can use the array's built-in `Clone` method.

Via an array (conventionally called `args`) of base type `string`, you can provide values to the program you are running from the command line by using command-line arguments.

Array elements can contain references to objects of any class type.

Review Questions

1. a. Declare an array variable called `distances` with elements of type `double`.

   b. Assign an array object with 5 elements to `distances`.

   c. Assign an array object to distances with the values `20.1`, `30.7`, `45.8`, `19.1`, `12.4`, and `34.5`.

2. Consider the following array:

   ```
   private int[] numbers = {10,5,3,15};
   ```

   a. What is the value of the following array element? `numbers[1]`

   b. What is the output from the following loop construct:

   ```
   for(int i = 3; i >= 0; i--)
   {
       Console.Write(" {0}", numbers[i])
   }
   ```

c. Write a loop using the **foreach** construct to traverse and print onscreen each element in **numbers**. This should result in the following output: 10 5 3 15.

d. What is wrong with the following code that attempts to traverse the numbers array? What will happen when it is executed?

```
for(int i = 0; i <= 4; i++)
{
    Console.WriteLine(numbers[i]);
}
```

3. A class contains the following array declaration:

```
private int[] heights = new int[3];
```

a. What is the value of each array element just after this array has been implicitly initialized?

b. A line in your class looks like the following

```
heights[4] = 10;
```

Is this a valid statement? What will happen when this line is executed?

4. Why is it not a good idea to use an array to represent accounts of a real world bank?

5. Consider the following array declaration (same as in question 2):

```
private int[] numbers = {10,5,3,15};
```

A fellow programmer has written the following method for retrieving values from the array:

```
int GetNumber(int index)
{
    return numbers[index];
}
```

Adjust for the zero-based array index so that `GetNumber(1)` will return the first element value of numbers instead of the second element value, as is the case with the currently shown method.

6. What is wrong with the following array declaration?

```
byte [] ages = new byte [4] {10, 34, 12, 19, 21, 56};
```

7. Write a method called **DisplayArray** that accepts an array reference of base type **int**. The method must be able to print the values of the array object referenced by the argument onscreen, regardless of the array length.

8. Write a method with the following header:

```
int [] AddNumber(int [] tempArray, int num)
```

that will add **num** to every element of **tempArray** and return this array back to the caller.

9. Consider the following two declarations:

   ```
   int [] myNumbers = {2,4,6,8};
   int [] yourNumbers;
   ```

   Suppose that we assign `myNumbers` to `yourNumbers` and add 10 to the first element of `yourNumbers`, as in the following lines

   ```
   yourNumbers = myNumbers;
   yourNumbers[0] += 10;
   ```

   What is the value of `myNumbers[0]` after these statements have been executed? Explain what is going on.

10. What is the fundamental difference between cloning an array with the array's `Clone` method and simply assigning the array variable value to another array variable?

11. Consider the two arrays from question 9, `myNumbers` and `yourNumbers`. Suppose each array variable references a different array object. Both these array objects contain exactly the same number of array elements and each pair of corresponding array elements have the same value. Will the following comparison be `true` or `false`? Explain why.

    ```
    (MyNumbers == YourNumbers)
    ```

12. Your program contains a class called `Planet`. You are writing another class called `SolarSystem`, which in this case must consist of 10 planets. You want to represent the 10 planets in an array of 10 planets. Write the declaration you must insert into the `SolarSystem` class to enable the representation of the 10 planets.

Programming Exercises

1. Implement a class called `ArrayMath`, containing the following methods to perform calculations on arrays:

   - A method called `ArrayAverage` that, as an argument, accepts an array of base type `double (of any length)` and returns the average of this array.
   - A method called `ArraySum` that accepts two arrays of base type `int`. The two arrays must have identical length. The method will add together each corresponding pair of array elements from the two arrays. Each sum is assigned to a corresponding element of a third array, which finally is returned to the caller.
   - A method called `ArrayMax` that finds and returns the maximum value in an array of base type `int`. The array argument can be of any length.

   Write the code to test this class and its methods.

2. Write the basic parts of a car game program. The program must include a `Car` class with the following members:

   - An instance variable called `position` of type `int`

- A method with the header `public void MoveForward(int distance)` that adds `distance` to the `position` instance variable
- A method with the header `public void Reverse(int distance)` that deducts `distance` from `position`
- A method called `GetPosition` that simply returns the value of `position` to the caller

Furthermore, the program must contain a class called `CarGame` that (by using an array) contains 5 objects of type `Car`. It must be possible to move each car (forward and reverse) and to get the position of each of the cars by providing an array index of the corresponding car.

Write a small test program to ensure that the two classes function correctly.

CHAPTER 11

ARRAYS PART II: MULTIDIMENSIONAL ARRAYS—SEARCHING AND SORTING ARRAYS

You will learn about the following in this chapter:

- Arrays with more than one dimension
- How to declare, define, and initialize multidimensional arrays
- How two-dimensional arrays form an invaluable data structure when
  - Constructing computer games involving boards or maps
  - Tracking information that is best presented in a table of rows and columns
- The differences between rectangular and jagged multidimensional arrays
- The invaluable relationship between nested loop constructs and multidimensional arrays
- How the `foreach` iteration statement can simplify the code significantly compared to other iteration statements when traversing a multidimensional array
- The most commonly used built-in array methods supplied by the .NET Framework
- Two classic computational problems associated with arrays—sorting and searching
- The famous Bubble Sort algorithm and how to apply it to sort a one-dimensional array
- The performance of the Bubble Sort algorithm compared with that of .NET's built-in array sorting method. This provides another example of why code reuse is so important in software development.
- Two classic search algorithms—The slow Sequential Search and the speedy Binary Search—and how to implement them
- How .NET's pre-built array methods can be used to search an array

Multidimensional Arrays

Just as a picture has two dimensions and the room you sit inside is three dimensional, a line only has one dimension and a dot zero dimensions. The five values represented by the array variable `accountBalances` of Listing 10.1 in Chapter 10, "Arrays Part I: Array Essentials," can be viewed as being positioned on a line one after the other, and each value can be accessed by specifying exactly one index. For those reasons, `accountBalances`, along with the remaining arrays used in the previous chapter, are called *one-dimensional arrays*.

C# allows you to specify arrays of two dimensions, requiring two indexes to identify an array element, and arrays of three dimensions calling for three indexes. In fact, C# lets you specify arrays with any number of dimensions you might require.

Dimensions

The number of dimensions indicates the number of extensions in a given direction. It is possible for us to visualize the implications of zero, one, two, and three dimensions, as shown in Figure 11.1.

FIGURE 11.1
Visualizing zero, one, two, and three dimensions.

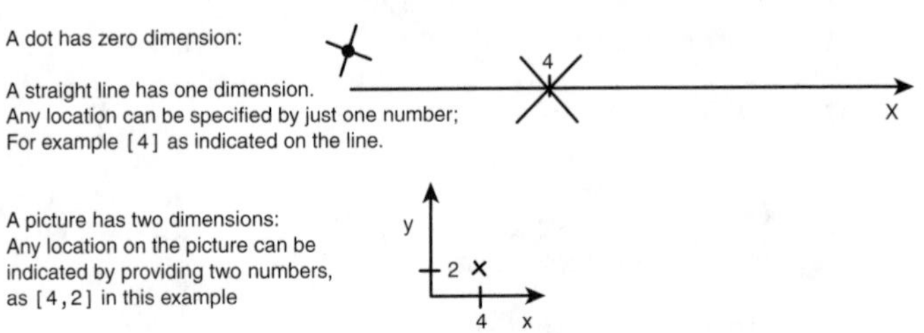

A dot has zero dimension:
A straight line has one dimension.
Any location can be specified by just one number;
For example [4] as indicated on the line.
4
X
A picture has two dimensions:
Any location on the picture can be
indicated by providing two numbers,
as [4,2] in this example
y
2
4
x

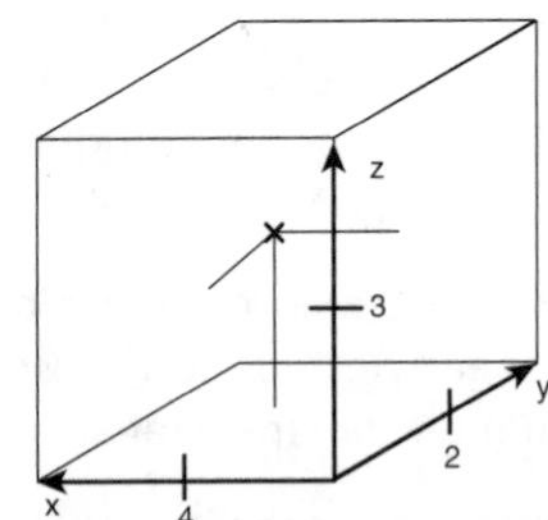

The space in a box has three dimensions
Any location (point) inside the box can
be specified by providing three numbers as
[4,2,3] in this example.
z
3
y
2
x
4

Even though it is difficult (near impossible) to visualize more than three dimensions, it is possible and sometimes useful to include arrays with four or more dimensions in a program. To avoid headaches and sleepless nights wondering about the warped and weird worlds of many dimensions, all you need to know here is that the number of indexes needed to reference an array element is equal to the number of dimensions of the array.

Note

An array is n-dimensional if it has n indexes.

Consequently, you could regard phone numbers of seven digits, such as 8327881, to be seven dimensional in that the seven indexes give you access to exactly one telephone that can be viewed as an array element. In a C# program that simulates phones and phone calls, we could even declare an array variable called `phone` and access a specific phone with the command `phone[8, 3, 2, 7, 8, 8, 1]`.

In this section, you will see how we declare and work with multidimensional arrays.

Two-Dimensional Arrays

Rather than looking at seven dimensional arrays, let's start with an example that utilizes an array of two dimensions.

Recall our elevator simulation program from Chapter 5, "Your First Object-Oriented C# Program." A floor request was defined as a "person" requesting to be taken to a particular "floor" by "pressing" a "button" in the "elevator." Suppose we intend to track the number of floor requests given to an elevator over a seven-day period on an hourly basis. If done manually by simply sitting inside a real elevator, a person could write these statistics down in a table similar to that shown in Table 11.1. In this particular case, she has already recorded the first two hours of the first day; the elevator here received 89 and 65 requests, respectively.

To specify any particular hour, we need to provide two indexes—the day and the hour. For that reason, the table is two-dimensional. In this case `(day:1, hour:0)` is equal to 89.

Table 11.1 Manually Recording Floor Requests Hourly for Seven Days

	Hour 0	Hour 1	Hour 2	Hour 3	...	Hour 23
Day 1	89	65		...		
Day 2				...		
...	...	...	...	...	...	...
Day 7						

Note: Hour 0 is the hour from midnight 00:00 until one o'clock 01:00.

Declaring and Defining Two-Dimensional Arrays

How can we effectively implement the equivalent of a floor request tracking system in a C# program? For starters, we need a data structure to contain the data shown in Table 11.1. We could attempt to use a one-dimensional array with 168 (7 × 24) entries, but it would be a cumbersome task to determine which statistic goes with which index, not to mention the difficulty of interpreting this array. For example, who would know that index [79] is equivalent to day 4/hour 7? If, instead, we apply a two-dimensional array, we can allow one index for the row and one index for the column, letting us express day 4, hour 7 as [3,7]. (Note that day 4 becomes index 3 due to the zero-based index, whereas hour 7 remains index 7 because the first hour is hour 0, as shown in Table 11.1)

Note

Just as the first entry of a one-dimensional array has index zero, multidimensional arrays also begin their indexes with zero. Consequently, the first element in a two-dimensional array is at [0,0].

If we call our two-dimensional array **`requests`** with the base type **`ushort`**, we can declare and define it as shown in Figure 11.2.

FIGURE 11.2
Declaring and defining the two-dimensional requests array.

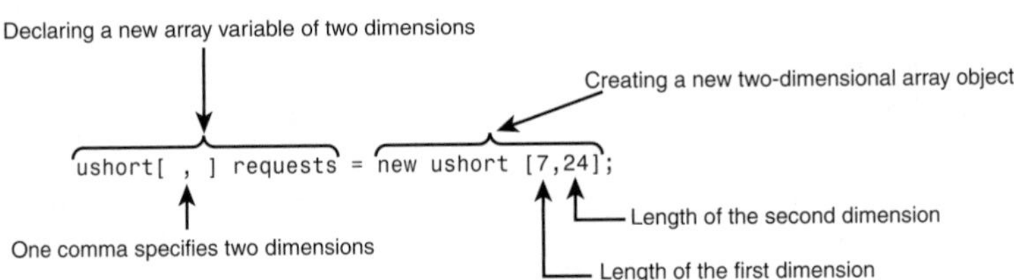

The above statement can as with one-dimensional arrays be broken up into two lines and written as:

```
ushort[ , ] requests;
requests = new ushort [7,24];
```

This is very similar to declaring a one-dimensional array. However, one comma is needed inside the otherwise empty pair of square brackets of the declaration, and two numbers (7 and 24 in this case) separated by a comma are needed to specify the lengths of the two dimensions when creating a new array with the `new` keyword.

The array variable declaration, the creation of the new array object, and the assignment of the array object's reference to the array variable (shown as the first source code line in Figure 11.2) can (as with a one-dimensional array) be broken up into two statements. The result of this break up is shown in the lower part of Figure 11.2.

Our new array can be depicted as shown in Figure 11.3.

The first dimension, specifying a particular day, has index values ranging from 0 to 6, and the second dimension, indicating the hour, ranges from 0 to 23. To access the fourth hour of the third day, you need to write the following:

```
requests[2,3]
```

where 2 signifies the third day, and 3 signifies the fourth hour.

FIGURE 11.3
The two dimensional array: *requests*.

requests[0,0]	requests[0,1]	requests[0,2]	requests[0,3]	...	requests[0,23]
89	65				

requests[1,0]	requests[1,1]	requests[1,2]	requests[1,3]	...	requests[1,23]

...

requests[6,0]	requests[6,1]	requests[6,2]	requests[6,3]	...	requests[6,23]

Note

By convention, the first index of a two-dimensional array denotes the row of its corresponding table and the second index corresponds to the column.

Accessing the Elements of a Two-Dimensional Array

After declaring the array variable and assigning it a two-dimensional array object reference, we are ready to access the individual array elements.

Apart from the extra indexes needed to identify an array element of a two-dimensional array, an array element of a two-dimensional array is applied in the same fashion and acts in the same way as that of a one-dimensional array. Consequently, it can be used in the same context as a single variable with the same type as its base type. For example, we could assign the value 89 to the first hour of the first day by writing the following:

```
requests[0,0] = (ushort) 89;
```

Notice the cast (`ushort`) applied in this line. In our case, the base type of `requests` is `ushort`. Because 89 is of type `int`, and because there is no implicit conversion path specified from `int` to `ushort`, we need to apply the cast operator `(ushort)`.

We can also involve the array elements in calculations. The following line assigns the total number of requests for the first three hours of the fourth day to a variable called `subTotal`:

```
subTotal = (ushort) (requests[3,0] + requests[3,1] + requests[3,2]);
```

As you will see in Listing 11.3, a two nested loop construct is primordial for traversing the elements of a two dimensional array. For that reason, I will spend a bit of time on the inner logic of this symbiotic relationship.

Recall that a one-dimensional array can be traversed with just one `for` loop, as shown in Listing 11.1.

LISTING 11.1 A Single `for` Loop Traversing a One-Dimensional Array

```
...
int [] myArray = new int [24];
```

LISTING 11.1 continued

```
for (int j = 0; j < 24, j++)
{
        ...
        ... myArray[j] ...
        ...
}
...
```

Note that the source code of Listing 11.1 does not compile.

The effect of this loop body is illustrated in Figure 11.4, which shows flow of control in the `for` loop and how this relates to which array element is being visited. During the first loop, `myArray[0]` is accessed because `j` is zero, the second execution of the loop body accesses `myArray[1]`, and this cycle continues until the loop body has been repeated 24 times. When `j` is 24, the for `loop` is terminated because the loop condition `j < 24` is `false`. Notice that if `myArray` in this example represented the hours of one single day, we would visit every single hour through the `for` loop shown in Listing 11.1.

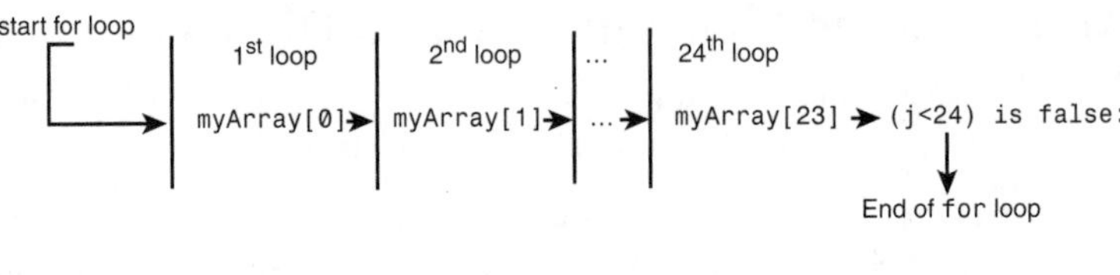

FIGURE 11.4
Single *for* loop traversing a one dimensional array.

The array variable `requests` not only represent the hours of one day but seven days. Thus, by repeating the process of Figure 11.4 seven times, we can visit all hours of not just one day but seven days. We can construct this functionality by inserting the previous `for` loop into another `for` loop that repeats itself seven times. This has been done in the source code extract found in Listing 11.2.

LISTING 11.2 Two Nested *for* Loops Traversing a Two- Dimensional Array

```
...
ushort [ , ] requests = new ushort [7,24];
...
for (int i = 0; i < 7; i++)
{
    ...
    for (int j = 0; j < 24 ; j++)
    {
        ...
            //this block is repeated seven times
        ... requests[i, j] ...
        ...
```

LISTING 11.2 continued

```
        }
    ...
    }
    ...
```

Note that the source code of Listing 11.2 does not compile.

The flow of control when executing the nested `for` loop construct of Listing 11.2 is illustrated in Figure 11.5, and as in Figure 11.4, it shows which array element is visited during which loop. Execution starts in the upper-left corner of the figure where the execution of the loop body of the outer loop is commenced. Because this outer loop body consists of the `for` loop presented in Listing 11.2, its execution is similar to that of Figure 11.4. The only difference being that an index (`i`) indicating the day being processed is added. The first execution of the outer loop body is more or less a repeat of Figure 11.4. In fact, all seven executions of the outer loop body have this appearance. By the time `i` is 24 and `j` is 7, all array elements have been visited once and the nested loop is terminated.

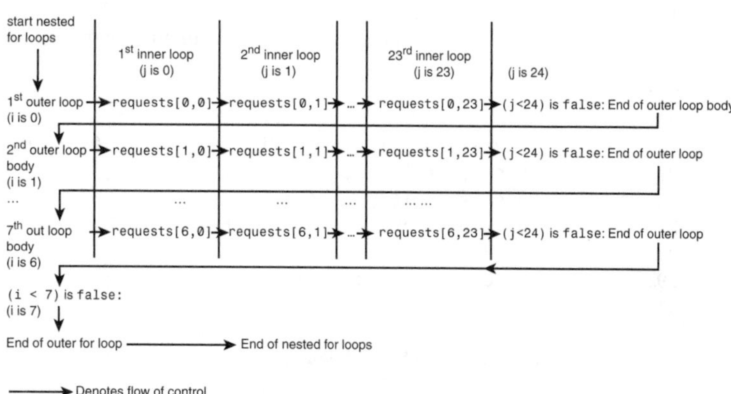

FIGURE 11.5
Nested *for* loops to traverse an entire two-dimensional array.

Listing 11.3 utilizes the `requests` array to hold the number of requests given to an elevator during each hour over a seven-day period. For simplicity, the program generates the number of requests per hour randomly by applying the `System.Random` class you have met previously (see lines 8, 18, and 20). The elevator is assumed to be the busiest between 8 in the morning and 6 in the evening when the number of requests will be between 20 and 99 (see line 20). If outside these hours, the number of requests will be between 1 and 10 (see line 18).

The numbers of requests are stored in `requests` (see line 7) and printed in a table with 7 rows and 24 columns, as shown in the sample output after Listing 11.3. `requests` is then used to calculate the total requests per day and the average requests per hour. Both statistics are also displayed in the sample output.

LISTING 11.3 `ElevatorRequestTracker.cs`

```
using System;

class ElevatorRequestTracker
{
    public static void Main()
    {
        ushort[,] requests = new ushort [7,24];
        Random randomizer = new Random();
        int sum;

         // Randomly generate number of requests received for every
         // hour of the day and every day of the week.
        for (int i = 0; i < 7; i++)
        {
            for (int j = 0; j < 24 ; j++)
            {
                if ((j < 8) || (j > 18))
                    requests[i,j] = (ushort)randomizer.Next(1,10);
                else
                    requests[i,j] = (ushort)randomizer.Next(20,99);
            }
        }

         //Print out table showing requests of all hours of every day
        Console.WriteLine("                                       Hour\n");
        Console.Write("    ");
        for (int i = 0; i < 24; i++)
        {
            Console.Write("{0,2} ",i);
        }

        Console.Write("\nDay");
        for (int i = 0; i < 7; i++)
        {
            Console.Write("\n{0}   ", (i + 1));
            for (int j = 0; j < 24; j++)
            {
                Console.Write("{0,2} ", requests[i,j]);
            }
        }

         // Calculate and print total number of requests on a daily basis
        Console.WriteLine("\n\nTotal number of request per day:\n");
        for (int i = 0; i < 7; i++)
        {
            sum = 0;
            for (int j = 0; j < 24; j++)
                sum += requests[i,j];
            Console.WriteLine("Day {0}: {1}", (i + 1), sum);
        }

         // Calculate and print average requests on an hourly basis
```

LISTING 11.3 continued

```
53:         Console.Write("\nAverage requests per hour:\n\nHour:");
54:         for (int i = 0; i < 24; i++)
55:         {
56:             Console.Write("{0,2} ",i);
57:         }
58:         Console.Write("\nAver:");
59:         for (int j = 0; j < 24; j++)
60:         {
61:             sum = 0;
62:             for (int i = 0; i < 7; i++)
63:                 sum += requests[i,j];
64:             Console.Write("{0,2} ", (sum / 7));
65:         }
66:     }
67: }
```

```
        Hour

     0  1  2  3  4  5  6  7  8  9 10 11 12 13 14 15 16 17 18 19 20 21 22 23
Day
1    7  8  3  6  8  2  2  5 92 67 37 38 87 53 96 29 96 96 35  7  3  2  8  1
2    7  7  2  1  5  6  4  9 34 58 39 88 28 76 58 88 80 68 40  2  7  7  2  6
3    6  4  5  5  6  3  8  5 98 38 86 31 22 36 20 40 37 44 23  4  2  1  1  3
4    5  3  9  7  9  6  4  1 59 61 49 29 34 90 43 93 69 76 88  8  8  4  8  6
5    6  1  9  4  7  8  5  5 50 37 20 42 39 33 67 49 88 84 71  5  8  8  1  3
6    1  2  7  5  3  2  4  2 58 54 26 93 74 20 44 73 24 86 78  9  8  1  7  5
7    2  5  1  1  7  4  7  7 92 68 47 66 26 20 43 38 86 87 83  8  1  7  7  8

Total number of request per day:

Day 1: 788
Day 2: 722
Day 3: 528
Day 4: 769
Day 5: 650
Day 6: 686
Day 7: 721

Average requests per hour:

Hour: 0  1  2  3  4  5  6  7  8  9 10 11 12 13 14 15 16 17 18 19 20 21 22 23
Aver: 4  4  5  4  6  4  4  4 69 54 43 55 44 46 53 58 68 77 59  6  5  4  4  4
```

Note:

- Because the numbers of requests are generated randomly, they will vary between different test runs of the program.

Line 7 declares the two-dimensional array variable `requests` as shown earlier. Line 8 declares `randomizer` to hold a reference to an object of type `Random` (or `System.Random`) and assigns it a reference to a new object of type `Random`. `randomizer` is now ready to generate random numbers. Lines 13–22 contain two nested `for` loops. The outer `for` loop lets `i` move from 0 to 6 by increments of one (see line 13); the inner `for` loop dictates `j` to move from 0 to 23 (see line 15), also by increments of one. As a result, the nested `for` loop construct is able to traverse our two-dimensional array and access every single element when `i` and `j` are used as indexes to specify an element in `requests` as in `requests[i, j]`. Lines 18 and 20 do exactly this by positioning requests[i,j] in the loop body of the innermost `for` loop and assigns a random number to every array element of `requests`. Notice that an `if` statement (beginning in line 17) is applied to determine the size of the random number assigned to each element. If `j` is outside the hours between 8 and 18 (`if ((j < 8) || (j > 18))`, assign a random number between 1 and 10 (line 18). If `j` is inside the hours between 8 and 18, assign a random number between 20 and 99 to the `requests` element (line 20). Recall that the argument of the `Next` method of `randomizer` takes two arguments—the former sets the lower limit for the random value returned, and the latter sets the upper limit.

Lines 24–40 are concerned with printing the full table of request numbers contained in requests. Lines 25–30 simply print the headings for the hours. Lines 32–40 once again uses a nested `for` loop; this time to print the full contents of requests.

Lines 44–50 calculate the total number of requests given for each day. For every day processed, we need to set the `sum` variable to zero (line 46), add together all requests for the 24 hours of that day (lines 47 and 48), and print this result to the console (line 49).

Lines 53–65 calculate and print the average number of requests for each hour during the seven days. Instead of calculating the sum of the entries in an entire row of the requests table, as in lines 44–50, we need to sum the entries in an entire column and then divide this result by seven to find the average (line 64). The inner `for` loop of lines 44–50 becomes the outer `for` loop, and the outer `for` loop becomes the inner `for` loop, as shown in lines 59–65.

Consider accessing an element of the array `requests` with the following command (as in Listing 11.3):

```
requests[i, j]
```

If `i` is held fixed and `j` is varying (for example, during a loop), programmers often say that a *row of the array is being accessed*. Conversely, if `j` is fixed and `i` varied, we say that a *column is being accessed*.

Note

In general, to traverse an entire n-dimensional array, use n nested loops and access the array elements from the loop body of the innermost loop.

Viewing the Two-Dimensional Array As an Array of Arrays

It is possible to think of the two dimensional array `requests` as an array of arrays. If we focus for a moment on the first dimension of `requests` (representing days), we can view the seven days as a one-dimensional array (see Figure 11.6). If we then include the hours, each "day" element can be regarded as consisting of a one dimensional "hour" array.

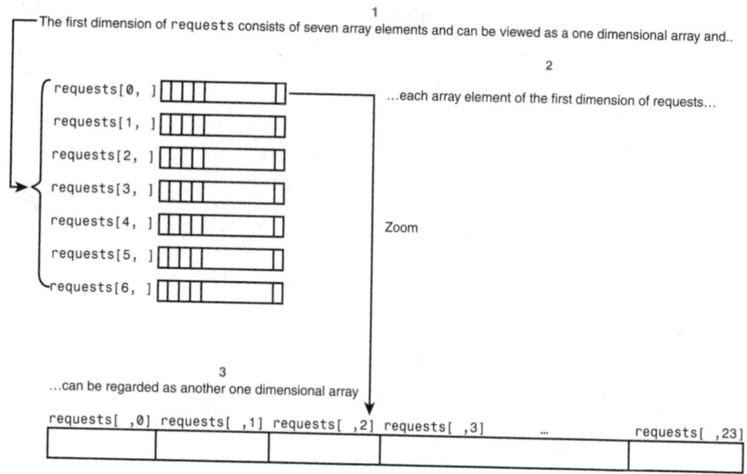

FIGURE 11.6
A two dimensional array can be viewed as an array of arrays.

Notice that every "hour" array in **requests** is of the same length (24); in other words, every row as viewed in Figure 11.3 is of the same length. Consequently, **requests** can be called a rectangular array.

When the rows of a two-dimensional array are all of the same length, the array is said to be *rectangular*.

This term can also be used to describe an array of multiple dimensions. An array for which it is true that any dimension can be viewed to contain one dimensional arrays all with the same length is said to be a *rectangular array*.

Case Study: The "Find the Tropical Island" Game

For a moment, let's put the banks, account balances, and elevators to rest. Instead, the game presented here lets you "travel" to an exotic tropical island…if you can find it. You are flying an airplane and are on your way to this paradise when the navigation system suddenly breaks down and looses part of its ability to communicate with you (due to a software bug). The only way to navigate now is through trial (qualified guessing) and error, accompanied by feedback from the navigation system, which now only provides a hint of the island's location relative to that of each guess. A guess consists of two numbers (a row and a column) specifying a point on a map. When the guess is entered into the navigation system, it will tell you whether the island is

- To the East or the West of the point (guess)
- To the North or the South of the point (guess)
- If the row of the point (guess) is the same as that of the island's location (on the same horizontal line)
- If the column of the point (guess) is the same as that of the island's (on the same vertical line)

The trial and error will continue until you enter the coordinates that match those of the island's location.

Note

True story: A specific type of fighter plane was found to flip upside down every time it crossed the equator during its first test flights, providing quite a shock to its pilot. The software bug causing this problem was fortunately detected and rectified soon after.

Software specification:

We want to write a program to simulate the situation just described. The user is initially shown a map on the console of the area where the island is located, but, due to the faulty navigation system, only water (in the form of the symbol ~) can be seen here initially. The user determines the size of the map at the start of the game by entering the number of rows and columns. Each point on the map can be identified with a row index and a column index. Figure 11.7 indicates the location of point [1,4] in a map of size 5 rows × 10 columns.

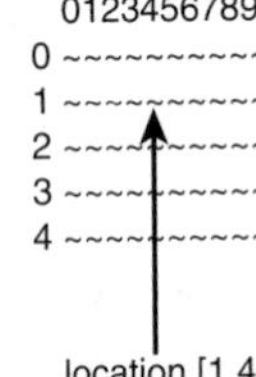

FIGURE 11.7
The map of the faulty navigation system.

The location of the island is chosen randomly and secretly by the program. The island is thus hiding behind one of the "waves" (~) shown in Figure 11.7.

The user is now ready to enter guesses. Each guess must consist of a location with a row and a column number. The feedback accompanying each guess is to be provided in the following way.

Every second guess is evaluated in terms of whether the island is located to the north or the south of the provided guess. All other guesses are evaluated in terms of east/west.

After each guess, a new map is printed on the console with a new letter printed in the location of the guess. An N on the map indicates that the island is to the north of the guess, an S to the south, an E to the east, and a W to the west. If the guess happens to have the same row as the island during a north/south evaluation, an R (for Row) is printed on the map. Similarly, if the guess during an east/west evaluation is found to have the same column as the island, a C is printed on this location. When the pilot (user) through luck (and hopefully clever logical deductions) finally enters a location matching that of the island, an I is printed in this position and the pilot is congratulated along with a message telling her how many (or few) guesses she used in total. The game is then terminated and the user is asked if she cares to play yet another. To see an example of this user interface, please have a look at the sample output after

Listing 11.4, which contains the complete Find the Island program. In this sample, the island is located at position [2,4], indicated by an `I` shown on the last map of the sample output.

The code references in the following section can be found in Listing 11.4 displayed later.

Software design:

Identifying the classes of the program

Two classes can be identified—`NavigationSystem` (lines 51–135) and `FindTheIslandGame` (lines 3–49). The latter is a container for the `Main()` method and controls the main flow of the game.

Identifying the instance variables of the classes:

- *The* `NavigationSystem` *class*—This class utilizes a two-dimensional map. It further holds the secret location of the island and also keeps track of the number of guesses entered by the user. Thus, we need to declare the following four instance variables (see lines 53–56):

```
char [,] map;
byte secretRow = 0;
byte secretColumn = 0;
int guessCounter = 0;
```

- *The* `FindTheIslandGame` *class*—All variables are kept within the `Main()` method (lines 5–48), so there are no instance variables in this class.

Identify the methods in each class:

NavigatorSystem class:

A constructor (lines 58–72) is imperative for the `NavigatorSystem` class to perform the following tasks:

- Create a new map (two-dimensional array object declared in line 53) with the number of rows and columns specified by the user and assign its reference to the `map` instance variable (line 60).
- Randomly generate the secret location of the island and store the coordinates in two variables (here called `secretRow` and `secretColumn`) for later guess evaluations (lines 63 and 64).
- Fill the `map` with "waves" (~) because this is the first view the user gets of the map (lines 66–70).
- Set the `guessCounter` to zero (line 71).

Printing out the `map` with the same style as that shown in the following sample output requires quite a few lines of code due to headings, alignments, and a nested `for` loop. As a result, this procedure deserves its own method, called `PrintMap()` (lines 74–94). Notice that this method is called from outside the `NavigatorSystem` object (line 34), as well as from within (line 127).

The `Main()` method must be able to present the guesses of the user to the `NavigatorSystem` for evaluation and feedback. A method called `EvaluateGuess` (lines 96–129) exposes this functionality. It is equipped with two formal parameters to receive and hold the guess (line 96) during the execution of `EvaluateGuess`. The method will provide most of the feedback by printing the new map onscreen (line 127), but the caller (located in line 41) needs to know whether the guess is correct or not to direct its flow accordingly. Consequently, `EvaluateGuess` must return a `bool` value reflecting whether the guess is correct or not.

The number of guesses should be updated automatically as guesses are received by the `EvaluateGuess` method (see line 100). However, we need an accessor method to retrieve this value. In this case, it is called `GetNumberOfGuesses` (lines 131–134).

`FindTheIslandGame` *class*

Only the `Main()` method is needed in the `FindTheIslandGame` class. It controls the overall flow of the program. It starts a new game, lets the user enter guesses until the island is found, and will repeat these two program segments until the user quits the program.

Internal method design:

1) `Main()` *of the* `FindTheIslandGame` *class:*

The user must be able to play as many games as he or she wishes without having to start the program over and over again. This is a repeated action and calls for a loop construct, and, because the user is always expected to play at least one game, the preferred iteration statement is the `do-while` loop. The loop body of this construct stretches from lines 15–47 and is repeated until the `answer` provided by the user in line 46 is different from "y" (or "Y") (line 47), in which case, the `Main()` method and thereby the program is terminated.

Every individual game is also of a repetitive nature—the user provides guess…the program responds…the user provides guess…the program responds…and so on, until the user provides a correct guess. Because the user will always provide at least one guess, we again apply the `do-while` loop spanning from lines 35–41. The only task of the loop body is to fetch the guess from the user. It is then presented to `navigator` (the `NavigatorSystem` object declared in line 7), which takes care of the evaluation and feedback required. Observe that only when the guess (consisting of `rowGuess` and `columnGuess`) is correct will

```
navigator.EvaluateGuess(rowGuess, columnGuess)
```

of line 41 be `true`; otherwise, it is `false`. The reason why `EvaluateGuess` manages to return `true` only if `rowGuess` and `columnGuess` form a correct guess is explained in Figure 11.8. The arguments `rowGuess` and `columnGuess` are passed along when `EvaluateGuess` is called in line 41, and are assigned to their corresponding formal parameters with the same names (line 96). Only if both `rowGuess` is equal to `secretRow` and `columnGuess` is equal to `secretColumn` in line 104 will the otherwise `false` `islandFound` variable (see line 98) be set to `true` in line 107 before its value is returned in line 128.

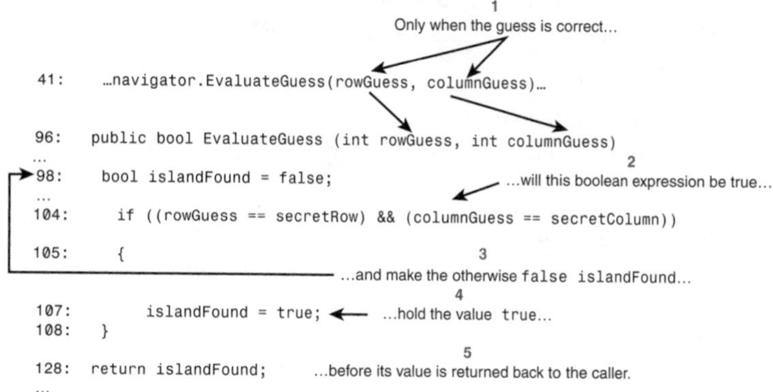
1
Only when the guess is correct...
41: ...navigator.EvaluateGuess(rowGuess, columnGuess)...
96: public bool EvaluateGuess (int rowGuess, int columnGuess)
...
98: bool islandFound = false;
2
...will this boolean expression be true...
...
104: if ((rowGuess == secretRow) && (columnGuess == secretColumn))
105: {
3
...and make the otherwise false islandFound...
4
107: islandFound = true;
...hold the value true...
108: }
5
128: return islandFound;
...before its value is returned back to the caller.
...

FIGURE 11.8
When the guess is correct *`EvaluateGuess`* returns the value *`true`*.

We want the `do-while` loop to repeat itself until the guess is correct. Because a `do-while` loop repeats its loop body until the loop condition (see line 41) is `false`, we must negate the Boolean value returned by the `EvaluateGuess` method by using the not operator (symbolized by `!`) as in the following:

```
!navigator.EvaluateGuess(rowGuess, columnGuess)
```

We thereby terminate the stream of guesses requested, received, and processed when the guess is correct.

2) *The constructor of the* `NavigatorSystem` *class (lines 58–72):*

An important feature of the program is to let the user choose the number of rows and columns of the map at the beginning of every game. All parts of the program relying on the size of the map must adjust to these changing requests from the user. One effective and relatively simple way of doing this is to first create the `map` with its specified measurements (see lines 58 and 60) and then use `System.Array`'s built-in method `GetLenth(`*`<dimension>`*`)` whenever the total number of rows or columns is needed in the program.

Note

The `GetLength(`*`<dimension>`*`)` is another of `System.Array`'s handy built-in methods. It provides the length of the specified dimension of a given multidimensional array. For example, if we declare map as follows:

```
char [ , ] map = new char [5,10];
```

then

```
map.GetLength(0)
```

will return the length of the first dimension, in this case, 5, and

```
map.GetLength(1)
```

returns the length of the second dimension, which is 10.

This strategy is not only used in lines 63, 64, 66, and 68 of the constructor, but also in other parts of the program (lines 79, 87, and 90).

In lines 63 and 64, the secret row and column numbers cannot be any greater than the number of rows and columns respectively in the map. To provide the correct restrictions to the random number generator `randomizer`, the upper limits are then set to `map.GetLength(0)-1` and `map.GetLength(1)-1`, respectively.

In many regards, a constructor is similar to a normal method. For example, it might contain formal parameters in its header, as shown in line 58. So whenever a new `NavigationSystem` object is created, as in line 22 (see Figure 11.9), the arguments provided in the parentheses after the classname must match the formal parameters of the constructor (line 58). The values of these arguments will then be transferred to the formal parameters, which then can be applied during the execution of the constructor body.

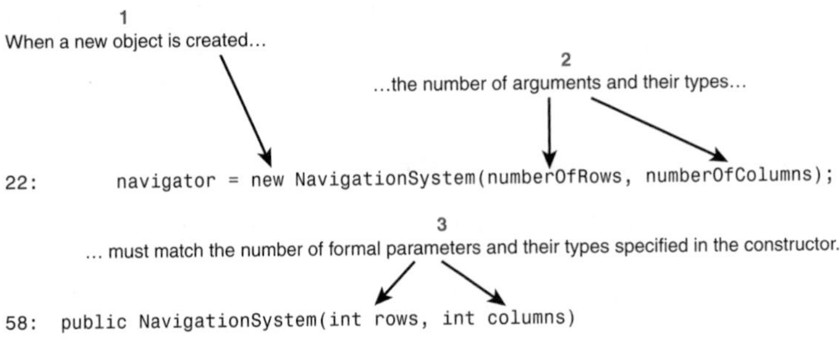

FIGURE 11.9
Formal parameters of a constructor.

3) Evaluating a guess in the `EvaluateGuess` *method (lines 96–129):*

If the guess is correct (making the Boolean expression of line 104 true), there is no need to conduct any further analyses; we only need to assign the letter I to the location (line 106), print out the map (line 127), and return the value `true` (lines 107 and 128).

On the other hand, if the guess is incorrect, `EvaluateGuess` needs to relate `guess` to the secret position of the island. For every second guess, the guess must be evaluated in terms of north/south direction, all other guesses in terms of east/west. The north/south analysis is performed in lines 111–116 if `guessCounter` is found to be even in line 109, and the east/west analysis in lines 120–125 is performed if `guessCounter` is odd.

Figure 11.10 illustrates the directions used in the game. An island has been positioned arbitrarily in a map at location [2,4]. Thirteen locations and their corresponding letters are shown along with their meaning. A corresponding `true` Boolean expression is further shown for each letter. For example, according to the first row of the table, an N is equivalent to `(rowGuess > secretRow)` being `true`.

We now can implement this logic in our `EvaluateGuess` method that spans lines 104–126.

FIGURE 11.10
Navigating the map.

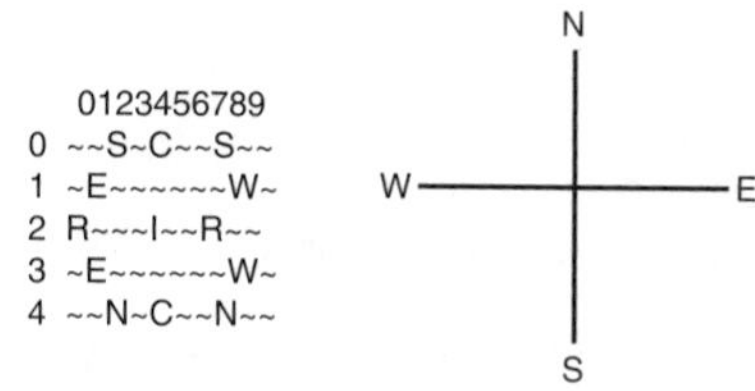

Letter in the map and its meaning	Corresponding true boolean expression
N: Island is to the north of location	(RowGuess > secretRow)
S: Island is to the south of location	(RowGuess < secretRow)
E: Isand is to the south of location	(ColumnGuess < secretColumn)
W: Island is to the west of location	(ColumnGuess > secretColumn)
R: location is on the correct row but wrong row	(rowGuess == secretRow)&& (rowColumn !=secretColumn)
C: Location is on the correct column but wrong row	(columnGuess == secretColumn) && (rowGuess !== secretRow)
I: Correct location	(rowGuess ==secretRow) && (ColumnGuess == secretColumn)

N, S and R result from north/south evaluations
E,W and C result from east/west evaluations

LISTING 11.4 `FindTheIslandGame.cs`

```
using System;

class FindTheIslandGame
{
    public static void Main()
    {
        NavigationSystem navigator;
        int numberOfRows = 0;
        int numberOfColumns = 0;
        byte rowGuess = 0;
        byte columnGuess = 0;
        string answer;

        do
        {
             //Let user determine the size of the map
            Console.WriteLine("First Choose size of map: ");
            Console.Write("Enter number of rows: ");
            numberOfRows = Convert.ToInt32(Console.ReadLine());
            Console.Write("Enter number of columns: ");
            numberOfColumns = Convert.ToInt32(Console.ReadLine());
            navigator = new NavigationSystem(numberOfRows,
            ➥ numberOfColumns);

            Console.WriteLine("\nBelow is a map of the ocean:\n" +
                "There is a hidden island behind one of the waves\n" +
```

LISTING 11.4 continued

```
                    "Can you find it?\n" +
                    "Make a (qualified) guess by entering a row and
                    ➥ a column\n" +
                    "Every second guess is evaluated in East West
                    ➥ direction\n" +
                    "The remaining guesses in North South direction\n" +
                    "An E in the map means the Island is to the East of
                    ➥ this point\n" +
                    "W means to the west; N to the North and S to the
                    ➥ South\n" +
                    "R means correct row but wrong column\n" +
                    "C means correct column but wrong row\n");
                navigator.PrintMap();
                do
                {
                    Console.Write("\nEnter row: ");
                    rowGuess = Convert.ToByte(Console.ReadLine());
                    Console.Write("Enter column: ");
                    columnGuess = Convert.ToByte(Console.ReadLine());
                } while (!navigator.EvaluateGuess(rowGuess, columnGuess));
                Console.WriteLine("\nWell done! The letter I marks
                ➥ the island");
                Console.WriteLine("You found the island in {0} guesses",
                navigator.GetNumberOfGuesses());
                Console.WriteLine("\nCare to play another game? Y)es N)o");
                answer = Console.ReadLine().ToUpper();
            } while (answer == "Y");
        }
}

class NavigationSystem
{
    char [,] map;
    byte secretRow = 0;
    byte secretColumn = 0;
    int guessCounter = 0;

    public NavigationSystem(int rows, int columns)
    {
        map = new char [rows, columns];
         //Randomly choose a secret location for the island.
        Random randomizer = new Random();
        secretRow = (byte)randomizer.Next(0, map.GetLength(0)-1);
        secretColumn = (byte)randomizer.Next(0, map.GetLength(1)-1);
         // Fill the map with ~ to symbolize waves
        for (int i = 0; i < map.GetLength(0); i++)
        {
            for(int j = 0; j < map.GetLength(1); j++)
            map[i,j] = '~';
        }
        guessCounter = 0;
    }
```

LISTING 11.4 continued

```

    public void PrintMap()
    {
        byte count = 0;

        Console.Write("  ");
        for (int i = 0; i < map.GetLength(1); i++)
        {
            if (count == 10)
                count = 0;
            Console.Write(count);
            count++;
        }
        Console.WriteLine();
        for (int j = 0; j < map.GetLength(0); j++)
        {
            Console.Write(j + ((j < 10) ? " " : ""));
            for(int i = 0; i < map.GetLength(1); i++)
            Console.Write(map[j,i]);
            Console.WriteLine();
        }
    }

    public bool EvaluateGuess (int rowGuess, int columnGuess)
    {
        bool islandFound = false;

        guessCounter++;
         //If location is not found and guessCounter is even
         //then check guess for North South direction
         //otherwise check for East West direction
        if ((rowGuess == secretRow) && (columnGuess == secretColumn))
        {
            map[rowGuess, columnGuess] = 'I';
            islandFound = true;
        }
        else if (guessCounter % 2 == 0)
        {
            if (rowGuess < secretRow)
                map[rowGuess, columnGuess] = 'S';
            else if (rowGuess > secretRow)
                map[rowGuess, columnGuess] = 'N';
            else
                map[rowGuess, columnGuess] = 'R';
        }
        else
        {
            if (columnGuess < secretColumn)
                map[rowGuess, columnGuess] = 'E';
            else if (columnGuess > secretColumn)
                map[rowGuess, columnGuess] = 'W';
            else
```

LISTING 11.4 continued

```
                map[rowGuess, columnGuess] = 'C';
        }
        PrintMap();
        return islandFound;
    }

    public int GetNumberOfGuesses()
    {
        return guessCounter;
    }
}
```

```
First Choose size of map:
Enter number of rows: 5<enter>
Enter number of columns: 10<enter>

Below is a map of the ocean:
There is a hidden island behind one of the waves
Can you find it?
Make a (qualified) guess by entering a row and a column
Every second guess is evaluated in East West direction
The remaining guesses in North South direction
An E in the map means the Island is to the East of this point
W means to the west; N to the North and S to the South
R means correct row but wrong column
C means correct column but wrong row

  0123456789
0 ~~~~~~~~~~
1 ~~~~~~~~~~
2 ~~~~~~~~~~
3 ~~~~~~~~~~
4 ~~~~~~~~~~

Enter row: 3<enter>
Enter column: 7<enter>
  0123456789
0 ~~~~~~~~~~
1 ~~~~~~~~~~
2 ~~~~~~~~~~
3 ~~~~~~~W~~
4 ~~~~~~~~~~

Enter row: 1<enter>
Enter column: 2<enter>
  0123456789
0 ~~~~~~~~~~
1 ~~S~~~~~~~
2 ~~~~~~~~~~
3 ~~~~~~~W~~
4 ~~~~~~~~~~
```

```
Enter row: 2<enter>
Enter column: 3<enter>
  0123456789
0 ~~~~~~~~~~
1 ~~S~~~~~~~
2 ~~~E~~~~~~
3 ~~~~~~~W~~
4 ~~~~~~~~~~

Enter row: 4<enter>
Enter column: 5<enter>
  0123456789
0 ~~~~~~~~~~
1 ~~S~~~~~~~
2 ~~~E~~~~~~
3 ~~~~~~~W~~
4 ~~~~~N~~~~

Enter row: 3<enter>
Enter column: 4<enter>
  0123456789
0 ~~~~~~~~~~
1 ~~S~~~~~~~
2 ~~~E~~~~~~
3 ~~~~C~~W~~
4 ~~~~~N~~~~

Enter row: 2<enter>
Enter column: 4<enter>
  0123456789
0 ~~~~~~~~~~
1 ~~S~~~~~~~
2 ~~~EI~~~~~
3 ~~~~C~~W~~
4 ~~~~~N~~~~

Well done! The letter I marks the island
You found the island in 6 guesses

Care to play another game? Y)es N)o
N<enter>
```

Jagged Arrays

A two- (or more) dimensional array does not need to be rectangular, meaning the rows of the array do not need to be of the same length. An array of this kind where different rows have different numbers of columns is called a *jagged array*. To illustrate a jagged array, let's recollect the rectangular `requests` array from Listing 11.3 that was used to collect elevator requests for seven days, and for 24 hours every day. Line 7 declared and defined it as follows:

```
ushort [ , ] requests = new ushort [7,24];
```

If, instead of collecting elevator requests for 24 hours every single day, you want to collect data for say, 18 hours during the fourth and the fifth day, and merely for 12 hours the sixth and seventh day, you can tailor make the array to mirror this need. The corresponding array would be jagged and declared as

```
ushort [] [] requests;
requests = new ushort [7][];
requests[0] = new ushort [24];
requests[1] = new ushort [24];
requests[2] = new ushort [24];
requests[3] = new ushort [18];
requests[4] = new ushort [18];
requests[5] = new ushort [12];
requests[6] = new ushort [12];
```

arrays of length 24 assigned to first three array elements

arrays of length 18 assigned to fourth and fifth array element

arrays of length 12 assigned to sixth and seventh array element

The fact that a two-dimensional array is an array of arrays becomes particularly obvious during the declaration just shown. The first line

```
ushort [] [] requests;
```

contains two empty pairs of square brackets to symbolize this characteristic, and the next line

```
requests = new ushort [7][];
```

assigns an array object reference to **requests** with the following characteristics—it contains 7 array elements (the length is 7), where each array element represents an array of **ushorts** that can be of any length.

We are now free to assign a one-dimensional array of any length to each of these seven array elements. This is done in the next seven lines. For example,

```
requests[4] = new ushort [18];
```

assigns a one-dimensional array of length 18 to the fifth element of **requests**. After the last seven lines shown previously have been executed, **requests** can be illustrated as shown in Figure 11.11.

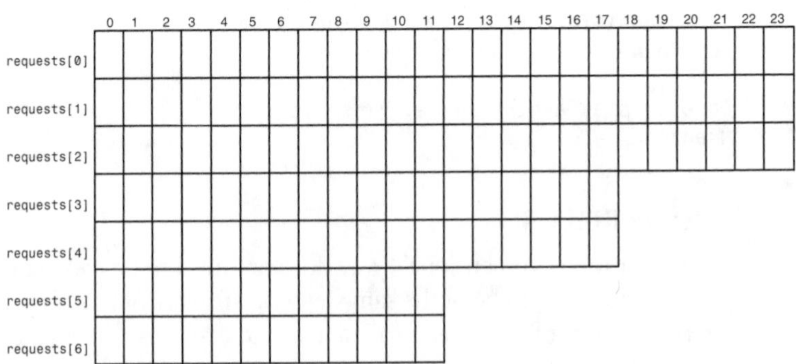

FIGURE 11.11
The jagged array *requests*.

When the rows of a two-dimensional array are not all of the same length, programmers refer to it as a *jagged array*. This can be extended to an array of multiple dimensions. An array for which it is true that one of the dimensions contain one-dimensional arrays of differing lengths, the array is said to be *jagged*.

Sometimes jagged arrays are referred to as *ragged arrays*.

You cannot use the same syntax to access an individual array element of a jagged array as that used for a rectangular array. Instead of providing one pair of square brackets containing two numbers separated by a comma, as in

```
request [3,5]     //only valid for accessing element of a rectangular array
```

you need to provide two pairs of square brackets, each containing an index, as in the following:

```
requests[3][5]    //valid when accessing element of array of arrays
```

Working with Jagged Arrays

If you want to visit every single element of a jagged array, you need to slightly adjust the nested `for` loops used previously to traverse a rectangular array. This is not so much for syntactic reasons as for logic reasons. The outer `for` loop remains untouched. However, because the number of inner loops now varies and is dependant on the loop counter of the outer loop (`i` in this case), we need to involve this variable in the loop condition of the inner loop. This is shown in the next piece of code:

```
for (int i = 0; i < requests.Length; i++)
{
      ...
      for (int j = 0; j < requests[i].Length; j++)
      {
        ...
          requests[i][j]
        ...
      }
```

i is the row index; j the column index

i of the outer loop chooses the correct row length for the loop condition of the inner loop

As the outer loop traverses through each row via the `i` counter, the inner loop is able to constantly adjust to the correct length.

Listing 11.5 puts these pieces together. It is similar to Listing 11.3, but this time utilizes a jagged array to suit a data collection timetable with varying numbers of hours monitored on different days, as shown in Table 11.2.

TABLE 11.2 Timetable for Elevator Requests Monitoring

Day	Number of hours monitored
1	24
2	24
3	24
4	18

TABLE 11.2 continued

Day	Number of hours monitored
5	18
6	12
7	12

The number of requests are generated randomly and assigned to all array elements of `requests`. The resulting jagged table is then printed out (see sample output).

LISTING 11.5 `JaggedElevatorRequests.cs`

```
using System;

class JaggedElevatorRequests
{
    public static void Main()
    {
        Random randomizer = new Random();
        ushort [][] requests;
        requests = new ushort [7][];
        requests[0] = new ushort[24];
        requests[1] = new ushort[24];
        requests[2] = new ushort[24];
        requests[3] = new ushort[18];
        requests[4] = new ushort[18];
        requests[5] = new ushort[12];
        requests[6] = new ushort[12];

         //Insert randomly generated number of requests for each array
         //element of requests.
        for (int i = 0; i < requests.Length; i++)
        {
            for (int j = 0; j < requests[i].Length; j++)
            {
                if ((j < 8) || (j > 18))
                    requests[i][j] = (ushort)randomizer.Next(1,10);
                else
                    requests[i][j] = (ushort)randomizer.Next(20,99);
            }
        }

         //Print out table showing requests of all hours of every day
        Console.WriteLine("                                        Hour\n");
        Console.Write("    ");
        for (int i = 0; i < 24; i++)
        {
            Console.Write("{0,2} ",i);
        }
```

LISTING 11.5 continued

```
        Console.Write("\nDay");
        for (int i = 0; i < requests.Length; i++)
        {
            Console.Write("\n{0}    ", (i + 1));
            for (int j = 0; j < requests[i].Length; j++)
            {
                Console.Write("{0,2} ", requests[i][j]);
            }
        }
    }
}
```

```
                                   Hour
     0  1  2  3  4  5  6  7  8  9 10 11 12 13 14 15 16 17 18 19 20 21 22 23
Day
1    2  7  1  3  4  5  6  9 62 86 39 92 54 65 89 60 62 97 63  4  6  9  4  8
2    2  2  4  5  1  9  3  2 32 75 46 69 47 29 40 76 59 71 97  5  4  7  1  1
3    8  9  7  2  8  4  8  3 49 34 31 36 27 31 89 67 65 30 79  7  3  3  2  4
4    7  8  9  9  9  8  5  4 25 49 73 27 36 29 42 80 85 27
5    3  2  9  1  6  4  7  4 96 38 21 46 83 61 84 44 53 20
6    5  9  3  5  7  7  2  7 57 82 51 55
7    8  9  9  2  9  9  5  7 36 63 33 61
```

All parts of the source code have been explained prior to the source code listing.

The individual rows of a jagged array can, like a one-dimensional array, be initialized at the time the array is created with values written explicitly in the source code. Recall how the one-dimensional array `ages` was initialized by writing:

```
byte [] ages  = {23, 27, 21, 30, 19, 34};
```

Each individual row of a jagged array can be initialized in a similar fashion. If `rainfall` is a jagged array with 4 rows of base type `double` and declared as

```
double [] [] rainfall = new double [3] [];
```

each row can be initialized as shown

```
rainfall[0] = new double[] {23.5, 44.1, 87.3, 89.1};
rainfall[1] = new double[] {22.1, 51.3, 76.2, 12.2, 45.0, 11.9};
rainfall[2] = new double[] {9.0, 13.5};
```

assigning four, six, and two elements to each row, respectively.

Arrays of More Than Two Dimensions

As mentioned earlier, C# lets you work with arrays of more than two dimensions. For example, if you want to collect elevator requests from 10 elevators instead of just one, and for 7 days/24 hours, you can match this requirement with a three-dimensional rectangular array declared as shown in Figure 11.12. The number of commas in the square brackets of the declaration must now be two instead of one; and three numbers, each specifying the length of a dimension, are needed when creating the three-dimensional array object.

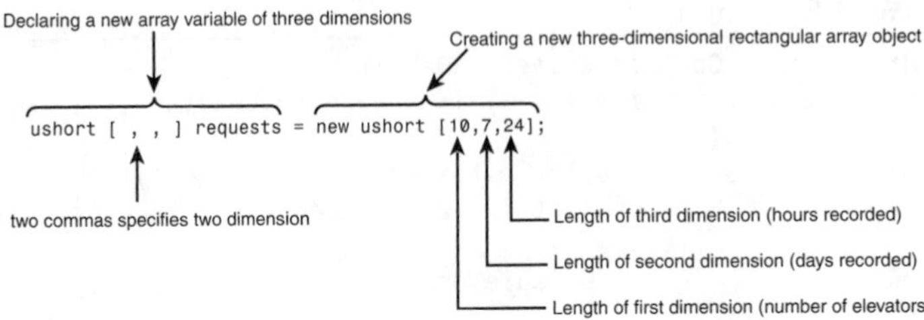

FIGURE 11.12
Declaring and defining the three-dimensional rectangular `requests` array.

To traverse an entire three-dimensional array calls for three nested loops (see Figure 11.13) with the indexed array element positioned in the loop body of the innermost loop.

FIGURE 11.13
Three nested `for` loops traversing three-dimensional array `requests`—incomplete code.

```
for (int i = 0; i < requests.GetLength(0); i++)
{
    ...
    for (int j = 0; j < requests.GetLength(1); j++)
    {
        ...
        for (int k = 0; k < requests.GetLength(2); k++)
        {
          ...
          ...requests[i,j,k]... // positioned in innermost loop.
          ...
        }
        ...
    }
    ...
}
```

Syntax Box 11.1 Declaring and Creating Rectangular Multidimensional Arrays

Multidimensional_rectangular_array_variable_declaration::=
`<Base_type> [ , [ ,..., ] ] <Array_identifier>;`

Note:

- The number of commas in the square brackets `<Base_type>` is one less than the number of dimensions.

Multidimensional_rectangular_array_object_creation::=
`new <Base_type> [<Length_0>, <Length_1> [ , <Length_2> ..., <Length_n>] ]`

Note:

- `<Length_0>` is the length of the first dimension.

```
Assigning reference of new multidimensional rectangular array object
➥ to array variable::=
<Array_identifier> = new <Base_type>
➥ [<Length_0>, <Length_1> [ , <Length_2> ..., <Length_n> ] ];
```

Arrays of three or more dimensions can be jagged. To understand how they are specified, we can imagine them as arrays of arrays of arrays of...and so on. For example, a three-dimensional array can be viewed as an array of two-dimensional arrays, and each two-dimensional array can again be viewed as an array of arrays. Consequently, the previously mentioned rectangular array could be regarded as an array with ten array elements each holding a two-dimensional array. Each of these two-dimensional arrays could again be viewed as an array with 7 array elements, each representing an array of 24 entries. Specifying `requests` to be a jagged array with ten two-dimensional arrays can be done with the following line:

```
ushort [] [] [] requests = new [10] [] [];
```

If we wanted the first dimension of the first two-dimensional array to have seven entries, we could write the following line:

```
requests [0] = new ushort [7][];
```

In our elevator statistics analogy, it means that the first elevator will have space for seven days worth of `requests` numbers.

Finally, we could specify the third day of the first elevator to have, say, 18 entries, and thereby allow us to record 18 hours:

```
requests [0] [2] = new ushort [18];
```

As you can imagine, it is an elaborate job to explicitly write out all the sizes of the different parts of a multidimensional jagged array. However, if the various sizes are determined by a logic system, it is possible to automate the array object creation process with suitable loops.

Syntax Box 11.2 Declaring and Creating Jagged Multidimensional Arrays

```
Multidimensional_jagged_array_variable_declaration::=
<Base_type> [ ] [ ]  [ [ ]...[ ] ] <Array_identifier>;
```

Note:

- The number of square bracket pairs is equal to the number of dimensions of the array.
- As usual, [ ] denotes the square brackets that you see in the source code, whereas *[ ]* encloses optional source code parts.

```
Multidimensional_jagged_array_object_creation::=
new <Base_type> [<Length_0>] [<Length_1>]
➥ [  [<Length_2>] [<Length_3>]...[<Length_n>]  ]
```

Note:

- *<Length_0>* is the length of the first dimension.

```
Assigning reference of new multidimensional jagged
➥ array object to array variable:
<Array_identifier> = new <Base_type> [<Length_0>] [<Length_1>]
➥  [ [<Length_2>] [<Length_3>]...[<Length_n>] ]
```

Accessing Multidimensional Arrays with the `foreach` Statement

Earlier, you saw how a single `foreach` statement could be used to traverse an entire one-dimensional array. A `foreach` statement can also be applied to access multidimensional arrays. When the `foreach` statement is used to traverse a rectangular array, the syntax is extremely simple compared to the nested `for` loops. For example, to traverse the entire three-dimensional `requests` array declared and defined as follows

```
ushort [ , , ] requests = new ushort [10,7,24];
```

so the program can calculate the sum of the values of all its array elements, we merely need to write one `foreach` statement:

```
foreach (ushort temp in requests)
{
    totalSum += temp;
}
```

No, I didn't miss anything, that's all there is to it.

The `foreach` statement will access the array elements in a sequence equivalent to reading through the following lines.

```
requests[0,0,0]  requests[0,0,1]...requests[0,0,23]
requests[0,1,0]  requests[0,1,1]...requests[0,1,23]
...
requests[0,6,0]   requests[0,6,1]...requests[0,6,23]
requests[1,0,0]   requests[1,0,1]...requests[1,0,23]

...

requests[9,0,0] requests[9,0,1]….requests[9,0,23]
...
requests[9,6,0] requests[9,6,1]….requests[9,6,23]
```

Note

The `foreach` statement does not give any indication of which part of the array is being accessed at a particular moment. This information is sometimes vital. For example, when printing the content of an array to the screen, rows and columns often have to be printed out in accordance with how they are organized in the array. Under those circumstances, you must employ your own counters in the `foreach` statement to keep track of which part of the array is being accessed.

If `foreach` is used to access a jagged multidimensional, you cannot get away with writing just one `foreach` statement. You will need to nest them in a similar fashion to that of the `for` loops to access each dimension separately. For example, if you want to traverse the elements of `jaggedRequests`, defined as

```
ushort [][][] jaggedRequests = new ushort [10][][];
```

you need to write

```
foreach (ushort [][] outerTemp in jaggedRequests)
{
    foreach (ushort [] middleTemp in outerTemp)
    {
        foreach (ushort innerTemp in middleTemp)
        {
            totalSum += innerTemp;
        }
    }
}
```

which will calculate the total sum of the values of all elements in `jaggedRequests`.

The Built-In Methods of `System.Array`

Recall how the `System.String` class provides any object of type `string` with a large number of methods and properties. The `System.Array` class also has numerous built-in methods and properties, providing useful functionality when working with arrays. You have already met a couple of these in the form of the `Length` property and the `GetLength` method. As usual, we apply the dot `.` operator to reach this built-in functionality

```
accountBalances.Length    //Returns the length of accountBalances
```

which calls the `Length` property of `accountBalances`.

The complete collection of methods and properties is listed in the .NET Frameworks Reference, along with their descriptions. Table 11.3 merely presents a few of the most commonly used methods.

Some of the examples in Figure 11.3 contain specific arrays that are described after the table.

TABLE 11.3 Selected Methods and Properties from `System.Array`

Method / Property	Explanation	Example
`System.Array.IndexOf` ➥`(`*`<Array_identifier>`*`,` *`<Value>`*`)` Notes: —*`<Value>`* must be identical to the base type of *`<Array_identifier>`*. —`IndexOf` is overloaded. Two other overloaded versions of `IndexOf` are shown next.	Returns the index of the first array element holding a value equal to *`<Value>`*. `-1` is returned if no matching values were found.	`System.Array.IndexOf(myArray,4)` Returns the value `2`. `System.Array.IndexOf(myArray,32)` Returns the value `-1`.

TABLE 11.3 continued

Method / Property	Explanation	Example

`System.Array.IndexOf`
➥ (*<Array_identifier>*,
➥ *<Value>*, *<Start_Index>*)
	Returns the index of the first array element holding a value equal to *<Value>*. The search will commence at the array element with index *<Start_Index>* and finish at the end of the collection.	`System.Array.IndexOf(myArray,4,3)`
		Returns the value `5`.
		`System.Array.IndexOf`
		➥ `(myArray,15,5)`
		Returns the value `-1`.

`System.Array.IndexOf` ➥(*<Array_identifier>*, ➥*<Value>*, *<Start_index>*, ➥*<Finish_index>*)	Returns the index of the first array element holding a value equal to *<Value>*. The search will commence at the array element with index *<Start_index>* and end at *<Finish_index>*.	`System.Array.IndexOf` ➥`(myArray,2,1,4)` Returns the value `3`.

`System.Array.IndexOf`
➥(*<Array_identifier>*, *<Value>*,
➥*<Start_index>*, *<Finish_index>*)
	Returns the index of the last array element holding a value equal to *<Value>*. The search will commence at the array element with index *<Start_Index>* and move backwards towards the *<Finish_index>*.	`ystem.Array.LastIndexOf`
		➥`(myArray,2,5,1)`
		Returns the value `3`.
		`System.Array.LastIndexOf`
		➥`(myArray,2,5,4)`
		Returns the value `-1`.

`System.Array.Clear`
➥(*<Array_identifier>*,
<Start_index>, *<Length>*)
	Sets `<Length>` number of array elements to their default initialization value, beginning at *<Start_index>*.	`System.Array.Clear(myArray,1,4)`
		Sets the elements of `myArray` to:
		`{2, 0, 0, 0, 0, 4, 2}`

`System.Array.Sort`
➥(*<Array_identifier>*)
	Sorts the elements of the array in ascending order.	`System.Array.Sort(myArray)`
		Sets the elements of `myArray` to:
		`{1, 2, 2, 2, 4, 4, 15}`

`System.Array.Reverse`
➥(*<Array_identifier>*)
	Reverses the order of the array elements of the given array.	`System.Array.Reverse(myArray)`
		Sets the elements of `myArray` to:
		`{2, 4, 15, 2, 4, 1, 2}`

`System.Array.Reverse`
➥(*<Array_identifier>*,
➥*<Start_index>*,
➥*<Finish_index>*)
	Reverses the order of the elements of an array in a given interval beginning at *<Start_index>* and finishing at *<Finish_index>*.	`System.Array.Reverse`
		➥`(myArray,1,4)`
		Sets the elements of `myArray` to:
		`{2, 15, 2, 4, 1, 4, 2}`

TABLE 11.3 continued

Method / Property	Explanation	Example

`System.Array.Copy`
`➥(`*`<Array_identifier1>`*`,`
`➥`*`<Array_identifier2>`*`, `*`<Length>`*`)`
	Copies *`<Length>`* amount of elements from *`<Array_identifier1>`* to *`<Array_identifier2>`* starting at index `0`.	`System.Array.Copy`
		`➥(myArray,myCopy,4)`
		Leaves `myArray` untouched and sets the elements of `myCopy` to:
		`{2, 1, 4, 2, 0, 0, 0}`

`System.Array.Copy`
`➥(`*`<Array_identifier1>`*`,`
`➥`*`<Start_index1>`*`,`
`➥`*`<Array_identifier2>`*`,`
`➥`*`<Start_index2>`*`, `*`<Length>`*`)`
	Copies *`<Length>`* amount of elements from index *`<Start_index1>`* of *`<Array_identifier1>`* to *`<Array_identifier2>`* beginning at *`<Start_index2>`*.	`System.Array.Copy`
		`➥(myArray,1,myCopy,2,3)`
		Leaves `myArray` untouched and sets the elements of `myCopy` to:
		`{0, 0, 1, 4, 2, 0, 0}`

`<Array_identifier1>` `=`
`➥(`*`<Array_Type>`*`)`
`➥`*`<Array_identifier2>`*`.Clone()`
	Creates a shallow copy of the array object referenced by *`<Array_identifier2>`* and assigns its reference to *`<Array_identifier1>`*.	`myClone = (int[])myArray.Clone();`
		Leaves `myArray` untouched and assigns a reference to a shallow copy of the object referenced by `myArray`.

`System.Array.LastIndexOf`
`➥(`*`<Array_identifier>`*`,`*`<Value>`*`)`
Note: This method is overloaded. Another overloaded version is shown next.
	Returns the index of the *last* array element holding a value equal to *`<Value>`*. -1 is returned if no matching values were found.	`System.Array.LastIndexOf`
		`➥(myArray,2)`
		Returns the value 6.

`System.Array.LastIndexOf`
`➥(<Array_identifier>, <Value>,`
`➥<Start_Index>)`
	Returns the index of the *last* array element holding a value equal to `<Value>`. The search will commence at the array element with index `<Start_Index>` and move backwards towards the beginning of the array.	System.Array.LastIndexOf
		`➥(myArray,2,2)`
		Returns the value 0

Notes:

- `myArray` used in the examples of the table is declared and defined as

  `int [] myArray = new int[7] {2, 1, 4, 2, 15, 4, 2};`

- `myCopy` used in a few examples is an array declared and defined as

  `int[] myCopy = new int[7];`

- `myClone` is used in the cloning example and is declared as

  `int[] myClone;`

- Programs including the line

  ```
  using System;
  ```

  can omit the reference to `System` when calling the static methods of `System.Array`, so, for example, instead of writing

  ```
  System.Array.IndexOf(<Array_identifier>, <Value>);
  ```

  You can simply write

  ```
  Array.IndexOf(<Array_identifier>, <Value>);
  ```

Special Array Techniques

This section introduces some supplementary techniques for solving problems often encountered when working with arrays. In particular, this section

- Presents a sorting program based on a famous sorting algorithm called Bubble Sort
- Compares the speed of the Bubble Sort program with that of the sorting program found in the .NET Framework
- Introduces a couple of algorithms to search for a particular value in an array
- Compares the speed of our implementation with that of the search method found in the .NET Framework

Sorting

The next couple sections introduce you to the simple bubble sort algorithm and compares its speed to the much faster, built-in sorting program found in the .NET Framework.

Presenting Bubble Sort

With the simple sorting program introduced in Chapter 7, "Types Part II: Operators, Enumerators and Strings," we were able to sort just three words in alphabetic order. By comparing and swapping values repeatedly (if necessary), smaller values would rise upward and larger values sink downward in a list of three words. The idea behind this algorithm can be applied to sort arrays of varying length, and is then commonly known as the *bubble sort* technique, because smaller values, like bubbles in water, gradually drift to the "top" (beginning) of the array.

Note

The bubble sort technique is also referred to as the *sinking sort* technique because large values sink to the "bottom" (end) of the array.

In the following description of the bubble sort algorithm, `testScores` is a one-dimensional array containing ten elements. It is declared/defined as follows:

```
int [] testScores = {300, 90, 50, 120, 100, 10, 290, 85, 90, 120};
```

Our aim is to sort the ten elements in ascending order (meaning smaller values first).

The algorithm traverses through the entire array (referred to as a *pass*) several times. During each pass, the algorithm repeatedly compares consecutive pairs of adjacent array element values as illustrated in Figure 11.14. The first pair compared is the pair with index 0 and 1. The second pair has indexes 1 and 2. This repeated action is continued until the end of the array is reached. In our case, the last pair to be compared has indexes 8 and 9. Observe that in an array with ten elements, there are nine (10–1) comparable pairs, and in an array with `length` number of elements, there are `length`–1 comparable pairs. During each comparison, the value of the array element with the lower index (called 1st value in the figure) is compared to that of the array element with the higher index (called 2nd value in the figure). If the 1st value is greater than the 2nd value, the two values are swapped; otherwise, nothing happens. If no elements were swapped during one full pass, it indicates that the array is sorted in the desired order and the algorithm is terminated. Notice in Figure 11.14 that 300 is the largest value in the list, and that during the first pass, it is moved to the last position. During the first comparison, it is moved to the second position because it is greater than 90. During the second comparison, it is moved to the third position because it is greater than 50, and so on until it is placed in the last position.

Let's now turn to the actual implementation of the algorithm. First of all, we need the ability to swap two elements of an array. The swapping technique used here employs a temporary variable and is identical to that of our simple word sorter program from Chapter 7. However, in this case, the swap takes place in a separate method that receives a reference to the array and two indexes specifying which two elements to swap. We will look closer at the swap method later in the finished program of Listing 11.8.

We can now concentrate on the core parts of the sorting algorithm. First, an outer loop is needed that will repeat itself as long as the last pass performed at least one swap. This can be expressed with pseudocode as in Listing 11.6.

LISTING 11.6 Pseudocode for Outer Framework Bubble Sort Algorithm—Initial Design

```
let swapped be a variable of type bool. Set it to true.
while swapped is true
{
    set swapped equal to false
    make one full pass, if any swaps are made set swapped to true
}
```

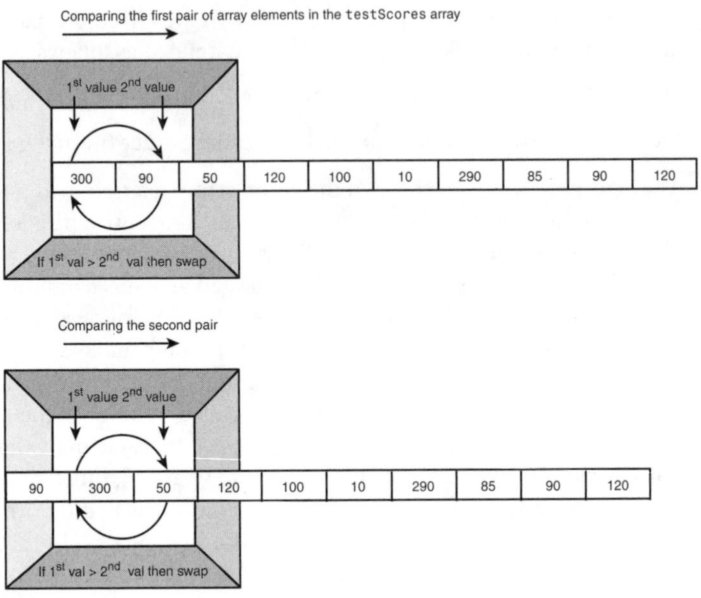

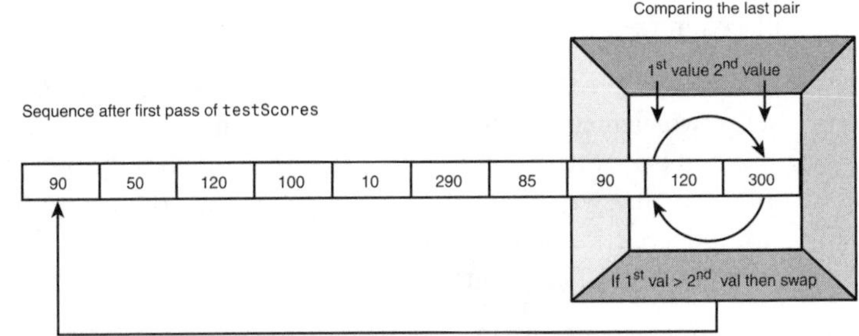

FIGURE 11.14
One pass through the *testScores*.

We now have an initial design of the outer framework that holds the code for what constitutes one pass. Let's then have a closer look at the pass part of the algorithm. As already mentioned, an array of length n has n–1 comparable pairs. Consequently, we need to perform n–1 comparisons. If `bubbles` is the name of the array we want to sort, we can express the loop part of the pass with a `for` loop:

```
for (int j = 0; j < (bubbles.Length-1); j++)
{
    // comparisons
}
```

If `j` is the loop counter and moves from index 0 to the largest index minus one, we can specify a pair of comparable array elements to have the indexes `j` and `j + 1`, respectively. Each comparison would look like the following:

```
if (bubbles[j] > bubbles[j + 1])
```

```
{
    Swap the two elements.
    Set swapped equal to true
}
```

By putting the pieces already presented together, we end up with the pseudocode of a valid bubble sort algorithm, as presented in Listing 11.7.

LISTING 11.7 Pseudocode for Bubble Sort—Slow Version

```
let swapped be a variable of type bool. Set it equal to true.
while swapped is true
{
    set swapped equal to false
    for (int j = 0; j < (bubbles.Length-1); j++)
    {
        if (bubbles[j] > bubbles[j + 1])
        {
            Swap the two elements.
            Set swapped equal to true
        }
    }
}
```

Listing 11.7 represents a fully working algorithm, but by observing a subtle point about the nature of this algorithm, we can make it faster. Recall how the largest value (300) of `testScores` during the first pass was brought all the way to the last position. During the next pass, the second largest value (290) is brought to the second-to-the-last position. After n passes, the n last positions of the array will be sorted in the correct order and contain the largest values of the array. Consequently, any attempt to let the comparison algorithm move into this territory is a waste of time. By equipping the outer loop with a pass counter, here called `i`, we can gradually let `i` reduce the number of comparisons performed by the inner for statement, as more passes are carried out.

The resulting pseudocode is shown in Figure 11.15.

FIGURE 11.15 Pseudocode for bubble sort algorithm—faster version.

```
let swapped be a variable of type bool. Set it equal to true.
for (int i = 0; swapped; i++)
{
      set swapped equal to false
      for (int j = 0; j < (bubbles.Length - (i + 1); j++)
      {
          if (bubbles[j] > bubbles[j + 1])
          {
              //Swap the two elements.
              //Set swapped equal to true
          }
      }
}
```

as `i` increases fewer comparisons are performed during one pass

Listing 11.8 presents the final C# source code for the bubble sort method (called `BubbleSortAscending` of lines 6–22) along with its helper method `Swap` (lines 25–32). The `Main()` method (lines 43–54) utilizes `BubbleSortAscending` to sort its `testScores` array (line 45). The result of the sorting is shown in the sample output after Listing 11.8.

LISTING 11.8 `BubbleSort.cs`

```
01: using System;
02:
03: class BubbleSorter
04: {
05:      // Sort the elements of an array in ascending order
06:     public static void BubbleSortAscending(int [] bubbles)
07:     {
08:         bool swapped = true;
09:
10:         for (int i = 0; swapped; i++)
11:         {
12:             swapped = false;
13:             for (int j = 0; j < (bubbles.Length - (i + 1)); j++)
14:             {
15:                 if (bubbles[j] > bubbles[j + 1])
16:                 {
17:                     Swap(j, j + 1, bubbles);
18:                     swapped = true;
19:                 }
20:             }
21:         }
22:     }
23:
24:      //Swap two elements of an array
25:     public static void Swap(int first, int second, int [] arr)
26:     {
27:         int temp;
28:
29:         temp = arr[first];
30:         arr[first] = arr[second];
31:         arr[second] = temp;
32:     }
33:
34:      //Print the entire array
35:     public static void PrintArray (int [] arr)
36:     {
37:         for (int i = 0; i < arr.Length; i++)
38:         {
39:             Console.Write("{0}, ", arr[i]);
40:         }
41:     }
42:
43:     public static void Main()
44:     {
45:         int [] testScores = {300, 90, 50, 120, 100, 10, 290, 85, 90, 120};
```

LISTING 11.8 continued

```
46:
47:         BubbleSortAscending(testScores);
48:         Console.WriteLine("The test scores sorted in ascending order:\n");
49:         for (int i = 0; i < testScores.Length; i++)
50:         {
51:             Console.Write("{0}  ", testScores[i]);
52:         }
53:     }
54: }
```

The test scores sorted in ascending order:

```
10  50  85  90  90  100  120  120  290  300
```

The method `Swap` (lines 25–32) declares in its header three formal parameters—`first`, `second`, and `arr`. The latter is of type reference-to-array-object-of-base-type-`int`. During the execution of this method, `arr` is referencing exactly the same array object as the reference that was passed as an argument. Any changes made to `arr` will be reflected as changes in the array argument. `first` and `second` specify the indexes of the array elements to be swapped. The swap follows the same technique as the swapping algorithm presented in Listing 7.10 of Chapter 7.

The `BubbleSortAscending` method (lines 6–22) receives a reference to the array object, which must be sorted. The formal parameter containing this reference is called `bubbles`. During the execution of `BubbleSortAscending`, `bubbles` is referencing the same array object as `testScores` declared in line 45. Any changes made to `bubbles` inside `BubbleSortAscending` is reflected in `testScores`.

If you have read the previous section, the source code of this method should be comprehensible.

The bubble sort is simple to implement, but very inefficient. Its use is limited to relatively short arrays or arrays that are nearly sorted. Other more sophisticated algorithms with names like Quick sort, Shell sort, Merge sort, and Heap sort should be applied to solve more elaborate sorting problems. These algorithms are beyond the scope of this book, but more information can be found in books and courses with names containing words like "algorithms" or "data structures."

If you want the functionality of a very fast sorting method, but have no interest in implementing it yourself, why not utilize what other highly-skilled programmers have already created and tested? You can do this by calling `System.Array`'s built-in `Sort` method presented briefly in Table 11.3 in the next section.

Sorting with `System.Array`'s `Sort` Method

The predefined `Sort` method of `System.Array` is static and is called by applying the dot operator to the classname `System.Array`. To sort the array `testScores` declared/defined as

```
int [] testScores = {300, 90, 50, 120, 100, 10, 290, 85, 90, 120};
```

we simply write

```
System.Array.Sort (testScores)
```

Listing 11.9 investigates how fast the `Array.Sort` method is compared to the `BubbleSortAscending` method. The implementation of the `BubbleSortAscending` and `Swap` methods are identical to that of Listing 11.8. The `Main()` method (lines 43–73) utilizes the `System.DateTime` structure to time the full sort of the `testScores` array (line 45) by using the bubble sort method and the `Array.Sort` method. By changing the length of `testScores` in line 45, it is possible to test how the two algorithms fare on small and large collections. The sample output displayed after Listing 11.9 shows the results I got on my computer when testing two arrays of length 1000 and 40000, respectively. As expected, both methods took less than a second to sort 1000 array elements. However, at 40000, the limitations of the bubble sort appears. While `Array.Sort` still took less than a second, bubble sort spent a staggering 23 seconds.

LISTING 11.9 `SortingCompetition.cs`

```
01: using System;
02:
03: class SortingCompetition
04: {
05:      // Sort the elements of an array in ascending order
06:     public static void BubbleSortAscending(int [] bubbles)
07:     {
08:         bool swapped = true;
09:
10:         for (int i = 0; swapped; i++)
11:         {
12:             swapped = false;
13:             for (int j = 0; j < (bubbles.Length - (i + 1)); j++)
14:             {
15:                 if (bubbles[j] > bubbles[j + 1])
16:                 {
17:                     Swap(j, j + 1, bubbles);
18:                     swapped = true;
19:                 }
20:             }
21:         }
22:     }
23:
24:      //Swap two elements of an array
25:     public static void Swap(int first, int second, int [] arr)
26:     {
27:         int temp;
28:
29:         temp = arr[first];
30:         arr[first] = arr[second];
31:         arr[second] = temp;
32:     }
33:
```

LISTING 11.9 continued

```
     //Print the entire array
    public static void PrintArray (int [] arr)
    {
        for (int i = 0; i < arr.Length; i++)
        {
            Console.Write("{0}, ", arr[i]);
        }
    }

    public static void Main()
    {
        int [] testScores = new int [1000];
        DateTime sortStart;
        DateTime sortEnd;

        for (int i = 0; i < testScores.Length; i++)
        {
            testScores[i] = testScores.Length - i;
        }

        Console.WriteLine("Now timing the bubble sort method
        ➥ please wait...");
        sortStart = DateTime.Now;
        BubbleSortAscending(testScores);
        sortEnd = DateTime.Now;
        Console.WriteLine("Seconds elapsed bubble sorting an array
        ➥ of length {0}: {1}",
            testScores.Length, ((sortEnd - sortStart).Ticks/10000000));

        for (int i = 0; i < testScores.Length; i++)
        {
            testScores[i] = testScores.Length - i;
        }

        Console.WriteLine("\nNow timing the built in sort method" +
            " of System.Array. Please wait...");
        sortStart = DateTime.Now;
        Array.Sort(testScores);
        sortEnd = DateTime.Now;
        Console.WriteLine("Seconds elapsed .NET sorting an array
        ➥ of length {0}: {1}",
            testScores.Length, ((sortEnd - sortStart).Ticks/10000000));
    }
}
```

Sample output 1. `testScores` containing 1000 elements:

```
Now timing the bubble sort method please wait...
Seconds elapsed bubble sorting an array of length 1000: 0

Now timing the built in sort method of System.Array. Please wait...
Seconds elapsed .NET sorting an array of length 1000: 0
```

Sample output 2. `testScores` containing 40000 elements:

```
Now timing the bubble sort method please wait...
Seconds elapsed bubble sorting an array of length 40000: 23

Now timing the built in sort method of System.Array. Please wait...
Seconds elapsed .NET sorting an array of length 40000: 0
```

Note:

- Results will vary according to the speed of your computer. You might want to use array lengths other than those shown here to get similar results.

After line 45, `testScores` has been initialized by the runtime to contain a long list of zeros. Both the sorting methods will sort the arrays in ascending order, so to challenge them, lines 49–52 assigns values of descending order to `testScores`. The value of `testScores[0]` will be `testScores.Length` (here 1000), and the value of `testScores[testScores.Length]` will be 1.

Lines 46 and 47 declare two variables of type `System.DateTime`. This structure type is useful when dealing with dates and time. The computer has an internal clock that keeps track of the date and time of the day down to milliseconds. With `DateTime`'s `static Now` property, we are able to access the time of the computer clock right now. The time returned via `Now` is in the form of a `DateTime` value. Thus, the following line assigns the time right now of the computer clock to `sortStart`:

```
sortStart = DateTime.Now;
```

If we assign the current time to `sortStart` immediately before beginning a sorting process, and to `sortEnd` instantly after the process has been terminated, it is possible to estimate the time elapsed during the process by deducting `sortStart` from `sortEnd`. This is done in lines 59 and 72. `DateTime` offers several different formats when printing a time interval on the console. In this case, I chose to express the interval in seconds. The `Ticks` property is suitable for this purpose. It returns a time interval as the amount of 100-nanosecond-intervals it contains. A nanosecond is one billionth (10^{-9}) of a second. 100 nanoseconds is 10 millionth of a second. Converting the amount returned by `Ticks` to seconds requires us to divide it by ten million, as displayed in lines 59 and 72.

When you run Listing 11.9 as it is displayed here, you will see sample output 1 appear onscreen. To run the program with 40,000 elements instead, you need to exchange 1000 in line 45 with 40000. The elapsed seconds will vary among different computer systems. If you have a very fast computer, you might have to increase to 40,000 to see a visible delay.

Searching

Looking up a person in the phone book, finding a specific topic in the index of a book, looking for that empty spot in the car park, or those lost keys at home are all examples of the process called searching.

Searching is the process of locating a data item in a collection of data items that matches certain criteria.

Searching is an important computer task. It allows us to let the computer sift through millions of data items in databases to find the requested information.

A *database* is a collection of related data items, organized to allow convenient access.

Computers, Searching, and the Human Genome Project

The Human Genome Project began in 1990 and is expected to last for thirteen years. The goals of the project are to identify the 30000 or so genes in human DNA, and to determine the sequence of three billion "data" items (chemical base pairs) found here. An important part of the project has been to record the information on computer databases, and thereby allow researchers to let computers search for specific patterns in this maze of information. At the heart of many of the data analysis tools employed, we find fast sophisticated searching algorithms without which the Human Genome Project would have been an impossible task to accomplish.

The mixture of computer science and biology/medicine has become so important that a new science called *bioinformatics*, which combines these disciplines, has emerged.

In the next couple of sections, we will concentrate on the problem of locating a specific number, called a key value, in an array. If the number is found, the position of the number is returned. If the number occurs more than once, the algorithm can return any one of those positions. If the number is not found, a signal saying "Not found" must be returned. The array cannot be altered during the search.

The next two sections look at two different search algorithms to solve the specified problem—the sequential search, which is simple but slow, and the more sophisticated and significantly faster binary search.

Sequential Search

The sequential search simply begins searching at the first item of the database (in this case, an array) and moves through the collection of items one by one. It is accordingly described as being *linear*. Each item visited is compared to the data item to be located. When a match is found, the position of the data item is reported and the process terminated. If no match is found, the process stops when the end of the array is reached, accompanied by an indication saying "Not found."

The *search key* is the data item to be located. The search key is used for comparisons during the searching process.

If the array is not sorted, the linear sequential search is more or less the only search method available. Other faster and more sophisticated search algorithms presume, during their hunt for the key value, that the array is sorted. When we discuss the binary search method, it will become clear why this particular technique only works on a sorted array.

A Phone Book Analogy

The numbers in a phone book are not sorted, so if you only have a phone number and want to find the person with this number, you have to perform a sequential search, sifting through all the numbers until a match is found.

The names of the phone book, on the other hand, are sorted in alphabetical order. Thus, if you have a name, you can perform a much faster search, which would be more closely related to the binary search technique presented in the next section.

Listing 11.10 presents an example of a sequential search method. The user can search the array `testScores` (line 19) by entering an integer value. If the value is found, the index containing the value is returned; otherwise, the program will let the user know that no matching value was found.

LISTING 11.10 `SequentialSearcher.cs`

```
01: using System;
02:
03: class SequentialSearcher
04: {
05:     public static int SequentialSearch (int key,int[] arr)
06:     {
07:         for (int i = 0; i < arr.Length; i++)
08:         {
09:             if (arr[i] == key)
10:                 return i;
11:         }
12:         return -1;
13:     }
14:
15:     public static void Main()
16:     {
17:         int searchKey;
18:         int searchResult;
19:         int [] testScores = {23, 6, 20, 12, 20, 34, 10, 5, 14, 30};
20:
21:         do
22:         {
23:             Console.Write("Please enter the test score you
                ➥ would like to locate: ");
24:             searchKey = Convert.ToInt32(Console.ReadLine());
25:             searchResult = SequentialSearch(searchKey, testScores);
26:             if (searchResult >= 0)
27:                 Console.WriteLine("The score was found in
                    ➥ position: {0}\n", searchResult);
28:             else
29:                 Console.WriteLine("The score was not found\n");
30:             Console.Write("Would you like to do another
                ➥ search? Y)es N)o ");
```

LISTING 11.10 continued

```
31:         } while (Console.ReadLine().ToUpper() == "Y");
32:     }
33: }
```

```
Please enter the test score you would like to locate: 30<enter>
The score was found in position: 9

Would you like to do another search? Y)es N)o Y<enter>
Please enter the test score you would like to locate: 20<enter>
The score was found in position: 2

Would you like to do another search? Y)es N)o Y<enter>
Please enter the test score you would like to locate: 15<enter>
The score was not found

Would you like to do another search? Y)es N)o N<enter>
```

The `SequentialSearch` method (lines 5–13) performs a sequential search on its formal parameter `arr`, an array of base type `int`. The search key is represented by the formal parameter named `key`. If the search key is found to match the value of an array element, the position of this element will be returned to the caller (lines 9 and 10); otherwise, the value `-1` is returned.

The linear search might be too slow for large collections of data. If those data are sorted, we can resort to the efficient binary search technique instead.

Binary Search

The following example illustrates the fundamental idea behind the binary search technique. Consider the array presented in Figure 11.16 called `myArray`. It contains fifteen array elements with values sorted in ascending order. Our task is to find the index of the search key value `22`. During this thought experiment, we can only, like the computer, access one array element at a time. Let's first look at the number in the middle of the array (called *middle-index*), in this case index 7 with value 16 (see Step 1 of Figure 11.16). What conclusions can we make by comparing this value to our search key `22`? Well, because `22` is greater than 16, and because the array is sorted in ascending order, `22` must exist (if it does exist) somewhere in the upper half of the array—more precisely, in an index for which it is `true` that `Middle-index + 1 <= index <= 14` that is equivalent to `8 <= index <= 14`, as illustrated with the horizontal arrows and in Figure 11.16. Observe that we have suddenly reduced the number of values we need to search by more than half (eight values in this case) simply by accessing one array element.

During Step 2 in Figure 11.16, we find the middle-index (index 11) of the new smaller array interval, and compare its associated value (24) with the search key `22`. Because the search key this time is smaller than the value of the middle-index (24), the key value must be located somewhere between index 7 and index 11. This can be expressed as `8 <= index <= middle-index–1` or shorter, `8 <= index <= 10`.

In Step 3, the middle-index of this new smaller interval is 9, and the search key is greater than its associated value (20). The new interval that can contain the key value 22 has shrunk to just one array element with index `10`. Expressed as `middle-index + 1 <= index <= 10` or shorter, `10 <= index <= 10`.

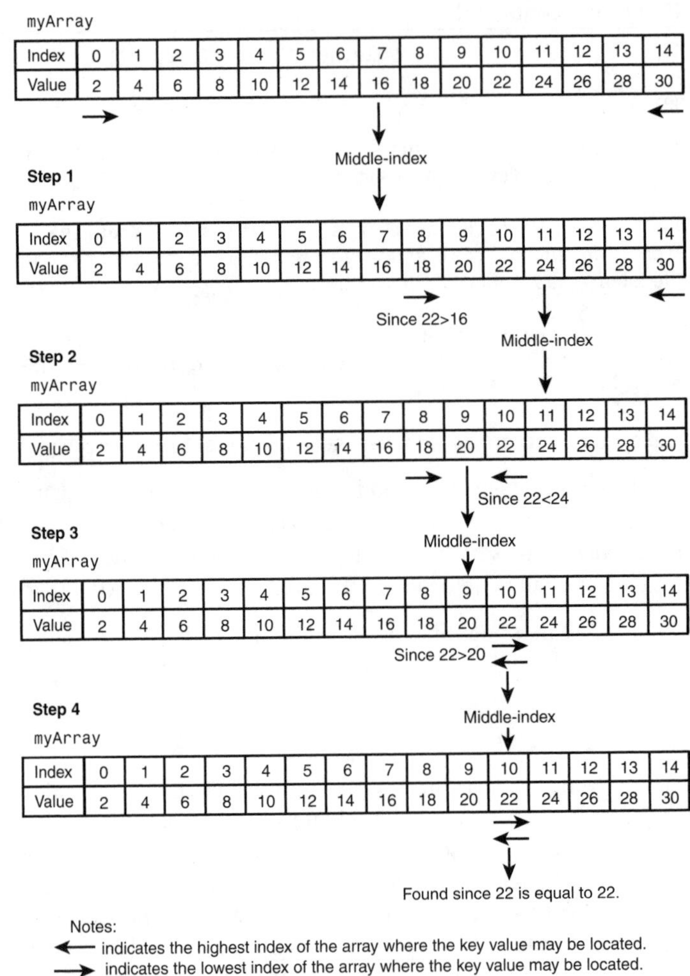

FIGURE 11.16
Finding value `22` in *`myArray`* using the binary search technique.

Step 4 finds the value of the new corresponding middle-index to be equal to the search key. We can thus conclude that index `10` contains the key value.

Figure 11.17 explicitly shows how fast the segments searched in the previous example shrink.

The Binary Search Technique in a Nutshell

The binary search method repeatedly compares the search key with the value of the middle-index of an array segment. Initially, this array segment consists of the entire array, but, by combining the result of the comparison with the knowledge that the array is pre-sorted, the algorithm is able to divide the array into two halves—one that must be searched further, and one that can be eradicated from any future searches.

FIGURE 11.17
Segments of *myArray* searched.

```
Step 1:  2   4   6   8  10  12  14  16m 18  20  22  24  26  28  30
Step 2:                                 18  20  22  24m 26  28  30
Step 3:                                 18  20m 22
Step 4:                                         22m
```

Note:

- `m` indicates the middle value of each segment.

Listing 11.11 implements the binary search algorithm in the **`BinarySearch`** method (lines 3–24). The `Main()` utilizes its functionality to search the **`testScores`** array (line 53) for values entered by the user (lines 55–65).

The **`PrintArray`** method is merely included for illustrative purposes. It lets you track the specific segments of the array searched by the **`BinarySearch`** method and provides similar output to that of Figure 11.17. However, to employ the **`PrintArray`** method correctly, it needs to be called from within the **`BinarySearch`** method. This call has not been included in Listing 11.11 to keep the initial source code uncluttered. Later in this chapter, I will explain how to utilize `PrintArray` correctly.

LISTING 11.11 `BinarySearcher.cs`

```
01: using System;
02:
03: class BinarySearcher
04: {
05:      //Search for the key value in the arr array
06:      //using the binary search algorithm.
07:     public static int BinarySearch (int key, int[] arr)
08:     {
09:         int low = 0;
10:         int high = arr.Length - 1;
11:         int middle;
12:
13:         while (low <= high)
14:         {
15:             middle = (low + high) / 2;
16:             if (key > arr[middle])
17:                 low = middle + 1;
18:             else if (key < arr[middle])
19:                 high = middle - 1;
20:             else
21:                 return middle;
22:         }
23:         return -1;
24:     }
25:
26:      //PrintArray is used merely for illustrative purposes.
27:      //It will print the segment of the array arr commencing
28:      //with the low index and up to the high index.
29:      //The middle element will be marked with an m.
```

LISTING 11.11 continued

```
    public static void PrintArray(int low, int middle,
    ➥ int high, int [] arr)
    {
        for (int i = 0; i <= high; i++)
        {
            if (i < low)
            {
                Console.Write("     ");
            }
            else
            {
                if (i == middle)
                    Console.Write("{0,2}m ", arr[i]);
                else
                    Console.Write("{0,2}  ", arr[i]);
            }
        }
        Console.WriteLine();
    }

    public static void Main()
    {
        int searchKey;
        int searchResult;
        int [] testScores =
        ➥ {2,4,6,8,10,12,14,16,18,20,22,24,26,28,30,32,34,36,38};

        do
        {
            Console.Write("Please enter the test score
            ➥ you would like to locate: ");
            searchKey = Convert.ToInt32(Console.ReadLine());
            searchResult = BinarySearch(searchKey, testScores);
            if (searchResult >= 0)
                Console.WriteLine("The score was found in
                ➥ position: {0}\n", searchResult);
            else
                Console.WriteLine("The score was not found\n");
            Console.Write("Would you like to do
            ➥ another search? Y)es N)o ");
        } while (Console.ReadLine().ToUpper() == "Y");
    }
}
```

```
Please enter the test score you would like to locate: 30<enter>
The score was found in position: 14

Would you like to do another search? Y)es N)o Y<enter>
Please enter the test score you would like to locate: 3<enter>
The score was not found

Would you like to do another search? Y)es N)o N<enter>
```

The `BinarySearch` method (lines 3–24) performs a binary search on the formal parameter `arr` (line 7), which must represent a one-dimensional array of base type `int` sorted in ascending order. The formal parameter `key` (line 7) is the search key. If the `key` is found in `arr`, the method returns the index containing this value; otherwise, `-1` is returned. To keep track of the current array segment where the key value (if present) must reside, the method declares two variables called `low` and `high` (lines 9 and 10). The key value (if present) must exist in the array segment enclosed by these two variables. Thus, they are the source code counterparts to the two small horizontal arrows (➔ and ←) from Figure 11.16. Initially, the entire array might contain the key value, so `low` is set to zero (line 9) and `high` to `arr.Length–1` (line 10). To represent the middle-index, we use a variable called `middle` (line 11).

The repetitive nature of the four steps of Figure 11.16 is represented by a `while` loop (lines 13–22). It should be terminated if either `low` is greater than `high`, or if `middle` is equal to `key`. The former termination condition is taken care of by the `while` loop condition `(low <= high)` (line 13). The latter by the statement `return middle;` (line 21) that terminates the loop and the method and returns the value of `middle` back to the caller. This statement is only executed if both of the following comparisons fail—`(key > arr[middle])` (line 16) and `(key < arr[middle])`, which means only if `key` is equal to `arr[middle]`, thus satisfying our termination condition.

During each repetition of the `while` loop body we need to

1. Find the middle-index: `middle` (line 15).
2. If `key` is greater than the array value pointed at by the middle-index, set `low` equal to `middle` plus one (lines 16 and 17).
3. If key is smaller than the array value pointed at by the middle-index, set `high` equal to `middle` minus one (lines 18 and 19).
4. If both 2 and 3 fail, terminate the loop and return the value of `middle` as discussed previously (line 21).

If the `while` loop is terminated due to the loop condition (`low <= high`) being `false`, it means that `key` could not be found in `arr`, in which case, `-1` is returned (line 23).

To print the array segments analyzed during each repeated execution of the `while` loop body, you can call the `PrintArray` method from within the `BinarySearch` method, as done in line 11 of Listing 11.12. Notice that a couple of `WriteLine` calls have been inserted in lines 7, 18, and 22 to make the output more presentable. By exchanging the `BinarySearch` version of Listing 11.11 with that of Listing 11.12, you will be able to produce the output shown after the listing.

LISTING 11.12 The `BinarySearch` Method Calling `PrintArray`

```
01: public static int BinarySearch (int key, int[] arr)
02: {
03:     int low = 0;
04:     int high = arr.Length - 1;
05:     int middle;
```

```

    Console.WriteLine("\nSegments of array searched:\n");
    while (low <= high)
    {
        middle = (low + high) / 2;
        PrintArray(low, middle, high, arr);
        if (key > arr[middle])
            low = middle + 1;
        else if (key < arr[middle])
            high = middle - 1;
        else
        {
            Console.WriteLine();
            return middle;
        }
    }
    Console.WriteLine();
    return -1;
}
```

```
Please enter the test score you would like to locate: 14<enter>

Segments of array searched:

 2   4   6   8  10  12  14  16  18  20m 22  24  26  28  30  32  34  36  38
 2   4   6   8  10m 12  14  16  18
                    12  14m 16  18

The score was found in position: 6

Would you like to do another search? Y)es N)o Y<enter>
Please enter the test score you would like to locate: 22<enter>

Segments of array searched:

 2   4   6   8  10  12  14  16  18  20m 22  24  26  28  30  32  34  36  38
                                        22  24  26  28  30m 32  34  36  38
                                        22  24m 26  28
                                        22m

The score was found in position: 10

Would you like to do another search? Y)es N)o N<enter>
```

The high efficiency of the binary search might not be apparent by searching a very short array, such as `testScores` in Listing 11.11. However, the extreme speed associated with this technique becomes apparent if we look at much larger collections of data items. Because the binary search eliminates half of the array elements searched after each comparison, we can find the maximum number of comparisons required for any array length by determining how many times we need to divide this length by two before we get a number equal to or smaller than 1. For example, to search 1,024 elements requires a maximum 10 searches because 2^{10} is equal to 1,024, and 1,024 divided by 2 ten times is equal to 1. To search a collection of one billion array elements merely requires 30 comparisons; an extraordinarily low number compared to the up to one billion comparisons required by the linear search presented in the previous section.

Searching with `System.Array`'s `IndexOf` Method

Instead of writing your own search method, you can apply the search functionality provided by the methods `IndexOf` and `LastIndexOf` (see Table 11.3 presented earlier). There are several overloaded versions of both of these methods, but this section will only provide an example of how to use one version of `IndexOf`. Please refer to the .NET Framework Documentation and Table 11.3 for information on the remaining overloaded methods. The `IndexOf` version applied in this section takes two arguments—the array to be searched and the search key value, as illustrated in the following line:

```
System.Array.IndexOf(<Array_identifier>, <Search_Key_Value>)
```

It either returns the index of the first array element containing the search key value, or `-1` one if not found. Notice that the array need not be sorted for the method to work.

The `IndexOf` method is utilized in Listing 11.13 to search the `testScores` array for search key values entered by the user.

LISTING 11.13 `DotNETSearcher.cs`

```
using System;

class DotNETSearcher
{
    public static void Main()
    {
        int searchKey;
        int searchResult;
        int [] testScores = {32, 2, 87, 23, 2, 51, 101, 22, 45, 33, 10};

        do
        {
            Console.Write("Please enter the test score you would
            ➥ like to locate: ");
            searchKey = Convert.ToInt32(Console.ReadLine());
            searchResult = Array.IndexOf(testScores, searchKey);
            if (searchResult >= 0)
                Console.WriteLine("The score was found in
                ➥ position: {0}\n", searchResult);
            else
                Console.WriteLine("The score was not found\n");
            Console.Write("Would you like to do another
            ➥ search? Y)es N)o ");
        } while (Console.ReadLine().ToUpper() == "Y");
    }
}
```

```
Please enter the test score you would like to locate: 2<enter>
The score was found in position: 1

Would you like to do another search? Y)es N)o Y<enter>
Please enter the test score you would like to locate: 20<enter>
The score was not found

Would you like to do another search? Y)es N)o N<enter>
```

Just one call to `Array.IndexOf` (line 15) is required to search `testScores`.

The search methods `IndexOf` and `LastIndexOf` search an unsorted array, and will not be as fast as the binary search method searching a sorted array for larger data collections. Consequently, you might want to conduct your own speed tests equivalent to those performed on the covered sorting methods with data similar to those searched by the final application before you choose which methods to apply.

Summary

This chapter extended your knowledge about one-dimensional arrays from Chapter 10 to include arrays with several dimensions. In particular, the use of two- and three-dimensional arrays were discussed, along with their close connection to nested loops. The chapter further looked at selected useful built-in array properties, methods, and important algorithms for sorting and searching an array.

The essential points discussed in this chapter are reviewed in this section.

It is difficult to visualize more than three dimensions, but we don't need this ability, because the number of indexes required to reference an array element is equal to the number of dimensions of the array.

The values in a two-dimensional array can be thought of as a table with rows and columns. The first element in a two-dimensional array is at [0,0]. Conventionally, the elements of two-dimensional arrays are accessed as `<Array_identifier>[<row>, <column>]`.

Array elements belonging to arrays of many dimensions can be used in expressions, just like other variables.

Use n nested loops to access all the elements of an n-dimensional array.

You can think of a two-dimensional array as an array of arrays. A rectangular array consists of a one-dimensional array with elements containing one-dimensional arrays of the same length. An array of two or more dimensions where every dimension consists of arrays of identical length is also a rectangular array.

A jagged array is an array with two or more dimensions where at least one of the dimensions consists of arrays that are not all of the same length.

A two-dimensional array is useful for representing the board (like the map in the Find the Island Game) of a board game.

The `foreach` construct makes it very simple to access a rectangular array of any dimension, it can be done with a non-nested `foreach` construct. However, this construct does not let you exert the same detailed control as the traditional loop statements (such as the `for` loop).

The `foreach` construct must be nested when used for accessing jagged arrays.

The array contains many useful built-in methods exerting functionality, such as sorting and searching.

Sorting and searching algorithms are used widely in the programming community.

The bubble sort algorithm is simple but slow and, therefore, is only useful to sort sets with a limited number of elements. The name bubble sort originates from the fact that smaller values gradually drift to the top (beginning) of an array during this search technique's execution.

The array's built-in sorting method is significantly faster than the bubble sort algorithm, especially when larger numbers of items are sorted.

The sequential search algorithm is simple and can be used on any set of items, but it is slow.

The binary search algorithm is very fast, but the set of items must be sorted prior to this search.

The array contains built-in search methods called `IndexOf` and `LastIndexOf`.

Review Questions

1. a. How many dimensions does the array `warpedWorld` have if accessing one of its elements requires a line of code like the following:

   ```
   warpedWorld[2,4,1,6,4]
   ```

   b. How many nested `for` loops would be required to access all elements in the `warpedWorld` array?

2. You are considering writing a chess-playing program. How many dimensions would the array representing the chessboard need to have?

3. a. Declare a rectangular three-dimensional array called `observations` with base type `uint`. Assign to it a reference to a new array object with the following numbers of elements in each dimension—5, 10, 20.

   b. Write a statement that assigns the value 100 to the observations element with indexes 3, 2, 10.

   c. What happens if you attempt to access the element with indexes 1, 12, 14?

   d. Write nested `for` loops to access and print onscreen the value of each element in the `observations` array.

   e. Use the `foreach` loop to perform the same operation as in question d.

4. a. Declare a jagged two-dimensional array called `numbers` of base type `int`, in which the first dimension contains 7 elements.

   b. Declare the third element of the first dimension to contain a one-dimensional array of length 20.

   c. Assign the value 100 to the fourth element in the array contained in the third element of the first dimension.

5. Suppose an array called `numbers` is declared as follows:

   ```
   int [] numbers = {2, 4, 6, 8, 10, 12, 6};
   ```

   Which values do the following method calls return?

   a. `System.Array.IndexOf(numbers, 6)`

   b. `System.Array.IndexOf(numbers, 7)`

   c. `System.Array.IndexOf(numbers, 2, 3)`

   d. `System.Array.LastIndexOf(numbers, 6)`

   e. `System.Array.Reverse(numbers)` followed by `System.Array.IndexOf(numbers, 12)`

6. Suppose that your program is searching an array containing one million data items by using the binary search algorithm. How many data items does it discard (and need not to look at again) from the search during the first search loop?

7. Your program needs to search for a value in an array of length 2048. What is the maximum number of loops required to find the value by using a

   a. Sequential search

   b. Binary search

Programming Exercises

1. Sometimes, the number of cars passing a certain point on a highway needs to be counted. Suppose a person needs to count the cars passing by every hour for one full week. Write a program that can assist this person in storing, retrieving, and analyzing this information. In particular the program must be able to

   - Store car count entries on an hourly basis for 24 hours a day and for 7 days.
   - Let the user enter a specific count by specifying the day, hour, and count.
   - Let the user retrieve a specific count by specifying the day and hour.
   - Calculate and display the total number of counts for the whole week.

- Determine the number of hours it takes before a given number of cars have passed by. For example, if the first five hours contain the following counts 30, 40, 10, 50, and 100, it takes 3 hours to reach 75 or more cars, and 5 hours to reach 226 or more cars.

  Notice that the user expects the day indexes to be 1–7 (this requires an adjustment to the zero-base array access) and the hour indexes to be 0–23.

2. Write a program containing a three-dimensional array of type `int` called `numbers` with the following dimensions: 5, 10, and 8. The user must be able to enter and retrieve individual values from this array by entering a chosen set of indexes. Further, the program must be able to calculate the sum of all numbers stored in all elements of the `numbers` array.

CHAPTER 12

CLASS ANATOMY PART I: `static` CLASS MEMBERS AND METHOD ADVENTURES

You will learn about the following in this chapter:

- The different class members
- `static` instance variables
- `static` methods
- Reference parameters
- Output parameters
- The parameter array
- Method overloading
- The keyword `this`

Recall that a class provides a blueprint for creating an object, just like an architectural drawing specifies how to build a house. The class is an abstraction of a real-world (tangible or conceptual) object that belongs to, for our program, a relevant problem domain. A single class template can be used to create numerous objects (instances) that all share the features specified by this particular class.

In previous chapters, we saw how to solve several different computational problems by letting suitable objects of different classes collaborate, each contributing with its unique abilities. The class construct allows us to combine data (collectively referred to as the *state* of the object) with functions (representing the *behavior* of the object) to form useful objects that fit into our overall software design. So far, our classes have consisted of instance variables and methods as shown in Figure 12.1.

Class members are the language elements constituting the class body. Instance variables and methods are two fundamental class members, but because the classes we write as so diverse and via their objects interact in many different situations, C# contains several other class members that allow you to make each class more agile, intuitive and easier to use for other classes and programmers and tailor fitted for its particular role in a program. We will focus on these other class members in this and the next two chapters and also look more closely at important aspects of the method construct we have not yet discussed.

FIGURE 12.1
A class with instance variables and methods.

```
class <Class_identifier>
{
    <Instance_variables>
    <Methods>
}
```

The Anatomy of a Class: Overview

Before we discuss each class member in detail, let's get an overview of the members we have available.

Syntax Box 12.1 expands the syntax shown in Figure 12.1 by including the total set of members we can include in the class definition. The first few lines displays the familiar class definition syntax consisting of the `class` keyword followed by the name of the class (identifier) and the set of curly braces that forms the class body where the class members reside. Further down, the class members have been divided into three broad categories—data members, function members, and nested types. The following provides a brief introduction to the members of each of these categories, which also have been listed in the syntax box. Data members consist of member variables, constants, and events.

- Member variables (also called fields) are used to represent data. A member variable can either belong to a particular instance (object) of a class, in which case it is called an instance variable, or it can belong to the class itself (by declaring it `static`), in which case it is called a `static` variable (or a class variable). Recall that a `static` method is called through its class (not its object) and belongs to a class not an object. Similarly, a `static` variable belongs to a class not any specific object.
- A member variable can also be declared `readonly` (with the `readonly` keyword). `readonly` member variables are closely related to the constant data member, but holds an important difference—the constant member's value is set to the value specified in the source code when the program is compiled and represents this value throughout the lifetime of the compiled program. In contrast, the `readonly` member is assigned its value when an object is created and only keeps this value during the lifetime of the object.
- *Events* are declared in a similar fashion to that of member variables, but their use is very different. When you click a button (perhaps an OK button) on your graphical user interface (GUI), a corresponding object inside the program you are running generates (or fires) an event (perhaps called `OKButtonClick`) that will cause another part of the program to react and execute a piece of code. This type of program is called an *event-driven program*, because the next action taken by the program depends on the next event fired in the program. Consequently, the notion of a program executed in the sequence by which its statements are written is more or less gone. This asynchronous ability is necessary when running a GUI application, because the user at any one particular time has the choice between pointing and clicking many different buttons onscreen and the keyboard. Event-driven programming is not only needed for GUI application, but also for other important types of applications.

Event-driven programming is an advanced subject, so the events discussion is deferred until Chapter 20, "Delegates and Events."

Syntax Box 12.1 Overview of the Class Members

```
Class_definition::=

class <Class_identifier>
{
    <Class_members>
}
```

where

```
<Class_members>
            ::= <Data_members>
            ::= <Function_members>
            ::= <Nested_types>

<Data_members>
            ::=    <Member_variables>
            ::=    <Constants>
            ::=    <Events>

<Function_members>
                ::= <Methods>
                ::= <Constructors>
                ::= <Destructor>
                ::= <Properties>
                ::= <Indexers>
                ::= <Operators>

<Nested_types>
                   ::= <Nested_classes>
                   ::= <Nested_structs>
                   ::= <Nested_enums>
```

Notes:

- The class definition provided here concentrates on the insides of the class and omits the syntax elements related to access modification, inheritance, and interfaces of the class itself.
- The class members can be written inside the class in any order you want without changing the semantics.
- A `<Function_member>` can either be an `<Instance_function>` or a `<Static_function>` (also called `<Class_function>`). An instance function is executed in relation to a particular object and, as opposed to the `static` function, needs an object to be called through.

Function members consist of methods, constructors, destructors, properties, indexers, and operators:

- The *method* is already a familiar construct, but it still contains a number of unexplored facets, such as reference and output parameters, parameter arrays, method overloading, and the `this` keyword. A large part of this chapter is devoted to those important concepts.

- *Constructors* have been informally presented previously and are thoroughly discussed in Chapter 13, "Class Anatomy Part II: Object Creation and Garbage Collection."
- The *destructor* (also called *finalizer*) is a new concept that deserves a brief introduction here before we look closer at it in Chapter 13. We know that objects are created and allocated a piece of memory where the values of their instance variables and other data are stored. When an object is no longer needed in the program, it must be disposed of and its memory released for use by new objects being created; otherwise, the program could quickly run out of memory. A destructor, like its sibling the constructor, can contain a set of programmer-specified statements that are called by the runtime (it cannot be called directly from the source code) when this reclamation takes place.
- *Properties* are accessed as if they are member variables, but contain statements, just like a conventional method, that are executed when the property is accessed. They are often used instead of accessor and mutator methods (that conventionally have names like `GetDistance` and `SetDistance`) to access `private` member variables and, therefore, support the encapsulation principle.
- *Indexers* are used with classes that represent an array as their main purpose. Whereas properties allow convenient access to individual member variables, indexers allow convenient array-like access to an array residing inside a class.
- Sometimes, it makes sense (and the code more readable) if two objects can be combined with an operator to form a well-defined result. For example, this could allow us to write statements like `totalTime = myTime + yourTime;` where all three values are objects of class `TimeInterval`. We can achieve this kind of behavior by including *operator* class members in our classes that specify the code to be executed when two objects are combined with the indicated operator. This process is often referred to as *operator overloading*.

Nested types are classes, structs, enums, and interfaces defined within the class body. They allow the programmer to hide types that are only needed within a class. Just like helper methods are kept `private` to lessen the complexity faced by the user of the class, nested types help us to reduce the number of classes to which an assembly user needs to look.

Data Members

The following sections look closer at the data members. Previous chapters have already covered instance variables, so the bulk of this part is about `static` variables and their use.

Instance Variables

When an object is created, its instance variables are filled with values specific to that object, and their values stay specific to this object throughout its lifetime. This mechanism is familiar territory, but worth recapturing to contrast it with `static` variables discussed in the next section.

Recall our `BankSimulation.cs` program in Chapter 10, "Arrays Part I: Array Essentials." It consisted of a `Bank` object referencing a number of `Account` objects through an array called `accounts`. The `Account` class defined, among others, an instance variable called `balance` as shown in the following:

```
class Account
{
      ...
      private decimal balance;
      ...
}
```

The user could specify the `Bank` object to contain any number of `Account` objects (in our sample, seven accounts were created). Subsequently, it was possible to alter (by depositing and withdrawing) the instance variable `balance` of any particular `Account` object by specifying the account number of the account with which it was associated. In our example, only the `balance` of the second account was altered to be equal to $110,000.00. The `balance` of each of the other `Account` objects remained zero. However, by continuing our simulation, we could also have ended up with seven accounts containing the following balances:

```
Account 1: balance equal to 10000
Account 2: balance equal to 110000
Account 3: balance equal to 35000
Account 4: balance equal to 55000
Account 5: balance equal to 300
Account 6: balance equal to 2000
Account 7: balance equal to 3500
```

This state of affairs has been depicted in Figure 12.2. The `Bank` object references seven different `Account` objects, each with its *own unique* `balance` value.

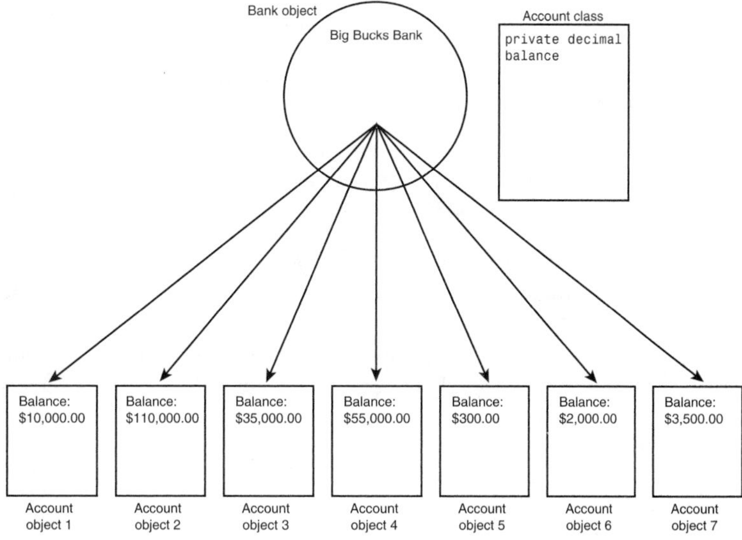

FIGURE 12.2
Different *balance* values for different *Account* objects.

The next section makes the important contrast between the instance variables (illustrated in Figure 12.2) and `static` variables.

`static` Variables

Instance variables are used to hold data relevant for an individual object, but what if we have a piece of information that is associated with the whole group of objects belonging to the same class? Let's illustrate what this means by returning to the `BankSimulation.cs` program in Chapter 10. Recall that we had to decide on the number of accounts initially and that this number would stay fixed for the duration of the program. Suppose we relaxed this condition and could open (create) and close accounts at any time during the execution of this program and wanted to keep track of the total number of `Account` objects created. Such a data element would not, like the instance variable `balance`, describe any `Account` object in particular, but would be associated with the whole group of `Account` objects. We could attempt to represent the data element by declaring an instance variable called `totalAccountsCreated` in the `Account` class:

```
class Account
{
    ...
    public uint totalAccountsCreated;    //inefficient
    ...
}
```

It would then be possible to increment `totalAccountsCreated` by one every time a new `Account` object is created. However, this approach contains two inefficiencies:

- *Duplication of data*—`totalAccountsCreated` describes one attribute about the `Account` objects as a group. Consequently, only one `totalAccountsCreated` variable is needed. However, the declaration of `totalAccountsCreated` shown before causes every single `Account` object to hold a `totalAccountsCreated` value identical to all other `Account` objects. Figure 12.3 shows the duplicated values—seven instance variables all containing the value seven after seven `Account` objects have been created. This is not only a waste of computer memory, but also is confusing for programmers to deal with. Which of the `Account` objects should we consult to find the total accounts created? The first one? What if no objects were created yet? Then there wouldn't be any objects to provide us with an answer.

- *Inefficient code due to required update of all* `Account` *objects*—The `Bank` object would have to update (increment `totalAccountsCreated` by one) all `Account` objects every time a new `Account` object is created. This is acceptable for a small number of accounts, but imagine a bank with hundreds of thousands of bank accounts. Every time a new `Account` is added, an iteration statement will have to traverse the entire collection of `Account` objects to perform the many updates.

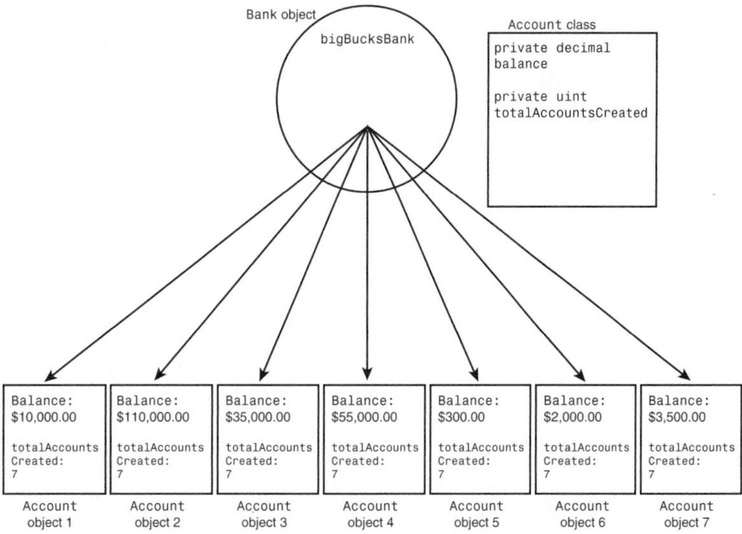

FIGURE 12.3
totalAccountsCreated contains duplicated values in all *Account* objects.

How can we solve these inefficiency issues? We need to store `totalAccountsCreated` in just one place, which is removed from each object but still related to the `Account` objects as a group. Because there is only one `Account` class and it defines attributes common to all `Account` objects, the `Account` class is the natural place to put `totalAccountsCreated`. The `static` keyword lets us do exactly that. By declaring `totalAccountsCreated` to be `static` as in the following

```
class Account
{
    ...
    public static uint totalAccountsCreated;  //Efficient
    ...
}
```

we are specifying that

- Only one copy of `totalAccountsCreated` exists, which belongs to the whole `Account` class rather than its individual objects.
- `totalAccountsCreated` is shared between all `Account` objects.
- `totalAccountsCreated` has a value, even if no `Account` objects have been created yet.
- `totalAccountsCreated` can be accessed through the `Account` class or from within any `Account` object.

The impact of the `static` keyword is illustrated in Figure 12.4.

Even though `totalAccountsCreated` is not held by any particular `Account` object, it can still be accessed and modified from within each object as if it is a standard instance variable. This is demonstrated in the following code snippet where there is no difference between accessing the instance variable `accountCreationNumber`, and the static variable `totalAccountsCreated`.

FIGURE 12.4
A *static* member variable is shared by all objects of the same class.

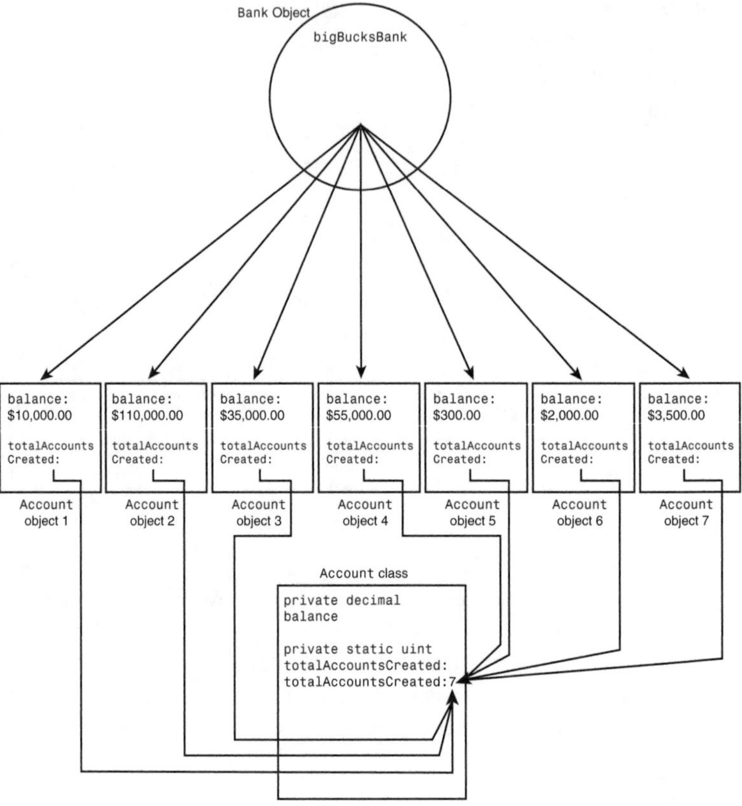


```
class Account
{
    ...
    private uint accountCreationNumber;
    public static uint totalAccountsCreated;
    ...
    public void accountsCreatedAfterMe()
    {
        Console.WriteLine("Number of accounts created after me: {0}",
            totalAccountsCreated - accountCreationNumber);  //Identical syntax
    }
    ...
}
```

Accessing `totalAccountsCreated` from outside an `Account` object must be done by applying the dot operator to the classname `Account` as in the following:

```
class Bank
{
```

```
    ...
    ...Account.totalAccountsCreated...
    ...
}
```

This way of accessing `totalAccountsCreated` is not valid if `totalAccountsCreated` is `private`, but is valid if it is declared `public`.

Note

Two of the access modifiers available to declare a `static` member variable are `public` and `private`. As a rule of thumb, all `static` member variables should, like their instance variable cousins, be declared `private` to abide with the encapsulation principles. For demonstration purposes, I have broken this rule and declared `totalAccountsCreated` to be `public` in this section. If a `static` member variable is declared `private`, it is only possible to access and modify it through the standard kind of methods we have met so far, or through `static` methods that, like `static` member variables, are associated with a class instead of its objects. `static` methods are discussed later in this chapter.

Note

A `static` member variable (like `totalAccountsCreated`) cannot be accessed by applying the dot operator to the name of an individual object (like `Account`) as in the following:

```
class Bank
{
    ...
    Account myAccount = new Account();
    ...myAccount.totalAccountsCreated...      //invalid
    ...
}
```

Listing 12.1 demonstrates how the `public static` member variable `totalAccountsCreated` (line 6) can be accessed, modified, and thereby utilized. The program called `DynamicBankSimulation.cs` contains stripped down versions of the three classes `Account`, `Bank`, and `BankSimulation` found in the `BankSimulation.cs` program of Chapter 10. Whereas the `BankSimulation.cs` program obliged us to specify a fixed number of accounts at the beginning of the program, `DynamicBankSimulation.cs` allows us to add and remove bank accounts during the runtime of the program. The program also keeps track of the total number of bank accounts created (held in `totalAccountsCreated`) and the current amount of accounts held by the `bigBucksBank`.

LISTING 12.1 `DynamicBankSimulation.cs`

```
01: using System;
02: using System.Collections;
```

LISTING 12.1 continued

```

class Account
{
    public static uint totalAccountsCreated = 0;

    public Account()
    {
        totalAccountsCreated++;
    }
}

class Bank
{
    private ArrayList accounts;

    public Bank()
    {
        Console.WriteLine("Congratulations! You have created a new bank");
        accounts = new ArrayList();
    }

    public void AddNewAccount()
    {
        accounts.Add(new Account());
        Console.WriteLine("New account added!");
        PrintStatistics();
    }

    public void RemoveFirstAccount()
    {
        if (accounts.Count > 0)
        {
            accounts.RemoveAt(0);
            Console.WriteLine("Account removed!\n");
            PrintStatistics();
        }
        else
        {
            Console.WriteLine("Sorry no more current accounts");
        }
    }

    public void PrintStatistics()
    {
        Console.WriteLine("Number of current accounts:" + accounts.Count +
            "\nNumber of new accounts created: " +
            ➥Account.totalAccountsCreated);
    }
}

class DynamicBankSimulation
{
```

LISTING 12.1 continued

```
    private static Bank bigBucksBank;

    public static void Main()
    {
        string command;

        bigBucksBank = new Bank();
        do
        {
            PrintMenu();
            command = Console.ReadLine().ToUpper();
            switch (command)
            {
                case "A":
                    bigBucksBank.AddNewAccount();
                    break;
                case "E":
                    Console.WriteLine("Bye Bye!");
                    break;
                case "R":
                    bigBucksBank.RemoveFirstAccount();
                    break;
                case "P":
                    bigBucksBank.PrintStatistics();
                    break;
                default:
                    Console.WriteLine("Invalid choice");
                    break;
            }
        } while (command != "E");
    }

    private static void PrintMenu()
    {
        Console.WriteLine("\nWhat would you like to do?\n" +
            "A) Add new account\n" +
            "R) Remove account\n" +
            "P) Print statistics\n" +
            "E) End session\n");
    }
}
```

```
Congratulations! You have created a new bank

What would you like to do?
A) Add new account
R) Remove account
P) Print statistics
E) End session

P<enter>
Number of current accounts: 0
Number of new accounts created: 0
```

```
What would you like to do?
...

A<enter>
New account added!
Number of current accounts: 1
Number of new accounts created: 1

What would you like to do?
...

A<enter>
New account added!
Number of current accounts: 2
Number of new accounts created: 2

What would you like to do?
...

R<enter>
Account removed!

Number of current accounts: 1
Number of new accounts created: 2

What would you like to do?
...

E<enter>
Bye Bye!
```

Note:

- For space reasons, the menu has only been shown once and then replaced by three dots (`...`).

For space reasons, the `Account` class has no `balance` instance variable or the likes. Line 6 declares `totalAccountsCreated` to be a `static` member variable of type `uint`. It is initialized to zero as soon as the program is started, which allows us to access it even before any `Account` objects are created. This is demonstrated with the **`P<enter>`** command in the first part of the sample output, letting the user know that zero accounts have been created and zero accounts currently exist. The `P` command triggers, via the `switch` section in lines 76–78, the `PrintStatistics` method (lines 45–49) of the `Bank` object called `bigBucksBank` to be executed.

`totalAccountsCreated` is accessed in line 48 by applying the dot operator to the classname `Account` as in `Account.totalAccountsCreated`.

`totalAccountsCreated` can be accessed and modified from within an `Account` object as if it is a standard instance variable; this is demonstrated by the constructor (lines 8–11) of `Account`. Recall that the constructor is called every time a new object is created, in this case, causing `totalAccountsCreated` to be incremented by one (line 10) every time a new `Account` object is created.

The standard C# array introduced in Chapter 10 has a fixed, unchangeable length after it is created. In our demonstration, we need an array-like construct that can hold a collection of objects but with an ability to grow and shrink during its lifetime. The `ArrayList` class found in the namespace called `System.Collections` of the .NET Framework contains this functionality. The fully-qualified name for `ArrayList` is `System.Collections.ArrayList` but, due to line 2 (`using System.Collections;`), we can use the shortcut `ArrayList`, as in lines 16 and 21. Like the `string` and `Array` classes, `ArrayList` contains a useful assortment of built-in methods. However, our program merely uses its two methods—`Add` (line 26) and `RemoveAt` (line 35), along with the property `Count` (lines 33 and 47). When the `accounts` instance (declared in line 16) is created in the constructor of a `Bank` object (line 21), its length is 0.

An `ArrayList` object will hold any object, so we do not, as with the `Array`, need to specify its base type. We can add a new `Account` object to accounts with the `Add` method by providing it an `Account` object reference as an argument (see line 26). When an object is added to accounts with the `Add` method, it is added to the end of the already existing list of objects, just as when people arrive at a queue. `RemoveAt` lets us specify the index (passed as an argument) of the particular object we want to remove (as in line 35), which happens to remove the first object in the list.

The `Count` property provides us with the current number of objects held by the `ArrayList`.

There is a difference between the number `Count` represents and the number `totalAccountsCreated` represents—`totalAccountsCreated` counts the number of times the event: "Create a new account" has taken place. On the other hand, `Count` keeps track of the actual number of objects stored inside accounts. Thus, whereas `Count` moves up when account objects are added and down when they are removed, `totalAccountsCreated` only moves up when an account is added, but is not affected by any `Account` object removals.

Constant Members

I have already discussed constant members in Chapter 6, "Types Part I: The Simple Types." However, now that you are familiar with `static` variables, this is an appropriate place to mention that constant members are `static` variables by default. Let's illustrate the implications with an example. Imagine that you are constructing a simple computer model of the solar system. You are particularly interested in how light travels between the sun and the other planets. To this end, you create a class called `Light`. Specific objects of `Light` can then be used to represent particular sunrays. You need the constant speed of light (approximately 299792 kilometers per second) for many of your calculations, and so you include it in your `Light` class as in the following lines:

```
class Light
{
    ...
    public const double Speed = 299792;
    ...
}
```

Even though there is no `static` keyword in sight, `Speed` is now not only constant but also `static`, and it can be accessed from another object simply by applying the dot operator to the class name `Light`:

```
...Light.Speed...
```

`readonly` Members

Because `readonly` members are closely connected to the constructor concept, their discussion is deferred until after the section about constructors in Chapter 13, "Class Anatomy Part II: Object Creation and Garbage Collection."

Declaring Data Members: An Overview

This section provides a brief overview of the syntax for declaring each of the mentioned data members.

Syntax Box 12.2 only shows the most important parts of a data member declaration. The declaration in this syntax box is spread over four lines because one line was too wide for the page, so the definition should be read as if the four lines were one line.

If, for a moment, we disregard the second line

```
[static] [const  |  readonly]
```

(this is possible because it only consists of optional elements), we can, with the remaining parts, form the following familiar instance variable declaration:

```
private decimal amount = 0;
```

and by including the optional `static` keyword as in

```
private static int counter = 0;
```

we declare `counter` to be a `static` member variable.

A constant is, as we have seen earlier, declared by including the `const` keyword, as in the following line:

```
const uint SpeedOfLight = 299792;
```

The `static` keyword cannot be applied in a constant declaration, because a constant is `static` by default. For reasons of simplicity, this has not been expressed in Syntax Box 12.2.

A constant must have its value defined by compile time and must have a value assigned to it as part of its declaration.

The `readonly` member variable is declared with the `readonly` keyword, as in the next line of code. As opposed to a constant, a `readonly` member variable is not `static` by default and can be declared `static` as shown here.

```
private static readonly int counter = 0;
```

Syntax Box 12.2 Declaring a Data Member

```
Data_member_declaration::=

[<Access_modifier>]
➥[static] [const | readonly]
➥<Type> <Member_variable1_identifier> [= <Expression1>]
➥[, <Member_variable2_Identifier> [= <Expression2> ] ...];
```

where

```
<Access_modifier>
          ::= public
          ::= private
          ::= protected
          ::= internal
          ::= protected internal
```

Notes:

- A simplified version of the syntax for a member variable declaration was shown in Syntax Box 6.1 in Chapter 6. This syntax box expands this initial definition.
- So far, we have only discussed the `public` and `private` access modifiers. `protected`, `internal`, and `protected internal` have merely been included here for completeness. These latter modifiers will be discussed in Chapter 15, "Namespaces, Compilation Units, and Assemblies," and Chapter 16, "Inheritance Part I: Basic Concepts," and can safely be ignored at this point.

Function Members

C# has a rich set of function members, as you saw in the introduction of this chapter, but even though they are called different names and are meant for different purposes, they all contain a block of statements that are executed when called, just like our conventional method, which we will focus on in the next section.

Methods

Methods can be divided into two main groups—*instance methods* (defined without the `static` keyword) that belong to the group of instance functions (see the note in Syntax Box 12.2) and `static` methods (defined with the `static` keyword) that belong to the group of `static` functions. An instance method is executed in relation to a specific object; it needs an object to be executed. In contrast, a `static` method is executed in relation to the class and does not need any particular object to be invoked, but is invoked through the classname.

All Objects of a Class Share Just One Copy of Each Instance Method

Because each instance method is executed in relation to a specific object, it seems that there exists one particular instance method copy in the memory per object. However, this is not the case, because it would consume far too much memory. Instead, all objects of the same class share just one copy of each instance method.

The **Rocket** class shown next illustrates this point. Two **Rocket** objects are created and their references assigned to **rocketA** and **rocketB**, respectively (lines 30 and 31). Even though there is only one copy of the **Launch** method, **rocketA.Launch()** (line 40) still executes **Launch** in relation to **rocketA**, and **rocketB.Launch()** (line 41) executes **Launch** in relation to **rocketB**.

```
01: class Rocket
02: {
03:     private double speed;
    ...
10:     public void Launch()
11:     {
            ...
15:         speed = 3000.9;
            ...
20:     }
        ...
25:   }

30: Rocket rocketA = new Rocket();
31: Rocket rocketB = new Rocket();

40: rocketA.Launch();
41: rocketB.Launch();
```

How can C# make this possible? The compiler secretly passes the reference of the object for which the method is called along as an argument to the instance method. If you could look down into the engine room of the compiler, it might look like the following lines:

```
Rocket.Launch (rocketA);
Rocket.Launch (rocketB);
```

The compiler then (also secretly) attaches the object reference to any code inside the method that is specific to the object. For example, during the **Rocket.Launch(rocketA)** call, the following line

```
speed = 3000.9
```

becomes equivalent to

```
rocketA.speed = 3000.9
```

A method definition consists of a method header and a method body (see Syntax Box 12.3). The method header specifies important attributes that determine how other parts of the program can access and invoke this method (for example, methods of other objects or methods of the same class). The method body consists of the statements executed when the method is invoked.

The accessibility of a method is specified by an optional access modifier in the method header (see Syntax Box 12.3) and has, in the examples we have seen so far, been comprised of the `public` and `private` keywords. `public` specifies that any part of the program has access to the method; `private` indicates that the method only can be reached from within the class itself. As you can see in Syntax Box 12.3, C# offers other ways to control the access of methods (and class members in general) in the form of the access modifiers `protected`, `internal`, and `protected internal`. However, because they are relevant in the context of assemblies and an important OO mechanism not yet discussed called inheritance, we will defer their discussion until these elements have been discussed sufficiently.

Syntax Box 12.3 The Method Definition

```
Method::=
      <Method_header>
      <Method_body>
```

where

```
<Method_header>::=
 [<Method_modifiers>] <Return_type> <Method_identifier>

➥ ([<Formal_parameter_list>])

<Method_body>::=
{
    <Statements>
}

            ::=
   ;

<Method_modifiers>
                  ::= <Access_modifier>
                  ::= new
                  ::= static
                  ::= virtual
                  ::= sealed
                  ::= override
                  ::= abstract
                  ::= extern

<Access_modifier>
                  ::=  public
                  ::=  private
                  ::=  protected
                  ::=  internal
                  ::=  protected internal

<Return_type>
              ::= void
              ::= <Type>
```

Notes:

- The method modifiers `new`, `static`, `virtual`, `sealed`, `override`, and `abstract` are related to the object-oriented mechanism called inheritance and will be discussed along with this important concept in Chapter 16.
- A *<Method body>* can either consist of a block of statements or simply a semicolon representing the empty statement.

A method is called by writing the method name followed by a pair of parentheses enclosing an argument list (see Syntax Box 12.4) that must match the formal parameter list specified in the method header of the method definition shown in Syntax Box 12.3.

Syntax Box 12.4 The Method Call

```
Method_call::=
[<Class_identifier>.|<Object_identifier>.]<Method_identifier>([<Argument_list>])
```

Notes:

- The optional `<Class_identifier>` (for calling a static method) and `<Object_identifier>` (for calling an instance method) trailed by the dot operator are only needed when the method is called from outside the class where it resides.
- The type of each individual argument in `<Argument_list>` must have an implicit conversion path leading to the type specified by the corresponding formal parameters in `<Formal_parameter_list>` that is part of the method header shown earlier in Syntax Box 12.3.

`static` Methods

Recall that a program is started by the .NET runtime with an initial call to the `Main()` method. The runtime does not create any objects and must invoke `Main()` without relating it to any particular object. When we declare `Main()` to be a **`static`** method, we specify that it belongs to a class, rather than an object of this class, and thereby allow the runtime to call `Main()` directly through the classname:

```
MyClass.Main()
```

where `Main()` belongs to the class `MyClass` specified in:

```
class MyClass()
{
    ...
    public static void Main()
    {
        ...
    }
    ...
}
```

Syntax Box 12.5 Declaring a `static` Method

A **`static`** method is defined by adding the reserved word **`static`** before the return type of the method header as in the following:

```
Static_method_definition::=
<Method_modifier> static <Return_type> <Method_identifier>
➥ ([<Formal_parameter_list>])
<Method_body>
```

Note:

- The **`static`** method definition must be positioned inside the class body, just like any other method.

Calling a static Method

A static method can be called in three different ways:

- From within an object of the class it belongs to, in which case it doesn't need any classname or object name as a prefix.

```
class Rocket
{
    public static void Average(...)
    {
            ...
    }

        ...Average(...) ... <—— call to Average from within the same class
}    ↑
     no need for class name or object name
```

- From outside the class in which it resides. Two possibilities then exist:
- If any objects of the class exist where the method is defined, it can be called by applying the dot operator to the name of the object followed by the name of the method:

```
Rocket rocketA = new Rocket();
...
...rocketA.Average(...)...
```

- Disregarding the existence of any objects of the class where the method is defined, it can be called by applying the dot operator to the classname followed by the name of the method:

```
...Rocket.Average(...)...
```

In general, it is better to use the class name `Rocket.Average(...)` than the object name `Rocket.Average(...)`, because the class name format clearly signals that we are calling a static method.

When to Use static Methods

There is one compelling reason for making the `Main()` method `static`—the program won't execute if you don't. Unfortunately, the choice is not that easy for the rest of the methods in our programs. However, what follows are a couple of examples where you should consider making the methods `static`.

1) Methods that cannot be pinpointed to belong to a specific object should be `static`.

Consider a method used to calculate the average of a list of numbers provided to it as arguments. This method does not interact with any instance variables/instance methods, but merely mingles with its own confined world (read method body) where it follows its own little average-calculation-algorithm. So, theoretically, it doesn't belong to any particular class.

Several different classes and objects throughout your program might need to use the functionality of this method. If it resided inside the MyMath class and was declared non-static as follows

```
class MyMath
{
    ...
    public double Average (params double[] numbers)
    {
        ...
    }
    ...
}
```

Then every method calling Average would have to first create an object of class MyMath and then call Average through this object as in the following:

```
MyMath mathObject = new MyMath();  <—— An object of type MyMath must be created before...
...
...mathObject.Average(...)  <—— ...the Average method can be called. This is
                                cumbersome and inefficient.
```

So the only reason for creating the mathObject is to call Average. As soon as we are finished with Average, the mathObject is forgotten and never used again. Not only did we waste time writing the extra line of source code to create the object, this same line also cluttered our code and the runtime had to waste time and memory creating an object with its instance variables and its accompanying reference variable. Had we instead declared Average to be static, as in the following

```
    ...
    public static double Average (params double[] numbers)
    ...
```

then our call to Average would have been simplified to

```
...MyMath.Average(...) ...
```

static methods are used throughout the .NET Framework and often for the reason already given. For example, the System.Math class contains 24 static math-related methods, and the System.Console class contains the well-known Read, ReadLine, Write and WriteLine methods that allow us to simply write

```
Console.WriteLine(…)
```

Tip

If your program contains several methods not related to any particular object but that provide functionality belonging to the same category, create a special class for these methods and let them all be static. For example, if you had other statistics related methods apart Average from those already discussed, you could create a class called Statistics and equip it with a range of static methods, all providing various statistics calculations. Any programmer in your project in need of calculating various statistics will then first look inside this class before he or she spends time writing his or her own methods.

2) In some cases, use a **static** *method to access a* **static** *member variable.*

In general, all **static** variables should, as mentioned earlier in this chapter, be declared **private**. When accessed from outside its class, a **private static** variable can only be accessed via a **static** method or via instance methods defined inside the same class as the variable. To use an instance method requires an object, so to access a **private static** variable at all times, even when no objects of the relevant class are created, you need a **static** method. For example, suppose that the **static** variable **totalAccountsCreated** of the **Account** class in Listing 12.1 presented earlier more appropriately was declared **private** instead of **public**. The **Account** class would then look like the code shown in Figure 12.5 and need the **static** method **GetTotalAccountsCreated** to be accessed at all times.

FIGURE 12.5
Accessing a *static* variable with a *static* method.

```
class Account          1 totalAccountsCreated is now private instead of public so...
{
    private static uint totalAccountsCreated = 0;

    public Account()
    {                                  2
        totalAccountsCreated++;     ...an accessor method is needed...
    }

    public static uint GetTotalAccountsCreated ()        3
    {                                        ...which must be declared static...
        return totalAccountsCreated;
    }
}
    ...
class Bank
{
      ...
    public void PrintStatistics()
    {
        Console.WriteLine("Number of current accounts: " + accounts.Count +
            "\nNumber of new accounts created: " +
            Account.GetTotalAccountsCreated());
    }
      ...
}                                          4
...                 ...in order to call it through the class name Account.
                 GetTotalAccountsCreated() can thus be called even if zero
                    Account objects have been created.
```

Tip

Some programmers believe that **static** methods are non-object-oriented because they don't belong to a specific object and, hence, become global in nature. This is a valid point, but most programmers still find that they need **static** methods from time to time. However, if you find yourself using many **static** methods, you might need to review your overall software design.

You cannot directly access and invoke instance variables and instance methods from within a **static** method of the same class.

static methods are associated with a class and not any particular object. Instance methods and instance variables belong to a particular object of a class. A practical consequence of this gap between **static** and instance class members is the inability of directly calling an instance method, or directly accessing an instance variable from within a **static** method of the same class. Let's illustrate this by continuing our previous story about the Solar system model and the **Light** class.

Listing 12.2 contains a simple **Light** class with the speed-of-light constant in line 6 called **Speed**. Remember that any constant by default also is **static**. **Light** further contains two instance variables (lines 7 and 8), two **static** methods (lines 10–20) and four instance methods (lines 22–40). By mixing **static** and instance methods and variables in the same class, we can explore the boundaries for the kind of calls we can validly make between these entities.

LISTING 12.2 SolarSystem.cs

```
01: using System;
02:
03: class Light
04: {
05:      // Speed of light in kilometers per second
06:     public const double Speed = 299792;
07:     private double timeTraveled;
08:     private double distanceTraveled;
09:
10:     public static double CalculateDistance (double seconds)
11:     {
12:         return seconds * Speed;
13:     }
14:
15:     public static double CalculateTime (double distance)
16:     {
17:         Light someLight = new Light();
18:         someLight.SetDistanceTraveled(distance);
19:         return someLight.GetTimeTraveled();
20:     }
21:
22:     public void SetTimeTraveled (double newTimeTraveled)
23:     {
24:         timeTraveled = newTimeTraveled;
25:     }
26:
27:     public void SetDistanceTraveled (double newDistanceTraveled)
28:     {
29:         distanceTraveled = newDistanceTraveled;
30:     }
31:
32:     public double GetDistanceTraveled ()
33:     {
34:         return CalculateDistance (timeTraveled);
35:     }
36:
37:     public double GetTimeTraveled ()
38:     {
39:         return distanceTraveled / Speed;
```

LISTING 12.2 continued

```
40:     }
41: }
42:
43: class SolarSystem
44: {
45:     public static void Main()
46:     {
47:         Light sunRay = new Light();
48:
49:         Console.WriteLine("Speed of light: {0}kilometers per hour",
            ➥Light.Speed);
50:         sunRay.SetTimeTraveled(240);
51:         Console.WriteLine("The sunray has traveled {0} kilometers after
            ➥240 seconds",
52:             sunRay.GetDistanceTraveled());
53:         Console.WriteLine("Light travels {0} kilometers after 480 seconds",
54:             Light.CalculateDistance(480));
55:         Console.WriteLine("It takes {0:N2} seconds for a ray of sunshine",
56:             Light.CalculateTime(150000000));
57:         Console.WriteLine("to travel from the sun to the earth");
58:     }
59: }
```

```
Speed of light: 299792 kilometers per hour
The sunray has traveled 71950080 kilometers after 240 seconds
Light travels 143900160 kilometers after 480 seconds
It takes 500.35 seconds for a ray of sunshine
to travel from the sun to the earth
```

The **static** method **CalculateDistance** (lines 10–13) is able to call **Speed** because **Speed** is a **const** and, therefore, a **static** variable by default. However, an attempt to use the instance variable **timeTraveled** (line 8) inside **CalculateDistance**, as suggested in the following lines, would be absurd and trigger an error message from the compiler.

```
public static double CalculateDistance ()
{
    return timeTraveled * Speed    // Invalid
}
```

The **CalculateDistance** method is not associated with any particular object, so the compiler does not know to which instance **timeTraveled** belongs.

On the other hand, the **SetTimeTraveled** method (lines 22–25) is an instance method. It is called through a particular instance object and can be used to access the **timeTraveled** instance variable of that same object, as shown in line 24.

It is also possible to call a **static** method from an instance method. The **GetDistanceTraveled** method defined in lines 32–35 calls the **static** method **CalculateDistance** with the argument **timeTraveled**. **CalculateDistance** does not have to determine which object **timeTraveled** belongs to, this has already been determined by the **GetDistanceTraveled** method. **CalculateDistance** just receives **timeTraveled** as an argument and does not care about its origin as long as its type matches that of its formal parameter.

Is it possible to invoke an instance method from within a **static** method? Yes, but only indirectly by first creating an instance of the class and then calling the non-**static** method through this particular object. The **CalculateTime** method of lines 15–20 performs this trick. It first creates an instance of **Light** called **someLight** in line 17 and can then call the non-**static** method **SetDistanceTraveled** through this object by applying the dot operator, as shown in line 18. At the same time, it also accesses the non-**static** variable **distanceTraveled** by assigning the argument **distance** to it. By finally calling the non-**static** method **GetTimeTraveled** and returning this method's return value back to the caller, **CalculateTime** is able to indirectly utilize the functionality of two non-**static** methods to calculate the time it takes light to travel a certain distance.

Had we inside **CalculateTime** attempted to call **SetDistanceTraveled** and **GetTimeTraveled** instead, without creating **someLight** and called them through this object, **CalculateTime** would have looked like the following lines and triggered a compiler error.

```
15:     public static double CalculateTime (double distance)
16:     {
17:         SetDistanceTraveled(distance);  // Invalid. Cannot call instance
18:         return GetTimeTraveled();       // methods directly from within
19:     }                                   // a static method.
```

Invalidly attempting to directly call instance methods and variables from within **static** methods is a common mistake made by programmers.

Note

The distance from the sun to the earth is approximately 150,000,000 kilometers (equivalent to approximately 3409 times around the earth). According to the sample output from Listing 12.2 (and modern scientific calculations), it takes a little more than 500 seconds (eight minutes and twenty seconds) for a sunray to reach the earth.

Little wonder the sun needs a good sleep like the rest of us after a long day.

Reference Parameters

Recall from Chapter 6 that C#'s types can be divided into value and reference types. When a value of a reference type is passed to a method, the changes made to this value within the confines of the method are reflected in the original value that was passed as an argument. This fact was utilized by the **Swap** method in the **BubbleSort.cs** program contained in Chapter 11, "Arrays Part II: Multidimensional Arrays—Searching and Sorting Arrays", which contained an array (a reference type) as a formal parameter, allowing it to swap array elements of the original array that was passed to it.

On the other hand, if a variable of a value type, such as one of the simple types, is passed as an argument to a method, the variable's value is copied to the corresponding formal parameter. Consequently, the original variable value and the value accessed inside the method are totally separate and changes made within the confines of the method are not reflected on the original variable value. This prevents us from performing the same act on a value type as **Swap** did on the array. We have lived happily without this ability so far because any value calculated by a method has been returned to the caller with the return value of the method. But what if we need to return more than one value of a value type back to the caller? With the return value, we can only return one value. Fortunately, reference parameters allow us to implement this functionality by letting any changes made to it be reflected in the original argument of a value type. A reference parameter is declared with the `ref` keyword, as in the following method header

```
public static void Swap(ref int a, ref int b)
```

which declares `a` and `b` to be reference parameters. To ensure that the programmers who write calls to the `Swap` method are aware that `Swap` contains reference parameters that likely will change the arguments passed to it, a method call must also include the `ref` keyword. It must be positioned in front of any argument passed to a reference parameter:

```
Swap(ref myValue, ref yourValue)
```

Failure to comply with this protocol will trigger the compiler to issue an error message alerting the unaware or forgetful programmer.

Listing 12.3 provides the full source code accompanying the previous two lines of code. The `Swap` method is used to swap `myValue` with `yourValue` and prints out the result.

LISTING 12.3 Swapper.cs

```
01: using System;
02:
03: class Swapper
04: {
05:     public static void Main()
06:     {
07:         int myValue = 10;
08:         int yourValue = 20;
09:
10:         Swap(ref myValue, ref yourValue);
11:         Console.WriteLine("My value: {0}   Your value: {1}",
            ➥myValue, yourValue);
12:     }
13:
14:     public static void Swap(ref int a, ref int b)
15:     {
16:         int temp;
17:
18:         temp = a;
19:         a = b;
20:         b = temp;
21:     }
22: }
```

```
My value: 20   Your value: 10
```

The `Swap` method (lines 14–21) uses the familiar swapping algorithm applied in previous examples to swap `a` and `b`. Because `a` and `b` are reference parameters, their swap will cause any original pair of arguments passed along with a method call to **Swap** to be swapped. This is verified through the sample output of this listing.

Note

Any argument passed to a reference parameter must be an assignable variable. For example, the following call to the **Swap** method of Listing 12.3 would be invalid

```
Swap(ref 10, ref 20)
```

because it is impossible to assign a value to **10** or **20**.

Output Parameters

Up until now, it has been a requirement that any variable used as an argument in a method call must be initialized prior to this call. For example, the following source code will not execute because the unassigned variable **distance** is used as an argument when **Initialize** is invoked.

```
01: class MyCalculator
02: {
03:   public static void Main()
04:   {
05:     int distance;
06:
07:     Initialize(distance);
08:   }
09:
10:     public static void Initialize(int newDistance)
11:     {
12:       newDistance = 100;
13:     }
14: }
```

distance is not initialized before being used as...
...an argument in the call to Initialize making...
...this call invalid.

If you attempt to compile the preceding code, you will get an error message similar to the following line

```
Use of unassigned local variable 'distance'
```

Sometimes, you might want a method to set the initial value of a variable by might it as an argument to this method. You need exactly the same functionality as a reference parameter but with the additional ability to use an uninitialized variable as an argument. The *output parameter* provides us with this ability. You declare an output parameter by including the **out** keyword in front of the type of the parameter in the method header

```
public static void Initialize(out int newDistance)
```

which states that **newDistance** is an output parameter. If you substitute this line with line 10 in the previous source code and insert the Keyword **out** before **distance** in line 7, the program becomes valid and the call to initialize in line 7 will cause **distance** to hold the value 100.

Note

An output parameter is the same as a reference parameter with one difference—the output parameter accepts unassigned variables.

Note

An output parameter must be assigned a value before control leaves its method.

Accommodating for Varying Number of Arguments: The Parameter Array

Recall the method called `Sum` from the `SimpleCalculator.cs` program in Chapter 4, "A Guided Tour Through C#: Part II," shown next:

```
     // Sum calculates the sum of two int's
    public static int Sum(int a, int b)
    {
        int sumTotal;

        sumTotal = a + b;
        return sumTotal;
    }
```

`Sum` calculates the sum of exactly two arguments. Suppose you also needed to calculate the sum of three arguments and four arguments and even ten arguments. You could attempt to cater to this need by writing a sum method for each number of arguments. Their headers could look like the following:

```
public static int SumThree(int a, int b, int c)

public static int SumFour(int a, int b, int c, int d)

public static int SumTen(int a, int b, int c, int d, int e, int f, int g, int h,
➥int i, int j)
```

Hmm…this is starting to look cumbersome, and I haven't even included the method bodies. It would be much easier if we could write a single method that would accept any number of arguments and still perform the correct calculations. The parameter array provides a solution to our problem. A *parameter array* is declared by writing the `params` keyword in front of a one-dimensional array in the method header

```
public static int Sum(params int [] numbers)
```

which is identical to line 20 of Listing 12.4 shown shortly. It allows us to call `Sum` and include any number of arguments as demonstrated in lines 10–12 of Listing 12.4.

Note

The parameter array must be one-dimensional, so you cannot use arrays of this format with the `params` keyword `int [ , ]`. However, arrays of the format `int []`, `int [] []`, or even `int [] [] []`, and so on are valid because they all contain one-dimensional arrays within them.

By including the `params` keyword, we ask the runtime to automatically insert the arguments provided into the `numbers` array in the order they are written in the method call. If the `Sum` method, for example, is called with the following line (see line 11 of Listing 12.4)

```
...Sum(10,20,30)
```

the `numbers` array will be of length 3 and have the following content when the execution of `Sum`'s method body is about to begin:

`numbers` array:

Index	0	1	2
Value	10	20	30

The `numbers` array is of base type `int`, so all arguments provided must be of a type implicitly convertible to type `int`.

The call to `Sum` can also contain zero arguments as demonstrated in line 14, which simply results in `numbers` being of length zero during the execution of `Sum`.

Finally, the argument provided to `Sum` can be a one-dimensional array of a base type implicitly convertible to the base type of `numbers`. This is demonstrated by line 8, which declares the array `myNumbers` and line 13 where `myNumbers` is provided as an argument for the call to `Sum`. As execution of `Sum` begins, `numbers` will have the same array element values as `myNumbers`.

LISTING 12.4 `SumCalculator.cs`

```
01: using System;
02:
03: class SumCalculator
04: {
05:     public static void Main()
06:     {
07:         int result1, result2, result3, result4, result5;
08:         int[] myNumbers = {4, 10, 6, 8, 2};
09:
10:         result1 = Sum(3,5);
11:         result2 = Sum(10,20,30);
12:         result3 = Sum(1,2,3,4,5,6,7,8,9,10);
13:         result4 = Sum(myNumbers);
14:         result5 = Sum();
15:
16:         Console.WriteLine("\nEnd results: {0}, {1}, {2}, {3}, {4}",
17:             result1, result2, result3, result4, result5);
18:     }
19:
```

LISTING 12.4 continued

```
20:     public static int Sum(params int[] numbers)
21:     {
22:         int sum = 0;
23:
24:         Console.Write("\nThe numbers array contains {0} elements:",
        ➥numbers.Length);
25:         foreach (int number in numbers)
26:         {
27:             Console.Write(" {0}", number);
28:             sum += number;
29:         }
30:         Console.WriteLine("\nThe sum is: {0}", sum);
31:         return sum;
32:     }
33: }
```

```
The numbers array contains 2 elements: 3 5
The sum is: 8

The numbers array contains 3 elements: 10 20 30
The sum is: 60

The numbers array contains 10 elements: 1 2 3 4 5 6 7 8 9 10
The sum is: 55

The numbers array contains 5 elements: 4 10 6 8 2
The sum is: 30

The numbers array contains 0 elements:
The sum is: 0

End results: 8, 60, 55, 30, 0
```

The relevant points regarding the parameter array have already been discussed.

It is worth noticing how the `Sum` method (lines 20–32) adapts to any number of parameters provided through the use of the `foreach` statement (lines 25–29) that traverses through the entire `numbers` array.

Note

It is not possible to use the `ref` and `out` keywords with the `params` keyword.

Note

If the list of formal parameters in the method header needs to include other parameters apart from the parameter array, the parameter array must be last in the list, rendering the following method header invalid

```
public static int Sum (params int[] numbers, int a, int b) //Invalid
```

whereas the following is valid

```
public static int Sum (int a, int b, params int[] numbers) //Valid
```

Another immediate consequence of this rule is that only one parameter array can be included in any one method header.

Method Overloading: Calling Different Methods with the Same Name, Different Arguments

Before I attempt to explain what method overloading is, take a look at the following example. It gives you an idea of why method overloading was ever invented in the first place.

Chapter 4 presented you with Pythagoras's formula for calculating the distance between two locations in a `Map` class. The following is a brief refresher of the formula:

> If L1(x1, y1) and L2(x2, y2) are two locations on a map, the distance between them can be calculated as:
>
> $$\text{distance} = \sqrt{(x1 - x2)^2 + (y1 - y2)^2}$$

We never wrote the code for a `Distance` method in Chapter 4, so let's write a version now:

```
class Map
{
    ...
    public double DistanceInt (int x1, int y1, int x2, int y2)
    {
        return Math.Sqrt(Math.Pow(x1 - x2, 2) + Math.Pow(y1 - y2, 2));
    }
    ...
}
```

The formal parameter list of `DistanceInt` accepts four arguments of type `int` or of types that are implicitly convertible to `int`. However, if we also need to calculate the distance between two locations defined by four arguments of, say, type `double`, we must write another method in the `Map` class. If we call it `DistanceDouble`, it could look like

```
class Map
{
    ...
    public double DistanceDouble (double x1, double y1, double x2, double y2)
    {
        return Math.Sqrt(Math.Pow(x1 - x2, 2) + Math.Pow(y1 - y2, 2));
    }
    ...
}
```

Another programmer then tells us about her newly created class called `Location` (shown next) that is used to represent locations. Each `Location` object represents a location with the `private` instance variables `x` and `y`. They can be accessed and modified with the accompanying accessor and mutator methods.

```
class Location
{
    private int x = 0;
    private int y = 0;

    public void setX(int newX)
    {
        x = newX;
    }

    public void setY(int newY)
    {
        y = newY;
    }

    public int getX()
    {
        return x;
    }

    public int getY()
    {
        return y;
    }
}
```

The programmer needs to perform distance calculations and would like to use the functionality of the methods we have already written. However, instead of providing four numeric arguments as required by the previously defined methods, she would find it more convenient to pass two `Location` objects. To accommodate the request of our fellow programmer, we then set out to write a method called `DistanceLocationObjects`. It looks as follows:

```
public double DistanceLocationObjects (Location L1, Location L2)
{
    return Math.Sqrt(Math.Pow(L1.getX() - L2.getX(), 2) +
    ➥Math.Pow(L1.getY() - L2.getY(), 2));
}
```

We now have three different methods with three different names. However, every method essentially does the same thing—*calculate a distance*. So even though the code works fine as is, it would be easier and more natural if each method call, whether providing arguments of type `int`, `double`, or `Location`, could use the same method name—`Distance`. If this was possible, the following three method calls would be valid

```
myMap.Distance(10, 10, 20, 30)←——Four arguments of type int

myMap.Distance(10.4, 20.3, 12.9, 10.0)←——Four arguments of type double

myMap.Distance(location1, location2)←——Two arguments of type Location.
```

and the compiler would automatically choose the correct way to handle the provided arguments. This scenario is made possible with *method overloading*, which allows us to define several methods in the same class with the same name but with different sets of formal parameters and different implementations. To implement method overloading in our case and make the three previous method calls valid and with correct return values, we simply need to change our three methods to have the same name—**`Distance`**. Their method headers now look like the following lines, while their original method bodies stay unchanged:

```
public double Distance(int x1, int y1, int x2, int y2)

public double Distance(double x1, double y1, double x2, double y2)

public double Distance(Location L1, Location L2)
```

When the compiler now meets the following call

```
myMap.Distance(10, 10, 20, 30)
```

it will go through the following process to determine which method to execute. First it looks for a method in `myMap` with a name that matches **`Distance`**. It finds three. Of those three, it chooses the method with the set of formal parameters that matches the set of arguments provided. A match requires that

- The amount of arguments provided fit the number of arguments accepted.
- Each argument must have a type compatible with its corresponding formal parameter. Thus, the first argument must have the same type as specified by the first formal parameter, the second argument must have the same type as specified by the second formal parameter, and so on.

By following this procedure, the compiler chooses to execute the **`Distance`** method with the header

```
public double Distance (int x1, int y1, int x2, int y2)
```

because it matches the four **`int`** arguments we provided in the method call. This is illustrated in Figure 12.6.

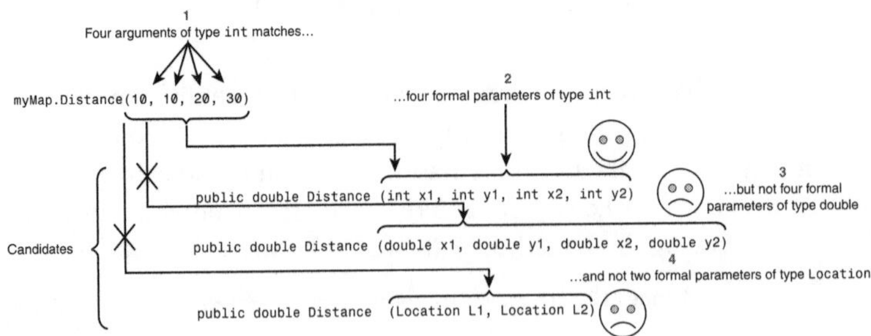

FIGURE 12.6
Finding the appropriate *`Distance`* method to execute .

The complete source code of the example is provided in Listing 12.5, where all three overloaded methods are being called in lines 17, 19, and 21.

LISTING 12.5 DistanceCalculator.cs

```
using System;

class DistanceCalculator
{
    public static void Main()
    {
        Map myMap = new Map();
        Location location1 = new Location();
        Location location2 = new Location();

        location1.setX(10);
        location1.setY(10);
        location2.setX(10);
        location2.setY(20);

        Console.WriteLine("Distance integers: " +
            myMap.Distance(5,10,5,30));
        Console.WriteLine("Distance doubles: " +
            myMap.Distance(15.4, 20.6, 15.4, 30.60));
        Console.WriteLine("Distance location objects: " +
            myMap.Distance(location1, location2));
    }
}

class Map
{
    public double Distance (int x1, int y1, int x2, int y2)
    {
        Console.WriteLine("\nUsing the integer version");
        return Math.Sqrt(Math.Pow(x1 - x2, 2) + Math.Pow(y1 - y2, 2));
    }

    public double Distance (double x1, double y1, double x2, double y2)
    {
        Console.WriteLine("\nUsing the double version");
        return Math.Sqrt(Math.Pow(x1 - x2, 2) + Math.Pow(y1 - y2, 2));
    }

    public double Distance (Location L1, Location L2)
    {
        Console.WriteLine("\nUsing the Location objects version");
        return Math.Sqrt(Math.Pow(L1.getX() - L2.getX(), 2) +
            Math.Pow(L1.getY() - L2.getY(), 2));
    }
}

class Location
{
    private int x = 0;
    private int y = 0;

    public void setX(int newX)
```

LISTING 12.5 continued

```
53:     {
54:         x = newX;
55:     }
56:
57:     public void setY(int newY)
58:     {
59:         y = newY;
60:     }
61:
62:     public int getX()
63:     {
64:         return x;
65:     }
66:
67:     public int getY()
68:     {
69:         return y;
70:     }
71: }
```

```
Using the integer version
Distance integers: 20

Using the double version
Distance doubles: 10

Using the Location objects version
Distance location objects: 10
```

Three methods with the same name but different sets of formal parameters are defined in the `Map` class (lines 25–45). Three method calls are made to `Distance` (lines 17, 19, and 21), each containing a different set of arguments matching different sets of formal parameters and, therefore, different overloaded methods. Each overloaded method has been equipped with a `WriteLine` statement indicating when this particular method is being executed (lines 29, 35, and 41). The resulting sample output confirms our claims that each distinct `Distance` method version is being called.

An important concept directly related to method overloading is the method signature concept.

The name of a method, along with its amount, types, and sequence of formal parameters, constitute the *signature* of a method. The following is an example.

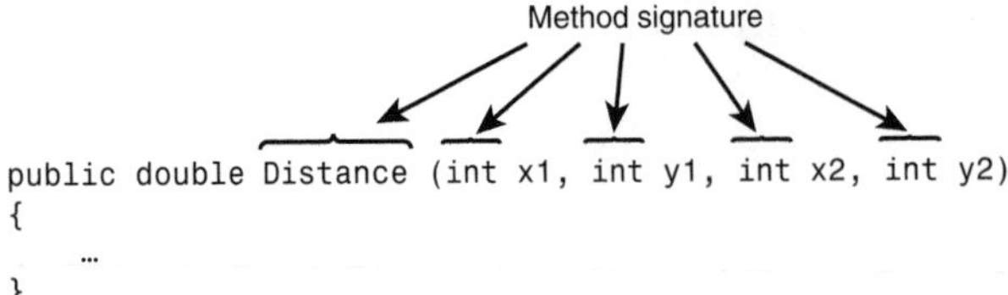

Notes:

- The return type of a method is not included in the method signature. Thus, the following three method headers represent the same signatures, even though the first method returns a `double` value, the second method an `int` value, and the third is `void`:

  ```
  public double Sum (double a, double b)
  public int Sum (double a, double b)
  public void Sum (double a, double b)
  ```

  The `params` keyword is ignored when establishing a methods signature. Consequently, the following two method headers have exactly the same signature:

  ```
  public double Sum (params double[] numbers)
  public double Sum (double[] numbers)
  ```

- The names of the formal parameters are not included in the method's signature, so the two displayed method headers have the same signature.

  ```
  public int Sum (double x, double y)
  public int Sum (double a, double b)
  ```

All methods in a class must have different signatures, but because the method name is just one of several attributes defining the method signature, it is possible to define many methods in the same class with the same name, as long as the rest of their signature differs. These methods are referred to as *overloaded methods*.

The pre-defined classes in the .NET Framework makes heavy use of method overloading. For example, the familiar `IndexOf` method of the `String` class has nine overloaded versions. Their method headers are listed next. The meaning of each overloaded method is described in the .NET Framework Reference, but we can recognize the second header, which simply takes a string as an argument and returns the index of the first match of this string.

```
public int IndexOf(char[])
public int IndexOf(string)
public int IndexOf(char)
public int IndexOf(string, int)
public int IndexOf(char, int)
public int IndexOf(char[], int)
public int IndexOf(char, int, int)
public int IndexOf(char[], int, int)
public int IndexOf(string, int, int)
```

Unknowingly, we have in many instances made use of the method overloading mechanism by simply calling the methods of the .NET Framework and by providing a list of arguments compatible with just one of these signatures.

Overloaded Methods and Implicit Conversions

For every argument in a method call that does not have a type exactly matching that specified by its corresponding formal parameter, the compiler will try to find an implicit conversion pathway that leads from the type of the argument to the type of the formal parameter.

The following example illustrates. As discussed in Chapter 6, a value of type `float` is implicitly convertible to a value of type `double`. With this in mind, let's inspect what happens if we attempt to call `Distance` in Listing 12.5 with four arguments of type `float`, as in the last call of the following lines:

```
float myX1 = 10f;
float myY1 = 15f;
float myX2 = 20f;
float myY2 = 25f;
...myMap.Distance (myX1, myY1, myX2, myY2)...
```

No direct match is found in any of the three method signatures (lines 27, 33, and 39) for any of the arguments, so C# moves to the next step where it attempts to find a match by implicitly converting the types of `myX1`, `myY1`, `myX2`, and `myY2` to the types present in the given formal parameters of one of the overloaded methods. Because `float` is implicitly convertible to `double`, a match is found in the method with the header:

```
33:     public double Distance (double x1, double y1, double x2, double y2)
```

Consequently, the compiler chooses to execute this particular overloaded method. Each of the values contained in `myX1`, `myY1`, `myX2`, and `myY2` are implicitly converted to `double` and assigned to `x1`, `y1`, `x2`, and `y2`, respectively, before execution of the method commences.

During the process of finding a matching type for an argument through implicit type conversion, the compiler follows three important rules worth keeping in mind. The next three sections focus on these rules.

Overloaded Methods and Implicit Conversion—Rule One

If two or more overloaded methods contain formal parameters specifying types along the implicit conversion path of the argument type, the compiler evidently has to choose from several possible matches. Rule one then says: Choose the type that is closest to the argument type in the conversion hierarchy.

Remember the implicit conversion hierarchy from Chapter 6 where it is possible to implicitly convert an `sbyte` to not only a `short`, but also to an `int`, `long`, `float`, `double`, and `decimal`. This is illustrated with highlighted arrows in Figure 12.7.

Listing 12.6 contains two overloaded methods called `DoIt` to demonstrate the effect of this first rule.

FIGURE 12.7
Implicit conversion path for *sbyte*.

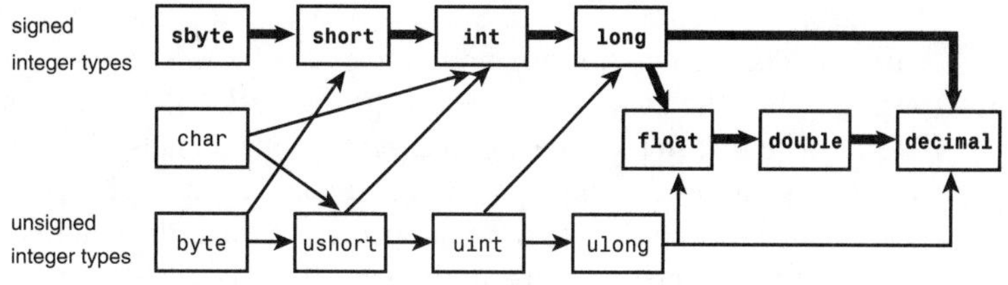

Where:

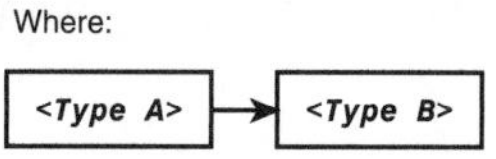

Means: It is possible to implicitly convert from Type A to Type B

Listing 12.6 MethodMatcher.cs

```
using System;

class MethodMatcher
{
    public void DoIt (int x)
    {
        Console.WriteLine("Executing int: " + x);
    }

    public void DoIt (double x)
    {
        Console.WriteLine("Executing double: " + x);
    }
}

class Tester
{
    public static void Main()
    {
        MethodMatcher myMatcher = new MethodMatcher();
        sbyte sbyteValue = 10;
        int intValue = 1000;
        long longValue = 30000;

        Console.Write("Calling with an sbyte value --> ");
        myMatcher.DoIt(sbyteValue);
        Console.Write("Calling with an int value --> ");
        myMatcher.DoIt(intValue);
        Console.Write("Calling with a long value --> ");
        myMatcher.DoIt(longValue);
    }
}
```

```
Calling with an sbyte value --> Executing int: 10
Calling with an int value --> Executing int: 1000
Calling with a long value --> Executing double: 30000
```

The first `DoIt` method (lines 5–8) contains a formal parameter that accepts an argument of type `int`. The second `DoIt` method in lines 10–13 accepts an argument of type `double`. Which overloaded method will then be executed if we call `DoIt` with an argument of type `sbyte`, as in line 26? The first step of finding an exact type match fails. The second step reveals that both method signatures contain types (`int` and `double`) that exist along the implicit conversion path of `sbyte`. According to the rule specified earlier, the compiler chooses the type closest to `sbyte` in the conversion path—in this case, `int`. This is confirmed by the sample output.

Line 28 calls `DoIt` with an argument of type `int`. This call is easily resolved because the `DoIt` method of lines 5–8 contains the signature `DoIt (int x)`, constituting an exact match to this call.

Finally, `DoIt` is called with an argument of type `long`. No exact match is found, so the compiler must resort to implicit conversion. The compiler moves along the implicit conversion path from `long` (see Figure 12.7) and finds a match between the last type on the path (`double`) and the signature `DoIt (double x)` of line 10, resulting in the execution of the corresponding method.

Overloaded Methods and Implicit Conversion—Rule Two

Two arrows leave the `long` box of Figure 12.7. One points to `float`, the other to `decimal`. In other words, a value of type `long` can either be implicitly converted to a value of type `float`, or to a value of type `decimal`. Now, consider a situation where we substitute the two `DoIt` methods of Listing 12.6 with two other `DoIt` methods containing the following two headers:

```
void DoIt (float x)
```

```
void DoIt (decimal x)
```

If we now make the call shown in the second line

```
sbyte mySbyte = 10;
DoIt (mySbyte)
```

how can the compiler choose which overloaded method to execute once the search reaches the `long` box? It can't. There is no rule stating which of the two arrows the compiler should follow as it leaves the `long` box to find an appropriate match. The method call is deemed unambiguous and triggers a compiler error.

Rule 2 generalizes the `DoIt` example just mentioned. Consider two overloaded methods called `MyMethod`. The two signatures of these two methods are identical, apart from two corresponding formal parameters of which one is a `float` type and the other a `decimal` type, as shown in the following two lines.

```
void MyMethod (…, float value, …)
                    ↕
void MyMethod (…, decimal value, … )
```

We then zoom in on the argument called `myArgument` included in a call to `MyMethod`, which corresponds to the highlighted formal parameters in the two `MyMethods`:

```
MyMethod (..., myArgument, ...)
```

The call to `MyMethod` will be deemed ambiguous if `myArgument` is of any of the `sbyte`, `short`, `int`, `long`, `byte`, `ushort`, `uint`, `ulong`, or `char` types. This is because any of these types will lead the compiler's search for a matching type through either the `long` or the `ulong` type boxes of the implicit conversion pathway. Two arrows leave from both the `long` and the `ulong` type boxes, as mentioned before and shown in Figure 12.7, so the compiler can only resolve the call if, during its search through the implicit conversion path, it does not have to travel through the types `long` or `ulong`. The method call is only acceptable if `myArgument` is of type `float`, `double`, or `decimal`.

Exactly the same conditions as described before hold if the two method headers look like the following:

```
void MyMethod (…, double value, …)

void MyMethod (…, decimal value, … )
```

where the formal parameter of type `float` has been substituted with a formal parameter of type `double`.

Overloaded Methods and Implicit Conversion—Rule Three

We have seen how two arrows leaving both the `long` and the `ulong` boxes cause certain method calls to be ambiguous. But two arrows also leave the `char`, `byte`, `ushort`, and `uint` boxes; doesn't this then cause the same problems? No! This time, C# has a rule (here called rule three) to remove the apparent ambiguousness.

Rule three: If the compiler on its search for a matching method signature moves through the implicit conversion pathway and finds two equally suited signatures, one containing a *signed* integer type, the other containing an *unsigned* integer type, it chooses the signature containing the signed integer type. The program of Listing 12.7 illustrates.

LISTING 12.7 `MethodMatcherTwo.cs`

```
using System;

class MethodMatcherTwo
{
    public void DoIt (uint x)
    {
        Console.WriteLine("Executing uint: " + x);
    }

    public void DoIt (int x)
    {
        Console.WriteLine("Executing int: " + x);
    }
}

class Tester
```

```
17: {
18:     public static void Main()
19:     {
20:         MethodMatcherTwo myMatcher = new MethodMatcherTwo();
21:         byte byteValue = 10;
22:
23:         Console.Write("Calling with a byte value --> ");
24:         myMatcher.DoIt(byteValue);
25:     }
26: }
```

```
Calling with a byte value --> Executing int: 10
```

`MethodMatcherTwo.cs` is similar to `MethodMatcher.cs` in that the overloaded method `DoIt` residing in the `MethodMatcherTwo` class is called from the `Main()` method. This time, the two overloaded methods contain a formal parameter of the unsigned type `uint` (line 5) and a formal parameter of the signed type `int` (line 10), respectively. `DoIt` is called with an argument of type `byte` (line 24). The compiler cannot find any exact match to `byte` in any of the overloaded methods, so the next step is to move along the implicit conversion path beginning at the `byte` box of Figure 12.7. When it arrives at the `ushort` box, it has two options. It can either choose the signature with the unsigned `uint` or the signed `int`. Rule three then dictates that the compiler choose the signed `int` as confirmed by the sample output.

Often, overloaded methods provide flexibility and convenience for the programmer calling them. A programmer only has to remember one method name and can then just pass whatever information he or she has available along as arguments. C# then automatically works out which particular overloaded method is suitable to be executed. Hmm...so the more overloaded methods we provide for one method name, the better, right? Not necessarily! Method overloading can be your good friend if implemented properly, or your great enemy if misused or overused. The next Common Pitfall gives an example of the latter.

Avoid overloading methods that essentially perform different actions. Instead call them different names.

Recall that 10 is an `int` and 10.0 is a `double`. Then consider the following two headers of overloaded methods:

1. `public int Sum (int a, int b)`
2. `public double Sum (double a, double b)`

The call

```
Sum (10, 10)
```

containing two `int`'s causes the method in 1 to be executed, but

```
Sum (10.0, 10.0)
```

with two `double`s causes the method in 2 to be executed. A minute detail like .0 decides which method is executed. This is fine here because the two methods essentially perform the same action. Apart perhaps concerns regarding precision, we don't care whether (10 + 10) or (10.0 + 10.0) is being calculated. However, if the two methods are performing significantly different actions, it is not advisable to let the type of a number (read a decimal point) decide which action is taken.

Listing 12.8 shows how things can go wrong when a method is over-overloaded. A programmer, who has just read about method overloading (but who skipped the Common Pitfall boxes), is working on the underlying computer program for a new virtual bookshop on the Internet. At the moment, he or she is writing the prototype for a `Book` class (lines 3–44) that eventually will hold all the relevant information about a book in the final program. The analysis of Listing 12.8 reveals the flaws of the `Book` class design.

LISTING 12.8 `VirtualBookshop.cs`

```
01: using System;
02:
03: class Book
04: {
05:     private string title;
06:     private uint numberOfPages;
07:     private double weight;
08:
09:     public void Set(string newTitle)
10:     {
11:         title = newTitle;
12:     }
13:
14:     public void Set(uint newNumberOfPages)
15:     {
16:         numberOfPages = newNumberOfPages;
17:     }
18:
19:     public void Set(double newWeight)
20:     {
21:         weight = newWeight;
22:     }
23:
24:     public void Set(string newTitle, uint newNumberOfPages,
        ➥ double newWeight)
25:     {
26:         title = newTitle;
27:         numberOfPages = newNumberOfPages;
28:         weight = newWeight;
29:     }
30:
31:     public void Set(string newTitle, double newWeight,
        ➥ uint newNumberOfPages)
32:     {
33:         title = newTitle;
34:         numberOfPages = newNumberOfPages;
35:         weight = newWeight;
36:     }
37:
38:     public void PrintDetails ()
```

LISTING 12.8 continued

```
39:     {
40:         Console.WriteLine("\nTitle: " + title);
41:         Console.WriteLine("Number of pages: " + numberOfPages);
42:         Console.WriteLine("Weight: {0} pounds", weight);
43:     }
44: }
45:
46: class VirtualBookshop
47: {
48:     public static void Main()
49:     {
50:         Book myBook = new Book();
51:
52:         myBook.Set("The latest tourist attraction: Planet Blipos");
53:         myBook.Set(1.3);
54:         myBook.Set(300);
55:         myBook.PrintDetails();
56:
57:         myBook.Set("Great places to visit on planet Blipos", 0.1, 4);
58:         myBook.PrintDetails();
59:         myBook.Set("Traveling to planet Blipos: A survival guide",
            ➥ 2000, 10.0);
60:         myBook.PrintDetails();
61:
62:         myBook.Set(11);
63:         myBook.PrintDetails();
64:
65:         //myBook.Set("Program your own space rocket", 8070, 3);
66:     }
67: }
```

```
Title: The latest tourist attraction: Planet Blipos
Number of pages: 300
Weight: 1.3 pounds

Title: Great places to visit on planet Blipos
Number of pages: 4
Weight: 0.1 pounds

Title: Traveling to planet Blipos: A survival guide
Number of pages: 2000
Weight: 10 pounds

Title: Traveling to planet Blipos: A survival guide
Number of pages: 11
Weight: 10 pounds
```

The program is still in its infancy, so only three pieces of information are represented in the `Book` class (lines 5–7)—the title, number of pages, and the weight (used when calculating shipping cost). As usual, the instance variables are declared `private`, so mutator methods must be provided to set their values. Excited about method overloading, the programmer believes it will be easier for the user of the class to apply just one method name called **Set** and, through overloading (headers in lines 9, 14, 19, 24, and 31), let C# second guess the intention of the method call and automatically choose the correct method. Calling **Set** with a single argument of type **uint** (or **int**) will assign the argument to **numberOfPages** (lines 14–17). An argument of type **double** will set the **weight** of the book (lines 19–22), and a single argument of type **string** will set the **title** (lines 9–12). This makes reasonable sense because the number of pages is always an integer number (an **int** or **uint**), weight most often contains a fraction (**double**), and a title consists of text (string).

Line 53 with the argument 1.3 correctly executes the **double** version of the overloaded methods, and line 54 with the argument 300 executes the **uint** version. Smooth sailing so far.

The programmer further wrote two overloaded **Set** methods containing three formal parameters (lines 24–29 and lines 31–36). They enable a programmer to assign values to all instance variables with just one method call, and lets him or her choose between inserting the number of pages before the weight (line 24) or vice versa (line 31) when specifying the arguments of a call to **Set**. Line 57 takes advantage of this facility and provides the weight (0.1) as the second argument, whereas line 59 positions the weight as the third argument (10.0). Both statements are correctly executed.

However, the first problem is encountered in line 62 where we intend to set the weight to 11.0 pounds, but forget to include the .0. As a result, C# sees an **int** (11), which is interpreted as the number of pages and is assigned as such with the method spanning lines 14–17. The sample output reveals the problem—a book with eleven pages weighing 10 pounds.

The double slash of line 65 has been included to avoid a compiler error. Removing them causes the following compiler error:

```
VirtualBookshop.cs(65,9): error CS0121: The call is ambiguous between
the following methods or properties:'Book.Set(string, double, uint)'

 and 'Book.Set(string, uint, double)'
```

We intended to assign 3 to **weight** but forgot to include .0 and thereby confused the compiler that no longer can choose between the signatures of line 24 and line 31.

To avoid the shown problems the programmer should have done the following:

- Limited the number of overloaded methods and instead created methods with names reflecting their essential actions, such as

  ```
  public void SetTitle(string newTitle)
  public void SetNumberOfPages (uint newNumberOfPages)
  public void SetWeight (double newWeigth)
  ```

- Limited the number of multi-assignment methods to one instead of two. The header of the remaining method accepting three arguments could look as follows:

  ```
  public void SetAll (string newTitle, uint newNumberOfPages,
  ➥ double newWeight)
  ```

Self-Referencing with the `this` Keyword

Every method of an object is automatically equipped with a reference called `this` that refers to the current object for which the method has been called. `this` is a keyword and is written inside a method body when a reference to the current object is needed.

Figure 12.8 illustrates the meaning of `this`. Two classes— `Book` and `VirtualBookshop`—are defined. A new `Book` object is created in line 70 of the `VirtualBookshop` class and its reference is assigned to `myBook`. `myBook` now references this new `Book` object (See 1 in Figure 12.8). `AnyMethod` (lines 20–40) is invoked through `myBook` in line 75. During the execution of `AnyMethod`, `this` holds a reference identical to that of `myBook`, and so is referencing the same object as `myBook` (See 2 in Figure 12.8). `this` can be applied like any other object reference, such as `myBook` with the small difference that `this` can also access `private` class members. For example, we can refer to an instance variable of the current object by applying the dot operator to `this` followed by the name of the instance variable, as shown in line 30.

FIGURE 12.8
The *`this`* reference.

```
10: class Book
11: {
15:     private string title;
20:     public void AnyMethod(…)
21:     {
        ...
30:         …this.title…
        ...
40:     }
    ...
50: }
    ...
60: class VirtualBookshop
61: {
    ...
70:     Book myBook = new Book();
        ...
75:     myBook.AnyMethod(…)
        ...
80: }
```

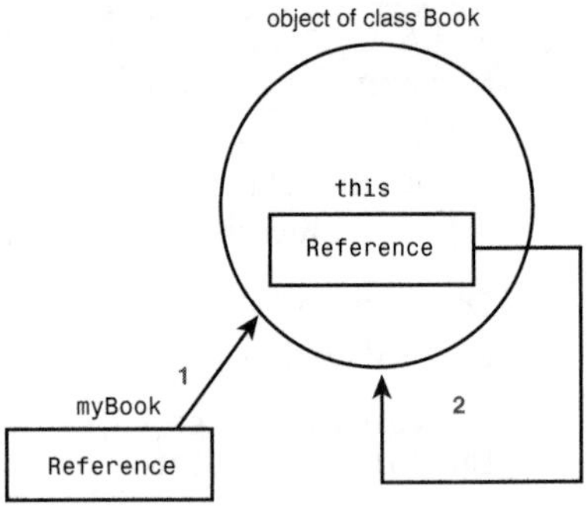

object of class Book
this
Reference
1
myBook
Reference
2

But wait a minute, previous examples only needed to use the name itself (`title`, in this case) when specifying an instance variable from within its class, so

```
30:          this.title
```

would be the same as

```
30:          title
```

This has been correct for the examples presented so far in this book, but Listing 12.9 provides a scenario where this is not the case and where `this` is needed to clarify our intentions. Listing 12.9 is similar to Listing 12.8 in that it contains a `Book` class with three instance variables (lines 5–7). Only one mutator method is provided for simplicity (lines 9–14). Instead, the class has been equipped with the accessor method `GetWeight` (lines 16–19) and a method called `PrintShippingCost` to print the shipping cost (lines 21–25). The `GetHeavierBook` (lines 27–33) compares the weight of the book represented by the current object with a `Book` object referenced by the argument passed to it. A reference to the heavier book is returned to the caller.

The `Dispatcher` class contains a method to calculate the cost of shipping a particular `Book` passed to it as an argument. The functionality provided by the `Book` class methods is applied by the `Main()` method of the `VirtualBookshop` class.

`this` is used for three different purposes in `VirtualBookShopTwo.cs`. We zoom in on those in the analysis after the sample output.

LISTING 12.9 `VirtualBookshopTwo.cs`

```
using System;

class Book
{
    private string title;
    private uint numberOfPages;
    private double weight;

    public void SetAll(string title, uint numberOfPages, double weight)
    {
        this.title = title;
        this.numberOfPages = numberOfPages;
        this.weight = weight;
    }

    public double GetWeight()
    {
        return weight;
    }

    public void PrintShippingCost()
    {
        Console.WriteLine("\nCost of shipping \"{0}\": {1:C}",
            title, Dispatcher.ShippingCost(this));
    }

    public Book GetHeavierBook (Book aBook)
    {
        if (weight > aBook.GetWeight())
            return this;
        else
            return aBook;
    }
}

class Dispatcher
{
    public static decimal ShippingCost (Book bookToSend)
    {
        return 5m + (decimal)(bookToSend.GetWeight() * 3);
    }
}

```

LISTING 12.9 continued

```
class VirtualBookshop
{
    public static void Main()
    {
        Book myBook = new Book();
        Book yourBook = new Book();
        Book heavierBook;

        myBook.SetAll("The Bliposians: Customs and Etiquette", 400, 2.3);
        Console.WriteLine("Shipping cost: {0:C}",
        ➥Dispatcher.ShippingCost (myBook));
        myBook.PrintShippingCost();

        yourBook.SetAll("Speak Blipolish in twenty days", 610, 3.1);
        heavierBook = yourBook.GetHeavierBook(myBook);
        heavierBook.PrintShippingCost();
    }
}
```

```
Shipping cost: $11.90

Cost of shipping "The Bliposians: Customs and Etiquette": $11.90

Cost of shipping "Speak Blipolish in twenty days": $14.30
```

Note

You might see another currency symbol than the dollar sign ($) in the sample output. The displayed symbol depends on the settings of your Windows operating system.

Listing 12.9 demonstrates three common uses for `this`.

- *To differentiate formal parameters and local variables from instance variables*—The scope of a method is part of the scope of the class within which this method is defined. Therefore, the formal parameters and local variables defined for a method are in the same scope as the instance variables of the class where the method resides, as illustrated in Figure 12.9. Usually, C# does not permit two variables belonging to the same scope to have the same name (see the "The Scope of Variables" section in Chapter 8). However, when one is an instance variable and the other a formal parameter or local variable, the compiler accepts it.

  Sometimes, we might want to take advantage of this possibility and declare formal parameters and local variables with the same names as their similarly scoped instance variables. Formal parameters in mutator methods used to assign new values to instance variables is a typical scenario exemplified in Listing 12.9 shown before. Before we look closer at Listing 12.9, we need to briefly revisit the `Set` mutator method in lines 24–29 of the `VirtualBookshop.cs` program in Listing 12.8. Its formal parameter names (`newTitle`, `newNumberOfPages`, and `newWeight`) were constructed by adding `new` in front of each of the corresponding instance variables to avoid a name clash with those. Name clashes would have resulted in problems that could only have been solved by the then unknown `this` keyword. That was then. Armed with the knowledge of `this`, we can now apply another line of thought saying, "Give the name to the formal parameter/local variable that is most suitable, disregarding name-clashes with instance variables." I have decided that `title` is a better name than `newTitle` (otherwise, I couldn't demonstrate the use of `this`), so we end up with the names written in line 9 of Listing 12.9. And here is the problem I alluded to before. How does the compiler know what `title` refers to when written inside the method body of `SetAll`. Is it the instance variable `title` or the formal parameter `title`? Because local variables and formal parameters take precedence over instance variables, `title` represents the formal parameter. But how do we then specify the instance variable `title`? Because `this` is a reference to the object containing the instance variables,

```
this.title
```

refers to the instance variable `title`. Line 11 thus instructs the compiler to assign the formal parameter `title` to the instance variable `title`.

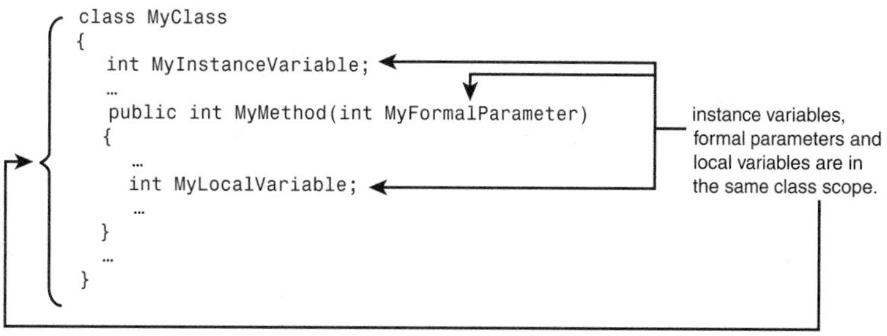

FIGURE 12.9
The scope of local variables, formal parameters, and instance variables.

```
class MyClass
{
    int MyInstanceVariable;
    ...
    public int MyMethod(int MyFormalParameter)
    {
        ...
        int MyLocalVariable;
        ...
    }
    ...
}
```

instance variables, formal parameters and local variables are in the same class scope.

- *To pass the reference of the current object as an argument to another method*—The `ShippingCost` method in lines 38–41 of the `Dispatcher` class takes an argument of type `reference-to-Book-object` and calculates the shipping cost of the book represented by the referenced object. It uses a simple formula saying "Fixed cost ($5.00) plus the `weight` in pounds times $3.00." Mathematically expressed, it looks as follows:

  ```
  5 + (weight x 3)
  ```

  The `weight` is obtained by calling the accessor method `GetWeight` of the `Book` object that is referenced by the formal parameter `bookToSend`.

  `ShippingCost` is used in line 53 as part of a statement that uses `WriteLine` to print out the shipping cost of `myBook`. `ShippingCost` is a `static` method, so it is called through the `Dispatcher` class itself. `myBook` holds a reference to a `Book` object (see line 48) and is used as an argument in line 53 for the call to `ShippingCost`. We manage to print out all the information we want with line 53; however, it requires us to fiddle around with the `WriteLine` method along with appropriate text and shipping cost to make the output look nice onscreen. So why not let the `Book` object take care of this? Then we can simply call a method like `PrintShippingCost` through `myBook`, as in line 54, everything else is taken care of. Let's look closer at how the `PrintShippingCost` method is designed in lines 21–25. `PrintShippingCost` needs to obtain the shipping cost of the current `Book` object. Luckily, the `ShippingCost` method of the `Dispatcher` class provides this information. But the argument must be a book object reference, so we need the reference of the object we are currently working inside as an argument. This argument is identical to the reference held by `myBook`. However, because `myBook` is in a different scope and not accessible from within the object it is referencing, `myBook` is useless for our purposes. Fortunately, `this` is the equivalent to `myBook` when inside `Book`, just as illustrated in Figure 12.8 shown earlier, so `this` is provided as a suitable argument in line 24.

- *To return the reference of the current object back to the caller of the method*—The `GetHeavierBook` method of the book class compares the `weight` of the current object (represented by the instance variable `weight` in line 29) and the `weight` (represented by `aBook.GetWeight()`) of a book object referenced by the formal parameter `aBook`. `GetHeavierBook` must return a reference to the `Book` object representing the heavier book. If `aBook` is heavier than the current object, the task is easy. We just return `aBook` (line 32). But what if the current object is heavier? Then we need to return a reference to the current object, in other words, we need to return `this` (line 30).

  The `Main()` method utilizes the `GetHeavierBook` method in line 57 to find the heavier book of `myBook` and `yourBook`. The `GetHeavierBook` is invoked by applying the dot operator to `yourBook`. Thus, `yourBook` is referencing the same object as `this` inside the `GetHeavierBook` method during the execution of this call. Because `myBook` is passed as an argument to `GetHeavierBook`, it holds the same reference as the formal parameter `aBook`. Line 30 is executed if `weight` is greater than `aBook.GetWeight()`, causing `this` to be returned and thereby assigned to `heavierBook`. Because `this` is equal to `yourBook`, `heavierBook` will, in this case, reference the same object as `yourBook`. Conversely, if line 32 is executed because `weight` is smaller than or equal to `aBook.GetWeight()`, `aBook` is returned and causes `heavierBook` to reference the same object as `myBook`.

Note

Some programmers adhere to the following rule: Don't change the names of local variables or formal parameters to avoid name clashes with instance variables. Instead, use the `this` keyword to indicate which of the variables are instance variables.

Other programmers will actively avoid name clashes to avoid the use of `this`.

Whichever side you belong to, remember to be consistent.

Avoid Cluttering the Code With `this`

To call a method of a class from within another method of the same class, we have been used to simply write the name of the method we are calling. For example, in the following code snippet, the method `Average` in lines 20–30 is called from line 42 of the `PrintAverage` method by writing the following:

```
Average(numbers)
```

The compiler is clever enough to figure out that it must look for the method within the confines of the current object. In fact, it automatically inserts `this.` in front of the method call during compilation. Consequently, the two method calls

```
Average(numbers)
```

and

```
this.Average(numbers)
```

have the same meaning when residing inside the `Calculator` class shown here. However, from a style point of view, you should avoid cluttering the code with unnecessary `this`s. So stick with the style used in line 42 and use `this` only when you explicitly need to specify the reference to the current object.

```
10: class Calculator
11: {
        ...
20:     private double Average (params int[] numbers)
21:     {
            ...
30:     }

40:     private PrintAverage (params int[] numbers)
41:     {
42:         Console.WriteLine("The average is: {0} ", Average(numbers));
43:     }
44: }
```

Summary

This chapter is divided into three main parts. The first part provides an overview of the different kind of members a class can contain. The second part focuses on data members and, in particular, `static` instance variables. The third part zoomed in on the parts of the method construct we haven't yet discussed in previous parts of the book. These are reference and output parameters, parameter arrays, method overloading and the `this` keyword.

Some of the most important points discussed in this chapter are as follows.

The class construct can contain members of three different categories—data members, function members, and nested types. Data members represent the data of the class, function members contain blocks with series of statements that are executed in a sequential fashion, and a nested type can be one of the `class`, `enum`, `struct`, and `interface` types.

An instance variable is associated with a specific object. A `static` variable is associated with a class. `static` variables allow us to represent data that are associated with a class (and, therefore, associated with all class objects as a group) in a memory- and execution-efficient manner.

Constant members are, by default, `static`.

Methods can be divided into two main groups—instance methods that are executed in relation to a particular object and `static` methods that are associated with the class in which they've been defined.

A `static` method can be called in three different ways. If called from outside the class in which it resides, it can be called either through an object or through the classname. If called from within the class in which it resides, it is called through the static method's name alone.

A method should be declared `static`:

- When the method does not belong to any particular object
- To access a `static` member variable

If you find that a large portion of the methods in your program are `static`, your overall design might be flawed.

You can declare a formal parameter of a method to be a reference parameter. The argument passed to a reference parameter and the reference parameter itself represent the same value, so any changes made to a reference parameter during the execution of its method are reflected in the argument.

An output parameter is the same as a reference parameter with one difference, the output parameter accepts uninitialized variables.

If a formal parameter is declared to be a parameter array with the `params` keyword, it accepts a varying number of arguments and will store those values in a dedicated array that can be accessed, like a conventional array, during the execution of the method.

Method overloading allows us to define two (or more) methods inside the same class with the same name. If two methods are to be correctly overloaded, they must have the same name and at least one of the following two points must be true:

- The number of formal parameters must be different between the two methods.
- At least one of the formal parameter types of one method must be different from the corresponding formal parameter of the other method.

When many methods are overloaded and contain the same name, they must all differ from each other as described in the two points.

The method signature is an important concept related to method overloading. The method signature consists of the name of the method and the sequence and number of the formal parameter types. The return type and the formal parameter names are not part of the signature.

Method overloading is frequently used to create methods with the same name that perform similar operations but on different data types.

If no direct match is found between the types of the arguments in a method call and a set of overloaded methods, the compiler will use implicit conversion paths to find a close match.

When the keyword `this` is positioned inside a method, it references the object instance in which the method resides. The keyword `this` is often used in the following three scenarios:

- To differentiate formal parameters and local variables from instance variables
- To pass the reference of the current object as an argument to another method
- To return the reference of the current object back to the caller of the method

Review Questions

1. You are writing a `Planet` class for a solar system simulation program. You need to keep track of the number of instantiated `Planet` objects. If you were to store this data as a variable inside `Planet`, should it be an instance variable or a `static` variable? Why?
2. Can you assign a value to a `static` variable even if no objects have been created?
3. Can a `static` variable be accessed from within an object of the class in which it is declared?
4. The following declaration was found inside a class:

   ```
   public static const double MassOfElectron = 9.0e-28;
   ```

   Is it correct? Why or why not?
5. Does it go against encapsulation principles to declare a `const` to be `public`?
6. A class called `Planet` contains the following declarations:

   ```
   class Planet
   {
       private static uint numberOfPlanetsCreated;
       private double mass;
       ...
       public static double CalculateGravity(...)
       {
           ...
       }

       public double Density(...)
       {
           ...
       }
   }
   ```

   Is it possible to

   a. Access `numberOfPlanetsCreated` from within the `CalculateGravity` method
   b. Access `mass` from within the `CalculateGravity` method
   c. Access `numberOfPlanetsCreated` from within the `Density` method

d. Access `mass` from within the `Density` method

e. Access `numberOfPlanetsCreated` from outside the `Planet` class by writing `Planet.numberOfPlanetsCreated`

f. Access mass from outside the `Planet` class by writing `Planet.mass`

7. Among other methods, your class `Planet` contains two methods of approximately the same length. One is a `static` method related to the `Planet` class, the other is an instance method related to a particular `Planet` object. Suppose 100 objects of type `Planet` exist inside your running solar system simulation. Is the following statement true or false? "All the instance methods of the Planet class take up approximately 100 times more memory than the `static` method." Why?

8. Consider the following method definition:

```
public void MyMethod(ref int myValue, int yourValue)
{
    myValue = 100;
    yourValue = 200;
}
```

Which of the following calls to `MyMethod` are correct and, if correct, what is the value of `myArgument` and `yourArgument` after `MyMethod` returns (`myArgument` and `yourArgument` are both of type `int` and initially both contain the value 0)?

a. `MyMethod(myArgument, yourArgument)`

b. `MyMethod(ref myArgument, ref yourArgument)`

c. `MyMethod(ref 10, ref yourArgument)`

9. Is the following method correct? Why or why not?

```
public int Sum(out int x, int y)
{
    return x + y;
}
```

10. Consider the following method header:

`public double Average(params int[] numbers)`

Which of the following calls to this method are valid? (`myArray` is an array of base type `int` with 100 elements.)

a. `Average()`

b. `Average(10)`

c. `Average(10,20)`

d. `Average(10,20,30.0)`

e. `Average(myArray)`

11. The following two method headers were found inside the same class. What can you call the methods?

```
public int Sum(int number1, int number2)
public double Sum(double number1, double number2)
```

12. a. Are the methods with the following method headers correctly overloaded? Why or why not?

```
public double Average(int x, int y)
public int Average(int x, int y)
```

    b. Are the methods with the following method headers correctly overloaded? Why or why not?

```
public double Average(int myX, int myY)
public int Average(int yourX, int yourY)
```

13. A class contains the following method header:

```
public uint Sum(uint x, uint y)
```

Is the following method call valid? Why or why not? (`myByte` and `yourByte` are both of type `byte`, which is different from `Sum`'s parameter types `uint`.)

```
Sum(myByte, yourByte)
```

14. Consider the following class called `Planet`:

```
class Planet
{
    private double myMass = 2000000;

    public double DoSomething(double myMass)
    {
        return (myMass * this.myMass) + myMass;
    }
}
```

What value will the following method call have when `DoSomething` returns (if the value of the instance variable `myMass` is still 2000000)?

```
DoSomething(20.0)
```

Programming Exercises

1. Write a class called `SportsCar` containing the two instance variables `maxSpeed` and `horsepower` of type `int`. Both these instance variables must, in any `SportsCar` object, hold values that are greater than certain pre-specified values; otherwise, they do not qualify as proper `SportsCar` objects. In our case, the minimum value for `maxSpeed` is 200 kilometers/hour, and the minimum value for horsepower is 250 hp. Include suitable member variables in the `SportsCar` class to hold these values (called `maxSpeedRequirement` and `horsepowerRequirement`) and write a method called

SportsCheck that returns true if both of the maxSpeed and horsepower for a particular SportsCar object are above the minimum requirements; otherwise, false. Write accessor and mutator methods for maxSpeed, horsepower, maxSpeedRequirement, and horsepowerRequirement.

Include another class containing a Main method to demonstrate the SportsCar class.

Please keep this program available for exercise 2.

2. Each object instantiated from the SportsCar class you wrote in exercise 1 can only be driven by certain people. Include a method in the SportsCar class that will read in any number of driver names (first names); call it SetLegalDrivers. So, if you have a SportsCar object in your program called sportsCar1, you can set the legal drivers by, for example, the following call:

   ```
   sportsCar1.SetLegalDrivers("Tom", "Julie", "Teddy", "Mary")
   ```

   or the call

   ```
   sportsCar1.SetLegalDrivers("Peter")
   ```

   Write a method called DriverCheck that lets you provide a first name as an argument and then returns true if the driver is allowed to drive the SportsCar object; otherwise, it returns false.

   Please keep this program handy for exercise 3.

3. Add a static method called GetMinimumRequirements containing two ref parameters of type int called newMaxSpeed and newHorsepower. This should allow other objects of other classes to call this method and obtain the values of both maxSpeed and horsepower held by the SportsCar class with just one method call. Write a tester class called Calculator with a static method called NumberCruncher that makes a call to GetMinimumRequirements and simply prints out the two values obtained from this call.

   Keep the source code intact for the exercise 4.

4. Equip the SportsCar class with an instance method called MostPowerful that has one formal parameter of type SportsCar called carCompare. Enable the MostPoweful method to compare the SportsCar, referenced by the formal parameter carCompare, with the SportsCar object the MostPowerful method is called for. The most powerful SportsCar object contains the greater horsepower instance variable. Return from the method a reference to the most powerful object.

   Allow not only one SportsCar to be passed as an argument to the MostPowerful method, but also two SportsCar objects. In case two arguments of type SportsCar are passed to MostPowerful, three objects are compared and the most powerful SportsCar object returned (hint: use method overloading to implement this functionality).

CHAPTER 13

CLASS ANATOMY PART II: OBJECT CREATION AND GARBAGE COLLECTION

You will learn about the following in this chapter:

- The three different ways of initializing instance variables—automatic initializations, initialization declarations, and constructors
- The `new` keyword's ability to call a constructor
- Overloading instance constructors
- The constructor initializer
- `private` instance constructors
- `static` constructors
- The `readonly` class member
- Garbage collection—freeing the memory occupied by unreachable objects
- The "Dispose design pattern"—freeing other scarce, non-memory resources occupied by unreachable objects
- Destructors and their limited use

Living organisms are conceived; they live for a certain period of time during which they occupy scarce resources (organic substances forming their tissues, water, and so on) so they can function, and eventually they die. Similarly, objects are created inside the computer memory; they have a lifetime where they occupy a part of the memory (and perhaps other scarce resources) so they can act and hold data, and then also they die.

Nature has a neat ecological system where dead bodies and debris are meticulously consumed by animals, such as hyenas, vultures, beetles, ants, worms, and microorganisms (natures garbage collectors). Not only does this system keep any area clear from debris, it also recycles otherwise trapped resources.

Unless dead objects are garbage collected and their memory freed, in a fashion similar to that of nature's painstaking reuse of every organic molecule, object corpses will soon fully occupy the computer memory, making it impossible for new objects to live here. As a consequence the computer eventually crashes—unable to support the memory required to keep the new objects of the program alive. (Hmm...this turned out to be quite a morbid introduction, but I guess nothing less could be expected for a chapter carrying the number 13).

This chapter is about the creation and destruction of the objects that live inside a running computer program.

Instance Constructors

You have already briefly been introduced to constructors in Chapter 5, "Your First Object-Oriented C# Program," and since then you have seen simple implementations of them in several source code examples. The following section elaborates on this earlier introduction and looks at why constructors are needed and how they are used.

Why Do We Need Instance Constructors?

When an object is created, the underlying computer memory representing its instance variables are allocated as part of this process. But just after this allocation procedure (and before any automatic or manual initializations have taken place), the memory and, hence, the instance variables only holds arbitrary garbage left over from last time this memory was used. Using this garbage as part of a computation can lead to detrimental results. Consider the following assignment statement:

```
distance = time * speed;
```

It is acceptable for `distance` to contain garbage before this assignment because it will be substituted by the result of the expression on the right side. However, if either `time` or `speed` contains garbage, `distance` will also be assigned garbage. As you can imagine, non-initialized instance variables can easily cause havoc during the execution of a program.

Fortunately, C# has many features to assist you with the initialization process. The instance variable declaration allows you to specify an initialization value for the instance variables (by using the familiar assignment operator to form initialization declarations), and any instance variables that have not been assigned a value explicitly are assigned a default value automatically by the runtime. So in C#, it is impossible to have any non-initialized instance variables roaming your programs. Doesn't this then cover all our initialization needs? No. The following looks closer at automatic initialization and initializing declarations and explains why we also need instance constructors to perform initializations.

Automatic Initializations

The runtime automatically initializes any instance variables that are not initialized explicitly in a declaration statement or by an instance constructor in the source code. The default values provided depend on the instance variable type:

- Numerical values of type `short`, `int`, `float`, `decimal` and so on, are assigned the value zero.
- Values of type `char` are assigned the Unicode character `'\u0000'`.

- Values of type `bool` are initialized to the value `false`.
- Values of reference types are initialized to `null`.

As a rule of thumb, it is not recommended that you let the runtime perform the initializations of instance variables automatically for the following two reasons:

- A programmer reading through the code cannot see the initialization values. He or she might not be aware of the previously shown default values.
- The default values might vary among different compilers and in different versions of a compiler shipped by the same software company.

Moreover, the default value is often different from the value we want to assign to the instance variable. Performing the initialization as part of the instance variable declaration can often fulfill our need to perform manual initializations.

Assign a Value to the Instance Variable As Part of Its Declaration

The following instance variable declaration sets the initial value of `balance` to 100:

```
class Account
{
    private decimal balance = 100;
      ...
}
```

Recall that the C# syntax rules allow us to position an expression after the assignment operator. With our syntax notation, this could be expressed as follows:

```
private decimal balance = <Expression>;
```

which initializes `balance` to the value of *<Expression>*. This is sufficient for many purposes, but what if we need to employ an `if` statement, say, to find the correct initialization value? For example, a bank might run a special promotion with the headline "If you open an account before the 1st of June 2001, the opening balance is $200 (paid by us); if you open it between 1st of June and 1st of July it's $100, and after 1st of July $0, so don't miss this special offer!" (A utopian example, but let's say the bank has its headquarters on planet Blipos). Without going into the details about how dates are represented and compared (I have used a bit of pseudocode for those `if` conditions as shown in the next code snippet), an attempt from a novice programmer to perform this initialization might look like the following lines.

```
class Account
{
    private decimal balance;
      if (OpeningDate is earlier than 1st of June)                       ⎫
            balance = 200;                                               ⎪
      else if (OpeningDate is between 1st of June and 1st of July)       ⎬ Invalid
            balance = 100;                                               ⎪
      else                                                               ⎭
            balance = 0;

      ...
}
```

These lines look promising but are invalid. C# only allows `if` statements and the like inside the bodies of function members. So let's try another avenue following this lead. Let's insert the initialization code in a method called `Initialize`:

```
class Account
{
    private decimal balance;

    public void Initialize()
    {
        if(OpeningDate is earlier than 1st of June)
            balance = 200;
        else if (OpeningDate is in between 1st of June and 1st of July)
            balance = 100;
        else
            balance = 0;
    }
}
```

This is valid, apart from the pseudocode representing the conditions of the `if` statements, of course. One downside, though, is that we must remember to call the `Initialize` method immediately after the creation of the `Account` object as in the following lines:

```
Account myAccount = new Account();
myAccount.Initialize();
```

It would be easier and less error prone if the `Initialize` statements were executed automatically simply by writing

```
Account myAccount = new Account();
```

This is made possible by the ability of the *instance constructor* to contain statements that are executed automatically when a new object is created.

Note

Strictly speaking, the `Initialize` method just shown is not initializing the `balance` variable. By the time `Initialize` is called, `balance` has already been initialized to the default value zero by the runtime.

Note

I chose three options ($200, $100, and $0) instead of just two in the bank promotion example, because the latter would have caused the attentive reader to protest and say: "Wait a minute, this could have been implemented by combining the declaration statement with the conditional operator, because the conditional operator can be positioned anywhere an expression is expected." For example, if the bank's headline was "Open an account before the 1st of June and $100 will be the opening balance; otherwise, $0" it could have been solved by writing the following lines:

```
class Account
{
        private decimal balance = (OpeningDate earlier than 1st July) ? 100 :
        ➥0;
        ...
}
```

Other Important Actions Performed at the Time of Object Creation

When an object is created, it might need to perform other actions apart from those related to instance variable initializations. For example, this could be to notify other parts of the program about its creation. A bank application might contain a `Statistician` class (see Figure 13.1), say, that keeps track of the number of accounts created (`accountsCreated`) and their total opening balances (`totalOpeningBalance`), allowing it to calculate things such as the average opening balance. If the `Statistician` class was equipped with a method called `AccountAdded` to update those statistics, it could be called from an `Account` objects during its initialization process as illustrated in Figure 13.1.

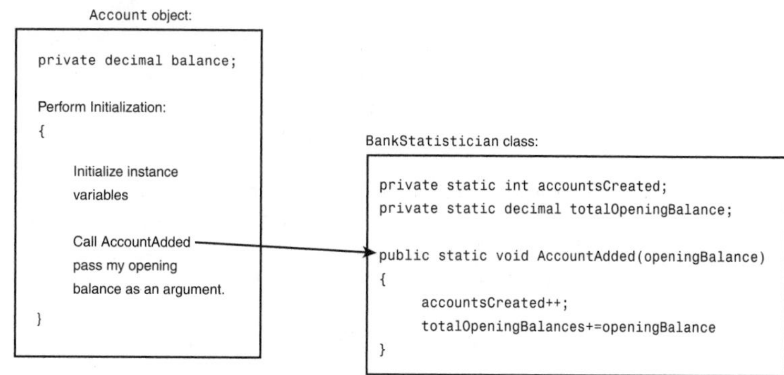

FIGURE 13.1
The *`Account`* object calls a method of the *`BankStatistician`* class as part of its initial actions.

But like the `if` statement shown before, C# only allows method calls within the body of a function member. We could include the method call in an `Initialization` method as previously suggested, but an instance constructor would be a better solution again. The following section shows how to apply instance constructors appropriately and demonstrates how to implement the scenario put forth in Figure 13.1.

Working with Instance Constructors

An *instance constructor* of a class is a specialized method that is invoked when the `new` keyword is used to create an object of that class. Instance constructors are used to perform instance variable initializations and other actions needed as part of the creation of an object.

Defining an Instance Constructor

Syntax Box 13.1 shows the definition of an instance constructor. To include an instance constructor in a class, you must write the instance constructor definition within the block of that class alongside its other members.

An optional constructor modifier, such as `private` or `public`, can be positioned in front of the identifier of the instance constructor. This allows you to control the accessibility of the instance constructor in the same fashion as that of methods and instance variables. The implications are markedly different, though, which is demonstrated later in this section. For the moment, we will just use the `public` modifier.

Syntax Box 13.1 The Instance_Constructor

```
Instance_Constructor_Definition::=
[<Constructor_modifier>] <Constructor_Identifier> ( [ <Formal_parameter_list> ] )
[ <Constructor_initializer> ]
<Constructor_body>
```

where:

```
<Constructor_modifier> ::= private
                       ::= public
                       ::= protected
                       ::= internal

<Constructor_initializer> ::= : base ( [<Argument_list>] )
                          ::= : this ( [<Argument_list>] )

<Constructor_body>::=
               {
                   <Statements>
               }

                 ::=
               ;
```

Notes:

- The <*Constructor_identifier*> must be identical to the class identifier in which the constructor resides. For example the constructor in a class called Dog must itself be called dog as illustrated in the example shown in a moment.
- The instance constructor cannot return a value so no return type is specified, not even the `void` keyword is used.
- The <*Constructor_initializer*> causes another instance constructor to be executed before the statements of this instance constructor.

Example:

```
class Dog
{
        private int age;
        private string name;

        public Dog (string initialName) : this()
        {
                name = initialName;
        }

        public Dog()
        {
                age = 0;
        }

}
```


Just like a conventional method header, the instance constructor definition must have parentheses positioned after the constructor identifier to contain an optional list of formal parameters. Argument values are passed to these parameters when a new object is created with the `new` keyword, as demonstrated in a moment.

Similar to its method siblings, an instance constructor can be overloaded by declaring several constructors in the same class, each with a different formal parameter list. The example in Syntax Box 13.1 contains two overloaded instance constructors—one has a formal parameter list with one formal parameter of type `string`, and the other has an empty parameter list.

If the class contains two or more instance constructors (which then consequently must be overloaded), you can optionally specify an instance constructor of the same class to be executed before the statements of the instance constructor you are declaring. This can be done by positioning the constructor initializer `: this ( [<Argument_list>] )` after the formal parameter list. The runtime will then execute the instance constructor of the same class that has a formal parameter list matching that of the constructor-initializer's argument list. In the example in Syntax Box 13.1, the instance constructor with an empty argument list (`Dog()`) is consequently always executed before `Dog(string initialName)`.

The constructor initializer `: base ( [<Argument_list>] )` is related to the object-oriented concept inheritance and, for that reason, will not be discussed until this important concept has been presented.

The instance constructor contains a constructor body identical to that of a conventional method body, meaning that it can either consist of an empty statement (a single semicolon) or a group of statements enclosed within a pair of braces. The statements are executed in the same fashion as those of a method when the instance constructor is invoked. However, they should only contain statements directly related to initialization and object creation.

Calling an Instance Constructor

C#'s syntax rules force us to append parentheses after the classname when we create a new object with the `new` keyword as in the following:

```
Cat myCat = new Cat();
```

The parentheses seem to clutter the code unnecessarily, so why must we include them? We already know that `new Cat()` creates a new object of the `Cat` class and returns a reference to this object, which, in this case, is assigned to `myCat`. However, `new Cat()` has another purpose only briefly mentioned before; it invokes an instance constructor in the same way that a conventional method call invokes a method. Remember that any method call must have parentheses appended after the method name as in the following:

```
MyMethod()
```

By adhering to this syntax and its associated semantics, the next line:

```
Cat()
```

must mean "call the method named `Cat`." As a result, the special method `Cat` we call an instance constructor is invoked.

The parentheses after the classname (in this case, `Cat`) can enclose a list of arguments (see Syntax Box 13.2) just like a conventional method call. This argument list must match a corresponding formal parameter list in an instance constructor. If there are two or more instance constructors (which are then overloaded) the instance constructor with the formal parameter list that matches the argument list will be invoked.

So, if the `Cat` class contains just one instance constructor with an empty parameter list, such as in the following source code snippet:

```
class Cat
{
      private int age;
      public Cat()
      {
            age = 0;
      }
}
```

the parentheses following the class must always be empty, as in

```
Cat myCat = new Cat();
```

The general syntax for instantiating an object is shown in Syntax Box 13.2.

Syntax Box 13.2 Instantiating a New Object

```
Object_instantiation::=

          new <Class_identifier> ( [<Argument_list>] )
```

Notes:

- There is only one way to create a new object—by using the `new` keyword as shown here.
- The shown expression returns a reference to the new object, which must be assigned to a reference variable of type reference-to-object-of-class <*Class_identifier*>. The expression is typically used as part of an assignment statement or as an argument in a method call.

An instance constructor with an empty formal parameter list is called a *default instance constructor*. Another term for a default instance constructor is a no-argument instance constructor.

In many of our previous examples, a class didn't even contain one instance constructor, such as the `Tree` class:

```
class Tree
{
      private int age = 0;
      ...
}
```

but we were still able to create a class as if it contained a an explicitly defined default instance constructor as in the following line:

```
Tree myTree = new Tree();
```

This is possible because, in the absence of any programmer-specified constructors in the source code, C# automatically creates a default instance constructor (meaning with zero formal parameters) that essentially does nothing apart from allowing you to create a new object. Thus, the following `Tree` class is semantically identical to the `Tree` class shown before:

```
class Tree
{
    private int age = 0;
    public Tree()
        ;       //this is an empty statement doing nothing
    ...
}
```

Caution

If you write one or more non-default instance constructors, you must write your own default instance constructor if you need one.

The C# compiler will not include a default instance constructor in a class if you include one or more instance constructors in this class. For example, if you include an instance constructor with one formal parameter, as in the following `Car` class:

```
class Car
{
      private int odometer;

      public Car (int initialOdometer)
      {
            odometer = initialOdometer;
      }
}
```

the following call to the default instance constructor becomes invalid because the default instance constructor does not exist:

```
Car yourCar = new Car(); //Invalid. Default instance constructor is nonexistent
```

In this case, you can only call the instance constructor by including the value, which you want to assign to the `odometer` initially, as an argument. For example, to assign the value 100 as an initial value to the `odometer` instance variable, you can write the following statement:

```
Car yourCar = new Car (100);
```

Tip

If you include one or more instance constructors in your class, it is often a good idea to also include a default instance constructor.

Even if you don't think your class needs a default constructor at the time you write it, a class is frequently reused for slightly different purposes and circumstances, and often with a sudden need for calling its default constructor. It's much easier to include a default instance constructor while you are constructing your class. The class is then fresh in your mind and you can design the rest of the class to fit in with the default instance constructor.

Overloading Instance Constructors

The arguments you pass to the formal parameters of an instance constructor from the object instantiation expression (shown here as *<Argument_list>*)

```
new <Class_identifier> ( [<Argument_list>] )
```

are often used to initialize the instance variables of the new object. For example, the following `Car` class includes an instance constructor that allows you to pass the initial values to its `brandName` and `odometer` instance variables.

```
class Car
{
      private string brandName;
      private int odometer;

      public Car (string initialBrandName, int initialOdometer)
      {
            brandName = initialBrandName;
            odometer = initialOdometer;
      }
      ...
}
```

This allows us to assign the initial values `"BMW"` and `1000` to the `brandName` and `odometer` instance variables with the following statement:

```
Car yourCar = new Car ("BMW", 1000);
```

However, depending on where in our program we create a new `Car` object, we might only have one of the required arguments or perhaps none of them. To accommodate for this need, we can write several different instance constructors with different formal parameter lists accepting different sets of arguments. For example, the following instance constructor accepts just one argument to initialize the `brandName`:

```
public Car (string initialBrandName)
{
      brandName = initialBrandName;
      odometer = 0;
}
```

Note

To distinguish between the different formal parameter lists included in each overloaded instance constructor, the compiler follows the same procedure as that of conventional overloaded methods. It looks for the number of formal parameters included and their types.

The way an argument list of an instance constructor call is matched with a formal parameter list of an overloaded instance constructor also follows the same rules as that of conventional overloaded methods.

For more details, please refer to the "Method overloading" section in Chapter 12, "Class Anatomy Part I: `static` Class Members and Method Adventures."

The program presented in Listing 13.1 contains an `Account` class with three overloaded instance constructors (lines 10–36). They provide flexibility in terms of which arguments we can pass along when a new `Account` object is created (see lines 106–107, 112, and 115).

Apart from initializing the instance variables of a new `Account` object, each instance constructor also calls the `AccountAdded` method of the `BankStatistician` class (see lines 16, 25, and 34). We thereby implement the idea discussed earlier and illustrated in Figure 13.1 of letting the instance constructor take care of actions, not related to instance variable initializations, that must also be performed when a new `Account` object is created. Each instance constructor has further been equipped with a unique print statement (lines 17, 26, and 35) so you can monitor when each instance constructor is called.

LISTING 13.1 `OpeningNewBankAccounts.cs`

```
01: using System;
02: using System.Collections;
03:
04: class Account
05: {
06:     private decimal balance;
07:     private decimal interestRate;
08:     private string holderName;
09:
10:     public Account(decimal initialBalance, decimal initialInterestRate,
11:         string initialHolderName)
12:     {
13:         balance = initialBalance;
14:         interestRate = initialInterestRate;
15:         holderName = initialHolderName;
```

LISTING 13.1 continued

```
        BankStatistician.AccountAdded(balance);
        Console.WriteLine("New account opened! All info was supplied\n");
    }

    public Account(string initialHolderName)
    {
        balance = 0;
        interestRate = 0;
        holderName = initialHolderName;
        BankStatistician.AccountAdded(balance);
        Console.WriteLine("New account opened! Only the
        ➥ holder name was supplied\n");
    }

    public Account()
    {
        balance = 0;
        interestRate = 0;
        holderName = "Not assigned yet";
        BankStatistician.AccountAdded(balance);
        Console.WriteLine("New account opened! No info was supplied\n");
    }

    public void SetBalance (decimal newBalance)
    {
        balance = newBalance;
    }

    public void SetInterestRate (decimal newInterestRate)
    {
        interestRate = newInterestRate;
    }

    public void PrintDetails()
    {
        Console.WriteLine("Account holder: " + holderName);
        Console.WriteLine("Balance: {0:C}", balance);
        Console.WriteLine("Interest rate: {0:C}\n", interestRate);
    }
}

class BankStatistician
{
    private static int accountsCreated;
    private static decimal totalOpeningBalance;

    public static void AccountAdded(decimal openingBalance)
    {
        accountsCreated++;
        totalOpeningBalance += openingBalance;
    }

```

LISTING 13.1 continued

```
    public static void PrintAccountStatistics ()
    {
        Console.WriteLine("Number of accounts created: {0}",
        ➥ accountsCreated);
        Console.WriteLine("Average opening balance: {0:N2}",
            ((accountsCreated == 0) ? 0 : (totalOpeningBalance
            ➥ / accountsCreated)));
    }
}

class Bank
{
    private ArrayList accounts;

    public Bank()
    {
        Console.WriteLine("Congratulations! You have created a new bank");
        accounts = new ArrayList();
    }

    public void OpenNewAccount ()
    {
        int choice;
        decimal initialBalance;
        decimal initialInterestRate;
        string initialHolderName;

        Console.WriteLine("Enter the number matching the
        ➥ information you have now");
        Console.WriteLine("1) Balance, interest rate
        ➥ and name of account holder");
        Console.WriteLine("2) Only the name of the account holder");
        Console.WriteLine("3) No information available");
        choice = Convert.ToInt32(Console.ReadLine());
        switch (choice)
        {
            case 1:
               Console.Write("Enter opening balance: ");
               initialBalance = Convert.ToDecimal(Console.ReadLine());
               Console.Write("Enter initial interest rate: ");
               initialInterestRate = Convert.ToDecimal(
               ➥Console.ReadLine());
               Console.Write("Enter name of account holder: ");
               initialHolderName = Console.ReadLine();
               accounts.Add(new Account(initialBalance,
               ➥ initialInterestRate,
                  initialHolderName));
               break;
            case 2:
                Console.Write("Enter the name of the account holder: ");
                initialHolderName = Console.ReadLine();
                accounts.Add(new Account(initialHolderName));
```

LISTING 13.1 continued

```
                break;
            case 3:
                accounts.Add(new Account());
                break;
            default:
                Console.WriteLine("Invalid input");
                break;
        }
    }

    public void PrintCurrentAccounts ()
    {
        foreach (Account tempAccount in accounts)
        {
            tempAccount.PrintDetails();
        }
    }
}

class BankTester
{
    public static void Main()
    {
        string answer;

        Bank myBank = new Bank();
        Console.WriteLine("Would you like to open an account? Y)es N)o");
        answer = Console.ReadLine().ToUpper();
        while (!(answer == "N"))
        {
            myBank.OpenNewAccount();
            Console.WriteLine("Would you like to
            ➥ open another account? Y)es N)o");
            answer = Console.ReadLine().ToUpper();
        }
        myBank.PrintCurrentAccounts();
        BankStatistician.PrintAccountStatistics();
    }
}
```

```
Congratulations! You have created a new bank
Would you like to open an account? Y)es N)o
Y<enter>
Enter the number matching the information you have now
1) Balance, interest rate and name of account holder
2) Only the name of the account holder
3) No information available
1<enter>
Enter opening balance: 1000<enter>
Enter initial interest rate: 0.05<enter>
Enter name of account holder: Donald Duck<enter>
New account opened! All info was supplied
```

```
Would you like to open another account? Y)es N)o
Y<enter>
Enter the number matching the information you have now
1) Balance, interest rate and name of account holder
2) Only the name of the account holder
3) No information available
2<enter>
Enter the name of the account holder: Mickey Mouse<enter>
New account opened! Only the holder name was supplied

Would you like to open another account? Y)es N)o
Y<enter>
Enter the number matching the information you have now
1) Balance, interest rate and name of account holder
2) Only the name of the account holder
3) No information available
3<enter>
New account opened! No info was supplied

Would you like to open another account? Y)es N)o
N<enter>
Account holder: Donald Duck
Balance: $1,000.00
Interest rate: $0.05

Account holder: Mickey Mouse
Balance: $0.00
Interest rate: $0.00

Account holder: Not assigned yet
Balance: $0.00
Interest rate: $0.00

Number of accounts created: 3
Average opening balance: 333.33
```

The program is only aimed at demonstrating instance constructor overloading. Consequently, the `Account` and `Bank` classes (lines 75–130) are stripped-down versions of the more elaborate classes shown in earlier bank simulation examples of this book. However, the `Bank` class still provides a simple user interface in its `OpenNewAccount` method to open new accounts. By repeatedly calling this method in line 143 until the user is finished opening new accounts, the `Main()` method of the `BankTester` program has an easy job of controlling the overall flow of the program.

Every new `Account` object is stored in the `ArrayList` object accounts in the `Bank` object. This allows us to print out the details of the three accounts we opened during the sample run.

The updates from the instance constructors to the `BankStatistician` makes it possible for the `BankStatistician` to print out the number of accounts created and the average opening balance in the last two lines of the output.

The `Add` method of the `ArrayList` object accounts accepts arguments of type `reference`-to-`Account`-object. Because `new Account(...)` returns a reference to a new `Account` object, we can insert this expression directly as an argument in the method call (see lines 106–107, 112, and 115).

Only one `BankStatistician` is ever needed to keep track of the new accounts opened. Thus, by declaring all the methods and variables of the `BankStatistician` class `static`, we can call its `AccountAdded` method directly through the classname without ever having to go through the trouble of creating a `BankStatistician` object.

As mentioned earlier, dividing by zero is an invalid calculation and will cause the runtime to generate an exception. If no `Account` objects are ever opened, `accountsCreated` will be zero, causing the average calculating expression `totalOpeningBalance / accountsCreated` (see line 71) to trigger an exception. The conditional operator has been applied in line 71 to effectively prevent the execution to ever reach this far if `accountsCreated` is equal to zero. In that case, a simple zero is returned.

The Constructor Initializer

We have already briefly described the basic mechanism of the constructor initializer:

```
: this ( [<Argument_list>] )
```

Why would you want to use this C# feature? The short answer is that it prevents you from being forced to include the same set of statements in several overloaded instance constructors.

Suppose a class requires a core set of initializations to be performed disregarding which overloaded instance constructor is invoked. We could first try to include the same set of statements performing those initializations in each instance constructor and then add the statements particular to this instance constructor on top. This would work, but it would burden every single instance constructor with a copy of these core statements and burden you with the tedious job of copying and pasting them. As an alternative, it might be possible to gather only the core statements in the default instance constructor and then let each overloaded instance constructor call it through the constructor initializer. It would then be possible to remove all the redundant code found in the initial design.

It doesn't always have to be the default instance constructor that is called by the constructor initializer, as the following example illustrates. Take another look at Listing 13.1. Are any of the statements found in all three instance constructors? Yes, the call to the `BankStatistician` method `AccountAdded`:

```
BankStatistician.AccountAdded(balance);
```

clearly belongs to this category. Furthermore, even though the assignment statements in each constructor that assign values to the `balance`, `interestRate`, and `holderName` instance variables differ in terms of the values assigned, they can all be regarded as special versions of the following three assignment statements (contained in the instance constructor of lines 10–18)

```
balance = initialBalance;
interestRate = initialInterestRate;
holderName = initialHolderName;
```

By passing suitable arguments to the instance constructor in lines 10–18, we can set `initialBalance`, `initialInterestRate`, and `initialHolderName` to represent the same values as that of the instance constructors of lines 20–27, or that of the default instance constructor in lines 29–36. This means we can let the instance constructor of line 10–18 take care of the assignments and the call to the `BankStatistician` method as long as we call this instance constructor with the constructor initializer from the other instance constructors and pass along suitable arguments. The result is shown in Listing 13.2, where two of the instance constructors (lines 17–20 and 22–25) have had all their redundant code removed. This functionality has now been taken over by the instance constructor in lines 7–15 through the constructor initializers in lines 17 and 22, respectively.

Please notice that the code in Listing 13.2 does not compile.

LISTING 13.2 Part of `Account` Class with Redundant Code of Instance Constructors Removed

```
01: class Account
02: {
03:     private decimal balance;
04:     private decimal interestRate;
05:     private string holderName;
06:
07:     public Account(decimal initialBalance, decimal initialInterestRate,
08:           string initialHolderName)
09:     {
10:         balance = initialBalance;
11:         interestRate = initialInterestRate;
12:         holderName = initialHolderName;
13:         BankStatistician.AccountAdded(balance);
14:         Console.WriteLine("New account opened");
15:     }
16:
17:     public Account(string initialHolderName) : this (0,0,initialHolderName)
18:     {
19:         Console.WriteLine("Note: Only initial holder name supplied");
20:     }
21:
22:     public Account() : this (0, 0, "Not assigned yet")
23:     {
24:         Console.WriteLine("Note: No initial information supplied");
25:     }
```

What You Can and Cannot Include in the Argument Expressions of the Constructor Initializer

In line 17 of Listing 13.2, we use the formal parameter `initialHolderName` as an argument in the constructor initializer. This is acceptable because the constructor initializer is within the scope of the formal parameter of its instance constructor.

On the other hand, it is not possible for the argument expressions of the constructor initializer to access any parts of the object created by the instance constructor to which it is attached. Consequently, any reference to instance variables is invalid and the `this` keyword cannot be applied in this part of the program, as illustrated in the following line:

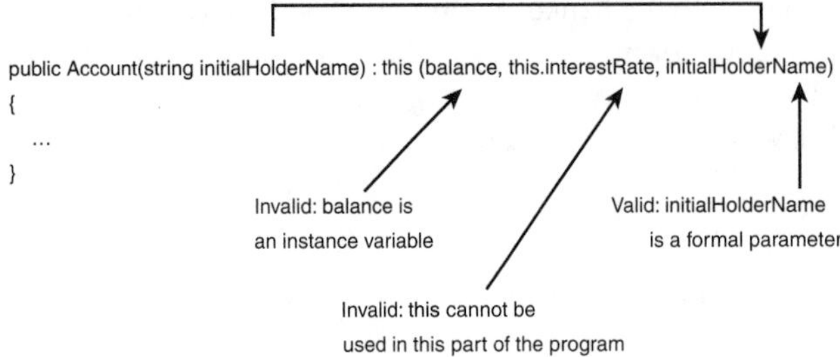
public Account(string initialHolderName) : this (balance, this.interestRate, initialHolderName)
{
...
}
Invalid: balance is
an instance variable
Valid: initialHolderName
is a formal parameter
Invalid: this cannot be
used in this part of the program

Note

The argument list of the constructor initializer cannot match the formal parameter list of the instance constructor to which it is applied.

Take a look at the constructor initializer of this example. It contains an argument list that matches the formal parameter list of the instance constructor to which it is applied:

```
class House
{
    ...
    public House (int initialAge) : this (10)
    {
        ...
    }
    ...
}
```

The argument list of the constructor initializer...

...is invalid because it...

...matches the formal parameter list of the instance constructor it is applied to

The instance constructor is, in effect, asking itself to be executed before its own method body in a recursive fashion. This next instance constructor execution would again ask itself to be executed before itself and so on, creating an infinite chain of calls to itself.

Recursion is a powerful technique when applied to conventional methods, but it doesn't make much sense if attempted on instance constructors. Consequently, the argument list of the constructor initializer cannot match the formal parameter list of the instance constructor to which it is applied.

Calling Other Conventional Methods of the same Class from Within an Instance Constructor

You have already seen how a `static` method like `AccountAdded` of the `BankStatistician` class can be called from within an instance constructor of the `Account` class in Listing 13.1. You can also call a method from within the same class as if you were calling it from a conventional method. However, it is important to keep the actions (whether they are statements executed inside the instance constructor or residing inside any other method called from an instance constructor) strictly related to the creation of the object.

`private` Instance Constructors

You can substitute the first keyword `public` (used in the previous instance constructor examples) of the instance constructor declaration with the keyword `private` to make your instance constructor `private`. A `private` instance constructor cannot be called from anywhere outside the class. This resembles the characteristics of `private` methods and instance variables. In effect, a `private` instance constructor cannot be used to create an object, so a class containing only `private` instance constructors effectively prevents any objects of this class to be instantiated from outside the class. This mechanism is often used to prevent classes that only contain `static` members, which were never meant to be instantiated, from accidentally being instantiated in other parts of the program.

Our `BankStatistician` class in Listing 13.1 is an example of a `static` members-only class. It would be illogical and not fit in with the overall design of the program to instantiate this class. To effectively prevent this from happening, we simply need to insert a `private` default instance constructor in the `BankStatistician` class, as the following lines demonstrate.

```
class BankStatistician
{
    private static int accountsCreated;
    private static decimal totalOpeningBalance;

    private BankStatistician ()
    {
    }
    ...
```

The only instance constructor is `private` effectively preventing any instantiation.

`static` Constructors

As opposed to an instance constructor, a `static` constructor of a class cannot be called explicitly in the source code. Instead, it is called automatically by the runtime sometime between the start of the program and the instantiation of the first object of the class. The `static` constructor is declared by writing the `static` keyword in front of the name of the class and by ending the line with empty parentheses (see Syntax Box 13.3). The statements are positioned in a block after this header.

There are a couple of notable differences between the declaration of a `static` constructor and an instance constructor. First, because the `static` constructor can only be accessed by the runtime, it makes no sense to specify an access modifier. Second, because the runtime wouldn't know which arguments to provide, no formal parameters can be specified.

The `static` constructor is not only typically used to initialize `static` variables (see the example in Syntax Box 13.3), but also used to perform other tasks that must be done once before the first instance of a class is created.

Syntax Box 13.3 The static Constructor

```
static <Constructor_identifier> ( )
{
    <Statements>
}
```

Notes:

- The <*Constructor_identifier*> must be identical to the name of the class in which the `static` constructor resides.
- No arguments can be specified for the `static` constructor.
- No access modifiers can be specified for the `static` constructor.

Example:

```
class Fish
{
    private static int numberOfFishCreated;

    static Fish()
    {
        numberOfFishCreated = 0;
    }
    ...
}
```

Tip

The call to the `static` constructor of a class could take place right after the start of the program, just before the creation of the first instance of the class, or somewhere in between. It all depends on the runtime's frame of mind. Because of this timing uncertainty, you should not let the `static` constructor contain any statements that are sensitive to timing.

The readonly Member

Like the constant member, (declared with the `const` keyword) the `readonly` member is used to represent an unchanging value. But, whereas the value assigned to the constant must be written in the source code, as demonstrated in the following line

```
const decimal MassOfElectron = 9.0E-28m;
```

the value of the `readonly` member does not have to be known until the program is running. The value of a `readonly` member is initialized in a constructor and cannot be altered after that moment. So, while the constant member remains unchanged throughout the lifetime of a compiled program, the `readonly` member merely stays unchanged during the lifetime of an object.

Syntax Box 13.4 shows how a `readonly` member is declared. Apart from the `readonly` keyword, the overall declaration and the meaning of its different parts resemble that of a conventional instance variable declaration.

Syntax Box 13.4 Declaring a `readonly` Member

```
readonly_member_declaration::=
[ <Access_modifier> ] [static] readonly <Type> <Identifier> [ = <Expression> ];
```

where:

```
<Access_modifier>
                ::= private
                ::= public
                ::= protected
                ::= internal
                ::= protected internal
```

Notes:

- The *<Access_modifier>* has the same meaning as when applied in a conventional instance variable declaration, except that the `readonly` member can only be accessed to read from, not assign to.
- The `readonly` member is not `static` by default like its constant counterpart, but must explicitly be declared `static` to achieve this status.
- The type of a constant member is restricted to one of the predefined types—`byte`, `sbyte`, `short`, `ushort`, `int`, `uint`, `long`, `ulong`, `float`, `double`, `decimal`, `char`, `bool`, `enum`, or `string`. In contrast, the *<Type>* of a `readonly` member can be any type.
- You can optionally initialize a `readonly` member with the assignment operator followed by an expression (shown as *[= <Expression>]*). However, this does not prevent you from assigning a value to this `readonly` member in a constructor.

The following example illustrates the use of the `readonly` member. Usually when a bank account of a real-world bank is opened, a unique account number is assigned to it that must stay unchanged throughout the lifetime of the account. We can reflect this fact in our `Account` class by declaring the representation of the `Account` number to be `readonly`, as in line 5 of Listing 13.3. The instance constructor in lines 7–10 can then initialize this account number, and no further changes are then possible throughout the lifetime of the new object.

LISTING 13.3 `PermanentAccountNumber.cs`

```
01: using System;
02:
03: class Account
04: {
05:     public readonly string AccountNumber;
06:
07:     public Account (string permanentAccountNumber)
08:     {
09:         AccountNumber = permanentAccountNumber;
10:     }
11: }
12:
13: class SimpleBank
14: {
```

LISTING 13.3 continued

```
15:     public static void Main()
16:     {
17:         Account yourAccount = new Account("8487-9873-9938");
18:         Console.WriteLine("Your account number: "
19:             + yourAccount.AccountNumber);
20:     }
21: }
```

```
Your account number: 8487-9873-9938
```

Notice that `AccountNumber` is declared `public` in line 5. We can safely do this without breaking any encapsulation principles because, even though `AccountNumber` can be accessed directly without the use of an accessor method, its value cannot be changed.

The constant member would be unsuited to represent the account numbers because the account number would not be known at the time the program is compiled.

Note

The conventional capitalization style used for writing `readonly` identifiers is Pascal Casing.

Garbage Collection: Automatic Dynamic Memory Management

Whereas classes are written in the source code before a program is executed, their object counterparts are created dynamically during runtime by using the `new` operator as described earlier. Every instantiated object occupies a certain amount of memory needed to store items, such as the object's instance variables. Because memory is a scarce resource, it is important to reclaim and thereby recycle the memory representing objects that are no longer used in the program to make space for newly instantiated objects coming into use.

How Do Objects Get Out of Reach?

Before we look at how C# performs this reclaim, it is worth looking closer at what we mean by "an object no longer used." Briefly explained, it is an object that can no longer be reached from the program, meaning that no references to it exist anymore. The program in Listing 13.4 contains four different examples of how an object can lose all its references and thereby get out of reach.

LISTING 13.4 `AccountsReclaiming.cs`

```
using System;

class Account
```

LISTING 13.4 continued

```
04: {
05:
06: }
07:
08: class Bank
09: {
10:     private Account bankAccount;
11:
12:     public void SetAccount (Account newAccount)
13:     {
14:         bankAccount = newAccount;
15:     }
16: }
17:
18: class Tester
19: {
20:     public static void Main()
21:     {
22:         Bank bank1;
23:
24:         Account account1;
25:         Account account2;
26:
27:         account1 = new Account();
28:
29:         account1 = null;
30:
31:         account1 = new Account();
32:         account2 = new Account();
33:
34:         account1 = account2;
35:
36:         bank1 = new Bank();
37:         bank1.SetAccount(new Account());
38:
39:         bank1 = null;
40:
41:         DoingAccountStuff();
42:     }
43:
44:     public static void DoingAccountStuff()
45:     {
46:         Account localAccount;
47:         localAccount = new Account();
48:     }
49: }
```

No output from this listing.

To make the code shorter I have left the `Account` class (lines 3–6) empty and the `Bank` class (lines 8–16) with only one `Account`.

The `Main()` method of the `Tester` class demonstrates four ways that an object can get out of reach.

- Assigning the null reference to all references of an object.

  Line 27 creates an object and assigns its reference to `account1`. In line 29, the `null` reference is assigned to `account1`, which then no longer contains a reference to the original object, as illustrated in Figure 13.2. The original `Account` object has gone out of reach because its only previous reference is not referencing it anymore.

FIGURE 13.2
Assigning the null reference to the only reference of an object.

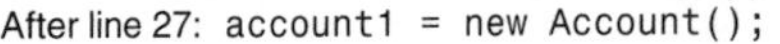

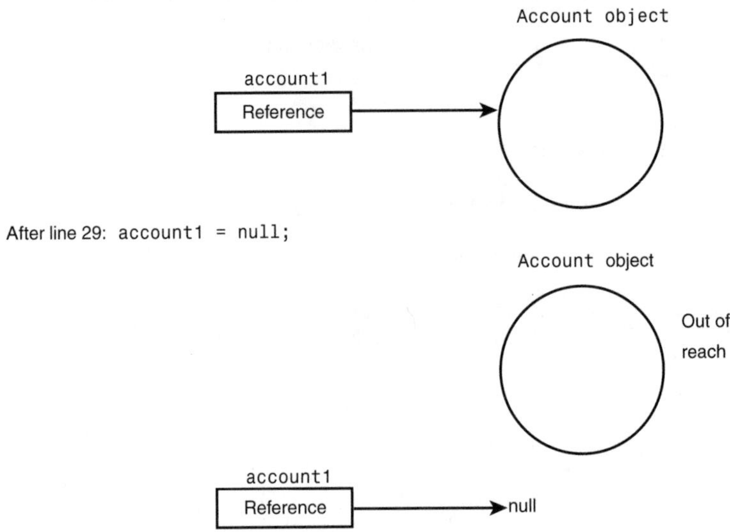

- When a reference variable holding the only reference to an object A is assigned a different reference object, A goes out of reach.

  Lines 31 and 32 assign two different `Account` objects to `account1` and `account2`. After line 34, both `account1` and `account2` are referencing the `Account` object originally referenced by just `account2` (see Figure 13.3). As a result, the object originally referenced by `account1` has gone out of reach.

- When an object A contains the only reference to an object B, both object A and B go out of reach when object A goes out of reach.

  In line 36, `bank1` is assigned a reference to a new `Bank` object. This `Bank` object contains an `Account` object reference, which is assigned a reference to a new `Account` object through the call to its `SetAccount` method in line 37. After line 39, `bank1` is no longer referencing the `Bank` object (see Figure 13.4). Consequently, the `Bank` object is out of reach. But because the `Bank` object is out of reach, the `Account` object it was referencing is also out of reach.

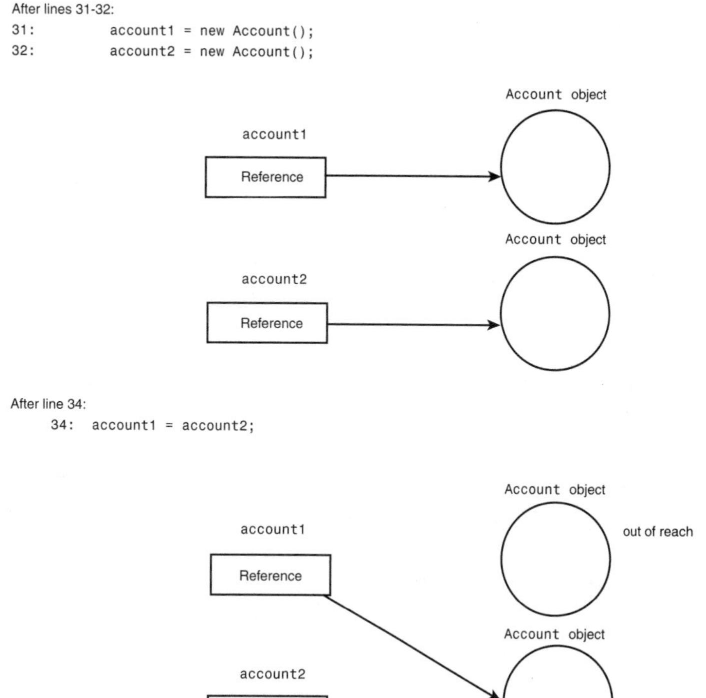

FIGURE 13.3
Assigning the reference of another object to the only reference of an object.

If the `Account` object had referenced yet another object and this object yet another object and so on, a chain of objects connected by references would be formed, all dependent on the references in front of them in the chain to stay within reach.

- When a local variable containing the only reference to an object goes out of scope, the object goes out of reach.

  The `Tester` class contains another method apart from `Main()` called `DoingAccountStuff` (lines 44–48). When this method is executed, its local `Account` reference variable called `localAccount` comes into scope after its declaration in line 46. In line 47, it is assigned a reference to a new `Account` object. However, `localAccount` goes out of scope when the method returns to the caller. Thus `localAccount` is out of reach, and so is the `Account` object it was referencing.

Note

If you attempt to use a reference variable that does not reference an object, but that instead references `null`, the runtime will generate a `NullReferenceException`.

FIGURE 13.4
When the `Bank` object referencing the `Account` object goes out of reach.

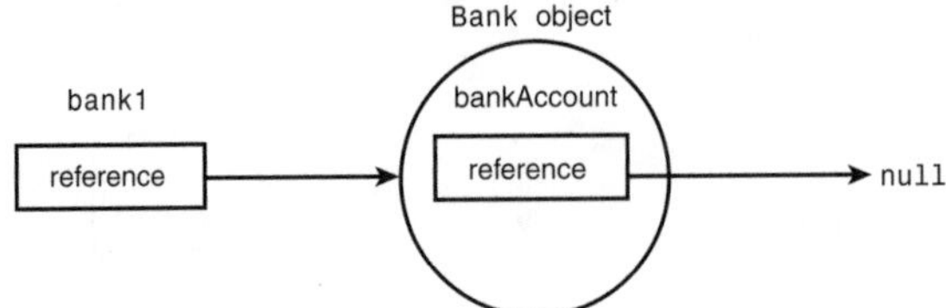

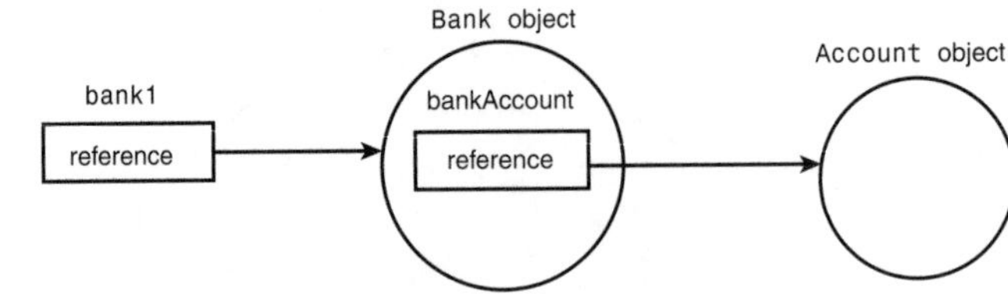

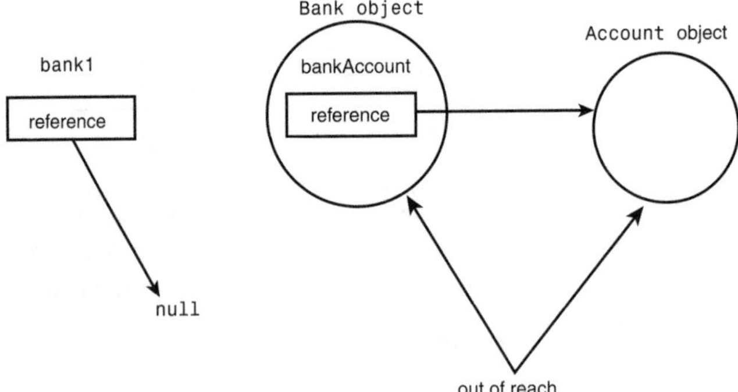

The Tasks of the Garbage Collector

To reclaim the memory of objects that are no longer reachable, C# relies on a mechanism supported by the .NET runtime called a garbage collector (GC).

The runtime's method of automatically managing memory is called *garbage collection (GC)*. The term garbage collection and its associated technique can be traced all the way back to the Lisp language (see Chapter 2, "Your First C# Program").

The GC has two main functions—detecting unreachable objects and reclaiming their memory. To perform these important cleanup functions, the GC employs highly complex algorithms that are beyond the scope of this book. However, there are a few aspects you need to be aware of, which are a result of the way these algorithms work:

- The .NET GC promises not to reclaim any objects that are reachable. For example, the GC will not suddenly gobble up one of the useable `Account` objects from our previous examples.
- The .NET GC works in the background of every C# program you run and will *eventually* and *automatically* detect and reclaim all objects that are unreachable. Consequently, you don't need to worry about starting it up or shutting it down; in fact, you can just forget it is even there under most circumstances.
- Notice the highlighted word "eventually" in the previous bullet. Isn't an object reclaimed in the same instant it becomes unreachable? Maybe, but probably not.
- Let's look a little closer at the circumstances for this likely time lag: Whenever the GC is running to perform its tasks, it occupies scarce processing time on the CPU, which would otherwise be used to execute your program, thus resulting in your program being temporarily frozen. Therefore, the GC must strike a balance between making sure that, on one hand, enough memory is reclaimed to allow new objects to be created and, on the other hand, perform this task by using as little CPU time as possible. If the GC had to fulfill a promise saying: "I will reclaim all objects in the same instant they become unreachable," it would have to occupy a disturbingly large percentage of the CPU's processing time. For that reason, the GC only promises us the following: "I will do what I can to always have enough memory available for your objects while minimizing the time I occupy the CPU. However I cannot promise when I will reclaim the unreachable objects; it could be immediately after they become unreachable, it might not occur until the program is about to close down after it has finished interacting with the end user, or it might occur sometimes in between these two timing extremes."
- The GC algorithms are based on a technique called the *"lazy" technique*, that lets the garbage collector work only at irregular intervals and in short spurts. These spurts of activity are often triggered by low memory combined with an immediate need to free up memory for new objects.

Giving a "Run Now" Suggestion to the GC

You might encourage the GC to run by calling the `static` method `Collect` of the `System.GC` class with the following line:

```
System.GC.Collect();
```

However, the GC might or might not follow this suggestion. Programmers often call the `GC.Collect` method after many objects have become unreachable or before parts of the program that are sensitive to being frozen by the activity of the GC are executed. In Listing 13.5, shown later in this chapter, you get a chance to test how responsive the GC is to the `GC.Collect` call in practice.

GCs and Real Time Applications Do Not Mix Well

When an application controls a series of events that must take place in real time, the application is said to be a *real time application*. For example, if the program is performing an animation of a cartoon character walking across the screen, each movement (event) of arms, legs, and so on, must happen not only in a certain sequence, but also in a well-timed manner. If the cartoon character makes a jump but then suddenly freezes in midair, the sense of real time has disappeared. A temporarily frozen cartoon character could easily be the result of the GC suddenly interrupting the general execution of the program with a spurt of activity. So, because of our current inability to control the GC, you should think twice before building a real time application based on the .NET GC version available at this time of writing.

Fortunately the GC's algorithms are constantly evolving, so we might soon see a GC with the ability to support real time applications.

Most of the time we don't need to be concerned about the time lag between an object becoming unreachable and the reclaiming of its memory by the GC. However, it is important to keep in mind when we look at different strategies for freeing other scarce resources than memory.

Freeing Scarce Resources Other Than Memory

Sometimes an object occupies scarce resources other than memory. For example, they could be

- *Files*—An object might, during its existence, need to access a file to read and/or write its contents. This access is usually obtained by letting the object hold a file handle, which is then opened. But only one file exists and, to avoid the chaotic situation of having the same file being changed at the same time by different entities (such as objects), only one object can access the file at any one time. Consequently, it is important that the file handle be closed as soon as the object is not used anymore to allow other objects access.
- *Network/Database connections*—There are usually only a limited number of network and database connections available that, like files, can be accessed by only one user at a time. It is important that any such connections be freed immediately after the user has finished with them to allow other users access.

How can we ensure that an object promptly frees the scarce resources it is occupying at the moment it becomes unreachable? Before we look at the recommended technique for solving this problem, called the *Dispose design pattern*, the next section looks at another tempting but incorrect (due to the time lag already described) approach using a destructor.

Note

The garbage collector only reclaims memory. It does not free up any other resources.

Note

Not all object-oriented languages include a garbage collector. In C++, for example, the programmer must manually write the source code that detects when an object is no longer needed and must explicitly call a special method called a *destructor* (which is semantically different from C#'s destructors) to reclaim the associated memory. This destructor method will execute immediately when called and can include code to terminate access to scarce non-memory resources (files, network connection, and so on) mentioned earlier. Consequently, the C++ programmer has very tight control over when memory and other scarce resources are released by an object.

This control unfortunately comes with a high price. Not only does the C++ programmer spend precious time writing the code needed to implement this detection and reclaim system, but it comes with some of the nastiest and well hidden bugs known in the industry: They cause two main types of problems:

- *Dangling pointers*—The program mistakenly reclaims an object still in use, leading to a problem known as dangling pointers. (Note: A pointer in C++ is the equivalent to a reference in C#).
- *Memory leaks*—The program does not detect all objects that should be reclaimed, often causing a program to eventually run out of memory and crash.

The Limited Use of the Destructor

As mentioned in the note preceding this section, C++ contains a language feature called a destructor that is called explicitly in the source code to reclaim the resources occupied by an object. C# contains a vaguely similar construct in the form of a special method also called a *destructor*. Just like every class (not containing any explicit constructors) is equipped with a default constructor, every C# class is also equipped with a default destructor. However, whereas you must explicitly call a constructor with the `new` keyword to create a new object, only the GC can call the destructor when a C# program is running. The syntax for specifying the statements you want the destructor to execute is shown in Syntax Box 13.5.

Syntax Box 13.5 The Destructor

```
Destructor_declaration::=
                          ~ <Destructor_identifier> ( )
                          {
                              <Statements>
                          }
```

Example:

```
class Account
{
    ...
    ~Account()
    {
        Console.WriteLine("I'm only called by the GC " +
            "and I might never be called during the execution of the program");
    }
    ...
}
```

Notes:

- The <*Destructor_identifier*> must, like a constructor, be identical to the class identifier.
- No formal parameters can be specified for the destructor.
- The following syntax has exactly the same meaning as the destructor declaration shown in the beginning of this Syntax Box:

```
protected override void Finalize ()
{
    <Statements>
}
```

This is because destructors in C# are known as finalizers in the .NET runtime, so both kinds of syntax have found their way into C#.

The GC calls the destructor of an object when the GC happens to detect that the object is unreachable (see the following Note for further details). Superficially, the destructor sounds like the perfect place to put the code used to free scarce non-memory resources, but, due to the time lag previously discussed, the destructor could be called at any point between the time it becomes eligible for reclaim and after the program has ended. A destructor might never be called during the execution of a program. Consequently, the destructor is not suited for freeing up scarce non-memory resources. There are several other reasons why you should think twice before declaring destructors in your classes. They are discussed in the next section.

The Resource Hungry Mechanics Behind Destructors

Here is a brief overview of how the GC works with destructors and highlights some of their inefficiencies.

When collecting garbage, the GC distinguishes between objects containing a destructor declaration explicitly specified by you, as in Syntax Box 13.5 (called objects with destructors) and objects without destructor declarations.

When the GC during a spurt of activity detects an object to be unreachable and without a destructor, it is reclaimed immediately. In contrast, when an unreachable object with a destructor declaration is detected, its reference is put in a special list with other objects of the same fate, all waiting to have the statements of their destructors executed. When the GC has finished its spurt of activity detecting unreachable objects, it starts up another process to execute the statements of each destructor in the objects of the special list. Each object reference is then finally positioned in another list ready to be reclaimed. However, this will not take place until the next time the GC has a spurt of activity.

It is evident from this GC portrayal that handling objects with destructors is a costly process both in terms of memory and CPU time. An object with a destructor needs two full GC spurts to be fully reclaimed, consequently occupying the memory for a longer period of time, and special processes are needed along with space occupied by references in special lists. But these are not the only reasons why you should avoid using destructors. The following are a few other points to take into consideration:

- The order in which the destructors of the objects are executed is not guaranteed.
- There is no guarantee as to when or if the destructors will be called.
- Not only do objects with destructors occupy memory for a longer period, but also might have references to other objects (with or without destructors) and also force those to lengthen their stay.

Putting the Destructor to Good Use

By now, you might wonder if the C# destructor can be used for anything at all. It turns out it has a couple of uses:

- To release non-scarce resources occupied by an object. For example, this could be a file access to a file that is only accessed by one object.
- To investigate the process of garbage collection.

We use this second ability in Listing 13.5 to give you a practical view of the GC's activity spurts and their timing during the execution of a program preoccupied with constructing new objects that become unreachable and eligible for garbage collection immediately after their creation.

LISTING 13.5 `GCAnalyzer.cs`

```
using System;

class Bacterium
{
    private static int bacteriaCreated;
    private static int tempBacteriaDestructed;
    private static int totalBacteriaDestructed;
    private static bool showBacteriaDestructed;
    private static bool hasGCJustRun;

    private int number;
    private string name;
    private string shape;
    private string growthMethod;
    private string group;

    public Bacterium ()
    {
        if (hasGCJustRun)
        {
            Console.WriteLine("Bacterium objects destructed during GC
            ➥Run: {0}",
                tempBacteriaDestructed);
            Console.WriteLine("Difference between bacteria created " +
                "and bacteria destructed {0}",
                (bacteriaCreated - totalBacteriaDestructed));
            Console.WriteLine("Resuming creating bacteria from number:
           ➥{0}\n",
```

LISTING 13.5 continued

```
                bacteriaCreated);
            hasGCJustRun = false;
        }

        bacteriaCreated++;
        number = bacteriaCreated;
        name = "Streptococcus";
        shape = "round";
        growthMethod = "chains";
        group = "alpha";
    }

    static Bacterium ()
    {
        bacteriaCreated = 0;
        tempBacteriaDestructed = 0;
        totalBacteriaDestructed = 0;
        showBacteriaDestructed = false;
        hasGCJustRun = false;
    }

    ~Bacterium()
    {
        if(!hasGCJustRun)
        {
            Console.WriteLine("Creation temporarily stopped " +
                "at bacteria number: {0} to perform destruction",
                ➥bacteriaCreated);
            hasGCJustRun = true;
            tempBacteriaDestructed = 0;
        }
        if (showBacteriaDestructed)
        {
            Console.WriteLine("Bacteria: {0} destructed", number);
        }
        tempBacteriaDestructed++;
        totalBacteriaDestructed++;
    }

    public static void SetShowBacteriaDestructed (bool showIt)
    {
        showBacteriaDestructed = showIt;
    }

    public static int GetTotalBacteriaDestructed ()
    {
        return totalBacteriaDestructed;
    }

    public static int GetTotalBacteriaCreated ()
    {
        return bacteriaCreated;
```

LISTING 13.5 continued

```
    }
}

class Body
{
    public static void Main()
    {
        int bacteriaCreatedBeforeCollect;
        int maxBacteria;
        Bacterium newBacterium;

        Console.Write("How many bacteria do you want to create? ");
        maxBacteria = Convert.ToInt32(Console.ReadLine());
        Console.Write("Enter amount of bacteria to create " +
            "before asking GC to run: ");
        bacteriaCreatedBeforeCollect = Convert.ToInt32(
        ➥Console.ReadLine());
        Console.Write("Do you want to see each " +
            "bacterium number when destructed? Y)es N)o ");
        if (Console.ReadLine().ToUpper() == "Y")
            Bacterium.SetShowBacteriaDestructed (true);
        else
            Bacterium.SetShowBacteriaDestructed (false);
        Console.WriteLine("\nCreation commencing\n");

        for (int i = 0; i < maxBacteria; i++)
        {
            newBacterium = new Bacterium();
            if (i == (bacteriaCreatedBeforeCollect - 1))
            {
                Console.WriteLine("Initiating GC to run " +
                    "after bacteria number: {0} has been created",
                    ➥(i + 1));
                GC.Collect();
            }
        }

        Console.WriteLine("\nCreation stopped at bacterium number: {0}",
            Bacterium.GetTotalBacteriaCreated());
        Console.WriteLine("Total Bacteria objects destructed " +
            "during execution of program: {0}",
            Bacterium.GetTotalBacteriaDestructed());
    }
}
```

Notes:

- You will likely get the following four warnings when compiling the source code of Listing 13.5.

```
GCAnalyzer.cs(12,20): warning CS0169: The private field 'Bacterium.name'
➥ is never used
```

```
GCAnalyzer.cs(13,20): warning CS0169: The private field 'Bacterium.shape'
➥ is never used
GCAnalyzer.cs(14,20): warning CS0169: The private field
➥ 'Bacterium.growthMethod' is never used
GCAnalyzer.cs(15,20): warning CS0169: The private field 'Bacterium.group'
➥ is never used
```

You can safely ignore these warnings. The four instance variables (`name`, `shape`, `growthMethod`, and `group`) of the `Bacterium` class have only been included to let each object occupy more memory and thereby require the creation of fewer `Bacterium` objects to run low on memory and trigger a GC spurt of activity.

- The timing and duration of each GC spurt depends on several variables, including the memory size of your computer, other programs you have running that might take up memory, and so on. As a result, the output, concerned with GC timing and duration, will vary between different runs of the program and will certainly not be identical to the following output.

Sample output 1:

```
How many bacteria do you want to create? 1000000<enter>
Enter amount of bacteria to create before asking GC to run: 1000001<enter>
Do you want to see each bacterium number when destructed? Y)es N)o N<enter>

Creation commencing

Creation temporarily stopped at bacterium number: 15759 to perform destruction
Bacteria objects destructed during GC Run: 8701
Difference between bacteria created and bacteria destructed 7058
Resuming creating bacteria from number: 15759

Creation temporarily stopped at bacterium number: 18367 to perform destruction
Bacteria objects destructed during GC Run: 9031
Difference between bacteria created and bacteria destructed 635
Resuming creating bacteria from number: 18367
Creation temporarily stopped at bacterium number: 899227 to perform destruction
Bacteria objects destructed during GC Run: 87700
Difference between bacteria created and bacteria destructed 4642
Resuming creating bacteria from number: 899227

Creation temporarily stopped at bacterium number: 982952 to perform destruction
Bacteria objects destructed during GC Run: 87699
Difference between bacteria created and bacteria destructed 668
Resuming creating bacteria from number: 982952


Creation stopped at bacterium number: 1000000
Total Bacteria objects destructed during execution of program: 982284
```

Sample output 2:

```
How many bacteria do you want to create? 1000<enter>
Enter amount of bacteria to create before asking GC to run: 1001<enter>
```

```
Do you want to see each bacterium number when destructed? Y)es N)o N<enter>
Creation commencing

Creation stopped at bacterium number: 1000
Total Bacteria objects destructed during execution of program: 0
```

Sample output 3:

```
How many bacteria do you want to create? 5000<enter>
Enter amount of bacteria to create before asking GC to run: 3000<enter>
Do you want to see each bacterium number when destructed? Y)es N)o N<enter>

Creation commencing

Initiating GC to run after bacterium number: 3000 has been created
Creation temporarily stopped at bacterium number: 3000 to perform destruction
Bacteria objects destructed during GC Run: 3000
Difference between bacteria created and bacteria destructed 0
Resuming creating bacteria from number: 3000


Creation stopped at bacterium number: 5000
Total Bacteria objects destructed during execution of program: 3000
```

At the heart of Listing 13.5 is a loop (see lines 102–111, you can ignore lines 105–110 for now) creating new `Bacterium` objects in line 104. Each time a new `Bacterium` object reference is assigned to `newBacterium` in line 104, the `Bacterium` object referenced by `newBacterium` just prior to this assignment becomes unreachable and is pushed into the unknown. So the loop gradually fills the memory up with unreachable objects that sooner or later must be reclaimed by the GC to create space for new `Bacterium` objects. If we, for example, set `maxBacteria` to one million (see sample output 1) in line 90, line 104 is repeated one million times and will likely create objects occupying memory many times your computer's memory capacity. Consequently, the GC will have to run many spurts during the course of the one million loops. While the GC is running, the runtime keeps the program frozen. The only lines of your code being executed during these periods are the destructors (lines 48–63) of the unreachable objects eligible for execution.

The runtime switches back and forth between two modes:

- *The main program is running*—New `Bacterium` objects are being created in line 104 causing their `Bacterium` constructor in lines 17–37 to be executed.
- *The GC is running (main program temporarily stopped)*—Unreachable objects are detected and reclaimed. The `Bacterium` destructors (lines 48–63) of these objects are executed.

One of the aims of this program is to detect and display when the runtime switches between these two modes. The main ingredient used for this purpose is the `bool` variable `hasGCJustRun` declared in line 9. `hasGCJustRun` is `static`, so only one `hasGCJustRun` exists; it belongs to the `Bacterium` class and is shared by all `Bacterium` objects. Both the constructor and destructor of any `Bacterium` object can reach the same `hasGCJustRun` variable. Initially, `hasGCJustRun` is set to `false` in line 45 (in the `static` constructor of the `Bacterium` class) and the only place where `hasGCJustRun` is ever set to `true` is in the destructor (line 54). As long as no destructors have been called, no constructor will execute lines 20–29 (due to the `if` statement in line 19).

After a number of objects have been created (and become unreachable) the GC might decide to run (switching from mode 1 to mode 2) and execute a number of destructors. When the first destructor is executed, the condition of line 50 is `true` so that lines 52–55 will be executed setting `hasGCJustRun` to `true` in line 54. The second time the destructor is called, line 50 is `false`, preventing lines 52–55 from being executed. In fact, as long as no constructor has been executed to set `hasGCJustRun` back to `false`, lines 52–55 will not be executed by any of the trailing destructor executions. After the GC spurt is stopped, the main program commences (switching from mode 2 to mode 1). This time, `hasGCJustRun` is equal to `true` causing lines 21–28 to be executed, but only the first constructor in this batch of constructor calls will execute those lines.

So briefly, the overall behavior of the program can be described as—when the GC switches from mode 1 to mode 2, lines 52–55 are executed once, and when the GC switches back from mode 2 to mode 1, lines 21–28 are executed once.

To keep track of the number of `Bacterium` objects created, the constructor increments the `static` variable `bacteriaCreated` by one every time it is called. This enables lines 52–53 to report the number of bacteria created when every GC spurt commences. Similarly, the destructor keeps track of the total number of bacteria destructed (line 62) over the course of the program and the number of bacteria destructed in any one spurt (line 61). The latter amount is reported by lines 21 and 22 of the constructor, along with the difference between the total number of bacteria created and the total number of bacteria destructed. The difference gives us an idea of how many unreachable objects the GC allows the memory to contain. Keep in mind, though, that objects that have had their destructors called are not reclaimed until the next time the GC runs.

The first sample output involves the creation of one million `Bacterium` objects. Notice how the GC spurts keeps the number of unreachable objects in check. Also note that many destructors (1000000 – 982284 = 17716) were never called during the execution of the program.

The second sample output makes it evident that destructors might never be called during the course of a program.

As mentioned earlier, you can attempt to wake up the GC by calling the `System.GC.Collect` method. Listing 13.5 allows you to test just how responsive the GC is to this call. As demonstrated in sample output 3, you need in the second question to enter at which number-of-bacteria-created you wish the program to make the `System.GC.Collect` call. The number is stored in `bacteriaCreatedBeforeCollect` (declared in line 85, assigned in line 93) and checked during each loop in line 105. The actual call is made in line 109. To avoid having the `GC.Collect` call being made, simply enter a number larger than the total number of bacteria the program will create (`maxBacteria`). The GC was 100 percent responsive in sample output 3. It started exactly at 3000, created objects as requested, and destructed all of them. However, during the testing of this program, I experienced several instances where the GC either didn't respond at all, or responded by collecting just a few `Bacterium` objects.

Controlling the Garbage Collector

There are other ways to control the GC than with the `GC.Collect` method. For more details, please refer to the `System.GC` class of the .NET Framework Documentation.

From time to time, your program might benefit from using these tools. However, the GC has been constructed and optimized to work behind the scenes and undisturbed. If you interfere with this finely-tuned mechanism by calling the `GC.Collect` method or any of the other methods described in the .NET Framework Reference, you might compromise the overall performance of the GC and your program.

The program lets you view the total list of all `Bacterium` objects that have had their destructor executed. This is simply done by printing out the number of each bacterium in a (probably very long) list. By answering Y to the third question after the program is started, you can initiate this option. For space reasons, no sample output has been provided for this option.

Freeing Scarce Non-Memory Resources with the `Dispose` Method

If we can't use the destructor method to free up scarce non-memory resources what is the alternative? Microsoft encourages programmers to use what they call the "`Dispose` design pattern." The following is a simplified description of how it works.

Every object occupying scarce non-memory resources must be equipped with a `public` method called `Dispose` with statements to free the object's resources. When the user (for example, an object in another part of the program) is finished using the object, the `Dispose` method must be called. This ensures an immediate return of the resources and avoids the time lag we would otherwise experience had the destructor been entrusted to accomplish the task. Executing the `Dispose` method renders the object useless; to avoid any later use of this object and to allow the GC to reclaim its memory eventually, all its references must be released immediately after calling `Dispose`. Microsoft also suggests writing the same reclaiming statements of the `Dispose` method in the destructor. This allows the GC to free the resources of an object eventually, even if the `Dispose` method for some reason is never called. However, it poses a small problem—unless instructed otherwise, the GC will call the destructor of an object even if its `Dispose` method has been called previously. This means trouble, because freeing the same resources twice is an error. Fortunately, there is an easy solution to the problem. Let the `Dispose` method instruct the GC (by calling `System.GC.SuppressFinalize`) not to call the destructor of its object.

Listing 13.6 provides a simplified example of how the `Dispose` design pattern can be implemented. It leaves out issues related to inheritance and interfaces but still amply demonstrates the important ideas behind this design pattern.

Note

For a more advanced account of the `Dispose` design pattern, please refer to "Common Design Patterns" of ".NET Framework Design Guidelines" in the .NET Framework documentation.

The following gives an overview of the main parts of the program. For a more detailed treatment, please see the analysis after the sample output.

The `MyFile` class (lines 3–64) of Listing 13.6 simulates a file. Like most files, it only allows access to one user at a time. This is accomplished through a virtual key. Only one virtual key exists in the whole program. `MyFile` initially holds this key. The only way for an object to gain temporary exclusive access to `MyFile` is by obtaining the key from `MyFile` through a call to its `Open` method. If an object asks for the key while it is in the hands of another object, `MyFile` is unable to fulfill the request and access is denied. An object terminates access to `MyFile` by calling the `MyFile.Close` method; the key is then returned to `MyFile`.

The main task of an object of `FileAccessor` class (lines 66–128) is simply to print the content of `MyFile` (contained in line 5). This cannot be accomplished without accessing `MyFile`, so access to `MyFile` is already made in the constructor of each `FileAccessor` object. Consequently, `MyFile` is a precious resource and `FileAccessor` is, for that reason, equipped with a `Dispose` method and a destructor, both containing statements (in accordance with the Dispose design pattern) to release `MyFile` by returning the key to `MyFile`.

The `Main()` method of the `TestFileAccess` class creates and destructs several `FileAccessor` objects attempting to access `Myfile`, and it shows how the `Dispose` method should and should not be applied.

LISTING 13.6 `FileAccessSimulation.cs`

```
01: using System;
02:
03: class MyFile
04: {
05:     private static string fileContent = "Once upon a time a
        ➥beautiful princess...";
06:     private const int accessKey = 321;
07:     private static int mobileKey = accessKey;
08:
09:     public static int Open (int accessorNumber)
10:     {
11:         if (mobileKey == accessKey)
12:         {
13:             mobileKey = 0;
14:             Console.WriteLine("Access established to accessor number:
                ➥{0} ",
15:                 accessorNumber);
16:             return accessKey;
17:         }
18:         else
19:         {
20:             Console.WriteLine("File occupied! Access attempt failed");
21:             return 0;
22:         }
23:     }
24:
```

LISTING 13.6 continued

```
    public static void Close (int returnKey, int accessorNumber)
    {
        if (accessKey == returnKey)
        {
            mobileKey = returnKey;
            Console.WriteLine("File closed successfully by accessor
            ➥number: {0} ",
                accessorNumber);
        }
        else
        {
            Console.WriteLine("Could not close file, invalid return key");
        }
    }

    public static string Read (int readKey)
    {
        if (readKey == accessKey)
        {
            return fileContent;
        }
        else
        {
            Console.WriteLine("Access denied! Invalid key provided");
            return "";
        }
    }

    public static bool IsOccupied ()
    {
        if (mobileKey == accessKey)
            return false;
        else
            return true;
    }

    public static void Reset ()
    {
        mobileKey = accessKey;
    }
}

class FileAccessor
{
    private bool fileAccessEstablished;
    private bool disposed;
    private int accessKey;
    private int number;
    private static int objectCounter = 0;

    public FileAccessor ()
    {
```

LISTING 13.6 continued

```
        objectCounter++;
        number = objectCounter;
        if (!MyFile.IsOccupied())
        {
            accessKey = MyFile.Open(number);
            fileAccessEstablished = true;
            disposed = false;
        }
        else
        {
            Console.WriteLine("Error! Accessor {0} could not access
            ➥MyFile", number);
            fileAccessEstablished = false;
        }
    }

    private void FreeState ()
    {
        if (!disposed)
        {
            MyFile.Close(accessKey, number);
            fileAccessEstablished = false;
            disposed = true;
        }
        else
        {
            Console.WriteLine("Error! Attempt to dispose accessor {0}
            ➥more than once",
                number);
        }
    }

    public void Dispose ()
    {
        FreeState ();
        GC.SuppressFinalize(this);
    }

    public void PrintFileContent ()
    {
        if (!disposed)
        {
            if (fileAccessEstablished)
                Console.WriteLine("Content printed by accessor {0}: {1}",
                    number, MyFile.Read(accessKey));
            else
                Console.WriteLine("Accessor {0} has no access to MyFile",
                ➥number);
        }
        else
        {
            Console.WriteLine("Access impossible. Accessor {0} has
            ➥already been disposed",
```

LISTING 13.6 continued

```
                    number);
            }
        }
    }

    class TestFileAccess
    {
        public static void Main()
        {
            FileAccessor accessor1;
            FileAccessor accessor2;
            FileAccessor accessor3;
            FileAccessor accessor4;
            FileAccessor accessor5;
            FileAccessor accessor6;

            accessor1 = new FileAccessor ();
            accessor1.PrintFileContent ();
            accessor1.Dispose();
            accessor1 = null;

            accessor2 = new FileAccessor ();
            accessor2.PrintFileContent ();

            accessor3 = new FileAccessor ();
            accessor3.PrintFileContent();

            accessor2.Dispose();
            accessor2 = null;
            accessor3 = null;

            accessor4 = new FileAccessor ();
            accessor4.PrintFileContent ();
            accessor4 = null;

            accessor5 = new FileAccessor ();

            MyFile.Reset();
            accessor5 = null;

            accessor6 = new FileAccessor ();
            accessor6.PrintFileContent ();
            accessor6.Dispose();
            accessor6.Dispose();
            accessor6 = null;
        }
    }
```

```
Access established to accessor number: 1
Content printed by accessor 1: Once upon a time a beautiful princess...
File closed successfully by accessor number: 1
Access established to accessor number: 2
Content printed by accessor 2: Once upon a time a beautiful princess...
```

```
Error! Accessor 3 could not access MyFile
Accessor 3 has no access to MyFile
File closed successfully by accessor number: 2
Access established to accessor number: 4
Content printed by accessor 4: Once upon a time a beautiful princess...
Error! Accessor 5 could not access MyFile
Access established to accessor number: 6
Content printed by accessor 6: Once upon a time a beautiful princess...
File closed successfully by accessor number: 6
Error! Attempt to dispose accessor 6 more than once
```

The virtual key mentioned in the previous overview is represented in the program by the number `321` and held by the `const accessKey` declared in line 6. When `mobileKey` is equal to `321`, `MyFile` has the key; when `mobileKey` is zero, it doesn't have it. The `Open` method (lines 9–23) will give the key away (line 16) if `MyFile` holds the key (checked in line 11), after which it is set to not have it (line 13). If `MyFile` does not hold the key, the opening attempt fails (lines 20 and 21).

The key is given back to `MyFile` by calling the `Close` method (lines 25–37).

To read the contents of `MyFile`, the `Read` method (lines 39–50) must be called and the caller must provide the correct key (see formal parameter in line 39); the string of line 5 will then be returned.

Before attempting to `Open MyFile`, it can be handy to know whether it is occupied. The `IsOccupied` method (lines 52–58) provides us with that answer. The last method of `MyFile`, called `Reset`, can be called in case of gridlocks, for example, if the key has been lost by an object that became unreachable before it got the chance to give back the key.

The main task of the `FileAccessor` constructor (lines 74–89) is to establish access to `MyFile`. This is possible if `IsOccupied` is `false` (checked in line 78). The `FileAccessor` object then temporarily gets to hold the key in the `accessKey` variable (line 80). The `bool` variable `disposed` (line 69) is used to prevent the `Dispose` method from cleaning up more than once for the same `FileAccessor` object. This is achieved by preventing `Dispose` (lines 106–110) from invoking the cleaning up part of `FreeState` (lines 95–97) if `dispose` is `true` (line 93) combined with letting `dispose` be `false` after the constructor's successful connection (line 82) and by letting `dispose` be `true` when cleanup has taken place once (line 97).

Both the `Dispose` method and the destructor contain calls to `FreeState` in accordance with the Dispose design pattern, so to prevent `FreeState` from being called twice (once by `Dispose` and once by the destructor when called by the GC), the `Dispose` method calls the GC `SuppressFinalize` method (line 109) and asks for `this` object to be taken off the list of object destructors called by the GC.

The `Main` method of the `TestFileAccess` class creates six `FileAccessor` objects. Only one of those (`accessor1` in lines 141–144) is correctly disposed and released. The `Dispose` method must always be called on an object (line 143) immediately after we have finished using it and must be made unreachable (line 144) immediately after the `Dispose` method has been called. *Reversing this sequence will not work.* The correctness of lines 141–144 is supported by the sample output, reporting that `accessor2` has trouble-free access to `MyFile` in line 146. `accessor3` is less fortunate during its access attempt in line 149 because of the missing call to the `Dispose` method of `accessor2`. This problem is rectified in lines 152 and 153.

A `FileAccessor` object can only connect to `MyFile` in its constructor, rendering `accessor3` useless. Thus, line 154 releases the reference to `accessor3`.

The attempt to rely solely on the GC to clear `accessor4`'s access to `MyFile` by simply making its referenced object unreachable in line 158 is likely to fail (as in this sample output) due to the infamous time lag previously discussed. Thus, `accessor5`'s attempt to connect in line 160 fails. `accessor4` brought the key with it into the unknown. Therefore, we must call the `MyFile.Reset` method to give back the key to `MyFile`.

Lines 165–168 demonstrate how the `disposed` variable of the `FileAccessor` class effectively prevents an instance from being cleaned up twice. The second call to `Dispose` in line 168 triggers the error message shown in the last line of the sample output.

Summary

In this chapter, you learned about object creation and, in particular, about constructors and their ability to perform useful actions when a new object is created. The chapter also looked at how memory, otherwise occupied by an object that no longer can be reached, is released with garbage collection, and how other scarce resources can be released with the Dispose design pattern.

The following paragraphs review the important points covered in this chapter.

An instance variable can be initialized in three different ways:

- Automatically by the runtime. In which case, the instance variable is assigned a default value. The default value depends on the type of the instance variable.
- Using a declaration initialization, which allows the programmer to specify the initialization value.
- Using a constructor, which is a function member that allows the programmer to include any number of statements that are to be executed when the object is created.

Constructors are often needed to perform initializations that involve the execution of several statements. They are also suited to perform other actions than initializations that are required when the object is created.

An instance constructor is called when the keyword `new` is used to create a new object.

If you don't specify any constructors for a class, a default constructor will automatically be included by the compiler. A default constructor takes no arguments.

Several constructors can be included in the same class, in which case, they become overloaded in a similar fashion to that of overloaded methods. The formal parameters of overloaded constructors must, like their overloaded method cousins, differ in terms of their types or their amount, or both.

The constructor initializer allows you to specify that a constructor, on its initiation, calls another constructor prior to the execution of its own method body. This can save you from including the same set of statements in several overloaded instance constructors.

You can prevent any objects to be instantiated from a class by declaring all its instance constructors (usually just one) to be `private`. This can be useful with classes that only contain `static` members.

A `static` constructor is not called directly from the source code, but is called automatically by the runtime sometime between the start of the program and the instantiation of the first object of the class. The `static` constructor is most commonly used to initialize `static` variables.

The value of a constant variable must be written in the source code, so it remains unchangeable from the time a program is compiled. In contrast, a `readonly` variable is initialized during runtime when its object is created and remains unchangeable during the lifetime of the object.

When no references exist to an object, it is out of reach and becomes eligible for garbage collection. Four examples of objects becoming unreachable were discussed:

- When all references to an object are assigned the `null` reference, this object goes out of reach.
- When a reference variable (holding the only reference to an object A) is assigned a different reference, object A goes out of reach.
- When an object A contains the only reference to an object B, both object A and B go out of reach when object A goes out of reach.
- When a local variable, which contains the only reference to an object, goes out of scope the object becomes unreachable.

The garbage collector works by default behind the scenes on every C# program; it is managed automatically by the runtime. It detects unreachable objects and reclaims their memory. The garbage collector is finely tuned to work in the background, and should only be interfered with in rare cases.

The garbage collector does not promise when it collects an unreachable object. It might not occur until after the program has finished interacting with the user.

A destructor is a class member containing executable statements that are executed as part of the garbage collector's memory reclamation.

Objects can occupy other scarce resources than memory, such as files and network connections. The garbage collector does not free these types of resources, and the destructor is not suited to carry out this task because of the garbage collector's timing uncertainties.

The programmer should implement his or her own system to detect when scarce non-memory resources must be freed and write the actual code that frees those resources. Microsoft recommends programmers to use the "Dispose design pattern" for this purpose.

Review Questions

1. A class called `Robot` contains the following two instance variable declarations:

   ```
   private ushort age;
   private bool isConnected;
   ```

   What is the value of `age` and `isConnected` immediately after their object has been instantiated?

   Improve the style of the declarations without changing the semantics of the code.

2. The users of your `Robot` class would like to assign a value to `age` at the same time as they are instantiating a `Robot` object. How would you accommodate for this request?

3. What constructor names can you use for a class called `Robot`?

4. Are constructors only used to initialize instance variables?

5. What is the return type of a constructor?

6. a. A `Dog` class contains no constructor definitions in the source code. Is the following statement (found inside a method of another class) valid?

   ```
   Dog myDog = new Dog();
   ```

   b. You decide to include a constructor with the following header in the `Dog` class:

   ```
   public Dog(int initialAge)
   ```

   Is the previous statement valid now? Why or why not?

7. a. You find the following two constructor headers in a class called `Cat`:

   ```
   public Cat(short initialAge, string initialName) : this (initialAge)
   public Cat(short initialAge)
   ```

   Are these headers valid? If so, what do they mean? What is `: this (initialAge)` used for?

   b. A fellow programmer changes those headings to become

   ```
   public Cat() : this ()
   ```

   Is this header valid? Why or why not?

8. The following line creates a new `Cat` object. What do the parentheses after `Cat` signify?

   ```
   Cat myCat = new Cat();
   ```

9. How can overloaded constructors make a class more flexible to use?

10. Why would you ever want a constructor that cannot be called from outside its class? How do you declare this kind of constructor? What is it called?

11. When is a `static` constructor called?

    a. From where is a `static` constructor called? When is a `static` constructor called?

    b. What's wrong with the following header of a static constructor?

    ```
    static Cat (int initialNumberOfCats)
    ```

12. Could you design a program that allows the end user to assign a value to a:

    a. Constant instance member?

    b. A `readonly` instance member?

    Hint: What is the lifetime of a constant member? What is the lifetime of a `readonly` instance member?

13. Briefly explain what it means for an object to be out of reach.

14. What are the two main tasks of the garbage collector?

15. Why does the garbage collector not just garbage collect any object that goes out of reach immediately?

16. What is a destructor? Why is it not useful for freeing up scarce non-memory resources?

17. A program contains a class called `Book` that contains 10 instance variables all of a simple type. During the execution of the program, 50 `Book` objects are created and most of them are destroyed. Is the garbage collector likely to run during the execution of your code?

18. Why should you be careful when using C# (at this time of writing) for real time applications?

19. Briefly explain why it is a good idea to use the `Dispose` design pattern to free scarce non-memory resources.

Programming Exercises

Exercises 2–5 each build on the code written in the previous exercise, so please keep the code from each exercise handy for the next exercise. As you progress through the questions, you should write a `Main` method containing code to demonstrate the classes you write.

1. Write a class called `Robot` with the following three instance variables: `name` (of type `string`), `age` (of type `ushort`), and `isOn` (of type `bool`). Make the program initialize these three instance variables to `"unknown"`, `0`, and `false`, respectively (without using constructors). Include accessor and mutato methods to assign and retrieve the values of these instance variables.

   Write a `Main` method that tests the `Robot` class.

2. Allow the users of the `Robot` class to set the initial values of the three instance variables when a `Robot` object is created. To this end, declare one constructor with three formal parameters and one default constructor.

3. Include a member variable called `robotsCreated` that keeps track of the number of `Robot` objects created. Make the constructors update `robotsCreated` so this variable is always up-to-date. Implement the following logic in the default constructor: If `robotsCreated` is less than five when this constructor is called, set `isOn` to `true`; otherwise, set it to `false`.

4. The `Robot` is able to perform a few simple calculations. For example, it can find the average of three `int` numbers. This ability is provided through a method with the following header:

   ```
   public int Average (int x, int y, int z)
   ```

   This method does not itself perform the average calculation but uses a `static` method named `Average` contained inside a class called `RobotMath`. The `RobotMath` class only contains `static` methods and `static` variables and should never be instantiated. Ensure that `RobotMath` is never instantiated.

CHAPTER 14

CLASS ANATOMY PART III: WRITING INTUITIVE CODE

You will learn about the following in this chapter:

- How to implement and work with properties
- How to implement and work with indexers
- Indexers and overloading
- User-defined operator overloading
- User-defined conversions
- Nested types

The constructs (properties, indexers, operator overloading, and user-defined conversions) discussed in this chapter do not enable us to write programs that could not easily be implemented by using the familiar method construct. In fact, some of these constructs are compiled into MSIL code that looks nearly identical to that generated for methods. Nevertheless, if we implement them when suitable in our classes, they allow the users of these classes to write cleaner and more intuitive code.

Properties provide elegant and robust support for the encapsulation principle introduced in Chapter 3, "A Guided Tour through C#: Part I." They allow the users of your classes to access `private` instance variables as if they were `public`, without using the cumbersome accessor and mutator methods presented earlier. This is achieved without jeopardizing the protection and data hiding that is required for `private` instance variables, because properties are implemented in a method-like fashion inside the class.

Indexers allow you to access a collection (for example an array) kept within an object from outside this object as if the object itself was an array. So, instead of using a method to access an array of, say, rainfall data inside an object called `rainfallInCalifornia` as shown here

```
rainfallInCalifornia.GetRainfallInMonth(6)
```

indexers allow you to simply use the square brackets used with arrays as in the following line:

```
rainfallInCalifornia[6]
```

Through operator overloading, you can apply operators like + and - on your own user-defined types instead of using the, at times, ugly looking methods. For example, you might have written a Fraction class to represent fractions. Without operator overloading, you would likely write a method called Add to add two fraction objects together (here called thisFraction and thatFraction) and assign the result to a third fraction object (called sumFraction). This would look like the following line:

```
sumFraction = thisFraction.Add(thatFraction);
```

Instead of operator overloading, let us write the cleaner looking and more intuitive line

```
sumFraction = thisFraction + thatFraction;
```

User-defined conversions also provide elegant substitutes for methods. Suppose you have written two classes called TempFahrenheit and TempCelsius both representing temperatures. You could then write a conversion method in the TempFahrenheit class called ConvertToCelsius. This would allow you to convert from the object myTempFahrenheit to myTempCelsius by writing the following:

```
myTempCelsius = myTempFahrenheit.ConvertToCelsius();
```

Alternatively, user-defined conversions allow us to perform an implicit conversion between the two types simply by writing the following:

```
myTempCelsius = myTempFahrenheit;
```

Of all the language elements in C#, the constructs presented in this chapter can easily be overused and misused, resulting in cryptic and unclear code. So when you read through the chapter, make sure you understand the problems each construct was meant to solve and—even more important—not meant to solve. This information is often presented in Tip and Common Pitfall boxes.

The chapter ends with a discussion of the last main class member category (the other two were data and function members) called nested types. Nested types allow us to insert type definitions in a class block. As a result, we can avoid exposing types to the outside world, which are only of interest to one particular class.

Properties

Even though a property presents itself as a public instance variable to the world outside the class where it is defined, it is still implemented somewhat like a method inside the class (it has an ability to execute statements). This double life makes them highly suited for replacing accessor and mutator methods. Our path to understanding properties and why they provide more consistent, clearer, and intuitive code begins with a look at accessor and mutator methods.

Properties Versus Accessor and Mutator Methods

According to the encapsulation principle, discussed in Chapter 3, instance variables of an object must be hidden from source code written outside the object. In C#, this is typically implemented by declaring all instance variables to be `private`. In the examples presented so far, access from outside an object has been provided indirectly via the `public` accessor and mutator methods that conventionally carry names like `GetDistance` and `SetDistance`. These methods are also able to carry out actions that either protect the instance variables from being assigned incorrect values or actions that must be performed in connection with setting and getting an instance variable. Listing 14.1 demonstrates the typical use of accessor and mutator methods.

LISTING 14.1 `BicyclingWithAccessorMethods.cs`

```
using System;

class Bicycle
{
    const byte MaxSpeed = 40;
    private byte speed = 0;
    private int speedAccessCounter = 0;

    public byte GetSpeed()
    {
        speedAccessCounter++;
        return speed;
    }

    public void SetSpeed(byte newSpeed)
    {
        if (newSpeed > MaxSpeed)
            Console.WriteLine("Error. {0} exceeds the speed limit {1}",
                newSpeed, MaxSpeed);
        else if (newSpeed < 0)
            Console.WriteLine("Error. {0} is less than 0", newSpeed);
        else
            speed = newSpeed;
    }

    public int GetSpeedAccessCounter()
    {
        return speedAccessCounter;
    }
}

class BicycleTester
{
    public static void Main()
    {
        byte speedInMilesPerHour;
```

LISTING 14.1 continued

```
37:         Bicycle myBike = new Bicycle();
38:
39:         myBike.SetSpeed(60);
40:         myBike.SetSpeed(30);
41:         Console.WriteLine("Current speed of myBike: {0}",
            ➥myBike.GetSpeed());
42:         speedInMilesPerHour = (byte)(myBike.GetSpeed () * 0.621);
43:         Console.WriteLine("Number of times speed of myBike has been
            ➥retrieved: {0}",
44:             myBike.GetSpeedAccessCounter());
45:     }
46: }
```

```
Error. 60 exceeds the speed limit 40
Current speed of myBike: 30
Number of times speed of myBike has been retrieved: 2
```

The `Bicycle` class contains two `private` instance variables—`speed` and `speedAccessCounter`, declared in lines 6 and 7. In this example, we want to prevent any outside user from assigning a value to `speed` that is smaller than zero or greater than `MaxSpeed`. This is accomplished by `SetSpeed`'s `if...else` statement in lines 17–23.

`speed` can be accessed via the `GetSpeed` method, which also counts of the number of times `speed` has been retrieved (line 11).

The `Main` method in the `BicycleTester` class represents the source code outside the `Bicycle` object and must use the `GetSpeed` and `SetSpeed` methods as a means to access `speed`. In the output sample, `Main`'s invalid attempt of assigning 60 to `speed` (see line 39) is appropriately denied by the `SetSpeed` method.

The number of times `speed` has been accessed (two, in this case—once in line 41 to print out information and once in line 42 as part of a standard arbitrary calculation) is correctly counted by `GetSpeed` and stored in the `speedAccessCounter`. This value is accessed with `GetSpeedAccessCounter` in lines 43 and 44 and printed on the console as shown in the sample output.

Accessor and mutator methods fulfill their tasks adequately from a functional point of view (they get the work done), and they are commonly used throughout the programmer community in languages like Java and C++ that do not feature constructs similar to C#'s properties. However, they cause syntactical inconsistencies between the way instance variables are modified and retrieved when called from within the object in which they reside and the way they are modified and retrieved from an outside object. To modify and retrieve an instance variable from within its object, we simply need to write the name of the instance variable as follows:

```
distance = 10;      or      time = distance / speed;
```

If the syntax was consistent, we should be able to write the following line instead of line 40 in Listing 14.1:

```
myBike.speed = 30;
```

which uses the assignment operator, not a `Set`- method as in line 40.

Similarly, we should be able to write line 42 as follows:

```
speedInMilesPerHour = (byte)(myBike.speed * 0.621);
```

where `speed` is simply retrieved by writing its name after `myBike`, not by calling `GetSpeed` as in line 42.

Unfortunately, this would require us to declare `speed` to be `public` and to throw away the important statements belonging to the accessor and mutator methods, were it not for the properties. C#'s *property construct* allows the outside user of an object to access an instance variable by using the consistent instance variable (non-method) syntax shown previously, while permitting all instance variables inside the object to remain `private`. At the same time, the property contains statements, otherwise held by accessor, and mutator methods that are executed when appropriate.

Listing 14.2 uses properties to accomplish exactly the same functionality as Listing 14.1.

LISTING 14.2 `BicyclingWithProperties.cs`

```
using System;

class Bicycle
{
    const byte MaxSpeed = 40;
    private byte speed = 0;
    private int speedAccessCounter = 0;

    public byte Speed
    {
        get
        {
            speedAccessCounter++;
            return speed;
        }

        set
        {
            if (value > MaxSpeed)
                Console.WriteLine("Error. {0} exceeds the speed limit {1}",
                    value, MaxSpeed);
            else if (value < 0)
                Console.WriteLine("Error. {0} is less than 0", value);
            else
                speed = value;
        }
    }

    public int SpeedAccessCounter
    {
        get
        {
            return speedAccessCounter;
```

LISTING 14.2 continued

```
34:         }
35:     }
36: }
37:
38: class BicycleTester
39: {
40:     public static void Main()
41:     {
42:         byte speedInMilesPerHour;
43:         Bicycle myBike = new Bicycle ();
44:
45:         myBike.Speed = 60;
46:         myBike.Speed = 30;
47:         Console.WriteLine("Current speed of myBike: {0}", myBike.Speed);
48:         speedInMilesPerHour = (byte)(myBike.Speed * 0.621);
49:         Console.WriteLine("Number of times speed of myBike has been retrieved:
{0}",
50:             myBike.SpeedAccessCounter);
51:     }
52: }
```

```
Error. 60 exceeds the speed limit 40
Current speed of myBike: 30
Number of times speed of myBike has been retrieved: 2
```

Note that the output is identical to that of Listing 14.1

Please refer to Syntax Box 14.1, shown later in this section, during this analysis.

The `Bicycle` class contains two properties. One is called `Speed` (lines 9–27) and provides access to the `speed` instance variable declared in line 6. The other, named `SpeedAccessorCounter` (lines 29–35) provides access to `speedAccessCounter`. Let's first look at the `Speed` property. A property consists of a header (line 9) and a block (lines 11–26) enclosed by braces (lines 10 and 27). In the header, we can specify the access modifier (in this case `public`), the type of the property (`byte`), and its name (`Speed`). The property block consists of a `get` statement block (lines 11–15) containing the statements equivalent to those found in an accessor method (compare with lines 11 and 12 of Listing 14.1) and a `set` statement block (lines 17–26) containing statements equivalent to those found in a mutator method (compare with lines 15–24 of Listing 14.1). The client side (which simply is the user of the class; in this case, it is the `Main method`) can now call the `Speed` property as if it is an instance variable. This is demonstrated in lines 45, 46, 47, and 48. When `Speed` is being assigned a value as in line 46

```
myBike.Speed = 30;
```

the statements of the `set` statement block are executed. The special parameter `value`, found in lines 19, 21, 22, 23, and 25, represents the value assigned, 30 in this case. `value` is automatically assigned the value 30 by the runtime. Line 25 thus passes 30 over to the instance variable `speed`.

Retrieving a value from `Speed`, as in line 48

```
speedInMilesPerHour = (byte)(myBike.Speed * 0.621);
```

triggers the statements of the `get` statement block to be executed. When a statement containing the `return` keyword is executed (line 14), the `get` statement block is terminated and the expression following `return` is returned to the retrieving call. The meaning of `return` in this context is identical to that of a conventional method.

If you only need to either set the value of an instance variable (`write-only`) or retrieve it (`read-only`), you can specify either just the `set` statement block or the `get` statement block; but at least one must be included. The `SpeedAccessCounter` property (lines 29–35) is an example of a read-only property that only allows its user to retrieve the value of an instance variable because of its missing `set` statement block.

Syntax Box 14.1 Property Declaration

```
Property_declaration::=
    [<Access_modifier>] [override | new [ virtual | abstract | static ] ] <Type>
➥<Identifier>
    {
        [<get_statement_block>]
        [<set_statement_block>]
    }
```

where

```
<Access_modifier>
                ::= public
                ::= private
                ::= protected
                ::= internal
                ::= protected internal

<get_statement_block> ::=
          get
          {
              [<Statements>]
              return <Expression>
          }

<set_statement_block> ::=
          set
          {
              [<Statements (using the keyword value)>]
          }
```

Notes:

- The type of the `<Expression>` positioned after the `return` keyword in the `<get_statement_block>` must be of the same type as specified by the `<Type>` of the property declaration header.
- The parameter `value` in the `<set_statement_block>` represents the value assigned to the property and is of the same type as `<Type>` of the property declaration header. The name `value` is set by the compiler and cannot be changed.

- A property can either have one *<get_statement_block>* or one *<set_statement_block>* or both. It cannot have zero statement blocks.
- The *<get_statement_block>* is often called *<get_accessor>* or simply *<getter>*. The *<set_statement_block>* is often called *<set_accessor>* or *<setter>*.
- The optional keyword `new` of the property declaration header is semantically different to `new` when you use it for creating new objects. It is, like the keywords `override`, `virtual` and `abstract`, related to OO concepts we haven't yet to discussed. I have included them here for completeness; they can safely be ignored for now.
- A property does not need to represent a specific instance variable (even though this is a common use); it only *pretends* to be an instance variable. A property can, for example, be called `Average` and calculate the average of several instance variables in its `get` statement block.

Note

Properties are easier for the client to use (a client is the part of a program that calls the properties and methods of a class or object) than accessor and mutator methods because

- Properties provide for consistent syntax between accessing an instance variable residing within an object and accessing an instance variable in another object.
- Properties save the programmer from checking whether an instance variable is `public` or `private` and whether accessor or mutator methods exist for this instance variable and save him from determining their formats.
- There is usually one accessor and one mutator method per instance variable (which needs to be accessible), but only one property is needed per instance variable. So, instead of sifting through, for example, forty accessors and mutators, the user only needs to look at twenty properties.

Note

Properties fit accessor and mutator parts into the same construct. An accessor and a mutator method work as a pair because they access the same instance variable. Consequently, a change in the source code in one of the methods often triggers the need for a change in the other. However, they are not treated as if they were a pair by the syntax, they could be two unrelated methods for that matter, floating around in the soup of other methods and instance variables. The property construct solves this problem by including both the accessor part (`get` statement block) and the mutator part (`set` statement block) in the same construct.

Use Pascal Casing for Properties and Camel Casing for Instance Variables

Microsoft recommends the Pascal casing style for properties (example: `Speed`) and camel casing for instance variables (example: `speed`). It is important to distinguish between the two styles in your source code, because the name of an instance variable and its associated property are often so similar that casing is the only thing that differentiates them. Failure to comply will cause the compiler to mix up the two, often leading to serious errors.

Let's investigate the effect of changing `speedAccessCounter` in line 33 of Listing 14.2 from its current (correct) camel casing style referring to the instance variable, to the (incorrect) Pascal casing style (`SpeedAccessCounter`), referring to the property. After this change, the compiler will, during the execution of line 33, interpret `SpeedAccessCounter` as another call to the `get` statement block of the `SpeedAccessCounter` property, and thus call itself. This new execution of the `get` statement block will again meet the statement containing `SpeedAccessCounter` and call the `get` statement block yet again. In fact, the `get` statement block will call itself infinitely many times and thereby crash your program.

Note

Properties can, like accessor and mutator methods, be called from within an object.

Properties Are Speedy

A property is executed as fast as its mutator and accessor counterparts and, in some instances, a property is executed as fast as a direct call to the instance variable it is accessing. Let's have a closer look at these two claims:

Properties are executed as fast as their equivalent accessor and mutator methods.

Both the `get` statement block and the `set` statement block of a property are turned into methods when compiled into MSIL. In MSIL, the `get` statement block is represented with a method called `get_<Property_identifier>:...` and the `set` statement block is represented with a method called `set_<Property_identifier>:...`. For example, the `get` statement block of the `Distance` property in Figure 14.1 is represented by a method equivalent construct with the header `get_Distance:float64()` in MSIL. It turns out that a method with the header `public double get_Distance()` is represented with an identical header, as illustrate in Figure 14.1. If the property and its twin methods are included in the same class (as in the `Light` class shown here), the result is a name clash. Consequently, if you tried to compile the `Light` class, you would get the following compiler error message:

```
    ...Class 'Light' already defines a member called 'get_Distance'
with the same parameter types
```

Because of the similarity between properties and methods in MSIL, there is no performance difference between using accessor and mutator methods and their equivalent properties.

A simple `get` *or* `set` *statement block is executed as fast as a direct call to the instance variable.*

If a `get` statement block only contains one statement consisting of the `return` keyword followed by the name of the instance variable, it is called a *simple* `get` statement block. Similarly, if a `set` statement block only has one statement that assigns the value of the `value` parameter to the associated instance variable, it is called a *simple* `set` statement block. The following property `Distance` contains two simple statement blocks:

```
...
private int distance;
public int Distance
{
    get
    {
        return distance;
    }
    set
    {
        distance = value;
    }
}
...
```

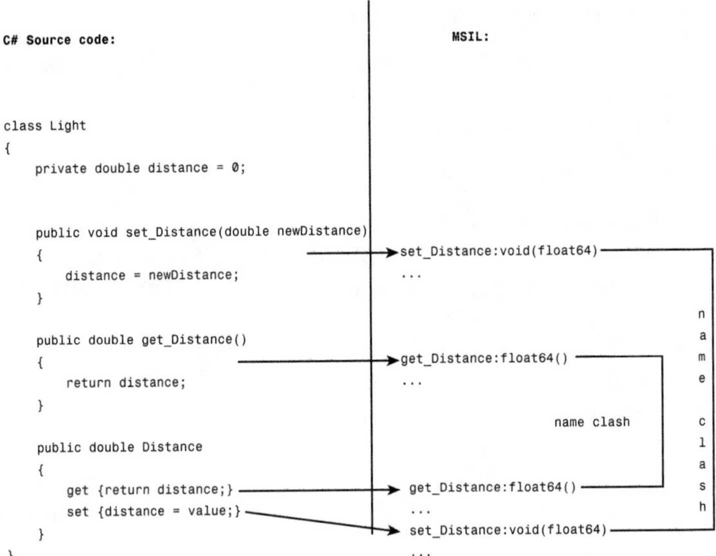

FIGURE 14.1
Example of identical properties and methods when compiled to MSIL.

When a simple `get` or `set` statement block is called, as in the following line:

```
time = moon.Distance / speed;
```

the compiler performs a special optimization called ***inlining***, whereby it replaces `moon.Distance` with the equivalent of a direct call to the `distance` instance variable. As a result, there is no performance difference between the last line and the following line (had `distance` been `public`):

```
time = moon.distance / speed;
```

where `distance` in `moon.distance` represents direct access to the instance variable `distance`.

Implementing Delayed Initialization and Lazy Updates with Properties

By using properties, it is possible to delay the initialization of an instance variable until its associated `get` statement block is called for the first time. This can improve the performance of a program when applied on instance variables that are rarely used and are time- and resource-consuming to initialize. Delayed initialization is a special case of another technique called lazy updates. Both techniques are discussed and demonstrated in the following discussion and example.

Sometimes, instance variables need to be updated regularly because they represent a value received from an exterior resource that changes within regular intervals. Some values might be valid for just a couple of seconds (stock prices) and others for weeks (economic indicators). Whenever this type of instance variable is needed in a calculation, it is possible to let the `get` statement block decide whether the program should use the old value stored in the instance variable object or whether it is time to go out and fetch a new value. This will minimize the number of times the program needs to use costly resources for updates. I will refer to these types of updates as ***lazy updates***. The following scenario provides an example of using lazy updates.

You are writing a program for a sophisticated commodity trader (trading in oranges, wheat, and so on). The program must be able to forecast, with reasonable precision, the volume and quality of future crops in different regions of America. A rainfall prediction ten days ahead in the relevant region is one of the many parameters needed in the complex calculations that form the base of the program, so you must include a sophisticated weather forecasting component in your program to generate these data. This component provides forecasts for fifty different regions throughout the country. Each rainfall forecast is CPU intensive and can take several minutes to calculate. The component does not remember its calculations and will always need to start from scratch, no matter how many times the same parameter has been requested. Every twenty seconds, the component provides a newer, more accurate forecast; so, the same calculation will give the same result during each twenty-second interval.

Different grains and fruits have different seasons, so the user only needs to forecast a few grains or fruits at any specific time during the year, and only a limited number of regions are involved in each forecast. Some of the instance variables in your program are used to hold rainfall forecasts for the different regions. You decide to use lazy updates for each of those instance variables because of their high update costs combined with the twenty-second lifespan.

Listing 14.3 contains a simplified crop-forecasting program to illustrate the principles just discussed.

LISTING 14.3 `CropForecaster.cs`

```
using System;
using System.Timers;

```

LISTING 14.3 continued

```
class WeatherForecaster
{
    public static double CalculateRainfallDay10RegionA()
    {
         //Simulated complex calculations takes 5000 milliseconds
        System.Threading.Thread.Sleep(5000);
        Random randomizer = new Random();
        return (double)randomizer.Next(40,100);
    }
}

class CropForecaster
{
    private double rainfallDay10RegionA;
    private bool rainfallDay10RegionANeedUpdate = true;

    public CropForecaster()
    {
        Timer aTimer = new Timer();
        aTimer.Elapsed += new ElapsedEventHandler(OnTimedEvent);
        aTimer.Interval = 20000;
        aTimer.Enabled = true;
    }

    public double RainfallDay10RegionA
    {
        get
        {
            if (rainfallDay10RegionANeedUpdate)
            {
                rainfallDay10RegionA =
              ➥ WeatherForecaster.CalculateRainfallDay10RegionA();
                rainfallDay10RegionANeedUpdate = false;
                return rainfallDay10RegionA;
            }
            else
            {
                return rainfallDay10RegionA;
            }
        }
    }

    private double ComplexResultA()
    {
         //Arbitrary calculation involving lots of
        ➥ calls to rainfallDay10RegionA
        return ((RainfallDay10RegionA / 2) + (RainfallDay10RegionA / 3) +
            (RainfallDay10RegionA / 4));
    }

    private double ComplexResultB()
    {
```

LISTING 14.3 continued

```
            //Arbitrary calculation involving even more calls
        ➥ to rainfallDay10RegionA
        return (RainfallDay10RegionA / 10 - 100) +
        ➥ (RainfallDay10RegionA / 100);
    }

    public double WheatCropSizeInTonsInRegionA ()
    {
        //More arbitrary calculations returning a nice big result
        Console.WriteLine("Commencing forecast calculations.
        ➥ Please wait...");
        return (ComplexResultA() / 2 + ComplexResultB() / 4 +
            ComplexResultA()) * 100000;
    }

    public void OnTimedEvent(object source, ElapsedEventArgs e)
    {
        //This method is currently called automatically every 20 seconds
        Console.WriteLine("\n\nNew Update Needed\nPerform
        ➥ another forecast?");
        rainfallDay10RegionANeedUpdate = true;
    }
}

class ForecastTester
{
    public static void Main()
    {
        string answer;
        CropForecaster myForecaster = new CropForecaster();

        Console.Write("Would you like to perform a crop
        ➥ forecast? Y)es N)o ");
        answer = Console.ReadLine().ToUpper();
        while (!(answer == "N"))
        {
            Console.WriteLine("Wheat crop size in tons: {0:N2}",
                myForecaster.WheatCropSizeInTonsInRegionA());
            Console.Write("Would you like to perform another
            ➥ crop forecast? Y)es N)o ");
            answer = Console.ReadLine().ToUpper();
        }
    }
}
```

Note

The numbers in the sample output are based on randomly produced values and will vary between different sample outputs.

```
Would you like to perform a crop forecast? Y)es N)o Y<enter>
Commencing forecast calculations. Please wait...
Wheat crop size in tons: 10,389,500.00
Would you like to perform another crop forecast? Y)es N)o Y<enter>
Commencing forecast calculations. Please wait...
Wheat crop size in tons: 10,389,500.00
Would you like to perform another crop forecast? Y)es N)o Y<enter>
Commencing forecast calculations. Please wait...
Wheat crop size in tons: 10,389,500.00
Would you like to perform another crop forecast? Y)es N)o

New Update Needed
Perform another forecast? Y<enter>
Commencing forecast calculations. Please wait...
Wheat crop size in tons: 13,694,500.00
Would you like to perform another crop forecast? Y)es N)o N<enter>
```

Listing 14.3 contains the `CropForecaster` class (lines 15–72) that, through the `WheatCropSizeInTonsInRegionA ()` method in lines 58–64, provides what pretends to be a forecast of a wheat crop in region A. This method utilizes the results of two other methods—`ComplexResultA` (lines 45–50) and `ComplexResultB` (lines 52–56). The calculations in all three methods are arbitrary and are not meant to resemble a real forecast; their important role in the program is simply to call the `RainfallDay10RegionA` property (lines 28–43) a few times, just as their serious counterparts would.

The `RainFallDay10RegionA` property performs lazy updates and minimizes the times the `WeatherForecaster`'s costly (it pretends to take 5 seconds to perform its calculations, see line 9) method `CalculateRainFallDay10RegionA` needs to be called. Lazy updates are achieved by the `RainFallDay10RegionA` in the following fashion: Every 20 seconds, the `OnTimedEvent` method (lines 66–71) will, regardless of what happens in the rest of the program, automatically be called and executed by the .NET runtime (it has been instructed to do so by lines 22–25, but we don't need to worry about why or how here). As a result, the `rainfallDay10RegionANeedUpdate` variable is automatically assigned the value `true` (in line 70) every 20 seconds. This, in turn, allows the `get` statement block to perform its lazy updates, because it only calls the `WeatherForecaster` the first time `rainfallDay10RegionA` is requested after `rainfallDay10RegionANeedUpdate` has been set to `true` (`rainfallDay10RegionANeedUpdate` is set to `false` in line 35 when `RainfallDay10RegionA` is accessed).

When you run the program, try to make several forecasts quickly, one after the other. You will see that only the first one is slow and the rest are swift…that is, until the following text is printed onscreen:

```
New Update Needed...
```

The first calculation after this message will be slow again, and the following ones will again be faster.

You don't need to know the meaning of the code in lines 22–25. You can simply regard it as a special way of instructing the runtime to call the `OnTimedEvent` (lines 66–71) method automatically every twenty seconds. You can adjust this time interval in line 24, if you want.

By substituting 20000 with 30000, for example, you are telling the runtime to make the call every thirty seconds instead of every twenty seconds. To convince yourself that lines 66–71 are automatically called, you can try not to interact with the program for at least twenty seconds after you have started it. You should see the following text written onscreen every twenty seconds (printed by line 69):

```
New Update Needed
Perform another forecast? Y<enter>
```

No, I haven't forgotten the delayed initialization. Even though the `true` initialization of `rainfallDay10RegionA` is performed automatically by C# (it is initially set to `0.0`), the first call to `RainfallDay10RegionA` can be regarded as a delayed initialization, and every call after that can be regarded as a lazy update.

Indexers: Using Objects Like Arrays

As we have seen earlier, an array contains many useful built-in methods and properties, such as `Sort` and `Length`. Sometimes, however, we need other abilities than those offered by the `Array` class. Perhaps we want an array that can find the sum and the average of its elements or display their values on a graphical user interface in a specific style. In those cases, we can write a class that essentially is an array (it would likely have an array or another collection as an instance variable) but with the extra functionality included.

Remember that to access a specific element of an array, we insert the element's index number in square brackets after the name of the array as follows:

```
...accounts[4]...
```

So if an object essentially represents an array, as described here, shouldn't we be able to access the elements of this "array" object in the same manner (with the index and the square brackets) as a conventional array? The C# design team answered yes to this question, and included the indexer construct to support this ability.

Note

Indexers offer an intuitive syntax to access the elements of a collection encapsulated by an object. The syntax consists of square brackets enclosing an *index argument* written after the name of the object, as shown in the following example:

```
...myArrayObject[4]...
```

The indexer concept is similar to that of the property. A property pretends to be a field, but, in reality, executes `get` and `set` statement blocks—an indexer pretends to be an array, but, in reality, also executes `get` and `set` statement blocks. Consequently, the syntax for implementing the two constructs is closely related.

Lines 7–17 of Listing 14.4 show a simple indexer positioned inside the `BirthsList` class. The indexer allows the `Main` method (lines 22–35) to access the `births` array (line 5) by treating the `BirthsList` object `bLDenmark` like an array (lines 27–30 and line 32).

LISTING 14.4 BirthsList.cs

```
01: using System;
02:
03: class BirthsList
04: {
05:     private uint[] births = new uint[4];
06:
07:     public uint this [uint index]
08:     {
09:         get
10:         {
11:             return births[index];
12:         }
13:         set
14:         {
15:             births[index] = value;
16:         }
17:     }
18: }
19:
20: class BirthListTester
21: {
22:     public static void Main()
23:     {
24:         BirthsList bLDenmark = new BirthsList();
25:         uint sum;
26:
27:         bLDenmark[0] = 10200;
28:         bLDenmark[1] = 20398;
29:         bLDenmark[2] = 40938;
30:         bLDenmark[3] = 6894;
31:
32:         sum = bLDenmark[0] + bLDenmark[1] + bLDenmark[2] + bLDenmark[3];
33:
34:         Console.WriteLine("Sum the four regions: {0}", sum);
35:     }
36: }
```

```
Sum the four regions: 78430
```

The following analysis should be read in conjunction with Syntax Box 14.2.

The indexer of the `BirthsList` class includes a `get` statement block (lines 9–12) and a `set` statement block (lines 13–16). Line 27 resembles the syntax of assigning a value to an array element and triggers the `set` statement block to be executed. Just prior to this execution, two assignments are automatically performed by the runtime. First, the value of the index argument specified in line 27 (`0`, in this case) is automatically assigned to the parameter `index` specified in line 7. Second, the implicitly defined parameter `value` of the `set` statement block is assigned the value on the right side of the assignment statement in line 27 (`10200`, in this case). At the time line 15 is being executed, it can be written as follows:

```
births[0] = 10200;
```

which assigns `10200` to the first element of the array `births`.

`bLDenmark[0]` (line 32) is retrieving a value, from index 0 in this case. This triggers the **`get`** statement block of the indexer to be executed. The runtime automatically inserts the specified index argument `0` into the parameter **`index`** prior to the execution of line 11, which then can be written as follows:

```
return births[0];
```

This returns the value of the first element of the **`births`** array back to `bLDenmark[0]`.

Even though similar, indexers hold several important differences from their property siblings, as you will discover if you look closer at Syntax Box 14.2:

- An indexer cannot be declared **`static`**. It must be an instance member, so only objects and not classes can be accessed with the square bracket notation.
- An indexer is identified through the object in which it resides and through the combination of arguments provided to it in the square bracket pair following the object name. Consequently, an indexer has no name in itself. Because we treat the object like an array and the indexer remains anonymous, the keyword **`this`** is always used as the identifier in the declaration of the indexer.
- The indexer declaration header must include a formal parameter list with at least one formal parameter.

Sytax Box 14.2 Indexer Declaration

```
Indexer_declaration::=
[<Access_modifier>] [override | new [ virtual | abstract ] ] <Type> this
➥ [<Formal_parameter_list>]
{
      [<get_statement_block>]
      [<set_statement_block>]
}
```

where

```
<Access_modifier>
                ::= public
                ::= private
                ::= protected
                ::= internal
                ::= protected internal

<get_statement_block> ::=
          get
          {
              [<Statements>]
              return <Expression>
          }

<set_statement_block> ::=
          set
          {
              [<Statements (using the keyword value)>]
          }
```

Notes:

- The optional keyword `new` of the property declaration header is semantically different than when you use it for creating new objects. Like the keywords `override`, `virtual`, and `abstract`, it is related to OO concepts we haven't discussed yet. I have included them here for completeness; they can safely be ignored for now.
- The `get` and `set` statement blocks are often collectively referred to as *accessors*.
- The formal parameter list can include parameters of any type. For example, it is possible to declare a formal parameter to be of type `string`. The corresponding index argument would then also be of type `string`. This is significantly different from the conventional array that only permits an index argument that either is or can be implicitly converted to one of the following types: `uint`, `int`, `ulong`, or `long`.

Implementing the Illusion of an Array

Although an object with an indexer seems to represent an array (from the object user's perspective), it is up to you how this illusion is implemented inside the class. Instead of using an array to store the list of data (as in line 5 of Listing 14.4), you could, for example, use an `ArrayList` or another more suitable collection class. The most important is that the object behaves according to the client's expectations.

Note

Even though an object is accessed as an array, it does not feature the methods and properties of a conventional array. For example, it would be invalid to access the length of `bLDenmark` in Listing 14.4 with the following call:

```
...bLDenmark.Length...
```

Calling an Indexer from within the Object It Inhabits

We already know how to call a method from within the object where it resides. This is done by writing the name of the method together with the appropriate arguments, as follows:

```
class MyClass
{
  ...
  private void PrintMenu()
  {

  }

  ...
  ...PrintMenu()...
  ...
}
```

The call to `PrintMenu` and the method itself exist within the same object.

Sometimes, we might also want to use the functionality of an indexer from within the object it inhabits. Because the indexer is nameless and is identified through its object, writing a name equivalent to `PrintMenu()` will not work. Fortunately, we can use the `this` keyword's ability to reference the object in which it resides. By positioning the square brackets enclosing suitable arguments after the `this` keyword, as shown in the following example code, we can refer to an indexer of the same object.

```
class Matrix
{
    ...
    public int this[int index]
    {
        get
        ...
        set
        ...
    }
    ...
    ...this[10]...
    ...
}
```

Calling an indexer from within the same object.

Listing 14.5, presented in the next section, provides a complete program that utilizes the ability to call an indexer with the `this` keyword.

Indexer Overloading: Multiple Indexers in the Same Class

It is possible to include several indexers in the same class, but, because they all have the same name (`this`), each indexer must have a unique indexer signature. The meaning of indexer signature is nearly equivalent to that of the method signature discussed in Chapter 12, "Class Anatomy Part I: `static` Class Members and Method Adventures."

The amount, types, and sequence of the indexer's formal parameter list constitute the *indexer's signature*. It does not include any name, as does the method signature.

For example, the next indexer has `int`, `int` as its signature:

```
public int this [int idxRow, int idxColumn]
{
    get
     ...
    set
    ...
}
```

It is important to keep the following points in mind when using the signature concept.

- The element type is not included in the indexer signature. Thus, the following two indexers represent the same signatures even though the first element type is `double` and the second element type is `int`:

```
public double this [int idxRow, int idxColum]
public int this [int idxRow, int idxColumn]
```

- The names of the formal parameters are not included in the method's signature, so the two displayed method headers have the same signature:

```
public int this [int idxRow, int idxColumn]
public int this [int a, int b]
```

When several indexers exist in the same class, each with a unique signature, those indexers are called *overloaded indexers*.

The discussion about method overloading in Chapter 12 showed you how the arguments of a method call are used to determine which of several overloaded methods to execute. This process matches the types, number, and sequence of the arguments provided in a method call with a suitable method signature. The compiler uses exactly the same process (including the rules involving implicit conversion paths mentioned in Chapter 12) for determining which indexer to execute by matching the given index arguments with a suitable indexer signature. Figure 14.2 shows a simple example with two overloaded indexers residing inside the `RainfallList` class. Both indexer signatures consists of one parameter, but they are distinguished by their types: `string` and `int`, respectively. The `rainInUSA[10]` and `rainInUSA["California"]` calls to the indexer trigger the execution of two different indexers because they involve different index argument types.

Listing 14.5 demonstrates the use of two overloaded indexers (lines 18–43 and lines 45–55) as well as how indexers can be called from within their own object by using the `this` keyword (lines 49 and 53) as mentioned earlier in this section. It also shows that properties do not necessarily have to access a particular instance variable but can return a calculated value instead.

LISTING 14.5 `AdvancedBirthsList.cs`

```
01: using System;
02:
03: class BirthsList
04: {
05:     private int[] births;
06:     private string[] birthsRegionNames;
07:
08:     public BirthsList(params string[] regionNames)
09:     {
10:         birthsRegionNames = regionNames;
11:         births = new int[regionNames.Length];
12:         for (int i = 0; i < regionNames.Length; i++)
13:         {
14:             births[i] = 0;
15:         }
```

LISTING 14.5 continued

```
    }

    public int this [int index]
    {
        get
        {
            if (index >= 0 && index < births.Length)
            {
                return births[index];
            }
            else
            {
                Console.WriteLine("Incorrect index provided");
                return -1;
            }
        }
        set
        {
            if (index >= 0 && index < births.Length)
            {
                births[index] = value;
            }
            else
            {
                Console.WriteLine("Incorrect index provided");
            }
        }
    }

    public int this [string indexName]
    {
        get
        {
            return this [NameToIndex(indexName)];
        }
        set
        {
            this[NameToIndex(indexName)] = value;
        }
    }

    private int NameToIndex(string indexName)
    {
        for (int i = 0; i < birthsRegionNames.Length; i++)
        {
            if (birthsRegionNames[i].ToUpper() == indexName.ToUpper())
                return i;
        }
        Console.WriteLine("Could not find region name");
        return -1;
    }

    public int TotalBirths
```

LISTING 14.5 continued

```
69:     {
70:         get
71:         {
72:             int sum = 0;
73:             foreach (int amount in births)
74:             {
75:                 sum += amount;
76:             }
77:             return sum;
78:         }
79:     }
80:
81:     public int Average
82:     {
83:         get
84:         {
85:             return TotalBirths / births.Length;
86:         }
87:     }
88: }
89:
90: class BirthListTester
91: {
92:     public static void Main()
93:     {
94:         BirthsList birthsListUSA = new BirthsList("California",
            ➥"New York", "Texas");
95:
96:         birthsListUSA["California"] = 10200;
97:         birthsListUSA[1] = 20398;
98:         birthsListUSA[2] = 40938;
99:
100:        Console.WriteLine("Number of births in Texas: {0}",
            ➥birthsListUSA["Texas"]);
101:        Console.WriteLine("Total births: {0}   Average births: {1}",
102:            birthsListUSA.TotalBirths, birthsListUSA.Average);
103:    }
104: }
```

```
Number of births in Texas: 40938
Total births: 71536   Average births: 23845
```

The `BirthsList` class (lines 3–88) is a sophisticated version of the `BirthsList` class found in Listing 14.4. During its creation, `tt` allows us to specify the names of the regions for which we can store a births count. This ability is utilized in line 94. Each births count can be accessed either by specifying the name of the region (lines 96 and 100) or by specifying the index number (lines 97 and 98). The `BirthsList` class will even calculate the total births of all regions with its `TotalBirths` property (lines 68–79) and the average regional births count with the `Average` property (81–87). Both properties are called in line 102.

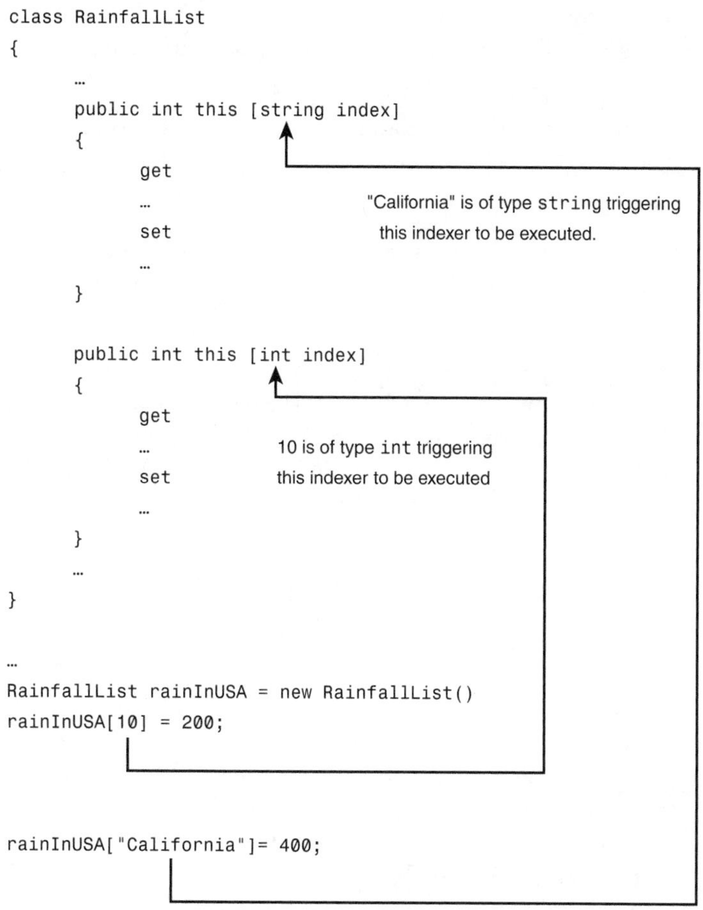
class RainfallList
{
...
public int this [string index]
{
get
...
set
...
}
"California" is of type string triggering
this indexer to be executed.
public int this [int index]
{
get
...
set
...
}
10 is of type int triggering
this indexer to be executed
...
}
...
RainfallList rainInUSA = new RainfallList()
rainInUSA[10] = 200;
rainInUSA["California"]= 400;

FIGURE 14.2
Two overloaded indexers.

The `BirthsList` class relies on two arrays to provide its services. `births` (line 5) is used to hold the births count, and `birthsRegionNames` represents the region name of each array element. The latter is used by the `NameToString` method (lines 57–66) to convert a region name to a corresponding index number in the `births` array.

The familiar `params` keyword of the constructor header (line 8) lets the user include any number of region names when constructing a new `BirthsList` object, as demonstrated in line 94. The amount of region names provided determines the length of the `births` array in line 11.

Lines 12–16 are merely used to initialize all elements of the births array to zero.

The indexer contained in lines 18–43 has one formal parameter of type `int`, so it is called when the index argument is of type `int` as in lines 97 and 98. Both the `set` and the `get` statement blocks of this indexer contain code to verify that the given index argument is within the ranges of the `births` array. An invalid argument triggers the program to print an error message on the screen. A professional solution would probably generate an exception instead, but since we haven't discussed this mechanism yet, our current approach will suffice.

The indexer in lines 45–55 applies the keyword `this` in lines 49 and 53 to call its overloaded sibling of lines 18–43. According to our earlier discussion about the `this` keyword, a statement such as the following:

```
this[1] = 10,
```

will, if written inside the `BirthsList` class, call the `set` statement block in lines 32–42. As a result, it will assign 10 to the `births` array element of index 1. Similarly, the following line:

```
return this[1];
```

will call the `get` statement block in lines 20–31, causing `this[1]` to represent the value of the second element in the `births` array. The `NameToIndex(indexName)` method call, found inside the square brackets of lines 49 and 53, returns the index or the `births` element corresponding to the `indexName`. Consequently, line 49 causes the value of the `births` element that corresponds to `indexName` to be returned to the original indexer call (line 100), and line 53 assigns the value represented by `value` to the births element corresponding to `indexName`.

Encapsulating the `births` collection in a class like `BirthsList` gives us free hands to include whatever functionality is needed when dealing with an object representing a list of births counts. Providing the total number of births in all regions and their average are just a couple of simple possibilities that, in this case, are calculated by using the two properties `TotalBirths` (lines 68–79) and `Average` (lines 81–87). Properties are often used to access instance variables, as you have seen earlier. However, a property can also return a purely calculated value that has no connection to any specific instance variable. `TotalBirths` and `Average` are both examples of those types of properties.

Avoid Overusing Indexers

There are two fundamental guidelines you should keep in mind before you implement indexers in your class:

- Indexers should only be used in classes that essentially represent a collection.
- The indexer should only be used to represent data that are part of the collection in a class and not any other instance variables.

Let's look at an example to illustrate the meaning of the last point. A programmer might decide to equip our now-familiar `BirthsList` class with two additional instance variables:

- `averageAge` To hold the average age of the population that spans the area covered by the entire array of regions represented by a specific `BirthsList` object
- `marriedCouples` To represent the number of married couples in this same area

The first part of the `BirthsList` class would then look like the following lines:

```
class BirthsList
{
        private int[] births;
        private string[] birthsRegionNames;
        private int averageAge;
        private int marriedCouples;
        ...
}
```

A programmer writing this class might now incorrectly decide to use the indexer to access not only the `births` array (the true collection) but also the other instance variables `averageAge` and `marriedCouples`. He or she decides on a convention saying "`averageAge` is accessed when the client provides the index argument 0 and `marriedCouples` is accessed with the index argument `1`."

```
...birthsListUSA[0]...<— Accesses averageAge       }
                                                   } Error prone design
...birthsListUSA[1]...<— Accesses marriedCouples   }
```

This design is destined to fail. The user of the `BirthsList` class must remember what `0` and `1` represent. Was `0` the `averageAge` or was it `marriedCouples`? It's easy to mix up the two and, as a result, this is an error-prone path to follow. In general you should adhere to the following general guideline:

There should be as few literals in a program as possible. Evaluate every literal in your program and, if possible, replace it with something more descriptive.

We can remedy the disastrous approach and adhere to the guideline by using properties with proper names (`AverageAge` and `MarriedCouples`) for our instance variables instead. This would remove the doubt in anyone's mind as to how the two instance variables are accessed:

```
birthsListUSA.AverageAge

birthsListUSA.MarriedCouples
```

Operator Overloading

You have already seen how the + operator can have different meanings in different contexts. For example, when we position the + operator between two values of type `int`, as in the following:

```
int distance1, distance2;
...
totalDistance = distance1 + distance2;
```

the compiler will recognize the `int` types and perform the familiar addition operation we know from arithmetic. However, if we apply the + operator with two values of type `string`:

```
string myText, yourText, fullText;
myString = "The boy was ";
yourString = "walking in the park";
fullText = myString + yourString;
```

myString and yourString are concatenated and assigned to fullText, which contains the following text:

```
"The boy was walking in the park"
```

So in the latter case the compiler performs another familiar but very different operation called concatenation, which combines the two texts in a meaningful way. Because the + operator can be applied to values of the two different types int and string, and in each case have different semantics, we say that the + operator is overloaded.

Note

An *overloaded* operator is an operator symbol that can be applied to different values of different types.

The operator overloading concept was conceived to make the code look more natural and to make expressions more compact and easier to write. To illustrate, let's pretend for the moment that operator overloading is unavailable in C#. The C# designers might then decide to reserve the + operator for adding int values together, thereby making it unavailable for any other simple type. Now, the designers would have to equip each simple type with a method called say, Add, that would take two arguments of the corresponding type and return the result to the caller. Adding two double values together would then look like the second line of the following code:

```
double distance1, distance2;
totalDistance = Double.Add(distance1, distance2);
```

which is less intuitive and more cumbersome than the natural and compact syntax we are used to.

```
totalDistance = distance1 + distance2;
```

Apart from the overloaded + operator, C# contains many other built-in cases of operator overloading. Implementing operator overloading, however, is not confined to the designers of C#. You can also implement it in your own classes and thereby allow them to be used with operator syntax. The next section looks more closely at this possibility.

User-Defined Operator Overloading

When you use a property or an indexer, you are in reality, behind the convenient syntax, triggering a block of statements to be executed (either in a get or set statement block). Operator overloading follows the same principle. When you apply an overloaded operator to one object (with a unary operator) or two objects (with a binary operator), you are calling a method behind this syntax, which contains statements that make it seem as if it is the operator itself that provides the expected result.

Operator Overloading Is Syntactic Sugar

Operator overloading is just another (often convenient) way of calling a method and is, for that reason, frequently referred to as *syntactic sugar*.

To implement operator overloading in your class, you must write this underlying method (called the *operator method*) just as you wrote the underlying **get** and **set** statement blocks for the properties and indexers. Before we look at how this is done, let's have a look at the `TimeSpan` class (lines 3–53) in Listing 14.6. The `TimeSpan` class is an obvious candidate for operator overloading, but does not yet support it. An object of `TimeSpan` represents a time interval.

LISTING 14.6 TimeSpanNoOverloading.cs

```
01: using System;
02:
03: class TimeSpan
04: {
05:     private uint totalSeconds;
06:     private const uint SecondsInHour = 3600;
07:     private const uint SecondsInMinute = 60;
08:
09:     public TimeSpan()
10:     {
11:         totalSeconds = 0;
12:     }
13:
14:     public TimeSpan(uint initialHours, uint initialMinutes,
15:         uint initialSeconds)
16:     {
17:         totalSeconds = initialHours * SecondsInHour +
18:             initialMinutes * SecondsInMinute + initialSeconds;
19:     }
20:
21:     public uint Seconds
22:     {
23:         get
24:         {
25:             return totalSeconds;
26:         }
27:         set
28:         {
29:             totalSeconds = value;
30:         }
31:     }
32:
33:     public void PrintHourMinSec()
34:     {
35:         uint hours;
36:         uint minutes;
```

LISTING 14.6 continued

```
37:         uint seconds;
38:
39:         hours = totalSeconds / SecondsInHour;
40:         minutes = (totalSeconds % SecondsInHour) / SecondsInMinute;
41:         seconds = (totalSeconds % SecondsInHour) % SecondsInMinute;
42:         Console.WriteLine("{0} Hours  {1} Minutes  {2} Seconds",
43:             hours, minutes, seconds);
44:     }
45:
46:     public static TimeSpan Add(TimeSpan timeSpan1, TimeSpan timeSpan2)
47:     {
48:         TimeSpan sumTimeSpan = new TimeSpan();
49:
50:         sumTimeSpan.Seconds = timeSpan1.Seconds + timeSpan2.Seconds;
51:         return sumTimeSpan;
52:     }
53: }
54:
55: class TimeSpanTest
56: {
57:     public static void Main()
58:     {
59:         TimeSpan totalTime;
60:         TimeSpan myTime = new TimeSpan(1,20,30);
61:         TimeSpan yourTime = new TimeSpan(2,40,45);
62:
63:         totalTime = TimeSpan.Add(myTime, yourTime);
64:
65:         Console.Write("My time:    ");
66:         myTime.PrintHourMinSec();
67:         Console.Write("Your time:  ");
68:         yourTime.PrintHourMinSec();
69:         Console.Write("Total time: ");
70:         totalTime.PrintHourMinSec();
71:     }
72: }
```

```
My time:    1 Hours  20 Minutes  30 Seconds
Your time:  2 Hours  40 Minutes  45 Seconds
Total time: 4 Hours  1 Minutes  15 Seconds
```

The time interval of each `TimeSpan` object is held by its instance variable `totalSeconds` (line 5). When a new object is created, the provided duration in hours, minutes, and seconds is converted into a single value and assigned to `totalSeconds` in the `TimeSpan` constructor (lines 14–19).Two `TimeSpan` objects will often need to be added together, so I have included a `static` method called `Add` (lines 46–52) to provide this functionality. `Add` specifies two formal parameters in its header called `timeSpan1` and `timeSpan2`. In line 50, the `totalSeconds` of each of these two objects are added together and their sum is assigned to the `totalSeconds` of the new `TimeSpan` object called `sumTimeSpan`, which is returned to the caller in line 51.

Line 63 of the `Main()` method (lines 57–71) is used to test the `Add` method. Notice in the sample output how the tedious task of adding different times together, consisting of hours, minutes and seconds, is correctly handled by `Add`.

The `TimeSpan` class and its `Add` method perform their jobs correctly, but wouldn't it be more intuitive and convenient if we could add the `totalSeconds` of two `TimeSpan` objects together by using the following syntax instead of the syntax shown in line 63 of Listing 14.6?

```
totalTime = myTime + yourTime;
```

We can support this syntax with operator overloading simply by substituting the word `Add` in the method header of the `Add` method (line 46, Listing 14.6) with the keyword `operator` followed by +, as shown in Figure 14.3, while the rest of the method remains untouched. This new method is commonly called an `operator+` method.

FIGURE 14.3
Changing the `Add` method to an operator method.

substituting the Add method with operator+

```
...
46:     public static TimeSpan operator+ (TimeSpan timeSpan1, TimeSpan timeSpan2)
47:     {
48:         TimeSpan sumTimeSpan = new TimeSpan();
49:
50:         sumTimeSpan.Seconds = timeSpan1.Seconds + timeSpan2.Seconds;
51:         return sumTimeSpan;
52:     }
...
63:         totalTime = myTime + yourTime;
```

using the + operator instead of calling the Add method

The new `operator+` method gives the compiler precise instructions on how to execute the following expression:

<Object1_Of_Type_TimeSpan> + <Object2_Of_Type_TimeSpan>

Whenever it encounters an expression with this fingerprint, consisting of two `TimeSpan` objects surrounding a plus symbol, it will execute our newly created `operator+` method. Just prior to executing its statements, it assigns the reference of the `TimeSpan` object that is positioned on the left side of the + symbol to the `timeSpan1` parameter of the `operator+` method (see 2 in Figure 14.4). Similarly, `timeSpan2` will be assigned the reference of the `TimeSpan` object on the right side of the + symbol. After the `operator+` method has terminated, the original expression takes the value returned from the `operator+` method (see 3 in Figure 14.4).

The general syntax for declaring an operator method is shown in Syntax Box 14.3. In general, the operator method looks like any `public static` (it must be `public static`) method with its name substituted by the keyword `operator` followed by an operator symbol. The return type cannot be `void`, and you must specify either one or two formal parameters, depending on whether you are overloading a unary or a binary operator. For more detailed information regarding the declaration, please refer to the notes in Syntax Box 14.3.

FIGURE 14.4

Executing two *TimeSpan* objects surrounding a + symbol.

1
When the compiler encounters an expression with two `TimeSpan` objects surrounding a + symbol...

```
<Object1_Of_Type_TimeSpan> + <Object2_Of_Type_TimeSpan>
```

2
...it executes the `operator+` method and inserts the left and the right operand into the first and the second formal parameter and...

```
public static TimeSpan operator+ (TimeSpan timeSpan1, TimeSpan timeSpan2)
{
      TimeSpan sumTimeSpan = new TimeSpan();

      sumTimeSpan.Seconds = timeSpan1.Seconds + timeSpan2.Seconds;
      return sumTimeSpan;
}
```

...the value returned from the operator+ method
3 becomes the value of the original expression.

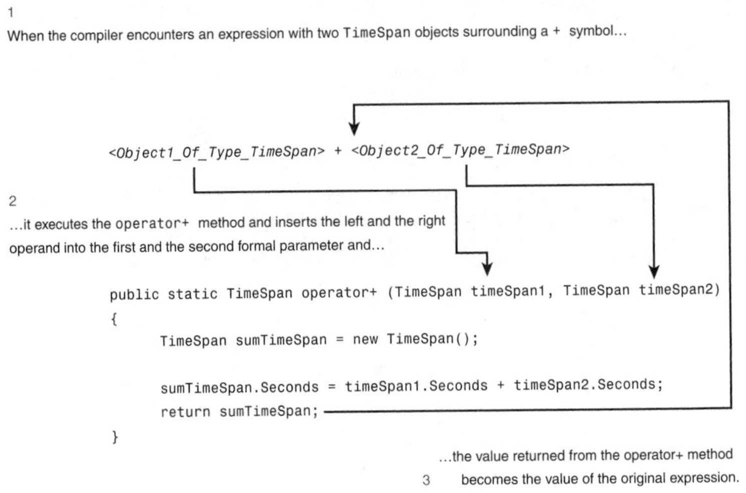

Syntax Box 14.3 Operator Method Declaration

```
Operator_method_declaration::=
public static <Return_Type> operator <Operator_symbol>
➥( <Type> <Formal_parameter1> [, <Type> <Formal_parameter2>] )
{
    <Statements>
}
```

where

```
<Operator_symbol>
          ::=  (one of the unary operators: ) +  -  !  ~  ++  --  !
                                              true  false

          ::= (one of the binary operators: ) +  -  *  /  %  &  |  ^
              <<  >>  ==  !=  <  >  <=  >=
```

Notes:

- Only the specific operators shown here can be overloaded. You cannot create your own operator symbol, such as <+, to be overloaded.
- The *<Return_type>* cannot be `void` and, as a consequence, the *<Statements>* in the method body must use the `return` keyword to return a value of a type that matches *<Return_type>*.
- The *<Return_type>* can be any type (apart from `void`), but the operators `true` and `false`, along with all the comparison operators, should always return a Boolean type value. The other operators should, as a rule of thumb, always return a type that is identical to the type (class) in which the operator method is residing.
- The operator method must have either one or two formal parameters in its formal parameter list. If a unary operator is overloaded, exactly one formal parameter must be specified; if a binary operator is overloaded, exactly two formal parameters must be overloaded.

- If the overloaded operator is a unary operator, the single formal parameter must be of the same type as the type (class) in which the operator method is residing.
- If the overloaded operator is a binary operator, the first formal parameter must be of the same type as the type (class) in which the operator method is residing; the second formal parameter can be of any type.
- The operator method must always be declared `public` and `static`.
- If you overload one of the comparison operators (<, <=, or ==), you must also overload its matching counterpart (>, >=, or !=).
- You cannot overload the cast operator (*<Type>*) in this context. However, the next section describes a technique similar to cast operator overloading (had it been possible) called conversion operators.
- An operator's precedence and associativity cannot be changed.
- It is not possible to turn a unary operator into a binary operator or vice versa.

The programmers that utilize our `TimeSpan` class enjoy the new intuitive `TimeSpan` addition syntax. However, they further request the ability to compare two `TimeSpan` objects with each of the operators <, >, ==, and != and to increment an object's `totalSeconds` instance variable by one with the ++ operator. So we go back to the drawing board to create a new improved `TimeSpan` class with the desired capabilities.

Before implementing the operator methods that will allow this extra syntax, it is important to define the meaning of <, >, ==, and != when applied to two `TimeSpan` objects as in the following:

```
<TimeSpanObject1> <Comparison_operator> <TimeSpanObject2>
```

In our case, the two `TimeSpan` objects being compared are defined to have their `totalSeconds` instance variables compared by the specified operator. For example, the `operator<` method will return the result of the following comparison (see line 69 of Listing 14.7).

```
<TimeSpanObject1>.Seconds  <  <TimeSpanObject2>.Seconds
```

The resulting improved `TimeSpan` class is shown in lines 3–81 of Listing 14.7.

LISTING 14.7 `TimeSpanWithOverloading.cs`

```
01: using System;
02:
03: class TimeSpan
04: {
05:     private uint totalSeconds;
06:     private const uint SecondsInHour = 3600;
07:     private const uint SecondsInMinute = 60;
08:
09:     public TimeSpan()
10:     {
11:         totalSeconds = 0;
```

LISTING 14.7 continued

```
    }

    public TimeSpan(uint initialHours, uint initialMinutes,
        uint initialSeconds)
    {
        totalSeconds = initialHours * SecondsInHour +
            initialMinutes * SecondsInMinute + initialSeconds;
    }

    public uint Seconds
    {
        get
        {
            return totalSeconds;
        }
        set
        {
            totalSeconds = value;
        }
    }

    public void PrintHourMinSec()
    {
        uint hours;
        uint minutes;
        uint seconds;

        hours = totalSeconds / SecondsInHour;
        minutes = (totalSeconds % SecondsInHour) / SecondsInMinute;
        seconds = (totalSeconds % SecondsInHour) % SecondsInMinute;
        Console.WriteLine("{0} Hours  {1} Minutes  {2} Seconds",
            hours, minutes, seconds);
    }

    public static TimeSpan operator+ (TimeSpan timeSpan1,
    ➥ TimeSpan timeSpan2)
    {
        TimeSpan sumTimeSpan = new TimeSpan();

        sumTimeSpan.Seconds = timeSpan1.Seconds + timeSpan2.Seconds;
        return sumTimeSpan;
    }

    public static TimeSpan operator++ (TimeSpan timeSpan1)
    {
        TimeSpan timeSpanIncremented = new TimeSpan();

        timeSpanIncremented.Seconds = timeSpan1.Seconds + 1;
        return timeSpanIncremented;
    }

    public static bool operator> (TimeSpan timeSpan1, TimeSpan timeSpan2)
```

LISTING 14.7 continued

```
    {
        return (timeSpan1.Seconds > timeSpan2.Seconds);
    }

    public static bool operator< (TimeSpan timeSpan1, TimeSpan timeSpan2)
    {
        return (timeSpan1.Seconds < timeSpan2.Seconds);
    }

    public static bool operator== (TimeSpan timeSpan1, TimeSpan timeSpan2)
    {
        return (timeSpan1.Seconds == timeSpan2.Seconds);
    }

    public static bool operator!= (TimeSpan timeSpan1, TimeSpan timeSpan2)
    {
        return (timeSpan1.Seconds != timeSpan2.Seconds);
    }
}

class TimeSpanTest
{
    public static void Main()
    {
        TimeSpan someTime;
        TimeSpan totalTime = new TimeSpan();
        TimeSpan myTime = new TimeSpan(2,40,45);
        TimeSpan yourTime = new TimeSpan(1,20,30);

        totalTime += yourTime;
        totalTime += myTime;

        Console.Write("Your time:       ");
        yourTime.PrintHourMinSec();
        Console.Write("My time:         ");
        myTime.PrintHourMinSec();
        Console.Write("Total race time: ");
        totalTime.PrintHourMinSec();

        if (myTime > yourTime)
            Console.WriteLine("\nI spent more time than you did");
        else
            Console.WriteLine("\nYou spent more time than I did");

        myTime++;
        ++myTime;

        Console.Write("\nMy time after two increments: ");
        myTime.PrintHourMinSec();

        someTime = new TimeSpan(1,20,30);
        if (yourTime == someTime)
```

LISTING 14.7 continued

```
115:             Console.WriteLine("\nSpan of someTime is equal to
                 ➥ span of yourTime");
116:         else
117:             Console.WriteLine("\nSpan of someTime is NOT equal to
                 ➥ span of yourTime");
118:     }
119: }
```

Note

When you compile Listing 14.7, you will likely see the following compiler warnings:

```
TimeSpanWithOverLoading.cs(3,7): warning CS0660: 'TimeSpan' defines operator
== or operator != but does not override Object.Equals(object o)

TimeSpanWithOverLoading.cs(3,7): warning CS0660: 'TimeSpan' defines operator
== or operator != but does not override Object.Equals(object o)
```

These warnings are related to inheritance and method overriding, which we have not yet discussed. You can ignore these warnings for now and run the program without problems. Inheritance and method overriding is discussed in Chapter 16, "Inheritance Part I: Basic Concepts," and Chapter 17, "Inheritance Part II: `abstract` Functions, Polymorphism, and Interfaces."

```
Your time:       1 Hours  20 Minutes  30 Seconds
My time:         2 Hours  40 Minutes  45 Seconds
Total race time: 4 Hours  1 Minutes  15 Seconds

I spent more time than you did

My time after two increments: 2 Hours  40 Minutes  47 Seconds

Span of someTime is equal to span of yourTime
```

The `operator>` method (lines 62–65) enables us to compare two `TimeSpan` objects with the > operator. The method (see line 64) closely follows the definitions put forth earlier for what we mean by comparing two `TimeSpan` methods. It has a `bool` return type instead of the `TimeSpan` type of the `operator+` method, to match the `bool` value returned from line 64. The `operator<` method follows the same logic as the `operator>` method.

The ability to compare two `TimeSpan` objects with the == and != operators is achieved through the `operator==` method (lines 72–75) and the `operator!=` method (lines 77–80) in a similar fashion to that of the `operator<` and > methods.

In contrast to the four previously mentioned operator methods, the `operator++` method (lines 54–60) only has one formal parameter because it is a unary operator. As prescribed in Syntax Box 14.3, the formal parameter is of the same type as the class in which it resides (`TimeSpan`). Observe in lines 107 and 108 of the `Main` method that the `operator++` method allows us to apply both the post- and pre-increment syntax version of the ++ operator.

Similarly, when we specify the `operator+` method, we can also use the combination assignment `operator +=`, as demonstrated in lines 92 and 93.

Recall that generally when two standard objects (except for objects of type `string`) are compared with the == operator (and the == operator has not been overloaded for these objects), their references and not their internal instance variables are compared. Had we not included the `operator==` method, the condition `yourTime == someTime` of line 114 would have been `false` instead of `true`, because the two `yourTime` and `someTime` objects that are being compared are situated in different locations and have different references.

Only Use Operator Overloading When It Is Natural and Makes the Program Clearer

Most people intuitively understand the meaning of the following line:

```
totalTime = myTime + yourTime;
```

but what about the next line, where `combinedPlanet`, `venus`, and `mars` all represent objects of class `Planet`?

```
combinedPlanet = venus + mars;
```

Are we adding together the volumes of the two planets, their circumference, their distance from the sun, or perhaps one of the other numerous instance variables that could be used to describe a planet (or perhaps it is the programmer's way of expressing eternal peace between the two sexes)? Nobody, apart perhaps the programmer who originally included the `operator+` method (who might have forgotten this six months later) in the `Planet` class, knows this answer intuitively. Instead of making the program clearer, it becomes cryptic and hard to read. The line would be much clearer if we applied a conventional `static` method with a visible name, as in the following line:

```
combinedPlanet = Planet.AddVolumes(venus, mars);
```

User-Defined Implicit and Explicit Conversions

Most programs operate on data of a diverse set of types, ranging from the predefined simple types (`int`, `double`, and so on) over the derived predefined .NET types (in the Framework class library) to your own custom made types. If an operation adds two `int` values together and assigns the result to an `int` variable, the operation stays within the same type (if the result stays within the range of an `int`). Sometimes, however, we combine different types in the same operations with an accompanying need to convert data from one type to another. As discussed in Chapter 6, "Types, Part I: The Simple Types," typical circumstances that require conversions are as follows:

- A value of one type is assigned to a variable of another type.
- Values of different types are combined in the same expression.
- The type of an argument in a method call is different from the type of its corresponding formal parameter in the method being called.

As long as the conversions only involve the simple types, the compiler feels at home. It follows predefined, exact rules and instructions, discussed at length in Chapter 6, that tell it

- If an implicit conversion path exists (as specified in the implicit conversion path for simple types) and, if so, how it is performed
- If an explicit conversion (using the cast operator `(<Type>)`) is possible and, if so, how it is performed

However, if we involve our own user-defined types in operations that either require conversions among user-defined types and simple types or among different ***unrelated*** user defined types, the compiler is clueless unless we explicitly specify, through user-defined (implicit or explicit) conversions, how these conversions are performed.

Inheritance and Assignments

A programmer can, via inheritance discussed in Chapter 16, relate different classes to each other and form class hierarchies. Classes with these special relationships may or may not, depending on the context, be assigned to each other without requiring explicitly specified conversion paths. For that reason, I have emphasized that the classes involved in the conversions discussed in this section are *unrelated*.

Two Cases in Need of User-Defined Conversions

This section presents two typical examples that call for the implementation of user-defined conversions.

In the first scenario, we attempt to assign a variable called `simpleTimeSeconds` of type `uint` to an object of the user-defined `TimeSpan` class, presented in the previous section:

```
class TimeSpan
{
    private uint totalSeconds;
    ...
}
...
class TimeSpanTest
{
    public static void Main()
    {
        ...
        uint simpleTimeSeconds = 30;
        TimeSpan myTime;
        myTime = simpleTimeSeconds;
}
    ...
}
```

However the line:

```
myTime = simpleTimeSeconds;
```

is invalid because the compiler does not know how to convert a value of type `uint` to a value of type `TimeSpan`.

To us humans an obvious conversion would be to assign the value of `simpleTimeSeconds` to `myTime`'s `totalSeconds`, but the compiler does not (yet) show many signs of artificial intelligence, and cannot possibly know how to perform this conversion. Later you will see how the compiler can be instructed to perform the needed conversion by including a user defined implicit conversion in `TimeSpan`.

The compiler also faces a problem if we try to convert from one user-defined object to another user-defined object. The next example illustrates this.

We are writing a computer program for the space shuttle that will bring us to planet Blipos. Among other things, the program manipulates times on Earth along with times on Blipos. According to Chapter 6, a day on planet Blipos consists of 65535 minutes, a minute is 256 seconds, and a second is exactly the same duration as a second here on Earth. The differences between time measuring on Earth and Blipos prompts us to include two classes called `BliposTimeSpan` and `EarthTimeSpan` to represent time spans on Blipos and Earth, respectively. (The `EarthTimeSpan` is similar to the `TimeSpan` class previously presented in Listing 14.7). Both time span classes represent a time span internally with an instance variable called `totalSeconds`, which is of the same type `uint`, as illustrated in the next code snippet.

```
class EarthTimeSpan
{
    private uint totalSeconds;
    ...
}

class BliposTimeSpan
{
    private uint totalSeconds;
    ...
}

    EarthTimeSpan myTime = new EarthTimeSpan(1, 20, 30);
    BliposTimeSpan alienTime;
    alienTime = myTime;
```

Both classes represent time spans
and both store this data in instance variables
of the same type...
...but the compiler cannot perform the required
conversion rendering this assignment statement invalid

However, the last line cannot be performed without any rules for how to convert from one object type to another. In a moment, we will look at how this problem can be solved by specifying a user-defined conversion.

Using Non-User-Defined Conversion Techniques

The problems related to both examples described in the previous section can be solved by including conventional methods or properties to take care of the assignments. For example, instead of writing:

```
myTime = simpleTimeSeconds;
```

we could use the already existing `Seconds` property and assign the `uint` value to `myTime` by writing the following:

```
myTime.Seconds = simpleTimeSeconds;
```

In the second example, we could specify a method inside the `EarthTimeSpan` class called `GetAsBliposTimeSpan` that would create a new `BliposTimeSpan` object and return it to the caller. It might look like the following:

```
public BliposTimeSpan GetAsBliposTimeSpan()
{
    BliposTimeSpan returnBlipos = new BliposTimeSpan();
    returnBlipos.Seconds = totalSeconds;
    return returnBlipos;
}
```

allowing us to write

```
alienTime = myTime.GetAsBliposTimeSpan();
```

and validly achieve what we initially attempted with the following line:

```
alienTime = myTime;
```

However, just like operator overloading allows us to sprinkle syntactic sugar on our code and substitute method and property calls with arithmetic operators, ***user-defined conversions*** allow us to make our code look even sweeter by removing properties and conversion methods, such as those shown in this section, and support the following cleaner looking lines:

```
myTime = simpleTimeSeconds;
alienTime = myTime;
```

The next section looks more closely at how we can specify our conversions in the source code of a C# program.

The Syntax of User-Defined Conversions

When we specify our user-defined conversions, we provide the instructions needed for the compiler to perform type conversions that involve user-defined types. These instructions are similar to those followed by the compiler when it converts from one simple type to another; they answer the following questions:

- Is an implicit conversion possible from one type to the other and, if so, how is it performed?
- Is an explicit conversion possible, using the cast operator `(<Type>)` and, if so, how is it performed? (Note: If an implicit conversion is possible, an explicit conversion is also possible).

The instructions (or statements) are held by a language construct that looks somewhat similar to an operator method, but with either the keyword `implicit` or the keyword `explicit` added in the header. Listing 14.8 demonstrates how we can the define an implicit conversion path from a value of type `uint` to a value of type `TimeSpan` and, thereby, allow us to write the following line:

```
myTime = simpleTimeSeconds;
```

as shown in line 34.

LISTING 14.8 `ImplicitConversionTester.cs`

```
01: using System;
02:
03: class TimeSpan
04: {
05:     private uint totalSeconds;
06:
07:     public TimeSpan(uint initialTotalSeconds)
08:     {
09:         totalSeconds = initialTotalSeconds;
10:     }
11:
12:     public void PrintSeconds()
13:     {
14:         Console.WriteLine("Total seconds: {0}", totalSeconds);
15:     }
16:
17:     public static implicit operator TimeSpan(uint convertFrom)
18:     {
19:         TimeSpan newTimeSpan;
20:
21:         newTimeSpan = new TimeSpan(convertFrom);
22:         Console.WriteLine("Converting from uint to TimeSpan");
23:         return newTimeSpan;
24:     }
25: }
26:
27: class ImplicitConversionTester
28: {
29:     public static void Main()
30:     {
31:         uint simpleTimeSeconds = 30;
32:         TimeSpan myTime;
33:
34:         myTime = simpleTimeSeconds;
35:         myTime.PrintSeconds();
36:     }
37: }
```

```
Converting from uint to TimeSpan
Total seconds: 30
```

This analysis should be read in conjunction with Syntax Box 14.4, shown after this analysis.

For space reasons, only a bare minimum version of `TimeSpan` is defined in lines 3–25.

A user-defined implicit conversion from `uint` to `TimeSpan` is contained in lines 17–24. The keywords `implicit` and `operator` in line 17 indicate a user-defined implicit conversion. (As shown in Syntax Box 14.4, we can substitute `implicit` with the keyword `explicit` to define a user-defined explicit conversion).

A user-defined conversion must always be declared `public` and `static`, as shown in line 17.

The type to which we are converting (in this case, `TimeSpan`) must follow the operator keyword and the following parentheses must enclose a parameter identifier (here called `convertFrom`) with the type from which we are converting.

During the assignment of `simpleTimeSeconds` to `myTime` in line 34, the implicit converter method is called and the parameter identifier `convertFrom` (line 17) is assigned the value held by `simpleTimeSeconds`. Line 17 promises that lines 19–23 create and return a `TimeSpan` object based on the value in `convertFrom`; this object is assigned to `myTime` in line 34. The statements for creating a suitable `TimeSpan` object in lines 19–23 are based on the following observation: `convertFrom` is equivalent to a `TimeSpan` object with its instance variable `totalSeconds` equal to `convertFrom`. We follow this recipe by passing `convertFrom` to the `TimeSpan` constructor in line 21. `newTimeSpan`'s `totalSeconds` is thereby set to `convertFrom`.

Line 22 is merely inserted for demonstration purposes to ascertain for ourselves that this conversion method is, in fact, being called. This is confirmed by the sample output. The `return` keyword asks the `newTimeSpan` reference to be returned and, thereby, assigned to `myTime` in line 34. Line 35 finally causes `totalSeconds` of `myTime` to be printed. As expected, the sample output confirms that its value is equal to the value held by `simpleTimeSeconds`.

Syntax Box 14.4 contains the formal syntax for specifying a user-defined implicit conversion and a user-defined explicit conversion.

Syntax Box 14.4 User Defined Implicit Conversion

```
User_defined_implicit_conversion::=

public static implicit operator <Type_convert_to> ( <Type_convert_from>
➥ <Parameter_identifier> )
{
      <Statements>
}

User_defined_explicit_conversion::=

public static explicit operator <Type_convert_to> ( <Type_convert_from>
➥ <Parameter_identifier> )
{
      <Statements>
}
```

Notes:

- The keywords `public`, `static`, and `operator` are always required.
- Exactly one parameter identifier must be included.
- The class in which the user-defined conversion resides must be involved in the conversion, because we are either specifying how to convert from a value of this class type or to a value of this class type. As a result either *<Type_convert_to>* or *<Type_convert_from>* must have the name of the class in which the conversion resides.
- Any pre-defined conversions, such as the implicit conversion path for simple numeric types, cannot be redefined.
- *<Statements>* must include a `return` statement that returns a value with the same type as that specified by *<Type_convert_to>*.
- The *<Type_convert_to>* and *<Type_convert_from>* form the signature of the user-defined conversion. Because the `implicit` and `explicit` keywords are not part of the signature, you cannot define an implicit and an explicit conversion with identical signatures within the same class.

Note

Any user-defined implicit conversion automatically allows you to apply the cast operator in an explicit type conversion. For example, we could have written the following instead of line 34 in Listing 14.8:

```
34:          myTime = (TimeSpan) simpleTimeSeconds;
```

However, it is not possible to perform an implicit conversion with a user-defined explicit conversion path.

Only Specify User-Defined Implicit Conversions for Safe Conversions

Recall that the simple types only specify implicit conversion paths when there is no risk of data loss and no risk of executing operations that would cause exceptions to be generated. When these risks are present, C# forces you to perform explicit conversions instead by using the cast operator, which acts as a warning sign in the source code. You should follow this same approach when implementing your own conversions. In Listing 14.8, there was no danger of data loss because we were essentially assigning a value of type `uint` (`simpleTimeSeconds`) to a variable also of type `uint` (`totalSeconds` from inside `TimeSpan`). On the other hand, if we specify a conversion path from `TimeSpan` to a variable of, say, type `ushort` (as in Listing 14.9), there is a clear risk of data loss caused by `ushort`'s narrower range. Consequently, an explicit conversion is suitable here as demonstrated next.

Listing 14.9 contains the recommended user-defined explicit conversion from `TimeSpan` to `ushort` in lines 20–24. As a result, we can apply the type cast in line 34, where `myTime` is assigned to `simpleTimeSeconds`, but any implicit conversions are impossible.

LISTING 14.9 `ExplicitConversionTester.cs`

```
01: using System;
02:
03: class TimeSpan
04: {
05:     private uint totalSeconds;
06:
07:     public TimeSpan(uint initialTotalSeconds)
08:     {
09:         totalSeconds = initialTotalSeconds;
10:     }
11:
12:     public uint TotalSeconds
13:     {
14:         get
15:         {
16:             return totalSeconds;
17:         }
18:     }
19:
20:     public static explicit operator ushort(TimeSpan convertFrom)
21:     {
22:         Console.WriteLine("Converting from TimeSpan to ushort");
23:         return (ushort)convertFrom.TotalSeconds;
24:     }
25: }
26:
27: class ExplicitConversionTester
28: {
29:     public static void Main()
30:     {
31:         ushort simpleTimeSeconds;
32:         TimeSpan myTime = new TimeSpan(130);
33:
34:         simpleTimeSeconds = (ushort) myTime;
35:         Console.WriteLine("Value of simpleTimeSeconds: {0}",
36:             simpleTimeSeconds);
37:     }
38: }
```

```
Converting from TimeSpan to ushort
Value of simpleTimeSeconds: 130
```

Instead of being the <*Type_convert_to*>, as in line 17 of Listing 14.8, `TimeSpan` (in line 20) is the <*Type_convert_from*>, `ushort` is the <*Type_convert_to*>, and the `implicit` keyword has been substituted with the `explicit` keyword in line 20.

Listing 14.10 demonstrates how we can specify a user-defined implicit conversion between the two user-defined types, `EarthTimeSpan` and `BliposTimeSpan` and allow the last of the following three lines to be executed:

```
EarthTimeSpan myTime = new EarthTimeSpan(130);
BliposTimeSpan alienTime;
alienTime = myTime;
```

LISTING 14.10 ConvertingUserDefinedTypes.cs

```
using System;

class EarthTimeSpan
{
    private uint totalSeconds;

    public EarthTimeSpan(uint initialTotalSeconds)
    {
        totalSeconds = initialTotalSeconds;
    }

    public uint TotalSeconds
    {
        get
        {
            return totalSeconds;
        }
    }

    public static implicit operator BliposTimeSpan
    ➥(EarthTimeSpan convertFrom)
    {
        BliposTimeSpan newBliposTimeSpan = new BliposTimeSpan
        ➥(convertFrom.TotalSeconds);
        Console.WriteLine("Converting from EarthTimeSpan to
        ➥ BliposTimeSpan");
        return newBliposTimeSpan;
    }
}

class BliposTimeSpan
{
    private uint totalSeconds;

    public BliposTimeSpan(uint initialTotalSeconds)
    {
        totalSeconds = initialTotalSeconds;
    }

    public void PrintTimeSpan()
    {
        Console.WriteLine("Blipos time span: {0} seconds", totalSeconds);
    }
}

class ExplicitConversionTester
{
    public static void Main()
    {
        EarthTimeSpan myTimeSpan = new EarthTimeSpan(200);
        BliposTimeSpan alienTimeSpan;

```

LISTING 14.10 continued

```
50:         alienTimeSpan = myTimeSpan;
51:         alienTimeSpan.PrintTimeSpan();
52:     }
53: }
```

```
Converting from EarthTimeSpan to BliposTimeSpan
Blipos time span: 200 seconds
```

Both the `BliposTimeSpan` and the `EarthTimeSpan` classes are stripped-down versions designed for demonstration purposes.

Lines 20–25 specifies the user-defined implicit conversion. `BliposTimeSpan` is the `<Type_convert_to>`, and `EarthTimeSpan` is the *`<Type_convert_from>`*.

Note that any one of the two classes can be equipped with the user-defined conversion definition. Removing lines 20–25 from inside `EarthTimeSpan` and positioning them inside `BliposTimeSpan` instead would still allow exactly the same the implicit conversion in line 50 to take place.

Combining User-Defined and Implicit Conversions

In Chapter 6, I mentioned the compiler's ability to move through several simple numeric types on the pre-defined implicit conversion path to perform a requested conversion. For example, the compiler will convert a `byte` value to a `ulong` value by moving along the following path, which is an extract from Figure 6.17 in Chapter 6.

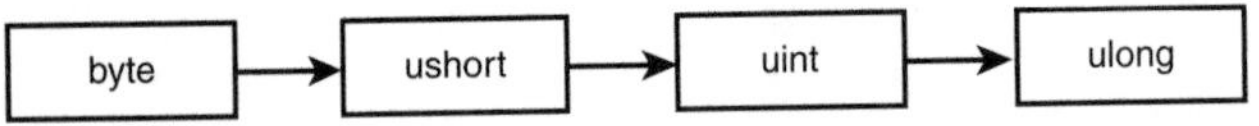

This is old news, but it forms the basis for understanding an interesting fact relevant to user-defined conversions: The compiler will combine any implicit conversion path (whether predefined or user-defined) with your user-defined conversions to convert from one type to another. Consequently, if you attempt to convert between two types and a user-defined conversion only specifies part of this path, the compiler will look for an implicit path that completes the journey between the two types. The `TimeSpan` class and its user-defined explicit conversion in lines 20–24 of Listing 14.9 can be used to illustrate this.

```
20:     public static explicit operator ushort(TimeSpan convertFrom)
21:     {
22:         Console.WriteLine("Converting from TimeSpan to ushort");
23:         return (ushort)convertFrom.TotalSeconds;
24:     }
```

This user-defined conversion not only allows us to cast the `TimeSpan` class into the `ushort` type, but we can also convert `TimeSpan` to a `uint` and a `ulong`, as specified in Figure 14.5 (or any other type along this implicit conversion path that can be seen in its entirety in Figure 6.17 in Chapter 6), because the compiler will complete the journey along the implicit conversion path from `ushort` to `ulong`.

This allows us to write the following

```
TimeSpan myTime = new TimeSpan(120);
ulong simpleTime;
simpleTime = (ushort)myTime;
```

which converts `myTime` of type `TimeSpan` to `simpleTime` of type `ulong` in the third line.

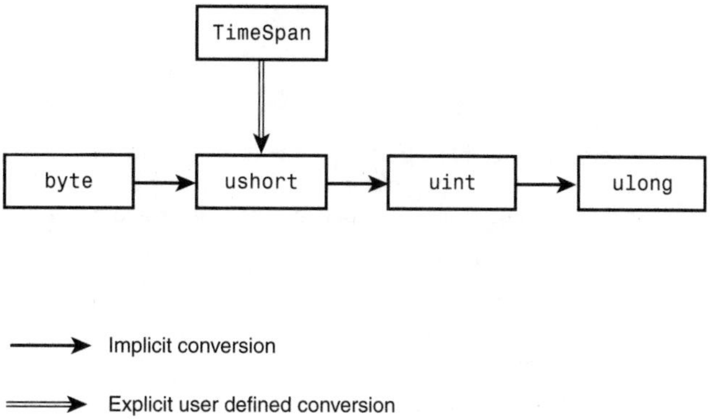

FIGURE 14.5
Converting from `TimeSpan` to `ulong`.

Had we defined another class called `GalaxyTimeSpan` containing a user-defined implicit conversion from `ulong` to `GalaxyTimeSpan`, the implicit conversion path could be depicted as shown in Figure 14.6. We could then convert from `TimeSpan` to `GalaxyTimeSpan`, as demonstrated in line three of the following lines:

```
TimeSpan myTime = new TimeSpan(500);
GalaxyTimeSpan milkyWayGalaxyTime;
milkyWayGalaxyTime = (ushort)myTime;
```

FIGURE 14.6
Converting from `TimeSpan` to `GalaxyTimeSpan`.

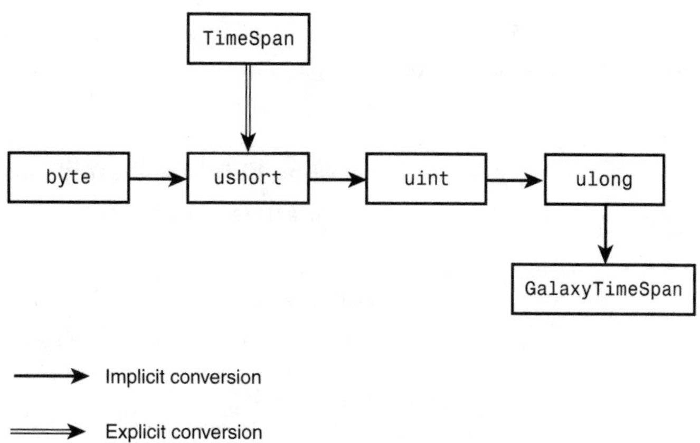

Even though both `TimeSpan` and `GalaxyTimeSpan` contains `totalSeconds` instance variables of the types `uint` and `ulong`, with the ability to represent values of considerable magnitude, the conversion always moves through the `ushort` type where numbers exceeding `ushort`'s range (0–65535) will cause an overflow or underflow. For example, if you initialize `totalSeconds` of the `TimeSpan` value `myTime` to 70000 (as in the next three lines of code), a conversion to `milkyWayTime` of type `GalaxyTimeSpan`, shown in line three, results in `milkyWayTime` with a `totalSeconds` instance variable holding the value 4464 (70000–65536).

```
TimeSpan myTime = new TimeSpan(70000);
GalaxyTimeSpan milkyWayTime;
milkyWayTime = (ushort)myTime;
```

Do Not Overuse User-Defined Conversions

It is sometimes tempting to include user-defined conversions that support and promote obscure and unintuitive code. For example, if we specified a user-defined implicit conversion from our program's `Dog` class to its `Cat` class, we would allow the following mysterious assignment statement:

```
myCat = myDog;
```

Are we assigning the name of the dog to the cat, or perhaps its age, maybe its color, or perhaps a combination of the three? If we happen to transfer the age, it would be much clearer to do it through properties and write the following:

```
Cat myCat = new Cat();
myCat.Age = myDog.Age;
```

Nested Types

Classes are not restricted to holding data and function members. They can also contain the definitions of types like classes, structs, enums, and interfaces, which then are referred to as *nested* types. This section only deals with nested classes, but the syntax is so similar and straightforward that it easily can be adjusted to work with the remaining three kinds of types (see the notes in Syntax Box 14.5).

As Syntax Box 14.5 shows, a class is nested inside an outer class by simply writing the class header and its associated block as usual, but inside the block of the outer class.

Syntax Box 14.5 The Nested Class

```
[<Access_modifier>] class <Identifier_outer_class>
{
    [<Outer_class_data_members>]
    [<Outer_class_function_members>]

    [<Access_modifier>] class <Identifier_nested_class>
    {
        [<Inner_class_data_members>]
        [<Inner_class_function_members>]
        [<Inner_class_nested_types>]
    }
}
```

Notes:

- A nested class can itself contain other nested classes, which again can contain other nested classes, and so on.
- Structs, enums and interfaces are turned into nested types by following the same principle as with classes; just write the definition as usual but place it inside the class block of the outer class.

By nesting a class, we can confine its visibility to the scope of its outer class. This is done with the same access modifiers that are used with the other class members (`private`, `public`, and so on) and with similar consequences. A `private` nested class can only be accessed from within the block of its outer class, whereas `public` exposes it beyond the class scope. Just as a method is made `private` because it is only needed within its class, a class is nested and declared `private` because it is so specialized and integrated with its outer class that no other part of the program would ever request its services.

Note

Nested classes often form composition relationships with their outer classes.

The Advantages of Nested Classes

Nested classes effectively say "Not for reuse purposes." Consequently they help reduce the number of classes on which programmers need to focus when they sift through the code to find classes for use in their own program parts.

Nested classes also let you organize your code effectively, because the inner class always follows its outer class. It is easier to move and keep count of one main class with its nested classes inside instead of several classes floating around independently in the source code.

A Simple Nested Class Example

It's time to have a look at a simple example to illustrate nested classes. Recall the `Elevator` class from our elevator simulation in Listing 5.1 of Chapter 5, "Your First Object-Oriented C# Program." We might decide to expand this program to contain an `ElevatorEngine` class that has the ability to control the exact speed of the `Elevator`, while enabling us to simulate the wear and tear of some of the `ElevatorEngine`'s inner parts. Its relationship with the `Elevator` is intimate, and its services are so specialized that we decide to make the `ElevatorEngine` a nested `private` class inside the `Elevator` class. The important code fragments for doing this are shown in Figure 14.7.

The `Person` class is an arbitrary class that has merely been included to illustrate the inability to use the `ElevatorEngine` class from outside the `Elevator` class.

In most cases, however, classes are not as closely related as the `ElevatorEngine` and the `Elevator` classes of our example, so access is needed to the majority of classes. To organize our classes in an orderly, systematic, hierarchical fashion providing easy access, we can use namespaces. The next chapter takes a closer look at how you can create and use your own namespaces.

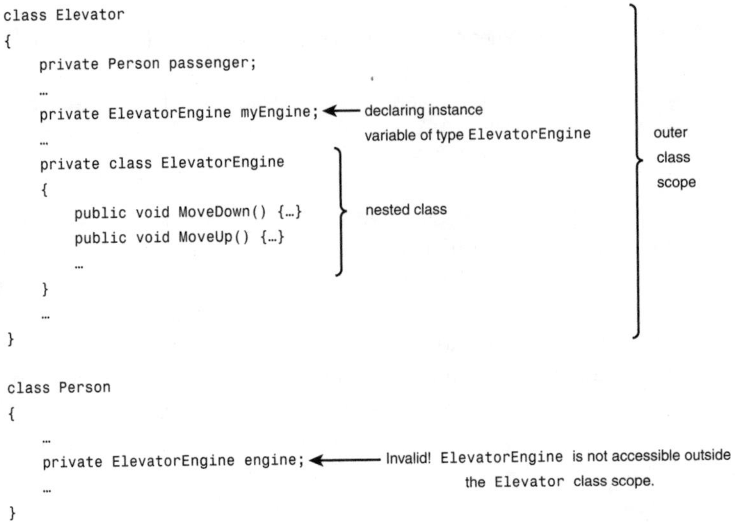

FIGURE 14.7
A nested class and its outer class.

```
class Elevator
{
    private Person passenger;
    …
    private ElevatorEngine myEngine;  ← declaring instance variable of type ElevatorEngine
    …
    private class ElevatorEngine      } nested class
    {
        public void MoveDown() {…}
        public void MoveUp() {…}
        …
    }
    …
}                                     } outer class scope

class Person
{
    …
    private ElevatorEngine engine;   ← Invalid! ElevatorEngine is not accessible outside
    …                                           the Elevator class scope.
}
```

Summary

In this chapter, you learned about the following function class members: properties, indexers, user-defined operator overloading, and user-defined conversions. We also looked at another kind of class member called nested types. The most important points in this chapter are noted in the following paragraphs.

Properties are better suited than accessor and mutator methods to access instance variables. The property is accessed in the same way as a public instance variable, but when a value is assigned or retrieved via the property, programmer defined `set` statement blocks and `get` statement blocks are executed. A property does not have to represent any particular instance variable but can merely return a calculated value.

Properties are as fast as accessor and mutator methods, because properties and methods look very similar when compiled into MSIL. Under the right circumstances, properties become as fast as directly accessing the instance variable. This is accomplished through an optimization technique called inlining.

If an instance variable is resource demanding to initialize and update, you can use properties together with two techniques called delayed initialization and lazy updates to delay and reduce the number of initializations and updates required.

Indexers allow you to access the data inside the array of an object by applying an array-like syntax (square brackets enclosing an index) to the object name itself.

The keyword `this` can be used to call an indexer from within the object in which the indexer is defined.

Several indexers can be included in the same class if they have different signatures. They are then called overloaded indexers.

User-defined operator overloading allows you to, for example, specify the + operator to perform your own tailor-made operation on the objects of a user-defined class, and thereby extend the + operator's use beyond the predefined numerical addition and `string` concatenation. C# only allows you to overload a restricted set of operators and does not permit you to create your own operators (such as ^*).

User-defined conversions let you extend the predefined implicit and explicit conversion paths already defined for the simple types to include your own user-defined types.

It is easy to overuse properties, indexers, operator-overloading, and user-defined conversions. Each construct has its own rules for when it is appropriately applied. However, there is one general question you should always ask yourself before implementing any of the constructs, "Viewed from the class users point, does the inclusion of the construct make the class more intuitive or more cryptic to use?" Only go ahead if you are convinced the answer is more intuitive.

C# allows you to insert the definition of a type (`class`, `enum`, `interface`) into a class block. They help organize your types and reduce the number of types through which programmers inspecting your code for reuse purposes need to sift.

Review Questions

1. (a) If `Speed` is a property defined inside an object called `myRocket`, what is the general name for the block of statements defined for the `Speed` property that are executed when the following line is executed?

   ```
   myRocket.Speed = 40;
   ```

   (b) When the following line is executed?

   ```
   travelTime = distance / myRocket.Speed;
   ```

2. Which capitalization style is recommended for

   (a) Instance variables?

   (b) Methods?

   (c) Properties?

3. The following lines specify an instance variable declaration and what is meant to be a property with the task of allowing access to the instance variable `speed` from outside the object. However, the property definition has four problems that need to be fixed before it will work correctly. Find and fix the problems.

```
private double speed;
private int Speed()
{
    get
    {
        return Speed;
    }
}
```

4. What is delayed initialization? When would you use it? Could delayed initialization also be implemented with accessor and mutator methods?

5. The header of the following indexer declaration has three problems. What are they?

```
static int myIndexer this [ ]
{
    ...
}
```

6. The `Rainfall` class contains an array with twelve elements. It also contains an indexer to access the array elements, which, like its array, is zero-based (first element is zero). A `rainfallParis` object is instantiated from the `Rainfall` class.

    (a) Write a statement that assigns the value of the third element of `rainfallParis` to the variable `rainfallMarch`.

    (b) Write a statement that assigns the value `rainfallJuly` to the seventh element of `rainfallParis`.

    (c) You are extending the `Rainfall` class with another method. Among other things in this method, you need to assign the third element of the indexer to your `myMarchRainfall` variable. Write the statement.

7. You have just finished implementing your `Car` class and are satisfied with the end result. During a quiet moment of contentment, your colleague suddenly suggests that to make the `Car` class perfect, you should include operator overloading for the class so it can be used with the `+` and `-` operators and support code like `car3 = car1 + car2`. Is this a good idea? Why or why not?

8. Why is operator overloading sometimes referred to as syntactic sugar?

9. Recall the `TimeSpan` class from Listing 14.7. It already includes an operator `+` method to add two `TimeSpan` objects together and assign the result to a `TimeSpan` reference variable. Your colleague decides to include an operator `-` method so that `TimeSpan` objects can be subtracted. The following is the code he initially inserted into the `TimeSpan` class. It contains several flaws. Find them.

```
private TimeSpan - (TimeSpan timeSpan1, TimeSpan timeSpan2)
{
    return (timeSpan1.Seconds - timeSpan2.Seconds)
}
```

10. Among other program elements, your program contains the two classes `EarthTimeSpan` and `BliposTimeSpan`. Each class still contains an instance variable called `totalSeconds` of type `uint`. In this case, `EarthTimeSpan` contains a user-defined explicit conversion to the type `short`, and `BliposTimeSpan` contains a user-defined implicit conversion from the type `decimal` to `BliposTimeSpan`. `myShort` is a variable of type `short` and `myDecimal` is a variable of type `decimal`, `earthTimeSpan1` is of type `EarthTimeSpan` and `bliposTimeSpan1` is of type `BliposTimeSpan`. Determine whether each of the following statements is valid:

    a. `myDecimal = bliposTimeSpan1;`

    b. `myDecimal = (decimal) bliposTimeSpan1;`

    c. `myShort = (short) bliposTimeSpan1;`

    d. `myShort = earthTimeSpan1;`

    e. `myShort = (short)earthTimeSpan;`

    f. `myDecimal = earthTimeSpan;`

    g. `myDecimal = (decimal)earthTimeSpan;`

    h. `bliposTimeSpan1 = earthTimeSpan1;`

    i. `bliposTimeSpan1 = (short)earthTimeSpan1;`

    j. `bliposTimeSpan1 = (decimal)earthTimeSpan1;`

    k. `earthTimeSpan1 = bliposTimeSpan1;`

    l. `earthTimeSpan1 = (short)bliposTimeSpan1;`

    m. `earthTimeSpan1 = (decimal)bliposTimeSpan1;`

11. You are writing a program that will assist architects in drawing architectural plans. The program contains many classes that rely on manipulating two-dimensional drawings. One of these classes is called `Bathroom`, and it represents and manipulates drawings of bathrooms. It needs a class called `Point` to represent a point consisting of two coordinates. Would it be a good idea to nest this class in the `Bathroom` class? Why or why not?

Programming Exercises

1. Expand the `Bicycle` class of Listing 14.2 to contain an instance variable called `age` that represents the age of a `Bicycle`. Write a property that allows users of the `Bicycle` class to `set` and `get` the `age` instance variable. Include code that prevents the `age` instance variable from being assigned a negative value or a value greater than 200. Equip the `Bicycle` class with an instance variable called `numberOfAgeAccesses` to represent the number of times the `age` instance variable has been accessed. Include a property to access `numberOfAgeAccesses`. Should this latter property contain both a `set` and a `get` statement block?

2. Write a class called `Rainfall` containing a one-dimensional array with 12 elements representing monthly rainfall measurements. Include the following features:

   - Allow the users of the `Rainfall` objects to access the 12 array elements with an index of type `int` as if these objects themselves were arrays. Let the first month be identified with index `1` (not zero). Make the program check that all indexes provided are within the correct bounds. Have the program count the number of times a rainfall reading has been accessed. Store this number in an instance variable called `numberOfRainAccesses`.
   - Include a property called `Average` that calculates the average monthly rainfall.
   - Please keep this class for use in exercise three.

3. Allow two `Rainfall` objects to be added together with the `+` symbol. This should allow you to write the following:

   ```
   totalRainfall = rainfallA + rainfallB;
   ```

   where all three objects are of type `Rainfall`. `totalRainfall` should now hold an array where the first element holds the result of adding the first element of the array in `rainfallA` together with the first element of the array in `rainfallB`; the second element holds the result of adding the second element of the array in `rainfallA` together with the second element of the array in `rainfallB`, and so on.

   Allow two `Rainfall` objects to be compared with the `<` and `>` comparison operators. Let the average of the 12 elements in each of the two compared objects be the deciding factor. So, if `rainfallA`'s average rainfall is greater than that of `rainfallB`, the following expression will be `true`:

   ```
   rainfallA > rainfallB
   ```

   and the next expression will be `false`:

   ```
   rainfallA < rainfallB
   ```

   Use the `Average` property that you have already written in exercise 2 to provide the necessary information for the comparison.

   Please save the code for use in exercise 4.

4. Write a class called `RainfallQuarterly` containing an array with four elements to store rainfall information on a quarterly basis. Write user-defined conversions between `RainfallQuarterly` and `Rainfall` going in both directions. A `Rainfall` object is converted to a `RainfallQuartely` object by adding together the first four array elements and assigning that value to the first array element of the `RainfallQuarterly` object, and so on. A `RainfallQuartely` object is converted to a `Rainfall` object by dividing the first array element by four and assigning this value to each of the first four elements in the `Rainfall` array, and so on. Should both conversions be explicit or just one of them, or perhaps both of them should be implicit? Why? Hint: In which conversion is data lost? In which conversion is it not lost?

CHAPTER 15

NAMESPACES, COMPILATION UNITS, AND ASSEMBLIES

You will learn about the following in this chapter:

- How to define and use namespaces
- How namespaces relate to compilation units and assemblies
- The `using` directive
- How to split compilation units up into smaller compilation units without changing the overall semantics
- Important compiler commands that allow you to
  - Create DLL and EXE assemblies
  - Control the name of a new assembly
  - Include namespaces from other assemblies in your own programs
- The intermediate language disassembling utility called Ildasm

Chapter 4, "A Guided Tour through C#: Part II," introduced you to the idea of using namespaces to organize classes in hierarchies of class containers and thereby keep the classes neatly ordered and easily accessible. So far, you have mainly been exposed to the namespace concept by using a few of the predefined namespaces (`System` and `System.Collections`) contained in the .NET Framework. This section looks at how you can define and use your own namespaces and how they relate to source files (also called compilation units) and assemblies.

Defining Your Own Namespaces

The syntax for defining a namespace of your own making is straightforward. Simply write the keyword `namespace` followed by a namespace name you've chosen. Below this header, include a pair of curly braces; they delimit the scope of your namespace. You can then include the classes you want this namespace to contain by writing their definitions between these curly braces. The source code of Listing 15.1 for example, defines a namespace called `ElevatorSimulation` that contains an `Elevator` and a `Person` class. The scope of the `ElevatorSimulation` namespace spans from line 2 to line 36.

LISTING 15.1 Defining the `ElevatorSimulation` namespace

```
01: namespace ElevatorSimulation
02: {
03:     using System;
04:
05:     class Elevator
06:     {
            <Class_members>
20:     }
21:
22:     class Person
23:     {
            <Class_members>
35:     }
36: }
```

Note: For space reasons the class members of the `Elevator` and `Person` classes have not been included. This explains the gaps in the line numbering. Line numbers 20 and 35 have been chosen somewhat arbitrarily. This listing does not compile.

Tip

Pascal casing is, per convention, used for namespace names.

The Source File Constitutes a Compilation Unit

The C# source code you write with Notepad (or another editor) becomes a C# source file when it is saved with the `.cs` extension. Each source file constitutes a *compilation unit*. So far, we have written programs consisting of just one compilation unit, but a program can consist of two or more compilation units. Later, we will see how this is made possible by the compiler.

You can define an unlimited number of namespaces in one compilation unit. The ways by which they can be arranged are numerous, but they are all based on a couple of simple rules:

- Zero or more namespaces can be positioned beside each other in a compilation unit.
- Zero or more namespaces can be positioned beside each other inside another namespace.

So, not only can namespaces be written next to each other in the compilation unit or inside another namespace, they can also be nested inside each other to any depth you might require. In a moment, we will see examples of the different overall structures.

The Global Nameless Namespace

None of the compilation units you have created from the examples shown so far in this book defined any namespaces explicitly. Classes and other types that are not defined inside an explicitly defined namespace are automatically set to belong to the same global nameless namespace. A type belonging to the global nameless namespace can be used in any other namespace merely by specifying its short name.

The previous examples in the book avoided explicit namespaces for two reasons; first, because the namespace concept was not yet fully introduced, and second, because the use of namespaces would be distractive and make the code samples longer. However, you should always organize your types by using namespaces.

Namespaces and Compilation Units

Listing 15.2 shows the most important code fragments for defining two namespaces called `ElevatorSimulation` (spanning lines 3–61 and containing the `Elevator`, `Person`, and `Building` classes) and `BankSimulation` (in lines 63–101 and containing the `Account`, `Bank`, and `Building` classes). The two namespaces are positioned beside each other in the same compilation unit. The class `MyGlobalNamespaceClass` (lines 103–120) has been thrown in to demonstrate a class that exists beside two namespaces and outside any namespace. The latter fact, as discussed in the previous section, causes it to belong to the global nameless namespace.

LISTING 15.2 Two Namespaces Written Beside Each Other in a Compilation Unit

```
001: using System;
002:
003: namespace ElevatorSimulation
004: {
005:     class Elevator
006:     {
             ...
010:         private Person passenger;
             ...
020:     }
         ...
030:     class Person
031:     {
             ...
040:     }
         ...
042:     class Building
043:     {
             ...
049:     }
050: }
051:
```

LISTING 15.2 continued

```
052: namespace BankSimulation
053: {
054:     using System.Collections;
055:     class Account
056:     {
057:         private ElevatorSimulation.Person accountholder;
             ...
060:     }
061:     class Bank
062:     {
             ...
070:         public void PrintBankDetails()
071:         {
                 …
075:             Console.WriteLine("Bank name: …");
080:         }
090:     }
091:     class Building
092:     {
             ...
100:     }
101: }
102:
103: class MyGlobalNamespaceClass
104: {
         ...
120: }
```

Note: The line numbers are somewhat arbitrary (but always increasing) because of the code fragments that are not shown. This code does not compile.

There are a few important points to notice about the source code in Listing 15.2:

- Compilation units can consist of `using` directives (see line 1), namespace definitions (lines 3–50 and 52–101) and class (or any other type) definitions (lines 103–120) written outside any explicitly specified namespaces. The `using` directives existing beside the namespaces must always precede the namespaces and the classes.
- By placing a class in a namespace, we effectively change its name to a long name, which consists of the namespaces within which it resides separated by periods (`.`). For example, the class defined as `Building` in lines 42–49 is called `ElevatorSimulation.Building`, which distinguishes it from the `BankSimulation.Building` class defined in lines 91–100. This clearly demonstrates the namespace's ability to avoid name clashes.
- Any `using` directive specified outside of any explicitly defined namespace (like `using System;` in line 1) covers all the classes written inside this compilation unit whether they belong to an explicitly defined namespace or not. So line 1 allows any of the methods inside any of the classes in the `ElevatorSimulation` and `BankSimulation` namespaces and inside the `MyGlobalNamespaceClass` to use, for example, the `Console` class as in line 75 without using its fully qualified name—`System.Console`.

- Any `using` directive specified inside an explicitly specified namespace only covers code that is written within the scope of this namespace. For example, only the classes defined within the `BankSimulation` namespace are affected by line 54 and can use the classname shortcuts from the `System.Collections`.
- To reference a class in code that is written outside of the namespace where the referenced class is defined, you must either import the namespace name with the `using` directive into the namespace where the code you are writing resides, or you must write its fully qualified name, as in line 57 (`ElevatorSimulation.Person` refers to the `Person` class of the `ElevatorSimulation` namespace). To save you from writing `ElevatorSimulation.` in line 57, you could have inserted the following line after line 54:

  ```
  using ElevatorSimulation;
  ```
- If you want to reference a class from code written inside of the namespace where this class has been defined, you merely need to write the name of the class. This is demonstrated in line 10, which refers to the `Person` class defined in the same `ElevatorSimulation` namespace.

Nested Namespaces

Apart from writing namespaces beside each other, as demonstrated in Listing 15.2, you can also nest namespaces inside other namespaces as mentioned earlier. The following scenario provides an example of a typical situation where namespace nesting would be convenient.

Suppose the editors at Sams Publishing wanted to provide a convenient way for programmers to reuse the code written in several of their C# books, including this one. An overall namespace hierarchy for doing this could look like that shown in Listing 15.3. An outermost namespace called `Sams` contains namespaces beside each other, named after each of Sams C# books (for brevity sake, only the two namespaces `CSharpPrimerPlus` and `SamsTeachYourselfCSharpIn21Days` have been shown). Each book namespace again contains namespaces beside each other with different projects of the book, such as the `ElevatorSimulation` and `BankSimulation` programs contained in this book.

LISTING 15.3 Providing Convenient Access to Code from Sams C# Books

```
namespace Sams
{
    namespace CSharpPrimerPlus
    {
        namespace ElevatorSimulation
        {
            class Elevator
            {
                private AllRounder mrUseful;
                ...
```

LISTING 15.3 continued

```
            }

            class Building
            {
                ...
            }

            <Other_Sams.CSharpPrimerPlus.ElevatorSimulation
           _ classes_and_types>

        }

        namespace BankSimulation
        {
            class Building
            {
                ...
            }

            <Other Sams.CSharpPrimerPlus.BankSimulation classes_and_types>
        }

        <Other_namespaces nested inside the Sams.CSharpPrimerPlus
         namespace>

    }

    namespace SamsTeachYourselfCSharpIn21Days
    {
        <Sams.SamsTeachYourselfCSharpIn21Days_namespace with namespaces
        ➥similar to ElevatorSimulation and BankSimulation>
    }

    <Other_Sams C Sharp Book namespaces positioned here>

    class AllRounder
    {
        ...
    }
}
```

The following points are important in relation to Listing 15.3:

- As per convention, you should use your company or product name for the outermost namespace, such as `Sams` in Listing 15.3. Not only does this effectively prevent name clashes between classes located in namespaces written by different companies, it also gives you an idea of who wrote the code you are reusing (and lets you get a bit of free advertising when other programmers use your own namespaces).

Note

The .NET SDK documentation contains more guidelines about how to name and define namespaces.

- A namespace name is made up of the names of the namespaces within which it resides and its own short name (such as `ElevatorSimulation` in line 5). The top-level namespace name is the first part of the name, and its own short name is the last part. Each part is separated from the other parts with periods. So the `Elevator` class in lines 7–20 of Listing 15.3 is written inside a namespace called `Sams.CSharpPrimerPlus.ElevatorSimulation`, and its own proper long name is `Sams.CSharpPrimerPlus.ElevatorSimulation.Elevator`.
- You can use the same syntax as specified in the previous point to define a namespace instead of using the intermittently cumbersome syntax shown in Listing 15.3, which uses curly braces and indenting. I will demonstrate this syntax in the next point.
- If you define the same namespace in several different parts of the compilation unit (and even in different compilation units, as you will see later) each of these namespace definitions are in effect contributing its code to this same namespace. For example, if, apart from the `Elevator` and `Building` classes, you wanted to add a class called `Person` to the `Sams.CSharpPrimerPlus.ElevatorSimulation` namespace in Listing 15.3, you could do so by using the syntax suggested in the previous point. Write the following lines after the last closing brace (in line 99) of Listing 15.3.

```
Sams.CSharpPrimerPlus.ElevatorSimulation
{
    class Person
    {
        ...
    }
}
```

  The `Sams.CSharpPrimerPlus.ElevatorSimulation` namespace would now contain the `Elevator`, `Building`, and `Person` classes exactly as if the `Person` class definition had been inserted in between the `Elevator` and `Building` class definitions (after line 20) in the `Sams.CSharpPrimerPlus.ElevatorSimulation` namespace.
- Notice that you cannot nest the longer qualified namespace names inside other namespaces when you define namespace parts. For example, you could not have inserted the `Sams.CSharpPrimerPlus.ElevatorSimulation` namespace part containing the `Person` class definition anywhere inside the `Sams` namespace.
- When we involve assemblies a little later in this namespace discussion, you will see how you can contribute code (in the form of namespace parts) to the same namespace, even from different compilation units.
- The code you write in an inner namespace can refer to a class defined in one of this namespace's outer namespaces by using this class's short name. For example, the

`Sams.CSharpPrimerPlus.ElevatorSimulation.Elevator` class (lines 7–20) can, as illustrated, simply specify the `Sams.AllRounder` class (in line 9) by writing the short name `AllRounder`. However, the contrary is not true. If you wanted to specify the `Sams.CSharpPrimerPlus.ElevatorSimulation.Elevator` class in the `Sams.AllRounder` class, you would have to specify this class by including the namespace names that would bridge the `Sams` namespace to this inner namespace. In this case, the specification inside the `Sams.AllRounder` class would look like the following:

```
CSharpPrimerPlus.ElevatorSimulation.Elevator
```

Notice that we don't need to include `Sams` as in:

```
Sams.CSharpPrimerPlus.ElevatorSimulation.Elevator
```

because `AllRounder` exists inside `Sams`.

Namespace Syntax

On the basis of our previous namespace discussion, we can deduce the syntax for writing compilation units, using statements, and namespaces. This has been done in Syntax Box 15.1, which makes heavy use of the optional *[ ]* brackets because the `using` statements, namespace definitions, and type definitions in a compilation unit and inside a namespace are optional.

Syntax Box 15.1 Compilation Units, Using Statements and Namespaces

```
Compilation_unit::=

        [[<using_statement_1>]
         [<using_statement_2>]
          ...]

        [[<Namespace_definition_1>]
         [<Namespace_definition_2>]
          ...]

        [[<Type_definition_1>]
         [<Type_definition_2>]
          ...]
```

where

```
<using_statement> ::=
             using <Namespace_name> ;

<Namespace_definition>::=
             <Short_namespace_name>
             {
                 [[<using_statement_1>]
                  [<using_statement_2>]
                   ...]
```

```
        [[<Namespace_definition_1>]
         [<Namespace_definition_2>]
          ...]

        [[<Type_definition_1>]
         [<Type_definition_2>]
         ...]
}
```

```
<Type_definition>
        ::= <class_definition>
        ::= <struct_definition>
        ::= <enum_definition>
        ::= <interface_definition>
        ::= <delegate_definition>
```

Notes:

- All `<using_statements>` must be positioned before any `<Namespace_definitions>` and any `<Type_definitions>` within a particular compile unit or namespace.
- Because a namespace definition can contain other namespace definitions, namespaces can be nested inside each other to any depth you might require.
- Instead of having to nest namespaces inside each other to write a namespace part, you can write the fully qualified namespace name with each short namespace name part separated from the other parts with periods (`.`) followed by a pair of curly braces, as shown in the following lines:

```
<short_namespace_name_1>.<short_namespace_name_2>....<short_namespace_name_n>
{
    <Content_of namespace_part>
}
```

However, this construct cannot be nested inside another namespace.

More About the `using` Directive

As you know, the `using` keyword, followed by a suitable namespace name, allows us to abbreviate a class's long fully-qualified name when we refer to it in the source code. Consequently, if we were to use the classes from the two namespaces `Sams.CSharpPrimerPlus.ElevatorSimulation` and `Sams.CSharpPrimerPlus.BankSimulation` (defined in Listing 15.3) in the source code of Figure 15.1, we could use the short classnames of the classes belonging to these namespaces by including lines 1 and 2 shown in Figure 15.1.

But what if both namespaces referenced by the `using` directive contain a class of the same name, as is the case with the `Building` class that is defined both in lines 22–38 of the `Sams.CSharpPrimerPlus.ElevatorSimulation` namespace and in lines 47–57 of the `Sams.CSharpPrimerPlus.BankSimulation` namespace in Listing 15.3? We would then have to specify the fully-qualified name of the `Building` class we wanted to use, despite the `using` directives in lines 1 and 2, to clear up this uncertain situation for the compiler. For example, if we wanted to specify the `Sams.CSharpPrimerPlus.ElevatorSimulation.Building` class, we would have to exchange `Building` in line 20 with this long name.

FIGURE 15.1
The compiler cannot know to which namespace `Building` belongs.

```
01: using Sams.CSharpPrimerPlus.ElevatorSimulation;
02: using Sams.CSharpPrimerPlus.BankSimulation;
    ...
10: namespace MySoftwareCoLtd
11: {
12:     class Town
13:     {
            ...
20:         private Building myBuilding;
30:     }
        ...
50: }
```

Does Building refer to `Sams.CSharpPrimerPlus.ElevatorSimulation.Building` or `Sams.CSharpPrimerPlus.BankSimulation.Building`?

Invalid. Exchange `Building` with `Sams.CSharpPrimerPlus.ElevatorSimulation.Building` to clarify intent.

Class and Namespace Aliases

Apart from employing the `using` keyword to allow shortcuts when specifying classnames, you can also use it to declare aliases for classes (and other types like enums, structs, interfaces, and delegates) and namespaces. The syntax for performing this declaration is specified in Syntax Box 15.2. The alias is positioned after the `using` keyword, which is followed by the = symbol and the name of the namespace or type name you want to assign to this alias.

Syntax Box 15.2 Declaring Namespace and Type Aliases

```
Namespace_alias_declaration::=
          using <Namespace_alias> = <Namespace_name>;

Type_alias_declaration::=
          using <Type_alias> = <Type_name>;
```

Note:

You can specify an alias for any of the following general types: classes, enums, interfaces, delegates, and structs.

The next example shows you how aliases are specified and why they can be convenient to use. In Figure 15.1 (shown earlier), we were, for ambiguity reasons, obliged to use the long name `Sams.CSharpPrimerPlus.ElevatorSimulation.Building` instead of just `Building` to specify this class, despite the `using` directive in line 1. Specifying this class many times in our code requires many keystrokes with an increased risk of typing errors and bulkier looking code. Line 1 of Figure 15.2 declares the leaner word `ElevatorBuilding` to be an alias for the awkward classname `Sams.CSharpPrimerPlus.ElevatorSimulation.Building` and allows us to use this shorter name in line 20 and anywhere else in the code affected by line 1.

Line 2 further illustrates how we can specify a namespace alias. In this case, `ElevatorSimulation` is stated to be an alias for the namespace `Sams.CSharpPrimerPlus.ElevatorSimulation`. This permits us to specify the `Person` class from the `Sams.CSharpPrimerPlus.ElevatorSimulation` namespace by writing `ElevatorSimulation.Person` in line 21 and declare a new variable of this type. In this case, the variable is arbitrarily called `pedestrian`.

FIGURE 15.2
Class alias and namespace alias.

```
01: using ElevatorBuilding = Sams.CSharpPrimerPlus.ElevatorSimulation.Building;
02: using ElevatorSimulation = Sams.CSharpPrimerPlus.ElevatorSimulation;
03: using Sams.CSharpPrimerPlus.BankSimulation;
    ...
10: namespace MySoftwareCoLtd
11: {
12:     class Town
13:     {
            ...
20:         private ElevatorBuilding myBuilding;
21:         private ElevatorSimulation.Person pedestrian;
30:     }
        ...
50: }
```

Class alias specified in line 1.

Namespace alias specified in line 2

Avoid Specifying Aliases for the Types of the .NET Framework Class Library

Most programmers are familiar with the names of the .NET Framework classes, so creating new aliases for these names can make the code less self-documenting. For example if you saw the following in another programmer's code

```
TxtInOut.Write("What does this mean?");
```

you would probably be confused about its meaning until you saw the following alias specification in the beginning of the code:

```
using TxtInOut = System.Console;
```

Do Not Over-Abbreviate the Alias Names

Choose meaningful alias names in your source code to improve clarity and readability.

For example, if, instead of the alias `ElevatorBuilding` specified in the following line of Figure 15.5

```
using ElevatorBuilding =
Sams.CSharpPrimerPlus.ElevatorSimulation.Building;
```

we had used the alias `ElBld` as follows

```
using ElBld = Sams.CSharpPrimerPlus.ElevatorSimulation.Building;
```

we would have saved some typing, but we would have made the code more cryptic.

Compile Units, Namespaces, and Assemblies

This section brings the assembly into our discussion that so far has concentrated on compile units and namespaces. The following discussion is built around a few simple examples whose goal is to give you an idea of the many ways you can configure and structure your classes (and other types) and programs around these three important elements.

Before beginning, you might want to refresh your memory about some of the more theoretical assembly aspects by looking at the "The Assembly, the Basic Unit of Code Reuse in .NET" section in Chapter 2, "Your First C# Program."

Compiling Several Compile Units into One Assembly

The routine of creating and running a program has so far consisted of the following steps:

1. Write the source code in a text editor, such as Notepad.
2. Save the text as a source code file (a compilation unit) with the `.cs` extension.
3. Compile the `.cs` file with the `csc` command to create an executable file with the `.exe` extension (also called a Portable Executable (PE) assembly).
4. Run the PE assembly by typing its name (without the `exe` extension).

In effect, we have written one source file and created one PE assembly in each example, as illustrated in Figure 15.3.

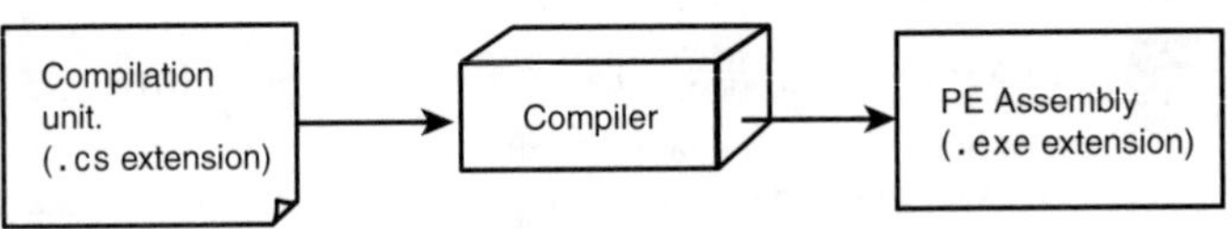

FIGURE 15.3
Compiling one compilation unit into one PE assembly.

This process has purposefully been kept simple and works well when focusing on and learning about most of C#'s language elements. However, for real-life projects that often contain many hundred of pages of code with a myriad of classes and other user-defined types involving several developers, this way of writing software is too rigid. The thought of one source code file with hundreds of pages surrounded by several developers pasting code in and out from here is like looking straight down into a pot of spaghetti. Instead, we need the ability to write many physically independent source files but, at the same time, let all source files contribute with type definitions to the same namespace hierarchy if needed. Figure 15.4 shows three compilation units being turned into one PE assembly by the compiler; C# allows us to combine an unlimited number of compilation units.

The following example shows how you can use the compiler to create an assembly from three source code files. Suppose that we are writing the elevator simulation program for this book that is going to be part of the `Sams` namespace presented earlier in Listing 15.3. For simplicity, we assume that there are only three classes in this program called `Elevator`, `Person`, and `ElevatorSimulation` (containing the `Main` method), and that all classes are cut down to the bones only. Conventionally, each class is written in its own source file that is named after the class. In this case, then, you need to create the three source code files shown in the next three listings (Listing 15.4, 15.5, and 15.6). Each source code file is created in the usual manner with the `.cs` extension. To indicate that the three source code files are related, you should insert them into a folder called `ElevatorSimulation`.

Tip

Conventionally, each class has its own source file. The source file is then usually named after the class it represents. If you are constructing a file called `Elevator`, save it in a file called `Elevator.cs`.

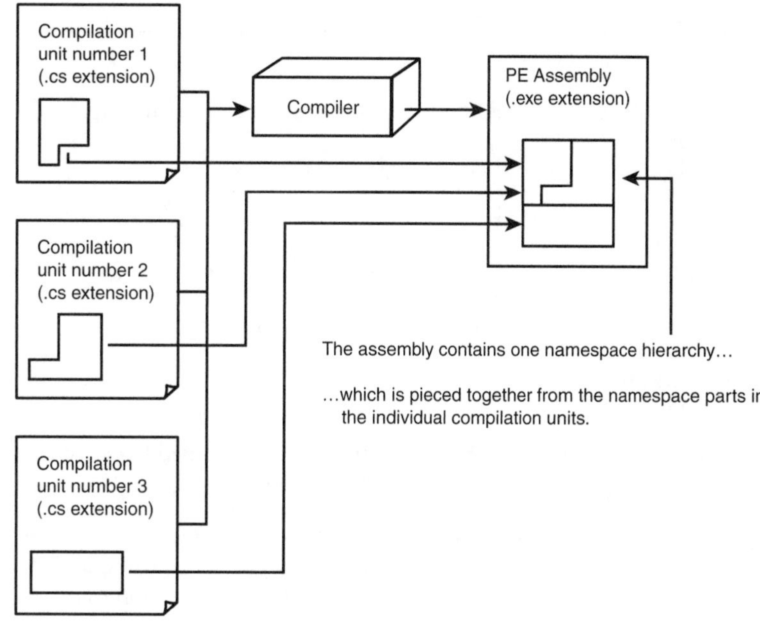

FIGURE 15.4
Compiling three compilation units into one PE assembly.

LISTING 15.4 `Elevator.cs`

```
using System;

namespace Sams.CSharpPrimerPlus.ElevatorSimulation
{
    internal class Elevator
    {
        public static void PrintClassName()
        {
            Console.WriteLine("This class is called Elevator");
        }
    }
}
```

LISTING 15.5 `Person.cs`

```
using System;

namespace Sams.CSharpPrimerPlus.ElevatorSimulation
{
    public class Person
    {
        public void Talk()
        {
            Console.WriteLine("Blah blah");
        }
    }
}
```

LISTING 15.6 `ElevatorSimulator.cs`

```
01: using System;
02:
03: namespace Sams.CSharpPrimerPlus.ElevatorSimulation
04: {
05:     public class ElevatorSimulator
06:     {
07:         public static void Main()
08:         {
09:             Person somePerson = new Person();
10:             somePerson.Talk();
11:             Elevator.PrintClassName();
12:         }
13:     }
14: }
```

You should now have three source code files named `Elevator.cs`, `Person.cs`, and `ElevatorSimulator.cs` in the `ElevatorSimulation` folder.

All three source code files specify the same namespace `Sams.CSharpPrimerPlus.ElevatorSimulation` (see line 3 in all three listings) so, in effect, each source file is contributing with one class definition to this same namespace.

The `ElevatorSimulator.cs` source file can refer to the `Person` and `Elevator` classes (see lines 9–11) without providing their long qualified names, because the `ElevatorSimulator` class is being specified inside the same namespace as `Person` and `Elevator`.

Notice that the `Elevator` class has been declared `internal` (line 5 of Listing 15.4), and `Person` has been declared `public` (line 5 Listing 15.5). Both `internal` and `public` are access modifiers but, whereas `public` allows a class to be used outside the assembly where it resides, `internal` restricts the use of a class to its own assembly. In a moment, when our source code has been turned into an assembly and reused by another program, we will experience the difference between the two access modifiers. There is no direct motive for declaring `Elevator` `internal` in this example other than to demonstrate its effect.

The `internal` Access Modifier

A class that does not have any access modifier is, by default, declared `internal` and cannot be used outside of its own assembly. You can also declare a class member to be `internal`. This allows you to let part of a class be accessible outside the assembly by declaring the class `public` but then restrict access to some of the members by declaring them `internal`.

Before we compile these three source files into the same assembly, it is worth introducing the few compiler commands shown in Table 15.1. They are all optional and, if used, must be positioned between the `csc` command and the source file names you provide. I will only present the `/out:` command now, but examples will be provided of all the commands as we continue our story about the three source files presented before. Don't worry if parts of Table 15.1 do not make sense to you now.

By default, the compiler uses the name of your source code file to name the assembly it created. To specify a different name for the assembly and to avoid any confusion as to which of the names the compiler chooses when several source files are compiled simultaneously, you can include the `/out:` compiler command followed by a filename of your choice, as shown in Table 15.1.

TABLE 15.1 A Few Selected Compiler Options

Compiler command	Description
`/out: <File_name>`	You can specify the name of the output file (the assembly) by writing this name after the `/out:` command.
`/t[arget]: exe`	This command creates a PE (portable executable) assembly with the `.exe` extension, which constitutes an executable console application that will automatically open the console. This is the default setting of the compiler. (Tip: For Windows-based GUI applications, use the `/t[arget]: winexe` command instead. This will prevent the console window from opening.)
`/t[arget]: library`	This will create a class library that cannot be executed on its own but that is only meant for reuse in other applications. The assembly created will have the extension `.dll`.
`/r[eference]:<Assembly_list>`	This references one or more assemblies (with extension `.exe` or `.dll`) by specifying the name of each referenced assembly separated by semicolons. By referencing an assembly, its namespaces and their types are made available for the assembly we are creating. Note: Each assembly included must be separated from other included assemblies with semicolons (see the example in the notes).

Notes:

- All the mentioned commands are optional.
- `/t[arget]:` means that `arget` is optional, so `/t:` and `/target:` have the same meaning. The same logic applies to `/r[eference]:`.
- The commands are part of the `csc` command given at the command line in the console window. The commands must be positioned in between the `csc` command and the C# source code files as specified next with our familiar syntax notation.

```
csc [/out: <File_name>] [/t[arget]: exe | /t[arget]: library]
 ➥[ /r[eference]: <Assembly_list>] <Source_file1>
➥[<Source_file2> <Source_file3>...]
```

To create a `.dll` assembly called `MyClassLibrary.dll` that references `ClassLib1.dll` and `ClassLib2.dll` and compiles the source files `Planet.cs` and `Rocket.cs`, we need to write the following after the command prompt:

```
csc /out:MyClassLibrary.dll /target:library /reference:ClassLib1;
➥ ClassLib2 Planet.cs Rocket.cs
```

It is time to compile the three source code files from Listings 15.4, 15.5, and 15.6. We decide to create an executable application called `ElevatorSimulation.exe`, which is done by giving the following command:

```
csc /out:ElevatorSimulation.exe /t:exe Elevator.cs Person.cs
    ➥ ElevatorSimulator.cs
```

Note that we could have omitted the `/t:exe` command because this command specifies the default option.

You can now run the `ElevatorSimulation.exe` program in the usual manner by typing its name, to create the following output:

```
Blah blah
This class is called Elevator
```

This example is continued in the next section, so please keep the source code in your `ElevatorSimulation` folder handy.

Reusing the Namespaces Contained in an Assembly

A couple of programmers are working on a `SpaceShuttle` class and need a `Person` class with the ability to say `Blah blah` (to presumably test the acoustics inside a `SpaceShuttle`). They want to reuse our `Sams.CSharpPrimerPlus.ElevatorSimulation.Person` class that has this ability. To give them this privilege, they need to know two fundamental things (apart from how to use the class, which we assume has been taken care of):

- The long, fully-qualified name of the class, so they can refer to the class in their source code. In other words, the short name of the class and the namespace where it resides.
- The name and location of the assembly where the namespace of the class resides, so they can reference this assembly with the `/reference:` command (see Table 15.1 shown earlier) during the compilation of their source code.

The programmers initially write a quick piece of source code, shown in Listing 15.7, to verify that they can, in fact, reuse our `Sams.CSharpPrimerPlus.ElevatorSimulation.Person` class. If you want to compile the `SpaceShuttle.cs` program, please insert this source file in the same folder as the `ElevatorSimulation.exe` assembly and call it `SpaceShuttle.cs`. I will provide instructions on how to compile it after the analysis of the code.

LISTING 15.7 `SpaceShuttle.cs`

```
using Sams.CSharpPrimerPlus.ElevatorSimulation;

namespace SpaceShuttleSimulation
```

LISTING 15.7 continued

```
04: {
05:     class SpaceShuttle
06:     {
07:         private static Person astronaut;
08:
09:         public static void Main()
10:         {
11:             astronaut = new Person();
12:             astronaut.Talk();
13:         }
14:     }
15: }
```

Just like we include `using System;` in the source code to let us write convenient shortcut names of the classes contained in the `System` namespace of the .NET Framework class library, the programmers insert line 1 in `SpaceShuttle.cs` to get convenient access to the classes of the `Sams.CSharpPrimerPlus.ElevatorSimulation` namespace that we created with the source code in Listings 15.4, 15.5, and 15.6.

Because of line 1, we can use the short name `Person` in line 7 and 11 to refer to the class with the long qualified name—`Sams.CSharpPrimerPlus.ElevatorSimulation.Person`.

When you compile the `SpaceShuttle.cs` source file, you need to specify to the compiler in which assemblies it can look for the namespaces you refer to in the source code. This is done with the `/r[eference]:` command. In our case, the namespace resides in the single assembly we called `ElevatorSimulation.exe`. This leads us to the following command that compiles the `SpaceShuttle.cs` source file into the executable assembly `SpaceShuttle.exe`:

```
csc /r:ElevatorSimulation.exe SpaceShuttle.cs
```

When you run the program, by writing the name of the program as usual, you should see the following output:

```
Blah blah
```

Note

You can reference several assemblies in the compiler command if the namespaces you use in your source code exist in several assemblies. You will see a demonstration of this in a moment.

Note

You might have been wondering why you do not need to reference any assemblies to use the classes of the `System` namespace. This is not necessary because the compiler, by default, references the `mscorlib.dll` assembly where the core namespaces, such as `System`, exist.

Note

The .NET Framework class library is spread over many different DLL assemblies. To find out which particular DLL you need to reference to access a specific class, look at the .NET Framework Documentation page for this class. At the bottom of this page, you will see the following information, which is provided for the `System.Windows.Forms.Form` class in this case (used to create `Windows GUI` applications):

Requirements:

Namespace: `System.Windows.Forms`

Assembly: `System.Windows.Forms.dll`

It clearly states that the fully qualified name of the `Form` class is `System.Windows.Forms.Form`, and that you have to reference the `System.Windows.Forms.dll` assembly if you are using the `Form` class in your program.

Recall that the `Sams.CSharpPrimerPlus.ElevatorSimulation.Elevator` class in Listing 15.4 is declared with the `internal` keyword. The `SpaceShuttle.exe` assembly we have just created is clearly outside the confines of the `ElevatorSimulation.exe` assembly where `Sams.CSharpPrimerPlus.ElevatorSimulation.Elevator` now resides. Consequently, if we tried to use the `Sams.CSharpPrimerPlus.ElevatorSimulation.Elevator` class in the `SpaceShuttle.cs` to create the `SpaceShuttle.exe`, we would see an error message. Let's confirm this theory. Insert the following line after line 12 in Listing 15.7

```
Elevator.PrintClassName();
```

and attempt to compile the `SpaceShuttle.cs` yet again with the same command as before:

```
csc /r:ElevatorSimulation.exe SpaceShuttle.cs
```

In response, we now get the following compiler error:

```
SpaceShuttle.cs(13,13): error CS0122: 'Sams.CSharpPrimerPlus.ElevatorSimulation.
Elevator' is inaccessible due to its protection level
```

which clearly confirms our speculation.

Note

The `SpaceShuttle.exe` depends on the existence of the `ElevatorSimulation.exe` to be executed. Removing `ElevatorSimulation.exe` from its folder causes the .NET runtime to generate a `System.TypeLoadException` whenever you try to run `SpaceShuttle.exe`.

Separating Namespaces into Several Assemblies

From the `SpaceShuttle.cs` code, our story returns to the source files `Elevator.cs`, `Person.cs`, and `ElevatorSimulator.cs` in Listings 15.4, 15.5, and 15.6. Suppose these source code listings grow to become more than just demonstration tools. Suppose we work hard to develop the `Elevator` and `Person` classes to feature state-of-the-art simulation capabilities, and that a whole namespace hierarchy of other related classes appear that surrounds the

Elevator class and a similarly large but separate set of classes appear around the Person class. As a result, the source files representing the classes and namespaces grow to hundreds of pages. However, despite this large mass of classes and namespaces, we are still combining all our compilation units into one single assembly called ElevatorSimulation.exe. Further, let's assume that the programming community is becoming as interested in reusing our Elevator and Person (and associated) classes as elevator specialists are in running ElevatorSimulation.exe as a normal program. As a result, we find ourselves selling a third of the ElevatorSimulation.exe assemblies to programmers only interested in reusing the Elevator-related classes (see Figure 15.5), another third to programmers interested in reusing Person-related classes, and the last third to the simulation experts who are interested in running the full-blown application.

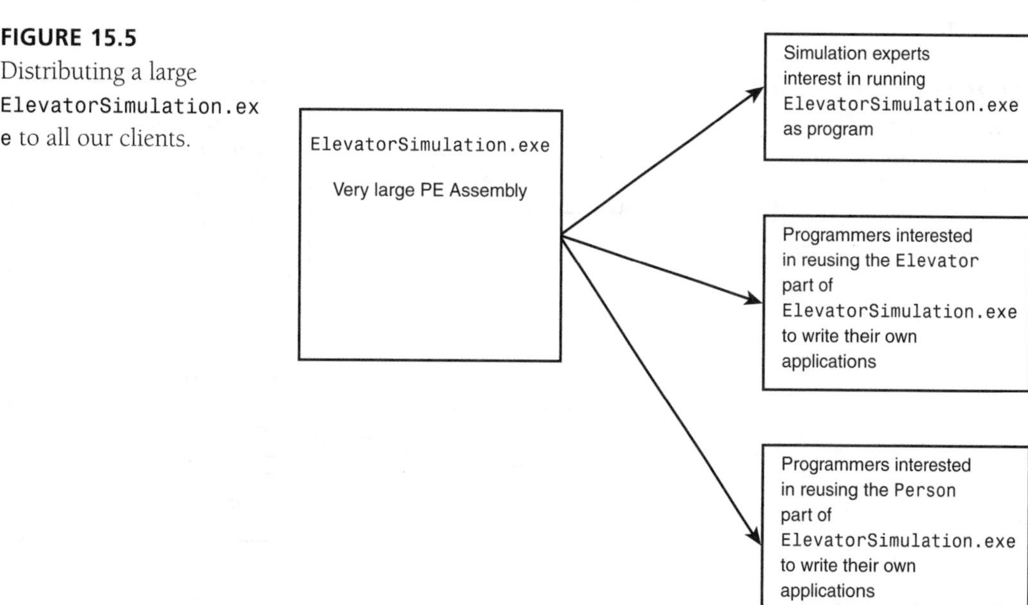

FIGURE 15.5
Distributing a large ElevatorSimulation.exe to all our clients.

However, this rigid distribution system, which sells the same ElevatorSimulation.exe product to all our customers, contains at least three problems, all related to our programmer customers who are only interested in reusing either the Person part or the Elevator part. Their main complaints are as follows:

- Even though they only use a part of the ElevatorSimulation.exe assembly, they have to store all parts of this large program and occupy scarce memory.
- Even though they only use part of ElevatorSimulation.exe assembly, they have to pay as much for the package as the simulation experts who get the full-blown benefits from this assembly.

- New versions of the Person and Elevator parts of the program are likely generated at a faster pace than versions of the whole ElevatorSimulation.exe assembly. Consequently, our programmer customers have to wait longer to get new versions than if they had been sold the Person or the Elevator parts independently.

The pressure mounts on us to change the much criticized distribution system. Fortunately, the way we can organize our compilation units, namespaces, and assemblies in C# and .NET is very flexible. To satisfy all parties, we decide to break our large ElevatorSimulation.exe into three smaller assemblies, as illustrated in Figure 15.6—a lean Elevator.dll representing the Elevator- related classes, a lean Person.dll, and a lean ElevatorSimulation.exe that does not itself carry the Elevator- and Person-related classes on which it depends. Instead, it references the Elevator.dll and Person.dll to run exactly as before. Let's see how this can be done.

FIGURE 15.6
Distributing leaner DLLs to programmers for reuse purposes.

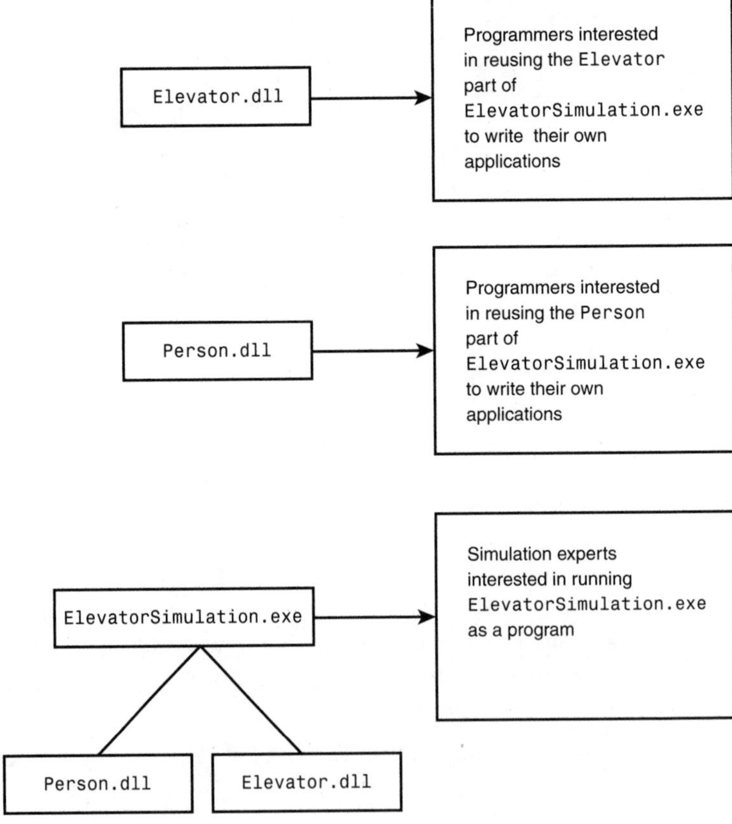

To keep matters simple, we won't try to make Elevator.cs, Person.cs, or ElevatorSimulator.cs any larger. You just have to imagine that each represents a large number of source files. Before we begin, you need to ensure that the

`Sams.CSharpPrimerPlus.ElevatorSimulation.Elevator` class from Listing 15.4 can be used outside its assembly by changing it from being an `internal` class to a `public` class. Not only does this allow other programmers to reuse this class, it also allows the `ElevatorSimulation.exe`, which now will be in a separate assembly, to reuse it.

To keep this venture separate from the previous source files created in this chapter, create a new folder called `ElevatorSimulationPro` and copy the three source files (`Elevator.cs`, `Person.cs`, and `ElevatorSimulator.cs`) over into this folder. It's now time to put the compiler to work. According to our plans, we need to create one EXE and two DLL assemblies. A DLL assembly is created by including the `/t[arget]: library` command, shown earlier in Table 15.1. To create the two `Elevator.dll` and `Person.dll` assemblies, you need to give the following two compiler commands:

```
csc /out:Elevator.dll /t:library Elevator.cs
```

```
csc /out:Person.dll /t:library Person.cs
```

The previous version we created of `ElevatorSimulation.exe` included all three source files. This time, we only include `ElevatorSimulator.cs` and instruct the `ElevatorSimulation.exe` assembly to look for the `Elevator` and `Person` classes in the `Elevator.dll` and `Person.dll` assemblies. The latter is done by including `/r[eference]:`*`<Assembly_list>`* as shown in the following command:

```
csc /out:ElevatorSimulation.exe /r:Elevator.dll;Person.dll ElevatorSimulator.cs
```

By running `ElevatorSimulation.exe` in the usual manner, you should see this output once again confirming that nothing has changed in terms of its functionality.

```
Blah blah
This class is called Elevator
```

Note

Somewhere in its namespace hierarchy, an executable assembly must have one `Main` method from where the program commences. A DLL does not need a `Main` method because it cannot be executed on its own; it is only created for reuse purposes.

The programmers developing the `SpaceShuttle.exe` who are among the group of programmers only interested in using the `Same.CSharpPrimerPlus.ElevatorSimulation.Person` class related functionality, now only need to reference and carry around the much leaner `Person.dll` when creating and running their assembly. To create a new `SpaceShuttle.exe` by referencing the `Person.dll`, copy the `SpaceShuttle.cs` source file over into the `ElevatorSimulationPro` folder and write the following command:

```
csc /r:Person.dll SpaceShuttle.cs
```

Running the `SpaceShuttle.exe` program in the usual manner confirms its unchanged capability to write

```
Blah blah
```

Exploring Assemblies with the Ildasm Utility

The .NET SDK ships with a built-in *i*ntermediate *l*anguage *d*is*as*se*m*bling utility program (`ildasm.exe`) that allows you to investigate the contents of any assembly in a simple, user-friendly GUI. This straightforward program gives you an overview of the namespaces, types, and type members of an assembly of your choice, along with the ability to scrutinize its intermediate language instructions and metadata.

You can start the ildasm application by typing the following after the command prompt:

```
ildasm<enter>
```

You should then see an empty window appear called ILDASM. To choose the EXE or DLL assembly you want to inspect, click Open on the File menu. Use the File Open dialog box to navigate to the assembly of your choice. After you have located it, simply double-click its name.

If we choose to examine the `Elevator.dll`, we see a window somewhat similar to that shown in Figure 15.7, with a tree view of this assembly's structure. Each tree branch represents a part (namespace, class, method, property, or other) of the assembly and has an icon attached that tells us whether we are looking at a class, method, or something else. In our case, we see a cyan colored diamond displayed next to the `Elevator.dll` path and, further down, a blue shield (symbolizing a namespace) next to the familiar name of the namespace where the `Sams.CSharpPrimerPlus.ElevatorSimulation.Elevator` class resides. Expanding the namespace node reveals the content of this namespace—the `Sams.CSharpPrimerPlus.ElevatorSimulation.Elevator` class and an associated blue rectangle with three connectors (symbolizing a class). To see the same tree view shown in Figure 15.7 you must also expand this class node. We can now recognize the name `PrintClassName`, which is `Elevator`'s `static` method (symbolized by a magenta rectangle marked 'S'). A magenta rectangle without an S, such as that shown above `PrintClassName`, symbolizes a non-static method. `ctor` written next to the rectangle stands for constructor and represents the default constructor that was automatically generated by the C# compiler for the `Elevator` class because no explicit constructors were specified in the source code.

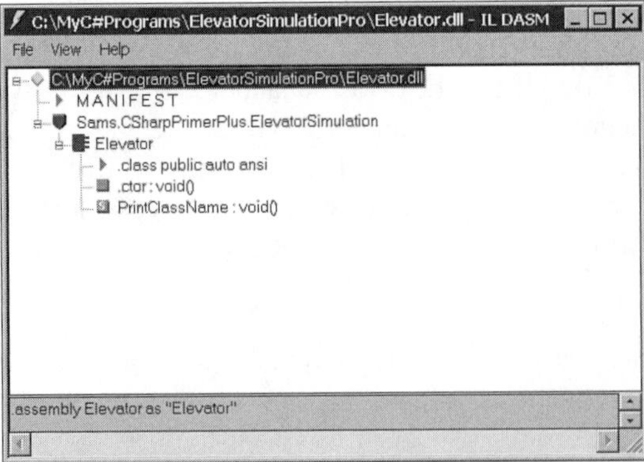

FIGURE 15.7
The ildasm window displaying the `Elevator.dll` assembly.

Notice the red right-pointing triangles next to `MANIFEST` and `.class public auto ansi`. This symbol signifies that more information (metadata) is held about a particular assembly or type. As we discussed in Chapter 2, the manifest holds information about the `Elevator.dll` assembly, and the red right-pointing triangle under the blue rectangle indicates that more information is held about the `Elevator` class.

By double-clicking any of the class members, another window appears containing the intermediate language instructions that the source code of this construct was turned into during its compilation. Useful information can be found by probing these more cryptic looking codes, but this discussion is beyond the scope this book.

Note

To see the meaning of all symbols used in the tree view of the Ildasm, click Help on its Help menu and double-click the Tree View Icons item.

As a second Ildasm demonstration, we will take a brief look at the advanced `mscorlib.dll` that contains important `System` namespace. `mscorlib.dll` on my computer is located at `C:\WINNT\Microsoft.NET\Framework\v1.0.2914\mscorlib.dll`. You might have it on a disk drive other than C, and the version number (v1.0.2914) will likely, vary depending on the .NET SDK version you have installed. After you see its initial tree view in the Ildasm window, try to open the `System` namespace to expose the `System.Collections` namespace where the familiar `ArrayList` class resides. By expanding the `System.Collections` namespace node, you should see a window similar to that shown in Figure 15.8. Notice that the details in this window are likely to vary between different versions of the .NET SDK.

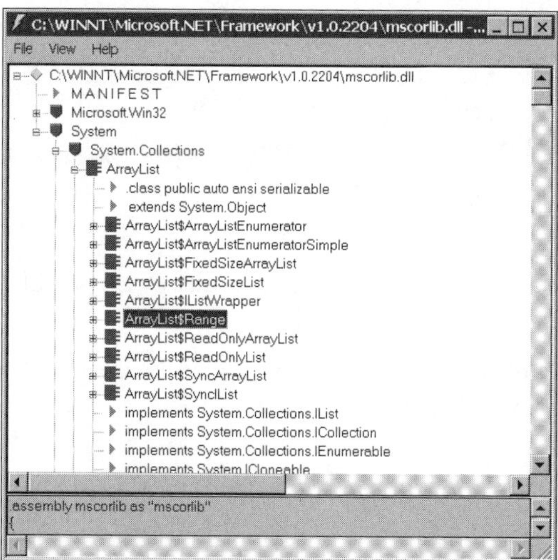

FIGURE 15.8
Ildasm displaying a tree view of `mscorlib.dll`.

Summary

This chapter looked at compilation units, namespaces, and assemblies and discussed different fundamental ways to configure these important C# and .NET elements.

The following are the important points mentioned in this chapter.

Namespaces are used for two main purposes:

- To organize our classes and other types into logical hierarchies when we write our own programs
- As a convenient way to access classes and other types in other components

When a class is inserted into a namespace, its name becomes a combination of the namespace name and the class's short name. This fact prevents name clashes.

A namespace is a logical entity that transcends physical source files and assemblies. A namespace can span over several compilation units and several assemblies.

Zero or more namespaces can be positioned beside each other in a compilation unit or in another namespace. Consequently, namespaces can be nested inside each other to any required depth.

Classes and other types defined outside any explicitly defined namespace automatically belong to a global nameless namespace.

The `using` directive can be used in two ways. First, it allows us to write shorter convenient names in our source code when we reference classes with otherwise long qualified names. Second, it allows us to create aliases for namespaces and classes (or other types).

It is possible to compile many compilation units into the same assembly.

By using the `/t[arget]:` compiler command, you can choose whether an assembly will be a DLL (by writing `library` after the command) for reuse only or a standalone executable (by writing `.exe` after the command).

The namespaces and the classes (types) contained in an assembly can be made available to another EXE or DLL created by the compiler by using the `/r[eference]:` command.

It is often more convenient to have several smaller DLL assemblies than one large DLL (or EXE).

The `Ildasm.exe` utility that ships with the .NET SDK is a simple tool for inspecting the contents of a DLL or EXE assembly.

Review Questions

1. What is the full name of the class defined inside these two namespaces?

```
namespace BliposSoft
{
    namespace RocketSimulation
    {
        class Rocket
        {
            ...
        }
    }
}
```

2. A programmer in an uncontrolled moment of vanity gave the following name to a class:

`ThisIsTheBestRocketClassInTheWholeWideWorldAndTheWholeWideBliposAsWell`

The claim in the name is true, so you need to use this class extensively in your program, but you don't want to write the long name. How can this be avoided?

3. The following class is found in a compilation unit that will be part of a DLL assembly.

```
class Bicycle
{
    double CalculateAirResistance()
    {
        ...
    }

    double WheelRotationsPerMinute()
    {
        ...
    }
}
```

The access modifiers in front of the class and the two methods are missing. Which access modifiers should we put in front of the class and the methods to:

a. Allow all of the class and both methods to be used in another assembly.

b. Prohibit any part of the class to be used in another assembly, but allow the methods to be used within their own assembly.

c. Allow the `CalculateAirResistance` method to be accessed from another assembly, but not the `WheelRotationsPerMinute` method.

d. Allow all of the class to be used in another assembly along with `CalculateAirResistance`, while `WheelRotationsPerMinute` must only be accessed from within the class.

4. You are working for a software company called BikeTech that is planning to write a class library containing the classes from the three main compartments in the company: Bicycle Design, Health and Fitness, and Computer Mapping. Use C# code to illustrate the overall namespace layout you would suggest for this class library.

5. Three different compilation units contain each of the following namespace definitions:

   Compilation unit 1:

```
namespace MyCompany
{
    public class Bicycle
    {
        ...
    }
}
```

   Compilation unit 2:

```
namespace MyCompany.Design
{
    public class Drawer
    {
        ...
    }
}
```

   Compilation unit 3:

```
namespace MyCompany.Design.Tools
{
    public class Cutter
    {
        ...
    }
}
```

   The compilation units are to be compiled into the same assembly. Instead of having three compilation units, write one compilation unit with namespace definitions matching those contained in the three displayed compilation units. Use the nested C# namespace definition format that looks like the following:

```
namespace <outer_namespace>
{
    namespace <inner_namespace>
    {
        etc.
```

6. You have written two source files called `Bicycle.cs` and `Person.cs`. You want to compile them and create a DLL assembly called `healthlib.dll`. You must also reference the following two assemblies to the compiler for this compilation: `mathlib.dll` and `anatomylib.dll`. Write the compiler command you would give to the compiler.

7. What can you use Ildasm for?

Programming Exercises

1. Recall your first object-oriented source code `SimpleElevatorSimulation.cs` in Listing 5.1 of Chapter 5, "Your First Object-Oriented C# Program." It contained three classes in the same compilation unit. In hindsight, it didn't follow the standard convention of one class per compilation unit. Rectify this problem and rewrite the program so that it more correctly contains three compilation units, each with its own class (`Elevator`, `Person`, and `Building`) and all classes properly structured inside a neat namespace hierarchy. Turn these three compilation units into a DLL assembly. (Hint: You should rename the `Main` method from the `Building` class, because this new DLL is for reuse only). Write another source file that performs an `Elevator` simulation similar to that performed by our original program, but this time it uses the namespaces and their classes located in the DLL assembly you created before from the three classes.

2. Perform the same type of exercise as exercise one, but this time use the `BankSimulation.cs` source file in Listing 10.14 of Chapter 10, "Arrays Part I: Array Essentials," as the basis. Write one compilation unit for each of the two classes `Account` and `Bank` and put them in a suitable namespace hierarchy. Compile this part into a DLL assembly. Write the source code for a bank simulation program that uses the namespaces and classes of the created DLL assembly. The functionality of this program should be identical to that of the program we originally created from Listing 10.14.

CHAPTER 16

INHERITANCE PART I: BASIC CONCEPTS

You will learn about the following in this chapter:

- The connection between taxonomical type hierarchies and object-oriented class hierarchies
- Why inheritance is advantageous when implementing classes that naturally fit into a class hierarchy
- The syntax needed for implementing a class hierarchy in C# and, in particular, how to derive a class from a base class
- Virtual functions
- The difference between overriding a method (using the `override` keyword) and re-implementing a new method (using the `new` keyword)
- How access modifiers and class hierarchies interact
- How to preserve the rules of encapsulation while implementing inheritance
- The `protected` and `internal protected` access modifiers
- Constructors and inheritance
- The base-access construct
- The importance of inheritance when reusing class libraries in general and the .NET Framework class library in particular
- Method overriding versus method overloading

An important aspect of object-oriented programming is its extensive support for code reuse, which keeps programmers from the time-consuming and error-prone process of re-implementing software functionality that has already been written and thoroughly tested, often by highly competent programmers.

You have already seen many examples of code reuse in this book, especially of the components in the .NET Framework class library. One of the underlying concepts for the type of code reuse you have experienced so far is called *aggregation*, which was discussed as part of the `SimpleElevatorSimulation.cs` source code in Listing 5.1 of Chapter 5, "Your First Object-Oriented C# Program." You might remember that aggregation let us piece together a class from other types. In our example, the `Elevator` class was composed of three `int` types and one `Person` class. Later, in Chapter 10, "Arrays Part I: Array Essentials," you saw how we could reuse .NET's `Array` class (line 55 of the `BankSimulation.cs` program in Listing 10.14) to create a bank with an array of bank accounts.

Inheritance is another important mechanism found in object-oriented programming to facilitate code reuse. Inheritance allows us to define a new class by *extending* an already existing class. The *derived class* inherits the class members from the old class for free; it is then up to the programmer to specify the differences between the old class and the new class. This is done by

- Adding new class members (function members and data members) to the derived class, which will then consist of the new members plus the members inherited from the old class
- Modify, if needed, how some of the inherited function members behave in the derived class by providing new implementations for those function members

So, whereas aggregation let us compose a `Car` class from its parts (`Engine`, `Wheel`, `Gear-box`, `SteeringWheel`, and other classes), inheritance let us extend a general `Car` class to, for example, create a more specialized `SportsCar` class by stating the differences between a `Car` and a `SportsCar` (better suspension, engine more powerful, and so on) while reusing the parts they have in common (four wheels, steering wheel, front seats, and so on). Often, the `Car` class *has an* `Engine`, has a `Wheel`, and so on, whereas `SportsCar` *is a* `Car`.

Inheritance forms the basis of another powerful object-oriented concept called *polymorphism*, which allows a program to access objects of different types through just one reference variable. This allows the same function name to have several different implementations during one runtime.

Inheritance and polymorphism have profoundly changed software construction and put tremendous power in the hands of the programmer.

This chapter introduces the basic concepts of inheritance. Chapter 17, "Inheritance Part II: Abstract Functions, Polymorphism, and Interfaces," builds on this knowledge.

The Need for Inheritance

The Greek philosopher Aristotle was the first well-known taxonomist in that he began to categorize the objects that surrounded him. When taxonomists categorize part of the world, they create hierarchies of categories that move from the general to the specific.

Note

When working with inheritance, it is useful to view the world through the glasses of a taxonomist.

For example, by using this approach, we can divide transportation vehicles into three broad categories: surface, airborne, and water vehicles, as shown in Figure 16.1; and when moving down the hierarchy, the categories become more specialized.

There are a couple of interesting things to note about the hierarchy in Figure 16.1, which can be generalized to hold for any hierarchy constructed in this manner.

- The relatively few attributes and actions that can be attached to the general category transportation vehicle on the top of the hierarchy are shared among all categories in the hierarchy. For example any car, bicycle, sledge, and so on can be described by the attributes `maximumNumberOfPassengers` and `approximateMaxSpeed` and contain the actions `MoveForward` and `Stop`.
- As we move down the hierarchy to the specialized categories, we can attach specialized attributes and actions that are not associated with the more general categories. For example, a car attribute such as `recommendedTireSize` could not be used on a surface vehicle because surface vehicles also include sledges that usually do not use tires.
- In general, we can say the following about any two categories that are connected by an arrow: The category that the arrow points away from contains the same attributes and actions as the category that the arrow is pointing at, plus some added attributes and actions. For that reason, we can say that the category that the arrow points away from *is* what the arrow points to. For example, bicycle is a surface vehicle, and sports car is a car. However, the contrary is not true. A surface vehicle is not necessarily a bicycle, it could also be a car, a train, or something else.

Note

At first, the arrows in Figure 16.1 seem to point in the wrong direction. A surface vehicle, for example, passes attributes and actions to a car. Shouldn't the directions of the arrows be reversed to illustrate this? Perhaps, but, per convention, the arrows are turned in the other direction for the following reason: Car knows about (or contains) all the attributes and actions that exist in surface vehicle, the reverse is not true.

Life Without Inheritance

Suppose that in our program we need to create objects with the attributes and functionality of a `SportsCar`. We also need objects with the attributes and functionality of a `FamilyCar`, and we need objects that have the attributes and functionality of a `RacingCar` (notice that these all belong to the car category in Figure 16.1). If we hadn't yet been introduced to inheritance, we could go about implementing this in two ways:

- We could reason that all three kinds of objects are car objects and therefore share numerous class members. Consequently, we could write just one class from which all the three kinds of car objects are instantiated.
- We could also reason that the three kinds of objects are so different that three different classes are needed—a `SportsCar` class, a `FamilyCar` class, and a `RacingCar` class.

It is possible to make both approaches work, but each has its own set of serious drawbacks. Let's look closer at the pros and cons of these two approaches.

FIGURE 16.1
Specialization/generalization hierarchy for vehicles.

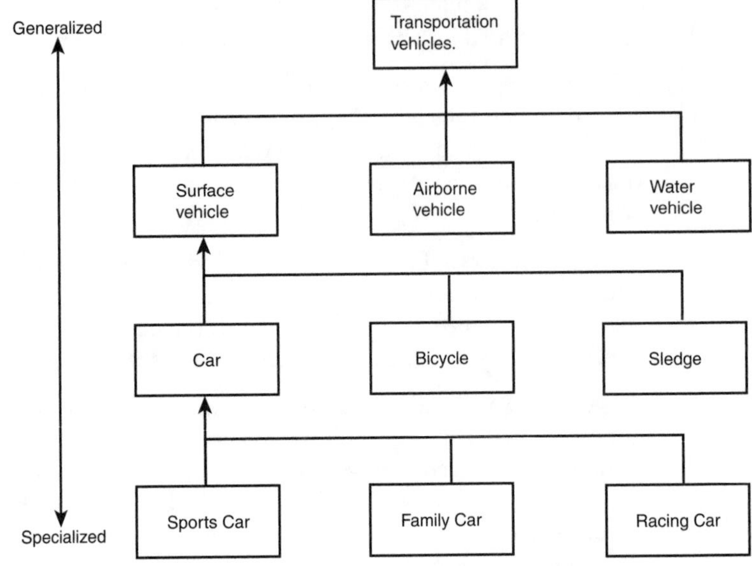

Approach Number 1: One Class

The `SportsFamilyRacingCar` class in Listing 16.1 contains fragments of source code that illustrate the way we would have to go about designing a class to represent objects that could act as the three different kinds of cars.

LISTING 16.1 One Class to create `SportsCar`, `FamilyCar`, and `RacingCar` Objects

```
class SportsFamilyRacingCar
{
    public SportsFamilyRacingCar(string initialTypeOfCar)
    {
        typeOfCar = initialTypeOfCar;
    }
    private readonly string typeOfCar;
    private uint odometer;
    private double engineTemperature;
    private byte NumberOfBabySeats;
    private bool hasBuiltInDogNet;


    private string highPressureFuelPumpSystem;
    ...

    public void StartOnBoardCamera()
    {
        //Start transmitting back to television station.
        //So people can watch race on TV.
    }
```

LISTING 16.1 continued

```
            ...
40:         public void MoveForward()
41:         {
42:             if (typeOfCar == "SportsCar")
43:             {
                    //Move medium fast
50:             }
51:             else if (typeOfCar == "FamilyCar")
52:             {
53:                 //Move slowly
60:             }
61:             else if (typeOfCar == "RacingCar")
62:             {
                    //Move very fast
70:             }
71:             else
72:             {
                    //Invalid type of car
80:             }
81:         }
82:         public double CalculateFuelConsumptionPerKilometer()
83:         {
                ...
90:         }
        ...
99: }
```

Note: The line numbers are somewhat arbitrary (but always increasing) because of the code fragments that are not shown. This code does not compile.

The `SportsFamilyRacingCar` class in Listing 16.1 is loaded with problems, but it also contains a few positive features.

Problem 1: Finding an appropriate name for the class is difficult.

Our problems already start with the naming of the class. It is more than a general car, so the name `Car` seems inappropriate. It is a sports car but not always; it can also be a family or a racing car. So we finally decide on the name `SportsFamilyRacingCar`.

Problem 2: An instance variable must be dedicated to keep track of which car type an object represents.

We need a way to determine what type of car a particular object is representing. This information is kept in the `typeOfCar` instance variable (see line 7), which is meant to hold one of the three strings `"SportsCar"`, `"FamilyCar"`, and `"RacingCar"` (this would better be represented by an `enum`, but we are trying to keep the code short). `typeOfCar` is assigned its value by the constructor in lines 3–6. When we start to fiddle around with instance variables that are meant to keep track of which type a particular object is supposed to be, it is usually a sign that we need to redesign our code. There should be a class for each type of object we want to create.

Advantage 1: Instance variables that are found in all three types of cars are kept in one place, so these variables do not need to be copied and are easy to maintain.

For example, all three types of cars have an `odometer` and an `engineTemperature`, as shown in lines 8 and 9. Had we written three different classes instead, as shown a little later, `odometer` and `engineTemperature` would have to be repeated in the three different classes.

Problem 3: Instance variables that are used in only one of the car types waste memory, bloat the code, and are error prone.

For example, only the family car and perhaps the sports car would need information about the number of baby seats and whether there is a built-in dog net. A `RacingCar` object would carry around these instance variables but never use them. Similarly, the racing car needs to carry information about the type of high-pressure fuel pumping system (to allow for fast refueling during a race) with which it is compatible (see line 15), but this is not needed for any of the other two types.

Problem 4: Function members that are only used in one of the car types bloat the code and are error prone.

For example the `StartOnBoardCamera` method (lines 20–30) is only relevant for a racing car. This method is needed to start its built-in camera that transmits pictures back to the television station during a televised race. However, family car objects still have to carry this method around bloating the code and making the code complex and therefore error prone.

Problem 5: Function members that carry the same name in all three car types but are implemented differently in each car type must contain complicated `if...else` *statements to execute only the code relevant to one type when the function member is called.*

The `MoveForward` method in lines 40–81 is used to illustrate this point. Every time `MoveForward` is called, it has to check which type of car the object is representing with an `if...else` construct to execute the corresponding piece of code. In our example, `MoveForward` causes a `SportsCar` to move medium fast, a `FamilyCar` to move slowly, and a `RacingCar` to move very fast.

Advantage 2: Function members that are identical in all three car types are kept in one place from where maintenance is easy.

The `CalculateFuelConsumptionPerKilometer` in lines 82–90 is an example of a method that is found in all three car types. Any upgrades to this method can be performed in one place, and the upgrades will affect each kind of car object.

Trying to represent three different kinds of car objects with one class has a couple of advantages, as the analysis in this section discussed. But overall, it is a disastrous approach because it is a burdensome task to squeeze all aspects of all three car types into one class. This is illustrated in Figure 16.2.

Writing three different classes is a slightly better approach but still contains inherent problems, as you will see in the next section.

FIGURE 16.2
Squeezing class members of three different car categories into one chaotic class.

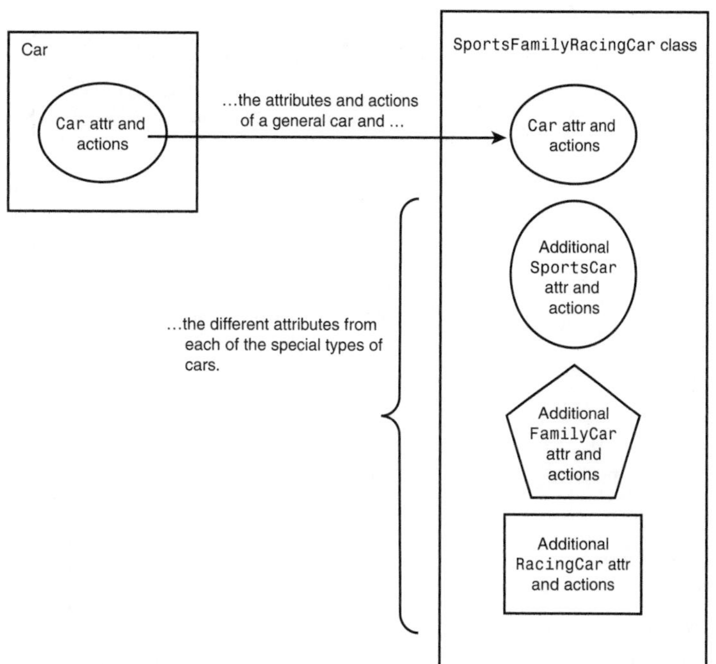

Approach Number 2: Writing Three Classes

Suppose we write three different classes called `SportsCar`, `FamilyCar`, and `RacingCar`. The illustrative parts of the `FamilyCar` class are shown in Figure 16.3. I have not shown the `SportsCar` and `RacingCar` versions because the `FamilyCar` class amply demonstrates the problems and advantages of this approach, which are similar in the two other classes.

The `FamilyCar` class is considerably more peaceful to look at than the contorted `SportsFamilyRacingCar` class from Approach 1.

It is interesting to note that the parts of the code that caused problems 3, 4, and 5 in our previous analysis, give rise to the advantage sections this time, whereas the code that gave rise to the two advantages in the previous approach are causing us problems here. Let's look closer at this phenomenon.

Problem 1: Attributes and actions that belong to a general car must be copied to all three classes.

The class members that are associated with a general car (for example, `odometer`, `engineTemperature`, and the `CalculateFuelConsumptionPerKilometer` method) must be copied around to all three classes, as illustrated in Figure 16.4. This provides a maintenance problem. If a programmer needs to upgrade the `CalculateFuelConsumptionPerKilometer` method, he or she needs to perform this upgrade in all three classes. If instance variables that belong to the general car category need to be added, they must be added to all three classes.

FIGURE 16.3
The `FamilyCar` class.

```
class FamilyCar
{
    private uint odometer;
    private double engineTemperature;

    private byte numberOfBabySeats;
    private bool hasBuiltInDogNet;

    MoveForward
    {
        //Move slowly
    }

    public double CalculateFuelConsumptionPerKilometer()
    {
        ...
    }
    ...
}
```

Copies of these instance variables also exist in the `SportsCar` and `RacingCar` classes

These instance variables are unique to `FamilyCar`.

`MoveForward` also exists in `SportsCar` and `RacingCar` but each with a different implementation

Copies of this method also exist in `SportsCar` and `RacingCar`.

FIGURE 16.4
All three classes contain copies of the attributes and actions of a general car.

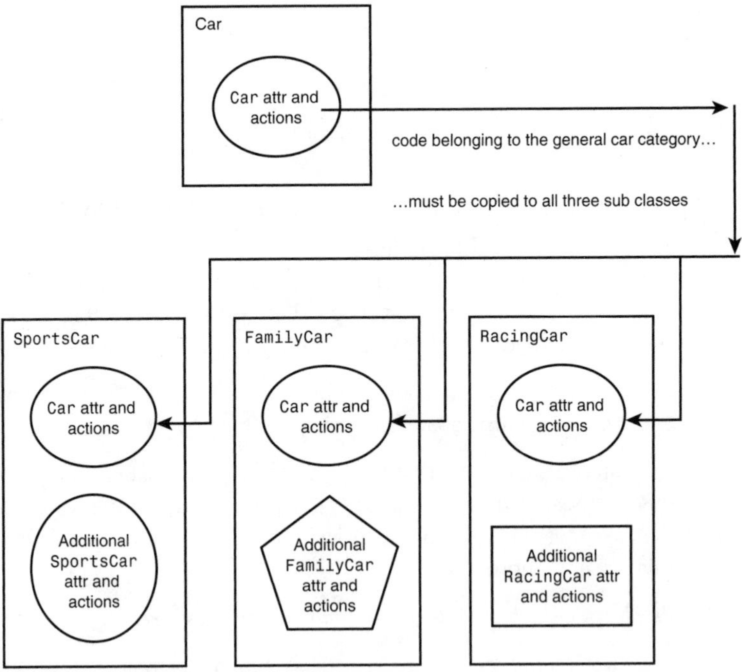

Advantage 1: Unique attributes and actions are seamlessly inserted into each class.

The unique attributes and actions associated with each of the three car categories (illustrated with different shapes in Figure 16.4) are, in stark contrast to the previous approach, elegantly inserted into the class where they belong and do not interfere with any of the other two classes. Similarly, the `MoveForward` method does not need the cumbersome `if...else` statements because we already know at the time the method is being written in which type of object this method will reside.

Our assessments of the two approaches lead us to the following dilemma: Class members that are common to the three car categories are handled correctly by Approach Number 1, but cause us problems in Approach Number 2. Class members that are unique to each car category causes us problems by Approach Number 1, but are handled correctly by Approach Number 2.

Both approaches cause us problems, so let's introduce a third approach that handles both the common and the unique class members correctly, and thereby takes the best from the two approaches while leaving the problems behind.

Approach Number 3: Towards Inheritance. Leaving the Problems Behind

First, we must create a `Car` class and insert the common class members, as shown in Figure 16.5. Then we write three specialized classes `SportsCar`, `FamilyCar`, and `RacingCar`; each containing only the class members that are unique to the class. Finally, we need a mechanism that supports the following statement: Apart from the unique features held by each of the specialized classes, each of these classes must also hold the class members held by the `Car` class. In other words, define three new and more specialized classes by extending the existing `Car` class. Then let the three derived classes *inherit* the class members from the existing `Car` class for free, and add the class members that are unique for each of these new three classes.

The inheritance mechanism provides support for the suggested third approach. Consequently, inheritance is called for when we need to create objects that share a group of class members as well as containing class members that are unique.

Before we look at how inheritance is implemented in C#, it is worth introducing some of the basic terminology used in connection with inheritance.

When `SportsCar` inherits the class members of the `Car` class, we say that `SportsCar` is *derived* from `Car` and that `SportsCar` is a *direct subclass* of the `Car` class. The `Car` class is called the *base class* (and sometimes a *superclass* or a *parent class*) of the `SportsCar` class, because it forms the base of the `SportsCar` class.

FIGURE 16.5
Unique class members in different classes.

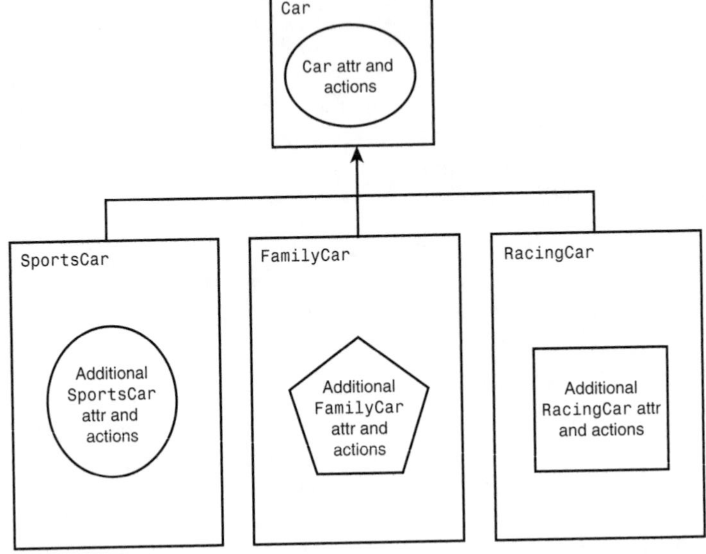

Where:

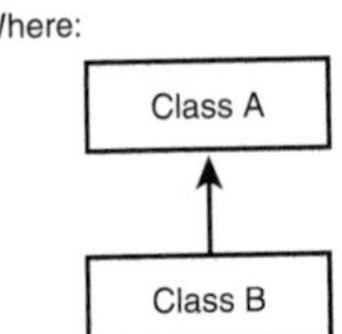

means class B contains the same attributes and actions as class A plus the attributes and actions specified in class B.

Inheritance Fundamentals

The basic syntax for deriving a class from a base class is shown in Syntax Box 16.1. We write the class header of the derived class as usual by specifying any optional modifiers followed by the **`class`** keyword and the classname. The different and important bit in this context is the semicolon (**`:`**) followed by the name of the class we want as a base class for the derived class. The meaning of the semicolon could consequently be "is derived from."

Syntax Box 16.1 Class Definition with Optional Derivation

```
Class_definition_with optional_derivation::=
[<Access_modifier>] class <Derived_class_name> [ : <Base_class_name>]
{
    <Class_members_of_derived_class>
}
```

Note:

The colon followed by the base classname (`: <Base_class_name>`) is called a *class-base specification*.

Example where `SportsCar` is derived from `Car`:

```
class Car
{
    <Car_class_members>
}
class SportsCar : Car
{
    <SportsCar_class_members>
}
```

Listing 16.2 continues the car example introduced previously. Apart from demonstrating the basic syntax for deriving the `RacingCar` class (lines 26–46) from the `Car` class (lines 3–24), it also gives a practical view of why inheritance provides an elegant solution to the problems we encountered in Approach 1 and 2 presented earlier.

LISTING 16.2 SimpleRacingCar.cs

```
01: using System;
02:
03: class Car
04: {
05:     private string brandName;
06:
07:     public string BrandName
08:     {
09:         get
10:         {
11:             return brandName;
12:         }
13:         set
14:         {
15:             brandName = value;
16:         }
17:     }
18:
19:     public double CalculateFuelConsumptionPerKilometer()
20:     {
21:         Console.WriteLine("Now calculating the fuel consumption");
22:         return 0.15;
23:     }
24: }
25:
26: class RacingCar : Car
27: {
28:     private string highPressureFuelPumpSystem;
29:
30:     public string HighPressureFuelPumpSystem
31:     {
32:         get
```

LISTING 16.2 continued

```
33:         {
34:             return highPressureFuelPumpSystem;
35:         }
36:         set
37:         {
38:             highPressureFuelPumpSystem = value;
39:         }
40:     }
41:
42:     public void StartOnBoardCamera()
43:     {
44:         Console.WriteLine("Now filming and transmitting pictures");
45:     }
46: }
47:
48: class CarTester
49: {
50:     public static void Main()
51:     {
52:         Car myGeneralCar = new Car();
53:         RacingCar yourRacingCar = new RacingCar();
54:
55:         myGeneralCar.BrandName = "Volvo";
56:         Console.WriteLine("General car name: " + myGeneralCar.BrandName);
57:         Console.WriteLine("Fuel consumption of normal car: " +
58:             myGeneralCar.CalculateFuelConsumptionPerKilometer());
59:
60:         yourRacingCar.BrandName = "Ferrari";
61:         Console.WriteLine("\nRacing car name: " + yourRacingCar.BrandName);
62:         Console.WriteLine("Fuel consumption of racing car: " +
63:             yourRacingCar.CalculateFuelConsumptionPerKilometer());
64:         yourRacingCar.HighPressureFuelPumpSystem = "MaxPressureLtd";
65:         Console.WriteLine("High pressure fuel pump system: " +
66:             yourRacingCar.HighPressureFuelPumpSystem);
67:         yourRacingCar.StartOnBoardCamera();
68:     }
69: }
```

```
General car name: Volvo
Now calculating the fuel consumption
Fuel consumption of normal car: 0.15

Racing car name: Ferrari
Now calculating the fuel consumption
Fuel consumption of racing car: 0.15
High pressure fuel pump system: MaxPressureLtd
Now filming and transmitting pictures
```

The `Car` class contains class members that are common to all cars. In this case, we have merely included the instance variable `brandName` (line 5), its associated property `BrandName` (lines 7–17), and the `CalculateFuelConsumptionPerKilometer` method (lines 19–23).

Only class members that are specific to the `RacingCar` are written as part of the `RacingCar` class definition. In this case, I have included the `highPressureFuelPumpSystem` (line 28), containing information about the high pressure fuel pumping system with which the racing car is compatible, and the associated `HighPressureFuelPumpSystem` property (lines 30–40). Finally, the `StartOnBoardCamera` method in lines 42–5 have been included.

Because a `RacingCar` is a `Car`, it must also contain the class members of a `Car.` But instead of physically writing these definitions inside `RacingCar`, we simply tell the C# compiler to include them from the `Car` class by writing the semicolon (`:`) followed by `Car` in line 26. Consequently, the `RacingCar` class contains all the class members of the `Car` class, plus the class members written in the `RacingCar` definition. The `Main` method of the `ClassTester` class is used to test this claim. First, it demonstrates the class members of the `Car` class (lines 55–58) through `myGeneralCar` of type `Car` declared in line 52. It then verifies with lines 60–63, and the sample output that we can, in fact, use the `BrandName` property (and therefore also the `brandName` instance variable) and the `CalculateFuelConsumptionPerKilometer` method as if these class members had been defined as part of the `RacingCar` class definition.

We didn't include the `MoveForward` method in this listing, because you need to understand a concept related to inheritance-called method overriding before you can understand how `MoveForward` can be correctly implemented in the `Car` and `RacingCar` classes. Method overriding is the subject of the next section.

Overriding Function Definitions

Recall that the `MoveForward` method was part of each of the three individual car classes, but was implemented differently in each of them (the `FamilyCar` was slow, the `SportsCar` was medium fast, and the `RacingCar` was very fast). We also concluded that `MoveForward` is an action taken by any car, so the `MoveForward` method must, according to our taxonomy-based transportation vehicle hierarchy presented earlier, be part of the `Car` class. This gives rise to the following (solvable) problem when we derive the `RacingCar` (and any of the other two subclasses) from the `Car` class: `MoveForward` will be one of the methods inherited by `RacingCar`. Unfortunately, the implementation of `MoveForward` in `Car` differs from what a correctly implemented `MoveForward` method looks like in `RacingCar`. Instead of adding one kilometer to the odometer, as in the `Car` class (for the moment we assume that this is how the `MoveForward` method is implemented in the `Car` class), we want it to add thirty kilometers in the `RacingCar` class (and five kilometers in the `FamilyCar` class and twenty kilometers in the `SportsCar` class). To solve our problem, we need the ability to *override* the `Car` class's implementation of the `MoveForward` method in each of the subclasses with an implementation that is suitable for each of the three classes. This is illustrated in Figure 16.6.

Note

An `abstract` method does not have any implementation; instead, it forces any derived class to provide the implementation. Most programmers would argue that `MoveForward` should be implemented as an `abstract` method in the `Car` class, because even though it must be part of `Car`, we don't know exactly what it is supposed to do (we don't know the speed of a general `Car`). We only have a better idea of this when `MoveForward` exists in a more specialized class, such as `SportsCar` (medium fast). `abstract` methods and the `abstract` keyword are elements closely related to inheritance. These concepts are discussed in the beginning of Chapter 17, "Inheritance Part II: `abstract` Functions, Polymorphism, and Interfaces."

`MoveForward` has been implemented as a normal non-abstract method in the `Car` class for demonstration purposes and because we haven't yet introduced `abstract` methods.

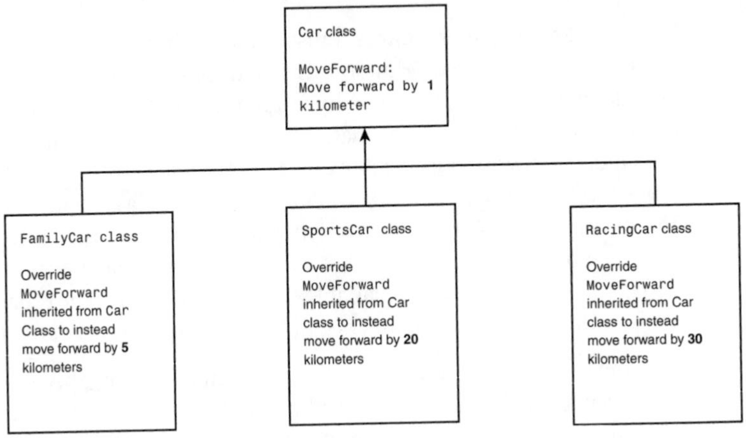

FIGURE 16.6
Overriding the *`MoveForward`* method of the *`Car`* class.

Car class

MoveForward:
Move forward by **1**
kilometer

FamilyCar class

Override
MoveForward
inherited from Car
Class to instead
move forward by **5**
kilometers

SportsCar class

Override
MoveForward
inherited from Car
class to instead
move forward by **20**
kilometers

RacingCar class

Override
MoveForward
inherited from Car
class to instead
move forward by **30**
kilometers

Listing 16.3 demonstrates how overriding is implemented in C#.

LISTING 16.3 `OverridingMoveForward.cs`

```
using System;

class Car
{
    private uint odometer = 0;

    protected uint Odometer
    {
        set
        {
            odometer = value;
        }
        get
        {
            return odometer;
        }
    }

    public virtual void MoveForward()
    {
        Console.Write("Moving forward... ");
        odometer += 1;
        Console.WriteLine("Odometer reading: {0}", odometer);
    }
}

class RacingCar : Car
{
```

LISTING 16.3 continued

```
29:     public override void MoveForward()
30:     {
31:         Console.Write("Moving dangerously fast forward... ");
32:         Odometer += 30;
33:         Console.WriteLine("Odometer in racing car: {0}",
34:             Odometer);
35:     }
36: }
37:
38: class FamilyCar : Car
39: {
40:     public override void MoveForward()
41:     {
42:         Console.Write("Moving slowly but safely forward...");
43:         Odometer += 5;
44:         Console.WriteLine("Odometer in family car: {0}",
45:             Odometer);
46:     }
47: }
48:
49: class CarTester
50: {
51:     public static void Main()
52:     {
53:         RacingCar myRacingCar = new RacingCar();
54:         FamilyCar myFamilyCar = new FamilyCar();
55:         myRacingCar.MoveForward();
56:         myFamilyCar.MoveForward();
57:     }
58: }
```

```
Moving dangerously fast forward... Odometer in racing car: 30
Moving slowly but safely forward...Odometer in family car: 5
```

Listing 16.3 contains a `Car` class (lines 3–25) with a `MoveForward` method, which as described before advances the `odometer` instance variable (declared in line 5) by 1 in line 22. The `RacingCar` (lines 27–36) and the `FamilyCar` classes (lines 38–47) both contain overriding definitions (lines 29–35 and 40–46, respectively) of the `MoveForward` method that are suited for each of these two classes.

To allow the `MoveForward` method (defined in lines 19–24) of the `Car` class to be overridden in a derived class, it must be declared to be a `virtual` method, as in line 19.

If a derived class is to `override` a method found in its base class, the derived class must include a method with the same name as the overridden method. In our case, this is accomplished by including a method called `MoveForward` in the `RacingCar` and `FamilyCar` classes. Further, this overriding method definition must have the same number and types of parameters as in the base class. This is also fulfilled in the method headers of lines 29 and 40, because the number of parameters is zero, like the `MoveForward` method defined in the `Car` class.

When you derive a new class from a base class, you might, while you are writing the derived class, define a method with the same name and parameter types as a method in the base class by pure chance. In this case, your intent is not to override the method but simply to create a new method. It is important for programmers reading through your code to know whether you are creating a new method or whether you are overriding a method in the base class. This is because an overridden method in the base class has the same basic interpretation as the method that is overriding it in a sub class, but with a different implementation. On the other hand, a new method that coincidentally has the same name and parameters can be related to something completely different. For example, if we purposefully override the `MoveForward` method in the derived class, this method will be implemented differently but will most certainly be related to how the vehicle is moving around physically. A coincidental `MoveForward` might, on the other hand, deal with time and perhaps increase the age of the car instead of the odometer, or perhaps move the car forward through different design stages.

For those reasons, the compiler reminds you with a warning to state whether you are overriding or creating a new method. Consequently, if you define a method with the same name and parameter types as a method in the base class, you will see a warning. To remove this warning you need to state your intent:

- If you are overriding the method, you must include the `override` keyword, as in lines 29 and 40.
- If your name and parameter types are matching those of the base type only by coincidence, you must include the `new` keyword.

Note

If you remove the `override` keyword in line 40, you will get the following warning:

```
OverridingMoveForward.cs(39,17): warning CS0114: 'FamilyCar.MoveForward()'
 hides inherited member 'Car.MoveForward()'. To make the current method
override that implementation, add the override keyword. Otherwise add the
 new keyword.
```

The `protected` keyword in line 7 is an access modifier that provides the same access as the `private` access modifier with one difference: `protected` also allows access from classes that are derived from `Car`. In this case, we declare the `Odometer` property to be `protected`, because the overriding `MoveForward` methods in the derived classes need access to this property (lines 32, 34, 43, and 45), and at the same time, we are ensuring that no other classes get access to `Odometer`.

Note

Some programmers would, with good reason, argue that the `Odometer` property should be declared `public` because other classes will need to get at least read-only access to the `odometer` instance variable.

As expected, the sample output generated by the calls to `MoveForward` in lines 55 and 56 confirms that we are calling two different methods, each suited for the object for which it is called.

Syntax Box 16.2 describes the formalities of overriding a base class method in a derived class. There are two obvious things you must do to make overriding work properly:

- Include the `virtual` keyword in the base class method (shown first in the syntax box).
- Include the `override` keyword in the overriding method of the derived class method (shown second).

However, there are a couple of other points you need to be aware of, as mentioned in the syntax box notes.

Syntax Box16.2 Base Class Identifier

```
class <Base_class_identifier>
{
    ...
    <Access_modifier> virtual <Return_type> <Method_identifier>
    ➥([<Formal_parameter_list>])
    {
        <Statements>
    }
    ...
}

class <Derived_class_identifier>
{
    ...
    <Access_modifier> override <Return_type> <Method_identifier>
    ➥([<Formal_parameter_list>])
    {
        <Statements>
    }
    ...
}
```

where

```
<Access_modifier>::=
                 public
                 protected
                 internal
                 protected internal
```

Notes:

- A `virtual` method cannot be `private`.
- If a method in a derived class is to override a method in the base class, it must have the same name and parameter types (number and sequence of types must match) as the base class.
- An overriding method must have the same access modifier and return type as the overridden method in the base class.

- In addition to `non-static` methods, `non-static` properties and `non-static` indexers can also be declared `virtual`. No other function members can be declared `virtual` and, as a result, can never be overridden.

virtual Functions

As mentioned previously, you omit the `virtual` keyword to prevent a function from being overridden. You are likely to declare most of your functions to be `virtual`.

sealed Classes

You can prevent a whole class from being used as a base class by declaring the class to be `sealed`. For example, you cannot derive a class from the following class:

```
sealed class MyMath
{
    ...
}
```

which makes the following class definition invalid:

```
class MoreMath : MyMath
{
    ...
}
```

Three common reasons for declaring a class `sealed` are as follows:

- The class is comprised of only static class members. For example, the .NET Framework's Math class is a sealed class because it only contains static class members.
- The class design is not suitable as a base class, perhaps because its inner structure is delicate, which could easily cause derived classes to create fatal mistakes. The .NET Framework's String class belongs to this category and is, for that reason, sealed.
- Non-virtual functions and sealed classes provide faster execution because the compiler knows more about how they will be used.

Access Modifiers and Inheritance

The `private` and the `protected` access modifiers are especially important in connection with inheritance. This section looks closer at these modifiers, along with the ability to declare a class member `protected`, `internal`, or `internal protected`.

The `protected` Access Modifier

As mentioned in the analysis of Listing 16.3, a `protected` class member can be accessed only from within its own class (like a `private` member) and from its subclasses. You should avoid declaring data members to be `protected` because it breaks with the encapsulation principles discussed in Chapter 3, "A Guided Tour Through C#: Part I." The next section looks more closely at this issue.

Accessing `private` Base Class Members

The `Car` class presented in Figure 16.7 is slightly different from the `Car` class presented in Listing 16.3, in that it does not contain the `protected` property `Odometer` to provide access to its `private` instance variable `odometer`. Consequently, `odometer` has to be accessed by referring to its own name. This is fine as long as we are accessing `odometer` from inside the `Car` class, as is done in its `MoveForward` method (see Figure 16.7). However, a `private` class member cannot be referenced by its name outside the class where it is declared. So `odometer` cannot be accessed from any derived classes, such as `RacingCar`, even though `odometer` is one of `RacingCar`'s inherited class members.

Observe that if we had not overridden the `MoveForward` method of the `Car` class in the `RacingCar` class, `MoveForward` would have been passed on to the `RacingCar` class containing the original implementation specified in the `Car` class. This would allow us to call `MoveForward` for an object of the `RacingCar` class because this inherited method, even though now called through `RacingCar`, was originally defined in the `Car` class.

FIGURE 16.7
`private` base class members cannot be directly accessed in subclasses.

```
using System;

class Car
{
    private uint odometer = 0;

    public virtual void MoveForward()
    {
        Console.Write("Moving forward... ");
        odometer += 1;
        Console.WriteLine("Odometer reading: {0}",
            odometer);
    }
}

class RacingCar : Car
{
    public override void MoveForward()
    {
        Console.Write("Moving dangerously fast forward... ");
        odometer += 30;
        Console.WriteLine("Odometer in racing car: {0}",
            odometer);
    }
}
```

1 `odometer` is declared `private`. `private` class members can *only* be accessed from within its own class, making...

2 ...these two statements valid, but...

3 ...these two statements invalid...

4 ...even though `odometer` is inherited by the `RacingCar` class.

Our discussion in this section does not change the fact that all instance variables should be declared `private`. So the correct way to provide access to a `private` instance variable of a base class from a derived class is through a property or method that is defined in the base class and declared either `protected` (such as the `Odometer` property in Listing 16.3), `internal`, or `public`.

Why do we need to insist that all instance variables should be declared `private` and not `protected` so they are not even accessible in subclasses? After all, a `RacingCar` is a `Car`; so it should have as much right to access an odometer as a `Car`. Why can't we at least make instance variables accessible to subclasses with the `protected` keyword? The problem is this: If we declare an instance variable of a base class `protected`, anybody who wants to gain access to this instance variable merely needs to derive a class from this base class and is immediately granted access. The `protected` variable then becomes highly accessible for anybody who is willing to put in the extra effort.

Do Not Declare Any Function That Could Be of Value to a Subclass as *`private`*

Even though `private` instance variables are only accessible through a function member defined in the base class, private instance variables are, as we have seen earlier, still inherited from the base class. Similarly, `private` base class function members (except for constructors and destructors) are also inherited from the base class and can only be accessed from function member definitions that were written in the base class and then inherited by the derived class. It is impossible to write new or overriding function members in the derived class that call the `private` methods (properties and indexers) inherited from the base class.

So, functions that you think could be of value to a derived class should not be declared `private`; they should be made available with one of the other access modifiers.

The `internal protected` Access Modifier

Recall the `internal` access modifier presented in Chapter 15, "Namespaces, Compilation Units, and Assemblies." It grants access to all classes within the same assembly. It is possible to combine `internal` with the `protected` access modifier to form the `internal protected` access modifier, which is demonstrated in the following line:

```
internal protected int myNumber;
```

`myNumber` is now accessible from

- Within the class where it is declared
- Within a class that has been derived from the class where `myNumber` is declared
- Within a class that belongs to the same assembly as `myNumber`'s class

Briefly stated, `internal protected` provides `internal` or `protected` access.

Note

The `internal protected` access modifier does *not* provide `internal` access AND `protected` access, (meaning access only from within its own class and from within a derived class that belongs to the same assembly). You can, however, implement this by declaring your class `internal` and the class member `protected`.

C#'s Access Modifiers: An Overview

Presenting the `internal protected` access modifier concludes our journey through the access modifiers found in C#. Table 16.1 provides a brief overview of C#'s access modifiers.

TABLE 16.1 Overview of C#'s Access Modifiers

Access Modifier	Meaning
`private`	A `private` type member is only accessible from within the type where it is defined. Class and struct members are `private` by default.
`public`	A `public` type or type member is accessible from any part of the program.
`internal`	An `internal` type or type member is accessible only from within the assembly where it is defined.
`protected`	A `protected` class member is accessible only from within the class where it is defined or from within a class that is derived from that class.
`internal protected`	An `internal protected` class member is accessible only from within the class where it is defined or from within a class that is derived from that class or from within the assembly where it is defined.

Derived Class Constructors

Regardless of their access modifiers, the constructors of a base class are never inherited by the derived class. Despite this fact, they can still be called from the constructors of the derived class and, in certain cases, the compiler will implicitly provide the necessary call back to a base class constructor. After all, a part of the derived class is from the base class, so the base class constructors are highly suited to initialize the base class part of the derived class.

Note

Like their constructor siblings, destructors are not inherited by the derived class.

Recall from Chapter 13, "Class Anatomy Part II: Object Creation and Garbage Collection" that we can invoke one constructor B from a constructor A of the same class. This will cause the statements of constructor B to be executed before the statements of constructor A. Syntactically, this was done by attaching the constructor initializer shown in the following line

```
: this (<Argument_list>)
```

to the header of the constructor to, for example, form the following construction:

```
class Dog
{
    ...
    public Dog (string initialName) : this()
    {
        ...
    }
    ...
    public Dog()
    {
        ...
    }
    ...
}
```

The constructor initializer will invoke...

...this constructor to be executed before the statements of its own constructor are executed.

Similarly, it is possible to invoke a constructor residing in a base class from a constructor in a derived class by attaching the following constructor initializer instead of the `: this` (<*Argument_list*> constructor initializer:

```
: base (<Argument_list>)
```

Like its sibling, it will look for a constructor that has a formal parameter list that matches that of the <*Argument_list*> in terms of their number and types; but this time, it will look in the base class instead of the same class.

Listing 16.4 illustrates this scenario and demonstrates why it makes sense to call base class constructors from constructors of derived classes. To this end the two constructors of the `RacingCar` class both use a constructor initializer (line 34 and line 39) to execute a constructor from the `Car` class.

LISTING 16.4 `DerivedClassConstructors.cs`

```
01: using System;
02:
03: class Car
04: {
05:     private string brandName;
06:
```

LISTING 16.4 continued

```
    public Car(string initialBrandName)
    {
        brandName = initialBrandName;
    }

    public Car()
    {
        brandName = "unknown";
    }

    public string BrandName
    {
        get
        {
            return brandName;
        }
        set
        {
            brandName = value;
        }
    }
}

class RacingCar : Car
{
    private string onBoardCameraName;

    public RacingCar() : base()
    {
        onBoardCameraName = "unknown";
    }

    public RacingCar(string initialBrandName, string initialCameraName)
    ➥ : base(initialBrandName)
    {
        onBoardCameraName = initialCameraName;
    }

    public string OnBoardCameraName
    {
        get
        {
            return onBoardCameraName;
        }
        set
        {
            onBoardCameraName = value;
        }
    }
}

class CarTester
```

LISTING 16.4 continued

```
58: {
59:     public static void Main()
60:     {
61:         Car myNoNameCar = new Car();
62:         Car myCar = new Car("Volvo");
63:         RacingCar myNoNameRacingCar = new RacingCar();
64:         RacingCar yourRacingCar = new RacingCar("Ferrari", "Sony");
65:         Console.WriteLine("The name of myNoNameCar: "
66:             + myNoNameCar.BrandName);
67:         Console.WriteLine("The name of myCar: " + myCar.BrandName);
68:         Console.WriteLine("The name of myNoNameRacingCar: "
69:             + myNoNameRacingCar.BrandName);
70:         Console.WriteLine("The camera name of myNoNameRacingCar: "
71:             + myNoNameRacingCar.OnBoardCameraName);
72:         Console.WriteLine("The name of yourRacingCar: "
73:             + yourRacingCar.BrandName);
74:         Console.WriteLine("The camera name of yourRacingCar: "
75:             + yourRacingCar.OnBoardCameraName);
76:     }
77: }
```

```
The name of myNoNameCar: unknown
The name of myCar: Volvo
The name of myNoNameRacingCar: unknown
The camera name of myNoNameRacingCar: unknown
The name of yourRacingCar: Ferrari
The camera name of yourRacingCar: Sony
```

The `Car` class spanning lines 3–28 contains one instance variable called `brandName`. Two constructors have been defined to initialize this instance variable. The first constructor (lines 7–10) has one formal parameter of type `string`, the other (lines 12–15) takes no arguments. The property in lines 17–27 has simply been written so we can check the contents of `brandName`.

The `RacingCar` class (lines 30–55) is derived from the `Car` class. Therefore, it contains two instance variables—the `brandName` variable inherited from the `Car` class and the `onBoardCameraName` declared within its own class body. Both instance variables need to be initialized. `onBoardCameraName` can be initialized with constructors in the usual way, but `brandName` is more problematic because it is `private`. Furthermore, the correct code for initializing it has already been written in the `Car` class, so let's reuse it. The constructor initializer, described earlier, lets us do exactly this.

The first constructor of the `RacingCar` class (lines 34–37) does not take any arguments, so it simply assigns the string `"unknown"` to the `onBoardCameraName` and, because we also don't have any value to assign to the `brandName` variable, we call the default constructor (that takes no arguments) of the `Car` class, as shown in Figure 16.8. It assigns the value `"unknown"` to the `brandName` variable.

The second constructor takes two arguments. The first argument is meant for `brandName` and the second is for `onBoardCameraName`. This time, we call the `Car` class constructor that takes one argument because we know the value (`initialBrandName`) that should be assigned to `brandName`, and we know that this base class constructor does exactly what we want—it assigns the `initialBrandName` to the `brandName` variable (see line 9).

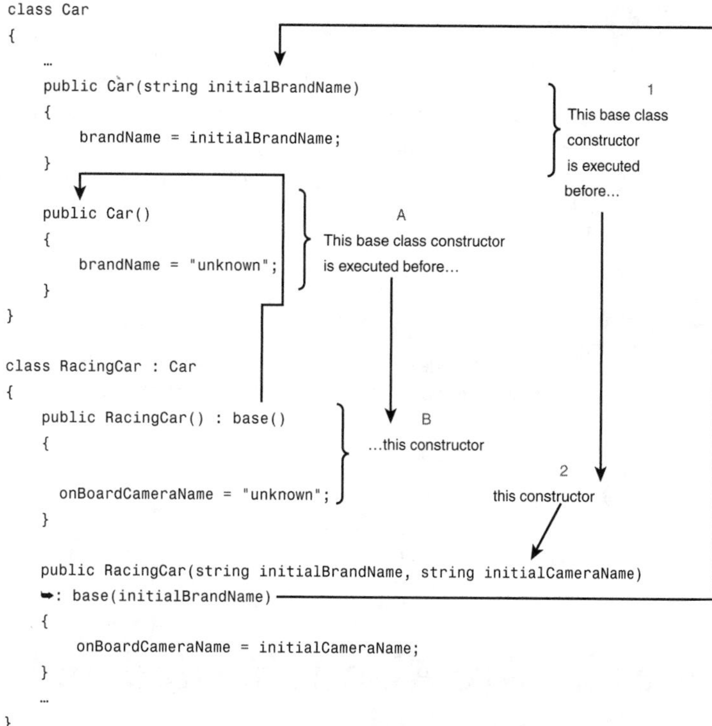

FIGURE 16.8
Invoking a base class constructor with the constructor initializer.

The `Main` method of the `CarTester` class verifies the constructors of the `Car` and the `RacingCar` classes. It uses the properties `BrandName` and `OnBoardCameraName` to access the `brandName` and `onBoardCameraName` instance variables.

Any constructor in a derived class that does not include one of the two constructor initializers `:this(`<*Argument_list*>`)` or `:base(`<*Argument_list*>`)` will, by default, get a constructor initializer attached by the compiler, which will call the default base class constructor. So the following constructor from the `RacingCar` class in Listing 16.4

```
public RacingCar() : base()
{
    onBoardCameraName = "unknown";
}
```

is identical to the following constructor, which has had the constructor initializer removed:

```
public RacingCar()
{
    onBoardCameraName = "unknown";
}
```

The compiler will insert this constructor initializer, even if no default constructor has been defined for the base class. If no default constructor exists in the base class under these circumstances, the compiler will report an error.

Note

Here are a couple of important reminders from Chapter 13:

A default constructor is a constructor without any formal parameters.

As soon as you define your own constructor in a class, the compiler assumes that you are taking care of the constructor side of things and will not supply any default constructor. It is then up to you to define one.

Tip

As a general guideline, a constructor in a derived class should always include a constructor initializer that calls an appropriate constructor in the base class.

Note

Only one constructor initializer can be attached to a constructor.

Indexers Are Also Inherited and Can Be Overridden

Even though Chapter 14, "Class Anatomy III: Writing Intuitive Code," told us that indexers do not carry a name, like its method and property siblings, but instead are called by referring to an object name followed by a pair of square brackets enclosing an indexer, they are still inherited and can be overridden like methods and properties. Listing 16.5 demonstrates how an indexer can be overridden and also introduces a new use for the `base` keyword (other than when used as part of the constructor initializer discussed earlier), which allows you to call the indexer of a base class.

LISTING 16.5 `SeasonalAdjustment.cs`

```
using System;

class ProductionList
{
    private uint[] production = new uint[4];

    public virtual uint this [uint index]
    {
```

LISTING 16.5 continued

```
        get
        {
            return production[index];
        }

        set
        {
            production[index] = value;
        }
    }
}

class ProductionSeasonAdjust : ProductionList
{
    public override uint this [uint index]
    {
        get
        {
            if(index < 2)
               return base[index] + 50;
            else
                return base[index] - 30;
        }

        set
        {
            base[index] = value;
        }
    }

    public uint TotalSeasonalAdjusted
    {
        get
        {
            uint tempTotal = 0;

            for(uint i = 0; i < 4; i++)
            {
                tempTotal += this[i];
            }
            return tempTotal;
        }
    }
}

class Tester
{
    public static void Main()
    {
        ProductionSeasonAdjust prodAdjust = new ProductionSeasonAdjust();

        prodAdjust[0] = 100;
```

LISTING 16.5 continued

```
61:             prodAdjust[1] = 300;
62:             prodAdjust[2] = 200;
63:             prodAdjust[3] = 500;
64:             Console.WriteLine("Production in first quarter season adjusted: " +
65:                 prodAdjust[0]);
66:             Console.WriteLine("Total production seasonally adjusted: " +
67:                 prodAdjust.TotalSeasonalAdjusted);
68:         }
69: }
```

```
Production in first quarter season adjusted: 150
Total production seasonally adjusted: 1140
```

The `ProductionList` class (lines 3–19) is meant to hold quarterly industrial production figures from part of the economy in a country. The class represents the `production` array declared in line 5, so an indexer is implemented in lines 7–18 to provide convenient access to this array. Notice that line 7 declares the indexer to be `virtual`.

We want to create another class that also represents quarterly industrial production figures, but that instead will return a seasonally adjusted production figure. To simplify matters, seasonally adjusted here simply means that if the production figure is from the first or the second quarter (index `0` or `1` in the `production` array), add 50 to its value when requested; otherwise, deduct 30. We also want to include a property called `TotalSeasonAdjusted`, which returns the sum of the values in the `production` array with each of the quarterly figures being seasonally adjusted before it is added to the total.

To implement these functionalities, we create a new class called `ProductionSeasonAdjust` (lines 21–37) and derive it from the `ProductionList` class. The indexer defined in lines 23–37 overrides the indexer in `ProductionList`. If the requested index is less than two, it must return the value of the `production` array plus 50; if greater than or equal to 2, it must return the value of the `production` array minus 30. This poses a problem: Even though the `production` array is inherited by the `ProductionSeasonAdjust`, it was declared `private` in the `ProductionList` class, so we cannot access it directly from `ProductionSeasonAdjust`. The problem could be resolved if we could somehow call the indexer of the base class, because this indexer accesses `production`. Fortunately, the *base-access* construct does exactly this.

The base access construct consists of the keyword `base` followed by a pair of square brackets that encloses an index. It must be positioned in a function member of a derived class. The base access construct will invoke the indexer in the base class that has an index of the same type as the index of the base access construct. In our case, the following part of line 28 and 30

```
base[index]
```

calls the indexer in lines 7–18 of the base class and passes along the value of its `index` parameter. Consequently `base[index]` becomes equal to the value returned from line 11 `(production[index])`. Thus, according to our seasonal adjustment requirements we need to add 50 to `base[index]` if `index` is less than 2; otherwise; we must deduct 30 from base[index] before the value is returned to the caller. This functionality is implemented in lines 27–31.

The TotalSesonalAdjusted property sums up the seasonally adjusted figures by calling the indexer of the class it resides inside (because it already returns seasonally adjusted figures as we have just seen) with the following call:

```
this[i]
```

Notice its similarity to the base access construct base[index]. Whereas this[i] calls an indexer from the same class, base[index] calls an indexer defined in the base class.

The Main method inserts the value 100 into production[0] in line 60. It is then printed in lines 64 and 65, but with a seasonal adjustment of plus 50, which correctly results in 150 being printed. The TotalSeasonalAdjusted property correctly returns the result 1140, which is calculated as follows

$$(100+50)+(300+50)+(200-30)+(500-30) = 1140$$

The base access construct not only allows you to access base class indexers but also base class members, as you will see in the next section.

Calling an Overridden Function in the Base Class

Listing 16.5 demonstrated our ability to call an indexer of a base class from a derived class with the base access construct. You can also call a method or a property of a base class from a derived class in a similar fashion. Listing 16.6 gives an example of how a method of a base class method can be called with the base access construct from a derived class and why it sometimes can be useful.

LISTING 16.6 CallingOverriddenMethod.cs

```
using System;

class Car
{
    private string brandName;
    private uint odometer;

    public Car(string initialBrandName, uint initialOdometer)
    {
        brandName = initialBrandName;
        odometer = initialOdometer;
    }
```

LISTING 16.6 continued

```

    public Car()
    {
        brandName = "unknown";
        odometer = 0;
    }

    public virtual void PrintAllInfo()
    {
        Console.WriteLine("Brand name: " + brandName);
        Console.WriteLine("Odometer: " + odometer);
    }
}

class RacingCar : Car
{
    private string onBoardCameraName;

    public RacingCar(string initialBrandName, uint initialOdometer,
        string initialCameraName) : base(initialBrandName, initialOdometer)
    {
        onBoardCameraName = initialCameraName;
    }

    public RacingCar() : base()
    {
        onBoardCameraName = "unknown";
    }

    public override void PrintAllInfo()
    {
        base.PrintAllInfo();
        Console.WriteLine("On board camera name: " + onBoardCameraName);
    }
}

class CarTester
{
    public static void Main()
    {
        RacingCar yourRacingCar = new RacingCar("Lotus", 2000, "Nikon");
        yourRacingCar.PrintAllInfo();
    }
}
```

```
Brand name: Lotus
Odometer: 2000
On board camera name: Nikon
```

The `RacingCar` class (lines 27–47) contains three instance variables—the two instance variables it inherits from the `Car` class (declared in lines 5 and 6) and `onBoardCameraName` (declared in line 29). (As mentioned earlier, an on-board camera is often used in a professional racing car to film and transmit pictures from the racing car to a television audience).

The `PrintAllInfo` method simply prints the values of all the instance variables of an object. In the `Car` class, it prints out the `brandName` and the `odometer` variables. In the `RacingCar` class, `PrintAllInfo` needs to print the `onBoardCameraName` as well as `brandName` and `odometer`. Because the requirements of `PrintAllInfo` in `RacingCar` are different from `PrintAllInfo` in `Car`, we need to override `PrintAllInfo` in the `RacingCar` class. We now encounter two incentives to use the base access construct to call `PrintAllInfo` of `Car` from within `PrintAllInfo` of `RacingCar`. First, we somehow need access to the `brandName` and `odometer` instance variables from `PrintAllInfo` in the `RacingCar` class, but direct access is not possible because they are both declared `private`. Second, `PrintAllInfo` of `Car` is providing part of the functionality needed by `PrintAllInfo` of `RacingCar` in that it prints two of the three instance variables that `PrintAllInfo` of `RacingCar` needs to print. So, if we can somehow call `PrintAllInfo` of the `Car` class from within `PrintAllInfo` in `RacingCar`, all that is left to do is to print the `onBoardCameraName`. This is done in lines 42–46. Line 44 calls `PrintAllInfo` for `RacingCar`'s base class `Car` with the keyword `base` followed by `PrintAllInfo`. `RacingCar`'s `PrintAllInfo` method then only needs to include line 45, which prints out the `onBoardCameraName`.

Syntax Box 16.3 contains the base access syntax for calling a method, property, or indexer of a base class from a derived class.

Syntax Box 16.3 Base Access

```
Base_access(method)::=
                base.<Base_class_method_name> (<Argument_list>);

Base_access(property)::=
                base.<Base_class_property_name>;

Base_access(indexer)::=
                base[<expression1> [, <expression2>, <expression3>…] ]
```

Notes:

- The <Argument_list> provided for the `Base_access(method)` must match the formal parameter list (their number and types) of the method called in the base class.
- The expression list provided for the `Base_access(indexer)` must match (their number and types) an indexer of the base class.
- Any of the three base access constructs can only be written inside the block of a constructor, an instance method, or a `get` or `set` accessor of a property or indexer.

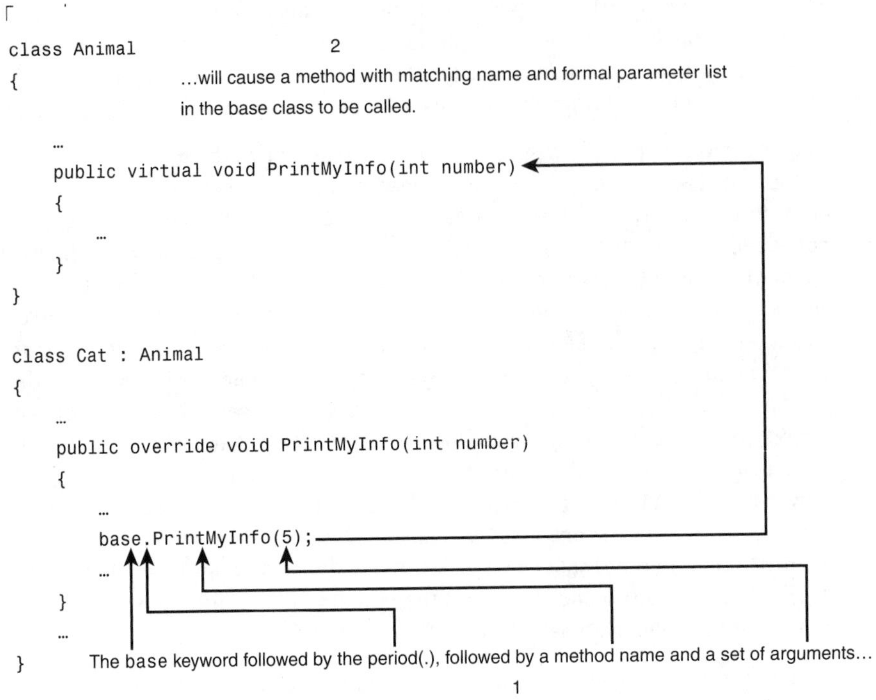

```
class Animal
{
    ...
    public virtual void PrintMyInfo(int number)
    {
        ...
    }
}

class Cat : Animal
{
    ...
    public override void PrintMyInfo(int number)
    {
        ...
        base.PrintMyInfo(5);
        ...
    }
    ...
}
```

1 The base keyword followed by the period(.), followed by a method name and a set of arguments...

2 ...will cause a method with matching name and formal parameter list in the base class to be called.

Reusing the .NET Framework Class Library with Inheritance

Many of the classes in the .NET Framework class library have been designed to be base classes from which we are meant to derive new classes in our code. The `System.Windows.Forms.Form` (from now on simply referred to as `Form`) class is a core class for writing Windows GUI applications in .NET. Anybody who wants to write Windows GUI applications must derive classes from this base class.

Listing 16.7 demonstrates how easy it is to draw a window similar to that shown in the sample output after the listing by deriving a class from the `Form` class. Even though the displayed window looks a bit empty, it nevertheless has all the capabilities that we have come to expect from a standard window. For example, you can resize it by dragging its borders and it can be minimized, maximized, closed and dragged around on the screen; an impressive amount of functionality in return for a program taking only 15 lines of code. Furthermore, it forms the basis for any window that could contain buttons, text fields, special graphics, and so on.

Note

The Form class resides in a dll called `System.Windows.Forms.dll`. At this time of writing, the compiler automatically references this library, so there is no need to explicitly reference this library when you compile the code in Listing 16.7.

LISTING 16.7 MyFirstGUI.cs

```
01: using System.Windows.Forms;
02:
03: public class frmMain : Form
04: {
05:     public frmMain()
06:     {
07:         this.Text = "My First Form";
08:     }
09:
10:     public static void Main()
11:     {
12:         frmMain myFirstForm = new frmMain();
13:         Application.Run(myFirstForm);
14:     }
15: }
```

The `Form` class is a highly complex class with many functions and data members that enable it to create and support a fully functioning window. By deriving the `frmMain` from the `Form` class as in line 3, `frmMain` inherits all these capabilities. This allows us to, for example, write a constructor (lines 5–8) that assigns the text “My First Form” to one of `frmMain`'s inherited properties called `Text`, which controls the title on the title bar as confirmed by the appearing window.

Line 12 creates a new instance of `frmMain` called `myFirstForm`, which is then passed as an argument to the `Run` method. `Run` is a `static` method contained in the `Application` class of the `System.Windows.Forms` namespace. Passing `myFirstForm` to `Run` displays it onscreen and enables it to react to events, such as mouse clicks on its maximize, minimize, and close buttons.

Multiple Levels of Derived Classes

It is possible to use a derived class as a base class for another derived class. In other words, you can create as many levels of derived classes as you want. For example, you could create a general `TransportationVehicle` class in line with Figure 16.1 and, from this class, derive a `SurfaceVehicle` class. This again could be a base class for a `Car` class that finally could become the base class for our well-known `SportsCar`, `FamilyCar`, and `RacingCar` classes, as illustrated in Figure 16.9.

FIGURE 16.9
Multiple levels of inheritance.

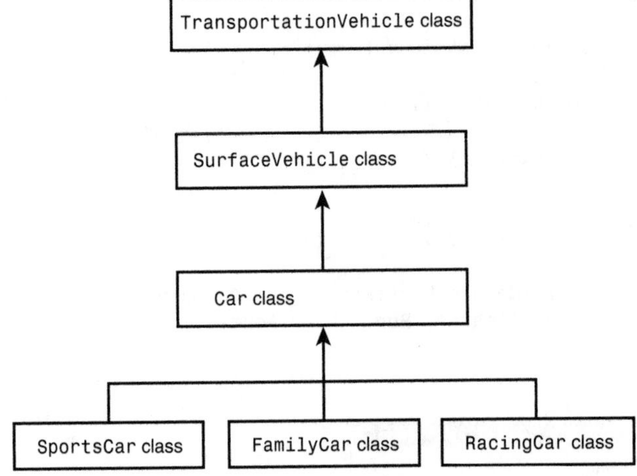

Listing 16.8 demonstrates how a part of Figure 16.9 can be implemented by implementing the three classes `SurfaceVehicle`, `Car`, and `FamilyCar` and shows that class members are inherited across several levels.

LISTING 16.8 `ThreeInheritanceLevels.cs`

```
using System;

class SurfaceVehicle
{
    private float weight;

    public SurfaceVehicle()
    {
        weight = 0;
    }

    public SurfaceVehicle(float initialWeight)
    {
        Console.WriteLine("Now initializing weight");
        weight = initialWeight;
    }
```

LISTING 16.8 continued

```

    public float Weight
    {
        get
        {
            return weight;
        }

        set
        {
            weight = value;
        }
    }
}

class Car : SurfaceVehicle
{
    private uint odometer;

    public Car() : base ()
    {
        odometer = 0;
    }

    public Car(uint initialOdometer, float initialWeight)
    ➥ : base(initialWeight)
    {
        Console.WriteLine("Now initializing odometer");
        odometer = initialOdometer;
    }

    public uint Odometer
    {
        get
        {
            return odometer;
        }

        set
        {
            odometer = value;
        }
    }
}

class FamilyCar : Car
{
    private byte numberOfBabySeats;

    public FamilyCar() : base()
    {
        numberOfBabySeats = 0;
```

LISTING 16.8 continued

```
    }

    public FamilyCar(byte initialNumberOfBabySeats, uint initialOdometer,
        float initialWeight) : base (initialOdometer, initialWeight)
    {
        Console.WriteLine("Now initializing numberOfBabySeats");
        numberOfBabySeats = initialNumberOfBabySeats;
    }

    public byte NumberOfBabySeats
    {
        get
        {
            return numberOfBabySeats;
        }

        set
        {
            numberOfBabySeats = value;
        }
    }
}

class Tester
{
    public static void Main()
    {
        FamilyCar myCar = new FamilyCar(1,10000,1500);

        Console.WriteLine("\nWeight: {0}\nOdometer: {1}
        ➥\nBaby Seats: {2}\n",
            myCar.Weight, myCar.Odometer, myCar.NumberOfBabySeats);
        myCar.Weight = 1800;
        myCar.Odometer = 4000;
        myCar.NumberOfBabySeats = 2;
        Console.WriteLine("Weight: {0}\nOdometer: {1}\nBaby Seats: {2}",
            myCar.Weight, myCar.Odometer, myCar.NumberOfBabySeats);
    }
}
```

```
Now initializing weight
Now initializing odometer
Now initializing numberOfBabySeats

Weight: 1500
Odometer: 10000
Baby Seats: 1

Weight: 1800
Odometer: 4000
Baby Seats: 2
```

Each of the classes in Listing 16.8 declares one instance variable and one associated property. The `Car` class is derived from the `SurfaceVehicle` class, and, consequently, inherits the instance variable `weight` and the property `Weight`. The `FamilyCar` is derived from the `Car` class and not only inherits the `odometer` instance variable and `Odometer` property declared in `Car`, but also the two class members that `Car` inherited from `SurfaceVehicle`. This is demonstrated in the `Main` method of the `Tester` class, where `myCar` (lines 99–103) is able to use the three properties `Weight` (and therefore, also the instance variable `weight`), `Odometer`, and `NumberOfBabySeats`.

Both the `Car` and `FamilyCar` class constructors apply constructor initializers to call a constructor of their base class (see lines 36, 41, 65, and 71). For example, when `FamilyCar`'s constructor (lines 70–75) is called, it will, as a first step, call the `Car` constructor (lines 41–45). When called, the `Car` constructor will, as a first step, call the `SurfaceVehicle` constructor (lines 12–16), which will have its statements executed, followed by those of the `Car` class constructor, followed finally by those of the `FamilyCar` class constructor. I have inserted the print statements in lines 14, 43, and 73 for demonstration purposes only, so you can follow the series of events just described. The first three lines of the sample output are a result of these print statements and are initiated by the creation of a `FamilyCar` object in line 95, which makes a call to the `FamilyCar` constructor in lines 70–75.

Notice how efficiently the three classes reuse the code in this program. For example, not only are `Weight` and `weight` reused in `Car`, but also in `FamilyCar`. In general, and if suitable, large hierarchies of classes result in large amounts of reused code.

Ancestor and Descendant Classes

Sometimes a derived class is referred to as a *child class*, and a base class is referred to as a *parent class*. This logic is extended to chains of derived classes where a base class of a base class (and so on) is called an *ancestor class*, and a derived class of a derived class (and so on) is called a *descendant class*.

Note

You can use the base access construct (defined in Syntax Box 16.3) to call a method, property, or indexer in a base class, but there is no construct available to call an ancestor further up the chain of base classes. For example, the following kind of syntax is invalid:

```
base.base.<Ancestor_method_name>;
```

Method Overriding and Overloading Are Different Mechanisms

It is important to distinguish between method overloading presented in Chapter 12, "Class Anatomy Part I: `static` Class Members and Method Adventures," and method overriding presented in this chapter. As noted in Syntax Box 16.2, an overriding method must have the same name and the same set of formal parameter types as the `virtual` base class method. In contrast, an overloading method has the same name but a different set of formal parameter types.

So if you included a method in your derived class that had the same name as a method in the base class but different formal parameter types, the method of the base class would not be overridden by the derived class method because of the differing number of formal parameters. The derived class would inherit this base class method instead.

It is important to notice, though, that this inherited base class method is not treated exactly like a method defined in the derived class. Consider a scenario where a base class and its derived class both contain methods with the same name (let's call it `MyMethod`) but different formal parameters. If `MyMethod` is called through an object of the derived class, the compiler will first try to match the arguments provided with this method call to any of the `MyMethod` definitions written in the derived class and, at this stage, ignore the `MyMethod` methods inherited from the base class. It will even perform implicit conversions if necessary to find a match before it considers the `MyMethod` methods inherited from the base class. Only if this also fails will it consider the methods inherited from the base class. If a chain of derived classes exists containing `MyMethod` methods with different formal parameters, then the compiler will move up through the hierarchy from the class for which the method was called. On each level, it will try to find a match in a similar fashion to that described for the class for which it was called originally.

Listing 16.9 illustrates this scenario. It contains an `Animal` class with two methods called `Move`. The `Dog` class is derived from the `Animal` class and also contains two methods called `Move`. Both of the `Move` methods in the `Animal` class have different formal parameters from the `Move` methods in the `Dog` class. They are not overridden but inherited (for that reason we don't need to include the `override` keyword when defining the two `Move` methods in the `Dog` class).

LISTING 16.9 `OverridingOverloading.cs`

```
using System;

public class Animal
{
    public virtual void Move(short distance)
    {
        Console.WriteLine("Animal.Move(short). Distance: {0}", distance);
    }

    public virtual void Move(double distance, string direction)
    {
        Console.WriteLine("Animal.Move(double, string). Distance:
        ➥ {0} Direction: {1}",
            distance, direction);
    }
}

public class Dog : Animal
{
```

LISTING 16.9 continued

```
19:     public void Move(int distance)
20:     {
21:         Console.WriteLine("Dog.Move(int). Distance: {0}", distance);
22:     }
23:
24:     public void Move(byte distance)
25:     {
26:         Console.WriteLine("Dog.Move(byte). Distance: {0}", distance);
27:     }
28: }
29:
30: class Tester
31: {
32:     public static void Main()
33:     {
34:         Dog fido = new Dog();
35:
36:         int myInt = 45;
37:         short myShort = 25;
38:         double myDouble = 5.6;
39:
40:         fido.Move(myInt);
41:         fido.Move(myDouble, "North");
42:         fido.Move(myShort);
43:     }
44: }
```

```
Dog.Move(int). Distance: 45
Animal.Move(double, string). Distance: 5.6 Direction: North
Dog.Move(int). Distance: 25
```

Not surprisingly, the call in line 40 calls the `Move(int)` method of the `Dog` class.

The compiler cannot find any `Move` parameter lists among the `Move` methods defined in the `Dog` class that matches this argument combination (`double, string`) provided with the call to `Move` in line 41. Consequently, it moves its focus to the `Move` methods inherited from the `Animal` class where it finds the matching `Move(double..., string...)` method.

Line 42 reveals that the compiler will use implicit conversion to find a matching parameter list before it will consider methods inherited from a base class. Even though the single argument of type `short` has a perfect match in the inherited method `Move(short...)` (defined in lines 5–8), the compiler uses implicit conversion to choose the less perfect match in `Move(int...)` (defined in lines 19–22).

Summary

This chapter discussed basic inheritance concepts and how these are implemented in C#. The following are some of the important points that were covered.

Aggregation implements *has a* relationship, inheritance implements *is a* relationship.

Class hierarchies are formed after the same principles as those used by taxonomists. They move from the topmost general categories to the lowermost specialized categories.

Through inheritance, class members in general classes can be reused in specialized classes. Without inheritance, we have two options for creating objects that have unique as well as common class members. Write one class from which all the individual objects are instantiated, or write one class for each distinguishable type of objects. Both approaches have serious drawbacks. Inheritance takes the best from both approaches while leaving their problems behind.

A derived class extends its base class by adding new class members while inheriting the class members of the base class. The derived class can modify the inherited base class members as required. A `virtual` function member of a base class can be modified in the derived class by overriding it with the use of the `override` keyword.

A derived class is also called a parent class, and a base class is called a child class. A base class of a base class, and so on, is called an *ancestor class*. A derived class of a derived class, and so on, is called a *descendant class*.

It is important to show whether your intent is to `override` or re-implement a function member with the `override` and `new` keywords.

A class cannot be derived from a `sealed` class.

A `protected` class member can only be accessed from within its own class and any descendant class.

Even though a derived class inherits the `private` class members of its base class, it cannot access those class members directly from within its own class definition.

The `internal protected` access modifier provides `internal` access or `protected` access.

A derived class never inherits the constructors of its base class, but they can be called with a constructor initializer from the derived class's constructors. The compiler automatically attaches constructor initializers (that call the default base class constructor) to any constructor in a derived class, which do not contain an explicitly specified constructor initializer.

An indexer of a base class can be called with the following syntax

```
base[indexer]
```

Class members in a base class can be called from the derived class with the keyword `base`. This is referred to as base access.

Inheritance is necessary for reusing large parts of the .NET Frameworks class library.

Method overriding and method overloading are different mechanisms. An overriding method in a derived class must have the same signature, return type, and access modifier as the method it is overriding in the base class. In contrast, an overloading method has the same name but a different set of formal parameter types than the method it is overloading.

Review Questions

1. You have just started working on two software projects and identified the following classes in the two programs:

   Program 1: Airplane, jet engines, wings, airplane body, passenger seats, and cockpit

   Program 2: Person, student, employee, undergraduate, graduate, secretary, cleaner, and director

   Which program seems able to benefit the most from inheritance? Why? Which concept is the other program likely to benefit from?

2. Consider the following class hierarchy.

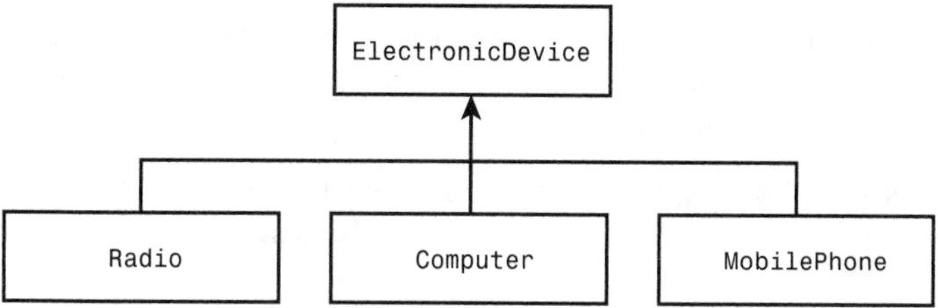

   In which class would you include each of the following class members:

   a. The `brandName` instance variable

   b. The `Autodial` method

   c. The `Start` method

   d. The `Tuning` method

   e. The `purchasePrice` instance variable

3. Suppose a class named `Animal` has a `public` method called `Move`. If the `Dog` class is derived from the `Animal` class, can you call the method `Move` for an instance of the `Dog` class as in `myDog.Move();`, even if you don't specify any such method in the `Dog` class?

4. This is what the `Move` method header looks like in the `Animal` class:

   ```
   public void Move()
   ```

   Can you `override` this method in the `Dog` class? Why or why not?

5. `Animal` also contains a `private` instance variable called `name`. Can you access `name` from within the `Dog` class definition? Is this an advantage or a disadvantage?

6. `Animal` further contains a `private` function member. Can you call this function member from within the definition of the `Dog` class?

7. `Animal` contains another method with the following header:

   ```
   protected virtual void MoveADistance(int distance)
   ```

   A fellow programmer has written the following method header in the derived `Dog` class to override `Animal`'s method:

   ```
   public override int MoveADistance(double distance)
   ```

   This method header contains several mistakes. Locate and correct the mistakes.

8. Can you prevent a class from acting as a base class? If so, how?

9. Why does it usually make sense to call a base class constructor from a constructor of a derived class?

10. Our `Animal` class from the previous questions has exactly one constructor that takes one parameter of type `int`. A fellow programmer has implemented the `Dog` class with a constructor that does not contain any explicitly defined constructor initializer. Why does this setup give rise to a compiler error?

11. The `Animal` class is also equipped with a complex method that returns the metabolic rate of a basic animal cell. Its method header in the `Animal` class looks like the following:

    ```
    public virtual double MetabolicRateCell()
    ```

    After the `MetabolicRateCell` for an `Animal` has been calculated, it is easy to calculate the `MetabolicCellRate` for a `Dog`; simply add 100 to this figure.

    You need to override `MetabolicRateCell()` in the `Dog` class and write its implementation. Write the code for the overriding method in the `Dog` class so that you use the figure returned from the `MetabolicRateCell` method in the base class.

12. You now derive a class from the `Dog` class called `Poodle`. Does the `Poodle` class contain the method originally defined in `Animal` called `Move`?

Programming Exercises

Exercises 2–4 build on the code of each previous exercise.

1. Write four classes called `ElectronicDevice`, `Radio`, `Computer`, and `MobilePhone`. Let `ElectronicDevice` be the base class for the other three classes and include the following three class members in its definition:

   - A private instance variable called `brandName` (of type `string`)
   - A public property called `BrandName` to access `brandName`
   - A private instance variable called `isOn` (of type `bool`)

   Also include two methods called `SwitchOn` (which must write "On" and set `isOn` to `true`) and `SwitchOff` (which must write "Off" and set `isOn` to `false`). The three subclasses remain empty for now.

Write the appropriate code to test that even though the three subclasses have empty definitions, you can utilize their inherited class members.

2. Override the `SwitchOn` and `SwitchOff` methods in each of the subclasses so that they apart from the actions they perform in the `ElectronicDevice` also write the name of the device that is being switched on or off. For example when you call the `SwitchOn` method for Radio you should see the following output on the screen

```
On
```

Radio and `isOn` should still be assigned the value `true.` (Hint: Use the base access to achieve this functionality.)

3. Equip the `ElectronicDevice` class with two constructors:

   - A default constructor that sets `brandName` to "unknown" and `isOn` to `false.`
   - A constructor that takes one argument of type `string` that is used to initialize `brandName` while `isOn` also is set to `false`.

   Add the following instance variables to the program:

   - Add `currentFrequency` of type `double` to `Radio`.
   - Add `internalMemory` of type `int` to `Computer`.
   - Add `lastNumberDialed` of type `uint` to `MobilePhone`.

   Add the following two constructors to each of the `Radio`, `Computer` and `MobilePhone` classes:

   - A default constructor that not only initializes the instance values defined in the particular class but also the instance variables inherited (`brandName` and `isOn`) from `ElectronicDevice`.
   - A constructor that takes two arguments—one to set the value defined for the class (either `currentFrequency`, `internalMemory`, or `lastNumberDialed`) and one to set the value of `brandName`. (Hint: Call the appropriate constructor initializers to implement this.)

4. Write a class called `LaptopComputer` that is derived from the `Computer` class. Define the instance variable `maxBatteriLife` of type `uint` for this class and provide two constructors:

   - One default constructor that assigns appropriate values to `maxBatteriLife` as well as the other class members `LaptopComputer` inherits.
   - One constructor with which you can pass initial values to `maxBatteriLife` as well as the class members `LaptopComputer` inherits from its descendants.

CHAPTER 17

INHERITANCE PART II: `abstract` FUNCTIONS, POLYMORPHISM, AND INTERFACES

You will learn about the following in this chapter:

- `abstract` functions and `abstract` classes
- Polymorphism and why `abstract` functions and `abstract` classes are important for implementing polymorphic software
- The dynamic binding mechanism, which is fundamental to polymorphism
- The advantages of polymorphism and examples of how it empowers programmers
- How type information is lost through up casting and how it can be regained through down casting by the use of the cast operator, the `is` operator and the `as` operator
- The `System.Object` class, from which all classes are ultimately derived
- Method hiding and method overriding
- Versioning and how it is supported in C#
- Multiple inheritance and why C# does not support it, but instead uses interfaces
- Interfaces
- How interfaces extend our ability to implement polymorphic code across the class hierarchies
- How inheritance, interfaces and polymorphism allow us to implement generic programs

Not only does inheritance allow us to arrange our classes in neat taxonomical hierarchies and to reuse the code of these classes effectively, as shown in Chapter 16, "Inheritance Part I: Basic Concepts," it also allows us to implement a powerful concept called polymorphism. When polymorphism is applied on a class hierarchy, it involves one ancestor class and several of its descendant classes. However, sometimes we want to apply polymorphism to a group of classes that do not have a common ancestor. Interfaces presented later in this chapter help us to break free from the class hierarchy structure and apply polymorphism to groups of classes without common ancestors.

Before we look at polymorphism, we need to introduce **abstract** functions that play an important role for implementing polymorphism in class hierarchies.

abstract Methods, Properties, Indexers, and Classes

The **Car** class in Listing 16.3 of Chapter 16 contained a definition (shown next) for the **MoveForward** method that added 1 to the **odometer** variable.

```
    public virtual void MoveForward()
    {
        Console.Write("Moving forward... ");
        odometer += 1;
        Console.WriteLine("Odometer reading: {0}", odometer);
    }
```

However, as noted in the same section, **MoveForward** could mean anything in the **generic Car** class for which it was defined. The implementation of **MoveForward** in the **Car** class was merely meant to be a dummy implementation waiting to be overridden in the **FamilyCar**, **SportsCar**, and **RacingCar** classes where we had a better idea of how to implement it (**FamilyCar** is slow, **SportsCar** is medium fast, and **RacingCar** is very fast).

If we plant incorrect methods (like **Car**'s **MoveForward** method) in our programs, we obviously face a serious problem. Anybody could just call this method and believe they were invoking a correct method.

We could attempt to eliminate this problem simply by removing the **MoveForward** method from **Car** and only implement it in the more specialized classes. However, this goes against our taxonomical class hierarchy and, even worse, it prevents us from using an important mechanism we will look at in a moment called polymorphism.

To solve our problem, C# allows us to specify a method to be **abstract** with the **abstract** keyword. An **abstract** method only contains the method header and no implementation. Instead, it requires a descendant to provide the implementation. As a result, we can throw away the dubious **MoveForward** implementation of the **Car** class and still express that any class derived from the **Car** class contains a **MoveForward** method. When a class contains one or more **abstract** methods, the class itself must be declared **abstract**. An **abstract** class cannot be instantiated because it contains methods that are not implemented.

Listing 17.1 provides a simple example of how an **abstract** method and an **abstract** class are defined. The source code is nearly identical to Listing 16.2 of Chapter 16, but this time **MoveForward** has been declared **abstract** in line 19 and the **Car** class declared abstract in line 3.

LISTING 17.1 AbstractMoveForward.cs

```
using System;

abstract class Car
{
    private uint odometer = 0;

    protected uint Odometer
    {
        set
        {
            odometer = value;
        }
        get
        {
            return odometer;
        }
    }

    public abstract void MoveForward();
}

class RacingCar : Car
{
    public override void MoveForward()
    {
        Console.Write("Moving dangerously fast forward... ");
        Odometer += 30;
        Console.WriteLine("Odometer in racing car: {0}", Odometer);
    }
}

class FamilyCar : Car
{
    public override void MoveForward()
    {
        Console.Write("Moving slowly but safely forward...");
        Odometer += 5;
        Console.WriteLine("Odometer in family car: {0}", Odometer);
    }
}

class CarTester
{
    public static void Main()
    {
        RacingCar myRacingCar = new RacingCar();
        FamilyCar myFamilyCar = new FamilyCar();
        myRacingCar.MoveForward();
        myFamilyCar.MoveForward();
    }
}
```

```
Moving dangerously fast forward... Odometer in racing car: 30
Moving slowly but safely forward...Odometer in family car: 5
```

The combination of applying the `abstract` keyword (shown in line 19) and substituting the method body with a semicolon at the same time (positioned at the end of the line) is required to make `MoveForward` an `abstract` method. Because the `Car` class now contains an `abstract` method, it too must be declared `abstract`, as shown in line 3.

The way an `abstract` method is overridden in a derived class is identical to that of a `virtual` method. In fact, an `abstract` method is implicitly also a `virtual` method. Consequently, none of the code in the `RacingCar` or the `FamilyCar` classes needed to be changed from Listing 16.3 of Chapter 16 and, as you can see, the sample output is also unchanged. However, by making `MoveForward` and `Car abstract`, we cause a few important changes that are not revealed by our source code example. First, it is impossible to create an instance of the `Car` class, because an `abstract` class cannot be instantiated. Second, had we not overridden the `MoveForward` method in, say, the `RacingCar` class, but just inherited it untouched, `RacingCar` would have inherited `MoveForward` from `Car`. Because this `MoveForward` method is `abstract`, `RacingCar` would then contain an `abstract` method. This would oblige us to declare `RacingCar` `abstract` and thereby prevent it from being instantiated. Sometimes, several levels in a chain of derived classes consist of `abstract` classes for this same reason. This is legitimate and can easily be part of a superbly designed class hierarchy.

Note

Even though we cannot instantiate an `abstract` class, we can still declare a variable to be of this type. For example, we could use our `abstract Car` class to make the following declaration:

```
Car myCar;
```

As you will see in a moment, this is an important ability needed to use polymorphism.

Non-`abstract` classes that can be instantiated are called *concrete classes*.

The `get` and `set` accessors of properties and indexers can also be declared `abstract`, with the same implications as those found for `abstract` methods. The syntax for declaring methods, properties, indexers, and classes `abstract` is shown in Syntax Box 17.1.

Syntax Box 17.1 Abstract Method

```
Abstract_method::=
[<Method_modifiers>] abstract <Return_type> <Method_identifier>
    ➥ ( [<Formal_parameter_list>] );

Abstract_property_1::=
    [<Property_modifiers>] abstract <Return_type> <Property_identifier>
    {
        [get;]
        [set;]
```

```
    }

Abstract_indexer_1::=
    [<Indexer_modifiers>] abstract [<Return_type>] this [<Parameter_list>]
    {
        [get;]
        [set;]
    }



Abstract_class::=
    <Class_modifiers> abstract <Class_name>
    {
        <Class_members>
    }
```

Notes:

- An abstract method is declared with the abstract keyword. It does not have a method body, it has a semicolon after the two parentheses enclosing the formal parameter list instead. The following line provides an example:

  ```
  public abstract void MoveForward();
  ```

- You can declare an entire property to be abstract by including the abstract keyword in the property header (*Abstract_property_1*). The get and set blocks must then be substituted by a semicolon as follows:

  ```
  public abstract int MyProperty
  {
      get;
      set;
  }
  ```

  Both the get and the set accessors are now abstract.

- abstract methods and accessors cannot also be declared private, static, or virtual.
- An abstract method and accessor is implicitly virtual.
- An abstract method and accessor can only reside inside an abstract class. On the other hand, an abstract class can contain non-abstract methods and accessors.
- An abstract class cannot be instantiated.
- If you derive a class from a class containing abstract methods, abstract accessors, or both, the derived class also becomes abstract unless you override and provide implementations for all the abstract methods and accessors inherited from the base class.
- You can override a virtual method (or accessor) with an abstract method (or abstract accessor) in a derived class. Any classes derived from this abstract class must override these abstract methods and provide new implementations for them to become non-abstract.

The same rules for overriding a virtual method or accessor also apply for overriding an abstract method or accessor.

An overriding method must contain the same name, return type, and formal parameters (number and types) as the abstract method it is overriding. It also must include the override keyword and be declared with the same access modifier.

To make a property accessor overriding, you must include it in a property, whose header contains the `override` keyword. The following property contains both an overriding `set` and `get` accessor:

```
protected override int Odometer
{
    set
    {
        <Statements>
    }
    get
    {
        <Statements>
    }
}
```

Polymorphism

In general, polymorphism means the ability to have many forms. Before we look closer at its meaning in computer science, we need to make a couple of important observations that are related to the inheritance hierarchy.

An Object of a Descendant Class Has More Than One Type

Consider our chain of derived classes in Figure 16.9 of Chapter 16. In everyday life, most people agree that a racing car is a car, a car is a surface vehicle, and a surface vehicle is a transportation vehicle. However, the contrary is not true, a car is not necessarily a racing car. In computer science and in C#, this is also the case. An object of type `SportsCar` is therefore also of type `Car` and of type `SurfaceVehicle` and of type `TransportationVehicle`. Consequently, a variable of type `Car` can hold a reference to an object of type `SportsCar`, making the following two lines valid:

```
Car myCar;
myCar = new RacingCar();
```

However, the opposite is not true. A variable of type `RacingCar` cannot hold an object of type `Car`, because a `Car` is not necessarily a `RacingCar`. So, the following code is not valid:

```
RacingCar myRacingCar;
myRacingCar = new Car();    //Invalid
```

We can extend this logic to the whole inheritance hierarchy, meaning that `myCar` of type `Car` can also hold a reference to either a `FamilyCar` object or a `SportsCar` object, and a variable of type `TransportationVehicle` can hold a reference to an object of a type of any of its descendants.

When you assign an object of a descendant type (such as `RacingCar`) to a variable of an ancestor type (such as `Car`) as follows:

```
Car myCar = new RacingCar();
```

you can only call the method (and property and indexer) names defined for the ancestor type through the ancestor type variable (here called myCar). For example, if your Car class contains the MoveForward method, and its derived class RacingCar, apart from inheriting this method, also defines the StartOnBoardCamera method, you can still only make the following call through myCar:

```
myCar.MoveForward();
```

but the following is invalid:

```
myCar.StartOnBoardCamera();     //invalid
```

because StartOnBoardCamera() is not defined in Car.

Dynamic Binding of Virtual Methods and (get, set) Accessors

Let's continue our small Car and RacingCar example from the previous section where we performed the following assignment:

```
Car myCar;
myCar = new RacingCar();
```

Suppose we make a call to MoveForward from myCar as follows:

```
myCar.MoveForward();
```

Both the Car class and the RacingCar class contain an implementation for the MoveForward method, so the runtime must now make an important choice: It can either invoke the MoveForward implementation of the Car class or the MoveForward implementation of the RacingCar class. If MoveForward is declared virtual in the Car class and overridden in the derived RacingCar class with the override keyword, the runtime will call the method defined for the RacingCar.

When the program with the declaration

```
Car myCar;
```

is compiled, the compiler cannot possibly know whether myCar will contain a Car object or a RacingCar object or perhaps a SportsCar or FamilyCar object when it meets the following line

```
myCar.MoveForward();
```

How, then, is it possible to execute the MoveForward implementation for the RacingCar class if myCar contains a RacingCar object; or execute the MoveForward implementation for the SportsCar class if it contains a SportsCar object; or the implementation for the Car class if it contains a Car object? C# uses a mechanism called *dynamic binding*, *late binding* (or virtual dispatch) that has taken these names for the following reason: Even though we know the name of the method being called at compile time, with the following line

```
myCar.MoveForward();
```

the actual implementation this name represents is determined dynamically (hence the name dynamic binding) and later than compile time (hence the name late binding) while the program is being executed. Figure 17.1 provides an overview of the dynamic binding mechanism. It says that if, for example, `myCar` has been assigned a `SportsCar` object with the following line:

```
myCar = new SportsCar();
```

then the line

```
myCar.MoveForward();
```

will execute the `SportsCar` class's version of `MoveForward`.

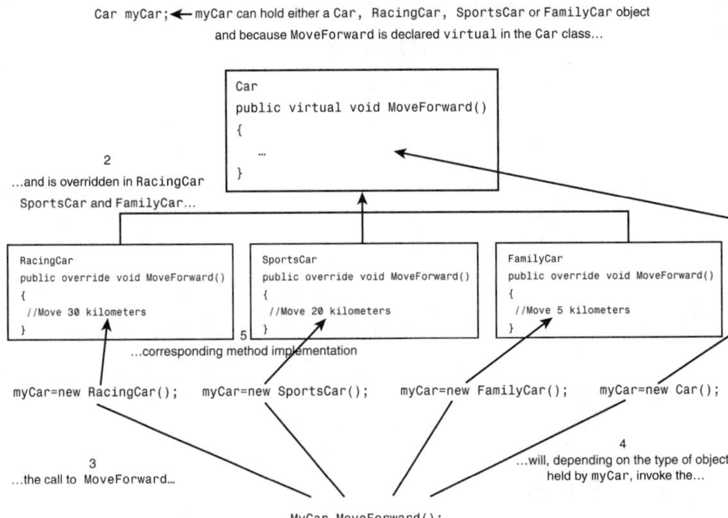

FIGURE 17.1
Dynamic binding in action.

Directly translated, *polymorphism* means the ability to have many forms. In computer science, it means using a single variable to reference objects of different classes and, through the dynamic binding mechanism, letting the method that is implemented for the class of the referenced object be called automatically. So, dynamic binding and polymorphism are more or less different words for the same thing. However, whereas dynamic binding refers to the mechanical process that takes place in the computer, polymorphism is a concept used for more abstract discussions about objects and classes.

Note

A computer language must at least support the notion of classes and objects along with encapsulation, inheritance, and polymorphism to deserve the label of being an object-oriented language.

Note

Sometimes, method overloading is also referred to as polymorphism because different method signatures with the same name have different implementations. However, as object-oriented programming has matured, polymorphism is used most commonly in connection with the dynamic binding mechanism.

Case Study: Using Polymorphism to Create a Simple Drawing Program

An architectural drawing can be viewed as a collection of shapes, where a shape can be a circle, a square, a triangle, and so on. Suppose we were asked to write an architectural drawing program so that architects could create their drawings on the computer screen. One of the fundamental requirements of this program would be to represent a drawing and to draw this representation onscreen whenever requested. Most of this case study is concerned with finding an elegant way to solve this problem and designing a simplified version of a program with this fundamental ability.

First, we set out in the usual manner to determine the classes we need to include in our program by rephrasing the first sentence of this case study and highlighting the nouns: A *drawing* consists of a *collection* of *shapes*. A shape can be (or *is*) a *circle*, a *rectangle*, a *triangle*, and so on. Accordingly, we need to implement a `Shape` class and, just like the `Car` class had three different subclasses, a `Shape` class also has several subclasses. In this case, we will limit the program to contain the three `Shape` subclasses `Circle`, `Rectangle`, and `Triangle`, as shown in Figure 17.2.

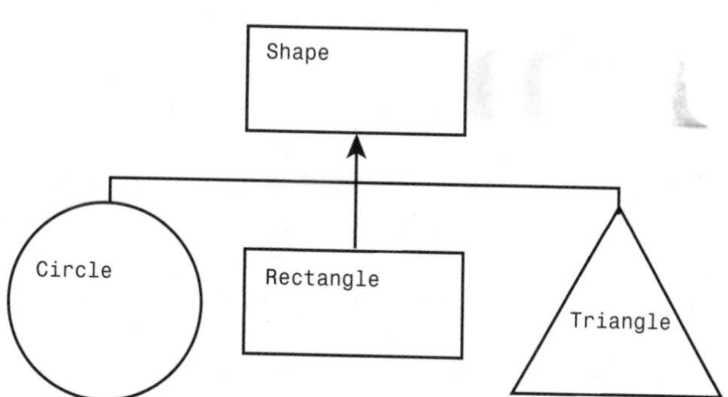

FIGURE 17.2
`Circle`, `Rectangle`, and `Triangle` are subclasses of `Shape`.

Apart from the `Shape` class and its three subclasses, we need to implement a collection of shapes. To this end, we will use the well-known array.

Note

After an array has been defined, it has a fixed length. This is not an optimal behavior in this case because a drawing, in most cases, consists of an unknown number of shapes at the time it is begun. An `ArrayList`, which can grow and shrink dynamically, would be more appropriate. However, whether we use an array or an `ArrayList` does not interfere with our ability to demonstrate the power of polymorphism.

As the architect adds shapes to the drawing, different kinds of corresponding `Shape` objects (in our case, `Circles`, `Rectangles`, and `Triangles`) are created in the program. Each `Shape` object's details, such as position on the drawing, its size, color, and so on, are stored inside the individual object. It is then added to our collection of objects, as shown in Figure 17.3.

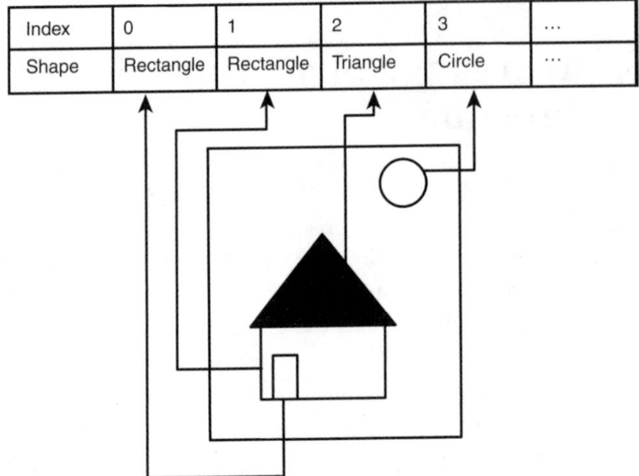

Index
0
1
2
3
...
Shape
Rectangle
Rectangle
Triangle
Circle
...

FIGURE 17.3
An array of shapes represents a drawing.

How can different shape types be inserted into the same array when all elements of the array must have the same type? Because `Circle`, `Square`, and `Triangle` are all descendants of `Shape`, any objects of one of those three types can be referenced by a variable of type `Shape`. Consequently, if we declare our array to be of type `Shape`, each element can store a `Circle`, `Square`, or a `Triangle`.

After the array of shapes has been created, we need the ability to draw its collection of `Shape` objects onscreen. To draw an object, we could attempt to write a method in a separate class called `DrawingMachine` that might contain a method called `MakeDrawing`. This method would look at each object in the array and at the instance variables of each object to determine its position, size, and shape. However, this approach would be cumbersome because each object requires different parameters and different algorithms to be drawn. For example, a circle needs a radius and a center point, whereas a rectangle needs a height and a width, and other more intricate shapes have many more parameters. Instead of using this tedious and cumbersome technique, we turn to polymorphism, which provides an elegant way to solve this problem.

Polymorphism allows us to support the following scenario: Instead of trying to figure out how each object is drawn from outside of the object, it makes more sense to let the object carry its own implementation for how it is drawn. Each object then forms a neat encapsulated package with the data as well as the implementation needed to draw itself. Let's call the method that draws the object `DrawYourself`. Any shape object contains a `DrawYourself` method, so the `Shape` class would also have a `DrawYourself` method. However, just as we didn't know the implementation for the `MoveForward` method in the `Car` class, we also don't know the implementation of the `DrawYourself` method in the `Shape` class. We must declare `DrawYourself` to be `abstract` in the `Shape` class and then write its implementations in the three subclasses.

Recall that an `abstract` method is also `virtual`, so if we override the `DrawYourself` method in each of the classes derived from `Shape`, the dynamic binding mechanism will be applied on them. This means that we can now simply draw the drawing by iterating through the collection of shapes and asking each shape to `DrawYourself`. The dynamic binding mechanism will determine which kind of shape object is stored in each array element and automatically call the appropriate `DrawYourself` method.

Listing 17.2 contains a simple implementation of the `Shape` class (lines 3–6) and its three subclasses. Notice that `DrawYourself` is declared `abstract` in the `Shape` class and is overridden in each of the three subclasses. The `Shape` classes have been kept simple and do not contain any information about position or size. They always produce just one shape, which is drawn on the console.

Please note that the source code in Listing 17.2 lacks a `Main` method and does not compile. In a moment, we will look at the code that puts the four classes to good use.

LISTING 17.2 ThreeShapes.cs

```
01: using System;
02:
03: public abstract class Shape
04: {
05:     public abstract void DrawYourself();
06: }
07:
08: public class Triangle : Shape
09: {
10:     public override void DrawYourself()
11:     {
12:         Console.WriteLine("         *     ");
13:         Console.WriteLine("        * *    ");
14:         Console.WriteLine("       *   *   ");
15:         Console.WriteLine("      *     *  ");
16:         Console.WriteLine("     *_______* ");
17:     }
18: }
19:
20: public class Circle : Shape
21: {
22:     public override void DrawYourself()
23:     {
24:         Console.WriteLine("        ***     ");
25:         Console.WriteLine("     *       *  ");
26:         Console.WriteLine("    *         * ");
27:         Console.WriteLine("    *         * ");
28:         Console.WriteLine("     *       *  ");
29:         Console.WriteLine("        ***     ");
30:     }
31: }
32:
33: public class Rectangle : Shape
34: {
```

LISTING 17.2 continued

```
    public override void DrawYourself()
    {
        Console.WriteLine(" ------------------ ");
        Console.WriteLine("|__________________|");
    }
}
```

To ascertain ourselves that dynamic binding is in fact taking place when we call the `DrawYourself` method through a variable of type `Shape`, I have written the code snippet in Listing 17.3. You need to attach this listing at the end of Listing 17.2 to make it work. Your output should then resemble the output shown in the output sample after Listing 17.3.

LISTING 17.3 `ShapesTester.cs`

```
01: class ShapeTester
02: {
03:     public static void Main()
04:     {
05:         Shape myShape;
06:
07:         myShape = new Circle();
08:         myShape.DrawYourself();
09:         myShape = new Triangle();
10:         myShape.DrawYourself();
11:         myShape = new Rectangle();
12:         myShape.DrawYourself();
13:     }
14: }
```

```
       ***
    *       *
   *         *
   *         *
    *       *
       ***
        *
       * *
      *   *
     *     *
    *_______*
 ------------------
|__________________|
```

`myShape` is declared to be of type `Shape` in line 5 of Listing 17.3. Consequently, `myShape` can reference any object of type `Circle`, `Triangle`, and `Rectangle` because they are descendants of the `Shape` class.

Even though lines 8, 10, and 12 in Listing 17.3 contain the same call to `DrawYourself` from the `myShape` variable, each call results in the execution of a different implementation of `DrawYourself` because of the dynamic binding mechanism. Line 8 results in the execution of the `Circle` version of `DrawYourself` because `myShape` at that moment contains a `Circle` object. The sample output confirms this by first drawing a circle. Line 10 results in the `Triangle` implementation of the `DrawYourself` method being executed because `myShape` has just been assigned a `Triangle` object in line 9. Line 12 follows the same logic.

The simple test in Listing 17.3 gives us a glimpse of the tremendous expressive capability polymorphism provides us with. Each time we call `myShape.DrawYourself()`, we do not have to concern ourselves with which object is being stored in `myShape` or any other details related to this object. All we need to care about is that a shape is being drawn. In other words, polymorphism allows us to draw a drawing on a high level of abstraction.

Let's use this tremendous power to complete our drawing program, as shown in Listing 17.4.

Note

Please remove Listing 17.3 from the program you ran before and insert the code in Listing 17.4. To test this new program, you can use the code provided in Listing 17.5, which can be inserted after the code in Listing 17.4.

LISTING 17.4 DrawingEngine.cs

```
public class DrawingEngine
{
    public Shape [] CreateDrawing()
    {
        int numberOfShapes = 0;
        int shapeCounter = 0;
        string choice;
        Shape [] drawing;

        Console.Write("How many shapes do you want in your drawing? ");
        numberOfShapes = Convert.ToInt32(Console.ReadLine());
        drawing = new Shape[numberOfShapes];
        do
        {
            Console.Write("Choose next shape: C)ircle R)ectangle
            ➥ T)riangle: ");
            choice = Console.ReadLine().ToUpper();
            switch(choice)
            {
                case "C":
                    drawing[shapeCounter] = new Circle();
                    break;
                case "R":
                    drawing[shapeCounter] = new Rectangle();
                    break;
                case "T":
                    drawing[shapeCounter] = new Triangle();
                    break;
```

LISTING 17.4 continued

```
28:                 default:
29:                     Console.WriteLine("Invalid choice");
30:                     shapeCounter—;
31:                     break;
32:             }
33:             shapeCounter++;
34:         } while (shapeCounter < numberOfShapes);
35:         return drawing;
36:     }
37:
38:     public void DrawDrawing(Shape [] drawing)
39:     {
40:         for(int i = 0; i < drawing.Length; i++)
41:         {
42:             drawing [i].DrawYourself();
43:         }
44:     }
45: }
```

The purpose of the `CreateDrawing` method (lines 3–36) of Listing 17.4 is to let the user create any sequence of `Shape` objects and return this collection of objects in an array of `Shape` elements.

Line 8 declares an array called `drawing` with elements of type `Shape`. This allows the user to insert either a `Circle` (line 20), a `Rectangle` (line 23), or a `Triangle` (line 26) into the next element of this array. After each of the `drawing` elements holds a reference to a shape object, `drawing` is returned to the caller in line 35.

The `DrawDrawing` method (lines 38–44) takes as an argument an array of `Shapes` and prints the contents of this array onscreen. `DrawDrawing` shows the advantages of using polymorphism. To draw every shape contained in the `drawing` array passed to it, `DrawDrawing` merely needs to iterate through the array and call the `DrawYourself` method for each of its elements. We don't need to worry about which object is stored in which element and how it is drawn; we just ask it to draw itself.

Notice how easy it is to extend our drawing program with other `Shape` classes. For example, to add an `Octagon` class, we merely need to derive it from the `Shape` class and provide an implementation for the `DrawYourself` method. We then need to allow the user to add `Octagon` objects to the drawing, but the `DrawDrawing` method remains unchanged; it doesn't care whether the shape is an octagon, a hexagon, or something else, as long as it is derived from the `Shape` class, because it is then guaranteed to have a `DrawYourself` method.

Listing 17.5 demonstrates Listing 17.2 and Listing 17.4 and must, as stated before, be combined with those two listings to work.

LISTING 17.5 TestDrawingEngine.cs

```
01: class TestDrawingEngine
02: {
03:     public static void Main()
04:     {
05:         Shape [] myDrawing;
06:         DrawingEngine myCAD = new DrawingEngine();
07:         string choice;
08:
09:         do
10:         {
11:             Console.WriteLine("Please prepare to create drawing");
12:             myDrawing = myCAD.CreateDrawing();
13:             do
14:             {
15:                 Console.WriteLine("Here is your beautiful drawing\n");
16:                 myCAD.DrawDrawing(myDrawing);
17:                 Console.Write("\nDo you want to see it again? Y)es N)o ");
18:                 choice = Console.ReadLine().ToUpper();
19:             } while(choice != "N");
20:             Console.Write("Do you want to create another drawing?
                ➥Y)es N)o ");
21:             choice = Console.ReadLine().ToUpper();
22:         } while(choice != "N");
23:     }
24: }
```

```
Please prepare to create drawing
How many shapes do you want in your drawing? 3
Choose next shape: C)ircle R)ectangle T)riangle: t
Choose next shape: C)ircle R)ectangle T)riangle: r
Choose next shape: C)ircle R)ectangle T)riangle: c
Here is your beautiful drawing

         *
        * *
       *   *
      *     *
     *_______*
 ------------------
|__________________|
        ***
     *       *
    *         *
    *         *
     *       *
        ***

Do you want to see it again? Y)es N)o n
Do you want to create another drawing? Y)es N)o n
```

Listing 17.5 uses the `CreateDrawing` method in line 12 to create a new array of shapes and assigns it to the `myDrawing` array. It then provides this array as an argument to `DrawDrawing` in line 16 to draw the shapes contained in `myDrawing` onscreen.

Polymorphism allows us to concentrate on generalities and lets us leave the specifics to the runtime engine. Even without knowing the exact types of a group of objects, we can still give commands to those objects and have them executed in manners appropriate to those objects. Polymorphism also facilitates extensibility, because polymorphic method calls are type independent to a certain degree.

Inheritance and polymorphism have revolutionized the way software is written. What follows are a couple of examples where polymorphism could be used.

Computer games include different objects that move, act, and are displayed onscreen. These can be spaceships, aliens, cars, monsters, and so on. We can create a common base class for the game participants called, say, `GameElement`, which can, among other methods, contain an `abstract` method called `DrawYourself`. Even though we have a collection of very different `GameElements`, each with a specific way of being drawn onscreen, we simply need to iterate through this collection and call the `DrawYourself` method when we want the pieces to be drawn onscreen.

An employee database system contains many different kinds of employees, such as programmers, secretaries, marketing researchers, cleaners, directors, and so on. Even though all these employees have differences, they all share many attributes, such as name, address, and birth date. They also have common methods, such as a method for calculating the salary (here called `CalculateSalary`). We can create a base class called `Employee` from which all the different employee classes are derived. By equipping `Employee` with common employee attributes and methods, such as `CalculateSalary`, it becomes possible to iterate through the collection of employees and simply call the `CalculateSalary` method when salary payments are due. We don't need to know whether the actual employee called is a `secretary` object or `cleaner` object because behind the scenes, through dynamic binding, an appropriate method is being called—a method that matches the particular object type referenced by the `Employee` variable that `CalculateSalary` was called through.

Losing and Regaining Type Information

If we assign an object of a derived class (`Rectangle`) to a variable of type base class (`Shape`) as in the following:

```
Shape myShape = new Rectangle();
```

the `Rectangle` object looses part of its identity. It is impossible to tell by looking at `myShape` in the source code whether it references an object of type `Rectangle`, `Circle`, or `Triangle`; we only know it's a `Shape`.

Even if we happen to know that `myShape` contains a `Rectangle` object in a particular place in our code and want to access its `Height` property (assuming that `Rectangle` contains a `Height` property) with the following call:

```
myShape.Height = 20.4;      //Invalid
```

the compiler returns an error message, because it cannot determine at compile time whether `myShape` will reference an object of type `Rectangle`, `Triangle`, or `Circle`. If it happens to, for example, be a `Circle`, havoc would break loose because `Circle` does not contain a `Height` property (it would, instead, contain a `Radius` property). We can only call functions defined in the `Shape` class, even if its variable contains an object of a subclass with other added functions.

As long as we only need to call the class members of the `Rectangle` class that also are defined in the `Shape` class, the information loss and limited access do not pose a problem. For example, in our code in the drawing program case study, we were happy to let the `drawing` array with the `Shape` elements hide their real content because the only call we needed to make was `DrawYourself`, which was channeled through `Shape` and, via dynamic binding, brought to the `DrawYourself` method of the right subclass.

However, the story is different if we need to call a function member specific to the `Rectangle` class. For example, what if we want to calculate the total height of all the `Rectangles` in our `drawing` (again assuming that `Rectangle` contains a `Height` property)? Our first attempt

```
double totalHeight;
for(int i = 0; i < drawing.Length; i++)
{
    totalHeight += drawing[i].Height;     //Invalid
}
```

fails, because the `drawing` elements are of type `Shape` and do not support a call to `Height`. If we could somehow detect whether an element contains a `Rectangle` object and then somehow transform it back into a full-blown `Rectangle`, we could then call its `Height` property.

Fortunately, C# keeps a close eye on which object (and its type) a variable is referencing at any point in time. (Otherwise, it wouldn't be able to support, for example, the dynamic binding mechanism.) It is possible to access this information programmatically with the `is` and `as` operators that are presented in the following sections.

The `is` Operator

The `is` operator can test whether a variable (such as `myShape`) is referencing an object of a specific type (such as `Rectangle`). The result of this test is one of the `bool` values—`true` or `false`. To test whether `myShape` holds a `Rectangle` object, we can write the following Boolean expression:

```
(myShape is Rectangle)
```

which returns `true` if `myShape` is referencing a `Rectangle` object; otherwise, it returns `false`.

If `myShape` is, in fact, holding a `Rectangle` object, we might want to transform `myShape` into a variable of type `Rectangle` because this will allow us to use the `Height` property. To do this, we can use the cast operator as described in the next section.

Casting Objects

The following assignment from earlier

```
Car myCar = new FamilyCar();
```

demonstrates our ability to assign an object of class `FamilyCar` to a variable `myCar` that is declared to reference objects of type `Car`. This is possible without further ado because `FamilyCar` is a descendant of `Car`, which means that all the class members that `Car` allows us to call will also be available to call in a `FamilyCar`. Because `Car` is higher up in the inheritance hierarchy than `FamilyCar`, this type of assignment requires what is called an *up cast*, as shown in Figure 17.4.

If we move in the opposite direction and cast a variable type into a descendant type, it is called *down casting*. However, down casting is more problematic. For example, we can't just write

```
FamilyCar myFamilyCar = myCar;    //Invalid
```

because `myCar` could also contain a `SportsCar` or a `RacingCar`, of which neither contain the same class members as can be called through a `FamilyCar`. However, if we are certain that `myCar` is, in fact, referencing a `FamilyCar` object, we can explicitly cast `myCar` into a `FamilyCar` object, as shown in the following line:

```
FamilyCar myFamilyCar = (FamilyCar) myCar;
```

FIGURE 17.4
Down casting and up casting.

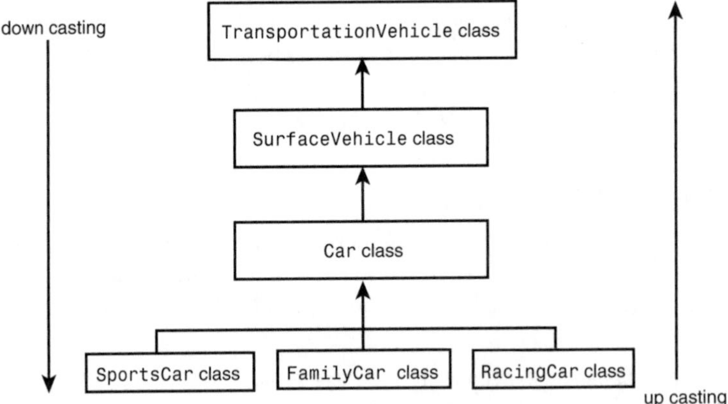

Note

If you cast an object of class A to class B and class A is a descendant of class B, it is called an up cast. An up cast does not need an explicit cast operator.

If class A is an ancestor of class B, it is called a down cast. A down cast requires an explicit cast operator such as `(<Type>)`.

Armed with the `is` operator to check whether a reference variable is referencing a particular kind of object type and the cast operator to perform down casts, we can solve our `Rectangle` problem stated earlier and sum up the total height of the `Rectangle` objects contained in the `drawing` array. This has been done in Listing 17.6.

LISTING 17.6 `DownCastingRectangles.cs`

```
using System;

abstract public class Shape
{
    public abstract void DrawYourself();
}

public class Rectangle : Shape
{
    private double height;

    public Rectangle(double initialHeight)
    {
        height = initialHeight;
    }

    public override void DrawYourself()
    {
        Console.WriteLine("Draw a rectangle");
    }

    public double Height
    {
        get
        {
            return height;
        }
        set
        {
            height = value;
        }
    }
}

class Circle : Shape
{
    public override void DrawYourself()
    {
        Console.WriteLine("Draw a circle");
    }
}

class Tester
{
    private static Shape[] drawing;

    public static void Main()
```

LISTING 17.6 continued

```
48:     {
49:         Rectangle myRectangle;
50:         double totalHeight = 0;
51:         drawing = new Shape[3];
52:
53:         drawing[0] = new Rectangle(10.6);
54:         drawing[1] = new Circle();
55:         drawing[2] = new Rectangle(30.8);
56:
57:         for(int i = 0; i < drawing.Length; i++)
58:         {
59:             if(drawing[i] is Rectangle)
60:             {
61:                 myRectangle = (Rectangle)drawing[i];
62:                 totalHeight += myRectangle.Height;
63:             }
64:         }
65:         Console.WriteLine("Total height of rectangles: {0}", totalHeight);
66:     }
67: }
```

```
Total height of rectangles: 41.4
```

To keep the source code short, the `Triangle` subclass has not been included, and each of the overriding `DrawYourself` methods only contain one simple call to the `WriteLine` method. This does not interfere with how the `is` operator and the cast operator are demonstrated in the `Main` method of the `Tester` class.

The drawing array (lines 53–55) assigned three objects, two of which are of type `Rectangle`. The `i` loop counter of the `for` loop (lines 57–64) iterates through each index of the `drawing` array. Line 59 utilizes the `is` operator to ask the question, "Does the drawing element with index `i` reference a `Rectangle` object?" Only if this is `true` will lines 61 and 62 be executed. Consequently, we can confidently perform the down cast in line 61 that lets us call the `Height` property in line 62 and add the height of `myRectangle` to `totalHeight`.

Tip

In general, you should only perform up casts (and thereby loose type information) if the lost type information will not be needed again. In most parts of your program, you should not need to use the `is` and the down cast operators. If you find the `is` and down cast operators in many places of your program, it is likely because of a design flaw.

Not only is the object type of the drawing element checked by the `is` operator, it is once again checked by the cast operator in line 61, even though it is needless (this is done automatically for any cast). This is a waste of computer resources. By using the `as` operator presented in the next section, we can avoid this redundant check.

The as Operator

The **as** operator is tailor-made to perform the type of down casts demonstrated in Listing 17.6. It combines the `is` operator object type check, the `if` statement, and the cast operator into one simple operation, as demonstrated in the following lines that can replace lines 57–64 of Listing 17.6:

```
for(int i = 0; i < drawing.Length; i++)
{
    myRectangle = drawing[i] as Rectangle;
    if(myRectangle != null)
    {
        totalHeight += myRectangle.Height;
    }
}
```

By positioning **as** between `drawing[i]` and `Rectangle` in the third line, we are asking to have the `drawing[i]` element down cast to class `Rectangle`. If this is possible (because `drawing[i]` contains an object of class `Rectangle`, which is automatically checked by the **as** operator), the `Rectangle` object is returned and, in this case, is assigned to the `myRectangle` variable. On the other hand, if the request fails because `drawing[i]` does not contain a `Rectangle` object, the `null` value is returned from the **as** operator and assigned to `myRectangle`. So, before we can call `Height` on `myRectangle`, we must check (as in line 4) that it does not hold the value `null`.

System.Object: The Ultimate Base Class

The .NET Framework class library contains a class called `System.Object` from which all classes are ultimately derived. This is due to two facts. First, whenever you create a class without specifying a base class for it, C# automatically specifies `System.Object` to be its base class. Second, any chain of derived classes will always have a topmost class (like `TransportVehicle` in Figure 16.9 of Chapter 16) that does not have any base class specified. This topmost class will then automatically get `System.Object` as its base class, and any descendants will inherit the class members from `System.Object`.

`System.Object` deserves a closer look, because any class inherits its useful class members. Table 17.1 provides an overview of each of `System.Object`'s methods. The method declaration column displays how each of the methods are declared inside `System.Object`.

TABLE 17.1 `System.Object`'s Methods

Method declaration	Description
`public virtual` ➥`string ToString()`	Returns a `string` representation of the current object by returning its namespace name and classname. This method is `virtual` and can be `overridden` to return any `string` you might find suitable. Often, `ToString()` is overridden to return information about the state of an object.

TABLE 17.1 continued

Method declaration	Description
`public virtual bool ➥Equals(object obj)`	Returns `true` if the current object is the same instance as `obj`; otherwise, returns `false`. Thus, `Equals` does not compare the state of the two objects (value-based equality) but tests for reference equality. Often though, `Equals` is overridden in a derived class to support value-based comparisons.
`public Type GetType()`	The `Type` class returned from the `GetType` method provides access to the metadata of the current object type. `GetType` was presented in Chapter 7, "Types Part II: Operators, Enumerators, and Strings."
`public virtual int ➥GetHashTable()`	Returns an `int` representation of the object called a hash, which is used for fast access to the object in special collections of objects called hash tables.
`protected object ➥MemberwiseClone()`	Returns a shallow copy of the current object, which means a copy of the current object is returned. Shallow refers to the fact that if this object is referencing other objects, only the references are copied, not the referenced objects.
`public static bool Equals ➥(object objA, object objB)`	Performs a value-based comparison between `objA` and `objB`.
`public static bool ➥ReferenceEquals ➥(object objA, object objB)`	Returns `true` if `objA` is referencing the same object as `objB`.
`protected virtual ➥void Finalize()`	This method is also called a destructor. If you override this method, as discussed in Chapter 13, "Class Anatomy Part II: Object Creation and Garbage Collection," the overriding method is called when the object is garbage collected. `Finalize` is of little practical use.

You can use the functionality of the instance methods inherited by your classes in Table 17.1 simply by calling them through your objects like any other function member, as demonstrated in Listing 17.7.

LISTING 17.7 `SystemObjectTest.cs`

```
using System;

namespace Animals
{
    class Dog
    {
        private string name;

```

LISTING 17.7 continued

```
        public Dog()
        {
            name = "unknown";
        }

        public Dog(string initialName)
        {
            name = initialName;
        }

        public string Name
        {
            get
            {
                return name;
            }
        }
    }
}

class ObjectTester
{
    public static void Main()
    {
        Type dogType;
        Animals.Dog myDog = new Animals.Dog("Fido");
        Animals.Dog yourDog = new Animals.Dog("Pluto");
        Animals.Dog sameDog = myDog;

        Console.WriteLine("ToString(): " + myDog.ToString());
        dogType = myDog.GetType();
        Console.WriteLine("Type: " + dogType.ToString());

        if(myDog.Equals(yourDog))
            Console.WriteLine("myDog is referencing the same object
            ➥ as yourDog");
        else
            Console.WriteLine("myDog and yourDog are referencing
            ➥ different objects");

        if(myDog.Equals(sameDog))
            Console.WriteLine("myDog is referencing the same object
            ➥ as sameDog");
        else
            Console.WriteLine("myDog and sameDog are referencing
            ➥ different objects");

        if(object.ReferenceEquals(myDog, yourDog))
            Console.WriteLine("myDog and yourDog are referencing the
            ➥ same object");
        else
```

LISTING 17.7 continued

```
55:             Console.WriteLine("myDog and yourDog are referencing
                ➥ different objects");
56:     }
57: }
```

```
ToString(): Animals.Dog
Type: Animals.Dog
myDog and yourDog are referencing different objects
myDog is referencing the same object as sameDog
myDog and yourDog are referening different objects
```

According to Table 17.1, the `ToString` method returns a `string` of the general form:

<Namespace_name>.<Class_name>

The `Dog` class exists in a namespace called `Animals`, so we should expect the following output from the call to `ToString` in line 38:

```
Animals.Dog
```

which is confirmed by the first line of the sample output.

Note

Often, as demonstrated in Listing 17.8 shown in a moment, `ToString()` is overridden in the derived class to return a `string` that represents the object's state.

The `Type` class returned from `myDog.GetType()` lets you access valuable (metadata) information about the `Dog` class. In this simple demonstration, we restrict ourselves to asking for the `string` representation of the type (line 40), which is identical to the format provided by the `ToString()` method.

Line 42 evaluates whether `myDog` and `yourDog` are referencing the same instance.

Line 36 assigns the reference held by `myDog` to `sameDog`, so `myDog` and `sameDog` are referencing the same object, which is correctly assessed by `Equals` in line 47.

C# contains the keyword `object`, which is an alias for the `System.Object` classname. Recall that we need to use the classname when we call a `static` method. Therefore, we can use `object` in line 52 to call the `static` `ReferenceEquals` method and test whether `myDog` and `yourDog` are referencing the same object instance. In effect, we are performing the same test in line 42 as in line 52.

As shown in Table 17.1 most of the methods contained in `System.Object` are `virtual` and can therefore be overridden. Listing 17.8 shows how the `ToString` method can be overridden to provide information about the state of an object and how `Equals` can be overridden to perform a value-based comparison between two objects instead of the default reference-based comparison we saw in Listing 17.7.

Note

Any class that overrides the **Equals** method, such as **Dog** in Listing 17.8, should also override the **GetHashCode** method to produce a unique numerical value that identifies the object in a hashtable collection. I have omitted the **GetHashCode** override to keep the code brief. As a result you will see a warning when you compile Listing 17.8.

Listing 17.8 *ObjectOverrideTest.cs*

```
using System;

namespace Animals
{
    class Dog
    {
        private string name;

        public Dog()
        {
            name = "unknown";
        }

        public Dog(string initialName)
        {
            name = initialName;
        }

        public string Name
        {
            get
            {
                return name;
            }
        }

        public override string ToString()
        {
            return "Dog name: " + name;
        }

        public override bool Equals(object obj)
        {
            Dog tempDog = (Dog) obj;

            if(tempDog.Name == name)
            {
                return true;
            }
            else
            {
                return false;
```

Listing 17.8 continued

```
43:             }
44:         }
45:     }
46: }
47:
48: class ObjectTester
49: {
50:     public static void Main()
51:     {
52:         Animals.Dog myDog = new Animals.Dog("Fido");
53:         Animals.Dog yourDog = new Animals.Dog("Fido");
54:
55:         Console.WriteLine(myDog);
56:
57:         if(myDog.Equals(yourDog))
58:             Console.WriteLine("myDog has the same name as yourDog");
59:         else
60:             Console.WriteLine("myDog and yourDog have different names");
61:     }
62: }
```

```
Dog name: Fido
myDog has the same name as yourDog
```

Lines 27-30 override the `ToString` method to output the content of the instance variable `name`.

The `Equals` method is overridden in lines 32-44 to compare the instance variable `name` of the current `Dog` object to a `Dog` object passed to it as an argument.

Recall that a variable of class `TransportVehicle` in our inheritance hierarchy of Figure 16.1 of Chapter 16, "Inheritance Part I: Basic Concepts" could be used to reference an object of any of the types in the hierarchy, because `TransportVehicle` was at the top of the hierarchy. Similarly because `System.Object` implicitly is at the top of any hierarchy, a variable of type `System.Object` can be used to reference an object of any type whether this be a `Car`, `Shape`, `Account`, `Elevator`, `Bacterium` or other. As a result the formal parameter `obj` declared in line 32 to be of type `object` is able to reference any object type that may be passed to it. However, just like the variable of type `Shape` restricted us to access only class members defined in the `Shape` class even though it referenced the subclass `Rectangle`, `obj` will only let us use the few `System.Object` members presented in Table 17.1, even if it like in this case stores a `Dog` object. To access the `Name` property of the `Dog` object referenced by `obj` we need to perform a down-cast as shown in line 34 where the `Dog` object is assigned to `tempDog`. Notice that to keep the code brief we are not checking with the `is` or `as` operators (presented earlier) whether `obj` actually holds a `Dog` object. So if anybody provides a different type of object the down cast will generate an exception. `tempDog` allows us in line 36 to access the `Name` property of the `Dog` object and thereby perform the comparison between the name of the `Dog` object provided as an argument and the name of this current object.

The `WriteLine` method in line 55 automatically calls `ToString` of `myDog` and prints the `string` returned on the screen. Even though it was impossible for the implementers of `WriteLine` to predict the object types passed to `WriteLine` they knew that they all inherited `ToString` and could therefore confidently let `WriteLine` call this method on any object argument without causing any problems.

According to lines 52 and 53 both `myDog` and `yourDog` are called `Fido`, so the Boolean expression in line 57 returns `true`.

NOTE

Any class like `Dog` in Listing 17.8 that overrides the `Equals` method, such as `Dog` in Listing 17.8, should also override the `GetHashCode` method to produce a unique numerical value that identifies the object in a hash-table collection.

Method hiding

Even if a function member (here referring to a method, property or indexer) is not declared `virtual` in a base class you can still write a function with the same signature and return type in its derived class. However, the dynamic binding mechanism will never be activated for this function. Consequently if you call a non-`virtual` function for a variable of a base class which references an object of the derived type it will invoke the version implemented in the base class not the version implemented in the derived class (as had been the case if the function was declared `virtual`). Instead of overriding the non-`virtual` base class function the new function is said to *hide* the base class function. Listing 17.9 demonstrates the difference between overriding and hiding a base class method.

Listing 17.9 *Source code of* `MethodHidingTest.cs`

```
using System;

class Car
{
    public virtual void MoveForward()
    {
        Console.WriteLine("Move Car forward by 1 kilometer");
    }

    public void Reverse()
    {
        Console.WriteLine("Reverse Car by 50 meters");
    }
}

class FamilyCar : Car
{
```

Listing 17.9 continued

```
18:     public override void MoveForward()
19:     {
20:         Console.WriteLine("Move Family Car forward by 5 kilometers");
21:     }
22:
23:     public new void Reverse()
24:     {
25:         Console.WriteLine("Reverse the Family Car by 200 meters");
26:     }
27: }
28:
29: class Tester
30: {
31:     public static void Main()
32:     {
33:         Car myCar;
34:
35:         myCar = new FamilyCar();
36:         myCar.MoveForward();
37:         myCar.Reverse();
38:     }
39: }
```

```
Move Family Car forward by 5 kilometers
Reverse Car by 50 meters
```

To demonstrate the difference between a `virtual` and a non-`virtual` method the `Car` class is equipped with one of each kind. The `virtual` method `MoveForward` and the non-`virtual` method `Reverse`. The `FamilyCar` class is derived from `Car`. It overrides the `MoveForward` method in lines 18-21 and hides the `Reverse` method in lines 23-26.

Whenever you hide a function you should include the keyword `new` as in line 23 (which in this context has a different meaning than the keyword `new` that we use to instantiate new objects). We will return to the `new` keyword in a moment. For now simply regard it as necessary to keep the compiler from generating a warning.

In usual fashion we declare a variable of the base class `Car` in line 33 and assigns it a reference to an object of its derived class `FamilyCar` in line 35. As the output confirms dynamic binding is activated (in line 36) for the `virtual` `MoveForward` method resulting in the execution of the implementation residing in the derived class `FamilyCar`. In contrast dynamic binding is not applied (in line 37) to the non-`virtual` method `Reverse` resulting in the `Reverse` implementation residing in `myCar`'s type `Car` to be executed. So no matter which type of object `myCar` is referencing this call:

```
myCar.Reverse()
```

will always cause the `Reverse` implementation found in the `Car` class to be executed because `myCar` is of type `Car`. This causes a serious problem. If `myCar` is referencing an object of a derived class we clearly want the derived class implementation of `Reverse` to be executed. To resolve this problem the `Reverse` method should be declared `virtual` like `MoveForward`.

Most of the functions declared for a base class are analogous to the `MoveForward` and `Reverse` methods in that they need to be declared `virtual` to avoid the kind of problems experienced with the non-`virtual` method `Reverse` in Listing 17.9. If `virtual` functions are much more common than non-`virtual` functions why does a function (without the `virtual` keyword) then default to become a non-`virtual` method? One of the main reasons has to do with a concept called versioning presented in the next section.

Versioning with the `new` and `override` keywords

A large proportion of the software written today is, as mentioned earlier developed by using class libraries often written by other remote programmers. Just like most standalone software applications are upgraded to versions with more features and less bugs, class libraries undergo a similar evolving process. It is a fairly painless process to upgrade to the latest version of the Doom game, but what if you want to upgrade the .NET Framework class library on which your application is heavily dependent. What if the library developers for example didn't like the name `WriteLine` anymore and changed it to `PrintLine` in the latest upgrade? You would then have to painstakingly substitute all the `WriteLine` calls in your code to `PrintLine` calls.

The problems and solutions related to class library upgrades are generally termed *versioning*. In this section we will deal with one particular versioning issue related to inheritance, which is elegantly handled by C#. This will make you appreciate why C# encourages us to use the `new` keyword (as shown in line 23 of Listing 17.9 if we are hiding a function member in a derived class and the keyword `override` if we are overriding it. It further shows you why non-`virtual` methods are the default and why the `virtual` keyword is explicitly required to declare a function to be `virtual`.

Often class library classes are reused by deriving your own classes from them. This was demonstrated earlier where we extended the `System.Windows.FormsWinForms.Form` class to display a simple GUI window.

Suppose you in a similar way, as illustrated in Listing 17.10 are writing a `SpaceShuttle` class by extending the `Rocket` class found in a class library written by a company called BlipSoft. Usually classes and class libraries exist inside dll assemblies as discussed in Chapter 15 and their code cannot be viewed, but for demonstration purposes I have inserted the `Rocket` class as part of the code shown in Listing 17.10.

Listing 17.10 *Source code of* `SpaceShuttle.cs`

```
using System;

class Rocket
{
      // Rocket is part of a class library developed
      // and maintained by the BlipSoft software company
```

Listing 17.10 continued

```
    private int age = 0;

    public int Age
    {
        get
        {
            return age;
        }

        set
        {
            age = value;
        }
    }
}

class SpaceShuttle : Rocket
{
     //SpaceShuttle is written by you
    private int distanceTravelled = 0;

    public int DistanceTravelled
    {
        get
        {
            return distanceTravelled;
        }
    }

    public void MoveForward(int distanceAdded)
    {
        distanceTravelled += distanceAdded;
    }
}

class Tester
{
    public static void Main()
    {
        SpaceShuttle columbia = new SpaceShuttle();

        columbia.MoveForward(30);
        Console.WriteLine("Distance travelled: {0}",
            columbia.DistanceTravelled);
    }
}
```

```
Distance travelled: 30
```

The Rocket class from BlipSoft does not include an instance variable to keep track of the distance traveled so you have included it in the SpaceShuttle class (line 26) along with the MoveForward method (lines 36-39) that adds a certain distance to the distanceTravelled instance variable. This all works fine until you receive a new upgrade of the class library from BlipSoft. By pure coincidence they have in this version added a virtual method to the Rocket base class with exactly the same name, return type and parameter types as your MoveForward method in the SpaceShuttle class. It looks like this:

```
public virtual void MoveForward(int daysAdded)
{
    age += daysAdded;
}
```

You have no connection with BlipSoft other than the use of their class library so you have no idea that this method has been included. If the compiler, as is the case for several other programming languages, automatically assumed that a virtual method in a base class should be overridden by a method of the same signature in a descendant class then MoveForward of SpaceShuttle would override MoveForward of Rocket. This would be an error because the two methods perform completely unrelated actions: Rocket's MoveForward is adding days to the age instance variable whereas SpaceShuttle's MoveForward is adding a distance to the distanceTravelled instance variable. the compilers of these other languages give no hint to the programmer of the error, which could stay undetected for a period of time. This error however does not prevent the program from running and the error could stay undetected for a period of time.

NOTE

If the code had been written in C++ then SpaceShuttle's MoveForward would automatically override Rocket's MoveForward without any warning. Any call to MoveForward through a variable of type Rocket containing an object of type SpaceShuttle would through dynamic binding call SpaceShuttle's MoveForward method.

If the code was written in Java and the two MoveForward methods contained different return types the program would fail to compile because an overriding method must return the same type as the type it is overriding.

The C# compiler prevents these problems by alerting you about the issue through the following warning when you compile your program with the upgraded class library:

```
SpaceShuttle.cs(40,17): warning CS0114: 'SpaceShuttle.MoveForward(int)' hides
inherited member 'Rocket.MoveForward(int)'. To make the current method
override that implementation, add the override keyword. Otherwise add the
new keyword.
```

You now get the opportunity to show your intent either by declaring SpaceShuttle's MoveForward to be an overriding method or just to be a new method hiding Rocket's MoveForward method. In our case we must declare it new as shown here:

```
    public new void MoveForward(int distanceAdded)
    {
        distanceTravelled += distanceAdded;
    }
```

Notice that even if you don't follow the advice in the compiler's warning and refrain from including the `new` or the `override` keywords the program will still compile and `SpaceShuttle`'s `MoveForward` method defaults to become a `new` hiding method. However the `new` and `override` keywords convey important information to people reading through your code so use them with care and make sure you eliminate all the compiler warnings.

Suppose the `MoveForward` method of the upgraded `Rocket` class was not suitable to be overridden and its designers accordingly declared it a non-`virtual` method by leaving out the `virtual` keyword and that this method would be shipped with the upgrade instead of the `virtual MoveForward` version shown before. Then there would be no doubt that `SpaceShuttle`'s `MoveForward` was merely hiding `Rocket`'s `MoveForward` because a non-`virtual` method can never be overridden. Furthermore there would be no issues regarding different return types and other details concerning overriding. In other words the two methods would be totally separate. `Rocket`'s non-`virtual MoveForward` would not be able to "reach in" and create confusion in `SpaceShuttle`'s `MoveForward` method like `Rocket`'s `virtual MoveForward` sibling.

In general you can create more havoc in derived classes by adding `virtual` methods rather than non-`virtual` methods to your base classes especially when these are part of a class library used by separate programmers where the communication is limited. So even though the majority of your methods in general needs to be declared `virtual`, C# still requires you to explicitly declare a method to be `virtual` to avoid any non-intended `virtual` methods roaming in your code.

NOTE

Virtual functions are slightly slower to execute than their non-`virtual` siblings, because the runtime dynamically need use a bit of processing power to determine which `virtual` method implementation to execute. In contrast the execution of a non-`virtual` method is determined and hardwire at compile time. This slight performance difference is another argument for making non-`virtual` functions the default.

Multiple inheritance

Multiple inheritance allows a class to have more than one base class. For example a particular kind of `car` may be a `jeep` and a family car at the same time as illustrated in Figure 17.5. The `FamilyCarJeep` is thus derived from the `FamilyCar` as well as the `Jeep`.

Even though multiple inheritance is a powerful concept, which is supported by languages like C++ and Eiffel it also involves several subtleties that can make its implementation tricky.

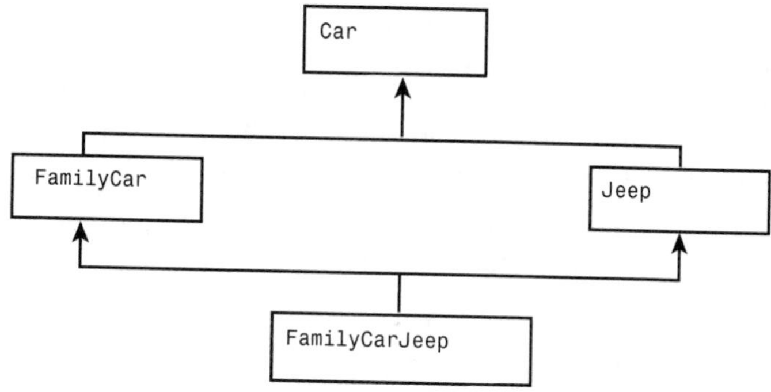

FIGURE 17.5
An example of multiple inheritance

NOTE

Multiple inheritance is a heavily debated concept in the programming community where pros and cons are thrown back and forth between its supporters and detractors.

One of the problems often mentioned by the detractors includes a scenario where the two base classes both contain a method with the same signature but different implementations. Which of the two versions should the derived class then inherit? For example, suppose both the `FamilyCar` and the `Jeep` classes implement the method `ToString`. The `FamilyCar` version returns the values of the `brandName` and `odometer` instance variables (in a `string`) whereas the `Jeep` returns the `numberOfSeats` and the `suspensionSystemName`. If the `FamilyCarJeep` does not override the `ToString` method, which `ToString` version should it inherit?

A similar problem is encountered when the two base classes contain two data members with the same name. Each data member might hold different kinds of information in each of the two base classes and both be important for the derived class. Should both data members be inherited and if so how are they distinguished?

Some computer languages that allow their classes to engage in multiple inheritance attempt to solve the mentioned problems in more or less elegant ways. The designers of C# decided to deal with the problems by disallowing multiple inheritance and instead provide an alternative language construct called an interface.

Interfaces

Recall the `Shape` class from the drawing program case study presented earlier. It contained the `abstract` method `DrawYourself`, which obliged any class derived from `Shape` to implement a `DrawYourself` method with the same signature and return type. In other words any class derived from `Shape` had to fulfill a contract saying: "I the derived class of `Shape` hereby promise to implement any `abstract` method contained in `Shape` or I shall be `abstract` myself". This guarantee enabled us to call the different `DrawYourself` implementations in `Circle`, `Triangle` and `Rectangle` through dynamic binding. Notice that the `Shape` class didn't contain any data members or function member implementations and therefore didn't offer any code reuse benefits to its sub classes; the main reason for creating the `Shape` class was instead to call `DrawYourself` with dynamic binding.

The *interface* language construct can be viewed as the ultimate `abstract` class in that it only contains `abstract` functions. Even syntactically an interface resembles a purely `abstract` class that only contains `abstract` functions.

A class can *implement* an interface. The class then promises to implement the interface's `abstract` function members just like a derived class promises to implement the `abstract` functions of its base class. So an interface offers an alternative to a purely `abstract` base class for implementing functions that can be called through dynamic binding. We could for example, in our previous drawing program, have exchanged the `Shape` class with an equivalent `Shape` interface also containing an `abstract DrawYourself` method. The `Circle`, `Triangle` and `Rectangle` classes would then implement the `Shape` interface instead. This would not affect our ability to call the `DrawYourself` method via dynamic binding and would thus leave the functionality of the program unchanged. However this experiment fails to demonstrate the true power of interfaces and their proper use.

Even though interfaces and `abstract` classes are closely related syntactically and semantically they have one important difference: Interfaces can only contain `abstract` functions whereas `abstract` classes apart from `abstract` functions also may contain data members and fully implemented non-`abstract` functions. Consequently implementing multiple interfaces does not pose the same potential problems as multiple inheritance because clashing data members and implementations are nonexistent. As a result a class can have at most one base class but implement an unlimited number of interfaces.

An interface can itself implement one or more interfaces and thereby inherit the `abstract` functions of these interfaces. This allows interfaces to form interface hierarchies similar to those formed by classes.

Commonly classes form the sturdy taxonomical class hierarchies presented earlier where each pair of base class/derived class represents an is-a relationship. These hierarchies provide tremendous benefits as discussed earlier, however they also restrict our ability to benefit from polymorphism somewhat. Let's see why: To benefit from polymorphism in a class hierarchy we must have a group of classes with the same ancestor. This ancestor then specifies the function headers (in the form of `abstract` classes) and thereby the protocols for communicating with the individual implementations in the derived classes. But what if the classes we want to group together in this generic construct do not have the same ancestor? What if they are scattered throughout our program and even located in separate class hierarchies? Suppose for example we are writing a space invaders game containing the two class hierarchies A and B as shown in Figure 17.6.

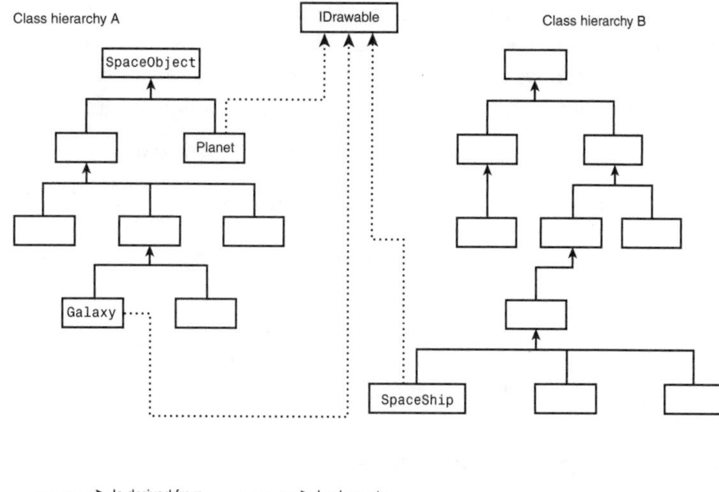

FIGURE 17.6
IDrawable let three unrelated classes implement the same *abstract* method

Like `Circle`, `Rectangle`, and `Triangle` in the drawing case study, we want to draw objects of the three classes `Planet`, `Galaxy` and `SpaceShip` on the screen. Each class has its own distinct way of drawing itself on the screen so we decide to equip each class with a `DrawYourself` method and hope to group them together under a common ancestor that contains an `abstract DrawYourself` method. This poses a major problem because the three classes are located in separate parts of the program and do not have a common ancestor. We could attempt to solve the problem by inserting another class sitting on top of both hierarchies and let this class contain the `abstract DrawYourself` method. This could work but it would distort the hierarchy. Furthermore if we applied this same strategy to other groups of disparately located classes with the same polymorhic needs we would end up with a topmost class containing all kinds of non-related `abstract` methods.

A much more elegant solution would be to create an interface called, say, `IDrawable` (Conventionally an interface name commences with an uppercase I) containing the `abstract` method `DrawYourself`, and let the three classes implement this interface as illustrated in Figure 17.6. The `IDrawable` interface could be implemented as follows (more about interface syntax in the following section):

```
public interface IDrawable
{
    void DrawYourself();
}
```

NOTE

It would not be possible to substitute the `IDrawable` interface with a class because `Galaxy`, `SpaceShip` and `Planet` would then each have two base classes, which is invalid.

`IDrawable` provides a common interface through which we can execute the different implementations of the three classes. So similar to Lines 38-44 in Listing 17.4 that accepted an array of type `Shape` we can now write a method called `DrawSpaceScene` which accepts an array with elements of type `IDdrawable` as shown in the following lines:

```
public void DrawSpaceScene(IDrawable [] drawing)
{
    for(int i = 0; i < drawing.Length; i++)
    {
        drawing [i].DrawYourself();
    }
}
```

This provides the same benefits in terms of generic programming as described in the drawing program case study.

Defining an interface

The syntax for defining an interface is shown in Syntax Box 17.2. It consists of an optional access modifier followed by the keyword `interface`, and the interface identifier. The optional *<Base_interface_list>* specifies >the list of interfaces that are implemented by the interface. As mentioned earlier this list can consist of an unlimited number of interfaces.

Syntax Box 17.2 The Interface

```
Interface_definition::=
[<Access_modifier>] interface <Interface_identifier> [:
<Base_interface_list>]
{
    [<Abstract_methods>]
    [<Abstract_properties>]
    [<Abstract_indexers>]
    [<Events>]
}
```

Where:

```
<Abstract_method>::=
<Return_type> <Method_identifier> ([<Parameter_list>]);

<Abstract_property>::=
<Property_type> <Property_identifier> { [get;] [set;] }

<Abstract_indexer>::=
<Indexer_type> this [<Parameter_list>] { [get;] [set;] }

<Event>::=
event <Event_type> <Event_identifier>;
```

Notes:

Conventionally the interface identifier should commence with a capital `I` (for interface) and because an interface en*able*s a class to perform additional actions by forcing it to implement its `abstract` members, the interface identifier often ends with –`able` as in `IComparable`, `ICloneable`, `Istorable` and so forth. None of the interface members (`abstract` methods, properties, indexers and events) can include an access modifier. The members are implicitly declared `public` because they are meant to be accessible from outside the class that implements the members of interface. Properties and indexers defined in an interface can either have one `abstract get` accessor or one abstract `set` accessor or both. Accessors are implicitly declared abstract.

Recall the built-in `string` method called `CompareTo` presented in Chapter 7. It allows us to compare two strings lexicographically. For example, we can compare `myString` and `yourString` by writing the following:

```
myString.CompareTo(yourString)
```

If `myString` is greater than `yourString`, `CompareTo` returns a positive value; if the two strings are identical, `CompareTo` returns zero; and if `myString` is smaller than `yourString`, a negative value is returned.

As we realized in Chapter 7, the `CompareTo` method allowed us to sort a list of strings in alphabetical order. Thus, any class with an equivalent `CompareTo` method can have its objects sorted. This allows us to construct a sorting method, which can sort not only strings but any list of objects instantiated from a class, guaranteeing to contain a `CompareTo` implementation. How can a class guarantee this—by implementing an interface that declares an `abstract` `CompareTo` method. We will continue our story about the generic sorting method in a moment; for now, let's assume that the previous discussion has convinced us that the following interface is needed to construct this generic sorting method.

```
public interface IComparable
{
    int CompareTo(IComparable comp);
}
```

By implementing this interface, a class guarantees to provide an implementation for a `public` method called `CompareTo` with an `int` return type and one formal parameter of type `IComparable`. Furthermore, if the `CompareTo` method is implemented correctly and returns negative, zero, and positive values following the same scheme as that of the `string` class, we know its objects are comparable. The next section demonstrates how a class implements an interface in general, and demonstrates in particular how the `TimeSpan` class (originally introduced in Chapter 14, "Class Anatomy III: Writing Intuitive Code") can implement the `IComparable` interface to make objects of this class comparable.

Implementing an Interface

The syntax for specifying that a class implements an interface is, as shown in Syntax Box 17.3, similar to deriving it from a base class. A colon separates the class identifier from the optional base class and list of interfaces implemented by the class.

Syntax Box 17.3 Class Definition

```
Class_defintion::=
<Access_modif> class <Class_identifier> [: [<Base_class>][, <Interface_list>]]
{
    <Class_members>
}
```

where

```
<Interface_list>::=
<Interface_identifier_1> [, <Interface_identifier_2> ...]
```

Notes:

- A class can have zero or one base classes.
- A class can implement an unlimited number of interfaces. Commas must separate all implemented interfaces.

Example:

The `SportsCar` class is derived from the `Car` class and implements the `ITunable` and `IInsurable` interfaces.

```
public class SportsCar : Car, ITunable, IInsurable
{
    <Class_members>
}
```

The `SportsCar` class must implement all `abstract` members in `Car`, `ITunable`, and `IInsurable`; otherwise, `SportsCar` becomes `abstract`.

By letting the `TimeSpan` class implement the `IComparable` interface from the previous section, and by writing the method body for the `CompareTo` method in `TimeSpan` as required, you can make any two `TimeSpan` objects comparable, as demonstrated in Listing 17.11.

LISTING 17.11 ComparableTimeSpans.cs

```
using System;

public interface IComparable
{
    int CompareTo(IComparable comp);
}

public class TimeSpan : IComparable
{
    private uint totalSeconds;

    public TimeSpan()
    {
        totalSeconds = 0;
    }

    public TimeSpan(uint initialSeconds)
    {
```

LISTING 17.11 continued

```
19:         totalSeconds = initialSeconds;
20:     }
21:
22:     public uint Seconds
23:     {
24:         get
25:         {
26:             return totalSeconds;
27:         }
28:
29:         set
30:         {
31:             totalSeconds = value;
32:         }
33:     }
34:
35:     public int CompareTo(IComparable comp)
36:     {
37:         TimeSpan compareTime = (TimeSpan) comp;
38:
39:         if(totalSeconds > compareTime.Seconds)
40:             return 1;
41:         else if(compareTime.Seconds == totalSeconds)
42:             return 0;
43:         else
44:             return -1;
45:     }
46: }
47:
48: class Tester
49: {
50:     public static void Main()
51:     {
52:         TimeSpan myTime = new TimeSpan(3450);
53:         TimeSpan worldRecord = new TimeSpan(1239);
54:
55:         if(myTime.CompareTo(worldRecord) < 0)
56:             Console.WriteLine("My time is below the world record");
57:         else if(myTime.CompareTo(worldRecord) == 0)
58:             Console.WriteLine("My time is the same as the world record");
59:         else
60:             Console.WriteLine("I spent more time than the world record
            ➥ holder");
61:     }
62: }
```

```
I spent more time than the world record holder
```

The `IComparable` interface is defined in lines 3–6. Notice that we can use `IComparable` to specify the type of `CompareTo`'s formal parameter in line 5. Thus, any object of a class that implements the `IComparable` interface can be passed to this method as an argument. Had we declared the formal parameter to be of type TimeSpan instead, the interface would lose its general appeal and only be useful for the TimeSpan class, which defeats our original purpose of creating a generic sorting method.

The colon in line 8, followed by the word IComparable, specifies that TimeSpan is implementing the IComparable interface.

Lines 35–45 provide the required implementation of the CompareTo method. The method signature and the return type in line 35 are identical to that specified in the definition of the IComparable interface, as required, and the access modifier is public because CompareTo is implicitly specified to be so in the interface definition. The CompareTo method's task in TimeSpace's case is to compare the totalSeconds instance variable contained in the TimeSpan object, which is referenced by the comp parameter, with the totalSeconds instance variable of the current object.

Note

A CompareTo method implemented by a Circle class might compare radiuses. An Account class might compare balances, while TimeSpan compares totalSeconds.

totalSeconds of the current object is readily available, but totalSeconds of the comp object must be accessed via the Seconds property. Even though comp references an object of type TimeSpan the Seconds property is inaccessible through the comp parameter. Only the CompareTo method can be called through comp, because this is the only method specified in the IComparable interface. To access the Seconds property, we must down cast comp to type TimeSpan as in line 37. We can then reach the Seconds property through compareTime in lines 39 and 41.

Just as it would be possible in the drawing program case study to call the DrawYourself method directly through an object of one of Shape's subclasses without the need for dynamic binding, as in

```
Circle myCircle;
myCircle.DrawYourself();      //Does not require dynamic binding
```

it is also possible to call the CompareTo method directly through a TimeSpan object as demonstrated in lines 55 and 57. However, just like the myCircle.DrawYourself call doesn't expose polymorphism and its power, the calls to CompareTo in lines 55 and 57

```
myTime.CompareTo(worldRecord)       //Does not require dynamic binding
```

are merely useful to illustrate how the CompareTo method works. They could even have been implemented without applying the IComparable interface.

Notice that even though worldRecord is defined to be of type TimeSpan in line 53, it can still (in lines 55 and 57) be used as an argument to the CompareTo method (which accepts arguments of type IComparable) because TimeSpan implements the IComparable interface.

Listing 17.11 was meant to illustrate the syntax of defining and implementing an interface, but it didn't illustrate the true power of interfaces. We make up for this in the next section.

Generic Programming with Interfaces

Suppose we manually need to sort a list of numbers in ascending order. It takes us a while to work out a good sorting system, but eventually we get the hang of it. Soon after, we need to sort a list of students according to their grades. It turns out we can use exactly the same system we used to sort the numbers; the only difference is that instead of comparing pairs of numbers, we compare pairs of students. In fact, we can sort any list of objects with this method, as long as we can compare the pairs of the involved objects. When somebody asks us to describe the technique, we tell them the following (with large chunks cut out): "First you do the following…and if object x is greater than object y, …otherwise…later you…finally you…." We are able to explain the sorting technique in general terms without mentioning the kind of object we are sorting. We simply say "If object X is greater than object Y" instead. The person must work out how to compare pairs of the particular objects he or she is sorting.

We can use the same principle in computer programming to support code reuse. If the fundamental implementation of our sorting algorithm is independent of the object type we are sorting, we can write a *generic implementation* for this sorting routine—an implementation that can be reused to sort any (comparable) object type.

This section demonstrates how we can apply interfaces to write a generic version of the `BubbleSortAscending` method that was first presented in Chapter 11, "Arrays Part II: Multi-Dimensional Arrays. Searching and Sorting Arrays," and shown in Listing 17.12 to refresh your memory. Notice that Listing 17.12 does not compile.

LISTING 17.12 `BubbleSortAscending.cs`

```
 // Sort the elements of an array in ascending order
public static void BubbleSortAscending(int [] bubbles)
{
    bool swapped = true;

    for (int i = 0; swapped; i++)
    {
        swapped = false;
        for (int j = 0; j < (bubbles.Length - (i + 1)); j++)
        {
            if (bubbles[j] > bubbles[j + 1])
            {
                Swap(j, j + 1, bubbles);
                swapped = true;
            }
        }
    }
}

 //Swap two elements of an array
```

LISTING 17.12 continued

```
21: public static void Swap(int first, int second, int [] arr)
22: {
23:     int temp;
24:
25:     temp = arr[first];
26:     arr[first] = arr[second];
27:     arr[second] = temp;
28: }
```

At the moment, the `BubbleSortAscending` method can only be used to sort arrays with elements of type `int` (see line 2). If we needed to sort an array of `doubles`, we would need to write another bubble sort method meant for an array of element type `double`. Each class of objects with the need to be sorted requires its own dedicated bubble sort method. For example, 30 classes would require 30 sorting methods. This is clearly an inefficient avenue to follow. Instead, we set out to make the `BubbleSortAscending` implementation generic. The end result is shown in Listing 17.13, and the logic behind the code is discussed next.

The `BubbleSortAscending` method in Listing 17.12 is highly suited to become generic because only line 11 of this implementation cares about the changing array element type; the rest of the sorting logic remains unchanged. Line 11 asks the question, "Is element `j` greater than element `j+1`?" If we can somehow guarantee that the array element type of the array passed to the bubble sort method contains a method with the name `CompareTo` that only return a positive value if `j` is greater than `j+1`, we can compare two objects in the array with the following call:

```
(objectA.CompareTo(objectB) > 0)
```

and we can exchange line 11 of Listing 17.12 with the following line:

```
if (bubbles[j].CompareTo(bubbles[j + 1]) > 0)
```

How can we guarantee the existence of a `CompareTo` method? Any class that implements the `IComparable` interface defined in the previous section commits to implementing a `CompareTo` method. Consequently, any array element type that implements `IComparable` can be sorted by our sorting method. By declaring the formal parameter of the generic bubble sort method to be an array of type `IComparable`, as stated in its header in line 51 of Listing 17.13, we are assured that only arrays with comparable objects are passed to the method.

The only differences between our non-generic bubble sort in Listing 17.12 and the generic version in lines 51–57 of Listing 17.13 are found in the method header (line 51 of Listing 17.13) and the object comparison in line 60.

The `TimeSpan` class merely needs to implement the `IComparable` interface as specified in line 13 and provide an implementation for `CompareTo` (lines 35–45) to become "sortable." However, this privilege is not restricted to the `TimeSpan` class. We can make `Account`, `RacingCar`, `Circle`, `Bacterium`, and any other suitable classes "sortable" simply by letting the class implement the `IComparable` interface and by adding a few lines of code to implement the `CompareTo` method. Every "sortable" class reuses the same bubble sort code written just once.

Again, the dynamic binding mechanism is at work behind the scenes (in line 60 of Listing 17.13) to make this powerful scenario work. Even though the **bubbles** array contains **IComparable** elements, the call in line 60 to **CompareTo** automatically, via dynamic binding, calls the implementation for **CompareTo** that matches the object type stored in the element when the call takes place.

The **Main** method demonstrates our sorting method's ability to sort an array of four **TimeSpan** objects. Notice that even though the **raceTime** array is of type **TimeSpan**, it is still accepted by the sorting method because **TimeSpan** implements the **IComparable** interface.

LISTING 17.13 GenericBubbleSort.cs

```
01: using System;
02:
03: public interface IComparable
04: {
05:     int CompareTo(IComparable comp);
06: }
07:
08: public class TimeSpan : IComparable
09: {
10:     private uint totalSeconds;
11:
12:     public TimeSpan()
13:     {
14:         totalSeconds = 0;
15:     }
16:
17:     public TimeSpan(uint initialSeconds)
18:     {
19:         totalSeconds = initialSeconds;
20:     }
21:
22:     public uint Seconds
23:     {
24:         get
25:         {
26:             return totalSeconds;
27:         }
28:
29:         set
30:         {
31:             totalSeconds = value;
32:         }
33:     }
34:
35:     public virtual int CompareTo(IComparable comp)
36:     {
37:         TimeSpan compareTime = (TimeSpan) comp;
38:
39:         if(totalSeconds > compareTime.Seconds)
```

LISTING 17.13 continued

```
            return 1;
        else if(compareTime.Seconds == totalSeconds)
            return 0;
        else
            return -1;
    }
}

class Sorter
{
     // Sort the comparable elements of an array in ascending order
    public static void BubbleSortAscending(IComparable [] bubbles)
    {
        bool swapped = true;

        for (int i = 0; swapped; i++)
        {
            swapped = false;
            for (int j = 0; j < (bubbles.Length - (i + 1)); j++)
            {
                if (bubbles[j].CompareTo(bubbles[j + 1]) > 0)
                {
                    Swap(j, j + 1, bubbles);
                    swapped = true;
                }
            }
        }
    }

     //Swap two elements of an array
    public static void Swap(int first, int second, IComparable [] arr)
    {
        IComparable temp;

        temp = arr[first];
        arr[first] = arr[second];
        arr[second] = temp;
    }
}

class Tester
{
    public static void Main()
    {
        TimeSpan [] raceTimes = new TimeSpan[4];

        raceTimes[0] = new TimeSpan(153);
        raceTimes[1] = new TimeSpan(165);
        raceTimes[2] = new TimeSpan(108);
        raceTimes[3] = new TimeSpan(142);

        Sorter.BubbleSortAscending(raceTimes);
```

LISTING 17.13 continued

```

            Console.WriteLine("List of sorted time spans:");
            foreach (TimeSpan time in raceTimes)
            {
                Console.WriteLine(time.Seconds);
            }
        }
}
```

```
List of sorted time spans:
108
142
153
165
```

Interfaces Can Only Be Instantiated Indirectly

Just like `abstract` classes, it doesn't make sense to instantiate an interface as in the following:

```
IComparable icComp = new IComparable();        //Invalid
```

You can only instantiate classes that provide implementations for all the `abstract` classes specified by ancestor classes and by implemented interfaces.

Building Interface Hierarchies

It is possible to extend an existing interface `A` by letting an interface `B` implement interface `A`. Interface `B` then contains the members from interface A, plus the members specified inside its own definition. A class can then either implement interface `A` or `B` according to its needs. If a class implements interface `A`, it must implement its `abstract` functions; if a class implements interface `B`, it must implement not only the `abstract` functions specified by `B` but also the `abstract` functions it inherits from `A`.

For example, we can extend the `IComparable` interface from the previous section by a new interface called `IComparableAdvanced`, as shown in the following lines:

```
interface IComparableAdvanced : IComparable
{
    bool GreaterThan(IComparableAdvanced comp);
    bool LessThan(IComparableAdvanced comp);
}
```

Any class implementing `IComparableAdvanced` must implement not only `GreaterThan` and `LessThan` but also `CompareTo`. Several interfaces can extend each other to form interface hierarchies.

Interface Conversions

If an object of class `C` implements an interface `I`, you can assign an instance of class `C` to a variable of interface `I` without using any explicit casts. For example, you can assign `TimeSpan` to `icTime` in the following line:

```
IComparable icTime = new TimeSpan(392);
```

because `TimeSpan` implements the `IComparable` interface.

If we need to go in the opposite direction (as in line 37 of Listing 17.13) and convert `icTime` to a variable of type `TimeSpan`, we need to perform the equivalent of a down cast, described earlier. (The down cast will allow us to access all the members of the `TimeSpan` object, rather than just those specified for the `IComparable` interface.) This requires a cast

```
TimeSpan myTime = (TimeSpan) icTime;
```

If `icTime` does not contain a `TimeSpan` object (but an object of another type that also implements the `IComparable` interface), the system will generate an exception. If you don't know in advance whether `icTime` contains a `TimeSpan` object, you can use the `is` and `as` operators described previously to ensure that `icTime` is of type `TimeSpan` before any conversions are attempted:

In the following, we use the `is` operator:

```
TimeSpan myTime;
if (icTime is TimeSpan)
    myTime = (TimeSpan) icTime;
else
    Console.WriteLine("Could not assign icTime to myTime");
```

and next the `as` operator

```
TimeSpan myTime;
myTime = icTime as TimeSpan;
if (myTime == null)
    Console.WriteLine("Could not assign icTime to myTime");
```

In this context, the `as` operator is also more efficient than the `is` operator.

Note

Sometimes, you might just want to check the object type in the variable of an interface type (like `icTime`) without performing a cast. The `is` operator is better suited for this scenario than the `as` operator, because the `is` operator does not automatically perform a cast.

Overriding Virtual Interface Implementations

Any function that a class implements from an interface can optionally be declared `virtual`. For example, the `CompareTo` method of `TimeSpan` was declared `virtual` in line 35 of Listing 17.13. A class derived from `TimeSpan` can `override` this `virtual` method in standard fashion or provide a `new` implementation.

For example, we could design a **TimeSpanAdvanced** class that overrides the **CompareTo** method of the **TimeSpan** class to provide more detailed feedback (see Listing 17.14). In this case, the new **CompareTo** returns 2 (line 10) if the **TimeSpan** object **A** is more than 50 seconds greater than object **B**. Conversely, if object **A** is more than 50 seconds below object **B**, minus 2 is returned.

Note

The code in Listing 17.14 does not compile independently. You can insert the **TimeSpanAdvanced** class beside the **TimeSpan** class in Listing 17.13 and make a couple of calls to its **CompareTo** method to give it a test run.

LISTING 17.14 TimeSpanAdvance.cs

```
01: public class TimeSpanAdvanced : TimeSpan
02: {
03:     public override int CompareTo(IComparable comp)
04:     {
05:         TimeSpan compareTime = (TimeSpan) comp;
06:
07:         if(base.Seconds > compareTime.Seconds)
08:         {
09:             if(base.Seconds > (compareTime.Seconds + 50))
10:                 return 2;
11:             else
12:                 return 1;
13:         }
14:         else if(base.Seconds < compareTime.Seconds)
15:         {
16:             if(base.Seconds < (compareTime.Seconds - 50))
17:                 return -2;
18:             else
19:                 return -1;
20:         }
21:         else
22:             return 0;
23:     }
24: }
```

Implementing Interface Functions Explicitly

When we implemented the **CompareTo** method in the **TimeSpan** class, it was implicitly understood by the compiler that we were implementing the **CompareTo** method specified by the **IComparable** interface. Generally, we simply need to include a function header in our implementing class with the same signature, return type, and access modifier (**public**) as that of the **abstract** function in the interface we are implementing; we don't need to explicitly state which interface we are implementing.

However, if a class implements two interfaces each containing `abstract` functions with the same signature, the compiler is not able to determine which of these two interfaces we are implementing simply by looking at the method header in our implementing class.

For example, if our space invader game presented at the introduction to this interface section contained not only an `IDrawable` interface with the `abstract` method `DrawYourself` meant to allow a game piece (like the `Planet`, `SpaceShip` or other mentioned previously) to draw itself onscreen

```
interface IDrawable
{
    void DrawYourself();
}
```

but also an interface called `IPrintable` with an `abstract` method called `DrawYourself` meant to allow an object to print itself on a printer

```
interface IPrintable
{
    void DrawYourself();
}
```

then it would be impossible for the compiler to determine which of the interfaces for which the following `DrawYourself` implementations are implemented.

```
public class SpaceShip : IDrawable, IPrintable
{
    ...
    public void DrawYourself()      Does this method implement DrawYourself from
    {                               IDrawable or IPrintable?
        ...
    }

    public void DrawYourself()      Does this method implement DrawYourself from
    {                               IDrawable or IPrintable?
        ...
    }
    ...
}
```

To resolve this problem, we can use explicit implementation for one or both of the implementations by inserting the name of the interface in front of the function name, as in the following code fragment.

```
public class SpaceShip : IDrawable, IPrintable
{
    ...
    void IDrawable.DrawYourself()
    {
        ...
    }

    public void DrawYourself()
    {
        ...
    }
    ...
}
```

This method explicitly implements DrawYourself from IDrawable

This method implicitly implements DrawYourself from IPrintable

In this case, we only applied explicit implementation to the IDrawable implementation. The compiler is then able to implicitly determine that the other DrawYourself method is implementing IPrintable's DrawYourself method. Alternatively, we could have applied explicit implementation on both method implementations.

Explicit implementations are implicitly public, so this access modifier cannot be used on explicit implementations. Furthermore, explicit implementations cannot be declared abstract, virtual, or new.

An explicitly implemented function cannot be accessed through its object as follows:

```
SpaceShip mySpaceShip = new SpaceShip();
...
mySpaceShip.DrawYourself()     // Calls the implicitly implemented DrawYourself
                               // not the explicitly implemented DrawYourself
```

Instead, we can call the DrawYourself implementation for IDrawable through a variable of type IDrawable (using dynamic binding) as in the following:

```
IDrawable idShip = mySpaceShip;
IdShip.DrawYourself()
```

Explicit implementation can be useful, even when we are not trying to resolve method signature clashes from different interfaces. Sometimes, we might want to implement an interface only with the intent of calling some or all of those methods through dynamic binding and not from the object itself. For example, if we only wanted the TimeSpace implementation of the CompareTo method to be called via dynamic binding and not be part of the TimeSpan object's directly accessible functions, we could define it as follows:

```
public class TimeSpace
{
    ...
    int IComparable.CompareTo(IComparable comp)
    {
        ...
```

```
    }
}
```

The third line in the following code fragment is now invalid:

```
TimeSpan myTime = new TimeSpan();
TimeSpan yourTime = new TimeSpan();
myTime.CompareTo(yourTime)     //Invalid
```

whereas the following is valid:

```
IComparable icTime = myTime;
icTime.CompareTo(yourTime)
```

Note

As mentioned earlier, it is impossible to declare an explicit interface implementation to be `virtual`, so a derived class cannot `override` this function but must re-implement it. For example, the `TimeSpanAdvanced` class defined in Listing 17.14 could not use the keyword `override` in line 3 if `CompareTo` was explicitly implemented in `TimeSpan`.

Summary

This chapter introduced you to `abstract` functions, polymorphism and interfaces. A review of the important points in this chapter follows.

An `abstract` method consists of a method header but has no method body and, therefore, no implementation. Properties and indexers can also be declared `abstract`.

A class with one or more `abstract` functions must itself be declared `abstract`. An `abstract` class can contain non-`abstract` function members.

An `abstract` class cannot be instantiated.

A class derived from an `abstract` class must provide implementations for all the `abstract` methods contained in this base class; otherwise, it also becomes `abstract`. `abstract` functions are implicitly `virtual`, so providing an implementation for an inherited `abstract` class is done in the same way as overriding a `virtual` method.

Polymorphism generally means the ability to have many forms. In computer science, it means the ability of a variable to reference different object types and call different method implementations with the same method call. The underlying mechanism that makes this scenario possible is called dynamic binding.

Polymorphism is a powerful concept because it allows programmers to program against a general interface (set of method calls) while the specific implementations called are determined by the runtime.

A polymorphic variable, through which polymorhic calls are made to methods of different classes, can reference objects of different descendant classes. When an object of a descendant class is assigned to such a variable of an ancestor class, the object loses part of its identity. This is called up casting. Only the class members defined for the ancestor class can be called, even though the object the variable is referencing contains additional class members. It is possible to determine the identity of the hidden object with the `is` operator. A down cast using the cast operator or the `as` operator can be applied to regain the lost type information.

All classes are ultimately derived from the `System.Object` class of the .NET Framework class library. Consequently, all classes inherit its six non-`static` methods.

When you write a function in a derived class with the same signature and return type as a non-`virtual` function in the base class, you are hiding the method in the base class. Dynamic binding is not applied to hidden functions. Even if the function in the base class is `virtual`, you can still hide it by applying the `new` keyword to the function in the derived class.

Upgrading the class libraries on which your program depends can lead to a number of problems and several possible solutions. Collectively, these issues are referred to as versioning. By using the keywords `virtual`, `new`, and `override` wisely, you can prevent several problems often encountered in connection with inheritance when class libraries are upgraded.

Even though most of your functions are likely to be `virtual`, a function defaults (without the `virtual` keyword) to be a non-`virtual` function. This is because `virtual` functions can create more problems in descendant classes than non-`virtual` methods, and because they are slightly slower than non-`virtual` methods.

In multiple inheritance, a class can have more than one base class. C# does not support multiple inheritance. Instead, it applies interfaces.

An interface only contains `abstract` function members and events. This avoids the conflicting instance variable names and implementations found with multiple inheritance. Consequently, whereas a class only can have one base class, it can implement many interfaces.

Use interfaces when you need several classes to have common function headers that are not present in a common ancestor class. This will allow you to apply polymorphism to a group of classes independently of where these classes are located in their class hierarchies.

When several implementations are identical apart from the types the implementation is applied on, we can write a generic implementation instead. Generic implementations are made possible through polymorphism.

Review Questions

1. Consider an `Animal` class from which the `Dog`, `Cat`, and `Duck` classes are derived. Suppose that any `Animal` can make a sound. Where would you locate the `Sound` method? Would you provide an implementation for this method or declare it `abstract`? Why?

2. If the `Sound` method of the `Animal` class was declared `abstract`, would you be able to instantiate an object from this class? Why or why not?

3. You want to implement a Sound method in each of Animal's three subclasses and call these three methods polymorphically. Which keywords would you use to declare the Sound method in Animal and in the three subclasses to allow this scenario to take place? Write the method headers in the Animal class and the three subclasses.

4. What's wrong with the following piece of code?

```
public abstract void Sound()
{
    Console.WriteLine("Quaaakkk quaaakkk");
}
```

5. If you want to call the Sound method of the three different subclasses polymorphically, would you need to do this for a variable of type Animal or for three variables of the types Cat, Dog, and Duck?

6. Suppose the Sound method has been declared in the Animal class and implemented in the three subclasses so each of these three subclass implementations can be called through dynamic binding. Which of the three implementations are called in the second line of the following code:

```
Animal myAnimal = new Dog();
myAnimal.Sound;
```

7. You have another animal class called Lion also containing a Sound method that you want to call polymorphically through a variable of type Animal. What do you need to do for this to be possible?

8. You need to find out if the variable myAnimal (declared as Animal myAnimal;) is referencing an object of type Dog. How can you find out?

9. You need to cast myAnimal into an object of type Cat, but only if myAnimal does contain a Cat. Show two different ways to do this.

10. Consider the Cat class from the previous questions. You have only defined the Sound method for it. Another programmer is using your Cat class and writes the following calls in his code (lines 2 and 3):

```
Cat myCat = new Cat();
myCat.Jump();
Console.WriteLine(myCat.ToString());
```

Are both these calls valid? If any of them are valid, what is the outcome of the call? Explain what is going on here.

11. If most methods are likely to be declared virtual, why is a method not virtual by default?

12. Why doesn't C# support multiple inheritance?

13. What's the problem with the following interface definition:

```
interface IRecoverable
{
    public void Recover()
    {
        Console.WriteLine("I am recovering");
    }
}
```

14. A programmer suggests that you can improve your code by exchanging the **Animal** class introduced in questions 1–3 with an interface called **IArticulateable**. Is he or she right? Why or why not?

Programming Exercises

1. Write a simple **Account** class containing an instance variable called **balance** and a property called **Balance** to provide access to **balance**. Allow the **Account** class to be sorted by the generic **BubbleSortAscending** contained in the **Sorter** class of Listing 17.13 by letting it implement the **IComparable** interface. Test your **Account** class by creating an array of **Accounts** with different **balance**s and pass this as an argument to the **BubbleSortAscending** method.

2. Write three classes called **Secretary**, **Director**, and **Programmer**. Each of the classes contains a **CalculateSalary** method. For simplicity, let each of these methods write "Now calculating the salary for…" followed by the name of the class in which the method resides.

   Suppose there are many objects of these classes in your program, and that they need to be stored in a collection, such as an array. How can you store them all in one array and also call the **CalculateSalary** of each object simply by iterating through the array and making the same method call for all objects? Write the code that implements this scenario.

3. Extend the code of question 2 by implementing the following separate hierarchy: A base class named **Building** containing two instance variables called **age** of type **int** and **currentValue** of type **decimal**. Derive two classes from **Building** called **House** and **OfficeBuilding**. **House** contains an instance variable called **numberOfBedrooms** of type **ushort** and **OfficeBuilding** an instance variable called **floorSpace** of type **uint**.

   You want to write and read objects of type **Secretary** and **House** to a file. So both of these classes must contain methods called **Read** and **Write** that (for simplicity make the **Read** methods write "Now reading House" and "Now reading **Secretary**" on the console and similarly for the **Write** methods) save these objects to and from a file. You want to construct just one method that accepts any object containing the **Read** and **Write** methods and will call these methods polymorphically, regardless of which type the object is. Write the code that implements this functionality.

CHAPTER 18

STRUCTS

You will learn about the following in this chapter:

- What a struct is
- The similarities and differences between classes and structs
- How to define and use structs
- Boxing and unboxing structs

According to Chapter 6, "Types, Part I: The Simple Types," C#'s types can be divided into reference types (such as `string`, `Elevator`, and `Car`) and value types (such as `short`, `int` and the other simple types). Until now, we have designed our own reference types with the `class` keyword to form classes. In a similar way, we can define our own value types by using the `struct` keyword to form structs as discussed in this chapter.

Classes are useful to represent most of the objects in a typical C# program. However, structs represent a lightweight alternative to classes, which, as the simple intrinsic types (`byte`, `short`, `int` and so on) demonstrate, are preferred over classes when we need to construct types that are simple and only need to represent one or a few related data items. Typical examples where structs usually have an edge over classes are when we need to represent

- A point in a coordinate system consisting of just two values, x and y
- A temperature
- A time span
- A fraction consisting of two numbers, a numerator and a denominator

Structs and classes have many similarities and a few significant differences. Like classes, structs can contain methods, properties, indexers, constructors, data members, operator methods, nested types, and they can implement interfaces. As opposed to classes, they don't support inheritance (but they still implicitly inherit from `System.Object`). They don't contain destructors, and parts of how their constructors are implemented are different.

Defining a Struct

Defining a new value type with the `struct` keyword is nearly identical to defining a new class as indicated in Syntax Box 18.1; you simply need to substitute the `class` keyword with the `struct` keyword.

Syntax Box 18.1 The `struct` Definition

```
[<Acess_modifier>] struct <Struct_identifier> [: <Interface_list>]
{
    <Struct_members>
}
```

Recall our `TimeSpan` class from Chapter 14, “Class Anatomy III: Writing Intuitive Code.” It was represented with a class because we hadn’t yet introduced structs at that point. However, it would be more effectively represented by a struct in most cases. This struct alternative is shown in lines 3–40 of Listing 18.1.

LISTING 18.1 `TimeSpanStruct.cs`

```
01: using System;
02:
03: public struct TimeSpan
04: {
05:     private uint totalSeconds;
06:     private const uint SecondsInHour = 3600;
07:     private const uint SecondsInMinute = 60;
08:
09:     public TimeSpan(uint initialSeconds)
10:     {
11:         totalSeconds = initialSeconds;
12:     }
13:
14:     public uint Seconds
15:     {
16:         get
17:         {
18:             return totalSeconds;
19:         }
20:
21:         set
22:         {
23:             totalSeconds = value;
24:         }
25:     }
26:
27:     public override string ToString()
28:     {
29:         uint hours;
30:         uint minutes;
```

LISTING 18.1 continued

```
31:         uint seconds;
32:
33:         hours = totalSeconds / SecondsInHour;
34:         minutes = (totalSeconds % SecondsInHour) / SecondsInMinute;
35:         seconds = (totalSeconds % SecondsInHour) % SecondsInMinute;
36:
37:         return String.Format("{0} Hrs {1} Mins {2} Secs",
38:             hours, minutes, seconds);
39:     }
40: }
41:
42: class Tester
43: {
44:     public static void Main()
45:     {
46:         TimeSpan myTime = new TimeSpan(43403);
47:         TimeSpan yourTime = new TimeSpan();
48:
49:         Console.WriteLine("My time: " + myTime);
50:         Console.WriteLine("Your first time: " + yourTime);
51:         yourTime.Seconds = 310;
52:         Console.WriteLine("Your second time: " + yourTime);
53:     }
54: }
```

```
My time: 12 Hrs 3 Mins 23 Secs
Your first time: 0 Hrs 0 Mins 0 Secs
Your second time: 0 Hrs 5 Mins 10 Secs
```

Overall, the class and the struct versions of `TimeSpan` look very much alike except that the `class` keyword has been exchanged with the `struct` keyword in line 3. However, as this analysis reveals, there are a few more or less obvious differences to the class version.

There is no explicit default (parameter-less) constructor defined because structs can only contain explicit constructors with at least one parameter, as in lines 9–12.

A struct is automatically equipped with a default constructor that initializes all data members to their default initialization values (an `int` is initialized to zero, a `bool` to `false`, and so forth). This is demonstrated in line 47, which calls `TimeSpan`'s default implicit constructor and assigns the new struct to `yourTime`. This results in `totalSeconds` being assigned the value zero, as shown in the sample output.

Constants can be initialized, as in lines 6 and 7. However, it is not possible to combine declaration and initialization statements for instance variables. For example, if we had exchanged line 5 with the following line:

```
private uint totalSeconds = 0;
```

we would have encountered a compiler error.

Any explicit constructor we write must initialize all the struct's data members. In this case, we only need line 11 to perform this task.

Even though structs generally cannot inherit from other structs and classes, any struct is implicitly derived from `System.Object` and inherits the members from this ultimate base class, which was presented in Chapter 17, "Inheritance Part II: Abstract Functions, Polymorphism, and Interfaces." Consequently, it is possible to override `System.Object`'s `ToString` method (lines 27–39) and let `WriteLine` call this method as part of executing lines 49 and 50.

In line 49, we are clearly passing the value type `myTime` to `WriteLine`. However, `WriteLine` is only able to process reference types, not value types like `myTime`. How is this apparent contradiction possible? C# has a built-in mechanism by which a value type is boxed into a corresponding reference type based object (box), which can then be processed by `WriteLine`. Due to the box metaphor, this mechanism is referred to as boxing in C# terminology. Boxing, along with the reverse process called unboxing, are discussed in more detail in a moment.

Note

To keep their structs as simple as possible, some programmers abolish the encapsulation rules we have abided by and declare the data members of the struct `public`. This permits direct access to these data members and allows the programmers to free the struct of the properties and methods that would otherwise have been needed to access these data members. This might be a legitimate design avenue to follow and is supported by C#. An example of a struct with a public data member is provided in Listing 18.3, presented later in this chapter.

Boxing and Unboxing

As mentioned in the previous analysis, C# automatically transforms a value type into a reference type when required. This process is called *boxing* while the reverse is called *unboxing*.

In line 46 of Listing 18.1, we created the `myTime` struct of type `TimeSpan` with the value 43403. To allow `WriteLine` to call `myTime`'s `ToString` method, C# boxed `myTime` inside an instance of type `System.Object` as illustrated in Figure 18.1. `WriteLine` then called `ToString` for this instance, which, through dynamic binding, invoked the `ToString` method we defined in lines 27–39 of Listing 18.1.

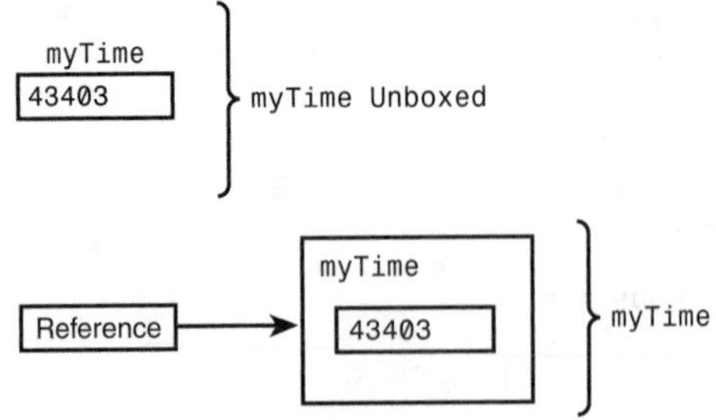

FIGURE 18.1
Boxing the `TimeSpan` structure.

Boxing allows us to assign not only class but also struct-based values to a variable of type `System.Object`. For example, we can assign `myTime` to the following variable `obj` of type `System.Object`:

```
System.Object obj = myTime;
```

We can then call the `ToString` method of `obj`, which will call `ToString` of `TimeSpan` through dynamic binding

```
string myTimeString = obj.ToString();
```

This is a powerful scenario that has many uses. For example, we can declare an array of type `System.Object` and thereby store any value (whether reference or value based) in the elements of the array. We could also define a method with a formal parameter of type `System.Object`. This method would accept any argument, whether value or reference based.

It is possible to unbox a value type, but, whereas boxing is implicit, unboxing must be done explicitly with the cast operator, as demonstrated in Listing 18.2.

LISTING 18.2 `UnboxingTest.cs`

```
01: using System;
02:
03: class TestUnboxing
04: {
05:     public static void Main()
06:     {
07:         int myInt = 3422;
08:         int yourInt;
09:
10:         object obj = myInt;
11:         yourInt = (int)obj;
12:
13:         Console.WriteLine("Value of yourInt: {0}", yourInt);
14:     }
15: }
```

```
Value of yourInt: 3422
```

Line 10 implicitly boxes `myInt` into `System.Object`, whereas the cast operator must be used explicitly in line 11 to unbox `myInt` and assign its value to `yourInt`. Notice that if `obj` in line 11 didn't contain an `int`, the runtime would generate an `InvalidCastException`.

Note

In general, structs are more efficient in their use of memory than classes. However, to box and unbox a struct requires a bit of additional computer resources. It is more expensive to assign a struct value than a class instance to a variable of type `System.Object`, because the class instance does not involve boxing during this assignment process. So, if you are likely to, for example, store many values of a particular struct in an array with elements of type `System.Object`, you should consider changing this struct to a class to improve the performance.

Creating Structs with and without `new`

As shown in lines 46 and 47 of Listing 18.1, a new struct object can, like a class object, be created with the keyword `new`. As opposed to classes, though, it is also possible to create a struct without using the `new` keyword. This procedure is demonstrated in Listing 18.3.

LISTING 18.3 `SimpleTimeSpanStruct.cs`

```
01: using System;
02:
03: public struct TimeSpan
04: {
05:     public uint totalSeconds;
06:
07:     public TimeSpan(uint initialTotalSeconds)
08:     {
09:         totalSeconds = initialTotalSeconds;
10:     }
11: }
12:
13: class Tester
14: {
15:     public static void Main()
16:     {
17:         TimeSpan myTime;
18:
19:         myTime.totalSeconds = 8383;
20:         Console.WriteLine("My time: {0}", myTime.totalSeconds);
21:     }
22: }
```

```
My time: 8383
```

When a new struct object is created without the `new` keyword, none of the constructors for this struct are called. Instead, all data members must be initialized by assigning the initialization values directly to the data members through the struct object name, as in line 19. It is not possible to perform these initializations through properties or methods, because none of the function members can be called until all data members have been initialized. Consequently, the data members must be declared `public`, as shown in line 5.

Value Types and Reference Types

Structs are value types, so when a struct object is assigned to a variable, the whole value is assigned, as opposed to reference-based values where only the reference is passed along. This can often lead to significantly different behavior between reference and value types.

Note

It is generally more efficient to pass class instances around in a program than struct-based values because the former only involves a simple reference whereas the latter involves the whole value.

Consider, for example, the method called **UpdateTime** defined in lines 37–42 of Listing 18.4. It has one formal parameter of type **TimeSpan**. When we pass a **TimeSpan** argument to this type, the **timeUpdate** parameter is not assigned a copy of a reference as would have been the case with a class object, but is assigned a copy of the full value of the argument instead. So **myTime** (line 32) is totally independent from **timeUpdate** in line 37 (had they been reference-based, they would both have referenced the same object). This is confirmed by the sample output where **myTime** clearly is not affected by the update that is taking place in line 39.

LISTING 18.4 TimeSpanMethod.cs

```
01: using System;
02:
03: public struct TimeSpan
04: {
05:     private uint totalSeconds;
06:
07:     public TimeSpan(uint initialTotalSeconds)
08:     {
09:         totalSeconds = initialTotalSeconds;
10:     }
11:
12:     public uint Seconds
13:     {
14:         get
15:         {
16:             return totalSeconds;
17:         }
18:
19:         set
20:         {
21:             totalSeconds = value;
22:         }
23:     }
24: }
25:
26: class Tester
27: {
28:     public static void Main()
29:     {
30:         TimeSpan myTime = new TimeSpan(480);
31:
32:         UpdateTime(myTime);
33:         Console.WriteLine("Time outside UpdateTime method: {0}",
34:             myTime.Seconds);
35:     }
36:
37:     public static void UpdateTime(TimeSpan timeUpdate)
38:     {
39:         timeUpdate.Seconds = timeUpdate.Seconds + 50;
40:         Console.WriteLine("Time inside UpdateTime method: {0}",
41:             timeUpdate.Seconds);
42:     }
43: }
```

```
Time inside UpdateTime method: 530
Time outside UpdateTime method: 480
```

Summary

This chapter discussed structs, how they compare with classes, and how they are defined and used.

The following important points were covered in this chapter.

Structs are similar to classes in many ways but also have important differences.

Structs are lightweight alternatives to classes. They are advantageous for representing one or a few related data items.

Structs do not support inheritance, but all structs are implicitly derived from `System.Object`.

The execution engine implicitly transforms a value type into a reference type when needed. This is called boxing. The reverse process of transforming this reference type back to a value type is called unboxing and requires an explicit cast.

All the data members of a struct must be initialized before any functions of this struct can be called.

Review Questions

1. List three kinds of data abstractions where structs should be considered instead of classes.
2. Mention the important similarities and differences between classes and structs.
3. If `myStruct` is a value type, how is the following call possible if `WriteLine` only accepts reference types?

   ```
   Console.WriteLine("Details of myStruct" + myStruct);
   ```
4. Can a struct have an explicit default constructor?
5. Why is boxing called boxing?
6. Suppose the struct `Fraction` contains the two public data members `numerator` and `denominator`. `Fraction` does not contain any explicitly defined constructors. You now write the following code:

   ```
   Fraction myFraction;
   myFraction.ToString();
   ```

   Is the second line valid? Why or why not?

Programming Exercises

1. Implement a struct called `Fraction` that contains two `private` data members of type `int` called `numerator` and `denominator`. Equip `Fraction` with the following elements:
    - A constructor that takes two arguments to initialize `numerator` and `denominator`
    - Properties to get and set `numerator` and `denominator`
    - A property called `Value` that simply returns the value of the fraction, which is calculated as `(numerator / denominator)`
    - Override the `ToString` method (implicitly inherited from `System.Object`) to return the following `string`: "Fraction value: xxx" where xxx represents the fraction value as a `string`.

    Write suitable code to test the `Fraction` struct.

CHAPTER 19

EXCEPTION HANDLING

You will learn about the following in this chapter:

- What an exception is
- How an uncaught exception abruptly terminates a program
- How to use the `try` and `catch` blocks to catch and handle exceptions
- How you can use the `finally` block to ensure a particular block of code is always executed
- How multiple `catch` blocks allow you to catch and handle different exception types thrown from the same block of code
- Nested `try` blocks
- How to explicitly throw and rethrow an exception with the `throw` keyword
- How to define your own exception types

The .NET execution engine generates an exception when a special condition arises during the runtime of a program. Special conditions are violations of the C# language rules and .NET execution environment. Dividing by zero, invalid casts, calling a non-existent file, and running out of memory are examples of special conditions. The ability to generate exceptions is not limited to the execution engine, you can also generate your own exceptions.

Exception handling allows you to deal with exceptions in a graceful manner by preventing the program from going down and let's you divide your code into two separate parts—the code that provides the expected functionality of the program and the code that deals with the exceptional cases. This effectively prevents the, often, large amounts of exception handling code from intermingling with and thereby contaminating the normal case code, which then remains (relatively) easy to read.

Exception Handling: A Brief Overview

C#'s exception handling is object-oriented in that the exception generated by the execution engine in response to a special condition is an object that contains information about the corresponding abnormal condition. Any such exception object is either of class

`System.Exception` or a subclass thereof. Typical predefined subclasses, found in the .NET Framework class library, are `System.DivideByZeroException`, `System.InvalidOutOfRangeException`, and `System.NullReferenceException`.

When an exceptional condition is encountered in a function, an exception object is created and *thrown* in that function. The function can *catch* (handle) the exception object itself or pass it on.

To implement code that monitors and handles exceptions in functions, C# contains the three keywords `try`, `catch`, and `finally`, displayed in Syntax Box 19.1. The `try` keyword followed by a block of code (enclosed by a pair of curly braces) is called a `try` block. Similarly, `catch` forms a `catch` block (also called an *exception handler*), and `finally` forms a `finally` block.

Any exception objects thrown inside the `try` block are, as shown in Syntax Box 19.1, compared with each of the following `catch` blocks to determine if any of these `catch` blocks were meant to catch this particular exception. This is the case if the exception object is of an exception class that is identical to or a descendant of the `catch` block parameter type (exemplified with the two placeholders *`<Exception_class_1>`* and *`<Exception_class_2>`* and the specific class `DivideByZeroException` in Syntax Box 19.1). If a suitable `catch` block is found, the exception handling code for this `catch` block is executed. For example, the exception object of class `DivideByZeroException` in Syntax Box 19.1 is of the same class as that specified by the third `catch` block. The code block of this `catch` block is therefore executed, followed by the execution of the `finally` block.

If no `catch` blocks match the `DivideByZeroException` class, none of the `catch` blocks are executed and the exception object is passed on. An uncaught exception object is handled by the runtime's default exception-handler, in which case the program is abruptly terminated.

The code in the `finally` block is always executed. Either `finally` is executed just before the execution flow exits the `try` block or, in case a `catch` block is being executed, just before execution exits that `catch` block.

Notice that a `try` block can either

- Have one or more associated `catch` blocks and no `finally` block
- Have one `finally` block attached and no `catch` blocks
- Include both one or more `catch` blocks as well as one `finally` block

Syntax Box 19.1 The `try` and `catch` Blocks and the `finally` Block

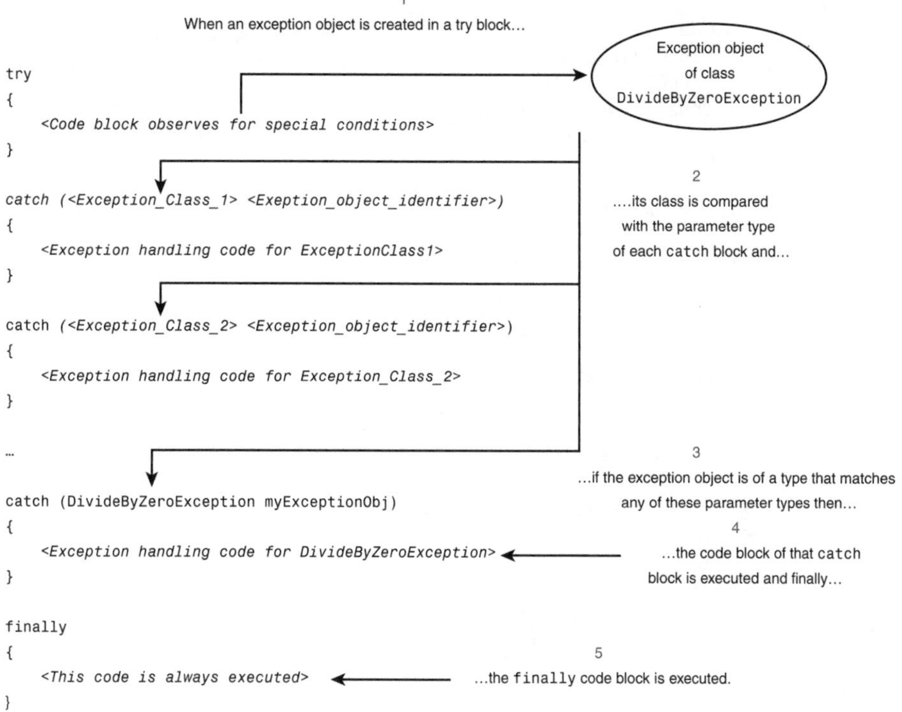

Life without `try-catch-finally`

Before we look at examples that implement the **`try-catch-finally`** trio introduced in the previous section, let's see what happens when an exception remains uncaught in your code. Listing 19.1 demonstrates this scenario.

Note

To see the same output as that shown in the sample output after Listing 19.1, you must compile the listing with the debug compiler switch on as follows:

```
csc /debug UncaughtException.cs<enter>
```

LISTING 19.1 `UncaughtException.cs`

```
using System;

class MyClass
```

LISTING 19.1 continued

```
04: {
05:     public static void Main()
06:     {
07:         Console.WriteLine("Entering MyClass.Main");
08:         YourClass yourObject = new YourClass();
09:         yourObject.Method1();
10:         Console.WriteLine("Leaving MyClass.Main");
11:     }
12: }
13:
14: class YourClass
15: {
16:     public void Method1()
17:     {
18:         Console.WriteLine("Entering YourClass.Method1");
19:         Method2();
20:         Console.WriteLine("Leaving YourClass.Method1");
21:     }
22:
23:     public void Method2()
24:     {
25:         Console.WriteLine("Entering YourClass.Method2");
26:         int myInt = 0;
27:         int yourInt;
28:          //Dividing by zero
29:         yourInt = 10 / myInt;
30:         Console.WriteLine("Leaving YourClass.Method2");
31:     }
32: }
```

```
Entering MyClass.Main
Entering YourClass.Method1
Entering YourClass.Method2

Exception occurred: System.DivideByZeroException: Attempted to divide by zero.
   at YourClass.Method2() in C:\Temp\TempC#Programs\UncaughtException.cs:line 29

   at YourClass.Method1() in C:\Temp\TempC#Programs\UncaughtException.cs:line 19

   at MyClass.Main() in C:\Temp\TempC#Programs\UncaughtException.cs:line 19
```

Note

You might see a window labeled Common Language Runtime Debugging Services as you run Listing 19.1. Debugging services provide help when looking for bugs. It is beyond the scope of this book to discuss the various debuggers available in .NET.

The three methods `Main`, `Method1`, and `Method2` are equipped with `WriteLine` statements (lines 7, 10, 18, 20, 25, and 30), so we can follow the program's execution flow in the sample output.

Execution flow initially enters the `Main` method as confirmed by the first line of the sample output. The `Main` method calls `Method1` in line 9, which again calls `Method2` in line 19. Under normal circumstances, `Method2` would finish executing its block of code (including the call to `WriteLine` in line 30) and return back to `Method1`, which again would execute line 19 before returning to the `Main` method where line 10 finally would be executed before the program was terminated.

However, an abnormal condition arises in line 29 of `Method2` where `10` is divided by zero. This causes the runtime to create and throw an exception object of type `System.DivideByZeroException` and the normal flow of execution is immediately stopped. Because line 29, which gave rise to the exception, is not placed inside a `try` block, `Method2` cannot handle the exception object. The exception object is then sent on a journey back through the method call hierarchy, which, in this case, consists of `Main` calling `Method1` and `Method1` calling `Method2`. During this journey, it looks for a `try` block with a matching `catch` block, so the execution object is passed over to `Method1` (without calling line 30). No `try` and `catch` blocks are found here either, so the execution object is passed on to the `Main` method (without executing line 20), which also lacks any exception handling code. Finally, the exception object is passed to the runtime's default exception handler, which prints the error message.

Notice how the error message of the sample output traces the journey of the exception object through the three methods by the three lines commencing with `at`.

The `try` and `catch` blocks

The exception message provided by the default exception handler, as demonstrated in the sample output from Listing 19.1, is useful for a programmer analyzing his or her source code. However, most end users would be baffled by a program that abruptly terminates and writes out, for them, a cryptic message.

To avoid this kind of behavior and let the program take corrective actions instead without terminating the program, we can enclose the code we want to monitor for special conditions inside a `try` block. After the `try` block, we can insert one or more `catch` blocks that specify the different exception object types we want to handle. I have used this approach on Listing 19.1 to form Listing 19.2, where the division by zero block in line 32 has been enclosed inside a `try` block that is immediately followed by a matching `catch` block.

LISTING 19.2 `SimpleTryCatch.cs`

```
01: using System;
02:
03: class MyClass
04: {
05:     public static void Main()
06:     {
07:         Console.WriteLine("Entering MyClass.Main");
08:         YourClass yourObject = new YourClass();
```

LISTING 19.2 continued

```
        yourObject.Method1();
        Console.WriteLine("Leaving MyClass.Main");
    }
}

class YourClass
{
    public void Method1()
    {
        Console.WriteLine("Entering YourClass.Method1");
        Method2();
        Console.WriteLine("Leaving YourClass.Method1");
    }

    public void Method2()
    {
        Console.WriteLine("Entering YourClass.Method2");
        int myInt = 0;
        int yourInt;
        try
        {
            Console.WriteLine("Entering try block");
             //Dividing by zero
            yourInt = 10 / myInt;
            Console.WriteLine("Leaving try block");
        }
        catch(DivideByZeroException exObj)
        {
            Console.WriteLine("Entering catch block");
            Console.WriteLine("Exception: " + exObj.Message);
            Console.WriteLine("Unable to automatically assign value
            ➥to yourInt");
            Console.Write("Please manually enter number to be
            ➥assigned yourInt: ");
            yourInt = Convert.ToInt32(Console.ReadLine());
            Console.WriteLine("Leaving catch block");
        }
        Console.WriteLine("Leaving YourClass.Method2");
    }
}
```

```
Entering MyClass.Main
Entering YourClass.Method1
Entering YourClass.Method2
Entering try block
Entering catch block
Exception: Attempted to divide by zero.
Unable to automatically assign value to yourInt
Please manually enter number to be assigned yourInt: 34<enter>
Leaving catch block
Leaving YourClass.Method2
Leaving YourClass.Method1
Leaving MyClass.Main
```

After an exception is thrown inside a `try` block, the execution flow is immediately transferred outside the `try` block into a following `catch` block that matches the thrown exception; the flow is never returned to the `try` block. For this reason, line 33 is never executed.

The purpose of the `catch` block is to resolve the special condition and then let the program continue in its usual manner. In our case, the `catch` block notifies the user of the problem in a user-friendly manner and lets him or her assign a value to `yourInt` manually because the program is unable to perform this task automatically.

As part of transferring the flow of execution to the matching `catch` block, a reference to an appropriate exception object is automatically assigned to `exObj` of line 35. This exception object contains functions that let you access the information (about the special condition that caused the creation of this object) encapsulated by this object. One of these functions is a property called `Message`, which provides a short description of the exception. We utilize this functionality in line 38 to inform the user about the problem at hand. In our case, the `Message` property returns the following string:

```
Attempted to divide by zero
```

as shown in the sample output.

You can find further information about `Message` and the other useful functions exposed by the `System.Exception` class and its subclasses in the .NET Framework Documentation.

Observe how the `try-catch` unit allows us to separate the special case code in the `catch` block from the normal case code of the `try` block that provides the expected functionality of the program. As a result, we effectively prevent the special case code from polluting the normal case code.

The matching `catch` block prevents the program from being abruptly terminated. Instead, the program flow continues to the statement following the `catch` block, which, in this case, is line 44. From here, the program continues as if no exception was ever thrown.

If we exchanged `DivideByZeroException` in line 35 of Listing 19.2 with, say, `ArgumentNullException`, the `catch` blocks would no longer have matched the thrown `DivideByZeroException` exception. As a result, the execution object would have moved up through the chain of method calls similar to that of Listing 19.1. If, on the other hand, we substituted the `DivideByZeroException` with the ancestor class `System.Exception`, the `catch` block would match any possible exception object thrown.

To catch any possible exception object, you could also insert a generic `catch` block (see Figure 19.1), which doesn't carry any pair of parentheses after the `catch` keyword enclosing the parameter.

However this approach does not give you access to the execution object and its useful functions.

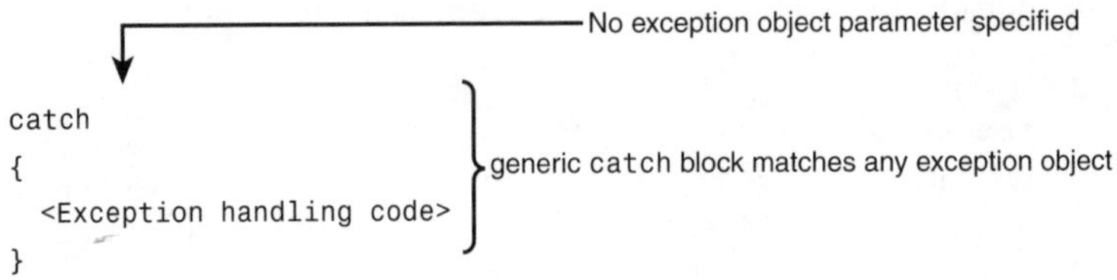

FIGURE 19.1
The generic `catch` block.

No exception object parameter specified

```
catch
{
  <Exception handling code>
}
```

generic `catch` block matches any exception object

Catching the Exception Object Farther up the Function Call Chain

As mentioned previously, an exception object travels up the function call chain until it finds a matching `catch` block. Consequently, it is possible to `catch` an exception object thrown in one function (like `Method2`) in a different function farther up the calling chain (like `Method1`). This is demonstrated in Listing 19.3, where the `try-catch` blocks of `Method2` in Listing 19.2 have been moved to `Method1`. So, instead of enclosing the divide by zero statement as in the previous listing, the `try` block in lines 19–24 now encloses the call to `Method2` in line 22.

LISTING 19.3 `CaughtInOtherFunction.cs`

```
01: using System;
02:
03: class MyClass
04: {
05:     public static void Main()
06:     {
07:         Console.WriteLine("Entering MyClass.Main");
08:         YourClass yourObject = new YourClass();
09:         yourObject.Method1();
10:         Console.WriteLine("Leaving MyClass.Main");
11:     }
12: }
13:
14: class YourClass
15: {
16:     public void Method1()
17:     {
18:         Console.WriteLine("Entering YourClass.Method1");
19:         try
20:         {
21:             Console.WriteLine("Entering the try block of Method1");
22:             Method2();
23:             Console.WriteLine("Leaving the try block of Method1");
24:         }
25:         catch(DivideByZeroException exObj)
26:         {
27:             Console.WriteLine("Entering catch block of Method1");
```

LISTING 19.3 continued

```
28:             Console.WriteLine("Exception: " + exObj.Message);
29:             Console.WriteLine("Exception was generated in Method2");
30:             Console.WriteLine("Leaving catch block of Method1");
31:         }
32:         Console.WriteLine("Leaving YourClass.Method1");
33:     }
34:
35:     public void Method2()
36:     {
37:         Console.WriteLine("Entering YourClass.Method2");
38:         int myInt = 0;
39:         int yourInt;
40:          //Dividing by zero
41:         yourInt = 10 / myInt;
42:         Console.WriteLine("Leaving YourClass.Method2");
43:     }
44: }
```

```
Entering MyClass.Main
Entering YourClass.Method1
Entering the try block of Method1
Entering YourClass.Method2
Entering catch block of Method1
Exception: Attempted to divide by zero.
Exception was generated in Method2
Leaving catch block of Method1
Leaving YourClass.Method1
Leaving MyClass.Main
```

When the divide-by-zero-exception is thrown in line 41, no exception handler is found, so the normal execution is immediately stopped, exactly as in Listing 19.1 (line 42 is not executed). However, as opposed to Listing 19.1, the exception object is brought to line 22 from where `Method2` was called. Because a `try` block encloses line 22 and the associated `catch` block matches the thrown exception object, this `catch` block now handles the exception. Notice how the execution flow returns to normal after the `catch` block has been executed, allowing line 32 and line 10 to be executed.

Multiple `catch` Blocks

If a `try` block contains code that can throw more than one type of exception object, (for example, `DivideByZeroException` as well as `IndexOutOfRangeException`), you can specify more than one `catch` block relating back to the same `try` block (as shown in Syntax Box 19.1). When an exception object is looking for a matching `catch` block, the possible `catch` blocks are inspected in the sequence in which they appear in the source code. The first matching `catch` block will handle the exception. After this matching `catch` block has been executed, all other related `catch` blocks are ignored, and the execution commences after the end of the last `catch` block.

Note

When multiple `catch` blocks are applied, the exception subclasses specified for the `catch` block parameters must precede any of their base classes in the sequence of `catch` blocks. Otherwise, these subclass `catch` blocks become unreachable, which is invalid in C#. For example, the second `catch` block in the following lines of code contains the parameter exception class `System.DivideByZeroException`, which is a subclass of `System.Exception`—the parameter class of the first `catch` block. As a result, any exception that is matched by `System.DivideByZeroException` is also matched by `System.Exception`. Consequently, the flow of execution will never reach the second `catch` block making the code invalid.

```
try
{…}
catch(System.Exception exObj)
{…}
catch(System.DivideByZeroException exObj)
{…}
```

Invalid, because the second `catch` block will never be executed.

The `finally` Block

Consider a method that opens a file in its first statements and closes the file just before the method exits. If the flow of execution due to a thrown exception (that substitutes normal execution flow with an abrupt non-sequential path as shown previously) never reaches the end of the method, the file is left unclosed, which can create serious problems in a program. Consequently, we must ensure that, regardless of whether an exception is thrown or not, the file is closed. This can be achieved by inserting the file closing code inside a `finally` block, which is always executed regardless of the circumstances. A `finally` block is executed just after the `try-catch` blocks have completed (regardless of whether an exception is thrown or whether a matching `catch` block is found) and just before the code following the `try-catch` blocks is to be executed.

Listing 19.4 demonstrates three different scenarios where the `finally` block is executed regardless of the circumstances.

LISTING 19.4 `TestFinally.cs`

```
using System;

class Tester
{
    public static void Main()
    {
        try
        {
            Console.WriteLine("Entering Main's try block");
```

LISTING 19.4 continued

```
            MyClass myObject = new MyClass();
            myObject.MethodA();
            myObject.MethodB();
            Console.WriteLine("Leaving Main's try block");
        }
        catch(Exception exObj)
        {
            Console.WriteLine("Entering Main's catch block");
            Console.WriteLine(exObj.Message);
            Console.WriteLine("Leaving Main's catch block");
        }
    }
}

class MyClass
{
    public void MethodA()
    {
        try
        {
            Console.WriteLine("Entering MethodA's try block");
            int myInt;
            int inputInt;

            Console.WriteLine("Opening file in MethodA");
            Console.Write("Please enter number: ");
            inputInt = Convert.ToInt32(Console.ReadLine());
            myInt = 10 / inputInt;
            Console.WriteLine("Leaving MethodA's try block");
        }
        catch(DivideByZeroException exObj)
        {
            Console.WriteLine("Entering MethodA's catch block");
            Console.WriteLine("Exception: " + exObj.Message);
            Console.WriteLine("Leaving MethodA's catch block");
        }
        finally
        {
            Console.WriteLine("Closing file in MethodA's finally block");
        }
        Console.WriteLine("Leaving MethodA");
    }

    public void MethodB()
    {
        try
        {
            Console.WriteLine("Entering MethodB's try block");
            int[] myArray = new int[10];
            Console.WriteLine("Opening file");
             //Index of bounds
            myArray[34] = 10;
```

LISTING 19.4 continued

```
62:                 Console.WriteLine("Leaving MethodB's try block");
63:             }
64:             finally
65:             {
66:                 Console.WriteLine("Closing file in MethodB's finally block");
67:             }
68:             Console.WriteLine("Leaving MethodB");
69:         }
70: }
```

Sample output 1: User enters zero and causes a divide by zero exception in `MethodA`.

```
Entering Main's try block
Entering MethodA's try block
Opening file in MethodA
Please enter number: 0<enter>
Entering MethodA's catch block
Exception: Attempted to divide by zero.
Leaving MethodA's catch block
Closing file in MethodA's finally block
Leaving MethodA
Entering MethodB's try block
Opening file
Closing file in MethodB's finally block
Entering Main's catch block
An exception of type System.IndexOutOfRangeException was thrown.
Leaving Main's catch block
```

Sample output 2: User does not enter zero and avoids the divide by zero exception in `MethodA`.

```
Entering Main's try block
Entering MethodA's try block
Opening file in MethodA
Please enter number: 34
Leaving MethodA's try block
Closing file in MethodA's finally block
Leaving MethodA
Entering MethodB's try block
Opening file
Closing file in MethodB's finally block
Entering Main's catch block
An exception of type System.IndexOutOfRangeException was thrown.
Leaving Main's catch block
```

The `Main` method calls `MethodA` and `MethodB` from within its `try` block. Any uncaught exceptions passed on from these two method calls will be handled by `Main`'s `catch` block in lines 15–20, because its parameter class `System.Exception` is the ultimate base class for any exception class.

`MethodA` and `MethodB` both simulate opening a file on their entry (lines 34 and 59) and each file must be closed before each of the methods exits. For that reason, the lines of code that (pretends to) close the files are positioned in `finally` blocks (lines 46–49 and lines 54–57).

In sample output 1, we cause a divide by zero exception to be generated in line 37 by assigning zero to `inputInt`. As expected, execution is immediately transferred to the `catch` block followed by the `finally` block, after which the execution flow returns to normal.

`MethodB` demonstrates that even though the `try` block has no associated `catch` blocks, its associated `finally` block is still executed just before the execution flow returns from `MethodB`. After the `finally` block has been executed, the exception object is passed over to the `Main` method where a matching `catch` block is found. Notice that `MethodB` causes an `IndexOutOfRangeException` to be generated and thrown in line 61 because we are attempting to assign 10 to index 34 of `myArray`, which only has 10 indices.

Sample output 2 shows that even though no exceptions are thrown this time in `MethodA`, the `finally` block is still executed. Execution of `MethodB` in sample output 2 is similar to that of sample output 1.

Note

A `try` block without any `catch` blocks (as in `MethodB` of Listing 19.4) but just a `finally` block cannot be used to handle exceptions. Instead, this construct is often used with functions that have code, which must be executed before the function exits and that have several `return` statements dispersed throughout its code. No matter which `return` statement the method exits with, the `finally` block is always guaranteed to be executed.

Nested `try` Blocks

You can insert a `try` block inside another `try` block to form nested `try` blocks. An unlimited number of nested `try` blocks can be written inside each other. Any uncaught exceptions of an inner `try` block moves through each of its outer `try` blocks one by one from innermost to outermost in search of a matching `catch` block. If no match is found, the runtime's default exception handler will handle the exception as shown earlier.

Listing 19.5 provides a simple example of one `try-catch` block nested inside another `try` block.

LISTING 19.5 `NestingTryBlocks.cs`

```
using System;

class TryNestTester
{
    public static void Main()
    {
        try
        {
            try
```

LISTING 19.5 continued

```
10:             {
11:                 int[] myArray = new int[10];
12:
13:                 myArray[50] = 498;
14:             }
15:             catch(DivideByZeroException exObj)
16:             {
17:                 Console.WriteLine("Inside inner catch block");
18:                 Console.WriteLine("Exception: " + exObj.Message);
19:             }
20:         }
21:         catch(IndexOutOfRangeException exObj)
22:         {
23:             Console.WriteLine("Inside outer catch block");
24:             Console.WriteLine("Exception: " + exObj.Message);
25:         }
26:     }
27: }
```

```
Inside outer catch block
Exception: An exception of type System.IndexOutOfRangeException was thrown.
```

The code of the inner `try` block (lines 9–14) throws an `IndexOutOfRangeException` in line 13, but no match is found in the corresponding `catch` block (lines 15–19). Consequently, the exception object is passed to the outer `try` block where a matching `catch` block is found in lines 21–25.

Note

Even though it is less obvious, Listing 19.4 also contains nested `try` blocks. When a function call (such as the calls to `MethodA` and `MethodB` in lines 11 and 12) is enclosed in a `try` block and the function that is called also contains a `try` block (as `MethodA` and `MethodB`), this latter `try` block is nested inside the `try` block from where its function is called.

`throw`: Explicitly Throwing Exceptions

In the previous sections, we have experienced the runtime's ability to automatically throw an exception when an abnormal condition arises. With the `throw` keyword, you can also throw an exception explicitly in your code, as in the following line:

```
throw new System.Exception();
```

This line creates and throws a new exception object of class `System.Exception`. You can alternatively provide a suitable `string` argument to the new object as follows:

```
throw new System.Exception("Invalid set of parameters");
```

This `string` can be accessed via the exception object's `Message` property presented earlier.

You can only throw objects that are of class **System.Exception** or a subclass thereof.

An explicitly thrown exception object has the same effect on execution flow and is caught in the same way as an implicitly thrown exception object.

The syntax for throwing an exception is shown in Syntax Box 19.2.

Syntax Box 19.2 Explicitly Throwing an Exception

```
throw <Exception_object>;
```

Notes:

You can either create a new exception object as you are throwing it:

```
throw new <Exception_class_identifier> ( [<String_message>] );
```

or you can throw an exception object that has already been created:

```
System.Exception myExceptionObject = new System.Exception( [<String_message>] );
throw myExceptionObject;
```

The ability to throw exceptions explicitly not only gives you more control over when exceptions are thrown and their types, it also allows you to let inner **catch** blocks rethrow exceptions to outer **try** blocks. The inner **catch** block can then take initial corrective actions, followed by further actions in outer **catch** blocks. Listing 19.6 demonstrates how to explicitly throw and rethrow exceptions.

LISTING 19.6 LogException.cs

```
using System;

class Tester
{
    public static void Main()
    {
        try
        {
            double number;
            double result;

            Console.Write("Calculate Log for the following number: ");
            number = Convert.ToDouble(Console.ReadLine());
            result = MyMath.CalculateLog(number);
            Console.WriteLine("The result is: {0}", result);
        }
        catch(ArithmeticException exObj)
        {
            Console.WriteLine("Inside Main's catch block");
            Console.WriteLine("Message: " + exObj.Message);
            Console.WriteLine("Help Link: " + exObj.HelpLink);
            Console.WriteLine("Method call trace: " + exObj.StackTrace);
        }
```

LISTING 19.6 continued

```
    }
}

class MyMath
{
    public static double CalculateLog(double num)
    {
        try
        {
            if(num < 0.0)
            {
                throw new ArithmeticException("Logarithm of a negative number cannot be calculated");
            }
            if(num == 0.0)
            {
                ArithmeticException arithEx = new ArithmeticException("Logarithm of zero is -infinity");
                arithEx.HelpLink = "http://www.themathwizards@#$.com";
                throw arithEx;
            }
            return Math.Log(num);
        }
        catch(ArithmeticException exObj)
        {
            Console.WriteLine("Inside CalculateLog's catch block");
            throw exObj;
        }
    }
}
```

Sample output 1:

```
Calculate Log for the following number: 10<enter>
The result is: 2.30258509299405
```

Sample output 2:

```
Calculate Log for the following number: 0<enter>
Inside CalculateLog's catch block
Inside Main's catch block
Message: Logarithm of zero is -infinity
Help Link: http://www.themathwizards@#$.com
Method call trace:    at MyMath.CalculateLog(Double num)
   at Tester.Main()
```

Sample output 3:

```
Calculate Log for the following number: -5<enter>
Inside CalculateLog's catch block
Inside Main's catch block
Message: Logarithm of a negative number cannot be calculated
Help Link:
Method call trace:    at MyMath.CalculateLog(Double num)
   at Tester.Main()
```

The `CalculateLog` method in lines 29–50 calculates and returns the logarithm of a given argument. The logarithm of 0 is minus infinity, and the logarithm of a negative number is not defined. Line 35 reflects this by throwing a new exception object of type `System.ArithmeticException` if `num` is less than zero. Similarly, if `num` is equal to zero an exception of the same class is created and thrown in lines 39–41, albeit in a slightly different way. This time, we first create the exception object `arithEx` in line 39 and, before it is thrown in line 41, we assign a `string` value to its `HelpLink` property. As soon as either line 35 or line 41 is executed, the normal execution is immediately stopped. A matching `catch` block is found in lines 45–49 where the exception object is rethrown in line 48. Consequently, this `catch` block does not bring execution flow back to normal, the search for a matching `catch` block to this rethrown exception object continues in an outer `try` block instead. A match is found in `Main`'s `catch` block, which accesses the `Message`, `HelpLink`, and `StackTrace` (providing a method call trace) properties and prints their return values on the console.

Notice how two `catch` blocks in this case are involved in handling one exception.

Writing Custom Exceptions

The .NET Framework's built-in exception classes will accommodate most abnormal conditions you encounter. However, when you need additional capabilities, you can write your own custom-made exception classes by using `System.ApplicationException` as a base class.

Lines 3–26 of Listing 19.7 illustrate this possibility by defining a new exception class called `LogarithmicException`.

LISTING 19.7 `CustomException.cs`

```
01: using System;
02:
03: public class LogarithmicException : System.ApplicationException
04: {
05:     private uint errorNumber;
06:
07:
08:     public LogarithmicException() : base("Logarithmic exception")
09:     {
10:         errorNumber = 1000;
11:     }
12:
13:
14:     public LogarithmicException(string message, uint initErrorNumber)
        ➥: base(message)
15:     {
16:         errorNumber = initErrorNumber;
17:     }
18:
19:     public uint ErrorNumber
20:     {
```

LISTING 19.7 continued

```
        get
        {
            return errorNumber;
        }
    }
}

class MyMath
{
    public static double CalculateLog(double num)
    {
        try
        {
            if(num < 0.0)
            {
                throw new LogarithmicException("Logarithm of a negative
                ➥ number cannot be calculated", 1001);
            }
            if(num == 0.0)
            {
                throw new LogarithmicException("Logarithm of zero is
                ➥ -infinity", 1002);
            }
            return Math.Log(num);
        }
        catch(LogarithmicException exObj)
        {
            Console.WriteLine("Message: " + exObj.Message);
            Console.WriteLine("Error number: " + exObj.ErrorNumber);
            throw new ArithmeticException("Invalid number for Logarithm
            ➥ calculation");
        }
    }
}

class Tester
{
    public static void Main()
    {
        try
        {
            double number;
            double result;

            Console.Write("Calculate Log for the following number: ");
            number = Convert.ToDouble(Console.ReadLine());
            result = MyMath.CalculateLog(number);
            Console.WriteLine("The result is: {0}", result);
        }
        catch(ArithmeticException exObj)
        {
            Console.WriteLine(exObj.Message);
```

LISTING 19.7 continued

```
70:         }
71:     }
72: }
```

Sample output 1:

```
Calculate Log for the following number: 10<enter>
The result is: 2.30258509299405
```

Sample output 2:

```
Calculate Log for the following number: 0<enter>
Message: Logarithm of zero is -infinity
Error number: 1002
Invalid number for Logarithm calculation
```

Sample output 3:

```
Calculate Log for the following number: -5<enter>
Message: Logarithm of a negative number cannot be calculated
Error number: 1001
Invalid number for Logarithm calculation
```

Suppose we have developed a number system for the different exceptions in our program, so that a unique number represents each exception. For example, divide by zero has number 1004, and passing a negative value to a logarithmic calculation has number 1001. Thus, apart from storing an exception message in an exception object, we also want to store an exception number. This latter functionality is not supported by any of the intrinsic exception classes, so we decide to derive our own exception class with this ability (called `LogarithmicException`) from the `System.ApplicationException` class as specified in line 3. The `errorNumber` instance variable in line 5 represents the exception number. The class has two constructors:

- A default constructor in lines 8–11 automatically assigns 1000 to the `errorNumber` and, by calling the base class constructor, assigns "Logarithmic exception" to the built-in `string` message.
- A two-parameter constructor in lines 14–17 passes the first `string` parameter to the base constructor, while the second `uint` parameter is assigned to `errorNumber` in line 16.

`errorNumber` can be accessed through the read-only property in lines 19–25.

New objects of `LogarithmicException` are created and thrown in lines 36 and 40, where we not only pass the usual `string` argument, but also a second argument of type `uint`, (1001 and 1002, respectively) which represents the error number.

The `errorNumber` is printed to the console in line 47 of the `catch` block by accessing the `ErrorNumber` property.

Notice that instead of rethrowing `exObj` (as in line 48 of Listing 19.6), line 48 in Listing 19.7 demonstrates our ability to create and throw a new exception object here (of class `ArithmeticException`) to be handled by the outer `try-catch` blocks in the `Main` method.

Summary

This chapter introduced exceptions, what they are, and how to handle them. The important points discussed in this chapter are as follows.

An exception represents an abnormal condition in your program.

An exception is an object of the class `System.Exception` or of a subclass derived thereof. The .NET Framework contains several intrinsic exception classes derived from `System.Exception`.

An exception object can either be implicitly created and thrown by the runtime, or explicitly created and thrown by applying the `throw` keyword in your source code.

An uncaught exception causes a program to stop abruptly and display (to many) an obscure message on the console.

Three different but closely related language elements are used to deal with exceptions:

- `try` blocks are positioned inside functions enclosing code that may throw exceptions but which, otherwise, perform the normal operations of your program.
- `catch` blocks contain the code that performs the corrective actions necessary to resolve the problems caused by an exception.
- `finally` blocks guarantee that the code they contain is executed before execution exits from its associated `try-catch` construction.

Each `catch` block matches a particular type of exception. A `try` block can have several associated `catch` blocks, each dealing with a different exception type thrown from within the `try` block.

`try` blocks can be nested inside each other.

The `throw` keyword can be used from within a `catch` block to either rethrow an exception or throw a new exception. This allows several `catch` statements to handle the same original exception.

Custom exception classes can be written by deriving them from the `System.ApplicationException` class.

Review Questions

1. List three examples of typical exceptions.
2. What are the advantages of handling exceptions with `try-catch-finally`?
3. Which class is at the top of the exceptions class hierarchy?
4. How many `catch` and `finally` blocks can be attached to a `try` block?
5. What happens to normal execution flow when an exception is thrown inside a `try` block?

6. How can a **catch** block match an exception?
7. If no abnormal conditions were experienced, where is the flow of execution transferred after a **try** block has finished executing?
8. What happens if an exception is thrown in a **try** block but no matching **catch** blocks are found?
9. What happens if a **catch** block throws an exception?
10. What is the purpose of the **finally** block?
11. Which class must you derive from to write your own custom-made exception classes?
12. Is the following **try-finally** construct valid? If so, why would you ever want to implement it?

```
try
{...}
finally
{...}
```

13. Is the following **try-catch** construct valid? Why or why not?

```
try
{...}
catch (System.Exception exObj)
{...}
catch (System.IndexOutOfRangeException exObj)
{...}
```

14. What happens if an exception finds no matching **catch** blocks in your program?

Programming Exercises

1. Implement the necessary exception handling code in Listing 19.1 to prevent the program from stopping abruptly and allow (in a user-friendly manner) the user to assign a value to `yourInt` in `Method2`.

   Programming exercises 2–4 build on the same program, so please save the program in each exercise.

2. Write a class called `Meteorologist` that contains an array named `rainfall` containing 12 elements (of type `int`). Write a constructor for the class that assigns an arbitrary number to each of the 12 elements in `rainfall`. Include a method with the following header in `Meteorologist`:

   ```
   public int GetRainfall(int index)
   ```

   This method must return the value of the element in `rainfall` that corresponds to the given `index`. Include the necessary code in `GetRainfall` to handle any out-of-range exceptions thrown from within the `GetRainfall` method. Implement code to test the `Meteorologist` class and its method.

3. During each month, a reading is made for the total amount of pollution absorbed into the rainwater from the air and brought to the ground. Include another array in `Meteorologist` called `pollution`, also with 12 elements of type `int`. Use the constructor from exercise 2 to assign arbitrary values to these 12 elements. Write a method with the header

   ```
   public int GetAveragePollution(int index)
   ```

   which calculates the average amount of pollution in each unit of rainfall for a given month. For example, to calculate the average pollution in month 4 per rainfall unit, perform the following calculation:

   ```
   averagePollution = pollution[3] / rainfall[3]
   ```

   Implement the necessary exception handling code for `GetAveragePollution`. Notice that both an index out-of-range exception as well as a divide by zero exception can be thrown in this method.

4. The `GetAveragePollution` method from exercise 3 opens a file on its entry. This file must always be closed before the method exits. Make sure that this is the case. You can pretend the file is being closed with the following line:

   ```
   Console.WriteLine("Closing WeatherXYZ file");
   ```

CHAPTER 20

DELEGATES AND EVENTS

You will learn about the following in this chapter:

- What a delegate is
- Defining and instantiating delegates
- Using delegates as arguments to method calls and creating arrays of delegates
- Multicast delegates and why they are useful for implementing event-driven programs
- What an event is and how it can be implemented with a delegate
- The basic architecture of a typical event-driven program

Recall from Chapter 17, "Inheritance Part II: `abstract` Functions, Polymorphism, and Interfaces" how inheritance enabled us to reference objects of different subclasses (such as `Circle`, `Rectangle` and `Triangle`) with the same variable of a common ancestor class (such as `Shape`). Through dynamic binding (by calling `DrawYourself` in `Shape`), this allowed us to automatically call the method implementation for the object that the variable was referencing at the moment of the call. We could, in effect, let the same method call invoke different implementations during runtime. This was powerful because we, as programmers, didn't know in advance which particular subclass objects the ancestor type variable (`Shape` in our case) would reference during runtime (we didn't know the particular shapes a drawing would contain). So we were able to postpone this decision until runtime.

Delegates, like inheritance, interfaces, and polymorphism, also help us to postpone decisions concerning method implementations until runtime.

A *delegate* is similar to an `abstract` method in that it specifies the return type and formal parameter types of a method but not the implementation. The same delegate can, like an abstract method, represent different method implementations during runtime, as long as these methods have the same return type and formal parameters as those specified for the delegate. During runtime, a suitable method is assigned to the delegate, which then encapsulates this method. When the delegate is called, it will delegate the actual execution to the method it encapsulates.

Delegates are useful when we, at the time of writing our source code, only know that an action (along with its return type and formal parameters) must happen at a particular place, but don't know its implementation. This computational problem is often encountered in modern computer programs. One example is event-driven, graphical user interfaces (GUI). As mentioned in Chapter 12, "Class Anatomy Part I: Static Class Members and Method Adventures" the next action in an event-driven program depends on the next event fired in the program. An event could be a mouse click on a button or a key pressed on the keyboard. Often, we know that a button must perform some kind of action when it is clicked, but we don't know the implementation before compile time. If we let the button click call a delegate, we can postpone the decision of which particular method this button click is invoking until runtime. At runtime, we can assign the particular method to the delegate, which then will be called every time the button is clicked. Events and delegates are closely related, as you will see later in this chapter. Both these concepts are pivotal for implementing event-driven programs in C#.

Delegates

A delegate is a class and, therefore, a reference type. It is derived from the base class `System.Delegate`. Just like any other class, a delegate must be defined and can then be instantiated.

Note

In OOP terminology, we distinguish between the term class as being the definition of a class you can read in the source code, whereas its instantiation that takes place during runtime is called an object. Unfortunately, delegates don't have a similar terminology. Both the delegate definition and the delegate's instantiations are referred to as delegates.

Even though delegates are derived from `System.Delegate`, we don't use the familiar class-derivation syntax (a colon `:`, as described in Chapter 16, "Inheritance Part I: Basic Concepts") for deriving and defining a new delegate (class); instead, we use the keyword `delegate` as in the following line:

```
public delegate double Calculation(int x, int y);
```

This line defines a delegate called `Calculation`, which can encapsulate any method that returns a `double` and takes two parameters both of type `int`.

The general syntax for defining a delegate is shown in Syntax Box 20.1.

Syntax Box 20.1 Delegate Definition

```
Delegate_definition::=
[<Access_modifier>] delegate <Return_type> <Identifier>
➥ ( [<Formal_parameter_list>] );
```

where

```
<Access_modifier>
        ::= public
        ::= protected
        ::= internal
        ::= private
```

Notes:

Delegates are classes, so their definitions can be positioned at the same locations as conventional class definitions.

You can use the same access modifiers on delegates as on classes, and they have the same meaning.

Our delegate definition called **`Calculation`** represents a user-defined type, just like any other conventional class definition. We can use this type to declare new variables of type **`Calculation`**, as in the following line, which declares **`myCalculation`** to be of type **`Calculation`**:

```
Calculation myCalculation;
```

`myCalculation` can reference any instances of type **`Calculation`**. A new delegate instance is created in the usual way with the **`new`** keyword followed by the name of the delegate class as shown in the following line:

```
myCalculation = new Calculation (<Method_name>);
```

`<Method_name>` represents the method this delegate instance will encapsulate. This method must, as mentioned earlier, have the same return type (**`double`** in this case) and formal parameters (two **`int`**s in this case) as that specified by the delegate definition. However, the method name is irrelevant.

`myCalculation` can then be called like a normal method in the following way:

```
result = myCalculation(15, 20);
```

`myCalculation` delegates this call to the method it encapsulates, by invoking it (while passing the parameters along to this method) and thereby causing its statements to be executed. The return value from the encapsulated method will be passed back through **`myCalculation`** and, in this case, assigned to **`result`**. Listing 20.1 puts the pieces together into one program, which is only meant to demonstrate the mechanics of delegates, not their virtues.

LISTING 20.1 `Calculator.cs`

```
using System;

class Calculator
{
    public delegate double Calculation(int x, int y);

    public static double Sum(int num1, int num2)
    {
        return num1 + num2;
```

LISTING 20.1 continued

```
10:     }
11:
12:     public static void Main()
13:     {
14:         double result;
15:         Math myMath = new Math();
16:
17:         Calculation myCalculation = new Calculation(myMath.Average);
18:         result = myCalculation(10, 20);
19:         Console.WriteLine("Result of passing 10,20 to
            ➥ myCalculation: {0}", result);
20:
21:         myCalculation = new Calculation(Sum);
22:         result = myCalculation(10, 20);
23:         Console.WriteLine("Result of passing 10,20 to
            ➥ myCalculation: {0}", result);
24:     }
25: }
26:
27: class Math
28: {
29:     public double Average(int number1, int number2)
30:     {
31:         return (number1 + number2) / 2;
32:     }
33: }
```

```
Result of passing 10,20 to myCalculation: 15
Result of passing 10,20 to myCalculation: 30
```

Line 5 defines the delegate `Calculation`. The program defines two different methods called `Sum` (lines 7–10) and `Average` (lines 29–32), which both have return types and formal parameters that match those specified by the `Calculation` delegate and, therefore, can be encapsulated by an instance of type `Calculation`. Observe that the name of the methods (`Sum` and `Average`) and the name of their formal parameters do not match that of `Calculation` or `myCalculation`. These names are not taken into account when the compiler determines if a particular delegate can encapsulate a method.

Line 17 creates a new `Calculation` instance with the `new` keyword and passes as an argument the `Average` method of the `myMath` object. Thus, after line 17, `myCalculation` encapsulates the `Average` method of the `myMath` object. Notice that any instance method passed as an argument to the delegate constructor must be referenced with both its object name and its method name as in `myMath.Average`.

In line 18, `myCalculation` delegates the call to `myMath.Average` because it was assigned this method in line 17 and, therefore, returns the average of 10 and 20 as shown in the output.

Line 21 creates a new instance of `Calculation`, this time encapsulating `Sum`. `Sum` is `static` and is found within the `Calculator` class, so we don't need any further reference for this method than just `Sum` when passing it as an argument to `Calculator`'s constructor.

Even though the call to myCalculation in line 22 is identical to line 18, it produces a different result because myCalculation encapsulates a different method at each call. Instead of finding the average, it now sums up the two numbers as specified in Sum.

Syntax Box 20.2 Delegate Instantiation

```
Delegate_instantiation::=

        new <Delegate_identifier> (<Method>)
```

Notes:

<Method> identifies the method the delegate instance will encapsulate. Exactly one argument must always be passed to the delegate constructor.

If <Method> is an instance method of another class, it must be identified as <Object_identifier>.<Method_identifier>.

If it is a static method of another class, it must be identified as <Class_identifier>.<Method_identifier>.

Arrays of Delegates and Delegates as Arguments to Method Calls

Even though Listing 20.1 demonstrates the mechanics of delegates, it fails to demonstrate the advantages of using delegates. The following sections attempt to give you a glimpse of the possibilities provided by delegates.

Sometimes, we need to bring an item through a series of different operations, but we don't know in advance the number of operations or their sequence. For example, chemists might have an arsenal of different treatments (operations) they can apply to rinse polluted water (filtering, different chemicals, heating, cooling, and so on). A water-cleansing simulation program can perhaps help chemists find the best combination of treatments by letting them experiment and put together different treatment sequences. However, these chemists must be able to decide the sequence of the treatments during runtime by picking and choosing among the different operations, and, for each combination, see the end result. As programmers, we don't know these sequences in advance. Delegates can help us solve this type of computational problem.

Listing 20.2 implements a similar scenario to that of a water-cleansing simulation program. However, to simplify, instead of polluted water the start item is simply a number. We have three different operations that can be applied to a number: "deduct 20", "time by 2," and "add 10," but we don't know in advance in what order these operations are applied and how many operations are included (the same operation can be applied multiple times). For example, if the start number is 10 and the following operations have been chosen

```
Times two       (returns 20)
Times two       (returns 40)
Minus twenty   (returns 20)
```

```
Plus ten            (returns 30)
Times two        (returns 60)
```

the end result is 60.

I have called the program `RocketCalculator` because rocket scientists have a reputation of playing around with parts of mathematical formulas and putting them together in different ways, like the program allows us to do.

Listing 20.2 demonstrates a couple of important points—our ability to create arrays of delegates (lines 7 and 13) and to write methods, which can be passed a delegate as an argument (line 16). More about this in the analysis after the sample output.

LISTING 20.2 `RocketCalculator.cs`

```
01: using System;
02:
03: delegate double DoCalculate(double num);
04:
05: class RocketCalculator
06: {
07:     private DoCalculate[] calculations;
08:     private int calculationCounter;
09:
10:     public RocketCalculator()
11:     {
12:         calculationCounter = 0;
13:         calculations = new DoCalculate[10];
14:     }
15:
16:     public void AddCalculation(DoCalculate newCalculation)
17:     {
18:         calculations[calculationCounter] = newCalculation;
19:         calculationCounter++;
20:     }
21:
22:     public double StartCalculation(double tempValue)
23:     {
24:         Console.WriteLine("Start value: {0}", tempValue);
25:         for (int i = 0; i < calculationCounter; i++)
26:         {
27:             tempValue = calculations[i](tempValue);
28:         }
29:         return tempValue;
30:     }
31: }
32:
33: class Math
34: {
35:     public static DoCalculate DoMinusTwenty = new
        ➥ DoCalculate(MinusTwenty);
36:     public static DoCalculate DoTimesTwo = new DoCalculate(TimesTwo);
```

LISTING 20.2 continued

```
    public static DoCalculate DoPlusTen = new DoCalculate(PlusTen);

    public static double MinusTwenty(double number)
    {
        Console.WriteLine("Minus twenty");
        return number - 20;
    }

    public static double TimesTwo(double number)
    {
        Console.WriteLine("Times two");
        return number * 2;
    }

    public static double PlusTen(double number)
    {
        Console.WriteLine("Plus ten");
        return number + 10;
    }
}

public class Tester
{
    public static void Main()
    {
        double startValue;
        double endResult;
        string response;

        RocketCalculator calculator = new RocketCalculator();

        Console.Write("Enter start value: ");
        startValue = Convert.ToDouble(Console.ReadLine());
        Console.WriteLine("Create sequence of operations by repeatedly");
        Console.WriteLine("choosing from the following options");
        Console.WriteLine("M)inus twenty");
        Console.WriteLine("T)imes two");
        Console.WriteLine("P)lus ten");
        Console.WriteLine("When you wish to perform
        ➥ the calculation enter C\n");

        do
        {
            response = Console.ReadLine().ToUpper();
            switch(response)
            {
                case "M":
                    calculator.AddCalculation(Math.DoMinusTwenty);
                    Console.WriteLine("Minus twenty operation added");
                break;
                case "T":
                    calculator.AddCalculation(Math.DoTimesTwo);
```

LISTING 20.2 continued

```
 88:                         Console.WriteLine("Times two operation added");
 89:                     break;
 90:                     case "P":
 91:                         calculator.AddCalculation(Math.DoPlusTen);
 92:                         Console.WriteLine("Plus ten operation added");
 93:                     break;
 94:                     case "C":
 95:                         endResult = calculator.StartCalculation(startValue);
 96:                         Console.WriteLine("End result: {0}", endResult);
 97:                     break;
 98:                     default:
 99:                         Console.WriteLine("Invalid choice please try again");
100:                     break;
101:                 }
102:         } while (response != "C");
103:     }
104: }
```

```
Enter start value: 10<enter>
Create sequence of operations by repeatedly
choosing from the following options
M)inus twenty
T)imes two
P)lus ten
When you wish to perform the calculation enter C

t
Times two operation added
t
Times two operation added
m
Minus twenty operation added
p
Plus ten operation added
t
Times two operation added
c
Start value: 10
Times two
Times two
Minus twenty
Plus ten
Times two
End result: 60
```

Line 3 defines a delegate called `DoCalculate`. Its return type and formal parameter match those of the three methods `MinusTwenty`, `TimesTwo`, and `PlusTen` found in the `Math` class (lines 39–55). Thus, a delegate instance of `DoCalculate` can encapsulate any of these three methods.

We want to construct sequences of the three `Math` methods as described before, and we need a place to store such a sequence. To this end, we declare an array of `DoCalculate` elements in line 7 called `calculations`. It is assigned an array object of ten elements in line 13 of the `RocketCalculator` constructor (thus our sequence can have a maximum ten `Math` methods). Ten is an arbitrary number.

Each element in the `calculations` array can reference a `DoCalculate` instance that encapsulates one of the three `Math` class methods.

We then need the ability to add `DoCalculate` delegate instances that encapsulate the `Math` class methods we want in the sequence. This is achieved with the `AddCalculation` method in lines 16–20. `AddCalculation`'s formal parameter `newCalculation` of type `DoCalculate` allows us to pass an instance of type `DoCalculate` to `AddCalculation` that encapsulates a particular `Math` method. `newCalculation`, which references this `DoCalculate` instance, is assigned to an element of the `calculations` array (line 18). The first time we call `AddCalculation`, the `calculationCounter` is equal to zero, so the first `newCalculation` parameter is assigned to the array element with index zero. As we add more `newCalculation` parameters, `calculationCounter` is incremented by one in line 19. This configuration allows us to fill the `calculations` array up with `DoCalculate` instances encapsulating `Math` methods of our choice.

We need to pass `DoCalculate` delegate arguments to the `AddCalculation` method, but how do we get hold of these instances? To facilitate this, three `DoCalculate` delegate instances have been created in lines 35–37 of the `Math` class. Each delegate instance encapsulates a different `Math` method. Notice that these delegates have been declared `static` to save us from creating an instance of the `Math` class every time we need access to one of these delegates.

The `Tester` class contains user interaction code that allows the user to create a sequence of methods. Line 66 creates a new instance of `RocketCalculator` called `calculator`. By choosing one of the letters M, T, and P, the user can assign either a `Math.DoMinusTwenty` (line 83) delegate instance, a `Math.DoTimesTwo` (line 87) delegate instance, or a `Math.DoPlusTen` (line 91) delegate instance to the next array element.

If you attempt to assign more than 10 calculations, the system will throw an `IndexOutOfRangeException`. To simplify the code, no index checks are being made and no exception handling has been implemented.

After a satisfactory combination has been assembled, the sequence can be applied on the `startValue` (assigned in line 69) by pressing C, which triggers the `StartCalculation` method of the calculator instance to be called (line 95).

`calculations[i]` represents a `DoCalculate` delegate instance that encapsulates a `Math` method. So, `calculations[i](tempValue)` (line 27) represents a call to this delegate instance. This call will be delegated to the particular `Math` method that it encapsulates and return the result back to be assigned to `tempValue`.

Multicast Delegates

The delegates presented so far only encapsulate one method each. It is also possible to define *multicast* delegates that can encapsulate one or more methods. When a multicast delegate is called, it invokes all the methods it encapsulates one by one. Multicast delegates are particularly useful for event handling purposes, as shown later in this chapter. For example, a button click event in an event-driven GUI program might want to invoke more than one method. Although this could also be achieved through a collection of delegates similar to the `calculations` array declared in line 7 of Listing 20.2, the multicast delegates are custom made for this situation, which they handle elegantly.

A delegate with the return value `void` is automatically a multicast delegate. In a moment, we will look at why a multicast delegate cannot return any value. The following line, taken from line 5 in Listing 20.3 defines a multicast delegate called `Greeting`:

```
delegate void Greeting();
```

A multicast delegate is declared and can be assigned a new delegate instance, (just like a single-cast delegate) as in the following line (see line 9 of Listing 20.3):

```
Greeting myGreeting = new Greeting(SayThankYou);
```

which declares `myGreeting` to be of class `Greeting` and assigns it a `new Greeting` instance that encapsulates the `SayThankYou` method defined in lines 34–37 of Listing 20.3.

Line 13 similarly declares and assigns a `new Greeting` instance to `yourGreeting`:

```
Greeting yourGreeting = new Greeting(SayGoodMorning);
```

Two multicast delegates can be combined with the `+` operator and the result assigned to a multicast delegate of the same type. This new multicast delegate will encapsulate all the methods of the two multicast delegates that were added together. Thus, the following line

```
Greeting ourGreeting = myGreeting + yourGreeting;
```

causes `ourGreeting` to encapsulate all the methods encapsulated by `myGreeting` (one, in this case) as well as all the methods encapsulated by `yourGreeting` (one, in this case).

You can also use the `+=` operator to add a multicast delegate to another multicast delegate, as in line 21

```
ourGreeting += new Greeting(SayGoodnight);
```

which, as usual, is the same as writing (see line 21)

```
ourGreeting = ourGreeting + new Greeting(SayGoodNight);
```

This causes `ourGreeting` to also include the `SayGoodNight` method among its encapsulated methods.

In a similar way, the `-` and `-=` operators can be used to remove a multicast delegate from another multicast delegate.

For example, to remove `yourGreeting` from `ourGreeting`, we can write (as in line 25):

```
ourGreeting = ourGreeting - yourGreeting;
```

which is similar to writing

```
ourGreeting -= yourGreeting;
```

Listing 20.3 uses the four operators +, +=, -, and -= on delegates and verifies their operations by printing to the console after each operator has been applied.

LISTING 20.3 MulticastTester.cs

```
using System;

class MulticastTester
{
    delegate void Greeting();

    public static void Main()
    {
        Greeting myGreeting = new Greeting(SayThankYou);
        Console.WriteLine("My single greeting:");
        myGreeting();

        Greeting yourGreeting = new Greeting(SayGoodMorning);
        Console.WriteLine("\nYour single greeting:");
        yourGreeting();

        Greeting ourGreeting = myGreeting + yourGreeting;
        Console.WriteLine("\nOur multicast greeting:");
        ourGreeting();

        ourGreeting += new Greeting(SayGoodnight);
        Console.WriteLine("\nMulticast greeting which includes
        ➥ Goodnight:");
        ourGreeting();

        ourGreeting = ourGreeting - yourGreeting;
        Console.WriteLine("\nMulticast greeting without your greeting:");
        ourGreeting();

        ourGreeting -= myGreeting;
        Console.WriteLine("\nSingle greeting without your greeting and
        ➥ my greeting:");
        ourGreeting();
    }

    public static void SayThankYou()
    {
        Console.WriteLine("Thank you!");
    }

    public static void SayGoodMorning()
    {
        Console.WriteLine("Good morning!");
    }

    public static void SayGoodnight()
    {
        Console.WriteLine("Goodnight");
```

```
    }
}
```

```
My single greeting:
Thank you!

Your single greeting:
Good morning!

Our multicast greeting:
Thank you!
Good morning!

Multicast greeting which includes Goodnight:
Thank you!
Good morning!
Goodnight

Multicast greeting without your greeting:
Thank you!
Goodnight

Single greeting without your greeting and my greeting:
Goodnight
```

Note

The operators `+`, `+=`, `-`, `-=` can only be used with multicast delegates, that is, delegates that return `void`.

Why Must Multicast Delegates be *void*?

If a delegate is specified to have a return value, the method it encapsulates will also have a return value. When a delegate only encapsulates one method, this works fine because the one return value from the encapsulated method is channeled back out through the delegate's return value and back to the caller. However, if a delegate encapsulates more than one method, it is impossible for us to control where these return values end up and how they are processed. Consequently, multicast delegates cannot return any value; they must be `void`.

Events

An *event* represents a signal that something noteworthy has happened in a program. Examples of events are a button click, a key press, a timer lapsing one minute, and a printer finishing printing. An object with the ability to generate events is called a *publisher* and is a *source* of events. To generate an event is also called to *fire* an event.

One or more objects can *subscribe* (or *register*) to be notified about a certain event fired from another object. These objects are called *subscribers* or *listeners*. Each subscriber must contain a method called an *event handler* to handle the event the subscriber has subscribed to be notified about. All subscribing event handlers are invoked one after the other when the corresponding event is fired. A subscriber can subscribe to several different event types and can contain several event handlers. Multicast delegates are highly suited to implement the event handling process and, thus, to form a link between subscribers and publishers.

What is the advantage of separating certain programs into publishers and subscribers? Why can't the publishers just react to the events themselves? Event handling allows us to write programs with lower coupling. The programmers writing the publisher objects don't need to know much about the subscriber objects and vice versa. Furthermore, subscriber type objects can easily subscribe or unsubscribe to certain events during runtime because this aspect has not been hardwired in the code.

Writing Event-Driven Programs

An event in C# is nothing more than a slightly specialized multicast delegate, tailor-made for the event handling process. As a result, events are easier to use and more robust for this purpose than normal multicast delegates.

Note

The following discussion refers to the delegates, events and event handlers from Listing 20.4 displayed later. The line numbers are provided as a quick reference to this listing.

An event is declared by applying the `event` keyword to a multicast delegate. For example, if we define the following multicast delegate called `MoveRequest` (line 25) (you can ignore the two parameters `sender` and `e` for now, they are discussed later)

```
public delegate void MoveRequest(object sender, MoveRequestEventArgs e);
```

then, instead of declaring a normal multicast delegate called `MyMoveRequest`, say, as shown next

```
public MoveRequest MyMoveRequest;
```

we can add the `event` keyword as shown in the following line (line 27) to declare an event called `OnMoveRequest`

```
public event MoveRequest OnMoveRequest;
```

`OnMoveRequest` is so similar to a normal multicast delegate like `MyMoveRequest` that you, for most purposes, can regard it as being a multicast delegate.

Note

Any event name by convention starts with `On`.

The delegate definition and its associated event declaration are positioned in the publisher class (the `GameController` class in lines 23–99). The event handler for this delegate and event is positioned in the subscribing class (the **Car** class in lines 101–147). As usual, the event handler must have the same return value and formal parameter types as the delegate (**MoveRequest**, in this case). This enables the event handler to be encapsulated by the event **OnMoveRequest** (by subscribing to this event), and it will consequently be called when the event is fired.

Note

Firing an event in C# is done by calling the event, just as when we call a delegate, as shown in the previous sections. In this case, it would mean to execute a line similar to the following (see lines 81, 85 and 89) inside the publisher:

```
OnMoveRequest(senderObject, someEventArguments);
```

In our case, the event handler could have the following header (line 124):

```
public void MoveRequestHandler(object sender, MoveRequestEventArgs e)
{
    ...
}
```

Suppose the delegate and the event it implements are defined in a class called **GameController** (lines 23–99) and are currently sitting in an instance of **GameController** called **controller**. It is now possible for the subscriber to subscribe to the event by encapsulating its **MoveRequestHandler** (event handler) method in the **OnMoveRequest** event in the familiar multicast fashion (line 116):

```
controller.OnMoveRequest += new GameController.MoveRequest(MoveRequestHandler);
```

In a similar fashion, the **MoveRequestHandler** can unsubscribe to the event by being un-encapsulated, as in the following line (line 121):

```
controller.OnMoveRequest -= new GameController.MoveRequest(MoveRequestHandler);
```

Note

One of the major differences between a normal multicast delegate and an event is that only the operators += and -= can be used with an event from outside the object in which it resides. For example, the following line is invalid because **OnMoveRequest** is an event:

```
controller.OnMoveRequest = new GameController.MoveRequest(
Â MoveRequestHandler);     //Invalid
```

This is a good thing because this line would cause havoc by removing all other event handlers encapsulated by **OnMoveRequest** and, instead encapsulate just the one **MoveRequestHandler** method specified in the line. If this statement was valid, one subscriber could effectively wipe out all other subscriptions.

When the compiler encounters the **event** keyword, it implicitly declares this event **private** and creates two **public** properties (only visible in the MSIL) called **add_<Event_name>** and **remove_<Event_name>** that are accessible with the += and -= operators.

For a moment, we need to return to the parameters (`object sender and MoveRequestEventArgs e`) of the `MoveRequest` delegate with which our event is implemented. Delegates that events are implemented with always have, per convention, two parameters of type `System.Object` (alias is `object` in C#) and type `System.EventArgs` (or a subclass thereof) as shown here (where `MoveRequestEventArgs` is a subclass of `System.EventArgs`):

```
public delegate void MoveRequest(object sender, MoveRequestEventArgs e);
```

The `object` parameter allows the publishing object to inform the subscribing object's event handler where (in what object) the event was fired (and is therefore often called `sender`). The event is fired from the object itself. A reference to the object itself is found in the `this` keyword, which, consequently, is the first argument, as in the following line (see line 81):

```
OnMoveRequest(this, new MoveRequestEventArgs(MoveRequestType.FastForward));
```

The second parameter, `MoveRequestEventArgs` (subclass of `System.EventArgs`), allows the publisher to pass particular information along to the subscriber about the event. To fully explain and exemplify the use of this parameter, we need to look closer at Listing 20.4. We do this in the analysis after the sample output.

LISTING 20.4 `CarGameEvents.cs`

```
01: using System;
02:
03: enum MoveRequestType {FastForward, SlowForward, Reverse};
04:
05: class MoveRequestEventArgs : EventArgs
06: {
07:     private MoveRequestType request;
08:
09:     public MoveRequestEventArgs(MoveRequestType initRequest) : base()
10:     {
11:         request = initRequest;
12:     }
13:
14:     public MoveRequestType Request
15:     {
16:         get
17:         {
18:             return request;
19:         }
20:     }
21: }
22:
23: class GameController
24: {
25:     public delegate void MoveRequest(object sender,
        ➥ MoveRequestEventArgs e);
26:
27:     public event MoveRequest OnMoveRequest;
```

LISTING 20.4 continued

```

    Car[] gameCars = new Car[10];
    string carName;
    int speedParam = 0;
    int carCounter = 0;
    int carNumber = 0;

    public void Run()
    {
        string answer;
        Console.WriteLine("Please select from the following menu: ");
        Console.WriteLine("A)dd new car");
        Console.WriteLine("C)ar. Subscribe to events");
        Console.WriteLine("U)nsubscribe from events");
        Console.WriteLine("L)ist cars in current game");
        Console.WriteLine("F)ast forward");
        Console.WriteLine("S)low forward");
        Console.WriteLine("R)everse");
        Console.WriteLine("T)erminate");

        do
        {
            Console.WriteLine("Select new option:");
            answer = Console.ReadLine().ToUpper();

            switch(answer)
            {
                case "A":
                    Console.Write("Enter name of the new car: ");
                    carName = Console.ReadLine();
                    Console.Write("Enter car speed parameter of
                    ➥ the new car: ");
                    speedParam = Convert.ToInt32(Console.ReadLine());
                    gameCars[carCounter] = new Car(speedParam, carName);
                    carCounter++;
                break;
                case "C":
                    Console.Write("Enter array index of car you want to
                    ➥ subscribe to events: ");
                    carNumber = Convert.ToInt32(Console.ReadLine());
                    gameCars[carNumber].Subscribe(this);
                break;
                case "U":
                    Console.Write("Enter array index of car you want to
                    ➥ unsubscribe from events: ");
                    carNumber = Convert.ToInt32(Console.ReadLine());
                    gameCars[carNumber].Unsubscribe(this);
                break;
                case "L":
                    for(int i=0; i < carCounter; i++)
                    {
                        Console.WriteLine(gameCars[i]);
```

LISTING 20.4 continued

```
                    }
                break;
                case "F":
                    if (OnMoveRequest != null)
                        OnMoveRequest(this, new MoveRequestEventArgs
                        ➥(MoveRequestType.FastForward));
                break;
                case "S":
                    if (OnMoveRequest != null)
                        OnMoveRequest(this, new MoveRequestEventArgs
                        ➥(MoveRequestType.SlowForward));
                break;
                case "R":
                    if (OnMoveRequest != null)
                        OnMoveRequest(this, new MoveRequestEventArgs
                        ➥(MoveRequestType.Reverse));
                break;
                case "T":
                break;
                default:
                    Console.WriteLine("Invalid choice.
                    ➥ Please try again");
                break;
            }
        } while(answer != "T");
    }
}

class Car
{
    private int distance;
    private int speedParam;
    private string name;

    public Car(int initSpeedParam, string initName)
    {
        speedParam = initSpeedParam;
        distance = 0;
        name = initName;
    }

    public void Subscribe(GameController controller)
    {
        controller.OnMoveRequest += new GameController.MoveRequest
        ➥(MoveRequestHandler);
    }

    public void Unsubscribe(GameController controller)
    {
        controller.OnMoveRequest -= new GameController.MoveRequest
        ➥(MoveRequestHandler);
    }
```

LISTING 20.4 continued

```

    public void MoveRequestHandler(object sender, MoveRequestEventArgs e)
    {
        switch (e.Request)
        {
            case MoveRequestType.SlowForward:
                distance += speedParam;
                Console.WriteLine("Car name: " + name + " Moving slowly.
                ➥ Distance: " + distance);
            break;
            case MoveRequestType.FastForward:
                distance += speedParam * 2;
                Console.WriteLine("Car name: " + name + " Moving fast.
                ➥ Distance: " + distance);
            break;
            case MoveRequestType.Reverse:
                distance -= 5;
                Console.WriteLine("Car name: " + name + " Reversing.
                ➥ Distance: " + distance);
            break;
        }
    }

    public override string ToString()
    {
        return name;
    }
}

class Tester
{
    public static void Main()
    {
        GameController controller = new GameController();
        controller.Run();
    }
}
```

```
Please select from the following menu:
A)dd new car
C)ar. Subscribe to events
U)nsubscribe from events
L)ist cars in current game
F)ast forward
S)low forward
R)everse
T)erminate
Select new option:
A<enter>
Enter name of the new car: Volvo<enter>
Enter car speed parameter of the new car: 20<enter>
Select new option:
```

```
F<enter>
Select new option:
C<enter>
Enter array index of car you want to subscribe to events: 0
Select new option:
F<enter>
Car name: Volvo Moving fast. Distance: 40
Select new option:
A<enter>
Enter name of the new car: Lotus<enter>
Enter car speed parameter of the new car: 40<enter>
Select new option:
C<enter>
Enter array index of car you want to subscribe to events: 1<enter>
Select new option:
S<enter>
Car name: Volvo Moving slowly. Distance: 60
Car name: Lotus Moving slowly. Distance: 40
Select new option:
U<enter>
Enter array index of car you want to unsubscribe from events: 0<enter>
Select new option:
R<enter>
Car name: Lotus Reversing. Distance: 35
Select new option:
L<enter>
Volvo
Lotus
Select new option:
C<enter>
Enter array index of car you want to subscribe to events: 0<enter>
Select new option:
R<enter>
Car name: Lotus Reversing. Distance: 30
Car name: Volvo Reversing. Distance: 55
Select new option:
T<enter>
```

Listing 20.4 is an event-driven car game. Overall, it simply contains a list of cars that can move forward or backward. Their movements are controlled by an instance of the `GameController` class, which again is controlled by the end user. Even though simplified, the game has the same overall architecture as most event-driven programs.

The `GameController` class publishes the event `OnMoveRequest` (line 27), to which one or more `Car` objects can subscribe. A subscribing `Car` object will have its event handler invoked (lines 124–141) when `OnMoveRequest` is fired. The event handler will, depending on the content of the `MoveRequestEventArgs` (line 124) parameter, either move the `Car` a certain distance forward (the actual amount is determined by its `speedParam` instance variable, see lines 104, 109, 129 and 133) or reverse the `Car` 5 kilometers (line 137). To pass along the necessary information, `MoveRequestEventArgs` is defined in lines 5–21, to contain the instance variable `request` of type `MoveRequestType`, which is an enum defined in line 3. Consequently, `request` can contain one of the three values—`MoveRequestType.FastForward`,

MoveRequestType.SlowForward, or MoveRequestType.Reverse. One of these values is assigned to the new MoveRequestEventArgs instance in lines 81, 85 or 89, and, through the switch statement in Car's event handler (lines 126, 128, 132 and 136), controls the particular action taken by the event handler. As required, MoveRequestEventArgs is derived from System.EventArgs (line 9).

The array gameCars (line 29) can hold ten Car objects. Car objects can be added (lines 55–61), subscribed to events (lines 63–66), un-subscribed from events (lines 68–71) and current Car objects be listed (lines 73–77). Notice from the sample output that only Car objects that subscribe to the event are moved.

The program does not check the array indexes you provide and does not provide any exception handling for out of range exceptions.

Observe that other classes, such as Motorbike, Pedestrian, and so on, could easily be written and added to the program and, if equipped with a suitable event handler, become active game participants by subscribing to the OnMoveRequest event.

Summary

This chapter discussed delegates and events and their importance for implementing event driven programs in C#. The important points mentioned in this chapter are as follows.

A delegate is a subclass of System.Delegate. It specifies the return and parameter types for the methods it can encapsulate. When a delegate is called, it delegates this call to the method implementation of the method is encapsulates.

Delegates let us postpone method implementation decisions until runtime. For example, arrays of delegates let us decide on sequences of operations during runtime, and method implementations can be passed around as arguments to methods.

A multicast delegate can encapsulate more than one method. Any delegate with the return type void is automatically a multicast delegate. Multicast delegates are particularly useful for event-driven programs.

An event signals that something noteworthy happened in the program. In C#, an event is implemented with a multicast delegate. An event-driven program consists of publisher objects firing events and subscriber objects containing event handlers that are invoked by these notifications.

Review Questions

1. What are the similarities and differences between delegates and abstract methods?
2. Why is delegate a good name for the delegate construct?
3. Where in a program can a delegate definition be positioned?

4. Consider the following delegate definition:

   `public delegate int Filtering(string str);`

   Which of the following methods can instances of this delegate encapsulate?

   a. `protected int Filtering(string myString, double x) {...}`

   b. `internal static int FilteringOp(string myStr) {...}`

   c. `public double Filtering(string str) {...}`

   d. `public short Sum(int x, int y) {...}`

5. Why must multicast delegates have the return type `void`?

6. a) Which arithmetic operators can be used with multicast delegates?

   b) Which arithmetic operators can be used with events when called from outside the object where they reside?

7. What is an event handler?

Programming Exercises

1. Add a `static` method called `Product` to the `Math` class in Listing 20.1. This method must calculate the product of two parameters and be encapsulated by instances of the `Calculation` delegate. Write the code for testing this method with the delegate.

2. Write a program similar to Listing 20.2. This time, instead of letting a number be manipulated by three different math operations, let the program allow an initial single letter to be manipulated by the three following string operations: `"Add an 'A' to the string"`, `"Add a B to the string"`, and `"Add a C to the string"`. Allow the user to put together any sequence of string operations with a maximum of twenty operations.

3. Expand Listing 20.4 with another subscriber class called `Motorbike`. Allow `Motorbike` objects to subscribe to the events fired by the `GameController` object by equipping it with a suitable event handler and so forth, similar to the `Car` class. Program the event handler so that when one of the signals `MoveRequestType.FastForward` or `MoveRequestType.SlowForward` are received, the `Motorbike` object moves forward by 30. If the `MoveRequestType.Reverse` is received, reverse the `Motorbike` object by 3 kilometers. Allow the user to add and remove `Motorbike` objects similar to that of the `Car` objects.

CHAPTER 21

PREPROCESSING, XML DOCUMENTATION, AND ATTRIBUTES

You will learn about the following in this chapter:

- C#'s preprocessor directives
- How to mark different parts of your code with preprocessor directives
- How to easily exclude code from being compiled with preprocessor directives
- A brief introduction to automated program documentation
- What a documentation comment is
- How to let the compiler turn documentation comments into well-formed XML program documents
- What an attribute is
- How to add additional declarative information to C#'s elements by using attributes

Even though the three subjects discussed in this chapter (preprocessor directives, XML documentation, and attributes) are not directly related, they are similar in that they are all separate from the core logical constructs that provide the main functionality of a C# program.

Preprocessor directives can be viewed as controlling the compilation process rather than being part of what is being compiled. The documentation comments used to produce XML documents are, like conventional comments, completely ignored by the compiler; and attributes are not compiled into MSIL but are added to an assembly's metadata instead.

Preprocessor directives is a relatively simple and limited subject of which the key aspects are discussed in this chapter.

XML documentation is a larger subject and only a brief introduction is provided here.

Attributes is a vast and advanced subject with many exciting possibilities. Even though this chapter only shows you a glimpse of what you can do with them, I hope it will inspire you to continue exploring this fascinating subject.

Preprocessor Directives

You can *view* the C# compiler as containing a separate *preprocessor* that processes and prepares the source code for the compiler before the actual compilation takes place. Programmers can use *preprocessor directives* to mark parts of the source code and thereby instruct the preprocessor to treat these parts in a certain way.

Note

Several of C#'s predecessors, including the C language, contain preprocessors that are separate from the compiler. This is not the case for C# where the preprocessor directives are processed as part of the lexical analysis (this explains the highlighted word view in the first line of this section). Nevertheless, the terms are used with C# for historical reasons and because it helps us to better understand what preprocessor directives do. You can ignore this note while you read through the rest of this section.

Exclude and Include Code with `#define`, `#if`, and `#endif`

The most common use of preprocessor directives is to exclude parts of the source code from being compiled. For example, you might, during the testing of your source code, include several `WriteLine` statements to print out variable values that otherwise could not be verified. You obviously don't want the end user to see these test printouts, so you must prevent them from being compiled into the finished program. Furthermore, you might want to switch back and forth between the program's testing and end user version. There are several ways to achieve this.

You can manually insert and manually delete `WriteLine` statements every time you need to switch from one version to another. However, this can be a cumbersome process.

You can insert the `WriteLine` statements and then hide them from the compiler by commenting them out. This is easier than the previous method, but you must still move around in the code and manually insert and delete the required `//` and `/* */` symbols.

These two procedures might work well for small programs, but larger programs sometimes have many test `WriteLine`s and related test statements scattered around in the source code, making it a tedious, time-consuming task to test your programs.

The preprocessor directives allow you to include and exclude test code (that is sprinkled around in your program) from compilation by changing just one line of code. Before we look at Listing 21.1, which demonstrates this ability, we need to briefly introduce the preprocessor directives to understand how this can be achieved.

All preprocessor directives, of which `#define` and `#if` are typical examples, begin with the pound sign (`#`) symbol. Fundamentally, the directives presented in this and the next two sections allow you to put identifiers into and out of existence (by defining and undefining them) at one point in the code and then test for their existence in other parts of the code.

The `#define` preprocessor directive is used to define and thereby put an identifier into existence. For example, the following line

```
#define TEST
```

defines the identifier `TEST`. You can choose any name for an identifier, but conventionally it is written with uppercase letters. `#define` must, as the only directive, be written before any other source code.

The preprocessor directives `#if` and `#endif` work as a pair and enclose one or more lines of code as shown in the following:

```
#if TEST
    <Enclosed source code is only compiled if TEST is defined>
#endif
```

An identifier (`TEST` in this case) must follow the `#if` directive. The enclosed code is only compiled if this identifier is defined. The `#if-#endif` pair can be positioned in an unlimited number of places in your code.

Listing 21.1 demonstrates the `#define`, `#if`, and `#endif` directives.

LISTING 21.1 `CarTesting.cs`

```
#define TESTING

using System;

class Car
{
    int odometer = 0;
    int moveCounter = 0;

    public double MoveForward(int distance)
    {
        moveCounter++;
        odometer += distance;
        Console.WriteLine("Car is moving forward by {0} kilometers",
        ➥ distance);
      #if TESTING
        Console.WriteLine("Testing. Odometer: {0}", odometer);
      #endif
        return (odometer / moveCounter);
    }
}

class Controller
{
    public static void Main()
    {
        double averageMoveDistance;
        Car myCar = new Car();

```

LISTING 21.1 continued

```
29:         averageMoveDistance = myCar.MoveForward(20);
30:         averageMoveDistance = myCar.MoveForward(10);
31:       #if TESTING
32:         Console.WriteLine("Testing. averageMoveDistance: {0}",
33:             averageMoveDistance);
34:       #endif
35:     }
36: }
```

Sample output 1: If line 1 contains the code `#define TESTING`

```
Car is moving forward by 20 kilometers
Testing. Odometer: 20
Car is moving forward by 10 kilometers
Testing. Odometer: 30
Testing. averageMoveDistance: 15
```

Sample output 2: If line 1 is deleted; meaning `TESTING` is undefined and you recompile the code

```
Car is moving forward by 20 kilometers
Car is moving forward by 10 kilometers
```

Suppose the `WriteLine` statements in line 16 and lines 32 and 33 exist purely for testing purposes. We want, with little effort, the ability to switch between a test version and an end user version, so we have enclosed these `WriteLine` statements between `#if` and `#endif` directives. Line 1 defines the `TESTING` identifier with the `#define` directive. If you include line 1 in your code, both of the test `WriteLine` statements will be included in the compilation, as you can see in sample output 1. However, if you simply erase line 1, none of the `WriteLine` statements are included, as verified by sample output 2.

`#undef`: Undefining Identifiers

Instead of deleting the first line of Listing 21.1 to undefine `TESTING`, you can explicitly undefine `TESTING` by using the `#undef` directive, as shown in the following line:

```
#undef TESTING
```

`#undef`, like its `#define` sibling, must appear before any statements in your code that is not also preprocessor directives.

`#elif` and `#else`

With `#elif` and `#else`, you can implement the same type of logic for the preprocessor as the corresponding familiar `else-if` constructs we have used in previous chapters for constructing branching statements in C#. Their impact is illustrated in the following lines:

```
#define DEBUGGING
#define TESTING
    ...
#if DEBUGGING
```

```
    <This code is only compiled if DEBUGGING is defined>
#elif TESTING
    <This code is only compiled if TESTING is defined and DEBUGGING is un-defined>
#else
    <This code is only compiled if both DEBUGGING and TESTING are un-defined>
#endif
    ...
```

`#elif` (corresponding to `else if`) and `#else` are used together with the `#if` and `#endif` directives. If `DEBUGGING` (written after the `#if` directive in the example) is defined, only the code between `#if` and `#elif` is compiled. The `#elif` directive only gets a chance to verify the existence of `TESTING` if `DEBUGGING` is not defined. Thus, only if `DEBUGGING` is undefined and `TESTING` is defined, will the code between `#elif` and `#else` be compiled. If both `TESTING` and `DEBUGGING` are un-defined, only the code between `#else` end `#endif` is compiled.

#error and #warning

`#error` and `#warning` don't exclude or include code from being compiled. Instead, `#error` causes the compiler to report an error and `#warning` triggers a warning. The text inserted after any of these two directives decides the text written as part of the error or warning message. For example, the warning inserted in the following lines causes the text "Remember to remove these lines of code" to be written on the console:

```
#define DEBUG
    ...
#if DEBUG
    ...
    #warning "Remember to remove these lines of code"
#endif
```

#region and #endregion

`#region` and `#endregion` let's you mark a certain portion of the code and provide a name for it. These directives are only relevant when you use editors, such as the C# editor in Visual Studio. NET, that can recognize these directives.

#line

You have probably noticed that whenever the compiler returns an error or warning message, it always passes the source code filename and line/character numbers along. You can alter this part of the message with the `#line` directive. For example, you can tell the compiler that a particular line is line number 59 and that the name of the file is `SpaceInvaders.cs` by using the following line:

```
#line 59 "SpaceInvaders.cs"
```

You will hardly ever need to use the `#line` directive.

XML Documentation

The familiar commenting symbols // and /* */ allow you to insert comments in the source code to facilitate the reader's understanding of the code. Comments are read in conjunction with the source code. Apart from commenting your code, it is also important to document it. Program documents are, as opposed to source code comments, viewed separately and independently from the source code. A good example of program documentation is the .NET Frameworks class library documentation. Here you can find specific class and struct descriptions, along with descriptions of their members and examples of how to use them; but you won't find any of the underlying source code.

You could set out to write your program documentation as a completely separate document in an editor like Notepad. This is what programmers of older languages, such as C and Pascal, had to do. C# offers a better alternative, it allows you to insert special *documentation comments* in the code that are recognized by the compiler. Documentation comments can automatically be transformed into Extensible Markup Language (XML) files by giving suitable commands to the compiler. These XML files can then be transformed into viewable documents similar to those seen in the .NET Frameworks documentation. However, this latter transformation is not supported by the compiler and is beyond the scope of this book.

There are several advantages associated with this way of documenting your code:

- You can automatically extract the documentation from the documentation comments in your code.
- The compiler can validate some of the document details by comparing them with the actual code.
- The compiler can automatically insert information into the documentation.
- The compiler can enforce a standard documentation format.
- XML is a powerful format in which to keep your documents.

A Simple Documentation Example

The following section is only meant to provide a brief introduction to XML documentation in C#.

The documentation comments can be applied to any class or struct or their members (methods, instance variables, and so on) and must be positioned just before one of these language element definitions. A documentation comment starts with three forward-slashes /// and consists of XML tags and descriptive text. The C# compiler recognizes a set of pre-defined XML tags, but you can also define your own tags.

A couple of commonly used pre-defined XML tags are `<summary>` and `<remarks>`. The `<summary>` tag is meant to contain a brief overview of the language element, whereas `<remarks>` can contain a longer description or special remarks.

Note

At this time of writing, the C# compiler recognizes 16 pre-defined XML tags. It is beyond the scope of this book to describe these. However, you can find more information about them in the .NET Framework SDK Documentation if you search for "XML documentation" and "tags for comments."

Listing 21.2 provides a simple example to illustrate the use of the <summary> and <remarks> tags. As you can see, a <summary> comment must commence with <summary> and end with </summary> to be well formed. The compiler will report an error if you divert from this standard XML syntax.

LISTING 21.2 RacingCar.cs

```
using System;

///<summary>The Car class represents a car in the car game </summary>
///<remarks>The car can be moved forward and backward</remarks>
class Car
{
     ///<summary> distance represents the amount
     ///of kilometers the car has driven </summary>
    private uint distance = 0;

     ///<summary> Used to move the car forward and backward </summary>
     ///<remarks> To reverse the car you must pass a
    ➥ negative argument </remarks>
    public void Move(uint addDistance)
    {
        distance += addDistance;
        Console.WriteLine("Moving {0} kilometers", addDistance);
    }
}

class Tester
{
    public static void Main()
    {
        Car myCar = new Car();
        myCar.Move(100);
    }
}
```

To generate a well-formed XML document from Listing 21.2, you need to provide the following command to the compiler:

```
csc /doc: RacingCar.xml RacingCar.cs
```

This will cause the compiler to generate a file called RacingCar.xml (you can view this file with Notepad) with the following contents:

```
<?xml version="1.0"?>
<doc>
    <assembly>
        <name>RacingCar</name>
    </assembly>
    <members>
        <member name="T:Car">
            <summary>The Car class represents a car in the car game </summary>
            <remarks>The car can be moved forward and backward</remarks>
        </member>
        <member name="F:Car.distance">
            <summary> distance represents the amount
            of kilometers the car has driven </summary>
        </member>
        <member name="M:Car.Move(System.UInt32)">
            <summary> Used to move the car forward and backward </summary>
<remarks> To reverse the car you must pass a negative
            ➥ argument </remarks>
        </member>
    </members>
</doc>
```

Apart from the XML tags we provided and their associated text, the compiler has automatically added an `<assembly>` tag and a `<member>` tag for each member preceded by a documentation comment. Each `<member>` tag is associated with a `name` attribute, which commences with a capital letter. `T` stands for type, `F` for field, and `M` for method.

Attributes

When you declare a variable to of type `int`, specify a method to be `public`, or specify a class to be a subclass of another class called, say, `Shape`, you are adding declarative information to each of these elements (the variable, method, and class). As mentioned in Chapter 6, "Types Part I: The Simple Types," declarative information can be compared to telling someone *what* to do, whereas the following imperative statement:

```
sum = number1 + number2;
```

is similar to telling someone *how* to do something (how to calculate the sum of two numbers). The "what" is significantly more expressive than the "how," so your ability to decorate code elements with additional information (adding declarative information) is a powerful concept.

Rather than restricting your ability (like most other languages) to decorate code elements with only the predefined C# language constructs and keywords like `int` and `public` and a colon `:` (for declaring a subclass), C# allows you to extend this ability through the use of attributes.

An *attribute* allows you to add declarative information to C#'s code elements beyond that already made possible by C#'s predefined keywords and constructs. All attributes are derived from the abstract class `System.Attribute`.

Generally, you can decorate the following code elements with attributes: assemblies, classes, structs, class and struct members, formal parameters, and return values. Each attribute is often meant to target only one or a few of these elements.

The .NET Framework contains many predefined attributes you can apply. The following are just three examples with a short description of their impact on your code:

- Prevent selected elements from being compiled and called, by decorating them with the `System.Diagnostics.ConditionalAttribute`. In some ways, this is similar to what you can achieve with the preprocessor directives.
- Mark selected elements obsolete with the `System.ObsoleteAttribute` and triggering the compiler to return a warning or an error if any of these elements are used by other parts of the program. This is useful, for example, when your program contains an old and a new version of a method for performing a certain function, and you want to entice other programmers to use the new version.
- Mark selected methods with the `System.Runtime.InteropServices.DllImportAttribute` to call functions outside of .NET that, for example, exists within the basic Windows Application Programming Interface.

Note

You can define your own custom-made attributes, but most programmers will rarely make use of this ability. As a result, this topic is not discussed in this book.

To decorate an element with a particular kind of attribute, you must enclose the attribute name in square brackets and position this construct just before the element you want to decorate. For example, to decorate the `StartSteamEngine` method with the `System.ObsoleteAttribute`, you can write the following:

```
[System.ObsoleteAttribute]
public void StartSteamEngine()
{
    ...
}
```

This will cause the compiler (during the compilation) to report the following warning for every method that attempts to call `StartSteamEngine`:

```
...Warning CS061 "...StartSteamEngine() is obsolete
```

Note

The attribute decorations of an element are stored as part of this element's metadata in the assembly. As discussed in Chapter 7, "Types Part II: Operators, Enumerators, and Strings," metadata (including the attribute decorations) can be inspected during runtime through an advanced mechanism called reflection.

Conventionally, an attribute name ends with `Attribute`. All the intrinsic .NET attributes follow this naming style.

The compiler allows you to omit the Attribute part of the attribute name when you specify its name in the square brackets. You can substitute [System.ObsoleteAttribute] with [System.Obsolete] or even [Obsolete] if you include the usual line using System; in your program.

The sheer presence of an attribute often provides sufficient declarative information on the target element. However, some attributes, like ObsoleteAttribute, allow you to supply extra information in the form of arguments, similar to those provided to a conventional constructor when you create a new object. For example, you might want the ObsoleteAttribute (annotated on the StartSteamEngine before) to cause the compiler to write the message "StartSteamEngine is obsolete: Use the StartJetEngine method instead" instead of just "StartSteamEngine is obsolete:" as before, and to cause an error instead of just a warning, when a call to this method is encountered by the compiler in the source code. This is accomplished as follows:

```
[System.ObsoleteAttribute("Use the StartJetEngine method instead", true)]
public void StartSteamEngine()
{
    ...
}
```

The second parameter true, enclosed by the parentheses, is assigned to a variable called IsError in the ObsoleteAttribute, which is false by default. When IsError is true, the Obsolete attribute will trigger a compiler error instead of a warning.

You must position the text ("Use the StartJetEngine...") first, and the Boolean value (true) second for the attribute annotation to be correct. For this reason, these arguments are often referred to as *positional parameters*.

Some attributes also allow you to assign values to *named parameters*. These named parameters refer to properties in the corresponding attribute's definition containing set accessors. For example, the XmlArrayAttribute attribute in the System.Xml.Serialization namespace contains the read-write (get, set) property called ElementName (it is not relevant in this context what this attribute does). You assign values to named parameters by naming them followed by an equals sign followed by the value, as shown in the following example:

```
[XmlArrayAttribute("YourString", ElementName = "MyDouble")]
```

which assigns "MyDouble" to XmlArrayAttribute's property ElementName. Notice that the named parameter must come after any positional parameters.

You can annotate one element with several attributes. The syntax for doing this is flexible, you can either list each attribute enclosed in square brackets one after the other before the target element as follows:

```
[Obsolete]
[Conditional("TEST")]
[Serializable]
class MyClass
{
    ...
```

```
}
```

Alternatively, you can list all attributes inside one pair of square brackets and separate them by commas:

```
[Obsolete, Conditional("TEST"), Serializable]
class MyClass
{
    ...
}
```

Finally, you can combine these two styles:

```
[Obsolete]
[Conditional("TEST"), Serializable]
class MyClass
{
    ...
}
```

A Simple Attribute Annotation Example

Listing 21.3 demonstrates the two intrinsic attributes `System.ObsoleteAttribute` and `System.Diagnostics.ConditionalAttribute`. The former has already been described in some detail, and the latter needs a further introduction here.

Like the `#if` preprocessor directive, the `ConditionalAttribute` tests whether a specified identifier exists (has been defined by the `#define` directive). For example, the following construct tests whether the `TEST` identifier exists:

```
[ConditionalAttribute("TEST")]
```

The `ConditionalAttribute` can only be used to annotate methods with return type `void`. If the specified identifier (`TEST` in this case) is undefined, the target method is announced non-callable, and all calls to this method are cancelled during compilation.

You could achieve the same effect by enclosing all calls to the target method inside the familiar `#if-#endif` pair. However, if the target method is called from twenty different parts of a program, this requires you to insert twenty different `#if-#endif` pairs, compared with only one `ConditionalAttribute`.

The `ConditionalAttribute` is, like the preprocessor directives, useful for including and excluding code inserted for testing purposes.

LISTING 21.3 Apollo13.cs

```
#define TEST

using System;
using System.Diagnostics;

class Rocket
```

LISTING 21.3 continued

```
{
    private double speed;
    private double fuel;
    private double distanceFromMoon;

    public Rocket(double initSpeed, double initFuel,
    ➥ double initDistanceFromMoon)
    {
        speed = initSpeed;
        fuel = initFuel;
        distanceFromMoon = initDistanceFromMoon;
    }

    [Obsolete("Please use Rocket.CurrentState instead")]
    public void CurrentSituation()
    {
        if (fuel > 5000)
            Console.WriteLine("Everything seems OK");
        else
            Console.WriteLine("Houston, I think we've got a problem");
    }

    public void CurrentState()
    {
        Console.WriteLine("Current speed: {0}  Current fuel left: {1}",
        ➥ speed, fuel);
    }

    [Conditional("TEST")]
    public void TestWriteAllDetails()
    {
        Console.WriteLine("Testing: Instance variables: speed: {0},
➥ fuel: {1}, distanceFromMoon: {2}", speed, fuel, distanceFromMoon);
    }
}

class ControlCenter
{
    public static void Main()
    {
        Rocket apollo13 = new Rocket(10000, 2000, 20000);

        apollo13.CurrentSituation();
        apollo13.CurrentState();
        apollo13.TestWriteAllDetails();
    }
}
```

Compiler warning during compilation:

```
Apollo13.cs(47,9): warning CS0618: 'Rocket.CurrentSituation()' is obsolete:
➥'Please use Rocket.CurrentState instead'
```

Sample output 1: No changes made to Listing 21.3:

```
Houston, I think we've got a problem
Current speed: 10000  Current fuel left: 2000
Testing: Instance variables: speed: 10000, fuel: 2000, distanceFromMoon: 20000
```

Sample output 2: With line 1 removed and the program recompiled

```
Houston, I think we've got a problem
Current speed: 10000  Current fuel left: 2000
```

Line 19 decorates the method `CurrentSituation` with the `Obsolete` attribute. The additional positional parameter of type `string` asks the compiler to write the text "Please use `Rocket.CurrentState` instead" as part of its warning message. Consequently, whenever the compiler during the compilation encounters a call to `CurrentSituation`, it issues the warning message shown in the sample output. The single warning message displayed is caused by line 47.

If, despite the warning, you run the program, you will see sample output 1. The third line of this sample output is the output from `TestWriteAllDetails`, which was called from line 49. The `Conditional` attribute decorating the `TestWriteAllDetails` method in line 33 didn't deter the compiler from including the calls to this method, because `TEST` exists at line 33. `TEST` is defined in line 1.

If you remove line 1 and recompile the program, you will see sample output 2. With an undefined `TEST` in line 33 the compiler prevented the call to `TestWriteAllDetails` from being made.

The formal syntax for specifying an attribute annotation is shown in Syntax Box 21.1.

Syntax Box 21.1 Attribute Annotation

```
Attribute_annotation::=
[[<Target_element>:] <Attribute_name> ( [<Positional_parameter_list>],
➥[<Named_parameter_list>] ) ]
```

Where

```
<Named_parameter_list> ::= <Named_parameter_1> = <Expression_1>,
➥ <Named_parameter_2> = <Expression_2>...
```

Note:

Generally, the attribute target is the element immediately following the attribute annotation. However, sometimes this rule is not sufficient to pinpoint the actual element we want to annotate. Then we must resort to the `<Target_element> :` specification included in the attribute annotation definition shown earlier in this syntax box. For example, it is impossible to position an attribute annotation in front of an assembly. To decorate an assembly with the `CLSCompliantAttribute`, we must instead include the following line in one of the source code files that are compiled to this assembly:

```
[assembly: CLSCompliantAttribute(true)]
```

Summary

This chapter discussed three vaguely related subjects—processor directives, XML documentation, and attributes. Whereas most of the important aspects of processor directives were presented, the XML documentation and attributes discussions were only introductory. A review of the most important points mentioned in this chapter follows.

Preprocessor directives can be used to mark parts of the source code for the compiler to treat these parts in a special way. Preprocessor directives are commonly used to exclude source code from being compiled; this is especially handy for testing purposes. In general, they allow you to produce different versions of a program from the same source code just by defining or undefining one or more identifiers.

A few of the preprocessor directives are used for purposes other than excluding source code from the compilation process. Instead, these directives can make the compiler report warnings and errors, mark regions of a program to be recognized by a C# editor, or change the line numbers used by the compiler.

Whereas standard source code comments must be read together with the source code, program documentation is viewed separately and independently from the source code.

The C# compiler can automatically extract XML documentation for your program from documentation comments you insert into the source code. Like standard comments, the compiler otherwise ignores the documentation comments.

A documentation comment starts with three forward slashes `///` and consists of XML tags and descriptive text. The compiler recognizes 16 XML tags, but you can expand this number with your own tags.

An attribute allows you to add declarative information to C#'s code elements (assemblies, classes, structs, class and struct members, formal parameters, and return values). Declarative information is highly expressive.

The .NET Framework contains many predefined attributes that can be used for many different purposes. You can also define your own predefined attributes. Any attribute, whether intrinsic or custom designed, must be a subclass of the abstract class `System.Attribute`.

The additional information provided by an attribute on its target element is stored as part of that element's metadata. This metadata can be viewed through a process called reflection.

Review Questions

1. How can you make the code between `#if` and `#endif` of the following lines be included in the compilation

```
#if TRIALEDITION
    <Some code>
#endif
```

2. Is the second line in the following two lines of code valid? Why or why not?

```
using System;
#define
```

3. Add the necessary preprocessor directives and identifiers to the following lines of code, so that `<Code part 1>` is excluded from the compilation and `<Code part 2>` is included.

```
...
#if
    <Code part 1>
#endif
...
#if
    <Code part 2>
#endif
...
```

4. What is the major difference between standard comments and program documentation?
5. What does a documentation comment consist of? Give an example.
6. Which command must you give to the compiler to let it transform the documentation comments into a separate XML document?
7. What is the main purpose of attributes?
8. Can any attribute be used to decorate any code element?
9. Name a couple of .NET's predefined attributes and briefly describe what they are used for.
10. As mentioned earlier, .NET contains an attribute called `XmlArrayAttribute`; it exists in the `System.Xml.Serialization` namespace. Which of the following annotations are correct (there can be more than one). (Assume the line `using System.Xml.Serialization;` is included at the beginning of the source):

    a. `[System.Xml.Serialization.XmlArrayAttribute]`

    b. `[XmlArrayAttribute]`

    c. `[XmlArray]`

    d. `[Xml]`

    e. `[Array]`

11. What is an attribute's positional parameter? Give an example.
12. Suppose your source code contains a method with the following header:

```
public void StartOperation()
{
    ...
}
```

Which attribute can you use to prevent any methods from calling this method? Provide the necessary annotation.

13. Can you use the same procedure as in question 12 to prevent any calls to the following method? Why or why not?

```
public int Sum(int x, int y)
{
    ...
}
```

14. What is a named parameter?

Programming Exercises

1. Assume that you are writing the source code from which three different program versions will be compiled—a Standard Version, a Professional Version, and an Enterprise Version. In this case, the program simply contains three different `WriteLine` statements that write the following three lines:

```
A:  "This is the standard version"
B:  "This is the professional version"
C:   "This is the enterprise version"
```

The Standard Version only prints line A, the Professional Version only prints line B, and the Enterprise Version only prints line C. Use preprocessor directives so that you can easily control (without deleting and adding `WriteLine` statements, but instead by defining and undefining identifiers) which of the three `WriteLine` statements is being included in the program.

2. Use document comments and the `<summary>` and `<remarks>` tags to document the following program. Make sure you provide descriptions for all classes and methods. Use the compiler to extract the corresponding XML document.

```
using System;

class Calculator
{
    public static int Sum(int x, int y)
    {
        return x + y;
    }

    public static int Product(int x, int y)
    {
        return x * y;
    }
}

class RocketScientist
```

```
{
    public static void Main()
    {
Console.WriteLine("Estimated time to go to Mars: {0}",
        ➥ EstimatedTimeToMars(23));

    }

    public static uint EstimatedTimeToMars(int x)
    {
        return (uint) (Calculator.Sum(x, 24) + Calculator.Product(x, 21));
    }
}
```

3. Consider the source code in Listing 21.4.

LISTING 21.4 Train.cs

```
using System;

class Train
{
    private uint distance = 0;

    public void MoveBySteam(uint addDistance)
    {
        Console.WriteLine("Moving {0} kilometers by steam", addDistance);
        distance += addDistance;
    }

    public void MoveByElectricity(uint addDistance)
    {
        Console.WriteLine("Moving {0} kilometer by electricy", addDistance);
        distance += addDistance;
    }

    public void TestingDistance()
    {
        Console.WriteLine("Testing. distance instance variable: {0}", distance);
    }
}

class Tester
{
    public static void Main()
    {
        Train orientExpress = new Train();

        orientExpress.MoveBySteam(100);
        orientExpress.MoveByElectricity(200);
        orientExpress.TestingDistance();
    }
}
```

a. The `Train` class's `MoveBySteam` method in Listing 21.4 has become obsolete and you want the compiler to report a warning whenever it encounters a call to this method during compilation. The warning must announce that the programmer should instead use the `MoveByElectricity` method.

b. The `TestingDistance` method should only be called during the testing of the program. Use an attribute to enable you to switch on and off any calls to this method in an easy fashion.

c. You want to test what happens to the program if no calls are made to `MoveBySteam` method, while still maintaining the warning introduced in exercise a. You want to easily be able to switch this test on and of and do this independently of the calls to `TestingDistance`. In other words, you want the possibility of switching off the calls to `MoveBySteam` while the `TestingDistance` method is still being called, and vice versa.

d. Because of the information you gain from the experiment you make in exercise c, you now want to make sure that no one is calling the `MoveBySteam` method. Make the compiler report an error instead of just a warning when it encounters a method call to this method in the source code.

CHAPTER 22

FILE I/O BASICS

You will learn about the following in this chapter:

- Input streams and output streams
- Text files and character streams
- Binary files and binary streams
- Four classes from the `System.IO` namespace that are commonly used to handle files and streams
- How to represent a file in your program with the `FileInfo` class
- The character stream classes `StreamWriter` and `StreamReader`
- The binary stream class `FileStream`

I/O is short for program input and program output. Program input refers to data (numbers, characters, and bytes) flowing into a program from a source (keyboard, file, remote computer, or something similar). Program output refers to data flowing out from a program to a destination (screen, file, remote computer, or something similar).

This chapter provides a brief presentation of important file I/O concepts and introduces you to a few selected classes located in the .NET Framework that are commonly used to perform file I/O in C#.

The Need for Files

Why do we need files? You have already used the `Console.ReadLine` and `Console.WriteLine` methods numerous times to receive input from the keyboard and send output to the screen. However, the keyboard and screen data are only very temporary; as soon as the program terminates, all the data is lost. On the other hand, files allow you to store data permanently after the program has ended and after the computer is switched off. A file's content can be used repeatedly by the same or by different programs, and files allow you to handle large amounts of data in a convenient fashion.

Stream Basics and File I/O

In general, streams handle program input and program output. An *input stream* can be viewed as a sequence of bytes flowing into your program from a source device from which your program can read data. In contrast, an *output stream* can be regarded as a sequence of bytes to which your program can write that flows out from your program and are delivered to a destination device.

In C# and .NET, streams are represented by objects instantiated from stream classes located in the `System.IO` namespace.

You Have Already (Unknowingly) Used Streams

By default, our familiar `Console.ReadLine` method reads from a standard input stream (an object of one of the `System.IO` stream classes) that brings characters written onscreen (with the keyboard) to your program. Similarly, the `Console.WriteLine` method writes, by default, to a standard output stream that sends characters to the screen.

The `System.IO` stream classes encapsulate and effectively shield you from underlying complexities related to hardware devices and the operating system. Not only does this make it much simpler to perform I/O operations, it provides a standard way to perform stream operations regardless of the destination devices involved. Furthermore, software maintenance becomes much easier; there is no need to change your C# programs just because an underlying technology has changed whether this be hardware or software related.

Text Files and Binary Files

Even though, technically speaking, all files consist of sequences of bits, any one file can either be regarded as being a text file or a binary file. A *text file* consists of a sequence of bits and bytes that contains a sequence of characters, when deciphered correctly. (Some text files are for example encoded using the Unicode standard.) We humans read text files. For example, the files you create, save, and open with the Notepad editor are text files. On the other hand, *binary files* are mostly generated and processed by computer programs.

C# programs provide output to and get input from binary files via *binary streams*. Similarly, text files are accessed and manipulated through *character streams*.

Binary files can be read from and written to a program efficiently because the data of a program are stored in the binary file exactly as it is stored in the computer memory; no processor hungry transformations are needed. This is not the case for the less efficient character streams. For example, all numeric data requires a processor-intensive process to be transformed into a text file.

File I/O Classes: An Overview

The stream classes are located in the `System.IO` namespace, together with other classes that can be used to manage the directories and files on your computer. To get an overview of these classes, you can briefly browse through the .NET Framework documentation of the `System.IO` namespace.

As you gradually get to know the stream classes, you will see that there are usually several ways (perhaps involving different classes) to accomplish the same end result. In this brief presentation, I have chosen a few frequently used ways to get some simple jobs done and will only look at a small subset of the many available classes in the `System.IO` namespace.

Table 22.1 contains the classes we will look at in the following sections. A `FileInfo` instance encapsulates a file in a directory on your computer's file system. It contains numerous methods for manipulating a file and for discovering details about it. The `FileInfo` class is discussed in more detail in the next section.

Table 22.1 Fundamental `System.IO` Classes

`System.IO` class	Description
`FileInfo`	An instance of `FileInfo` represents a file in your computer's file system. It lets you modify and gather details about the file it represents, and it enables you to create new files and delete existing files.
`StreamReader`, `StreamWriter`	Character-based input and output streams.
`FileStream`	Used to read and write to binary files.

Instances of the `StreamReader` and `StreamWriter` classes represent character streams by which you can read and write text to a text file.

An instance of the `FileStream` will read and write both text and binary files. However, if you are certain that you are dealing with a text file, the `StreamReader` and `StreamWriter` classes contain facilities that make this task easier to accomplish.

Notice that a `FileInfo` object does not represent a stream object. Instead, you can use its `OpenText` and `CreateText` methods to return `StreamReader` and `StreamWriter` objects, providing stream access to the file represented by the `FileInfo` object.

Similarly, you can use a `FileInfo` object's `OpenRead` and `OpenWrite` methods to return a `FileStream` object that can be used to read and write to either the associated binary file or text file.

The `FileInfo` Class

When you create a new `FileInfo` object, you must associate this object with a file by passing a `string` representation of a filename to the `FileInfo` constructor. This filename can either represent an already existing file, or a non-existing file that you want to create. We will look at how you can create a new file with `FileInfo` later.

Suppose that `C:\MyTestFiles\MyFairytale.txt` is an already existing file. The following line (taken from line 10 in Listing 22.1)

```
FileInfo existingFile = new FileInfo(@"C:\MyTestFiles\MyFairytale.txt");
```

creates a `FileInfo` object called `existingFile` that represents the file `MyFairytale.txt` located in the `C:\MyTestFiles` directory.

Why Use @ in Front of Filenames?

Why does the previous line of source code include the symbol `@` in front of the `string` containing the filename? You might recall from Chapter 7, "Types Part II: Operators, Enumerators, and Strings," that the `@` symbol turns a `string` into a verbatim `string`, which lets us write `\` instead of the cumbersome `\\` when we specify pathnames.

We can now use the various `FileInfo` class members, a selected few of which are displayed in Table 22.2, to manipulate and ask questions about the underlying file (`MyFairytale.txt`, in this case).

Table 22.2 A Few `FileInfo` Class Members

`FileInfo` class member	Description
`CopyTo`	Copies the file represented by the `FileInfo` object to a new file
`Delete`	Deletes the file represented by the `FileInfo` object
`FullName`	Returns the full name (including the full path) of the file represented by the `FileInfo` object
`Length`	Returns the size (in bytes) of the file represented by the `FileInfo` object
`Name`	Returns the short name (excluding the path) of the file represented by the `FileInfo` object

Note

To see the entire list of `FileInfo` class members, please consult the .NET Framework documentation.

Note

Before you start using `FileInfo` and the rest of the classes in `System.IO`, be aware that many of these classes have the potential to wipe out or damage important files on your computer in case, for example, you provide the wrong filename or the wrong command. To protect your important files, you should keep any test files separate from other files by creating a test directory called, say, `MyTestFiles`. All the files used in coming examples are supposed to exist in a `C:\MyTestFiles` directory (where C is an arbitrary letter), but you can use any directory you prefer, as long as you remember to adjust the directory letters and the rest of the file path in your source code accordingly.

Whether you are experimenting with files or not, you should always keep backup files of the important files on your computer.

Listing 22.1 demonstrates how to use the `FileInfo` class members shown in Table 22.2 on an existing file, which in this case is called `MyFairytale.txt`. To run the program successfully, you must first create and save a file called `MyFairytale.txt` in the `MyTestFiles` directory by using the Notepad editor. The contents of this file, which you can simply write in the Notepad window, should be

```
Once upon a time
there was a beautiful princess
```

You are now ready to compile and run the source code of Listing 22.1.

LISTING 22.1 `SimpleFileInfo.cs`

```
using System;
using System.IO;

class FileInspector
{
    public static void Main()
    {
        try
        {
            FileInfo existingFile = new FileInfo
            ➥(@"C:\MyTestFiles\MyFairytale.txt");

            Console.WriteLine("File name: " + existingFile.Name);
            Console.WriteLine("Full file name: " + existingFile.FullName);
            Console.WriteLine("File length: {0} bytes",
            ➥ existingFile.Length);
            Console.WriteLine("Date creation time: " +
            ➥ existingFile.CreationTime);

            Console.WriteLine("Making a copy of MyFairyTale.txt
            ➥ called YourFairytale.txt");
            existingFile.CopyTo(@"C:\MyTestFiles\YourFairytale.txt", true);
            Console.WriteLine("Deleting MyFairytale.txt");
            existingFile.Delete();
        }
```

LISTING 22.1 continued

```
22:         catch (IOException exObj)
23:         {
24:             Console.WriteLine(exObj);
25:         }
26:     }
27: }
```

```
File name: MyFairytale.txt
Full file name: C:\MyTestFiles\MyFairytale.txt
File length: 48 bytes
Date creation time: 24/08/2001 11:08:54 PM
Making a copy of MyFairyTale.txt called YourFairytale.txt
Deleting MyFairytale.txt
```

Line 2 has been included to save us from prefixing `FileInfo` with its namespace name `System.IO`.

A file is often kept over a long period of time, during which several programs and programmers might have access to this same file. As a result, the file is prone to be mistakenly deleted, renamed, or reformatted. For example, if you try to access a non-existent file, the runtime will throw an exception. As a result, exceptions can be thrown relatively easily when you work with files, so it is important to use C#'s exception handling mechanisms for dealing with these exceptions appropriately, as discussed in Chapter 19, "Exception Handling." Accordingly, Listing 22.1 contains the familiar `try-catch` construct.

Line 10, discussed earlier, creates the `FileInfo` object `existingFile` that represents the `C:\MyTestFiles\MyFairyTale.txt` file. Lines 12–15 simply access and print out information about the represented file by using some of the `FileInfo` members listed in Table 22.2.

Line 18 makes a copy of the file called `C:\MyTestFiles\YourFairytale.txt`. The second argument, `true`, provided to `CopyTo`, allows the copy to overwrite any existing file with the same name.

Finally, line 20 deletes the file `C:\MyTestFiles\MyFairytale.txt` represented by `existingFile`.

After running this program, your `MyTestFiles` directory should contain only one file called `YourFairytale.txt` with the same two lines of text we originally included in `MyFairytale`.

`FileInfo` Versus `File`

`System.IO` contains another class called `File` that represents much of the same functionality as the `FileInfo` class. However, in contrast to `FileInfo`, all the `File` class members are `static`. So by using `File` instead of `FileInfo`, you can save yourself from instantiating a new `FileInfo` object. For example, to copy the file `C:\MyTestFiles\MyFairytale.txt` to `C:\MyTestFiles\YourFairytale.txt`, you can use `File's Copy` method and simply write the following:

```
File.Copy(@"C:\MyTestFiles\MyFairytale.txt",
➥ @"C:\MyTestFiles\YourFairytale.txt");
```

without any prior object creation, as would have been necessary with `FileInfo`. Why then bother using `FileInfo`? Every time you call a method with the `File` class, a processor-intensive security check must be performed, even if you access the same file repeatedly with different `File` methods. In contrast, the `FileInfo` class only performs one security check when the `FileInfo` object is created. After that, all processing related to the underlying file can be performed without security checks.

Full and Relative Filenames

A filename that includes the root directory and the full path to the file is called a *full* (or fully qualified) filename. For example, `C:\MyTestFiles\MyFairytale.txt` is a full filename. If the path is omitted, as in `MyFairytale.txt`, the filename is interpreted *relative* to the current directory. For example, if the program in Listing 22.1 was running from the `C:\MyC#Programs\Ch22` directory, and line 18 only specified the relative filename `YourFairytale.txt`, the program would save `YourFairytale.txt` in the `C:\MyC#programs\Ch22` directory.

Text File Input and Output with StreamReader and StreamWriter

The `StreamReader` and `StreamWriter` classes are specially designed to represent character streams and contain members that make reading from and writing to text files convenient. These streams can only be used with text files. A few of their methods are shown in Tables 22.3 and 22.4.

Both stream classes contain a method called `Close` that closes the related stream. This releases the resources allocated to the stream and allows other parts of the program access to the underlying file (usually only one stream can access a file at any one time). Furthermore, a stream that is left unclosed without an associated running program is prone to be damaged.

Even if you don't close a stream explicitly with the `Close` method, the system automatically closes the file when the program ends in a normal fashion. However, if the program ends abnormally (crashes), the runtime does not get the chance to close the files. Thus, you should always close a stream as soon as possible, after you have finished using it.

TABLE 22.3 A Few Selected `StreamWriter` Class Members

`StreamWriter` class member	Description
`Close`	Closes the output stream and releases any associated resources.
`Write`	Writes one or more characters to the stream without inserting a newline character.
`WriteLine`	Writes one or more characters to the stream and inserts a newline character.

TABLE 22.4 A Few Selected `StreamReader` Class Members

`StreamReader` class member	Description
`Close`	Closes the input stream and releases any associated resources.
`Read`	Reads the next character (or number of characters) from the input stream.
`ReadLine`	Reads the next line of characters and returns this as a string. Returns `null` when the end of the file is reached.

Note

To see the remaining class members of `StreamWriter` and `StreamReader`, please consult the .NET Framework documentation.

The `WriteLine` method is convenient for writing a line of text (in the form of a `string`) to a `StreamWriter` stream. The `WriteLine` method automatically inserts a newline character after each string argument it writes to the file. For example, if we use a `StreamWriter` instance called `myStreamWriter` to write to a file called `myFile` and call the `WriteLine` method three times as in the following lines:

```
MyStreamWriter.WriteLine("Three lines");
MyStreamWriter.WriteLine("but all");
MyStreamWriter.WriteLine("in one file");
```

`myFile` will contain three newline (NL) characters, one after each of the three string arguments, as illustrated in Figure 22.1.

FIGURE 22.1
Content of *`myFile`*.

T	h	r	e	e		l	i	n	e	s	NL	b	u	t		a	l	l	NL	i	n		o	n	e		f	i	l	e	NL	EOF

Note: EOF is an acronym for "End of file".

Correspondingly, the `ReadLine` method reads to the next newline character in the file and returns the characters in this segment of the file as a `string`. For example, the first time we call the `ReadLine` method on an input stream accessing `myFile` shown in Figure 22.1, it returns the string `"Three lines"`, the second time `"but all"`, and so on. When the end of the file is reached, the `ReadLine` method returns `null`.

The `StreamWriter`'s `Write` method is heavily overloaded. You can use this method to write a single character, a `string`, an array of characters, and many other data elements to the stream. You can view all seventeen overloaded `Write` methods in the .NET Framework documentation.

As opposed to the `WriteLine` method, `Write` does not automatically insert a newline character after its argument has been inserted in the file.

The `StreamReader`'s `Read` member represents two overloaded methods. The first version takes one argument and simply reads in the next character from the stream. The second version allows you to specify how many characters you want to read from the stream.

Listing 22.2 illustrates how to use the `StreamWriter` and `StreamReader` classes. The program (in lines 6–36) reads in three lines (`strings`) supplied by the user via the console. Each line is through a `StreamWriter` output stream written to a file called `C:\MyTestFiles.MyStory.txt`, which is subsequently closed. The program (in lines 38–67) then opens `MyStory.txt` and, via a `StreamReader` input stream, reads and outputs the contents of the file to the console.

LISTING 22.2 `TextInOut.cs`

```
01: using System;
02: using System.IO;
03:
04: class TextReaderWriter
05: {
06:     public static void WriteTextToFile()
07:     {
08:         string textLine;
09:         StreamWriter outStream = null;
10:
11:         try
12:         {
13:             FileInfo textFile = new FileInfo
                ➥ (@"C:\MyTestFiles\MyStory.txt");
14:
15:             outStream = textFile.CreateText();
16:
17:             Console.WriteLine("Writing to text file");
18:             Console.WriteLine("Please write three lines of text\n");
19:
20:             for (int i = 0; i < 3; i++)
21:             {
22:                 textLine = Console.ReadLine();
23:                 outStream.WriteLine(textLine);
24:             }
25:         }
26:
27:         catch (IOException exObj)
28:         {
29:             Console.WriteLine(exObj);
30:         }
31:
32:         finally
33:         {
34:             outStream.Close();
35:         }
36:     }
37:
38:     public static void ReadTextFromFile()
39:     {
```

LISTING 22.2 continued

```
            string textLine;
            StreamReader inStream = null;

            try
            {
                FileInfo textFile = new FileInfo
                ➥ (@"C:\MyTestFiles\MyStory.txt");

                inStream = textFile.OpenText();
                Console.WriteLine("\nReading from text file: \n");
                textLine = inStream.ReadLine();

                while (textLine != null)
                {
                    Console.WriteLine(textLine);
                    textLine = inStream.ReadLine();
                }
            }

            catch (IOException exObj)
            {
                Console.WriteLine(exObj);
            }

            finally
            {
                inStream.Close();
            }
        }
}

class Tester
{
    public static void Main()
    {
        TextReaderWriter.WriteTextToFile();
        TextReaderWriter.ReadTextFromFile();
    }
}
```

```
Writing to text file
Please write three lines of text

It was a rainy night.<enter>
The thunder was rumbling in the distance.<enter>
Suddenly a bat flew across the graveyard.<enter>

Reading from text file:

It was a rainy night.
The thunder was rumbling in the distance.
Suddenly a bat flew across the graveyard.
```

First a new `FileInfo` instance called `textFile` is created in line 13. To `FileInfo`'s constructor, the program passes the name of the new file we want to create (`C:\MyTestFiles\MyStory.txt`).

In line 15, the program calls `FileInfo`'s `CreateText` method, which returns a `StreamWriter` instance that writes to the new file `C:\MyTestFiles\MyStory.txt`; this `StreamWriter` reference is assigned to `outStream`. When we connect a file to a stream, as in line 15, we say the file is being *opened*. If the file did not exist (as is the case with `MyStory.txt`) a new file is created; if an old file with the same name already did exist, its contents are erased and substituted by the contents of the new file. So in either case, we start with an empty file.

The `for` loop in lines 20–24 loops three times. During each loop, `textLine` is assigned a `string` entered by the user (line 22) and in the next line passed as an argument to the output stream `outStream`. At the end of the three loops, `MyStory.txt` contains the characters of the three `string`s entered by the user.

It is important to close `outStream`, so in accordance with Chapter 19, "Exception Handling," we include the call to `Close` in a `finally` block (lines 32–35) associated with the `catch-try` statements. This guarantees that `outStream` is closed, even if an exception is thrown.

A `finally` block (lines 32–35 and 63–66) can, in case of an abnormal situation, be invoked at any time during the execution of its associated `try` block. Consequently, the compiler requires that all variables contained in the `finally` block and declared outside the `try` block (`outStream` in line 34 and `inStream` in line 65) are initialized prior to entering the `try` block. To avoid a compiler error, the program initializes `outStream` and `inStream` to `null` in lines 9 and 41, respectively.

The `WriteTextToFile` method (lines 6–36), is called from the `Main` method in line 74. So by the time the `ReadTextFromFile` method is called in line 75, `MyStory.txt` has been created and we can use it to demonstrate the `StreamReader` class. Let's have a closer look at `ReadTextFromFile`.

Line 45 creates an instance of `FileInfo` called `textFile`. Again, we pass the filename as an argument to the constructor but, as opposed to line 13, this time the file already exists.

In line 47, `FileInfo`'s `OpenText` method returns a reference to a `StreamReader` instance with access to `FileInfo`'s associated file—`MyStory.txt`. This reference is assigned to `inStream`, which can be used to read from `MyStory.txt`.

As stated earlier, the `ReadLine` method reads to the next newline character and returns the encountered characters as a `string`; conversely, if the end of the file has been reached, it returns `null`. We utilize this knowledge to construct lines 49–55. Line 49 assigns `ReadLine`'s return value to `textLine`. The result is checked in the `while` statement that only loops if `textLine` is not equal to `null`; this is only the case if the end of the file has not been reached. Thus, if `textLine` is not `null`, its contents are sent to the console in line 53. `ReadLine` is repeatedly called in line 54 until the end of the file is reached and `null` is assigned to `textLine`. This construct ensures that each segment of `MyStory.txt` surrounded by newline characters is sent to the console in line 53.

You can check the contents of `MyStory.txt` with Notepad.

Binary Input and Output with the FileStream Class

FileStream is a commonly used and versatile binary stream class that can be used to read and write individual bytes and blocks of bytes. Because characters are merely encoded bytes, the FileStream class can also be used to stream characters. However, it does not contain the same convenient methods targeted at character streams as do the StreamReader and StreamWriter classes.

The FileStream class can be used to create new files as well as open existing files.

Table 22.5 lists a few of FileStream's class members.

TABLE 22.5 A Few Selected FileStream Class Members

FileStream class member	Description
Close	Closes the stream and releases any associated resources
ReadByte	Reads one byte from the stream
WriteByte	Writes one byte to the stream
Length	Returns the length (in bytes) of the stream

Note

Please consult the .NET Framework documentation to view the rest of the FileStream class members.

The WriteBytes method in lines 6–30 of Listing 22.3 demonstrates how the FileStream class can be used to create a file and write ten numbers of type byte to this file. The ReadBytes method in lines 32–65 uses FileStream to read the contents from this new file.

LISTING 22.3 ByteWritingReading.cs

```
01: using System;
02: using System.IO;
03:
04: class TestBytesInOut
05: {
06:     public static void WriteBytes()
07:     {
08:         FileStream outStream = null;
09:
10:         try
```

LISTING 22.3 continued

```
        {
            FileInfo bytesFile = new FileInfo
            ➥ (@"C:\MyTestFiles\numbers1.dat");
            outStream = bytesFile.OpenWrite();

            for (byte i = 0; i < 10; i++)
            {
                outStream.WriteByte(i);
            }
        }

        catch (IOException exObj)
        {
            Console.WriteLine(exObj);
        }

        finally
        {
            outStream.Close();
        }
    }

    public static void ReadBytes()
    {
        int totalSum = 0;
        int temp = 0;
        FileStream inStream = null;

        try
        {
            FileInfo numberFile = new FileInfo
            ➥ (@"C:\MyTestFiles\numbers1.dat");
            inStream = numberFile.OpenRead();

            Console.WriteLine("Length: " + inStream.Length);
            Console.WriteLine("List of numbers in file:");

            for (int i = 0; i < inStream.Length; i++)
            {
                temp = inStream.ReadByte();
                Console.WriteLine(temp);
                totalSum += temp;
            }

            Console.WriteLine("\nTotal sum of numbers in
            ➥ file: {0}", totalSum);
        }

        catch (IOException exObj)
        {
            Console.WriteLine(exObj);
        }
```

LISTING 22.3 continued

```
60:
61:         finally
62:         {
63:             inStream.Close();
64:         }
65:     }
66: }
67:
68: class Tester
69: {
70:     public static void Main()
71:     {
72:         TestBytesInOut.WriteBytes();
73:         TestBytesInOut.ReadBytes();
74:     }
75: }
```

```
Length: 10
List of numbers in file:
0
1
2
3
4
5
6
7
8
9

Total sum of numbers in file: 45
```

You can use `FileStream`'s own constructor to create a new `FileStream` object, or you can use one of `FileInfo`'s methods. The latter approach is applied in Listing 22.3, which uses `FileInfo`'s `OpenWrite` (line 13) and `OpenRead` (line 41) methods to return a binary output stream and a binary input stream, respectively, both of type `FileStream`.

Lines 12 and 13 create a new file called `C:\MyTestFiles\numbers1.dat` that allows the `outStream` object of type `FileStream` to write to this file. `outStream`'s method `WriteByte` takes one argument of type `byte` and writes it to the new file. In our case, the first ten numbers (starting with zero) are written to the file in lines 15–18.

Notice that `C:\MyTestFiles\numbers1.dat` is a binary file not a text file, so it's contents cannot be properly viewed by a text editor, such as Notepad. Instead, we can use a binary input stream of type `FileStream` as returned by `FileInfo`'s `OpenRead` method in line 41.

We use `FileStream`'s `Length` property in line 46 to determine the number of times the `for` loop should be repeated. This makes sense because:

- `Length` returns the number of bytes in `inStream`

- The loop will be repeated `Length` times
- Each loop reads one `byte` in line 48, starting from the first `byte` in the file

Thereby we ensure that every single `byte` of `numbers1.dat` is assigned to `temp` in line 48 and written to the console in line 49.

We can also involve the data in `numbers1.dat` in numeric calculations. In this case (lines 48 and 50), we simply add `temp` to `totalSum` for every loop to calculate the total sum of all numbers kept in the `numbers1.dat` file; the result is written to the console in line 53.

Summary

This chapter provided a brief introduction to input and output streams and how they are used to write to and read from files.

The important points discussed are reviewed in this section.

I/O stands for program input and program output.

Program input refers to data flowing into a program and is handled by input streams from which the program can read.

Program output refers to data flowing out of a program and is handled by output streams to which the program can write.

In C# and .NET, streams and files can be abstracted into objects of classes that reside in the `System.IO` namespace. This makes it easier to perform file I/O.

Any file consists of one long sequence of bits positioned one after the other. Depending on their interpretation, some files are named text files (accessed via character streams or binary streams) while other files are named binary files (only accessed via binary streams).

The `FileInfo`, `StreamWriter`, `StreamReader`, and `FileStream` classes are commonly used for manipulating files and for performing file I/O. `FileInfo` represents a file in your computer's file system, `StreamWriter` and `StreamReader` represent character streams, and `FileStream` represents binary streams. The `System.IO` namespace contains many other useful classes targeted at interacting with the underlying file system and for performing I/O.

Review Questions

1. What is the main reason for using files?
2. How are streams represented in C# and .NET?
3. In what context have you already used streams in previous chapters?
4. In which direction is the data moving when we talk about input—from the program to a destination device or from a destination device to the program?

5. In what ways are text files and binary files similar? In what ways are they different?
6. Can you read a text file with a binary stream?
7. Suppose that you need to call just a single method only once in your program to manipulate a particular file in your file system. Which class would you use—`File` or `FileInfo` (given that the method exists in both classes)? Why?
8. Suppose that you need to call several methods one after the other to manipulate one particular file in your file system. Which class would you use—`File` or `FileInfo` (given that the methods exist in both classes)?
9. Consider the following two lines:

   ```
   FileInfo newFile = new FileInfo(@"C:\MyTestFiles\HorrorStory.txt");
   Console.WriteLine("Length of file: {0}", newFile.Length);
   ```

   What will happen in the second line if `C:\MyTestFiles\HorrorStory.txt` does not already exist?
10. Briefly explain the difference between a file's full name and a file's relative name.
11. If a C# program ends normally, any unclosed files are automatically closed. Why then bother closing a file with the `Close` method?
12. How do you know that the `ReadLine` method of the `StreamReader` class has reached the end of the corresponding file?
13. Give another term for connecting a file to a stream.
14. What does the `OpenWrite` and `OpenRead` methods of the `FileInfo` class return?

Programming Exercises

1. Create a text file with Notepad called `C:\MyTestFiles\ShortStory.txt` with the contents:

   ```
   This text
   Only contains
   Three lines
   ```

   Write a program that tells the user the full name of the file and when it was created.

   Please keep this program handy for exercise 2.
2. Extend the program in exercise 1 so that the program also counts the number of lines in `C:\MyTestFiles\ShortStory.txt` and shows this number on the console.
3. Write a program that contains an array called `rainfall`, containing twelve elements of type `byte`. Each element represents a monthly rainfall reading and can have a value between 0 and 200. Include a simple user interface so that the user can view the element values of `rainfall` and assign values to any one of its elements.

Expand the user menu so that the user can choose to save the contents of `rainfall` to a file called `C:\MyTestFiles\Rainfall.dat`. Furthermore, include an option in the user menu that allows the user to load the data contained in `C:\MyTestFiles\Rainfall.dat` back into the `rainfall` array. This must permit the user to save the rainfall data kept in the `rainfall` array, end the program, and later restart the program and load the `Rainfall.dat` data back into the `rainfall` array of the program.

CHAPTER 23

RECURSION FUNDAMENTALS

You will learn about the following in this chapter:

- Recursive methods and recursion
- The ability of C# to support pending method instances of the same method, and why this is an imperative ability when implementing recursive methods
- The key ingredients of a successful recursive method
- The fundamental reasons why recursion works
- Recursion versus iteration
- Binary search implemented using recursion instead of iteration

In this book, you have seen many examples of methods calling other methods. For example `MethodA` might, from within its method body, call `MethodB` to help `MethodA` accomplish a certain task. C# also allows a method to call itself. If `MethodA`'s body contains a call to `MethodA`, `MethodA` is said to call itself. A method that calls itself is called a *recursive method*. The general concept of using recursive methods is called *recursion*.

Direct and Indirect Recursion

There are two kinds of recursion—direct and indirect. When `MethodA` calls itself from within its own method body, we call it direct recursion. When `MethodA` calls itself by calling a different method (`MethodB` that calls `MethodA`), we call it indirect recursion. In this chapter, we will only look at direct recursion.

Even though recursion at first sounds like paradoxical circular logic, it is an important computer science topic. When applied correctly, recursion results in compact and clear algorithms that can be used to solve significant computational problems, such as sorting and searching.

Pending Method Instances of Different Methods

To understand how recursion works, it is important to first understand the mechanics of chains of method calls. Listing 23.1 does not contain any recursive method calls and does not solve any particular problem, it merely demonstrates what happens when one method calls a second method that calls a third method that calls a fourth method.

LISTING 23.1 `MethodCallDemo.cs`

```
using System;

class MethodCallDemo
{
    public static void Main()
    {
        MethodA(3);
    }

    public static void MethodA(int level)
    {
        Console.WriteLine("First part of MethodA. Level: {0}", level);
        MethodB(level - 1);
        Console.WriteLine("Last part of MethodA.  Level: {0}", level);
        return;
    }

    public static void MethodB(int level)
    {
        Console.WriteLine("First part of MethodB. Level: {0}", level);
        MethodC(level - 1);
        Console.WriteLine("Last part of MethodB.  Level: {0}", level);
        return;
    }

    public static void MethodC(int level)
    {
        Console.WriteLine("              MethodC. Level: {0}", level);
        return;
    }
}
```

```
First part of MethodA. Level: 3
First part of MethodB. Level: 2
              MethodC. Level: 1
Last part of MethodB.  Level: 2
Last part of MethodA.  Level: 3
```

Apart from the `Main` method, Listing 23.1 contains three similar methods called `MethodA`, `MethodB`, and `MethodC`. Each method accepts an argument of type `int` that is assigned to a formal parameter called `level`. Furthermore, the methods contain `WriteLine` calls to help us track the flow of execution in the program. Finally, each method (excluding `MethodC`) contains a call to another method. This call is positioned between the two `WriteLine` statements and provides an argument that is equal to `level` minus 1.

As illustrated in Figure 23.1 the `Main` method starts a chain of method calls by calling `MethodA` in line 7 with the argument 3 that is assigned to `MethodA`'s parameter called `level`. The flow of execution then moves through line 12 that contains a call to `WriteLine`. `MethodB` then is called in line 13 with the argument 2 `(level-1)` . It is important to notice that even though execution at this point continues at `MethodB`, `MethodA` is still waiting to have its last part executed; only when execution reaches `MethodA`'s `return` statement will `MethodA` terminate. In the meantime, while the flow of execution is at another method, `MethodA` (containing its local variable `level` with the value 3) is considered to be a *pending method instance*, kept in memory for use when flow of execution returns back to this method. The runtime makes sure that all local variables and formal parameters for this method are stored until the method is properly finished. In this case, the parameter `level` with the value 3 is stored in memory.

During the execution of `MethodB`, a call is made to `MethodC`. While `MethodC` is being executed, the program contains three pending method instances (see Figure 23.1)—one of `Main`, one of `MethodA`, and one of `MethodB`. Notice that `MethodA`'s local variable `level` has the value 3, and `MethodB`'s local variable `level` has the value 2, while `MethodC`'s `level` has the value 1.

`MethodC` does not call any other methods but, instead, simply returns. This causes execution to re-enter `MethodB`, which continues from where the call to `MethodC` was made and, thus, has its last part executed. The same happens when `MethodB` returns execution to `MethodA`. Finally, execution returns to `Main` that only contains the one method call to `MethodA`, so the program ends.

Pending Method Instances of the Same Method

While `MethodC` was being executed in the program of Listing 23.1, each of the methods `Main`, `MethodA`, and `MethodB` had exactly one associated pending method instance. It also is possible for one single method to have many associated pending method instances in C#. This ability is one of the fundamental requirements for writing recursive methods in a particular computer language. To demonstrate this ability, let's look at Listing 23.2 that generates four pending method instances similar to those in Listing 23.1, but this time the pending method instances (apart from `Main`) are all of the same method. It is our aim with the single method in Listing 23.2 to get as close as possible to the functionality of Listing 23.1.

FIGURE 23.1
Four method instances.

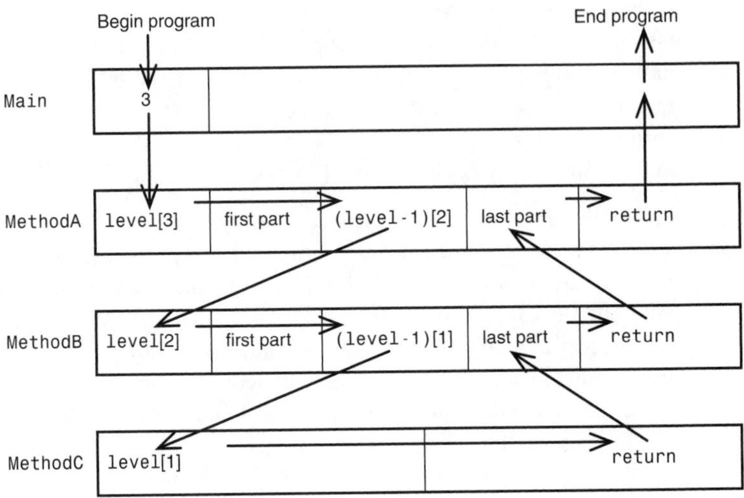

Notes:

⟶ Indicates flow of execution

Each rectangular box (called `Main`, `MethodA`, `MethodB`, and `MethodC`) indicates a method instance.

Numbers enclosed in square brackets indicate the value of the variable it suffixes. For example `level` [1] means that `level` has the value 1.

LISTING 23.2 `SimpleRecursion.cs`

```
using System;

class TestRecursive
{
    public static void Main()
    {
        Recurs(3);
    }

    public static void Recurs(int level)
    {
        Console.WriteLine("First part of Recurs. Level: {0}", level);

        if (level == 1)
            return;
        else
            Recurs(level - 1);

        Console.WriteLine("Last part of Recurs.  Level: {0}", level);
    }
}
```

```
First part of Recurs. Level: 3
First part of Recurs. Level: 2
First part of Recurs. Level: 1
Last part of Recurs.  Level: 2
Last part of Recurs.  Level: 3
```

Instead of the three methods (`MethodA`, `MethodB` and `MethodC`) in Listing 23.1, this listing contains a single method `Recurs` (lines 10–20). To get the same chain of calls as those in Listing 23.1, we must make `Recurs` act like `MethodA` and `MethodB` when `level` is equal to 3 and 2, and make `Recurs` act like `MethodC` when `level` is equal to 1. This is achieved with the `if` statement in lines 14–17. If `level` is equal to 1, the method simply returns (line 15) as `MethodC`; if `level` is different from 1 (as when `level` is equal to 2 or 3), the method makes another method call with the argument `(level–1)` (as `MethodA` and `MethodB`). In this case, the call is made to `Recurs` itself, which makes `Recurs` a recursive method. However, because one method can have numerous pending method instances, we can trace the program in a very similar fashion to that in Listing 23.1, which is illustrated in Figure 23.2. In line 7, `Main` calls `Recurs` and passes it the argument 3. Thus, `level` is equal to 3 in the first method instance of `Recurs`, as illustrated in Figure 23.2. Because `level` is different from 1 in line 14, line 17 is executed, which is a call to `Recurs` with the argument 2 (`level–1` = 3 - 1). Another method instance of `Recurs` is generated, and we have one pending `Recurs` method with `level` equal to 3. In the new `Recurs` instance, `level` is equal to 2, so line 17 is executed again, this time passing along the argument `1 (2–1)`. In the new method instance, which corresponds to the lowest rectangle in Figure 23.2, `level` is equal to 1, so this time line 15 is executed (acting like `MethodC`). Control is returned to the previous pending `Recurs` method instance, which executes its last `WriteLine` statement before returning control to the previous method instance, which finally returns control to the `Main` method where the program is terminated.

`Recurs` does not repeatedly call itself infinitely many times because every time `Recurs` calls itself, the new generated method instance contains a `level` value that is closer to the value 1 than the previous method instance that (due to line 14) will stop the chain of calls with a `return` statement (line 15) instead of another method call (line 17).

The following method called `RecursCountUp` is somewhat similar to `Recurs`, but with a couple interesting differences. The `if` condition is `true` when `level` is equal to 10, instead of equal to 1, and every time `RecursCountUp` calls itself, it provides the argument `(level + 1)` instead of `(level–1)`. Thus, if our initial call to `RecursCountUp` contains the argument 1, new method instances of `RecursCountUp` will be created with `level` values gradually increasing until 10 is reached, at which time the `return` statement is executed causing all pending `RecursCountUp` methods to be closed one by one.

If you want to run the `RecursCountUp` method, you simply can insert it into Listing 23.2 instead of the `Recurs` method, and substitute the call `Recurs(3)` in the `Main` method with `RecursCountUp(1)`.

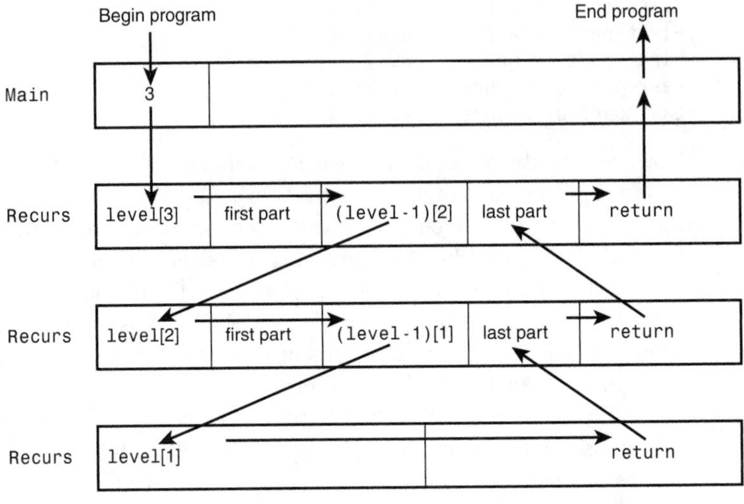

FIGURE 23.2
Recurs's three method instances.

```
public static void RecursCountUp (int level)
{
    Console.WriteLine("First part of Recurs. Level: {0}", level);

    if (level == 10)
        return;
    else
        RecursCountUp(level + 1);

    Console.WriteLine("Last part of Recurs.  Level: {0}", level);
}
```

The value, which causes the `return` statement to be called, (1 in `Recurs` and 10 in `RecursCountUp`) is called the *base case*. The call to the method itself ((`Recurs (level–1)` or `RecursCountUp (level + 1)`) is called the *recursive call* or the *recursive step*. To avoid an infinite number of calls, the recursive call in a recursive method must give rise to a new method instance that is closer to the base case. For example, `(level–1)` made `level` closer to 1 in the next method instance of `Recurs`, and `(level + 1)` made `level` closer to 10 in the next method instance of `RecursCountUp`. There are many different variations on this theme; in the following sections, we present just a couple of them..

Putting Recursion to Work: Calculating n Factorial

Our previous recursive methods have not presented us with any useful abilities. Before we look at examples of how we can exploit the mechanisms demonstrated so far to solve computational problems, let's line up the main ideas of how recursion can help us solve a problem.

Recursion is suited to solve problems that can be solved by repeatedly dividing a task into two smaller (or simpler) but similar problems. When the task has been divided a number of times (through recursive calls), a base case (see earlier) task will present itself and break the chain of recursive calls. The recursive method only knows the direct answer to the base case, but by combining the partial answers to the subtasks (held by pending method calls) with the answer to the base case (all being combined while the pending method calls returns), the full answer to the original problem emerges, and a total answer can be provided by the initial method instance of the recursive method. This is an exotic series of events that is probably best explained through examples.

The first recursive method presented in the following example has the ability to calculate the factorial of a number.

Note

The ability to calculate the factorial of a number is not confined to recursive methods. Any problem that can be solved recursively also can be solved iteratively. This fact is discussed later in the chapter.

The factorial of a number n is an important mathematical function written as *n!* (and called *n factorial*) and is defined as follows:

$n! = n \times (n - 1) \times (n-2) \times \ldots \times 1$

where n must be a positive integer or zero, and where 0! is defined to be equal to 1.

Examples: 4 factorial can be written as

$4! = 4 \times 3 \times 2 \times 1 = 24$

1 factorial is

$1! = 1$

and 0 factorial is

$0! = 1$

To see why n! can be found recursively, observe that the following is true:

$n! = n \times (n-1)!$

This becomes evident if we write:

$4! = 4 \times (3 \times 2 \times 1) = 4 \times 3!$

From this observation, we see that the factorial can be calculated by being separated into two sub-problems where one part is known (the n on the left of the multiplication sign) and the other ((n–1)!) is a smaller version of the original problem n!. We also notice that n–1 can be used similarly to `(level–1)` in line 17 of Listing 23.2, so it allows us to move closer to a base case that can be calculated directly as (0! = 1). Listing 23.3 presents the method `Factorial`, a recursive method for calculating factorials based on the observations we've just made.

LISTING 23.3 `Factorial.cs`

```
01: using System;
02:
03: class MyMath
04: {
05:     public static long Factorial (long number)
06:     {
07:         if (number == 0)
08:             return 1;
09:         else
10:             return (number * Factorial (number - 1));
11:     }
12: }
13:
14: class TestFactorial
15: {
16:     public static void Main()
17:     {
18:         Console.WriteLine("4 factorial is {0}", MyMath.Factorial(4));
19:     }
20: }
```

```
4 factorial is 24
```

The `Factorial` method's base case is when `number` is equal to zero, because we know that 0! is equal to 1. This is reflected in lines 7 and 8 that collectively say that if `number` is equal to 0, return 1. If `number` is larger than zero, we can use our earlier definition for factorial.

$n! = n \times (n-1)!$

The `Factorial` method returns the value for a factorial, so we can write the earlier definition as follows:

```
number * Factorial (number–1)
```

as shown in line 10. The last part of line 10 is a recursive call. Observe that `(number–1)` makes every recursive call to `Factorial` get closer to the base case. If this was not the case, the method would (attempt to) perform an infinite amount of recursive calls.

In our test run, we asked the **Factorial** method to calculate 4 factorial. The resulting flow of execution has been illustrated in Figure 23.3. The **Factorial** keeps calling itself until **number** reaches the base case, which happens when five **Factorial** method instances have been generated. The last **Factorial** method instance returns 1 (because **number** is 0) to the previous pending **Factorial** method, where this value (1) is substituted for **Factorial** (1–1) to calculate 1 * **Factorial** (1–1) = 1 * 1 = 1. The result of this calculation (1) is again returned to the previous pending **Factorial** method where it is substituted for **Factorial** (2–1) to calculate 2 * **Factorial** (2–1) = 2 * 1 = 2. This series of events keeps repeating until the topmost **Factorial** method instance is reached. At this level, we now know that the value of **Factorial** (4–1) is 6, because this value has been returned from the underlying mass of **Factorial** method instances. This finally allows us to calculate 4! as 4 * 6 = 24, which is returned to the **Main** method from where the initial call to **Factorial** was made.

FIGURE 23.3
Five **Factorial** instances.

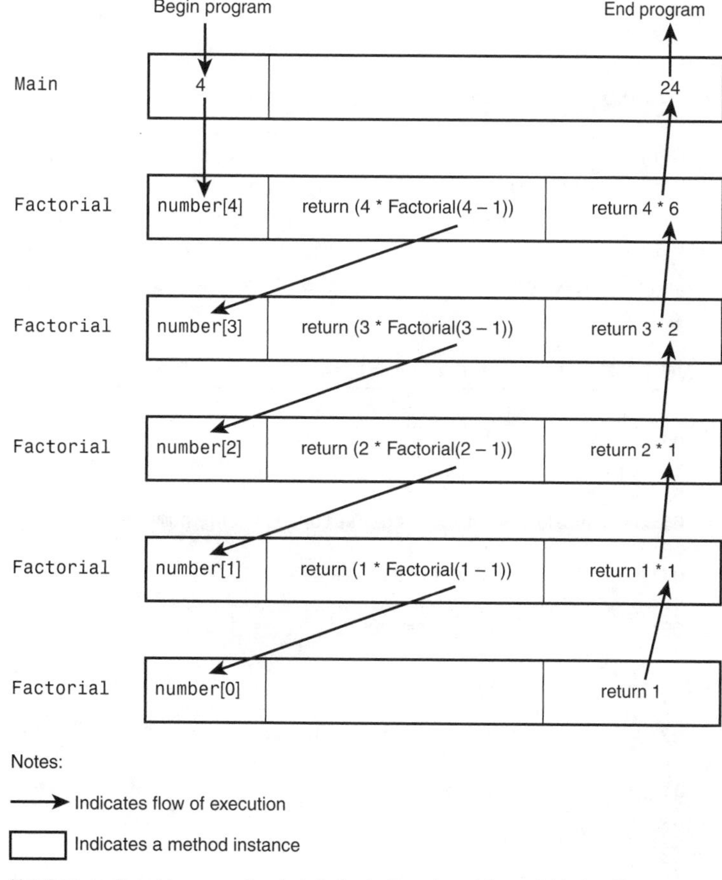

Common Ingredients Found in Correct Recursive Methods

It is hard to provide a simple recipe for writing correct recursive methods, but most successful recursive methods contain the following ingredients:

- A branching statement, such as an if-else statement or a switch statement.
- One or more of the branches of the branching statement contains recursive calls that must bring the generated method instance closer to the base case.
- One or more of the branches of the branching statement contains base cases that do not contain recursive calls but simple return statements instead that might or might not return a value.

Advanced programmers often use a mathematical technique called mathematical induction to construct recursive methods and to prove that they are correct. However, this technique is beyond the scope of this book.

Recursion and Iteration

Iteration uses one of the language constructs `for`, `while`, or `do-while`, as discussed in Chapter 9, "Flow of Control Part II: Iteration Statements." Any computational problem that can be solved by using recursion also can be solved solely through iteration. For example, the `Factorial` method contained in Listing 23.4 uses a `for` loop construct to calculate the factorial and, thereby, uses iteration instead of recursion as in Listing 23.3.

LISTING 23.4 `IterativeFactorial.cs`

```
using System;

class Math
{
    public static long Factorial(long number)
    {
        long factorial = 1;

        for(long i = number; i >= 1; i--)
        {
            factorial *= i;
        }
        return factorial;
    }
}

class Tester
{
    public static void Main()
    {
        Console.WriteLine("4! = {0}", Math.Factorial(4));
    }
}
```

```
4! = 24
```

We want to calculate the factorial of `number` defined as `Factorial`'s formal parameter in line 5. The counter `i` defined in line 9 will initially have the value `number`. Line 11 is repeatedly executed until `i` is less than 1. Every time line 11 is executed, `i` is multiplied by `factorial` and decremented by one, so by the time `i` is one, `factorial` contains the value `number`!.

Both recursion and iteration use repetition. Recursion involves repeated method calls that gradually bring method instances closer to a base case. This process stops when the base case is reached. Iteration often entails counters that are incremented or decremented until the loop condition becomes `false`.

Whereas iteration often involves just one method instance, recursion, as we have seen previously, relies on the creation of many method instances (and their associated local variable values) to solve a problem. It is costly for the runtime to keep track of and store method instances both in terms of memory and CPU time. Consequently, iteration is usually more efficient than recursion.

If all computational problems can be solved with iteration, and iteration is more efficient than recursion, why then ever use recursion? Sometimes a recursive solution is more apparent and elegant as well as being simpler, cleaner to write, and easier to understand than an iterative solution. This is usually the case when the computational problem can naturally be expressed in recursive terms.

The next section shows an example of an iterative solution that can be implemented by using recursion.

Binary Search Using Recursion

Recall from Chapter 11, "Arrays Part II: Multidimensional Arrays. Searching and Sorting Arrays," how we used the binary search technique to locate a number in a sorted array of numbers. The implementation in Chapter 11 made use of iteration. In this section, we will use the same basic ideas of binary search, but this time implemented with a recursive method. Because the underlying ideas are the same whether we use iteration or recursion, you might want to revisit the binary search section in Chapter 11 before beginning the recursion example described next.

The binary search technique can be viewed as a series of searches where each search is a smaller version of the previous search. Each search can briefly be described as follows. First, find the middle element of the part of the array we are searching and then compare this element with the search key (the number for which we are looking to find a match). If they match, we are done. The middle element's index then contains a value that matches the search key, so this index value is returned (this is the base case). Otherwise, if the search key is less than the middle element value, search in the sub-array (this is a smaller version of the previous search) that is situated to the left of the middle element. Otherwise, if the search key is greater than the middle element, search in the sub-array (this is also a smaller version of the previous search) that is situated to the right of the middle element. If at any point we are searching an empty array, the search key does not exist anywhere in the entire array.

Notice how we can define the binary search in terms of smaller versions of itself and a base case. Listing 23.5 contains the recursive method `BinarySearch` in lines 13–28 that implements the presented logic.

LISTING 23.5 RecursiveBinarySearch.cs

```
01: using System;
02:
03: class Searcher
04: {
05:     private static int[] arr;
06:
07:     public static int StartSearch(int[] newArray, int searchKey,
        ➥ int low, int high)
08:     {
09:         arr = newArray;
10:         return BinarySearch(searchKey, low, high);
11:     }
12:
13:     public static int BinarySearch(int key, int low, int high)
14:     {
15:         if(low > high)
16:             return -1;
17:         else
18:         {
19:             int mid = (low + high) / 2;
20:
21:             if(key == arr[mid])
22:                 return mid;
23:             else if (key < arr[mid])
24:                 return BinarySearch(key, low, mid - 1);
25:             else
26:                 return BinarySearch(key, mid + 1, high);
27:         }
28:     }
29: }
30:
31: class Tester
32: {
33:     public static void Main()
34:     {
35:         int searchKey;
36:         int searchResult;
37:         int[] testScores = {2,4,6,8,10,12,14,16,18,20,22,24,26,28,30,32,
            ➥ 34,36,38};
38:
39:         do
40:         {
41:             Console.Write("Please enter the test score you would
                ➥ like to locate: ");
42:             searchKey = Convert.ToInt32(Console.ReadLine());
43:             searchResult = Searcher.StartSearch(testScores, searchKey,
```

LISTING 23.5 continued

```
                 ➥ 0, 18);
44:              if(searchResult >= 0)
45:                  Console.WriteLine("The score was found in
                   ➥ position: {0}\n", searchResult);
46:              else
47:                  Console.WriteLine("The score was not found\n");
48:              Console.Write("Would you like to do another search?
                 ➥ Y)es N)o ");
49:          } while (Console.ReadLine().ToUpper() == "Y");
50:      }
51: }
```

```
Please enter the test score you would like to locate: 4<enter>
The score was found in position: 1

Would you like to do another search? Y)es N)o Y<enter>
Please enter the test score you would like to locate: 11<enter>
The score was not found

Would you like to do another search? Y)es N)o Y<enter>
Please enter the test score you would like to locate: 38<enter>
The score was found in position: 18

Would you like to do another search? Y)es N)o N<enter>
```

The array we are searching must be sorted for the binary search to work correctly. In this case, we are searching the array `testScores` declared in line 37 that, via the `StartSearch` method (called in line 43), is assigned (in line 9) to the `arr` array (declared in line 5).

The recursive `BinarySearch` method contains the classic elements of a recursive method—`if-else` statements (lines 15–27 and lines 21–26) with two base cases (line 16 and 22) and two recursive calls (lines 24 and 26).

The `key` parameter (declared in line 13) contains the value we are searching for, while the parameters `low` and `high` represent the index values (not the score values themselves) that enclose the part of the `arr` array we are searching. `BinarySearch`'s return value (of type `int`) contains the index of the `arr` array where an element value matching that of `key` was located; if a match to `key` is not found, `-1` is returned.

For a moment, let's concentrate on lines 19–26 that are processed as long as there is still a part of the array we haven't searched.

First, the middle index (represented by `mid`) of the `arr` array we are searching is determined (line 19). Line 21 then checks if `key` is located in this middle element. If this is the case, this index value is returned to the caller in line 22. If not, we must continue our search either in line 24 or line 26. If `key` is less than the middle element (checked in line 21), the `key` value for which we are searching must be located between the `low` index and the `(mid–1)` index. Consequently, we ask `BinarySearch` to search this part of the `arr` array by invoking it with these arguments in line 24.

Observe that the `low` argument is assigned to the `BinarySearch`'s `low` parameter, and the `mid–1` argument is assigned to `BinarySearch`'s `high` parameter. With this call, we have eliminated half or so of the array part we need to search, and is, consequently, moving towards a base case.

If `key` is greater than the middle element, it makes sense instead to search the part of the array located between index `mid + 1` and `high`, as reflected in the call to `BinarySearch` in line 26. Notice that with both the calls to `BinarySearch`, we simply take for granted that `BinarySearch` performs its job correctly of locating an index with the matching element. If an element does exist with a value that matches that of `key`, we are moving toward the base case in lines 21 and 22 with every recursive call. However, if no element value matches that of `key`, an infinite number (was it not for lines 15 and 16) of recursive calls will occur. To realize why lines 15 and 16 properly detect that the key value cannot be found and that they effectively prevent an infinite number of recursive calls to take place, consider the following logic. In each recursive call, either the value of `low` is increased or the value of `high` is decreased. If `low` ever becomes greater than `high`, it means that there are no elements left to check in the array and that the `key` value did not exist in `arr`. Thus, according to our convention from earlier, `-1` is returned to the caller in line 16.

Note

To see an example where recursion is used to convert numbers between different number systems, please consult Appendix D, "Number Systems," located on this book's Web site at `www.samspublishing.com`.

Summary

In this chapter, you learned about the essentials of recursion. Apart from looking at the theoretical foundation for recursion, you also were presented with a couple of typical recursion examples.

The important points covered in this chapter are reviewed in this section.

When a method calls itself from within its own method body, the method is called a recursive method. The use of recursive methods is called recursion.

Recursive method calls result in pending method instances of the recursive method.

A successful recursive method contains a branching statement, one or more base cases, and one or more recursive calls. Each recursive call must move toward the base case to avoid infinitely many recursive calls.

Recursion is suited to solve computational problems that can be solved by solving simpler versions of an original problem. Eventually, the problem becomes so simple (base case) that the recursive method knows the direct answer. By possibly combining the values kept in several pending method instances, an answer to the original problem can be found.

Any problem that can be solved with recursion also can be solved without recursion, using iteration instead. Recursion is not as effective as iteration, but sometimes provides clearer more compact algorithms, especially if the problem at hand is expressed recursively naturally.

Factorial and binary searches are two typical problems that can be solved recursively.

Review Questions

1. What is the output from the following method if you call it with the argument `1`?

```
public static void Recurs(int number)
{
    if(number > 8)
        return;
    else
    {
        Console.WriteLine("Number: {0}", number);
        Recurs(number * 2);
    }
}
```

2. Identify in the **Recurs** method of question 1 the main ingredients found in most successful recursive methods.

3. Rewrite the **Recurs** method in question 1 so that it (by still using recursion) provides the following output if called with the argument `16`.

```
Number: 16
Number: 8
Number: 4
Number: 2
Number: 1
```

4. Which technique provides for the most efficient solution recursion or iteration? Why?

5. The following **Sum** method is supposed to calculate the sum of a series of numbers starting at the argument passed to **Sum** and decrementing until `1` is reached. For example, **Sum** of 4 is supposed to be 4 + 3 + 2 + 1 = 10, and **Sum** of 1 is 1. However, **Sum** has a couple of missing parts. Make the corrections.

```
public static int Sum(int number)
{
    return number + Sum(number-1);
}
```

6. Consider the ruler in Figure 23.4. Describe the fundamental logic behind a recursive method that can draw this ruler.

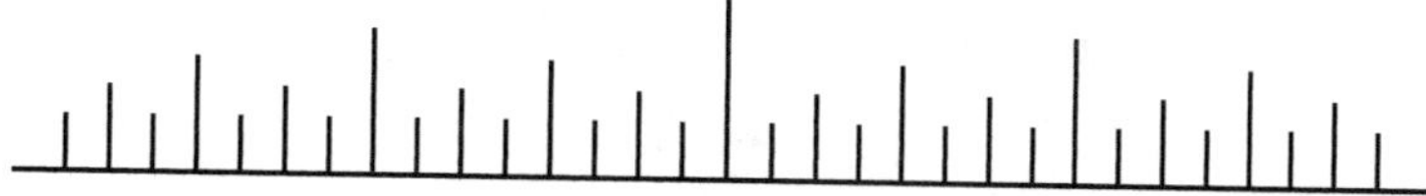

FIGURE 23.4
A recursive ruler.

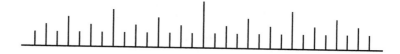

Programming Exercises

1. Write a recursive method call `Count` that takes a positive argument of type `int`. The `Count` method must be able to count the number of digits in the provided argument. For example, 2319 has four digits. Hint: If the number is less than 10, we have a base case (one digit); if the number of digits is 10 or greater, we can express the number of digits as 1+ the count of (`number/10`).

2. Write a recursive method that prints out the name (with text) of each digit in a number provided. For example, if the number 2319 is provided, the method should print: two three one nine. hint: To print 2319, we can print 231 followed by the last digit 9. We can isolate 231 with the calculation `2319/10`, and we can isolate 9 with `2319 % 10`. A seperate method can be used to print a single digit as a word.

APPENDIX A

ANSWERS TO QUIZZES AND EXERCISES

Chapter 1

Answers to Chapter 1 Review Questions

1. Computers are versatile and can be programmed to solve a wide range of problems.
2. The computer programmer uses a programming language to write the exact instructions that make up the computer program the end user will apply.
3. The object-oriented world consists of objects that interact to solve various tasks.
4. Hardware and software.
5. Software consists of instructions the computer executes.
6. The user provides data (called input) to the computer (via a keyboard or something similar) which the computer processes. The computer responds to the user with output (for example, via the screen).
7. The processor is an important piece of computer hardware that executes a computer program's instructions.
8. Auxiliary memory and main memory. Auxiliary memory stores data permanently, whereas the main memory represents temporary storage containing the running program parts and its associated intermediate calculation results.
9. The total rainfall during year 2000, which then can be divided by 12 to find the average.
10. A bit can have one of two values, often referred to as 1 and 0. A byte consists of eight bits.
11. Each of the eight bits in a byte can represent two values. So a byte can represent $2 \times 2 \times 2 \times 2 \times 2 \times 2 \times 2 \times 2 = 256$ different numbers.
12. Through a list of numbered locations called bytes. Each location has an address for easy reference.
13. To permanently store different kinds of data.

14. A source program consists of text with high-level instructions that are translated into machine level instructions executed by the computer. The source program is kept in a source program file.

15. A C# source program file has the extension `.cs` (for c sharp) as in `YourProgram.cs`.

16. A compiler translates the high-level instructions of the source program file into low-level machine language that can be executed by the computer processor.

17. Among many other services, .NET:

    - Contains an execution engine that can execute the MSIL instructions that represent the high-level instructions of a C# program
    - Holds a vast selection of pre-written program parts that you can utilize in your programs
    - Manages the computer memory used by your computer program

18. Microsoft Intermediate Language (MSIL) provides a middle layer between the high-level source program and the low-level machine language and is thereby able to decouple these two parts.

Chapter 2

Answers to Chapter 2 Review Questions

1. The four core activities of the software development process are

    - *Software specification*—Specifying the requirements of the software
    - *Software design*—Specifying how the software specification can be turned into a fully-functioning program
    - *Writing the software*—Writing the text of the source code program, which in our case consists of C# language constructs
    - *Software validation and debugging*—Checking that the program does what is specified in its software specification

2. An algorithm is a set of precise instructions that the computer follows to accomplish a task. For example, algorithms can be expressed using pseudocode or a high-level language like C#.

3. Computers are very fast but extremely dumb when trying to understand a computer program. They do not make assumptions and need to be told exactly what to do.

4. Execution begins with the topmost line and moves through the lines one by one as they appear in the pseudocode or the C# code. Execution ends at the last line.

5.
   - Syntax errors appear when the source code program does not follow the (grammatical) rules (the syntax) put forth in the C# language for how to write instructions.
   - Logic errors represent flaws in the logic of a program.
   - Runtime errors range from errors directly caused by the programmer to difficult-to-prevent problems, such as attempting to access corrupted or non-existing files.

6. Most computer programs are so complex that it is impossible to test all the different scenarios the program will endure. Logic errors can still occur in programs without any syntax errors.

7. Process-oriented programming focuses on actions rather than on the related data.

8. Object-oriented programming combines actions and their related data to form self-contained units called classes, with equal emphasis on actions and data. Objects are instantiated from classes. Objects collaborate to solve tasks by sending messages to each other. One main advantage of object-oriented programming is that it allows programmers to divide a program into smaller, simpler, self-contained units with a resulting reduction in complexity.

9. An object is a fairly self-contained module containing data and actions that act on those data.

10. A class is a blueprint for generating objects. A class can be viewed in the source code, whereas an object is created on the basis of a class during the execution of a program.

11. By describing the programming problem in a spoken language like English and then identifying the nouns used in this description.

12. A software component.

13. The assembly is the basic unit of reuse in .NET. It is a self-describing element that consists of MSIL, metadata, and resources.

14. The .NET Frameworks class library.

15. The designers wanted C# to be an evolutionary step forward from previous powerful languages (C and C++, in particular) by building on the strengths of these languages and to allow programmers an easy migration to C#. At the same time, they wanted C# to be simpler, safer, and more productive than its predecessors. C# is the first true component-oriented language, it provides full support for RAD, and it is a true object-oriented language where everything can be viewed as being an object.

16. The C# source code is written with a text editor. The source code is compiled into MSIL using a C# language compiler. The .NET execution engine executes the MSIL to run the program.

17. Yes, the compiler checks for syntax errors, but it cannot know what you want your program to do, so it is unable to check for logical errors.

Answers to Chapter 2 Programming Exercises

Exercise 1:

```
Take a piece of paper and a pencil.
Write number1 on the left side of the paper and number2 on the right
 ➥ side of the paper and Greatest number below on the middle of the page.
Write the number that number1 represents underneath number1.
Write the number that number2 represents underneath number2.
If the number associated with number1 is greater than the number associated
➥ with number2 write this former number underneath Greatest number
➥ otherwise write the number associated with number2 under
➥ Greatest number.
```

Exercise 2:

```
1. Take a piece of paper and a pencil.
2. Write maxSoFar with a zero underneath.
3. Repeat the following action (3.a) for each value in the list:
3.a. If the current value we are focusing at in the list is greater than the
     ➥ value written under maxSoFar then put a line through this
     ➥ previous number and write the greater value under the old
     ➥ crossed out number.
4. The value written furthest down that is not crossed out is the largest
   ➥ number in the list of numbers.
```

Exercise 3: Change point 4 of the pseudocode to the following:

```
4. If the ListSize is greater than 0 then
        divide the Sum by the ListSize and write the number down
    otherwise if the ListSize is 0 then simply write the 0 down.
```

Exercise 4:

```
using System;
public class StoryTeller
{
    public static void Main()
    {
        Console.WriteLine("Our alien friend");
        Console.WriteLine("lives on planet Blipos");
        Console.WriteLine("far far away");
    }
}
```

Chapter 3

Answers to Chapter 3 Review Questions

1. Abstraction allows programmers to simplify the problem domain they are attempting to turn into a computer program and allows them to focus only on its relevant parts.
2. No, the idea behind encapsulation is not confined to software design. Example: Even though a car engine can be adjusted in numerous ways, the driver can only regulate it in

a few simple areas; the rest are encapsulated from the driver and are either preset from the factory or controlled by on-board computers. If the driver could make all possible adjustments, it would lead to two problems. It would be complicated to drive a car, and the likelihood of the driver harming the engine would increase manifold.

3. Encapsulation allows an object to expose only the parts that are relevant to the outside world. This prevents outside users from tampering with the internal parts of an object. At the same time, it becomes simpler to operate the object because irrelevant complicating parts are not part of the object's interface.
4. `private` and `public`.
5. A class is a passive blueprint (existing in the source code) for its active object counter parts.
6. The class interface is what the outside world uses to communicate with the objects of this class.
7. With two double forward slash characters `//`.
8. People reading through the source code look at comments to understand the source code better.
9. A keyword has a distinct predefined meaning in the C# language. It is part of the C# vocabulary, just as "you" is part of the English vocabulary and has a special predefined meaning.

   An identifier is another word for a name. Identifiers are used to identify C# elements, such as classes, methods, and variables, that must all have an associated identifier.
10. A block is enclosed by the curly braces `{}`. It represents a logical unit in C#. For example, a block can belong to a class or a method.
11. No, because the runtime always calls the `Main` method of a program to begin its execution.
12. Its identifier, its type, and its value.
13. It is called a statement and must be terminated by a semicolon.
14. The `Write` (or `WriteLine`) method of the `System.Console` class can be used to print text onscreen, as in the following:

```
System.Console.WriteLine("My dog is brown");
```

15. By writing the method identifier and by providing the arguments the method requires. If the method is called from outside the object where it resides, the object name must also be specified.

    When a method is invoked, the flow of execution enters the method body and the statements contained here are executed. Then execution returns to the caller.
16. The mechanism of giving a new value to a variable is called assignment. The equals sign (=) is used to denote an assignment.

17. It ensures that the program only contains properly declared variables. This prevents stray variables, mistakenly created due to misspellings and the like, from appearing in a C# program.

18. By using an `if` statement.

19. Whitespace is comprised of blank lines, space characters, tab characters, and carriage returns. The compiler ignores whitespace in most cases, but tokens cannot be broken up by whitespace.

20. No, many different valid styles are applied in the programmer community.

Answers to Chapter 3 Programming Exercises

The following listing provides answers to Exercises 1–5.

```
// This is a simple C# program
class Hello
{
    // The program begins with a call to Main()
   public static void Main()
   {
       string userInput;
       string userName;

       System.Console.WriteLine("Please enter your name");
       userName = System.Console.ReadLine();
       System.Console.WriteLine("Hello " + userName);
       System.Console.WriteLine("Do you want me to write the two
       ➥ famous words?");
       System.Console.WriteLine("Type Yes or No. Then <enter>");
       userInput = System.Console.ReadLine();
       if (userInput == "Yes")
           System.Console.WriteLine("Hello World!");
       System.Console.WriteLine("Bye Bye. Have a good day");
       System.Console.WriteLine("The program is terminating");
   }
}
```

Chapter 4

Answers to Chapter 4 Review Questions

1. Namespaces act as containers for classes. They help us organize the classes of our programs and to provide easy access to them (when reused) by outside parties.

2. It allows us to write short names instead of long, fully-qualified names when we refer to classes in a namespace. This makes it easier to type the names and improves the readability of the source code.

3. The `System` namespace.

4. Like salt in your food, excessive amounts of comments are as damaging as too few comments.

5. A variable of type `int` occupies 32 bits of memory and can represent whole numbers between –2147483648 and 2147483647.

6. The identifiers `x` and `y` do not convey any information about what kind of value they represent, as opposed to names like `accountBalance` and `height`. However, `x` and `y` in Listing 4.1 represent a variety of values that cannot be pinpointed to a specific name, so the generic names `x` and `y` are acceptable.

7. A method header and its method body that is enclosed by curly braces.

8. Classes generally represent items (tangible or conceptual) so nouns constitute better names for classes than verbs. Verbs, such as `MoveLeft`, are better suited to methods that take actions.

9. By writing the keyword `void` in front of the method identifier in the method header.

10. By writing the keyword `int` in front of the method identifier in the method header.

11. The value of a method argument is passed along to the called method.

12. A formal parameter is part of the method header and has a certain value as the execution of the method commences.

13. Each argument of a method call is assigned to its corresponding formal parameter during a method call.

14. It has the potential (through operator overloading) to perform many different operations, depending on the types involved. We have seen examples of arithmetic addition and `string` concatenation.

15. By separating a few complex actions into several simpler actions (methods).

16. A method that accomplishes one clear task.

Answers to Chapter 4 Programming Exercises

The following program contains answers to Exercise 1 and 2. The parts related to Exercise 1 and Exercise 2 are marked Ex.1 and Ex.2 respectively.

```
using System;

//Ex. 1
 //This class finds the sum, product, difference,
 //min and max of two numbers

public class SimpleCalculator
{
    public static void Main()
    {
        int x;
        int y;
```

```
            Console.Write("Enter first number: ");
            x = Convert.ToInt32(Console.ReadLine());
            Console.Write("Enter second number: ");
            y = Convert.ToInt32(Console.ReadLine());
            Console.WriteLine("The sum is: " + Sum(x, y));
            Console.WriteLine("The product is: " + Product(x, y));
            Console.WriteLine("The maximum number is: " + Math.Max(x, y));
            Console.WriteLine("The minimum number is: " + Math.Min(x, y));
            Console.WriteLine("The difference is: " + Subtract(x, y)); //Ex. 2
        }

        // Sum calculates the sum of two int's
        public static int Sum(int a, int b)
        {
            int sumTotal;

            sumTotal = a + b;
            return sumTotal;
        }

        // Product calculates the product of two int's
        public static int Product(int a, int b)
        {
            int productTotal;

            productTotal = a * b;
            return productTotal;
        }

        // Ex.2
        // Subtract calculates the difference between two int's
        public static int Subtract(int a, int b)
        {
            int difference;

            difference = a - b;
            return difference;
        }
    }
```

The following program constitutes answers to Exercises 3 and 4. It allows the calculations to be performed on three values and implements the `MyMax` and `MyMin` methods:

```
using System;

//This class finds the sum, product, difference,
//min and max of three numbers

public class SimpleCalculator
{
    public static void Main()
    {
        int x;
        int y;
```

```
    int z;
 // Ex.3
    Console.Write("Enter first number: ");
    x = Convert.ToInt32(Console.ReadLine());
    Console.Write("Enter second number: ");
    y = Convert.ToInt32(Console.ReadLine());
     // Ex. 3
    Console.Write("Enter third number: ");
    z = Convert.ToInt32(Console.ReadLine());
    Console.WriteLine("The sum is: " + Sum(x, y, z));
    Console.WriteLine("The product is: " + Product(x, y, z));
     // Ex. 4
    Console.WriteLine("The maximum number is: " + MyMax(x, y, z));
    Console.WriteLine("The minimum number is: " + MyMin(x, y, z));
     // Ex.3
    Console.WriteLine("The difference is: " + Subtract(x, y, z));
}

 // Ex. 3
 // Sum calculates the sum of two int's
public static int Sum(int a, int b, int c)
{
    int sumTotal;

    sumTotal = a + b + c;
    return sumTotal;
}

 // Ex. 3
 // Product calculates the product of two int's
public static int Product(int a, int b, int c)
{
    int productTotal;

    productTotal = a * b * c;
    return productTotal;
}

 // Ex. 3
 // Subtract calculates the difference between two int's
public static int Subtract(int a, int b, int c)
{
    int difference;

    difference = a - b - c;
    return difference;
}
 //Ex. 4
 // Find max value of three parameters
public static int MyMax(int a, int b, int c)
{
    int max;
```

```
            max = Math.Max(a, Math.Max(b, c));
            return max;
        }
         // Ex. 4
         // Find min value of three parameters
        public static int MyMin(int a, int b, int c)
        {
            int min;

            min = Math.Min(a, Math.Min(b, c));
            return min;
        }
    }
```

Chapter 5

Answers to Chapter 5 Review Questions

1. Lexical analysis is a process performed by the compiler to distinguish the atomic parts (in the source code of a computer language) from each other.

2. The atomic C# parts constitute the unbreakable parts, such as keywords, identifiers, curly braces, parentheses, semicolon, and so on.

3. If an identifier is written with Pascal casing, all words within this name begin with an uppercase character, as in `CalculateMaxDistance`.

   Camel casing is nearly identical to Pascal casing, the only difference being that identifiers written with camel casing do not contain an uppercase letter in its first word. `numberOfElevators` is written with camel casing.

   Pascal casing should be used for class and method identifiers and camel casing for variables.

4. A literal has the fixed value that is written in the source code. For example, the literal 10 always has the value 10. In contrast a variable called `myNumber` can represent different values.

5. Operators act on operands.

6. `50` and `(50 + x)` are both expressions, but the keyword `public` is not an expression.

7. `if`, `public`, `private`.

8. Pseudocode is highly suited to express a set of detailed actions (an algorithm) that must be executed sequentially to solve a task. However, classes break free from this sequential execution form. This renders the pseudocode incapable of describing overall class designs.

9. An association relationship, which in UML is illustrated with a simple line.

10. A composition relationship, which in UML is illustrated with a line that has a black diamond attached.

11. An aggregation relationship, which in UML is illustrated with a line that has a white diamond attached.

12. Through instance variables that reference other objects.

13. Instance variables can be initialized as part of their declaration statement or in a constructor.

14. The instance variable `passenger` can hold a reference to a `Person` object.

Answers to Programming Exercises in Chapter 5

The following program contains answers to all six programming exercises presented in Chapter 5. Lines that are added or altered compared to Listing 5.1 in Chapter 5 due to an exercise are marked with a comment. For example, a line affected by exercise 1 is marked `//Ex.1`.

```
// A simple elevator simulation

using System;

class Elevator
{
    private int currentFloor = 0; //Ex.4
    private int requestedFloor = 0;
    private int totalFloorsTraveled = 0;
    private int totalTripsTraveled = 0; //Ex.6
    private Person passenger;

    public void LoadPassenger()
    {
        passenger = new Person();
    }

    public void InitiateNewFloorRequest()
    {
        requestedFloor = passenger.NewFloorRequest();
        Console.WriteLine("Departing floor: " + currentFloor
            + " Traveling to floor: " + requestedFloor);
        totalFloorsTraveled = totalFloorsTraveled +
            Math.Abs(currentFloor - requestedFloor);
        totalTripsTraveled = totalTripsTraveled + 1; //Ex.6
        currentFloor = requestedFloor;
    }

    public void ReportStatistic()
    {
        Console.WriteLine("Total floors traveled: " + totalFloorsTraveled);
        Console.WriteLine("Total trips traveled: "
            + totalTripsTraveled); //Ex.6
```

```
    }
}

class Person
{
    private System.Random randomNumberGenerator;

    public Person()
    {
        randomNumberGenerator = new System.Random();
    }

    public int NewFloorRequest()
    {
         // Return randomly generated number
        return randomNumberGenerator.Next(0,50); //Ex.3
    }
}

class Building
{
    private static Elevator elevatorA;

    public static void Main()
    {
        Console.WriteLine("The simulation has commenced"); //Ex.1
        elevatorA = new Elevator();
        elevatorA.LoadPassenger();
        elevatorA.InitiateNewFloorRequest();
        elevatorA.InitiateNewFloorRequest();
        elevatorA.InitiateNewFloorRequest();
        elevatorA.InitiateNewFloorRequest();
        elevatorA.InitiateNewFloorRequest();
        elevatorA.InitiateNewFloorRequest();//Ex.5
        elevatorA.InitiateNewFloorRequest();//Ex.5
        elevatorA.InitiateNewFloorRequest();//Ex.5
        elevatorA.InitiateNewFloorRequest();//Ex.5
        elevatorA.InitiateNewFloorRequest();//Ex.5
        elevatorA.ReportStatistic();
        Console.WriteLine("The simulation has ended"); //Ex.2
    }
}
```

Chapter 6

Answers to Chapter 6 Review Questions

1. The distinction "Simple types versus derived types" is used for historical reasons and because it is convenient, but it is strictly speaking not correct. In contrast "Value types versus reference types" is correct but perhaps less intuitive.

2. Different types are needed to represent different kinds of data.

3. The kind of data the type can represent, the memory use, the kind of operations in which it will take part, and in case it can hold simple numbers: the range and precision.
4. A strongly typed language attempts to prohibit types from being involved in processes in which they are not meant to participate.
5. No, because assigning a value of type `int` to a variable of type `short` potentially results in loss of magnitude. Any assignment with the potential risk of data loss (magnitude or precision) requires an explicit conversion.
6. By appending an `f` (or `F`) to the number. Thus, `6.89f` is a literal of type `float`.
7. `private float distance = 100.5f;`.
8. If the compiler switch is set to `unchecked`, the variable overflows to make its value equal to 0. If it is set to `checked` a runtime error occurs.
9. The simple type `float`.
10. The simple type `decimal`.
11. `myIntValue = (int)myNumber + (int)yourNumber;`.
12. The expression is of type `string`.
13. `0.2f` is not exactly 0.2. This inaccuracy is exposed when `(10 * 0.2f)` is compared to a value of type `double`, such as 2.0, resulting in the expression to be `false`.
14. Use constants when your source code contains values that are constant throughout the lifetime of the program. The advantages of using constants are
    - It is easier to understand the meaning of a name like Pi instead of a literal like 3.14.
    - The use of constants allow you to change a value in one place (where it is declared) rather than in every place it is used in the source code.
15. `Console.WriteLine(30000000.326m.ToString("C"));`.

Answers to Chapter 6 Programming Exercises

The following source code provides answers to programming Exercises 1–4. The code parts related to a particular exercise have been marked with a comment, such as `// Ex.1` or `// Exercise 1`.

```
using System;

class BliposClock
{
    private byte seconds;
    private short minutes;
     //Exercise 2
    private byte days;
    private ulong years;
```

```
public BliposClock()
{
    seconds = 0;
    minutes = 0;
     // Exercise 2
    days = 0;
    years = 0;
}

public void OneForward()
{
    byte originalSeconds = seconds;
    short originalMinutes = minutes; //Ex. 2
    byte originalDays = days; //Ex. 2

    seconds++;
    if (originalSeconds > seconds)
         // Overflow of seconds variable
        minutes++;
     // Exercise 2
    if (originalMinutes > minutes)
         // Overflow of minutes variable
        days++;
    if (originalDays > days)
         // Overflow of days variable
        years++;
}

public void OneBackward()
{
    byte originalSeconds = seconds;
    short originalMinutes = minutes; //Ex. 2
    byte originalDays = days; //Ex. 2

    seconds--;
    if (originalSeconds < seconds)
         // Underflow of seconds variable
        minutes--;
     // Exercise 2
    if (originalMinutes < minutes)
         // Underflow of minutes variable
        days--;
    if (originalDays < days)
         // Underflow of days variable
        years--;
}

public void FastForward()
{
    byte originalSeconds = seconds;
    short originalMinutes = minutes; //Ex. 2
    byte originalDays = days; //Ex. 2
```

```
    seconds = (byte)(seconds + 50);
    if (originalSeconds > seconds)
         // Overflow of seconds variable
        minutes++;
     // Exercise 2
    if (originalMinutes > minutes)
         // Overflow of minutes variable
        days++;
    if (originalDays > days)
         // Overflow of days variable
        years++;
}

public void FastBackward()
{
    byte originalSeconds = seconds;
    short originalMinutes = minutes; //Ex. 2
    byte originalDays = days; //Ex. 2

    seconds = (byte)(seconds - 50);
    if (originalSeconds < seconds)
         // Underflow of seconds variable
        minutes--;
      // Exercise 2
    if (originalMinutes < minutes)
         // Underflow of minutes variable
        days--;
    if (originalDays < days)
         // Underflow of days variable
        years--;
}

 // Exercise 1
public void HundredForward()
{
    byte originalSeconds = seconds;
    short originalMinutes = minutes; //Ex. 2
    byte originalDays = days; //Ex. 2

    seconds = (byte)(seconds + 100);
    if (originalSeconds > seconds)
         // Overflow of seconds variable
        minutes++;
     // Exercise 2
    if (originalMinutes > minutes)
         // Overflow of minutes variable
        days++;
    if (originalDays > days)
         // Overflow of days variable
        years++;
}

 // Exercise 1
```

```
public void HundredBackward()
{
    byte originalSeconds = seconds;
    short originalMinutes = minutes; //Ex. 2
    byte originalDays = days; //Ex. 2

    seconds = (byte)(seconds - 100);
    if (originalSeconds < seconds)
         // Underflow of seconds variable
        minutes--;
     // Exercise 2
    if (originalMinutes < minutes)
         // Underflow of minutes variable
        days--;
    if (originalDays < days)
         // Underflow of days variable
        years--;
}

// Exercise 3
public void AddOneDay()
{
    byte originalDays = days;

    days++;
    if (originalDays > days)
         // Overflow of days variable
        years++;
}

 // Exercise 3
public void DeductOneDay()
{
    byte originalDays = days;

    days--;
    if (originalDays < days)
         // Underflow of days variable
        years--;
}

 // Exercise 3
public void AddOneYear()
{
    years++;
}

 // Exercise 3
public void DeductOneYear()
{
    years--;
}
```

```
    public void SetSeconds(byte sec)
    {
        seconds = sec;
    }

    public void SetMinutes(short min)
    {
        minutes = min;
    }

     // Exercise 2
    public void SetDays(byte newDays)
    {
        days = newDays;
    }

     // Exercise 2
    public void SetYears(ulong newYears)
    {
        years = newYears;
    }

    public void ShowTime()
    {
        Console.WriteLine("Sec: " + seconds + " Min: " + minutes);
         // Exercise 2
        Console.WriteLine("Day/year: " + days + "/" + years);
         // Exercise 4
        if (days == 100)
            Console.WriteLine("Happy Birthday Emperor!");
    }
}

class RunBliposClock
{
    public static void Main()
    {
        string command;

        Console.WriteLine("Welcome to the Blipos Clock. " +
            "256 seconds per minute " +
            "65536 minutes per day");
        BliposClock myClock = new BliposClock();
        Console.WriteLine("Please set the clock");
        Console.Write("Enter Seconds: ");
        myClock.SetSeconds(Convert.ToByte(Console.ReadLine()));
        Console.Write("Enter Minutes: ");
        myClock.SetMinutes(Convert.ToInt16(Console.ReadLine()));
        Console.Write("Enter Days: "); //Ex.2
        myClock.SetDays(Convert.ToByte(Console.ReadLine())); //Ex.2
        Console.Write("Enter Years: "); //Ex.2
        myClock.SetYears(Convert.ToUInt64(Console.ReadLine())); //Ex.2
        Console.WriteLine("Enter command: F) Forward B) Backward " +
            "A) Add fifty ");
```

```
            Console.WriteLine("D) Deduct fifty H) Add hundred " + //Ex.1
                "M) Deduct hundred "); //Ex.1
            Console.WriteLine("Q) Add one Day  Y) Add one year " + //Ex.3
                "U) Deduct one day \n  W) Deduct one year  T) Terminate"); //Ex.3
            do
            {
                command = Console.ReadLine().ToUpper();
                if (command == "F")
                    myClock.OneForward();
                if (command == "B")
                    myClock.OneBackward();
                if(command == "A")
                    myClock.FastForward();
                if(command == "D")
                    myClock.FastBackward();
                 //Exercise 1
                if(command == "H")
                    myClock.HundredForward();
                if(command == "M")
                    myClock.HundredBackward();
                 //Exercise 3
                if(command == "Q")
                    myClock.AddOneDay();
                if(command == "Y")
                    myClock.AddOneYear();
                if(command == "U")
                    myClock.DeductOneDay();
                if(command == "W")
                    myClock.DeductOneYear();
                myClock.ShowTime();
            } while (command != "T");
            Console.WriteLine("Thank you for using the Blipos Clock");
        }
    }
```

The following source code constitutes the answer to Exercise 5.

```
using System;

class AgeCalculator
{
    public double AverageAge(byte age1, byte age2, byte age3)
    {
        double average;

        average = (double)(age1 + age2 + age3) / 3;
        return average;
    }
}

class Tester
{
    public static void Main()
    {
```

```
            byte ageA;
            byte ageB;
            byte ageC;

            AgeCalculator myCalculator = new AgeCalculator();

            Console.Write("Enter age 1: ");
            ageA = Convert.ToByte(Console.ReadLine());
            Console.Write("Enter age 2: ");
            ageB = Convert.ToByte(Console.ReadLine());
            Console.Write("Enter age 3: ");
            ageC = Convert.ToByte(Console.ReadLine());

            Console.WriteLine("Average age: " +
                myCalculator.AverageAge(ageA, ageB, ageC).ToString("N3"));
        }
    }
```

Chapter 7

Answers to Chapter 7 Review Questions

1. a. 5 + (10 * 2) = 5 + 20 = 25

   b. (5 * 6) / 3 = 30 / 3 = 10

   c. (12 / 4) * 6 = 3 * 6 = 18

   d. 20 % 8 = 4

   e. The value of `myIntVariable` is incremented by one. If `myIntVariable++` is part of a longer expression, this increment will take place after other operations in the expression.

   f. The value of `myIntVariable` is decremented by one. If `--myIntVariable` is part of a longer expression this decrement will take place before other operations in the expression.

2. Add a pair of parentheses, as in the following line:

   ```
   (number1 + number2) * number3
   ```

3.

   ```
   (num1 + ((num2 / num3) * num4)) - ((num5 * num6) / num7)
   ```

4.

   ```
   if ((myNumber % 2) == 0)
       Console.WriteLine("The number is even")
   ```

5. It is of type `int`.

6.

```
bacteriaInBody1++;
totalBacteria = bacteriaInBody1 + bacteriaInBody2;
bacteriaInBody2++;
```

7.

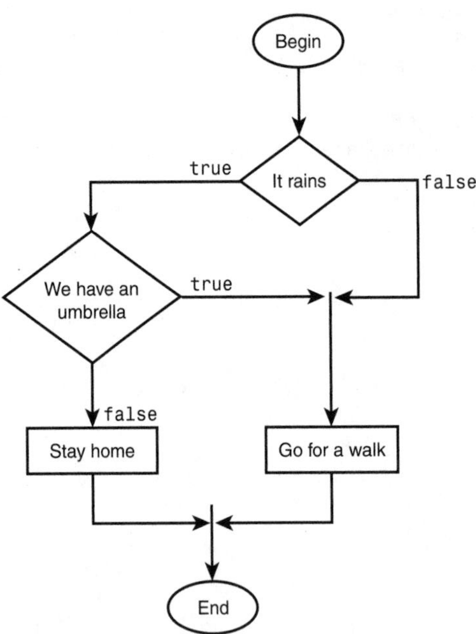

8. The enumerator construct.

9.

```
Console.WriteLine("And then he said: \"This is a great moment\"");
```

10.

```
myString.Substring(9,5)
```

11.

```
Console.WriteLine("The first distance is {0} meters, the second distance
➥ is {1} meters, and the third distance is {2} meters", distance1,
➥ distance2, distance3);
```

Answers to Chapter 7 Programming Exercises

The following source code contains answers to Exercises 1 and 2. The relevant parts are marked `// Exercise 1` or `// Ex. 1` or similar.

```
using System;

class DayCounter
{
    public static void Main()
    {
        uint dayCounter = 0;
        uint maxSimulationDays;
        uint weeks;
        uint years; // Exercise 2
        byte remainderDays;
        byte remainderDaysSaturday; //Exercise 1

        Console.Write("Please enter the number of days " +
            "the simulation should run for ");
        maxSimulationDays = Convert.ToUInt32(Console.ReadLine());
        while(dayCounter < maxSimulationDays)
        {
            dayCounter++;
            weeks = dayCounter / 7;
            years = weeks / 52; //Exercise 2
            remainderDays = (byte)(dayCounter % 7);
             //Exercise 1
            remainderDaysSaturday = (byte)((dayCounter + 1) % 7);
             //Exercise 2
            Console.WriteLine("Weeks: {0} Days: {1} Years: {2}",
                weeks - (years * 52), remainderDays, years);
            if(remainderDays == 0)
                 // TODO send "it's Sunday" message to controller
                Console.WriteLine("\t\tHey Hey It's Sunday!");
             //Exercise 1
            if(remainderDaysSaturday == 0)
                Console.WriteLine("\t\tHey It's Saturday");
             // TODO start simulation lasting for one day.
             // Let the program pause for 200 milliseconds
            System.Threading.Thread.Sleep(200);
        }
        Console.WriteLine("Simulation ended");
    }
}
```

The following source represents an answer to Exercise 3:

```
using System;

class BliposClock
{
     //A time in the BliposClock is represented by just one value: totalSeconds.
     //All displayed times are derived from this basic value.
    private ulong totalSeconds;

    public BliposClock()
    {
        totalSeconds = 0;
```

```
    }

    public void AddSeconds(ulong secondsToAdd)
    {
        totalSeconds = totalSeconds + secondsToAdd;
    }

    public void DeductSeconds(ulong secondsToDeduct)
    {
        totalSeconds = totalSeconds - secondsToDeduct;
    }

     //initialMinutes can be between -32768 and 32767 so to convert this value
     //to totalSeconds we must add 32768 and multiply by 256 before we add this
     //value to initialSeconds as shown in the statement of the following method.
    public void SetTime(byte initialSeconds, short initialMinutes)
    {
        totalSeconds = (ulong)initialSeconds + (ulong)((initialMinutes + 32768) *
        ➥256);
    }

    public void ShowTime()
    {
        byte secondsToShow;
        int secondsPassedBy; // Total number of seconds the day is old
        short minutesToShow;

        secondsToShow = (byte)(totalSeconds % 256);
        secondsPassedBy = (int)(totalSeconds % (256 * 65536));
         //By dividing secondsPassedBy by 256 in the next line we find the
         //number of whole minutes the day is old. This number can be
         //between 0 and 65535. However we need a number
         // between -32768 and 32767, which we can get by
         //subtracting 32768 as shown in the next line.
        minutesToShow = (short) ((secondsPassedBy / 256) - 32768);

        Console.WriteLine("Sec: {0}  Min: {1}", secondsToShow, minutesToShow);
    }
}

class RunBliposClock
{
    public static void Main()
    {
        string command;
        byte tempSeconds;
        short tempMinutes;

        Console.WriteLine("Welcome to the Blipos Clock. " +
            "256 seconds per minute " +
            "65536 minutes per day");
        BliposClock myClock = new BliposClock();
        Console.WriteLine("Please set the clock");
        Console.Write("Enter Seconds: ");
        tempSeconds = Convert.ToByte(Console.ReadLine());
```

```
            Console.Write("Enter minutes: ");
            tempMinutes = Convert.ToInt16(Console.ReadLine());
            myClock.SetTime(tempSeconds, tempMinutes);

            Console.WriteLine("Enter (F)orward ackward " +
                "(A)dd fifty educt fifty (T)erminate");
            do
            {
                command = Console.ReadLine().ToUpper();
                if (command == "F")
                    myClock.AddSeconds(1);
                if (command == "B")
                    myClock.DeductSeconds(1);
                if(command == "A")
                    myClock.AddSeconds(50);
                if(command == "D")
                    myClock.DeductSeconds(50);
                myClock.ShowTime();
            } while (command != "T");
            Console.WriteLine("Thank you for using the Blipos Clock");
        }
    }
```

Chapter 8

Answers to Chapter 8 Review Questions

1. a. The branching statement `if-else`.

   b. An iteration statement.

2.

   a.

```
if(rainfall > 100)
    Console.WriteLine("Heavy rainfall");
```

   b.

```
if((rainfall > 100) || (wind > 120))
    Console.WriteLine("Bad weather");
```

   c.

```
if((rainfall == 0) && (wind < 10) && (temperature >= 23) && (temperature
➥<= 27))
    Console.WriteLine("Nice weather");
```

   d.

```
if(rainfall == 0)
    Console.WriteLine("It is not raining");
else
    Console.WriteLine("It is raining");
```

3. The semicolon after the first line represents an empty statement, so the `if` statement could also be written as follows. If rainfall is greater than 0, the empty statement is executed; otherwise not. The last line is always executed.

```
if(rainfall > 0)
;
Console.WriteLine("It's raining");
```

4. It allows a program to choose among more than two alternative branches.

5.

   a. `((rainfall > 100) && (rainfall < 150))`

   b. `((number % 2 != 0) && (number != 23))`

   c. `((number % 2 == 0) || (weight < 100))`

6. `!(IsEven(someNumber))`.

7. Scope refers to the section of the source code where a particular variable identifier can be used. The scope of a variable begins at the point where it is declared and ends where the block in which it is declared terminates. The scope includes the blocks that might be nested inside this block.

8. To direct control to another `switch` section in a `switch` statement.

9.

```
switch(timeOfDay)
{
    case "morning":
        Console.WriteLine("Good Morning");
    break;
    case "midday":
        Console.WriteLine("Good Day");
    break;
    case "evening":
        Console.WriteLine("Good Evening");
    break;
    default:
        Console.WriteLine("Invalid time");
    break;
}
```

10. Falling through is when the flow of execution moves from one `switch` section directly to the next `switch` section. This can be prevented by either a `break` or a `goto` statement.

11. `minimumCost = (cost1 < cost2) ? cost1 : cost2;`

Answers to Chapter 8 Programming Exercises

Exercise 1:

```
using System;

class TaxCalculator
```

```
{
    public static void Main()
    {
        double income;
        double tax;

        Console.Write("Enter income: ");
        income = Convert.ToDouble(Console.ReadLine());

        if(income <= 10000)
            tax = 0;
        else if((income > 10000) && (income <= 25000))
            tax = (income - 10000) * 0.05;
        else if((income > 25000) && (income <= 50000))
            tax = (15000 * 0.05) + ((income - 25000) * 0.1);
        else if((income > 50000) && (income <= 100000))
            tax = (15000 * 0.05) + (25000 * 0.1) + ((income - 50000) * 0.15);
        else
            tax = (15000 * 0.05) + (25000 * 0.1) + (50000 * 0.15)
            ➥ + ((income - 100000) * 0.2);

        Console.WriteLine("The tax is: {0}", tax);
    }
}
```

Exercise 2:

```
using System;

class ExamScoreConverter
{
    public static void Main()
    {
        string score;

        Console.WriteLine("Enter score you wish to convert");
        score = Console.ReadLine().ToUpper();

        switch(score)
        {
            case "A":
                Console.WriteLine("90-100 percent score");
            break;
            case "B":
                Console.WriteLine("80-89 percent score");
            break;
            case "C":
                Console.WriteLine("70-79 percent score");
            break;
            case "D":
                Console.WriteLine("60-69 percent score");
            break;
            case "E":
                Console.WriteLine("0-59 percent score");
```

```
                break;
                default:
                    Console.WriteLine("Invalid exam result provided");
                break;
            }
        }
    }
```

Exercise 3:

```
using System;

class NumberFinder
{
    public static void Main()
    {
        int maxNumber = 100;
        int minNumber = 0;
        bool found = false;
        int guessCounter = 0;
        string reply;

        do
        {
            guessCounter++;
            Console.WriteLine("My guess is: {0}",
            ➥ ((maxNumber + minNumber) / 2));
            Console.WriteLine("Enter H for H)igher or L for L)ower
            ➥ C for C)orrect?");
            reply = Console.ReadLine().ToUpper();
            if(reply == "H")
                minNumber = (maxNumber + minNumber) / 2;
            else if (reply == "L")
                maxNumber = (maxNumber + minNumber) / 2;
            else
                found = true;
        } while (!found);
        Console.WriteLine("I found the number in {0} guesses", guessCounter);
    }
}
```

Chapter 9

Answers to Chapter 9 Review Questions

1. The `while` statement is an entry condition loop statement; the `do-while` is an exit condition loop statement. The entry condition loop may never be executed, whereas the `do-while` condition will be executed at least once. The entry condition loop is better suited to generate and traverse data sequences because perhaps the expected set of data is empty or perhaps no data should be generated in a particular run of the program.

2.

```
1 2 3 4
```

3.

```
4 3 2 1
Value of counter: 0
```

4.

```
0 2 4 6
```

5.

```
for(int i = 12; i >= -3; i -= 3)
{
    Console.Write(i + "  ");
}
```

6. It is valid. The output is as follows:

```
1  6  15  28
```

7.

```
2 3 4 5
3 4 5 6
4 5 6 7
```

8. A `break` statement has been inserted between the two `WriteLine` statements. It is executed whenever `counter` is greater than 3.

```
for(int counter = 1; ; counter++)
{
    Console.WriteLine("Value of counter: {0}", counter);
    if(counter > 3)
        break;
    Console.WriteLine("Value of counter * 10: {0}", counter);
}
```

9.

```
for(int i = 0; i <= 20; i++)
{
    if(!(i % 4 == 0))
        Console.Write(i + ", ");
}
```

10. An arrow in a flowchart represents a movement of control from one part of the program to another. It is easy to draw arrows on a chart that goes to any place. However, sometimes the only way this can be implemented is through the error-prone `goto` statement. On the other hand, the format of pseudocode is very similar to C# source code (you write one line at a time and lines are mostly executed sequentially) and is highly compatible with the compact structured C# constructs, such as `while` loops, `if` statements, and so on.

Answers to Chapter 9 Programming Exercises

Exercise 1:

```
using System;

class Calculator
{
    public static void Main()
    {
        string answer;
        long factorial;
        int number;

        do
        {
            Console.Write("Please enter number: ");
            number = Convert.ToInt32(Console.ReadLine());
            factorial = 1;

            if(number >= 0)
            {
                for(int i = number; i >= 1; i--)
                {
                    factorial *= i;
                }
            }
            else
            {
                factorial = -1;
            }
            Console.WriteLine("{0} factorial = {1}", number, factorial);
            Console.WriteLine("Perform another calculation Y)es N)o");
            answer = Console.ReadLine().ToUpper();
        } while(answer != "N");
        Console.WriteLine("Thank you for using the factorial calculator");
    }
}
```

Exercise 2:

```
using System;

class StarTriangle
{
    public static void Main()
    {
        for(int i = 1; i <= 8; i++)
        {
            for(int j = 1; j <= i; j++)
            {
                Console.Write("*");
            }
            Console.WriteLine();
```

```
        }
    }
}
```

Exercise 3:

```
using System;

class MixedTriangles
{
    public static void Main()
    {
        for(int i = 1; i <= 8; i++)
        {
            for(int j = 1; j <= i; j++)
            {
                Console.Write("*");
            }
            Console.WriteLine();
            for(int k = 1; k <= 9 - i; k++)
            {
                Console.Write("#");
            }
            Console.WriteLine();
        }
    }
}
```

Chapter 10

Answers to Chapter 10 Review Questions

1.

   a. `private double[] distances;`

   b. `distances = new double[5];`

   c. `private double[] distances = {20.1, 30.7, 45.8, 19.1, 12.4, 34.5};`

2.

   a. The value of `numbers[1]` is 5

   b. 15 3 5 10

   c.

```
foreach(int temp in numbers)
{
    Console.Write(" {0}", temp);
}
```

   d. The `for` loop repeats itself one time too many, so `i` becomes larger than 3 in the last loop and causes an `IndexOutOfBoundsException`. The loop condition should be `i < 4` instead of `i <= 4`.

3.

   a. Array elements of type `int` are implicitly initialized to 0.

   b. No, it is not a valid statement. The index 4 is out of range. When this line is executed, an `IndexOutOfRangeException` will be generated.

4. A bank has a constant need to delete and add new accounts. This calls for an array-like structure that dynamically can have new elements added and deleted. Arrays are not suited for this task because they have a fixed length once they are created.

5.

```
int GetNumber(int index)
{
    return numbers[index - 1];
}
```

6. `[4]` (positioned after `byte`) states that the length of the array is 4. However, the same line is attempting to assign six values at the same time; this difference is invalid.

7.

```
void DisplayArray(int[] tempArray)
{
    for(int i = 0; i < tempArray.Length; i++)
    {
        Console.WriteLine(tempArray[i]);
    }
}
```

8.

```
int [] AddNumber(int [] tempArray, int num)
{
    for(int i = 0; i < tempArray.Length; i++)
    {
        tempArray[i] += num;
    }
    return tempArray;
}
```

9. `myNumbers` and `yourNumbers` are referencing the same array object, so adding 10 to `yourNumbers[0]` is the same as adding 10 to `myNumbers[0]`. As a result, `myNumbers[0]` is equal to 12.

10. The `Clone` method creates an entire new array object with copies of array element values that are separate from those of the array for which the `Clone` method is called. In contrast, a simple assignment from one array variable to another only passes a reference along, which will cause the two array variables to reference the same array object.

11. It is `false` because the comparison operator (==) tests whether the compared array variables are referencing the same object (reference-based comparison).

12.

```
Planet [] planets = new Planet[10];
```

Answers to Chapter 10 Programming Exercises

Exercise 1:

```
using System;

class ArrayMath
{
    public static double ArrayAverage(double [] tempArray)
    {
        double sum = 0;

        foreach(double temp in tempArray)
        {
            sum += temp;
        }
        return sum / tempArray.Length;
    }

    public static int [] ArraySum(int [] tempArray1, int [] tempArray2)
    {
        int [] sumArray = new int [tempArray1.Length];

        for(int i = 0; i < tempArray1.Length; i++)
        {
            sumArray[i] = tempArray1[i] + tempArray2[i];
        }
        return sumArray;
    }

    public static int ArrayMax(int [] tempArray)
    {
        int maxValue = -2147483648;

        foreach(int temp in tempArray)
        {
            if(temp > maxValue)
                maxValue = temp;
        }
        return maxValue;
    }
}

class Tester
{
    public static void Main()
    {
```

```
        double [] distances = {100, 200, 300};
        int [] agesTeam1 = {10, 20, 30};
        int [] agesTeam2 = {34, 38, 31};
        int [] sumArray;

        Console.WriteLine("Average distance of distances array: {0}",
        ➥ ArrayMath.ArrayAverage(distances));
        Console.WriteLine("Max age in agesTeam1 array: {0}",
        ➥ ArrayMath.ArrayMax(agesTeam1));
        sumArray = ArrayMath.ArraySum(agesTeam1, agesTeam2);
        Console.WriteLine("sumArray's element values: {0} {1} {2}",
        ➥ sumArray[0], sumArray[1], sumArray[2]);
    }
}
```

Exercise 2:

```
using System;

class Car
{
    private int position = 0;

    public void MoveForward(int distance)
    {
        position += distance;
    }

    public void Reverse(int distance)
    {
        position -= distance;
    }

    public int GetPosition()
    {
        return position;
    }
}

class CarGame
{
    private Car [] cars;

    public CarGame()
    {
        cars = new Car [5];
        for(int i = 0; i < cars.Length; i++)
        {
            cars[i] = new Car();
        }
    }

    public int GetCarPosition(int carIndex)
    {
        return cars[carIndex].GetPosition();
```

```
    }

    public void MoveCarForward(int carIndex, int distance)
    {
        cars[carIndex].MoveForward(distance);
    }

    public void ReverseCar(int carIndex, int distance)
    {
        cars[carIndex].Reverse(distance);
    }
}

class CarGameTester
{
    public static void Main()
    {
        CarGame testGame = new CarGame();
        testGame.MoveCarForward(0, 100);
        testGame.MoveCarForward(1, 40);
        Console.WriteLine("Position of car 0: {0}",
        ➥ testGame.GetCarPosition(0));
        Console.WriteLine("Position of car 1: {0}",
        ➥ testGame.GetCarPosition(1));
    }
}
```

Chapter 11

Answers to Chapter 11 Review Questions

1.

    a. 5 dimensions

    b. 5 nested `for` loops

2. 2 dimensions.

3.

    a. `uint [ , , ] observations = new uint [5,10,20];`.

    b. `observations[3,2,10] = 100;`.

    c. The second index (12) is out of range and will trigger the runtime to generate an `IndexOutOfRangeException`.

    d.

    ```
    for(int i = 0; i < 5; i++)
    {
        for(int j = 0; j < 10; j++)
    ```

```
        {
            for(int k = 0; k < 20; k++)
            {
                Console.WriteLine(observations(i, j, k));
            }
        }
    }
```

e.

```
foreach(uint temp in observations)
{
    Console.WriteLine(temp);
}
```

4.

a. `int [][] numbers = new int [7][];`

b. `numbers [2] = new int [20];`

c. `numbers[2][3] = 100;`

5.

a. 2

b. –1

c. –1

d. 6

e. 1

6. Half of one million: 500000

7.

a. If the sequential search begins at the beginning of the array and the key value is located at the end of the array, a maximum number of loops is required that amounts to 2048.

b. After each loop of the binary search, half of the previous array segment is eliminated. Consequently, a maximum of 11 searches are needed because 2048 divided by 2 11 times is equal to 1. In other words, $2^{11} = 2048$.

Answers to Chapter 11 Programming Exercises

Exercise 1:

```
using System;

//From user's point of view the first day has number 1 because
//its index has been adjusted for the zero based index and the
//the first hour has number 0. So days has indexes from 1-7,
```

```
 //hours has indexes from 0-23
class CarCounter
{
    private int [,] hourCarCounts = new int [7,24];

    public CarCounter()
    {
         //Initialize all hourCarCounts elements to zero
        for(int i = 0; i < 7; i++)
        {
            for(int j = 0; j < 24; j++)
            {
                hourCarCounts[i,j] = 0;
            }
        }
    }

     //Display a menu,
     //let the user enter a command and respond accordingly
    public void Run()
    {
        string answer;

        Console.WriteLine("I Input another value");
        Console.WriteLine("G Get count for specific hour");
        Console.WriteLine("S Calculate the total cars counted");
        Console.WriteLine("H Calculate number of hours to reach a
        ➥ given car count");
        Console.WriteLine("T Terminate");

        do
        {
            Console.Write("\nPlease choose an option: ");
            answer = Console.ReadLine().ToUpper();

            switch(answer)
            {
                case "I":
                    InputCarCount();
                break;
                case "G":
                    GetHourCount();
                break;
                case "S":
                    Console.WriteLine("The total number of cars counted {0}",
                    ➥ TotalCarsCounted());
                break;
                case "H":
                    HoursToReachCount();
                break;
                case "T":
                    Console.WriteLine("Bye Bye!");
                break;
```

```
                default:
                    Console.WriteLine("Invalid reply. Please try again");

                break;
            }
        } while (answer != "T");
    }

     //Let the user input a car count into a given day and hour
    public void InputCarCount()
    {
        int day;
        int hour;
        int carCount;

        Console.Write("Input day: ");
        day = Convert.ToInt32(Console.ReadLine());
        Console.Write("Input hour: ");
        hour = Convert.ToInt32(Console.ReadLine());
        Console.Write("Input car count: ");
        carCount = Convert.ToInt32(Console.ReadLine());
         // 1 is deducted from day in the next line to adjust
         // for zero based index
        hourCarCounts[day - 1,hour] = carCount;
    }

     //Finds the car count of a specific day and hour
    public void GetHourCount()
    {
        int day;
        int hour;

        Console.Write("Enter day: ");
        day = Convert.ToInt32(Console.ReadLine());
        Console.Write("Enter hour: ");
        hour = Convert.ToInt32(Console.ReadLine());
         // 1 is deducted from day in the next line to adjust
         // for zero based index
        Console.WriteLine("Car count: {0}", hourCarCounts[day - 1, hour]);
    }

     //Finds the sum of all hourly car counts in hourCarCounts
    public int TotalCarsCounted()
    {
        int sum = 0;

        foreach(int temp in hourCarCounts)
        {
            sum += temp;
        }
        return sum;
    }

     //Calculates the hours it takes to reach a given car count
    public void HoursToReachCount()
```

```
    {
        int reachCarCounts = 0;
        int hourCount = 0;
        int sumCarCounts = 0;

        Console.Write("Input number of cars to be reached: ");
        reachCarCounts = Convert.ToInt32(Console.ReadLine());

        for(int i = 0; i < 7; i++)
        {
            for(int j = 0; j < 24; j++)
            {
                hourCount++;
                sumCarCounts += hourCarCounts[i,j];
                if(sumCarCounts > reachCarCounts)
                {
                    Console.WriteLine("Number of hours: {0}", hourCount);
                    return;
                }
            }
        }
        Console.WriteLine("The given count: {0} was never reached",
        ➥ reachCarCounts);
    }
}

class Tester
{
    public static void Main()
    {
        CarCounter myCarCounter = new CarCounter();
        myCarCounter.Run();
    }
}
```

Exercise 2:

```
using System;

class BoxOfNumbers
{
    private int [,,] numbers = new int [5,10,8];

    public BoxOfNumbers()
    {
         //Initialize all numbers
        for(int i = 0; i < 5; i++)
        {
            for(int j = 0; j < 10; j++)
            {
                for(int k = 0; k < 8; k++)
                {
                    numbers[i,j,k] = 0;
                }
            }
```

```
        }
    }

    //Display a menu,
    //let the user enter a command and respond accordingly
    public void Run()
    {
        string answer;

        Console.WriteLine("I Input another number");
        Console.WriteLine("G Get number for specific indexes");
        Console.WriteLine("S Calculate the sum of the numbers");
        Console.WriteLine("T Terminate");

        do
        {
            Console.Write("\nPlease choose an option: ");
            answer = Console.ReadLine().ToUpper();

            switch(answer)
            {
                case "I":
                    InputNumber();
                break;
                case "G":
                    GetNumber();
                break;
                case "S":
                    Console.WriteLine("Sum of all numbers {0}", NumbersSum());
                break;
                case "T":
                    Console.WriteLine("Bye Bye!");
                break;
                default:
                    Console.WriteLine("Invalid reply. Please try again");
                break;
            }
        } while (answer != "T");
    }

    //Lets the user input a number for a given set of indexes
    public void InputNumber()
    {
        int indexDimension1;
        int indexDimension2;
        int indexDimension3;
        int number;

        Console.Write("Enter index for 1st dimension: ");
        indexDimension1 = Convert.ToInt32(Console.ReadLine());
        Console.Write("Enter index for 2nd dimension: ");
        indexDimension2 = Convert.ToInt32(Console.ReadLine());
        Console.Write("Enter index for 3rd dimension ");
        indexDimension3 = Convert.ToInt32(Console.ReadLine());
```

```
            Console.Write("Enter number: ");
            number = Convert.ToInt32(Console.ReadLine());
            numbers[indexDimension1, indexDimension2, indexDimension3] = number;
        }

         //Finds and displays the number for a given set of indexes
        public void GetNumber()
        {
            int indexDimension1;
            int indexDimension2;
            int indexDimension3;

            Console.Write("Enter index dimension 1: ");
            indexDimension1 = Convert.ToInt32(Console.ReadLine());
            Console.Write("Enter index dimension 2: ");
            indexDimension2 = Convert.ToInt32(Console.ReadLine());
            Console.Write("Enter index dimension 3: ");
            indexDimension3 = Convert.ToInt32(Console.ReadLine());
            Console.WriteLine("Number: {0}",
                numbers[indexDimension1, indexDimension2, indexDimension3]);
        }

         //Finds the sum of all numbers
        public int NumbersSum()
        {
            int sum = 0;

            foreach(int temp in numbers)
            {
                sum += temp;
            }
            return sum;
        }
    }

    class Tester
    {
        public static void Main()
        {
            BoxOfNumbers myNumberBox = new BoxOfNumbers();
            myNumberBox.Run();
        }
    }
```

Chapter 12

Answers to Chapter 12 Review Questions

1. As a `static` variable, because the variable describes the `Planet` objects as a group.

2. Yes.

3. Yes.
4. No. A `const` is implicitly `static`, so it is not valid to also explicitly declare it `static`.
5. No, because the `const` value cannot be changed.
6.
   a. Yes.
   b. No.
   c. Yes.
   d. Yes.
   e. Yes.
   f. No.
7. The statement is `false` because the instance methods share the same code. The `static` method and the instance methods take up approximately the same memory.
8.
   a. Invalid. `ref` must suffix both arguments.
   b. Valid.
   c. Invalid. `10` is not an assignable variable.
9. Incorrect. Any `out` parameter must be assigned a value inside its method.
10.
    a. Valid.
    b. Valid.
    c. Valid.
    d. Invalid, `30.0` is not of type `int`.
    e. Valid.
11. Overloaded.
12.
    a. No, only the return type differs (one is `double`, the other `int`). However, the return type is not part of a method's signature, so the two method signatures are identical, which is invalid.
    b. No, the parameter names are not part of a method's signature, so even though they differ between the two methods, the two signatures are identical, which is invalid.
13. Yes, the method call is valid. `myByte` and `yourByte` are implicitly converted to `uints` during the method call.

14. In the line

```
return(myMass * this.myMass) + myMass;
```

`myMass` accesses the value of formal parameter `myMass` (here equal to 20.0), whereas `this.myMass` accesses the value of the instance variable `myMass` (here equal to 2000000). So the return value is

```
(myMass * this.myMass) + myMass =
(20.0 * 2000000) + 20.0 = 40000020
```

Answers to Chapter 12 Programming Exercises

Answers to all programming exercises are contained in the following program. Program parts relating to particular exercises are marked in the code.

```
using System;

class SportsCar
{
    private int maxSpeed = 0;
    private int horsepower = 0;
    private static int maxSpeedRequirement = 0;
    private static int horsepowerRequirement = 0;

    private string [] legalDrivers = new string [0]; //Exercise 2

    public bool SportsCheck()
    {
        if((maxSpeed >= maxSpeedRequirement) && (horsepower >=
        ➥ horsepowerRequirement))
            return true;
        else
            return false;
    }

    public void SetMaxSpeed(int newMaxSpeed)
    {
        maxSpeed = newMaxSpeed;
    }

    public int GetMaxSpeed()
    {
        return maxSpeed;
    }

    public void SetHorsepower(int newHorsepower)
    {
        horsepower = newHorsepower;
    }

    public int GetHorsepower()
    {
        return horsepower;
```

```
}

public static void SetMaxSpeedRequirement(int newMaxSpeedRequirement)
{
    maxSpeedRequirement = newMaxSpeedRequirement;
}

public static int GetMaxSpeedRequirement()
{
    return maxSpeedRequirement;
}

public static void SetHorsepowerRequirement(int newHorsepowerRequirement)
{
    horsepowerRequirement = newHorsepowerRequirement;
}

public static int GetHorsepowerRequirement()
{
    return horsepowerRequirement;
}

 //Exercise 2
public void SetLegalDrivers(params string [] newLegalDrivers)
{
    legalDrivers = newLegalDrivers;
}

 //Exercise 2
public bool DriverCheck(string name)
{
    foreach(string tempName in legalDrivers)
    {
        if(tempName == name)
            return true;
    }
    return false;
}

 //Exercise 3
public static void GetMinimumRequirements(ref int newMaxSpeed,
➥ ref int newHorsepower)
{
    newMaxSpeed = maxSpeedRequirement;
    newHorsepower = horsepowerRequirement;
}

 //Exercise 4
public SportsCar MostPowerful(SportsCar carCompare)
{
    if(carCompare.GetHorsepower() > this.horsepower)
        return carCompare;
    else
        return this;
```

```
    }
     //Exercise 4
    public SportsCar MostPowerful(SportsCar carCompare1,
    ➥ SportsCar carCompare2)
    {
        if(MostPowerful(carCompare1).GetHorsepower() >
           ➥ carCompare2.GetHorsepower())
            return MostPowerful(carCompare1);
        else
            return carCompare2;
    }
}

 //Exercise 3
class Calculator
{
    public static void NumberCruncher()
    {
        int sportsCarMaxSpeedReq = 0;
        int sportsCarHorsePowerReq = 0;
        SportsCar.GetMinimumRequirements(ref sportsCarMaxSpeedReq,
        ➥ ref sportsCarHorsePowerReq);

        //number crunch...number crunch...number crunch

        Console.WriteLine("Value of sportsCarMaxSpeedReq: {0}",
        ➥ sportsCarMaxSpeedReq);
        Console.WriteLine("Value of sportsCarHorsePowerReq: {0}",
        ➥ sportsCarHorsePowerReq);
    }
}

class Tester
{
    public static void Main()
    {
          //Exercise 1
        SportsCar myCar = new SportsCar();
        SportsCar yourCar = new SportsCar();
          //Calling static methods through class name
        SportsCar.SetMaxSpeedRequirement(200);
        SportsCar.SetHorsepowerRequirement(250);
          //Calling instance methods through object names
        myCar.SetMaxSpeed(170);
        myCar.SetHorsepower(110);
        yourCar.SetMaxSpeed(270);
        yourCar.SetHorsepower(300);

        Console.WriteLine("It is {0} that my car is a sports car",
        ➥ myCar.SportsCheck());
        Console.WriteLine("It is {0} that your car is a sports car",
        ➥ yourCar.SportsCheck());
```

```
            //Exercise 2
            myCar.SetLegalDrivers("Peter", "Ann", "Eric");
            Console.WriteLine("It is {0} that Peter can drive myCar",
            ➥ myCar.DriverCheck("Peter"));
            Console.WriteLine("It is {0} that Josephine can drive myCar",
            ➥ myCar.DriverCheck("Josephine"));

            //Exercise 3
            Calculator.NumberCruncher();

            //Exercise 4
            SportsCar mostPowerfulCar;
            SportsCar herCar = new SportsCar();
            herCar.SetMaxSpeed(290);
            herCar.SetHorsepower(320);
            mostPowerfulCar = myCar.MostPowerful(yourCar);
            Console.WriteLine("The most powerful car of your car and my car
            ➥ has {0} horsepowers", mostPowerfulCar.GetHorsepower());
            mostPowerfulCar = myCar.MostPowerful(yourCar, herCar);
            Console.WriteLine("The most powerful car of your car, my car and her
            ➥ car has {0} horsepowers", mostPowerfulCar.GetHorsepower());
        }
    }
```

Chapter 13

Answers to Chapter 13 Review Questions

1. `age` has the value `0` and `isConnected` the value `false`.

   Improved code would be as follows:

   ```
   private ushort age = 0;
   private bool isConnected = false;
   ```

2. By equipping the `Robot` class with the following constructor:

   ```
   public Robot(ushort initAge)
   {
       age = initAge;
   }
   ```

3. All constructors of the class `Robot` must be called `Robot`.

4. No, they can be used to perform any actions necessary when a new object is created.

5. There is no return value, so there is no return type.

6.

   a. When no constructors are explicitly defined for a class, the compiler automatically includes a default constructor for this class, making the call valid.

b. The previous statement is not valid now because the compiler does not automatically include a default constructor when any explicit constructors are specified for a class.

7.

a. Yes, both headers are valid. `: this (initialAge)` is a constructor initializer, which in this case causes the constructor with the header `public Cat(short initialAge)` to be called before the statements residing in the constructor to which the constructor initializer is attached.

b. This header is not valid because the constructor initializer is calling the constructor to which it is attached. The result is an infinite number of calls to the constructor.

8. The parentheses signify that the method-like language element called a constructor is being called.

9. Overloaded constructors contain different formal parameters, so a class with several constructors accepts several different combinations of arguments when a new object is created.

10. A constructor that is declared `private` cannot be called from outside its class. If a class only contains `private` constructors, a class cannot be instantiated from outside the class. This technique is sometimes used for classes containing only `static` members.

11.

a. A `static` constructor is called by the runtime sometime between program startup and the first instance of the class for which it is designed is created.

b. A `static` constructor cannot contain any parameters because the runtime never provides any arguments when it calls the `static` constructor.

12.

a. No. The constant instance member value is decided before the program is compiled—at the time when the program is written—so the programmer must know its value. A constant member cannot change value after its program has been compiled, and it is not possible to change its value until the next time the program is compiled.

b. Yes. A `readonly` instance member has its value determined at the time the object is created, after which it cannot be altered. A `readonly` instance member has the same lifetime as the object in which it resides.

13. An object is out of reach when no reference variables are referencing the object.

14. To identify objects that are out of reach. To reclaim the memory allocated for objects that are out of reach.

15. This is an inefficient approach. A better approach is to collect a group of reclaimable objects and then process them all at once.

16. A destructor is defined explicitly for a class, in which case it contains statements written by a programmer. The destructor can only be called by the garbage collector during its collection of an unreachable object.

    The destructor is not useful to free up scarce non-memory resources because we don't know when it is called; in fact, it may never be called during the runtime of a program.

17. No.

18. When the garbage collector is activated, the rest of the program is frozen, so a real-time application is not on real time during this period. When we combine this fact with the inability to control when the garbage collector is running, it becomes difficult to write a real-time application with a GC-based programming language like C#.

19. The `dispose` design pattern gives full control to the programmer of when to dispose of scarce resources held by an object.

Answers to Chapter 13 Programming Exercises

Exercise 1:

```
class Robot
{
    private string name = "unknown";
    private ushort age = 0;
    private bool isOn = false;

    //Accessor and mutator methods
}
```

Exercises 2 and 3:

```
class Robot
{
    private string name;
    private ushort age;
    private bool isOn;
    private static int robotsCreated;

    static Robot()
    {
        robotsCreated = 0;
    }

    public Robot(string initName, ushort initAge, bool initIsOn)
    {
        name = initName;
        age = initAge;
        isOn = initIsOn;
        robotsCreated++;
    }

    public Robot()
    {
```

```
        name = "unknown";
        age = 0;
        robotsCreated++;
        if(robotsCreated < 5)
            isOn = true;
        else
            isOn = false;
    }

    //accessors and mutator methods
}
```

Exercise 4:

```
class Robot
{
    ...
    public int Average(int x, int y, int z)
    {
        return RobotMath.Average(x, y, z);
    }
    ...
}

class RobotMath
{
     //private constructor prevents any instances to be created from
     //outside the RobotMath class.
    private RobotMath()
    {
    }

    public int Average(int x, int y, int z)
    {
        return (x + y + z) / 3;
    }
}
```

Chapter 14

Answers to Chapter 14 Review Questions

1.

   a. `set` statement block or `set` accessor

   b. `get` statement block or `get` accessor

2.

   a. Camel casing

   b. Pascal casing

c. Pascal casing

3. Change `private` to `public`, change `int` to `double`, remove the parentheses after `Speed`, and return `speed` not `Speed`.

```
 private double speed;
public double Speed
{
    get
    {
        return speed;
    }
}
```

4. Delayed initialization—When a program does not initialize an instance variable until its associated `get` statement block is called the first time. Delayed initialization is used with instance variables that are resource demanding to update and rarely used.

   Delayed initialization can also be implemented with accessor and mutator methods.

5. An indexer cannot be `static` and does not have a name (as `myIndexer`); only the keyword `this` is used. At least one parameter must be specified inside the square brackets. The following is a valid indexer header:

```
public int this [int index]
{
    ...
}
```

6.

   a) `rainfallMarch = rainfallParis[2];`

   b) `rainfallParis[6] = rainfallParis;`

   c) `myMarchRainfall = this[2];`

7. This is not a good idea. We don't know intuitively how the `Car` objects are being added together, so including operator overloading for the `Car` class is likely to make the code more cryptic.

8. Operator overloading changes the code's appearance syntactically (sometimes it looks sweeter), but underneath the syntax surface, operator overloading is just another way of calling a method.

9. The operator - method must be `public` and `static` and include the `operator` keyword in front of the minus symbol. Furthermore, it must return a `TimeSpan` object not a value of type `uint`.

   The correct operator - method looks as follows:

```
public static TimeSpan operator- (TimeSpan timeSpan1, TimeSpan timeSpan2)
{
    TimeSpan differenceTimeSpan = new TimeSpan();
```

```
        differenceTimeSpan.Seconds = timeSpan1.Seconds - timeSpan2.Seconds;
        return differenceTimeSpan;
    }
```

10.

   a. Invalid

   b. Invalid

   c. Invalid

   d. Invalid

   e. Valid

   f. Invalid

   g. Valid

   h. Invalid

   i. Valid

   j. Valid

   k. Invalid

   l. Invalid

   m. Invalid

11. If there is a class called `Bathroom`, there are also likely to be classes with names such as `Kitchen`, `Bedroom`, and so on. All these classes have a fundamental need to manipulate two-dimensional drawings and therefore a need to use the `Point` class. Consequently, it is not a good idea to isolate the `Point` class inside `Bathroom`. Instead, it should be positioned where all these classes can access it and share the functionality provided by the `Point` class.

Answers to Chapter 14 Programming Exercises

The following code could be inserted into the `Bicycle` class to answer Exercise 1. Note: This code does not compile separately.

```
const byte MaxAge = 200;
private byte age;
private uint numberOfAgeAccesses = 0;

public byte Age
{
    get
    {
        numberOfAgeAccesses++;
        return age;
    }
```

```
        set
        {
            if (value > MaxAge)
                Console.WriteLine("Error. {0} exceeds the age limit {1}",
                ➥ value, MaxAge);
            else if (value < 0)
                Console.WriteLine("Error. {0} cannot be less than 0", value);
            else
                age = value;
        }
    }

    public uint NumberOfAgeAccesses
    {
        get
        {
            return numberOfAgeAccesses;
        }
    }
```

The following code could be an answer to Exercises 2–4. Note: This code does not compile independently.

```
// This class is an answer to questions 2 and 3.
class Rainfall
{
    private uint[] rainfall = new uint[12];
    private uint numberOfRainAccesses = 0;

     //Initialize the rainfall array
    public Rainfall()
    {
        for(int i = 0; i < 12; i++)
        {
            rainfall[i] = 0;
        }
    }

    public uint this [int index]
    {
        get
        {
            if (index < 1 || index > 12)
            {
                Console.WriteLine("Index is out of bounds");
                return 0;
            }
            else
            {
                numberOfRainAccesses++;
                return rainfall[index - 1];
            }
        }

        set
```

```
        {
            if (index < 1 || index > 12)
                Console.WriteLine("Index is out of bounds");
            else
                rainfall[index - 1] = value;
        }
    }

    public uint NumberOfRainAccesses
    {
        get
        {
            return numberOfRainAccesses;
        }
    }

    public uint Average
    {
        get
        {
            uint sum = 0;

            for (int i = 0; i < 12; i++)
            {
                sum += rainfall[i];
            }
            return (sum / 12);
        }
    }

    public static Rainfall operator+ (Rainfall rainfall1, Rainfall rainfall2)
    {
        Rainfall sumRainfall = new Rainfall();

         //Add each corresponding month pair of the two
         //Rainfall objects together and assign the result
         //to the corresponding month of sumRainfall.
        for (int i = 1; i < 13; i++)
        {
            sumRainfall[i] = rainfall1[i] + rainfall2[i];
        }
        return sumRainfall;
    }

    public static bool operator> (Rainfall rainfall1, Rainfall rainfall2)
    {
        if (rainfall1.Average > rainfall2.Average)
            return true;
        else
            return false;
    }

    public static bool operator< (Rainfall rainfall1, Rainfall rainfall2)
    {
```

```
            if (rainfall1.Average < rainfall2.Average)
                return true;
            else
                return false;
        }
    }

    //This class is written as an answer to programming exercise 4.
    class RainfallQuarterly
    {
        private uint[] rainQuarterly = new uint[4];

        public uint this [int index]
        {
            get
            {
                if (index < 1 || index > 4)
                {
                    Console.WriteLine("Index is out of bounds");
                    return 0;
                }
                else
                {
                    return rainQuarterly[index - 1];
                }
            }

            set
            {
                if (index < 1 || index > 4)
                    Console.WriteLine("Index is out of bounds");
                else
                    rainQuarterly[index - 1] = value;
            }
        }

        //Implicit because no data is lost: For each quarter the three corresponding
        //months are added together and the sum assigned to this quarter.
        public static implicit operator RainfallQuarterly (Rainfall convertFrom)
        {
            RainfallQuarterly newRainQuarterly = new RainfallQuarterly();
            uint tempSum;
            int tempIndex = 1;
            //For each quarter add the corresponding months together and
            //add this value to the quarter
            for (int i = 1; i < 5; i++)
            {
                tempSum = 0;
                for (int j = 1; j < 4; j++)
                {
                    tempSum += convertFrom[tempIndex];
                    tempIndex++;
                }
                newRainQuarterly[i] = tempSum;
```

```
        }
        return newRainQuarterly;
    }

    //Explicit because data is lost when each quarterly amount is turned into
    //three monthly values all of the same size.
    public static explicit operator Rainfall (RainfallQuarterly convertFrom)
    {
        Rainfall newRainMonthly = new Rainfall();
        int tempIndex = 1;
        uint tempAverage;
         //For each quarter calculate a monthly average rainfall
         //Assign this value to the months of this quarter
        for (int i = 1; i < 5; i++)
        {
            tempAverage = convertFrom[i] / 3;
            for (int j = 1; j < 4; j++)
            {
                newRainMonthly[tempIndex] = tempAverage;
                tempIndex++;
            }
        }
        return newRainMonthly;
    }
}
```

Chapter 15

Answers to Chapter 15 Review Questions

1. `BliposSoft.RocketSimulation.Rocket`
2. You can create a shorter alias, such as `Rocket` for `ThisIsTheBestRocketClassInTheWholeWideWorldAndTheWholeWideBliposAsWell` with the following line:

   ```
   using Rocket = ThisIsTheBestRocketClassInTheWholeWideWorldAndTheWhole
   ➥WideBliposAsWell;
   ```

   You can now use the name `Rocket` in your code instead of the long cumbersome name.
3.
   a. Declare both the class and the two methods for `public`.

   b. Declare both the class and the two methods for `internal`.

   c. Declare the class and `CalculateAirResistance` to be `public`, but `WheelRotationsPerMinute` to be `internal`.

   d. Declare the class and `CalculateAirResistance` to be `public` and `WheelRotationsPerMinute` to be `private`.

4.

```
namespace BikeTech
{
    namespace BicycleDesign
    {
        ...
    }
    namespace HealthAndFitness
    {
        ...
    }
    namespace ComputerMapping
    {
        ...
    }
}
```

5.

```
namespace MyCompany
{
    public class Bicycle
    {
        ...
    }

    namespace Design
    {
        public class Drawer
        {
            ...
        }

        namespace Tools
        {
            public class Cutter
            {
                ...
            }
        }
    }
}
```

6.

```
csc /out:healthlib.dll /t: library /r:mathlib.dll;anatomylib.dll
➥ Bicycle.cs Person.cs
```

7. Ildasm let's you inspect the contents of any assembly by displaying its ingredients in a user-friendly GUI.

Answers to Chapter 15 Programming Exercises

Exercise 1: Create the following three compilation units. (The contents of the individual classes have been omitted for space reasons. You can simply insert the code from Listing 5.1 here.)

Compilation unit one with the following overall content is called `Elevator.cs`:

```
using System;
namespace ElevatorSimulation
{
    public class Elevator
    {
        ...
    }
}
```

Compilation unit two with the following content is called `Person.cs`:

```
using System;
namespace ElevatorSimulation
{
    public class Person
    {
        ...
    }
}
```

Compilation unit three with the following content is called `Building.cs`. (The `Building` class contains the `RunSimulation` method instead of the `Main` method.)

```
using System;
namespace ElevatorSimulation
{
    public class Building
    {
        ...
        public void RunSimulation()
        {
            ...
        }
    }
}
```

Compile the three compilation units into a DLL called `ElevatorSimulation.dll` with the following compiler command:

```
csc /out: ElevatorSimulation.dll /t:library Elevator.cs Person.cs Building.cs
```

You can now write a separate small program (called, for example, `Simulator.cs`) that calls the `RunSimulation` method of the `Building` class. Its main ingredients are as follows:

```
using System;
using ElevatorSimulation;
```

```
class Simulator
{
    public static void Main()
    {
        Building aBuilding = new Building();

        aBuilding.RunSimulation();
    }
}
```

When you compile `Simulator.cs`, you must reference the `ElevatorSimulation.dll` as in the following command that generates an `.exe` file called `Simulator.exe`.

```
csc /r:ElevatorSimulation.dll Simulator.cs
```

To run the program, you can now simply type

```
Simulator
```

which should result in the familiar output from Listing 5.1.

Observe that you could alternatively compile just the `Elevator.cs` and `Person.cs` compilation units into a `.dll` and then create your own simulation similar to that contained in the `Building` class. This latter class would have to be compiled with the `.dll` containing the code of `Elevator.cs` and `Person.cs`. This approach is used in the next answer.

Exercise 2: First create the following two compilation units. (The contents of the individual classes have been omitted for space reasons. You can simply insert the code from `BankSimulation.cs`.)

Compilation unit one with the following general content is called `Account.cs`:

```
using System;
namespace BankSimulation
{
    public class Account
    {
        ...
    }
}
```

Compilation unit two with the following content is called `Bank.cs`:

```
using System;
namespace BankSimulation
{
    public class Bank
    {
        ...
    }
}
```

Let the compiler generate a `.dll` called `Banklib.dll` with the following command:

```
csc /out: Banklib.dll /t:library Bank.cs Account.cs
```

Write a compilation unit with the contents of the `BankSimulation` class from Listing 10.14 and call it `BankSimulation.cs` with the following content:

```
using System;
using BankSimulation;
{
    public class BankSimulator
    {
        public static void Main
        {
            ...
        }
    }
}
```

Compile this compilation unit into an `.exe` assembly called `BankSimulation.exe` with the following compiler command:

```
csc /r:Banklib.dll BankSimulation.cs
```

You can now run the bank simulation with the following command:

```
BankSimulation
```

This should generate the same output as that of Listing 10.14.

Chapter 16

Answers to Chapter 16 Review Questions

1. Program 1 contains an airplane and the parts of an airplane. We can say airplane has-a jet engine and airplane has-a wing and so on. Consequently, it seems the aggregation concept will play an important role when implementing program 1.

   In program 2, we find many is-a relationships. For example, student is-a person, employee is-a person, and secretary is-an employee. Consequently, the program seems to be able to benefit from the inheritance concept.

2.
   a. `ElectronicDevice`
   b. `MobilePhone`
   c. `ElectronicDevice`
   d. `Radio`
   e. `ElectronicDevice`

3. Yes, you can make the call `myDog.Move()`. The `Move` method is inherited by the `Dog` class from the `Animal` class.

4. No, you cannot override this method. To enable this, `Move` must be declared `virtual`.
5. No, you cannot access name from within the `Dog` class definition. This is an advantage because it supports the encapsulation principle.
6. No.
7. The following is the correct header:

   ```
   protected override void MoveADistance(int distance)
   ```
8. Yes, by sealing it with the `sealed` keyword.
9. A part of the derived class is made up of the base class. The base class constructors know how to initialize this part.
10. Any constructor of a derived class that does not contain an explicit constructor initializer automatically gets an implicit constructor initializer attached, which calls the default constructor of the base class. This happens, even if the default constructor of the base class has not been defined.

    As soon as one constructor has been defined for a class, the default constructor is no longer supplied automatically. The base class in this case does not have a default constructor because it contains one explicitly defined constructor that takes one argument.

    The combination of the two described scenarios causes the compiler error.
11.

    ```
    public override double MetabolicRateCell()
    {
        return base.MetabolicRateCell() + 100;
    }
    ```
12. Yes. Class members are inherited across several inheritance levels.

Answers to Chapter 16 Programming Exercises

When you have written the code for all the programming exercises, your code should look somewhat similar to what is shown next. You might want to add additional `public` properties to access `private` instance variables and expand the test code further than what is shown here.

```
using System;

class ElectronicDevice
{
    private string brandName;
    private bool isOn;

    public ElectronicDevice()
    {
        brandName = "unknown";
        isOn = false;
    }
```

```
    public ElectronicDevice(string initBrandName)
    {
        brandName = initBrandName;
        isOn = false;
    }

    public string BrandName
    {
        get
        {
            return brandName;
        }

        set
        {
            brandName = value;
        }
    }

    public virtual void SwitchOn()
    {
        isOn = true;
        Console.WriteLine("On");
    }

    public virtual void SwitchOff()
    {
        isOn = false;
        Console.WriteLine("Off");
    }
}

class Radio : ElectronicDevice
{
    private double currentFrequency;

    public Radio() : base()
    {
        currentFrequency = 0;
    }

    public Radio(double initCurrentFrequency, string initBrandName)
    ➥ : base(initBrandName)
    {
        currentFrequency = initCurrentFrequency;
    }

    public override void SwitchOn()
    {
        base.SwitchOn();
        Console.WriteLine("Radio");
    }
```

```
    public override void SwitchOff()
    {
        base.SwitchOff();
        Console.WriteLine("Radio");
    }
}

class Computer : ElectronicDevice
{
    private int internalMemory;

    public Computer() : base()
    {
        internalMemory = 0;
    }

    public Computer(int initInternalMemory, string initBrandName)
    ➥ : base(initBrandName)
    {
        internalMemory = initInternalMemory;
    }

    public override void SwitchOn()
    {
        base.SwitchOn();
        Console.WriteLine("Computer");
    }

    public override void SwitchOff()
    {
        base.SwitchOff();
        Console.WriteLine("Computer");
    }
}

class MobilePhone : ElectronicDevice
{
    private uint lastNumberDialled;

    public MobilePhone() : base()
    {
        lastNumberDialled = 0;
    }

    public MobilePhone(uint initLastNumberDialled, string initBrandName)
    ➥ : base(initBrandName)
    {
        lastNumberDialled = initLastNumberDialled;
    }

    public override void SwitchOn()
    {
        base.SwitchOn();
```

```
            Console.WriteLine("Mobile Phone");
        }

        public override void SwitchOff()
        {
            base.SwitchOff();
            Console.WriteLine("Mobile Phone");
        }
    }

    class LaptopComputer : Computer
    {
        private uint maxBatteriLife;

        public LaptopComputer() : base()
        {
            maxBatteriLife = 0;
        }

        public LaptopComputer(uint initMaxBatLife, int initInternalMemory, string
        ➥ initBrandName) : base(initInternalMemory, initBrandName)
        {
            maxBatteriLife = initMaxBatLife;
        }
    }

    class Tester
    {
        public static void Main()
        {
            Radio myRadio = new Radio(100, "Bang & Olufsen");
            Console.WriteLine("BrandName: " + myRadio.BrandName);

            LaptopComputer myLaptop = new LaptopComputer(12, 256, "IBM");
            Console.WriteLine("BrandName: " + myLaptop.BrandName);
        }
    }
```

Chapter 17

Answers to Chapter 17 Review Questions

1. The `Sound` method should be positioned in the `Animal` class because any animal can make a sound. We don't know the sound an `Animal` makes (it could be meow, vrooff, or something else), so `Sound` should be declared `abstract` in `Animal`.

2. No. The `Animal` class must be declared `abstract` because it contains the `abstract` `Sound` method. An `abstract` class cannot be instantiated, because otherwise it would be possible to call methods without any implementation.

3. Method header of `Sound` in the `Animal` class is as follows:

   ```
   public abstract void Sound();
   ```

   `Sound`'s header is the same in all three derived classes:

   ```
   public override void Sound()
   ```

4. An `abstract` method cannot have an implementation.
5. For a variable of type `Animal`.
6. The implementation of the `Sound` method written in the `Dog` class is called and executed.
7. Let the `Lion` class be derived from the `Animal` class. Make sure the `Sound` method is defined with the `override` keyword.
8. By using the `is` operator as follows:

   ```
   (myAnimal is Dog)
   ```

   which returns `true` if `myAnimal` is referencing an object of type `Dog`.
9. You can use the `is` operator as shown in the following lines:

   ```
   if (myAnimal is Cat)
       myCat = (Cat) myAnimal
   ```

   or the `as` operator as in the following line:

   ```
   myCat = myAnimal as Cat;
   ```

10. `myCat.Jump()` is not valid because `Cat` does not contain any `Jump` method.

    However, `myCat.ToString()` is valid because `Cat` implicitly inherits the `ToString` method from the `System.Object` class. The call returns the name of the class in a string (`"Cat"`).
11. The `virtual` methods of a base class can create more havoc in derived classes than non-`virtual` methods. `virtual` methods are executed slightly slower than non-`virtual` methods.
12. Several subtle problems are associated with multiple inheritance.
13. First, the access modifier `public` cannot be applied to the method `Recover`. Second, `Recover` is `implicitly` abstract, so it cannot have an implementation. A semicolon must be inserted instead of the implementation.
14. You can create the same functionality with `IArticulateable`, but you cannot improve the code. The power of interfaces is realized when you want to implement polymorphism on a group of classes that do not have a common ancestor (`Animal` is a common ancestor).

Answers to Chapter 17 Programming Exercises

Exercise 1:

```
using System;

public interface IComparable
{
    int CompareTo(IComparable comp);
}

public class Account : IComparable
{
    private decimal balance;

    public Account(decimal initBalance)
    {
        balance = initBalance;
    }

    public decimal Balance
    {
        get
        {
            return balance;
        }

        set
        {
            balance = value;
        }
    }

    public virtual int CompareTo(IComparable comp)
    {
        Account compareAccount = (Account) comp;

        if(balance > compareAccount.Balance)
            return 1;
        else if(compareAccount.Balance == balance)
            return 0;
        else
            return -1;
    }
}

class Sorter
{
     // Sort the comparable elements of an array in ascending order
    public static void BubbleSortAscending(IComparable [] bubbles)
    {
        bool swapped = true;

        for (int i = 0; swapped; i++)
```

```
            {
                swapped = false;
                for (int j = 0; j < (bubbles.Length - (i + 1)); j++)
                {
                    if (bubbles[j].CompareTo(bubbles[j + 1]) > 0)
                    {
                        Swap(j, j + 1, bubbles);
                        swapped = true;
                    }
                }
            }
        }

         //Swap two elements of an array
        public static void Swap(int first, int second, IComparable [] arr)
        {
            IComparable temp;

            temp = arr[first];
            arr[first] = arr[second];
            arr[second] = temp;
        }
    }

    class Tester
    {
        public static void Main()
        {
            Account [] accounts = new Account[4];

            accounts[0] = new Account(100);
            accounts[1] = new Account(200);
            accounts[2] = new Account(50);
            accounts[3] = new Account(75);

            Sorter.BubbleSortAscending(accounts);

            foreach(Account tempAccount in accounts)
            {
                Console.WriteLine(tempAccount.Balance);
            }
        }
    }
```

Exercise 2: Create a base class called `Employee`. Derive each of the three classes from this base class as shown in the following code:

```
using System;

abstract class Employee
{
    public abstract void CalculateSalary();
}
```

```
class Secretary : Employee
{
    public override void CalculateSalary()
    {
        Console.WriteLine("Calculate salary for secretary");
    }
}

class Director : Employee
{
    public override void CalculateSalary()
    {
        Console.WriteLine("Calculate salary for director");
    }
}

class Programmer : Employee
{
    public override void CalculateSalary()
    {
        Console.WriteLine("Calculate salary for programmer");
    }
}

class Tester
{
    public static void Main()
    {
        Employee [] employees = new Employee[3];

        employees[0] = new Secretary();
        employees[1] = new Director();
        employees[2] = new Programmer();

        foreach(Employee tempEmployee in employees)
        {
            tempEmployee.CalculateSalary();
        }
    }
}
```

Exercise 3: The following code contains an interface called `IStorable` that has two abstract methods—`Read` and `Write`. The `Secretary` and `House` classes both implement this interface. The `Transfer` method takes an argument of `IStorable`. We can thus send both an instance of type `Secretary` and of type `House` to this method. This is done in the `Tester` class. Notice that this code results in a few warnings when compiled because none of the instance variables of the classes are used (to keep the code brief).

```
using System;

abstract class Employee
{
    public abstract void CalculateSalary();
```

```
}

class Secretary : Employee, IStorable
{
    public override void CalculateSalary()
    {
        Console.WriteLine("Calculate salary for secretary");
    }

    public void Read()
    {
        Console.WriteLine("Now reading secretary");
    }

    public void Write()
    {
        Console.WriteLine("Now writing secretary");
    }
}

class Director : Employee
{
    public override void CalculateSalary()
    {
        Console.WriteLine("Calculate salary for director");
    }
}

class Programmer : Employee
{
    public override void CalculateSalary()
    {
        Console.WriteLine("Calculate salary for programmer");
    }
}

interface IStorable
{
    void Read();
    void Write();
}

class Building
{
    private int age;
    private decimal currentValue;

}

class House : Building, IStorable
{
    private ushort numberOfBedrooms;
```

```
    public void Read()
    {
        Console.WriteLine("Now reading house");
    }

    public void Write()
    {
        Console.WriteLine("Now writing house");
    }
}

class OfficeBuilding
{
    private uint floorSpace;

}

class Tester
{
    public static void Main()
    {
        House myHouse = new House();
        Secretary mySecretary = new Secretary();

        Transfer(myHouse);
        Transfer(mySecretary);
    }

    public static void Transfer (IStorable tempStore)
    {
        tempStore.Read();
        tempStore.Write();
    }
}
```

Chapter 18

Answers to Chapter 18 Review Questions

1.

   a. To represent fractions (with a numerator and a denominator

   b. To represent points on a map (2D) or points in space (3D)

   c. To represent a time span

2. Similarities: structs and classes can both contain methods, properties, indexers, constructors, data members, operator methods, nested types; both can implement interfaces; and they both implicitly inherit from the `System.Object` class.

Differences: Structs cannot contain destructors; their constructors work in a slightly different way. Structs form value types, whereas classes form reference types; structs don't support inheritance, and structs are stored more efficiently in memory.

3. As part of the process of being passed as an argument to `WriteLine`, `myStruct` is boxed into a reference value, which then can be processed by `WriteLine`.
4. No.
5. One can imagine boxing as the process of putting a struct value into a box that is of a reference type.
6. No, the second line is not valid. `Fraction` does not contain any explicitly defined constructors, so the numerator and denominator values have not been initialized by the time `ToString` is called in the second line. This is invalid because no methods, properties, or indexers can be called for a struct value that contains uninitialized data members.

Answers to Chapter 18 Programming Exercises

Exercise 1:

```
using System;

struct Fraction
{
    private int numerator;
    private int denominator;

    public Fraction(int initNumerator, int initDenominator)
    {
        numerator = initNumerator;
        denominator = initDenominator;
    }

    public int Numerator
    {
        get
        {
            return numerator;
        }

        set
        {
            numerator = value;
        }
    }

    public int Denominator
    {
        get
        {
            return denominator;
        }
```

```
            set
            {
                denominator = value;
            }
        }

        public double Value
        {
            get
            {
                return (double)numerator / (double)denominator;
            }
        }

        public override string ToString()
        {
            string returnString;

            returnString = "Fraction value: " + Value;

            return returnString;
        }
    }

    class Tester
    {
        public static void Main()
        {
            Fraction myFraction = new Fraction(1, 3);
            Console.WriteLine(myFraction);
        }
    }
```

Chapter 19

Answers to Chapter 19 Review Questions

1. Dividing by zero, running out of memory, accessing a non-existent file.
2. The normal case code and exception handling code can be kept separate. Exceptions can be handled gracefully without exposing the end user to cryptic looking code.
3. `System.Exception`
4. Zero, one or many `catch` blocks, and zero or one `finally` block. However, at least one block (it can either be a `catch` or a `finally` block) must be attached to a `try` block.
5. Normal execution is terminated. The program will move quickly out through the various method calls looking for a matching `catch` statement. If a matching `catch` block is found, normal execution continues from here; otherwise, the exception is caught by the runtime and the program is abruptly terminated.

6. By being the same class or an ancestor class of the exception object class that was thrown.

7. If the `try` block has an associated `finally` block, this block will be executed. If no `finally` block exists for the `try` block, execution begins after the last `catch` block.

8. Then the runtime will look for a matching `catch` statement by unraveling the current method call chain. If none is found, the runtime will handle the exception itself.

9. The search will continue for a `catch` block that matches the exception thrown in the `catch` block.

10. It guarantees to execute the code contained in its block, regardless of whether or not an exception has been thrown.

11. `System.ApplicationException`

12. Yes, it is valid. This construct is sometimes used when a method has many return statements but a core set of statements must be executed before the method ends, regardless of the return statement the method exits with.

13. No, it is invalid. The last `catch` statement will never be executed because `System.Exception` is an ancestor to `System.IndexOutOfRangeException`.

14. The runtime's default exception handler will handle the exception and abruptly terminate the program.

Answers to Chapter 19 Programming Exercises

Exercise 1: See Listing 19.2 for the answer.

Exercises 2–4:

```
using System;

class Meteorologist
{
    private int[] rainfall;
    private int[] pollution;

    public Meteorologist()
    {
        rainfall = new int[12];
        pollution = new int[12];

         //Assign an arbitrary number to each
         //rainfall and pollution element.
         //In this case rainfall is set to
         //i * 5 and pollution to i + 10
        for(int i = 0; i < 12; i++)
        {
            rainfall[i] = i * 5;
            pollution[i] = i + 10;
```

```
        }
    }

    public int GetRainfall(int index)
    {
        try
        {
            return rainfall[index];
        }
        catch(IndexOutOfRangeException exObj)
        {
            Console.WriteLine("The index must be between 0 and 11");
            Console.WriteLine(exObj.Message);
            return -1;
        }
    }

    public int GetAveragePollution(int index)
    {
        Console.WriteLine("Opening WeatherXYZ file");
        try
        {
            return pollution[index] / rainfall[index];
        }
        catch(IndexOutOfRangeException exObj)
        {
            Console.WriteLine("The index must be between 0 and 11");
            Console.WriteLine(exObj.Message);
            return -1;
        }
        catch(DivideByZeroException exObj)
        {
            Console.WriteLine("The rainfall element was zero");
            Console.WriteLine(exObj.Message);
            return -1;
        }
        finally
        {
            Console.WriteLine("Closing WeatherXYZ file");
        }
    }
}

class Tester
{
    public static void Main()
    {
        Meteorologist aMeteorologist = new Meteorologist();
        Console.WriteLine("Rainfall in January: {0}",
        ➥ aMeteorologist.GetRainfall(0));
         //Triggering IndexOutOfRangeException
        Console.WriteLine("Rainfall next year: {0}",
        ➥ aMeteorologist.GetRainfall(13));
```

```
            //Triggering DivideByZeroException
            Console.WriteLine("Average pollution: {0}",
            ➥ aMeteorologist.GetAveragePollution(0));
        }
    }
```

Chapter 20

Answers to Chapter 20 Review Questions

1. Similarities:

   - They both specify a return type and parameters for a method that they are able to represent and invoke at runtime.
   - They both allow you to postpone the decision of which method to invoke until runtime.

   Differences:

   - The method name must match that of the abstract class. The method name is irrelevant for the delegate.
   - Abstract methods work through inheritance, interfaces, and dynamic binding.
   - Generally, delegates are more suited for event handling purposes.

2. A delegate is called like a method, but unlike the method, it does not execute the call itself. Instead, it delegates the execution to the method it encapsulates at the time the delegate is called.
3. A delegate is just another class, so a delegate definition can be positioned in the same location as a class definition.
4. b.
5. A multicast delegate can encapsulate several methods. If the multicast delegate specified a return type other than `void`, the methods it encapsulates would all return a value. It is impossible to specify how these return values should be processed.
6.

   a. `+, -, +=, -=`

   b. `+=, -=`
7. An event handler is a method that resides in the subscribing object. When the event (that this event handler is handling) is fired in the publisher, the event handler is invoked.

Answers to Chapter 20 Programming Exercises

Exercise 1: Insert the following method in the `Math` class:

```
public static double Product(int number1, int number2)
{
    return (number1 * number2);
}
```

To test this method, insert the following lines in the `Main` method:

```
myCalculation = new Calculation(Math.Product);
result = myCalculation(10, 20);
Console.WriteLine("Result of passing 10, 20 to myCalculation: {0}", result);
```

Exercise 2:

```
using System;

delegate string DoStringProcessing(string text);

class CharacterProcessor
{
    private DoStringProcessing[] processingList;
    private int stringProcessingCounter;

    public CharacterProcessor()
    {
        stringProcessingCounter = 0;
        processingList = new DoStringProcessing[20];
    }

    public void AddStringOperation(DoStringProcessing newStringProcess)
    {
        processingList[stringProcessingCounter] = newStringProcess;
        stringProcessingCounter++;
    }

    public string StartProcessing(string tempString)
    {
        Console.WriteLine("Start string: " + tempString);
        for (int i = 0; i < stringProcessingCounter; i++)
        {
            tempString = processingList[i](tempString);
        }
        return tempString;
    }
}

class StringOperator
{
    public static DoStringProcessing DoAddA = new DoStringProcessing(AddA);
    public static DoStringProcessing DoAddB = new DoStringProcessing(AddB);
    public static DoStringProcessing DoAddC = new DoStringProcessing(AddC);
```

```
    public static string AddA(string text)
    {
        Console.WriteLine("Add A to string");
        return text + "A";
    }

    public static string AddB(string text)
    {
        Console.WriteLine("Add B to string");
        return text + "B";
    }

    public static string AddC(string text)
    {
        Console.WriteLine("Add C to string");
        return text + "C";
    }
}

public class Tester
{
    public static void Main()
    {
        string startText;
        string endResult;
        string response;

        CharacterProcessor processor = new CharacterProcessor();

        Console.Write("Enter start string: ");
        startText = Console.ReadLine();
        Console.WriteLine("Create sequence of operations by repeatedly");
        Console.WriteLine("choosing from the following options");
        Console.WriteLine("A) Add A");
        Console.WriteLine("B) Add B");
        Console.WriteLine("C) Add C");
        Console.WriteLine("When you wish to perform the processing
        ➥ enter P\n");

        do
        {
            response = Console.ReadLine().ToUpper();
            switch(response)
            {
                case "A":
                    processor.AddStringOperation(StringOperator.DoAddA);
                    Console.WriteLine("Add A operation added");
                break;
                case "B":
                    processor.AddStringOperation(StringOperator.DoAddB);
                    Console.WriteLine("Add B operation added");
                break;
                case "C":
```

```
                    processor.AddStringOperation(StringOperator.DoAddC);
                    Console.WriteLine("Add C operation added");
                break;
                case "P":
                    endResult = processor.StartProcessing(startText);
                    Console.WriteLine("End result: {0}", endResult);
                break;
                default:
                    Console.WriteLine("Invalid choice please try again");
                break;
            }
        } while (response != "P");
    }
}
```

Exercise 3: The enum `MoveRequestType`, the `MoveRequestEventArgs` class, the `Car` class, and the `Tester` class all remain unchanged and have not been displayed here. You can merely paste them in from Listing 20.4 to run the program.

```
using System;

class GameController
{
    public delegate void MoveRequest(object sender, MoveRequestEventArgs e);

    public event MoveRequest OnMoveRequest;

    Car[] gameCars = new Car[10];
    Motorbike[] gameMotorbikes = new Motorbike[10];

    string name;
    int speedParam = 0;
    int motorbikeCounter = 0;
    int carCounter = 0;
    int carNumber = 0;
    int motorbikeNumber = 0;

    public void Run()
    {
        string answer;
        Console.WriteLine("Please select from the following menu: ");
        Console.WriteLine("A)dd new car");
        Console.WriteLine("B) Add new motorbike");
        Console.WriteLine("C) Subscribe car to events");
        Console.WriteLine("M) Subscribe motorbike to events");
        Console.WriteLine("U)nsubscribe car from events");
        Console.WriteLine("V) Unsubscribe motorbike from events");
        Console.WriteLine("L)ist cars and motorbikes in current game");
        Console.WriteLine("F)ast forward");
        Console.WriteLine("S)low forward");
        Console.WriteLine("R)everse");
        Console.WriteLine("T)erminate");

        do
```

```
        {
            Console.WriteLine("Select new option:");
            answer = Console.ReadLine().ToUpper();

            switch(answer)
            {
                case "A":
                    Console.Write("Enter name of the new car: ");
                    name = Console.ReadLine();
                    Console.Write("Enter car speed parameter of the
                    ➥ new car: ");
                    speedParam = Convert.ToInt32(Console.ReadLine());
                    gameCars[carCounter] = new Car(speedParam, name);
                    carCounter++;
                break;
                case "B":
                    Console.Write("Enter name of the new motorbike: ");
                    name = Console.ReadLine();
                    gameMotorbikes[motorbikeCounter] = new Motorbike(name);
                    motorbikeCounter++;
                break;
                case "C":
                    Console.Write("Enter array index of car you want to [sr]
                    ➥subscribe to events: ");
                    carNumber = Convert.ToInt32(Console.ReadLine());
                    gameCars[carNumber].Subscribe(this);
                break;
                case "M":
                    Console.Write("Enter array index of motorbike you want to
                    ➥subscribe to events: ");
                    motorbikeNumber = Convert.ToInt32(Console.ReadLine());
                    gameMotorbikes[motorbikeNumber].Subscribe(this);
                break;
                case "U":
                    Console.Write("Enter array index of car you want to
                    ➥unsubscribe from events: ");
                    carNumber = Convert.ToInt32(Console.ReadLine());
                    gameCars[carNumber].Unsubscribe(this);
                break;
                case "V":
                    Console.Write("Enter array index of motorbike you want to
                    ➥unsubscribe from events: ");
                    motorbikeNumber = Convert.ToInt32(Console.ReadLine());
                    gameMotorbikes[motorbikeNumber].Unsubscribe(this);
                break;
                case "L":
                    Console.WriteLine("Cars currently listed:");
                    for(int i=0; i < carCounter; i++)
                    {
                        Console.WriteLine(gameCars[i]);
                    }
                    Console.WriteLine("Motorbikes currently listed:");
                    for(int i=0; i < motorbikeCounter; i++)
```

```
                    {
                        Console.WriteLine(gameMotorbikes[i]);
                    }
                break;
                case "F":
                    if (OnMoveRequest != null)
                        OnMoveRequest(this, new MoveRequestEventArgs
                        ➥(MoveRequestType.FastForward));
                break;
                case "S":
                    if (OnMoveRequest != null)
                        OnMoveRequest(this, new MoveRequestEventArgs
                        ➥(MoveRequestType.SlowForward));
                break;
                case "R":
                    if (OnMoveRequest != null)
                        OnMoveRequest(this, new MoveRequestEventArgs
                        ➥(MoveRequestType.Reverse));
                break;
                case "T":
                break;
                default:
                    Console.WriteLine("Invalid choice. Please try again");
                break;
            }
        } while(answer != "T");
    }
}

class Motorbike
{
    private int distance;
    private string name;
    const int speedParam = 30;

    public Motorbike(string initName)
    {
        distance = 0;
        name = initName;
    }

    public void Subscribe(GameController controller)
    {
        controller.OnMoveRequest += new GameController.MoveRequest
        ➥(MoveRequestHandler);
    }

    public void Unsubscribe(GameController controller)
    {
        controller.OnMoveRequest -= new GameController.MoveRequest
        ➥(MoveRequestHandler);
    }
```

```
        public void MoveRequestHandler(object sender, MoveRequestEventArgs e)
        {
            switch (e.Request)
            {
                case MoveRequestType.SlowForward:
                    distance += speedParam;
                    Console.WriteLine("Motorbike name: " + name +
                    ➥" Moving forward. Distance: " + distance);
                break;
                case MoveRequestType.FastForward:
                    distance += speedParam;
                    Console.WriteLine("Motorbike name: " + name +
                    ➥" Moving forward. Distance: " + distance);
                break;
                case MoveRequestType.Reverse:
                    distance -= 3;
                    Console.WriteLine("Motorbike name: " + name +
                    ➥" Reversing. Distance: " + distance);
                break;
            }
        }

        public override string ToString()
        {
            return name;
        }
    }
```

Chapter 21

Answers to Chapter 21 Review Questions

1. By letting the following line be the first line in the source code:

   ```
   #define TRIALEDITION
   ```

2. No, it is invalid. `#define` and `#undef` must precede any non-preprocessor directives in the source code.

3.

   ```
   #undef PART1
   #define PART2
   #if PART1
       <Code part 1>
   #endif
   ...
   #if PART2
       <Code part 2>
   #endif
   ```

4. Standard comments are read in conjunction with the source code. Program documentation is read separately and independently from the source code. Standard comments start with // or are surrounded by /* */, whereas documentation comments begin with /// and contain XML tags.

5. A documentation comment starts with /// and consists of XML tags and descriptive text. For example

```
///<summary>The Rocket class represents a rocket in a rocket simulation
</summary>
```

6. The following compiler command

```
csc /doc: <XML_FileName>.xml <FileName>.cs
```

generates an .xml documentation file called <*XML_FileName*>.xml based on the source code file <*FileName*>.cs.

7. Attributes let you add declarative information to the elements in your source code beyond what is possible with the already existing C# keywords and language constructs.

8. No, many attributes are meant to decorate only one or a few types of source code elements, such as just methods or just classes.

9. System.Diagnostics.ConditionalAttribute: Prevent methods from being compiled and called.

   System.ObsoleteAttribute: Mark selected elements obsolete. Will produce warnings or errors if these elements are used by other parts of the code.

10. a, b, and c.

11. Some attributes accept arguments that must be positioned in a certain order to be assigned to the correct attribute parameters. These arguments are referred to as *positional parameters*.

   Example: "Use the Calculate method instead" and true are both positional parameters in the following attribute annotation:

```
[System.ObsoleteAttribute("Use the Calculate method instead", true)]
```

12. If TEST is undefined, the following annotation will prevent the StartOperation method from being compiled and called:

```
[ConditionalAttribute("TEST")]
public void StartOperation()
{
    ...
}
```

13. No, the ConditionalAttribute can only be applied on methods with the return type void.

14. As opposed to positional parameters, named parameters can be positioned in any order you might choose. However, the named parameter is assigned a value by including its name followed by an equals sign (=) followed by the value, as shown in the following:

    <Named_parameter_name> = *<Value>*

Answers to Chapter 21 Programming Exercises

Exercise 1: The following represents the professional version. By simply changing which of the three identifiers—STANDARDVERSION, PROFESSIONALVERSION, and ENTERPRISEVERSION—is defined, you can easily control which version is compiled.

```
#undef STANDARDVERSION
#define PROFESSIONALVERSION
#undef ENTERPRISEVERSION

using System;

class BliposExplorer
{
    public static void Main()
    {
      #if STANDARDVERSION
        Console.WriteLine("This is the standard version");
      #endif

      #if PROFESSIONALVERSION
        Console.WriteLine("This is the professional version");
      #endif

      #if ENTERPRISEVERSION
        Console.WriteLine("This is the enterprise version");
      #endif
    }
}
```

Exercise 2: To extract the documentation, remember to use the /doc: compiler switch.

```
using System;

///<summary> Calculator contains methods for solving arithmetic
➥ calculations </summary>
///<remarks> Contains the Sum and Product methods </remarks>
class Calculator
{
     ///<summary> Sum calculates the sum of two ints </summary>
    public static int Sum(int x, int y)
    {
        return x + y;
    }

     ///<summary> Product calculates the product of two ints </summary>
    public static int Product(int x, int y)
```

```
    {
        return x * y;
    }
}

///<summary> RocketScientist can perform sophisticated calculations
➥ related to rockets </summary>
class RocketScientist
{
    public static void Main()
    {
        Console.WriteLine("Estimated time to go to Mars: {0}",
        ➥ EstimatedTimeToMars(23));
    }

     ///<summary> Estimates the time it will take to go to Mars </summary>
    public static uint EstimatedTimeToMars(int x)
    {
        return (uint) (Calculator.Sum(x, 24) + Calculator.Product(x, 21));
    }
}
```

Exercise 3:

a. Insert the following line just before the `MoveBySteam` method header:

   ```
   [Obsolete("Use MoveByElectricity instead")]
   ```

b. Include the following line just before the `TestingDistance` method header:

   ```
   [System.Diagnostics.Conditional("TEST")]
   ```

   If you want `TestingDistance` to be called, include the line

   ```
   #define TEST
   ```

   at the start of the source code; otherwise, don't write anything or include the following line:

   ```
   #undef TEST
   ```

c. The following shows what the code might look like after answering points a, b, and c. Defining `TEST` in the first line allows `TestingDistance` to be called. Undefining `STEAM` in the second line prevents `MoveBySteam` from being called.

   ```
   #define TEST
   #undef STEAM

   using System;

   class Train
   {
       private uint distance = 0;

       [System.Diagnostics.Conditional("STEAM")]
       [Obsolete("Use MoveByElectricity instead")]
   ```

```
  public void MoveBySteam(uint addDistance)
  {
Console.WriteLine("Moving {0} kilometers by steam", addDistance);
distance += addDistance;
}

               public void MoveByElectricity(uint addDistance)
    {
        Console.WriteLine("Moving {0} kilometer by electricy", addDistance);
        distance += addDistance;
    }

    [System.Diagnostics.Conditional("TEST")]
    public void TestingDistance()
    {
        Console.WriteLine("Testing. distance instance variable: {0}",
        ➥ distance);
    }
}

class Tester
{
    public static void Main()
    {
        Train orientExpress = new Train();

        orientExpress.MoveBySteam(100);
        orientExpress.MoveByElectricity(200);
        orientExpress.TestingDistance();
    }
}
```

d. You need to adjust the `Obsolete` attribute annotation of `MoveBySteam` to the following, which now includes the Boolean value `true`.

```
[Obsolete("Use MoveByElectricity instead", true)]
```

Chapter 22

Answers to Chapter 22 Review Questions

1. Files provide permanent means for storing data.
2. With objects of stream classes found in the `System.IO` namespace.
3. `Console.WriteLine` and `Console.ReadLine`.
4. From a destination device to the program.
5. They both consist of bits and bytes. The bits and bytes in text files are encoded into a list of characters. This is not the case for binary files.
6. Yes.

7. The `File` class contains `static` methods, so there is, as opposed to the `FileInfo` class, no need to first instantiate a `File` object before calling its methods. Because only a single call is needed, exactly one expensive security check is required whether we use `FileInfo` or `File`. So overall, `File` is the preferred class.

8. `FileInfo` is preferred, because it only requires one security check when objects of this class are instantiated. In contrast, `File` requires a security check for every method call.

9. The runtime will generate a `System.IO.FileNotFoundException`.

10. A file's full name includes the complete path to the file, from the root directory (A, B, C, and so on) through sub-directories to the short name of the file (Example: `C:\MyFiles\TextFiles\MyHorrorStory.txt`). A file's relative name does not contain the path (Example: `MyHorrorStory.txt`).

11. If the program crashes, the program cannot automatically close the file, leaving it exposed to possible damage.

12. It returns `null` when the end of the file is reached.

13. Opening a file.

14. A `FileStream` object.

Answers to Chapter 22 Programming Exercises

Exercises 1 and 2:

```
using System;
using System.IO;

class FileInspector
{
    public static void Main()
    {
         //Exercise 2
        string textLine;
        StreamReader inStream;
        int counter = 0;

        try
        {
             //Exercise 1
            FileInfo txtFile = new FileInfo(@"C:\MyTestFiles\ShortStory.txt");

            Console.WriteLine("File name: " + txtFile.FullName);
            Console.WriteLine("Creation time: " + txtFile.CreationTime);

             //Exercise 2
            inStream = txtFile.OpenText();
            textLine = inStream.ReadLine();
            while(textLine != null)
            {
```

```
                counter++;
                textLine = inStream.ReadLine();
            }
            Console.WriteLine("Number of lines in text: {0}", counter);
        }
        catch (IOException exObj)
        {
            Console.WriteLine(exObj);
        }
    }
}
```

Exercise 3:

```
using System;
using System.IO;

class Rainfall
{
    private static byte [] rainfall = new byte [12];
    private static FileStream outStream = null;
    private static FileStream inStream = null;

    public static void Main()
    {
        string answer;
        int index;
        byte rainfallReading;

        Console.WriteLine("Choose between the following options: ");
        Console.WriteLine("I)nput a rainfall reading");
        Console.WriteLine("L)ist the rainfall readings");
        Console.WriteLine("S)ave the rainfall readings");
        Console.WriteLine("R)ead the rainfall readings from file");
        Console.WriteLine("T)erminate program");

        do
        {
            Console.Write("\nEnter choice: ");
            answer = Console.ReadLine().ToUpper();
            switch (answer)
            {
                case "I":
                    Console.Write("Enter month (1-12): ");
                    index = Convert.ToInt32(Console.ReadLine());
                    Console.Write("Enter rainfall reading: ");
                    rainfallReading = Convert.ToByte(Console.ReadLine());
                    rainfall[index - 1] = rainfallReading;
                break;
                case "L":
                    Console.WriteLine("Rainfall readings:");
                    foreach(int temp in rainfall)
                    {
                        Console.Write("{0} ", temp);
```

```
        }
        Console.WriteLine();
    break;
    case "T":
        Console.WriteLine("Bye bye");
    break;
    case "S":
        try
        {
            Console.WriteLine("Saving rainfall data to
            ➥ Rainfall.dat");
            FileInfo byteOutFile = new FileInfo
            ➥(@"C:\MyTestFiles\Rainfall.dat");
            outStream = byteOutFile.OpenWrite();
            for(int i = 0; i < 12; i++)
            {
                outStream.WriteByte(rainfall[i]);
            }
        }

        catch (IOException exObj)
        {
            Console.WriteLine(exObj);
        }

        finally
        {
            outStream.Close();
        }
    break;
    case "R":
        try
        {
            Console.WriteLine("Reading data from Rainfall.dat");
            FileInfo byteInFile = new FileInfo
            ➥ (@"C:\MyTestFiles\Rainfall.dat");
            inStream = byteInFile.OpenRead();
            for (int i = 0; i < inStream.Length; i++)
            {
                rainfall[i] = (byte)inStream.ReadByte();
            }
            inStream.Close();
        }

        catch (IOException exObj)
        {
            Console.WriteLine(exObj);
        }

        finally
        {
            inStream.Close();
        }
```

```
                    break;
                    default:
                        Console.WriteLine("Invalid choice. Try again");
                    break;
                }
            } while(answer != "T");
        }
    }
```

Chapter 23

Answers to Chapter 23 Review Questions

1.

   Number: 1

   Number: 2

   Number: 4

   Number: 8

2. A branching statement (`if-else`) spanning lines 3–9. A base case in line 4, a recursive call (or recursive step) in line 8. Each recursive call moves towards the base case.

3. Two simple changes are needed in lines 3 and 8:

```
01: public static void Recurs(int number)
02: {
03:     if(number < 1)
04:         return;
05:     else
06:     {
07:         Console.WriteLine("Number: {0}", number);
08:         Recurs(number / 2);
09:     }
10: }
```

4. Iteration is more efficient than recursion because it does not require the generation of pending method instances (as opposed to recursion), which involves much overhead to store and manage by the runtime.

5. `Sum` is missing a branch statement and a base case. The following is the correct `Sum` method:

```
public static int Sum(int number)
{
    if(number == 1)
        return 1;
    else
    {
        return number + Sum(number - 1);
```

```
        }
    }
```

6. If line height is lower than the shortest lines shown in the figure return (base case). Otherwise draw a line in the middle of the part of the ruler you are drawing. Draw a slightly lower line in the part to the left of the line just drawn (recursive call) and a line in the part to the right of the line (recursive call). The process begins by setting the line height to the longest of the vertical lines.

Answers to Chapter 23 Programming Exercises

Exercise 1:

```
public static int Count(int number)
{
    if(number < 10)
        return 1;
    else
        return 1 + Count(number / 10);
}
```

Exercise 2:

```
using System;

class NumberProcessor
{
    public static void NumberToWord(int number)
    {
        if(number >= 10)
            NumberToWord(number / 10);
        Console.Write(DigitToText(number % 10) + " ");
    }

    public static string DigitToText(int digit)
    {
        switch (digit)
        {
            case 0:
                return "zero";
            case 1:
                return "one";
            case 2:
                return "two";
            case 3:
                return "three";
            case 4:
                return "four";
            case 5:
                return "five";
            case 6:
                return "six";
            case 7:
```

```
                return "seven";
            case 8:
                return "eight";
            case 9:
                return "nine";
            default:
                Console.WriteLine("Can only process single digits");
                return "Error";
        }
    }
}

class Tester
{
    public static void Main()
    {
        NumberProcessor.NumberToWord(3426);
    }
}
```

INDEX

Symbols

A

B

C

D

E

F

G-H

I

J-K

L

O

P

T

U

V-Z